Reconstructing Social Psychology

Edited by Nigel Armistead

Penguin Education

Penguin Education
A Division of Penguin Books Ltd,
Harmondsworth, Middlesex, England
Penguin Books Inc, 7110 Ambassador Road,
Baltimore, Md 21207, USA
Penguin Books Australia Ltd,
Ringwood, Victoria, Australia
Penguin Books Canada Ltd,
41 Steelcase Road West,
Markham, Ontario, Canada

First published 1974
Copyright © Nigel Armistead and contributors, 1974

Printed in Great Britain by
Richard Clay (The Chaucer Press), Ltd,
Bungay, Suffolk.
Set in Monotype Times

Contents

6 Contents

Introduction
Nigel Armistead

A book is not just a series of words: it is a part of people's lives. Probably a more significant part of the authors' lives than of the readers' insofar as the authors have put more of themselves into it. This book has arisen out of our dissatisfaction with much of what is called psychology. That dissatisfaction is felt most acutely in relation to the lives we are leading and the world that we see around us. We feel that social psychology should be making some sense of our experience and that it doesn't: we feel disappointed. Many people say that we hope for too much, that social psychology (or psychology or sociology) cannot provide all the answers or even raise all the questions. While agreeing that social psychology can never be, and should never be, a total solution to the problems of living, we have not given up hope that it can say a lot more to us than it says at present.

Before studying psychology, I was interested in two vague sets of questions: how the society around me operated and how I got to be the sort of person I was. I expected the two sets of questions to be related, although the former would be more characteristic of sociology and the latter more characteristic of social psychology. I got into psychology because Cambridge University didn't have much sociology and social psychology in 1963. Psychology at Cambridge seemed the next best thing. The social-psychology component of the course was very much an afterthought, and taught by a non-specialist, and I got more interested in brains, rats, monkeys and experiments. I convinced myself that this was the answer to human problems, steering a factual road between the unknown, but apparently vague, mysteries of philosophy and sociology.

However, this study of psychology had *nothing to do with my life* or with the issues of the world (about which I knew very little). As I see it now, I was only able to continue this study, given my initial interests, by postponing most of my life until after the final degree exams. This life, apart from psychology, consisted of the odd game of sport, not very deep or personal conversations, and trying rather unsuccessfully to learn how to get on with girls at the local hops. I had stopped asking the 'big' questions about life, morality, society, that I had been asking when I arrived. I was enclosed. I'm not blaming psychology for this, but psychology was instrumental in the process of enclosure and retreat, and I'm not sure that that is how it should be.

I was partially aware of all this and was glad to get a place to do research on 'social skills' at Oxford, where I hoped I could 'start living' and combine an experimental approach with a socially relevant topic that concerned people. I wanted to find out why some people found it easy to get on with others, whereas other people like myself didn't. However, my approach was reductionistic – the 'basic' explanation must be physiological. I pursued the line, cribbed from Eysenck, that individual differences in 'arousal' levels in the brain were responsible for individual differences in social skills. The reasoning was rather tortuous but it made sense on paper. I eventually got round to an experiment to see if there was any correlation between what I took to be behavioural measures of arousal and social skill. There weren't – but there were a few correlations between different measures of social skill. So there was something to 'follow up' in the second year.

Meanwhile, I had tried to 'start living', by doing more of the things I hadn't done at Cambridge: I spent more time with people, I vowed never to work in the evenings, I played a lot of cricket. After a while, I made some closer friends of both sexes than I had at Cambridge. Then, early in 1968, I fell in love at a distance, and made a complete mess of it. This experience turned me inside out, and all sorts of things took on meaning for me, which had never had much meaning before. I read Laing's *Divided Self* and it made sense, whereas I had not been able to get through it before; I got into Bob Dylan and into classical music, too; in general, I switched on to 'culture', whether literature, music or painting, and got interested in new ways of living without knowing what that implied. At the same time, the 'follow-up' experiment I was supposed to be doing lost all meaning and became a real burden: 'life' was catching up with my interest in social skills and making experiments on them seem pretty stupid.

I thought about 'dropping out' for a while. But before I'd really taken the idea seriously and worked it out, the 'May events' in France came along. Here were people actually *doing* some 'new ways of living' and getting put down for it. This raised in a much more urgent way the questions about why society is the way it is and how it might be different. So this began to replace culture as my central interest and I went along to some sociology lectures. Well, Parsons's theory of society was not exactly what I was looking for, and this put me off sociology and back, reluctantly, on to finishing my Ph.D. However, the follow-up experiment didn't work out at all, I met a girl who had been in Paris in May, and the Russian invasion of Czechoslovakia stifled a bit more freedom and made me very angry. So I looked into sociology again and found out that it *wasn't* all Parsons, and was told that sociologists *did* ask questions about values and changing society, and that it was possible to transfer to a B.Phil. in sociology. This time the wider world had caught up with me, and made the ideas of dropping out or getting a Ph.D. seem pretty stupid when there seemed so much to learn.

I got into sociology rather too single-mindedly and forgot about social psychology. Sociology didn't have the answers, though. After a training in experimental psychology, I found it incredibly abstract and inconclusive. Worst of all, it didn't seem to have much to say about people and their experience of living, nor about how society could be different, as opposed to explaining how it is. Again, I postponed things till after the exams: I would look into those questions later. Luckily, I got a job where I could do that, teaching social psychology in a sociology department. For the past three years, I've tried to look at people's experience in relation to the institutions of our society, and to put together a coherent course. It hasn't really worked since I lack a framework within which to do this. That is one reason for embarking on this book: to get together some ideas that will help me and other people who are dissatisfied with most social psychology and sociology.

Another reason is to do with social change. I had a flirtation with revolutionary politics in 1971 and found that, to an even greater extent than sociologists, most revolutionaries ignore people's experience both in their analyses and in their actions. Many questions that seemed important to me (for instance, about sex and sex roles, about psychiatry and about why people thought the way they did) were either not being asked, or being answered in a crude and dismissive way. Moreover, the personal relationships within these revolutionary groups appeared very cold and off-putting. So there were aspects of social change that were not being discussed on the Left, mostly, I thought, in the social-psychological area. These were either desirable components of social change in their own right (for example, the family, sex roles, mental illness, educational practice, personal relationships), or they were possible blocks to social change (i.e. if you don't bother to find out or take seriously what people think and why, you won't make the right proposal for action to change things). A second reason for editing the book, then, is to explore this whole area of the 'personal' and the 'political', and how we should analyse their relationship.

I see most social psychology as an alienated study by alienated people (I am guessing that my own alienation is not untypical). My original questions about 'how society operates' and about 'how I got to be the sort of person I was' were never really answered. In relation to social psychology, what was happening in my life and in the world around me made what I was studying seem trivial, boring and unrelated to the questions about values and social change that were concerning me. Now I think I would phrase the questions a different way: I want to know

1 Why we have the experiences we do have (we are probably not alone in our experience);

2 What the relationship is between those experiences and the way in which sets of people think and behave ('society' consisting of different sets of people affecting each other);

3 What might be done to change the situation, if necessary.

If we want to answer these questions, we need to have a developmental perspective on the individual (the accumulation of past experience), and a historical perspective on 'society' (the accumulation of other people's experience and ideas); we need to look at real-life behaviour and pay a lot of attention to people's experiences in real life; we need to look carefully at the social context of behaviour and experience; and we need to be involved in producing social change ourselves. I don't believe social psychology fills any of these needs adequately and I shall try to explain why that is a bit later in this introduction. The rest of the book contains other people's reason for these inadequacies and, more importantly perhaps, their suggestions for how we might do things better.

The account I have just given of my experience of social psychology does not fulfil the criteria in the previous paragraph. An adequate account would have to include, at least, my prior personal history and socialization; the relationship of these experiences to wider social norms, values and practices; and the function of those norms, values and practices in relation to the class structure and the institutions of a technocratic society. However, I have been self-indulgent enough as it is, and I don't want to involve other people directly in what I say for the purpose of criticizing social psychology.

A view of social psychology

There are, in my view, two main traditions in social psychology, between which there has been precious little contact, since they have been institutionalized in university psychology and sociology departments respectively: hence the most appropriate labels for these traditions are 'psychological social psychology' and 'sociological social psychology'. The former definitely has more influence on social-psychology courses, whether because its adherents have produced more and better work, or because sociological social psychologists often call themselves sociologists, or because psychology carries more 'scientific' prestige than sociology.

'Psychological social psychology' is an outgrowth of general psychology, and, like its parent, was formed as a reaction to 'heresies' current in the early 1900s. In the case of general psychology, this heresy was introspectionism, the idea that you could get at psychological truths by examining the contents of your own consciousness. The reaction to this was behaviourism, which maintained that the only reliable data are publicly observable pieces of behaviour. Psychological social psychology also repudiated introspectionism and emphasized publicly observable behaviour. Furthermore, it reacted against 'instinct' theories, which explained different sorts of social behaviour by means of different instincts, and against 'group-mind' theories, which suggested that there was some form of consciousness over and above the consciousnesses of individuals. Neither of these sorts of theories was felt to have any convincing evidence to support it.

These three reactions established characteristic features of psychological social psychology that are still with us, and can be illustrated from my own research. The emphasis on publicly observable behaviour has resulted in an external approach to people: it is what they do that is important, rather than what they think or say. So, for instance, I tried to measure social skill through ratings of video-tape recordings of people interacting with a stooge – I didn't ask the people how they experienced the situation or what they thought about their 'social skill'.

The reaction against 'instinct' theories resulted in a very cautious attitude towards motivation: many social psychologists were for a long time reluctant to think in terms of motives other than the basic hunger, thirst and comfort drives. When they were, these other motives were derived from the basic drives and were conceptualized as 'needs' inside the individual, rather than as motives generated by the social world or as spontaneous human capacities. Even Gestalt-influenced social psychologists, who did at least think of motivation as arising from the 'immediate psychological field', had a tension-reduction interpretation of how it operated, similar to that of Hull. My notion of social motivation was the ultimate in physiological reductionism: I conceived of the human organism as trying to maintain an 'optimal level of cortical arousal' in the brain, whereby an 'overaroused' person (introvert) would avoid social situations, whereas an 'underaroused' one (extravert) would seek them out.

Lastly, the reaction against 'group-mind' theories led to an atomistic approach to social psychology: even when examining groups of people, the unit of explanation is the individual and his individual characteristics. For example, my conception of social skill was of a characteristic located inside an individual, rather than of a feeling that was generated between two or more people and that itself reflected wider social norms and values. The external and individualistic approaches to people still remain within psychological social psychology, even if the approach to motivation has broadened in recent years.

Between the two World Wars, general psychology tried to get out of the problems of introspectionism by relying primarily upon the *experimental* study of the *behaviour* of *non-human organisms*. The *experiment* enabled the existence and direction of causality to be inferred; *behaviour* was publicly observable; *non-human organisms* could be experimented upon with impunity and would reveal the basic laws of behaviour in their stark simplicity. The fact that the experimental 'subjects' could not report back to the experimenter did not matter, since verbal reports amounted to unreliable introspection. These psychologists adopted the presumed natural- and physical-science methods of investigation that were being propagated at the time by the 'logical positivist' philosophers. Logical positivists maintained that the sciences, physical, natural and social, are all one and that the same basic approach was applicable to them all, namely the approach of the physical sciences; they also maintained that abstract statements that do not refer to concrete, verifiable physical entities should be inadmissible in scientific discourse – the meaning of a statement consists in the method by which it is verified. This was interpreted to mean that psychology should proceed by formulating specific predictions about observable behaviour that are falsifiable empirically: usually by doing an experiment. Scientific laws would be deduced gradually from the results of many such experiments. Furthermore, the meaning of psychological concepts is contained in the operations by which they can be measured – these 'operational definitions' are the stuff of psychological research. Consciousness, experience and inner states can only be studied if they can be 'operationally defined' in terms of measurable behaviour.

Practically speaking, this philosophical position meant that psychologists should proceed by operationalizing their concepts as measurable variables, and then including these variables in an experimental design. The independent variable(s) is to be varied by the experimenter with different groups of subjects to see if these variations have any effect upon the dependent variable(s), which is usually some aspect of the subjects' behaviour that can be measured. The results of such an experiment can be analysed in two basic ways – the difference between the mean scores of different groups of subjects on the dependent variable can be examined, or the researcher can attempt to account for the observed variation ('variance') in the dependent variable in terms of variations in the independent variables (the procedure known as 'analysis of variance'). Failing this ideal of an experimental investigation, the researcher should certainly concentrate upon measuring observable behaviour on some sort of scale and correlating his different measures with each other to try and locate where causal connections might exist to test experimentally.

This positivist way of doing things was adopted by psychological social psychologists, except that they concentrated upon the experimental study of the *social* behaviour of *human* organisms. However, the carry-over from general psychology was considerable, in particular affecting the way in which the crucial word 'social' was interpreted. From early on, psychological social psychology conceived of the 'social' as the *interaction between organisms* leading to differences in behavioural output, these organisms being abstracted from any ongoing real-life social context and processes. For instance, many of the first social-psychology experiments were on 'co-action' or 'social facilitation' as it is now called (i.e. the influence upon behaviour of the presence of other people); and out of twenty-three articles in the 1935 *Handbook of Social Psychology*, no fewer than eight were about non-human organisms, including bacteria and plants! Such an emphasis was only possible with a mechanical view of the 'social' as being to do with the influence of organisms upon each other in the manner of particles or molecules. Despite the presence of many broad-minded statements about social psychology, this 'interaction' conception of the 'social' runs through the influential first chapter of Murphy, Barclay and Newcomb (1937). This conception underlay Moreno's sociometry, which was about charting the likes and dislikes between people, and informs the way in which many psychological social psychologists still think. Argyle's recent text book on social psychology is entitled *Social Interaction* and one of the currently popular descriptions of social psychology is the 'study of social influence' (for example, Hollander, 1971; Wright *et al.*, 1970). Such a conception of the 'social' fits very well with the experimental study of behaviour along the lines of general psychology, since animal behaviour and social behaviour between people can both be studied by means of the public observation and measurement of the external behavioural characteristics of individuals.

So what is psychological social psychology trying to achieve with data obtained in this way? Despite a plea by Murphy, Barclay and Newcomb that social psychology should be concerned with the 'life history of the person socially defined', psychological social psychology has moved away from any such developmental approach, abandoning it to 'child' and 'developmental' psychology. Instead the quest has been for 'general laws of social behaviour', just as other psychologists seek 'general laws of behaviour'. These general laws were to be discovered on the basis of laboratory experiments that established generalizations about what produces what in social behaviour. It was hoped that these general laws would apply irrespective of culture and social situation, just as the general laws of psychology were to apply to all organisms and all situations.

There has been some difference of opinion amongst psychological social psychologists about the nature of these general laws of social behaviour. Some consider that any general laws of psychology should also apply to social behaviour and thus see social psychology as a special case of general psychology.[1] They often take the categories and concepts of general psychology and study 'social' factors in relation to them (for example, social learning, social motivation, social perception, social communication), usually using the explanatory frameworks of general psychology to do so (stimulus–response, learning theory, information theory, etc.). Other psychological social psychologists, probably the majority, believe that social behaviour requires laws of its own, which cannot be derived from the principles of general psychology. This, they feel, is especially true of small-group behaviour, and behaviour for which there are no obvious non-social parallels (for example, conformity and leadership). However, both sets of people are looking for laws about social behaviour that apply irrespective of social situation (bar, meeting, party), culture (ghetto, Chinese, heterosexual) or history (Elizabethan England, the depression, the McCarthy era). Hence the focus is upon general laws to do with such abstract general categories as attitude change, conformity, leadership, small-group interaction, integroup relations, rather than upon the 'contents' of social life: *what* attitudes people hold, *what* they are conforming to, *what* the group is trying to achieve, *what* the issues of contention are between groups. The interest is in the 'how' of social behaviour (its mechanics or form) rather than the 'what' (its substance or content). For instance, Lana (1969, pp. 162–3), a traditional social psychologist, remarks:

While working in the area of persuasive communication for several years, I became increasingly aware of what I thought to be a curious fact about research in this area, including my own work. We were almost always concerned with aspects

1. For example, Zajonc (1966); McGinnies (1970); McGinnies and Ferster (1971); Ulrich and Mountjoy (1972); Stotland and Canon (1972).

of the communicative situation which had little to do with the content, that is, with the empirical and logical aspects of the message that was being communicated. Most of us were interested in one or more of the following variables: the controversiality of the issue referred to in the communication, the awareness by the subject of the manipulatory intent of the communicator, the style used by the communicator, his prestige, the length of the communication, the medium used to transmit the communication. . . . This research focus was not an accident of the interest patterns of the various psychologists doing work in communication. Of that I was convinced. Was it a natural by-product of American behaviourist tradition to focus on just about anything but meaning . . . ?

In fact, Lana goes on to explain the situation in terms of McLuhan's ideas, but I think he was right first time.

When you combine the striving for general laws with a conception of the 'social' in terms of interaction between organisms and with the experimental, laboratory method, you end up with a social psychology that systematically ignores, both in its conceptualizations and in its predominant method, the social context in which social behaviour occurs. This is the main reason why psychological social psychology is up a blind alley. With the best of scientific intentions, it has left itself high and dry by ignoring social contexts which should not be taken for granted.

Two defences against these criticisms have been made by psychological social psychologists: firstly, that they ignore the work of Lewin and those he influenced (for example, Asch, Barker, Festinger, Sherif, Deutsch, Cartwright, Crutchfield, Newcomb); and secondly, that there is anyway plenty of work, especially recently, that does not ignore the social context or 'real-life' issues. It is true that the Gestalt school of social psychology, stemming especially from Lewin, has stressed the immediate social context acting upon the individual and has done some real-life research, *but*

1 Lewin himself, and most of the above-mentioned 'followers', still see social psychology as conforming to the same principles as general psychology (though those principles may be conceived rather differently from usual).

2 They still seek general laws, irrespective of social situation.

3 They have often been co-opted into laboratory experimentation, emphasizing the 'how' rather than the 'what' of social behaviour (especially Asch, Festinger, Deutsch and Crutchfield).

Lewin was also associated with the Society for the Psychological Study of Social Issues, which has been encouraging 'relevant' research by social psychologists since 1936 and publishing some of it in the *Journal of Social*

Issues. Personally, I welcome some of this material, while pointing out that a lot of the research is in the interests of the political status quo (especially in relation to industry and American foreign policy).[2] Recently, other journals have contained more 'real-life' and 'relevant' research, but most of it is couched within the positivist, organismic framework that I have outlined and manages to ignore the meaning of the situation to the participants and to depoliticize the social context.

'Sociological social psychology' is a more amorphous thing. It derives from the theoretical writings of Cooley, Thomas and Mead[3] in the same period which saw the establishment of psychological social psychology. These writings stemmed from a dissatisfaction with both the instinct/group-mind theories of social life and the behaviourist reaction to such theories. They emphasized that the crucial environmental influences on social behaviour were symbolic and derived primarily from language use in social interaction (hence the name 'symbolic interactionism', which is often seen as synonymous with sociological social psychology). Cooley and Mead concentrated on social interaction in developmental perspective, talking about the 'looking-glass self' and 'taking-the-role-of-the-other' in relation to the young child, while Thomas's 'definition of the situation' is more concerned with interaction in the here-and-now social situation. However, they all wanted to stress that the individual, his sense of self-identity and his behaviour are produced and moulded through social interaction. The symbolic interactionist tries to study these processes as they occur in social settings.

However, these writings did not at first throw up much in the way of research; rather, they were incorporated into the mainstream of American sociological thinking. A more important influence upon social psychology at this time was that of anthropologists studying the relationships between culture and personality. Margaret Mead's work, in particular, made a big impact, but we should note that personality was seen in predominantly Freudian terms and that the effects were seen as one-way and deterministic. These studies are always referred to in psychological social psychology texts, but their full implications concerning the 'social construction of personality' are not drawn out: instead they are taken to demonstrate, for example, the 'plasticity' of the human organism, and to sound a pious warning about possible cultural variability.

Theoretical developments in sociological social psychology had to wait until the Second World War and its aftermath, when we find various

2. See Beckman (1973). A recent exception is the funding by the SPSSI of the research for Fields (1973).
3. See articles by these authors in Manis and Meltzer (1967).

formulations of 'reference-group' theory, and of 'role' theory, which elaborate the conceptual apparatus for discussing and explaining social behaviour, and form a link with the social context in which behaviour occurs. In the early 1950s sociological social psychology became something of an adjunct to the dominant framework in American sociology, i.e. structural functionalism as propounded by Parsons. This is a rather deterministic way of looking at society, stressing how all the parts of society fit together to maintain the 'social system' in equilibrium. 'Roles' are parts of the social system into which individuals have to fit; 'attitudes' reflect the norms and values of the wider society; 'personality' is the product of adequate 'socialization' procedures necessary if society is to run smoothly.

After the war many sociologists were concerned with the reconstruction of shattered communities and the rehabilitation of shattered individuals. Small-scale community studies paying attention to 'social-psychological' factors, were very much in vogue, and a sub-discipline of 'small-group sociology' emerged. It is perhaps not surprising that much of this research was basically about how individuals fit, or in some cases do not fit, into the social system.

By and large, then, sociological social psychology has not contributed much to social psychology, and indeed, it is virtually ignored on most courses, with perhaps a passing reference to Mead and a nod in the direction of role theory.[4] One reason for this exclusion is that symbolic interactionism is considered 'interesting' but waffly and unempirical by psychological social psychologists. Its predominant method is 'participant observation', the attempt of the researcher to immerse himself in the social situation so as to understand it properly. Depending as it does on verbal reports and interpretation of the meaning of people's behaviour, this method is not trusted by most psychologists. Some symbolic interactionists have even moved in the direction of quantification. Other people who might call themselves sociological social psychologists spend their time measuring attitudes of one sort or another on scales or questionnaires. However, they tend to be indistinguishable from many empirical sociologists.

Instead of symbolic interactionism, the favourite import from sociology to social psychology courses has been 'exchange theory' as propounded by Homans. This is an attempt to ground sociology in the psychology of reward and punishment: people do things if the rewards are great enough and don't do them if the costs are too great. Rewards and costs are the

4. There are however some significant recent developments, discussion of which I am postponing till the final section of this introduction.

cement holding society together at every level. Whether or not this works for sociology some social psychologists have embraced the idea fervently. It connects conveniently with behaviouristic psychology; it provides a convenient interpretative framework for most behaviour; and it leads to convenient research designs, as exemplified by all the 'game theory' studies. Apart from this, there has been precious little convergence or even contact between psychological and sociological social psychologists. Most of the contributors to this book are more sympathetic towards sociological social psychology, especially present developments in it, but that does not exclude it from considerable criticism.[5]

Some similarities between the two traditions in social psychology

Although some qualifications will have to be made I think it is possible to identify important similarities between the traditions both in what they do and in what they don't do.

Positivist ways of thinking have had considerable influence on both sorts of social psychology: social facts, like other facts, are out there in the world and it's just a question of measuring them somehow. That is a difficult task, of course, but it's basically a technical problem of improving our measuring techniques and statistical analyses. Then we can test our hypotheses accurately. Psychological social psychology favours experiments for getting at the facts, and some sociological social psychologists use scales and questionnaires. In both cases the truth, significance and meaning of the facts that are produced by these methods are taken for granted. Perhaps these 'true' facts are themselves produced only by the methods designed to discover them. The artificiality of the experimental and questionnaire situations is not questioned too deeply, or when it is, it becomes an area for further research along similar lines (experiments on the 'social psychology of the psychology experiment'). Nor is it realized the extent to which people are constrained by these methods – in an experiment the subject is *provided* with a situation in which there are usually a limited number of things he can do; in a questionnaire, the respondent is answering prestructured questions, usually with a limited choice of replies. Moreover, it is the researcher who is determining the content of the experiment or questionnaire so that the facts produced may tell us more about him than about the subject! Can we ignore the meaning of these situations to the subject? How does he interpret the situation and what does this lead him to do? Can we accept that the social psychologist is not *creating* reality, rather than discovering it?

5. Other recent introductions to symbolic interactionism are Rose (1962); Lindesmith and Strauss (1968); Stone and Farberman (1970); Cardwell (1971).

Furthermore, is quantification suitable for much of the 'data' of social psychology? Psychological social psychology, in particular, but some sociological social psychology, too, tries to operationalize its concepts as variables, and then to account for all the variance in the dependent variable as the ultimate goal of research. But if you spend your time concentrating upon variations, aren't you likely to forget about the *nature* of what you are studying and why it is there in the first place? For instance, if you set about accounting for variations in prejudice, won't you tend to ignore the nature and meaning of prejudice as a social phenomenon and what this might tell us about why there is prejudice at all? Does not the quantification of behavioural indices make unjustified assumptions about the meaning of behaviour to the different actors displaying the 'same' behaviour? And can you capture all that is of significance in a social situation in a series of variables? Eysenck has recently tried to do this in relation to the I Q scores of black people – he quantifies education as 'number of years in school', and 'stigma' as 'rated self-esteem'. Does the educational experience of a black person amount to number of years in school? And does a lifetime's stigmatization reflect itself in where a black person marks a rating scale of self-esteem? In general, can you quantify the nature of a person's experience, his interpretation of his surroundings, the meaning of his statements, the nature of his emotions?

A *deterministic* bias can also be seen in much of social psychology. Psychological social psychologists imagine they are discovering laws of nature that explain the way people behave in social situations. Sociological social psychologists have looked for the roles and rules, the norms and values that govern people's social behaviour. Despite this important difference, however, both tend to see people's behaviour as determined, in the one case by laws to do with human nature, in the other case by man-made prescriptions. These laws and prescriptions are thought to act upon behaviour in a cause-and-effect manner, leaving the individual little room for manoeuvre. But are people pushed around by natural laws and social forces? Or do we choose what we do for our own good or bad reasons, *influenced* by our human nature and by social forces, but not determined by them? Do we not create meaning and construct our social worlds out of what is available to us?

Another similarity between both social psychologies rests in their refusal to recognize that values are mixed up in just about everything they do. To put it more generally, ideological influences on social psychology are denied. Social psychology is supposed to be a value-neutral, objective activity, and that is how it should be, for most social psychologists. If values *are* allowed into the picture, they are usually admitted only in the initial choice of research problem, and in the ways in which others may use the results. Ethical questions about research procedures (for example, deception, confidentiality) are also discussed. But this leaves out of account a whole host of value issues to do with the formulation of the problem (what questions are being asked, and who is asking them?), the concepts used (whose values are lurking in a concept like 'adjustment'?), the methodology used (do survey questions have values built into them?), the role of the social psychologist as researcher (does he get involved or stand back?) and the presentation of results (who has access to them?).

The last major similarity that I am going to try and bring out is the inadequate treatment of the 'social' in social psychology. I have already mentioned how psychological social psychology thinks of the 'social' as to do with observable social interaction. This definition of the 'social' has excluded a serious developmental or historical perspective. However, we need to follow the development and change of social behaviour and experience over time both in the individual and in society. Sociological social psychology does concern itself more with the development of the individual, but has also lacked a historical perspective, adopting a rather static view of society.

On the whole, though, sociological social psychology does have a richer conception of the 'social': stemming from Mead's work, it places much more emphasis upon how 'society' gets built into the 'mind' and the 'self' through socialization. Thus the 'social' is not just something that occurs when people meet, but is involved more deeply in our very thoughts and identities. However, even sociological social psychology tends to neglect many of the social influences at work in our society. It has concentrated upon the sub-institutional areas of life i.e. those areas that are relatively independent of the major social institutions, and upon unusual social situations. It also has concentrated upon the 'how' of interaction, rather than the 'what' – symbolic-interactionist books (see p. 18) are full of material on processes of interaction rather than on its contents and contexts. In fact, neither sort of social psychology has much to say about the ways in which people experience and are influenced by their jobs, their schools, their families, their skin colour, their religion. If they do deal with these institutional areas, they tend to assume that the way things are is inevitable in an industrialized society, rather than being the product of specific social conditions and values which could be changed, or at least responded to in different ways, by individuals.

Present developments

It would be ridiculous to imply that the ideas in this book are particularly new or startling: they must be seen against the background of what is happening in social psychology and sociology at the present time. Doubts are being felt in both disciplines about what we are doing and how we are doing it.

In psychological social psychology, Ring (1967) has protested about the 'fun and games' attitude of many social psychologists to their experiments and Kelman (1968) has worried about the dehumanizing effects of social-science research techniques in general, and their possible use in social control. Don Mixon has contributed to this line of thought and develops his ideas in this book. Quite a lot of people are worried about the laboratory experiment as a valid research procedure and are trying to broaden the basis of psychological social psychology.[6] John Rowan is one of these people, and in his essay here he takes the argument further by questioning the passive role of the researcher. Other people are worried about the validity of questionnaires and both Martin Roiser and John Heritage question that validity from a wider perspective than is usually adopted.

The philosophical assumptions of psychological social psychology have recently been discussed by Lana (1969) and criticized by Harré and Secord (1972). George Gross, John Shotter and Rom Harré continue this process in the present essays. Another recent publication, edited by Israel and Tajfel (1972), also includes several fairly wide-ranging criticisms of psychological social psychology: Moscovici complains that current theories neglect the social nature of man and his place in society, in particular symbolic communication and ideology; Tajfel points to the neglect of the social context in experiments and to the attempt to 'account causally for human social behaviour in terms of "general" laws of individual motivation' – instead, we should be studying 'psychological processes accompanying, determining and determined by social change'; both Israel and Asplund raise value issues in relation to social psychology and stress that they are intertwined both in the presuppositions and in the effects of our theories; Israel also draws a contrast between the view that theories reflect the facts of social reality and the view that theories construct reality both by conferring meaning upon the data and by actually bringing about changes in the world. Many of these issues will be taken up in the essays in this book, but why not also consult the fuller discussions in Israel and Tajfel?

6. See Bickman and Henchy (1972); Rowan (1973a, 1973b).

Another important development, at least in America, is the plea for 'social relevance' and significance. This can be seen in various forms, from the stirrings at conferences to the use of literature and social comment, to the concern with 'relevance' in some recent textbooks.[7] The result, in my view, has been that the existing concepts and methods have been applied to social issues and illustrated through literary extracts, rather than that these concepts and methods have been rethought. We try to address ourselves to that rethinking. Nowhere is this rethinking more important than in the vexed area of biological influences upon social characteristics such as 'intelligence', 'violence' and 'schizophrenia'. Martin Richards's essay begins the necessary reconstruction of the nature of these relationships.

Others of us make use of ideas that have developed within what is known as 'humanistic psychology' or 'third-force psychology'. This movement has grown in reaction to the dominant orthodoxies of behaviourism and psychoanalysis, both of which are seen as too deterministic. Instead, humanistic psychology stresses man's potential for change and growth and that he can be active and self-directed in bringing about such changes. Also, man must be seen as a whole, not in the bits and pieces into which behaviourism and role analysis divide him up. Although these ideas have had most influence upon therapy, they are thought to have a wider applicability.[8] Several of our essays are influenced by this model of man, especially those by John Shotter, John Rowan, Geoff Pearson and Denis Pym.

Another, related, strand of thinking that affects the contents of our book is *phenomenology*. Phenomenologists have been sniping away at psychology for a long time, especially in Europe. Now they seem to be making some impact. Phenomenology has been gaining more ground in sociology, however, with books like Berger and Luckman (1967) and Filmer *et al.* (1972) encouraging a renewal of interest in Schutz (1932). The motivation for this has been a dissatisfaction with the lifelessness, the statistical orientation and the sweeping generalizations of much of macro-sociology, which was felt to leave people out of account. In general, phenomenology stresses that we must 'get back to the phenomenon' we are examining, by trying to rid ourselves of all preconceptions about it. We must pay attention to the experience of the perceiver or actor, both the nature of the experience and how that experience is built up over time. 'Phenomena' are not events in the outside world, perceived by a passive observer, but *interpretations* by an active subject who invests his environment with

7. See Korten, Cook and Lacey (1970); Fernandez (1972); Wrightsman (1972); Swingle (1973).
8. See Maslow (1973); Rogers (1961).

meaning and acts intentionally in relation to that environment. Given this general perspective, social psychology begins to look rather different, and phenomenological influences can be seen in the essays by, for example, Tim Lang, Rom Harré and myself.

One particular development out of phenomenology has been 'ethnomethodology'. Ethnomethodologists are interested in the experience of the actor, too, but maintain that we can never actually get at that experience. Instead, we have to rely upon how the actor himself describes and accounts for his experience and for what he does. These descriptions and accounts are, or rather should be, the data of sociological investigation. Ethnomethodologists then try to study how these 'accounting procedures' make sense of the social world for participants by providing a sense of order and social structure. In doing this, a process of negotiation goes on between different participants' accounts of what is going on, and what should therefore be done, in social situations. Ethnomethodologists study these processes and hope thereby to arrive at the basic rules of everyday life – however, this involves a certain amount of interpretation, which ethnomethodologists recognize is just *their* interpretation of what is going on, rather than any final explanation of reality. This perspective has been very controversial in recent years, and seems to be gaining adherents.[9] In the present book, John Heritage outlines an ethnomethodological position on attitudes and assessment, while David Triesman criticizes the relatavistic approval of ethnomethodology of official statistics, and Henrietta Resler and Paul Walton briefly question their treatment of the 'social'.

In the last section, I did not mention Goffman or recent symbolic interactionists. This was because these writers appear to contain the germs of a rather different perspective, moving away from the idea that people are determined by their roles in society, as structural-functionalist sociology would have us believe. The notion of 'role' was being elaborated and refined in the 1950s by sociologists like Merton, Turner and Gross. People were seen as having some flexibility within their role-specifications, and, moreover, actively constructing their roles. Goffman noticed how people often stand back from their roles and indicate that they are not totally 'in' their roles (calling this 'role-distance'). More recently, the whole concept of role has come in for some heavy criticism (Jackson, 1972).

Goffman also placed a lot of emphasis upon the 'work' that people do to maintain the self-image that they are presenting in interaction. This, together with his concept of role-distance, implies a certain amount of

9. The best introduction I have been able to find is Douglas (1971), especially the articles by Zimmerman.

agency on the part of the individual – he is not totally determined by social forces. However, this aspect of Goffman's work became submerged in his later work, where he sees individuals as 'making out' precariously in relation to the overpowering weight of the social order (1969; 1972a; 1972b). Atkinson (1971) has recently tried to formulate this 'submerged strand' in sociology into an alternative that stresses how people see situations and act in them according to their own 'situational logic'. The structural concepts of macro-sociology are then reformulated to accommodate people's active construction of their social worlds.

The area of sociological social psychology in which the active, self-determining individual has been given most credit has been symbolic interactionist studies of deviants. One of the complaints against symbolic interactionism is that it has tended to concentrate on the 'bizarre', but at least in this area the problems of identity-formation and -maintenance have been thrown into sharp relief. If you study hipsters, dwarfs, nudists and marginal occupations of various sorts, you are sensitized to how people construct a world for themselves and make sense of it with each other (Truzzi, 1968). Perhaps, also, such people are *forced* to be more self-determining than most of us! At any rate, such studies have been disproportionately influential, and have led to a recognition of the importance of seeing the *actor's* point of view which has had profound effects upon criminology and the study of deviance in general (Cohen, 1971). This 'appreciative' stance is evident here in the essays by Tim Lang, Godfrey Harrison and myself.

Another recent move in sociology has been away from the assumption of a cohesive society where everyone is in basic agreement about values and consents to the existing social order, towards a view of society in which power, conflict and coercion are fundamental ingredients. However, a straightforward, 'vulgar Marxist' account of opposing class interests doesn't make a lot of sense in the face of the continued election of conservative governments in the West. We also need an understanding of 'ideology' – how the ideas of people in power get passed off as eternal truths and serve to disguise competing interests and justify what the powerful do. The domain of ideology concerns academic theories, including social-psychological ones, as well as the ideas of the 'man in the street'.

Marxism has never had much of a social psychology, seeing these issues as secondary to the macro-problems of social structure.[10] True, there is also a 'submerged tradition' in Marxism (which Marxists will argue isn't really submerged!) that stresses man as active producer and world-creator. Despite this, Marxists have not usually bothered to show how their

10. Except perhaps for Reich (1972) and Brown (1973).

analysis makes sense of what is going on at the interactional level in the various social institutions of our society. That is an important task for the future.[11] The essays in this book on ideology are not 'strictly' Marxist, but Marxist-influenced to different degrees: Martin Roiser, Joan Busfield, George Gross, Graham Murdock and David Ingleby all explore distortions of ideas in relation to social psychology that serve to maintain our present institutions, while Henrietta Resler, Paul Walton and David Triesman all try to conceptualize the relationship between micro- and macro-levels from a Marxist standpoint; and as an adjunct to this introduction Peter Sedgwick presents a short Marxist criticism of psychology as a whole.

Broadly speaking, then, I think we can identify three 'alternative' strands in the social sciences which we consider have something to contribute to a reconstructed social psychology: humanistic psychology, phenomenology and Marxism. There are many differences between these perspectives; nevertheless, they do all imply a view of man as constrained in various ways, but struggling to understand those constraints and to overcome them through intentional social action. We do not imagine that these strands of thinking will miraculously 'solve' the problems of social psychology, nor that they are enough by themselves. But they are at least a background against which we can view the current state of social psychology, and a source from which we can perhaps develop a social psychology that does not leave us dissatisfied and that helps to create a more human world.

11. See Lichtman (1970). Some vaguely Marxist assaults have been made on psychology and psychiatry as social institutions: see Agel (1971, 1973); the pamphlet *Rat, Myth and Magic* (Russell Press, 1972); and the magazines *Red Rat* and *Humpty Dumpty* (see p. 330).

References

AGEL, J. (1971), *The Radical Therapist*, Ballantine; Penguin, 1974.

AGEL, J. (1973), *Rough Times*, Ballantine.

ATKINSON, D. (1971), *Orthodox Consensus and Radical Alternative*, Heinemann.

BECKMAN, L. (1973), 'Psychology as a social problem: an investigation into the Society for the Psychological Study of Social Issues', in J. Agel, *Rough Times*, Ballantine, 1973.

BERGER, P., and LUCKMAN, T. (1967), *The Social Construction of Reality*, Allen Lane The Penguin Press; Penguin, 1972.

BICKMAN, L., and HENCHY, T. (eds.) (1972), *Beyond the Laboratory: Field Research in Social Psychology*, McGraw-Hill.

BROWN, P. (ed.) (1973), *Radical Psychology*, Tavistock.

CARDWELL, J. D. (1971), *Social Psychology: A Symbolic Interactionist Perspective*, Davis.

COHEN, S. (ed.) (1971), *Images of Deviance*, Penguin.

DOUGLAS, J. D. (ed.) (1971), *Understanding Everyday Life*, Routledge & Kegan Paul.

FERNANDEZ, R. (ed.) (1972), *Social Psychology through Literature*, Wiley.

FIELDS, R. (1973), *A Society on the Run: A Psychology of Northern Ireland*, Penguin.

FILMER, P. *et al.* (1972), *New Directions in Sociological Theory*, Collier-Macmillan.

GOFFMAN, E. (1969), *The Presentation of Self in Everyday Life*, Penguin.

GOFFMAN, E. (1972a), *Encounters*, Penguin.

GOFFMAN, E. (1972b), *Relations in Public*, Penguin.

HARRÉ, R., and SECORD, P. F. (1972), *The Explanation of Social Behaviour*, Blackwell.

HOLLANDER, E. (1971), *Principles and Methods of Social Psychology*, Oxford University Press.

ISRAEL, J., and TAJFEL, H. (eds.) (1972), *The Context of Social Psychology: A Critical Assessment*, Academic Press.

JACKSON, J. A. (ed.) (1972), *Role*, Cambridge University Press.

KELMAN, H. C. (1968), *A Time to Speak*, Jossey-Bass.

KORTEN, F. F., COOK, S. W., and LACEY, J. I. (eds.) (1970), *Psychology and the Problems of Society*, American Psychological Association.

LANA, R. E. (1969), *Assumptions of Social Psychology*, Appleton-Century-Crofts.

LICHTMAN, R. (1970), 'Symbolic interactionism and social reality: some Marxist queries', *Berkeley J. Sociol.*, vol. 15, p. 75.

LINDESMITH, A. R., and STRAUSS, A. L. (1968), *Social Psychology*, 3rd edn, Dryden.

Manis, J. G., and Meltzer, B. N. (eds.) (1967), *Symbolic Interaction: A Reader in Social Psychology*, Allyn & Bacon.

Maslow, A. (1973), *The Farther Reaches of Human Nature*, Penguin.

McGinnies, E. (1970), *Social Psychology: A Functional Analysis*, Houghton Mifflin.

McGinnies, E., and Ferster, C. B. (eds.) (1971), *The Reinforcement of Social Behavior*, Houghton Mifflin.

Murphy, G., Barclay, L. B., and Newcomb, T. M. (1937), *Experimental Social Psychology*, Greenwood.

Reich, W. (1972), *Mass Psychology of Fascism*, Souvenir Press.

Ring, K. (1967), 'Experimental social psychology: some sober questions about some frivolous values', *J. exp. soc. Psychol.*, vol. 3, pp. 113–23.

Rogers, C. (1961), *On Becoming a Person*, Houghton Mifflin.

Rose, A. M. (1962), *Human Behavior and Social Processes*, Routledge & Kegan Paul.

Rowan, J. (1973a), *The Science of You*, Davis-Poynter.

Rowan, J. (1973b), *The Social Individual*, Davis-Poynter.

Schutz, A. (1932), *The Phenomenology of the Social World*, Heinemann.

Stone, G. P., and Farberman, H. A. (eds.) (1970), *Social Psychology through Symbolic Interaction*, Ginn-Blaisdell.

Stotland, E., and Canon, L. K. (1972), *Social Psychology: A Cognitive Approach*, Saunders.

Swingle, P. G. (ed.) (1973), *Social Psychology in Everyday Life*, Penguin.

Truzzi, M. (ed.) (1968), *Sociology and Everyday Life*, Prentice–Hall.

Ulrich, R., and Mountjoy, P. (eds.) (1972), *The Experimental Analysis of Social Behaviour*, Appleton–Century–Crofts.

Wright, D. S., Taylor, A., Roy Davies, D., Sluckin, W., Lee, S. G. M., and Reason, J. T. (1970) *Introducing Psychology*, Penguin.

Wrightsman, L. (1972), *Social Psychology in the Seventies*, Brooks–Cole.

Zajonc, R. B. (1966), *Social Psychology: An Experimental Approach*, Wadsworth.

Ideology in Modern Psychology[1]
eter Sedgwick

t gives me special delight to address a session of psychologists held at the
niversity in whose Psychology Department I obtained my first-ever paid
ob, as a humble Demonstrator. This pleasure is enriched by the recollec-
on that it was during my work at this post, around fourteen years ago,
hat an early publication of mine, a satirical article which the student
magazine intended to print, provoked the ire of the then Vice-Chancellor
nd other senior academic authorities. Their foolish censorship was
nstrumental in detonating the first mass student explosion that occurred
n post-war Britain, well in advance of more recent manifestations. The
tudent response was, however, incapable of defending me against the
hreat, emanating from the topside of the university's power structure, to
eprive me of my non-tenured appointment. In this predicament, with a
amentable lack of support from my own department, I preferred, instead
f awaiting the sack, to leave the university for a succession of posts
ncluding a spell of teaching in the prison service, where a greater in-
ellectual freedom was afforded me. This particular encounter between
sychology and society formed a harsh but instructive lesson.

In beginning work on this talk, drafted as the opening for a discussion
n the relationship between psychology as a discipline and the pressures
r influences on it from the society which both includes and surrounds the
aboratory, Thomas Kuhn's celebrated concept of the scientific *paradigm*
eemed the most useful organizing motif. If one could identify a central
paradigm', in the sense of a governing theoretical standpoint associated
vith a body of scientific achievement, which was ascribable to psychology
t any one time, it might be possible to trace links between this specialist
antage-point and a particular social or historical context. However, it
eems that Kuhn's concept of the paradigm is insufficient for this purpose.
As well as the paradigm, the structuring body of scientific precedent, we
eed to consider two other categories of analysis, which I shall term the
erspective and the *problematic*.

. A talk given for the 'Psychology and Society' session of the 1973 Annual
Conference of the British Psychological Society held at the University of Liverpool.

By a 'perspective', I mean a vision of human possibility – including th
restrictions on human potential that flow from certain perspectives; by
'problematic', I mean the set of conceptual problems that one chooses t
start from. Psychology has many paradigms; but one paradigm may b
compatible with several perspectives. Thus we have the paradigm of, sa
Pavlovian or of Freudian theory: but either of these has been taken to b
conformable with either a Marxist or a liberal or indeed a conservativ
perspective on human nature and on the alternative social institution
within which man's nature may become fulfilled. And while psychology
admittedly a 'multi-paradigm science' (a category usefully discussed i
recent papers by Masterman, 1970, and Burgess, 1972), when we contras
it as a body of thought and achievement with other social-science dis
ciplines, such as economic history or anthropology, it is clearly distinguishe
from these by a very specific problematic of its own: namely, that it deal
with problems arising from observations that a suitably trained researche
may make in relation to a discrete subject, or to a plurality of such sub
jects, whether human or animal, within conditions designed to reduc
error. All the paradigms of psychology, including those belonging t
psychoanalysis and to social psychology, seem to occur within this centra
mode of posing problems. There are of course exceptions to it in socia
psychology, especially those areas dealing with social movements an
mass behaviour; but at this point the resulting cumulation of theory an
data can equally well be called social psychology or sociology, since ther
is a break with the special problematic of the psychological enterprise
and indeed with the psychologist's special training.

Paradigms in psychology may have covert moral or social implication
even when they are not overtly attached to a perspective by their followers
Thus, let us take the most spectacular paradigm-shift of psychology with
in the last twenty years: the replacement, in virtually all areas except th
clinical behaviour-therapy school, of stimulus–response behaviourism by
cognitive or central-process theories which emphasize the subject's ow
action in the structuring of perception and response. This movement, much
in line with Kuhn's portrayal of the process of change in scientific ideas,
has not occurred through the emergence of factual disproofs to the pre
viously reigning theoretical system, but through the switching of attention
by researchers to problems which could not be posed in the old language.
So great and so fundamental a conceptual shift, involving the most basic
specification of how any behaviour is produced at all, cannot be altogether
isolated from contemporary movements in moral and social thought.
Classical stimulus-response, drive-reduction behaviourism can be seen to
function in a loose affiliation with the conformist intellectual climate of the

ate 40s and 50s, a period of high Cold War abroad and a domestic stability founded on the acquiescence of the oppressed. It was the era of the so-called 'end of ideology' in which behaviourism maximally flourished.

Herbert Marcuse's denunciation of empirical psychology in *One-Dimensional Man* is based on serious ignorance both of general scientific method and of ongoing developments in psychological theory; nevertheless his identification of behaviourism as an anti-critical, socially repressive ideological tendency was substantially correct. Marcuse's 'one-dimensional character-type is a person whose sole intellectual plane lies in existing social reality; he cannot even conceive of alternative configurations to the civic order in which he occupies a place. In this sense, the classical behaviourist paradigm is deeply one-dimensional 'inasmuch as, focusing on the array of existing stimulation that is conceived to impinge on the subject, it allows the organism no opportunity to test or surpass the offerings of the stimulus-field. Cognitive models of action (by contrast) provide the subject with an alternative to present reality, i.e., with some means of monitoring and checking the impress of stimulation' (Sedgwick, 1966).

When I first reached this judgement on the politics of behaviourism, it seemed plausible that its converse was also true, i.e. that the cognitive paradigms of perception and action might express a relatively more critical and radical spirit, corresponding to the general crisis of authority recently characteristic of Western societies. It was tempting to suppose that the cognitive-cybernetic vision of the human subject as an active operator, manipulating in accordance with feedback from the stimulus-area selected by his sovereign attention, rather than manipulated by the experimenter's reinforcement-schedule, might mark some kind of opening to the Left in psychological theory. Or the contemporary interest in the subjective, purposive nature of cognition and action, common to both the cybernetic and the phenomenological currents of today's psychology, might point to the awakening of a new humanism in the profession. It would be a relief to believe so; but the newer developments in cognitive psychology are attended by uncertainties. The cybernetic view of man as an actively intervening operator does have some appealing parallels with the industrial, technical and practical perspective on man as a labouring species that is sketched by the early Karl Marx: but it has been found equally suitable as the theoretical backing for researches designed to improve the efficiency of bomber pilots. Eugene Galanter, the co-author of our most seminal treatise on the activist, cognitive psychology, *Plans and the Structure of Human Behaviour*, was indeed so absorbed in the project on aircraft control skills that occupied him in the midst of the Vietnam war that the very possibility of a hostile response to his endeavours, which became actual during the Columbia student demonstrations of 1968, came to him as an incredible surprise.

Nevertheless, the re-instatement of the purposive and the active into the definition of the psychological subject can hardly pass without some broader consequences. The questions 'What action?' and 'For what purpose?' have to be posed for that most cognitive of activities, psychological science itself. In emphasizing the link between theory and practice, modelling and correction through feedback, that lies at the heart of human knowledge, cybernetic psychology has lent itself, in a number of applied fields, to the implementation of a particular socio-political perspective which may be termed liberal or reformist. A cognitive paradigm of action, when allied with liberal politics, can motivate reform-minded psychologists to engage in such welfare activities as the training of the disabled in social skills or the reduction of fatigue in monotonous tasks. However, no psychological paradigm works by itself to analyse or criticize the institutions of society within which such tiny reforms are conducted. 'Industrial psychology', however liberal or sophisticated, operates for the purpose of increasing output, or the worker's satisfaction with his job or his class-position, within the industrial relations of assembly-line capitalism: not to challenge and still less to overturn those relations. More generally: in today's situation of urgent social tension, the demand for *relevance* to humanity's problems is getting voiced in many academic disciplines, and it is likely that psychologists will respond to this pressure – which is entirely proper, and not to be shirked – by enrolling as technical aides for social philosophies that are framed outside the purview of psychology. The maxim ' psychology in the service of – or for the benefit of – society' is more and more likely to form a motto for psychologists. Yet the question 'In the service of *whose* definition of society – that of employers or that of the trade-union rank and file; that of the bureaucracies of the welfare office, or that of their clients?' is scarcely ever likely to be considered; social consensus on the values within which he should work is on the whole assumed by the applied psychologist. If the paradigms of present-day psychology increasingly emphasize the link between theory and practice, the practitioner usually takes for granted official practice, working with the perspective of the moderate centre in an age where the ground occupied by this centre is only a middle between alternatives of several kinds.

The politicization of psychology, as dissensus over basic social goals becomes more manifest in society at large, thus appears to be inevitable. To those who would seek to maintain a position of apparent value-freedom for psychology (a position which customarily merely reflects the most received and banal of dominant social values), it must be retorted that the politicization of certain areas of psychology has already been set in hand, from the rightward end of the political spectrum. The recent dispute over the heritability of IQ among blacks of the United States forms one instance in which the choice of a particular paradigm of causation is linked with a partisan social perspective. To use, for the purpose of determining the relative roles of heredity and history, a comparison between two groups which display both genetic differentiation *and* an enormous cultural gulf, would appear to be the least promising of scientific procedures; for the causative effects of heredity and of history have clearly been confounded, over a time-span of centuries, from the moment when the first black slaves were assigned, on the basis of a genetically determined but environmentally significant index (skin-colour), to treatments that would inevitably widen the gap between them and any alternative control subjects: smashing of the family-structure, loss of original language, flogging, etc. The basis for using black-versus-white comparisons for the purpose of estimating the heritability of IQ among blacks cannot be justified by scientific canons. The emphasis on the role of heredity or the role of history in the apportionment of variability around the average of obtained scores must be dictated by non-scientific values. For the techniques and norms of science have nothing to tell us, on this evidence, as to what the average of yet-to-be obtained scores might be for the prospective descendants of either blacks or whites within a different societal environment; and the concept of heritability cannot be used in this context to estimate the likelihood of any genetically enforced constraints on future attainment. Only social and political values can force a choice in slanting the interpretation, on hereditarian or on environmental lines, of such fluid and ambiguous data. A right-wing, conservative ideology would suggest that the part of heredity be brought to the forefront, before cultural influences are included as a possible explanation. More liberal or radical beliefs will suggest that we subject the lower-scoring group to a transformed cultural environment, revolutionizing not merely their education but their housing, employment and life-chances generally, before we can begin to uncover what may be the special role of genetic variability. Right-wing values will, in short, endorse the favourable entertainment of the opinion that certain races are hereditarily inferior to others, an attitude which is usually termed 'racism' when it is expressed straightforwardly in ordinary English, but which gets called 'science' once it is uttered in the copious polysyllables of psychometric jargon. Values to the Left will, conversely, encourage programmes for large-scale social change since the responsibility for the inferior performance of the tested blacks will be seen as resting firmly with the social order.

The practical proposals offered by the leading hereditarians in this debate are thus of a conservative stamp, involving no major onslaught on the social structures of injustice: Eysenck wants vitamins to be administered to the poor blacks in the slum ghettoes to raise their I Qs, Jensen wants low-I Q people (mainly black, on his own admission) to be taken out of the normal educational system and streamed into a form of schooling that stresses mechanical learning, and Shockley wants them sterilized. The politics of these proposals are clear: change the victims individually, rather than change the slums and the job-structure. The lower classes should be ministered unto, kindly or sternly, but not mobilized.

More importantly, we must note that, with the contributions of Jensen and Eysenck to this debate, racism has now become a respectable psychological creed. Psychologists and educators in the United States have been quick to note the political implications of racially slanted conclusions like those of Jensen and Shuey. In this country, psychologists still treat the controversy as though it was a dispute between scientists about evidence, rather than a confrontation between political positions in which there is no neutral ground. The admission of racist hypotheses into the currency of scientific discussion in itself endows them with a certain status, and thus constitutes a serious concession to the racist pressures. How can an applied scientific profession like psychology pretend to neutrality on the question of racism, when the holding of racist beliefs is likely to influence a psychologist's policy in his selection or treatment of black children in educational screening?

The revival of academic racism coincidentally with a period of open and vulgar popular racialism is unsurprising. Racist theory in psychology became anathema only in a specific historical period, the prelude and aftermath to the fascist experience. In conformity with the anti-fascist values which temporarily became energized during the world-wide struggle against openly racist powers, many public declarations were made by official scientific bodies, asserting that racist hypotheses were unproven and that the biological equality of man had a rational scientific foundation. Unfortunately the actual practice of the victor-powers following the Second World War was far from this noble ideal, and it was inevitable that theory would catch up with the repressive actuality of domestic and colonial racism. Banished from the realm of mentionable issues within mainstream politics, racism was dragged from under the carpet and rendered into an open public philosophy by such figures as Powell and Wallace. In such a period of popularity for conscious, unashamed bigotry, it was only a matter of time before in the academies, too, someone would call the bluff of the liberal anathema, dragging racist doctrine from the fringe of the undiscussable on to the scientific community's theoretical agenda. Politics is here, in Eysenck's case in a classic Social-Darwinist philosophy which views the Irish nation as a sad example of the survival of the unfittest, and revives the hereditary vice that causes crime, in a form displayed nowadays by the questionnaire-response rather than the receding forehead of yore.

In this brief selection of ideological themes in modern psychology, I have touched on liberal and on conservative utilizations of psychological paradigm. What, then, of the possibility of a radical, or even of a revolutionary perspective for psychology? So far the output of those claiming to be 'radical psychologists' has been very disappointing. Even such a product as *Rat, Myth and Magic*, the most coherent work to date of any critics of psychology formed from within the discipline, lacks any positive viewpoint except a latching-on to shreds of phenomenology, anarchism, Women's Liberation and encounter-group theory. Other academic disciplines have their radical ideological caucuses, which (whatever their other failings) appear to be able to get started with a certain intellectual momentum. Why is this? Why should psychology be able to display clear conservative or liberal orientations, both in application and in basic theory, and yet – hitherto at least – be unable to accommodate a politically radical or revolutionary perspective?

This is the most important question that can be raised in the whole subject-matter of ideological perspective in psychology. For, if it is the case that the psychological enterprise has found room, intermittently, for all political perspectives except that of the far Left, it might be because the logic of psychological thinking was permanently skewed, loaded, biased against radicalism and revolution.

In reviewing this problem we have to go beyond particular paradigms or even perspectives and look at the central problematic of psychology, its orientation towards the discrete experimental S or subject. The reading that the psychologist works from may be grouped with other readings from the same S or from different Ss, averaged, squared, submitted to analysis of variance, refused by the journal editor, or lost in the waste-bin: but it is, fundamentally, the product of an observation on an individual subject. A radical or revolutionary approach, in contrast, starts off not with individual Ss but with systematically structured and historically specific aggregates of Ss, such as capitalism, apartheid, dock-strikes, the Peronist movement, the armed forces of the Crown, the rising cost of living, the Gestapo, etc. Radical social theories, in short, begin with the macro, though they may have some focus on micro-social phenomena; a knowledge of comparative economics will shed light, for example, on a face-to-face institution like the nuclear family. Psychology starts off with the micro, or even with the mini-micro like the eye-blink; it may work up to the mega-micro (small-group studies), but it does not contain the concepts that can get as far as the macro. Violence, for psychology, becomes translated into a discussion about 'aggression' displayed by individual Ss; it is never seen as a property of institutions like the police or the Mafia, or of historically contingent situations like a picket-line in a period of intense collision between the State and trade-union militancy. Another contrast can be drawn between the way in which psychologists discuss the reality or non-reality of 'the achievement motive', an ahistorical dimension supposed by its proponent, McClelland, to have been present within individuals across different epochs as the motivation for technical and economic enterprise, and the way in which social and economic historians discuss the validity of Weber's 'Protestant ethic' thesis. In the latter case we go beyond the summation of individual responses, into the analysis of cultural, economic and political complexes such as the banking system in a given country during the Reformation. Even if McClelland's achievement motive were conceded to be a real force at work in individuals, there would still have to be a suitable institutional setting for it to become manifest in behaviour; and yet, at the level of the institution, psychology is dumb.

The *problematic* of psychology in its historical development from the nineteenth-century laboratories of its founders like Wilhelm Wundt down to the present day is much too narrow to assist more than marginally in most questions requiring serious social analysis. Psychologists therefore have to go outside the logic of their own training and take up explicit political positions in order to master an outlook on the social order of which they form an indubitable part. There are three alternatives for a psychology which cannot itself incorporate activist and interventionist political values. Its practitioners may compartmentalize their 'professional status' and lead split lives, using a radically different problematic outside working hours; or they can try to find some modern equivalent of the 'psychology in the service of social goals' which functioned during a period of value-consensus such as the Second World War, but which cannot be propounded today without immediate and plausible accusations of partisanship; or they can grow out of being psychologists. This last alternative seems to have happened to me over the years; but I have enough attachment to my old discipline to hope that it is not a necessary choice for the members of this audience.

References

BURGESS, I. (1972), 'Psychology and Kuhn's concept of paradigm', *J. behav. Sci.*, vol. 1, pp. 193–200.

MASTERMAN, M. (1970), 'The nature of a paradigm', in I. Lakatos and A. Musgrave (eds.), *Criticism and the Growth of Knowledge*, Cambridge University Press.

SEDGWICK, P. (1966), 'Natural science and human theory: a critique of Herbert Marcuse', in R. Miliband and J. Saville (eds.), *Socialist Register*, Merlin Press.

Part One
Methodology

In the introduction I maintained that positivist ideas underlie most social-psychological methodology. In Part One, we have six essays which together expand on that theme and suggest extensions and alternatives to positivism. 'Methodology' is interpreted more broadly than is usual in social psychology, where it has become restricted to particular techniques for designing and carrying out research. Here, we try to treat methodology in relation to what are usually compartmentalized as 'philosophical' and 'theoretical' ideas. We begin to break down the barriers between these three areas, in the belief that such distinctions are both artificial and conservative. Artificial, in that philosophical assumptions permeate methodological prescriptions, and in that different theories imply and are subsequently 'proved' by different methodologies. Conservative, in that the compartmentalization hides these interrelationships and enables the conventional methodological wisdom to be passed off as unproblematic and necessarily the case.

A useful distinction that catches much of the difference in our approach from the conventional one is that between *praxis* and *process*. Praxis refers to the engagement of an active subject with his or her environment (literally 'a deed' in Greek), whereas process refers to the passive undergoing of an inevitable sequence of events by an object (literally 'having occurred' from the Latin). We are claiming that praxis is the more appropriate model for social psychology; and that conventional social psychology operates with an implicit process model. People are seen in social psychology as subject to processes which go on regardless of their own agency and powers of action. For instance, cognitive dissonance is seen as a process that is supposed to happen to a person under certain circumstances, rather than as the result of intentional human action on one's own psychological state; we can *choose* whether to 'reduce dissonance' depending upon what the issues are and how much they concern us. This distinction ties in with several of the defects in social psychology suggested in the introduction.

Positivism is process-oriented. This is made clear by George Gross in relation to Hobbes, and by John Shotter in relation to Descartes. These forefathers of positivism made mechanistic assumptions about humanity, which have become incorporated into the conventional approach to social psychology. The critique is also taken up by Rom Harré in the early part of his article in Part Three. Furthermore, positivism has led to a style of quantification and experimentation which is very restrictive. Don Mixon, John Rowan and Martin Roiser all explore these restrictions and suggest respectively that role-playing studies, the involvement of the researcher, and attitude scales based on the 'policies' of different groups would widen our horizons. Lastly, I try to get away from the positivist emphasis upon observable behaviour as *explanandum* in social science, and suggest that we could instead be explaining people's experience.

Determinism is also associated with a process model. Our behaviour is seen as being caused by natural and social forces, which are largely outside our control. By contrast, the praxis model recommends that our behaviour is intentional, albeit influenced by natural and social phenomena. However, the influence of the natural world is seen as being more crucial upon non-social behaviour, and the influence of the social world as restricting the *choices* available to a person and shaping the nature of such choices. George Gross brings out the determinism that links Hobbes, social psychology and technocratic ideology, and John Shotter is saying that to be human is to be a growing social agent with the power of responsible action, i.e. self-determining. Both Don Mixon and I sit on the fence as far as determinism is concerned: Don Mixon is keen on a rule-following model of human behaviour which smacks of social determinism, and my article reflects my feeling that most of us are more determined than we think.

Thirdly, the process model is conducive to an impoverished, technicized treatment of the social. When things are seen as *happening to* people, the way *they* see things and *their* involvement in the construction of events are ignored. By stressing the meaningfulness of behaviour to the actor and his or her active creation of the social world, the praxis model encourages a deeper and more sensitive analysis of social life. These issues are explored more fully in Parts Two and Three, but here we have George Gross criticizing the philosophical underpinnings of a technocratic, process-oriented social psychology, Martin Roiser asking us to look at the social groups to which people belong and refer, if we want to know about their attitudes, and myself exploring the links between an individual's experience and the wider society. Also, both John Shotter and John Rowan emphasize the involvement of people in creating the social world, which is seen to include new social-psychological principles and theories which may emerge from an ongoing involvement with people in 'research'.

The question of values does not fit so readily into the process/praxis distinction. However it comes up in most of the essays in this Part. George Gross, in particular, outlines how values get built into what subsequently appears as the 'facts of the matter'; the classic recipe for ideology-construction. Don Mixon clarifies the value-loadings in the origins and use of summary scores derived from batches of individuals and Martin Roiser suggests that the uniformity assumed in attitude-scale items reflects the 'one-nation' ideology that the powerful always push. John Rowan's whole essay can be seen as a plea for the recognition that values are mixed up in everything that a researcher does: instead of abhorring such a situation, we should rather welcome it as an indication that research need not be the alienating activity that many of us have found it to be.

Of course, there are more methodological issues that need to be taken up: for instance, participant observation is only treated briefly by John Rowan and tangentially by myself; the question of how social norms get built into measuring instruments is touched on by Martin Roiser, but is actually treated more fully by John Heritage in Part Three; the social context of the social-psychology experiment needs a more hard-hitting treatment than it has yet received (what assumptions about power, control, one-way communication are embedded in it?); and there are more technical criticisms of research designs and analyses that could reveal how presuppositions and values creep into so-called 'hard' research (David Ingleby has a few suggestions along these lines in Part Three). However, we hope there is enough here to both widen and deepen current conceptions of methodology.

2 Unnatural Selection[1]
George Gross

'The laws of Commerce are the laws of Nature, and therefore the laws of God.'
Edmund Burke, *Thoughts and Details on Society* (1800)

Introduction and summary

'That modern psychology has projected an image of man which is as demeaning as it is simplistic, few intelligent and sensitive non-psychologists would deny. To such men – whether they be scientist, humanist or citizen – psychology has increasingly become an object of derision.' Thus Sigmund Koch (1964), the distinguished editor of an authoritative six-volume work *Psychology: A Study of a Science*; the sentiment is echoed by Professor Liam Hudson (1972), who asserts that the fruits of 'hard' psychology 'unmistakably, have about them an air of triviality'. In this necessarily brief essay, I shall take up a similar point of view with respect to social psychology. I shall, furthermore, contend that there has been a principle of unnatural selection operating upon social psychology in particular and upon the social sciences in general. The principle is of an ideological kind and the function which it is intended to serve is that of social control. The principle of unnatural selection has had the disastrous effect of ensuring the survival, and indeed the dominance, of a positivist, reductionist paradigm in social psychology and (albeit to a lesser extent) in political theory: I am referring to the doctrines of behaviourism and 'behaviouralism'. The essence of such a *credo* is that the 'behavioural sciences' should be limited to methods and theories which view human beings from the outside, from the point of view of the observer. Such paradigms are *reductionist* in that they prescribe methods which reduce the true complexity of experience by imitating the physical and the natural sciences. Their aim is to predict and thus to be able to control behaviour. All such psychological theory and practice of individual and social engineering treat man as an object, with a lop-sided stress on man as organism: Locke and the early philosopher psychologists of English empiricism saluted 'the incomparable Mr Newton', and late nineteenth- and twentieth-century 'scientific psychology' is an excessive homage to Mr Darwin.

The essential ideological function of positivist social psychology and political science is to *depoliticize* social science and to present an image of

1. I would like to thank my friends and colleagues Jerry Cohen, David Ingleby, Jerry Palmer, Tim Shallice, Peter Sheldrake and Bob Young for valuable discussions relevant to this paper.

t as a neutral objective domain of technical expertise which is inaccessible o ordinary mortals and which is applied, to the benefit of the whole of ociety, by their democratically elected representatives guided in such natters by technocratic advisers. This is the force of technocratic ideology xpounded by a generation of functionalist social scientists – ideologues >f, first, the Cold War and 'the end of ideology', then, of peaceful, techno- :ratic co-existence, then of Vietnam and counter-insurgency. Following he analyses by Habermas (1963, 1971) and Schroyer (1970) I shall try to ndicate the real function of technocratic rhetoric and ideology, namely as a pseudo-justification for a particular distribution of power in industrial ociety.

Moreover, in outlining the way in which the (ideological) principle of nnatural selection dominates decisions as to what is regarded as an ppropriate paradigm, theory, field of research, methodology, etc., I hall of necessity touch on the history of social psychology, the philosophy >f science, and the sociology of knowledge in what is (again, of necessity) a highly schematic way. (Cf. the important article by Ingleby, 1972.)

Competing paradigms in contemporary social psychology

What has been hailed as scientific, empirical and even 'engineering' >sychology dominates research and teaching in academic psychology and social psychology. This same brand of psychology has other incarna- ions in the real world where it is known as clinical psychology, educational >sychology or industrial psychology. In both its academic and applied 'ersions psychology in Great Britain has increasingly come under the :ontrol of a professional guild which claims to represent it adequately – the Royally Chartered) British Psychological Society.

Thus established, psychology wishes to be defined as the science of >ehaviour. It is not behaviourist in the old crusading style which hoped forever to close the bloodshot inner eye of introspection'; but it satisfies ll the criteria referred to by Schroyer (1970) as characterizing the positivist view; namely, it holds '(1) that knowledge is inherently neutral; (2) that here is a unitary scientific method; (3) that the standard of certainty and exactness is the only explanatory model for scientific knowledge.' Schroyer :ontinues:

We refer to this conception of science ... as scientism. ... Scientism is the culmina- ion of the positivist tradition and has become dominant in both established ocial science of late capitalism and in the scientistic materialism of orthodox Marxism. ... The faith that men will be emancipated through the extension of neutral techniques of science and technology obscures the reality of research which serves and justifies technical control systems that accept power structures as given. . . . Thus the greatest problem that social theory faces is not whether behaviourism, game theory or systems analysis are theoretically valid, but whether they might not become valid through a self-fulfilling prophecy justified by a technocratic ideology.

It must be added, however, that this established, positivist and technocratic paradigm is being challenged by a competing paradigm which regards psychology not only as a biological science but also a social science *sui generis*. This *critical* perspective stresses man, not just as an object, but as a conscious (though also, in part, unconscious) *subject*; concerned not as a passive organism or black box, but as an agent; involved, not in a stimulus-response chain, but in intentional activity in a concrete sociohistorical and political world (not in a T-maze, or a Skinner box). Social psychology, with its mixed allegiance to sociology on the one hand and to academic psychology on the other, is one of the areas in which the conflict between the positivist and the critical frameworks is particularly sharp. At the end of a review which focuses on the confusion and incoherence of social-psychology text books, Giddens (1965) is surely right in maintaining that 'It is the responsibility of social psychologists to come to grips with some of the difficulties which arise in respect of the relationships between psychology and sociology. To date, by and large, they have shelved this responsibility in favour of *ad hoc* empiricism and piecemeal theory.' One might add that the theoretical parochialism of psychology acts as a ball-and-chain dragging upon the far more sophisticated discussions of theory, meaning and ideology which have been current in sociology for years (see, for example, a recent collection of papers edited by O'Neill, 1973, and the belated but welcome *Journal for the Philosophy of the Social Sciences* which began publication in 1972).

Paradigm, normal science and ideology

In this highly schematic outline, I have so far employed the term *paradigm*, the currency of which in the study of the history of science owes everything to Kuhn's *The Structure of Scientific Revolutions* and his later work. According to Kuhn the history of a science is characterized by a repeated sequence, as follows:

Paradigm dominance – or normal science;
Anomalous findings;
Paradigm switch – or revolution.

Normal science 'is not orientated so much to the pursuit of fundamental novelties of fact or theory, nor indeed to the testing of theory, as to the ingenious production of expectable or expected solutions to prescribed

problems according to standardized procedures' (Martins, 1972). The
constraining factor is the old paradigm in its obsolete and therefore restrictive phase. 'That there is normal science – and that it is exactly as
Kuhn says it is – is the outstanding and crashingly obvious fact which
confronts any philosophers of science who ... set out to do any actual
scientific research' (Masterman, 1970).

'Mannheim's sociology of knowledge explicitly excluded the domain
of mathematics, logic and natural science. Merton's view of the sociology
of science contributed to the separation of the latter from the sociology of
knowledge. But Kuhn has reopened a whole range of problems which
sociologists themselves seemed determined to avoid. Part of the shock
value of Kuhn's theory of science stems from his adoption of terms like
consensus, authority, dogma, tradition, faith, conversion ...' (Martins,
1972). Kuhn tackles the problem of the relation between the social and
psychological aspects of scientific practice, and its 'internal' development
in terms of established laws, theories – and paradigms.

Now, for the purposes of the present inquiry, the question is: are we
to be satisfied with the concept of paradigm in respect of the contradictory
frameworks in social psychology – namely, on the one hand the positivist
framework which has been outlined above, and on the other, a *critical
perspective*. Before trying to answer this question, permit me to focus down
on it by looking at it from a different angle, that taken by Winch (1958). I
quote from a paper by Hollis (1972), who states Winch's position succinctly
although he disagrees with it:

It is no good 'basing our understanding of societies on the methods of the natural
sciences'. Natural sciences trade in objective causes of objectively identifiable
events: whereas people perform acts, which are intelligible only by reference to
social institutions. Whereas natural science is busy with prediction on the basis of
natural laws, social science needs to consider the rules which people follow. In
short, '*the central concepts which belong to our understanding of social life are
incompatible with concepts central to the activity of scientific prediction*'.

This position is similar to that argued by Peters and Tajfel (1957): 'Misled
by the obvious fact that physiological theories are extremely *relevant* to
explanations of human actions, Hull, like Hobbes, thought that descriptions of human behaviour could be *deduced* from a physiological theory
alone. This, in our view, is the basic logical mistake in mechanistic
theories. . . .' In place of the reductionist view, Peters and Tajfel opt for a
theory of 'goal-directed and rule-following activities' in which 'an agent
is assumed to have an objective, and to have information about means
which will lead to this objective'. In these examples we are always faced
with conflicting frameworks; but it is not clear whether these are to be

understood as conflicting *theories*, conflicting *paradigms* (even allowing for the variety of uses which Kuhn makes of the term) or conflicting *ideologies*? Within a given *epistemic* field (Foucault, 1970) there is a hierarchy of structures in which ideology, the most complex of the structures, selects or rejects certain paradigms which in turn include or exclude certain theories which in turn influence problem selection, hypotheses, methodology, etc. To make this claim more precise and concrete will be my aim in what follows. In the next section I shall follow Habermas's historical approach to these problems, focusing the argument round Hobbes (and even earlier philosophers) and the concept of *praxis*. Before moving on to those matters, a remark concerning the philosophy of science: one might be tempted to think that the philosophy of science provides some guarantee of the correctness of the dominant paradigm in social psychology – and even in 'political science'. I believe that such confidence in the philosophy of science would be mistaken: the same principle of ideological selection is operative in the domain of the philosophy of science. More specifically, technocratic ideology has generated so blind an allegiance to the positivist versions of the philosophy of science that alternatives such as the hermeneutic–dialectic tradition (Radnitzky, 1968) remain more or less unknown to British philosophy of science. And yet it is precisely such other frameworks stemming from a preoccupation with the specific features that distinguish the cultural and human sciences from other disciplines which, in my view, will provide the necessary starting points for an adequate philosophy of science for social psychology. The failure of positivist philosophy of science in that domain is attributable to its cavalier extension to the social sciences of an epistemology derived from an overwhelming concentration on the physical and biological sciences.

Hobbes: positivist psychology, law and political philosophy

Why Hobbes? Hobbes's thought is an extremely significant point of confluence, and indeed, in part, source, of several traditions: he was among the first to try, systematically, to transfer the Newtonian and Galilean experimental and mathematical methods from the physical sciences where they rightly triumphed, not only to the domain of individual and social behaviour, but to that of political and legal philosophy where it forms an essential strand in what is later to become technocratic ideology. The fact that Hobbes was in the vanguard of the rationalist and scientific enlightenment (despite his distance from the members of what was to become the Royal Society) and the fact that Hobbes's technocratic blueprint was for a monarchy, does not, I believe, detract from this thesis.

As is well known, Hobbes's *Leviathan* (1651) was, in his own words, occasioned by the disorders of the present time'. What is perhaps less well known is that Hobbes was more royalist than the King. In *Behemoth* – and here I follow Watkins's account – Hobbes does not hide his conviction that the King, in giving

assent, in 1641, to an Act whereby Parliament could not be dissolved *without its own consent*, ... committed a grievous error: he allowed a rival power to become irremovable.... But the King signed away his sovereignty only under heavy pressure.... Among the *subversive doctrines* which he [Hobbes] singled out as primarily responsible were these: that private men are judges of good and evil; that it is a sin to do something against one's private conscience (Watkins, 1965 – my italics).

What of Hobbes the psychologist? Hobbes was one of the founders of the tradition which seeks to model psychology on the natural sciences. He believed that 'the cause of all things must be sought in the variety of motion' and thought of his own work in terms of his friend William Harvey's extension 'of the new science of motion to physiology' (Peters and Tajfel, 1957). Unlike Descartes, who believes that 'animal behaviour and the *involuntary* actions of man could be mechanically explained, but not distinctively human actions involving reason and will ... [Hobbes] was the first to attempt a systematic explanation of *all* human actions in the same terms as were used to explain the behaviour of inanimate bodies' (Peters and Tajfel, 1957). This is the force of:

Every man asks for what is good, and flees from what is bad for him; above all he flees the greatest of the natural evils, Death; and he does so as a consequence of *a natural necessity no less compelling than that according to which a stone falls to earth.*[2]

In his introduction to *De Cive* Hobbes states that he is searching for the constitutive causes of the rights and duties of subjects in the *quality of human nature'* (Peters, 1956 – my italics). Moreover, his 'geometrization of politics' (Wolin, 1960) led him to a method involving 'the deduction of politics from psychological postulates' (Peters, 1956). This has come to be known as *methodological individualism*, a characteristic of the paradigm dominated by technocratic ideology.

When Hobbes turns his attention to the 'matter, forme, and power of a commonwealth' we are no longer in the same domain as Aristotle's *Politics*, says Habermas (1963), but instead in that of 'social philosophy'. Politics in the classical sense, Habermas goes on, was the study of the just and good life, the continuation of ethics; it was concerned exclusively

2. Quoted by Habermas (1963). I have taken the liberty of translating Habermas's version of Hobbes.

with *praxis*; politics is built ultimately on character; it is not technica
Hobbes, on the contrary, holds that mankind's chief progress is a con
sequence of the correct application of techniques – and primarily that o
the administration of the State.

Furthermore, Habermas continues, Aristotle emphasizes that politic
and practical philosophy in general, cannot be measured by the standard
of the most rigorous criteria of knowledge. This is so, because the objec
of politics, namely the just and the excellent in the context of changing an
contingent praxis, lies outside the domain of permanence and of logica
necessity. The true riches of practical philosophy lie elsewhere, in *phrones*
– the art of the shrewd grasp of situations. Vico, too, rejects the enterpris
of the 'new philosophy' where it attempts to transfer the methods o
scientific evaluation to the practice of political wisdom.

There is already a quantum jump between classical political theory an
Machiavelli and Thomas More: for these two, Habermas points ou
politics is severed from ethics and becomes the morally neutral calculus o
military (Machiavelli) or economic (More) power. Hobbes, however, wa
the first to study the laws of 'civil society' with the explicit intention o
putting political action on the same unimpeachably accurate basis as thos
applied scientific techniques which he knew from contemporary mechanics
that is the force of 'men as they are Matter' in the following sentenc
from *Leviathan* (ch. 29):

When [men's Commonwealths] come to be dissolved, not by external violenc
but by intestine disorder, the fault is not in men as they are Matter, but as they ar
Makers and Orderers of them.

What of men as they are 'Makers and Orderers' of Commonwealths? A
they are matter, men are ruled by the laws of nature; as they are maker
they are to be ruled by the sovereign political power to which they bin
themselves – as a consequence of the fear of death – by means of a cove
nant, or social contract. The sovereign power is 'entrusted with the con
dition, and for this end, that men might have and secure their properties'
In exchange, the subject contracts legal obligations – obedience to the
laws pertaining to the public sphere of duties. Between external compulsio
to carry out duties and internalized, psychological compulsion to obey
what is absent in Hobbes's account is the dimension of praxis.

The postulate of the dominance of competitive material appetites is crucial t
Hobbes's theory of the state.... We need not be surprised, then, that to
Hobbes, all relations between men tend to be the relations of the market: 'Th
Value or Worth of a man is, as of all other things, his Price; that is to say, s
much as would be given for the use of his power' (Macpherson, 1965).

Technological rationality and technocratic ideology

From Hobbes to contemporary social psychology there are more than two hundred and fifty years of history – the 'internal' history of the evolution of scientific psychology from the English empiricist (and later American pragmatist) philosophy; and the wider social and political history – largely that of the various phases of industrialization. To outline the former would require a sketch of Saint-Simon and his Supreme Council of Newton; Comte, the systematizer of positivism; and Bentham, the Utilitarians and the felicific calculus. It would further require an appreciation of the birth of experimental psychology and the succession of competing doctrines that influenced its course, the victory of behaviourism, the growth of industrial psychology in the closest connection with the management ideology of social and human engineering. Here, I can do no more than indicate the essential continuities.

In the first place, there is a clear continuity between Hobbes's (uncritical) equation of a man's worth with his price, referred to above, and Marx's (critical) analysis of nineteenth-century industrialized man. In the early mercantile capitalism of Hobbes's day (emerging from feudalism and absolutism), as in Marx's time, and in the advanced technocratic capitalism of today, instead of things being means to man's ends, man is a means, a thing, whereby a system, the market, industrial production, imposes its ends. It is this reversal of ends and means which Marx called the 'fetishism of commodities'. The process whereby men ceased to determine their own ends in work, he called alienation. The quantification of relations between men, their reduction to cogs in machinery of production and the market, he called reification.

Hobbes's geometry of politics is homologous with the contemporary ideology of 'scientific' politics: the essence of both consists in a depoliticization of the majority of the population. For both, politics is a matter of laws governing nature and human nature. For centuries divine sanction was added to the formula (as in Burke's perfectly serious and perfectly mystifying syllogism quoted at the head of the present essay). But Burke, the umbilical *cordon bleu* of English ideological cuisine (which proposed deference, subordination and paternalism in place of liberty, equality and fraternity), did not overlook the secular ingredients in his recipe: everything, he foresaw for England, will remain 'locked fast as in a sort of family settlement; grasped as in a kind of mortmain forever'. The link between deference as a political ideology and the family process whereby it is reproduced and internalized as a character trait is well caught in the term 'family settlement'. The paternalism/deference syndrome colours relations between employer and employee, teacher and pupil, doctor and patient, magistrate and accused. At the same time, hierarchical power relations at work influence the behaviour of parents in the family. And the authority relationship between parents and children often generate a tendency to obedience which is more or less unconsciously built into the child's character which thus dovetails into the subordinate roles which educational and other institutions hold in store for them.

How does this relate to present-day political ideology? Part of the answer to this question is to be found in the following exerpt from a work on English political culture by two political scientists untainted by radical views:

One of the most pervasive conditions promoting the survival of deference is the modest role accorded to the people in British political culture. Although it is a commonplace of research on stable democracies that general electorates are typically uninvolved in politics and show low levels of interest and information, it is only in Britain that this is so largely consistent with the prevailing climate of political values. . . . No major political party suggests even rhetorically that ordinary people ought to play a continuously active role in determining government policy or that the electorate's views should, in principle, be decisive in the taking of major decisions. . . . The modest formal political role of the general population – restricted to choosing at general elections which set of political leaders shall exercise decisive power for a period of time – provides a context which has facilitated the survival of deference long into the age of universal franchise (McKenzie and Silver, 1968).

But, the authors hasten to add: 'This discussion *does not*, of course *assume that such a concept* of "the people's" role *is incompatible with democracy*' (my italics). Of course not. Perish the thought. All that such technocratic theoreticians require is that elected representatives of the people should have available the information and conclusions provided by the 'behavioural sciences', including political science, in order to be able adequately to control the affairs of the nation (whose interests, as a whole, conservative ideology has always claimed to have at heart).

But how do these considerations relate to technological rationality and technocratic ideology? In what must be the final section of this essay I shall try to answer that question, following the analysis made by Habermas (1971). Science and technology are real forces capable of transforming society. But they do not, and need never, in themselves automatically create a better world. And when they are used to mask or to justify the political status quo, the domination of a majority of the population by a minority, then this is the ideological and technocratic use of science which nothing in science itself can ever justify. That advanced industrial society depends upon science and technology is one thing. To claim that the present power structure of such society is in any way legitimated by that fact or is in any way necessitated by it is something else: ideological special pleading. Depoliticization is a necessary part of the technocratic ideology because 'public discussion could render problematic the framework within which the tasks of government action are presented as technical ones. Therefore the new politics of state interventionism requires a depoliticization of the mass of the population. . . . The quasi-autonomous progress of science and technology then appears as an independent variable on which . . . economic growth depends. Thus there arises a perspective in which the development of the social system *seems* to be determined by the logic of scientific technical progress. . . . [This] can become a background ideology that penetrates into the consciousness of the depoliticized mass of the population where it can take on legitimating power. . . . The manifest domination of the authoritarian state gives way to the manipulative compulsions of technical–operational administration . . .' (Habermas, 1971).

In a review of Chomsky's *American Power and the New Mandarins*, Raymond Williams (1969) made a point which surely bears repeating in the present context: 'The ordinary human recognitions and connections have been overlaid and suppressed by techniques of rational calculations within a pseudo-reality. But the duty of intellectuals is to remake the connections between humanity and reasoning.'

References

FOUCAULT, M. (1970), *The Order of Things*, Tavistock.

GIDDENS, A. (1965), 'The present position of social psychology', *Brit. J. Sociol.*, vol. 16, pp. 365–72.

HABERMAS, J. (1963), *Theorie und Praxis*, Luchterhand.

HABERMAS, J. (1971), 'Technology and science as "ideology"', in *Towards a Rational Society*, Heinemann.

HOLLIS, M. (1972), 'Witchcraft or winchcraft', *Phil. Soc. Sci.*, vol. 2, p. 89.

HUDSON, L. (1972), *The Cult of the Fact*, Cape.

INGLEBY, D. (1972), 'Ideology and the human sciences', in T. Pateman (ed.), *Counter Course*, Penguin.

KOCH, S. (1964), 'Psychology and emerging conceptions of knowledge as unitary', in T. W. Wann (ed.), *Behaviorism and Phenomenology*, University of Chicago Press.

MACPHERSON, C. B. (1965), 'Hobbes today', in K. Brown (ed.), *Hobbes Studies*, Blackwell.

MARTINS, H. (1972), 'The Kuhnian revolution and its implications for sociology', in T. J. Nossiter *et al.* (eds.), *Imagination and Precision in the Social Sciences*, Faber.

MASTERMAN (1970), 'The nature of a paradigm', in I. Lakatos and A. Musgrave (eds.), *Criticism and the Growth of Knowledge*, Cambridge University Press.

McKENZIE, R. R., and SILVER, A. (1968), *Angels in Marble*, Heinemann.

O'NEILL, J. (ed.) (1973), *Modes of Individualism and Collectivism*, Heinemann.

PETERS, R. S. (1956), *Hobbes*, Penguin.

PETERS, R. S., and TAJZEL, H. (1957), 'Hobbes and Hull', *B.J. Phil. Sci.*, vol. 29.

RADNITZKY, G. (1968), *Contemporary Schools of Metascience*, Akademiförlaget, Sweden.

SCHROYER, T. (1970), 'Toward a critical theory for advanced industrial society', in H. P. Dreitzel (ed.), *Recent Sociology, No. 2*, Collier-Macmillan.

WATKINS, J. W. N. (1965), *Hobbes's System of Ideas*, Hutchinson.

WILLIAMS, R. (1969), 'Changing the terms of reason', *Guardian*, 30 October.

WINCH, P. (1958), *The Idea of a Social Science and its Relations to Philosophy*, Routledge & Kegan Paul.

WOLIN, S. (1960), *Politics and Vision*, Little.

3 What Is It To Be Human ?
John Shotter

Whereas other animals cannot alter themselves except by changing their species, man can transform himself by transforming the world and can structure himself by constructing structures; and these structures are his own, for they are not eternally predestined either from within or from without.
Jean Piaget, *Structuralism*, pp. 118–19

Modern philosophy, it is said, begins with Descartes (1596–1650); it is largely from his proposals that modern science emerged – and with it all the problems we face in psychology today. Promising deep and effective knowledge of the natural world, Descartes's philosophy held out the great hope that:

... knowing the force and the actions of fire, water, air, the stars, the heavens, and all other bodies that surround us ... we should be able to utilize them for all the uses to which they are suited and thus render ourselves masters and possessors of nature.

Instead of victims, we may become masters of our fates.

Prior to Descartes, everything in the cosmos was characterized by greater or lesser degrees of value, of perfection according to a hierarchical scheme with matter at its foot and God at its summit. By excluding values and reducing everything tangible to matter in motion according to mathematically expressible laws, Descartes destroyed the older notions of the cosmos. God is no longer present in the world, nor for that matter is man, in the sense of having any obvious place assigned there for his own *self*. As a mind, quite separate from the world as matter, the role of man *himself* can only be that of dominating his surroundings and becoming master and possessor of the natural world, utilizing it for all the uses to which it is suited. And that world itself, containing as it does only matter in lawful and orderly motion, becomes, as we shall see, both a timeless and lifeless place.

If we are ever to study ourselves without emasculating ourselves in the process – without destroying our own ability to transform ourselves – it is Descartes's account of our being in the world (his ontology) and the accounts of how we came to know its nature (his epistemology) that we must replace.

And it is no use experimental psychologists denigrating this attempt as 'armchair psychology', thinking that clear *statements* describing alternative modes of being can be discovered by doing experiments. As they should know only too well, experiments have nothing to do with discovering statements; experiments are only meant to put the logically derived consequences of clear statements to the test. Such statements have to do with the frameworks of thought (see the reference to Berger and Luckman, 1967, on p. 63) *within* which scientific statements are formulated, and there is no straightforward way in which empirical facts could be said either to verify or falsify such frameworks. They lay down the ground-rules which scientists use in identifying what needs explaining and what would count as an intelligible explanation. Facts could not, for instance, falsify the laws of mechanics in any direct manner because the facts being what they are is itself something to be explained in terms of these laws (Hanson, 1958).

Lacking a clear and *adequate* statement of the nature of our own being in the world, modern psychology has floundered on, doing, wherever it has been effective, untold violence to our image of ourselves as self-determining beings, as beings able to be responsible for our own actions rather than being caused to behave by influences outside ourselves.

Here, then, I am trying to help in the reconstruction of social psychology by attempting to formulate a much richer conception of the nature of our being in the world than that deriving from Descartes. I have not attempted to lay out a whole blueprint for a new science, but Harré's blueprint (see p. 240) is not incompatible with my proposals; the interrelated issues I discuss may be taken as preliminaries to such a blueprint. There are four central issues:

1 That what seems to anchor me as a person in reality is the sense of responsibility that I can have for my own actions;

2 That treating *time* realistically as the medium through which people develop leads to the idea of an indeterministic contingent world in which, to a degree, what happens is up to us;

3 That men construct for themselves a human world from out of the natural world, and, in using it to express new forms of humanity, transform themselves;

4 That the source of responsibility for people's actions may not always be located *in* individuals: sometimes it is shared *between* them. Thus at first parents share with their babies responsibility for what their babies do, only later do babies become responsible for themselves. Shared responsibilities can become located solely in the individual, thus increasing his powers of self-determination.

It is only in an indeterminate world that men can have the power to determine themselves, to construct laws and choose to act in accordance with them – and remember, it is not the man wafted this way and that at the caprice of circumstance who shows order and principle in his behaviour, but the man who keeps a principle or plan firmly in mind, and refuses to be distracted by events.

The classical world and its investigation

I would like to introduce the idea of an indeterministic growing world by way of contrast with the classical picture of the world which psychology has inherited in large part from Descartes.

The publication in 1637 of Descartes's *Discours de la méthode* (the full title of which in translation is 'Discourse on the method of properly conducting one's reason and of seeking the truth in the sciences') engendered the great belief that it was possible to translate *methodically* all that is unknown into the realm of indisputable common knowledge. The method was to start from clear and distinct ideas and to proceed by way of those 'long chains of reasonings, quite simple and easy, which geometers are accustomed to using to teach their most difficult demonstrations'. Via the unity of mathematics – remember Descartes had shown how in coordinate geometry, geometry could be translated into algebra – such a method promised a unified view of the cosmos. For the nature of the world is such that with this method, Descartes said, 'there can be nothing so distant that one does not reach it eventually, or so hidden that one cannot discover it'. It is a world in which all that there is of it already exists.

When we speak of 'the method of the natural sciences', we can trace part of it back to the *Discours*; it was to this emphasis on mathematically expressible laws that Newton added the experimental method. In a letter to the secretary of the Royal Society of 1672 he wrote:

The best and safest method of philosophizing seems to be, first, to inquire diligently into the properties of things and to establish those properties by experiments, and to proceed later to hypotheses for the explanation of things themselves. For hypotheses ought only to be applied in the explanation of the properties of things, and not made use of in determining them.

But actually, it was only possible for him to assert this given the way in which Descartes had *idealized* the subject matter of Natural Philosophy – hypotheses *did* enter into the determination of 'things', for Descartes had written:

I resolved ... to speak only of what would happen in *a new world*, if God were to create, somewhere in *imaginary space*, enough matter to compose it, and if he were to agitate diversely and confusedly the *different parts* of this matter, so that he created a chaos as *disordered* as the poets could ever imagine, and afterwards did no more than to lend his usual preserving action to nature, and let her act according to his *established laws* (my italics).

Thus scientists must study the abstract stuff, *matter*, which is to be known in terms of its measurable properties, *spatial extent* and *motion*, and whose behaviour is investigated to yield God's established laws. All 'things' in the world, except, Descartes thought, men's rational souls, could be brought into the confines of such an investigation, for they could all be treated as identical in terms of the motion of matter moving according to mathematical laws.

Thus it was primarily from Descartes's metaphysics, his entirely speculative picture of the fundamental nature of the world that the modern natural sciences emerged. And as 'scientific' thought grew to be the ideal for all thought, it became imperative to bring within its confines what Descartes had left out: men's rational soul – for there was no other realm in which it could exist, except in the world of matter in motion. Men's actions must be reduced to the motions of their matter.

This then is the Cartesian world. It is a world which must be investigated for the laws regulating the motions of its elementary parts. It is an all-already-existing world in which the only changes are changes of rearrangement. Nothing in it passes into existence and out of it again; it is a world of being, not becoming. If we are unable to predict our future in it at the moment, that is not because it is in principle impossible – quite the contrary: it is because we are still too ignorant; we have not yet amassed enough knowledge; yet more research is needed. In such a world, as Laplace (1886) realized:

An intellect which at a given instant knew all the forces acting in nature, and the position of all things of which the world consists – supposing the said intellect were vast enough to subject these data to analysis – would embrace in the same formula the motions of the greatest bodies in the universe and those of the slightest atoms; nothing would be uncertain for it, and the future, like the past, would be present to its eyes.

It is a world in which the future is merely hidden like distant regions of space (for time is spatialized); and it seems possible, ultimately, to know everything!

Such hopes and beliefs as these still motivate, I feel, much of what is called scientific psychology today. It is surely possible, isn't it, to discover completely how man works?

Our fundamental sense of our own responsibility

While such a view as that above may capture all our significant experiences of what we call the 'external world' (Russell, 1914), the world which yields to our manipulations, it utterly fails to capture our experience of our own functioning in such a world. Because of this and also its frankly speculative character, I would like to suggest an alternative basis for our investigations in psychology: *a basis in the sense of responsibility which we all have for our own actions.*

We all distinguish, and indeed if we are to be accounted reasonable human beings we all *must* be able to distinguish, between that for which we as individual personalities are responsible and that which merely happens, irrespective of our agency. This distinction is *fundamental* not only in everyday life but also in science, where it is absolutely fundamental: it is only because we can sense, when acting in accord with theories of what the world might be like, whether the results of our actions accord with or depart from the expectations engendered by the theories, that we can ever put such theories to empirical test. No more fundamental basis for deciding the truth of empirical matters exists, nor will another ever be found – in the organizational complexity of matter, say, as some such as Sutherland (1970) suggest – for how could it ever be established as a true basis? It would still rest upon the basis of our ability to recognize the consequences of our own actions. Our sense of responsibility is, then, at the very basis of science itself; lacking any sense of their own functioning scientists would be unable to do experiments.

The distinction I have been making above is the distinction between *actions* and *events*, *doings* and *happenings* which has been explored extensively of late in the philosophy of human action (for example, Winch, 1958; Peters, 1958; Hampshire, 1959; Taylor, 1966; R. Bernstein, 1972). My aim in making this distinction and in exploring all that follows from it is to establish that there can be a distinct sphere of thought and investigation called (social) psychology – inherently social in character – which, because it has *its own goals* (and its own methods for achieving them), is irreducible to any other science. Its main theoretical goal is to make the experience of being a human self among other similar selves intelligible, to understand the idea of what it is to be human. In practice its goal will be to develop and expand the human *self*, to seek ways of expanding the sphere of genuine human action, to increase what people as individual personalities can do for themselves at the expense of what they just find happening to them whether they wish it or not.

Responsible action

If, when we are acting alone, we want others to say that we are acting not just intelligently, or even intelligibly, but *responsibly*, then we must make our actions intelligible to ourselves as we perform them *in other people's terms*, and understand how they relate to other people's needs and interests. In other words, if we are to be accepted by our fellows as reasonable people we are expected to show not just awareness (i.e. consciousness) of our circumstances, but *self*-awareness (i.e. self-consciousness); that is, we are expected not just to act in a manner appropriate to our circumstances but also to act in a manner appropriate to interests other than our own immediate and idiosyncratic ones. Responsible actions are related not to individual but to shared interests. We thus arrive at what may seem to some a paradox: as an individual personality, I can only be truly responsible for my own actions to the extent that I know how to respond to them as others do – the criterion George Mead proposed for such conduct:

Such is the difference between intelligent conduct on the part of animals and what we call a reflective individual. We say the animal does not think. He does not put himself in a position for which he is responsible; he does not put himself in the place of the other person and say in effect, 'He will act in such a way and I will act in this way' (1934, p. 73).

The paradox is resolved by realizing the inherently social nature of all man's *self*-conscious activity (activity in which *he* knows what he is doing, even if the action is as trivial as him moving his arm). I can only be a self in relation to others.

Now in explaining our actions to others, we have, ideally, to give our *reasons*, tell of our aims or *intentions*, say what we expect to result and why. In practice, however, our intentions are often as obscure to ourselves as to others – and this is where empirical investigation can prove effective (for example, Cicourel, 1973; Garfinkel, 1967; Schutz, 1972). Unlike actions, events just happen, they are no one's responsibility; and they are not, of course, to be explained by seeking their reasons. To explain them, we must seek collectively their causal principles, the laws of nature which seem to govern the structure of their appearances – the traditional task of the natural sciences. So we must be clear when investigating psychological phenomena whether it is *reasons* (or something having the logical structure of a reason) or *causal principles* that we seek; the two belong, as we shall see, to two distinct spheres of thought and investigation.

To sum up so far then: while classical science demands that we study everything as if, ultimately, it could be considered as elements of matter in motion according to natural (or to Descartes's absent God's established) laws, people seem able to act according to beliefs or interests, to mere *conceptions* of laws or rules, thus exempting themselves from this demand. But in acting thus, according to what others can recognize as rules or laws, people must make their own actions intelligible to themselves as they perform them in terms of their relations to other people – they can *monitor* their actions (Harré and Secord, 1972). But even more than this, and this is what makes psychology as the study of selves possible, men are aware that they are aware of what they are doing; they are capable of monitoring their own self-monitoring, and of criticizing the account they give of themselves. It is this sphere of responsible or accountable action, what selves can do, that is my central concern in this essay.

Now in attempting to act responsibly, people may fail; they may act rightly or wrongly, appropriately or inappropriately, legitimately or illegitimately. So besides being essentially a developmental social science in dealing with affairs of this sort – acting responsibly in relation to shared rules or criteria – psychology becomes a *moral* science. And its goal? To the extent that, as we shall see, human nature is essentially incomplete, it can only be concerned with discovering our next possible stages of development; it must be, as Bruner (1972) has termed it, a 'policy' science. Thus at its heart we shall not find, as in the natural sciences, *calculation* to do with the one true view, but forms of *negotiation* to do with possible alternatives to the current view.

In its guise as a moral science, psychology cannot, however, be made autonomous; it has to function in a state of exchange with psychology in its other guise as a natural science. For while there are some things we as individual personalities clearly do *do*, there are others which just as clearly we do not *do*. These distinctly different kinds of activity belong to two different but clearly related spheres of study. Below I shall distinguish between the man-made and the natural, between what *individual personalities* with their *personal powers* can do (using the term *powers* in Harré's (1970) sense which is related to the idea of a field of possibilities), and what *natural agents* with their *natural powers* do. In making such a distinction I shall take the *cultural world* as that for which man is responsible, and the *natural world* as that which is responsible for men, thus locating in the natural world at large *an agency* with the power, like men, to make things happen in and of itself (as does, for instance, Whitehead, 1929), a characteristic Descartes' deathly world certainly did not possess.

The distinction between nature and culture should not be taken as indicative of an objective characteristic of the world: it is after all man-made; it is a matter of how we intend it (and that is open to negotiation and re-negotiation). Artificial though it may be, it is nonetheless in its intentional sense a distinction of crucial importance for it will *prescribe* the form of our subject matter and the manner of our conduct in its investigation; it will prescribe in our investigation our goals and the manner of their achievement. The distinction leads to two different kinds of *regulative maxims*, as Kant termed them, rules for regulating one's conduct.

But we must do more than simply distinguish these maxims and their spheres of application; we must also appreciate the nature of their interplay and its sphere of application – the sphere within which man extracts his culture from nature. It is this interplay between the spheres distinguished below which is important.

The natural and the man-made in man

The distinction between the natural and the cultural world has also recently been drawn by Popper (1972). The natural world, the world of people's psychological states, and those parts of the natural world which are products of the human mind – such as works of art, ethical values, social institutions, libraries, scientific problems and scientific theories – he calls worlds 1, 2 and 3 respectively, in the order, he thinks, of their emergence into existence. It is the all-but-complete autonomy of world 3 which interests him. It is partially autonomous because, once we have produced it, it becomes an *object* outside ourselves, and as such is then open to investigation and inter-subjective criticism; and quite often we may discover in it *unintended consequences*, thus increasing our powers in unexpected ways. It is the introduction of world 3 into his philosophy that Popper thinks of as revolutionary. And he suggests that:

One day we will have to revolutionize psychology by looking at the human mind as an organ for interacting with the objects of the third world; for understanding them, contributing to them, participating in them; and for bringing them to bear on the first world (Popper, 1972, p. 156).

Now, within the cultural perspective, we would view men as individual personalities, responsible for their actions to their fellows, and monitoring or interpreting their own and one another's actions in relation to shared aims and interests, whose forms are in themselves humanly constructed – and it is worth remarking in this context that no other beings construct their own goals in such a way. It is being responsible for their own actions in this way that gives the structure of their behaviours a *man-made* aspect, and makes it possible for them to be interpreted for their *meaning*, for their relevence to shared aims and interests – it is also this 'constructed' aspect of their behaviour which, spuriously, makes it seem amenable to mechanistic explanation. An action can have its meaning in terms of the part it plays in furthering a culture's aims or in modifying its interests.

Alternatively, within the natural perspective, in contrast to man as a child of culture, we must view him as a child of nature, just as much a part of the natural order as the trees and the stars. Here we must view him as like an animal, living with his fellows as animals, aware of his circumstances in the sense of responding to them, but not self-consciously aware of them in the sense that 'he' can be said to be responsible for his responses to them; he acts as he must only in relation to his own bodily states. As men *themselves* are not responsible for their actions in this sphere, the structure of their behaviour does not have a man-made aspect to it. It has a distinctly different structure to it, one which does not render it amenable to ready explanation mechanistically at all. And what it is for a man to bring a set of circumstances under his own self-control is, I shall maintain, to impose upon the natural order of his behaviour in these circumstances, one way or another, a man-made structure.

In the man-made and the natural we have two distinct but related spheres of study needing two distinct but related modes of thought and methods of investigation. But this distinction is not in any sense new or original. It was proposed long ago by Giambattista Vico in his *Scienza Nuova* of 1744. Contrary to Descartes, he thought men could not fully understand nature, for, 'Is it not true', he said, 'that we can only know what we make? Then only God can understand nature, because it is his creation. Man, on the other hand, can understand civilization, because he has made it' (quoted in Magill, 1963, p. 478). While man makes culture, nature makes man; and, as we shall see, as there is an essential contingency always in the action of an agency, it is only in those spheres where man can reduce nature by his manipulations to the form of a machine, thus depriving it of its agency, that he gain any degree of control over it at all.

As this distinction between the man-made and the natural is so fundamental it is worthwhile at this point going a little more deeply into the structures of the two different kinds of system: even the most complex of man-made systems, machines for instance, are constructed piece-by-piece from objective parts; that is, from parts which retain their character unchanged irrespective of whether they are parts of the system or not. (And just as men may construct mechanisms for use in the affairs of their external world, so it is not inconceivable that they may construct mechanisms within themselves for use in the regulation of their personal affairs – see Shotter (1974) for a discussion of how mothers may help their infants in the execution of this task.) But whole men as natural systems are certainly not constructed piece-by-piece; on the contrary, they *grow*. They transform themselves from simple individuals into richly structured ones in such a way that their 'parts' at any one moment in time owe not just their character but their very existence both to one another, *and* to their relations with the 'parts' of the system at some earlier point in time – their *history* is just as important as their *logic* in their growth, and because of of this it is impossible to picture natural systems in spatial diagrams. As Čapek (1965, p. 162) remarks, 'any spatial symbol contemplated at a given moment is *complete*, i.e., all its parts are given *at once*, simultaneously, in contrast with the temporal reality which is by its own nature *incomplete* and whose "parts" – if we are justified in using such a thoroughly inadequate term – are by definition successive, i.e., nonsimultaneous.' There is always more to come of natural systems because as well as existing in space they realize themselves through time; true, if they contain *reversible* processes (see Piaget, 1971, 1972), it may be more of the same; but then again, if they contain *irreversible* processes – which they must if they are to be in any sense growing systems – then they may manifest genuine novelty.

Now it is clearly tempting, lacking any clear 'picture' of natural systems, to assimilate them to ones which we can picture, to assume in fact that they manifest the same 'constructional' properties as familiar man-made systems – we then know what we are all talking about. This is exactly the strategy of the classical analytic method in science. Sutherland (1970, p. 98), for instance, in discussing the question 'Is the brain a physical system?' equates natural (physical) and man-made (mechanistic) systems in saying that their main characteristic is that '. . . the principles used in explaining the behaviour of the whole system can be inferred from a knowledge of the laws governing the component parts of the system together with a knowledge of how these parts are organized'. And it is thus that he attempts to argue for the relevancy of computer studies to psychological issues: only if we can in fact make machines like man can we be said, truly, to understand him. But the two systems, the natural and the man-made, can only be equated if the natural systems do not contain 'structure-dependent' parts (Chomsky, 1968, 1972) and are in fact made up of objective parts: a feature which natural systems in their entirety clearly do not possess – as pointed out above, they are growing systems with *successive* as well as simultaneous parts. While such systems must contain some objective parts, and even something like mechanisms as they grow older, their 'parts' in general at some moment in time must only be *perceptually distinguishable* but not in any genuine sense *physically separable* – that is, if the system is to remain alive. For separation would destroy just that precise set of mutual influences by which a living system's 'parts' determine one another's functioning (and those in touch with its environment have their response determined) in relation to the whole. The analytic method, while appropriate to understanding man-made systems, destroys natural ones irretrievably. Sutherland's approach is appropriate for the world of man-made products, the products of man's productive processes, but not in accounting for the productive processes themselves.

In discussing the man-made world I have chosen to concentrate attention on the machine rather than upon rules and maxims, upon institutions and the socially constructed world in general, as one of my purposes is to attack mechanistic psychology and to show that there can be an objective alternative to it. I would not want it to be thought that in discussing machines I meant only *physically constructed* entities; I mean *socially constructed* ones too. But as Mumford (1967) argues, there is often not much of a distinction, for machines can be constructed from men, the *megamachines* constituting much of modern society being a case in point. Berger and Luckman (1967, pp. 77–8) state the character of world 3 very well:

An institutional world is experienced as an objective reality. It has a history that antedates the individual's birth and is not accessible to his biographical recollection. It was there before he was born, and it will be there after his death. . . . Since institutions exist as external reality, the individual cannot understand them by introspection. He must 'go out' and learn about them, just as he must learn about nature. . . . The paradox that man is capable of producing a world that he then experiences as something other than a human product will concern us later on. At the moment, it is important to emphasize that the relationship between man, the producer, and the social world, his product, is and remains a dialectical one. . . . The product acts back on the producer.

And, they continue, it is 'only with the transmission of the social world to a new generation [that] the fundamental social dialectic appears in its totality'; for each new generation of man is a social product (Shotter, 1974).

The reality of time and the contingency of action

The intention in classical thought, from the Greeks till now, has always been to seek the eternal and timeless. Little thought has been given to the idea of a growing world, or growing systems, or irreversible changes and the occurrence of genuine novelty. Indeed, within Descartes' world running on pre-established principles, genuine novelty would be unthinkable: it would seem to come out of nowhere, to be unprincipled and thus uncaused. In such a world, only regularities, only *reversible* changes qualify for a rational (i.e. logical) explanation. But as a growing system, I myself live in space *and through time*. At this moment, I myself am manifesting a particular spatial configuration *here*; then, I was manifesting another state of being *there*; next, I may or may not *be* here, I may or may be not *be* there, it all depends. Through time I can, if I try, realize different possible states of my being in space – and recognizing and recollecting them all together as mine is what gives me my own special sense of personal unity (a unity which can, of course, be lost by some deeply disturbed people). Possessing many possible modes of being, I can project myself in living from one to another – although sometimes I find myself being projected by agencies other than my own. Thus my life can have a directed quality to it, directed by *myself* or by others. My actions, in being directed from a past towards a future, can express an *intention*. I cannot, however, intend a novel action. Although I may *find* myself expressing an intention in a truly novel way, novelty is something which I simply find *happening* to me; it is not something *I* can do. But having it once happen to me, I may, under certain conditions (see Dreyfus, 1965, and Shotter, 1970, 1974, for brief discussion on the determination of intentions), make it, as something which now is not of course novel, happen again. And this is the nature of Piaget's concern in studying the growth of logico-mathematical knowledge, the nature of the child's increasing ability through a sequence of *irreversible* changes (stages) and novel actions to develop more and more extensive and co-ordinated schemes of *reversible* actions (operations).

Now as within the classical deterministic scheme of things a present state of affairs *necessitates* one and only one future state, the future has, thus, the same sort of unknown character to it as distant regions of space: it is simply hidden from human knowledge. If we were all not so ignorant, we could know all our future as Laplace once promised. Thus in this scheme of things, time loses its unique reality and becomes like a fourth dimension of space, and in a sense past and future coexist with the present. But the reality of time implies the reality of irreversible processes and the emergence of novelty, which is incompatible with the pre-existence of the future. In a world existing through real time, the only status the future can have is that of ambiguity, of real possibility. It is *contingent* not *necessary*; not because of our ignorance but because of a genuine ambiguity in events not yet realized. Such a world, to contrast it with the deterministic world of classical thought, may be called indeterministic. And for genuine human action to exist, this must be the character of the world in which we live: for in acting we do something; we make something take on a form other than that which it would have had if we had not acted; thus we determine the world. For this to be possible the world must be capable of being given a form which it did not already possess, that is, the world must be essentially indeterminate. Except that his 'sea of possibilities' metaphor again spatializes time, William James (1956, pp. 150–51) has produced one of the best characterizations of indeterminism of which I know. 'Indeterminism', he said:

... admits that possibilities may be in excess of actualities, and that things not yet revealed to our knowledge may in themselves really be ambiguous. Of two alternative futures which we conceive, both may now be really possible; and the one becomes impossible only at the very moment when the other excludes it by becoming real itself. Indeterminism thus denies the world to be one unbending unit of fact. It says there is a certain ultimate pluralism in it; and, so saying, it corroborates our unsophisticated view of things. To that view, actualities seem to float in a sea of possibilities from out of which they are chosen; and, *somewhere*, indeterminism says, such possibilities exist, and form a part of truth.

Usually we do seem able to intervene in ongoing processes and to make something happen in one way rather than another, as if both possibilities had been intrinsically available in the process. In a growing world, although each present event is not *necessitated* by its own past, it is undoubtedly *caused*; it is made to happen by an *act of selection or choice*. What had been an uncertain future is specifically realized now, by the exclusion of other possibilities. Thus to do anything in such a world is to do this *and not that*. This does not mean that action in such a world is *preceded* by choice, that some mysterious mental act of choosing precedes all our actual choosing. While reflection may precede action, it is only a theoretical, a possible choosing, as is clear from the fact that the 'action' so chosen need not be performed. *Actual choosing is intrinsic to the performance of human actions whether preceded by reflection or not.*

Now by insisting upon the reality of time, upon a growing world full of real possibility, we have implied a distinctly different image of man from the classical image of him as an isolated contemplative. Instead of thinking before he acts, our man in general must act before he thinks in order later to think before he acts – if this is not to be dangerous, there must be 'safe' areas in which he can play (Shotter, 1973). This is, of course, the image of man embodied in Piaget's slogan, 'thought is internalized action', but what Piaget needs to add to this is that in order to be intelligible the structure of such thought and action must be socially negotiated (Harré and Secord, 1972; Berger and Luckman, 1967).

Although this view – that action is primary and thought derived from it – is now becoming common, it is not usually realized what such a view implies. In speaking, for instance, we can and usually do speak grammatically without it first being necessary for us to think about how to do it. Reflecting upon possible grammatical continuations while speaking requires a high level of skill and usually leads to hesitancy (cf. B. L. Bernstein's (1972) 'elaborated code'); it is the exception rather than the rule. Rather than speaking as if one were a computer operating according to a pre-formed programme, one can structure one's speech by monitoring it for its meaning in relation to one's intention in the course of its production – and there are many ways of doing this (Shotter, 1973, 1974). In general we speak with feeling not with thought, and it is only as our intentions issue in performance that we are able to tell whether we are successfully executing them or not. While I usually (but not always) know what I intend, I am in no better position than anyone else for observing my own performances. They must be judged as they occur, both in space *and time* – it being the temporal sequencing of spatial possibilities that reveals a person's choice and thus manifests his intention. Lashley (1951) has been one of the few behaviourist psychologists to see in the temporal sequencing of behaviour any major problem.

Time, then, is the essential psychological medium; it is through time that we express ourselves. In the classical scheme, in which time has been spatialized, this possibility has been lost. There, if contingency was allowed to exist at all it would seem to destroy the possibility of necessity (but this is not necessarily so: see Piaget's (1971, 1972) discussions of this point). Treating time realistically suggests that our thoughts and feelings need not remain private, but that it is possible for us to *show* our thoughts, feelings, moods, beliefs, intentions, etc., in our actions, in our temporal trajectory through sets of contingencies. However, in our attempts to make sense of such expressions, in deciding into which public or trans-subjective category they should be assigned in order to specify them, we must refer not only to objective, to spatial criteria, but also to temporal ones. Such temporal criteria, however, would be essentially contingent; that is, they would be essentially *incomplete*, and determining them (i.e. making them complete) one way or another is itself a matter of choice. Thus, if they are to be made 'logically adequate', then *negotiation* with others is necessarily involved. Space prevents a full discussion of this most important issue here, but discussion of it can be found in Berger and Luckman (1967), Harré and Secord (1972) and Shotter (1974). Suffice it here to say this: to structure our perceptions of a person we must specify a set of both spatial and temporal categories, and place him in relation to them. In categorizing him spatially we can determine his objective structure and locate it, outside ourselves, in space; in categorizing him temporally we can determine his subjective structure (his mental state) ... but where in space should we locate it? This is what has always puzzled us about mental states: because there is nowhere precisely in space to locate them, neither in the observer nor the observed, they seem to float ethereally somewhere in between, and lacking any substantiality seem to have no real existence. In the classical world of matter in motion, they have no matter. But in an indeterministic world moving through real time, they have their location in a person's history, and it is that which is amenable to specification. It is via the structuring of our history that we can determine our future; but if we are concerned to act always responsibly, in a way intelligible to our fellows, how we do in fact structure it is not a matter entirely up to us – it must be negotiated with others.

We have now begun to move into deep waters. The discussion above will suffice if it conveys some of the unique properties of time, and shows that it may be quite incorrect to think of it as simply a fourth dimension of space. While the past is what has been determined (and determined by man in some degree), the future has not yet been so, and thus must be considered not as a single, fourth dimension, but multi-dimensional. It is the future, not this or that hidden region of space, which holds promise of rich possibilities.

By discussing time in this way, I have attempted to indicate that the fact that people are 'growing systems' is all of a piece with the fact that they can learn, express their intentions, pay attention, communicate, pursue goals, create novelty, and so on. In other words, I hope that by realizing in broad outline how it is that we live through time, it will be possible to see that the mental categories which we have called 'fictions' in the past are truly real. And that psychology can be seen as the science which, by operating in an indeterministic world in which both logic *and history* can function to determine our future, helps us make clear in detail the possibilities from which we may choose our next step.

What is it to be human?

What is it then, in the new psychology, to be human? It is to be a growing system which can, in interaction with other growing systems, increasingly localize within itself the power of responsible action. But a conception of man such as this is not so new. In 1487, the Renaissance humanist Pico della Mirandola (1965, p. 5) characterized man as one of God's works of 'indeterminate form', to whom God said:

Thou, like a judge appointed for being honourable, art the moulder and maker of thyself; thou mayest sculpt thyself into whatever shape thou dost prefer. Thou canst grow downward into the lower natures which are brutish. Thou shalt have the power out of thy soul and judgement to be reborn into the higher forms which are divine.

The goal of a new psychology would be to increase people's personal powers of responsible action; to increase not people's mastery over other people but their mastery over their own possible ways of life. It would have nothing to do with how we as 'mechanisms' work, for as growing systems we are not in fact mechanisms even though we may produce them. Its goal can be just as scientific a goal as the goal of the natural sciences, for I take it that what distinguishes those aspects of our lives which we designate as 'scientific' and mark off from the rest of what we do is that in them we attempt to discover general principles via which we can transform ourselves from being victims to being masters of our fates. As time, and thus contingency and choice are central to the new psychology, it will *make* as much as discover the principles via which we can increase our personal powers of responsible action, and the task will be essentially a prospective one, for our powers will remain essentially incomplete. The scientific process will itself involve a negotiated form of interaction with the subjects under study. Vygotsky (1962) discusses one such form of interaction as *instruction*. Via instruction, *spontaneous* actions are raised into the realm of the *deliberate*. But as Vygotsky (1962, p. 90) says, 'in order to subject a function to intellectual and volitional control, we must first possess it'. This point is most important, for it suggests that man can win, so to speak, his personal powers from nature; that what at first he only does spontaneously in response to a *particular* circumstance, he can, *via another person's agency*, come to do later, as he pleases, *irrespective* of his circumstances. The participation of another person in this process is crucial. By attending closely to another's spontaneous acts and selecting from them, he constructs an *ideal self* which he can hold out to the other as a challenge to be attained; he can help the other to come to do deliberately what he did at first only spontaneously.

Each to each a looking-glass
Reflects the other that doth pass
(Cooley, 1902)

Via *instruction* individuals can become responsible themselves for actions which initially arose only in the context of their interaction with others – such forms of instruction are explored more fully in Shotter (1974).

In the past, man has invented for himself many forms of expression, forms of language, writing, mathematics, forms of art, forms of war, forms of family and community organization; in short, he has invented for himself forms of life. And there is no reason to suppose that the process by which we transformed ourselves from cave-dwellers in the past is now at an end.

Cultural progress is surely still possible, and a science called *psychology* can surely assist in making the future transformations of man more responsible ones, so that we can all in the future enhance one another's growth. In the task ahead, the dignity, the self-respect, the confidence to believe that by acting freely we can out of our soul and judgement be reborn into higher forms is essential. Beyond freedom and dignity (Skinner, 1972) is the human termite colony – if, indeed, man's nature could really cease to be a growing one as Skinner's vision would demand.

References

BERNSTEIN, B. (1972), *Class, Codes and Control*, Routledge & Kegan Paul.

BERNSTEIN, R. (1972), *Praxis and Action*, Duckworth.

BERGER, P. L., and LUCKMAN, T. (1967), *The Social Construction of Reality*, Allen Lane The Penguin Press; Penguin, 1971.

BRUNER, J. S. (1972), Address to developmental psychology section of the British Psychological Society.

ČAPEK, M. (1965), *The Philosophical Impact of Contemporary Physics*, Van Nostrand.

CHOMSKY, N. (1968), *Language and Mind*, Harcourt, Brace & World.

CHOMSKY, N. (1972), *Problems of Knowledge and Freedom*, Barrie & Jenkins.

CICOUREL, A. V. (1973), *Cognitive Sociology*, Penguin.

COOLEY, C. H. (1902), *Human Nature and the Social Order*, Scribner.

DREYFUS, H. L. (1965), 'Why computers must have bodies in order to be intelligent', *Rev. Metaphysics*, vol. 21, pp. 13–32.

GARFINKEL, H. (1967), *Studies in Ethnomethodology*, Prentice-Hall.

HAMPSHIRE, S. (1959), *Thought and Action*, Chatto & Windus.

HANSON, N. R. (1958), *Patterns of Discovery*, Cambridge University Press.

HARRÉ, R. (1970), 'Powers', *Brit. J. Philos. Sci.*, vol. 21, pp. 81–101.

HARRÉ, R., and SECORD, P. (1972), *The Explanation of Social Behaviour*, Blackwell.

JAMES, W. (1956), *The Will to Believe*, Dover.

LAPLACE, P. S. (1886), *Introduction à la théorie analytic des probabilités*, Paris.

LASHLEY, K. S. (1951), 'The problem of serial order in behavior', in L. P. Jeffress (ed.), *Cerebral Mechanisms in Behavior*, Wiley.

MAGILL, F. N. (1963), *Masterpieces of World Philosophy*, Allen & Unwin.

MEAD, G. H. (1934), *Mind, Self and Society*, University of Chicago Press.

MUMFORD, L. (1967), *The Myth of the Machine*, Secker & Warburg.

PETERS, R. S. (1958), *The Concept of Motivation*, Routledge & Kegan Paul.

PIAGET, J. (1971), *Structuralism*, Routledge & Kegan Paul.

PIAGET, J. (1972), *The Principles of Genetic Epistemology*, Routledge & Kegan Paul.

PICO DELLA MIRANDOLA (1965), *The Dignity of Man*, Bobbs-Merrill.

POPPER, K. (1972), *Objective Knowledge*, Oxford University Press.

RUSSELL, B. (1914), *Our Knowledge of the External World*, Allen & Unwin.

SCHUTZ, A. (1972), *The Phenomenology of the Social World*, Heinemann.

SHOTTER, J. (1970), 'Men, the man-makers: George Kelly and the psychology of personal constructs', in D. Bannister (ed.), *Perspectives in Personal Construct Theory*, Academic Press.

SHOTTER, J. (1973), 'Prolegomena to an understanding of play', *J. Theory soc. Behav.*, vol. 3, pp. 47–89.

SHOTTER, J. (1974), 'The development of personal powers',
  in M. P. M. Richards (ed.), *The Integration of a Child into a Social World*,
  Cambridge University Press.
SKINNER, B. F. (1972), *Beyond Freedom and Dignity*, Cape; Penguin, 1973.
SUTHERLAND, N. S. (1970), 'Is the brain a physical system?', in R. Borger and
  F. Cioffi (eds.), *Explanation in the Behavioural Sciences*,
  Cambridge University Press.
TAYLOR, R. (1966), *Action and Purpose*, Prentice-Hall.
VYGOTSKY, L. S. (1962), *Thought and Language*, MIT Press.
WHITEHEAD, A. N. (1929), *Process and Reality*, Macmillan.
WINCH, P. (1958), *The Idea of a Social Science and its Relations to Philosophy*
  Routledge & Kegan Paul.

4 If You Won't Deceive, What Can You Do?
Don Mixon

When first encountered, the field of experimental social psychology can appear to be a confusing agglomerate of studies. My own initial reaction was to find many experiments curious, but few of them interesting or notable. One study stood out, for unlike most of the work, it dealt in striking and dramatic fashion with a problem of major and urgent importance. The subject of the study was destructive obedience, the phenomenon Stanley Milgram (1963) thought a central factor in the systematic slaughter of millions of civilians in the Second World War death camps. The fascination of the work was not diminished by the fact that Milgram's initial results were not encouraging: in one respect his New Haven subjects appeared to be behaving in a worse fashion than the Second World War Germans. That is, obedient Germans were presumably under penalty of dire consequences for defiance, while New Haven subjects ordered to give electric shock on command seemingly were free to leave the experiment at any time without penalty. Following instructions, 65 per cent of Milgram's subjects administered the most severe shock on the shock generator. It is disturbing indeed that men appear so ready to inflict harm on others. Yet my first reaction was not simple dismay; something in the hip, anti-establishment atmosphere of San Francisco State College (Summer, 1967) and in my own radical inclinations led me to take considerable satisfaction in having my worse fears concerning the 'true nature' of my fellow countrymen apparently confirmed.

Interest was stirred not simply by the fact that he dealt with important matters, but also by the *way* in which Milgram worked. At a time when most social psychologists were demonstrating their mastery of complex statistical design and were using considerable skill and ingenuity in attempts to test experimentally minor facets of jejune theories, Milgram's methodological guideline was simple, thorough and direct. In the series of studies that followed the 1963 report the device of patiently and systematically varying experimental conditions was used to discover and specify the kinds of situations in which obedience would or would not occur. Milgram's moral concern directed his research project toward the discovery of conditions in which a person might be expected to *defy* a command to harm another.

The more I read and thought about Milgram's work, the more convinced I became of its value and uniqueness. One year after I first heard of them, the Obedience Studies came up for discussion in graduate seminar and I responded with alacrity. I had become a Milgram advocate. But my enthusiasm was brought up short when the professor asked: 'Would you yourself conduct such an experiment?' I could give no immediate answer, not because I suddenly had changed my mind about the value of such work, but because the thought of actually performing the experiment myself forced me to consider aspects of the study I had managed to ignore. Much of the dramatic impact of Milgram's reports was due to the fact that many of his naïve subjects exhibited extremely nervous and agitated behaviour when asked to give increasingly severe shock to another person. That subjects twitched and stuttered and laughed nervously seemed good evidence that they were taking the business of shocking people seriously. But in addition, Milgram's report of the emotional strain evidenced by many of his naïve subjects brought about serious moral controversy (for example, Baumrind, 1964; Milgram, 1964) concerning the right of an experimenter to inflict such suffering.

While nothing may be wrong *per se* in a person finding himself emotionally involved in a situation, moral evaluation is greatly affected by how the person came to be in the stressful situation. Deceit played a very large part in bringing Milgram's subjects to the point of stress. The situation Milgram's naïve subjects found themselves in was carefully contructed around a basic deception. In order to create in the laboratory an analogue to Second World War situations of destructive obedience Milgram decided that he must deceive his naïve subjects concerning the true nature of his interests. In making this decision Milgram was doing no more than following what has become a standard social-psychological practice. But whereas social psychologists frequently attempt to deceive, seldom do their efforts succeed in producing such strong effects on the emotional equilibrium of subjects. Hence the moral protests. And so my dilemma. When asked if I myself would conduct Milgram's experiment I thought quite simply that it would be wrong for me to deceive people, particularly when a result of the deception might be a distressing emotional experience for the deceived. But in deciding that I would not deceive I seemed to be eschewing the possibility of doing significant work; for meaningful research, as represented by Milgram's studies, appeared to depend on, to be inseparable from, deception. If I wished to do serious work I seemed to

have to choose either to deceive people or find a methodological alternativ
to deception. The wish to find *an* alternative to deception was a reflectio
of my methodological naïveté, for I had accepted the notion that ther
exists *a* scientific method. Science, of course, is rich in methods: the histor
of science is replete with incidents in which methods have been devised t
solve problems as they arise. Social psychologists in recent years hav
tended to think in terms of a single experimental method. They in fac
have been content to let a complex and sophisticated methodology dictat
the very problems considered worthy of attention. Seduced perhaps by th
claim contained in the title of Fisher's *The Design of Experiments*, psy
chologists have been enamoured of the notion that relatively new researcl
techniques involving statistical methods supplant past methods; that ther
is in fact *a* way to design experiments.

In the search for alternatives to deception a primary obstacle is th
complacent assumption that the conventional research design is a goo
one, so good and so all-sufficient that alternative methods must produc
equivalent results. The remainder of this paper will be devoted to under
mining this assumption in various ways, one of which is suggesting alter
native methods based on other assumptions. I hope to demonstrate tha
deception is not inseparable from meaningful research, that it is in fact a
makeshift appended to a fundamentally unsatisfactory approach to socia
research.

Writers concerned with the immorality of deceiving subjects on occasior
have suggested role-playing as an alternative method. The role-playing
alternative has been rejected, at times with considerable passion: '... the
use of role-playing strikes at the very root of psychology as a science'
(Freedman, 1969, p. 108). Why should role-playing appear so threatening
and unacceptable? I suspect it is because role-playing makes open and
unabashed use of a basic human ability, an ability most experimenters
assume must be rendered impotent in the laboratory. Without the ability
to pretend, to feign, to dissemble, to fake, and to simulate, people could
not play roles – and experimenters could not deceive subjects. Without the
ability to pretend, social life would not take the forms so familiar to us all.

Man's ability to pretend has long posed problems for many people. If
we think a person might be pretending, what do we make of his actions?
The answer depends entirely on what we want to say about such actions.
The problem of a conventional experimentalist can be understood by
looking at what might be called the Tyrant's Nightmare. A tyrant looks
about him and sees his subjects bowing, scraping and smiling at all the
appropriate times and in all the correct places, but he feels no joy at the

ight. For suppose the subjects are simply feigning and in their hearts hate
and despise him? His crown does not rest easy, nor does his mind and
body during dream-tossed nights. How can he discover the 'true' sentiments of his subjects? Possibly by spying, eavesdropping and making use
of all manner of unusual and unexpected tests he can catch his subjects
off-guard and to some degree render impotent their ability to dissemble.
f such measures reassure him with their findings and if his need for cer-
ainty is not strong, he may convince himself that his subjects are un-
onditionally loving and loyal and so gain a few nights of uninterrupted
leep.

The conventional experimentalist sees his task as essentially similar to
hat of the tyrant. Since he cannot trust his subjects not to feign, he must
with ingenious tests catch the subject off-guard and so discover his 'true'
obedience, 'true' conformity, or even 'true' attitude. In effect conventional
experimentalists appear to be striving for tests of condition-free obedience,
onformity, attitudes.

An alternative way of conceiving experiments can be understood by
ooking at the nature of pretending. When a person pretends or dissembles
he says in effect that 'I am only doing this because of circumstances; if
onditions were otherwise I would behave differently'. For an initial
analysis of episodes it is unimportant whether a person is feigning or not.
The task is to find out how a person behaves under certain conditions,
not how he would behave were conditions otherwise. Such a task would
allow the sort of conditional statements common to all science. Un-
conditional or condition-free statements are ordinarily thought outside the
province of science.

The overall objective of both the tyrant and many social scientists can
be summarized with the same two words – prediction and control. A more
modest and defensible and less manipulative objective can also be described
with two words – foresight and understanding (Toulmin, 1961). In order to
exercise foresight and to understand what people do a social psychologist
an attempt to discover and specify the conditions and circumstances in
which actions do and do not occur. Actors playing roles can be used in
uch investigations.

A person who takes part in a conventional experiment is called a 'sub-
ect'. A person participating in a role-playing investigation is called an
actor'. The language of the conventional experiment is that of the sober,
manipulative scientist; the language of role-playing is forthrightly theatri-
al. I shall stress the differences between the orthodox experiment and
ole-playing, but certain basic similarities also exist. For example, consider
he question: 'Can a person *not* play a role?' A question so broad is

difficult to answer. But if narrowed to: 'Can an experimental subject no
play a role?' the answer seems clearly to be 'No'. Whatever else he may
do or have in mind to do, the behaviour of a subject is governed by hi
understanding of the role 'experimental subject'. Also influencing a sub
ject's behaviour is his understanding of the rules of the experimenta
situation. Of course, the actions of an actor in a role-playing study are
also governed by roles and rules – roles and rules specified in the scenario
The roles and rules of the orthodox experimental situation (as in much o
social life) are implicit; roles and rules of a role-playing scene can be
deliberately explicit.

Social psychologists study meaningful actions, not physical movements
For example, Milgram was not interested in the physical movement in
volved in pushing a lever on a shock generator; he studied an action called
'destructive obedience'. Pushing a lever on a shock generator can be
called 'destructive obedience' only in very particular circumstances. Socia
actions can be understood, indeed identified, only in context and essentia
to an understanding of social context are the concepts 'role' and 'rule'
For example, if I am ordered to administer severe electric shock to another
person the meaning of my subsequent action or inaction depends upon a
number of things. One vital factor is whether or not the order is given by a
person who occupies a role that carries with it the right to give such a
command. But since no role (even that of Dictator) carries with it the un-
conditional right to issue destructive commands, the meaning of the
command and my interpretation of its rightfulness also depend upon the
rules governing the situation or episode in which it occurs. In other words,
whether we like it or not, it is permitted and expected to harm a person in
one rule-context and *not* permitted or expected in other rule-contexts.

Social psychologists have long tended to treat everything a person does
as undifferentiated behaviour. This habit of mind can no doubt be traced
to the decision made early in the century to declare the subject matter of
psychology 'behaviour' and to treat what people do as 'responses'. Quite
obviously behaviour can be treated as undifferentiated responses – investigators have done so for years – but there is increasing doubt that
behaviour can be understood in this manner. Even the 'radical behaviourist' B. F. Skinner in a recent theoretical work (1969) has found it
necessary to distinguish in an admirably clear fashion between two types
of behaviour – 'contingency-governed' and 'rule-governed'. It is in fact
the increasing realization of the importance of the concept 'rule' (for
example, Harré and Secord, 1972) that prompted me to suggest (Mixon,
1972) that in order to understand a social episode it is necessary to make
distinctions between types of behaviour, in particular to distinguish be-

veen behaviour governed by social roles and rules and behaviour that best
ight be called 'performance'.

The difference between role/rule-governed behaviour and performance
an be illustrated with a game analogy. In the American game baseball, as
a any game, what the players do can be understood if one has a know-
dge of the roles of the players and the rules that govern their actions.
'or example, a knowledge of roles and rules will make it perfectly under-
andable (or even predictable if you like) that the batter on hitting a 'fair'
all will run toward first base. The action which to the uninformed might
e inexplicable is given meaning by reference to roles and rules. However,
ot everything that happens in a game can be explained by roles and rules.
Vhether the batter will be able even to hit the ball, how fast he will run if
e does, whether or not he will be 'safe', indeed the ultimate question of
hich team will win the game falls into another category altogether. *How*
ie players do what the roles and rules guide them to do can be called
erformance. While rule-governed behaviour can be understood by
eferring to rules, performance calls for a different type of explanation.
erformance comes to be understood ('predicted') by examining such
actors as past performance, current states and chance.

Social psychologists have shown a great deal of interest in performance,
ar less in what looks like their natural province, rule-governed behaviour.
he lack of work on rule-governed behaviour can be attributed to the
mitations inherent in the naturalistic experiment. Conventional methods
llow adherents to study people in but a single role (experimental subject)
nd in but a single rule-context (the psychological experiment). Moreover,
ie role/rule context of the psychological experiment cannot even be
onsidered representative: the experiment is a very special sort of social
ituation, at once curious and unique (for example, Orne, 1962; Mixon,
972). But if the naturalistic experiment is seriously limited in the study of
oles and rules, role-playing can be used to study any role in literally any
ile-context that can be imagined.

How can role-playing be used in research? In many ways. Role-playing
 an extremely flexible instrument of great potential. The uses I shall
iscuss are meant to be suggestive, not exhaustive. A most interesting use
 in aid of what Harré and Secord (1972) call 'explorations'. Exploration
ivolves extending common knowledge. Much of social behaviour, no
latter how well observed and reported, is not well understood. Suppose an
ivestigator is simply puzzled by a social scene or episode and wonders
hy people in particular roles in a particular context do what they do. A
:enario can be drawn up and actors can repeat the puzzling scene as
iany times and with as many modifications as are necessary to under-

stand the scene. The scenario method is a way of tinkering with wh
might be called a working model of a social episode. The importance
models to the practice of science has been forcefully pointed out in rece
years (for example, Hesse, 1963; Harré, 1970). What is not general
understood is that when constructing models social scientists have
distinct advantage over their physical-science counterparts. A role-playi
model permits the investigator to become quite literally one of its parts;
has the chance to look at the scene from the 'inside' by taking the vario
roles himself. A second advantage is that when other actors take the rol
(become parts in the model) the investigator can ask them what they thir
is going on in the scene.

I have done this sort of exploratory work (Mixon, 1972) with a sce
that has long fascinated me – Milgram's obedience study. The episo
Milgram created was a 'learning experiment' the design of which require
subjects ('teachers') to give increasingly severe electric shock to 'learners
Since Milgram's 'dependent variable' was a rule-governed action, tl
rule-governed behaviour of his subjects could have been uniform or pi
dictable. It was not. Why did some of his subjects obey and some defy
The situation has seemed perfectly clear to most commentators; the cor
mand appeared to be obviously immoral and all subjects therefore *shou*
have defied the experimenter. If defiance is so clearly called for whe
looking at the episode from the outside, why was it not clear to those takir
part on the inside? I found a complete script of the study and transforme
it into an active role-playing exercise. One of the first things I did was
take the role of the naïve subject in order to look at the scene through h
eyes. Later I took the roles of both experimenter and victim and repeate
the scene over and over again using a different person each time in tl
role of naïve subject. The repetition allowed me to become thorough
familiar with each detail of the scene and by changing actors I was able
question many people about what was going on. My subsequent inte
pretation of the scene thus draws on evidence from many sources.

Previous interpretations have rested on the assumption that obedie
subjects helplessly performed an obviously immoral act. From the outsic
the situation seemed clear, its definition obvious. It was otherwise to th
actors. They were not at all sure what was going on. The focus of much o
their puzzlement was the behaviour of the experimenter. They could no
understand why, when it looked as if something had gone seriously wron
with the experiment, the experimenter behaved as if nothing had happene
Far from being clear and obvious, the situation was mysterious an
ambiguous.

To understand what happened in Milgram's study it is necessary t take into account the rules and conventions of the psychological experiment. The experiment is a situation of almost unrivalled compliance; subjects do just about anything an experimenter tells them to do – including such seemingly inhumane and anti-social acts as throwing corrosive acid in a person's face. The reason for this is that people expect, and quite rightly, that the consequences of actions in an experiment are not necessarily the same as in everyday life, that acid thrown in the laboratory will not burn and scar. The fact that 65 per cent of Milgram's subjects were totally compliant was shocking to most people. When looked at in the context of the rules and conventions of the psychological experiment, what is interesting is that 35 per cent of his subjects defied the experimenter. If experimental subjects will throw corrosive acid on command, why should they refuse to administer severe shock? At one point, when Milgram did his pilot study, subjects did not refuse, but instead 'went blithely to the end of the board' (Milgram, 1965, p. 61). The pilot study contained no feedback from the 'victim' that would indicate the shocks were harming him. Milgram got people to disobey only when he introduced into the situation evidence that the consequences of administering the shock were real. Feedback from the 'victim' suggested that he had been hurt or possibly killed. Why then in the face of this evidence did so many people continue to administer more and more severe shock? I think that question can be answered by pointing out a piece of poor script-writing. The actors in my role-playing version could not understand why the experimenter behaved as if the feedback from the 'victim' was unimportant. The feedback suggested that something serious had occurred, that something had gone badly wrong with the experiment. The experimenter behaved as if nothing serious had or could happen. The experimenter in effect contradicted the evidence that otherwise seemed so clearly to suggest that the 'victim' was in serious trouble. Given the overall experimental context where things and consequences are often not what they appear to be, Milgram's situation was one that could be defined either as an experiment where expected safeguards had broken down, or as an experiment where expected safeguards only appeared to have broken down.

How might Milgram's episode be made clearly one thing or the other? We already know from his pilot study that so long as the 'victim' gives no indication that he is being hurt subjects defined the situation as an experiment – that is, an episode in which one follows instructions and occurrences are not necessarily what they appear to be. A general rule governing the experimental situation can be stated as follows: a subject will obey an apparently inhumane command so long as there is no reason to believe that expected experimental safeguards have broken down.

Suppose the evidence that safeguards have broken down is overwhelming – would subjects disobey? I think they would. For though past and current history provides ample evidence that men will obey the most vile commands when given by legitimate authority, men resist and resent illegitimate commands, unless they are transformed by means such as bribery. An experimenter has no authority to command a subject to *actually* hurt another. I reasoned that if the experimenter behaved as if *he* believes the 'victim' is being seriously hurt then his orders to inflict further hurt will be defied. Such a conjecture can be explored or given empirical substance by having the experimenter in the active role-playing study behave as if he believes the 'victim' is in danger. An alternative method, called nonactive role-playing, might also be used (Mixon, 1972). At this point, by suggesting that conjectures be tested we are no longer thinking solely in terms of exploration, but are beginning to think in terms of experimentation.

The problem is to find out when, in the context Milgram created, subjects will obey and when they will disobey. Given more general form, the task is to find out when an act will or will not occur. A method devised to implement this task is called on All and None investigation. The attempt to discover when an act will or will not occur follows a practice long used in experimental sciences, but reverses the procedure commonly followed in social psychology. Ordinarily a social-psychological investigator works from a known set of treatments to an unknown outcome. The All and None procedure works towards particular outcomes (criteria) by way of to-be-discovered scenario changes. A similar practice common in chemistry has been described by Lancelot Hogben (1968, p. 230) as follows: 'The statement that a solution of iodine in K I makes starch paste blue in $75 \pm 1 \cdot 5$ per cent of samples examined will not commend itself to a chemist. He will wish to know what impurities or what range of pH values, etc., determine when the reaction does or does not occur.' Using an analogous procedure a social-psychological investigator will want to know what it is in the components of a scene that determines when an act does or does not occur.

Using the All and None method I found that when it became perfectly clear that the experimenter believed the 'victim' was being seriously harmed all actors indicated defiance to experimental commands (Mixon, 1972). Briefly summarized, the All and None analysis suggests that people will obey seemingly inhumane experimental commands so long as there is no good reason to think experimental safeguards have broken down; people will defy seemingly inhumane experimental commands when it becomes clear that safeguards have broken down – when consequences may indeed be what they appear to be. When the experimental situation is confusing and mystifying as in Milgram's study, some people will obey and some defy experimental commands.

Role-playing then can be used to further understanding by exploring social episodes; interpretations based on the exploration can be tested by another form of role-playing. Because Milgram's episode dealt with a rule-governed act the analysis I have just sketched is outside the usual probability framework. When the purpose is to find out when an act will or will not occur, the language of statistics is inappropriate. Social science at times appears to be conceived, thought and written in statistical language. Statistics is important in the analysis of certain types of social phenomena, but like any other tool can be misapplied, misused. Misapplication and misuse is at times the case in social psychology.

Psychologists in recent years have directed their attention towards methodological questions of a particular sort. The questions are known by such names as generalization, reliability, validity, experimenter bias and demand characteristics. The primary aim of this sort of methodological work is to ensure the accuracy of statements made about experimental results. It hardly needs stating that this is a fundamental and necessary concern. But however important it is that what one says on the basis of an experiment be credible, other questions are vital too. For example, it is of basic importance that a chosen experimental design be appropriate to the question asked, and even more important that the question asked be interesting and meaningful. Interesting and meaningful studies are rarer than they should be, largely because psychologists have taken on faith the belief that a particular and limited type of experimental design exhausts the possibilities of systematic empirical investigation. In so doing, they have severely limited the types of questions that they can ask and answer.

The way to do experiments (according to orthodox teaching) was developed for agricultural research. If this view is correct, scientists have been unable to do proper experiments until quite recently, for the agricultural methods are only a few decades old. The technology accompanying statistical research design is quite formidable and allows adepts ample scope to exercise the most elaborate ingenuity in search of that holy grail 'accounting for all of the variance'. 'Analysis of variance' techniques permit subtle and quite complex questions of a particular type to be asked. If sampling is done correctly (as *seldom* seems to be the case in experimental social psychology) statistical theory has a widely accepted rationale that permits generalization from experimental samples to larger populations. Yet in spite of its complexity and seeming range the *type* of question posed is in fact of quite limited interest. Designs most often used deal with the effects of experimental treatments on average scores. ('Average' in its most general sense refers to any measure of central tendency.)

Average scores may or may not be interesting. In the everyday world of growing crops for money the average is not only interesting but is a very significant category. For example, in a competitive market the average number of bushels of wheat per acre harvested by a farmer has a marked effect on his fortunes. If his average yield is low he may impoverish himself and if it is consistently low he may even lose his farm. Therefore a technology addressed to assessing the effects of experimental treatments on average yield is of prepotent interest to those engaged in producing and selling agricultural products in a competitive market.

To take a simple case, if an agricultural technician wishes to assess the effects of two new fertilizers on the productivity of wheat, he may prepare identical plots A, B, and C and plant and cultivate them in a like manner. The only difference in the way he treats the plots is that A is given fertilizer AI and B is given fertilizer BI, while C (his control) is given no fertilizer. When the crop is harvested he measures the yield of grain and then does statistical tests to determine whether or not the observed differences were large enough to be attributed to treatment rather than chance. If for example he finds that fertilizer AI produced a significantly greater amount of grain he may after further tests wish to recommend that wheat farmers use it under certain specified conditions. It should be especially noted that when highest average yield is the prepotent concern it makes little difference how the treatments affected individual plants. For example, fertilizer BI may have stimulated uniform development so that each and every head of wheat in plot B was minutely but measurably heavier than each head of wheat in the unfertilized control plot; in contrast fertilizer AI, the big producer, may have stimulated some plants, had no effect on others, and even lessened the yield in still others. No matter; the crucial factor to a farmer interested in greater profits is average yield, not the state of individual wheat plants.

In contrast to agriculture where the average score is prepotent, the average, in spite of its overwhelming use in social research, is seldom a socially significant category. Many of the things that interest, or should interest, social psychologists cannot be understood without reference to the individual and an average score that masks individual performance does a positive disservice. Much of rule-governed behaviour is a matter of either doing something or not doing it. For example, reference to average conformity is meaningless. Milgram recognized the problem and did not report scores of mean obedience, but totals of obedient and defiant people. Communication and persuasion involve succeeding or not succeeding in getting through to individual people. If we want to persuade and thus move groups of people, we either get through to all members of the group or to those members of the group who can move the group. Merely to affect by treatment an average score which is by nature sensitive to inflation by unknown individuals may have no effect on group movement at all.

Instances in which an average score is inappropriate may become clear by pointing out a case in social life when it *is* appropriate. In studies of factory productivity an average score has much the same prepotency as in agricultural studies. The performance of an individual worker becomes as irrelevant as the productivity of an individual wheat plant. In order to make a profit in a competitive market factory owners are interested in increasing average output. Treatments that significantly increase this average are of interest no matter what they do to the performance of individual workers. It is interesting how handily statistical design lends itself to exploitation, whether of land or people.

A clearly inappropriate use of average scores can be demonstrated in relation to those social-psychological theories that are concerned with characteristics or characteristic behaviour shared by all people or all members of a particular group. For example, some social-psychological theories postulate a state present in *all* people under specifiable conditions. The much-researched cognitive dissonance theory holds that certain conditions produce in people a state of dissonance that in turn produces attitude change. The theory does not state that dissonance (and change) will occur in some people and not in others, yet when experiments are performed a design is chosen that detects only significant change in average scores. In other words investigators cite in support of a theory that postulates a state (and change) in all people a statistic that can mask the fact that even a highly 'significant' difference was due to a large change in some people, none in others, and even opposite results in still others. A statistical design based on averages seems clearly inappropriate to the testing of any theory concerned with making statements about *all* members of a particular group.

The 'treatment' design is but one of a number of statistical approaches. Social scientists also are interested in making general statements about groups of people and often base such statements on average scores. Generalizations about groups are extremely difficult and notoriously abused. For example, if a layman on the basis of observation claims that 'Blacks are more — than Whites', we label his statement an over-generalization and are likely to call *him* a bigot. His statement is an over-generalization because he assigns a characteristic to an entire group on the basis of the behaviour of some individual members of the group. A social scientist who makes general statements on the basis of average scores does essentially the same thing. His sampling is undoubtedly superior and his choice of characteristic behaviour more acute, but averages are affected by a few extreme individual scores. General statements based on average scores are liable to assign characteristics to an entire group on the basis of the scores of some individuals. A statistically significant difference in average scores is not sufficient warrant for a researcher to state, for example, 'Blacks are more (or less) — than Whites', or to make any other generalization that takes a similar form. Generalizations about groups are very important both socially and scientifically and need to be made with far greater care than is common today.

If you won't deceive, what can you do? I have only touched on possible answers to that question. One enormous task, scarcely begun, is the patient and critical observation and interpretation of the regularities of social life. Role-playing is a very flexible instrument particularly well adapted to the systematic exploration of social episodes that need repeating in order to be understood. Deception is not inseparable from meaningful research, but is simply part of an approach to research that is itself fundamentally un-satisfactory. The conventional social-psychological experiment, far from being a paradigm that all suggested alternatives must be equivalent to, is a limited instrument designed to pose and answer particular types of questions. Research designs that have become fashionable and orthodox are based on summary scores that very often have little or no social meaning. If social psychology is to become a serious and meaningful discipline we must begin to ask serious and meaningful questions. What do we want to know about people and their social life? What sorts of statements would we like to be able to make? Methods exist and methods can be devised to find answers to a wide range of questions. The social psychologist has been in serious error to allow a particular sophisticated, but limited, research instrument to dictate where his interest shall lie, what questions he shall ask, and what kinds of statements he shall make.

References

BAUMRIND, D. (1964), 'Some thoughts on ethics of research: after reading Milgram's "Behavioral Study of Obedience"', *Amer. Psychol.*, vol. 19, pp. 421–3.

FREEDMAN, J. L. (1969), 'Role-playing: psychology by consensus', *J. Personality soc. Psychol.*, vol. 13, pp. 107–14.

HARRÉ, R. (1970), *The Principles of Scientific Thinking*, Macmillan.

HARRÉ, R., and SECORD, P. (1972), *The Explanation of Social Behaviour*, Blackwell.

HESSE, M. (1963), *Models and Analogies in Science*, Sheed & Ward.

HOGBEN, L. (1968), *Statistical Theory: The Relationship of Probability, Credibility and Error*, Norton.

MILGRAM, S. (1963), 'Behavioral study of obedience', *J. abnorm. soc. Psychol.*, vol. 67, pp. 371–8.

MILGRAM, S. (1964), 'Issues in the study of obedience: a reply to Baumrind', *Amer. Psychol.*, vol. 19, pp. 848–52.

MILGRAM, S. (1965), 'Some conditions of obedience and disobedience to authority', *Human Relations*, vol. 18, pp. 57–76.

MIXON, D. (1972), 'Instead of deception', *J. Theory soc. Behav.*, vol. 2, pp. 145–77.

ORNE, M. T. (1962), 'On the social psychology of the psychological experiment: with particular reference to demand characteristics and their implications', *Amer. Psychol.*, vol. 17, pp. 776–83.

SKINNER, B. F. (1969), *Contingencies of Reinforcement*, Appleton-Century-Crofts.

TOULMIN, S. (1961), *Foresight and Understanding*, Hutchinson.

5 Research as Intervention
John Rowan

Bisociation is a word used by Arthur Koestler to mean the funny, witty, exciting or insightful thing that can happen when two separate fields of discourse are forced into one another.

Let's see what happens when we bisociate psychological research and change-agent intervention. Each of these has a quite different set of rules. And I want to look at this because it is happening to me now. I feel I am moving away from being a researcher and towards being a change agent.

The psychological researcher is usually aiming at an experiment. In an experiment everything has to be held constant, balanced out or randomized, except for the variables under consideration. In modern research, we often abandon the old ways of doing this, and adopt an approach which includes possible sources of bias into the design itself, using multivariate analysis to sort out the resulting confusion, but the basic idea of purity is still the same.

The change agent is usually aiming at solving some problem or associated set of problems in an organizational setting (Bennis *et al.*, 1970). In such an intervention the main constraints are ethical – the change agent must aim at objectivity, integrity, competence, confidentiality and the welfare of the people involved. This tends to be laid out in codes of ethics rather than in textbooks.

Yet obviously the researcher wants to be ethical, and the change agent often does research on the effects of his or her intervention. So what is the problem, and what is the advantage, in forcing them into one another? Aren't they perfectly compatible as they are? If we asked each person separately, they might say something like this:

Researcher: 'I don't like the way in which you involve yourself in the situations you study. I don't see how you can get any objective explanations out of that loose set-up. You seem prepared to accept constraints which make any real scientific approach impossible. I sometimes suspect you of using the findings of pure science for your own financial advantage, while actually taking the name of science in vain.'

Change Agent: 'I don't like the way in which you aim at a phony objectivity which only succeeds in trivializing your work and making it irrelevant.
I don't like the way in which you kid yourself you are not involved when
really you desperately care how the results come out. And if you *could* be
wholly cold and neutral, I would hate that too, because that indicates a
deep psychological defect, all too common amongst would-be scientists.'

Now, is that just misunderstanding or failure of communication, or is it a
deep difference? At any rate, it demonstrates that there may be something
worth scrutiny. Let's start our bisociation by looking at the social-
psychological researcher in more detail.

The researcher

All through the time of social psychology's rapid rise, it has become more
narrowly based. The typical experiment in social psychology is carried out
on a small and unrepresentative sample of students – usually second-year
(sophomore) students. For example, in the *Journal of Personality and Social
Psychology* for January 1972, there are about seventy people – almost
always students – in each experiment; and since there are several experimental conditions in each study, actually only ten to twenty subjects in
each experimental condition.

And large conclusions are often drawn from such narrow bases. For
example, one paper concludes that 'being crowded' is really equivalent to
receiving excessive stimulation from social sources'. The implication of
this is that in order to reduce crowding in public spaces it is not necessary
to provide more space, but only to provide more partitions, fewer door-
ways and more elongated rooms. The experiments on which this conclusion
is based were carried out using ten male and ten female undergraduates, and fibreboard models of rooms in which the subjects had to place
clothes-pins with arms made of pipe cleaners to represent people.

The vast majority of experimental social psychology takes no notice of
this kind of problem. There appear to be five questions which experimental
psychologists ask themselves before starting a particular investigation:

1 Is it cheap? Can I do it with no materials other than duplicated score
sheets – there is always plenty of paper about – and with existing apparatus?

2 Is it handy? Can I do it with the people I have on hand? Can I do it
without moving too far from my office? Can I use my computer?

3 Is it convenient? Can I fit it into the life of my students without dis-
rupting their habits in any way?

4 Is it brief? Can I get it over in twenty minutes – or an hour, if I can run several people at a time?

5 Is it publishable? Will it add to my book of records, whether it reveal anything worth knowing or not? Memo: interesting statistics can help poor sampling will not be penalized.

This may seem a very unfair catalogue of questions, but of course I am taking for granted that researchers are often both sincere and expert The pressures on them are to publish, to get their theses completed, to get another grant and so on. It is these pressures which ensure that bad conventions get set up and perpetuated.

One cannot help feeling that it would be better if these experimenters asked instead a different set of questions, which would be better adapted to getting something worthwhile out of their work, such as the following:

1 Is my method an adequate representation of what I am supposed to be studying? If I am studying anger, are my subjects really angry?

2 Is my sample representative? If so, what is it representative of? With how much confidence can I generalize to the parent population? Do I have any idea of what parent population I am talking about?

3 Is my work relevant? Who suffers and who benefit from the work I am doing? If nobody suffers and nobody benefits, how do I feel about that?

4 Is my work merely descriptive, or does it lead to change of some kind? Change in what direction, and in whose interest?

In an attempt to answer some of these criticisms, the concept of a research cycle has been introduced. The research cycle is a concept which can be interpreted in at least two different ways. It can be seen either as taking the old methods and using them in a more imaginative way, or as involving a number of new methods as well.

Research cycle – type one

The first type of research cycle starts with the experimenter's experience, moves straight into the laboratory, goes back to the experimenter's armchair, from there out into the field (real-life situation) and from there to the final report. A good example of this was a whole series of researches by Stanley Schachter and his associates on obesity. They did a number of laboratory experiments, and then a whole series of wide-ranging and very imaginative researches in real-life situations. The results were more convincing than any straight laboratory experiment would have been.

The November 1968 issue of the *Journal of Personality and Social Psy-*

ology was almost totally devoted to real-life research on important ssues, and was really exciting to read.[1] But no other issue up to the time of riting has fulfilled the promise that this was going to be the pattern for e future. This suggests that something is still wrong with this style of search.

And we do not have to look far to see what it is. Although the research far more imaginative, and takes in far more varied situations, it all still volves an alienated relationship between the experimenter and the bject. It is still the case that the experimenter is an intelligent prober into ature, while the subject is a thing to be studied. Maybe quite an interesting ing, but still on quite a different plane from the experimenter. It is not til we challenge this, that we start to challenge what is basically wong ith social psychology today.

What we are coming to here is not an ethical issue of how the psyologist should treat the subject, but the twofold issue of what the sychologist is doing to *himself and the subject* – the relationship which e psychologist is setting up; and the image of man which is implicit in at relationship (Israel and Tajfel, 1972).

An increasing body of criticism is arising to say that psychology can nly discover one-sided things if it insists on setting up one-sided relationips:

ou can only get answers to those questions you are asking. Questions of trust quality and dialogue between the investigator and his subject are not being asked, nce they offend against current conceptions of good methodology. But power ver people in a laboratory can *only* lead (if it leads anywhere) to a technology of ehaviour control. The results which flow from the unilateral inputs of the experienter are only applicable to those exercising unilateral inputs in our culture Iampden-Turner, 1971).

erhaps this is a criticism from outside, from someone who has never had) conduct experiments himself, and who therefore does not really under-:and the position. So here is an experienced professor of psychology ılking.

sychologists face a choice. We may elect to treat our subjects as objects of study or the benefit of some élite; or we may choose to learn about determiners of the uman condition in order to discover ways to overcome or subvert them. . . . We hall have to state openly whether we are psychologists-for-institutions or psychogists-for-persons. The trouble with scientific psychologists – among whom I umber myself – is that we have, in a sense, been 'bought' (Jourard, 1968).

. Two of these papers are reprinted in Swingle (1973).

Now obviously this line of thinking opens up wide vistas, affecting th' whole way in which society is run and operates, which are dealt wit' elsewhere in this volume. But here we are mainly interested in its implica' tions for research styles. What difference exactly does it make to ou' research if we take these points to heart, and see what the change agent approach has to offer?

The change agent

The second type of research cycle starts with the change agent's experienc' moves to some method-oriented interaction with people, which is the' revised in accordance with the actual responses obtained, a process i' which the people themselves take part; this leads to further metho' oriented interactions, and the process continues, resulting ultimately in body of shared experience. Depending on the type of experience which i' involved, it may or may not be appropriate to abstract the results a 'knowledge' which can be fixed in a scientific paper and used by others.

For example, Alan Sutter (1969) did research on drug use, and focuse' drug users' and addicts' own experiences, in their own language, which h' then wrote up into a research report. He checked the authenticity of hi' information by submitting his report to panels of drug users. This enable' him to validate his information and to collect more.

There are not very many good examples of the whole process in action the challenge in its fully realized form is too recent for that – but there are number of partial examples which will give something of the flavour o' this research style. They fall under two main headings – action researc' and intervention research.

Action research

This is a method which came into being in the 1930s and was pursued in . number of ways in the 1940s – partly due to the inspiration and example o' Kurt Lewin (1946), who led here, as in so many other ways. One of th' areas in which work was done was racial prejudice. The idea was that . community which was suffering from the effects of racial prejudice – any' thing from bad feelings and discrimination to riots and lynchings – coul' undertake a self-survey.

A community self-survey can be described as action research in which the *mem' bers of the community themselves*, under the expert guidance of applied socia' psychologists, are responsible for the collection and analysis of community data Three important objectives can be achieved by such community self-surveys first, the facts collected will permit the realistic planning of a programme of action ... Second, the facts thus uncovered by the citizens of the community will b' more readily accepted by the community than if those facts were supplied to them by an outside research agency. . . . Third, quite apart from the facts collected, the intimate contact with the problems of minority-group members may have a powerful motivating effect on the surveyors.

This account by Krech and Crutchfield (1948) makes the point that it is only when people actually get talking to minority-group members in a face-to-face situation that they realize just how bad things are. Action research has been well described by Zander (1942) and by Weaver (1945). It is quite capable of producing both knowledge and action of a remedial kind. It may be doubted, however, whether it is very powerful in changing the basic level of prejudice. In other words, the amount and kind of *discrimination* in a community can be charted and changed by action research at the community level, and this is of course highly beneficial and worth doing, but a great deal of *prejudice* may be left intact.

So action research is better for dealing with overt action, while leaving people's minds alone. And perhaps for this reason, it has become almost entirely a tool of management now. Whyte's (1949) classic study of the restaurant industry marks the transition, and a recent book by Clark (1972) shows the melancholy result over the past twenty years. One never hears of the community self-survey now.

Intervention research

Is intervention research any better? Let us go back to prejudice again, and see what this approach has to offer. It will make the difference in the two styles quite clear. Jønes and Harris (1971) have reported on the use of small groups to study racial attitudes. They used six to eight weekly sessions of an hour and a half, followed by a six-hour session, with groups of ten to fifteen people, some white and some black. There are two co-leaders, one black and one white. The research showed that certain phases seemed to be constant, and regularly arose to be worked through as the sessions progressed.

1 Introductory phase. The main theme is of white people claiming to be free from prejudice;

2 Information phase. Black members come back with details of how they have suffered. (This is as far as one would normally get with the former type of action research.)

3 Competitive phase. The whites come back with stories of how they, too, have experienced discrimination or persecution, because of being Jewish, Catholic, long-haired, revolutionary, female, etc.;

4 Competitive response. The blacks then emphasize how much worse their problem is, and it becomes clearer that it is white society which i responsible, in their eyes;

5 Dissociation. The whites then try to dissociate themselves from white society generally, and also accuse the blacks of exaggerating. One way or another, they avoid accepting the black statements as applying to them;

6 Impasse. It becomes clear that the blacks and the whites are on two different wavelengths. There is a feeling of being stuck. Evasions of different kinds are tried. It seems that nothing is going to change or happen;

7 Moment of truth. Eventually one of the blacks will express *anger*, strongly, honestly and unequivocally. The group by now knows him or her well, and cannot fail to be impressed;

8 Follow through. The other blacks in the group sooner or later support the member who has spoken out. The emotional reality of what it is like to be black comes through clearly;

9 Realization. The whites gradually and painfully see the contrast between sympathetic, understanding, warm-hearted liberalism, and the real awareness of the black experience. They see that they have been living in a different world, and systematically deceiving themselves about it;

10 Digestion. The whites start to go over their past experiences with blacks, in the light of the new consciousness they have now of what it means to be black. The blacks feel relief and surprised delight that the whites are really listening and struggling to understand;

11 Consensual validation. Both whites and blacks are able to work on their and each other's problems in an atmosphere which at last is relatively clear.

The process is of course not automatic, and many hitches and problems may occur along the way; but already it seems clear that the kind of deep emotional readjustment which is required to do anything important about racial prejudice takes a great deal of energy and social pressure to achieve. Even in these groups, there are a few people who seem to be unreachable. But this is much more recent research, and is still going on in a number of different places.

One thing about it needs pointing up, perhaps, and that is that the blacks in these groups had an experience of expressing deep anger, and seeing it work. Casriel (1971) distinguishes four types of anger, and says that it is only the fourth which is therapeutic. The first type is intellectual anger, quietly thought and expressed; the second is riddance anger, screaming but mixed with anxiety; the third is more in the chest, a murderous rage.

ndividuals have to feel that third level before they can get to the fourth level.
They have to feel secure enough for that third type of anger in order to feel the
fourth level, which I call 'identity anger'. People feel it in their belly, and it comes
out as a feeling that 'I'm angry because I've been hurt; it wasn't fair what happened to me, Godammit, and I'm angry, I'm angry and nobody is going to do
that to me again; no more. I'm not going to let *anybody* do that to me. *No more;
no more!*' You feel it in your total body, and you feel aware of a total you, a total
whole identity.

It seems, then, that groups like this may not only reduce prejudice in the
whites, but be an important therapeutic experience for the blacks, too.

It is important to see how this research procedure differs from participant
observation. Participant observation has been an important technique in
social psychology, as can be seen in the classic papers by Whyte on gangs in
an Italian slum, by Polsky on the life of the pool hustler, by Barker and
Wright in their study of behaviour settings, and so on. But in participant
observation, people are revealing themselves to the observer, while he is
not revealing himself to them. In the Jones and Harris study just described,
the researchers were themselves the group leaders, and exposed their
feelings and prejudices in just the same way as other members of the
group. The participant observer, on the other hand, can often remain
virtually unchanged and unchallenged by his experience, which thus
becomes of one-way benefit to him and his sponsors. Indeed, the basically
alienated nature of this technique is brought out in the following quote.

Festinger, Riecken and Schachter wanted to join a secret group preparing for the
end of the world. . . . When rebuffed in their initial effort to join, it was necessary
for these investigators to have a 'psychic experience' before they were acceptable
to the other members.

Karl Weick gives this account without remarking on what stands out – the
way in which the investigators were willing to stoop to an evil-smelling
deception in order to get their data. As it happens, they were 'punished',
in that their failure to confirm their original hypothesis was probably a
direct effect of their deception! But investigators do not always get their
come-uppance in this poetic way.

There is again a danger, as with action research, that intervention research may be used as a tool of management. This is already happening.
Argyris talks about 'organic research' in much the same way as I have
talked about intervention research. But certainly this style of research
seems to be less one-sided and therefore less alienating than other kinds,
and more defensible on those grounds.

In sociology the same process can be seen at work. The vast structural-functional analyses of Talcott Parsons have given way to the much more intimate and detailed studies of Goffman and Garfinkel. All these movements are in the direction of greater attention being paid to qualitative research.

Qualitative research

One of the traditional distinctions within the field of survey research has been the distinction between qualitative and quantitative research. Qualitative research, often taking the form of group discussions or depth interviews, would be carried out first, and then hypotheses emerging from it would be carried forward into the quantitative stage. For example, in a typical large-scale exercise, Bynner (1969) says:

The questionnaires used in the main investigation were designed on the basis of a series of exploratory and pilot studies. In the first of these, discussions were held with groups of boys and girls (smokers and non-smokers separately) from secondary modern schools to find out what their attitudes were towards smoking and, particularly, what they thought of the non-smokers and smokers among their peers. This study suggested a number of hypotheses about the influences prompting children to start smoking, and drawing upon the content of the children's remarks a large number of questions were designed to test and explore them further. After a pre-test these questions were modified and then tried out in a pilot survey in May 1965 of 1180 boys and girls in the first and fourth years of twenty secondary schools. (The final survey approached sixty schools and had a total sample of 5600 boys.)

Now this is the traditional use of qualitative research – it is left behind as soon as it is decently possible to do so. Yet it is crucially important, because any hypotheses which do not emerge at that stage are almost impossible to pick up later. Consequently, it is the base on which the whole later research edifice stands. And it is the only stage at which we are talking to 'real people'; at every subsequent stage we are talking to processed people, in the sense that they can only answer in terms of *our* questions and *our* categories. At the qualitative stage, they are using their own words and their own experience.

The main criticism of qualitative research has always been its subjectivity – its uncheckable character. At one level this is easy to refute – perhaps one cannot repeat the investigation exactly – can one ever? – but one can certainly set up similar investigations and compare notes. But at a deeper level, it raises the whole question of what we are doing in science. As soon as one gets amongst actual psychologists, and away from the textbooks, one finds them talking like this: 'That was a brilliant paper last month by

Crackerjack in the Journal.' 'Did you think so? It may look all right, but I don't trust him. I once worked in his lab, and he is not above fiddling his results.'

There is a whole lot going on in the scientific community besides science, and personal integrity is part of the story too. Rogers (1968) says about this:

Even in the realm of confirmation, the personal element enters. In a recent discussion with Lancelot Whyte, the physicist who became a historian of ideas and a philosopher of science, I was surprised to find that, for him, the truth value of a statement, even in science, could in the last analysis be evaluated by one criterion only. If I understood him correctly, that criterion is: how deeply acquainted with the phenomena, how non-defensive, how truly open to all facets of his experiencing, is the scientist who perceived the pattern and put it to the test?

If this is true in the hard world of empirical confirmation of hypotheses by empirical test, how much more true is it likely to be in the field of qualitative research? What we are really saying is that a fully functioning person in Rogers's sense is the only person who can be *objective*, and that this is the only kind of objectivity which really matters. It is the phenomenologists who have said this best, in their distinction between objectivity (in the sense in which we are talking about it now) and *objectivism*.

Objectivity, as a human attitude, is free man's recognition of his orientation to, and being normalized by, something which is not himself, insofar as this recognition finds expression, usually in an implicit fashion, in his words and deeds. It is the opposite of arbitrariness, prejudice and self-sufficient subjectivism.

On the other hand, says Strasser (1963), objectivism is a kind of reduction of psychology to the kind of experience which can be described accurately in the language of physical science. It trusts that there is some kind of method which in and of itself guarantees scientific truth. But there is in fact no such method. Polanyi (1968) gives this example.

The author of this letter [in *Nature*] had observed that the average gestation period of different animals ranging from rabbits to cows was an integer multiple of the number *pi* (3.14159 ...). The evidence he produced was ample, the agreement good. Yet the acceptance of this contribution by the journal was only meant as a joke. No amount of evidence could convince a modern biologist that gestation periods are equal to integer multiples of *pi*. Our conception of the nature of things tells us that such a relationship is absurd.

If in the face of incontrovertible evidence that there exists a significant relationship between two variables, we still prefer to trust our informed feeling that the whole thing is nonsense, that is the kind of decision which

we must be making all the time, without perhaps realizing it. We canno
avoid making such decisions, so we had better become more conscious of
what we are doing and how we do it, and not deceive ourselves into thinking that we are simply going by 'the facts' or by impersonal laws of proof
And it is at the level of qualitative research that our noses are rubbed most
explicitly in this conclusion.

And qualitative research enables us to keep in touch with the purpose
and meanings which lie behind people's actions. In other words, it enables
us to respect the praxis of our subjects – taking their own intentions
seriously, rather than interpreting them in alien forms.

One of the best researchers using the qualitative method is Peter Madison
(1969a, 1969b) who says:

Since 1952 I have been making detailed qualitative studies of college students,
using autobiographies, repeat interviews, student journals and personality tests.
... The student is studied early in his college career and followed year by year to
graduation and sometimes for as long as five to ten years after.... One can't
observe a person closely over a period of time without his being influenced by the
act of studying him. Any longitudinal study on such a personal level is, by definition, action research.

It can be seen that here, in its purest form, where it is freed from its
connection with quantitative research, qualitative research comes very
close to the style we have called intervention research. Madison's understanding and care and psychological knowledge render him a first-rate
observer and guide through the complex data, and his approach is
thoroughly objective in the phenomenological sense. One feels all the
way through that he is doing justice to the praxis of his subjects.

Experimenter effect

And this leads us straight into the whole question of experimenter effect,
which we must look at briefly before concluding. Orne started it all with
his paper on the social psychology of the social psychology experiment –
the reflexive area which we have seen continually arising in one way or
another as the most problematic.

Psychology is essentially a reflexive science: that is, the findings of the
psychologist about his subjects must also apply in some way to the psychologist himself and his own activities. This was what Orne tried to
follow up.

He was intrigued by the way in which subjects in experiments obeyed
orders in an almost hypnotic way (in fact, he had already done experiments
on the role-playing of hypnotic states) and did some very striking things.

For example, he asked students who had come as subjects to the laboratory to tear up paper into small pieces, without giving any more reason than that. He wanted to see how long they kept on doing it before getting angry with the experimenter for wasting their time. Six hours later he wanted to go home, and had to stop the subjects, who were only too willing to carry on.

It seemed clear that the experimental situation, which had been treated for all these years as a purely rational and 'clean' situation where accurate observations could be made free from bias, was actually a highly potent social field, with very strong forces at work. (One effect of this work was to make experimenters do more post-experimental interviewing.)

But the basic problem remains: the university psychological laboratory is a highly authority-structured situation, in which the experimenter has very high social status. This may be the last thing which the experimenter wants, but he has it, whether he wants it or not. The point is that the experimenter can vary the effect which he has, but not do away with it. For example, Hoffman found that people are more likely to sort photographs into emotionally positive categories with 'friendly' experimenters than they are when the same experimenters are 'neutral' in manner. So it is not enough for the experimenter to want to be democratic in his approach – the situation has such strong demands that it turns him into an authority anyway, only this time it is a *nice* authority. It looks very much as though the social relationship which the university has to the rest of the society (intellectual authority) is reproduced in little in the laboratory–subject situation. So we are not just talking about the laboratory, but about social relationships generally. Our society runs in forms of a dominant ideology, which is an ideology of domination. And we can see this ideology at work in almost every laboratory experiment – and for that matter in almost every social survey.

The identity of the researcher

The more we go into questions of research methodology, the more we find ourselves coming up against the problems of reflexivity – that is, the way in which the researcher is implicated in his own investigations, willy-nilly. The researcher is always either changing the status quo, or reinforcing it. And mostly he is reinforcing it. It is not just a question of designing better experiments – it is a question of what ground the psychologist is standing on when he conducts his experiments. As Jourard (1972) says:

The agencies which believe it worthwhile financing research into human behaviour typically believe that their interests will be furthered if man's behaviour becomes less unpredictable. They want men to be transparent to them (while they remain opaque to the others), and they want to learn how to make men's actions more amenable to control.

There are questions here which need to be answered by anyone who wants to do good research. Who is going to support him or her, and on what basis? Are social psychologists anything more than social engineers? Are they even engineers, or are they only maintenance men?

When psychologists use sensory-deprivation experiments to devise better interrogation procedures for the military, or use conflict theory to aid in the control of political internees, or use perceptual experiments to devise better noise machines for use against rioters, how do they describe their work when they come home?

And in the research laboratory? Are we engaging in a common endeavour with our subjects, or are we merely using them, and perhaps even lying to them systematically? I have myself been a subject in an experiment in which I was lied to and never debriefed. I only found out by talking to another subject in the lift as we left.

And in the survey field? What are the social relationships between researcher and interviewer? Between interviewer and respondent?

And when we have begun to answer all these questions, what do we actually do?

One thing which seems to be happening is that psychologists are combining work in psychotherapy or in personal growth with research. And the research tends to be in the area of finding out what enhances people and what diminishes people. In a discussion of many aspects of this kind of research, Heron (1972) says:

There is a dyadic and co-equal relation between facilitator and agent. These roles are reversible between the two persons involved; or each person may combine them at the same time. One may facilitate and be present for the self-experiment of the other.

So this research increasingly comes to be about shared experience. I have myself become involved both in co-counselling and in other work which involves an intervention orientation. There is no policy which can be laid down for everybody – having once faced the issues, each psychologist has to decide for himself or herself what to do. But it should at least be clear that there are social implications in whatever actions the psychologist takes. The psychologist is one of a small number of highly educated people who have great influence in our society, mainly at the level of intellectual communication. It matters very much what image of man he holds, and what model of man he propagates. It matters very much that he realizes that his research is a social intervention into the lives of other people.

We are entering into a period of more and more rapid change. The human being who is going to ride the surf is going to have to be more adaptable, less rigid than any previous human being has needed to be. And we are beginning to know how to encourage ourselves and other people to be more capable of this. As Rogers (1969) puts it:

I am suggesting that as the individual approaches the optimum of complete functioning his behaviour, though always lawful and determined, becomes more difficult to predict; and though always dependable and appropriate, more difficult to control.

It seems that it is possible for psychologists either to help in this process, by validating people, respecting their praxis, and confirming their reality as persons; or to hinder it by intentionally or unthinkingly reinforcing the rigidities which stem from the general alienation of society. It is intervention, either way.

If as psychologists we opt for the former alternative, we must not be too surprised if we meet opposition. On the other hand, we should not anticipate opposition in such a way that we produce it by the sheer force of our own expectations. Social psychology is a wide field, and there is room in it for many different ways of action, many styles of being.

We have to choose. We have to decide on our own projects. And we have to do all this under the pressure of many forces pushing or trying to push us. We have to be free, while knowing that we are determined. This is the paradox of transcendence – it is at one and the same time true that we are all creatures of our age and our society, down to the most minute particulars; and also that we are infinite and uncontainable. Psychology needs to study both; and to do that, it must respect both. Or it is not a human psychology at all.

References

BENNIS, W. G. *et al.* (eds.) (1970), *The Planning of Change*, Holt, Rinehart & Winston.

BYNNER, J. M. (1969), *The Young Smoker*, HMSO.

CASRIEL, D. H. (1971), 'The Daytop story and the Casriel method', in L. Blank *et al.* (eds.), *Confrontation: Encounters in Self and Interpersonal Awareness*, Collier-Macmillan.

CLARK, P. A. (1972), *Action Research and Organizational Change*, Harper & Row.

HAMPDEN-TURNER, C. (1971), *Radical Man*, Duckworth.

HERON, J. (1972), *Experience and Method*, BPS Conference.

ISRAEL, J., and TAJFEL, H. (eds.) (1972), *The Context of Social Psychology: A Critical Assessment*, Academic Press.

JONES, F., and HARRIS, M. W. (1971), 'The development of interracial awareness in small groups', in L. Blank *et al.* (eds.), *Confrontation: Encounters in Self and Interpersonal Awareness*, Collier-Macmillan.

JOURARD, S. M. (1968), *Disclosing Man to Himself*, Van Nostrand.

JOURARD, S. M. (1972) *Psychology for Control, and for Liberation of Humans*, BPS Conference.

KRECH, D., and CRUTCHFIELD, R. S. (1948), *Theory and Problems of Social Psychology*, McGraw-Hill.

LEWIN, K. (1946), 'Action research and minority problems', *J. soc. Issues*, vol. 2.

MADISON, P. (1969a), 'Complex behavior in natural settings', in T. Mischel (ed.), *Human Action: Conceptual and Empirical Issues*, Academic Press.

MADISON, P. (1969b), *Personality Development in College*, Addison-Wesley.

POLANYI, M. (1968), 'The growth of science in society', in W. R. Coulson and C. R. Rogers (eds.), *Man and the Science of Man*, Bobbs-Merrill.

ROGERS, C. R. (1968), 'Some thoughts regarding the current presuppositions of the behavioral sciences', in W. R. Coulson and C. R. Rogers (eds.), *Man and the Science of Man*, Bobbs-Merrill.

ROGERS, C. R. (1969), *Freedom to Learn*, Bobbs-Merrill.

STRASSER, S. (1963), *Phenomenology and the Human Sciences*, Duquesne University Press.

SUTTER, A. (1969), 'Worlds of drug use in the street scene', in D. R. Cressey and D. A. Ward (eds.), *Delinquency, Crime and Social Process*, Harper & Row.

SWINGLE, P. (ed.) (1973), *Social Psychology in Everyday Life*, Penguin.

WEAVER, R. C. (1945), *Community Relations Manual*, American Council for Race Relations.

WHYTE, W F (1949), *Human Relations in the Restaurant Industry*, McGraw-Hill.

ZANDER, A. (1942), *Centerville Studies Itself*, University of Michigan Press.

6 Asking Silly Questions
Martin Roiser

This article takes as its starting point the frustration that many people feel
when they try to answer attitude questionnaires. It attempts to do justice
to those who have laboriously tried to reassert their own attitudes, feeling
them unrepresented, or even caricatured by the items offered. For the
most part these criticisms, added as comments at the end, or expressed in
other ways, have been ignored by psychologists. For one thing they are not
easy to score, but more importantly the subject is not considered qualified
to criticize the questionnaire designed and standardized by the expert
psychologist.

A personal experience is relevant here. Some time ago I was asked, as a
subject, to fill in a questionnaire drawn up by a well-known social psychologist. It was entitled 'The Student and Society'. I recall a feeling of
intense annoyance on finding the following item: 'I am in favour of
destroying the present political system even without knowing what will
replace it'. My pencil hovered nihilistically over the response 'strongly
agree', then wavered uneasily between 'mildly agree' and 'cannot answer'.
In vain did I search the questionnaire for a reasonable expression of my
views. Caricatures of extremity and moderation predominated, intermingled with potted homilies and laughable simplifications. I added a
side of my own views on the back, but I doubt whether they were quantifiable, as that term is generally understood by psychologists.

In this article the theory underlying conventional attitude measures is
examined. The efforts of psychologists to avoid ambiguity and bias in the
design of attitude statements are criticized. Three examples of objections
from subjects to attitude questionnaires are examined. Finally it is asked
whether an alternative rationale for the measurement of attitude is needed,
and its implications discussed.

Attitude scales typically comprise a number of brief statements gathered
and standardized by the psychologist. For instance, the subject may be
asked to register degrees of agreement or disagreement with the phrase:
'Everyone in this country should be treated equally regardless of colour',
and so on. From his pattern of responses a numerically precise score on a
scale can be calculated to mark the subject's racial attitude. Often subjects,

unappreciative of the rationale of psychology, have complained that such statements are too brief and the response categories too limited. Despite the brevity of the statements subjects have claimed them to be frequently ambiguous or biased.

Psychologists have generally been agreed that an attitude item should be precise, since otherwise its measuring ability is impaired. Ideally it is seen as having a fixed, externally ascertainable value, just like a physical stimulus, a weight or a light. Thus the response made can be checked against the real value. In fact one of the founding fathers of attitude measurement, Leon Thurstone, began as a psychophysicist, transferring physical judgemental concepts to the study of attitude (Thurstone and Chave, 1929). This helps to explain why the objections that subjects have made to items have been undervalued. The subject cannot, after all, 'disagree with' a stimulus. He either perceives it correctly or incorrectly. The subject is asked to express agreement or disagreement with the attitude 'behind' the stimulus item. That the item adequately represents the attitude in question is left to the psychologist and his standardizing procedures. To bring together the attitude behind the statement and the statement itself could involve viewing the attitude as a communication, since the statement of attitude clearly has these properties. This would complicate the simple view of the statement as stimulus. The idea that social and behavioural phenomena, like attitudes and attitude statements, should be dealt with as discrete, quantifiable, stimulus-objects, is of course a basic tenet of behaviourist theory.

In addition to evoking objections from subjects these stimulus-like attitude items have run into other difficulties. Unlike physical stimuli they have no external referent; their referent is the 'internal' attitude. The determination of the value of such stimuli must thus be done through the judgement of subjects. But experiments have shown that subjects of different attitudes make different evaluations of attitude statements (Hovland and Sherif, 1952). Moreover the differences are complex and do not conform to a simple formula (Selltiz, Edrich and Cook, 1965; Zavalloni and Cook, 1965). More recently it has been shown that subjects themselves can be aware that there is an intrinsic lack of precision in the perceived values of attitude statements; that is, they not only make different judgements from other subjects, but know that they are doing it (Dawes *et al.*, 1972).

Thus the criticisms raised by subjects do find a parallel in studies on the judgement of attitude statements. Maybe the subjects have realized, much sooner than the psychologists, that there is an inevitable ambiguity attached to many, if not most, statements of attitude, and their criticisms should be taken seriously. To examine this criticism is not easy. Data have often been discarded and never, to the writer's knowledge, sought systematically. But there are enough examples to at least start the discussion.

The first concerns a judgemental study rather than an attitude survey. Subjects were asked not whether they agreed with items, but what attitudes they thought the items signified. The psychologist, E. D. Hinckley, was in fact constructing a scale for measuring 'attitudes toward the social position of Negroes'. Subjects were asked to rate items on a 1–11 scale according to their favourability–unfavourability. The study was strictly carried out: 'every student was required to stay in the classroom until the end of the hour, even though he had finished rating' (Hinckley, 1932, p. 287). Thus there was perhaps little room for objection. But, in the final sample, there was a group, mainly black, whose ratings were considered deviant. These subjects had rated many items as extremely unfavourable, many as extremely favourable, and few in the middle categories. They had 'polarized' their ratings. The others had spread their items evenly. These subjects were considered to show poor discrimination and carelessness and were excluded from the sample. In addition, as might be expected, Hinckley also excluded items that could be said to be faulty:

It is necessary that the statements which are used in the final scale be clear, concise and unambiguous, and that they contain no irrelevant elements. . . . The care which was taken in this refining process cannot be overemphasized. The search for statements and the reduction of the original list extended over a year (1932, p. 286).

Subsequent work suggests that he was not only wrong in excluding the 'objecting' subjects, but that he was also wrong in including some of the items that he did, particularly in the light of more recent studies. Readers may like to judge for themselves whether the following of Hinckley's items meet the criteria 'clear, concise and unambiguous':

A wide-awake Negro is physically superior and in other respects equal to the white man.
The Negro is fully capable of social equality with the white man, but he should not be so recognized until he is better trained.
The rich spiritual life of the Negro compensates adequately for the defects in his nature.[1]

Subjects in the early sixties recorded substantial shifts in the unfavourable direction in the rating of these statements. They were, with many others, removed from the item pool on the grounds that 'Many of the supposedly

1. I am grateful to Professor Selltiz for making available a list of the items used in the original study by Hinckley, together with ratings gained in that and later studies.

favourable items had a strong derogatory or condescending undertone' (Selltiz, Edrich and Cook, 1965, p. 409). But what remains to be explained is how the items got included in the first place. The solidly favourable ratings that they gained among white subjects, and blacks if those excluded are forgotten, and their survival of the elimination procedures, suggest that their derogatory overtones, their ambiguity and bias may really have been hard to detect in the racialist culture of the times. (Many of the colleges used in the study came from Georgia, Virginia, Florida and Carolina.) The disparity in ratings of different attitude groups, the obvious presence of bias in the items, seems to have appeared much more markedly later on. If this is the case then the 'loading' of these items has come about through the social investment of certain phrases with derogatory affect; 'wide-awake', 'better trained', 'rich spiritual life'. If bias in an item can result from the change in meaning of a couple of words then the attitude item, brief as it may be, becomes a complex phenomenon. Hinckley's subjects only objected in an indirect sense, as has been said. But, partly through their actions, at the time written off as 'careless and showing poor discrimination', it has been shown that ratings of statements can differ markedly between people of different attitudes. This rating difference which effectively denotes ambiguity in the statement can, it seems likely, appear at different stages in time. Thus the task of producing unbiased, unambiguous statements becomes more difficult. So in one instance, subjects making awkward evaluations of attitude statements, who were removed from the sample, were subsequently found to be justified.

A more obvious example of objection to a questionnaire, and of the psychologist's response, is to be found in Eysenck (1954). He says:

[some] respondents claimed that the questionnaire forced them to record complex attitudes as simple dichotomies; many said that they could 'write a book' on each of the statements.... In a number of cases the writer himself discussed questionnaire answers with respondents.... When asked to amplify their answers, either in writing or verbally, the response was very scant; the elaborations put forward did not justify the claims of the respondents. Nor would they, in the writer's opinion, have altered the position on the attitude scale marked by the respondents. Often remarks were frankly irrelevant: sometimes they merely restated in a slightly bombastic fashion what the questionnaire statement had said more simply; frequently they consisted of unimportant quibbles over wording (pp. 125–6).

Examination of Eysenck's list does, in the writer's view, evoke some sympathy for the critical respondents. Without knowing which items they found objectionable, or what the content of their objections was, here are some of the items which might strike people as unsatisfactory. The response categories allowed were; 'strongly agree', 'agree on the whole', 'cannot decide', 'disagree on the whole', 'strongly disagree':

Ultimately private property should be abolished and complete socialism introduced.

All human beings are born with the same potentialities.

The dropping of the first atom bomb on a Japanese city, killing thousands of innocent women and children, was morally wrong and incompatible with our kind of civilization (1954, p. 278).

In the first sentence the words 'abolish' and 'introduce' have a kind of legalistic ring which seems out of key with the general sentiment. The second statement really appears to be a trick one. In fact it is very reminiscent of the jibe about '100 per cent environmentalists' that is heard in the debate about heredity and environment. The third sentence appears to have an internal contradiction since it was 'our civilization' that dropped the bomb. The trouble is that the sentences do form a recognizable caricature. If the subject is tempted away from the 'cannot decide' category and puts 'agree on the whole' then according to Eysenck's method of scoring the response is treated precisely the same as if he had marked 'strongly agree' (1954, p. 276). As previous results suggest, the perception of ambiguity and bias is by no means universal. Others might find the statements above quite lucid expressions of opinion, with which they can agree or disagree unambiguously.

As with Hinckley, Eysenck cannot be accused of completely ignoring the problem of bias. He quotes examples of different answers obtained from variations of the same basic question. But he does treat the problem as less than severe, as can be seen from the statement: 'fortunately it is usually easy to detect biased wording by simple inspection' (1954, p. 57).

For the third example of objections to attitude items it was possible to acquire a sample of completed questionnaires and examine the comments written in by the respondents.[2] Though this is a somewhat unsystematic way of collecting data it was thought possible to test the three following rival explanations of objections to items. If objections are based on some characteristic unrelated to attitude, like 'awkwardness', then there should be an even distribution of objections. If it is based on strength of attitude then those at both ends of the scale will object most. If it is based on subjects of a particular attitude objecting to particular items then a more complex picture may emerge. The forty-two objectors were sub-divided into three groups according to the attitude under examination, pro-

2. I am grateful to Judith Gould and Margaret McCourt for giving me access to this data.

religious, neutral and anti-religious. This was done on the basis of measured attitude and indices of church membership and attendance. Within the total sample the anti-religious objectors numbered 17 out of 166, or 10·2 per cent, the neutral objectors numbered 14 out of 160 (8·8 per cent) and the pro-religious objectors numbered 11 out of 51 (21·6 per cent).

Table 1 Characteristics of subjects objecting to religious attitude survey

	subjects' own attitudes		
	anti-religious	neutral	pro-religious
raw score	40–63	64–103	104–127
total subjects in each category	166	160	51
number of objectors in each category	17	14	11
percentage of objectors	10.2	8.8	21.6
memberships of objectors[a]	0	4	17
church attendances in a month of objectors	0	8	88
percentage of items criticized	20.5	17.7	25.0

[a] Memberships included denominations and other groups. Many of the pro-religious sample had two memberships

The picture that emerges suggests that although there are subjects of all attitudes who write comments, and that neutral subjects are, marginally, the least critical, the pro-religious subjects are far more prone to write comments than anyone else. When quantity of commentary is allowed for this effect becomes more pronounced. The writing of long explanatory scripts was entirely restricted to this category.

The further questions that should be asked is how valid are these criticisms. Criteria of validity are difficult, but it can be asked whether the objections appear to rise above the level of 'irrelevant', 'bombastic' and 'unimportant quibbles over wording'. Beyond that it can be asked whether there are any agreed criticisms of particular items within or across groups.

An item-by-item analysis shows that the pro-religious subjects have most comments to make per questionnaire, followed by the anti-religious and the neutral subjects. Furthermore the pro-religious subjects concentrate their criticisms on certain items while the other subjects spread their comments evenly. Six items (out of twenty-one) received comment from at least half of the pro-religious subjects, and five items received from them no comment at all. In both the other groups no item was criticized by more than half the subjects and all the items received some comment. Thus the pro-religious group was much more 'agreed' on its criticisms than the other groups. Further, of interest to the present argument is the fact that the criticism of an item by one group was no guarantee that it would be criticized by another. Two items were criticized by all groups: 'If you lead a good and decent life it is not necessary to go to church' and 'Parents have a duty to teach elementary Christian truths to their children'; and one neutral item went virtually uncommented. But many items received uneven criticism. At least two were heavily criticized by the pro-religious but not by the others: 'The existence of disease, famine and strife in the world makes one doubt some religious doctrines' and 'International peace depends on the world-wide adoption of religion'. Two items were criticized by the non-religious, but not by the religious: 'Jesus Christ was an important and interesting historical figure, but in no way divine' and 'Religious faith is merely another name for belief which is contrary to reason'. This last finding is important since it suggests that there would be difficulties in redesigning the questionnaire to suit all groups. Also relevant to this are differences of criticism made about the use of the term 'religious', illustrated by these quotes from pro and anti subjects respectively, one finding the term too broad, the other too narrow:

'. . . does the term religious mean Christian belief or the wide spectrum of religious belief?'

'. . . the term "religion" is very narrow. . . . The survey does not allow for mystical or spiritual experiences outside the framework of religion.'

In terms of content of criticism the most frequent complaint was that items were vague and ambiguous. Following these were comments concerning items being 'weighted', 'loaded', 'awkward' or 'biased'. In many instances subjects complained about items with which they might have been expected to agree. One highly religious subject commented that an item favouring religious education implied 'a sort of Sunday School network dominating society'. He responded 'uncertain'. The isolated situation of the subject and the way in which the subject wished to treat the questionnaire as communication was well illustrated by the comment: 'In general debate I would not contemplate many of the statements as phrased, but there is little room for discussion with a survey'.

In general the criticisms put forward were serious and coherent, though a few were flippant and merely hostile. In particular the comments of the pro-religious subjects were strenuously argued and backed up with Bible references. The broad point which, in the writer's opinion, the criticisms succeeded in making, was that the framework of the questionnaire did not satisfactorily allow the subjects concerned to express their own viewpoint. Neither this discussion, nor of course the questionnaire, is concerned with the justification or consistency of the attitudes being measured. But what is claimed by attitude scales, and what in this case was not accomplished, was an adequate description of all the attitudes concerned. The objectors certainly formed a minority of the respondents, but if the behavioural indices of attitude shown in the table are considered, for the pro-religious at least, they consist of a minority whose attitudinal involvement and activity merit recognition beyond their numbers. The criticisms were not generally trivial or bombastic, points of considerable interest were made, and, particularly among the pro-religious group, there was agreement on a number of points of criticism.

These three examples of studies of different attitudes have registered, in one way or another, dissatisfaction with items on attitude scales. But they cannot be said to be conclusive. Data was not directly sought and the nature of the objection was not always clear. The crucial hypotheses have not yet been put to systematic test. However, the indications are there and further studies are clearly needed in which respondents have adequate opportunity to be involved in the designing of the questionnaire.

In what direction could these studies lead, beyond confirming the results already suggested? There are two broad points which are suggested and need further elaboration. The first is the distinction between *ambiguity* and *bias*. The second is the role of the social group in the generation of meaning. For both these points there are important leads from the data surveyed already.

It was quite noticeable, though no one remarked on this distinction, that there were two kinds of objection, made both by psychologists and by subjects. Hinckley warned of the problem of ambiguity and Eysenck of bias (though neither avoided them, as has been seen). Among the subjects many complained of vagueness and imprecision (i.e. ambiguity) and there were also complaints of 'loading', 'weighting' and 'bias' (though probably both ambiguity and bias occur in the subjects' everyday expression of attitude). It is possible to suggest here a distinction between *ambiguity* and *bias*, conceptually, experimentally and in terms of social usage.

Ambiguity is taken as denoting imprecision in a broad sense. In its simplest form an ambiguous statement is two-sided: it might mean one thing or it might mean another. Bias, an attitudinally more pointed form of ambiguity, has a superficial two-sidedness which contains within it an indication of the dominant intended meaning. The *two-sidedness* becomes the *two-faced*. A crude analogy is that of a dice whose numbers have been partly worn away in comparison to one which is loaded.

Thurstone gave an effective way of denoting the ambiguous statement. This type of statement receives widely differing evaluations from subjects, some seeing it as unfavourable, some as favourable. This property can be given a simple numerical index, the 'Q-value' or ambiguity rating (1929, p. 37). An example from his study is: 'I do not believe in any kind of church but have never given the matter serious thought'. What attitude lies behind this statement is unclear: it is rather neutral, vague and ambiguous. Neither Thurstone, nor his junior co-worker Hinckley, investigated the problem of bias, which involves the different evaluation of statements by people of different attitude. They thought it did not occur. The biased statement has two sides which are differently perceived by those of different attitude. Experimentally it is likely to receive a higher Q-rating than the simply ambiguous statement. This is certainly the case for the items from the Hinckley study quoted earlier. Evaluations of these statements were shifted three or four points on the eleven-point scale of favourability. This confirmed their apparent quality of 'derogatory undertones'. The shift in evaluation was especially marked for the groups of black subjects, understandably. Here the distinction between ambiguity and bias becomes clear. Ambiguity can be denoted by differences in evaluation irrespective of the attitudes of the judges. Bias, on the other hand, is denoted by differences in evaluation which have particular reference to the attitudinal groups from which the judges are drawn. The black subjects in the study quoted were thus particularly aware of the unfavourable connotations of the statements concerned. The prejudiced white subjects, on the other hand, were not that aware of them and so gave much more favourable ratings. They were not, apparently, aware of any internal inconsistency in the statement which was obvious to the other subjects, and to the experimenters. It can be said that this very inconsistency within the statement prompts the unfavourable rating. If a person attempts to dress up an unfavourable attitude in favourable terms then he can be assumed to be doubly unfavourable. It is interesting to note in passing that most examples of biased statements seem to be phrased in this direction. They involve the partial covering up of an unfavourable attitude in pleasant words, though there is no reason why it should not be done the other way round.

It may have been noticed that this discussion of ambiguity and bias has leant strongly on the very tradition of attitude measurement that it seeks to bring into question. Obviously the existing tradition of research has to be studied, but a further discussion is needed. This concerns the social groups within which attitudes are developed. That attitudes are generated within social groups is hardly a controversial point to make. However, when it is examined carefully it does come into conflict with the techniques of attitude measurement used to date. In the data examined previously it was very noticeable that the pro-religious group is distinguished as clearly, if not more so, from other groups by the behavioural criteria of religious membership as by the scalar index of attitude. Furthermore in the studies by Zavalloni and Cook (1965) and by Selltiz *et al.* (1965), it made very little difference to the results whether the subjects were divided up according to measured attitude or according to the groups to which they belonged. Indeed in one study the results were more marked when subjects were divided according to membership (Zavalloni and Cook, 1965, p. 46). If it is the case that subjects' own group-membership patterns are as informative about their behaviour as their measured attitudes then the whole effort of constructing an attitude scale has not accomplished a great deal. Since membership of given groups appears, in these instances, to provide an adequate alternative metric of attitude, a more 'natural' scale moreover, then perhaps psychologists should pay more attention to the attitudinal consequences of membership than they have done traditionally.

Further it can be pointed out that membership of groups often provides quite specific information as to attitudes held. Zavalloni and Cook quote as one of their membership groups college fraternities that had taken 'pledges' in campaigns against the admission of Negro students. If the content of such a pledge were incorporated into an attitude inventory it would presumably evoke maximum agreement from the signatories. Likewise the other organizations in their study would have been likely to require some degree of formal adherence to attitudinal conditions of membership. Examples are numerous. In the religious sphere it could be presumed that clergymen would 'strongly agree' with the 'Thirty-nine Articles' were they included in a questionnaire. In Eysenck's political-attitudes study there are items more or less resembling the policy statements of political groups to which his subjects could be expected to belong.

In a sense then an attitude questionnaire can be seen as selections from the policy statements of the groups whose attitudes are being surveyed. But in practice it does not work like this. This is because one of the main reasons for forming an attitude group is that the attitudes involved are not those of the world at large, either in content or style, and thus are precisely those attitudes which are *not* likely to be included in a questionnaire. The more distant from consensus thinking is the group then the less likely is it that its own statements of attitude will find their way onto a 'general' questionnaire.

Any group will, of course, formulate its programme, pledge or conditions of membership in a form which is internally favourable and consistent. Correspondingly it will portray opposing groups in terms which are unfavourable, and internally inconsistent, self-discrediting and biased. To try to construct an attitude questionnaire from statements drawn from the programmes, say, of the John Birch Society and the Black Panther Party, covering equivalent ranges of content in each case, would be difficult. But if an attitude scale claims generality then this is what it must try to do. If, on the other hand, the questionnaire seeks to avoid group-specific terminology (or 'jargon') and aims solely at consensus viewpoints, then it will effectively omit, or at least misrepresent, attitudinally significant groups.

If this outline is correct then an explanation can be offered for a puzzling feature of the criticisms of the religious-attitude survey discussed above. The anti-religious subjects offered fewer criticisms of the questionnaire than the pro-religious subjects, though in scalar terms they were as far from the neutral attitude. An explanation of this may be that there were among this sample no relevant membership organizations from which particular formulations of anti-religious attitude could be developed. Indeed the absence of such organizations is reflected in the very structure of the anti-religious attitudes which have been found to be more vague, more fragmented and 'less probing' than those at the pro-religious end (Poppleton and Pilkington, 1963; Fraser and Stacey, 1973). Such dimensional asymmetry should not, ideally, occur in a scale of attitude. But in this instance it finds a simple explanation in terms of the lack of anti-religious membership groups.

It may be objected that only a minority of people in any sample are likely to belong to appropriate membership groups. In a sense this is true, though many studies have found widespread membership among subjects. However, membership is only the most formal and extreme form of a more general phenomenon. A person need not be a 'card-carrying member' to share the attitudes of a given group. It has been pointed out that membership groups and reference groups act as psychological perspectives (Shibutani, 1967). They create an internal consensus, a 'universe of discourse', within which their own view of the world pertains. Those sharing that view are 'members'. The membership group is the most socially obvious form of this phenomenon. It represents the point at which attitudes begin to form frameworks for action, to implement the 'aims and objects' of the group.

The relationships between groups are communicated by attitudes. In this sense, as was suggested earlier, the attitude can be seen as a communicative act, aimed at defining the relationship between people or groups. Each group will attempt to 'define the situation' in such a way as to make its own attitudes the most consistent. It will attempt to capture the consensus to its own way of thinking. Seen in this way the attitude statement cannot have the property required of a stimulus, a publicly observable, unambiguously quantifiable value. It is intrinsically part of a debate. Likewise the attitude itself cannot be seen as some inaccessible entity in the 'black box' of the individual. Statements 'emanating' from it cannot thus be seen as simple stimuli from which the larger attitude is inferred. The attitude and its statements are all part of the debate. This approach might appear to put attitude wholly in the realm of ideas, divorcing it from the solid biological reality in which many psychologists have attempted to ground the concept. A debate after all does concern ideas and is, theoretically, quite swiftly resolved. But the debates between attitudinal groups are grounded in the real problems of the social world. The resolution is thus an extremely slow process, depending on the ability of particular groups to succeed in overcoming the problems they set themselves. This view of social groups as collective attempts to overcome real problems is well outlined by Hans Toch (1971) in his book on social movements.

What the psychologist has done traditionally in measuring attitude is to take the line of least resistance among the groups battling to define the situation. He has, without justification, suggested this as an objective measure of attitude. In reality all he has achieved is a consensus measure, unable to cope with the alternative perspectives, with the sub-consensual.[3]

The thesis that attitudes can be objectively measured on a precise interval scale (Thurstone and Chave, 1929) can be derived from behaviourist theory, which treats attitude statements as quantifiable stimuli. This has already been discussed. But a very similar thesis can also be derived from a socio-political theory, one which maintains that there is only a single valid consensus of meaning within a given society, that from the point of view of the community of meanings we are 'all one nation'. Though there are differences of attitude these exist within an agreed framework; they can be measured on the same scale. Deviant perspectives are denied, so the plurality of attitudes does not offend the accepted structure of meaning. The socio-political theory concerned is conservative and constitutional. It admits only of gradual change from recognized differences of viewpoint.

This convenient coincidence of academic and political ideology has distorted the study of attitudes in quite a marked way, I would suggest. But more serious is the way in which measurements of attitude have been used under the slogan of 'public opinion counts'. Opinion polls, containing the

3. This distinction between the consensual (of generally agreed meaning) and the sub-consensual (of specific meaning to the individual) is well illustrated by Kuhn and McPartland's study of self-attitudes (1967). There is no reason why the term 'sub-consensual' should not apply to the group also.

most limited and biased selection of items, administered doorstep by doorstep, are presented as 'the voice of the people'. No doubt the designers of 'proper' attitude scales would deny connection with the opinion pollsters. I hope that enough evidence has been presented here to show that such connection cannot be denied, and that the failure of psychologists to critically evaluate their subject has opened the way for manipulative exercises of this sort.

Finally, I return to the starting-point, the respondent in a survey, confronted with a questionnaire. Any person asked to participate in a survey has the right to expect that it will contain an unambiguous and unbiased statement of his own attitude. Maybe this expectation will make it very difficult to continue to design questionnaires of general applicability in their present form. In the meantime the infuriated fillers-in of questionnaires should be recommended not only to write in what they find wrong with which statements, but they should also insist that their objections be treated seriously by the psychologist concerned. This may serve to impress on him that attitudes are really part of a debate, from which the psychologist himself is not free to withdraw, and convince him that it is a caricature and a prejudice to foist on people consensual formulations.

References

DAWES, R. H., SINGER, D., and LEMONS, F. (1972), 'An experimental analysis of the contrast effect and its implications for intergroup communication and the indirect assessment of attitudes', *J. Personality soc. Psychol.*, vol. 21, pp. 281–93.

EYSENCK, H. J. (1954), *The Psychology of Politics*, Routledge & Kegan Paul.

FRASER, B. S., and STACEY, B. G. (1973), 'A psychophysical investigation of the influence of attitude in the judgement of social stimuli', *Brit. J. soc. clin. Psychol.*, vol. 12, pp. 337–52.

HINCKLEY, E. D. (1932), 'The influence of individual attitude on the construction of an attitude scale', *J. soc. Psychol.*, vol. 3, pp. 282–96.

HOVLAND, C. I., and SHERIF, M. (1952), 'Judgemental phenomena and scales of attitude; item displacement in Thurstone scales', *J. abnormal soc. Psychol.*, vol. 47, pp. 822–32.

KUHN, M. H., and MCPARTLAND, T. S. (1967), 'An empirical investigation of self-attitudes', in J. G. Manis and B. N. Meltzer (eds.), *Symbolic Interaction*, Allyn & Bacon.

POPPLETON, P. K., and PILKINGTON, G. W. (1963), 'The measurement of religious attitudes in a university population', *Brit. J. soc. clin. Psychol.*, vol. 2, pp. 20–36.

SELLTIZ, C., EDRICH, H., and COOK, S. W. (1965), 'Ratings of statements of favourableness about a social group as an indicator of attitude toward the group', *J. Personality soc. Psychol.*, vol. 5, pp. 408–15.

SHIBUTANI, T. (1967), 'Reference groups as perspectives', in J. G. Manis and B. N. Meltzer (eds.), *Symbolic Interaction*, Allyn & Bacon.

THURSTONE, L. L., and CHAVE, E. J. (1929), *The Measurement of Attitude*, University of Chicago Press.

TOCH, H. (1971), *The Social Psychology of Social Movements*, Methuen.

ZAVALLONI, M., and COOK, S. W. (1965), 'Influence of judges' attitudes on ratings of favourableness of statements about a social group', *J. Personality soc. Psychol.*, vol. 1, pp. 43–54.

7 Experience in Everyday Life
Nigel Armistead

The function of the novel seems to be changing; it has become an outpost of journalism; we read novels for information about areas of life we don't know – Nigeria, South Africa, the American Army, a coal-mining village, coteries in Chelsea, etc. We read *to find out what is going on*. One novel in five hundred or a thousand has the quality a novel should have to make it a novel – the quality of philosophy. I find that I read with the *same kind of curiosity* most novels, and a book of reportage. Most novels, if they are successful at all, are original in the sense that they report the existence of an area of society, a type of person, not yet admitted to the general literate consciousness. The novel has become a function of the fragmented society, the fragmented consciousness. Human beings are so divided, are becoming more and more divided, and *more sub-divided in themselves*, reflecting the world, that they reach out desperately, not knowing they do it, for information about other groups inside their own country, let alone about groups in other countries. It is a blind grasping out for their own wholeness, and the novel report is a means towards it. Inside this country, Britain, the middle class have no knowledge of the lives of the working people, and vice versa; and reports and articles and novels are sold across the frontiers, are read as if savage tribes were being investigated. Those fisherman in Scotland were a different species from the coalminers I stayed with in Yorkshire; and both come from a different world than the housing estate outside London.
Doris Lessing, *The Golden Notebook*

I am going to suggest that social psychologists should be filling the gap to which Doris Lessing is pointing: that would involve focusing on people's experience in order to study the way they live and make sense of their lives. Sociologists have been commenting upon this apparent fragmentation of society and of people for a long time, and arguing about its extent and its causes and consequences. What hasn't been done, in my opinion, is to follow through the implications of this fragmentation for how we should go about social psychology.

In such a context, the fundamental task of any social psychology should be to help us understand other people's experience both for its own sake and to compare it with our own. To do this, we need to examine people's past and present experiences in and of everyday social situations: some of these will be experiences of a long-standing and general nature (for example, what's your marriage like?), while others will be experiences of specific situations (for example, what was going on in that meeting?). Of course, there's been a lot of work done in such areas by sociologists and social psychologists, but by and large this work does not tell us much about people's experience. The focus has usually been on regularities in people's behaviour and on making generalizations about that behaviour in relation to aspects of the environment or the person that can be quantified (neighbourhood characteristics, income, self-esteem, cognitive complexity, etc). Now I am not necessarily trying to put this down completely, but it does worry me when people's experience of situations only appears, if at all, as 'illustrative material' and 'anecdotal evidence', rather than as the focus of the study.

All of us spend our conscious lives with a continuous stream of thoughts, feelings and impressions going through our minds. Some of these are related to the immediate situation, others are related to the past or the future. Many of them are not particularly rational, respectable, or well-formulated, but nonetheless make up the stuff of our daily lives. All of this is what I mean by experience, and to my mind it is just as important as what we *do*. Ideally, of course, we want to know about both. However, behaviourists argue that experience is only important insofar as it leads to differences in behaviour. On this argument, it doesn't matter if someone is unhappy; what counts is whether he shows it in his behaviour. This is a very dangerous position, when some people can gain by ignoring other people's experience. It is quite possible for someone to go through the motions of their job and hate every minute of it: behaviourists would only become interested if he became inefficient or threw a spanner in the works. Instead, I think we should study that man's experience of work as an important topic in its own right.

However, there is another argument for the importance of experience, which is that even if we want to explain social *behaviour*, we shall have to study experience. This assertion rests on the distinction between behaviour as movement and behaviour as motivated action (cf. Shotter, pp. 53–71). Movements are to be explained in terms of physiology or the structure of the nervous system, whereas motivated actions are to be explained in terms of what the person was trying to do, as embodied in his reasons. Most of the behaviour studied in social psychology falls in the 'motivated action' category. People are capable of 'monitoring' their own reasons and of reporting them. As Harré (pp. 240–59) suggests, we can relate these reports to the person's situational definitions, chosen social 'persona', prior rehearsal and adherence to rules. The point is that these are all to do with a person's experience, which we will therefore have to explore if we are to explain his behaviour.

What we have here is an insistence, that we can all confirm from our own experience, that what people 'have in mind' is a crucial influence upon what they do. Of course, they may not do exactly what they had in mind, and we have to allow for habitual action and subconscious influences, where there may have been nothing 'in mind' corresponding to the action. But these exceptions have scared off social psychologists from letting people explain their own behaviour, while there remains a large field of actions where this is just what we should be doing. In any case, asking people is a necessary part of the investigation – they may know why they didn't do what they intended; their lack of reasons for their action may indicate that it was a habit; and if we want to appeal to subconscious motivation, we shall have to show that their conscious (reported) motivations are inadequate.

Furthermore, when social behaviour is measured, social psychologists implicitly assume that the meaning of that behaviour is the same for all the participants in an experiment or social situation, and for the 'subject' and the researcher. To avoid making such unjustified assumptions, we should examine people's experience as well as observing their behaviour.

For a long time, social scientists have concentrated on explaining behaviour, and this is especially true of social psychology. People have even started using 'the behavioural sciences' as a synonym for 'the social sciences'. The argument for this approach is always that behaviour is relatively unambiguous and is publicly observable, whereas experience is essentially unreliable and inaccessible. Well, I agree that experience appears harder to get at than behaviour, but is this any reason for not trying if we consider that experience is important? We shall just have to find ways of studying experience which aren't based on intuition or guesswork (see first two sections of this essay).

Another argument for the 'behavioural science' approach is that people's experiences are essentially idiosyncratic, whereas in science we are trying to make generalizations (in social psychology, this point usually gets made under the heading of idiographic *v.* nomothetic approaches). But experience is no more idiosyncratic than behaviour – lots of us have similar experiences, and much of our conversation consists of identifying and discussing them – whereas behavioural regularities are also abstractions from individually different pieces of behaviour – no two people ever perform exactly the same movement. So perhaps we should not despair of making generalizations about experience (see third section of this essay).

However, if we were able to generalize about people's experience, that would not be enough. Let us suppose we have established an 'experiential map' of our society (or rather of the people who constitute it). We still have to explain why the map looks as it does. Why do people have these particular experiences? Why do some groups have different experiences from others? What produces any apparent patterns of experience (see section four of this essay)?

Getting at experience

How, then, are we to get at people's experience: their thoughts and feelings about life in general and about particular situations they are in?

The first answer that comes to psychologists' heads is probably introspection. Now, as far as I am aware, introspection was found to be inadequate as a way of investigating *non-social* experiences and questions, such as 'imageless thought', and the categories of consciousness. But in relation to social experience, I think we should reconsider introspection. We do know what we are thinking and feeling about our lives and the situations we are in. We do know how we perceive and interpret our social environment. We do know the reasons for most of our actions. So we should not rule out evidence that depends upon introspection. What we should rule out is reliance upon the introspection of the researcher for the gathering of evidence about other people's experience, even of the same social situation. And the argument against the researcher's introspection becomes even stronger when we consider the experience of people in completely different situations from himself.

One step removed from the researcher's introspection are the insights of novelists, playwrights and film-makers. Now we are considering the fruits of another person's experience, and the way he imaginatively portrays the experience of other people. For me, Doris Lessing's novels have more to say about women and men than any social psychology I have read. Similarly, four TV plays by John Hopkins called *Talking to a Stranger* had more to say about the family even than Laing. But the 'validity' of these statements depends upon my response of recognition to what the author is portraying. They may not be valid and revealing for some other reader or viewer. The same applies to diaries and autobiographies, although they do have the advantage of being about an actual life and not just fictitious characters. In addition, they make no claim to representativeness as some of the better artistic productions do. So a social psychology that aspires to produce evidence and explanations that will be agreed upon by all needs to go further, without necessarily ignoring such personal insights as part of the evidence at hand.

The crucial move in getting outside one person's experience is surely to ask other people about their experience. It is true that other people's experience, especially their emotions, can be revealed in their non-verbal behaviour. But this conveys only rather gross aspects of their experience – for instance, that they are upset, rather than *why*. We can infer why a person is upset, if we know the circumstances, but that is our interpretation, not a description of his experience. By contrast, what people say about their experience is richer, more revealing and less dependent upon the observer's interpretations. Any misinterpretations can be corrected and gaps can be filled in. All this is not to say that verbal accounts are the last word: people do distort, conceal and lie. But we need good evidence for disbelieving what they report as their experience. As Laing has shown, that experience may be intelligible, even if it is not what we might consider an adequate or truthful account of a situation. And in any case 'distorted' or 'incorrect' experience needs to be adequately explained, not dismissed as irrelevant.

Our primary data, then, should be people's accounts of their experience. How are we to go about that in practice, so as to ensure maximum validity? There are various means available for obtaining samples of another person's experience, ranging from more to less structured methods. However, the more structured methods such as questionnaires tend to define and limit the expression of experience by the use of predefined categories (see Roiser, Heritage, pp. 101–14, pp. 260–81). There may be a case for questionnaires that are formulated on the basis of the respondents' informal accounts. This is what many researchers do in the 'pilot' stage, but it is important to remember that such questionnaires are designed for that specific situation and that the questionnaire will only be as good as the qualitative pilot work (see Rowan, pp. 86–100). Another possibility is for rating scales to be devised for which the categories are chosen by the subject and explicitly given the meaning that the subject himself attributes to them (as they usually are without the researcher realizing). This might be useful for exploring changes in individual experience over time or in different situations.

Such modifications of standard techniques have their point where one is interested in quantification and in relatively circumscribed aspects of people's experience. There are also at least two total methodologies that try to see the world from the actor's point of view and allow him to structure his own experience. Stephenson (1953) claims that Q methodology is a way of empirically studying an individual's experience and can be adapted for use with several people so that the similarities or differences in their experience can be demonstrated (Stephenson, 1967). Secondly, Bannister and Fransella (1971) claim that Kelly's repertory-grid technique enables one to 'map the unique psychological space of the individual' via eliciting the constructs he typically uses in categorizing his environment. Again the technique can be adapted for use with groups and in particular situations. With both these methodologies, statistics and factor analysis can be used and hypotheses tested. While they may therefore be more acceptable to experimental social psychologists, they are nevertheless limited in several ways: they only collect one type of information, the operations required by the method constrain the subject, and may themselves distort his experience. In other words, they may be providing a more partial and inaccurate sample of experience than is necessary. Furthermore, neither of them pay much attention to how the experience is constructed over time and to explaining why the experience has those particular contents. Who constructs the constructs?

Towards 'participant dialogue'?

The alternative that I want to outline and defend involves the use of the less structured methods: open-ended questionnaires, interviews and discussions. Here it is possible to let people speak for themselves, except insofar as the researcher structures things via his questions. Ideally, then, the researcher should let people say what they want, and then follow up with specific questions. This should provide a record of what people wish us to know about their experience. But how do we know we are not being fooled? Experiences which are personal or which cast the subject in a bad light are not likely to be revealed, and most people try to create favourable impressions. The usual answer to this is to establish some sort of fake 'rapport'. But there is a broader question at issue: what right have we to just drop in with our tape-recorders and disappear again, using the information for our own purposes? Genuine trust and confidence are likely to exist only when the researcher fully explains the reasons for the research and those reasons are accepted by the subject. Such an outcome is more likely where the researcher is involved or identified in some way with those he is researching. In such circumstances of ongoing relationship and trust, it is also possible for the researcher to check that the account of experience offered is consistent with the person's social behaviour – where it is not, the actor can, without affront, be asked to explain the apparent discrepancy. Thus research can, and perhaps should, involve a two-way relationship, even though it will usually be asymmetrical. (Incidentally, the most valid 'knowledge' about other people's experience is lying around untapped by social scientists, in the heads of trusted friends – perhaps it should be left that way.)

A second difficulty is that people may not know what their experience is or was – it may be confusing, or they may be vague about it, or even have forgotten it. But this is only a problem if we suppose that all experience is clear-cut and known clearly by people. It is surely more important to know the areas where people are confused or 'don't know'. For instance, confusion about sex-role identity and vagueness about old age and death would be important things to know about, and it would be expecially revealing to know what sort of experiences people remember and which they forget!

Two examples of research which go some way towards meeting these requirements are provided by Toch and by Cohen and Taylor. Toch and his associates (1972) were trying to understand and explain the behaviour of violent men from a social-psychological perspective:

Our assumption is that if we want to explain why men are driven to acts of destruction, we must examine these acts, and understand the contexts in which they occur. We must know how destructive acts are initiated and developed, how they are conceived and perceived, and how they fit into the lives of the perpetrators (p. 38).

And this can only be achieved by exploring the experience of the participants in violent acts:

We must also assume that we cannot make sense of violent acts by viewing them as outsiders. Ultimately, violence arises because some person feels that he must resort to a physical act, that a problem he faces calls for a destructive solution. The problem a violent person perceives is rarely the situation as we see it, but rather some dilemma he feels he finds himself in. In order to understand a violent person's motives for violence, we must thus step into his shoes, and reconstruct his unique perspective, no matter how odd or strange it may be. We must recreate the world of the violent man, with all its fears and apprehensions, with its hopes and ambitions, with its strains and stresses (p. 38).

These two quotes sum up the approach to social psychology I am recommending, even though the focus of explanation is specific behavioural acts. As you might expect, the main source of evidence was extensive interviews with violent offenders and policemen involved in violent incidents – first, the interviewees described their violent involvements in general, then they were taken through each incident, step by step, by the interviewer. But the interviewers were 'peers' rather than 'social scientists':

Convicted offenders produced and administrated our prison interview; paroled inmates negotiated with the parolees in our sample; police professionals conducted our police study (p. 41).

As a result, Toch claims greater honesty and sensitivity in the interview data. He also claims that this 'circumvents ethical problems' to do with the researcher–researched relationship (pp. 46–7). But this is surely not the case: all the problems he mentions about one-way communication, the subject as informer, the uses to which research is put, are merely disguised by the use of peers, not solved. These 'lay' researchers were also involved in the subsequent analysis of the data, where their familiarity with the situations under study was a considerable help (see next section).

The second example (Cohen and Taylor, 1972) focuses upon more general experience – the experience of long-term imprisonment:

Starting with the group members' perception of this environment we have tried to construct, with their help, a phenomenology of the security wing: how life there is given meaning, how one passes time, how friends are made and lost, how one resigns oneself to the environment and how one resists it (p. 59).

Again, some basis of trust existed between the researchers and the researched in that the study emerged out of successful discussion classes taken by two social-science lecturers in Durham prison. The research methods were less structured than Toch's, consisting of conversations, unstructured group interviews, the men's own writings (essays, poems, letters) and the response of the men to various literary works describing other people's experiences in extreme situations. Here, the subjects, not just the subjects' peers, were more genuinely involved in the research, and the communication has been more two-way and lasting. This way of doing research (and the results) contrasts favourably with the traditional sort of psychological research sponsored by the Home Office into the psychological changes associated with long-term imprisonment and evaluated by Cohen and Taylor in an appendix.

On the basis of these two examples, I should like to tackle the question of validity. Broadbent (1973), in attacking non-behaviouristic psychology, has said:

Given massive economic interdependence, our own intentions can only be translated into action in the light of other people's intentions and needs, and we cannot judge those by examining our own consciousness. We shall need to become continuously aware that the perceptions, thoughts and motives of others really are inaccessible by looking inside ourselves. Communication can be established only through the neutral ground of public events (p. 118).

But what people say about their experience is just as much a public event as reaction times and questionnaire responses. There are no differences between them in principle as valid evidence. The operations that produce them are repeatable – someone else can ask the same questions or go through the same procedure. They all depend on the trustworthiness of the subject – that he is trying to react quickly, that he is not fiddling the questionnaire (and the lie scale), that he is not distorting his experience. And they are assessed by agreement amongst observers – about the reading on a dial, the ticks on a questionnaire or the meaning of a statement. The dif-

erences arise from the fact that accounts are more ambiguous than physical events in that they involve the dimension of meaning – but this is a fact
of social life that we shouldn't run away from. The crucial question for
Broadbent to answer is: how is he going to gain access to 'the perceptions,
thoughts and motives of others'? Using his methodology, it is impossible.

Generalizing about experience

Having obtained a record of experience in the social situations we wish to
investigate, can we make any generalizations or are we stuck with the idiosyncratic accounts of particular individuals? While it is true that even the
most idiosyncratic account will only make sense in the light of general
ideas current in society, generalizations that draw together common
themes from different people's accounts are surely an empirical matter:
perhaps they are possible, perhaps they are not. It will depend upon the
uniqueness of the experiences, and upon our ability to see the similarities
between different accounts. Drawing out such similarities can only be
achieved through an informed selection and interpretation that relates the
meanings of the accounts to the purposes of the investigation. Several bases
for classification may be possible, but some will be made more convincing
by the nature of the data, and will be more appropriate to the questions
being asked, even implicitly, in the research. For instance, the material
reproduced by Toch cries out for classifications to do with pride, power
and the handling of emotions, but he could probably have done a valid
classification on the basis of such factors as clothing and language. Many
psychologists will consider this 'subjective', but like any other classifica-
tory procedure in psychology (for example, what is a 'stimulus'?) it involves the choice of a basis for classification in relation to the purpose of
the psychologist.

Here is how Toch went about it. Each violent incident from an interview was analysed into a summary form depicting the sequence of events.
Then the summaries of all the violent incidents were discussed by a group
of both professional and non-professional researchers to prepare 'a summary of the interpersonal pattern of the interviewee's violent involvements':

The group is a 'pattern analysis' tool, in the sense that it functions to isolate
common denominators in samples. It does so by focusing logic, social-science
analysis and practical experience on a group of incidents in an effort to characterize the violent person's contribution to them as far as this may be possible
without going beyond the information he has provided (p. 68, my emphasis).

The next stage involved constructing a typology that accommodated the
interpersonal patterns of different violent men:

The typology . . . was derived through a process of grouping and content analysis. Preliminary definitions came into existence deductively, were revised through cumulative classification of pattern summaries, and were then conceptually refined. The final definitions were applied in a formal analysis of the sample, with each interview assigned to the category which appeared to best describe it (p. 174).

This, unfortunately, is all we are told about the procedure for arriving at an overall typology, e.g. how many people were involved, or how much disagreement took place. However, half the cases were independently coded and Toch defends the procedure's validity and reliability (pp. 214–25).

By contrast, Cohen and Taylor used a far less structured procedure in making their classifications and generalizations. Their samples of the men' experience were interpreted, organized and written up, and then shown to the prisoners for their confirmation and comments. The predictive value of their classification of the likely success of different strategies of adaptation to long-term imprisonment can, somewhat morbidly, be tested over the next few decades.

I think we can be rather more systematic than these three authors in trying to devise valid generalizations from experiential data. First, the meaning of each account has to be established. In order to improve accuracy at this stage, I suggest the following safeguards:

1 The meaning of each account ideally should be established by different people, independently of each other;

2 Any ambiguities in an account should be resolved by discussion and 'negotiation', rather than arbitrarily, so that several people may have to be involved;

3 Whatever meaning is decided should be checked back with the person who gave the original account;

4 The people involved should be familiar with the situation to which the account refers and in which it was given.

This stage amounts to summarizing and systematizing the original account. When the meanings of different accounts have been established, we can try to classify and generalize. Accuracy safeguards might include:

1 Several people should classify independently;

2 Ambiguities and differences should be resolved by negotiation, in which justifications can be produced, and further evidence sought, where necessary;

3 The classification should be checked and, if necessary, negotiated with the originators of the accounts;

The sample of account-givers and situations described should be ade-
ate to support the generalizations being made;

The classification should remain faithful to the original accounts;

The original accounts should be reproduced, or at least made available
r the reader to scrutinize;

The whole process could be repeated using different classifiers;

Predictions could be formulated on the basis of the classification; for
ample, about what experiences a different group of people would report,
even about how this group would be expected to behave.

ch safeguards mean that 'reliability', 'validity' and the ability to gen-
alize are not the exclusive property of conventional social psychology, as
so often claimed.

xplaining patterns of experience

far I have been recommending a descriptive approach to people's
perience, and trying to argue my way round some of the objections that
e usually raised. Now I am envisaging that we have a classification that
ay include some relatively widespread patterns of experience that ap-
oach the status of a generalization, while other classes of experience may
relatively unique. How are we to explain these classes of experience?

In the case of the widespread patterns, I suggest there are two major
rections to consider. One is to make a link with the 'social structure' and
explain people's experience in terms of power relations. The other is to
ake a link with 'culture' and to explain people's experience as an instance
widely held norms and values. It might be possible in some cases to
ow a link between the norms and values and power relations. The usual
sumption is that people have similar experiences because they are in a
milar situation. But why are they in similar situations and what deter-
ines the nature of that situation? Let me illustrate.

In Cohen and Taylor's book, the nature of the men's experience is largely
efined by the conditions imposed by the prison authorities and the Home
ffice, although there are different ways of adapting which the authors re-
te to the men's previous experiences. Here is an extreme and obvious
ample of how a general pattern of experience can be explained in relation
power (whether or not one approves of such arrangements). But the
ower to define the nature of situations exists in other, less deviant spheres
f social life. Whether we like it or not, a large part of our experience is
ructured for us by those who can control the physical and social situa-
ons we are in, whether it is planners, landlords, management, school

authorities or parents. And not only can the situation be structured, bu the nature of our experience can itself be structured, in that the very cate gories and concepts we use to experience the world are influenced by th people around us and, through them, by the culture of which we are, pe haps unwittingly, members. Our experience of the world is not a represen tation of 'reality', but one possible description amongst many. Howeve one particular description has been built into us from our earliest years This is particularly true of our interpretations of the social world, wher parents have the power to influence the way we interpret the world throug their comments and reactions, especially over sensitive and contentiou issues like sex and politics.

However, defining of experience is not all done at first hand. The mas media do a lot of it at second hand – whose experience counts at this level In both Toch and Cohen and Taylor, instances of violence are describe from the actors' points of view. In both cases, two accounts of the violenc are offered – that of the offender and that of the police or guards. Yet it i always the account of the latter that sticks: they have the authority, an often the equipment, to make their definitions of the situation count (fo example, by arrest and in the courts), never mind what 'actually' occurrec These definitions are then widely diffused through the media – they becom part of the 'rising tide of violence' – and structure the experience of a whol population. Again, the power to make one's own definition stick and to ge that definition diffused throughout a social group exists in other sphere Parents have this power over children, teachers over pupils, organizationa seniors over juniors, doctors over patients, psychiatrists and social wor kers over clients.

So here is one direction for our explanations of patterns of experience who defines and structures experience for whom, and whose experienc counts and is diffused? An attempt to examine such explanations empiri cally would involve asking people to identify the sources of their exper ience and studying at first hand situations where the supposed processe were going on, e.g. committee meetings, classrooms, interactions with th media. The result might be a rather different perspective on power in ou society.

The second direction is to appeal to norms and values. Throughout th last few paragraphs, I could have been looking at *how* experience was struc tured, and this would probably have been in terms of widely accepte ideas. But this may also be true of experience where the power to define i not obviously involved. For instance, Toch's typology of 'approaches to

1. Geoff Pearson suggests that the introduction to Castaneda (1973) provides a pene trating illustration of this point.

interpersonal structures that promote violence' (p. 175) includes many categories (self-image promoting, self-image defending, reputation defending) that look like widely held ideas about 'being a man' in our society. This interpretation is reinforced by the lengthy case studies in chapters 3 and 4, where masculine pride and socialization into toughness are the recurrent themes. Further documentation could be provided by comparing the original accounts with some independently derived characterization of masculine attitudes. This sort of explanation sees the experience leading up to violence as the 'deviant' tip of an iceberg of masculine attitudes stressing the importance of self-image, toughness, superiority and the suppression of feelings for other people. In the same way, other patterns of experience could be related to other norms and values that shape our experience (e.g. ideas about justice, normality, decency, property, sociability). Again, empirical investigation is possible by asking the subject to explain or justify the account he has given – very likely he will start referring to such norms and values before long.

The link between the norms and values and power relations could be made in at least two ways. Firstly, the norms and values could be instrumental in upholding power relations. For instance, the above stereotype of masculinity seems to be derived from the Wild West tradition and preserves the same brand of competitive individualism today (Toch's respondents frequently use the word 'dude', and use 'firing on' to mean 'punching'). The relationship to an aggressively capitalist economy should be clear. Secondly, the norms and values could themselves be the result of power relations. To continue with the example, the exaggerated form of masculinity (assertive physical toughness) could be viewed as the only viable mode of self-assertion and identity-maintenance in the economically and politically deprived circumstances of the urban proletariat – the people at the bottom of the political power pyramid compensate with an emphasis on physical power. I am not saying that I have demonstrated these links, only that they could and should be investigated for a sufficient explanation of Toch's 'experiential' typology. Empirical work could involve examining the communications of the 'experience-definers' to see if they contain the said norms and values, since one would expect the powerful to push ideas that bolstered their own position, and seeing if the norms and values are referred to in situations where power is being challenged.

Another direction for the explanation of experience might be in terms of the history of the individual. This would include individuals with relatively unique experiences as well as those whose experience falls into a widespread pattern. For instance, Schatzman (1973) shows how the schizophrenic experience of Schreber, a famous textbook psychiatric case, can be explained as a result of the socializing practices of his father, an equally famous German 'educationalist'. However, the matter does not stop there:

Nearly everyone who has studied families of persons labelled paranoid or schizophrenic agrees that the irrationality of the schizophrenic finds its rationality in the context of his first family. In what context does that family context find its rationality? What is the social network round the family of a paranoid or a schizophrenic, and what are its properties? ... Where do the patterns of thought, word and deed of parents of mad offspring fit in? (p. 141)

In this last chapter, Schatzman shows the relationship between Schreber senior's childbearing beliefs and the more general norms and values of nineteenth-century German society. Then the links with Nazism and the implications for our own society are drawn, especially the parallels with the views of psychologists like Skinner.

A similar treatment could be used for explaining patterns of more normal experience: one would then look for common past experiences that make sense of a common present experience and try to relate that past experience to the norms, values and power structure of the previous period. With both widespread and unique experience, then, we should be looking at the nature of the experience, and be trying to understand why it takes that form and to trace what social processes were involved in its construction.

Afterthoughts

I have argued that we can have a social psychology that concerns itself with people's experience in everyday life: that asking people is the crucial methodology; that people's accounts constitute public evidence; that classification, generalization and explanation will involve some interpretation of meaning, albeit with the suggested checks and safeguards; and that explanation of experience should move in a societal direction.

In doing all this, I have emphasized the centrality of listening to what people say. However, I am not saying that nothing else is important. Some experience is not easily open to verbal organization and communication; the factors that influence experience are not always immediately obvious to the person giving the account. While accepting these possibilities, I want to insist that people's accounts should always be sought and should themselves be explained by any explanation that presumes to discount them. People's accounts should be both starting-point and finishing-point for explanations, even if they are not sufficient by themselves.

The examples I have given come from studies of deviants. However, to return to the introduction, modern societies create an awareness of fragmented social worlds where in a sense we are all deviants. We need, therefore, to carry out the same sort of research with the 'normal' population: people's thoughts and feelings in everyday social life. There are many important questions that would be amenable to this approach – being a woman, being a man, being old, being married, being a child, being poor, being in business (or any other occupation) together with more specific experiences in particular types of situation. We cannot assume that our stereotypes, or what the media and the 'experts' tell us, are correct. Most of the time we operate upon implicit assumptions that are more convenient for our own particular view of the world than they are representations of other people's experience. Even if people's accounts of their experience are distorted, they are likely to be less distorted than our assumptions about it.

It could be objected that all this is merely a social-science ideology for the interests of students and middle-class youth: it depends upon a certain amount of articulateness about one's experience, it appears to derive from the 'experience ethic' and suggests a questioning of received wisdoms. I hope this is all true, but can't we distinguish between the origins of a set of ideas and their consequences? I expect my concerns are shared by many young middle-class people and derive from a fairly standard educational and cultural experience. But is it not also true that other people are becoming more articulate about their experience, and would be more so, given the chance, the motivation and the right conditions? And is it not possible for an interest in people's experience to be translated into a careful analysis of that experience, where we attempt to find out and explain what is the case, rather than to reinforce our own prejudices?

Whether this sort of social psychology requires any professional expertise, I am not sure. Certainly the skills would not be those of technical competence so much as of interpersonal sensitivity. There is plenty of this outside social-science departments; what is lacking there are the time and the facilities (tape-recorders, access to subjects). Social psychology would become much more like what we do every day of our lives – talking to people, finding out what they think and why. The 'social psychologist' would be doing these things in a rather more formal and systematic way and attempting to make generalizations and explanations that are valid and widely acceptable.

This is the sort of study I half hoped for when I started social science ten years ago, and now find myself having to argue for, because there isn't much of it around. I think the reason for this lies in the development of positivist methodology which may itself be influenced by politics and ideology (Armistead, 1972). However, one of the consequences of the emphasis on behaviour seems clear, which is that people's experience can be ignored, unless they create a fuss. If those in power want to do something, the wrong *behaviour* can mess things up, whereas the wrong *experience* doesn't get in the way. So I see the study of experience as a political act, at a time when people's experiences of the world are diversifying rapidly, and more and more of them are likely to be ignored by those who run centralized states. It could also be political in the stronger sense that it could reveal the ways in which people's experience is structured by political and economic conditions, but that is something we should demonstrate rather than assume. It is also a 'humanistic' act in that it encourages us to understand other people's experience and to become aware of the limitations of our own. Hopefully, this could not only counteract the fragmentation of our society and our selves, but also enable us to see the extent to which we are social products, and to sense the possibilities for further development and change.

References

ARMISTEAD, N. (1972), 'The values on which psychology rests', in *Rat, Myth and Magic: A Political Critique of Psychology*, Russell Press.

BANNISTER, D., and FRANSELLA, F. (1971), *Inquiring Man: The Theory of Personal Constructs*, Penguin.

BROADBENT, D. (1973), *In Defence of Empirical Psychology*, Methuen.

CASTANEDA, C. (1973), *Journey to Ixtlan: Last Lessons of Don Juan*, Bodley Head.

COHEN, S., and TAYLOR, L. (1972), *Psychological Survival*, Penguin.

SCHATZMAN, M. (1973), *Soul Murder: Persecution in the Family*, Allen Lane The Penguin Press.

STEPHENSON, W. (1953), *The Study of Behavior: Q Technique and its Methodology*, University of Chicago Press.

STEPHENSON, W. (1967), *The Play Theory of Mass Communications*, University of Chicago Press.

TOCH, H. (1972), *Violent Men*, Penguin.

Further Reading

ATKINSON, D., *Orthodox Consensus and Radical Alternative*, Heinemann, 1971.
An attack on sociological theory; the 'alternative' is quite social-psychological (especially chapter 7).

BERGER, J., *A Fortunate Man*, Penguin, 1969.
Though not strictly social psychology it asks the right sort of questions about the life of a country doctor.

BERGER, P., and LUCKMAN, T., *The Social Construction of Reality*, Penguin, 1971.
A more sophisticated, theoretical attempt than mine to marry 'everyday life' and 'society'.

BRUYN, S., *The Human Perspective in Sociology*, Prentice-Hall, 1966.
Although it concerns participant observation, much of Part 4 and the Appendixes is relevant for developing an 'experiential methodology'.

GOFFMAN, E., *Asylums*, Penguin, 1968.
Links the experience of the mental patient to the institution of which he is part, especially in the 'moral career of the mental patient'.

HAMPDEN-TURNER, C., *Radical Man: The Process of Psycho-Social Development*, Duckworth, 1971.

A slam at psychological theory and a humanistic-cum-radical alternative.

LAING, R., and ESTERSON, A., *Sanity, Madness and the Family*, Penguin, 1970.
Links the experience of schizophrenia to the family situation without the over-interpretation of other work.

SEVERIN, F. (ed.), *Discovering Man in Psychology*, McGraw-Hill, 1973.
Part 4 concerns the interpretation of 'science' in psychology, and there is a short section on phenomenological methodology.

TRISELIOTIS, J., *In Search of Origins*, Routledge & Kegan Paul, 1973.
A study of adopted people searching for their biological parents – their experiences of adoption and of identity, their motivations and expectations for the search.

Part Two
Topics

Conventional social psychology has become more and more out of touch with the world it is supposed to be explaining. Where it does not totally ignore issues in the real world, it still treats them in a narrow and conservative way that abstracts the issues from their social context. This is particularly true of the relationship between values and topics dealt with by social psychology. Part Two consists of six essays which explore this relationship.

The world does not wait for social psychology: people's ideas move and change, and social psychology gets left behind. In the last few years there have been important challenges to the social order, and these are reflected in the following essays. The family, reputedly our most stable social institution, is and has always been changing. Currently, new cracks are beginning to appear: some of these are picked up in the first three essays, where assumptions in social psychology about the fixed nature of the family are criticized. As women and children in particular are challenging the family, so other minority groups are challenging racial prejudice and discrimination. Godfrey Harrison describes what may be learnt from black people's literature, and Graham Murdock uses race as an example of the ideological content of the media. Finally, the work ethic has been challenged by various types of 'drop-outs' (beatniks, hippies, the idle rich), as well as by automation and by the daily resistance of workers and strikers. Denis Pym questions the relevance of a 'work' model to what is going on in 'employment'. In the face of these changes in the world, the media subtly reinforce the status quo, in the way they treat such issues: they act as part of the 'soft machine' that absorbs dissent and regurgitates it as part of the accepted order of things. This cooling out of alternative realities and reinforcement of the dominant reality is illustrated in Graham Murdock's essay.

If we are to grasp the moving, changing world and its values, we should place our social psychology in historical perspective. As John Shotter has argued in Part One, we need a time dimension. Conventional social psychology is often static in two senses: it ignores the historical context and it freezes the individual in time. Here, the historical context to social psychological topics is presented by Geoff Pearson, Joan Busfield, Tim Lang and Godfrey Harrison, while Denis Pym looks more towards the future. The importance of the development of the individual over time is brought out particularly by Tim Lang and Geoff Pearson.

The infusion of values into social psychology is firmly resisted by most social psychologists. But this is a Canute-like exercise: social psychology is already suffused with values, the values of the societies of which it is itself a product. It is not enough just to study value-related topics, or to study values themselves after the fashion of Allport, Rokeach and Brown. We are asking social psychologists to recognize that their 'objectivity' masks fundamental value assumptions about human nature, about what the 'problems' are, about how they are to be conceptualized and investigated, about the nature of our society and its influence upon individuals within it. Instead, we should have a social psychology which accepts that values *cannot be ruled out*, either of what we study or of the way we study it. This is because the social psychologist is himself a part of the world he studies and is subject to the same biases and influences he detects in other people: he has a class position, a sex role, a racial identity, an occupational situation, a set of beliefs and values; and he is operating as part of a specific social system: technocratic, Western capitalism. This will be explored more in Part Three, but here some of these rather sweeping assertions are backed up by the six 'topical' essays.

Geoff Pearson outlines the values in and around psychiatry in general and family therapy in particular: even when the individualizing bias of 'fossil psychiatry' is corrected by family theory, the family is still not seen as an arena of ongoing values and conflicts situated in a social matrix that extends beyond the home. Joan Busfield begins to specify the wider values surrounding the family, attributing particular importance to the conflict between the individualism of the wider society and the collectivist ideology of the family. Tim Lang shows the hidden values in conventional explanations of school phobia, and goes on to explore the values concerning childhood and school that provide the assumed framework within which such explanations operate. His own explanation stresses the unresolved conflict between compulsory attendance and anti-school values. Godfrey Harrison reveals how White, Anglo-Saxon, Male, Middle-Class, Protestant values have resulted in a bias in the social psychology of prejudice that ignores the experience of the victims in favour of contrastive studies that compare groups of people or some characteristic significant to the WASMMCPs. Graham Murdock identifies the values conveyed through the media and misunderstood by Mary Whitehouse and conventional social psychology alike: both are asking the same question are there any harmful effects?), although Mary Whitehouse probably has a better grasp of the generalized effects of the media. The present essay explores what values are being constructed and diffused *overall* by the media, especially via the news. Lastly, Denis Pym takes a personal trip around the horizons of occupational psychology, the area of social psychology where there is the most dissatisfaction with conventional approaches. He indicates some of the shaky value premises upon which occupational psychology has been built. All these essays illustrate the ways in which values set the terms of reference within which conventional social psychology goes blindly about its business.

The value theme does not adequately encompass another strand running through these essays, namely the active–passive, praxis–process distinction referred to in the introduction to Part One. A shared rejection of the billiard-ball, blotting-paper, plasticine model of humanity is apparent here. Geoff Pearson and Tim Lang see family members as asserting their independence and autonomy to various degrees, and in any case *producing* the situations they are in. Denis Pym claims that 'the winners' in the world of employment are the self-propelled individuals who carve out their own style of work; while Godfrey Harrison points out the value of accounts written by people actively engaged in situations and struggle. Together with this emphasis on praxis, the subsidiary themes are also continued here: the questioning of positivism and determinism, and the search for a fuller treatment of the 'social'. For instance, Denis Pym is very critical of positivism, and Joan Busfield, Geoff Pearson and Graham Murdock are particularly keen to put the individual into the full social context from which the social psychologies of the family and the mass media abstract her or him.

Prisons of Love: the Reification of the Family in Family Therapy
Geoffrey Pearson

The case is typical – a psychiatrist had seen the boy, but no one else in the family. A psychiatric social worker had seen the mother, but not the boy or anyone else. The P.S.W. and the psychiatrist had seen each other at case conferences. No one had seen anyone else . . . no one had seen David's home, his school, the streets in which he played. . . . Is it not an odd way to go about things? If one has a referral, say, from a hockey team, because the left back is not playing properly, one wouldn't think only of getting the left back round to one's office, taking a history, and giving a Rorschach. At least I hope not. One would also go to see how the team plays hockey.

R. D. Laing, *The Politics of the Family and Other Essays*

Ronald Laing here is criticizing what I will call the 'fossil paradigm' of psychiatry: the idea that emotional problems are firmly rooted inside the patient's head, having nothing to do with what goes on between people. The alternative directs us to a *social* psychology of mental disorder, and if social psychologists have themselves neglected the 'clinical' field – the area of helping others in distress – the 'caring professions' or 'helping professions' have not neglected social psychology. They *consume* it avidly, and the social psychology of the family extends a growing influence, and helps shape their conception of social problems, their own 'helping' role and their whole professional world view. Doctors, social workers, clinical psychologists, health visitors, probation officers, nurses, psychiatrists, educational psychologists, magistrates and others are urged to understand their clientele not as 'individuals', but as members of a family, and to 'go along and see the team play'. This is commonly known as 'family therapy' and its theoretical underpinnings as 'family theory', and my purpose here is to look critically at some aspects of it, and how it aids, or inhibits, our understanding of how people make families and break families. A change of key reveals a second theme for this paper in a problem which is arguably the central theoretical *motif* of social psychology; the relationship of individual to group; personal identity and membership. It will bring us into contact with questions of order, freedom, responsibility and autonomy – moral and political issues, and very 'unscientific', but nevertheless vital if

we are to understand how social psychology relates to human distres
pain, and suffering.

Fossil psychiatry and the moral impulse of family therapy

In the days of 'pre-scientific' psychiatry, the madhouse was fully unde
stood as a potential resource for the resolution of *family* conflicts. Th
imagery which guided 'lunacy reform' in Britain in the late nineteenth ce
tury was not that of the 'poor, infirm madman' who required protectio
but of wicked uncles who might lock away in remote dungeons relativ
who stood in their way of inheritance. Hence the Lunacy Act of 1890, whic
dominated legislation for mental disorder in the United Kingdom until th
1960s, was informed not by any attempt to structure a law which would g
treatment to those who needed it, but by a concern to prevent the wrongf
detention of the sane. Psychiatry was inseparable from ideas of propriet
constraint and liberty.

This insight – that the madhouse could be a place to put some people i
order to benefit others – was undone by many patient years of work on th
fossil model which deemed psychiatry as neutral, scientific and unobje
tionable. Thus one eminent psychiatrist, working within the fossil par
digm, has argued that the psychiatrist is no more a moral agent than th
man you might hire to repair your TV set when it is faulty. Having adjuste
your set, he does not insist on which channel you watch. The question o
who decides when your TV set needs repair, however, is not explored i
the fossil paradigm. Indeed, the denial of the socio-ethical background t
human distress and social problems is sometimes quite complete in term
of the blunted moral sense of fossil psychiatry. Family therapy, howeve
secures the central insight that mental illness *must* be understood in inte
personal terms. Whatever the causes of mental disorder, and granted th
not all symptoms are necessarily interpersonally determined, they wi
have interpersonal consequences, thus requiring that a total theory be se
in a fully social context. A general theory of psychiatry *must* account fo
things such as labelling and the explusion of members from families, scap
goating, stigmatization, questions of agreed conduct, permissible oddities
sanctions against those who offend these codes, etc. The study of ment
illness, when grasped as a social-psychological enterprise, is also the stud
of the institutions of mental illness: what is taken by people (and by whic
people) to be sane, odd, insane, 'unsane', loco, barmy, or stupid; who de
fines, and who has the power to make their definitions stick.

Of one thing we can be certain: no one knows a great deal about th
nature of what we call 'mental illness', 'emotional distress', 'madness'
'personal problems', 'break-up', or 'break-down', or how to administer

'cure', offer 'help', give 'treatment', 'heal', or effect a 'solution'. The fact that we have so many words for 'it' and what to do about 'it' suggests that there are fundamental conflicts even about what the problem is, what a good solution should be, or who (priests, psychologists, psychiatrists, social workers) should have the healing function. There are a great many theories about the subject – too many even to mention – and each warring theoretical faction holds tenaciously to its own position, often in ignorance of other orientations. Different researchers fashion their research to meet the requirements of quite different theories, and it becomes impossible to correlate findings from one school with those of another. What emerges is a glut of 'facts' with no firm theoretical centre around which to order their interpretation: an embarrassment of 'answers' in fact which suggests that we have yet to learn to ask the right questions. In the absence of any compelling theoretical paradigm, psychiatric 'revolutions' are impotent squabbles: professional soldiers trudge wearily back and forth amassing data, battles are won and lost, but the war goes on.

But if mental-health professionals are confused, the man in the street, it seems, is not. Piedmont and Downey (1971) write that mental-health revolutions have been revolutions for professionals only, and the public conception of mental illness is still one couched in moral rather than scientific terms as a question of ethics, propriety and agreed rules of conduct and their enforcement. Popularly, we know, there is a dark side to the business: 'nut doctors', 'do-gooders', 'trick-cyclists' and 'shrinks' are not looked upon as unambiguous helpers. Revolutions in psychiatry are, as in the fairy tale of the Emperor's new clothes, there to be seen only by the initiated; that is, those who already *know* what they are going to 'see'.

Recently, however, even initiates have seen the nakedness of the Emperor. Thomas Szasz is foremost among those who argue that the mental-health professionals are secular moralists, enforcing codes of conduct while claiming that they are 'curing sickness'. Szasz quotes another psychiatrist, Menninger, who says of homosexuality:

We cannot, like Gide, extol homosexuality. We do not, like some, *condone* it. We regard it as a symptom with all the functions of other symptoms.

But then, Szasz asks, quite properly, *if* homosexuality is a 'symptom,' what is there to condone, or not condone? Menninger would not 'condone' the fever of pneumonia, say, or the spots of measles. Szasz writes:

My contention [is] that the psychiatric perspective on homosexuality is but a thinly disguised replica of the religious perspective which it displaced, and that efforts to 'treat' this kind of conduct medically are but thinly disguised methods for suppressing it. . . . [The psychiatrist's] medical role is but a cloak for that of the moralist and social engineer (Szasz, 1970).

Despite many shortcomings, Szasz's work is as important as any in psychiatry since the War if we are to begin to place psychiatry and psychology back in the world. Its main thrust suggests that issues of mental health are issues of human living and how 'proper living' is defined differently at different points in historical time and under different social, economic and cultural circumstances. There is ample evidence to support this, but mental-health ideology, argues Szasz, side-steps these matters – which are *moral* and *political*, having to do with how people negotiate their lives together, and the powerful definitions of 'normality' within which they do so – and makes them appear as value-neutral, and objective standards of 'health'. It de-fuses, de-politicizes and takes the moral guts out of problems of human conduct. To take an example offered by Szasz (1970, p. 229): in 1954 the United States Supreme Court argued that according to 'modern authority' on 'psychological knowledge' the segregation of black and white children in schools was psychologically harmful to black children. Racism is thus reduced to a neutral (de-politicized) pseudo-scientific issue, which is what it is not. Suppose 'psychological knowledge' had it that segregation was *good* for black children: would that justify apartheid? Or even, suppose that I *want* to harm blacks, or do not care what harms them: what then?

Here the mystification of what Szasz calls the 'medical model' stands transparent: social problems, whether crime, broken marriages, poverty, irresponsible statesmanship, adolescent conflicts with parents, homelessness, unemployment, or student protest, are seen as the result of some personal quirk, an 'illness' to be 'diagnosed' and 'treated' by a technician. Szasz objects: social problems he sees as true moral dilemmas, and he suggests that they be resolved, where they can be resolved, by a direct confrontation of the moral and political issues. Principally, and classically, he suggests that 'help' is fundamentally a moral act and will either tend towards consolidating social order (constraining individuals) or will be on the side of individual liberty. An outgrowth of critical thought in the helping professions similarly protests against this dominant medical model which one-sidedly sees social problems as personal 'sickness' and neglects wider social explanations. Its mood is easily indicated: giving alms to the poor man may help that man, but it will not rid us of poverty; giving psychotherapy, 'occupational guidance', or 'rehabilitative treatment' to the 'work-shy' similarly does not solve the problem of unemployment. Giving electric shocks to homosexuals may deflect their sexual bent, but it will not change a cultural structuring of sex roles which finds homosexuality obectionable and menacing. Counselling a 'disturbed adolescent' may help him to live more easily with the parents who could not live easily with him as he was. All in all, the criticism is that the fossil model provides the happy pills which enable people, hopefully, to go on living in a work situation, family, or world which itself remains unchanged and unproblematic. Family therapy constitutes a sharp break with the fossil model. In the fossil paradigm, mental disorder is an *individual's* complaint, irrespective of whether its causes are organic/biochemical, 'psychological', or 'behavoural'; in family theory, mental disorder is a property of *familial and social systems*.

I cannot here given a detailed and authoritative account of the many threads of family therapy. Roughly, however, the origins of family therapy are two-fold: 'communications-systems theory' (Ruesch and Bateson, 1951) and a struggle within and against psychoanalytical conceptions. In psychoanalysis symptoms are the fossilized remains inside the patient's head of his earlier relationships in childhood. The purpose of therapy is to exorcise these psychic demons, and except for the purposes of footing the bill the family is kept firmly at arm's length. Although its relationship with psychoanalysis has always remained tensional, family therapy explodes this vision. Ackerman, the grand old man of family therapy, writes:

When family conflict is sopped up and internalized, when it becomes locked inside the mind of one person, it cannot be solved. If a useful and healthful solution is to be found, intrapsychic conflict must be activated and re-projected into the field of family interaction (Ackerman, 1961).

We can point to two sources of dissatisfaction which precipitated this break. Experience with disturbed children and adolescents showed that their families were often as disturbed as the child and that working with the 'identified patient' alone was futile; the resolution of marriage conflicts posed a similar dilemma. Thus, Jack who is worried because he is always screaming at Jill – although he 'really' loves her – seeks help. 'Help' stops Jack screaming at his wife, but it also changes him and Jill finds herself living with someone whom she did not marry. In the words of the skit song, 'I can't get adjusted to the you who got adjusted to me'.[1] Jackson (1957) provided an early re-formulation of these dilemmas in the conception of 'family homeostasis', demonstrating how the improvement of the identified patient would often be followed by repercussions (psychosomatic attacks, depression, even psychotic episodes) in another family

1. The anecdote makes its point, but could be misleading in that Jill is as likely to scream at Jack. More significantly, given male–female power differentials in marriage, when Jack screams at Jill it is not unlikely that *she* will go for help, 'to make her into a more loving wife'.

member. Who, then, is the patient? With the tabling of this question grew
the notion that emotional problems should be confronted squarely by
looking at *whole* families in what was known as 'conjoint family therapy'.
More recently, Speck has developed the intriguing concept of 'network
therapy', relating personal distress to even wider social contexts and acting
therapeutically on *whole social networks* – that is, groups of thirty, forty
or even fifty people at a time, consisting of the patient's family and their
extended kin, friends, neighbours and other significant persons (doctors,
employers, teachers, even local shopkeepers). Speck sometimes speaks of
this work as 'retribalization' (Speck, 1967; Speck and Rueveni, 1969;
Speck and Attneave, 1973).

Family therapy's central thrust saw symptoms as orchestrated to family
contexts which were themselves 'crazy' in some kind of way: the patient's
behaviour, no matter how irrational, was appropriate given those social
and familial contexts. Lidz talked about the 'transmission of irrationality';
Laing and Esterson (1964) argued that schizophrenia was 'intelligible'
when attention was paid to contexts, while Wynne *et al.* (1958) described
psychotic episodes as attempts to grow up in families which could not
allow their children to grow up. They write:

The social organization in these families is shaped by a pervasive familial sub
culture of myths, legends and ideology which stress the dire consequences of
openly recognized divergences from a relatively limited number of fixed, engulfing
family roles.

A common theme in the literature on the family of the schizophrenic is
that under such circumstances a person could only 'be himself' at the
risk of being seen by the family as odd, bad, or mad, thereby growing up
with a sense of himself as defective. Plugged into a role which had become
more vital to the family equilibrium than its occupant ('I don't know what's
wrong – he's usually such a nice quiet boy'), if the family was to survive in
its accustomed state, any attempt to grow beyond that role, or re-negotiate
it, must be denied and invalidated as 'inexplicable' ('Why would you want
to do that to your *mother* – of all people!') and, in the final invalidation,
sickness ('He doesn't really mean it – he can't help it, you know, he's
ill'). What the family could not tolerate in its deviant member was often
seen to be what they found intolerable in themselves. The patient 'carried'
the burden of the family; he was their 'scapegoat', or as in Bernice
Rubens's novelistic account, *The Elected Member* (1969).

2. For detailed reference to the development of family theory and family therapy,
see Jackson (1968); Haley (1971); Handel (1968); and the journal *Family Process*,
first published in 1962.

The question of how families might go beyond making a member feel unwanted and uncomfortable, and actually drive someone crazy, is not yet satisfactorily answered. Nevertheless, family therapy suggested that crazy behaviour was rational in certain family contexts; there was, indeed, certain method in madness. Paranoid people, for example, might actually be persecuted (Schatzman, 1973). Family therapy seemed to side with the underdog, redressing an imbalance of power, and the patient was portrayed as the innocent victim of frightening confusion: 'knots, tangles, tangles, *impasses*, disjunctions, whirligogs, binds' (Laing, 1970). We see families placing their members in 'untenable situations', roles 'engulf' them, myths deny them: people are twisted *into* pre-given identities, and *out of* their selves. Therapists even reported that they felt themselves going mad if they stayed for too long in such families.

In the influential, but frequently misunderstood, theory of the 'double-bind', for example, madness was seen as the result of long-term exposure to bewildering, paradoxical messages (Bateson *et al.*, 1956). An example of *paradox* in communication would be the instruction 'Disobey me!' Here, if I am to comply, I must disobey you, although to do that is to obey, which is what I must not do. I must obey while disobeying; do what you instruct while going against that same instruction: I am instructed to do what I am not to do. Another example of paradoxical communication is, 'Be spontaneous!' which requires the victim to provide something which *by definition* cannot be provided to order: spontaneity. Add to this para-doxical element the formal requirements of a 'double-bind' which are that I can neither escape from the situation, nor comment on its absurdity, and there is a situation where I *must* respond although no response is possible. The victim is 'damned if he does and damned if he doesn't': he must respond without responding; remove himself without removing himself; communicate without saying anything. Literally, the logic of paradox demands that the victim must 'lose his mind', or 'go out of his mind'.

I have risked an uncritical appraisal of family therapy which over-emphasizes the internal consistency of both its theory and its therapeutic practice in order to grasp the core. First, family therapy promises, al-though it has not yet delivered, a fully interpersonal, social-psychological approach to mental disorder. Secondly, it offers the prospect of a moral–political theory of psychiatry in its insistence that we look at what people *do* to each other and with each other, rather than attending to the distorted interiorized representation of these goings on. The nineteenth-century view of the madhouse as a dumping ground seems to be recovered in family therapy's moral insight of psychiatric invalidation as a symbolic

dumping ground. In its focus on the family system/individual interface,
sort of moral drama is played out: patients are heroic little figures, strugg
ing to make sense of themselves in an uncanny syntactical jungle. Th
therapeutic enterprise requires grappling with the crazy logic of the famil
system which grinds up the members which comprise it. Those enjoyin
sanity and security at another's expense might have to go under in thi
endeavour, experience their own suffering, pain and madness. What i
inescapable is that therapists are *agents*, doing things to one person o
behalf of others: theirs is a moral and political enterprise. However, th
recognition of moral dilemmas does not guarantee their solution, and w
must turn now to how family therapy's moral impulse fares in its con
ceptual–technical realm.

The abstracted family and the family machine

Family theory suggests that there is no point in trying to understand famil
problems and family change in terms of the properties of unit-members
one must attend to the *structure of systems*. Taking an illustration of thi
from a quite different area, it can be observed how the value of poun
sterling fluctuates on the money market and the relationship of thes
fluctuations to rumour and selling. A vicious circle can operate whereb
rumour that the pound is weak leads to selling which leads to an objectiv
weakening of the pound, leading to more rumour, more selling, etc.

Rumour that $\rightarrow$ Selling $\rightarrow$ £ objectively $\rightarrow$ Rumour $\rightarrow$ More $\rightarrow$ etc.
£ is weak   of £   weakens   selling

We call such a process, of which I have offered a very crude mode
'positive feedback', a 'deviance-amplifying system', or a 'mutual multi
lateral causal system'. Such processes occur in a wide number of spheres
including families. Clearly, to account for the weakness of sterling b
blaming 'rumour' is absurd: we must give an adequate account of th
structure of the money market which allows rumour to take hold. Sig
nificantly, it is possible to reverse the deviance-amplification spiral – i
the sense of rumouring strength and encouraging buying – into a 'virtuou
cycle' because of the *same* features of structure.

Equally, it is inadequate to offer a familial theory of 'schizophrenia
which only says that it is caused by 'X' or 'Y': what is required is a
account of family structure which amplifies some events, while regulatin
or minimizing the effects of others, thus amplifying 'X' or 'Y' systemati
cally, but not other events ('P' or 'Q') which are also elements of th
family's way of life, and which in a different kind of family structure migh
be 'pathological'. Put into systems jargon, a family is a system charac

terized by the principle of *equifinality*: the same results may spring from different origins because of the nature of family organization. Results (e.g. 'schizophrenia') are independent of initial conditions (e.g. 'X', 'Y', 'P' or 'Q') although still rule-governed by the rules of structure and process. Under conditions of equifinality very large results can come from even very small or insignificant initial inputs.

Here is the rational kernel of family theory: families are to be understood as rule-governed systems which can sometimes run 'out of control', damaging member units. But here also is the danger that the family might be lost as a humanly intelligible enterprise in the theory of family therapy. To return for a moment to the fate of sterling, 'structure' must be understood as comprising not only the machinery of the money market, but also the *values* in which it is embedded. Ripping the money market out of these contexts, one might be able to construct models and theories which accurately *predict* what goes on within it, and one might embrace this as one version of *science*. However, decontextualized and separated from the system of values which it feeds from, operates on and implements, as a humanly intelligible enterprise the finance market can only appear as a crazy, childish, but harmful monster game of 'Monopoly'. Moreover, even to gain such an impoverished understanding of finance exchange as a party game would require some commonsense knowledge of the values of individualism, property and gain, without which 'Monopoly' is no game, and even less fun. When structure is decontextualized, it is also dehumanized in the sense of becoming *mechanism*.

Similarly, family therapy often strips away the contextualized meanings which surround family-system processes in its understanding both of family problems and their solution. Take, for example, a project by Langsley and others (1968) which has some bearing on the therapeutic effectiveness of the issues we have been discussing. Briefly, Langsley, using a technique called 'Family Crisis Therapy', managed to avoid the otherwise inevitable hospitalization of a sample of mentally disordered patients, and effect better all-round recovery rates. The core feature of his technique was to help family members re-define their problem as a problem for the whole family and not only for the sick member. The message was: your problems are problems in day-to-day living, not 'sickness' residing in one member, thus to some extent embracing the moral arguments of Szasz. The results for this short-term intensive and inexpensive technique were good, and the authors had reason to be enthusiastic. As they note, however, this cannot be taken as an indication of the success of conjoint family therapy; it simply offers, as they put it, comparison with traditional hospital-based methods. And perhaps even these modest claims go too far: perhaps

Langsley does no more than indicate what always lies, unmentioned, at the back of family therapy; namely, the avoidance of hospitalization, degradation ceremonies and the consequent blows to self-esteem suffered by mental-hospital inmates. Langsley does two things. First he makes a moral point – psychiatric problems are living problems; and secondly he demonstrates how *bad* mental hospitals are, rather than how *good* family therapy is.

To take the discussion to the heart of the matter, these hospital-based methods of treatment to a large extent reflect our cultural prescriptions for dealing with irrationality and crazy behaviour. Madness, quite apart from being conceived of as a 'condition' from which some suffer, also embodies a set of culturally institutionalized meanings. In our culture there are different representations of madness: madness is folly; madness flows from 'excess'; it is violence, innocence, ecstasy and doom all at one and the same time. In its contradictions it is ungovernable, but also inflexible and determined. What I am suggesting, but can only hint at here, is that madness means many things and is closely tied to a wider vocabulary of cultural meanings, and cannot be understood apart from those. Madness is not peripheral to our culture, but is a fundamental category of our experience. In a vital sense it is something we might fall into when in error.

We are given no clues in the literature of family theory as to how we should understand madness, or how madness is understood by those families which it visits. The matter is simply taken for granted as non-problematic; the arguments and insights of family theory thus rest finally on an unanalysed 'commonsense' world. True, a repeated observation of the families of schizophrenics has been that family members *feared* that 'madness' would appear in one member or another, not uncommonly the 'identified patient'. But how are we to understand this? In Esterson's extended study in *The Leaves of Spring* of the Danzig family, for example, we are simply left guessing as to what madness means to this family in spite of the author's 'insider-phenomenological' orientation. Is it this *particular* madness in their daughter Sarah? The 'madness inside us all'? The lurking beasts of our socialized imagination? Or, 'madness in general', that dark, terrible, reified madness which only happens to other people?

These would be the preliminary requirements of a *humanized* conception of madness and the family. Our culture prescribes how we shall deal with the unmentionable and the irrational: dismiss it as poetry, lock it away, knock it on the head and, if all else fails, ignore it. However, family theorists snatch the family out of the world and would deal with this as a problem of 'scapegoating' within the family, and would understand and treat as an aspect of *internal* family dynamics what are nothing more than straightforward applications of widely held myths about 'nutters' as *monsters* to be treated with suspicion, fear and contempt. Family therapy, assiduously ignoring those widely held, power-invested beliefs about madness and unlicensed human imagination, rips *family structure* out of wider *social structure* and proceeds to lay the fault at the door of the family itself, labelling it a 'sick' family which scapegoats, shuns and hides from its deviant member.

My intention is not to deny that one should attempt to understand the inner workings of the family, or that an important moment of the scapegoating process is to be found in internal dynamics, but is to point to the one-sidedness of this social psychology of the abstracted family which somehow seems to have defected from culture. Man lives not primarily in the family, but in the world. Even so, the world of his family may be important, even central. Men hide inside their family shells from the harshness of the outside world; there they cut its bewildering complexity down to size. Indeed, some argue that our culture insists that men should retreat from the public realm as an arena in which to fashion their identities into the private spheres of familism and sexuality as the proper place for finding and constructing life meanings. But this is no excuse for a social psychology: social science which only expresses further the dilemmas and contradictions of our world has lost its cutting edge. Above all, it has lost the conception of what it is to be human.

Abstracted from the world, the family in family therapy is where the action is. How does it construe the action? Family therapy has a sort of moral armoury of words (invalidate, disqualify, mystify, disconfirm) which indicate that 'sickness' and 'therapy' might sometimes have to do with conflicting interests, some of which are discredited while others are legitimated, transforming interpersonal conflicts into mental (inner) problems. It also has a technical armoury. Key words, signifying key concepts, are transaction, role, rule, complementarity, feedback, homeostasis and system. The question is: how does the development of the technical–theoretical aid the development of family therapy's moral sense? I will focus here on the concept cluster embodied in the notion of 'transaction'.

Transaction: not the dancers but the dance

Jackson's concept of 'family homeostasis', as I have already shown, demonstrates and attempts to grapple with the manner in which symptoms float in families. It urges that the question of who is 'It' at any point in time is of secondary importance in relation to the family system properties which require an 'It'. Put in a nutshell, there are some families who if they did not have a schizophrenic member, would have to invent one. What kind of an advance is this on earlier formulations of the nature of symptoms? In psychodynamic terms, a symptom is a sort of statement. For example, a child whose problem is that he soils himself is seen as having discovered a way of getting at his mother: it is 'angry soiling'. Symptoms are communication, albeit bad communication. They are ways of removing oneself, or others, from the stage: 'wishing the problem away'. They are a means of getting at someone or something, or a means of signalling distress: 'I find this family intolerable'. The discovery that symptoms can move around within a family could become a more solid formulation of this, but the matter is subtly rephrased: in family therapy the family *needs* symptoms. And while symptoms thus signal *family* imbalance, there is a danger of losing our understanding of them as *personal* expressions of distress; signals which say something about what a hell of a place this is to live are transformed into a 'family balance sheet'.

While this is uncharitable to many who are trying to grapple with these problems, I want to suggest that there is a *tendency* in family therapy to place the family's existence as the thing of primary importance over and above personal well-being. The place of theory here is crucial. Theoretical work, while it may often not be properly understood, provides the *imagery* which informs this tendency. The most powerful set of images is secured in the central notion of symptoms as a *family transaction*.

In what systems theorists would call 'crudely psychologistic' accounts of family pathology, people do things to each other, and some drive others crazy. We find this in some of Laing's work, and in the early work of the Bateson Group, for example. Thus the earliest formulation of the double-bind theory speaks of a *victim*. In a later contribution, however, Weakland (1960) writes that the use of the word 'victim' was only a convenience; in actual fact the double-bind always binds *both* parties and, strictly speaking, there is no binder and bound, but rather *two* victims each bound in a paradoxical system. To give an example which has often been used as a paradigm for this kind of problem, consider a married couple who are locked in an interminable conflict. Let 'W' stand for 'The wife nags the husband', and let 'H' stand for 'The husband withdraws from the wife'. Then this couple's relationship is characterized by a pattern in which the wife nags whereupon the husband withdraws, causing the wife to nag him, and the cycle starts again. Thus:

... H W H W H W H W H W ...

Asked why she nags her husband, the wife replies that he is always withdrawing from her. Asked why he withdraws, the husband states that he cannot tolerate her nagging. They have different perceptions of their shared reality; to employ a term suggested by Watzlawick *et al.* (1968) the couple 'punctuate' their conflicting transaction differently, thus:

Husband's punctuation: WH WH WH WH WH WH WH etc.

Wife's punctuation:　　　HW HW HW HW HW HW HW etc.

Jackson (1967), commenting on the same issue, writes that, 'it matters little how this got started, since once under way it tends to be self-perpetuating and mutually causative'. The effect of this kind of thinking is to belittle human conflict as irrelevant, and to assert over the conflict a unifying non-conflictual scheme which relates to *system properties*. Thus, Watzlawick also writes that, 'disagreement about how to punctuate the sequence of events is *at the root* of countless relationship struggles', suggesting that there is no *real* conflict at the base of these struggles, and that one should attend not to the conflicts and competing interests, but to patterns, forms and processes which are likened to games. As an imagery which guides action, the victim–victimizer paradigm suggests that here is moral dilemma. It does not resolve the conflict, but it suggests that someone is getting the rough end of a deal, and that we might have to take sides. As imagery, the system-transaction model has as a basic root the assumption that there is a *consensus* of interests, and that problems arise only from *misunderstandings*.

This imagery is informed by a very considerable theoretical enterprise in family therapy. And here we change gear in this paper, for family therapists claim, with some justification, to be in the vanguard of the attempt to construct a fully social-psychological, field-transactional model of the person which could act as a conceptual bridge between the personal and the social. They sense themselves to be not at all marginal to the theoretical concerns of social psychology, and for some it amounts to a crusade, and inscribed on their banner is 'Cybernetics'. They note that linear uni-directional causal thinking cannot grasp the flow and interchange in human systems; the urgent task is for the construction of a theoretical language adequate to the requirements of grasping *transaction* in families as opposed to interaction. Thus:

Interaction refers to the effect upon each other of organized, detached entities such as the behaviour of billiard balls or gas molecules. The notions of classical physics such as the Newtonian laws of gravity are based on interaction concepts. So is the term, interpersonal relations, insofar as it describes the effects upon each other's behaviour of discrete personalities. *Transaction* ... describes the inter-penetration and mutual, reverberating and reciprocal effects of processes which can no longer be referred to organized, detached entities. It is here rather a question of system in process with system. Biochemical systems have this characteristic, as do most of the processes which are denoted by the term homeostasis. The equilibrium-maintaining, self-correcting systems involved in cybernetics and communications engineering are also transactional in orientation (Group for the Advancement of Psychiatry, 1954).

In a more recent development of this tendency Shands (1971) has argued that when we pay attention to forms, shape and process certain kinds of difference and dichotomization become unimportant. In an expression of the field-transaction analysis of system he writes that conflicts are only the superficial face of a concealed unity:

In games and wars, protagonists and antagonists are both included under the general definition of reciprocal role-occupants whose mutually integrated behaviour is the game involved (Shands, 1971).

The universe in this account is originally whole; only our conceptual structures introduce categories and conflict. As one commentator has put the matter, for Shands 'person and group are dual aspects of a single process, separable only for the convenience of verbal description' (Ransom, 1972).

Here, on the edge of high theory, the distinction between self and other, individual and group, 'inner' and 'outer' – quite fundamental distinctions for any morally-reflexive social psychology – have become not only 'conveniences', but *handicaps* forced upon us by the structure of our language. *The* problem for this 'science', therefore, becomes the construction of a new language which can cut up the world in a different manner and help us to grasp the subtleties of 'reality' without damaging it, or casting the shadow of our discrete, uni-directional schemes of causality upon its structure and form.

Thus, family therapy can be seen in its 'transactionalism' to have confronted, if not resolved, the fundamental therapeutic problem of the relationship of the individual to the family. Moreover, it is not difficult to claim these questions of identity, membership and socialization, and the relationship of man to socius, individual to system – *psychology to sociology* – as the central problem of social psychology.

Such a task of integration will require theory, but not a theory such as this which on the one hand de-humanizes its subject, and on the other blunts its own moral–practical cutting face. As Adorno (1967) has remarked, writing critically of another grand systems theorist – Talcott

Parsons – the unification of sociology and psychology will not be executed by doing violence to the vital distinction between man and society. To attempt the *theoretical* unification of what is in actuality conflict – as some human relationships are – is to commit an absurd error: 'no future synthesis of the social sciences can unite what is inherently at odds with itself'. Adorno elaborates:

What compartmentalized disciplines project on to reality merely reflects back what has taken place in reality. False consciousness is also true: inner and outer life are torn apart. Only through the articulation of their difference, not by stretching concepts, can their relation be adequately expressed. . . . A psychology which turns its back on society and idiosyncratically concentrates on the individual . . . says more about the hapless state of society than one which seeks by its 'wholistic approach' or an inclusion of social 'factors' to join the ranks of a no-longer-existent *universitas literarum*.

This for Adorno is the price of conceptual harmony, and his words are borne out in the pages of family therapy. We find Bell, for example, writing of the 'arbitrariness of our distinctions between the family group and the individual members of the family'. He continues: 'Both the group and the individual are correlated open systems. To look at one or the other as independent is only a professional choice . . .' (quoted in Beels and Ferber, 1969).

Our funds of initiative and inspiration which were increased at a leap when field theory exploded the fossil paradigm are in danger of being lost. The *moral* point of the collapse of fossil psychology is buried in the philosophical–methodological debate of a new cybernetic scientism. Here the distinctions of individual, group, family, community and society are merged and obscured in the intellectually exciting, but morally bankrupt, cybernetic concepts of deviance-amplifying systems, self-correctional fields, step-functions, and Markovian analogies. The last shreds of moral engagement find their expression largely in some idea of a scientific Wonderland, and the enemies of this cybernetic scientism are no longer pathology-inducing social organizations, or person-invalidating psychiatric practices, but the errors and crudities of 'Newtonian Science'. The practical implications of this theoretical shift are easy to see: the question of how one negotiates the tricky problem of the relationship of the individual to his family is reduced to a 'professional decision' which is in the final analysis 'arbitrary'.

For a humanized conception of the family

This has been a very abridged paper, and it has been very unfair to many who call themselves family therapists or attempt some clinical application of social psychology to problems of human distress. Nevertheless, it draws attention to some bedrock issues in the application of social psychology, specifically its moral and political implications, and it charges social psychology and family therapy with a neglect of these implications. How, then, do we begin to formulate a *human* conception of the family?

When searching for an understanding of the family, the social psychologist often reaches for a book on small-group theory. We must object: the family is not only the playground of social psychologists; it is not only a 'small group'. It is also a legally enforceable living arrangement which embodies as a *necessary* feature conflicts of loyalties and priorities, in the sense of responsibilities and obligations to self and others. Nor should we neglect power-differentials in the family, principally concerning the place of women and children. Bettelheim (1971), in a comparison of the Western family and the Israeli kibbutz, for example, notes that the family is a socio-economic as well as a psychological entity. He asks could we even conceive of certain conflicts of childhood (principally the Oedipus complex) if it were not for the gross economic dependence of children, on specific, *and culturally defined*, parents. Equally, any fully human account of family conflicts would have to understand differences in marital power and marital quarrels in the context of the discrimination against women in larger society. A family can, of course, be a good place to be, and there are instances – probably numerous – where what is 'good' for the family as a whole can be judged 'good' for each individual member. But the more general case must be one where we assume that loyalties and constraints on individual autonomy and liberty give rise to conflicts of interest.

Any family theory must ground itself in the *reality* of the family as a social institution. The question of how responsibilities, obligations and other issues of 'contract' in the family weigh in the determination and resolution of human conflicts is ignored, however, in this morally ambiguous family therapy. In the absence of any serious attempt to understand how *adults* negotiate their moral commitments in and out of families, there is only the imagery of the psychology of parent–child relations to guide us, and the imagery is one of a heavy, if not total, interdependence and reliance of family members on each other. A further objection must be registered, and we must raise the question: why is this theory of the family unable to confront issues of adult conduct? Is the human actor merely something which 'mediates system events' (Ransom), or a 'nodal point' (Shands) in a communicational system? What kind of forgetfulness does this neglect of the person signify? Is the interdependence of self and others so complete that we cannot make any distinction between them which is not 'arbitrary'? Answers are found in how we understand and construct 'theory', and the bias which this introduces is in no sense arbitrary.

Theory has got what Gouldner (1971) calls its 'background assumptions' or 'domain assumptions'. They are the bits of theory not open to analysis and they contain assumptions such as: man is essentially rational or irrational; society is fundamentally precarious or stable; human action is unpredictable; etc. All social theory contains such assumptions, and they provide the root metaphors of social science which are often more powerful in their influence than the more carefully elaborated superficial face of theory. Theory is often only a cosmetic for these powerful belief systems.

Systematically in this 'deep structure' of large bodies of social science we are told how much human beings rely on each other. The message is: no man is an island; man is social, contextualized, 'situational', embedded; man is not free, he is literally *rooted*. However, if we learn anything from recent developments in 'self-help' groups and the organizations of some deviant groupings – Women's Liberation, Gay Liberation, Black Power, etc. – it is that man is not on his back. Man *is* dependent on others, but he is *not* embedded; *we can choose on whom to be dependent*, and how to fashion our lives, values and identities. Where we cannot choose, it is because we are prevented from choosing, either by external social constraints, or by interiorized socialization.

So family therapy theorizes a great deal, but it does not think what theory is. It is also unthinking of its place in the world. Therefore, it does not escape its embeddedness in culture, and can do little more than simply give expression to cultural problems (for example, the place of the family in society), exerting itself one way or the other, necessarily arbitrarily. A reflexive grasp of family therapy, or any other helping process directed to the lives of people, would see it as part of the attempt to grasp at our human (rule-governed) relatedness – order, freedom, responsibility.

Most of us do not know why we marry and start new families, other than that it is the normal thing to do. It is part of the 'taken-for-granted' world, and to ask of the taken-for-granted world 'Why?' is to expect the answer, 'Because that's how any self-respecting father, wife, doctor, lorry driver, clerk, would behave'. As Alfred Schutz has observed, it is in the nature of the taken-for-granted that it has an objective and anonymous character; it is conceived of as being independent of my personal biographical circumstances.

We forget that the family is *ours*. Instead it becomes something 'out there' in the world of objects, or in its reified mode it stares back at us as a fantastic spiritual edifice, and family therapy reflects this unthinking attitude of common sense. A theory and therapeutic practice of the family which attempts to deal with the *experience of persons* under *socially-structured conditions* – that is, a two-sided, fully human perspective – will not be built out of bits of common sense, but will require full-blooded cultural criticism. Its grounds will be a practice directed to helping people *conduct* their lives, rather than helping to keep down the divorce rate, keep the family together, gives the kids a home, or whatever. A family is not a mutually causal, multi-channelled, deviance-amplifying communication system; nor is it a *place* in which to bring up children. It is *people* attempting to live together, guided by rules of conduct and under varying degree of constraint and choice. The family is made by men and women. It is also defended by law, although whether it is men who are thereby defended, or the principles which men make, is not always clear. 'What some families need', goes an old therapist's joke about unhappy marriages, 'is a good lawyer.' To forget that is to forget all.

References

ACKERMAN, N. W. (1961), 'A dynamic frame for the clinical approach to family conflict', in N. W. Ackerman *et al.* (eds.), *Exploring the Base for Family Therapy*, Family Service Association of America.

ADORNO, T. W., (1967), 'Sociology and psychology', *New Left Review*, no. 46, pp. 67–80.

BATESON, G., JACKSON, D. D., HALEY, J., and WEAKLAND, J. (1956), 'Toward a theory of schizophrenia', *Behavioral Science*, vol. 1, no. 4, pp. 251–64; reprinted in Jackson (1968).

BEELS, C. C., and FERBER, A. (1969), 'Family therapy: a view', *Family Process*, vol. 8, no. 2, pp. 280–318.

BETTELHEIM, B. (1971), *The Children of the Dream*, Paladin.

ESTERSON, A. (1970), *The Leaves of Spring: A Study in the Dialectics of Madness*, Tavistock; Penguin, 1972.

GOULDNER, A. (1971), *The Coming Crisis of Western Sociology*, Heinemann.

Group for the Advancement of Psychiatry (1954), *Integration and Conflict in Family Behavior*, GAP Report, no. 27, New York, GAP.

HALEY, J. (ed.) (1971), *Changing Families*, Grune & Stratton.

HANDEL, G. (ed.) (1968), *The Psychosocial Interior of the Family*, Allen & Unwin.

JACKSON, D. D. (1957), 'The question of family homeostasis', *Psychiat. Quart. Suppl.*, vol. 31, no. 1, pp. 79–90; reprinted in Jackson (1968).

JACKSON, D. D. (1967), 'The individual and the larger contexts', *Family Process*, vol. 6, no. 2, pp. 139–47.

JACKSON, D. D. (ed.) (1968), *Human Communication* (2 vols.), Palo Alto, Science and Behavior Books.

LAING, R. D. (1970), *Knots*, Tavistock; Penguin, 1972.

LAING, R. D., and ESTERSON, A. (1964), *Sanity, Madness and the Family*, Tavistock; Penguin, 1970.

LANGSLEY, D. G., *et al.* (1968), 'Family crisis therapy – results and implications', *Family Process*, vol. 7, no. 2, pp. 145–58.

PIEDMONT, E. B., and DOWNEY, K. J. (1971), 'Revolutions in psychiatry: or, the emperor's new clothes', *Int. J. soc. Psychiat.*, vol. 17, no. 2, pp. 111–21.

RANSOM, D. (1972), 'Review of H. C. Shands, *The War With Words*', *Family Process*, vol. 11, no. 3, pp. 349–60.

RUBENS, B. (1969), *The Elected Member*, Eyre & Spottiswoode; Penguin, 1971.

RUESCH, J., and BATESON, G. (1951), *Communication: The Social Matrix of Psychiatry*, Norton.

SCHATZMAN, M. (1973), *Soul Murder: Persecution in the Family*, Allen Lane The Penguin Press.

SHANDS, H. C. (1971), *The War With Words: Structure and Transcendence*, Mouton.

SPECK, R. V. (1967), 'Psychotherapy of the social network of a schizophrenic family', *Family Process*, vol. 6, no. 2, pp. 208–14.

SPECK, R. V., and RUEVENI, U. (1969), 'Network therapy – a developing concept', *Family Process*, vol. 8, no. 2, pp. 182–91.

SPECK, R. V., and ATTNEAVE, C. (1973), *Family Networks*, Pantheon.

SZASZ, T. S. (1970), *The Manufacture of Madness*, Harper & Row; Paladin, 1973.

WATZLAWICK, P., BEAVIN, J. H., and JACKSON, D. D. (1968), *Pragmatics of Human Communication*, Faber.

WEAKLAND, J. H. (1960), 'The "double bind" hypothesis of schizophrenia and three-party interaction', in D. D. Jackson (ed.), *The Etiology of Schizophrenia*, Basic Books.

WYNNE, L. C., *et al.* (1958), 'Pseudo-mutuality in the family relations of schizophrenics', *Psychiatry*, vol. 21, no. 3, pp. 205–20; reprinted in Handel (1968).

9 Family Ideology and Family Pathology
Joan Busfield

I

A major weakness of social psychology is its failure to incorporate many aspects of the social into its framework.[1] Above all social psychologists have tended to ignore differences at the ideological level: to forget that ideas, values and beliefs are culturally and temporarily variable. This narrowness of focus is very apparent in their work on personality. Studies of intra-societal and cross-cultural variables in personality have made little attempt to consider how the very notion of personality is culturally relative. What it is to be a 'person' in contemporary industrial society is not the same as what it is to be a person in a so-called traditional society. It is even doubtful whether what we understand by terms such as person or personality has much relevance in cultures very different from our own (Lane, 1974).[2]

This weakness of social psychology is demonstrably manifest in the body of work on 'family pathology', which accounts for the mental sickness of one member of a family in terms of the dynamics and peculiarities of his or her family relations. Two approaches may be contrasted; the first accords with the conventional natural scientific paradigm: it suggests that pathological family processes cause one member of the family to manifest disturbed behaviour. Its *modus operandi* is therefore to pinpoint differences in family interaction between 'pathological' families with a mentally sick (usually schizophrenic) member and the 'normal' families without one (Bateson *et al.*, 1956; Singer and Wynne, 1965). Such an approach by its use of the notion of cause encounters a fundamental problem in showing that any difference between the normal and pathological families is cause rather than consequence of having a sick member (Fontana, 1966; Brown, 1967). The second approach, in contrast, stresses understanding rather than explanation; it regards the behaviour of the 'sick' member as intelligible if viewed in the context of what goes on in the family as a whole (Laing and Esterson, 1971). Such an approach appears to be (in

1. A problem that is exacerbated by disciplinary boundaries.
2. Nor should we assume that the individual's relation to society will be the same in all cultures.

part) a development from the first; for if the behaviour of the sick individual is the consequence of conflicts and contradictions within the family, it is readily viewed as a meaningful and intelligible response to the situation. This in turn makes application of terms such as sickness and pathology questionable, for if behaviour is rational and intelligible, how can it be deemed sick and disordered (Laing, 1967). I shall not, however, in this paper be able to consider the arguments on either side; the appropriateness of terms like mental illness, pathology and so forth are discussed in many other places (Szasz, 1960; Begelman, 1971; Ausubel, 1961).

All the work, however, whatever its approach, lacks a broader context of cultural ideas that would enhance its power and insight. We cannot hope to understand what goes on inside families if we study them in isolation from the wider society. Without such a setting much of the meaning and significance of what happens in the family is lost. If we do not know the social and cultural demands placed upon individuals in families, their behaviour within the family appears idiosyncratic: an individually created product of the members themselves. Those who have adopted the first approach have, it is true, looked at 'normal' families as well as those with mentally sick members, but because they have concentrated on *differences* between the two types of families, they have failed to examine the cultural beliefs and expectations that govern *all* family interaction. Those who adopt the second approach have tended to give up the comparative enterprise altogether and have concentrated on giving detailed case studies of schizophrenogenic families. Yet the task of making individual behaviour intelligible still needs to be set in the context of contemporary ideas about family life (Sedgwick, 1972). Much of what the authors of both approaches have described as the contradictions and conflicts that explain or make intelligible the pathology of a limited number of individuals, are contradictions and conflicts faced by all families in our society. As a hypothesis the idea of family pathogenesis is as yet insufficiently precise; it could account for far more widespread pathology than is observed.

Esterson's detailed description of the relations of the Danzig family provides an obvious example of the need for a broader cultural context (1972). The contradictions and conflicts that he so graphically depicts are often part of the very fabric of our culture and are not restricted to a narrow group of families. In general his account is psychologistic (at times very psychoanalytic) and ignores the implications of recognizing that the Danzig family are not alone in the conflicts they experience and manifest. Yet if these contradictions and conflicts are common to most families, numerous questions occur. What are the usual strategies, if any, for handling them? Do some families ignore these strategies, mishandle them, or what? What leads some persons to be labelled mentally ill when others in apparently comparable situations are not?

I cannot, however, in this paper hope to answer these questions. My aim is more modest; I want to begin to outline some aspects of the *ideological* context of family relationships in English society, and I shall only be able to touch upon some of the implications of this type of analysis for the study of family pathology.[3] I am not, of course, the first to attempt to describe the ideology of family relations, though there has been little study of English society specifically. Whilst developing some of these ideas, what I do here differs in emphasis, content and interpretation from other endeavours (Mitchell, 1971; Parsons, 1956). Furthermore other work has tended to occur in rather different contexts and to be almost totally ignored by social psychologists.

II

Within the culture a central, if not the central, interpretation of the term family is the so-called *nuclear* family, a unit of parents and children living together. Children are regarded as essential to family life. Without children a couple do not constitute a proper family. We talk of children 'making a family', of couples 'having a family' and of 'the family leaving home', and in many contexts the words 'family' and 'children' can readily be substituted. Esterson describing the Danzig family puts it this way: 'With the birth of the children the Danzigs became a family' (1972, p. 62). In view of this it is not surprising that studies of family pathology are usually studies of the nuclear family. Studies of mental illness focusing on the husband/wife relationship do not tend to be termed family studies; nor, somewhat more surprisingly, do studies of broken homes. The studies of maternal deprivation do not appear to be regarded as studies of *family* pathology: an incomplete family is hardly a family at all. In the subsequent discussion on the ideology of family relations in this society I use the term family in a somewhat broader sense to cover not only relations within an existing nuclear family but relations between persons who have at some time been members of the same nuclear family, although they no longer are: the so-called *elementary* family.[4]

What are the ideas, beliefs and values governing family relations in the society? It is my contention that they generally differ from and conflict with the beliefs and values that dominate other relations within the

3. I use the word ideology here to refer to any set of interrelated ideas and beliefs.
4. For a good discussion of the term family and its different interpretations see Harris (1909, ch. 3).

society.[5] They are therefore most clearly described by contrast. Let me emphasize: I am concerned with how we *think* about different types of social relations and with what we regard as *desirable*, and not with *behaviour*. Often there is a marked discrepancy between our thought and action; partly just because the contradiction in our ideas precludes any simple consistency between ideology and behaviour, and partly because the realms of thought and action have different properties. My emphasis here on oppositions and contrasts in our ideas reflects, I think, the categorical and often binary nature of our thinking.[6]

The distinction that is often made between individualist and collectivist ideologies provides the first two of the four points of contrast in our ideas about family and non-family relations that I shall discuss in this paper. Individualism is a vital feature of the ideology of contemporary capitalist societies. The term is, of course, used to refer to a number of different things; I shall mean by it that the individual is regarded as the important locus of action within the society; that the individual is attributed independence, autonomy, freedom of choice, and power over his own actions; and that the individual is deemed to have the right and authority to choose and to be capable of making decisions by himself and for himself. Hence individualism combines a number of different but closely related ideas (Lukes, 1973). In contrast what is dominant in collectivist ideologies is the sense of social being; of being a member of, and belonging to, some social group whether family, clan, tribe or class. It is the group that is regarded as the unit of action, and interdependence and lack of autonomy tend to characterize the individual's position within the group (Dumont, 1965). Traditional societies have been dominated by collectivist ideologies; individualism, in contrast, is the underlying assumption of capitalist institutions and reaches its zenith in laissez-faire liberalism and the idea of a free-market economy. It is reflected in our very notion of the individual and in our ideas of what it is to be a person. We take it for granted that a person is not only someone who can control his activities but someone who should control his actions as a free, autonomous being.

This contrast between the ideologies of individualism and collectivism is an important part of the difference between the ideological context of the family and other social relations. For although individualism is the dominant ethic of capitalist societies and is incorporated into numerous

5. In this my analysis develops Parsons's notion of a conflict of values (1956). In making this contrast I do not espouse any theory of structural differentiation between the family and other social institutions.
6. Much of the complexity of our thought comes from the intricate relations between the concepts we use.

institutions, the spheres in which the individual is seen to have, and is encouraged to have, individual control are to some extent both culturally and temporally variable. Whilst most institutions within our culture are based on individualist ideas, family relations are based on collectivist ones. This situation, not surprisingly, creates numerous problems and conflicts. Individuals are assumed and expected to act freely and autonomously when they are engaged in most non-familial relations, and to submerge their individuality and independence when participating in familial relations.

In comparing the collectivism that characterizes family ideology with the individualism of non-familial institutions two aspects of the contrast are especially salient. The first of these is that between dependence and autonomy. Emphasis on the autonomy of the individual is integral to individualist ideas and is perhaps the central linking feature of the numerous forms of individualism. Collectivism, as already suggested, emphasizes a sense of social being, of dependence on others. The second is that between collective and self-orientation. A collectivist ideology encourages a belief in, and a concern for, the importance and interests of the group, in contrast to the concern and importance of the individual that is emphasized by individualism.

There are two further differences that are important to the contrast in our ideas about family and non-family relations; they are not however integral to the individualist–collectivist contrast. The first is that we expect family relations to be based on emotion and personal concern, whilst we do not assume that other social relations will generally have such a basis (although such feeling and concern is not precluded). Second, the ideology of family relations is one of familiarity, rather than privacy: we expect family relations to be based on openness and trust, whereas privacy is the norm of non-family relations.

The institution of the family is, then, in an ideologically contradictory position based on values and beliefs that do not generally apply elsewhere in society. We can only understand the 'internal' dynamics of family relationships by realizing this.

III

The contrast between dependence and autonomy aptly describes the difference in what is expected of the individual when engaged in family relations and what is expected of the individual in other social relations. The problems arising from the attempt to reconcile these conflicting demands have been oft-noted. We hold an autonomous person to be one who has a sense of separateness from others and a sense of control over his own actions. He is essentially someone who feels himself to have a choice over what he does. As such autonomy is something that is at present especially highly valued. Many psychologists now emphasize the importance of the autonomous, creative capacities of man and feel, quite rightly, that they have been neglected in much academic psychology.[7] Social institutions in the culture generally assume such autonomy; they assume each individual makes decisions, negotiates, enters contracts, and so forth. And this is not only true of economic institutions; government institutions like the medical services are also based on such assumptions.[8] Medical services whilst not based on a free-market contract are nevertheless contractual. With family relations the situation is different, interdependence rather than individual choice is the norm. Position within the family is assigned without choice and there is no question of changing it. We are all born into a particular family and our place within that family is regarded as fixed; we cannot choose to be a member of a different family, nor can we change our role within it.

Of course, the situation is more complex than this. Although the individual has no personal choice as to who his parents are he is given choice over whom he marries. According to our current beliefs choice of spouse is a free choice by the individual. But this choice over whom one marries serves only to highlight the contrast between our ideas about family relations and other social relations. For although marriage is regarded as a contractual relationship as far as selection of marriage partner is concerned, and so is governed by individualistic values, the culture allows little choice either about entry into familial relationships (we assume both that individuals will get married and that they will have children, except in special circumstances)[9] or about breaking family bonds once they exist. We expect that individuals once they marry should remain married, and although it is possible to contract out of the marriage relationship this is not regarded as desirable. This is especially so if there are children of the marriage. However this is scarcely surprising in view of the fact that familial relationships are hardly said to exist unless there are children of the marriage. Moreover the apparent anomaly of free choice of marriage

7. This is amply reflected in the contributions to this volume. Unfortunately at times the ideological nature of this assertion seems to be forgotten.
8. Parsons (1956) contrasts familial values with those governing *economic* activities. This is surely the wrong division.
9. I discuss the non-discretionary nature of getting married and having children in more detail elsewhere (Busfield, 1974). The idea that for women getting married is an achievement does not conflict with this; it is a sense of achievement at accomplishing what will happen and has to happen, like the sense of achievement when a child learns to walk. It does not mean there is any choice in the matter.

partner becomes more explicable when we realize that marriage in itself does not fully establish *familial* relationships.

The contradiction between the 'spontaneous' choice of marriage partner in conformity with the norms of individual freedom and autonomy and the lasting and inescapable nature of familial obligations consequent on that choice is marked. We regard the love that is culturally deemed the necessary condition of marriage as a personal, individual matter; yet if the love does not last the maintenance of the marriage is no longer a personal, individual matter. The word love is interesting since we give it a number of divergent meanings yet use the same word. Our ideas of conjugal love or of love between parent and child are very different, for instance, from what we understand by romantic love. Our ideas about the love that is held to be the essential condition of marriage are very confused. Although marriage is believed to be a matter of choice, the love that is the basis of choosing one's spouse is itself viewed as something outside our control. As Juliet Mitchell puts it: 'There is a formal contradiction between the voluntary contractual character of "marriage" and the spiritual uncontrollable character of "love" – the passion that is celebrated for its involuntary force'! (1971, p. 114).

In practice, of course, marriage partners are chosen from a narrow range of persons, usually those from a similar social and educational background and geographical region (Berent, 1954) and may be little different from the marriages that would result if the choice were not deemed an individual one. However, the ideological shift is a major one. The development is brought out in a number of sources. The dominant theme of Shakespeare's *Romeo and Juliet* is the conflict between familial choice and individual choice, and this reflects the transition in values of the time. Lawrence Stone argues that 'it would seem that the doctrine of the absolute right of parents over the disposal of their children was slowly weakening in the late sixteenth and early seventeenth centuries'; he attributes the change to the growth of individualism (Stone, 1967, p. 279). The more recent counterpart deals not with the issue of individual choice versus familial choice but with the problem of successful versus unsuccessful choice; on the difficulties of making the personal choice the correct one. Literary sources tend to suggest that selection of someone with similar social characteristics is most likely to make a successful marriage. This is the theme of numerous novels and plays such as *Look Back in Anger, Room at the Top* and so forth. Moreover in so far as normative constraints currently influence the individual's choice of marriage partner, the situation is still very different from that in which the decision is held to be a parental matter, for the mechanisms of social control operate differently. In one situation choice is taken out of the hands of the individual altogether; in the other the individual has choice, but his choice is influenced both by practical constraints (whom he meets and so forth) and by norms that encourage him to look for personal and social compatibility.

In analysing the ideology of the family the different positions of men and women need to be considered. At first sight it appears that rather than both men and women being subject to conflicting demands of dependence and autonomy, men are attributed autonomy in all spheres and women denied it. Whilst there can be no doubt that men have more power, status and autonomy than women in all types of social relations, our ideology is far more egalitarian. Of course even at the level of ideas there are distinctions in the degree of autonomy that is attributed to men and women, but these differences do not completely outweigh the distinction between dependence and autonomy that contrasts family and other social relations. The point is that women are excluded (or discouraged) from participating in non-familial social relations. This reduces their sphere of autonomy and means that the balance of ideas and values is different for men and women. Women insofar as more of their interaction is with other family members are more dominated by the ideas that govern family relations. In this respect they are less constantly exposed to ideological conflict, especially when engagement in family relations is maximized, as during the period of bearing children and looking after them full time.[10] Men are more constantly exposed to ideological contradiction since they are more often involved in non-familial social relations.

This difference between men and women itself creates problems which can be handled in a number of ways. Maximizing engagement in family relations by all members of the family is one solution. The so-called 'privatization' of the family, the withdrawal from other social relations, presumably does this (Goldthorpe and Lockwood, 1963). An alternative strategy is segregation of male and female roles within the family, for, as customarily described, this is none other than minimization by the male of engagement within familial relations. In this light segregation is seen not as the 'traditional' (long-standing) pattern of (working-class) familial relations, but as a transitional phenomenon: the result of the differential exposure of men and women to individualistic values, that arose with the dominance of those values, and disappears with the rejection of those values.

It is, of course, integral to our understanding of the role of the child that he or she is in a position of dependence: to be a child is to be denied

10. There is considerable evidence that when children leave home (the family breaks up) women experience considerable stress and conflict.

the autonomy and independence of adulthood; the two are so closely linked in our minds that in other situations of dependence the position of the child is taken as a model. We tend, however, to wrongly assume that childhood has the same meaning in all societies. Ariès points to the relative newness of the term itself and suggests that part of our current understanding of the term is that of 'a training for life' (1962). Since training for life in an individualistic society demands training in independence from parents as well as others, yet a child is expected to be dependent, this is a source of much contradiction and conflict. It is a situation that provides almost the classic paradigm of a double bind in its irreconcileable demands. But the conflict is not universal; if childhood is not regarded as a period of *training* for adulthood, or if being an adult does not demand individual independence and autonomy, then the contradiction does not exist. It is a conflict that becomes especially strong in adolescence though it is not restricted to this period, and is especially powerful since the contradictory expectations are often expressed by the same people.

Many studies of family pathology bring out this particular conflict. Laing gives it theoretical importance in his *The Divided Self* (1965), where he suggests that it is parents' reluctance to allow a child to develop independence and autonomy that underlies the fragmentation of self that he sees as central to the schizophrenic experience. Not surprisingly it is a conflict that is brought out in the families described in *Sanity, Madness and the Family* (Laing and Esterson, 1971). The Danzig family manifest this contradiction very clearly. The theme of satisfying the demands of dependence and independence is one of the dominant conflicts of their family relations.

As adults they were expected to appear independent, and they depended on each other for this appearance. For the persons they were now required to appear to be were persons who had come of age, and marriage was a necessary part of this appearance. Marriage was less the expression of maturity than the public show necessary for their reputation. As the obedient children they felt they were publicly required to appear to be they, for the sake of their parents' reputation and their own, had to appear grown up and independent (Esterson, 1972, p. 64).

The conflict is also salient to the double-bind situation, not only as one example of a possible double bind, but also because the dependence of a child on the family facilitates the satisfying of the final necessary condition for a double-bind situation of a 'negative injunction prohibiting the victim from escaping from the field' (Bateson *et al.*, 1956, p. 24). A child cannot easily escape from his familial relations, and even marriage, whilst it gives the right to live outside the parental home and certain other features of independence, does not give the individual total freedom from ties to his family of origin. It is interesting in this context to note that in the studies of family pathology it is invariably a child who comes to be defined as the sick member. This seems to be a reflection of the dependent position of children within the family. If we regard the sick member as the scapegoat of a family it is likely that a child will play this role, given his or her social position.

The non-discretionary nature of familial ties has other important implications for family life. Studies of pathological families very often depict what appear to be very obviously 'bad' marriages: marriages that would seem better ended. That this does not happen is at times seen as a further sign of familial sickness. On the contrary I would suggest it is, rather, a realization of the cultural demand that familial ties once created cannot be broken. Such a situation may be further exacerbated by the fact that the very knowledge that the marriage was 'freely chosen' increases the scope for dissatisfaction.

The second related distinction that usefully contrasts the collectivism of family relations with the individualism that underlies other social relations is that between collectivity and self-orientation. An important and oft-noted feature of individualistic ideas is the encouragement of what is deemed important and desirable for the individual. Collectivism, on the other hand, encourages what is important and desirable for the group. Self-orientation when positively valued tends to be seen as a concern for self-development and self-fulfilment and as a concern for the creative aspects of the individual. Psychologists talk of self-actualization and self-realization. When negatively valued it becomes egoism, egocentrism and selfishness.

When engaged in family relations the individual is expected to put the family first; elsewhere he is generally assumed and expected to think first of his own interests. This presents numerous conflicts. One possible source of conflict that reflects this opposition may arise from a husband's job outside the home. If his work takes him away from home either for a longer time than his family regards as desirable or at the wrong times, this creates an obvious conflict of interests. The conflict is reduced somewhat, if the undesirable aspects of the work situation are agreed to be unavoidable or can be presented in the interests of the family. Where, however, a husband's interest and involvement in his job is considerable and this conflicts with the fulfilment of familial obligations difficulties may easily arise. The attempted legitimation of 'I do it for my family' has a hollow ring when additional income is patently unnecessary.

The contradiction between pursuing one's own interests and pursuing those of the family may also be important for children. A child's desire

TO KING JAMES THE SIXTH OF SCO[TLAND]

[AUGUST 7, 15...]

AMONG your many studies my dear Brother and Cousin, I wo[uld]
Isocrates's noble lesson were not forgotten, that wills the Emperor his
sovereign to make his words of more account than other men their oaths,
as meetest ensigns to show the truest badge of a Prince's arms. It
moveth me much to move you, when I behold how diversely sundry
wicked paths, and, like all evil illusions, wrapped under the cloak of your
best safety, endanger your state and best good. How may it be that you
can suppose an honourable answer may be made me when all your doings
gainsay your former vows. You deal not with one whose experience
can take dross for good payments, nor one that easily will be beguiled.
No, no, I mind to set to school your craftiest counsellor. I am sorry to
see you bent to wrong yourself in thinking to wrong others; there are
those which if they had not even then taken opportunity to let a ruin that
was newly begun, that plot would have perilled you more than a thousand
of such mean lives be worth, that persuade you to vouch such deeds to
deserve a soul's pardon. Why do you forget what you write to myself
with your own hand, showing how dangerous a course the Duke was
entered in, though you excused himself to think no harm therein, and yet
they that with your safety preserved you from it, you must seem to give
them reproach of guilty folk. I hope you more esteem your honour than
to give it such a stain, since you have protested so often to have taken
these Lords for your most affectionate subjects, and to have done all for
your best. To conclude, I beseech you pass no further in this cause till
you receive an express messenger, a trusty servant of mine, by whom you
shall see plainly how you may receive honour and contentment with
more surety to your rest and state, than all these dissembling coun-
sellors will or can bring you. As knoweth the Lord to whose most sage
keeping I do commit you, with my many commendations to your person.

TO LORD BURGHLEY

Right Honourable,

Since your Lordship's last being here in London there have been two great feasts, the one at the Grocer's Hall, the other at the Haberdashers' Hall. At the Haberdashers' feast was my Lord Mayor, and divers of his brethren with myself, where my Lord Mayor after the second course came in, did take the great standing-cup of the gift of Sir William Garrett, being full of hypocras (and silence being commanded through all the tables) all men being bare-headed, My Lord before all men did use these words, with a convenient loud voice: "Mr. Recorder of London, and you my good brethren the Aldermen, bear witness that I do drink unto Mr. Alderman Massam as Sheriff of London and Middlesex from Michaelmas next coming for one whole year; I do beseech God to grant him as quiet and peaceable a year, with as good and gracious favour of Her Majesty, as I myself and my brethren the Sheriffs now being have hitherto had, and as I trust shall have." This spoken all men desired the same. The sword-bearer in haste went to the Grocers' feast, where Mr. Alderman Massam was at dinner, and there did openly declare the words that my Lord Mayor had used. Whereunto, (silence made and all being hushed), the Alderman answered very modestly in this sort, "First, I thank God, who through his great goodness hath called me from a very poor and mean degree unto this worshipful estate. Secondly, I thank Her Majesty for her gracious goodness in allowing unto us these great and ample franchises. Thirdly, I thank my Lord Mayor for having so honourable an opinion of this my Company of Grocers as to make choice of me, being a poor member of the same." And this said, both he and the Company, pledged my Lord and gave him thanks.

Mr. Nowell of the Court hath lately been here in London. He

SIR FRANCIS DRAKE (c. 1540–96)

This was England's greatest seaman, the first of our nation to sail round the world, the man who, more than any other, helped to break the power of Spain. Drake was one of the greatest figures in Elizabethan England. In this letter he records the destruction of the Great Armada.

TO LORD WALSINGHAM

[July 31, 1588]

Most Honourable, I am commanded to send these prisoners ashore by my Lord Admiral, which had ere this been done long, but that I thought their being here might have done something which is not thought meet now.

Let me beseech your Honour that they may be presented unto her Majesty, either by your Honour, or by my honourable good Lord, my Lord Chancellor, or both of ye. The one, Don Pedro, is a man of greatest estimation with the King of Spain, and thought next in his army to the Duke of Sidonia. If they should be given [away] from me unto any other, it would be some grief to my friends. If her Majesty will have them, God defend [forbid] but I should think it happy.

We have the army of Spain before us and mind, with the Grace of God, to wrestle a pull with him. There was never anything pleased me better than the seeing the enemy flying with a southerly wind to the northwards. God grant you have a good eye to the Duke of Parma; for with the Grace of God, if we live, I doubt it not but ere it be long so to handle the matter with the Duke of Sidonia as he shall wish himself at St. Mary Port among his orange trees.

God give us grace to depend upon him; so shall we not doubt

victory, for our cause is good.   Humbly taking my leave, this last of
July, 1588.

> Your Honour's faithfully to be commanded ever,
>
> Fra. Drake

I crave pardon of your Honour for my haste, for that I had to
watch this last night upon the enemy.

> Yours ever,
>
> Fra. Drake

EDMUND SPENSER (c. 1552–99)

Among the many lights that made the galaxy of the Elizabethan Court none shone so brightly as Edmund Spenser. He was the incarnation of the Renaissance spirit in England, and something of his humour reveals itself in this letter to Gabriel Harvey, himself an author of repute.

TO GABRIEL HARVEY

[APRIL 1580]

GOOD MASTER H., I doubt not but you have some great important matter in hand, which all this while restraineth your pen and wonted readiness in provoking me unto that wherein your self now faults. If there be any such thing in hatching, I pray you heartily, let us know, before all the world see it. But if haply you dwell altogether in *Justinian's* court, and give yourself to be devoured of secret Studies, as of all likelihood you do, yet at least impart some of your old, or new Latin, or English, eloquent and gallant poesies to us, from whose eyes, you say, you keep in a manner nothing hidden. Little news is here stirred: but that old great matter still depending. His Honour never better. I think the *Earthquake* was also there with you (which I would gladly learn) as it was here with us: overthrowing divers old buildings and pieces of churches. Sure very strange to be heard of in these Countries, and yet I hear some say (I know not how truly) that they have known the like before in their days. *Sed quid vobis videtur magnis Philosophis?* I like your late English Hexameters so exceedingly well that I also enure my pen sometime in that kind: which I find, indeed, as I have heard you often defend in word, neither so hard nor so harsh that it will easily and fairly yield itself to our mother tongue.

For the only, or chiefest hardness which seemeth, is in the accent: which sometime gapeth, and as it were yawneth ill-favouredly, coming short of that it should, and sometime exceeding the measure of the number, as in *Carpenter*, the middle syllable being used short in speech, when it shall be read long in Verse, seemeth like a *lame Gosling that draweth one leg after her*: and *Heaven* being used short as one syllable, when it is in verse stretched out with a Diastole, is like *a lame Dog*

45

that holds up one leg. But it is to be won with custom, and rough words must be subdued with use. For, why a God's name may not we, as else the Greeks, have the kingdom of our own language, and measure our accents by the sound, reserving that Quantity to the Verse? But of that more hereafter. Now, my *Dreames,* and *dying Pellicane,* being fully finished (as I partly signified in my last letters) and presently to be imprinted, I will in hand forthwith with my "Faery Queene," which I pray you heartily send me with all expedition; and your friendly letters, and long expected judgement withal, which let not be short, but in all points such as you ordinarily use, and I extraordinarily desire. *Multum vale. Westminster. Quarto Nonas Aprilis,* 1580.

Yours always to command

Immerito

SIR RALPH LANE (d. 1603)

Sir Ralph was an English adventurer, one of that gallant band who accompanied Sir Richard Grenville in his expedition to the coast of North America, in 1585. He was left in command of the colony established by Grenville and shortly afterwards wrote from Virginia a letter to Hakluyt and another friend which is of interest as one of the earliest "letters home" ever written by a British colonist.

TO RICHARD HAKLUYT

[SEPT. 3, 1585]

IN the meanwhile, you shall understand that since Sir Richard Grenville's departure from us, as also before, we have discovered the main to be the goodliest isle under the cope of heaven, so abounding with sweet trees that bring such sundry rich and pleasant gums, grapes of such greatness, yet wild, as France, Spain, nor Italy have no greater, so many sorts of apothecary drugs, such several kinds of flax, and one kind like silk, the same gathered of a grass as common there as grass is here. And now within these few days we have found here maize or Guinea wheat, whose ear yieldeth corn for bread four hundred upon one ear, and the cane maketh very good and perfect sugar. Besides that, it is the goodliest and most pleasing territory of the world: for the continent is of a huge and unknown greatness and very well peopled and towned though savagely, and the climate so wholesome that we had not one sick since we touched the land here.

To conclude, if Virginia had but horses and kine in some reasonable proportion, I dare assure myself, being inhabited with English, no realm in Christendom were comparable to it. For this already we find that what commodities soever Spain, France, Italy or the east parts do yield unto us, in wines of all sorts, in oils, in flax, in rosins, pitch, frankincense, currants, sugars, and such-like, these parts do abound with the growth of them all, but being savages that possess the land, they know no use of the same. And sundry other rich commodities that no parts of the world, be they West or East Indies, have, here we find great abundance of.

47

The people naturally are most courteous and very desirous to have clothes, but especially of coarse cloth rather than silk; coarse canvas they also like well of, but copper carrieth the price of all, so it be made red.   Thus, good Mr. Hakluyt and Mr. H., I have joined you both in one letter of remembrance, as two that I love dearly well, and commending me most heartily to you both, I commit you to the tuition of the Almighty.   From the new fort in Virginia, this third of September, 1585.

Your most assured friend,
RALPH LANE

SIR WALTER RALEIGH (1552–1618)

Courtier, soldier, historian and poet, it is difficult to say in which of these lights Raleigh shined most. Brilliant at the Court of Elizabeth, the clouds settled on him when her mean-spirited successor came to the throne. Disgrace and imprisonment followed in rapid succession in 1603, and in the solitude of the Tower he wrote his "History of the World" and reflected on the precariousness of royal favour. Death was imminent and the night before he awaited execution he wrote this letter to his wife. He was reprieved, however, and for fifteen years longer tried to serve his sovereign. But the end came in 1618, when he went to the block.

TO HIS WIFE

You shall now receive, my dear wife, my last words, in these my last lines, my Love I send you, that you may keep it when I am dead, and my Counsel that you may remember it when I am no more. I would not by my will present you with Sorrows, dear Bess. Let them go into the grave with me, and be buried in the dust. And seeing it is not the will of God that I shall see you any more in this life, bear it patiently, and with a heart like thyself.

First I send you all the thanks which my heart can Conceive or my words can express for your many travails and care taken for me, which, though they have not taken effect, as you wished, yet my debt to you is not the less; but pay it I never shall in this world.

Secondly, I beseech you, for the love you bare me living, do not hide yourself many days after my death, but by your travails seek to help your miserable fortunes, and the right of your poor Child. Thy mournings cannot avail me, I am but dust.

Thirdly, you shall understand that my land was conveyed *Bona fide* to my child. The writings were drawn at Midsummer twelve months, my honest Cousin Brett can testify so much, and Dalberrie, too, can remember somewhat therein. And I trust my Blood will quench their malice that have thus cruelly murthered me; and that they will not seek also to kill thee and thine with extreme poverty.

To what friend to direct thee, I know not, for all mine have left me in the true time of trial; and I plainly perceive that my death was determined from the first day.

Most sorry I am, God knows, that being thus surprised with death, I can leave you in no better estate. God is my witness, I meant you all my office of wines, or all that I could have purchased by selling it, half my stuff, and all my jewels; but some on't for the boy. But God hath prevented all my resolutions, and even that great God that ruleth all in all. But if you can live free from want, care for no more; the rest is but vanity.

Love God, and begin betimes, to repose yourself on Him, and therein shall you find true and lasting riches, and endless comfort. For the rest, when you have travailled and wearied all your thoughts over all sorts of worldly cogitations, you shall but sit down by sorrow in the end.

Teach your son also to love and fear God whilst he is yet young, that the fear of God may grow up with him; and the same God will be a husband to you, and a father to him, husband and a father which cannot be taken from you.

Baylie oweth me £200 and Adrian Gilbert £600. In Jersey, I have also much money owing me, besides the arrears of the Wines will pay my debts. And howsoever you do, for my soul's sake, pay all poor men.

When I am gone, no doubt you shall be sought by many; for the world thinks that I was very rich. But take heed of the pretences of men, and their affections; for they last not but in honest, and worthy men; and no greater misery can befall you in this life than to become a prey, and afterwards to be despised. I speak not this, God knows, to dissuade you from marriage, for it will be best for you, both in respect of the world and of God.

As for me, I am no more yours, nor you mine. Death hath cut us asunder; and God hath divided me from the world, and you from me.

Remember your poor child, for his father's sake, who chose you, and loved you in his happiest times.

Get those Letters (if it be possible) which I wrote to the Lords, wherein I sued for my life. God is my witness, it was for you and yours I desired life. But it is true that I disdain myself for begging it; for know it, dear wife, that your son is the son of a true man, and one, who in his own respect, despiseth death and all his mishapen and ugly shapes.

I cannot write much. God knows how hardly I steal this time, while others sleep; and it is also high time that I should separate my thoughts from the world.

Beg my dead body, which living was denied thee; and either lay it at Shirbourne (if the land continue) or in Exeter Church by my Father and Mother.

I can say no more, time and death call me away.

The everlasting, powerful, infinite and omnipotent God, that Almighty God who is goodness itself, the true life, and true light, keep thee, and thine; have mercy on me, and teach me to forgive my persecutors and accusers, and send us to meet in His glorious kingdom.

My dear wife farewell. Bless my poor Boy, Pray for me, and Let my good God hold you both in His arms.

Written with the dying hand of sometime thy Husband but now (alas) overthrown

WA. RALEIGH

yours that was, But now not my own.

W. R.

GILBERT TALBOT, 7th EARL OF SHREWSBURY
(1553–1616)

Talbot's stepmother was the notorious Bess of Hardwick, and in league with her, while still a young man, he was engaged in countless quarrels and disputes. Later he became a prominent man under Elizabeth. It is in neither of these aspects, however, that we find him in this letter, which was prompted by that intense sympathy ever felt by sufferers from the gout with all in like case.

TO LORD BURGHLEY

MY SPECIAL GOOD LORD.   At this present I have no particular matter wherewith to trouble your Lordship, and yet I cannot satisfy my silence but hereby to recommend myself to your Lordship in all true affection of heart, being always more ready and desirous to express the same by any other means if it lay in my power.   I heard your Lordship was, of late, somewhat visited with the gout; I hope before this you are well rid thereof.   I would your Lordship would once make trial of my *Oil of Stagsblood* for I am strongly pursuaded of the rare and great virtue thereof.   In the beginning of this winter I was touched with the gout in the joint of my great toe, and it began somewhat sharply; and yet was I speedily eased and for that time cured by that oil only. I know it to be a most safe thing.   Some offence there is in the smell thereof; and yet it is written of it that the very smell thereof is comfortable, and yieldeth strength to the brain.   I am afraid to trouble your Lordship over long, therefore, with the remembrance of my wife's trouble and most hearty commendations to your lordship, and with both our prayers for your Lordship's health, honour, and happiness, I will for this time take my leave.

At Handsworth, this 23rd January, 1593.
GILBERT SHREWSBURY

JOHN MANNINGHAM (d. 1622)

Manningham was the Creevy of his day—an inveterate gossip and a chattering diarist. The following letter was scribbled in a leaf of his diary, probably ready to be sent to a friend. It contains one of the few contemporary anecdotes about Shakespeare, who at that time was known as the author of one or two plays. Manningham himself had been to "Twelfth Night" a few weeks previously.

UPON a time when Burbidge played Richard III there was a citizen grown so far in liking with him that before she went from the play she appointed him to come that night unto her by the name of Richard the Third. Shakespeare overhearing their conclusion went before, was entertained and at his game ere Burbidge came. Then, message being brought that Burbidge was at the door Shakespeare caused return [answer] to be made that William the Conqueror was before Richard the Third. Shakespeare's name William.

JOHN CHAMBERLAIN (1553-1627)

Chamberlain's sole interest in life was letter-writing. A man of comfortable private means, mixing in the best society, and intimate with some of the most eminent men in England, he spent a pleasant uneventful existence writing the news and gossiping on paper to all and sundry.

TO DUDLEY CARLETON

[DECEMBER 22, 1600]

GOOD MR. CARLETON, The letter you left for me was not delivered till Thursday at night, too late to send the enclosed for Mr. Allen by the way of Ascot as you wished, so that I thought best to convey it the next morning by the carrier of Oxford. The French King [Henry IV] kept the solemnity of his marriage [to Marie de Medicis] at Lyons, the 23rd of the last, and saw not the great Duchess nor the Duchess of Mantua, who went into Lorraine another way, because they espied his humour that he lingered at the camp for the nonce only to avoid charges and give them no presents. His ambition is much misliked of all, and the clergy will in no wise be well persuaded of him. He was so desirous and hasty to see his Queen that he went disguised as a private gentleman, with others (that he had appointed), to see her dine, and caused a letter from himself to be delivered her in his presence (unknown yet), which she received with such humbleness that it was praised of everybody and pleased him not a little. He could not tarry the solemnity, but went that night to her unknown, and one of his minions demanding what he meant, told him he went to do what he never did in his life, to lie that night with an honest woman.

But would you think that precedence for place is as much esteemed by women in France as in England, and that Madame de Fresne and Madame de Chambourg, two great ladies, at their first interview before the Queen fought and scratched one another cruelly? The King is in a manner possessed of all Savoy; the last place he took was St. Cateline, a fort built to bridle Geneva, whither Beza came to see him, in hope he would have left the fort to the town; but the King meant no such matter, yet used him well and gave him 300 crowns.

54

The Duke of Savoy, is retired into Piedmont to stay the inroads there, which the King hath procured by sending 3,000 French to harry the country and fortify some small places for this winter time. The Pope labours by all means to make peace for the Duke of Savoy, and is thought will effect it in this sort, that the King shall have 800,000 crowns for his charges, and render Savoy, and the Pope will become paymaster for the money, having (they say) contrived a marriage for his niece with the Duke's eldest son. It may be you have heard all or the most part of this already, but I measure you by myself that I am never cloyed with particulars. We hear out of Poland that the Chancellor, with an army of 20,000 choice men, should be *cæsus ad internecionem* by the Vaivode of Walachia, and not above eight escaped of all that number. The Moscovite Ambassador hath buried one of his men and sent him with a letter to seek St. Nicolas. Here is a whispering that Don Sebastian, the revived King of Portugal, should be secretly at the court, but *credat Judæus Apella.*

The Lord Deputy of Ireland is gone Northward, either to revictual his new fort or upon some other good intelligence. He lately made three new knights, a son of Sir John Fortescue's, Rotherham of Bedfordshire, and one Captain Berry. We have an uncertain rumour of treasure come hither out of Spain, with powder and munition and arms for 4,000 men. Some of the Queen's ships are making ready to look after the Spaniards that are coming for the Low Countries, but I think they will do no more to them, though they should fall in their mouth.

The Scottish King [James VI and I of England] hath another son [later Charles I]; we listen still for news from thence as if there were some tempest brewing. Sir William Evers hath been tampering that way whatsoever it is, whereupon he was sent for up and first committed to his own lodging, with a man of Mr. Secretary's to attend him; then was he set over to one Harvey Carew, and it is feared he will kiss the Tower in the end. Our East Indian business goes slowly forward; I doubt they will be forestalled, and their market marred by the Hollanders or Frenchmen that are setting forth four ships thither from St. Malos. We hear of divers ships laden with wines cast away coming from Bordeaux. The Court is settled here for all Christmas.

Mr. Secretary entertains the Queen this day to dinner at his lodging in the Savoy, if the appointment hold, as it hath already failed twice. He hath set his wits and friends to work to give her all contentment, and to receive her with all fine and exquisite curiosity. The Lord North's funeral is kept this day at Powles. The Countess of Essex is lately brought to bed of a daughter. Mrs. Pranell is like to make a wide stride, from that she was, to be Countess of Hertford; the world says they be assured already, if not married. Sir Henry Killegrew married a daughter the last week to one Seymour of Devonshire. There was a great commission at Lambeth the other day about the controversy between Alderman Banning and his wife; the Lord Archbishop, the Lord Admiral, the Lord Chamberlain, and divers other of the Council were of it. The world expected great matters of such an authentical hearing, but in conclusion the women escaped better than was looked for, having only sentence of separation *a mensa et thoro*. Sir Robert Drury is committed to the custody of Alderman Saltingstall for speaking and hearing certain buggswords [blustering talk] at his being in France, as is pretended, but this is rather thought to be colour than true cloth. Little Britain remembers you with all kindness. I am going to-morrow, God willing, to Knebsworth, where I know you wish us a merry Christmas, and we, *pour la pareille*, will wish you many good years.

　　　　　From London this 22nd December, 1600.

　　　　　　　　　　　Yours most assuredly,

　　　　　　　　　　　JOHN CHAMBERLAIN

TO MRS. ALICE CARLETON

　　　　　　　　　　LONDON, FEBRUARY 16, 1614

YESTERDAY I received your letter of the 29th January. It is no marvel if the post keeps not their ordinary days and times, for we have had such weather that I think they had much ado to come at all. Ever since Sunday was three weeks we have had continual frost and snow, whereof we have had such plenty as I never knew the like; for there hath not passed one day since that time but it hath snowed more or less, and Sunday last it began at seven o'clock in the morning, and never ceased till Monday after nine that night; so that it lay very deep, and we fear we shall hear of much harm. But the greatest part of it went away on Tuesday and yesterday with a kindly thaw, but this night it is frozen again, and grown very cold.

　　　The Lady Beauchamp, sister to the Earl of Dorset, and wife to the Earl of Hertford's grandchild, is brought a-bed of a son, and I hear the like of the Lady Haddington, daughter to the Earl of Sussex. Sir Edward Montagu's young lady brought him a son likewise of late, but it lasted not above two or three days. Mrs. Bartlett, Mr. Conyer's daughter, lies in now of a son at Highgate.

The Lady Cheke, Mr. Osborne's sister, of the Exchequer, would needs be let blood the last week, for a little heat or itching in her arm, but by mishap the queen's surgeon pricked her too deep, and cut an artery, which fell to rankle, and in a few days grew to a gangrene, whereof she died on Saturday, and was buried by night, with above thirty coaches and much torchlight attending her, which is of late come much into fashion, as it should seem, to avoid trouble and charge. But I rather think it was brought up by papists, which serve their turn by it many ways. She left no children, nor ever had any; so that it is thought her husband, Sir Thomas, will not be long unprovided of a new lady, for that his land, for want of heirs male, is to return to the crown, and some Scot or other hath begged the reversion.

Touching the Lady Edmonds' body, I know not whether it be yet come over, but I am sure he wrote to her mother to know where she would have it buried, yet giving his advice that he thought it best at Cambridge, as next to the place where it was to arrive. Whereunto the Lady Wood assented; so that it is done, or to be done there, without any solemnity.

Sir George Haywood, the Lady Scott's son by old Rowland, is fallen mad. The Lord of Somerset hath the government and custody of his land till he recover. His friends make all the means they can by physic to cure him, whereof there is the less hope, for that he hath a sister married to Sir Richard Sandys, now in the same case, and much about a year since was well recovered, but within this month fallen into a relapse. I never in my life heard of so many distracted people of good sort, as I have done within these two or three years.

Your neighbour, Bruckshaw, hath lain this month or five weeks in the Marshalsea, with six or seven of his companion brewers, for that they will not yield to have their drink taken to serve the king without money; for the king's brewer cannot get a groat of £16,000 that is owing to him for beer; so that he hath neither money nor credit to hold out any longer. This term they attempted by law to remove themselves and to try their case; but they could not be relieved, for that there came a mandate from the king, whereby it is become a matter of state, and out of the compass of law.

CHIDIOCK TICHBORNE (c. 1558–86)

> This young man threw in his lot with the Babington conspirators and at a meeting held in St. Giles's Fields agreed to be one of the six who should be responsible for assassinating the queen. When the plot fell through Tichborne was arrested and thrown into the Tower, and the night before he was beheaded he wrote the following letter to his young wife Agnes.

TO HIS WIFE

[1586]

To the most loving wife alive, I commend me unto her, and desire God to bless her with all happiness, pray for her dead husband, and be of good comfort, for I hope in Jesus Christ this morning to see the face of my maker and redeemer in the most joyful throne of his glorious kingdom. Commend me to all my friends, and desire them to pray for me, and in all charity to pardon me, if I have offended them. Commend me to my six sisters, poor desolate souls, advise them to serve God, for without him no goodness is to be expected. Were it possible, my little sister Bab, the darling of my race, might be bred by her, God would reward her; but I do her wrong I confess, that hath by my desolate negligence too little for herself, to add a further charge unto her. Dear wife forgive me, that have by these means so much impoverished her fortunes; patience and pardon good wife I crave— make of these our necessities a virtue, and lay no further burthen on my neck than hath already been. There be certain debts that I owe, and because I know not the order of the law, piteous it hath taken from me all, forfeited by my course of offence to her majesty, I cannot advise thee to benefit me herein, but if there fall out wherewithal, let them be discharged for God's sake. I will not that you trouble yourself with the performance of these matters, my own heart, but make it known to my uncles, and desire them, for the honour of God and ease of their soul, to take care of them as they may, and especially care of my sisters' bringing up the burthen is now laid on them. Now, Sweet-cheek, what is left to bestow on thee, a small jointure, a small recompense for thy deserving, these legacies following to be thine own.

58

God of his infinite goodness give thee grace always to remain his true
and faithful servant, that through the merits of his bitter and blessed
passion thou mayst become in good time of his kingdom with the
blessed women in heaven.   May the Holy Ghost comfort thee with
all necessaries for the wealth of thy soul in the world to come, where
until it shall please Almighty God I meet thee, farewell loving wife,
farewell the dearest to me on all the earth, farewell!

By the hand from the heart of thy most faithful loving husband,

CHIDEOCK TICHEBURN

FRANCIS BACON, BARON VERULAM AND VISCOUNT ST. ALBANS (1561–1626)

Philosopher, statesman and lawyer, Bacon is perhaps known nowadays best as a writer of essays. In this letter to the young Earl of Rutland he expounds with characteristic lucidity his views on travel and study.

TO THE EARL OF RUTLAND

MY LORD, I hold it for a principle in the course of intelligence of state, not to discourage men of mean sufficiency from writing unto me, though I had at the same time very able advertisers [news collectors]; for either they sent me some matter which the other had omitted, or made it clearer by delivering the circumstances, or if they added nothing, yet they confirmed that which coming single I might have doubted. This rule therefore I have prescribed to others, and now give it to myself. Your Lordship hath many friends who have more leisure to think and more sufficiency to counsel than myself; yet doth my love to you dedicate these few free hours to study of you and your intended course; in which study if I find out nothing but that which you have from others, yet I shall perhaps confirm the opinion of wiser than myself.

Your Lordship's purpose is to travel, and your study must be what use to make of your travel. The question is ordinary, and there is to it an ordinary answer; that is, your Lordship shall see the beauty of many cities, know the manners of the people of many countries, and learn the language of many nations. Some of these may serve for ornaments, and all of them for delights; but your Lordship must look further than these; for the greatest ornament is the inward beauty of the mind, and when you have known as great variety of delight as the world will afford, you will confess that the greatest delight is *sentire te indies fieri meliorem;* to feel that you do every day become more worthy; therefore your Lordship's end and scope should be that which in moral philosophy we call *cultum animi,* the tilling and manuring of your own minds. The gifts or excellencies of the mind are the same

60

as those are of the body; Beauty, Health, and Strength. Beauty of the mind is showed in graceful and acceptable forms, and sweetness of behaviour; and they that have that gift cause those to whom they deny anything to go better contented away than men of contrary disposition do them to whom they grant. Health consisteth in an unmovable constancy and a freedom from passions, which are indeed the sicknesses of the mind. Strength of mind is that active power which maketh us perform good things and great things, as well as health and even temper of mind keeps from those that are evil and base. All these three are to be sought for, though the greatest part of men have none of them; some have one and lack the other two; a few attain to have two of them and lack the third; and almost none have all.

The first way to attain experience of forms or behaviour, is to make the mind itself expert. For behaviour is but a garment, and it is easy to make a comely garment for a body that is itself well proportioned, whereas a deformed body can never be so helped by tailor's art but the counterfeit will appear; and in the form of our mind it is a true rule, that a man may mend his faults with as little labour as cover them.

The second way is by imitation, and to that end good choice is to be made of those with whom you converse; therefore your Lordship should affect their company whom you find to be worthiest, and not, partially, think them most worthy whom you affect.

To attain to health of mind, we must use the same means that we do for the health of our bodies; that is, to take observation what diseases we are aptest to fall into, and to provide against them, for physic hath not more medicines against the diseases of the body than reason hath preservatives against the passions of the mind. The Stoics were of opinion that there was no way to attain to this even temper of the mind but to be senseless, and so they sold their goods to ransom themselves from their evils; but not only Divinity, our schoolmistress, doth teach us the effect of grace, but even Philosophy, her handmaid, doth condemn our want of care and industry if we do not win very much upon ourselves. To prove which I will only use one instance: there is nothing in nature more general or more strong than the fear of death, and to a natural man there is nothing seems more impossible than to resolve against death. But both martyrs for religion, heathen for glory, some for love of their country, others for affection to one special person, have encountered death without fear,

and suffered it without show of alteration; and therefore, if many
have conquered passion's chiefest and strongest fortress, it is lack of
undertaking in him that getteth not an absolute victory. To set down
the ways how a man may attain to the active power mentioned in this
place (I mean strength of mind), is much harder than to give rules in
the other two; for behaviour or good form may be gotten by education,
and health or even temper of mind by observation. But if there be
not in nature some partner to this active strength it can never be
obtained by any industry; for the virtues which are proper unto it are
liberality or magnificence, and fortitude or magnanimity; and some are
by nature so covetous or cowardly, as it is as much in vain to seek to
enlarge or inflame their minds as to go about to plough the rocks.
But where these active virtues are but budding, they must be ripened
by clearness of judgment and custom of well doing. Clearness of
judgment makes men liberal, for it teacheth men to esteem of the
goods of fortune not for themselves, for so they are but jailors to them,
but for their use, for so they are lords over them; and it makes us to
know that it is *beatius dare quam accipere*, the one being a badge of
sovereignty, the other of subjection. Also it leadeth us to fortitude,
for it teacheth us that we should not too much prize life which we
cannot keep, nor fear death which we cannot shun; that he which dies
nobly doth live for ever, and he that lives in fear doth die continually;
that pain and danger be great only by opinion, and that in truth nothing
is fearful but fear itself; that custom makes the thing used natural as
it were to the user. I shall not need to prove these two things, since
we see by experience it holds true in all things, but yet those that give
with judgment are not only encouraged to be liberal by the return of
thankfulness from those to whom they give, but find in the very exercise
of that virtue a delight to do good. And if custom be strong to confirm
any one virtue more than another, it is the virtue of fortitude, for it
makes us triumph over the fear which we have conquered, and anew
to challenge danger which happily we have encountered, and hold
more dear the reputation of honour which we have increased.

I have hitherto set down what desire or wish I would have your
Lordship to take into your mind, that is to make yourself an expert
man, and what are the general helps which all men may use which
have the said desire. I will now move your Lordship to consider what
helps your travel may give you.

First, when you see infinite variety of behaviour and manners of
men, you may choose and imitate the best; when you see new delights

which you never knew, and have passions stirred in you which before you never felt, you shall both know what disease your mind is aptest to fall into, and what the things are that breed the disease. When you come into armies, or places where you shall see anything of the wars (as I would wish you to see them before your return), you shall both confirm your natural courage, and be made more fit for true fortitude, which is not given to man by nature, but must grow out of discourse of reason; and lastly, in your travel you shall have great help to attain to knowledge, which is not only the excellentest thing in man, but the very excellency of man.

In manners or behaviour, your Lordship must not be caught with novelty, which is pleasing to young men; nor infected with custom, which makes us keep our own ill graces, and participate of those we see every day; nor given to affection [affectation] (a general fault of most of our English travellers), which is both displeasing and ridiculous.

In discovering your passions and meeting with them, give not way to yourself nor dispense with yourself in little, though resolving to conquer yourself in great; for the same stream that may be stopped with one man's hand at the spring head, may drown whole armies of men when it hath run long. In your being in the wars, think it better at the first to do a great deal too much than anything too little; for a young man's, especially a stranger's, first actions are looked upon, and reputation once gotten is easily kept, but an evil impression conceived at the first is not quickly removed.

The last thing that I am to speak of, but the first that you are to seek, is conceived knowledge. To praise knowledge, or to persuade your Lordship to the love of it, I shall not need to use many words; I will only say, that where that wants the man is void of all good; without it there can be no fortitude, for all other darings come of fury, and fury is a passion, and passions ever turn into their contraries; and therefore the most furious men, when their first blaze is spent, be commonly the most fearful. Without it there can be no liberality, for giving is but want of audacity to deny, or of discretion to prize; without it there can be no justice, for giving to a man that which is his own is but chance, or want of a corrupter or seducer; without it there can be no constancy or patience, for suffering is but dullness or senselessness; without it there can be no temperance, for we shall restrain ourselves from good as well as from evil, for that they that cannot discern cannot elect or choose; nay without it there can be no true religion, all other devotion being but blind zeal, which is as strong in heresy as in truth. To reckon up all parts of knowledge, and to show the way to attain to every part, is a work too great for me at any time, and too long to discourse at this; therefore I will only speak of such knowledge as your Lordship should have desire to seek, and shall have means to compass. I forbear also to speak of divine knowledge, which must direct your faith, both because I hope your Lordship doth still nourish the seeds of religion which during your education at Cambridge were sown in you. I will only say this; as the irresolute man can never perform any action well, so he that is not resolved in soul and conscience, can never be resolute in anything else. But that civil knowledge, which will make you do well by yourself, and do good unto others, must be sought by study, by conference, and by observation. Before I persuade your Lordship to study, I must look to answer an argument drawn from the nobility of all places of the world, which now is utterly unlearned, if it be not some very few; and an authority of an English proverb, made in despite of learning, that the greatest clerks are not the wisest men. The first answer, that this want of learning hath been in good countries ruined by civil wars, or in states corrupted through wealth or too great length of peace. In the one sort men's wits were employed in their necessary defence, in the other drowned in the study of *artes luxuriæ*. But in all flourishing states learning hath ever flourished. If it seem strange that I account no state flourishing but that which hath neither civil wars nor too long peace, I answer, that politic bodies are like our natural bodies, and must as well have some exercise to spend their humours, as to be kept from too violent or continual outrages which spend their best spirits. The proverb I take to be made in that age when the nobility of England brought up their sons but as they entered their whelps, and thought them wise enough if they could chase their deer; and I answer it with another proverb made by a wise man, *Scientia non habet inimicum præter ignorantem.* All men that live are drawn either by book or example, and in books your Lordship shall find (in what course soever you propound to yourself) rules prescribed by the wisest men, and examples left by the wisest men that have lived before us. Therefore knowledge is to be sought by your private study, if you do not often remove from place to place, but stay some time and reside in the best. In the course of your study and choice of your books, you must first seek to have the grounds of learning, which are the liberal arts; for without them you shall neither gather other knowledge easily, nor make use of that you have; and then use studies of delight but sometimes for recreation, and neither drown yourself in them, nor omit those studies whereof you are to have continual use. Above all other books be conversant in the Histories, for they will best instruct you in matter moral, military, and politic, by which and in which you must ripen and settle your judgment. In your study you are to seek two things: the first to conceive or understand; the second to lay up or remember; for as the philosopher saith, *discere est tanquam recordari*. To help you to conceive, you may do well in those things which you are to read to draw yourself to read with somebody that may give you help, and to that end you must either carry over with you some good general scholar, or make some abode in the universities abroad, where you may hear the professors in every art. To help you to remember, you must use writing, or meditation, or both; by writing I mean making of notes and abridgments of that which you would remember. I make conference the second help to knowledge in order, though I have found it the first and greatest in profiting, and I have so placed them because he that hath not studied knows not what to doubt nor what to ask: but when the little I had learned had taught me to find out mine own emptiness, I profited more by some expert man in half a day's conference, than by myself in a month's study. To profit much by conference, you must first choose to confer with expert men, I mean expert in that which you desire to know; next with many, for expert men will be of diverse and contrary opinions, and every one will make his own probable, so as if you hear but one you shall know in all questions but one opinion; whereas by hearing many, you shall, by seeing the reasons of one, confute the reasons of the other, and be able to judge of the truth. Besides, there is no one man that is expert in all things, but every great scholar is expert in some one, so as your wit shall be whetted with conversing with many great wits, and you shall have the cream and quintessence of every one of theirs. In conference be neither superstitious, nor believing all you hear (what opinion soever you have of the man that delivereth it), nor too desirous to contradict. For of the first grows a facility to be led into all kinds of error; since you shall ever think that he that knows all that you know, and somewhat more, hath infinite knowledge, because you cannot sound or measure it. Of the second grows such a carping humour, as you shall without reason censure all men, and want reason to censure yourself. I do conclude this point of conference with this advice, that your Lordship shall rather go a hundred miles out of the way to speak with a wise man, than five to see a fair town.

E.L.   D

The third way to attain knowledge is observation, and not long life or seeing much; because, as he that rides a way often, and takes no care of marks or notes to direct him if he comes the same again, or to make him know where he is if he come unto it, shall never prove a good guide; so he that lives long and sees much, but observes nothing, shall never prove a wise man. The use of observation is in noting the coherence of causes and effects, counsels and successes, and the proportion and likeness between nature and nature, force and force, action and action, state and state, time past and time present. The philosopher did think that all knowledge doth much depend on the knowledge of causes; as he said, *id demum scimus cujus causam scimus;* and therefore a private man cannot prove so great a soldier as he that commands an army, nor so great a politique as he that rules a state, because the one sees only the events and knows not the causes, the other makes the causes that govern the events. The observation of proportion or likeness between one person or one thing and another, makes nothing without example nor nothing new: and although *exempla illustrant non probant,* examples may make things plain that are proved, but prove not themselves; yet when circumstances agree, and proportion is kept, that which is probable in one case is probable in a thousand, and that which is reason once is reason ever.

Your Lordship now seeing that the end of study, conference, and observation, is knowledge; you must know also that the true end of knowledge is clearness and strength of judgment, and not ostentation or ability to discourse; which I do the rather put your Lordship in mind of, because the most part of our noblemen and gentlemen of our time have no other use of their learning but their table-talk; and the reason is because they, before setting down their journey's end ere they attain to it they rest, and travel not so far as they should; but God knows they have gotten little that have only this discoursing gift; for though, like empty casks, they sound loud when a man knocks upon their outside, yet if you pierce into them you shall find them full of nothing but wind. This rule holds not only in knowledge, or in the virtue of knowledge, or in the virtue of prudence, but in all other virtues; that is, that we should both seek and love virtue for itself, and not for praise; for as one said, *turpe est proco ancillam sollicitare, est autem virtutis ancilla laus:* it is a shame for him that woos the mistress to court the maid, for praise is the handmaid of virtue.

I will here break off, for I have both exceeded the convenient length of a letter, and come short of such a discourse as this subject doth deserve. Your Lordship may perhaps find in this paper many things superfluous, most things imperfect and lame; I will, as well as I can, supply that defect upon a second advertisement, if you call me to account. What confusion soever you find in my order or method, is not only my fault, whose wits are confounded with too much business, but the fault of this season, this being written in Christmas, in which confusion and disorder hath by tradition not only been winked at but warranted. If there be but any one thing that your Lordship may make use of, I think my pain well bestowed in all; and how weak soever my counsels be, my wishes shall be as strong as any man's for your Lordship's happiness. And so I rest, your Lordship's very affectionate cousin and loving friend.

JAMES I (1566–1625)

To say that Papists were looked on askance in the England of James I would be to underestimate. They were hated, and the Law dealt with them firmly and cruelly. That James found his position difficult in this respect with regard to foreign ambassadors is shown by this letter to his son. Sir Thomas Lake had been Secretary of State, but at the same time he was a pensioner of Spain. Further troubles followed. In 1618 Lady Exeter brought Lake and his family before the Star Chamber on a charge of defaming her character. The Lakes lost and were sentenced to pay a fine of £10,000 and £1,000 damages to Lady Exeter. Hence this letter.

TO PRINCE CHARLES

MY ONLY SWEET AND DEAR CHILD, I pray thee haste thee home to thy dear dad by sunsetting, at the furthest; and forget not to make Digby give the Spanish Ambassador assurance that I will leave nothing undone that I may perform with justice and honour in holding a mild hand upon the Papists; only a way must be found to make their complaints come to my ears. But as for my Lady Lake, I must confess both to have pronounced an unjust sentence and break my promise to my Lady Exeter in a matter of justice if I grant her any ease at this time. Besides that this cause has no aspect to religion, except the Romish Religion be composed of the seven deadly sins, for I dare swear she is guilty of them all. If Spain trouble me with suits of this nature, both against my justice and honour, their friendship will be more burdensome than useful unto me; and so, Lord send me a comfortable and happy meeting with thee this night.

JAMES R.

ROBERT DEVEREUX, EARL OF ESSEX (1567–1601)

No man ever saw deeper into the heart of the Virgin Queen than Essex. These letters of his to her are of surpassing interest, breathing as they do the spirit and gallantry of an age long past. The ill-starred favourite of Elizabeth's later years fell into disgrace and was beheaded on Tower Green after a futile rebellion.

TO QUEEN ELIZABETH

[1594?]

MADAM, The delights of this place cannot make me unmindful of one in whose sweet company I have joyed as much as the happiest man doth in his highest contentment; and if my horse could run as fast as my thoughts do fly, I would as often make mine eyes rich in beholding the treasure of my love, as my desires do triumph when I seem to myself in a strong imagination to conquer your resisting will. Noble and dear lady, tho' I be absent, let me in your favour be second unto none; and when I am at home, if I have no right to dwell chief in so excellent a place, yet I will usurp upon all the world. And so making myself as humble to do you service, as in my love I am ambitious I wish your Majesty all your happy desires. Croydon, this Tuesday, going to be mad and make my horse tame. Of all the men the most devoted to your service.

R. ESSEX

TO THE SAME

SANDWICH, THIS 23RD JUNE, 1597

YOUR spirit I do invoke, my most dear and most admired sovereign, to assist me, that I may express that humblest and most due thankfulness, and that high and true joy which upon the reading of your Majesty's letter my poor heart hath conceived. Upon your spirit, I say, I call, as only powerful over me, and by his infinite virtue only able to express infinite things.

Or if I be too weak an instrument to be inspired with such a gift, or that words be not able to interpret for me, then to your royal dear heart I appeal, which, without my words, can fully and justly understand me.

Heavens and earth shall witness for me. I will strive to be worthy of so high a grace and so blessed a happiness. Be pleased, therefore, most dear Queen, to be ever thus gracious, if not for my merit yet for your own constancy. And so you shall bestow all those happinesses which in the end of your letter you are pleased to wish; and then, if I may hear your Majesty is well and well-pleased nothing can be ill with your Majesty's humblest and most affectionate vassal,

ESSEX

TO THE SAME

[1598]

MADAM, When I think how I have preferred your beauty above all things, and received no pleasure in life but by the increase of your favour towards me, I wonder at myself what cause there could be to make me absent myself one day from you. But when I remember that your Majesty hath, by the intolerable wrong you have done both me and yourself not only broken all laws of affection, but done against the honour of your sex, I think all places better than that where I am, and all dangers well undertaken, so I might retire myself from the memory of my false, inconstant and beguiling pleasures. I am sorry to write thus much for I cannot think your mind so dishonourable but that you punish yourself for it, how little soever you care for me. But I desire whatsoever falls out that your Majesty should be without excuse, you knowing yourself to be the cause, and all the world wondering at the effect. I was never proud till your Majesty sought to make me too base. And now since my destiny is no better, my despair shall be as my love was, without repentance. I will as a subject and an humble servant owe my life, my fortune, and all that is in me; but this place is not fit for me, for she which governs this world is weary of me, and I of the world. I must commend my faith to be judged by Him who judgeth all hearts since on earth I find no right. Wishing your Majesty all comforts and joys in the world, and no greater punishment for your wrongs to me than to know the faith of him you have lost, and the baseness of those you shall keep.

Your Majesty's most humble servant,
R. ESSEX

SIR HENRY WOTTON (1568–1639)

Sir Henry was one of the brilliant diplomatists who made England's power felt throughout the Continent. He was ambassador to Vienna when this letter was written and he describes an incident in one of the countless Continental wars.

[OCTOBER 1620]

RIGHT HONOURABLE, Of my purpose to depart from Vienna, and to leave the Emperor to the counsels of his own fortune, I gave his Majesty knowledge by my servant, James Vary.

I will now make you a summary account of what hath happened here, which is to be done both out of duty to your place, and out of obligation to your friendship.

The Count Tampier had some twelve days since taken from the Hungarians, by surprisal in the field, thirteen cornets of horse, and one ensign of foot, which here with much ostentation were carried up and down, and laid on Sunday was seven night under the Emperor's feet, as he came from the chapel.

Some note, that the vanity of this triumph was greater than the merit; for the Hungarians by their ordinary discipline, abound in cornets, bearing one almost for every twenty horse, so as flags are good cheap amongst them, and but slightly guarded. Howsoever the matter be made more or less, according to the wits on both sides, this was *breve gaudium*, and itself, indeed, some cause of the following disaster; for the Count Tampier, being by nature an enterprising man, was now also inflamed by accident, which made him immediately conceive the surprisal of Presburg, while the Prince of Transylvania was retired to the siege of Güns, some six or seven leagues distant. A project in truth, if it had prospered, of notorious utility.

First, by the very reputation of the place, being the capital town of Hungaria.

Next, the access to Comorn and Raab (which places only the Emperor retaineth, in that kingdom of any considerable value) had been freed by water, which now in a manner are blocked up.

Thirdly, the incursions into these provinces, and ignominious depredations had been cut off.

And lastly, the Crown of Hungaria had been recovered, which the Emperor Matthias did transport to the castle of Presburg, after the deposition of Rodolph, his brother, who always kept it in the castle of Prague; which men account one of the subtle things of that retired Emperor, as I hear by discourse. So as upon these considerations, the enterprise was more commendable in the design, than it will appear in the execution; being thus carried.

From hence to Presburg is in this month of October an easy night's journey by water. Thither on Thursday night of the last week, Tampier himself, accompanied with some four or five Colonels, and other remarkable men of this court, resolves to bring down in twenty-five boats, about 3,000 foot, or such a matter; having given order, and space enough before, for certain horse, partly Dutch, and partly Polonians, to be there, and to attend his coming about two hours before Friday morning. And to shadow this purpose, himself on Thursday in the afternoon, with affected noise goes up the river the contrary way, though no reasonable imaginations could conceive whither; for the lower Austria was then all reduced. By which artificial delay, and by some natural stops in the shallows of the water, when they fell silently down again, it was three or four hours of clear day before he arrived at Presburg the next morning: where his meaning was, first to destroy the bridge built upon boats, and thereby to keep Bethlem Gabor (as then on the Austrian side) not only from succouring the town, but from all possibility of repassing the Danube nearer than Buda. Next, to apply the petard to one of the gates of the citadel. Some wise say, he had like inward intelligence, that at his approach, the wicket of the castle should be opened unto him by one Palfy, an Hungarian gentleman; which conceit, though perchance raised at first to animate the soldier, yet hath gotten much credit, by seeing the enterprise against all discourse continued by daylight. Be that point how it will, his fatal hour was come: for approaching a sconce that lies by the castle gate, and turning about to cry for his men to come on, he was shot in the lowest part of his skull nearest his neck, after which he spake no syllable, as Don Carolo d'Austria (second base son to Rodolph the Emperor, and himself at that time saved by the goodness of his armour) doth testify. After which, some two or three soldiers attempting to bring away his body, and those being shot, the rest gave it over, and the whole troops transported themselves to the other side, leaving the boats behind them, as if they had meant to contribute new provision for the mending of the bridge, whereof they had only broken one little piece.

This was the end of the Count Tampier; by his father's side a Norman, by his mother's a Champaigne, a servant twenty-two years to the House of Austria. Himself captain of a thousand horse: but commander divers times in chief, especially before the coming of the Count Bucquoy, from whom he was severed to these nearer services, being of incompatible natures: a valiant and plotting soldier; in encounters more fortunate than sieges; gracious to his own, and terrible to the Hungarians; to the present Emperor most dear, though, perchance, as much for civil as military merit: for this was the very man that first seized upon the Cardinal Clesel, when he was put into a coach, and transported hence to Tirol; so as now we may expect some pamphlet the next mart from Ingolstadt, or Köln; that no man can end well who hath laid violent hands upon any of those Roman Purpurati.

To this point I must add two remarkable circumstances: the first, that Tampier, among other papers found in his pockets, is said to have had a memorial of certain conditions, whereon it should be fit to insist in his parley with the town, as having already swallowed the castle. The other, that his head having been cut off by a soldier, and sold for five dollars to another, who meant to have the merit of presenting it to the prince, the presenter was rewarded with a stroke of a sabre, for insulting over the dead carcass of a gentleman of honour.

JOHN DONNE (1573–1631)

Poet and divine, Donne occupies a place to himself in English litera-
ture. He was the first of the "metaphysical" poets, and in later life a
noted churchman and Dean of St. Paul's. He accompanied Essex on his
expedition to the Azores in 1597, *when he composed his poems of "The*
Storm" and "The Calm." One of the letters here printed was written
to the Sir Henry Wotton of the previous page; the other was to that
intimate friend of his to whom the beautiful poem "The Litany" was
addressed.

TO SIR HENRY WOTTON

[c. 1600]

SIR, I am no great voyager in other men's works: no swallower nor
devourer of volumes nor pursuant of authors. Perchance it is because
I find borne in myself knowledge or apprehension enough, for (without
forfeiture or impeachment of modesty) I think I am bond to God thankfully to acknowledge it to consider Him and myself: as when I have at
home a convenient garden I covet not to walk in others' broad meadows
or woods, especially because it falls not within that short reach which my
foresight embraceth, to see how I should employ that which I already
know; to travel for inquiry of more were to labour to get a stomach and
then find no meat at home. To know how to live by the book is a
pedantry, and to do it is a bondage. For both hearers and players are
more delighted with voluntary than with set music. And he that will
live by precept shall be long without the habit of honesty: as he that would
every day gather one or two feathers might become brawn with hard
lying before he make a feather bed of his gettings. That Earl of Arundel
that last died (that tennis ball whom fortune after tossing and banding
brick-walled into the hazard) in his imprisonment used more than much
reading, and to him that asked him why he did so he answered he read so
much lest he should remember something. I am as far from following
his counsel as he was from Petruccio's: but I find it true that after long
reading I can only tell you how many leaves I have read. I do therefore
more willingly blow and keep awake that small coal which God hath
pleased to kindle in me than far off to gather a faggot of green sticks which

consume without flame or heat in a black smother. Yet I read something. But indeed not so much to avoid as to enjoy idleness. Even when I begun so much to write these I flung away Dante the Italian, a man pert enough to be beloved and too much to be believed. It angered me that Celestine a pope [so] far from the manners of other popes that he left even their seat, should by the court of Dante's wit be attacked and by him thrown into his purgatory. And it angered me as much, that in the life of a pope he should spy no greater fault than that in the affectation of a cowardly security he slipped from the great burden laid upon him. Alas! what would Dante have him do? Thus we find the story related. He that thought himself next in succession, by a trunk [tube] thorough a wall whispered in Celestine's ear counsel to remove the papacy. Why should not Dante be content to think that Celestine took this for as immediate a salutation and discourse of the Holy Ghost as Abraham did the commandment of killing his son? If he will needs punish retiredness thus, what hell can his wit devise for ambition? And if white integrity merit this, what shall *Male* or *Malum* which Seneca condemns most, deserve? But as the chancellor Hatton being told after a decree made, that his predecessor was of another opinion, answered "he had his genius and I had mine." So say I of authors, that they think and I think both reasonably yet possibly both erroneously; that is manly. For I am so far from persuading yea counselling you to believe others that I care not that you believe not me when I say that others are not to be believed; only believe that I love you and I have enough.

I have studied philosophy, therefore marvel not if I make such accompt of arguments *qui trahuntur ab effectibus*.

TO SIR HENRY GOODYER

[*c.* 1608]

Sir, This letter hath no more merit than one of more diligence, for I wrote it in my bed, and with much pain. I have occasion to sit late some nights in my study, (which your books make a pretty library) and now I find that that room hath a wholesome emblematic use. For having under it a vault, I make that promise me that I shall die reading, since my book and a grave are so near. But it hath another as unwholesome, that by raw vapours rising from thence, (for I can impute it to nothing else) I have contracted a sickness which I cannot name nor describe. For it hath so much of a continual cramp that it wrests the sinews, so much of a tetanus, that it withdraws and pulls the mouth, and so much of the gout, (which they whose counsel I use, say it is) that it is not like to be cured, though I am too hasty in three days to pronounce it.   If it be the Gout, I am miserable; for that affects dangerous parts, as my neck and breast, and (I think fearfully) my stomach, but it will not kill me yet.   I shall be in this world, like a porter in a great house, ever nearest the door, but seldomest abroad.   I shall have many things to make me weary, and yet not get leave to be gone.   If I go, I will provide by my best means that you suffer not for me, in your bonds.   The estate which I should leave behind me of my estimation, is my poor fame in the memory of my friends, and therefore I would be curious of it, and provide that they repent not to have loved me.   Since my imprisonment in my bed, I have made a meditation in verse, which I call a Litany; the word you know imports no other than supplication, but all Churches have one form of supplication by that name.   Amongst ancient annals, I mean some 800 years, I have met two Litanies in Latin verse, which gave me not the reason of my meditations, for in good faith I thought not upon them then, but they give me a defence, if any man; to a layman, and a private, impute it as a fault to take such divine and public names to his own little thoughts.   The first of these was made by *Ratpertus*, a monk of *Suevia;* and the other by S. *Notker,* of whom I will give you this note by the way, that he is a private saint for a few parishes; they were both but Monks, and the Litanies poor and barbarous enough; yet Pope Nicolas V valued their devotion so much that he canonized both their poems, and commanded them for public service in their Churches.   Mine is for lesser chapels, which are my friends, and though a copy of it were due to you now, yet I am so unable to serve myself with writing it for you at this time (being some 30 staves of 9 lines), that I must intreat you to take a promise that you shall have the first, for a testimony of that duty which I owe to your love, and to myself, who am bound to cherish it by my best offices.   That by which it will deserve best acceptation, is, That neither the Roman Church need call it defective, because it abhors not the particular mention of the blessed Triumphers in heaven; nor the Reformed can discreetly accuse it of attributing more than rectified devotion ought to do.   The day before I lay down, I was at London, where I delivered your letter for Sir Edward Conway, and received another for you, with the copy of my book, of which it is impossible for me to give you a copy so soon, for it is not of much less than 300 pages.   If I die, it shall come to you in that fashion that your letter desires it.   If I warm again, (as I have often seen such beggars as my indisposition is, end themselves soon, and the patient as soon) you and I shall speak together of that, before it be too late to serve you in that commandment. At this time I only assure you, that I have not appointed it upon any person nor ever purposed to print it: which latter perchance you thought, and grounded your request thereupon. A gentleman that visited me yesterday told me that our Church hath lost Mr. Hugh Broughton, who is gone to the Roman side. I have known before, that Serarius the Jesuit was an instrument from Cardinal Baronius to draw him to Rome, to accept a stipend, only to serve the Christian Churches in controversies with the Jews, without indangering himself to change of his persuasion in particular deductions between these Christian Churches, or being enquired of, or tempted thereunto. And I hope he is not otherwise departed from us. If he be, we shall not escape scandal in it; because, though he be a man of many distempers, yet when he shall come to eat assured bread, and to be removed from partialities, to which want drove him, to make himself a reputation, and raise up favourers; you shall see in that course of opposing the Jews, he will produce worthy things: and our Church will perchance blush to have lost a soldier fit for that great battle; and to cherish only those single dualisms, between Rome and England, or that more single, and almost self-homicide, between the unconformed Ministers, and Bishops. Sir you would pity me if you saw me write, and therefore will pardon me if I write no more: my pain hath drawn my head so much awry, and holds it so, that mine eye cannot follow mine hand. I receive you therefore into my prayers, with mine own weary soul, and commend myself to yours. I doubt not but next week I shall be good news to you, for I have mending or dying on my side, which is two to one. If I continue this, I shall have comfort in this, that by Blessed Saviour exercising his Justice upon my two worldly parts, my fortune and body, reserves all his mercy for that which best tastes it, and most needs it, my soul. I profess to you truly, that my lothness to give over now, seems to my self an ill sign that I shall write no more.

Your poor friend, and God's poor patient,

Jo. DONNE

SIR DUDLEY CARLETON, VISCOUNT DORCHESTER
(1573–1632)

Sir Dudley was a diplomatist and saw considerable service on the Continent. Among the duties trusted to him was that of assisting the inept Duke of Buckingham, whose utter failure at La Rochelle crowned a misspent career. Carleton was with the Duke when Felton assassinated him, and in this letter to Queen Henrietta Maria he tells the story of what happened.

TO THE QUEEN

MADAM, I am to trouble your Grace with a most lamentable relation. This day betwixt nine and ten of the clock in the morning, the Duke of Buckingham then coming out of a parlour into a hall, to go to his coach and so to the King (who was four miles off), having about him divers lords, colonels, and captains, and many of his own servants, was by one Felton (once a Lieutenant of this our Army) slain at one blow, with a dagger-knife. In his staggering he turned about, uttering only this word, "Villain" and never spake word more, but plucking out the knife from himself, before he fell to the ground, he made towards the traitor, two or three paces, and then fell against a table, although he was upheld by divers that were near him, that (through the villain's close carriage in the act) could not perceive him hurt at all, but guessed him to be suddenly over-swayed with some apoplexy, till they saw the blood come gushing from his mouth and the wound, so fast that life and breath at once left his begored body.

Madam, you may easily guess what outcries were then made by us that were Commanders and Officers there present, when we saw him thus dead in a moment, and slain by an unknown hand. For it seems that the Duke, himself only, knew who it was that had murdered him, and by means of the confused press at the instant about his person, we neither did nor could. The soldiers fear his loss will be their utter ruin, wherefore at that instant the house and the court about it were full, every man present with the Duke's body, endeavouring a care of it. In the meantime Felton passed the throng, which was confusedly great, not so much as marked or followed; in so much that not knowing where nor who he was that had done that fact, some came to keep guard at the gates, and others went to the ramparts of the town. In all which time the villain was standing in the kitchen of the same house, and after the inquiry made by a multitude of captains and gentlemen then pressing into the house and court, and crying out amain "Where is the villain? Where is the butcher?" he, most audaciously and resolutely drawing forth his sword, came out and went amongst them, saying boldly, "I am the Man, here I am." Upon which divers drew upon him, with an intent to have then dispatched him; but Sir Thomas Morton, myself and some others, used such means (though with much trouble and difficulty) that we drew him out of their hands, and by order of my Lord High Chamberlain, we had the charge of keeping any from coming to him until a guard of musketeers were brought, to convey him to the Governor's house, where we were discharged.

My Lord High Chamberlain and Mr. Secretary Cooke who were then at the Governor's house, did there take his examinations, of which as yet there is nothing known, only whilst he was in our custody I asked him several questions, to which he answered; viz. he said, he was a Protestant in religion; he also expressed himself that he was partly discontented for want of eighty pounds pay which was due to him; and for that he, being Lieutenant of a company of foot, the company was given over his head unto another; and yet, he said that that did not move him to this resolution, but that he reading the Remonstrance of the house of Parliament it came into his mind that in committing the act of killing the Duke, he should do his country great good service. And he said that to-morrow he was to be prayed for in London. I then asked him at what church, and to what purpose; he told me at a church by Fleet-Street-Conduit, and, as for a man much discontented in mind. Now we seeing things to fall from him in this manner, suffered him not to be further questioned by any, thinking it much fitter for the lords to examine him, and to find out and know from him whether he was encouraged and set on by any to perform this wicked deed.

But to return to the screeches made at the fatal blow given. The Duchess of Buckingham and the Countess of Anglesey came forth into a gallery which looked into the hall where they might behold the blood of their dearest lord gushing from him. Ah poor ladies, such was their screechings, tears, and distractions, that I never in my life heard the like before, and hope never to hear the like again. His Majesty's grief for the loss of him was expressed to be more than great, by the many tears he hath shed for him, with which I will conclude this sad and untimely news.

Felton had sewed a writing in the crown of his hat, half within the lining, to shew the cause why he put this cruel act in execution; thinking he should have been slain in the place. And it was thus:

"If I be slain, let no man condemn me, but rather condemn himself; it is for our sins that our hearts are hardened, and become senseless, or else he had not gone so long unpunished.

JOHN FELTON"

"He is unworthy of the name of a gentleman, or soldier, in my opinion, that is afraid to sacrifice his life for the honour of God, his King, and Country.

JOHN FELTON"

Madam, this is the truth, the whole truth, and nothing but the truth, yet all too much too, if it had so pleased God. I thought it my bounden duty howsoever to let your Majesty have the first intelligence of it, by the hand of

Madam,
Your sorrowful servant,
DUDLEY CARLETON

LADY ARABELLA STUART (1575–1615)

Lady Arabella stood in the line of succession to the English throne next to James I, who was her cousin, and in the closing years of Elizabeth's reign there was a considerable party with no liking for the King of Scots— who urged her claims in preference to his. Shortly before Elizabeth's death Lady Arabella was arrested by her orders, in consequence of the talk about a marriage with Seymour, son of the heiress of the Suffolk line. In 1610 this gossip was renewed. She and Seymour were summoned before the Privy Council, and they solemnly promised not to marry without the king's consent. A couple of months later they did *marry, however, and in a day or two Lady Arabella was committed to the Tower, to begin the weary imprisonment that ended with her death. This letter was written when she was in prison.*

TO WILLIAM SEYMOUR

Sir, I am exceeding sorry to hear you have not been well. I pray you let me know truly how you do, and what was the cause of it. I am not satisfied with the reason Smith gives for it, but if it be a cold, I will impute it to some sympathy betwixt us, having myself gotten a swollen cheek at the same time with a cold. For God's sake, let not your grief of mind work upon your body. You may see by me what inconveniences it will bring one to; and no fortune, I assure you, daunts me so much as that weakness of body I find in myself; for, *si nous vivons l'âge d'un veau,* as Marot says, we may, by God's grace, be happier than we look for, in being suffered to enjoy ourself with his majesty's favour. But if we be not able to live to it, I, for my part, shall think myself a pattern of misfortune in enjoying so great blessing as you, so little awhile. No separation but that deprives me of the comfort of you. For wheresoever you be, or in what state soever you are, it sufficeth me you are mine! *Rachel wept and would not be comforted, because her children were no more.* And that, indeed, is the remediless sorrow, and none else! And therefore God bless us from that, and I will hope well of the rest, though I see no apparent hope. But I am sure God's book mentioneth many of his children in as great distress that have done well after, even in this world!

81

I do assure you nothing the state can do with me can trouble me so much as this news of your being ill doth; and you see when I am troubled, I trouble you too with tedious kindness; for so I think you will account so long a letter, yourself not having written to me this good while so much as how you do.   But, sweet sir, I speak not this to trouble you with writing but when you please.   Be well, and I shall account myself happy in being

Your faithfull loving wife,

ARB. S.

ROBERT TOUNSON (1575–1621)

Tounson was chaplain to King James and Dean of Westminster. It was in the latter capacity that he attended Raleigh to the scaffold, describing his "last behaviour" in a letter to his friend Sir John Isham. Some years later Tounson became Bishop of Salisbury, but he died "in a mean condition" leaving "thirteen poor children." One of his first actions as bishop was to forbid ladies in yellow ruffs to enter his church, but the King declared that the objection was not against ruffs as such but "other manly and unseemly apparel."

TO SIR JOHN ISHAM

WESTMINSTER, NOVEMBER 9, 1618

SIR, The last week was a busy week with me, and the week afore that was more; I would gladly have writ unto you but could find no time. Yet I hope you had the relation of Sir Walter Rawleigh's death; for so I gave order that it should be brought unto you. I was commanded by the Lords of the Council to be with him, both in prison and at his death, and so set down the manner of his death as near as I could. There be other reports of it but that which you have from me is true. One Craford, who was sometime Mr. Rodeknight's pupil, hath penned it prettily and meaneth to put it to the press and came to me about it, but I hear not that it is come forth. The sum of that which he spake at his death you have, I suppose, already. He never made mention of his offence for which he died, namely his former treason, but only desired to clear himself of new imputations there mentioned. Privately he told me in prison that he was charged to have broken the peace with Spain, but he put that, he said, out of the count of his offences, saving that he heard the king was displeased at it. For how could he brake peace with him who within these 4 years, as he said, took diverse of his men and bound them back to back and drowned them. And as for burning the town, he said it stood upon the king's own ground, and therefore he did no wrong in that. He was the most fearless of death that ever was known, and the most resolute and confident, yet with reverence and conscience. When I began to encourage him against the fear of death, he seemed to make so light of it

83

that I wondered at him; and when I told him that the dear servants of God, in better causes than his, had shrunk back and trembled a little, he denied not, but yet gave God thanks he never feared death, and much less then, for it was but an opinion and imagination. And the manner of death, though to others [it] might seem grievous, yet he had rather die so than of a burning fever; with much more to that purpose, with such confidence and cheerfulness, that I was fain to divert my speech another way and wished him not to flatter himself, for this extraordinary boldness, I was afraid, came from some false ground. If it sprang from the assurance he had of the love and favour of God, of the hope of his salvation by Christ and his own innocence, as he pleaded, I said he was an happy man; but if it were out of an humour of vainglory or carelessness or contempt of death, or senselessness of his own estate, he were much to be lamented. For I told him that heathen men had set as little by their lives as he could do, and seemed to die as bravely. He answered, that he was persuaded that no man that knew God and feared him could die with cheerfullness and courage except he was assured of the love and favour of God unto him; that other men might make shows outwardly, but they feel no joy within. With much more to that effect, very christianly, for he satisfied me then, as I think he did all the spectators at his death. After he had received the Communion in the morning, he was very cheerful and merry and hoped to persuade the world that he died an innocent man, as he said. Thereat, I told him that he should do well to advise what he said. Men in these days did not die in that sort innocent, and his pleading innocence was an oblique taxing the justice of the realm upon him. He confessed justice had been done, and by course of law he must die, but yet I should give him leave, he said, to stand upon his innocence in the fact. And he thought, both the king and all that heard his answers thought verily that he was innocent for that matter. I then pressed him to call to mind what he had done formerly, and though p'haps in that particular for which he was condemned he was clear, yet for some other matter it might be he was guilty, and now the hand of God had found him out, and therefore he should acknowledge the justice of God in it, though at the hands of men he had but hard measure. And here I put him in mind of the death of my L. of Essex, how it was generally reported that he was a great instrument of his death, which if his heart did charge him with, he should heartily repent, and ask God forgiveness. To which he made answer as is in the former relation; and said, moreover, that my L. of Essex was fetched by a trick, which he privately told me of. He was very cheerful that morning he died, ate his breakfast heartily and took tobacco and made no more of his death than if he had been to take a journey; and left a great impression in the minds of those that beheld him, in so much that Sir Lewis Stukely [1] and the Frenchman grow very odious: This was the news a week since; but now it is blown over and he almost forgotten. The news which I have is that the promoter of Rothwell hath gotten his charges of Sir Thomas Brooke [2] and Sir Thomas much checked, and hath entered into bond of a £100 to the promoter, never to molest or trouble him again, and the promoter triumpheth in his victory very much and Sir Thomas glad he hath escaped so. I once saw Henry Tremill and that is all. What is become of Robin Dallison I cannot tell, but he was here in great expectation of a place which I think now he is fallen from, for all officers here are much younger than himself. The business of the treasurer sleepeth; and that of my L. of Exeter and Sir Thomas Lake [3] will not be called upon this term. There be, as I hear, 17,000 sheets of paper in that book, which upon ordinary account cometh to eight hundred and fifty pound, the very writing. The king and the prince, thanks be to God, are very well; the Queen is still at Hampton Court and crazy, they say. You will remember me kindly to my lady and your mother, and if you have any imployment for me here, you shall find me always

At your service,

ROBERT TOUNSON

The following poem, in another hand, was found with the Tounson letter, to which it presumably formed an enclosure. It has been long known, with slight modifications, and is traditionally said to have been composed by Raleigh the night before his death.

> Euen soe is tyme, who takes in trust
>   Our youth our ioyes & all wee haue
> And payes us but with earth & dust
>   Whoe in the darke & sylent graue
> When wee haue wandered all our wayes
>   Shutts up the story of our dayes
>   And from which earth & graue & dust
>   The Lord will raise mee up, I truste
>   WALTER RALEIGH.

---

[1] Appointed keeper of Raleigh on his return from the Orinoco, in which capacity his supposed unfair conduct made him intensely unpopular.

[2] Presumably some dispute in regard to Jesus Hospital at Rothwell. Sir Thomas Brooke belonged to an old Northamptonshire family connected with the Ishams.

[3] Sir Thomas Lake was charged with defamation of character by the Countess of Exeter and found guilty. (See Letter, p. 68.)

JOSEPH MEAD (1586–1638)

Mead is best known to fame as the writer of a "Key to the Apocalypse," but he appears in this volume by virtue of letters written to his friend Sir Martin Stuteville describing happenings in London. His narrative of the arrival of Henrietta Maria is a wonderful little cameo of description.

TO SIR MARTIN STUTEVILLE

LONDON, JANUARY 11, 1621

THE Parliament having been full ten days in suspense whether to hold or not, was, on Wednesday, clean dissolved by Proclamation. The same day his Majesty rode by coach to Theobalds to dinner, not intending, it is said, to return till after Easter. After dinner, riding on horseback abroad, his horse stumbled and cast his Majesty into the New River, where the ice brake. He fell in so that nothing but his boots were seen. Sir Richard Young was next, who alighted, went into the water and pulled him out. There came much water out of his mouth and body. His Majesty rode back to Theobalds, went into a warm bed and, as we hear, is well, which God continue.

TO THE SAME

LONDON, JUNE 17, 1625

THE last night at 5 o'clock, there being a very great shower, the King and Queen in the Royal barge with many other barges of honour and thousands of boats, passed through London Bridge to Whitehall; infinite numbers, besides these, in wherries, standing in houses, lighters, western barges, and on each side of the shore. Fifty good ships discharging their ordnance as their Majesties passed along by; as, last of all, the Tower did such a peal as I believe she never before heard the like. The King and Queen were both in green suits. The barge windows, notwithstanding the vehement shower, were open; and all the people shouting amain. She

86

put out her hand and shaked it unto them. She hath already given some good signs of hope that she may ere long, by God's blessing, become ours in religion.

She arrived at Dover on Sunday about eight in the evening, lay there in the Castle that night; whither the King rode on Monday morning from Canterbury, came thither after 10 o'clock and she then being at meat, he stayed in the presence till she had done; which she, advertised of, made short work, rose, went unto him, kneeled down at his feet, took, and kissed his hand. The King took her up in his arms, kissed her, and talking with her, cast down his eyes towards her feet (she seeming higher than report was, reaching to his shoulders). Which she soon perceiving discovered [uncovered] and showed him her shoes, saying to this effect "Sir, I stand upon mine own feet. I have no helps by art. Thus I am, and am neither higher nor lower." She is nimble and quiet, black-eyed, brown-haired, and in a word a brave Lady, though perhaps a little touched with a green sickness.

One ship whereupon stood above an hundred people, not being balanced nor well tied to the shore, and they standing all upon one side, was overturned and sunk, all that were upon her tumbling into the Thames; and yet was not anyone lost that I can hear of, but all saved by the help of boats. The bells rang till midnight and all the streets were full of bonfires, and in this one street were above thirty.

At dinner (at Dover) being carved pheasant and venison by his Majesty (who had dined before) she ate heartily of both, notwithstanding that her confessor (who all this while stood by her) had forewarned her that it was the eve of St. John Baptist, and was to be fasted, and that she should take heed how she gave ill example or a scandal at her first arrival.

The same night, having supped at Canterbury, her Majesty went to bed; and, some space of time after, his Majesty followed her. And having entered his bedchamber, the first thing he did, he bolted all the doors round about (being seven), with his own hand, letting in but two of the bedchamber to undress him, which being done, he bolted them out also. The next morning he lay till seven of the clock, and was pleasant with the lords that he had beguiled them; and hath ever since been very jocund.

Yesterday I saw them coming up from Gravesend, and never beheld the King to look so merrily. In stature her head reached to his shoulder, but she is young enough to grow taller.

Yesterday betwixt Gravesend and London she had a beautiful and stately view of part of our Navy that is to go to sea, which gave her a volley of 1,500 great shot. So they arrived at Whitehall, where they continue till Monday, when they go to Hampton Court. On Sunday there is a great feast at Whitehall.

SIR EDMUND VERNEY (1590–1642)

Sir Edmund was standard-bearer of Charles I and followed his master into the field. His son Ralph took the opposite side. On the morning before Edge Hill Sir Edmund waited on the King at breakfast in a lonely little inn overlooking the field. Soon afterwards, when the battle was raging, he dashed into the thick of the fight bearing the standard. In an instant he was surrounded by enemies, who offered him his life if he would deliver the colours. Sir Edmund answered that his life was his own but the standard was the King's, and he would not deliver it while he lived. Faithful to the last, Sir Edmund's hand was found still grasping the standard though severed from his body, which was never found.

TO RALPH VERNEY

MAY 11, 1639

RALPH, Sir Peter Killigrew has stayed longer for the kings letter than he expected, and I having received a packet from you three hours since, I have broken up my packet again to insert this letter in answer to this last of yours, dated the 7th of May. For most of your letter I think I have received them, but I am sure many of mine to you have miscarried, for truly I have never failed sending twice a week at least, and some weeks oftener, but I much fear they are gotten into ill hands. I will hereafter keep a note of all I send or receive, and the date of them. But I shall not write often now, for we shall go into the field presently; nay, the king himself and all his army, after we go out of this town, will lodge in the fields every night, and no man must look into a village.

I sent Robin Leslie's business by Mr. Webb, my lord duke's secretary, who went from Durham on Monday last. If Mr. Leslie has a mind to come he may, for I do not see how he gives any assistance to the business; but, if he be there, I would have him deal so with the coachmen that as little clamour may be raised as possibly can be, and that must be by getting the 50 coachmen to take under them as many others of the poor men about the town as they can, that they may not complain. This must be done privately, for if the poorer sort discover a fear of complaining they will cry out the more.

I have received all my arms that you sent, and I have a long gauntlet, but I have never a short one, nor is it any matter, for I will never use more than back and breast. I pray haste away my pot, and take care it be wide enough, for this is so much too little that nobody but a mad man could have been so mad as to mistake so grossly; therefore take care it be wide enough now.

This afternoon there is news come for certain that 2,000 Scots are come within ten mile of Berwick. They say 8,000 more is coming after them, and 2,000 more are gone to lie near Carlisle. We shall soon have blows now, but I believe it will be skirmishes with the horse, and no battle till towards the end of summer. It is folly to think any longer of a peace. We shall be suddenly engaged now.

God of his mercy send us well to meet either here or hereafter. God of heaven and earth bless you and all yours. Farewell.

[*A day later*] I have tried my arms, and the headpiece is very much too little for me. If the pot I expect daily from him be so too I am undone. I pray send to him about it as soon as you receive this letter. This will come upon no part of my head, it is so very little. The rest of my arms are fit, but I shall never use more than back and breast.

As I was thus far in my letter, my lord chamberlain sent for me, and told me the sad news of sweet Mrs. Henslow's death, desiring me to break it to her father. Truly I cannot express my grief for the loss of her. She was one that I had an extraordinary esteem for, and to whose love I owe much. I have now lost her; if she had lived a few weeks longer she might have lost me. I will write to Mrs. Rogers, and inclose it in this. I pray send it to her. The God of heaven bless you and yours. Farewell,

YOUR LOVING FATHER

ROBERT HERRICK (1591–1674)

What need to say who Herrick was? Who that loves English has not read "Hesperides"? This letter was written from Cambridge when the poet was a young man, racking his brains to graduate. Whether "hopeful Herrick" got the money we cannot say, but he graduated in 1617.

CAMBRIDGE

SIR, that which makes my letter to be abortive and born before maturity is and hath been my Commencement, which I have now overgone, though I confess with many a throe and pinches of the purse; but it was necessary, and the prize was worthy the hazard; which makes me less sensible of the expense, by reason of a titular prerogative— *et bonum est prodire in bono.* The essence of my writing is (as heretofore) to entreat you to pay for my use to Mr. Arthur Johnson, bookseller in Paul's church yard the ordinary sum of ten pounds, and that with as much celerity as you may, though I could wish charges had leaden wings and Tortoise feet to come upon me; *sed votis puerilibus opto.* Sir, I fix my hopes on Time and you; still gazing for an happy flight of birds, and the refreshing blast of a second wind. Doubtful as yet of either Fortunes, I live, hoarding up provision against the assault of either. Thus I salute your virtues.

HOPEFUL R. HERRICK

GEORGE VILLIERS, DUKE OF BUCKINGHAM (1592–1628)

James I was not fastidious in his friendships, and when he selected young George Villiers to shower his favours upon, he chose a poor creature. Buckingham was sent to Spain with Prince Charles to court the Infanta for his bride and it is from Madrid that he wrote this letter. "Steenie" as James called him, treated his kingly master with a sort of good-natured contempt—but the letter speaks for itself.

TO KING JAMES I

[MADRID, APRIL 25, 1623]

DEAR DAD, GOSSIP, AND STEWARD, Though your baby himself hath sent word what need he hath of more jewels, yet will I by this bearer, who can make more speed than Carlile, again acquaint your Majesty therewith, and give my poor and saucy opinion what will be fittest more to send. Hitherto you have been so sparing that, whereas you thought to have sent him sufficiently for his own wearing, to present his mistress who I am sure shall shortly now lose that title, and to lend me, I, to the contrary, have been forced to lend him. You need not ask who made me able to do it. Sir, he hath neither chain nor hatband; and I beseech you consider first how rich they are in jewels here, then in what poor equipage he came in, how he hath no other means to appear like a king's son, how they are usefullest at such a time as this when they may do yourself, your son and the nation honour, and lastly how it will neither cost nor hasard you anything. These reasons, I hope, since you have ventured already your chief jewel, your son, will serve to persuade you to let loose these more after him. First your best hatband; the Portugal diamond; the rest of the pendant diamonds, to make up a necklace to give his mistress; and the best rope of pearl; with a rich chain or two for himself to wear, or else your dog must want a collar; which is the ready way to put him into it. There are many other jewels which are of so mean quality as they deserve not that name, but will save much in your purse and serve very well for presents. They had never so good and great an occasion to take the air out of their boxes as at this time. God

92

knows when they shall have such another: and they had need sometimes to get nearer the sun to continue them in their perfection. Here give me leave humbly on my knees to give your Majesty thanks for that rich jewel you sent me in a box by my Lord Vaughan, and give him leave to kiss your hands from me who took the pains to draw it. My reward to him is this; he spent his time well, which is the thing we should all most desire, and is the glory I covet most here in your service, which sweet Jesus grant me, and your blessing.

Your Majesty's most humble slave and dog,

STEENIE

JOHN HAMPDEN (1594–1643)

One of the choicest and noblest spirits of Stuart England, Hampden was more a man of action than a letter-writer. The following lines were written to another patriot, Sir John Eliot, who was at that time in the Tower of London for the cause of liberty. While there Eliot was writing "The Monarchy of Man" and borrowed books from Hampden for that purpose.

TO JOHN ELIOT

SIR, You shall receive the book I promised by this bearer's immediate hand; for the other papers I presume to take a little, and but little, respite. I have looked upon that rare piece only with a superficial view; and at first sight to take the aspect and proportion of the whole; after, with a more accurate eye, to take out the linaments of every part. It were rashness in me, therefore to discover any judgment before I have ground to make one. This I discern, that it is as complete an image of the pattern as can be drawn by lines; a lively character of a large mind; the subject, method, and expressions, excellent and homogenial, and, to say truth (sweet heart) somewhat exceeding my commendations. My words cannot render them to the life; yet (to show my ingenuity rather than wit), would not a less model have given a full representation of that subject? not by diminution, but by contradiction, of parts? I desire to learn; I dare not say. The variations upon each particular seem many; all, I confess, excellent. The fountain was full; the channel narrow; that may be the cause; or that the author imitated Virgil, who made more verses by many than he intended to write. To extract a just number, had I seen all his, I could easily have bid him make fewer; but if he had bade me tell which he should have spared I had been opposed. So say I of these expressions; and that to satisfy you, not myself, but that, by obeying you in a command so contrary to my own disposition, you may measure how large a power you over

JO. HAMPDEN

SIR BEVILL GRENVILLE (1595–1643)

This gallant Royalist soldier led the van at the Battle of Bradock Down in January, 1643, and a few months later fell in the attack on Sir William Waller's forces at Lansdown, near Bath. The first letter, written to his wife, describes the victory at Bradock; in the second he tells a friend why he left his wife and family to serve his King.

TO LADY GRACE GRENVIL

For the Lady Grace Grenvil,
    at Stow,
  The messenger is paid,
Yet give him a shilling more.

MY DEAR LOVE, It has pleased God to give us a happy victory on this present Thursday, being the 19th of January, for which pray join with me in giving God thanks. We advanced yesterday from Bodmin to find the enemy which we heard was abroad, or, if we missed him in the field, we were resolved to unhouse them in Liskerd, or leave our bodies in the highway. We were not above three miles from Bodmin when we had view of two troops of their horse, to whom we sent some of ours—which chased them out of the field, while our foot marched after our horse. But night coming on, we could march no farther than Boconnock Park, where (upon my Lord Mohun's kind motion) we quartered all our army that night by good fires under the hedges. The next morning (being this day) we marched forth, and, about noon, came in full view of the enemy's whole army upon a fair heath between Boconnock and Braddock church. They were in horse much stronger than we, but, in foot, we were superior I think. They were possessed of a pretty rising ground which was in the way toward Liskerd: and we planted ourselves upon such another against them within musket-shot; and we saluted each other with bullets about two hours or more, each side being willing to keep their ground of advantage and to have the other to come over to his prejudice. But after so long delay, they standing still firm, and being obstinate to hold

95

their advantage, Sir Ralph Hopton resolved to march over to them, and to leave all to the mercy of God and valour on our side. I had the van, and so, after solemn prayers at the head of every division, I led my party away, who followed me with so great courage both down the one hill and up the other, that it struck a terror in them, while the seconds came up gallantly after me, and the wings of horse charged on both sides. But their courage so failed as they stood not the first charge of the foot, but fled in great disorder; and we chased them diverse miles. Many are not slain, because of their quick disordering. But we have taken above 600 prisoners, and more are still brought in by the soldiers. Much arms they have lost; eight colours we have won, and four pieces of ordnance from them; and without rest we marched to Liskerd, and took it without delay, all their men flying from it before we came; and so I hope we are now again in the way to settle the country in peace. All our Cornish Grandees were present at the battle, with the Scotch General Ruthven, the Somerset Colonels, and the Horse-captains Pim and Tomson, and, but for their horses' speed, had been all in our hands. Let my sister, my cousins of Clovelly, with your other friends, understand of God's mercy to us; and we lost not a man. So I rest

Yours ever,

Bevill Grenvil

TO SIR JO. TRELAWNY

Most Honourable Sir, I have in many kinds had trial of your noble-ness, but in none more than in this singular expression of your kind care and love. I give also your excellent Lady humble thanks for respect unto my poor woman, who hath been long a faithful much obliged servant of your ladies. But, Sir, for my journey, it is fixed I cannot contain myself within my doors when the King of England's standard waves in the field upon so just occasion—the cause being such as must make all those that die in it little inferior to martyrs. And, for mine own, I desire to acquire an honest name, or an honour-able grave. I never loved my life, or ease so much as to shun such an occasion, which if I should, I were unworthy of the profession I have held, or to succeed those ancestors of mine, who have so many of them, in several ages, sacrificed their lives for their country.

Sir, the barbarous and implacable enemy (notwithstanding His Majesty's gracious proceedings with them) do continue their insolencies, and rebellion in the highest degree, and are united in a body of great strength; so as you must expect, if they be not prevented and mastered near their own homes, they will be troublesome in yours, and in the remotest places ere long.

I am not without the consideration (as you lovingly advise) of my wife and family; and as for her, I must acknowledge she has ever drawn so evenly in her yoke with me as she hath never pressed before or hung behind me, nor ever opposed or resisted my will. And yet truly I have not, in this or anything else, endeavoured to walk in the way of power with her, but of reason; and though her love will submit to either, yet truly my respect will not suffer me to urge her with power, unless I can convince with reason. So much for that, whereof I am willing to be accomptable unto so good a friend.

I have no suit unto you in mine own behalf, but for your prayers and good wishes, and that, if I live to come home again, you would please to continue me in the number of your servants.

I shall give a true relation unto my very noble friend Mr. Moyle of your and his aunt's loving respects to him which he has good reason to be thankful for; and so, I beseech God to send you and your noble family all health and happiness; and, while I live,

I am, Sir,

Your unfailing, loving, and faithful servant,

B. G.

JAMES HOWELL (1595–1666)

Howell's "Letters" (1645–55) are among the most interesting books of the period and describe with a marvellous vividness life as he saw it. Being in Spain upon diplomatic business he chanced to find himself in Madrid at the time when Prince Charles and Buckingham were courting the Infanta, and he wrote his impressions to his friend Captain Porter.

TO CAPTAIN THO. PORTER

MADRID, JULY 10, 1623

NOBLE CAPTAIN, My last unto you was in Spanish, in answer to one of yours in the same language, and amongst that confluence of English gallants which, upon the occasion of his Highness being here, are come to this Court, I fed myself with hopes a long while to have seen you, but I find now that those hopes were imped with false feathers. I know your heart is here and your best affections, therefore I wonder what keeps back your person; but I conceive the reason to be that you intend to come like yourself, to come commander-in-chief of one of the Castles of the Crown, one of the Ships Royal. If you come to this shore-side I hope you will have time to come to the Court. I have at any time a good lodging for you, and my landlady is none of the meanest, and her husband hath many good parts. I heard her setting him forth one day, and giving this character of him; "*Mi marido es buen musico, buen esgrimido, buen escrivano, excellente Arithmetico, salvo que no multiplica:* My husband is a good Musician, a good Fencer, a good Horseman, a good Penman, and an excellent Arithmetician, only he cannot multiply." For outward usage, all industry is used to give the Prince and his servants all possible contentment, and some of the King's own servants wait upon them at table in the palace, where I am sorry to hear some of them jeer at the Spanish fare, and use other slighting speeches and demeanour. There are many excellent poems made here since the Prince's arrival which are too long to couch in a letter, yet I will venture to send you this one Stanza of Lope de Vegas.

Carlos Estuardo Soy
Que siendo Amor mi guia
Al cielo d'Espana voy
Por ver mi Estrella Maria.

There are comedians once a week come to the palace, where, under a great canopy, the Queen and the Infanta sit in the middle, our Prince and Don Carlos on the Queen's right hand, the King and the little cardinal on the Infanta's left hand. I have seen the Prince have his eyes immovably fixed upon the Infanta half an hour together in a thoughtful speculative posture, which sure would needs be tedious unless affection did sweeten it: it was no handsome comparison of Olivares that he watched her as a cat doth a mouse. Not long since the Prince, understanding that the Infanta was used to go some mornings to the Casa de campo, a summer House the King hath the other side the River, to gather maydew, he did rise betimes and went thither, taking your brother with him. They were let into the house and into the garden, but the Infanta was in the orchard, and there being a high partition wall between, and the door doubly bolted, the Prince got on the top of the wall and sprung down a great height, and so made towards her. But she spying him first of all the rest, gave a shriek and ran back. The old Marquis, that was then her guardian, came towards the Prince and fell on his knees, conjuring his Highness to retire, in regard he hazarded his head if he admitted any to her company. So the door was opened and he came out under that wall over which he had got in. I have seen him watch a long hour together in a closed coach in the open street to see her as she went abroad. I cannot say that the Prince did ever talk with her privately, yet publicly often, my Lord of Bristol being interpreter; but the King always sat hard by, to overhear all. Our cousin Archy hath more privilege than any, for he often goes with his fool's coat where the Infanta is with her *meniñas* and ladies of honour, and keeps a blowing and blustering amongst them and flurts out what he list.

One day they were discoursing what a marvellous thing it was that the Duke of Bavaria, with less than 15,000 men, after a long toilsome march, should dare to encounter the Palgrave's Army, consisting of about 25,000, and give them an utter discomfiture, and take Prague presently after. Whereunto Archy answered, that he would tell them a stranger thing than that. "Was it not a strange thing," quoth he, "that in the year '88 there should come a fleet of one hundred and forty sails from Spain to invade England, and that ten of these could not go back to tell what became of the rest?" By the next opportunity I will send you the Cordovan pockets and gloves you writ for, of Francisco Moreno's perfuming. So, my dear Captain, live long, and love his

J. H.

MATTHEW HOPKINS (d. 1647)

A thriving trade was driven by this man in the detection of witches; indeed little is known of him except in this capacity. "Witch-finder General" he careered throughout East Anglia, riding from village to village and charging 20s. per witch. Poor old women were ducked, burnt and otherwise ill-treated, until eventually someone suggested submitting him to his favourite experiment of "swimming" suspects. Whereupon he was found guilty, and hanged accordingly, or as "Hudibras" has it:

> . . . *proved himself at length a witch*
> *And made a rod for his own breech.*

This letter to the local magnate of Houghton in Huntingdonshire, whose clergyman had spoken against him, is included as a literary curiosity.

My service to your worship presented.—I have this day received a letter to come to a town called Great Houghton to search for evil-disposed persons called witches (though I hear your minister is far against us, through ignorance). I intend to come, God willing, the sooner to hear his singular judgment in the behalf of such parties. I have known a minister in Suffolk as much against this discovery in a pulpit, and forced to recant it by the Committee [of Parliament] in the same place. I much marvel such evil men should have any (much more any of the clergy, who should daily speak terror to convince such offenders) stand up to take their parts against such as are complainants for the king, and sufferers themselves, with their families and estates. I intend to give your town a visit suddenly. I will come to Kimbolton this week, and it will be ten to one but I will come to your town first; but I would certainly know before whether your town affords many sticklers for such cattle, or is willing to give and allow us good welcome and entertainment, as others where I have been, else I shall waive your shire (not as yet beginning in any part of it myself), and betake me to such places where I do and may punish (not only) without control, but with thanks and recompense. So I humbly take my leave, and rest your servant to be commanded.

MATTHEW HOPKINS

HARRY LEIGHTON (*fl.* 1645)

Nothing is known of this worthy, except that he wrote various letters to Mr. Speaker Lenthall from the army. In this letter he tells the story of Naseby Fight.

TO WILLIAM LENTHALL

HONOURABLE SIR, This morning by daybreak we marched out of Guilsbourn after the enemy. After an hour's march we discovered their horse drawn up at Sibbertoft, three miles this side of Harborough. An hour after, their foot appeared. This was about eight in the morning. By ten we were disposed into a battalia on both sides. Both sides with mighty shouts expressed a hearty desire for fighting. Having for our parts recommended our cause to God's protection, and received the word, which was "God our Strength"—theirs "Queen Mary"—our forlorn hopes began. Both sides laboured for the hill and wind which, in conclusion was, as it were, equally divided. Our forlorn hope gave back, and their right wing of horse fell upon our left with such gallantry that ours were immediately routed. Above a thousand ran along with them. But such was the courage and diligence of the right wing backed by the foot, that they not only beat back the enemy from the train, but fell in with their foot; and after two hours' dispute won all their field-pieces (of which some are cannon) most of their baggage, mortar-pieces, boats, three thousand arms, much powder, match, etc., and nigh on four thousand prisoners. Their number was about twelve thousand. Some six hundred slain. Many commanders of note. The others not above a hundred. Our horses are still in pursuit and have taken many of theirs. The standard is ours; the king's wagon; and many ladies. God Almighty give us thankful hearts for this great victory, the most absolute as yet obtained. Lieutenant-General Cromwell and Major-General Skippon (who is shot in the side, but not dangerous) did beyond expression gallantly. So did all our other commanders and soldiers. We have lost but two captains. Though this come late, be pleased to accept it from

Your honour's most humble servant

HAR. LEIGHTON

NAZEBY, where the fight was this Saturday,
1 JUNE, 1645

Capt. Potter is dangerously wounded, but hopes of his recovery. So is Capt. Cook.

S. MEWCE (*fl.* 1653)

*This man was the London agent to the Royalist family of Hatton,
to whom he wrote the following account of the dissolution of the Rump
Parliament.*

TO LADY HATTON

21ST APRIL, 1653

MADAME, The long-sitting parliament was dissolved in a trice, without noise. The General and Harison came into the House, where, when he was set down and put on his hat, he made a sharp speech, and in particular reproached the Speaker, the Commissioner Whitlock, Sir Henry Vane, Col. Algernon Sydney, and some other members, and then commanded that bauble the mace to be taken away; which done, he commanded those prime men whom he had forementioned to go forth; which not readily obeying, he commanded Harison to call up the soldiers, who soon put out those that seemed unwilling; and the rest easily obeyed and all departed, and the doors are locked up after them. It is said that the Speaker is committed, and your Ladyship's acquaintance, Alderman Allon, and divers others secured. We must now every day look for new things. God knows what will follow, but generally this change is not unwelcome to the people.

Your Ladyship's friends here present their respects to you.

I am, Madame, Your Ladyship's humble servant,

S. MEWCE

OLIVER CROMWELL (1599–1658)

Few men are exhibited so clearly in their letters as Oliver Cromwell. Whether in the hour of victory, or writing to condole with a bereaved father, or scribbling a note to a loved daughter, the nature of the man shines out like a beacon. What need to say more?

TO SIR WILLIAM SPRING AND MAURICE BARROW

CAMBRIDGE, SEPT. 1643

I HAVE been now two days at Cambridge, in expectation to hear the fruit of your endeavours in Suffolk towards the public assistance. Believe it, you will hear of a storm in few days! You have no Infantry at all considerable; hasten your Horses;—a few hours may undo you, neglected.—I beseech you be careful what Captains of Horse you choose, what men be mounted: a few honest men are better than numbers. Some time they must have for exercise. If you choose godly honest men to be Captains of Horse, honest men will follow them; and they will be careful to mount such.

The King is exceeding strong in the West. If you be able to foil a force at the first coming of it, you will have reputation; and that is of great advantage in our affairs. God hath given it to our handful; let us endeavour to keep it. I had rather have a plain russet-coated Captain that knows what he fights for, and loves what he knows, than that which you call "a Gentleman" and is nothing else. I honour a *Gentleman* that is so indeed!—

I understand Mr. Margery hath honest men will follow him: if so, be pleased to make use of him; it much concerns your good to have conscientious men. I understand that there is an Order for me to have 3,000*l.* out of the Association; and Essex hath sent their part, or near it. I assure you we need exceedingly. I hope to find your favour and respect. I protest, if it were for myself, I would not move you. That is all, from

Your faithful servant,
OLIVER CROMWELL

P.S. If you send such men as Essex hath sent, it will be to little

105

purpose. Be pleased to take care of their march; and that such may come along with them as will•be able to bring them to the main Body; and then I doubt not but we shall keep them, and make good use of them.—I beseech you, give countenance to Mr. Margery! Help him in raising his Troop; let him not want your favour in whatsoever is needful for promoting this work;—and *command* your servant. If he can raise the horses from Malignants, let him have your warrant: it will be of special service.

TO VALENTINE WALTON

[LEAGUER BEFORE YORK] 5 JULY, 1644

IT's our duty to sympathize in all mercies; and to praise the Lord together in chastisements or trials, that so we may sorrow together.

Truly England and the Church of God hath had a great favour from the Lord, in this great Victory given unto us, such as the like never was since this War began. It had all the evidences of an absolute Victory obtained by the Lord's blessing upon the Godly Party principally. We never charged but we routed the enemy. The Left Wing, which I commanded, being our own horse, saving a few Scots in our rear, beat all the Prince's horse. God made them as stubble to our swords. We charged their regiments of foot with our horse, and routed all we charged. The particulars I cannot relate now; but I believe, of Twenty-thousand the Prince hath not Four-thousand left. Give glory, all the glory, to God.—

Sir, God hath taken away your eldest Son by a cannon-shot. It brake his leg. We were necessitated to have it cut off, whereof he died.

Sir, you know my own trials this way: but the Lord supported me with this, That the Lord took him into the happiness we all pant for and live for. There is your precious child full of glory, never to know sin or sorrow any more. He was a gallant young man, exceedingly gracious. God give you His comfort. Before his death he was so full of comfort that to Frank Russel and myself he could not express it, "It was so great above his pain." This he said to us. Indeed it was admirable. A little after, he said, One thing lay upon his spirit. I asked him, What that was? He told me it was, That God had not suffered him to be any more the executioner of His enemies. At his fall, his horse being killed with the bullet, and as I am informed three horses more, I am told he bid them, Open to the right and left, that he might see the rogues run.   Truly he was exceedingly beloved in the Army, of all that knew him.   But few knew him; for he was a precious young man, fit for God.   You have cause to bless the Lord. He is a glorious Saint in Heaven; wherein you ought exceedingly to rejoice.   Let this drink up your sorrow; seeing these are not feigned words to comfort you, but the thing is so real and undoubted a truth. You may do all things by the strength of Christ.   Seek that, and you shall easily bear your trial.   Let this public mercy to the Church of God make you to forget your private sorrow.   The Lord be your strength: so prays

Your truly faithful and loving brother

My love to your Daughter, and my Cousin Perceval, Sister Desborow and all friends with you.

TO HIS DAUGHTER, BRIDGET IRETON

London, 25th October, 1646

Dear Daughter, I write not to thy Husband; partly to avoid trouble, for one line of mine begets many of his, which I doubt makes him sit up too late; partly because I am myself indisposed [disinclined] at this time, having some other considerations.

Your Friends at Ely are well: your Sister Claypole is, I trust in mercy, exercised with some perplexed thoughts.   She sees her own vanity and carnal mind; bewailing it: she seeks after (as I hope also) what will satisfy.   And thus to be a seeker is to be of the best sect next to a finder; and such an one shall every faithful humble seeker be at the end.   Happy seeker, happy finder!   Who ever tasted that the Lord is gracious, without some sense of self, vanity, and badness? Who ever tasted that graciousness of His, and could go less in desire, —less than pressing after full enjoyment?   Dear Heart, press on; let not Husband, let not anything cool thy affections after Christ.   I hope he [thy husband] will be an occasion to inflame them.   That which is best worthy of love in thy Husband is that of the image of Christ he bears.   Look on that, and love it best, and all the rest for that.   I pray for thee and him; do so for me.

My service and dear affections to the General and Generaless. I hear she is very kind to thee; it adds to all other obligations.   I am, thy dear Father.

Oliver Cromwell

TO RICHARD MAYOR

ALNWICK, 17 JULY, 1650

THE exceeding crowd of business I had at London is the best excuse
I can make for my silence this way. Indeed, Sir, my heart beareth
me witness I want no affection to you or yours; you are all often in
my poor prayers.

I should be glad to hear how the little Brat doth. I could chide
both Father and Mother for their neglects of me: I know my Son
is idle, but I had better thoughts of Doll. I doubt now her Husband
hath spoiled her; pray tell her so from me. If I had as good leisure
as they, I should write sometimes. If my Daughter be breeding,
I will excuse her; but not for her nursery! The Lord bless them.
I hope you give my Son good counsel; I believe he needs it. He
is in the dangerous time of his age; and it's a very vain world. O,
how good it is to close with Christ betimes;—there is nothing else
worth the looking after. I beseech you call upon him,—I hope you
will discharge my duty and your own love: you see how I am employed.
I need pity. I know what I feel. Great place and business in the world
is not worth the looking after; I should have no comfort in mine but
that my hope is in the Lord's presence. I have not sought these
things; truly I have been called unto them by the Lord; and therefore
am not without some assurance that He will enable His poor worm
and weak servant to do His will, and to fulfil my generation. In this
I desire your prayers. Desiring to be lovingly remembered to my
dear Sister, to our Son and Daughter, to my Cousin Ann and the good
Family, I rest,

Your very affectionate brother

SAMUEL RUTHERFORD (1599–1661)

No letter in this book shows out so vividly the mind of the rigid old Scottish Presbyterians as this epistle from old Samuel Rutherford. His severe Calvinism lost him his living for some years, even in Calvinist Scotland; yet the affectionate and sympathetic nature of the man breathes in every line of this letter.

TO THE ELECT AND NOBLE LADY, MY LADY KENMURE

ANWOTH, JANUARY 15, 1629

MADAM, Saluting your ladyship with grace and mercy from God our Father, and from our Lord Jesus Christ. I was sorry, at my departure, leaving your ladyship in grief, and would still be grieved at it if I were not assured that you have One with you in the furnace, whose visage is like unto the Son of God.

I am glad that you have been acquainted, from your youth, with the wrestlings of God, being cast from furnace to furnace; knowing, if you were not dear to God, and if your health did not require so much of Him, He would not spend so much physic upon you. All the brethren and sisters of Christ must be conformed to His image in suffering (Rom. viii. 17), and some do more fully resemble the copy than others.

Think, madam, that it is a part of your glory to be enrolled among those whom one of the elders (Rev. vii. 14) pointeth out to John: "These are they which came out of great tribulation, and have washed their robes, and made them white in the blood of the Lamb." Behold your Forerunner going out of the world, all in a lake of blood; and it is not ill to die as He did. Fulfil, with joy, the remainders of the afflictions of Christ in your body.

You have lost a child; nay, she is not lost to you who is found to Christ; she is not sent away but only sent before, like unto a star which, going out of our sight, doth not die and vanish but shineth in another hemisphere. You see her not, yet she doth shine in another country. If her glass was but a short hour, what she wanteth of time, that she

109

hath gotten of eternity; and you have to rejoice that you have now some treasure laid up in heaven.

Build your nest upon no tree here; for you see God hath sold the forest to death; and every tree whereupon we would rest is ready to be cut down, to the end we may flee and mount up and build upon the rock, and dwell in the holes of the rock. What you love besides Jesus, your husband, is an adulterous lover. Now, it is God's special blessing to Judah that he will not let her find her paths in following her strange lovers (Hos. ii. 6), "Therefore, behold, I will hedge up thy way with thorns, and make a wall that she shall not find her paths" (ver. 7). "And she shall follow after her lovers, but she shall not overtake them." O, thrice happy Judah, when God buildeth a stone wall betwixt her and the fire of hell! The world and the things of the world, madam, are the lovers you naturally affect, beside your own husband Christ. The hedge of thorns, and the wall which God buildeth in your way to hinder you from these lovers, are the thorny hedge of daily grief, loss of children, weakness of body, iniquity of the times, uncertainty of estate, lack of worldly comfort, fear of God's anger for old unrepented-of sins. What lose you, if God twist and plait the hedge daily thicker? God be blessed, the Lord will not let you find your paths. Return to your first Husband; do not weary, neither think that death walketh towards you with a slow pace; you must be riper ere you be shaken; your days are no longer than Job's, that were "swifter than a post, and passed away as the ships of desire, and as the eagle that hasteth for the prey" (Job ix. 25, 26). There is less sand in your glass than there was yesternight; this span-length of ever-posting time will soon be ended. But the greater the mercy of God the more years you get to advise upon what terms and upon what conditions you cast your soul into the huge gulf of never-ending eternity.

The Lord hath told you what you should be doing till He come; wait and hasten, saith Peter, "for the coming of our Lord." All is night that is here, in respect of ignorance and daily ensuing troubles, one always making way to another, as the ninth wave of the sea to the tenth; therefore sigh and long for the dawning of that morning, and the breaking of that day of the coming of the Son of man, when the shadows shall flee away. Persuade yourself the King is coming; read his letter sent before him (Rev. iii. 11): "Behold I come quickly." Wait with the wearied night-watch for the breaking of the eastern sky, and think that you have not a morrow; as the wise father said,

TO MY LADY KENMURE

who, being invited against to-morrow to dine with his friends, answered,
For these many days I have had no morrow at all.

I am loth to weary you; show yourself a Christian by suffering
without murmuring, for which sin fourteen thousand and seven hundred were slain (Numb. xvi. 49). In patience possess your soul; they
lose nothing who gain Christ. I commend you to the mercy and
grace of our Lord Jesus, assuring you that your day is coming, and
that God's mercy is abiding you. The Lord Jesus be with your spirit.

CHARLES I (1600–49)

In April, 1646, Charles was obliged to leave Oxford, where the Parliament's army was pressing him hard, and repair northwards. He reached Newcastle, guarded by the Scottish army, on May 13, and found himself baited to take the Covenant, and wrote this letter to his wife.

TO HIS QUEEN

NEWCASTLE, 10 JUNE, 1646

THESE two last weeks I heard not from thee, nor any about thee, which hath made my present condition the more troublesome, but I expect daily the contentment of hearing from thee. Indeed I have need of some comfort, for I never knew what it was to be barbarously baited before, and these five or six days last have much surpassed, in rude pressures against my conscience, all the rest since I came to the Scotch army; for, upon I know not what intelligence from London, nothing must serve but my signing the covenant (the last was, my commanding all my subjects to do it), declaring absolutely, and without reserve, for Presbyterian government, and my receiving the Directory in my family, with an absolute command for the rest of the kingdom; and if I did not all this, then a present agreement must be made with the parliament, without regard of me, for they said that otherways they could not hope for peace or a just war. It is true they gave me many other fair promises in case I did what they desired (and yet for the militia they daily give ground); but I answered them, that what they demanded was absolutely against my conscience, which might be persuaded, but would not be forced by anything they could speak or do. This was the sum of divers debates and papers between us, of which I cannot now give thee an account. At least [last?] I made them be content with another message to London, requiring an answer to my former, with an offer to go thither upon honourable and just conditions. Thus all I can do is but delaying of ill, which I shall not be able to do long without assistance from thee. I cannot but again remember thee, that there was never man so alone as I, and therefore very much to be excused for the committing of any error, because I have reason to suspect everything that these advised me, and to distrust mine own single opinion, having no living soul to help me. To conclude, all the comfort I have is in thy love and a clear conscience. I know the first will not fail me, nor (by the grace of God) the other. Only I desire thy particular help, that I should be as little vexed as may be; for, if thou do not, I care not much for others. I need say no more of this, nor will at this time, but that I am eternally thine.

JOHN ELIOT (1604–90)

John Eliot was an apostle to the Indians of Massachusetts, and recently came into notice once more when his translation of Baxter's "Call to the Unconverted" was sold for £6,800. It was a grubby little book, but no other copy is known to exist. Eliot passed sixty years of his life as a pastor and missionary at Roxbury, New England. His Indian edition of the Bible was published in 1685. It was Eliot's enthusiasm that forced the Long Parliament, in 1649, to set up a corporation for prompting and propagating the Gospel in New England. Boyle was governor of this corporation.

TO THE HON. ROBERT BOYLE

[ROXBURY, OCTOBER 17, 1675]

RIGHT HONOURABLE, I must change my ditty now. I have much to write of lamentation over the work of Christ among our praying Indians, of which God hath called you to be nursing-fathers. The work in our Patent is under great sufferings; it is killed in words, wishes and expression but not in deeds as yet. It is, as it were dead, but not buried, nor, I believe, shall be. It is made conformable to Christ in some poor measure in dying, but I believe it shall rise again. We needed, through our corruptions and infirmities, all that is come upon us and when the Lord hath performed all his work, his purging work, upon us, he can easily—and will—lay by the rod. When the house is swept he will lay away the broom. My care and labour is to exhort them to humiliation and repentance; to be patient is meet in the sight both of God and men. I complain not of our sufferings, but meekly praise the Lord, that they be no worse. Yet I cannot but say they are greater than I can, or in modesty and meekness is fit for me to, express. Be it so, it is the Lord that hath done it, and shall living man complain? It is the appointed way of God, that through many tribulations we must enter into the heavenly Kingdom. A tried faith and a tried patience are precious in the sight of God.

114

There be 350 souls or thereabout, put upon a bleak bare island, the fittest we have, where they suffer hunger and cold. There is neither food nor competent fuel to be had, and they are bare in clothing, because they cannot be induced to work for clothing, as they were wont to do. Our Rulers are careful to order them food, but it is so hard to be performed that they suffer much. I beg your prayers, that the Lord would take care of them and provide for them. I cannot without difficulty, hardship, and peril, get unto them. I have been but twice with them; yet I praise God that they be put out of the way of greater perils and dangers and temptations. Capt. Gookins and I did this week visit another company (where be 59 souls) at Concord, whom we have ordered in as much safety as the difficulty of the times would permit us; and so we commit them to God, begging his protection over them. From there we went to Pentucket, to visit the poor Wameset Indians, who in a fright fled into the woods until they were half starved. The occasion of their flight was because some ungodly and unruly youth came upon them where they were ordered by Authority to be, called them forth from their houses, shot at them, killed a child of Godly parents, wounded his mother and four more. The woman lifted up her hands to heaven and said, "Lord, thou seest that we have neither done or said anything against the English that they thus deal with us" (or words to this effect). They are come back again, there be more than a hundred souls of them. We have advanced to quiet and settle matters there also, so well as we could, and so commit them to God's protection.

At another place there were a company making ready to go to the island but were surprised by the Enemy, and carried away captive, and we cannot hear anything of them. What is become of them, whether any of them be martyred, we cannot tell. We cannot say how many there be of them, but more than an hundred, and sundry of them right Godly, both men and women. Another great company of our new praying Indians of the Niepmuk fled at the beginning of the Wars, first to Connecticott, and offered themselves to Mr. Pinchon, one of our magistrates; but he (though willing) could not receive them. They fled from thence to Unkas (who is not in hostility against the English) and I hope they be there. This is the present state of the most of our praying Indians in our Jurisdiction. All in Plymouth Patent are still in quiet, and so are all our Vineyard Indians, and all the Nantuket Indians. I beg prayers that they may be still preserved. I shall give your honour no further trouble at present. I beseech you let it be acceptable to you, that I meddle not with anything else saving the present condition of your alumni. So commending your honour to the Lord, I rest.

Your honour's to serve you
in our Lord Jesus,
JOHN ELIOT

WILLIAM DENTON (1605–91)

This vigorous physician was appointed doctor to Charles I and attended him in his visit to Scotland. It is from there that he wrote to Ralph Verney, whose father was in arms for the king, as told on p. 89.

TO RALPH VERNEY

NEWCASTLE, 16TH [MAY], 1639

RALPH, I received your letter with news of my book. I shall defer my thanks for them until you send me a pair of barbing scissors, here being none that are either to be bought or set. Your father is yet well in body, and at a good distance from the borders. The king goeth towards Berwick on Thursday next, and intends to entrench himself within 5 or 6 miles of it, but on this side Tweed, and, so long as he keeps there, I presume we shall be in safety. I hope that the king doth not intend to fight this summer, but thinks, by drawing his forces so near them to tempt them to bring out their forces in a body, and by that means to exhaust them; but I fear he will be cozened, for I believe that they be as cunning as they be wicked. The news of their being 12,000 in a body within four miles of Berwick is false. This is the best cordial that I can send you at this distance. Be confident that I will leave no stone unmoved that I conceive may knock your father's fighting designs on the head, and preserve him. If I can but keep him from going out in parties I hope he will return with safety. I shall be very sensible of the least hazard that I shall think he may be in, and if all the wit and power I have or can make may prevent it, it shall be no fault of your assured loving uncle,

W. DENTON

JOHN MILTON (1608–74)

The author of "Paradise Lost" was one of the very greatest of English poets and a writer of magnificent prose. After some years of travel and study, he returned to England to identify himself with the Parliamentary cause, and it was not till after the Restoration that, a blind, ageing, and lonely man, he wrote his greatest works. Charles Diodati, his closest friend, died while Milton was abroad, and his loss is commemorated in the "Epitaphium Damonis."

TO CHARLES DIODATI

LONDON, SEPTEMBER 2, 1637

Now at length I see plainly that what you are driving at is to vanquish me sometimes in the art of obstinate silence; and, if it is so, bravo! have that little glory over us, for behold! we write first. All the same, if ever the question should come into contention why neither has written to the other *for so long*, do not think but that I shall stand by many degrees the more excused of the two,—*manifestly so indeed, as being one by nature slow and lazy to write*, as you well know; while you, on the other hand, whether by nature or by habit, are wont without difficulty to be drawn into epistolary correspondence of this sort. It makes also for my favour that I know your method of studying to be so arranged that you frequently take breath in the middle, visit your friends, write much, sometimes make a journey, whereas my genius is such that no delay, no rest, no care or thought almost of anything, holds me aside until I reach the end I am making for, and round off, as it were, some great period of my studies. Wholly hence, and not from any other cause, believe me, has it happened that I am slower in approaching the voluntary discharge of good offices; but in replying to such, O our *Theodotus*, I am not so very dilatory; nor have I ever been guilty of not meeting any letter of yours by one of mine in due turn. How happens it that, as I hear, you have sent letters to the bookseller, to your brother too not unfrequently, either of whom could, conveniently enough, on account of their nearness, have caused letters to have been delivered to me, if there had been any? What I complain

118

of, however, is that, whereas you promised that you would take up
your quarters with us for a passing visit on your departure from the
city, you did not keep your promise, and that, if you had but once
thought of this neglect of your promise, there would not have been
wanting necessary occasion enough for writing. All this matter of
deserved lecture, as I imagine, I have been keeping against you. What
you will prepare in answer see for your self. But, meanwhile, how is
it with you, pray? Are you all right in health? Are there in those
parts any smallish learned folk with whom you can willingly associate
and chat, as we were wont together? When do you return? How
long do you intend to remain among those *hyperboreans*? Please to
answer me these questions one by one: not that you are to make the
mistake of supposing that only now have I your affairs at heart,—for
understand that, in the beginning of the autumn, I turned out of my
way on a journey to see your brother for the purpose of knowing what
you were doing. Lately, also, when it had been fallaciously reported
to me in London by some one that you were in town, straightway and
as if by storm I dashed to your crib; but *'twas the vision of a shadow!*
for nowhere did you appear. Wherefore, if you can without inconvenience, fly hither all the sooner, and fix yourself in some place so
situated and I may have a more pleasant hope that somehow or other
we may be able at least sometimes to exchange visits,—though I would
you were as much our neighbour in the country as you are when in
town. *But this as it pleases God!* I would say more about myself
and my studies, but would rather do so when we meet; and now to-
morrow we are to return to that country-residence of ours, and the
journey so presses that I have hardly had time to put all this on the
paper. Farewell.

HENRIETTA MARIA (1609-69)

On January 10, 1642, Charles left Whitehall, never to return until that fatal day seven years later. On August 22 he raised his standard at Nottingham, and a week later his queen wrote him the letter that follows. Daughter of the king of France and herself a woman of strong feelings, she was her husband's able lieutenant and constant counsellor during the fateful days that were to follow.

TO HER HUSBAND

31 AUG. 1642

I HAD sent off a person to come to you, but the wind has not permitted. I am in extreme anxiety, hearing no tidings from you, and those from London are not advantageous to you. Perhaps by this they think to frighten me into an accommodation; but they are deceived. I never in my life did anything from fear, and I hope I shall not begin by the loss of a crown; as to you, you know well that there have been persons who have said that you were of that temper; if that be true, I have never recognized it in you, but I still hope, even if it has been true, that you will show the contrary, and that no fear will make you submit to your own ruin and that of your posterity. For my own part, I do not see the wisdom of these Messieurs rebels, in being able to imagine that they will make you come by force to their object, and to an accommodation; for as long as you are in the world, assuredly England can have no rest nor peace, unless you consent to it, and assuredly that cannot be unless you are restored to your just prerogatives: and if even in the beginning you should meet with misfortunes, you will still have friends enough who will assist you to replace yourself. I have never yet seen nor read an example which can make me doubt of it by any means. Resolution and constancy are two things very necessary to it, assisted by the justice of our cause. Neither God nor men of honour will abandon you, provided you do not abandon yourself.

You see that I do not even fear lest this should be opened. I will venture to say that although it be not thought good, it will not be printed; that would be just the contrary of what is now done, for what they find just and good they hide, and what is thought bad is printed. That shows that JUSTICE suffers with us. Always take care that we have her on our side: she is a good army, and one which will at last conquer all the world, and which has no fear. Although perhaps for a time she hide herself, it is only to strengthen herself to return with greater force. She is with you, and therefore you should not fear: you will both come out together, and will appear more glorious than ever. I am very sure of it. See the effects of a melancholy solitude, but not at all of vexation, for, when I reflect well on all these things that I have been writing to you, I find myself so satisfied that no ill-humour can have any power over me, not even the ordinances of Parliament, which are the effects of one of the worst humours in the world. Considering the style of this letter, if I knew any Latin, I ought to finish with a word of it; but as I do not, I will finish with a French one, which may be translated into all sorts of languages, that I am yours after death, if it be possible.

THE GAWDY LETTERS

The Gawdy family, settled for generations in West Harling, was one of the most considerable county families in Norfolk. In the early part of the seventeenth century Framlingham Gawdy was a prosperous land owner; sending no less that six of his sons to Cambridge. Each in turn sent home for money, clothes and so forth, and the two following letters from William and Bassingbourne Gawdy are fair examples of how a young man wrote to his father in the days of Charles I.

WILLIAM GAWDY TO HIS FATHER

GON. CAI. COL.
6 OF JULY 1621

DEAR FATHER, we did expect you here at Cambridge at your going to London. I was chosen by the proctors to be senior brother in the Commencement house this year, which is a place of great credit, but withall very chargeable; for I should have given the proctors each of them a satin doublet and should have invited all the doctors and chief men in the town to supper. My tutor took some time to consider of it, hoping you would have come this way, but you coming not I was constrained to refuse it. I desire you (if you buy a new hat before Easter) to bring down mine ready trimmed with you, for my old one begins to grow unfitting for a gentleman to wear, and I am loth to buy me a new one, because it will not be long ere I shall have that. I pray let it be new shagged though it be somewhat the thinner and (if it be possible) let it be made less in the head, and let the brims be cut somewhat narrower, as the fashion is. And I pray let me have a silver girdle of the best sort, and let Frank Gaudy bring it with him when you come into the country at Easter, and I will pay you for it again. I pray you let me receive your letter the next week by the Cambridge carrier. So with my duty remembered unto you, craving your blessing, and hoping to meet you at Harling a fortnight before Easter I rest

Yours dutiful son
WILLIAM GAWDY

WILLIAM GAWDY TO HIS MOTHER

DEAR MOTHER, in the last letter which I received from you by the carrier you promised me that you would send me the cakes and cheeses. I therefore hope to receive them from you upon Saturday, by this carrier, who is a very honest fellow, and hath promised me to call in our house always when he cometh into Norfolk, which is once a fortnight, and will bring up letter or anything for me which you will send. I would entreat you to make me some boothose tops and send me against Easter. So with my humble duty remembered unto you and my good father, and expecting you answer,

I rest your dutyful and obedient son

WILLIAM GAUDY

BASSINGBOURNE GAWDY TO HIS FATHER

SIR, I received your letter by Tho. Ship, and the other papers, and amongst them my Tutor's last bill, which truly at the first sight did amaze me as well as yourself. But after that I considered everything I began to fear that it was right, for this bill is an half-year bill, that which was behindhand was the bill from Midsummer to Michaelmas. He hath had but £7 for all this half year. My Tutor hath sent you the bill at large in his letter. The day after I came to town (Cambridge) I and Mr. Anderson, who presents his services to you, and Tho. Ship went to buy my gown, which comes to £7 12s. 6d., and the making 15s. I have paid it. Sir you wrote to me to forbear silver buttons, but both my Tutor and Mr. Anderson did persuade me to it: it did cost but 20s. the more: if you think it too much I will abate it in my allowance. I have sent you my hatcase, that you may send up my new hat: I have very much need of it. If you stand in need of money for the present I can stay for it this month. I pray send me word how my Grandfather doth. So I rest

Your most obedient son

BASS. GAUDY

JEREMY TAYLOR (1613–67)

Taylor was rector of Uppingham when the Civil War broke out, and as he gave the King his loyalty, he lost his living. After the Restoration he was given an Irish bishopric, but during the dark days— when this letter was written—he earned a livelihood by teaching.

PORTMORE, JUNE 4, 1659

HONOURED SIR, I have reason to take a great pleasure that you are pleased so perfectly to retain me in your memory and affections, as if I were still near you, a partner of your converse, or could possibly oblige you. But I shall attribute this so wholly to your goodness, your piety, and candour, that I am sure nothing on my part can incite or continue the least part of those civilities and endearments by which you have often and still continue to oblige me. Sir, I received your two little books, and am very much pleased with the golden book of St. Crysostom, on which your epistle hath put a black enamel and made a pretty monument for your dearest strangest miracle of a boy. And when I read it I could not choose but observe St. Paul's rule, *flebam cum flentibus.* I paid a tear at the hearse of that sweet child. Your other little Enchiridion is an emanation of an ingenious spirit; and there are in it observations the like of which are seldom made by young travellers; and though, by the publication of these, you have been civil and courteous to the commonwealth of learning, yet I hope you will proceed to oblige us in some greater instances of your own.

I am much pleased with your way of translation; and if you would proceed in the same method and give us, in English, some devout pieces of the father, and your own annotations upon them, you would do profit and pleasure to the public. But, Sir, I cannot easily consent that you should lay aside your "Lucretius," and having been requited yourself by your labour, I cannot perceive why you should not give us the same recreation, since it will be greater to us than it could be to you, to whom it was allayed by your great labour: especially you having given us so large an essay of your ability to do it; and the world having given you an essay of their acceptation of it.

124

Sir, that Pallavicini whom you mention is the author of the late "History of the Council of Trent," in two volumes in folio, in Italian. I have seen it, but had not leisure to peruse it so much as to give any judgment of the man by it. Besides this, he hath published two little manuals in 12mo. "Assertionum Theologicarum;" but these speak but very little of the man. His history, indeed, is a great undertaking, and his family (for he is of the Jesuit order) use to sell the book by crying up the man: but I think I saw enough of it to suspect the expectation is much bigger than the thing.

It is no wonder that Baxter undervalues the gentry of England. You know what spirit he is of, but I suppose he hath met with his match: for Mr. Piers hath attacked him: and they are joined in the lists. I have not seen Mr. Thorndike's book. You make me desirous of it, because you call it elaborate; but I like not the title nor the subject, and the man is indeed a very good and a learned man, but I have not seen much prosperity in his writings. But if he have so well chosen the questions, there is no peradventure but he hath tumbled into his heap many choice materials. I am much pleased that you promise to inquire into the way of the Perfectionists; but I think L. Pembroke and Mrs. Joy, and the Lady Wildgoose are none of that number. I assure you, some very learned and very sober persons have given up their names to it. Castellio is their great patriarch; and his Dialogue, "An per Spir. 'S. Homo possit perfectè obedire Legi Dei;" is their first essay. Parker hath written something lately of it, and in Dr. Gell's last book in folio there is much of it. Indeed, you say right that they take in Jacob Behmen, but that is upon another account, and they understand him as nurses do their children's imperfect language; something by use, and much by fancy.

I hope, Sir, in your next to me (for I flatter myself to have the happiness of receiving a letter from you sometimes), you will account to me of some hopes concerning some settlement or some peace to religion. I fear my peace in Ireland is likely to be short; for a Presbyterian and a madman have informed against me as a dangerous man to their religion; and for using the sign of the cross in baptism. The worst event of the information which I fear is my return into England; which, although I am not desirous it should be upon these terms, yet if it be without much violence, I shall not be much troubled.

Sir, I do account myself extremely obliged to your kindness and charity in your continued care of me and bounty to me. It is so much the more, because I have almost from all men but yourself, suffered some diminution of their kindness, by reason of my absence; for, as the Spaniard says, "The dead and the absent have but a few friends." But, Sir, I account myself infinitely obliged to you; much for your pension, but exceedingly much more for your affection, which you have so signally expressed. I pray, Sir, be pleased to present my humble service to your two honoured brothers; I shall be ashamed to make any address, or pay my thanks in words to them till my " Rule of Conscience" be public, and that is all the way I have to pay my debts; that and my prayers that God would. Sir, Mr. Martin, bookseller at the Bell in St. Paul's Church-yard, is my correspondent in London, and whatsoever he receives he transmits it to me carefully; and so will Mr. Royston, though I do not often employ him now. Sir, I fear I have tired you with an impertinent letter, but I have felt your charity to be so great as to do much more than to pardon the excess of my affections. Sir, I hope that you and I remember one another when we are upon our knees. I do not think of coming to London till the latter end of summer or the spring, if I can enjoy my quietness here; but then I do if God permit: but beg to be in this interval refreshed by a letter from you at your leisure, for, indeed, in it will be a great pleasure and endearment to,

Honoured Sir,
Your very obliged, most affectionate and humble Servant,
JER. TAYLOR

PHILIP, LORD WHARTON (1613–96)

One of the handsomest men of his time and the greatest beau about Court, to everyone's surprise Wharton turned Puritan and threw himself heart and soul into the Cause. He was an old man when he wrote this letter, but the zeal still burns bright.

TO RALPH THORESBY

WOBURN, OCTOBER 5, 1691

MR. THORESBY, There are eighty Bibles and Catechisms, which will be with you suddenly. I desire you (with the help of such friends as you think fit) to get the names of such children as you think most proper to deliver them to.

There are also with the said Bibles and Catechisms, eight of Lye's Catechisms, and eight of Allein's "Sure Guide to Heaven," which are to be delivered to one of each ten children who had books last year and who have made best proficiency in the repeating the Catechisms and Psalms appointed, together with 12d in money or coals for the parents or guardian of each such child. There is also a small encouragement allowed to each person who examines the said children, as to their said proficiency (that is to say) 2s. 6d. to each person who examines ten children. There being several books to be given out and in several places, this method of half-a-crown to each person who examines ten children is pitched upon, that those who are entrusted in this matter may with the more ease know what they are to expend.

If your health and business will give you leave to examine the said children herein, I would rather you did it than any else; but if otherwise, I shall refer it to you to examine so many tens as you think fit, and to name whom you please to examine the rest.

You are desired to preach a sermon at Leeds this year at the delivering out of the said books, and I desire there may be no mention of me, only I entreat you that then, and at other times, you remember me and mine in your prayers; the purport of the sermon in the next side is enclosed. I shall be willing to know, so soon as conveniently may be, if there will be a prospect whether probably there may be eighty children at Leeds, fit objects of charity, to deliver other eighty Bibles unto next year, that the books may be accordingly provided and sent thither, and if not that what shall not be sent thither may be delivered at some other place.

Mr. William Mortimer, of Helaugh, shall have order to deliver you 10s. for the sermon you preach this year, and 8s. for the parents of those children who have made best proficiency in repeating their Catechism and Psalms appointed, and 20s. for yourself, or such else as examined the said children as to their said proficiency, viz. 2s. 6d. for each ten children you or any else did examine: as also what the carriage of the box, with the said Bibles, &c. shall come to.

There should be notice given when you deliver out the Bibles, that there shall be the like encouragement next year to eight, who shall have made best proficiency, and that all the children be careful to keep their books, and not carelessly spoil them, and have them forthcoming next October. It is supposed the carrier was spoken to, to bring up the empty box gratis; and therefore you will do well to cause the same to be delivered to him, directed thus:

For Mr. John Clarke,
In Purse Court, in Paul's Chain, in Cheapside.

I desire your prayers for me and mine,

Your very loving friend,

P. Wharton

ABRAHAM COWLEY (1618–67)

One of the poetic lights of Stuart times, Cowley was a zealous Royalist and followed the widowed Queen Henrietta Maria to exile in Paris. It is from there that he wrote this letter, showing the plots and schemes with which the exiles occupied their time.

TO HENRY BENNET (LATER EARL OF ARLINGTON)

PARIS, NOVEMB. 18, 1650

SIR, It is not easy to give you an intelligible account of the business of Scotland, though we have much in the prints of it, and Sir Edward Walker with some others be newly arrived from thence in Holland. Things very strange and remarkable have happened within these two months, but what will be the issue of them is yet very doubtful, though they look as if they meant to do us good. About the beginning of October a great number of lords and gentlemen (both of the King's old party, and of the Engagers) weary of the oppression of the prevailing faction, and seeing the folly and blindness of it to the point of opposing the common enemy, resolved to take arms, and handled the matter so as that the King promised to come to them himself, for which a day of rendezvous was appointed. But the King, the night before communicating the counsel to some of his English company (my Lord Duke of Buckingham and Lord Wilmot are named), they had so little opinion of the solidity of the matter, that they persuaded the King to lay aside the resolution, and to send to the engaged persons not to assemble. At least the King seemed to be persuaded, but several of the Engagers met, and he, three days after, with very few in his company, under a pretext of hawking, was upon his way towards them. But (the thing being discovered too soon, I know not by what means) he was overtaken by a party of horse and beseeched (that is, forced) to return to St. Johnston's, and since to Sterling, which is the

head quarter of the army.   But for all this, whether out of fear of the
violence of the stream the other way, or out of desire to give him better
satisfaction, he found himself better treated than before, sat daily with
them in council (which he never did before) and the 30th of October
was appointed for his coronation.   In the meantime the other party
grew in strength, chose Middleton their General, and became a body
of about 5000 men.   To them was Sir John Brown sent with a party
of two regiments of horse to offer them an Act of Indemnity, and in
case of refusal, to reduce them by force.   He sent this message to them,
and added, that if they returned a dilatory answer, he would hang up
their messenger.   Their answer was very quick, for they fell presently
upon him, and took, slew, and dispersed the whole party.   This brought
down the pride of the violent faction to a treaty with them, and hostages
were given on both sides.   The treaty was but begun when Sir Edward
Walker came away, but it was generally believed that the issue of it
would be the union of all parties, and admission of all persons into the
service.   The lords risen in arms were Murray, Huntly, Earl of
Athol, Marshall, Arrall, Lindsey, Ogleby, Lord Sinclair, Nuburgh,
Plescarty, and many more: Mr. Long, Mr. Progers, Mr. Seymour,
and Dr. Fraser are again banished for having had a hand in this business.
In the mean time we have received a greater blow abroad than anything
at home can recompense, if we were to have never so good news;
that is, in the death of the Prince of Orange, who died last week of
the small-pox after a week's sickness, and was, I think, the most considerable man at this time (as to the consequences of his person) not
only to us, but to all this part of the world, that could have been
taken out of it.   The Princess Royal is in her 8th month, and if it
please God to give her a son [this was eventually William III of
England] it will be some consolation in this great misfortune.   The
D. of York is still at Brussels, in all extremities of want, having been
so far from receiving any support from the Archduke and the Duke
of Lorrain, that he has scarce had the ordinary civilities he might have
expected.   He wrote lately to the Queen to desire that he might by
her means be invited into Holland, but that is dashed by this misfortune,
and the greatest hopes of his subsistence lost by it.   I think he will be
forced to return hither at last, though his council rather design a journey
into Germany, or indeed Japan, or the West Indies.   Sir G. Ratcliff
is the controller of his household, and orders the whole business of two
dishes a meal for the Duke in his chamber.   My Lord gives you many
thanks for your treffles, and Mrs. Gardner for your care of her beauty;

the former I had some part in, the latter I am sure I never shall. This is a cruel long letter to begin our commerce withall, but I will not always be so troublesome,

I am, Sir,
Your most humble, and most faithful servant,
A. COWLEY

JOHN MAIDSTONE (*fl.* 1659)

Among the letters preserved in Thurloe's "State Papers" is the following from Maidstone to John Winthrop, governor of the colony of Connecticut in New England. Who Maidstone was, except that he was a distant relative of Winthrop, it is now difficult to say.

TO JOHN WINTHROP

WESTMINSTER, MARCH 24, 1659

SIR, Your kind remembrance of me in Mr. Hooke's letter covered me with no small shame, that I have neglected a person of so signal worth, as all reports I meet with present you in; especially when it is attended with the consideration of the obligations your father's memory hath left upon me.

Yet may I not be so injurious to myself as to acknowledge, that the long omission of writing to you proceeded from forgetfulness. The frequent discourse I have made of yourself and honoured father have created testimony sufficient to vindicate me from such ingratitude. But the perpetual hurry of distressing affairs, wherein for some years I have been exercised, deprived me of gaining a fit opportunity of conveying letters. And this is briefly and truly the cause of so long an intermission. For me now to present you with a relation of the unheard of dealing of God towards his people in these nations, is not my design; partly because I believe you have heard much of it, but principally because such a work would better become a voluminous chronicle, than a short epistle. For it would weary the wing of an eagle to measure out the ways, wherein God hath walked, with all the turnings and intricacies, that are found in them. The quarrel, at first commenced betwixt King and Parliament, was grounded upon a civil foundation; the King accusing them of invading his prerogative, and the house charging him with the breach of their privileges, and consequently the invassalaging the people represented by them. When this argument had for some time been agitated by as hot and bloody a war as this latter age hath seen, it fell at last to be managed (on the Parliament side) by instruments religiously principled, in whose hand it received so many evident testimonies of God's extraordinary presence and conduct, that in conclusion a period was put to it, the King made a prisoner, and all his expectation of rescue utterly defeated and cut off. While the matter stood in this posture, great debates, solicitous consultations and cabals are held, in order to settlement; for these transactions (according to the constant product of all such things) had created factions and divisions betwixt persons of equal worth in point of parts, and (as themselves thought) of balancing merit, to receive the reward of so great and hazardous an undertaking as they had gone through. The parties instantly divided themselves (or rather did appear divided, for they had been so before) under the heads of presbytery and independency. The former had the advantage in number, the ministry generally adhering to them; the latter in having been the active instrument, by whose valour and conduct the king was brought from a palace to a prison, and thereby were possessed of the military power of the nation; by help whereof, and having many friends in the House of Commons against the mind of the major part, they first secluded them, and then set aside the House of Lords; and by a co-operation with the House of Commons then sitting, (whom they owned as the supreme power of the nation) the king was brought to trial before an High Court of Justice (consisting of Members of Parliament, officers of the Army and others) and proceeded against to execution.

This act was highly displeasing to many, who with equal zeal and forwardness, had assisted in the war. Insomuch that the difference, which the King's party put between them that fought with him, and those that take away his life, they expressed in this proverb; that presbyterians held him by the hair, till independents cut off his head. Yet have the former struggled hard ever since, to do something, that might render them under a better character, as to their covenant and loyalty to the King. The peace of the nation being thus settled, and the King's family and offspring departed into foreign places, his eldest son the Prince of Wales travelled into the Netherlands, where (after some short time) application was made to him by the most serious and prudent party of Scotland (amongst whom I know some to be as choice men, as most I have been acquainted with, for wisdom and true holiness, for so it becomes me to judge) who presented to him the consideration of the stupendous judgments of God upon him and his father's house, and pressed upon him the sense of it, endeavouring to reduce him to Scotland, in order to restore him to his dominions, upon hope that he might be instrumental to honour God, and re-establish public peace. To this he gave very fair returns, and in a short time shipped himself

for Scotland, and arrived there, where he was honourably entertained
by that, which is called the Kirk Party and is indeed the religious party
of that nation: by them he was crowned King of Scotland, and so
brought into a capacity of action.

The Kirk Party had now the command of him and the nation,
but another party had a greater room in his heart, having been constant
to his father, when the other had raised war against him. These
divided under two heads called Resolutioners and Protesters.[1]

The Parliament of England by this time grew awakened, foreseeing that this whole action was calculated to the perfect capacity of
Scotland, imposing a king upon England, of which they were evinced
by more than probable arguments; to obviate which they resolve to
send a potent army under the command of general Cromwell (the Lord
Fairfax refusing that service upon the influence of presbyterians, as
was said) that Scotland might be rendered the seat of war, and so made
less able to annoy England. This accordingly was done, an invasion
made from England, Scotland put into arms to resist it, whereby they
wearied and wasted the English army and forced it (in a miserable
condition) to retreat for England, had they not at Dunbar, out of pure
necessity, enforced an engagement to their own destruction. For the
defeat then given to the Scotch army was as signal as anything in the
whole war. The advantage of number and men fit for fight was very
great; but that, which is most observable, is the quality of the persons:
for presbytery being the golden bal that day, I am credibly informed,
that thousands lost their lives for it (after many meetings, debates and
appeals to God betwixt our English officers and them) of as holy praying
people, as this island or the world affords.

The Lord General Cromwell was a person of too great activity
and sagacity to lose the advantage of such a victory and therefore marched
his army to Edinburgh, and possessed himself of that place, laid seige
to the strong castle in it, and distressed it till it submitted, being so
situated as not to be entered by onslaught, nor undermined, by reason
of the rock on which it is built. There he spent the winter, but was
not idle, for in that time many strong places became subject to him:
by this means the young king had opportunity to fall in with his beloved
party called the Resolutioners. His interest likewise wrought here
in England, carried on by the Presbyterian party; and in this quarrel,

[1] Resolutioners were of the more dissolute sort of people; Protesters a precise
party, called formerly Puritans. At this time they published a remonstrance, and
therefore were indefinitely called Protesters and Remonstrators.

honest Mr. Love, who doubtless was a godly man, though indiscreet, lost his head, and many of his brethren were endangered, being detained prisoners, till General Cromwell came home and procured their release. But before that, his continuance in Scotland was a time of great action, wherein he so distressed the King, as he enforced him to march with all the force he could make for England; but being close pursued by the English horse, under the command of General Lambert (a prudent, valiant commander, and a man of gallant conduct) and resisted by force raised in England, he was compelled to make a halt at Worcester city, till the Lord General, with a body of the army, advanced thither, and after a short time totally defeated his army, himself escaping very hardly, and afterwards, (with great difficulty) conveyed himself beyond the seas. The idea of the stock of honour, which General Cromwell came invested with to London, after this crowning victory (superadded to what God had before clothed him with not only by his achievements in England, but those in Scotland, which I pretermitted, because, being grounded on those barbarous massacres, the habitable world sounded with the noise of them) will in my silence present itself to your imagination. He had not long continued here, before it was strongly impressed upon him by those to whom he had no reason to be utterly incredulous, and strengthened by his own observation, that the persons then called the Parliament of the Commonwealth of England, as from whom he had derived his authority, and by virtue whereof he had fought so many holy men in Scotland into their graves, were not such as were spirited to carry the good interest to an end, wherein he and they had jeopardized all that was of concern to them in this world; and I wish cordially that there had not been too great a ground for those allegations. The result of them after many debates betwixt the members then sitting, and the General, with some who joined with him, was the dissolution of that Parliament by a military force, since called by a softer word, interruption. Great dissatisfaction sprung from this action, and such as is not yet forgotten amongst good men. For let the reasons and end be never so good, upon which the General acted this part; yet, say they, 'twas high breach of trust in him, to overthrow that authority, in defence of which God had appeared, and made him so significant an instrument; yet *factum valet*, say others, who were not well satisfied neither; and now care is used to settle fluctuating Britain.

In order to which the Lord General by his authority (which was but military) summons one hundred persons out of all parts of the nation (with competent indifferency and equality) to represent the nation, and invests them with legislative authority. They meet and accept it, assume the title of Parliament, and sit in the House of Commons, and enact sundry laws; but in a short time made it appear to all considering and unprejudiced men, that they were *huic negotio impares, non obstante* their godliness; of which the more judicious of them being sensible, contrived the matter so as to dissolve themselves by an act of their own, and resolve their authority, whence they first derived it, upon the general. It was not long before he was advised to assume the Government of this nation in his single capacity, limited with such restrictions as were drawn up in an instrument of Government framed to that purpose. This he accepted of, and (being by it with due ceremonies in Westminster-hall inaugurated, he) assumed it accordingly. According to one of the articles in it, he summoned a House of Commons at Westminster the September following, of which House I had the honour to be a member. The House consisting of many disobliged persons (some upon the king's account, and others upon a pretence of right to sit upon the former foundation, as not being legally, though forceably dissolved; and others judging that the powers given by the instrument of government to the protector were too large; professing that though they were willing to trust him, yet they would not trust his successors with so large a jurisdiction) fell into high animosities, and after five months spent in framing another instrument instead of the former (which they said they could not swallow without chewing) they were by the protector dissolved.

This was ungrateful to English spirits who deify their representatives; but the protector's parts and interest enabled him to stem this tide. Yet the weight of Government incumbing too heavily upon him, before many years passed he summoned another Parliament, and his experience guided him to concur with them in a new instrument to govern by. In it they would have changed his title and made him King, and I think he had closed with them in it, not out of lust to that title (I am persuaded) but out of an apprehension, that it would have secured (in a better way) the nation's settlement: but the party to whom the protector ever professed to owe himself (being the generality of his standing friends) rose so high in opposition to it (by reason of the scandal, that thereby would fall upon his person and profession) as it diverted him, and occasioned him to take investiture in his government, though from them, yet under his former title of protector.

As in former cases, this found acceptance with many, but was dissatisfactory to a greater number of them.

The instrument of government made in this Parliament, and to which the protector took his oath, was called the humble petition and advice.

In it provision was made for another House of Parliament, instead of the old Lords; that this might be a screen or balance betwixt the protector and commons, as the former lords had been betwixt the king and them.

This to consist of seventy persons, all at first to be nominated by the protector, and after as any one died, a new one to be nominated by him and his successors, and assented to by themselves, or without that consent not to sit: twenty of them was a quorum. It was no small task for the protector to find idoneous men for this place, because the future security of the honest interest, seemed (under God) to be laid up in them; for by a mortal generation (if they were well chosen at first) like foundationals in the gathering of a church, they would propagate their own kind, when the single person could not; and the Commons (who represented the nation) would not, having in them, for the most part, the spirit of those they represent, which hath little affinity with or respect to the cause of God. And indeed, to speak freely, so barren was the island of persons of quality, spirited for such a service, as they were not to be found, according to that of the Apostle, 1 Cor. i. 26. *Ye see your calling, not many wise nor noble*, &c. This forced him to make it up of men of mean rank, and consequently of less interest, and upon trial too light for balance, too thin for a screen, and upon the point ineffectual to answer the design, being made a scorn by the nobility and gentry, and generality of the people; the House of Commons continually spurning at their power, and spending large debates in controverting their title, till at length the protector (finding the distempers which grew in his Government, and the dangers of the public peace thereby,) dissolved the Parliament, and so silenced that controversy for that time. And that was the last that sat during his life, he being compelled to wrestle with the difficulties of his place, so well as he could, without parliamentary assistance, and in it met with so great a burden, as (I doubt not to say, it drank up his spirits, of which his natural constitution yielded a vast stock) and brought him to his grave; his interment being the seed time of his glory, and England's calamity. Before I pass further, pardon me in troubling you with the character of his person, which by reason of my nearness to him, I had opportunity well to observe.

His body was well compact and strong, his stature under 6 ft.

(I believe about two inches) his head so shaped as you might see it a storehouse and shop both of a vast treasury of natural parts. His temper exceeding fiery, as I have known, but the flame of it kept down, for the most part, or soon allayed with those moral endowments he had. He was naturally compassionate towards objects in distress, even to an effeminate measure; though God had made him a heart wherein was left little room for any fear, but what was due to himself, of which there was a large proportion, yet did he exceed in tenderness towards sufferers. A larger soul, I think, hath seldom dwelt in a house of clay than his was. I do believe, if his story were impartially transmitted, and the unprejudiced world well possessed with it, she would add him to her nine worthies, and make up that number a decemviri. He lived and died in comfortable communion with God, as judicious persons near him well observed. He was that Mordecai that sought the welfare of his people, and spake peace to his seed, yet were his temptations such, as it appeared frequently, that he that hath grace enough for many men may have too little for himself; (the treasure he had being but in an earthen vessel,) and that equally defiled with original sin, as any other man's nature is. He left successor in the protectorship his eldest son, a worthy person indeed, of an obliging nature and religious disposition, giving great respect to the best of persons, both ministers and others; and having to his lady a prudent, godly, practical christian. His entrance into the government was with general satisfaction, having acceptation with all sorts of people, and addresses from them importing so much. It was an amazing consideration to me (who out of the experience I had of the spirits of people did fear confusion would be famous Oliver's successor) to see my fears so confuted; though alas, the sin of England soon shewed that they were not vain fears. For in a short time some actings in the army appeared tending to divest the protector of the power of it. This bred some jealousy and unkindness betwixt him and the officers of it; but it was allayed, and things looked fair again. About this time writs were sent out to summons a parliament, which accordingly sat down in March following. The power of the protector and that of the other House was instantly controverted in the House of Commons, which House consisted of a tripartite interest, viz. the protector's, the commonwealth's (as it was so called by some, though groundlessly enough) and Charles the King of Scots; each party striving to carry to an end their own design, siding one while with one, another while with another obstructed settlement, and acted nothing but what tended to leave religion and sobriety naked of protection. The vigilant army observed this, and disposed themselves to prevent this growing evil: in order to it, keep general counsels, publish remonstrances, and make addresses. The Parliament fearing the co-ordinacy (at least) of a military power with the civil, forbid the meetings of the army. The army resent this so ill, as by a violent impression they prevail with the protector to dissolve the parliament. This he did *animo tam reluctanti*, that he could not conceal his repentance of it, but it break out upon all occasions. The army observing it reflected on him as a person true to the civil interest, and not fixed to them. ' And the officers keeping general counsels in a few days resolve to depose him, and restore the members of parliament dissolved by the first protector in the year 53, to the exercise of their government again, in order (as they ridiculously styled it) to the settling of a commonwealth. The nation resented this act of the army exceeding ill; the godly party being generally much dissatisfied with it, in regard the persons brought together, were for the most part disobliging to anything of reason or sobriety; so that they enslaved the people to the lusts of a few men; as it soon appeared from these the officers of the army, and all in civil power derived their authority, and they seemed to have brought all under perfect subjection. But their deportment waxed too swelling for the army to bear long; for upon an insurrection raised in the West by Sir George Booth, a secluded member, in behalf of a free parliament, forces were sent against him under General Lambert, by whom Sir George was soon reduced and made a prisoner. This so elevated the ruling men in parliament, as they began to increase the thickness of their fingers. The army, fearing they would not rest till they had brought them to Rehoboam's scantling, make complaint to them by way of remonstrance, out of which egg a bird sprang that made new division, or rather renewed the old betwixt them, till it came to another interruption. This put us into so great distemper, as one regiment marched against another, some for parliament, others against them, and drew up near Westminster-hall even to push of pike, but God in his mercy kept them from engaging; so that no blood was spilt. The House thus disturbed used its interest to redintegrate its power: members meet in private cabals about it. They send into Scotland to General Monk, who was placed there by the old protector, Commander in Chief of the force of that nation. To him they complain of the breach of trust by the army here, and by them of the violence offered to Parliament. This Monk resents ill, and declares for the Parliament against the army. The army in England meet in council; they choose the Lord Fleetwood Captain General of all the forces in England, Scotland and Ireland; send letters to Monk for accommodation; appoint a Committee of Safety for the public peace, made up of many chief officers of the army, and others of the best quality they could get: declare a resolution to call a new parliament, appoint a committee to draw a platform of government for the three nations. While this was acting, the nations grew into a flame, greatly hating any government introduced by the sword; so the officers of the army, and Committee of Safety, and all began to draw heavily, and in a few weeks by the revolt of the soldiery, which began first at Portsmouth, was seconded by the fleet, and generally fallen in with by the private soldiers, their wheels fell off, and left them on the ground. The Members of Parliament returned to sit, all the officers that were looked upon as having a hand in their interruption set aside, though to other things indemnified. Thus far was Jotham's parable in the Case of Abimelech and the men of Shechem realized in this matter also. General Monk advances now to London, and is there honourably entertained; he is invited into London, courted and caressed there upon hope he would introduce the King of Scots, whose interest grew all this while, and the generality of the people expressed intentness upon it; abuse the Parliament, and affront (to violence) the speaker at his lodgings, and the members walking in the streets.

In this interim the House dismisses Sir Henry Vane from sitting in it, as a person that had not been constant to parliament privileges; and Major Salaway, a person of great parts and Sir Henry Vane's second in most things, with some others who acted in the Committee of Safety. Yet were they greatly pressed by declarations from the people, who, though they were pleased with the dishonour put on Sir Henry Vane (he being unhappy in lying under the most catholic prejudice of any man I know) yet partly dissatisfied with the seclusion of the members of 48, and partly thirsting after their liberties in free parliament, were restless and impetuous.

General Monk is now earnestly applied to by the greatest part of the citizens of London, and the members of parliament who were secluded in the year 48, to restore them to the exercise of their trust. In that capacity, after some debate of some of the then sitting members concerning this matter, without further consent obtained from the then sitting members and without their privity, they were by the General brought into the House. They sat not three weeks before they, by Act of Parliament, dissolved themselves and made provision for a succeeding parliament, which is to sit down the 25th day of the next month. In this time they made sundry acts; one about the Ministry, to the advantage of Presbyterie; another, in which they settled a militia distinct from that of the army, put into such commissioners hands, for the most part, as are for the King's interest. They likewise settled a Council of State, consisting of one and thirty very prudent and sober men, and of good interest as to civil concernments.

But to draw to a period, and trouble you no longer with this discourse; the interest of religion lies dreadfully on the dust; for the eminent professors of it having achieved formerly great victories in the war and thereby great power in the army made use of it to make variety of changes in the government; and every one of those changes hazardous and pernicious and dissatisfactory in one considerable respect or other.

They were all charged upon the principles of the authors of them, who, being congregational men, have not only made men of that persuasion cheap, but rendered them odious to the generality of the nation; and that the rather because General Fleetwood who married the Protector's daughter, and the Lord Desborough who married his sister, were principal instruments (as is apprehended, though I think not truly of Fleetwood) in overthrowing the family, from which they had their preferment and so many signal kindnesses. It is not to be expressed what reproach it brought upon profession of religion by this means, and what a foundation laid to persecute it out of England, if that party prevails; for demonstration is made by experience that professors were not more troublesome and factious in times of peace, before the wars of England began, and the great instruments of them, than they have been imperious, self-seeking, trust-breaking and covenant-violating since they were invested with power. And whither this scandal will go, or what the effects of it will be, the Lord knows; but to be sure, as Solomon says, he that breaks a hedge, a serpent will bite him; and this is fulfilled upon them who have been the greatest hedge-breakers that I have known. And as there is a woe pronounced to the world by our Saviour because of offences, so there is a redundant woe to them by whom those offences come.

I have cause to believe that you have met with most of what I have here communicated to you, in a better dress, from some other hand; if so, I entreat the pardon of your stomach for my *crambe bis coctum*. I also entreat your advice by the next opportunity concerning friends here, what encouragement persons may have if times press them to transport their families into New England, with some general directions of doing to the best advantage.

I do promise my self this fruit of my writing, that as it may renew our intercourse and kindle the former coals of love, so it will provoke you with greatest fervency to lay the sad state of our affairs here before the Lord, whose name is greatly engaged in them; for the rage of the enemy is swelled to an intolerable height and his mouth set against the heavens. God hath great cause now to fear the enemy and the avenger. And this is our last refuge, for we have forfeited all to the utmost. I pray present me to my cousin, your wife, under the character of a person ready though unable to serve her. Accept of the like tender from, Sir,

                    Your real servant and unworthy kinsman,
                                        Jo. MAIDSTON

If you shall give yourself the trouble at any time of honouring me with a letter, you may please to direct it to Pondhouse, at Boxted in Essex, where my father lived; it is three miles from Colchester.

HENRY BENNET, EARL OF ARLINGTON (1618–85)

Cowley's friend, to whom the letter on page 129 was addressed, came into his own when Charles II was restored. He was one of the famous Cabal and was subsequently impeached in the House of Commons largely on account of his evil influence on the King. His letter to Ormond, in Ireland, tells of the Great Fire.

TO THE DUKE OF ORMOND

WHITEHALL, SEPT. 4TH, 1666

My LORD, I take this occasion to write to your Grace the saddest story that e'er befel a city. Sunday, at one of the clock in the morning, a fire broke out in Pudding Lane, which being fomented by a violent wind, burnt all ways to this very hour towards us, into the body of the city, and towards the Tower. We have often offered at remedies by cutting off some part of the town, but still too late; 'tis now past four in the afternoon, and we begin to despair of an attempt we were beginning at noon of a traverse beyond Somerset House. Just now we are beginning to work at Scotland Yard, to see whether by pulling down houses there we can save this palace. I am afraid this attempt will be as unsuccessful as all the rest, for the fire is far advanced in Fleet Street already; if the wind hold, God knows but it may overtake us before night, his Holy Will be done. Notwithstanding this submission it becomes us to do the best we can towards the preservation of the peace of the Kingdom; accordingly His Majesty assures himself your Grace will do your utmost to do the like in that kingdom [Ireland], which is all the advice that the hurry we are in will allow us to give you.

We had letters last night from the fleet from St. Helen's Point, where they put in, something disordered by the foul weather, but not so much as we feared. They suppose the enemy [the Dutch] suffered much more, whom they pursued as far as they could, but sheltering themselves in St. John's Road upon the coast of France near Boulogne, they durst follow them no farther. Both of the fleets are refitting.

ANNE, LADY NORTH (c. 1620–83)

She was the wife of Dudley, 4th Baron North, with whom she lived at their Suffolk estate of Tostock. This letter is to her son Roger, at that time twenty-four years of age, and the "little Miss" she mentions was her granddaughter Anne, child of her son Francis, at that time Chief Justice.

TO ROGER NORTH

TOSTOCK, 7TH JULY, 1679

DEAR SON ROGER, I praise God little Miss is pretty well again; her feverish distemper quite gone, but she is faint, [so] that if she stir but a little it puts her into a sweat. This day she took an opening julep by the Dr.'s direction which hath wrought very well without the least disturbance to her, so I hope she will quickly be perfectly well, but I have been and am still in sad fears for some of my family. My dog Tugg ran mad; but my servants did not believe it at first, and loved her so well they would try several things to her, so that they have all been slabbered and blooded. Some of them she bit, and two of my little dogs she tumbled about, but whether she bit any we know not, but I am in great fears and care about it. I have sent this day to Kirtling to fetch the coach that the keeper told me stood in the Barn and was scarce worth the fetching. Nobody would give 20s. for it, but I fancy when I have trim'd it up and used it a little about the fields to carry the children airing, it will look more to advantage than now it doth. I have written to my daughter Wyseman [1] that if you would have the £9 for your horse and what monies else you have laid out for me, that she would pay you.

From your most affectionate Mother,
A. NORTH

My most kind love to my son Ch: Justice.

[1] Elizabeth North. She married Sir Robert Wiseman, 24th September, 1672. Subsequently she married William, second Earl of Yarmouth.

144

EDWARD, EARL OF CONWAY (c. 1623–85)

Little is known of Conway except that, like a good many other country gentlemen, he frequented Court and kept a number of correspondents well aware of what was happening. His friend the Earl of Essex was Lord-Lieutenant of Ireland at the time this letter was written, and naturally interested to hear of what was going on at home.

TO THE EARL OF ESSEX

NOVEMBER 29, 1673

MAY IT PLEASE YOUR EXCELLENCY, I have presumed to write to your Excellency the 18th and the 22nd, and to Sir Arthur Forbes the 18th and the 25th, so that I have not omitted any post since I came to town, nor shall I omit any, if my letters are of any service or entertainment to your Excellency.

The Duchess of York came to Whitehall on Wednesday last. The King brought her up from the barge to the Queen's presence-chamber, and stopped in the outer-drawing-room till the Queen came to the door of the Presence Chamber to meet her; the Duke of York led up the Duchess of Modena, and as soon as they were entered the Presence-Chamber the King called for a chair for her, upon which my Lady Suffolk, my Lady Falmouth, and the rest of the Ladies to the number of 20 that were of the Nobility ran out of the room, as thinking themselves of equal quality to the Duchess of Modena; and that night the King sent to the Duke to desire that she might not be in the room when the Ladies came to kiss the Duchess of York's hand, which was ordered accordingly. I went with my Lord Keeper and my Lord Treasurer on Thursday morning, when they kissed her hand. She is a proper handsome Lady. She hath very good eyes, very good features, and a very good complexion, but she wants the air which should set off all this, and having been bred in a monastery knows not how to set one foot before another with any gracefulness. I observed that though many commended her in their discourse to the Duke, yet none wished him joy, nor would the City be brought to make bonfires.

What I writ last to Sir A. Forbes I had from Speaker and Treasurer

145

but Orrery is of opinion Parliament will sit, and that the King having made sure of the money of France, will endeavour to get more of Parliament.   Speaker and Treasurer are enemies to Herbert, and swore to me that from the day I was Secretary to Essex they would push at Essex. I have had many debates with myself whether I should write this to you or not, and at last I resolved that though it should ruin me in your favour, yet I would preserve my integrity and tell you the truth.

I cannot omit one passage which probably your Excellency will not have from any other hand; it is that upon Wednesday last, before the Lords Commissioners of the Admiralty, Sir Thomas Littleton reproached my Lord Treasurer, and called him a cheat, upon which all the Lords Commissioners rose up on great disorder.   The occasion of it was this; the Victuallers of the Navy were turned off, and a new contract made with others; the old ones were all admitted to speak to the King, except Sir Thomas Littleton, who, it is thought, will be sent to the Tower next Council day, which is not till Wednesday.

*   *   *   *   *

On Monday next the King hath appointed to hear it debated before the Committee for Foreign Affairs, whether the Office of Ministry of the Ordnance in Ireland shall stand, or fall into the office under Sir Thomas Chicheley of England.

Last night my Lord Treasurer carried me to my Lady Shrewsbury's, where there was Nell Gwyn, the Duke of Buckingham, and Mr. Speaker.   About three a clock in the morning we went to supper, were very merry, and drank smartly.   I wish I knew how to write your Excellency all our good discourse, for I assure your Excellency that I am with the greatest sincerity imaginable, &c.

THOMAS SYDENHAM (1624–89)

Dr. Sydenham, called "the English Hippocrates" on account of his eminence in clinical medicine, fought on the Parliamentary side in the Civil War. He saw the Great Plague of London; he distinguished scarlatina from measles; and wrote the classical account of gout (de podagra), from which complaint he suffered. Sydenham was in advance of his time; he advocated fresh air in the sick-room. "Sydenham's laudanum" is the vinum opii *of the British Pharmacopœia; and St. Vitus's Dance is often known as "Sydenham's chorea." The recipient of the following letter was the famous "Father of English Chemistry," the discoverer of "Boyle's Law."*

TO ROBERT BOYLE

PALL MALL, APRIL 2, 1688

SIR, It had become me to have begged your acceptance, when I took the boldness to tender to you the second edition of my book; but partly business and partly an unwillingness in me to give you two troubles at once, diverted me from writing. But now that you are pleased to give yourself the pains of a thanks, which I never thought myself capable of deserving from you, I hold myself obliged to return you my humble thanks, that you take in good part my weak endeavours, and are pleased to have a concern (as you have always done) for me.

I perceive my friend Mr. Locke hath troubled you with an account of my practice as he hath done himself in visiting with me very many of my variolous patients especially. It is a disease wherein, as I have been more exercised this year than ever I thought I could have been, so I have discovered more of its days than ever I thought I should have done. It would be too large for a letter to give you an account of its history; only in general I find no cause, from my best observation, to repent of anything said by me in my tract "De Variolis," but do greatly, that I did not say, that considering the practices that obtain, both amongst learned and ignorant physicians, it had been happy for mankind that either the art of physic had never been exercised, or the notion of malignity never stumbled upon. As it is palpable to all the world, how fatal that disease proves to

147

many of all ages, so it is most clear to me, from all the observations that I can possibly make, that if no mischief be done, either by physician or nurse, it is the most slight and safe of all other diseases. If it shall be your hap to be seized of that disease (as probably you never may) I should recommend to you, upon the word of a friend, the practice mentioned in the 155th page of my book.

I confess, some accidents there are incident to that disease which I never was able to master, till towards the end of last summer, and which, therefore, could not be mentioned by me, as a phrenitis coming on the eighth day, where the patient is in the vigour of his youth, hath not been blooded, and hath been kept in a dose from the first decumbiture; as likewise (which is wont to be no less fatal) a great dosing, accompanied with a choking respiration, coming on from the tenth day (reckoning from the rigour and horror, which is my way of accounting) and occasioned by the matter of a ptyalism in a flux-pox, baking and growing thick, as it declines and comes to a concoction in those days. But which is observable, the small-pox never fluxes or runs together, but it hath been thrust out before the fourth day; and where you see any eruption the first, second or third day from the decumbiture, you may safely pronounce it will be a flux-pox or a measle, for that sort, in its first appearance is like it. And, which is likewise observable in the highest flux of all, as that which comes out on the first or second day, it is in vain to endeavour the raising them to an height, for it is both impossible and unsafe to attempt, but all the discharge there can be, must be either from a ptyalism, in a grown person, or a diarrhœa, in an infant, to whom the same is no more dangerous than the other to the former; and, wherever they flux, their discharge must be made one of those two ways. But of these things I shall discourse to you more at large, when I shall have the happiness to see you, which I hope may be suddenly.

The town stands well in health, and at our end not anybody sick, that I hear, of the small-pox. I have much business about other things, and more than I can do, who yet am not idle. I have the happiness of curing my patients, at least of having it said of me, that few miscarry under me; but cannot brag of my correspondency with some other of the faculty, who, notwithstanding my profoundness in palmistry and chemistry, impeach me with great insufficiency, as I shall likewise do my tailor, when he makes my doublet like a hopsack, and not before, let him adhere to what hypothesis he will. Though yet, in taking fire at my attempts to reduce practice to a greater easiness, plainness, and in the meantime letting the mountebank at Charing Cross pass unrailed at, they contradict themselves, and would make the world believe I may prove more considerable than they would have me. But, to let these men alone to their books, I have again taken breath, and am pursuing my design of specifics which, if but a delusion, so closely haunts me, that I could not but indulge the spending of a little money and time at it once more. I have made a great progress in the thing, and have reason to hope not to be disappointed. My occasions will not suffer me give you more trouble and therefore be pleased to accept of those very unfeigned thanks, which I here make you, for all the singular kindnesses and favours whereby you have obliged me to be very uncomplimentary.

Sir, your most humble servant,
T. Sydenham

GEORGE FOX (1624–91)

The founder of the Society of Friends, or Quakers, was many times imprisoned for his religious beliefs. During the Commonwealth he addressed a bold letter to Cromwell, who seems to have appreciated his greatness, and gave him a sympathetic hearing on several occasions.

TO OLIVER CROMWELL

O Protector, Who hast tasted of the power of God, which many generations before thee have not so much, since the days of apostacy from the apostles—take heed that thou lose not thy power, but keep kingship off thy head, which the world would give thee, and earthly crowns under thy feet, lest with that thou cover thyself, and so lose the power of God. When the children of Israel went from that of God in them, they would have kings, as other nations had, as transgressors had, and so God gave them one; and what did they do then? And when they would have taken Christ, and made him a king, he hid himself from them; he was hid from that which would have made him a king, he who was king of the Jews in word. O Oliver, take heed of undoing thyself, by running into things that will fade—the things of this world that will change. Be subject and obedient to the Lord God.

GEORGE FOX

FRANCIS AUNGIER, LORD LONGFORD (*fl.* 1675)

The following is a very graphic account of a difference that arose between the two Houses of Parliament. In May, 1675, Sir John Churchill, Master of the Rolls, was appointed by the House of Lords senior counsel for Sir Nicholas Crisp on his appeal from a Chancery decree in favour of Thomas Dalmahoy, a member of the Lower House. This was considered a breach of privilege and led to the scene described in this letter.

TO THE EARL OF ESSEX

LONDON, JUNE 5, 1675

MY LORD, The scene being much altered in the difference between both Houses since my last, I presume to give your Excellency this short narrative of it. On Tuesday last the House of Commons ordered their Sergeant to take into custody Sir John Churchill, Mr. Sergeant Pemberton, Mr. Sergeant Peck and Mr. Charles Porter, as persons who had infringed the privileges of the House by appearing at the Lords' Bar in a case wherein Mr. Dalmahoy (a member of the House) was concerned. And to the intent that they might be the easier had, Mr. Speaker invited them to dinner, and after they had made good cheer, gave them very good advice to obviate and prevent any further disputes between both Houses, which they then seemed to comply with. But our Sergeant letting them have their liberty upon parole, they were the next day sent for by the Lords, and at their bar interrogated in all particulars concerning their commitment, and were, thereafter, given the protection of the House. The same day the Lords sent a message to us by my Lord Chief Justice of the Common Pleas and my Lord Chief Baron for a present conference upon matters of high importance, wherein his Majesty's and the safety of the Kingdom was concerned. And the Houses agreeing to the present conference, the enclosed paper was read with a very audible voice by my Lord Privy Seal. On Thursday the House sent their Sergeant to the Tower, for neglect of his duty in suffering his prisoners to escape, and ordered Mr. Secretary in their name to beseech his Majesty that we might have another Sergeant appointed to attend them; and accordingly my

151

Lord Chamberlain appointed one Topham, a very stout fellow, to attend to the House.

Yesterday morning, as Mr. Speaker was coming through Westminster Hall to the House, he met Mr. Sergeant Pemberton, whom he commanded his officers then attending to apprehend and secure in the Speaker's Chamber, of which he gave the House an account as soon as they sat, and received the thanks of the House for his zeal and care in thus asserting their privileges; and the House being then also informed that Sir John Churchill, Mr. Sergeant Peck, and Mr. Charles Porter were below in the Hall, they commanded instantly their Sergeant to carry his men with him down into the Hall and to apprehend the said persons, though they were pleading at the Bars of any of the Courts; and to go well attended, that he might not receive an affront from the Black Rod who, they understood, was in the Court of Requests armed with an order from the House of Lords to rescue the prisoners. This order of the House of Commons was very briskly executed, the said persons being taken from the several Bars of the Chancery, King's Bench and Common Pleas, and brought safe into the Speaker's Chamber, without opposition. But the House of Lords being informed of these proceedings, they immediately order their Black Rod to fetch out the said prisoners, wherever they should find them committed. They likewise order their Black Rod to apprehend the Sergeant of the House of Commons, and address to his Majesty, by word of the white-staves, that another Sergeant might be appointed to attend the House of Commons.

The House of Commons, after a long debate, vote the said persons to be sent to the Tower, and Sir John Robinson, Sergeant of the Tower, being then in the House, had directions not to set them at liberty without an order from the House.

By this time it was two of the clock and the House of Lords had adjourned for an hour or two, whose example in that particular the House of Commons thought fit to follow. And while the Speaker was at dinner the Sergeant hired three coaches at Westminster Hall Gate, pretending to carry his prisoners through the City to the Tower, being then informed that the Black Rod lay in wait for him in a house near the Palace Yard gate. But he went more discreetly to work, for he carried his prisoners through Sir John Cotton's house and took boat at his garden stairs, and by water delivered them safe into Sir John Robinson's hands; to whom in three minutes the Black Rod came to demand the prisoners, but the Lieutenant positively refused to deliver them. As soon as the House met they agreed upon the enclosed reasons in answer to the paper delivered the day before by the Lords at a conference, and sent up a message for a conference on the subject matter of the late conference, to which the Lords replied that they would send up an answer by messengers of their own. But their Black Rod being returned from the Tower and giving them an account that the Lieutenant of the Tower refused to deliver the prisoners, they voted a second address to his Majesty by the white-staves that the Lieutenant of the Tower should be removed and a new one appointed in his stead. To which his Majesty then answered that he would consider of it and give them an answer this day, by 5 in the afternoon. When the House of Commons met this morning, they found their Sergeant was changed, and while they were debating on it with some warmth, Mr. Secretary Coventry came in and from his Majesty told us that it was his Majesty's pleasure we should immediately adjourn till 4 of the clock in the afternoon, when it was his pleasure we should attend him in the Banqueting House, and that his Majesty had sent the same message to the Lords.

Accordingly we met, when his Majesty made us the enclosed gracious speech, after which, the Speaker returning to the House, we voted the enclosed votes and adjourned the debate of our Sergeant till Monday morning.

The Lords after met and the white-staves reporting to their lordships that his Majesty had considered of their address concerning the removal of the Lieutenant of the Tower, but saw no reason for it. Upon which their Lordships adjourned till Monday. My paper only now allows me room to beg your Excellency's pardon for this tedious narrative which is the true state of matters of fact between both Houses.

I am, my Lord, Yr Excellency's most humble servant

FRAN. AUNGIER

CHARLES HATTON (*fl.* 1689)

> *Here is another example of the chatty letter sent from London to friends in the country. History says little about Lady Griffin and her troubles; this was evidently nothing but a choice tit-bit of gossip of the day.*

TO SIR CHARLES LYTTELTON

OCTOBER 24, 1689

MY Lady Essex Griffin is sent to the Tower for a pewter pot plot, much more ridiculous than Mrs. Sellier's meal tub. My Lord Griffin's cook bespoke of a pewterer an oblong square pewter pot, to put brandy in; but it was to have a false bottom, in which was to be put some contraband goods to be sent into France. When the pot was made, yesterday morning, betwixt one and two of the clock in the morning, the cook and a foot boy went to call up the pewterer, to come to my Lord Griffin's house to solder in the false bottom. The pewterer told them he could not there do it so conveniently as at his own house, and bid them fetch the pot, and he would get ready his tools and solder in the bottom. They went, fetched the pot, and, as soon as the pewterer had received it, he told them he must know what was put into the false bottom. They pretended that there was jewels. But the pewterer, pulling what was in the false bottom, found letters to the King [James II] and several papers, apprehended the cook and footman, and, sending for a constable, carried them to the Secretaries' office; but, nobody being there, he secured them in the porter's lodge, went to Mr. Hampden, acquainted him, and early that morning they were examined. A messenger was sent to search the Lord Griffin's house and secure my Lord; but he was gone away. My Lady is sent to the Tower, and my Lady Eliz. Thatcher. Her first husband was De la Val. The pewter bottle was to have been sent by one Monsieur Busy, a Frenchman who married my Lady Newburgh: and Mr. Thatcher, my Lady Elizabeth's husband, was to go as his man with him into France, and from thence to carry the pewter bottle into Ireland. In the false bottom there is said to have been found a draft of a patent to create my Lord Griffin an earl, and in his letter he expressed a desire that it might bear date before the abdication was voted. What else of any

154

certainty I cannot hear. Some say there was lists of "worthy men" and "men worthy." This is for certain, there never was a more foolish contrivance, and whoever had any hand in it must be as blind of their understanding as my Lady Essex's eyes are.

It was thought my Lord Preston, Lord Forbes, Sir John Fenwick, Mr. Chomley, and others would by their writes of Habeas Corpus have been brought up to the Bench this day; but they not being willing to comply with my Lord Lucas in paying him the fees he demanded of them, to be as vexatious to them as he can, he will not bring them up till to-morrow.

I have enclosed yesterday's votes, and I hear the H. of C. have voted to-day that they will stand by and assist his Majesty in reducing Ireland, and joining with his allies abroad in a vigorous prosecution of the war against France. And to-morrow sennight is appointed to consider of a supply for his Majesty. All here give your Lordship and all at Kirby their very humble service, and more particularly your most humble servant,

C. HATTON

JOHN RAY (1627–1705)

Ray has been called the Father of English Natural History, and seems to have been one of the first systematic observers of plants and wild life. Sir Hans Sloane, that great patron of scientists, was his constant friend, and the following letter, written ten days before Ray's death, is a remarkable piece of dignified gratitude.

TO SIR HANS SLOANE

DEAR SIR, the best of friends. These are to take a final leave of you as to this world: I look upon myself as a dying man. God requite your kindness expressed anyways towards me a hundredfold; bless you with a confluence of all good things in this world, and eternal life and happiness hereafter; grant us a happy meeting in heaven. I am, Sir, eternally yours,

JOHN RAY

WILLIAM LLOYD

WILLIAM LLOYD (1627–1717)

A stout churchman, bishop in turn of St. Asaph, Lichfield and Worcester, Lloyd was one of the seven bishops who helped to lose James II's throne for him. The letter here printed tells the story of the last days of the ill-fated Duke of Monmouth.

TO DR. FELL (BISHOP OF OXFORD)

[JULY 16, 1685]

MY LORD, I received your Lordship's letter by the last post, with two enclosed, one to the Duke of Ormond, the other to the Lord Privy Seal; both which letters I delivered to their own hands, and they promised to answer them.

For the King's Inauguration, I know my Lord of Canterbury has made ready an office to be used every year, the 6th of February, so that there will need no question concerning it.

I was this day again at Sir H. Foxe's, to speak with him, but he was not at home. I will try again to-morrow.

I told your Lordship in my last that the Bishop of Ely was appointed by his Majesty to attend the Duke of Monmouth, and to prepare him to die the next day. The Duke wrote to his Majesty representing how useful he might and would be, if his Majesty would be pleased to grant him his life. But if it might not be, he desired a longer time, and to have another divine to assist him, Dr. Tennison or whom else the King should appoint. The King sent him the Bishop of Bath and Wells to attend, and to tell him he must die the next morning. The two Bishops sat up in his chamber all night, and watched while he slept. In the morning, by his Majesty's order, the Lords Privy Seal and Dartmouth brought him also Dr. Tennison and Dr. Hooper. All these were with him till he died.

They got him to own the King's title to the crown, and to declare in writing that the last King told him he was never married to his mother, and by word of mouth to acknowledge his invasion was sin; but could never get him to confess it was a rebellion. They got him to own that he

157

and Lady Harriet Wentworth had lived in all points like man and wife, but they could not make him confess it was adultery.

He acknowledged that he and his Duchess were married by the law of the land, and therefore his children might inherit, if the King pleased. But he did not consider what he did when he married her. He confessed that he had lived many years in all sorts of debauchery, but said he had repented of it, asked pardon, and doubted not that God had forgiven him. He said that since that time he had an affection for Lady Harriet, and prayed that if it were pleasing to God it might continue, otherwise that it might cease; and God heard his prayer. The affection did continue, and therefore he doubted not it was pleasing to God; and that this was a marriage, their choice of one another being guided not by lust but by judgment upon due consideration.

They endeavoured to show him the falsehood and mischievousness of this enthusiastical principle. But he told them it was his opinion, and he was fully satisfied in it. After all, he desired them to give him the Communion next morning. They told him they could not do it while he was in that error and sin. He said he was sorry for it.

The next morning he told them he had prayed that if he was in an error in that matter God would convince him of it; but God had not convinced him, and therefore he believed that it was no error.

When he was upon the scaffold he professed himself a Protestant of the Church of England. They told him he could not be so if he did not own the doctrine of the Church of England in the point of non-resistance, and if he persisted in that enthusiastic persuasion. He said he could not help it, but yet he approved the doctrine of the Church in all other things. He then spoke to the people in vindication of the Lady Harriet, saying she was a woman of great honour and virtue, a religious godly lady (those were his words). They told him of his living in adultery with her. He said, no; for these two years last past he had not lived in any sin that he knew of; and that he had never wronged any person, and that he was sure when he died to go to God, and therefore he did not fear death, which (he said) they might see in his face. Then they prayed for him, and he kneeled down and joined with them. After all they had a short prayer for the King, at which he paused, but at last said Amen. He spoke to the headsman to see he did his business well, and not use him as he did the Lord Russell, to give him two or three strokes; for if he did, he should not be able to lie still without turning. Then he gave the executioner six guineas, and four to one Marshall, a servant of Sir T. Armstrong's, that attended him with the King's leave: desiring Marshall to give them the executioner if he did his work well, and not otherwise.   He gave this Marshall overnight his ring and watch; and now he gave him his case of pickteeth: all for Lady Harriet.   Then he laid himself down, and upon the sign given, the headsman gave a light stroke, at which he looked him in the face.   Then he laid him down again, and the headsman gave him two strokes more, and then laid down the axe, saying he could not finish his work; till being threatened by the Sheriff and others then present, he took up the axe again and at two strokes more cut off his head.

All this is true as to matter of fact, and it needs no comment to your Lordship.   I desire your prayers, and remain,

Yours Lordship's most affectionate,

W. Asaph

LADY DOROTHY OSBORNE (1627–95)

Readers of Macaulay's history will remember this very delightful lady and the loss of her beauty by small-pox, her brilliant assistance to her husband in his diplomatic work, and the trials she suffered in her own home. These two letters were written a couple of years before she married Sir William Temple, the brilliant diplomatist at The Hague, who saw so much of the inner workings of the plot to supplant James II by the Prince of Orange. His letter to Lady Dorothy, written a year before their marriage, is that of a true lover.

TO SIR WILLIAM TEMPLE

[1653]

SIR, Your last letter came like a pardon to one upon the block. I had given over the hopes on't, having received my letters by the other carrier, who was always wont to be last. The loss put me hugely out of order, and you would have both pitied and laughed at me if you could have seen how woodenly I entertained the widow, who came hither the day before, and surprised me very much. Not being able to say anything, I got her to cards, and there with a great deal of patience lost my money to her;— or rather I gave it as my ransom. In the midst of our play, in comes my blessed boy with your letter, and, in earnest, I was not able to disguise the joy it gave me, though one was by that is not much your friend, and took notice of a blush that for my life I could not keep back. I put up the letter in my pocket, and made what haste I could to lose the money I had left, that I might take occasion to go fetch some more; but I did not make such haste back again, I can assure you. I took time enough to have coined myself some money if I had had the art on't, and left my brother enough to make all his addresses to her if he were so disposed. I know not whether he was pleased or not, but I am sure I was.

You make so reasonable demands that 'tis not fit you should be denied. You ask my thoughts but at one hour; you will think me bountiful, I hope, when I shall tell you that I know no hour when you have them not. No, in earnest, my very dreams are yours, and I have got such a habit of thinking of you that any other thought intrudes and

160

proves uneasy to me. I drink your health every morning in a drench that would poison a horse I believe, and 'tis the only way I have to persuade myself to take it. 'Tis the infusion of steel, and makes me so horribly sick, that every day at ten o'clock I am making my will and taking leave of all my friends. You will believe you are not forgot then. They tell me I must take this ugly drink a fortnight, and then begin another as bad; but unless you say so too, I do not think I shall. 'Tis worse than dying by the half.

I am glad your father is so kind to you. I shall not dispute it with him, because it is much more in his power than mine, but I shall never yield that 'tis more in his desire, since he was much pleased with that which was a truth when you told it him, but would have been none if he had asked the question sooner. He thought there was no danger of you since you were more ignorant and less concerned in my being in town than he. If I were Mrs. Chambers, he would be more my friend; but, however, I am much his servant as he is your father. I have sent you your book. And since you are at leisure to consider the moon, you may be enough to read Cléopâtre, therefore I have sent you three tomes; when you have done with these you shall have the rest, and I believe they will please. There is a story of Artemise that I will recommend to you; her disposition I like extremely, it has a great deal of practical wit; and if you meet with one Brittomart, pray send me word how you like him. I am not displeased that my Lord (Lisle) makes no more haste, for though I am very willing you should go the journey for many reasons, yet two or three months hence, sure, will be soon enough to visit so cold a country, and I would not have you endure two winters in one year. Besides, I look for my eldest brother and cousin Molle here shortly, and I should be glad to have nobody to entertain but you, whilst you are here. Lord! that you had the invisible ring, or Fortunatus his wishing hat; now, at this instant, you should be here.

My brother has gone to wait upon the widow homewards—she that was born to persecute you and I, I think. She has so tired me with being here but two days, that I do not think I shall accept of the offer she made me of living with her in case my father dies before I have disposed of myself. Yet we are very great friends, and for my comfort she says she will come again about the latter end of June and stay longer with me. My aunt is still in town, kept by her business, which I am afraid will not go well, they do so delay it; and my precious uncle does so visit her, and is so kind, that without doubt some mischief will follow. Do you know his son, my cousin Harry? 'Tis a handsome youth, and well-natured,

E.L.   .   G but such a goose; and she has bred him so strangely, that he needs all his ten thousand a year. I would fain have him marry my Lady Diana, she was his mistress when he was a boy. He had more wit then than he has now, I think, and I have less wit than he, sure, for spending my paper upon him when I have so little. Here is hardly room for

Your affectionate friend and servant

TO THE SAME

[1653]

SIR, If to know I wish you with me pleases you, 'tis a satisfaction you may always have for I do perpetually; but were it really in my power to make you happy, I could not miss being so myself, for I know nothing else I want towards it. You are admitted to all my entertainments; and 'twould be a pleasing surprise to me to see you amongst my shepherdesses. I meet some there sometimes that look very like gentlemen (for 'tis a road), and when they are in good humour they give us a compliment as they go by; but you would be so courteous as to stay, I hope, if we entreated you; 'tis in your way to this place, and just before the house. 'Tis our Hyde Park and every fine evening, anybody that wanted a mistress might be sure to find one there. I have wondered often to meet my fair Lady Ruthvin there alone; methinks it should be dangerous for an heir. I could find in my heart to steal her away myself, but it should be rather for her person than her fortune. My brother says not a word of you, nor your service, nor do I expect he should; if I could forget you, he would not help my memory. You would laugh, sure, if I could tell you how many servants he has offered me since he came down; but one above all the rest I think he is in love with himself, and may marry him too if he pleases, I shall not hinder him. 'Tis one Talbot, the finest gentleman he has seen this seven year; but the mischief on't is he has not above fifteen or sixteen hundred pound a year, though he swears he begins to think one might bate £500 a year for such a husband. I tell him I am glad to hear it; and if I was as much taken (as he) with Mr. Talbot, I should not be less gallant; but I doubted the first extremely. I have spleen enough to carry me to Epsom this summer; but yet I think I shall not go. If I make one journey, I must make more, for then I have no excuse. Rather than be obliged to that, I'll make none. You have so often reproached me with the loss of your liberty that to make you some amends I am contented to be your prisoner this summer; but you shall do one favour for me into the bargain. When your father goes into Ireland, lay your commands upon some of his servants to get you an Irish greyhound. I have one that was the General's; but 'tis a bitch, and those are always much less than the dogs. I got it in the time of my favour there, and it was all they had. Henry Cromwell undertook to write to his brother Fleetwood for another for me; but I have lost my hopes there. Whomsoever it is that you employ, he will need no other instructions but to get the biggest he can meet with; 'tis all the beauty of those dogs, or of any kind, I think. A masty (mastiff) is handsomer to me than the most exact little dog that ever lady played withal. You will not offer to take it ill that I employ you in such a commission, since I have told you that the General's son did not refuse it; but I shall take it ill if you do not take the same freedom with me whensoever I am capable of serving you. The town must needs be unpleasant now, and, methinks, you might contrive some way of having your letters sent to you without giving yourself the trouble of coming to town for them when you have no other business; you must pardon me if I think they cannot be worth it.

I am told that R. Spencer is a servant to a lady of my acquaintance, a daughter of my Lady Lexington's. Is it true? And if it be, what is become of the £2,500 lady? Would you think it, that I have an ambassador from the Emperor Justinian that comes to renew the treaty? In earnest, 'tis true, and I want your counsel extremely, what to do in it. You told me once that of all my servants you liked him the best. If I could do so too, there were no dispute in't. Well, I'll think on't, and if it succeed I will be as good as my word; you shall take your choice of my four daughters. Am not I beholding to him, think you? He says that he has made addresses, 'tis true, in several places since we parted, but could not fix anywhere; and, in his opinion, he sees nobody that would make so fit a wife for him as I. He has often inquired after me to hear if I were marrying, and somebody told him I had an ague, and he presently fell sick of one too, so natural a sympathy there is between us; and yet for all this, on my conscience, we shall never marry. He desires to know whether I am at liberty or not. What shall I tell him? Or shall I send him to you to know? I think that will be best. I'll say that you are much my friend, and that I have resolved not to dispose of myself but with your consent and approbation, and therefore he must make all his court to you; and when he can bring me a certificate under your hand, that you think him a fit husband for me, 'tis very likely I may have him. Till then I am his humble servant and your faithful friend.

SIR WILLIAM TEMPLE TO DOROTHY OSBORNE

IRELAND, MAY 18, 1654

... I AM called upon for my letter, but must have leave first to remember you of yours. For God's sake write constantly while I am here, or I am undone past all recovery. I have lived upon them ever since I came, but had thrived much better had they been longer. Unless you use to give me better measure, I shall not be in case to undertake a journey to England. The despair I was in at not hearing from you last week, and the belief that all my letters had miscarried (by some treachery among my good friends who, I am sorry, have the name of yours), made me press my father by all means imaginable to give me leave to go presently if I heard not from you this post. But he would never yield to that, because, he said, upon your silence he should suspect all was not likely to be well between us, and then he was sure I should not be in condition to be alone. He remembered too well the letters I writ upon our last unhappy differences, and would not trust me from him in such another occasion. But, withal, he told me he would never give me occasion of any discontent which he could remedy; that if you desired my coming over, and I could not be content without, he would not hinder me, though he very much desired my company a month or two longer, and that in that time 'twas very likely I might have his as well.

Now, in very good earnest, do you think 'tis time for me to come or no? Would you be very glad to see me there, and could you do it in less disorder, and with less surprise, than you did at Chicksands?

I ask you these questions very seriously; but yet how willingly would I venture to be with you. I know you love me still; you promised me, and that's all the security I can have in this world. 'Tis that which makes all things else seem nothing to it, so high it sets me; and so high, indeed, that should I ever fall 'twould dash me all to pieces. Methinks your very charity should make you love me more now than ever, by seeing me so much more unhappy than I used, by being so much farther from you, for that is all the measure can be taken of my good or ill condition. Justice, I am sure, will oblige you to it, since you have no other means left in the world of rewarding such a passion as mine, which, sure, is of a much richer value than anything in the world besides. Should you save my life again, should you make me absolute master of your fortune and your person too, I should accept none of this in any part of payment, but look upon you as one behindhand with me still. 'Tis no vanity this, but a true sense of how pure and how refined a nature my passion is, which none can ever know except my own heart, unless you find it out by being there.

How hard it is to think of ending when I am writing to you; but it must be so, and I must ever be subject to other people's occasions, and so never, I think, master of my own.   This is too true, both in respect of this fellow's post that is bawling at me for my letter, and of my father's delays.   They kill me; but patience,—would anybody but I were here. Yet you may command me ever at one minute's warning.   Had I not heard from you by this last, in earnest I had resolved to have gone with this, and given my father the slip for all his caution.   He tells me still of a little time; but, alas! who knows not what mischances and how great changes have often happened in a little time?

For God's sake let me hear of all your motions, when and where I may hope to see you.   Let us but hope this cloud, this absence that has overcast all my contentment, may pass away, and I am confident there's a clear sky attends us.   My dearest dear, adieu.

Yours

Pray, where is your lodging?   Have a care of all the dispatch and security that can be in our intelligence.   Remember my fellow-servant; sure, by the next I shall write some learned epistle to her, I have been so long about it.

THOMAS MAULE (*fl.* 1686)

Maule was another of Sir George Etherege's boon companions and correspondents. Here is a chatty letter from Paris telling of English friends there.

TO SIR GEORGE ETHEREGE

PARIS, 28 DECEMBER, 1686

SIR, Your enclosed in one to Mr. Corbet I have received, and sorry I cannot say so much of another you mention to have sent me formerly. I hope my not answering of it in all this time is a sufficient demonstration to you that I never received it; for you cannot think I understand my advantage so little as not to embrace the first opportunity of holding so good a correspondence with one whose friendship I ever valued at too high a rate to venture the losing of it by so unpardonable a neglect. And to tell you the truth I have been very often out of countenance, and somewhat out of humour, not to be able to give an account of Sir George Etherege, when inquired for amongst his friends, and have not drunk his health with that gusto I used to do, but have either spilt my wine or put on a sullen, grave face, thinking by that foolish means to be revenged on you. But now we are fully reconciled (and that is a word at this time of no small importance) I will confess to you that I am not so fond of my court employment as you imagine, because that either I grow old, or the set of maids do so, and consequently have not many charms to make any one sigh but poor Robin Sayers, who has blown (not in Sunderland's cant) Mrs. Yarburgh into the north, there to lead apes in hell; for she has left the court, and her court portion is paid without any obligation of marrying. Her place is not ill supplied by Mrs. Fairefax, who was once married, and I doubt not as good a maid as any of the whole set, to Lord Abergavenny, who released her for a thousand pound. The widow Swan, they say, is disposing of her person, whose place will not be ill filled by Mrs. Fragmorton, who has made Packe's eyes water a hundred times, even when Lady Dorset sat governess of his unruly passion. Mrs. Frazier will not declare herself till she knows whether Scarborough's passion will keep alive a year and a day at Lisbon. As for the Princess's

166

maids, I suppose you are not very solicitous to know what is become of them since Mrs. Nott's face was spoiled with the small-pox. However, I cannot forbear telling of you that Harry Wharton is no more the constant, and that gives great alarms to Ginee Deer lest the disease should run in a blood and infect poor Tom; for he has forsaken Mrs. Mary and makes violent love to Mrs. Drumar by the help of his friend Lord Scarsdale, who is contented at present with an amusement with Mrs. Ogle. The Lord you desire to be informed of deceived nobody's expectations, for ever since the first month of their marriage 'tis cross and pile [pitch and toss] but that before night they part and nothing hinders of his side but the two thousand per annum separate maintenance; but now the quarrels are so loud that "bitch" and "rogue" are words of very civil respect, so that very soon you will hear of an elopement which they say she did very lately for two or three days, and he, being very unwilling to part with any ready money, submitted and made peace; but it is no more expected to be kept than betwixt the Turks and Christians. I will now fill up my sheet and tell you that the King has taken away my Lord Shrewsbury's and my Lord Lumley's regiments for reasons best known to himself, though the town will have it because of their refusal to comply with the King's desires in taking of the Test. But of these matters of state I know you have a much better account, therefore will not further trouble you but to assure you I am,

Your most obedient and humble servant

T. MAULE

SIR EDWARD VAUDREY (*fl.* 1687)

In this letter a soldier narrates one of the incidents at the siege of Budapest, when the Turks were being finally ejected from that city.

TO SIR GEORGE ETHEREGE

FROM THE CAMP BEFORE BUDA,
FRIDAY, THE 16 OF AUGUST, 1687

HONOURED SIR, I observe so little what I write that I forgot whether I gave you an account in my last of the Grand Vizier's arrival, since which, the first days having passed in pure skirmishes, there happened on Wednesday last an action not unworthy your knowledge.

At the break of day we saw him detach from his army a body of men which, falling down from the hills into the plain which separates his from ours, passed it without opposition and gained those which command our lines upon the right hand. Their number as we have since been informed by prisoners was six thousand janizaries and four thousand horse, chosen men out of his whole army and the very flower of all his troops. Their design was either to force a way into the town upon our right whilst he drew his whole army into the plain to attack our left, or, if failing of that, to retrench themselves upon the hills and inconvenience by their cannon our camp, which lay at their foot.

The Duke of Lorraine, having penetrated their designs, kept the main body of his troops to oppose those of the Grand Vizier's in the plain, and sent seven regiments of horse, with some few Hungarians, to make head against the detachment upon the hills. 'Twas here they charged us with some salvoes from their cannon, and so furious a fire from their janizaries, that the Hungarians with the regiment of Cravats [Croats], which were drawn up at our head, fell into disorder upon their first shock; upon which the regiment of Taafe (at the head of which Mr. Fitzjames charged) advancing came timely up to retrieve the business, and, by the help of the other horse, forced the enemy headlong down the hills, with that confusion that above two thousand of their janizaries remained upon the place, and the rest, as we have since been informed by fugitives, thought fitter to return towards Constantinople than join the army. We brought back eight pieces of cannon, above fifty standards, and very near three hundred prisoners. A more vigorous action was perhaps never performed by horse alone with those disadvantages, both of ground and number. Having regained our first post after the pursuit of the enemy, which we made the shorter by not knowing but that the main body was engaged, the high hills having separated us from the sight of what passed at our left, we found the Grand Vizier had drawn his whole army into the plain, to which the Duke of Lorraine had opposed his; but that they both stood at a respectful distance from one another without action. After that our victorious body of horse had by a new order quitted its *champ de bataille* and joined the right wing of our army, that of the enemy's began to make several movements, which showed more the uneasiness of his mind and the irresolution of what he had to do than any design to attack us. So that by degrees, having withdrawn all his infantry to the foot of his own hills, our right wing received orders [to advance] towards some bodies of horse which had taken a familiar liberty of approaching too near to us. Proportionately as we advanced they withdrew, till, finding themselves at the foot of their mountains, and seeing that our wing had by much outmarched the rest of our army, they charged a small body of Hungarians upon our left, who yielding before them, had like to have discovered our flank and caused some disorder, but by the *fermeté* of our troops and skill of our officers, who immediately fronted some squadrons that way and covered our flank. The Turks at their turn retired, and we at the same time, it being already late, received orders to withdraw. The next morning, for what reason we yet know not, the enemy decamped and went some two or three hours' march further off. This is matter of fact and as near as I guess the truth. That which is doubtful is the report we have by fugitives of three bashas [pashas] having been killed in this action; some say the *seraskier* was likewise killed two days before in a skirmish. Certain it is we found letters in his pocket of that consequence which give just grounds for the suspicion.

As for the siege I own I was never so cheated in my life, not doubting we should have been masters of Buda long before this. Where the fault lies I dare not judge much less commit to paper. Certain it is we advance but slowly since our lodgment upon the towers.

The attack I told you in my last we prepared for was put off by the defect of our mines which sprung all to our disadvantage. I hope well of the success but we are neither yet in the town nor the Grand Vizier out of the country.

E. Vaudrey

JOHN LOCKE (1632–1704)

*One of the greatest philosophers this country has ever produced,
Locke was a very lovable man and enjoyed many close friendships.
That he could unbend with delightful grace is well shown in this letter
to one of his friends. He was already in failing health when these
lines were penned, and but a few months later was dead.*

TO LADY CALVERLEY
[1703]

MADAM, Whatever reason you have to look on me as one of the slow
men of London, you have this time given me an excuse for being so;
for you cannot expect a quick answer to a letter, which took me up
a good deal of time to get to the beginning of it. I turned and turned
it on every side; looked at it again and again, at the top of every page;
but could not get into the sense and secret of it till I applied myself
to the middle.

You, madam, who are acquainted with all the skill and methods
of the ancients, have not, I suppose, taken up with this hieroglyphical
way of writing for nothing; and since you were going to put into your
letter things that might be the reward of the highest merit, you would,
by this mystical intimation, put me into the way of virtue, to deserve
them.

But whatever your ladyship intended, this is certain, that in the
best words in the world, you gave me the greatest humiliation imaginable. Had I as much vanity as a pert citizen, that sets up as a wit
in his parish, you have said enough in your letter to content me; and
if I could be swoln that way, you have taken a great deal of pains to
blow me up, and make me the finest gaudy bubble in the world, as I
am painted by your colours. I know the emperors of the East suffer
not strangers to appear before them, till they are dressed up out of
their own wardrobes; is it so too in the empire of wit? and must you
cover me with your own embroidery, that I may be a fit object for
your thoughts and conversation? This, madam, may suit your great-

171

ness, but doth not at all satisfy my ambition. He, who has once flattered himself with the hopes of your friendship, knows not the true value of things, if he can content himself with these splendid ornaments.

As soon as I had read your letter, I looked in my glass, felt my pulse, and sighed; for I found, in neither of those, the promises of thirty years to come. For at the rate I have hitherto advanced, and at the distance, I see, by this complimental way of treatment, I still am, I shall not have time enough in this world to get to you. I do not mean to the place where you now see the pole elevated, as you say, 54 degrees. A post-horse, or a coach, would quickly carry me thither. But when shall we be acquainted at this rate? Is that happiness reserved to be completed by the gossiping bowl, at your grand-daughter's lying-in?

If I were sure that, when you leave this dirty place, I should meet you in the same star where you are to shine next, and that you would then admit me to your conversation, I might perhaps have a little more patience. But, methinks, it is much better to be sure of something, than to be put off to expectations of so much uncertainty. If there be different elevations of the pole here, that keep you at so great a distance from those who languish in your absence; who knows but, in the other world, there are different elevations of persons?

And you, perhaps, will be out of sight, among the seraphims, while we are left behind in some dull planet. This the high flights of your elevated genius give us just augury of, whilst you are here. But yet, pray take not your place there before your time; nor keep not us poor mortals at a greater distance than you need.

And when you have granted me all the nearness that acquaintance and friendship can give, you have other advantages enough still to make me see how much I am beneath you. This will be only an enlarge-ment of your goodness, without lessening the adoration due to your other excellences.

You seem to have some thoughts of the town again. If the par-liament, or the term, which draw some by the name and appearance of business; or if company, and music meetings, and other such enter-tainments, which have the attractions of pleasure and delight, were of any consideration with you; you would not have much to say for York-shire, at this time of the year. But these are no arguments to you, who carry your own satisfaction, and I know not how many worlds always about you.   I would be glad you would think of putting all these up in a coach and bringing them this way.

For though you should be never the better, yet there be a great many here that would, and amongst them

The humblest of your Ladyship's servants

JOHN LOCKE

SAMUEL PEPYS (1633–1703)

Pepys's youth was spent in the turbulent days of the Commonwealth, but as a young man he obtained the patronage of his cousin, Sir Edward Montague, later Earl of Sandwich. After the Restoration he was made "Clerk of the Acts" of the Navy and a clerk of the Privy Seal. The first letter printed below refers to the decision of the Navy to support the Restoration of Charles II, made at a council of War at which Pepys acted as secretary. It is given as it appears in the Diary, and is a very early example of a letter written solely to give publicity to the writer. The last of our letters was written to Lord Sandwich, when he was in danger of losing the King's favour by his absence from Court, and was being generally condemned for his way of life.

May 4th. I wrote this morning many letters, and to all the copies of the vote of the council of war I put my name, that if it should come in print my name may be *to* it. I sent a copy of the vote to Doling, inclosed in this letter:

Sir, He that can fancy a fleet (like ours) in her pride, with pendants loose, guns roaring, caps flying, and the loud "Vive le Roy's," echoed from one ship's company to another, he, and he only, can apprehend the joy this inclosed vote was received with, or the blessing he thought himself possessed of that bore it, and is

Your humble servant.

TO SIR W. COVENTRY

SEPTEMBER 4, 1666

Sir, The fire is now very near us as well on Tower Street as Fenchurch Street side, and we little hope of our escape but by that remedy to the want whereof we do certainly owe the loss of the City, namely, the pulling down of houses in the way of the fire. This way Sir W. Pen and myself have so far concluded upon the practising that he is gone to Woolwich and Deptford to supply himself with men and necessaries in order to the doing thereof, in case at his return our condition be not bettered and that he meets with his R.H.'s approbation, which I have thus undertaken to learn of you. Pray please to let me have this night (at whatever hour it is) what his R.H.'s directions are in this particular. Sir J. Minnes and Sir W. Batten having left us, we cannot add, though we are well assured, of their, as well as all the neighbourhood's concurrence.

Your obedient Servant,

S. P.

TO LORD SANDWICH

MY LORD, I do verily hope that neither the manner nor matter of this advice will be condemned by your Lordship, when for my defence in the first I shall allege my double attempt, since your return from Hinchinbrok, of doing it personally, in both of which your Lordship's occasions, no doubtfulness of mine, prevented me, and that being now fearful of a sudden summons to Portsmouth, for the discharge of some ships there, I judge it very unbecoming the duty which every bit of bread I eat tells me I owe to your Lordship to expose the safety of your honour to the uncertainty of my return. For the matter, my Lord, it is such as could I in any measure think safe to conceal from or likely to be discovered to you by any other hand, I should not have dared so far to own what from my heart I believe is false, as to make myself but the relater of other's discourse; but, so, your Lordship's honour being such as I ought to value it to be, and finding both in city and court that discourses pass to your prejudice too generally for mine or any man's controllings but your Lordship's, I shall, my Lord, without the least greatening or lessening the matter, do my duty in laying it shortly before you.

People of all conditions, my Lord, raise matter of wonder from your Lordship's so little appearance at Court; some concluding thence their disfavour thereby, to which purpose I have had questions asked me, and endeavouring to put off such insinuations by asserting the contrary, they have replied, that your Lordship's living so beneath your quality, out of the way, and declining of Court attendance, hath been more than once discoursed about the King. Others, my Lord, when the chief ministers of State, and those most active of the Council have been reckoned up, wherein your Lordship never used to want an eminent place, have said, touching your Lordship, that now your turn was served, and the King had given you a good estate, you left him to stand or fall as he would, and, particularly in that of the Navy, have enlarged upon your letting fall all service there.

Another sort, and those the most, insist upon the bad report of the house wherein your Lordship, now observed in perfect health again, continues to sojourn, and by name have charged one of the daughters for a common courtesan, alleging both places and persons where and with whom she hath been too well known, and how much her wantonness occasions, though unjustly, scandal to your Lordship, and that as well to gratifying of some enemies as to the wounding of more friends I am not able to tell.

Lastly, my Lord, I find a general coldness in all persons towards your Lordship, such as, from my first dependence on you, I never yet knew, wherein I shall not offer to interpose any thoughts or advice of mine, well knowing your Lordship needs not any. But with a most faithful assurance that no person nor papers under Heaven is privy to what I here write, besides myself and this, which I shall be careful to have put into your own hands, I rest confident of your Lordship's just construction of my dutiful intents herein, and in all humility take leave, may it please your Lordship,

Your Lordship's most obedient Servant,

S. P.

SIR GEORGE ETHEREGE (c. 1635–91)

Etherege personified the spirit of the Restoration. A close friend of Rochester and Sedley, "Easy Etherege," as he was called, lived the gay life of London, flaunting the conventions and even the decencies. On account of a disgraceful brawl he had to fly the country, but his interest at Court procured him diplomatic employment at The Hague and Ratisbon. As these letters show, however, his heart was ever in London.

TO MR. DRYDEN

RATISBON 10/20 MARCH 1686/7

SIR, You know I am no flatterer, and therefore will excuse me when I tell you I cannot endure you should arrogate a thing to yourself you have not the least pretence to. Is it not enough that you excel in so many eminent virtues but you must be a putting in for a vice which all the world knows is properly my province? If you persist in your claim to laziness you will be thought as affected in it as Montaigne is, when he complains of the want of memory. What soul has ever been more active than your own? what country, nay what corner of the earth has it not travelled into? whose bosom has it not dived into and informed itself there so perfectly of all the secrets of man's heart that only the Great Being, whose image it bears, knows them better? I, whose every action of *my* life is a witness of my idleness, little thought that you, who have raised so many immortal monuments of your industry, durst have set up to be my rival. But to punish you I will distinguish: you have no share in that noble laziness of mind which all I write make out my just title to, but as for that of the body I can let you come in for a snack without any jealousy. I am apt to think you have bated something of your mettle since you and I were rivals. in other matters, though I hope you have not yet obtained the perfection I have heard Sir Charles Sedley brag of: which is, that when a short youth runs quick through every vein and puts him in mind of his ancient prowess, he thinks it not worth while to bestow motion on his *et cætera muscle*.

Though I have not been able formerly to forbear playing the fool

177

in verse and prose I have now judgment enough to know how much I ventured, and am rather amazed at my good fortune than vain upon a little success; and did I not see my own error the commendation you give me would be enough to persuade me of it. A woman, who has luckily been thought agreeable, has not reason to be proud when she hears herself extravagantly praised by an undoubted beauty. It would be a pretty thing for a man who has learned of his own head to scrape on the fiddle to enter the list with the greatest master in the science of music.

It is not to contend with you in writing but to vie with you in kindness that makes me fond of your correspondence, and I hope my want of art in friendship will make you forget the faults it makes me commit in writing.

I have not time now to acquaint you how I like my employment. Nature no more intended me for a politician than she did you for a courtier, but since I am embarked I will endeavour not to be wanting in my duty. It concerns me nearly, for, should I be shipwrecked, the season is too far gone to expect another adventure. The conversation I have with the ministers here improves me daily more in philosophy than in policy, and shows me that the most necessary part of it is better to be learned in the wide world than in the gardens of Epicurus.

I am glad to hear your son is in the office; hoping now and then by your favour to have the benefit of a letter from him. Pray tell Sir Henry Shere, his honesty and good understanding have made me love him ever since I knew him. If we meet in England again he may find the gravity of this place has fitted me for his Spanish humour.

I was so pleased with reading your letter than I was vexed at the last proof you gave me of your laziness, the not finding it in your heart to turn over the paper. In that you have had the better of me; but I will always renounce that darling sin, rather than omit anything which may give you an assurance of my being faithfully yours, &c.

TO LORD MIDDLETON

[RATISBON, 4/14 APRIL, 87]

My LORD, My last to your Lordship of the 31st of March was about a business which concerns Abbot Fleming. He tells me when he was in England you would have advised him to ask his Majesty's letter to the Pope, rather than to the Elector of Bavaria, which cost him the trouble and charge of a long journey to no purpose. He hopes your

Lordship will think fit to move his Majesty in what he humbly desires now, it being only his Majesty's letter to the Cardinal of Norfolk to give him authority to use his Majesty's name to his Holiness in his behalf.

There has happened a difference between two Protestant princes of the Empire lately; the Elector of Brandenburg and the Duke of Zell, touching a commandery called Gartau, which lies on the Elbe. This commandery, as it is said, has always been held on the house of Brunswick, and when it was alienated by the Knights of Malta they were acknowledged as lords, and all into whose hands it has come since have ever owned them as such. The present possessor, a gentleman whose name is Beaulieu, is a subject of the Elector of Brandenburg, and was summoned by him to come and do him fealty for this commandery, the Elector pretending that all the commanderies in the Empire which are in the hands of Protestants depend on him as their great prior or master. Beaulieu, though strictly charged to the contrary by the Duke of Zell, has acknowledged the Elector his lord, and the Elector in a solemn hunting, according to the custom here, to set out his limits included these lands. The Duke of Zell, at the same time, put a company of foot into the house to keep the possession, and lodges three or four more companies thereabout to support them in case they should be attached. The Duke of Zell has since writ a letter to the Elector in such high terms that they have both given order to their troops to march towards the said commandery.

The Duchess of Hanover is now at Berlin, and it is thought she may facilitate the making up of this business. The occasion of her journey thither is to compose another difference, which is between the Prince Electoral and his wife, her daughter, which I am trusted with as a secret.

The French had some time been ill satisfied with the Elector of Brandenburg's conduct as to their affairs, and have broke off the secret alliance they had with him, and disappointed him of a sum of money which would have been welcome at this time, I am &c.

TO MR. CORBET

[RATISBON, 18/28 APRIL, 87]

SIR, Yesterday your letter of the 30th of March came to my hands, and gave me a pleasure which nothing but the like proof of your kindness can give me here. If my ghost be as restless when I am in the other world as my mind now I am in another country, my friends must expect to be much haunted; it will cost them some frights, and, it may be, some money to lay me.

There is not a day but my thoughts dog you from the coffee-house to the play, from thence to Marylebone, always concerned for your good luck, and in pain I cannot make one with you in the sports you follow. Some of the ancients have imagined that the greatest torment of the dead was an impatient longing after what they delighted most in while they were living, and I can swear by my damnation in Germany, this hell is no jesting matter. Now Mr. B—— is promoted I hope Mr. Swan will be mounted. I am sorry on so good an occasion I have not a quibble in my head which would pass muster. I pity Mrs. Debora's loss in Mr. Whitaker's being gone to board in another quarter; if he happens into a house with Mr. Crown John's songs and Joseph's voice will charm the whole family.

I find the colonel is resolved to blaze to the last as well as myself. Methinks I see in a triumph of our present loves a Cupid, for fear of burning his fingers, with a little piece of a torch on a saveall. He has beauty, the strongest Bavarian with her sandy coloured locks, brawny limbs, and a brick complexion, and yet I find myself often very hearty.

Pray remember me kindly to all my friends, and particularly to Tom Maule. I am very sensible of the trouble the correspondence you have had with me gives you. I shall not tire you with any tedious acknowledgments, but only assure you you oblige one who cannot be ungrateful and is extremely

Sir, &c.

TO LORD DORSET

[RATISBON, 25 JULY, 87]

MY LORD, When you consider I have been two years from England without letting you know I am sensible you are the person in the world I am most obliged to, you will have reason to think me ungrateful; but I know your humour so well you had rather forgive a debt than be troubled with acknowledgment. I hope therefore you will look upon the neglect as the mere effect of laziness, and will easily excuse that vice in me, who am in a country from whence I can send you nothing to contribute to your pleasure. All my business in this dull place is to give a bare account of what is done, which requires only a little plain sense. I have lost for want of exercise the use of fancy and imagination, and am grown so very stupid that when I read a new poem methinks the author should be invited to one of those reverend cells the hermit Lee [1] has quitted. Lovers have been metamorphosed by the ancient poets, though churches have not yet; you and I were ne'er so bold to turn the fair Castle when she fled us into a tree, not dreaming she would grow as big as one of Evelyn's oaks, nor ourselves into bulls when we carried the two draggle-tailed nymphs one bitter, frosty night over the Thames to Lambeth. Sertorius aimed to make a milk-white hind an immortal dame, but his hint's improved by the lady of the spotted muff's ingracious son. I cannot guess on whom the Duke of Buck's mantle is fallen, but it is MacFleckno with doubled portion of that prophet's art.

I am so glad of an occasion of laughing here; it is no wonder the ridicule gets the better of the heroic; a letter from Sheppard might get the better of both if he had as great an alacrity in writing as he has in talking; there would be many congratulations if he had liberty granted him in this point; I wish it him heartily, since I never knew he had any further malice in it than making the company split themselves with laughter.

I would gladly be a witness of the content you enjoy at Copt Hall now, and I hope to surprise you there one day, your gravity laid aside, teaching my Lord Buckhurst how to manage his hobby horse. I am, &c.

[1] Nathaniel Lee, the dramatist, was confined on two occasions in Bethlehem Hospital during periods of insanity.

LADY RACHEL RUSSELL (1636–1723)

Lady Rachel was the wife of the famous "Patriot Russell" who fell a victim to intrigue in the time of Charles II. She survived him many years, and was herself a woman of considerable parts. This letter to her friend, Doctor Fitzwilliam, throws a domestic light on a remarkable character.

TO DR. FITZWILLIAM

IF you have heard of the dismal accident in this neighbourhood, you will easily believe Tuesday night was not a quiet one with us. About one o'clock in the night, I heard a great noise in the square, so little ordinary, I called up a servant, and sent her down to learn the occasion. She brought up a very sad one, that Montague House was on fire; and it was so indeed; it burned with so great violence, the whole house was consumed by five o'clock. The wind blew strong this way, so that we lay under fire a great part of the time, the sparks and flames continually covering the house, and filling the court. My boy awaked, and said he was almost stifled with smoke, but being told the reason, would see it, and so was satisfied without fear; took a strange bedfellow very willingly, Lady Devonshire's youngest boy, whom his nurse had brought wrapped in a blanket. Lady Devonshire came towards morning, and lay here; and had done so still, but for a second ill accident. Her brother, Lord Arran, who has been ill of a fever twelve days, was despaired of yesterday morning, and spots appeared; so she resolved to see him, and not to return hither, but to Somerset House, where the queen offered her lodgings. He is said to be dead, and I hear this morning it is a great blow to the family; and that he was a most dutiful son and kind friend to all his family.

Thus we see what a day brings forth! and how momentary the things we set our hearts upon. O, I could heartily cry out: "When will longed-for eternity come!" but our duty is to possess our souls with patience.

I am unwilling to shake off all hopes about the brief, though I know them that went to the chancellor since the refusal to seal it, and his answer does not encourage one's hopes.   But he is not a lover of smooth language, so in that respect we may not so soon despair.

I fancy I saw the young man you mentioned to be about my son. One brought me six prayer-books as from you; also distributed three or four in the house.   I sent for him, and asked him if there was no mistake.   He said no.   And after some other questions, I concluded him the same person.   Doctor, I do assure you I put an entire trust in your sincerity to advise; but, as I told you, I shall ever take Lord Bedford along in all the concerns of the child.   He thinks it early yet to put him to learn in earnest; so do you, I believe.   My lord is afraid, if we take one for it, he will put him to it; yet I think perhaps to overcome my lord in that, and assure him he shall not be pressed.   But I am much advised, and indeed inclined, if I could be fitted to my mind, to take a Frenchman; so I shall do a charity, and profit the child also, who shall learn French.   Here are many scholars come over, as are of all kinds, God knows.

I have still a charge with me, Lady Devonshire's daughter, who is just come into my chamber; so must break off.   I am, sir, truly your faithful servant.

The young lady tells me Lord Arran is not dead, but rather better.

CHARLES SACKVILLE, 6th EARL OF DORSET (1638–1706)

Sackville was among the most famous wits and poets of the gay Restoration court. He was notorious as the lover of Nell Gwynne, and was a friend of Sir Charles Sedley, whose poems were published with his own in 1701. During the First Dutch War he was serving in the fleet, and sent to London his famous lines to the ladies of Whitehall.

TO THE LADIES OF WHITEHALL

To all you ladies now at land
    We men at sea indite;
But first would have you understand
    How hard it is to write:
The Muses now, and Neptune too,
We must implore to write to you—
    With a fa, la, la, la, la.

For though the Muses should prove kind,
    And fill our empty brain,
Yet if rough Neptune rouse the wind
    To wave the azure main,
Our paper, pen, and ink, and we,
Roll up and down our ships at sea—
    With a fa, la, la, la, la.

Then if we write not by each post,
    Think not we are unkind;
Nor yet conclude our ships are lost
    By Dutchmen or by wind:
Our tears we'll send a speedier way,
The tide shall bring them twice a day—
    With a fa, la, la, la, la.

The King with wonder and surprise
    Will swear the seas grow bold,
Because the tides will higher rise
    Then e'er they did of old:
But let him know it is our tears
Bring floods of grief to Whitehall stairs—
    With a fa, la, la, la, la.

Should foggy Opdam chance to know
    Our sad and dismal story,
The Dutch would scorn so weak a foe,
    And quit their fort at Goree:
For what resistance can they find
From men who've left their hearts behind?—
    With a fa, la, la, la, la.

Let wind and weather do its worst,
    Be you to us but kind;
Let Dutchmen vapour, Spaniards curse,
    No sorrow we shall find:
'Tis then no matter how things go,
Or who's our friend or who's our foe—
    With a fa, la, la, la, la.

To pass our tedious hours away
    We throw a merry main,
Or else at serious ombre play:
    But why should we in vain
Each other's ruin thus pursue?
We were undone when we left you—
    With a fa, la, la, la, la.

But now our fears tempestuous grow
    And cast our hopes away;
Whilst you, regardless of our woe,
    Sit careless at a play:
Perhaps permit some happier man
To kiss your hand, or flirt your fan—
    With a fa, la, la, la, la.

When any mournful tune you hear,
  That dies in every note
As if it sigh'd with each man's care
  For being so remote,
Think then how often love we've made
To you, when all those tunes were play'd—
  With a fa, la, la, la, la.

In justice you cannot refuse
  To think of our distress,
When we for hopes of honour lose
  Our certain happiness:
All those designs are but to prove
Ourselves more worthy of your love—
  With a fa, la, la, la, la.

And now we've told you all our loves,
  And likewise all our fears,
In hopes this declaration moves
  Some pity for our tears:
Let's hear of no inconstancy—
We have too much of that at sea—
  With a fa, la, la, la, la.

APHRA BEHN (1640–89)

*Mrs. Aphra Behn was one of the first—if not actually the first—
English woman novelist. She was the daughter of a barber named
Johnson, and married a Dutchman. Her novel "Oroonoko" was very
famous in its day and her plays were favourites of the Restoration stage.*

TO TONSON, THE BOOK-SELLER

DEAR MR. TONSON, I am mightily obliged to you for the service you
have done me to Mr. Dryden, in whose esteem I would choose to be
rather than anybody's in the world. And I am sure I never, in thought,
word, or deed, merited other from him, but if you had heard what was
told me, you would have excused all I said on that account. Thank
him most infinitely for the honour he offers, and I shall never think
I can do anything that can merit so vast a glory; and I must owe it
all to you if I have it. As for Mr. Creech, I would not have you
afflict him with a thing [that] can not now be helped, so never let him
know my resentment. I am troubled for the line that's left out of
Dr. Garth, and wish your man would write it in the margin, at his
leisure, to all you sell.

As for the verses of mine, I should really have thought them worth
thirty pound; and I hope you will find it worth £25; not that I should
dispute at any other time for 5 pound where I am so obliged; but you
cannot think what a pretty thing the Island will be, and what a deal
of labour I shall have yet with it. And if that pleases, I will do the
second voyage, which will compose a little book as big as a novel by
itself. But pray speak to your brother to advance the price to one
5 pound more, 'twill at this time be more than given me, and I vow
I would not ask it if I did not really believe it worth more. Alas I
would not lose my time in such low gettings, but only since I am about
it I am resolved to go through with it though I should give it. I pray
go about it as soon as you please, for I shall finish as fast as you can
go on. Methinks the Voyage should come last, as being the largest
volume. You know Mr. Cowley's "David" is last, because a large
poem, and Mrs. Philips her plays for the same reason. I wish I had

more time; I would add something to the verses that I have a mind too, but, good dear Mr. Tonson, let it be 5 pound more, for I may safely swear I have lost the getting of 50 pound by it, though that's nothing to you, or my satisfaction and humour: but I have been without getting so long that I am just on the point of breaking, especially since a body has no credit at the playhouse for money as we used to have, fifty or sixty deep, or more; I want extremely or I would not urge this.

Yours,
A. B.

Pray send me the loose papers to put to these I have, and let me know which you will go about first; the songs and verses or that. Send me an answer to-day.

ROBERT PLOT (1640–96)

Doctor Plot was a zealous antiquary and also one of the most eminent writers on natural history of his time. His letter to Doctor Charlett, himself a scientist of some repute, shows that Plot was not without a sense of humour.

TO DR. CHARLETT

ROCHESTER, AUGUST 18, 1693

GOOD MASTER, According to my promise I here send you word that I have reached this place, having been as successful in my journey as I could expect. But the greatest rarity that I met with has been here, viz., a medicine for the bite of a mad dog, which was applied here to Dr. de Langley, Prebend of Canterbury, his wife and fair daughter, who were all three dipped in salt-water a little below the bridge, without fig-leaves, last Friday morning by two lewd [common] fellows of this town, the spectators, you may be sure, being very numerous. That the Rev. Dr. was really mad I hope you will not doubt; but whether the medicine had its due effect I guess I shall hear by that time I reach Canterbury, when you shall be sure to hear again from

Your most faithful friend,

ROB. PLOT

RICHARD STRETTON (*fl.* 1695)

Who the Rev. Richard Stretton was, or what part he played in life, has escaped the makers of biographical dictionaries. He was, however, a friend of good Ralph Thoresby, the antiquary, and that he was a man of feeling is proved by these letters.

TO RALPH THORESBY

LONDON, MAY 4, 1695

DEAR SIR, This brings you the most sad disconsolate tidings that ever I had occasion to send you. It hath pleased the only wise God, with one stroke of his hand, to remove the desire of mine eyes, and the delight of my heart, my tender, loving, and dearly beloved wife from me yesterday between seven and eight at night (after four or five days of pain and sickness); with a cheerful, sweet, composed countenance, without so much as one sigh or groan, she resigned up her soul into the hands of a tender Redeemer, who loved her, and washed her from her sins in his own blood. She had no pangs in her death: she is got to rest, and I have not the least hesitation, or doubt in my own heart, but that she is as well as heart can wish; but we are left in a sad desolate and disconsolate estate. But God hath spoken, and he also hath done it, and what shall I say? I will be dumb and not open my mouth, because he hath done it; it is fit to be silent before God, when God puts us to silence. He had a greater right in her than I had; his did precede and excel mine, and he hath better provided for her than ever I could have done. My lease of her was expired and forfeited long before; and as a Sovereign he may dispose of his own as he pleaseth. She lived desired, and dies as much lamented as most women of her rank ever were. She will be missed by more than near relations. I have lost as loving, tender, prudent a wife, and my son as tender careful a mother, as ever any could enjoy. Oh! what arrears of thankfulness are due, that we enjoyed her so long, and so much sweetness and comfort in her; help us with your prayers (and engage all our friends to beg) for support under, and a sanctified use and improvement of this severe providence. I have known what it is to part with sweet hopeful

190

children, and it is hard enough to bear it; but to part with a wife, and such a wife, cuts deep and reacheth the very soul. Mine, and my son's hearty love and service to you and your's, and to all friends. I commit you to God and rest

Yours sorrowful, afflicted friend and servant,

RICHARD STRETTON

TO THE SAME

LONDON, FEBRUARY 25, 1695–6

DEAR SIR, These bring you the most amazing, surprising news of God's gracious care over us, and goodness to us, in the discovering, and thereby preventing an hellish cursed plot, as deeply and cunningly laid, and as near to execution, as the Powder-plot was. There were, some say fifty, others say three hundred, ruffians in a conspiracy, under an oath of secrecy and fidelity, to assassinate the King; and it was to have been executed last Saturday at Richmond, as he was shooting; or if that failed (for he did not go as he was wont), then on the Lord's-day, as he went to chapel; and the Duke of Berwick, it is said, is in town, ready to have headed the insurrection upon the news of the blow being given; and King James lay at Calais, where Boufflers was ready with twenty thousand men to embark (upon three or four hundred transport ships they had ready, and Du Bart's fleet to be their guard,) as soon as they heard of the King's death. But God hath detected, and thereby, we hope, disappointed their villainous wickedness, and caused their own tongues to fall upon themselves. It is said one of the conspirators discovered it to the King on Wednesday was se'nnight; and the King had two expresses from Flanders last week, one on Wednesday, and the other on Saturday, giving him an account of Boufflers' march to King James at Calais, and the Duke of Berwick and others being here and wishing the King to take care of his own person. They came from the Duke of Bavaria, or Wittenburgh, or both; and they had drawn down twenty thousand men towards Ostend, to be ready to embark if others did. On Saturday there was a great council sat, and warrants issued out to apprehend the conspirators, several of which are seized. It was said yesterday there were fourteen in Newgate, and the Lord Mohun sent to the Tower. They are in a close search for the Duke of Berwick, the Lord Powis, Middleton, and Parker, (that escaped out of the Tower,) and others, that they say are in town. On the Lord's-day, my Lord Mayor and his brethren were sent for to Kensington, and they have ordered the raising of the trained-bands; and auxiliaries to be ready. Yesterday, his Majesty came to the House, and made a speech to both Houses, (which is printed,) acquainting them with the discovery of this hellish conspiracy. Both Houses agreed on an address, wherein they acknowledge him the only rightful King of England, and congratulate his deliverance, and assure him they will stand by him with their lives and fortunes to secure his person and support his government, against King James, and all his enemies, at home or abroad; and if he should die an untimely death, (which God forbid!) they will revenge his death upon his enemies. The Commons ordered an association to be drawn up to the same purpose, which they agreed to, and were to subscribe this day; and have ordered a Bill to be brought in, that if any thing happen to his Majesty, the Parliament in being shall not be dissolved till the next rightful heir shall do it. They have addressed the King to take care of his sacred person, and to secure all them that he may suspect will disturb his government; and have ordered a Bill to be brought in to suspend the Habeas Corpus Bill, that he may secure them: and several other good things they did; the best day's work that ever they yet made. They sat till seven, and then went both Houses in a body with their address to Kensington. Our Common Council met twice this day to finish their address. The Earl of Romney is sent down into Kent to raise their militia, and the Earl of Scarborough into Sussex, to do the like. Admiral Russel is gone into the Downs, and all the men-of-war sent to sail with him. It is hoped there are forty or fifty men-of-war rendezvoused there by this time; we have good hopes their mischievous designs will be prevented. My hearty love and service to you and your's, and to all friends. I commit you to God, and rest, in haste, your's,

R. S.

THOMAS WILKINS (*fl.* 1695)

Wilkins was a little country curate who had a strange psychic adventure. His account of it, written to old Richard Bentley, makes good reading.

TO RICHARD BENTLEY

OXON, DEC. 11, 1695

AT Warblington, near Havant, in Hampshire, within 6 miles of Portsmouth, in the Parsonage house dwelt Thomas Perce, the tenant, with his wife and a child, and a manservant Thomas and a maidservant. About the beginning of August, anno 1695, on a Monday, about 9 or 10 at night, all being gone to bed except the maid with the child, the maid being in the kitchen, and having raked up the fire, took a candle in one hand and the child in the other arm, and turning about, saw a figure in a black gown walking through the room, and thence out of the door into the orchard. Upon this, the maid, hasting up stairs, having covered but two steps, cried out. On which the master and mistress ran down, found the candle in her hand, she grasping the child about its neck with the other arm. She told them the reason of her crying out. She would not that night tarry in the house, but removed to another belonging to one Henry Salter, farmer, where she cried out all the night from the terror she was in, and she could not be persuaded to go any more to the house upon any terms.

On the morrow, i.e. Tuesday, the tenant's wife came to me, lodging then at Havant, to desire my advice, and have me consult with some friends about it. I told her I thought it was a sham, and that they had a desire to abuse Mr. Brereton, the Rector, whose house it was. She desired me to come up. I told her I would come up, and sit up or lie there as she pleased; for then, as to all stories of ghosts and apparitions I was an infidel. I went thither, and sat up the Tuesday night with the tenant and his manservant. About twelve or one o'clock I searched all the rooms in the house to see if anybody were hid there to impose upon me. At last we came into a lumber-room; there I smiling told the tenant that was with me, that I would call for the apparition, if there was any, and oblige him to come. The tenant then seemed to be afraid, but I told him I would defend him from harm; and then I repeated "Barbara, Celarent, Darij," &c. On this the tenant's countenance changed, so that he was ready to drop down with fear. Then I told him I perceived he was afraid, and I would prevent its coming, and repeated "Baralipton," &c. Then he recovered his spirits pretty well, and we left the room, and went down into the kitchen, where we were before, and sat up there the remaining part of the night, and had no manner of disturbance.

Wednesday night, the tenant and I lay together, and the man by himself, and had no manner of disturbance.

Thursday night, the tenant and I lay together in one room, and the man in another room, and he saw something walk along in a black gown, and place itself against a window, and there stood for some time, and then walked off.

Friday morning, the man relating this, I asked him why he did not call me, and I told him that I thought that was a trick or sham. He told me the reason why he did not call me was that he was not able to speak or move. Friday night we lay as before, and Saturday night, and had no disturbance either of the nights.

Sunday night, I lay by myself in one room, (not that where the man saw the apparition), and the tenant and his man in one bed in another room: and betwixt 12 and 2 the man heard something walk in their room at their bed's foot, and whistling very well. At last it came to the bedside, drew the curtain, and looked on them: after some time it moved off. Then the man called to me, desired me to come; for that there was something in the room went about whistling. I asked him whether he had any light, or could strike one. He told me no. Then I leaped out of bed; and not staying to put on my clothes, went out of my room and along a gallery to their door, which I found locked and bolted. I desired him to unbolt the door, for that I could not get in. Then he got out of bed and opened the door, which was near, and went immediately to bed again. I went 3 or 4 steps; and, it being a moonshine night, I saw the apparition move from the bed's feet, and clap up against the wall that divided their room and mine. I went and stood directly against it, within my arm's length of it and asked it in the name of God what it was, what made it come disturbing of us. I stood some time expecting an answer, and receiving none; and thinking it might be some fellow hid in the room to fright me, I put out my arm to feel it, and my hand seemingly went through the body of it, and felt no manner of substance till it came to the wall. Then I drew back my hand, and still it [the figure] was in the same place. Till now I had not the least fear, and even now had very little. Then I adjured it to tell me what it was. When I had said those words, it, keeping its back against the wall, moved gently along toward the door; I followed it, and it going out at the door, turned its back toward me. It went a little along the gallery; I followed it a little into the gallery, and it disappeared where there was no corner for it to turn, and before it came to the end of the gallery, where was the stairs. Then I found myself very cold from my feet as high as my middle, though I was not in great fear. I went into the bed betwixt the tenant and his man, and they complained of my being exceeding cold. The tenant's man leaned over his master in the bed, and saw me stretch out my arm toward the apparition, and heard me speak the words, the tenant also heard the words. The apparition seemed to have a morning gown of a darkish colour, no hat nor cap, short black hair, a thin meagre visage, of a pale swarthy colour, seemed to be of about 45 or 50 years old: the eyes half shut, the arms hanging down, the hands visible beneath the sleeve; of a middle stature. I related this description to Mr. John Larner, Rector of Havant, and to Major Battin of Langstone, in Havant parish. They both said the description agreed very well to Mr. Pitfield, a former Rector of the place, who has been dead above twenty years. Upon this the tenant and his family left the house, which has remained void since.

The Monday after last Michaelmas day, a man of Chedson, in Warwickshire, having been at Havant fair, passed by the foresaid Parsonage house about 9 or 10 at night, and saw a light in most of the rooms of the house, his pathway being close by the house. He wondering at the light, looked into the kitchen window, and saw only a light; but turning himself about to go away, he saw the appearance of a man in a long gown. He made haste away; the apparition followed him over a piece of Glebe land of several acres, to a lane, which he crossed, and over a little meadow; then over another lane to some pales which belong to Farmer Henry Salter, my landlord, near a barn in which were some of the farmer's men and some others. This man went into the barn, told them how he was frighted and followed from the Parsonage house by an apparition, which they might see standing against the pales if they went out. They went out and saw it scratch against the pales, and make a hideous noise. It stood there some time, and then disappeared. Their description agreed with what I saw. This last account I had from the man himself whom it followed, and also from the farmer's men.

THO: WILKINS, Curate of W.

WILLIAM WYCHERLEY (c. 1640–1716)

Wycherley had already made his name as a dramatist, and was an old man, when he penned the following letter to Alexander Pope. His comments on the virtues of a long life are characteristic of his spirit.

TO ALEXANDER POPE

MARCH 29, 1705

YOUR letter of the twenty-fifth of March I have received, which was more welcome to me than anything could be out of the country, though it were one's rent due that day; and I can find no fault with it, but that it charges me with want of sincerity, or justice, for giving you your due, who should not let your modesty be so unjust to your merit, as to reject what is due to it, and call that compliment, which is so short of your desert, that it is rather degrading than exalting you. But if compliment be the smoke only of friendship, as you say, however, you must allow there is no smoke but there is some fire; and as the sacrifice of incense offered to the gods would not have been half so sweet to others if it had not been for its smoke, so friendship, like love, cannot be without some incense to perfume the name it would praise and immortalize. But since you say you do not write to me to gain my praise, but my affection, pray how is it possible to have the one without the other? We must admire before we love. You affirm, you would have me so much your friend as to appear your enemy, and find out your faults rather than your perfections; but, my friend, that would be so hard to do that I, who love no difficulties, cannot be persuaded to it. Besides, the vanity of a scribbler is such that he will never part with his own judgment to gratify another's, especially when he must take pains to do it: and though I am proud to be of your opinion, when you talk of any thing or man but yourself, I cannot suffer you to murder your fame with your own hand, without opposing you. Especially when you say your last letter is the worst, since the longest, you have favoured me with, which I therefore think the best, as the longest life, if a good one, is the best, as it yields the more variety, and is the more exemplary; as a cheerful summer's day, though longer

197

than a dull one in the winter, is less tedious and more entertaining. Therefore, let but your friendship be like your letter, as lasting as it is agreeable, and it can never be tedious, but more acceptable and obliging to your, &c.

SIR ISAAC NEWTON (1642–1727)

Our letter is characteristic of the great mathematician and natural philosopher. It was written but a few years after he had expounded to the world his theory of the Law of Gravity.

TO RICHARD BENTLEY

CAMBRIDGE, FEB. 25, 1692/3

SIR, Because you desire speed, I'll answer your letter with what brevity I can. In the six position you lay down in the beginning of your letter, I agree with you. Your assuming the *Orbis magnus* 7,000 diameters of the earth wide, implies the Sun's horizontal parallax to be half a minute. Flamsteed and Cassini have of late observed it to be but about 10", and thus the *Orbis magnus* must be 21,000, or, in a rounder number, 20,000 diameters of the earth wide. Either assumption will do well; and I think it not worth the while to alter your numbers.

In the next part of your letter you lay down four other positions, founded upon the six first. The first of these four seems very evident, supposing you take attraction so generally as by it to understand any force by which distant bodies endeavour to come together without mechanical impulse. The second seems not so clear: for it may be said that there might be other systems of worlds before the present ones, and others before those, and so on to all past eternity; and, by consequence, that gravity might be coeternal to matter, and have the same effect from all eternity as at present, unless you have somewhere proved that old systems cannot gradually waste and pass into new ones; or that this system had not its original from the exhaling matter of former decaying systems, but from a chaos of matter evenly dispersed throughout all space. For something of this kind, I think you say, was the subject of your sixth sermon; and the growth of new systems out of old ones, without the mediation of a divine power, seems to me apparently absurd.

The last clause of your second Position I like very well. 'Tis inconceivable that inanimate brute matter should (without the mediation of something else, which is not material) operate upon and affect other matter without mutual contact; as it must, if gravitation, in the sense of Epicurus, be essential and inherent in it. And this is one reason why I desired you would not ascribe innate gravity to me. That gravity would be innate, inherent, and essential to matter, so that one body may act upon another at a distance through a vacuum, without the mediation of anything else, by and through which their action or force may be conveyed from one to another, is to me so great an absurdity that I believe no man who has in philosophical matters any competent faculty of thinking can ever fall into it. Gravity must be caused by an agent acting constantly according to certain laws; but whether this agent be material or immaterial, is a question I have left to the consideration of my readers.

Your fourth assertion, that the world could not be framed by innate gravity alone, you confirm by three arguments. But, in your first argument you seem to make a *petitio principii*; for whereas many ancient philosophers and others, as well Theists and Atheists, have allowed that there may be worlds and parcels of matter innumerable or infinite; you deny this by representing it as absurd as that there should be positively an infinite arithmetical sum or number, which is a contradiction *in terminis*; but you do not prove it as absurd. Neither do you prove that what men mean by an infinite sum or number is a contradiction in nature; for a contradiction *in terminis* argues nothing more than an impropriety of speech. Those things which men understand by improper and contradictious phrases may be sometimes really in nature without any contradiction at all: a silver inkhorn, a paper lanthorn, an iron whetstone, are absurd phrases; yet the things signified thereby are really in nature. If any man should say that a number and a sum (to speak properly) is that which may be numbered and summed, but things infinite are numberless, or (as we usually speak) innumerable and sumless, or insummable, and therefore ought not to be called a number or sum, he will speak properly enough, and your argument against him will, I fear, lose its force. And yet, if any man shall take the words number and sum in a larger sense, so as to understand thereby things which, in the proper way of speaking, are numberless and sumless (as you do, when you seem to allow an infinite number of points in a line), I could readily allow him the use of the contradictious phrases of an innumerable number or sumless sum, without inferring from thence any absurdity in the thing he means by those phrases. However, if by this or any other argument you have proved the finiteness of the universe, it follows that all matter would fall down from the outsides, and convene in the middle. Yet the matter in falling might concrete into many round masses, like the bodies of the planets, and these, by attracting one another, might acquire an obliquity of descent, by means of which they might fall, not upon the great central body, but on one side of it, and fetch a compass about it, and then ascend again by the same steps and degrees of motion and velocity with which they descended before, much after the manner that Comets revolve about the Sun. But a circular motion in concentric orbs about the sun they could never acquire by gravity alone.

And though all the matter were at first divided into several systems, and every system by a divine power constituted like ours; yet would the outward systems descend towards the middlemost; so that this frame of things could not always subsist without a divine power to conserve it; which is your second argument: and to your third I fully assent.

As for the passage of Plato, there is no common place from whence all the Planets being let fall, and descending with uniform and equal gravities (as Gallileo supposes) would, at their arrival to their several Orbs, acquire their several velocities with which they now revolve in them. If we suppose the gravity of all the Planets towards the Sun to be of such a quantity as it really is, and that the motions of the Planets are turned upwards, every Planet will ascend to twice its height from the Sun. Saturn will ascend till he be twice as high from the Sun as he is at present and no higher; Jupiter will ascend as high again as at present, that is, a little above the orb of Saturn; Mercury will ascend to twice his present height, that is, to the orb of Venus; and so of the rest. And then, by falling down again from the places to which they ascended they will arrive again at their several orbs with the same velocities they had at first, and with which they now revolve.

But, if so soon as their motions by which they revolve are turned upwards, the gravitating power of the Sun, by which their ascent is perpetually retarded, be diminished by one half, they will now ascend perpetually, and all of them at all equal distances from the sun will be equally swift. Mercury, when he arrives at the orb of Venus, will be as swift as Venus; and he and Venus, when they arrive at the orb of the earth, will be as swift as the earth; and so of the rest. If they begin all of them to ascend at once, and ascend in the same line, they will constantly, in ascending, become nearer and nearer together, and their motions will constantly approach to an equality and become at length slower than any motion assignable. Suppose, therefore, that they ascended till they were almost contiguous, and their motions inconsiderably little, and that all their motions were all the same moment of time turned back again; or, (which comes almost to the same thing), that they were only deprived of their motions, and let fall at that time; they would all at once arrive at their several orbs, each with the velocity it had at first; and if their motions were then turned sideways, and, at the same time the gravitating power of the Sun doubled, that it might be strong enough to retain them in their Orbs, they would revolve in them as before their ascent. But if the gravitating power of the sun were not doubled, they would go away from their Orbs into the highest heavens in Parabolical lines. These things follow from my "Princip. Math." *lib.* i. *prop.* 33, 34, 36, 37.

I thank you very kindly for your designed present, and rest

Your most humble Servant to command,

Is. NEWTON

WILLIAM PENN (1644–1718)

The Quaker founder of the State of Pennsylvania was a man of considerable influence at Court, and, as shown in the first letter below, used it where possible to assist Friends when they got into trouble: George Fox, the founder of the Society, was in Worcester gaol suffering for his opinions, when the first letter was written, and his release soon followed as a result of Penn's exertions. The second letter was written to his wife and children on the eve of his departure for America.

TO GEORGE FOX

[1674]

DEAR GEORGE FOX, Thy dear and tender love in thy last letter received, and for thy business thus: A great lord, a man of noble mind, did as good as put himself in a loving way to get thy liberty. He prevailed with the king for a pardon, but that we rejected. Then he pressed for a more noble release, that better answered hath. It sticks with the Lord Keeper, and we have used, and do use what interest we have. The king is angry with him [the Lord Keeper] and promiseth very largely and lovingly, so that if we have been deceived, thou seest the grounds of it. But we have sought after a writ of error these ten days past, well-nigh resolving to be as sure as we can, and an *habeas corpus* is gone, or will go to-morrow night.

My dear love salutes thee and thy dear wife. Things are brave as to truth in these parts. Great conviction upon the people. My wife's love is to you all. I long and hope ere long to see thee. So, dear George Fox, am, etc.

WILLIAM PENN

TO HIS FAMILY

WORMINGHURST, 4TH OF THE 6TH MONTH, 1682

MY DEAR WIFE AND CHILDREN, My love, which neither sea, nor land, nor death can extinguish towards you, most endearedly visits

203

you with eternal embraces, and will abide with you for ever. My dear wife, remember thou wast the love of my youth and the joy of my life, the most beloved, as well as most worthy of all my earthly comforts. God knows and thou knowest it, it was a match of Providence's own making. Now I am to leave thee, and that without knowing whether I shall ever see thee more in this life.

Take my counsel to thy bosom:—

Firstly. Let the fear of the Lord dwell in you richly.

Secondly. Be diligent in meetings and worship and business, and let meetings be kept once a day in the family, and, my dearest, divide thy time and be regular. In the morning, view the business of the house. Grieve not thyself with careless servants, they will disorder thee, rather pay them and let them go. It is best to avoid many words, which I know wound the soul.

Thirdly. Cast up thy income and see what it daily amounts to, and I beseech thee live low and sparingly until my debts are paid. I write not as doubtful of thee, but to quicken thee.

Fourthly. My dearest, let me recommend to thy care the dear children abundantly beloved of me. Breed them up in the love of virtue. I had rather they were homely than finely bred. Religion in the heart leads into true civility, teaching men and women to be mild and courteous.

Fifthly. Breed them up in a love one of another. Tell them it is the charge I left behind me. Tell them it was my counsel, they should be tender and affectionate one to another. For their learning be liberal, spare no cost. Rather keep an ingenuous person in the house to teach them, than send them to schools, too many evil impressions being commonly received there. And now, dear children, be obedient to your dear mother, whose virtue and good name is an honour to you, for she hath been exceeded by none in integrity, industry, and virtue, and good understanding, qualities not usual among women of her worldly condition and quality. Be temperate in all things, watch against anger, and avoid flatterers, who are thieves in disguise. Be plain in your apparel, let your virtue be your ornament. Be not busy-bodies, meddle not with other folk's manners, and for you who are likely to be concerned in the Government of Pennsylvania, especially my first born, be lowly, diligent and tender. Keep upon the square, for God sees you. Use no tricks, but let your heart be upright before the Lord. So may my God, who hath blessed me with abundant mercies, guide you by His counsel, bless you, and bring you to His eternal glory. So farewell to my thrice beloved wife and children.

Yours as God pleaseth, which no waters can quench, no time forget, nor distance wear away, but remains for ever,

WILLIAM PENN

LADY RODES (*fl.* 1690)

These two letters are from a Quaker mother to her son, who had left her to go to London. Their virtue lies in an extreme simplicity and the intimate, homely light they throw on the times.

FOR SIR JOHN RODES

at William Meads in Fanshaw Street at the Sign of the Ship, London.

JUNE THE 14, 1690

MY DEAR LAMB, I received thine dated the 10 of this Instant. I was glad to hear thou wast recovered thy journey, and so willing to return home again so speedily. I hope there may be an opportunity fall out, when W. Penn returns back again, for thee to go to the Bath; for I am yet desirous thou should make a trial of the waters. But at present I am more willing thou shouldst be at home, because of W. Penn's coming into the country; for I would not have thee absent by no means when he comes. I hear by Francis Ludlame, my brother is come home, and was robbed upon his journey twenty miles this side of London. They took twenty guineas from him and what silver he had and his sword. He was in a hackney-coach, and there were three men besides him and one woman, and they took her watch from her and robbed them all; and there came a gentleman and his man by, whilst they were searching them, and they fell upon them and robbed them also. They would have persuaded them to have left them something to have borne their charges, but the thieves answered and said, such gentleman as they had credited upon the road. I would have thee forcast to have company down; but I trust and hope God Almighty will preserve thee and keep thee from the enemy, both outwardly and inwardly; it is him alone that I put my confidence in, for my expectation is from him only. Remember to inquire about my Sister Hussy's children—thou may tell S. Barker, his children are gone to Attercliffe. I would have thee mind him of speaking to Clark and sound him, that we may know what would stop his mouth, for I am very fearful of law suits, by reason of my large experience that I have had of the

206

charge and trouble they bring; which does much disquiet me, and I have been set very hard to bear them. But blessed be God, I have found him a present help in my needful time of trouble. If thou hear of any ships going to Virginia, I would have thee write to Charles Rodes, to give him an account we have written. This young S. Clarke told me when he was here, he would undertake to convey a letter safe to him; so, if thee can light on him, I would have thee write to C. Rodes and wish him to write speedily back, for I have a great desire to hear from him. I desire thee to tell S. Barker I would have him to buy me a silk dust-coat to ride in; for I find camlet is so thick for this hot weather, I cannot well endure it. I would have it a grave colour. It is a slight kind of a silk, and will not cost much. I would have as much as to make me a riding-coat and petticoat; if it be a yard broad, 3 breadths will be enough for the petticoat. If S. B. does not understand what silk I mean, he may call at Betty Ash and she can inform him what is used for dust-coats, what sort of silk. I write to thee since I received S. Barker's letter and the enclosed printed papers, and I have despatched one to Henry Jackson. R. Harrison and his wife were here yesterday to see me, and desired to have their dear loves and service to thee.

So with my own dear and tender love to my dear babe, I take leave of thee and remain thy affectionate Mother

M. RODES

Thy sisters remember their love to thee. I beseech God Almighty to bless and keep and preserve thee in thy journey and ever more, so saith my soul. My Love, my Love, farewell, farewell. Adieu.

I would have my coat partly of this colour, but rather sadder. My respects and kind love to S. Mead and Cousin Moris. . . .

TO THE SAME

THE 2ND MONTH, 1691

MY DEAR CHILD, I received thine by the Post by which I understand, Tom Bentley is got safe to London, and I approve of that way to have him be upon taking some time before he be bound. I did intend to put thee in mind of Joshua Kirby, for his mother is very desirous to have him out, and it will be a making to the boy; so I would have thee remember to get a place for him upon such reasonable terms as ten pound, and parents find him clothes and pay the moneys at twice.

I desire thee to get a handsome stuff suit and a good waistcoat. Thou knowst I did not like the last stuff suit, therefore remember and let it not be like that, but something more refined and finer. I wish that riding-coat of mine, the price I mean, had been bestowed on clothes for thee. As for me, its little matter what I wear. I cannot but take it kindly thou took such care for me, and it is a demonstration of thy love to me. Yet I should have certainly been satisfied of thy unfained love to me, without that chargable present. I cannot help confessing, how sweet and precious, and desirable and highly valuable thy love to me is, more than the gold of Ophir, and I hope nothing will be able to separate or withdraw thy affections from me, tho' formerly I believe, thou may remember some people were so wicked as they desired to see a breach betwixt us. But their hopes are frustrated, as the hope of the hypocrite will perish, and come to nothing; but the just shall be established and have an everlasting foundation which cannot be shaken by the blast and breath of wicked men. So, dear Babe, I commit thee to the keeping and protection of Him who alone can keep thee and me in safety and peace, so I hope he will keep us in unity with his good spirit and that will keep us in Peace and love one with another, which is the fervent and cordial desire of her that is thy unfained affec. Mother in the blessed truth of our God.

M. RODES

I have a mind to know if thou hast seen W.P. So, dear Babe, let nothing trouble thee, but still trust and hope in God for their safety in him both night and day which was an expression of thy dear father's upon his death bed. I do believe he came to witness and experience the sweetness of trusting and depending upon the God of his salvation, and I am satisfied he is at rest in the Lord.

JOHN WILMOT, EARL OF ROCHESTER (1647–80)

Rochester was one of the gayest and wildest of the gay and wild Restoration court. His wife, to whom the following letter was written, was wooed in characteristic style. Elizabeth Malet was, according to Pepys, "the great beauty and fortune of the north," though Gramont described her as "a melancholy heiress." When Rochester asked her to marry him she refused; shortly afterwards, on her return from supping with Frances Stewart, Rochester stopped her coach at Charing Cross, hauled her out of it forcibly, packed her into another that was waiting nearby, and whisked her off into the country. A hue and cry was started and they were caught at Uxbridge. Rochester was sent to the Tower, but after a while he was liberated and in due time married the lady.

TO HIS WIFE

I AM very glad to hear news from you, and I think it very good when I hear you are well; pray be pleased to send me word what you are apt to be pleased with, that I may shew you how good a hubsand I can be; I would not have you so formal as to judge of the kindness of a letter by the length of it, but believe of everything that it is as you would have it.

'Tis not an easy thing to be entirely happy; but to be kind is very easy, and that is the greatest measure of happiness. I say not this to put you in mind of being kind to me; you have practised that so long, that I have a joyful confidence you will never forget it; but to shew that I myself have a sense of what the methods of my life seemed so utterly to contradict, I must not be too wise about my own follies, or else this letter had been a book dedicated to you, and published to the world. It will be more pertinent to tell you, that very shortly the king goes to Newmarket, and then I shall wait on you at Adderbury; in the meantime, think of anything you would have me do, and I shall thank you for the occasion of pleasing you.

Mr. Morgan I have sent in this errand, because he plays the rogue here in town so extremely, that he is not to be endured; pray, if he behaves himself so at Adderbury, send me word, and let him stay till

I send for him.   Pray, let Ned come up to town; I have a little business with him, and he shall be back in a week.

Wonder not that I have not written to you all this while, for it was hard for me to know what to write upon several accounts; but in this I will only desire you not to be too much amazed at the thoughts my mother has of you, since, being mere imaginations, they will as easily vanish, as they were groundlessly erected; for my own part, I will make it my endeavour they may.   What you desired of me in your other letter, shall punctually be performed.   You must, I think, obey my mother in her commands to wait on her at Aylesbury, as I told you in my last letter.   I am very dull at this time, and therefore think it pity in this humour to testify myself to you any further; only, dear wife, I am your humble servant—ROCHESTER

JOHN RADCLIFFE (1650–1714)

Dr. Radcliffe, the benefactor of Oxford and of St. Bartholomew's Hospital, London, was a graduate of Oxford and a Fellow of Lincoln College. His London practice was very extensive and he made a large fortune. He correctly diagnosed smallpox as the fatal illness of Queen Mary, wife of William III. Subsequently he became physician to Queen Anne. In spite of his rough manners and intemperate habits he was a shrewd clinician. Radcliffe was the original owner of the "gold-headed cane" now in the library of the Royal College of Physicians. The following letter was found after his death.

TO HIS SISTER, MRS. MILLICENT RADCLIFFE

OCTOBER 22ND, 1714

MY DEAR, DEAR, MILLY, When this shall come to your hands, you will know that the writer of it is no longer in the land of the living where he has sojourned by the mercies of God to an advanced age and from whence, though an unworthy sinner, he has made his retreat in full confidence of Salvation by the precious Blood of his and of mankind's most Gracious Redeemer.

You will find by my will that I have taken better care of you than perhaps you might expect from my former treatment of you for which with my dying breath I most heartily ask pardon. I had, indeed, acted the brother's part much better in making a handsome settlement for you while living than after my decease; and can plead nothing in excuse but that the love of money, which I have emphatically known to be the root of all evil, was too predominant over me.

Though I hope I have made some amends for that odious sin of Coveteousness in my last dispositions of those worldly goods which it pleased the great dispenser of providence to bless me with.

It would be a great comfort to me, if departed souls have any sense of sublunary affairs, to know that the management of what I have bequeathed you for life shall be so laid out as to pave the way for you to a glorious immortality by acts of goodness and charity, since you will thereby be furnished with means of subsisting yourself and of

211

giving support to your indigent neighbour, whom you are commanded by the Gospel to *love as yourself*.

Your sister is under the necessity of being at much greater expenses than yourself; I have therefore left her a double portion, being well assured that it will create no misunderstanding between you from that uninterrupted affection which you have hitherto had for her and which she has reciprocally shown to you.

Since £500 per annum will enable you to live as handsomely and comfortably as £1,000 per annum will her, I have made the same disproportion between my nephews with the same hopes of their living amicably together, and desire you to let them know that I conjure them to live as becometh brethren that are of the same Household of Faith and of the same blood. I have nothing further than to beseech the Divine Being who is the God of the living to prosper you and all my relations with good and unblameable lives, that when you shall change the world you are now in for a better, we may all meet together in glory and enjoy these ineffable delights which are promised to all that love Christ's coming.

Till then, my dear, dear Milly, take this as a last farewell from

Your most Affectionate and Dying Brother

J. RADCLIFFE

N.B. The Jewels and Rings in my gilt cabinet, by my great scrutore, not mentioned in my will, I hereby bequeath to you.

JOHN CHURCHILL, DUKE OF MARLBOROUGH (1650–1722)

Marlborough was the finest soldier and diplomatist of his age, and commanded the English and Dutch armies against the French from 1702 to 1712. His desertion of James II at the Revolution gave him a character for treachery which his subsequent intrigues with his old master perpetuated. His letter to James, renouncing his service, suggests that he was at that time at least influenced by more than purely selfish motives.

TO KING JAMES II

[1689]

SIR, Since men are seldom suspected of sincerity when they act contrary to their interests, and though my dutiful behaviour to your Majesty in the worst of times (for which I acknowledge my poor services much overpaid) may not be sufficient to incline you to a charitable interpretation of my actions, yet I hope the great advantage I enjoy under your Majesty, which I can never expect in any other change of Government, may reasonably convince your Majesty and the world that I am actuated by a higher principle, when I offer that violence to my inclination and interest as to desert your Majesty at a time when your affairs seem to challenge the strictest obedience from all your subjects, much more from one who lies under the greatest obligations to your Majesty. This, Sir, could proceed from nothing but the inviolable dictates of my conscience, and a necessary concern for my religion (which no good man can oppose), and with which I am instructed nothing can come in competition. Heaven knows with what partiality my dutiful opinion of your Majesty has hitherto represented those unhappy designs which inconsiderate and self-interested men have framed against your Majesty's true interest and the Protestant religion; but as I can no longer join with such to give a pretence by conquest to bring them to effect, so I will alway with the hazard of my life and fortune (so much your Majesty's due) endeavour to preserve your royal person and lawful rights, with all the tender concerns and dutiful respect that becomes, Sir, your Majesty's most dutiful and most obliged subject and servant.

CHURCHILL

MARY II (1662–94)

Mary was one of the most lovable and charming characters in English history, and readers of Macaulay will recall with pleasure his happy tributes to her memory. For many years, both before and after her marriage, she kept up a constant correspondence with her friend, Frances Bathurst (née Apsley), whom she addressed as her "dear husband" and called, after the fashion of those times, by the high-sounding name of Aurelia. Herself she signed as Marie Clorinne.

TO AURELIA

MARCH 3RD, 1678

I NEVER repented writing to Mrs. Berkeley till now, that I find it was a trouble to you. I confess, it was a fault to write to anyone and not to my dearest, dearest, dearest dear husband; but you know I cannot have time enough any one day to write to all my friends, though you may be sure there is none I write to with more willingness and greater pleasure than I do to my dear Aurelia, who I love more than she can imagine or ever will believe. You know it has always been my choice to write to you when I could have seen you, and pray don't believe so ill of me to think [that] where I once love anything or anybody I can ever change my mind. For the picture, if there is anything in the world can make me sit, it shall be you, but you know what a pain it is; however, I shall, and that with as much haste as possible; though at this time I should sit with less pleasure than any other.

I suppose you know the Prince has gone to the Army; but I am sure you can guess of the trouble I am in. I am sure I could never have thought it half so much. I thought coming out of my own country, parting with my friends and relations the greatest that ever could, long as they lived, happen to me; but I am to be mistaken that now I find, till this time I never knew sorrow. For what could be more cruel in the world than parting with what one loves, and not only common parting but parting so as may be, never to meet again. To be perpetually in fear. For God knows when I may see him or whether he is not now at this instant in a battle. I reckon him now never

214

in safety, ever in danger. Oh, miserable life that I lead now. I do what I can to be merry when I am in company, but when I am alone, then it is that I remember all my griefs. I do not now wish to see any of my friends, for I should but be a trouble to them. Dear Aurelia, don't take it ill. With you I could be, because to you I should dare to speak, which to angels I dare not. Forgive me that I trouble you with this, but take it as a mark of my love. For I dare write this to you which I hardly dare think before another. Now I am in my closet I give myself up to my grief and melancholy thoughts, and you may believe it is a great comfort that I have a friend in the world to write them to.

I hope it won't be long now before I shall go to Breda, where I shall see the Prince. For he is so near the Army he can live in the town and go to it at any time at a quarter of an hour's warning. When I am there, if I don't write, don't wonder, for maybe I shan't have time, or twenty things may happen. However, be assured of this, that if I can I will. You shall still hear all my misfortunes, as a mark how much I love you.

MARIE CLORINNE

Pray remember me to Lady Apsley and Apsley, and my Lady Wentworth and Mrs. Legg. You can't doubt but I am very sorry to hear your sister has had the measles: I hope by this time she is quite well. Don't say anything of all I have writ to you, for I am ashamed of it; pray don't.

FRANCIS ATTERBURY (1662–1732)

Politician, controversialist and divine, Atterbury was one of the prominent characters during the first decades of the eighteenth century. Queen Anne made him Bishop of Rochester, but ten years later he fell into dire disgrace as a Jacobite, lost his bishopric and was forced into exile, where he died of a broken heart. The letter we print was written to Pope when Atterbury was at the height of his fame.

TO ALEXANDER POPE

SEPTEMBER 27, 1721

I AM now confined to my bed-chamber, and to the matted room wherein I am writing, seldom venturing to be carried down even into the parlour to dinner, unless when company to whom I cannot excuse myself comes, which I am not ill pleased to find is now very seldom. This is my case in the sunny part of the year: what must I expect when

Inversum contristat Aquarius annum?

"If these things be done in the green tree, what shall be done in the dry?" Excuse me for employing a sentence of Scripture on this occasion; I apply it very seriously. One thing relieves me a little under the ill prospect I have of spending my time at the Deanery this winter; that I shall have the opportunity of seeing you oftener; though, I am afraid, you will have little pleasure in seeing me there. So much for my ill state of health, which I had not touched on, had not your friendly letter been so full of it. One civil thing which you say in it made me think you had been reading Mr. Waller; and possessed of that image at the end of his copy, *à la malade*, had you not bestowed it on one who has no right to the least part of the character. If you have not read the verses lately, I am sure you remember them, because you forget nothing.

> With such a grace you entertain,
> And look with such contempt on pain, &c.

I mention them not upon account of that couplet, but one that follows; which ends with the very same rhymes and words (*appear*

216

and *clear*) that the couplet but one after that does; and therefore in my Waller there is various reading of the first of these couplets; for there it runs thus:

> So lightnings in a stormy air,
> Scorch more than when the sky is fair.

You will say that I am not very much in pain, nor very busy, when I can relish these amusements, and you will say true; for at present I am in both these respects very easy.

I had not strength to attend Mr. Prior to his grave, else I would have done it, to have shown his friends that I had forgot and forgiven what he wrote on me.   He is buried, as he desired, at the feet of Spenser, and I will take care to make good in every respect what I said to him when living; particularly as to the triplet he wrote for his own epitaph; while we were in good terms, I promised him should never appear on his tomb while I was Dean of Westminster.

I am pleased to find you have so much pleasure, and (which is the foundation of it) so much health at Lord Bathurst's: may both continue till I see you! May my Lord have as much satisfaction in building the house in the wood, and using it when built, as you have in designing it! I cannot send a wish after him that means him more happiness, and yet, I am sure, I wish him as much as he wishes himself.   I am, etc.

TOM BROWN (1663–1704)

Among the scurrilous coffee-house wits and hack writers at the end of the seventeenth century Tom Brown takes rank. He is little known now, except by those acquainted with the world of William and Mary; though quotation is often made of his famous rhyme beginning "I do not love thee, Doctor Fell."

TO A LADY WHO SMOKED TOBACCO

MADAM, Though the ill-natured world censures you for smoking, yet I would advise you, madam, not to part with so innocent a diversion. In the first place, it is healthful; and, as Galen rightly observes, it is a sovereign remedy for the toothache, the constant persecutor of old ladies. Secondly, tobacco, though it be a heathenish weed, is a great help to Christian meditations; which is the reason, I suppose, that recommends it to your parsons, the generality of whom can no more write a sermon without a pipe in their mouths, than a concordance in their hands; besides, every pipe you break may serve to put you in mind of mortality, and show you upon what slender accidents man's life depends. I knew a dissenting minister who, on fast-days, used to mortify upon a rump of beef, because it put him, as he said, in mind that all flesh was grass; but, I am sure, much more is to be learnt from tobacco. It may instruct you that riches, beauty, and all the glories of the world, vanish like a vapour. Thirdly, it is a pretty plaything. Fourthly, and lastly, it is fashionable, at least 'tis in a fair way of becoming so. Cold tea, you know, has been a long while in reputation at court, and the gill as naturally ushers in the pipe, as the sword-bearer walks before the lord mayor.

JOHN TOMKINS (1663-1706)

Tomkins was a Quaker annalist and the first biographer of the Society of Friends. The great storm which he here describes swept over the country on November 26, 1703. The loss sustained in London alone was calculated at £2,000,000. It is very graphically described by Defoe.

TO SIR JOHN RODES

LONDON, 2ND, 10M, 1703

DEARLY BELOVED FRIEND, It is now 9 days since thou left us, by which time we expected an account of thy safe arrival at home, being the more concerned by reason of a violent storm of wind, of which we have not known the like, not the oldest man that we know of. It began to blow so hard here from South-west, and by west, last 4th day, *viz.* 24 last mo., at which time one man-of-war was lost off Harwich and damage in divers other places—and so continued turbulent till last 6th day, 26, about 11th hour night, and held in an extreme manner, till past 7th hour next morning. The violence thereof, not only did infinite damage by Land and Sea, also Country as well as City, but killed many, and affrighted the whole City, bringing down to the ground some houses, and multitudes of Chimneys and Tileing; whereby several were killed, as appears by enclosed Bill of Mortality for last week. More will be inserted in the next. It will be endless to insert what we already hear of the dismal effects of this Storm, which we look upon as a Judgment upon the Nation, and will be found to be so. The merchants and trading part have not had such a scourge in their memory so general. One merchant ship at Plymouth, called the *Sarah Mary Hopewell*, outward bound for Barbadoes, value £40,000, is lost—where many Friends were concerned—and particularly N. Marks, many hundred pounds—besides sundry other ships of considerable effects, which affect Friends particularly. Bristol has felt the same smart; sundry of the Queen's ships lost there, and besides Merchant's ships, one particularly from Virginia, which had 900 hogsheads of tobacco on board; and withal such a mighty inundation of water occasioned by excessive height of tide, that great quantities of tobacco, sugar, salt, etc., was destroyed, and the loss thereby much surmounts the damage done by the wind.   Very great tides we have also had at London, since the storm, that has spoiled much goods on Southwark side especially, and much people and cattle drowned about Bristol, all along the Severn side, towards Gloster.   And the packet-boats, with 60 passengers we hear lost in their passage between Wales and Awre in Glostershire, near Oldston.   I refer thee to the enclosed printed daily courrant and most authentic of prints, except Gazette, to save transcribing, which may not be so complete; only I observe the charge of postage which upon so extraordinary occasion thou will pass by.   No business done here in respect to trade at Exchange, but relating and hearing accounts of losses abroad, etc.   The Lord's hand is in all this, and it will be well if people would bear the rod and Him that hath appointed it; for there is a voice which is teaching in this calamity.   I hope to hear from thee suddenly.   My true love and respects to the lady thy dear Mother, and to thyself, From thy faithful affectionate Friend

JOHN TOMKINS

Jo. Baines' dear love is to thee by dear love to Dr. J. G.   Let me know if you met with any Storm or had any of those bad effects in your Country.

WILLIAM WALSH (1663–1708)

*Walsh was a man of fashion, a poet, and a critic, who knew every-
body worth knowing in the world of his time. His chief title to fame,
perhaps, lies in his connexion with Pope, whom he encouraged and by
whom he was immortalized in letters of glowing gratitude.*

TO ALEXANDER POPE

Sept. 9, 1706

AT my return from the North I received the favour of your letter,
which had lain there till then. Having been absent about six weeks,
I read over your Pastorals again, with a great deal of pleasure; and to
judge the better, read Virgil's Eclogues, and Spenser's Calender, at
the same time; and I assure you, I continue the same opinion I had
always of them. By the little hints you take upon all occasions to
improve them it is probable you will make them yet better against
winter; though there is a mean to be kept even in that too, and a man
may correct his verses till he takes away the true spirit of them, especially
if he submits to the correction of some who pass for great critics by
mechanical rules, and never enter into the true design and genius of
an author. I have seen some of these that would hardly allow any
one good ode in Horace, who cry Virgil wants fancy, and that Homer
is very incorrect. While they talk at this rate, one would think them
above the common rate of mortals; but generally they are great admirers
of Ovid and Lucan, and when they write themselves, we find out all
the mystery. They scan their verses upon their fingers; run after
conceits and glaring thoughts; their poems are all made up of couplets,
of which the first may be last, or the last first, without any sort of
prejudice to their works, in which there is no design, or method, or
anything natural or just. For you are certainly in the right, that in
all writings whatsoever (not poetry only) nature is to be followed; and
we should be jealous of ourselves for being fond of similes, conceits,
and what they call saying fine things. When we were in the North,
my Lord Wharton showed me a letter he had received from a certain
great general in Spain. I told him I would be all means have that

general recalled and set to writing here at home, for it was impossible
that a man with so much wit as he showed could be fit to command an
army, or do any other business.   As for what you say of expression, it is
indeed the same thing to wit as dress is to beauty.   I have seen many
women over-dressed, and several look better in a careless night-gown
with their hair about their ears, than Mademoiselle Spanheim dressed
for a ball.

I do not design to be in London till towards the parliament: then
I shall certainly be there, and hope by that time you will have finished
your Pastorals as you would have them appear in the world and particularly the third, of Autumn, which I have not yet seen.   Your
last Eclogue being upon the same subject as that of mine on Mrs.
Tempest's death, I should take it very kindly in you to give it a little
turn, as if it were to the memory of the same lady, if they were not
written for some particular woman whom you would make immortal.
You may take occasion to show the difference between poets' mistresses
and other men's.   I only hint this, which you may either do or let
alone, just as you think fit.   I shall be very much pleased to see you
again in town, and to hear from you in the meantime.   I am, with
very much esteem, your, etc.

MATTHEW PRIOR (1664–1721)

This charming poetical epistle was written to the daughter of Lord Harley who in after years became Duchess of Portland. Her recollection of him was that he made "himself beloved by every living thing in the house—master, child, and servant, human creature, or animal."

MY NOBLE, LOVELY, LITTLE PEGGY,
  Let this my First Epistle beg ye
  At dawn of morn, and close of even,
  To lift your heart and hands to Heaven.
  In double duty, say your prayer:
  Our Father first, then Notre Père.

  And, dearest child, along the day,
  In everything you do and say,
  Obey and please my lord and lady,
  So God shall love and angels aid ye.

  If to these precepts you attend,
  No second letter need I send
  And so I rest
      your constant friend
        MATTHEW PRIOR

SIR JOHN VANBRUGH (1664–1726)

Vanbrugh has claims on fame both as a dramatist and an architect. His plays were for long favourites of the London stage, while mansions such as Blenheim still bear witness to his genius. Jacob Tonson, the publisher, went to Holland in 1703 to buy paper and engravings, and was evidently furnished by Vanbrugh with letters of introduction.

TO TONSON, THE BOOKSELLER

LONDON, JUNE THE 15, 1703

YOUR letter I had from Amsterdam. My brother bids me tell you he is extremely obliged to you, and desires you will let him be a little more so by improving (as it may lie in your way) the friendship he has begun with the gentleman at Rotterdam; though my hopes are, you'll be spueing at sea before this gets half way to the Brill. In short, the Kitt Catt wants you, much more than you ever can do them. Those who remain in Town are in great desire of waiting on you at Barne Elmes; not that they have finished their pictures neither; though to excuse them (as well as myself) Sir Godfrey [Kneller] has been most in fault. The fool has got a country house near Hampton Court, and is so busy about fitting it up (to receive nobody), that there's no getting him to work. Carpenter Johns, too, is almost as bad. I went up yesterday under a tilt (as everybody has done that has gone by water these three weeks, for the devil's in the sky); their's all in disorder still; every room is chips—up to your chin: they haven't been at work, you must know, this fortnight. There's a great deal done however—one week's sticking to it will fit it for the reception of a King; my room is finished, and a bed in it. The compass window, below and above, is made, but the sashes are not yet up; both the rooms are ten times better for it. Neighbour Burgess has been too honest; the peas and beans lie all languishing upon the earth; not a cod has been gathered. There will be a hundred thousand apricots ripe in ten days; they are now fairer and forwarder than what I saw at the Queen's table at Windsor on Sunday—and such strawberries as never were tasted: currants all as red as blood too; and gooseberries, peaches, pears, apples, and plums to gripe a nation.

The Duke of Somerset has had several letters from you; but do you know that the Torys (even the wisest of 'em) have been very grave upon your going to Holland. They often say (with a nod) that Caesar's Commentaries might have been carried through without a voyage to Holland. There were meanings in that subscription, and that list of names may serve for farther engagements than paying three guineas a piece for a book. In short, I could win a hundred pounds if I were sure you had not made a trip to Hanover, which you may possibly hear sworn when you come home again; so I'd advise you to bring a very exact journal, well attested.

Lord Carlisle went homeward yesterday, with wife and children, and has made Lord Essex Deputy Earl Marshall. To crown that, Harry St. George, Garter, and me, Herald Extraordinary (if the queen pleases), in order to be Clarencieux at his return to Town. But whether we shall carry either point at Court is not yet sure, though it stands home pressed at this moment, and will I believe be known to-night.

I have finished my purchase for the Playhouse [in the Haymarket], and all the tenants will be out by Midsummer-day; so then I lay the corner-stone; and though the season be thus far advanced, have pretty good assurance I shall be ready for business at Christmas.

I saw Captain Saunders just now. He sails to-morrow for Holland: that he may bring you back with him in health and good humour, is my most hearty prayer.

.J. V.

TO THE SAME

LONDON, JULY THE 30TH, 1703

I WRIT to you about a fortnight since, and have since spoke more than once to Lord Essex for his arms, which he said he would not fail to send you, and has done it for aught I know. He's always at Cashiobury, and Jack Dormer has kept him company there this month, by the help of Di Kirk, who has been there as long; but she's come away at last, and so is he. I said something to you of that matter in my last; my opinion is strengthened upon it since, by his staying there so long, and that in the soberest way in the world, playing at brag with the women every night, instead of drinking; and even my Lord Essex chimed into this way of living very contentedly. Dunch is overjoyed to see Dormer buzzing about the candle, and is great hopes he'll bob into it, at last, as he did.

Sir Roger Mosthyn is wedded to Lord Nottingham's daughter; and you have heard, no doubt, that that old prig Sir Steven Fox has tacked himself to a young wench of twenty. She was a parson's daughter, and a parson managed the match, a young dog; a smirk who, I suppose, has agreed with her how matters are to be when widowhood comes; but I hope she'll reward him with her Abigail. Mr. Fox and his wife have been sore upon this matter; my Lord Northampton and his folks were wiser, put on a gay air, and came immediately up to town to congratulate; I wish my Lord Cornwallis had done so too: but I don't yet hear what turn he gives it. I hear there is something on foot towards a match between Lord Hartford and Lady Mary Churchill, though that between her and Lord Mounthermer was thought fixed.

My Lord Wharton was got to Tolme Pierpoint in his way to York, and there fell very ill. His law business was however so much in his head that he fain would have gone on, but with much ado they prevailed with him to go back to Winchington, where he writ to Dr. Garth to meet him. Dr. Sloane too went down, and extreme ill they found him on Saturday last. On Monday he was so much worse that they had very little hopes for him, and he none at all of himself. He acted the hero, however, took formal leave of them all; talked to his son a good deal, and charged him with a good deal of duty and respect to his mother; said a great deal to Lord Vasseur about his education, and shewed a world of tenderness and regard to Madam, telling her he begged she would forgive him that he left the guardianship of his son to her only during her widowhood, he being fearful that if she married again it might prove to his prejudice. She melted down with all this, threw herself upon the ground, and was not to be comforted. Then came all the principal burgesses of Ailesbury to enquire after him, and he ordered them to be brought into his room, shook them every one by the hand, and by his usual treatment of honest Tom, Dick, and so forth, bid them farewell, and stick firm to their principles; then recommended himself heartily to the Kit-cat. He got a little sleep that night; by God's help and the doctor's was better next day; and on Wednesday Garth left him (he says) out of danger. He goes down to him again tomorrow, and is positive he will recover; but has as long a hill to climb up to health and strength again as he had before.

I have here sent you my own coat of arms, and have written to Lord Carlisle for his; but if you spend much more of your time about them in Holland, we all resolve never to subscribe to another book that must carry you beyond sea.

I have nothing to say about public affairs, but that our favourite Portugal treaty, when we were in great haste for it from Vienna, was left in a land-waiter's hands at Harwich about a week. The fellow swore 'twas no treaty but a bundle of Flanders lace, and so broke it open; upon which the gentleman that brought it refused to take it again, and came away without it. An order has been sent down for it since, and we have it at last. I had like to have forgot what I am to say to you from Mrs. Roach. She's in great fear you should forget her Flanders lace; you may draw a bill for the money, she says, when you please. I am most heartily yours.

J. V.

JONATHAN SWIFT (1667–1745)

While Swift was pursuing politics, writing, scheming and striving for advancement in London, he used to send home full accounts of his doings to the rectory of Laracor, where Stella and her friend Mrs. Dingley were following his career with loving eyes. The long letter to the latter tells of his hopes and disappointments about preferment.

TO MRS. DINGLEY

WINDSOR, SEPTEMBER 15, 1712

I HAVE been much out of order of late, with the old giddiness in my head. I took a vomit for it two days ago, and will take another about a day or two hence. I have ate mighty little fruit; yet I impute my disorder to that little, and shall henceforth wholly forbear it. I am engaged in a long work, and have done all I can of it, and wait for some papers from the ministry for materials for the rest; and they delay me, as if it were a favour I asked them; so that I have been idle here this good while, and it happened in a right time, when I was too much out of order to study. One is kept constantly out of humour by a thousand unaccountable things in public proceedings; and when I reason with some friends, we cannot conceive how affairs can last as they are. God only knows, but it is a very melancholy subject for those who have any near concern in it. I am again endeavouring, as I was last year, to keep people from breaking to pieces upon a hundred misunderstandings. One cannot withhold them from drawing different ways, while the enemy is watching to destroy both. See how my style is altered, by living and thinking, and talking among these people. Instead of my canal and river, walk and willows, I lose all my money here among the ladies; so that I never play when I can help it, being sure to lose. I have lost five pounds the five weeks I have been here. I hope you are luckier at picquet with the dean and Mrs. Wall. I wait here but to see what they will do for me; and whenever preferments are given from me, I will go over.

18th. I have taken a vomit to-day, and hope I shall be better. I have been very giddy since I wrote what is before, yet not as I used to be; more frequent, but not so violent. Yesterday we were alarmed with the

228

queen's being ill; she had an aguish and feverish fit; and you never saw such countenances as we all had, such dismal melancholy. Her physicians from town were sent for; but towards night she grew better, to-day she is on her feet and was up: we are not now in any fear; it will be at worst but an ague, and we hope even that will not return. Lord Treasurer would not come here from London, because it would make a noise, if he came before his usual time, which is Saturday, and he goes away on Mondays. The Whigs have lost a great support in the Earl of Godolphin.[1] It is a good jest to hear the ministers talk of him now with humanity and pity, because he is dead, and can do them no more hurt. Lady Orkney, the late king's mistress, who lives at a fine place five miles from hence (called Cliffden) and I, are grown mighty acquaintance. She is the wisest woman I ever saw; and Lord Treasurer made great use of her advice in the late change of affairs. I hear Lord Marlborough is growing ill of his diabetes; which, if it be true, may soon carry him off; and then the ministry will be something more at ease. The doctor tells me I must go into a course of steel, though I have not the spleen; for that they can never give me, though I have as much provocation to it as any man alive. Bernage's regiment is broke; but he is upon half-pay. I have not seen him this long time; but I suppose he is over-run with melancholy. My Lord Shrewsbury is certainly designed to be governor of Ireland; and, I believe, the duchess will please the people there mightily. I hear there are five or six people putting strongly in for my livings, God help them. But if ever the court should give me anything, I would recommend Raymond to the Duke of Ormond; not for any particular friendship to him, but because it would be proper for the minister of Trim to have Laracor. You may keep the gold studded snuff-box now; for Hill, governor of Dunkirk, has sent me the finest that ever you saw. It is allowed at court, that none in England comes near it, though it did not cost above twenty pounds. And the Duchess of Hamilton has made me a pocket for it, like a woman's, with a belt and buckle, (for I wear no waistcoat in summer) and there are several divisions, and one on purpose for my box. We have had most delightful weather this whole week; but illness and vomiting have hindered me from sharing in a great part of it. Lady Masham made the queen send to Kensington for some of her preserved ginger for me, which I take in the morning, and hope it will do me good. The queen will stay here about a month longer, I suppose; for Lady Masham will go in ten days to lie-in at Kensington. Poor creature she fell down in the court here the other day. She would

---

[1] He died September 15, 1712.

needs walk across it upon some displeasure with her chairmen, and was like to be spoiled, so near her time; but we hope all is over save for a black eye and a sore side; though I shall not be at ease till she is brought to bed. I find I can fill up a letter, some way or other, without a journal. If I had not a spirit naturally cheerful, I should be very much discontented at a thousand things. Pray God preserve your health, and that I may live free from the envy and discontent, that attends those, who are thought to have more favour at court than they really possess. Farewell.

TO THE SAME

London, April 7th, 1713

I DINED with Lord Treasurer, and though the business I had with him is something against Thursday, when the parliament is to meet, and this is Tuesday, yet he put it off till to-morrow. I dare not tell you what it is, lest this letter should miscarry, or be opened; but I never saw his fellow for delays. The parliament will now certainly sit, and everybody's expectations are ready to burst. At a council to-night, the Lord Chief Justice Parker, a Whig, spoke against the peace; so did Lord Cholmonde-ley, another Whig, who is Treasurer of the Household. My Lord Keeper was this night made Lord Chancellor. We hope there will soon be some removes.

April 8. Lord Cholmondeley is this day removed from his employment, for his last night's speech; and Sir Richard Temple, Lieutenant-General, the greatest Whig in the army, is turned out; and Lieutenant-General Palmer will be obliged to sell his regiment. This is the first-fruits of a friendship I have established between two great men. I dined with Lord Treasurer, and did the business I had for him to his satisfaction. I won't tell you what it was. The parliament sits to-morrow for certain. Here is a letter printed in Maccartney's name, vindicating himself from the murder of Duke Hamilton. I must give some hints to have it answered; 'tis full of lies, and will give an opportunity of exposing that party.. To-morrow will be a very important day. All the world will be at Westminster. Lord Treasurer is as easy as a lamb. They are mustering up the proxies of the absent lords, but they are not in any fear of wanting a majority, which death and accidents have increased this year.

9. I was this morning with Lord Treasurer, to present to him a young son of the late Earl of Jersey, at the desire of the widow. There I saw the mace and great coach ready for Lord Treasurer, who was going to parliament. Our society met to-day, but I expected the houses

would sit longer than I cared to fast; so I dined with a friend, and never enquired how matters went till eight this evening, when I went to Lord Orkney's, where I found Sir Thomas Hanmer. The Queen delivered her speech very well, but a little weaker in her voice. The crowd was vast. The order for an address was moved, and opposed by Lords Nottingham, Halifax, and Cowper. Lord Treasurer spoke with great spirit and resolution; Lord Peterborough flirted against the Duke of Marlborough, (who is in Germany, you know) but it was in answer to one of lord Halifax's impertinencies. The order for an address passed by a majority of thirty-three, and the houses rose before six. This is the account I heard at Lord Orkney's. The Bishop of Chester, a high Tory, was against the court. The Duchess of Marlborough sent for him some months ago to justify herself to him in relation to the Queen; and showed him letters, and told him stories, which the weak man believed, and was perverted.

10th. I dined with a cousin in the city, and poor Patty Rolt was there. I have got her rogue of a husband leave to come to England from Portmahon. The Whigs are much down, but I reckon they have some scheme in agitation. This parliament time hinders our court meetings on Wednesdays, Thursdays, and Saturdays. I had a great deal of business to-night, which gave me a temptation to be idle, and I lost a dozen shillings at ombre with Dr. Pratt and another. It rains every day, and yet we are all over dust. Lady Masham's eldest boy is very ill: I doubt he will not live, and she stays at Kensington to nurse him, which vexes us all. She is so excessively fond, it makes me mad. She should never leave the Queen, but leave everything, to stick to what is so much the interest of the public, as well as her own. This I tell her; but talk to the winds.

11th. I dined at Lord Treasurer's with his Saturday company. We had ten at table, all lords, but myself, and the Chancellor of the Exchequer. Argyle went off at six, and was in very indifferent humour, as usual. Duke of Ormond and Lord Bolingbroke were absent. I stayed till near ten. Lord Treasurer showed us a small picture, enamelled work, and set in gold, worth about twenty pounds; a picture, I mean of the Queen, which she gave to the Duchess of M. set in diamonds. When the duchess was leaving England, she took off all the diamonds, and gave the picture to one Mrs. Higgins, (an old intriguing woman, whom everybody knows) bidding her make the best of it she could. Lord Treasurer sent to Mrs. Higgins for this picture, and gave her one hundred pounds for it. Was ever such an ungrateful beast as that duchess? or did you ever hear such a story? I suppose the Whigs will not believe it. Pray, try them. She takes off the diamonds, and gives away the picture to an insignificant woman as a thing of no consequence; and gives it to her to sell, like a piece of old-fashioned plate.

12th. I went to court to-day, on purpose to present Mr. Berkeley,[1] one of your fellows of Dublin college, to Lord Berkeley of Stratton. That Mr. Berkeley is a very ingenious man, and a great philosopher, and I have mentioned him to all the ministers, and have given them some of his writings; and I will favour him as much as I can. This I think I am bound to, in honour and conscience, to use all my little credit towards helping forward men of worth in the world. The Queen was at chapel to-day, and looks well. I dined at Lord Orkney's with the Duke of Ormond, Lord Arran, and Sir Thomas Hanmer. Mr. St. John, secretary at Utrecht, expects every monent to return there with the ratification of the peace.

13th. This morning my friend, Mr. Lewis, came to me, and showed me an order for a warrant for the three vacant deaneries but none of them to me. This was what I always foresaw, and received the notice of it better, I believe, than he expected. I bid Mr. Lewis tell my Lord Treasurer, that I take nothing ill of him but his not giving me timely notice, as he promised to do, if he found the Queen would do nothing for me. At noon, Lord Treasurer hearing I was in Mr. Lewis's office came to me, and said many things, too long to repeat. I told him, I had nothing to do but go to Ireland immediately; for I could not, with any reputation, stay longer here, unless I had something honourable immediately given to me. We dined together at the Duke of Ormond's. He there told me he had stopped the warrants for the deans, that what was done for me, might be at the same time, and he hoped to compass it to-night; but I believe him not. I told the Duke of Ormond my intentions. He is content Sterne should be a bishop, and I have St. Patrick's; but, I believe, nothing will come of it; for stay I will not; and so I believe you will see me in Dublin before April ends. I am less out of humour than you would imagine; and if it were not that impertinent people will condole with me, as they used to give me joy, I would value it less. But I shall avoid company, and muster up my baggage, and send them next Monday by the carrier to Chester, and go see my willows, against the expectation of all the world.

14th. I dined in the City to-day, and ordered a lodging to be got ready for me against I came to pack up my things; for I will leave this

[1] Afterward Bishop of Cloyne.

end of the town as soon as ever the warrants for the deaneries are out, which are yet stopped. Lord Treasurer told Mr. Lewis, that it should be determined to-night; and so he will say an hundred nights; so he said yesterday, but I value it not. My daily journals shall be but short till I get into the City, and then I will send away this, and follow it myself; and design to walk it all the way to Chester, my man and I, by ten miles a day. It will do my health a great deal of good. I shall do it in fourteen days.

15th. Lord Bolingbroke made me dine with him to-day, (I was as good company as ever) and told me the Queen would determine something for me to-night. The dispute is Windsor, or St. Patrick's. I told him I would not stay for their disputes, and he thought I was in the right. Lord Masham told me, that Lady Masham is angry I have not been to see her since this business and desires I will come to-morrow.

16th. I was this noon at Lady Masham's, who was just come from Kensington, where her eldest son is sick. She said much to me of what she had talked to the Queen, and Lord Treasurer. The poor lady fell a-shedding tears openly. She could not bear to think of my having St. Patrick's, &c. I was never more moved than to see so much friendship. I would not stay with her, but went and dined with Dr. Arbuthnot, with Mr. Berkeley, one of your fellows, whom I have recommended to the Doctor, &c. Mr. Lewis tells me, that the Duke of Ormond has been to-day with the Queen; and she was content that Dr. Sterne should be Bishop of Dromore, and I dean of St. Patrick's; but then out came Lord Treasurer, and said, he would not be satisfied, but that I must be a prebendary of Windsor. Thus he perplexes things. I expect neither; but I confess, as much as I love England, I am so angry at this treatment that, if I had my choice, I would rather have St. Patrick's. Lady Masham says, she will speak to the purpose to the Queen to-morrow.

17th. I went to dine at Lady Masham's to-day, and she was taken ill of a sore throat, and is aguish. She spoke to the Queen last night, but had not much time. The Queen says she will determine to-morrow with Lord Treasurer. The warrants for the deaneries are still stopped, for fear I should be gone. Do you think any thing will be done? I don't care whether it is or no. In the meantime I prepare for my journey, and see no great people, nor will see. Lord Treasurer told Mr. Lewis, it should be done to-night; so he said five nights ago.

18th. This morning Mr. Lewis sent me word, that Lord Treasurer told him the Queen would determine at noon. At three Lord Treasurer sent to me, to come to his lodgings at St. James's, and told me the Queen was at last resolved that Dr. Sterne should be Bishop of Dromore and I Dean of St. Patrick's, and that Sterne's warrant should be drawn immediately. You know the deanery is in the Duke of Ormond's gift; but this is concerted between the Queen, Lord Treasurer, and the Duke of Ormond, to make room for me. I do not know whether it will yet be done; some unlucky accident may yet come. Neither can I feel joy at passing my days in Ireland, and, I confess, I thought the ministry would not let me go; but perhaps they can't help it.

19th. I forgot to tell you, that Lord Treasurer forced me to dine with him yesterday, as usual, with his Saturday company; which I did, after frequent refusals. To-day I dined with a private friend, and was not at court. After dinner, Mr. Lewis sent me word that the Queen stayed till she knew whether the Duke of Ormond approved of Sterne for a bishop. I went this evening, and found the Duke of Ormond at the Cockpit, and told him, and desired he would go to the Queen, and approve of Sterne. He made objections, and desired I would name any other deanery, for he did not like Sterne; that Sterne never went to see him; that he was influenced by the Archbishop of Dublin, &c., for all is now broken again. I sent out for Lord Treasurer, and told him this. He says all will do well; but I value not what he says. This suspense vexes me worse than anything else.

20th. I went to-day, by appointment, to the Cockpit, to talk to the Duke of Ormond. He repeated the same proposals of any other deanery, &c. I desired he would put me out of the case, and do as he pleased. Then, with great kindness, he said he would consent; but would do it for no man else but me, &c. And he will speak to the Queen to-day or to-morrow: so, perhaps, something will come of it. I can't tell.

21st. The Duke of Ormond has told the Queen, he is satisfied that Sterne should be bishop, and she consents I shall be dean; and I suppose the warrants will be drawn in a day or two. I dined at an alehouse with Parnell and Berkeley; for I am not in humour to go among the ministers, though Lord Dartmouth invited me to dine with him to-day, and Lord Treasurer was to be there. I said I would, if I were out of suspense.

22nd. The Queen says warrants shall be drawn, but she will dispose of all in England and Ireland at once, to be teased no more. This will delay it some time; and, while it is delayed, I am not sure of the Queen, my enemies being busy. I hate this suspense.

23rd. I dined yesterday with General Hamilton. I forgot to tell you. I write short journals now. I have eggs on the spit. This night

the Queen has signed all the warrants, among which Sterne is Bishop of
Dromore, and the Duke of Ormond is to send over an order for making
me Dean of St. Patrick's. I have no doubt of him at all. I think 'tis
now past. But you see what a condition I am in. I thought I was to
pay but six hundred pounds for the house; but the Bishop of Clogher
says eight hundred pounds; first-fruits about one hundred and fifty
pounds Irish, and so with a patent, &c., a thousand pounds in all; so that
I shall not be the better for the deanery these three years. I hope, in
some time, they will be persuaded here to give me some money to pay off
these debts. I must finish the book I am writing before I can go over;
and they expect I shall pass next winter here, and then I will drive them
to give me a sum of money. However, I hope to pass four or five
months with you. I received yours to-night; just ten weeks since I had
your last. I shall write next post to Bishop Sterne. Never man had so
many enemies of Ireland as he. I carried it with the strongest hand
possible. If he does not use me well, and gently, in what dealings I shall
have with him, he will be the most ungrateful of mankind. The Archbishop of York, my mortal enemy, has sent, by the third hand, that he
would be glad to see me. Shall I see him, or not? I hope to be over in
a month. I shall answer your rattle soon; but no more journals. I
shall be very busy. Short letters from henceforward. I shall not part
with Laracor. That is all I have to live on, except the deanery be worth
more than four hundred pounds a year. Is it? Pray write to me a good-
humoured letter immediately, let it be ever so short. This affair was
carried with great difficulty, which vexes me. But they say here, it is
much to my reputation, that I have made a bishop, in spite of all the world,
and to get the best deanery in Ireland.

24th. I forgot to tell you I had Sterne's letter yesterday, in answer
to mine. I dined in the City to-day with my printer, and came home
early, and am going to be busy with my work. I will send this to-
morrow, and I suppose the warrants will go then. I wrote to Dr.
Coghill, to take care of passing my patent: and to Parvisol, to attend him
with money, if he has any, or to borrow some where he can.

25th. Morning. I know not whether my warrant be got ready
from the Duke of Ormond. I suppose it will by to-night. I am going
abroad, and will keep this unsealed, till I know whether all be finished.

I had this letter all day in my pocket, waiting till I heard the warrants
were gone over. Mr. Lewis sent to Southwell's clerk at ten; and he said
the Bishop of Killaloe had desired they should be stopped till next post.
He sent again, that the Bishop of Killaloe's business had nothing to do

with ours.   Then I went myself, but it was past eleven, and asked the reason.   Killaloe is removed to Rapho, and he has a mind to have an order for the rents of Rapho, that have fallen due since the vacancy, and he would have all stop till he has gotten that.   A pretty request!   But the clerk, at Mr. Lewis's message, sent the warrants for Sterne and me; but then it was too late to send this, which frets me heartily.

26th.   I was at court to-day, and a thousand people gave me joy; so I ran out.   I dined with Lady Orkney.   Yesterday I dined with Lord Treasurer, and his Saturday people, as usual; and was so be-deaned, &c.   The Archbishop of York says, he will never more speak against me.   Pray see, that Parvisol stirs about getting my patent.   I have given Took D. D.'s note, to prove she is alive.

27th.   Nothing new to-day.   I dined with Tom Harley, &c.   I'll seal up this to-night.   Pray write soon.

TO STELLA (ESTHER JOHNSON)

NOVEMBER 15, 1712

BEFORE this comes to your hands you will have heard of the most terrible accident that hath almost ever happened.   This morning, at eight, my man brought me word that Duke Hamilton had fought with Lord Mohun and killed him, and was brought home wounded.   I immediately sent him to the duke's house, in St. James's Square; but the porter could hardly answer for tears, and a great rabble was about the house.   In short, they fought at seven this morning.   The dog Mohun was killed on the spot; and, while the duke was over him, Mohun shortened his sword, stabbed him in at the shoulder to the heart.   The duke was helped towards the cake-house by the ring in Hyde Park (where they fought), and died on the grass, before he could reach the house, and was brought home in his coach by eight, while the poor duchess was asleep. Macartney and one Hamilton were the seconds, who fought likewise, and both are fled.   I am told that a footman of Lord Mohun's stabbed Duke Hamilton, and some say Macartney did so too.   Mohun gave the affront, and yet sent the challenge.   I am infinitely concerned for the poor duke, who was a frank, honest, good-natured man.   I loved him well, and I think he loved me better.   He had the greatest mind in the world to go with me to France, but durst not tell it me; and those he did tell said I could not be spared, which was true.   They have removed the poor duchess to a lodging in the neighbourhood, where I have been with her two hours, and am just come away.   I never saw so melancholy a scene; for, indeed, all reasons for real grief belong to her; nor is it possible for anybody to be a greater loser in all regards. She has moved my very soul. The lodging was inconvenient, and they would have removed her to another; but I would not suffer it, because it had no room backward, and she must have been tortured with the noise of the Grub Street screamers mentioning her husband's murder in her ears.

WILLIAM CONGREVE (1670–1729)

Congreve had already made his name when he wrote this letter to his friend Kelly. It is full of the chatter and gossip of London and gives a vivid picture of the times.

TO MR. KELLY

LONDON, NOV. 30, 1703

DEAR KELLY, I think it a tedious while since I heard from you; and though, to the best of my remembrance, I answered your last, yet I write again to put you in mind of your old friends, every one of whom has very narrowly escaped the hurricane on Friday night last. The public papers will be full of particulars. 'Tis certain, in the memory of man, never was any thing like it. Most of the tall trees in the Park are blown down; and the four trees that stood distinct before St. James's, between the Mall and the Canal. The garden-wall of the priory, and the Queen's garden there, are both laid flat. Some great sash-windows of the banqueting-house have been torn from the frames, and blown so as they have never been found nor heard of. The leads of churches have some of them been rolled up as they were before they were laid on: others have been skimmed clever off, and transported cross the street, where they have been laid on other houses, breaking the roofs. The news out of the country is equally terrible; the roads being obstructed by the trees which lie cross. Anwick, Coventry, and most of the towns that my acquaintance have heard of, are in great measure destroyed, as Bristol, where they say a church was blown down. It is endless to tell you all. Our neighbour in Howard's-street 'scaped well, though frighted, only the ridge of the house being stripped; and a stack of chimneys in the next house fell luckily into the street. I lost nothing but a casement in my man's chamber, though the chimneys of the Blue Ball continued tumbling by piece-meal most part of the night at Mr. Porter's. The wind came down the little court behind the back parlour, and burst open that door, bolts and all, whirled round the room, and scattered all the prints; of which, together with the table and chairs, it mustered into one heap, and made a battery of 'em to break down the other door into the entry,

238

whither it swept 'em; yet broke not one pane of the window which join'd to the back-court door. It took off the sky-light of the stairs, and did no more damage there. Many people have been killed. But the loss at sea is inconceivable, though the particulars are not many yet confirmed; and I am afraid poor Beaumont is lost. Shovel, they say, and Fairholm, are heard of. I hope you have been less sufferers. One should be glad to hear so from your own hands. Pray give my service to all friends. The King's-Bench walk buildings are just as before their roofs were covered. Tell that to Robin. I am, dear Kelly, yours,

W. CONGREVE

HUMPHREY WANLEY (1672–1726)

Wanley was one of those dear old antiquaries of the eighteenth century who found so much to interest them and knew so little how to judge it aright. He was, however, a very talented man in the decipherment of manuscripts, and a keen connoisseur of books and manuscripts. In this letter he gives an account of an impostor who personated the Duke of Monmouth who had already been dead some fourteen years.

AUGUST 25, 1698

WE have an account from the Assizes of Horsham in Sussex that on Monday se'nnight last a fellow was indicted and tried there for personating and pretending himself to be the late Duke of Monmouth, and by that means drawing considerable sums of money out of the zealots of that country. It appeared that he lodged at the house of one Widow Wickard (tho' with seeming privacy), where his true friends visited him and were admitted to kiss his hand upon their knees. He said he was the true legitimate son of King Charles II, and that his Uncle King James had such honour for him as to execute a common criminal in his stead to satisfy the Priests and to send him out of the way. And that the Prince of Orange was a very honest Gentleman and his deputy, and would surrender the crown to him when things were ripe, etc. Happy was he that could by any interest be introduced to his Highness to have the honour of his hand. It happened that one of his trusty friends one morning coming to pay him a visit with a stranger with him found him in bed. At the sight of the stranger he seemed much surprised and offended, and turning himself quick to the wall, sighing, said "Oh! my friends will undo me." At which the Gentleman assured his Highness that the person he had brought with him was life and fortune in his interest. Upon which he returned about and gave him his hand to kiss. Presently after, came into his lodgings a wench with a basket of chickens as a present from her mistress, and another with a letter to him, at the reading of which he seemed a little discontented. Upon which they desired to know if his Highness had received any bad news. He answered, No, 'twas

240

indifferent, 'twas from Lord Russell to acquaint him that he was come with his fleet to Torbay and wanted some further direction. But that which troubled him was that he wanted a horse and money to carry him thither. At which they bid him not trouble for that he should be supplied immediately with both, which accordingly he was, and was away a fortnight, till he had spent both money and horse, and then returned. 'Tis said he has received above £500 thus, and lain with at least 50 of their wives. Upon his trial he declared himself to be the son of him that keeps the Swan Inn at Leicester, adding that he could not help it if the people would call him the Duke of Monmouth, he never bid them do so but told two Justices of the Peace, who had sent for him, his true name. He made so cunning a defence, and none of his zealots coming in against him (being prosecuted only by Mayor Brewer), that he was cleared of the indictment. Only the Lord Chief Justice afterwards bound him to good behaviour, for which he soon found bail amongst his party, who maintained him like a prince in prison, and three or four of the chief of them attended him to the Bar at his Trial and believe him still to be the true Duke of Monmouth. The Gaoler got, the first day he was committed, 40s. of people that came to see this impostor at 2d. a piece.

JOSEPH ADDISON (1672–1719)

These three letters which appeared in the "Spectator" are exceedingly characteristic of Addison's turn of humour, and show the man better, perhaps, than any of his private correspondence.

TO SPECTATOR

SALOP, MARCH 19, 1712

MR. SPECTATOR, Since there are scarce any of the arts or sciences that have not been recommended to the world by the pens of some of the professors, masters, or lovers of them, whereby the usefulness, excellence, and benefit arising from them, both as to the speculative and practical part, have been made public, to the great advantage and improvement of such arts and sciences; why should dancing, an art celebrated by the ancients in so extraordinary a manner, be totally neglected by the moderns, and left destitute of any pen to recommend its various excellencies and substantial merit to mankind?

The low ebb to which dancing is now fallen is altogether owing to this silence. The art is esteemed only as an amusing trifle; it lies altogether uncultivated, and is unhappily fallen under the imputation of illiterate and mechanic: and as Terence, in one of his prologues, complains of the rope-dancers drawing all the spectators from his play, so may we well say that capering and tumbling is now preferred to, and supplies the place of just and regular dancing, on our theatres. It is therefore, in my opinion, high time that someone should come in to its assistance, and relieve it from the many gross and growing errors that have crept into it, and overcast its real beauties; and to set dancing in its true light, would show the usefulness and elegancy of it, with the pleasure and instruction produced from it; and also lay down some fundamental rules, that might so tend to the improvement of its professors, and information of the spectators, that the first might be the better enabled to perform, and the latter rendered more capable of judging, what is (if there be anything) valuable in this art.

To encourage therefore some ingenious pen capable of so generous an undertaking, and in some measure to relieve dancing from the disadvantages it at present lies under, I, who teach to dance, have attempted a small treatise as an essay towards an history of dancing; in which I have enquired into its antiquity, original, and use, and shown what esteem the ancients had for it. I have likewise considered the nature and perfection of all its several parts, and how beneficial and delightful it is, both as a qualification and an exercise; and endeavoured to answer all objections that have been maliciously raised against it. I have proceeded to give an account of the particular dances of the Greeks and Romans, whether religious, warlike, or civil; and taken particular notice of that part of dancing relating to the ancient stage, and in which the pantomimes had so great a share. Nor have I been wanting in giving an historical account of some particular masters excellent in that surprising art; after which I have advanced some observations on the modern dancing, both as to the stage, and that part of it so absolutely necessary for the qualification of gentlemen and ladies; and have concluded with some short remarks on the origin and progress of the character by which dances are written down, and communicated to one master from another.

If some great genius after this would arise and advance this art to that perfection it seems capable of receiving, what might not be expected from it? For if we consider the origin of arts and sciences, we shall find that some of them took rise from beginnings so mean and unpromising that it is very wonderful to think that ever such surprising structures should have been raised upon such ordinary foundations. But what cannot a great genius effect? Who would have thought that the clangorous noise of a smith's hammers should have given the first rise to music? Yet Macrobius in his 2nd book relates, that Pythagoras, in passing by a smith's shop, found that the sounds proceeding from the hammers were either more grave or acute, according to the different weights of the hammers. The philosopher, to improve this hint, suspends different weights by strings of the same bigness, and found in like manner that the sounds answered to the weights. This being discovered, he finds out those numbers which produce sounds that were consonants: as, that two strings of the same substance and tension, the one being double the length of the other, give that interval which is called Diapason or an eighth. The same was also effected from two strings of the same length and size, the one having four times the tension of the other. By these steps, from so mean a beginning, did this great man reduce what was only before noise, to one of the most delightful sciences, by marrying it to the mathematics; and by that means caused it to be one of the most abstract and demonstrative of sciences. Who knows therefore but motion, whether decorous or representative, may not (as it seems highly probable it may) be taken into consideration by some person capable of reducing it into a regular science, though not so demonstrative as that proceeding from sounds, yet sufficient to entitle it to a place among the magnified arts.

Now, Mr. Spectator, as you have declared yourself visitor of dancing-schools, and this being an undertaking which more immediately respects them, I think myself indispensably obliged, before I proceed to the publication of this my essay, to ask your advice; and hold it absolutely necessary to have your approbation; and in order to recommend my treatise to the perusal of the parents of such as learn to dance, as well as to the young ladies to whom, as visitor, you ought to be guardian.

I am, Sir,

Your most humble servant,

LETTER FROM AN APE

MADAM, Not having the gift of speech, I have a long time waited in vain for an opportunity of making myself known to you; and having at present the conveniences of pen, ink, and paper by me, I gladly take the occasion of giving you my history in writing, which I could not do by word of mouth. You must know, Madam, that about a thousand years ago I was an Indian *brachman*, and versed in all those mysterious secrets which your European philosopher, called Pythagoras, is said to have learned from our fraternity. I had so ingratiated myself by my great skill in the occult sciences with a demon whom I used to converse with, that he promised to grant me whatever I should ask of him. I desired that my soul might never pass into the body of a brute creature; but this he told me was not in his power to grant me. I then begged that into whatever creature I should chance to transmigrate, I might still retain my memory, and be conscious that I was the same person who lived in different animals. This he told me was within his power, and accordingly promised on the word of a demon that he would grant me what I desired. From that time forth I lived so very unblameably, that I was made president of a college of *brachmans*, an office which I discharged with great integrity till the day of my death.

I was then shuffled into another human body, and acted my part so very well in it that I became first minister to a prince who reigned upon the banks of the Ganges. I here lived in great honour for several years, but by degrees lost all the innocence of the *brachman*, being obliged to rifle and oppress the people to enrich my sovereign; till at length I became so odious, that my master, to recover his credit with his subjects, shot me through the heart with an arrow, as I was one day addressing myself to him at the head of his army.

Upon my next remove I found myself in the woods under the shape of a jackal, and soon lifted myself in the service of a lion. I used to yelp near his den about midnight, which was his time of rousing and seeking after his prey. He always followed me in the rear, and when I had run down a fat buck, a wild goat, or a hare, after he had feasted very plentifully upon it himself, would now and then throw me a bone that was but half picked for my encouragement; but upon my being unsuccessful in two or three chases, he gave me such a confounded gripe in his anger that I died of it.

In my next transmigration I was again set upon two legs, and became an Indian tax-gatherer; but having been guilty of great extravagancies, and being married to an expensive jade of a wife, I ran so cursedly in debt that I durst not show my head. I could no sooner step out of my house, but I was arrested by some body or other that lay in wait for me. As I ventured abroad one night in the dusk of the evening, I was taken up and hurried into a dungeon, where I died a few months after.

My soul then entered into a flying-fish, and in that state led a most melancholy life for the space of six years. Several fishes of prey pursued me when I was in the water, and if I betook myself to my wings, it was ten to one but I had a flock of birds aiming at me. As I was one day flying amidst a fleet of English ships, I observed a huge seagull whetting his bill and hovering just over my head, upon my dipping into the water to avoid him I fell into the mouth of a monstrous shark that swallowed me down in an instant.

I was some years afterwards, to my great surprise, an eminent banker in Lombard Street; and remembering how I had formerly suffered for want of money, became so very sordid and avaricious that the whole town cried shame of me. I was a miserable little old fellow to look upon, for I had in a manner starved myself, and was nothing but skin and bone when I died.

I was afterwards very much troubled and amazed to find myself dwindled into an emmet. I was heartily concerned to make so insignificant a figure, and did not know but, some time or other, I might be reduced to a mite if I did not mend my manners. I therefore applied myself with great diligence to the offices that were allotted me, and was generally looked upon as the notablest ant in the whole molehill. I was at last picked up, as I was groaning under a burden, by an unlucky cock-sparrow that lived in the neighbourhood, and had before made great depredations upon our commonwealth.

I then bettered my condition a little, and lived a whole summer in the shape of a bee; but being tired with the painful and penurious life I had undergone in my two last transmigrations, I fell into the other extreme, and turned drone. As I one day headed a party to plunder a hive, we were received so warmly by the swarm which defended it, that we were most of us left dead upon the spot.

I might tell you of many other transmigrations which I went through, how I was a town rake, and afterwards did penance in a bay gelding for ten years; as also how I was a tailor, a shrimp, and a tom-tit. In the last of these my shapes I was shot in the Christmas holidays by a young jackanapes, who would needs try his new gun upon me.

But I shall pass over these and several other stages of life, to remind you of the young beau who made love to you about six years since. You may remember, Madam, how he masked, and danced, and sung, and played a thousand tricks to gain you; and how he was at last carried off by a cold that he got under your window one night in a serenade. I was that unfortunate young fellow, whom you were then so cruel to. Now long after my shifting that unlucky body, I found myself upon a hill in Æthiopia, where I lived in my present grotesque shape, till I was caught by a servant of the English factory, and sent over into Great Britain: I need not inform you how I came into your hands. You see, Madam, this is not the first time that you have had me in a chain; I am, however, very happy in this my captivity, as you often bestow on me those kisses and caresses which I would have given the world for when I was a man. I hope this discovery of my person will not tend to my disadvantage, but that you will still continue your accustomed favours to

Your most devoted humble servant,

PUGG

P.S. I would advise your little shock-dog to keep out of my way; for as I look upon him to be the most formidable of my rivals, I may chance one time or other to give him such a snap as he won't like.

SIR, You know very well that our nation is more famous for that sort of men who are called Whims and Humourists than any other country in the world, for which reason it is observed that our English comedy excels that of all other nations in the novelty and variety of its characters.

Among those innumerable sets of Whims which our country produces, there are none whom I have regarded with more curiosity than those who have invented any particular kind of diversion for the entertainment of themselves or their friends. My letter shall single out those who take delight in sorting a company that has something of burlesque and ridicule in its appearance. I shall make myself understood by the following example. One of the wits of the last age, who was a man of a good estate, thought he never laid out his money better than in a jest. As he was one year at the Bath, observing that in the great confluence of fine people there were several among them with long chins, a part of a visage by which he himself was very much distinguished, he invited to dinner half a score of these remarkable persons who had their mouths in the middle of their faces. They had no sooner placed themselves about the table, but they began to stare upon one another, not being able to imagine what had brought them together. Our English proverb says,

> 'Tis merry in the hall,
> When beards wag all.

It proved so in an assembly I am now speaking of, who seeing so many peaks of faces agitated with eating, drinking, and discourse, and observing all the chins that were present meeting together very often over the centre of the table, everyone grew sensible of the jest, and came into it with so much good humour, that they lived in strict friendship and alliance from that day forward.

The same gentleman some time after packed together a set of oglers, as he called them, consisting of such as had an unlucky cast in their eyes. His diversion on this occasion was to see the cross bows, mistaken signs, and wrong connivances that passed amidst so many broken and refracted rays of sight.

The third feast which this merry gentleman exhibited was to the stammerers, whom he got together in a sufficient body to fill his table. He had ordered one of his servants, who was placed behind a screen, to write down their table-talk, which was very easy to be done without the help of shorthand. It appears by the notes which were taken, that though their conversation never fell, there was not above twenty words spoken during the first course; that upon serving up the second, one of the company was a quarter of an hour in telling them that the ducklings and sparrow-grass were very good; and that another took up the same time in declaring himself of the same opinion. This jest did not, however, go off so well as either of the former; for one of the guests being a brave man, and fuller of resentment that he knew how to express, went out of the room, and sent the facetious inviter a challenge in writing, which though it was afterwards dropped by the inter-position of friends, put a stop to these ludicrous entertainments.

Now, Sir, I dare say you will agree with me, that as there is no moral in these jests, they ought to be discouraged, and looked upon rather as pieces of unluckiness than wit. However, as it is natural for one man to refine upon the thought of another, and impossible for any single person, how great soever his parts may be, to invent an art and bring it to its utmost perfection, I shall here give you an account of an honest gentleman of my acquaintance, who, upon hearing the character of the wit above mentioned, has himself assumed it, and endeavoured to convert it to the benefit of mankind.

He invited half a dozen of his friends one day to dinner, who were each of them famous for inserting several redundant phrases in their discourse, as "d'y'hear me," "d'y'see," "that is," and, "so, Sir." Each of the guests making frequent use of his particular elegance, appeared so ridiculous to his neighbour, that he could not but reflect upon him-self as appearing equally ridiculous to the rest of the company. By this means, before they had sat long together, everyone talking with the greatest circumspection, and carefully avoiding his favourite expletive, the conversation was cleared of its redundancies, and had a greater quantity of sense, though less of sound in it.

The same well-meaning gentleman took occasion, at another time, to bring together such of his friends as were addicted to a foolish habitual custom of swearing. In order to show them the absurdity of the practice, he had recourse to the invention above mentioned, having placed an Amanuensis in a private part of the room. After the second bottle, when men open their minds without reserve, my honest friend began to take notice of the many sonorous but unnecessary words that had passed in his house since their sitting down at table, and how much good conversation they had lost by giving way to such superfluous phrases. "What a tax," says he, "would they have raised for the poor, had we put the laws in execution upon one another?" Everyone of them took this gentle reproof in good part: upon which he told them that knowing their conversation would have no secrets in it, he had ordered it to be taken down in writing, and for the humour's sake would read it to them if they pleased. There were ten sheets of it, which might have been reduced to two, had there not been those abominable interpolations I have before mentioned. Upon the reading of it in cold blood, it looked rather like a conference of fiends than of men. In short, everyone trembled at himself upon hearing calmly what he had pronounced amidst the heat and inadvertency of discourse.

I shall only mention another occasion wherein he made use of the same invention to cure a different kind of men, who are the pests of all polite conversation, and murder time as much as either of the two former, though they do it more innocently; I mean that dull generation of story-tellers. My friend got together about half a dozen of his acquaintance, who were infected with this strange malady. The first day one of them sitting down, entered upon the Siege of Namur, which lasted till four o'clock, their time of parting. The second day a North Briton took possession of the discourse, which it was impossible to get out of his hands so long as the company stayed together. The third day was engrossed after the same manner by a story of the same length. They at last began to reflect upon this barbarous way of treating one another, and by this means awakened out of that lethargy with which each of them had been seized for several years.

As you have somewhere declared that extraordinary and uncommon characters of mankind are the game which you delight in, and as I look upon you to be the greatest sportsman, or, if you please, the Nimrod among this species of writers, I thought this discovery would not be unacceptable to you.

I am,
Sir, &c.

SIR RICHARD STEELE (1672–1729)

Steele was the father of the magazine and review, for he founded the "Tatler" and then the "Spectator." There is little doubt that the idea of Sir Roger de Coverley was his. The Mrs. Scurlock to whom these letters were addressed became his second wife and was, so they said, "a cried-up beauty." The other two letters are from the "Spectator."

TO MRS. SCURLOCK

AUGUST 30TH, 1707

MADAM, I beg pardon that my paper is not finer, but I am forced to write from a coffee-house, where I am attending about business. There is a dirty crowd of busy faces all around me, talking of money; while all my ambition, all my wealth, is love! Love which animates my heart, sweetens my humour, enlarges my soul, and affects every action of my life. It is to my lovely charmer I owe, that many noble ideas are continually affixed to my words and actions; it is the natural effect of that generous passion to create in the admirer some similitude of the object admired. Thus, my dear, am I every day to improve from so sweet a companion. Look up, my fair one, to that Heaven which made thee such; and join with me to implore its influence on our tender innocent hours, and beseech the Author of love to bless the rites He has ordained—and mingle with our happiness, a just sense of our transient condition, and a resignation to His will, which only can regulate our minds to a steady endeavour to please Him and each other,

I am for ever your faithful servant,

RICH. STEELE

TO THE SAME

SATURDAY NIGHT (AUG. 30, 1707)

DEAR LOVELY MRS. SCURLOCK, I have been in very good company, where your health, under the character of *the woman I loved best*, has been often drunk; so that I may say that I am dead drunk for your sake, which is more than *I die for you*.

RICH. STEELE

TO THE SAME

SEPT. IST, 1707

MADAM, It is the hardest thing in the world to be in love, and yet attend business. As for me, all who speak to me find out, and I must lock myself up, or other people will do it for me.

A gentleman asked me this morning, "What news from Lisbon?" and I answered, "She is exquisitely handsome." Another desired to know "when I had last been at Hampton Court?" I replied, "It will be on Tuesday come se'nnight." Pr'ythee allow me at least to kiss your hand before that day, that my mind may be in some composure. O Love!

> A thousand torments dwell about thee,
> Yet who could live, to live without thee?

Methinks I could write a volume to you; but all the language on earth would fail in saying how much, and with what disinterested passion,

I am ever yours,

RICH. STEELE

TO MRS. STEELE

OCT. 16, 1707

DEAREST BEING ON EARTH, Pardon me if you do not see me till eleven o'clock, having met a schoolfellow from India, by whom I am to be informed on things this night which expressly concern your obedient husband,

RICH. STEELE

FROM THE *SPECTATOR*

> . . . Longa est injuria, longe
> Ambages . . .
>   VIRGIL.

THE Occasion of this Letter is of so great Importance, and the Circumstances of it such, that I know you will but think it just to insert it, in Preference of all other Matters than can present themselves to your Consideration. I need not, after I have said this, tell you that I am in Love. The Circumstances of my Passion I shall let you understand as well as a disordered Mind will admit. That cursed Pickthank Mrs. *Jane*! Alas, I am railing at one to you by her Name as familiarly, as if you were acquainted with her as well as my self:

But I will tell you all as fast as the alternate Interruptions of Love and Anger will give me Leave. There is a most agreeable young Woman in the World whom I am passionately in love with, and from whom I have for some Space of Time received as great Marks of Favour as were fit for her to give or me to desire. The successful Progress of the Affair of all others the most essential towards a Man's Happiness, gave a new Life and Spirit not only to my Behaviour and Discourse, but also a certain Grace to all my Actions in the Commerce of Life in all things tho' never so remote from Love. You know the pre-dominant Passion spreads itself thro' all a Man's Transactions, and exalts or depresses it according to the Nature of such Passion. But alas, I have not yet begun my Story, and what is making Sentences and Observations when a Man is pleading for his Life? To begin then: This Lady has corresponded with me under Names of Love, she my *Belinda* I her *Cleanthes*. Tho' I am thus well got into the Account of my Affair, I cannot keep in the Thread of it so much as to give you the Character of Mrs. *Jane*, whom I will not hide under a borrowed Name; but let you know that this Creature has been since I knew her very handsome, (tho' I will not allow her even the *has been* for the Future) and during the Time of her Bloom and Beauty was so great a Tyrant to her Lovers, so overvalued her self and under-rated all her Pretenders, that they have deserted her to a Man; and she knows no Comfort but that common one to all in her Condition, the Pleasure of interrupting the Amours of others. It is impossible but you must have seen several of these Volunteers in Malice, who pass their whole Time in the most laborious way of Life, in getting Intelligence, running from Place to Place with new Whispers, without reaping any other Benefit but the Hopes of making others as unhappy as themselves. Mrs. *Jane* happened to be at a Place where I, with many others well acquainted with my Passion for *Belinda*, passed a *Christmas* Evening. There was among the rest a young Lady free in her Mirth, so amiable in a just Reserve that accompanied it, I wrong her to call it a Reserve, but there appeared in her a Mirth or Cheerfulness which was not a Forbearance of more immoderate Joy, but the natural Appearance of all which could flow from a Mind possessed of an Habit of Innocence and Purity. I must have utterly forgot *Belinda* to have taken no Notice of one who was growing up to the same womanly Virtues which shine to Perfection in her, had I not distinguished one who seemed to promise to the World the same Life and Conduct with my faithful and lovely *Belinda*. When the Company broke up, the fine young Thing permitted me to take Care of her Home; Mrs. *Jane* saw my particular Regard to her, and was informed of my attending her to her Father's House. She came early to *Belinda* the next Morning, and asked her if Mrs. *Such-a-one* had been with her? No. If Mr. *Such-a-one's* Lady? No; Nor your Cousin *Such-a-one*? No. Lord, says Mrs. *Jane*, what is the Friendship of Women—Nay they may well laugh at it. And did no one tell you any thing of the Behaviour of your Lover Mr. *What-d'ye-call* last night? But perhaps it is nothing to you that he is to be married to young Mrs. ―― on Tuesday next? *Belinda* was here ready to die with Rage and Jealousy. Then Mrs. *Jane* goes on: I have a young Kinsman who is Clerk to a Great Conveyance, who shall shew you the rough Draught of the Marriage-Settlement. The World says her Father gives him two thousand Pound more than he could have with you. I went innocently to wait on *Belinda* as usual, but was not admitted; I wrote to her, and my Letter was sent back unopened. Poor *Betty* her Maid, who is on my Side, has been here just now blubbering, and told me the whole Matter. She says she did not think I could be so base; and that she is now odious to her Mistress for having so often spoke well of me, that she dare not mention me more. All our Hopes are in having these Circumstances fairly represented in the *Spectator*, which, *Betty* says she dare not but bring up as soon as it is brought in; and has promised when you have broke the Ice to own this was laid between us: And when I can come to an Hearing, the young Lady will support what we say by her Testimony, that I never saw her but that once in my whole Life. Dear Sir, do not omit this true Relation, nor think it too particular; for there are Crowds of forlorn Coquets who intermingle themselves with other Ladies, and contract Familiarities out of Malice, and with no other Design but to blast the Hopes of Lovers, the Expectation of Parents, and the Benevolence of Kindred. I doubt not but I shall be,

Sir,

Your most Obliged Humble Servant,

CLEANTHES

MR. SPECTATOR, I am so great a Lover of whatever is *French*, that I lately discarded an humble Admirer, because he neither spoke that Tongue, nor drank Claret. I have long bewailed, in secret, the Calamities of my Sex during the War, in all which time we have laboured under the insupportable Inventions of *English* Tire-women, who, tho' they sometimes copy indifferently well, can never compose with that *Gout* they do in *France*.

I was almost in Despair of ever more seeing a Model from that dear Country, when last *Sunday* I over-heard a Lady, in the next Pew to me, whisper another, that at the *Seven Stars* in *King-street Covent-garden* there was a *Madamoiselle* completely dressed just come from *Paris*.

I was in the utmost Impatience during the remaining part of the Service, and as soon as ever it was over, having learnt the Milliner's *Address*, I went directly to her House in *King-street*, but was told that the *French* Lady was at a Person of Quality's in *Pall-Mall*; and would not be back again 'till very late that Night. I was therefore obliged to renew my Visit early this Morning, and had then a full view of the dear Moppet from Head to Foot.

You cannot imagine, worthy Sir, how ridiculously I find we have all been trussed up during the War, and how infinitely the *French*-dress excels ours.

The Mantua has no Leads in the Sleeves, and I hope we are not lighter than the *French* Ladies, so as to want that kind of Ballast; the Petticoat has no Whalebone, but fits with an Air altogether gallant and degagé; the *Coiffeure* is inexpressibly pretty, and in short, the whole Dress has a thousand Beauties in it, which I would not have as yet made too public.

I thought fit, however, to give you this Notice, that you may not be surprised at my appearing *a la mode de Paris* on the next Birth-Night.

I am, Sir,
Your Humble Servant,
Teraminta

ISAAC WATTS (1674–1748)

Most of us know Watts chiefly through his hymns and the famous little poem beginning "How doth the little busy bee." But there was another Watts, whose thoughts on life and friendship were worth the hearing. It was by this man that the following letter is written.

STOKE NEWINGTON, NEAR LONDON, JAN. 21, 1735

SIR, Your letter, dated about the middle of October, should have been answered long ago, had I not been withheld from my study by long illness; nor am I yet fully recovered. I take pleasure, Sir, to find your honest inquiries after truth, and that you are not willing either to put off your children, or to be contented yourself, with a mere set of words, instead of clear and intelligible doctrines.

I will, therefore, write you my thoughts in a few lines, of that impotency and inability of man to believe and repent, and return to God, which arises from the Fall, and which is, I think, the best and the only way to secure our thoughts from running into the extremes of Antinomian opinions on the one side, or Arminian on the other.

This impotency, though it may be called natural, or rather native, as it comes to us by nature in its present corrupted state, yet it is not a want of natural powers, either of understanding or will, to know or choose that which is good for if there were not natural powers sufficient for this purpose, I do not see how men could be charged as criminals in not receiving the gracious offers of the gospel. This impotence, therefore, is what our divines usually call a moral impotence, i.e., their mind will not learn divine things, because they shut their eyes; they will refuse the proposals of grace, they shut it out of their hearts, they have a delight in sin, and dislike to Christ and His salvation; they have a rooted obstinacy of will against the methods of divine mercy, and against the holiness which is connected with happiness. And yet this moral impotency is described in scripture by such methods as represent us "blind," or "dead in sin", and that we can no more change our nature than the Ethiopian can change his skin, or the leopard his spots; and the reason of these strong expressions is, because God knows

255

this natural aversion to grace and holiness is so strong and rooted in their hearts that they will never renounce sin and receive the salvation of Christ, without the powerful influence of the Spirit of God, even that same Spirit which can cure those who are naturally blind, or can raise the dead.

Now, that this weakness of man to do that which is good is a moral impotence, appears by the moral remedies which are applied to cure it: *viz.*, commands, promises, threatenings, which sort of methods would be useless and ridiculous to apply to natural impotence; that is, to make the blind see, or the dead arise. It must be concluded, therefore, that man has a natural ability, i.e. natural powers, to do what God requires, but at the same time such a native aversion of will that he will never do it without divine grace. Thus there is a fair way laid for the necessity of divine grace, and yet at the same time a just foundation laid for the condemnation of impenitent sinners. I have spoken more largely to this subject in the eleventh of the Bury Street Sermons, which were published last year in two volumes octavo.

May the wisdom and grace of our Lord Jesus Christ direct you to walk in a safe way to eternal life, and to lead your children therein. At the same time assuring you, that the happening to take a little different turn of thought in some of the difficult inquiries is not of so vast importance as some persons would make it to be, with respect to our salvation, provided we do but maintain a constant dependence upon the grace of the Spirit of God in all our duties to assist us, and on the perfect righteousness or obedience and sufferings of Christ as our atonement for sin, and the only effectual ground of our acceptance with God. I am, Sir, under frequent returning weaknesses, rendered unable to write much, and, therefore, subscribe

Your friend and humble servant,

I. WATTS

CHRISTIAN, LADY FOX (1677-1719)

In her twenty-sixth year Christian Hopes, daughter of a Lincoln-shire rector, married Sir Stephen Fox, who was then seventy-seven years of age. He was a prominent man of his time, and had done yeoman service for the Stuarts, both during their exile and after the Restoration. Of the four children of this marriage the two sons, to whom the letters below were addressed, became respectively Earl of Ilchester and Lord Holland. They were at Eton when these letters were written, Stephen being twelve and Henry just turned eleven.

TO STEPHEN AND HENRY FOX

SEPT. 28 (?1716)

I THINK you and your brother used to be fond of pigeon pie, and there-fore I have sent one with as many pigeons as you are years old. I hope it will be as good a guzzle as your loaves was. Be merry and wise. Don't make yourselves sick nor do anything you should not in the eating of it. . . . I am glad you like your writing-desks. Pray be careful not to spoil 'em. I have sent you something to wipe pens with and will send you a smoother very soon.

.   .   .   .   .   .

CHISWICK. OCT. 15

I HOPE my dear Harry is as good as brother Stephen, tho' he is so modest as not to brag of it; and to encourage him to continue so, I have sent him some little cakes because Bohee tea does not use to agree with you; and if I could but be sure that you really deserved it I would send some chocolate. Tell me, do you keep your promise of being very diligent at your books, and constantly say your prayers, and are respect-ful to Mrs. Snapes, and never say an ill word? If you do all this, then you may expect everything that is kind from, my dear, your very

Affectionate mother,

C. Fox

I will send your silk stockings, but I should think you wiser not to wear 'em till Easter, for 'tis very foolish to wear silk stockings, espe-cially such a light colour, this cold, dirty weather.

HENRY ST. JOHN, VISCOUNT BOLINGBROKE (1678–1751)

This eminent statesman counted Pope and Swift among his intimate friends, and many letters passed between them.

TO JONATHAN SWIFT

NOVEMBER 19, 1729

I FIND that you have laid aside your project of building in Ireland, and that we shall see you in this island, *Cum Zephyris, Hirundine prima.* I know not whether the love of fame increases as we advance in age; sure I am that the force of friendship does. I loved you almost twenty years ago, I thought of you as well as I do now, better was beyond the power of conception, or to avoid an equivoque, beyond the extent of my ideas. Whether you are more obliged to me for loving you as well, when I knew you less, or for loving you as well after knowing you so many years, I shall not determine. What I would say is this: whilst my mind grows daily more independent of the world and feels less need of leaning on external objects, the ideas of friendship return oftener, they busy me, they warm me more: is it that we grow more tender as the moment of our great separation approaches? Or is it that they who are to live together in another state (for *vera amicitiam non nisi inter bonos*) begin to feel more strongly that divine Sympathy which is to be the great band of their future society? There is no one thought which soothes my mind like this: I encourage my imagination to pursue it, and I am heartily afflicted when another faculty of the intellect comes boisterously in, and wakes me from so pleasing a dream, if it be a dream. I will dwell no more on Economics than I have done in my previous letter. This much only I will say, that *otium cum dignitate* is to be had with £500 a year as well as with £5,000: the difference will be found in the value of the man, and not in that of the estate.

I do assure you, that I have never quitted the design of collecting, revising, improving and extending several materials which are still in my power, and I hope that the time of setting myself about this last work of my life is not far off.

Many papers of much curiosity and importance are lost, and some of them in a manner that would surprise and anger you.   However, I shall be able to convey several great truths to posterity, so clearly and so authentically, that the Burnets and Oldmixons of another age may rail, but not be able to deceive.   Adieu my friend.   I have taken up more of this paper than belongs to me, since Pope is to write to you; no matter, for upon recollection the rules of proportion are not broken: he will say as much in one page, as I have done in three.   Bid him talk to you of the work [1] he is about, I hope in good earnest; it is a fine one; and will be in his hands an original.   His sole complaint is, that he finds it too easy in the execution.   This flatters his laziness, it flatters my judgment, who always thought that (universal as his talents are) this is eminently and peculiarly his, above all the writers I know living or dead; I do not except Horace.   Adieu.

[1] This was a scheme for a series of poems dealing with the various aspects of mankind, parts of which were later written as the "Essay on Man" and the four "Moral Essays."

AARON HILL (1685-1750)

Hill and Pope fell foul of one another in 1720, and a little later Pope pilloried his opponent in the "Dunciad." To this Hill retorted in "The Progress of Wit," but early in 1731 they patched up the quarrel and in the end Pope complained that Hill deluged him with letter after letter. That these were not without merit is shown by the two here printed.

TO ALEXANDER POPE

SEPT. 17, 1731

DEAR SIR, It will never be in my power to forget how compassionate you have been in calling and sending so often. It is plain, you have none of the fashionable want of feeling for the calamities of others; and when I reflect that you are kind enough to concern yourself for mine, it brings me nearer to comfort than either resignation or philosophy. The part you are pleased to take in my loss of a wife, who had the misfortune of being a stranger to you, would have been as just as it is generous, had you been qualified to measure it by an acquaintance with her virtues. It was one of those virtues, that she admired Mr. Pope, and knew why she admired him. She wished for nothing with more liveliness than the pleasure of seeing you, and (such is the illusion of our prospects) the very day on which she promised herself the enjoyment of that wish she became insensible to all wishes on this side eternity!

I chose a place for her in the Abbey cloister; the wall of the church above being so loaded with marble as to leave me no room to distinguish her monument. Give me leave to hope for the benefit of your advice on this mournful occasion. I cannot suffer her to lie unnoticed, because a monument in so frequented a place as Westminster Abbey, restoring her to a kind of second life among the living, it will be in some measure not to have lost her. But there is a low and unmeaning lumpishness in the vulgar style of monuments which disgust me as often as I look upon them; and, because I would avoid the censure I am giving, let me beg you to say whether there is significance in the draft of which

I inclose you an awkward scratch, not a copy. The flat table behind is black; the figures are white marble. The whole of what you see here is but part of the monument, and will be surrounded by pilasters, rising from a pediment of white marble, having its foundation on a black marble mountain; and supporting a cornice and dome that will ascend to the point of the cloister-arch. About half-way up a craggy path on the black mountain below will be the figure of Time in white marble, in an attitude of climbing, obstructed by little Cupids of the same colour; some rolling rocks into his path from above; some throwing nets at his feet and arms from below; others in ambuscade, shooting arrows at him from both sides; while the Death you see in the draft will seem, from an opening between hills in relievo, to have found admission by a shorter way, and prevented [forestalled] Time, at a distance.

I cannot forbear to inclose you an anonymous favour which I received in a penny post letter from some kind hand, disguised that I should not guess the obliger. I find in it a strong and touching simplicity; nature nervous and undressed; striking from and to the heart, without pomp or affectation. You will be pleased with these four verses, if my melancholy has not helped their impression on me. It is true, they seem rather the moving words of a wife while dying than the inscription of her monument after death; but I have never been able to read them without emotion, and being charmed with them myself I wished you a part of the pleasure.

I had heard of the obliging opinion you expressed of my tragedy, when you had lately an occasion of speaking to Mr. Wilks concerning the affairs of the stage. I assure you, without compliment, I had rather it should please you singly than a dozen crowded audiences. And one thing I can be sure of in its favour—it will be the better for some marks of your pencil. If you would have the goodness to allow me to put a copy of it into your hands, and speak of it occasionally, with the same kind partiality, to some of those who can give success to tragedies, that alone might determine me to venture it on the stage next winter.

I have thoughts, about the middle of this month, of taking your advice and Tully's; I will try what change of place, and the pleasure of being nearer you can do toward dispelling a grief that time seems to threaten increase. I will fly from it, if I can, but the *atra cura post equitem* will sit too close to be parted with. I am truly and unalterably, dear sir, your most affectionate and most obedient servant.

TO THE SAME

DEAR SIR, I ought sooner to have thanked you for the pleasure you have given me by that excellent Letter to Lord Burlington. If the title had been "Of False Taste," would it not have been properer?

We have poets whom heaven visits with a taste, as well as planters and builders. What other inducement could provoke some of them to mistake your epistolary relaxation of numbers for an involuntary defect in your versification?

We have printers, too, of better taste than morals, who like you so well that they cannot endure you should be made a monopoly. The hawker's wind is upon you already; and your last incense to the muses is blown about the streets in thinner and less fragrant expansion. The pictures of your mind, like those of other great men's persons, are to be multiplied and extended, that we may have you at whole length and in miniature.

I send you a piece that is safe enough from this danger. "Athelwold" will have nothing to fear from the pirates; I believe I need not inform you how it dragged itself along for two lean nights, after the first, as lame and as wounded as the snake in your poem; but not half so delightfully.

It would be affectation, not modesty, to deny that I am nettled at the monstrous reception which the town has given this tragedy. But I find there is a two-fold obligation upon a tragic writer, if he would engage attention at our theatres. He must make audiences as well as plays. He must become the solicitor of his own commendation. That is, in other words, if he desires to be known he must deserve to be forgotten.

Bating the reverence due to fashion, this is putting the poet upon the footing of the prize-fighter. He must not only submit himself to be wounded for the public diversion, but must also march about with his drum from one end of the town to the other, to stir up fools' curiosity and draw together the company.

I should feel the liveliest indignation upon such an occasion as this in the cause of another: but as the case is my own, I think,—and smile,—and am satisfied. I had rather be neglected to my mortification than become popular to my infamy.

It is possible, after all, that some persons of sufficient rank and distinction to bespeak plays and compel audiences, may be kind enough to "Athelwold" to introduce him now and then into civiler company, for the sake of the players. It were a downright shame, if these good people who gave the tragedy all its merits of fine dressing and scening should be suffered to lose their money, while the good for nothing author, who was guilty of the dull part of the entertainment, has lost nothing but his labour. But enough of this subject.

I hope the good lady [Pope's mother] whose illness hastened you home, found recovery on your return. Who can blame her for missing you in a world so few are like you? Believe me, with much acknowledgment and esteem, dear sir, your faithful and obedient servant.

GEORGE BERKELEY (1685–1753)

Berkeley was one of the prominent figures of the early eighteenth century; an eminent churchman and one of the leading philosophers of his time, he was the centre of more than one controversy. This letter was written when he was a young man and addressed to the famous Arbuthnott, physician, wit, and man of letters. It gives an account of one of the notable eruptions of Vesuvius.

TO DR. ARBUTHNOTT

APRIL 17, 1717

WITH much difficulty I reached the top of Mount Vesuvius, in which I saw a vast aperture full of smoke, which hindered the seeing its depth and figure. I heard within that horrid gulf certain odd sounds, which seemed to proceed from the belly of the mountain; a sort of murmuring, sighing, throbbing, churning, dashing (as it were) of waves, and between whiles a noise like that of thunder or cannon, which was constantly attended with a clattering like that of tiles falling from the tops of houses on the streets. Sometimes, as the wind changed, the smoke grew thinner, discovering a very ruddy flame, and the jaws of the pan or crater streaked with red and several shades of yellow. After an hour's stay, the smoke, being moved by the wind, gave us short and partial prospects of the great hollow, in the flat bottom of which I could discern two furnaces almost contiguous: that on the left, seeming about three yards in diameter, glowed with red flame, and threw up red-hot stones with a hideous noise, which, as they fell back, caused the fore-mentioned clattering.

May 8, in the morning, I ascended to the top of Vesuvius a second time, and found a different face of things. The smoke ascending upright gave a full prospect of the crater, which, as I could judge, is about a mile in circumference, and an hundred yards deep. A conical mount had been formed since my last visit, in the middle of the bottom: this mount, I could see, was made up of the stones thrown up and fallen back again into the crater. In this new hill remained the two mounts or furnaces already mentioned: that on our left was in the vertex of the hill which it had formed round it, and raged more violently than before, throwing up every three or four minutes, with a dreadful bellowing, a vast number of red-hot stones, sometimes in appearance above a thousand, and at least three thousand feet higher than my head as I stood upon the brink: but there being little or no wind, they fell back perpendicularly into the crater, increasing the conical hill. The other mouth to the right was lower in the side of the same new-formed hill. I could discern it to be filled with red-hot liquid matter, like that in the furnace of a glass-house, which raged and wrought as the waves of the sea, causing a short abrupt noise like what may be imagined to proceed from a sea of quicksilver dashing among uneven rocks. This stuff would sometimes spew over and run down the convex side of the conical hill; and appearing at first red-hot, it changed colour, and hardened as it cooled, shewing the first rudiments of an eruption, or, if I may say so, an eruption in miniature.

Had the wind driven in our faces, we had been in no small danger of stifling by the sulphureous smoke, or being knocked on the head by lumps of molten minerals, which we saw had sometimes fallen on the brink of the crater, upon those shots from the gulf at bottom. But as the wind was favourable, I had an opportunity to survey this odd scene for above an hour and a half together; during which it was very observable that all the volleys of smoke, flame, and burning stones, came only out of the hole to our left, while the liquid stuff in the other mouth wrought and overflowed, as hath been already described.

June 5th, after an horrid noise, the mountain was seen at Naples to spew a little out of the crater. The same continued the 6th. The 7th, nothing was observed till within two hours of night, when it began a hideous bellowing, which continued all that night and the next day till noon, causing the windows, and, as some affirm, the very houses in Naples to shake. From that time it spewed vast quantities of molten stuff to the south, which streamed down the mountain like a great pot boiling over. This evening I returned from a voyage through Apulia, and was surprised, passing by the north side of the mountain, to see a great quantity of ruddy smoke lie along a huge tract of sky over the river of molten stuff, which was itself out of sight. The 9th, Vesuvius raged less violently: that night we saw from Naples a column of fire shoot between whiles out of its summit.

The 10th, when we thought all would have been over, the mountain grew very outrageous again, roaring and groaning most dreadfully. You cannot form a juster idea of this noise in the most violent fits of it, than by imagining a mixed sound made up of the raging of a tempest, the murmur of a troubled sea, and the roaring of thunder and artillery, confused all together. It was very terrible as we heard it in the further end of Naples, at the distance of above twelve miles: this moved my curiosity to approach the mountain. Three or four of us got into a boat, and were set ashore at Torre del Greco, a town situated at the foot of Vesuvius to the south-west, whence we rode four or five miles before we came to the burning river, which was about midnight. The roaring of the volcano grew exceedingly loud and horrible as we approached. I observed a mixture of colours in the cloud over the crater, green, yellow, red, and blue; there was likewise a ruddy dismal light in the air over that tract of land where the burning river flowed; ashes continually showered on us all the way from the sea-coast: all which circumstances, set off and augmented by the horror and silence of the night, made a scene the most uncommon and astonishing I ever saw, which grew still more extraordinary as we came nearer the stream. Imagine a vast torrent of liquid fire bearing down and consuming vines, olives, fig-trees, houses; in a word, everything that stood in its way. This mighty flood divided into different channels, according to the inequalities of the mountain: the largest stream seemed half a mile broad at least, and five miles long. The nature and consistence of these burning torrents hath been described with so much exactness and truth by Borellus in his Latin treatise of Mount Etna, that I need say nothing of it.

I walked so far before my companions up the mountain, along the side of the river of fire, that I was obliged to retire in great haste, the sulphureous stream having surprised me, and almost taken away my breath. During our return, which was about three o'clock in the morning, we constantly heard the murmur and groaning of the mountain, which between whiles would burst out into louder peals, throwing up huge spouts of fire and burning stones, which falling down again, resembled the stars in our rockets. Sometimes I observed two, at others three, distinct columns of flames; and sometimes one vast one that seemed to fill the whole crater. These burning columns and the fiery stones seemed to be shot 1,000 feet perpendicular above the summit of the volcano. The 11th at night, I observed it, from a terrace in Naples, to throw up incessantly a vast body of fire, and great stones to a surprising height. The 12th, in the morning, it darkened the sun with ashes and smoke, causing a sort of eclipse. Horrid bellowings, this and the foregoing day, were heard at Naples, whither part of the ashes had reached. At night I observed it throwing up flame, as on the 11th.

On the 13th, the wind changing, we saw a pillar of black smoke shot upright to a prodigious height. At night I observed the mount cast up fire as before, though not so distinctly, because of the smoke. The 14th, a thick black cloud hid the mountain from Naples. The 15th, in the morning, the court and walls of our house in Naples were covered with ashes. The 16th, the smoke was driven by a westerly wind from the town to the opposite side of the mountain. The 17th, the smoke appeared much diminished, fat and greasy. The 18th, the whole appearance ended; the mountain remaining perfectly quiet without any visible smoke or flame. A gentleman of my acquaintance, whose window looked towards Vesuvius, assured me that he observed several flashes, as it were of lightning, issue out of the mouth of the volcano.

It is not worth while to trouble you with the conjectures I have formed concerning the cause of these phenomena, from what I observed in the Lacus Amsancti, the Solfatara, etc. as well as in Mount Vesuvius. One thing I may venture to say, that I saw the fluid matter rise out of the centre of the bottom of the crater, out of the very middle of the mountain, contrary to what Borellus imagines; whose method of explaining the eruption of a volcano by an inflexed syphon and the rules of hydrostatics, is likewise inconsistent with the torrent's flowing down from the very vertex of the mountain. I have not seen the crater since the eruption, but design to visit it again before I leave Naples. I doubt there is nothing in this worth showing the Society: as to that, you will use your discretion.

G. BERKELEY

WILLIAM STUKELEY (1687–1765)

In this very charming letter the famous old English antiquarian tells Sir Hans Sloane, founder of the British Museum, all about the Flood.

TO SIR HANS SLOANE

STAMFORD, OCT. 19, 1730

HONOURED AND DEAR SIR, Among the proofs of the Deluge of Noah visible to this day, whereof there are infinite numbers in your admirable museum, this stone likewise before me is one, of which I send you enclosed the exact drawing. The sight of the stone, and the day, put me in mind of that great judgment, which God Almighty brought upon our globe as on this day, whereof the stone is a monument. The appearances which you see in the cavity of it are, perhaps, a parcel of fruits like hazel-nuts, promiscuously jumbled together, and turned into stone; though they are pretty much like nuts, yet I suspect they are some other fruit. You, that are the great oracle of all natural knowledge, will probably at first sight resolve the doubt: and for that purpose I have drawn underneath two of them in their true shape and bulk. The fruits themselves are very distinct, the texture of the coat, rind, or shell of them is like that of our hazel-nuts and pistachios, and of the same bulk. There is in some of them a bit of the *pedunculus* or stalk; in others, the cavity from whence it is dropped off is very plain. This stone, among others full of shells, was taken out of a quarry near Aynho in Oxfordshire, and sent to Dr. Mead by the Rev. Mr. Wasse, minister there, about nine years ago. There were several small *cornua ammonis*, and other fossil shells, dug up in the same place, and are frequently so. The Doctor gave them to me. The stone is ten inches long between the two corners. A shell left in the stone, and there are other shells on the back of it.—It is commonly known that, upon digging in our fenny levels of Lincolnshire, on the edge of the high countries, they find very great quantities of antediluvian timber-trees, for such I do not scruple to call them. The like is observed on the marshy grounds at the mouth of all great rivers, and generally in all boggy and moorish ground, all the world over. Likewise among these trees they frequently find great quantities of hazel-nuts, acorns, and the like, crowded together on heaps. These appearances, as well as the stone before us, are, I suppose, not only a demonstrative proof of the veracity of the sacred records, whence we have the account of the Deluge; but likewise in my judgment, bring us to a very near approach to the time of the beginning of the Deluge; but different from what is assigned·in Authors.—I observe, they generally make the beginning of the Deluge to fall in winter. Scaliger fixes it to the 17th of November; Abp. Usher, the 17th of December; Whiston, the 28th of November; Shuckford, the 1st or 2nd of November. The Sacred Historian says, it began on the 17th day of the second month. The first month they begin with the autumnal equinox, as if Moses reckoned time by exact Julian years. But according to the calculations I have made of this matter, I find God Almighty ordered Noah to get the creatures into the Ark on Sunday the 12th of October, the very day of the autumnal equinox that year, and on this present day, on the Sunday se'nnight following (the 19th of October) that terrible catastrophe began, the moon being past her third quarter. If we would know how it answers to this year, in order to understand the season, it is parallel to the 19th September, when summer is over, and autumn begins. All the grain and fruits of the earth are now perfectly ripe, and fit to be gathered. The nuts began to drop off the trees, Holyrood day being past. The seeds of vegetables have all possible chance to escape in sufficient quantity, to clothe again the new world. Many trees were then torn up by the roots with the violence of the storm, hurried down from the high countries, and with the decreasing waters left in the mud, on the edge of the fens, mouths of great rivers, etc., where the turf has overgrown them. Along with them nuts and acorns were driven together in heaps, and are found at this day in their true form. The oil they abound with, and hardness of their shell, has enabled them to withstand a total change of parts, though the colour be lost, and the whole like dirt. They wanted the condition of the fruits in our stone, if such they be, which happening to fall into the cavity of a matter then beginning to turn into stone, by help of the petrifying juices, like insects in amber, have found a more durable tomb. It is just to suppose that, if the Deluge had begun at the latter end of November, or December, the nuts would have been sunk into the earth, which is generally soft in woods, or would have been eaten up by animals, or carried into their dens and holes by that time; and not so readily have been gathered together, to accompany the trees; as when beaten off the trees when first ripe, according to our assertion.

This assignment of the beginning of the Deluge may possibly be a week earlier, or the like, but not later, and is attended too with this advantage: that the Ark rested on the top of Mount Ararat on Monday the 23rd of March, and the earth generally appeared on the 5th of June; which answers to the beginning of our May, as to season. Here was the whole power of the summer's heat, to dry the earth, and call forth the benumbed vegetable world; and Noah went out of the Ark at the latter end of October, soon after the autumnal equinox, and there would be sufficient quantity of food for the creatures turned out. Whereas, by the other hypothesis, Noah quits the Ark at the very dregs of winter.—Thus the flood began and ended at the time of the year when the world was created, and in several respects there is a *par ratio* for it; though I believe God Almighty in this grand concern ordered it pursuant to many natural causes, and made use of the concurrence of all as far as they would extend; yet in the main it was purely miraculous; and to pretend to solve it by philosophical or astronomical principles is no less an impotent than an impious attempt; and among other things, has given a handle to the late sceptics, who doubt of the divine authority of the Scriptures; which, the more they are looked into, the more they discover their truth and beauties. I am, honoured and dear Sir, your most obedient and devoted servant,

WM. STUKELEY

ALEXANDER POPE (1688–1744)

Pope was a great letter writer, and his epistles are often gems of art. This description of an old English country seat has a vividness all its own, while the chatty letters to the Blounts, his life-long friends, breathe the whole spirit of the times.

TO JONATHAN SWIFT

JANUARY 13, 1714

WHATEVER apologies it might become me to make at any other time for writing to you, I shall use none now, to a man who has owned himself as splenetic as a cat in the country. In that circumstance, I know by experience a letter is a very useful as well as an amusing thing: if you are too busied in state affairs to read it, yet you may find entertainment in folding it into divers figures, either doubling it into a pyramidical, or twisting it into a serpentine form: or if your disposition should not be so mathematical, in taking it with you to that place where men of studious minds are apt to sit longer than ordinary; where, after an abrupt division of the paper, it may not be unpleasant to try to fit and rejoin the broken lines together. All these amusements I am no stranger to in the country, and doubt not, by this time, you begin to relish them in your present contemplative situation.

I remember, a man who was thought to have some knowledge in the world used to affirm, that no people in town ever complained they were forgotten by their friends in the country; but by increasing experience convinces me he was mistaken, for I find a great many here grievously complaining of you upon this score. I am told further, that you treat the few you correspond with in a very arrogant style, and tell them you admire at their insolence in disturbing your meditations, or even inquiring of your retreat; but this I will not positively assert, because I never received any such insulting epistle from you. My Lord Oxford says you have not written to him once since you went; but this perhaps may be only policy in him or you! and I, who am half a Whig, must not entirely credit anything he affirms. At Button's, it is reported you are gone to Hanover, and that Gay goes only on an embassy to you. Others apprehend some dangerous state treatise from your retirement; and a wit, who affects to imitate Balzac, says, that the ministry now are like those heathens of old, who received their oracles from the woods. The gentlemen of the Roman Catholic persuasion are not unwilling to credit me when I whisper, that you are gone to meet some Jesuits commissioned from the court of Rome, in order to settle the most convenient methods to be taken for the coming of the Pretender. Dr. Arbuthnot is singular in his opinion, and imagines your only design is to attend at full leisure to the life and adventures of Scriblerus. This, indeed, must be granted of greater importance than all the rest; and I wish I could promise so well of you. The top of my own ambition is to contribute to that great work; and I shall translate Homer by the by. Mr. Gay has acquainted you what progress I have made in it. I cannot name Mr. Gay without all the acknowledgments which I shall ever owe you on his account. If I writ this in verse, I would tell you, you are like the sun, and, while men imagine you to be retired or absent, are hourly exerting your influence, and bringing things to maturity for their advantage. Of all the world, you are the man—without flattery—who serve your friends with the least ostentation; it is almost ingratitude to thank you, considering your temper; and this is the period of all my letter which, I fear, you will think the most impertinent. I am, with the truest affection, yours, etc.

TO LADY MARY WORTLEY MONTAGU

DEAR MADAM, It is not possible to express the least part of the joy your return gives me; time only and experience will convince you how very sincere it is. I excessively long to meet you, to say so much, so very much to you, that I believe I shall say nothing. I have given orders to be sent for, the first minute of your arrival—which I beg you will let them know at Mr. Jervas's. I am fourscore miles from London, a short journey compared to that I so often thought at least of undertaking, rather than die without seeing you again. Though the place I am in is such as I would not quit for the town, if I did not value you more than any, nay, everybody else there; and you will be convinced how little the town has engaged my affections in your absence from it, when you know what a place this is which I prefer to it; I shall therefore describe it to you at large, as the true picture of a genuine ancient country-seat.

You must expect nothing regular in my description of a house that seems to be built before rules were in fashion; the whole is so disjointed, and the parts so detached from each other, and yet so joining again, one cannot tell how, that—in a poetical fit—you would imagine it had been a village in Amphion's time, where twenty cottages had taken a dance together, were all out, and stood still in amazement ever since. A stranger would be grievously disappointed who should ever think to get into this house the right way. One would expect, after entering through the porch, to be let into the hall; alas! nothing less, you find yourself in a brew-house. From the parlour you think to step into the drawing-room; but, upon opening the iron-nailed door, you are convinced, by a flight of birds about your ears, and a cloud of dust in your eyes, that it is the pigeon-house. On each side our porch are two chimneys, that wear their greens on the outside, which would do as well within, for whenever we make a fire, we let the smoke out of the windows. Over the parlour windows hangs a sloping balcony, which time has turned into a very convenient penthouse. The top is crowned with a very venerable tower, so like that of the church just by, that the jackdaws build in it as if it were the true steeple.

The great hall is high and spacious, flanked with long tables, images of ancient hospitality; ornamented with monstrous horns, about twenty broken pikes, and a matchlock musket or two, which they say were used in the civil wars. Here is one vast arched window, beautifully darkened with divers scutcheons of painted glass. There seems to be great propriety in this old manner of blazoning upon glass, ancient families being like ancient windows, in the course of generations seldom free from cracks. One shining pane bears date 1286. The youthful face of Dame Elinor owes more to this single piece than to all the glasses she ever consulted in her life. Who can say after this that glass is frail, when it is not half so perishable as human beauty or glory? For in another pane you see the memory of a knight preserved, whose marble nose is mouldered from his monument in the church adjoining. And yet, must not one sigh to reflect that the most authentic record of so ancient a family should lie at the mercy of every boy that throws a stone? In this hall, in former days, have dined gartered knights and courtly dames, with ushers, sewers, and seneschals; and yet it was but the other night that an owl flew in hither and mistook it for a barn.

This hall lets you up (and down) over a very high threshold, into the parlour. It is furnished with historical tapestry, whose marginal fringes do confess the moisture of the air. The other contents of this room are a broken-bellied virginal, a couple of crippled velvet chairs, with two or three mildewed pictures of mouldy ancestors. These are carefully set at the further corner; for the windows being everywhere broken, make it so convenient a place to dry poppies and mustard-seed in, that the room is appropriated to that use.

Next this parlour lies, as I said before, the pigeon-house, by the side of which runs an entry that leads, on one hand and the other, into a bed-chamber, a buttery, and a small hole called the chaplain's study. Then follow a brew-house, a little green and gilt parlour, and the great stairs, under which is the dairy. A little further on the right, the servants' hall; and by the side of it, up six steps, the old lady's closet, which has a lattice into the said hall, that, while she said her prayers, she might cast an eye on the men and maids. There are upon this ground floor in all twenty-four apartments, hard to be distinguished by particular names; among which I must not forget a chamber that has in it a large antiquity of timber, which seems to have been either a bedstead or a cider-press.

Our best room above is very long and low, of the exact proportion of a bandbox; it has hangings of the finest work in the world; those, I mean, which Arachne spins out of her own bowels; indeed, the roof is so decayed, that after a favourable shower of rain, we may, with God's blessing, expect a crop of mushrooms between the chinks of the floors.

All this upper story has for many years had no other inhabitants than certain rats, whose very age renders them worthy of this venerable mansion, for the very rats of this ancient seat are gray. Since these had not quitted it, we hope at least this house may stand during the small remainder of days these poor animals have to live, who are now too infirm to remove to another: they have still a small subsistence left them in the few remaining books of the library.

I had never seen half what I have described, but for an old starched grey-headed steward, who is as much an antiquity as any in the place, and looks like an old family picture walked out of its frame. He failed not, as we passed from room to room, to relate several memoirs of the family; but his observations were particularly curious in the cellar: he shewed where stood the triple rows of butts of sack, and where were ranged the bottles of tent for toasts in the morning: he pointed to the stands that supported the iron-hooped hogsheads of strong beer; then stepping to a corner, he lugged out the tattered fragment of an unframed picture: "This," says he, with tears in his eyes, "was poor

Sir Thomas, once master of the drink I told you of: he had two sons (poor young masters!) that never arrived to the age of this beer; they both fell ill in this very cellar, and never went out upon their own legs." He could not pass by a broken bottle without taking it up to shew us the arms of the family on it. He then led me up the tower, by dark winding stone-steps, which landed us into several little rooms, one above another; one of these was nailed up, and my guide whispered to me the occasion of it. It seems the course of this noble blood was a little interrupted about two centuries ago by a freak of the Lady Frances, who was here taken with a neighbouring prior; ever since which the room has been nailed up. The ghost of Lady Frances is supposed to walk here: some prying maids of the family formerly reported that they saw a lady in a fardingale through the keyhole; but this matter was hushed up, and the servants forbid to talk of it.

I must needs have tired you with this long letter; but what engaged me in the description was, a generous principle to preserve the memory of a thing that must itself soon fall to ruin; nay, perhaps, some part of it before this reaches your hands. Indeed, I owe this old house the same gratitude that we do to an old friend that harbours us in his declining condition, nay, even in his last extremities. I have found this an excellent place for retirement and study, where no one who passes by can dream there is an inhabitant, and even anybody that would visit me dares not venture under my roof. You will not wonder I have translated a great deal of Homer in this retreat; anyone that sees it will own I could not have chosen a fitter or more likely place to converse with the dead. As soon as I return to the living, it shall be to converse with the best of them. I hope, therefore, very speedily to tell you in person how sincerely and unalterably I am, madam, your, &c.

I beg Mr. Wortley to believe me his most humble servant.

TO MRS. BLOUNT

BATH, OCT. 6TH (1714)

MADAM, If I may ever be allowed to tell you the thoughts I have so often of you in your absence, it is at this time, when I neglect the company of a great number of ladies, to write this letter. From the window where I am seated I command the prospect of twenty or thirty, in one of the finest promenades in the world, every moment that I take my eye off from the paper. If variety of diversions and new objects be capable of driving our friends out of our minds, I have the best excuse imaginable for forgetting you: for I have slid, I cannot tell how, into all the amusements of this place: my whole day is shared by the pump-assemblies, the walks, the chocolate-houses, raffling-shops, plays, medleys, &c. We have no ladies who have the face, though some of them may have the impudence, to expect a lampoon. The prettiest is one I had the luck to travel with, who had found out so far as to tell me, that whatever pretences I make to gaiety, my heart is not at Bath. Mrs. Gage came hither the other day, and did me a double honour, in speaking to me, and asking publicly, when I saw you last? I endeavour (like all awkward fellows) to become agreeable by imitation; and observing who are most in favour with the fair, I sometimes copy the civil air of Gascoin, sometimes the impudent one of Nash, and sometimes for vanity, the silly one of a neighbour of yours, who had lost to the gamesters here that money of which the ladies only deserve to rob a man of his age. This mistaken youth is so ignorant as to imagine himself as agreeable in the eyes of the sex to-day, as he was yesterday, when he was worth three or four hundred pounds more. Alas! he knows not, that just as much is left of a mistress's heart, as is emptied from one's own pocket! My chief acquaintances of my own sex are the aforesaid Mr. Gascoin and Mr. Nash; of the other, Dame Lindsey and Jenny Man. I am so much a rake as to be ashamed of being seen with Dr. Parnelle. I ask people abroad who that Parson is? We expect better company here next week; and them a certain Earl shall know what ladies drink his health every day since his disgrace, that you may be in the public pamphlets, as well as your humble servant. They say, here are cabals held, under pretence of drinking waters; and this scandal, like others, refreshes me, and elevates my spirits. I think no man deserves a monument that could not be wrapped in a winding-sheet of papers writ against him. If women could digest scandal as well as I, there are two that might be the happiest creatures in the universe. I have in one week run through whatever they call diverting here; and I should be ashamed to pass two just in the same track. I will therefore take but a trip to Longleat, which is twelve miles hence, to visit my Lord Lansdown, and return to London. I must tell you a truth, which is not, however, much to my credit. I never thought so much of yourself and your fair sister as since I have been fourscore miles distant from you. At Binfield I look upon you as good neighbours, at London as pretty kind of women, and here as divinities, angels, goddesses, or what you will.

In like manner, I never knew at what a rate I valued your life, till you were upon the point of dying. If Mrs. Teresa and you will not fall sick every season, I shall certainly die for you. Seriously, I value you both so much, that I esteem others much the less for your sakes: you have robbed me of the pleasure of esteeming a thousand fine qualities in them by showing me so many in a superior degree in yourselves. There are but two things in the world which can make you indifferent to me, which I believe you are not capable of; I mean ill-nature and malice. I have seen enough of you not to resent any frailty you could have, and nothing less than a vice can make me like you less. I expect you should discover, by my common conduct towards you both, that this is true; and that therefore you should pardon a thousand things in me for that disposition. Expect nothing from me but truth and freedom, and I shall be always thought by you, what I always am, your faithful, obliged, humble servant.

TO MARTHA AND TERESA BLOUNT

DEAR LADIES, I think myself obliged to desire you would not put off any diversion you may find in the prospect of seeing me on Saturday, which is very uncertain. I take this occasion to tell you once for all, that I design no longer to be a constant companion when I have ceased to be an agreeable one. You only have had, as my friends, the privilege of knowing my unhappiness, and are therefore the only people whom my company must necessarily make melancholy. I will not bring myself to you at all hours like a skeleton, to come across your diversions and dash your pleasures. Nothing can be more shocking than to be perpetually meeting the ghost of an old acquaintance, which is all you can ever see of me.

You must not imagine this to proceed from any coldness, or the least decrease of friendship to you. If you had any love for me, I should be always glad to gratify you with an object that you thought agreeable. But as your regard is friendship and esteem, those are things that are well—perhaps better—preserved absent than present. A man that loves you is a joy to your eyes at all times. A man that you esteem is a solemn kind of thing, like a priest only wanted at a certain hour, to do his office. 'Tis like oil in a salad—necessary, but of no manner of taste.

And you may depend upon it, I will wait upon you on every occasion at the first summons as long as I live. Let me open my whole heart to you. I have sometimes found myself inclined to be in love with you, and as I have reason to know, from your temper and conduct, how miserably I should be used in that circumstance, it is worth my while to avoid it. It is enough to be disagreeable without adding food to it by constant slavery. I have heard, indeed, of women that have had a kindness for men of my make—I love you so well that I tell you the truth, and that has made me write this letter. I will see you less frequently this winter, as you'll less want company. When the gay part of the world is gone, I'll to ready to stop the gap of a vacant hour whenever you please. Till then I'll converse with those who are more indifferent to me, as you will with those who are more entertaining. I wish you every pleasure God and man can pour upon ye; and I faithfully promise you all the good I can do, which is the service of a friend who will ever be, ladies, entirely yours.

SAMUEL RICHARDSON (1689–1761)

Could anything be more characteristic of the author of "Pamela" than this letter to one of his countless women correspondents and admirers?

TO MRS. BELFOUR

OCTOBER 6TH, 1748

MADAM, There was no need to bespeak my patience, nor anything but my gratitude, on reading such a letter as you have favoured me with. Indeed, I admire it, and have reason to plume myself upon the interest you take in my story. I should be utterly inexcusable, in my opinion, if I took not early and grateful notice of it; yet cannot but say, that if there were no other reason but the condescending one you are pleased to mention in the latter part of your letter, to deny me, I should be proud to know to whom I have the honour of addressing myself by pen and ink.

You cannot imagine, how sensibly I am grieved for the pain the unexpected turn in my story has given you. God forbid that anything unhappy, or disastrous, should ever fall to the lot of a lady so generously sensible to the woes of others, as she must be who can thus be affected by a moral tale, though the character (however presumed to be in nature) existed not in life.

Indeed, you are not *particular* in your wishes for a happy ending, as it is called. Nor can I go through some of the scenes myself without being sensibly touched. (Did I not say that I was another Pygmalion?) But yet I had to show, for example sake, a young lady struggling nobly with the greatest difficulties, and triumphing from the best motives, in the course of distresses, the tenth part of which would have sunk even manly hearts; yet tenderly educated, born to affluence, naturally meek, although, where an exertion of spirit was necessary, manifesting herself to be a true heroine.

And what, madam, is the temporary happiness we are so fond of? What the long life we are so apt to covet?

The more irksome these reflections are to the young, the gay, and the healthy, the more necessary are they to be inculcated.

279

A verse may find him who a sermon flies,
And turn delight into a sacrifice.

Of this nature is my design. Religion never was at so low an ebb as at present. And if my work must be supposed of the novel kind, I was willing to try if a religious novel would do good.

And did you not perceive that in the very first letter of Lovelace, all those seeds of wickedness were thick sown, which sprouted up into action afterwards in his character? Pride, revenge, a love of intrigue, plot, contrivance! And who is it that asks, "Do men gather grapes of thorns, or figs of thistles?" On this consideration it has been matter of surprise to me, and indeed of some concern, that this character has met with so much favour from the good and virtuous, even as it stands from his two or three first letters; and in some measure convinced me of the necessity of such a catastrophe as I have made.

Had I drawn my heroine reconciled to relations unworthy of her, nobly resisting the attacks of an intrepid lover, overcoming her persecutors, and baffling the wicked designs formed against her honour; marrying her Lovelace, and that on her own terms; educating properly, and instructing her own children; what, however useful, however pleasing the lesson, had I done more than I had done in Pamela? And it is hoped, that there are many mothers, many wives, who, though they have not been called upon to many trials, thus meritoriously employ themselves in their families.

And as to reforming and marrying Lovelace, and the example to be given by it, what but this that follows, would it have been, instead of the amiable one your good nature and humanity point out? "Here," says another Lovelace, "may I pass the flower and prime of my youth, in forming and pursuing the most insidious enterprises. As many of the daughters and sisters of worthy families as I can seduce, may I seduce—scores perhaps in different climates; and on their weakness build my profligate notions of the whole sex. I may at last meet with, and attempt, a Clarissa, a lady of peerless virtue. I may try her, vex her, plague and torment her worthy heart. I may fit up all my batteries against her virtue; and if I find her proof against all my machinations, and myself tired with rambling, I may then reward that virtue; I may graciously extend my hand—she may give me hers, and rejoice, and thank heaven for my condescension in her favour. The Almighty, I may suppose, at the same time, to be as ready with his mercy, foregoing his justice on my past crimes, as if my nuptials with this meritorious fair one were to atone for the numerous distresses and ruins I have occasioned in other families; and all the good-natured, the worthy, the human part of the world, forgiving me too, because I am a handsome and a humorous fellow, will clap their hands with joy, and cry out,

> Happy, happy, happy pair!
> None but the rake deserves the fair!"

There cannot be a more pernicious notion, than that which is so commonly received, that a reformed rake makes the best husband. This notion it was my intent to combat and expose, as I mentioned so early as in the preface to my first volume. And how could I have answered this end, had I pursued the plan your benevolent heart wishes I had pursued? Indeed, indeed, madam, reformation is not, cannot, be an easy, a sudden thing, in a man long immersed in vice. The temptation to it, as from sex to sex, so natural; constitution, as in such a character as Lovelace, so promotive; a love of intrigue so predominant; so great a self-admirer; so much admired by others; and was it not nature that I proposed to follow?

You suppose me, madam, to be one who can believe that there is felicity in marriage. Indeed I honour the state; I have reason to do so. I have been twice married, and both times happily. But as to Clarissa, whom you wish to be joined to a man of her own reforming, "new modelled," as you say, "and by her made perfect as herself," let me say, if I had designed her to shine in the married life, I would have given her a man whose reflections upon his past life should have sat easier upon him; both for his sake, and for the sake of her pious heart, than those of a wicked man could do, who had been the ruin of many innocents before he became hers. Great abatements to a well-founded happiness surely in these reflections! I would not have confirmed the pernicious notions above-mentioned of the reformed rake.

A man who knows so much of his duty, as he is supposed to know, and who is, nevertheless, wicked upon principle, must be an abandoned man; and even should he reform, an uneasy, and therefore an unhappy one.

But why, as I asked in my former, is death painted in such shocking lights, when it is the common lot? If it is become so terrible to human nature, it is time to familiarize it to us. Hence another of my great ends, as I have hinted. "Don't we lead back," says Clarissa, on a certain occasion, which had shocked those about her, "a starting steed to the object he is apt to start at, in order to familiarize him to it, and cure his starting?"

Who but the persons concerned should choose for themselves what would make them happy? If Clarissa think not an early death an evil, but on the contrary, after an exemplary preparation, looks upon it as her consummating perfection, who shall grudge it her? who shall punish her with life? "There is no inquisition in the grave," as she quotes, "whether we have lived ten or an hundred years, and the day of death is better than the day of our birth."

But, after all, it is the execution must either condemn or acquit me. I am, however, discouraged and mortified at what you tell me, that you cannot think of accepting of the volumes when completed, if the catastrophe be not as you wish.

I am pained for your apprehended pain, were you to read to the end; and the more so, I own, that I have lost my aim, and judge wrongly from my own heart and eyes, if there are not scenes to come that will affect so tender a heart as yours.

That fifth volume is finished; I will send it directed to Mrs. Belfour (I must not dare to hope for the honour of a more welcome address) to the bookseller at Exeter. And if you will favour me with a letter upon it—yet you must take care how you favour me too—men are naturally encroachers. And it would be difficult in me to deny myself the hope of such a correspondent to the end of my life. I love Miss Howe next to Clarissa; and I see very evidently in your letters that you are the twin sister of that lady. And indeed I adore your spirit and your earnestness,

And am, Madam, with the greatest respect,
Your most sincere admirer and humble servant,
S. RICHARDSON

LADY MARY WORTLEY MONTAGU (1689–1762)

Lady Mary was one of the first of England's feminists. But what is of greater interest to her country was the fact that during her travels in the East, while her husband was ambassador to the Porte, she observed the practice of inoculation against smallpox and was one of the first to introduce it to England. The first letter is typical of the very amusing accounts she sent home of the then little-known life of Constantinople; the second is to her friend Lady Bute, with some sound advice on the education of girls.

TO THE COUNTESS OF MAR

Pera of Constantinople, March 10, O.S.

I have not written to you, dear Sister, these many months—a great piece of self-denial. But I know not where to direct, or what part of the world you are in. I have received no letter from you since that short note of April last, in which you tell me that you are on the point of leaving England, and promise me a direction for the place you stay in; but I have, in vain, expected it till now, and now I only learn from the Gazette that you are returned, which induces me to venture this letter to your house at London. I had rather ten of my letters should be lost than you imagine I don't write; and I think it is hard fortune if one in ten don't reach you. However, I am resolved to keep the copies, as testimonies of my inclination to give you, to the utmost of my power, all the diverting part of my travels, while you are exempt from all the fatigues and inconveniencies.

In the first place, then, I wish you joy of your niece; for I was brought to bed of a daughter five weeks ago. I don't mention this as one of my diverting adventures; though I must own that it is not half so mortifying here as in England; there being as much difference as there is between a little cold in the head, which sometimes happens here, and the consumption coughs so common in London. Nobody keeps their house a month for lying-in; and I am not so fond of any of our customs as to retain them when they are not necessary. I returned my visits at three weeks' end, and about four days ago crossed the sea which divides this place from Constantinople, to make a new one, where I had the good fortune to pick up many curiosities. I went to see the Sultana Hafiten, favourite of the late Emperor Mustapha, who, you know (or perhaps you don't know), was deposed by his brother, the reigning Sultan, and died a few weeks after, being poisoned, as it was generally believed. This lady was, immediately after his death, saluted with an absolute order to leave the Seraglio and choose herself a husband among the great men at the Porte. I suppose you may imagine her overjoyed at this proposal. Quite the contrary. These women who are called and esteem themselves queens look upon this liberty as the greatest disgrace and affront that can happen to them. She threw herself at the Sultan's feet, and begged him to poignard her rather than use his brother's widow with that contempt. She represented to him, in agonies of sorrow, that she was privileged from this misfortune by having brought five princes into the Ottoman family. But all the boys being dead, and only one girl surviving, this excuse was not received, and she was compelled to make her choice. She chose Bekir Effendi, then Secretary of State and above four-score years old, to convince the world that she firmly intended to keep the vow she had made of never suffering a second husband to approach her bed; and since she must honour some subject so far as to be called his, she would choose him as a mark of her gratitude, since it was he that had presented her at the age of ten years, to her last lord. But she never permitted him to pay her one visit though it is now fifteen years she has been in his house, where she passes her time in uninterrupted mourning, with a constancy very little known in Christendom, especially in a widow of one-and-twenty, for she is now but thirty-six. She has no black eunuchs for her guard, her husband being obliged to respect her as a queen and not to enquire at all into what is done in her apartment.

I was led into a large room with a sofa the whole length of it, adorned with white marble pillars like a Ruelle, covered with pale blue figured velvet on a silver ground, with cushions of the same, where I was desired to repose till the Sultana appeared, who had contrived this manner of reception to avoid rising up at my entrance, though she made me an inclination of her head when I rose up to her. I was very glad to observe a lady that had been distinguished by the favour of an emperor to whom beauties were, every day, presented from all parts of the world. But she did not seem to me to have ever been half so beautiful as the fair Fatima I saw at Adrianople; though she had the remains of a fine face, more decayed by sorrow than time. But her dress was something so surprisingly rich that I cannot forbear describing it to you. She wore a vest, called *dualma*, which differs from a *caftan* by longer sleeves, and folding over at the bottom. It was of purple cloth, strait to her shape, and thick set, on each side down to her feet and round the sleeves, with pearls of the best water, of the same size as their buttons commonly are. You must not suppose that I mean as large as those of my Lord ———, but about the bigness of a pea; and to these buttons, large loops of diamonds, in the form of those gold loops so common on birthday coats. This habit was tied at the waist with two large tassels of smaller pearls, and round the arms embroidered with large diamonds. Her shift was fastened at the bottom with a great diamond, shaped like a lozenge; her girdle as broad as the broadest English riband, entirely covered with diamonds. Round her neck she wore three chains, which reached to her knees; one of large pearl, at the bottom of which hung a fine coloured emerald as big as a turkey-egg; another, consisting of two hundred emeralds close joined together, of the most lively green, perfectly matched, every one as large as a half-crown piece, and as thick as three crown pieces; and another of small emeralds, perfectly round. But her ear-rings eclipsed all the rest. They were two diamonds shaped exactly like pears, as large as a big hazel nut. Round her *Talpoche* she had four strings of pearl, the whitest and most perfect in the world, at least enough to make four necklaces, every one as large as the Duchess of Marlborough's, and of the same shape, fastened with two roses consisting of a large ruby for the middle stone, and round them twenty drops of clean diamonds to each. Besides this, her head-dress was covered with bodkins of emeralds and diamonds. She wore large diamond bracelets, and had five rings on her fingers, except for Mr. Pitt's the largest I ever saw in my life. 'Tis for jewellers to compute the value of these things; but according to the common estimation of jewels in our part of the world her whole dress must be worth a hundred thousand pounds sterling. This I am sure of, that no European queen has half the quantity, and the Empress's jewels, though very fine, would look very mean near hers.

She gave me a dinner of fifty dishes of meat, which (after their fashion) were placed on the table but one at a time, and was extremely tedious. But the magnificence of her table answered very well to that of her dress. The knives were of gold, and the hafts set with diamonds. But the piece of luxury which grieved my eyes was the

table-cloth and napkins, which were all tiffany embroidered with silk
and gold, in the finest manner, in natural flowers. It was with the
utmost regret that I made use of these costly napkins, which were as
finely wrought as the finest handkerchiefs that ever came out of this
country. You may be sure that they were entirely spoiled before
dinner was over. The sherbet (which is the liquor they drink at
meals) was served in china bowls; but the covers and salvers massy gold.
After dinner, water was brought in gold basins, and towels of the
same kind with the napkins, which I very unwillingly wiped my hands
upon, and coffee was served in china with gold soucoups [saucers].

The Sultana seemed in a very good humour, and talked to me
with the utmost civility. I did not omit this opportunity of learning
all that I possibly could of the Seraglio, which is so entirely unknown
amongst us. She assured me that the story of the Sultan's throwing
a handkerchief is altogether fabulous; and the manner upon that occasion no other than this. He sends the Kyslir Aga to signify to the
lady the honour he intends her. She is immediately complimented
upon it by the others and led to the bath, where she is perfumed and
dressed in the most magnificent and becoming manner. The Emperor
precedes his visit by a royal present, and then comes into her apartment.
Neither is there any such thing as her creeping in at the bed's foot.
She said, that the first he made choice of was always after the first
rank, and not the mother of the eldest son, as other writers would
make us believe. Sometimes the Sultan diverts himself in the company of all his ladies, who stand in a circle round him. And she confessed, they were ready to die with envy and jealousy of the happy she
that he distinguished by any appearance of preference. But this
seemed to me neither better nor worse than the circles in most courts,
where the glance of the monarch is watched, and every smile is waited
for with impatience and envied by those who cannot obtain it.

She never mentioned the Sultan without tears in her eyes, yet
she seemed very fond of the discourse. "My past happiness," said
she, "apppears a dream to me. Yet I cannot forget that I was beloved
by the greatest and most lovely of mankind. I was chosen from all
the rest, to make all his campaigns with him; and I would not survive
him, if I was not passionately fond of the Princess, my daughter. Yet
all my tenderness for her was hardly enough to make me preserve my
life. When I left him, I passed a whole twelve-month without seeing
the light. Time has softened my despair; yet I now pass some days
every week in tears, devoted to the memory of my Sultan." There

was no affectation in these words. It was easy to see she was in a deep melancholy, though her good humour made her willing to divert me.

She asked me to walk in her garden, and one of her slaves immediately brought her a pellice of rich brocade, lined with sables. I waited on her into the garden, which had nothing in it remarkable but the fountains; and from thence she shewed me all her apartments. In her bed-chamber her toilet was displayed, consisting of two looking glasses, the frames covered with pearls, and her night *Talpoche* set with bodkins of jewels, and near it three vests of fine sables, every one of which is at least worth a thousand dollars (two hundred pounds English money). I don't doubt but these rich habits were purposely placed in sight, though they seemed negligently thrown on the sofa. When I took my leave of her I was complimented with perfumes, as at the Grand Vizier's, and presented with a very fine embroidered handkerchief. Her slaves were to the number of thirty, besides ten little ones, the eldest not above seven years old. These were the most beautiful girls I ever saw, all richly dressed; and I observed that the Sultana took a great deal of pleasure in these lovely children, which is a vast expense; for there is not a handsome girl of that age, to be bought under a hundred pounds sterling. They wore little garlands of flowers, and their own hair braided, which was all their head-dress; but their habits were all of gold stuffs. These served her coffee kneeling; brought water when she washed, etc. 'Tis a great part of the business of the older slaves to take care of these young girls, to learn them to embroider, and to serve them as carefully as if they were children of the family.

Now, do you imagine I have entertained you all this while with a relation that has, at least, received many embellishments from my hand? This, you will say, is but too like the Arabian Tales. These embroidered napkins! and a jewel as large as a turkey's egg! You forget, dear Sister, those very tales were written by an author of this country, and (excepting the enchantments) are a real representation of the manners here. We travellers are in very hard circumstances. If we say nothing but what has been said before us, we are dull and we have observed nothing. If we tell anything new, we are laughed at as fabulous and romantic, not allowing either for the difference of ranks which afford difference of company, or more curiosity, or the change of customs that happen every twenty years in every country, But the truth is, people judge of travellers exactly with the same candour, good nature, and impartiality, they judge of their neighbours upon all occasions. For my part, if I live to return amongst you, I am so well acquainted with the morals of all my dear friends and acquaintances, that I am resolved to tell them nothing at all, to avoid the imputation of my telling too much. But I depend upon your knowing me enough to believe whatever I seriously assert for truth; though I give you leave to be surprised at an account so new to you.

But what would you say if I told you that I have been in a Haram, where the winter apartment was wainscoted with inlaid work of mother-of-pearl, ivory of different colours, and olive wood, exactly like the little boxes, you have seen brought out of this country; and in whose rooms, designed for summer, the walls are all crusted with japan china, the roofs gilt, and the floors spread with the finest Persian carpets? Yet there is nothing more true; such is the palace of my lovely friend the fair Fatima, whom I was acquainted with at Adrianople. I went to visit her yesterday; and if possible, she appeared to me handsomer than before. She met me at the door of her chamber, and giving me her hand with the best grace in the world; "You Christian ladies," said she, with a smile that made her as beautiful as an angel, "have the reputation of inconstancy, and I did not expect, whatever goodness you expressed for me at Adrianople, that I should ever see you again. But I am now convinced that I have really the happiness of pleasing you; and if you knew how I speak of you amongst our ladies, you would be assured that you do me justice in making me your friend." She placed me in the corner of the sofa, and I spent the afternoon in her conversation with the greatest pleasure in the world. The Sultana Hafiten is what one would naturally expect to find a Turkish lady, willing to oblige, but no knowing how to go about it; and 'tis easy to see in her manner that she has lived excluded from the world. But Fatima has all the politeness and good breeding of a court, with an air that inspires at once respect and tenderness; and now that I understand her language I find her wit as agreeable as her beauty. She is very curious after the manners of other countries, and has not the partiality for her own so common to little minds. A Greek that I carried with me, who had never seen her before (nor could have been admitted now, if she had not been in my train) shewed that surprise at her beauty and manner which is unavoidable at the first sight, and said to me in Italian, "This is no Turkish lady, she is certainly some Christian." Fatima guessed she spoke of her, and asked what she had said. I would not have told her, thinking she would have been no better pleased with the compliment than one of a Turk, but the Greek lady told it to her, and she smiled, saying, "It is not the first time I have heard so; my mother was a Poloneze, taken at the siege of Caminiec; and my father used to rally me, saying he believed his Christian wife had found some Christian gallant; for that I had not the air of a Turkish girl." I assured her that if all the Turkish ladies were like her, it was absolutely necessary to confine them from public view for the repose of mankind; and proceeded to tell her what a noise such a face as hers would make in London or Paris. "I can't believe you," replied she, agreeably. "If beauty was so much valued in your country, as you say, they would never have suffered you to leave it." Perhaps, dear Sister, you laugh at my vanity in repeating this compliment, but I only do it as I think it very well turned, and give it you as an instance of the spirit of her conversation. Her house was magnificently furnished, and very well fancied; her winter rooms being furnished with figured velvet on gold grounds, and those for summer with fine Indian quilting embroidered with gold. The houses of the great Turkish ladies are kept clean with as much nicety as those in Holland. This was situated in a high part of the town; and from the window of her summer apartment we had the prospect of the sea, the islands, and the Asian mountains.

My letter is insensibly grown so long, I am ashamed of it. This is a very bad symptom. 'Tis well if I don't degenerate into a downright storyteller. It may be our proverb, that knowledge is no burden, may be true, as to one's self; but knowing too much is very apt to make us troublesome to other people.

I am, etc.

TO THE COUNTESS OF BUTE

LOVERE, JAN. 28, N.S., 1753

DEAR CHILD, You have given me a great deal of satisfaction by your account of your eldest daughter. I am particularly pleased to hear she is a good arithmetician; it is the best proof of understanding: the knowledge of numbers is one of the chief distinctions between us and brutes. If there is anything in blood, you may reasonably expect your children should be endowed with an uncommon share of good sense. Mr. Wortley's family and mine have both produced some of the greatest men that have been born in England; I mean Admiral Sandwich, and my grandfather, who was distinguished by the name of Wise William. I have heard Lord Bute's father mentioned

E.L.   L as an extraordinary genius, though he had not many opportunities of showing it; and his uncle, the present Duke of Argyll, has one of the best heads I ever knew. I will therefore speak to you as supposing Lady Mary not only capable, but desirous of learning; in that case, by all means let her be indulged in it. You will tell me I did not make it a part of your education; your prospect was very different from hers. As you had much in your circumstances to attract the highest offers, it seemed your business to learn how to live in the world, as it is hers to know how to be easy out of it. It is the common error of builders and parents to follow some plan they think beautiful—and perhaps is so—without considering that nothing is beautiful which is displaced. Hence we see so many edifices raised, that the raisers can never inhabit, being too large for their fortunes. Vistas are laid open over barren heaths, and apartments contrived for a coolness very agreeable in Italy, but killing in the north of Britain: thus every woman endeavours to breed her daughter a fine lady, qualifying her for a station in which she will never appear, and at the same time incapacitating her for that retirement to which she is destined. Learning, if she has a real taste for it, will not only make her contented, but happy in it. No entertainment is so cheap as reading, nor any pleasure so lasting. She will not want new fashions, nor regret the loss of expensive diversions, or variety of company, if she can be amused with an author in her closet. To render this amusement complete, she should be permitted to learn the languages. I have heard it lamented that boys lose so many years in mere learning of words: this is no objection to a girl, whose time is not so precious: she cannot advance herself in any profession, and has therefore more hours to spare; and as you say her memory is good, she will be very agreeably employed this way. There are two cautions to be given on this subject: First, not to think herself learned when she can read Latin, or even Greek. Languages are more properly to be called vehicles of learning than learning itself, as may be observed in many schoolmasters, who, though perhaps critics in grammar, are the most ignorant fellows upon earth. True knowledge consists in knowing things, not words. I would no further wish her a linguist than to enable her to read books in their originals, that are often corrupted, and are always injured, by translations. Two hours' application every morning will bring this about much sooner than you can imagine, and she will have leisure enough besides to run over the English poetry, which is a more important part of a woman's education than it is generally supposed. Many a young damsel has been ruined by a fine copy of verses, which she would have laughed at if she had known it had been stolen from Mr. Waller. I remember, when I was a girl, I saved one of my companions from destruction, who communicated to me an epistle she was quite charmed with. As she had naturally a good taste, she observed the lines were not so smooth as Prior's or Pope's, but had more thought and spirit than any of theirs. She was wonderfully delighted with such a demonstration of her lover's sense and passion, and not a little pleased with her own charms, that had force enough to inspire such elegances. In the midst of this triumph, I showed her that they were taken from Randolph's poems, and the unfortunate transcriber was dismissed with the scorn he deserved. To say truth, the poor plagiary was very unlucky to fall into my hands; that author being no longer in fashion, would have escaped anyone of less universal reading than myself. You should encourage your daughter to talk over with you what she reads; and as you are very capable of distinguishing, take care she does not mistake pert folly for wit and humour, or rhyme for poetry, which are the common errors of young people, and have a train of ill consequences. The second caution to be given her—and which is most absolutely necessary—is to conceal whatever learning she attains, with as much solicitude as she would hide crookedness or lameness: the parade of it can only serve to draw on her the envy, and consequently the most inveterate hatred, of all he and she fools, which will certainly be at least three parts in four of her acquaintance. The use of knowledge in our sex, beside the amusement of solitude, is to moderate the passions, and learn to be contented with a small expense, which are the certain effects of a studious life; and it may be preferable even to that fame which men have engrossed to themselves, and will not suffer us to share. You will tell me I have not observed this rule myself; but you are mistaken: it is only inevitable accident that has given me any reputation that way. I have always carefully avoided it, and ever thought it a misfortune. The explanation of this paragraph would occasion a long digression, which I will not trouble you with, it being my present design only to say what I think useful for the instruction of my granddaughter, which I have much at heart. If she has the same inclination—I should say passion —for learning that I was born with, history, geography, and philosophy will furnish her with materials to pass away cheerfully a longer life than is allotted to mortals. I believe there are few heads capable of making Sir Isaac Newton's calculations, but the result of them is not difficult to be understood by a moderate capacity. Do not fear this should make her affect the character of Lady ——, or Lady ——, or Mrs. ——; those women are ridiculous, not because they have learning, but because they have it not. One thinks herself a complete historian, after reading Echard's *Roman History*; another a profound philosopher having got by heart some of Pope's *unintelligible* essays; and a third an able divine, on the strength of Whitefield's sermons; thus you hear them screaming politics and controversy.

It is a saying of Thucydides, that ignorance is bold, and knowledge reserved. Indeed, it is impossible to be far advanced in it without being more humbled by a conviction of human ignorance than elated by learning. At the same time I recommend books, I neither exclude work nor drawing. I think it is as scandalous for a woman not to know how to use a needle, as for a man not to know how to use a sword. I was once extremely fond of my pencil, and it was a great mortification to me when my father turned off my master, having made a considerable progress for the short time I learned. My over-eagerness in the pursuit of it had brought a weakness in my eyes, that made it necessary to leave off; and all the advantage I got was the improvement of my hand. I see by hers that practice will make her a ready writer: she may attain it by serving you for a secretary, when your health or affairs make it troublesome to you to write yourself; and custom will make it an agreeable amusement to her. She cannot have too many for that station of life which will probably be her fate. The ultimate end of your education was to make you a good wife—and I have the comfort to hear that you are one; hers ought to be to make her happy in a virgin state. I will not say it is happier, but it is undoubtedly safer, than any marriage. In a lottery, where there is—at the lowest computation—ten thousand blanks to a prize, it is the most prudent choice not to venture. I have always been so thoroughly persuaded of this truth, that, notwithstanding the flattering views I had for you —as I never intended you a sacrifice to my vanity—I thought I owed you the justice to lay before you all the hazards attending matrimony: you may recollect I did so in the strongest manner. Perhaps you may have more success in the instructing your daughter; she has so much company at home, she will not need seeking it abroad, and will more readily take the notions you think fit to give her. As you were alone in my family, it would have been thought a great cruelty to suffer you no companions of your own age, especially having so many near relations, and I do not wonder their opinions influenced yours. I was not sorry to see you not determined on a single life, knowing it

was not your father's intention; and contented myself with endeavouring to make your home so easy, that you might not be in haste to leave it.

I am afraid you will think this a very long insignificant letter. I
hope the kindness of the design will excuse it, being willing to give
you every proof in my power that I am your most affectionate mother.

PHILIP DORMER STANHOPE, 4TH EARL OF CHESTER-
FIELD (1694–1773)

*Here is one of the famous letters to his illegitimate son, giving instruc-
tion in manners and morals and the method of "uniting wickedness and the
graces." Chesterfield was the mirror of politeness of his times; Johnson
acutely stigmatized his letters as inculcating "the manners of a dancing
master and the morals of a whore."*

TO HIS SON

LONDON, MARCH 6, 1747

DEAR BOY, Whatever you do, will always affect me, very sensibly, one
way or another; and I am now most agreeably affected by two letters,
which I have lately seen from Lausanne, upon your subject; the one was
from Madame St. Germain, the other from Monsieur Pampigny: they
both give so good an account of you, that I thought myself obliged, in
justice both to them and to you, to let you know it. Those who deserve
a good character ought to have the satisfaction of knowing that they have
it, both as a reward and as an encouragement. They write, that you are
not only *décrotté*, but tolerably well bred: and that the English crust of
awkward bashfulness, shyness, and roughness, (of which, by the bye, you
had your share) is pretty well rubbed off. I am most heartily glad of it;
for, as I have often told you, those lesser talents, of an engaging, insinuat-
ing manner, an easy good-breeding, a genteel behaviour and address, are
of infinitely more advantage, than they are generally thought to be,
especially here in England. Virtue and learning, like gold, have their
intrinsic value; but if they are not polished, they certainly lose a great
deal of their lustre: and even polished brass will pass upon more people
than rough gold. What a number of sins does the cheerful, easy good-
breeding of the French frequently cover? Many of them want common
sense, many more common learning; but, in general, they make up so
much, by their manner, for those defects, that frequently they pass
undiscovered. I have often said, and do think, that a Frenchman, who,
with a fund of virtue, learning, and good sense, has the manners and
good-breeding of his country, is the perfection of human nature. This

294

erfection you may, if you please, and I hope you will, arrive at.   You now what virtue is: you may have it if you will; it is in every man's ower; and miserable is the man who has it not.   Good sense, God has iven you.   Learning, you already possess enough of, to have, in a reason-ble time, all that a man need have.   With this, you are thrown out early nto the world, where it will be your own fault if you do not acquire all the ther accomplishments necessary to complete and adorn your character. ou will do well to make your compliments to Madame St. Germain and Monsieur Pampigny; and tell them, how sensible you are of their artiality to you, in the advantageous testimonies which, you are in-ormed, they have given of you here.

Adieu!   Continue to deserve such testimonies; and then you will not nly deserve, but enjoy, my truest affection.

WILLIAM CLARKE (1696–1771)

*There is something very refreshing about this early description of
Brighton beach. Clarke was a Sussex parson and an antiquarian of
some repute. His principal work was in coins and the antiquities of
Chichester, but it is evident from this letter that he viewed mankind with
a friendly and tolerant eye; and found as much to amuse him in his con
temporaries as in the antiquities of Romans and Saxons.*

JULY 22, 1736

WE are now sunning ourselves upon the beach at Brighthelmston, and
observing what a tempting figure this island must have made formerly in
the eyes of those gentlemen who were pleased to civilize and subdue us
The place is really pleasant; I have seen nothing in its way that outdoes
it: such a tract of sea, such regions of corn, and such an extent of fine
carpet, that gives your eye the command of it all. But then the mischief
is, that we have little conversation besides the *clamor nauticus*, which is
here a sort of treble to the plashing of the waves against the cliffs. My
morning business is, bathing in the sea, and then buying fish; the evening
is, riding out for air, viewing the remains of old Saxon camps, and count
ing the ships in the road—and the boats that are trawling. Sometimes
we give the imagination leave to expatiate a little—fancy that you are
coming down, and that we intend next week to dine one day at Dieppe
in Normandy; the price is already fixed, and the wine and lodging there
tolerably good. But, though we build these castles in the air, I assure you
we live here almost underground. I fancy the architects here usually
take the altitude of the inhabitants, and lose not an inch between the
head and the ceiling, and then dropping a step or two below the surface
the second story is finished—something under 12 feet. I suppose this
was a necessary precaution against storms, that a man should not be
blown out of his bed into New England, Barbary, or God knows where
But, as the lodgings are low, they are cheap: we have two parlours, two
bedchambers, pantry, &c. for 5s. per week; and if you really will come
down, you need not fear a bed of proper dimensions. And then the

oast is safe, the cannons all covered with rust and grass, the ships moored
—no enemy apprehended. Come and see,

"*Nec tela timeres
Gallica, nec Pictum tremeres, nec littore toto
Prospiceres dubiis venturum Saxona ventis.*"

My wife does not forget her good wishes and compliments upon this
occasion. How would you surprise all your friends in Fleet Street, to tell
them that you were just come from France, with a vivacity that everybody would believe to be just imported from thence!

Later.

We are now about taking our leave of that very variable element the
sea. After it had smiled upon us for a month, it is at present so black and
angry, that there is no seeing or approaching it. It is all either fog or
foam; and I truly pity everybody who cannot fly from it. We had this
morning some hopes of entertaining your Society with our discoveries
upon the beach. The sea had thrown up a piece of an old coin, grown
green with salt water: but, instead of an Otho's head, it proved only a
fragment of Charles I. Pray let me know which way your researches
run at present in that Society. We have here a very curious old font,
covered over with hieroglyphics, representing the two Sacraments, which
rise in very bold but bad relievos on each side of it.

FRANCIS DUFF *(fl.* 1738)

Francis Duff was a medical student and one of the thirty-six childre
of Patrick Duff of Craigston, Aberdeenshire. By this letter, written i
an elder brother, he appears to have been in the service of the Africa
Company.

TO PATRICK DUFF

WILLIAMS' FORT, WHYDAH, AFRIC
NOV. 14, 1738

SIR, Having this opportunity of returning you my most hearty thanks fo
the innumerable favours I have already received from you when I an
very sensible it was out of my power of repaying, I beg leave to offe
myself a Petitioner to you for this last favour which I hope you'll be s
good as grant, my unforeseen necessities obliging me to it, but be assure
that the former with this shall be faithfully remitted to Georg
Auchterlony merchant of London in six months time.

My delay betwixt Cape Coast and Whydah being so very long force
me to trouble you in this manner. A gentleman named Crabb and I i
our passage from Cape Coast to Whydah in a thirteen hand canoe wer
taken by three large canoes belonging to Champo off Quytal the 7th c
August, who stripped us of all our necessaries and detained us prisone;
for ten weeks three days. Champo being then defeated by the king c
Dahome, the Dahomes released us and carried us to their King wh
behaved in a very civil manner to us and sent us to Whydah. My nc
having so much as a shirt, stocking or shoe on my arrival at Whydah c
any necessary whatsomever, but two cloths the King of Dahome give u
to hide our nakedness forced me to draw upon you for sixty one pounc
fifteen shillings payable in three weeks after sight. The King c
Dahome promised to pay us for all our things we lost in two month
which amounts to two hundred and forty six pounds sterling which I d
assure you shall be remitted to George Auchterlony for the repaying c
you. I hope my necessities will make you take compassion upon m
and not allow my note of hand to lay unpaid. In compliance with thi
you will for ever infinitely oblige me. He to whom the note of han

becomes due, being an Englishman and knowing Geo. Auchterlony, makes me give the order upon him to whom I hope you'l be so good as order to pay.

My being very much indisposed after my long journey so far by land hinders me from writing my uncle and the rest of my relations, knowing you'll be so good as write them. How soon I am indifferently well I shall write you more fully. I now beg leave to offer my most dutiful respects to you, your lady and Lady Braco and all the rest of my relations. Wishing sincerely this may find them all in good health is the earnest desire of, Sir, your most obedient and most humble servant,

FRANCIS DUFF

WILLIAM WARBURTON (1698–1779)

One of Warburton's greatest friends and neighbours was William Stukeley, to whom the following letter is written. Warburton was, at the time, rector of Brant Broughton near Newark. Throughout a life of stormy controversy he was famous for giving hard hits to his opponents, and in the whole of English letters there are few writers of greater vigour.

TO THE REV. DR. STUKELEY

NEWARK, JAN. 19, 1736/7

DEAREST DOCTOR, I received the pleasure of yours of the 12th instant, with the entertaining poem on that encourager of the Orthodox Muse, *Tobacco*; to whose smoke neither the fire nor the water of Parnassus can stand in competition. There is a strength of reasoning, and flight of fancy, in your verses, that are not often to be met in poets by profession. The first manifests itself in the poem to Dr. Taylor, and the latter in this to me.

That which you tell me was Mr. Gale's advice to Professor Blackwell, was extremely prudent and friendly. But, I protest that, neither in his "Life of Homer," nor in the fine letter he did me the honour to write to me, can I find anything that looks at all like a disbelief of our Holy Religion. On the contrary, I am well persuaded, he is much a friend to it. He will shortly publish a "Life of Horace."

Dr. Taylor is as much yours as a man not his own can be. He is desperately in love with Miss S.; and though I do not find the old folks on either side approve his passion, yet he seems to have at all and marry her. He was talking in this heroic strain to me the other day; when I told him all the encouragement he was to expect from his hardy achievement was the applause of an opera hero; that I would say, *Bravo! bravo!* and I was sure his wife would call out, *Encore!* In a word, that edifice of Moral Stoicism, which I have been long labouring to erect on his treacherous bottom, is, like a beautiful kind of frost-work, melted down at once before the *ignis fatuus* of a pair of black eyes; and nothing, even, of the foundation left but that very natural principle, held in common by the ancient and

300

modern masters of Wisdom, *that all the virtues lie in the middle.*   In vain I tell him of his doom; appetite is too warm for the *icy precepts of respect,* as Shakespeare calls them.   I have found what our friend Horace says to be true, *Naturam expellas FURCA, tamen usque recurret.*   In English, "You may strive what you will, to keep down Nature *with the fears of Conjugal Infidelity,* she will at length be uppermost."

You are never to expect a reasonable conduct in the Stamford Antiquary [Peck].   The stale dregs of Literature have long intoxicated our Reverend Brother, and given his Microcosm a wrong ply.   Nature, all-wise in her operations, formed him with the guts and brains of an Alderman; and, by the richness of the low lands, and the poverty of that sterile promontory his front, pointed out which was fit for culture.   But, perverse letters misled him, and gave him the wretched ambition of furnishing the garret of his skull, which Nature, according to all the good rules of housekeeping, had designed for a lumber-room, and which yet, with all the aid of proud Science, will be *but* a lumber-room, while the capacious saloon below was not furnished as the principal apartment deserved.

But he struggles to no purpose; Nature is not to be overcome.   He will still have this in common with that great type of Nature's unsophisticated offspring, *the woodcock,* to have his guts better than his brains. Nor need this ungracious bird be ashamed of giving the pre-eminence where it is due: for it is according to the pure simple workings of Nature, whose excellencies all of themselves tend downwards, to seek, as it were, a foundation and root of stability and duration; and it is only an artificial ferment that makes things fly off from their centre of gravity, and unnaturally, aspire upwards.   The truth of this we see in garden plants. It is the preposterous heat of hot-beds that forces the mushroom and the melon upwards; while the fragrant turnip, the mild potato, and the brisk-tasted radish, left to themselves to follow Nature, like the beau, the dunce, and the coxcomb, her locomotive vegetables, all take a downward course.   I never could enough admire the sagacity and good sense of our ancestors in the appellation they gave a fool, which was that of *a Natural*; intimating thereby that he was the genuine unsophisticated product of Nature, whose essence, or rather quintessence of humanity, lay in his guts.   Of such a one they used to say, *he has no guts in his brains:* not by way of opprobrium, but commendation; only intimating, that his bodily taste was better than his mental; or, that his brains had not the high attic relish of his guts.   On this account they would call an *unnatural* fellow *a man of no bowels.*   This was their sense of a *Natural;*

while in the *unnatural* man, or one sophisticated by false science, they thought *wit*, like a forced plant, was, with great pains and labour raised up into the airy unsubstantial region of the brain; which, not above once in an age, makes a Philosopher; while it is the daily destruction of Aldermen and Justices; who, to make up this *pitiful extract of Reason*, are worse used than the Duke of Newcastle's cook used his Westphalia hams and gammons.

Well was it observed by an ancient Sage, that it is to education men owe all the happiness and misery of life. And our Philosophy, as it is explained above, shows how this was brought about. My Lady's eldest hope is educated, or transplanted, in the nursery, where Nature, according to the true course of things, is drawn gently downwards, by buttered crusts and candles: while younger Master Jack is kept, or rather chained to the oar, in a class at Westminster; where an unmeaning blockhead, with a *fasces* of birch, strains all his nerves to force unwilling *wit* preposterously *upwards*, at the other end. But see the difference!—I was going on, but happy for you, my paper forbids me.—Thus stands the case with these two rebels of Nature, the Doctor and Antiquary. The one neglects the Muses after he has possessed and enjoyed them; the other pursues them with frigid impotency. Good mother Nature then should use them like two *prodigal* sons, as they are, and turn them out of *doors*, the one to his *husks*, and the other to his *harlots*.

I am, dear Sir, with my very humble service to good Mrs. Stukeley, your most affectionate friend and humble servant,

W. WARBURTON

TO THE SAME

JUNE 19, 1738

MY DEAR FRIEND, I beg your acceptance of the enclosed. Our friend the Doctor told me he had the pleasure of seeing you. He told me you rejected the lines he shewed you as impostures. I do not wonder at it. You know best whether the thing be possible. But the family is so far above all suspicion of fraud, or having any ends to serve by it, that nothing but an absolute impossibility could make me disbelieve it.

I hope you are easier in your domestics than you was; that you have got servants that are honest, careful, and with a few brains. I very much wish to see you, and hope you will do me that pleasure at Broughton some time next month. However, do me the favour to let me know, that I may be at home; for this summer time I have some short excursion or other that I am every post making, but none half so interesting to me as the seeing you.   I hope the young ones are all well, and that Miss Fanny is grown woman enough now to make your coffee; a happiness, some years ago, you used to flatter yourself with the hopes of living to see.

You see the burthen of my song is hope, hope, hope; and how much I am obliged to live upon it.   But, that this may never fool you or me too long, I will tell you a story.   Sir Francis Bacon was walking out one evening near the Thames, where he saw some fishermen ready to cast in their nets: he asked them what they would have for their draught; they said, ten shillings; he bade them five; so, not agreeing, the fishermen threw in upon their own fortune, and took nothing.   On this, Bacon, seeing them look very blank, asked them why they were such blockheads as not to take his money?   They answered, they had been toiling all day, and had taken nothing, and they were in *hopes* that their last cast would have made amends for all.   On which he told them, they were unlucky dogs; but that he would give them something to carry home with them; and it was this maxim, which they should be sure never to forget, *that hope is a good breakfast, but a very bad supper*.   So far my story.   But I do not know how it is; but I should make but a bad meal of it, either at breakfast or supper.   I should like it well enough for a kind of second course, as cheese to digest a good substantial dinner.   And so the happy use it, while the unhappy, like the poor, are forced to make an eternal meal upon it.

I am, dear friend, yours most affectionately,

W. WARBURTON

JUNIUS (1769)

A mysterious series of letters, directed against the British ministry, Sir William Draper, and others, appeared in the "Public Advertiser" between 1768 and 1772. The authorship was the subject of ten thousand inquiries, it puzzled the wits and sages of London, and to this day has never been satisfactorily ascribed. In all probability Sir Philip Francis was Junius, but pace *Samuel Parr (see page 456), nobody really knows.*

TO THE KING

SIR, When the complaints of a brave and powerful people are observed to increase in proportion to the wrongs they have suffered; when, instead of sinking into submission, they are roused to resistance, the time will soon arrive at which every inferior consideration must yield to the security of the sovereign, and to the general safety of the state. There is a moment of difficulty and danger, at which flattery and falsehood can no longer deceive, and simplicity itself can no longer be misled. Let us suppose it arrived. Let us suppose a gracious, well-intentioned prince made sensible at last of the great duty he owes to his people, and of his own disgraceful situation; that he looks round him for assistance, and asks for no advice but how to gratify the wishes and secure the happiness of his subjects. In these circumstances, it may be matter of curious speculation to consider, if an honest man were permitted to approach a king, in what terms he would address himself to his sovereign. Let it be imagined, no matter how improbable, that the first prejudice against his character is removed; that the ceremonious difficulties of an audience are surmounted; that he feels himself animated by the purest and most honourable affection to his king and country; and that the great person whom he addresses has spirit enough to bid him speak freely, and understanding enough to listen to him with attention. Unacquainted with the vain impertinence of forms, he would deliver his sentiments with dignity and firmness, but not without respect:

Sir—It is the misfortune of your life, and originally the cause of every reproach and distress which has attended your government, that you should never have been acquainted with the language of truth till you

304

heard it in the complaints of your people. It is not, however, too late to correct the error of your education. We are still inclined to make an indulgent allowance for the pernicious lessons you received in your youth, and to form the most sanguine hopes from the natural benevolence of your disposition. We are far from thinking you capable of a direct deliberate purpose to invade those original rights of your subjects on which all their civil and political liberties depend. Had it been possible for us to entertain a suspicion so dishonourable to your character, we should long since have adopted a style of remonstrance very distant from the humility of complaint. The doctrine inculcated by our laws, "that a king can do no wrong," is admitted without reluctance. We separate the amiable good-natured prince from the folly and treachery of his servants, and the private virtues of the man from the vices of his government. Were it not for this just distinction, I know not whether your majesty's condition, or that of the English nation, would deserve most to be lamented. I would prepare your mind for a favourable reception of truth, by removing every painful offensive idea of personal reproach. Your subjects, sir, wish for nothing but that, as *they* are reasonable and affectionate enough to separate your person from your government, so *you*, in your turn, would distinguish between the conduct which becomes the permanent dignity of a king, and that which serves only to promote the temporary interest and miserable ambition of a minister.

You ascended the throne with a declared—and, I doubt not, a sincere —resolution of giving universal satisfaction to your subjects. You found them pleased with the novelty of a young prince, whose countenance promised even more than his words, and loyal to you not only from principle but passion. It was not a cold profession of allegiance to the first magistrate, but a partial, animated attachment to a favourite prince, the native of their country. They did not wait to examine your conduct, nor to be determined by experience, but gave you a generous credit for the future blessings of your reign, and paid you in advance the dearest tribute of their affections. Such, sir, was once the disposition of a people who now surround your throne with reproaches and complaints. Do justice to yourself. Banish from your mind those unworthy opinions with which some interested persons have laboured to possess you. Distrust the men who tell you that the English are naturally light and inconstant; that they complain without a cause. Withdraw your confidence equally from all parties; from ministers, favourites, and relations; and let there be one moment in your life in which you have consulted your own understanding.

When you affectedly renounced the name of Englishman, believe me, sir, you were persuaded to pay a very ill-judged compliment to one part of your subjects at the expense of another. While the natives of Scotland are not in actual rebellion, they are undoubtedly entitled to protection; nor do I mean to condemn the policy of giving some encouragement to the novelty of their affection for the house of Hanover. I am ready to hope for everything from their new-born zeal, and from the future steadiness of their allegiance. But hitherto they have no claim to your favour. To honour them with a determined predilection and confidence, in exclusion of your English subjects—who placed your family, and, in spite of treachery and rebellion, have supported it, upon the throne—is a mistake too gross for even the unsuspecting generosity of youth. In this error we see a capital violation of the most obvious rules of policy and prudence. We trace it, however, to an original bias in your education, and are ready to allow for your inexperience.

To the same early influence we attribute it that you have descended to take a share, not only in the narrow views and interests of particular persons, but in the fatal malignity of their passions. At your accession to the throne the whole system of government was altered; not from wisdom or deliberation, but because it had been adopted by your predecessor. A little personal motive of pique and resentment was sufficient to remove the ablest servants of the crown; but it is not in this country, sir, that such men can be dishonoured by the frowns of a king. They were dismissed, but could not be disgraced.

Without entering into a minuter discussion of the merits of the peace, we may observe, in the imprudent hurry with which the first overtures from France were accepted, in the conduct of the negotiation, and terms of the treaty, the strongest marks of that precipitate spirit of concession with which a certain part of your subjects have been at all times ready to purchase a peace with the natural enemies of this country. On your part we are satisfied that everything was honourable and sincere; and if England was sold to France, we doubt not that your majesty was equally betrayed. The conditions of the peace were matter of grief and surprise to your subjects, but not the immediate cause of their present discontent.

Hitherto, sir, you had been sacrificed to the prejudices and passions of others. With what firmness will you bear the mention of your own?

A man not very honourably distinguished in the world commences a formal attack upon your favourite; considering nothing but how he might best expose his person and principles to detestation, and the national character of his countrymen to contempt. The natives of that country, sir, are as much distinguished by a peculiar character, as by your majesty's favour. Like another chosen people, they have been conducted into the land of plenty, where they find themselves effectually marked and divided from mankind. There is hardly a period at which the most irregular character may not be redeemed; the mistakes of one sex find a retreat in patriotism; those of the other in devotion. Mr. Wilkes brought with him into politics the same liberal sentiments by which his private conduct had been directed; and seemed to think, that as there are few excesses in which an English gentleman may not be permitted to indulge, the same latitude was allowed him in the choice of his political principles, and in the spirit of maintaining them. I mean to state, not entirely to defend, his conduct. In the earnestness of his zeal, he suffered some unwarrantable insinuations to escape him. He said more than moderate men would justify, but not enough to entitle him to the honour of your majesty's personal resentment. The rays of royal indignation, collected upon him, served only to illumine, and could not consume. Animated by the favour of the people on one side, and heated by persecution on the other, his views and sentiments changed with his situation. Hardly serious at first, he is now an enthusiast. The coldest bodies warm with opposition; the hardest sparkle in collision. There is a holy mistaken zeal in politics as well as religion. By persuading others, we convince ourselves; the passions are engaged, and create a maternal affection in the mind, which forces us to love the cause for which we suffer. Is this a contention worthy of a king? Are you not sensible how much the meanness of the cause gives an air of ridicule to the serious difficulties into which you have been betrayed? The destruction of one man has been now for many years the sole object of your government; and if there can be anything still more disgraceful, we have seen for such an object the utmost influence of the executive power, and every ministerial artifice, exerted without success. Nor can you ever succeed, unless he should be imprudent enough to forfeit the protection of those laws to which you owe your crown; or unless your ministers should persuade you to make it a question of force alone, and try the whole strength of government in opposition to the people. The lessons he has received from experience will probably guard him from such excess of folly; and in your majesty's virtues we find an unquestionable assurance that no illegal violence will be attempted.

Far from suspecting you of so horrible a design, we would attribute the continued violation of the laws, and even this last enormous attack upon the vital principles of the constitution, to an ill-advised unworthy

personal resentment.   From one false step you have been betrayed into
another; and as the cause was unworthy of you, your ministers were
determined that the prudence of the execution should correspond with the
wisdom and dignity of the design.   They have reduced you to the necessity of choosing out of a variety of difficulties; to a situation so unhappy,
that you can neither do wrong without ruin, nor right without affliction.
These worthy servants have undoubtedly given you many singular proofs
of their abilities.   Not contented with making Mr. Wilkes a man of
importance, they have judiciously transferred the question from the rights
and interests of one man, to the most important rights and interests of the
people; and forced your subjects from wishing well to the cause of an
individual, to unite with him in their own.   Let them proceed as they
have begun, and your majesty need not doubt that the catastrophe will do
no dishonour to the conduct of the piece.

The circumstances to which you are reduced will not admit of a compromise with the English nation.   Undecisive qualifying measures will
disgrace your government still more than open violence; and without
satisfying the people, will excite their contempt.   They have too much
understanding and spirit to accept of an indirect satisfaction for a direct
injury.   Nothing less than a repeal as formal as the resolution [1] itself, can
heal the wound which has been given to the constitution; nor will anything less be accepted.   I can readily believe that there is an influence
sufficient to recall that pernicious vote.   The House of Commons undoubtedly consider their duty to the crown as paramount to all other
obligations.   To *us* they are indebted for only an accidental existence,
and have justly transferred their gratitude from their parents to their
benefactors; from those who gave them birth to the minister from whose
benevolence they derive the comforts and pleasures of their political life;
who has taken the tenderest care of their infancy, and relieves their necessities without offending their delicacy.   But if it were possible for their
integrity to be degraded to a condition so vile and abject, that, compared
with it, the present estimation they stand in is a state of honour and
respect, consider, sir, in what manner you will afterwards proceed.   Can
you conceive that the people of this country will long submit to be
governed by so flexible a House of Commons?   It is not in the nature of
human society that any form of government in such circumstances can
long be preserved.   In ours, the general contempt of the people is as fatal
as their detestation.   Such, I am persuaded, would be the necessary

[1] Of the House of Commons, on the subject of the election of John Wilkes to
Parliament and the refusal of the House to acknowledge his election.

effect of any base concession made by the present House of Commons; and, as a qualifying measure would not be accepted, it remains for you to decide whether you will, at any hazard, support a set of men who have reduced you to this unhappy dilemma, or whether you will gratify the united wishes of the whole people of England by dissolving the parliament.

Taking it for granted, as I do very sincerely, that you have personally no design against the constitution, nor any view inconsistent with the good of your subjects, I think you cannot hesitate long upon the choice which it equally concerns your interest and your honour to adopt.   On one side, you hazard the affections of all your English subjects; you relinquish every hope of repose to yourself, and you endanger the establishment of your family for ever.   All this you venture for no object whatever, or for such an object as it would be an affront to you to name. Men of sense will examine your conduct with suspicion; while those who are incapable of comprehending to what degree they are injured, afflict you with clamours equally insolent and unmeaning.   Supposing it possible that no fatal struggle should ensue, you determine at once to be unhappy, without the hope of a compensation either from interest or ambition.   If an English king be hated or despised, he must be unhappy; and this, perhaps, is the only political truth which he ought to be convinced of without experiment.   But if the English people should no longer confine their resentment to a submissive representation of their wrongs; if, following the glorious example of their ancestors, they should no longer appeal to the creature of the constitution, but to that high Being who gave them the rights of humanity, whose gifts it were sacrilege to surrender, let me ask you, sir, upon what part of your subjects would you rely for assistance?

The people of Ireland have been uniformly plundered and oppressed. In return, they give you every day fresh marks of their resentment. They despise the miserable governor you have sent them, because he is the creature of Lord Bute; nor is it from any natural confusion in their ideas that they are so ready to confound the original of a king with the disgraceful representation of him.

The distance of the colonies would make it impossible for them to take an active concern in your affairs, even if they were as well affected to your government as they once pretended to be to your person.   They were ready enough to distinguish between you and your ministers. They complained of an act of the legislature, but traced the origin of it no higher than to the servants of the crown; they pleased themselves with the hope that their sovereign, if not favourable to their cause, at least was impartial. The decisive personal part you took against them has effectually banished that first distinction from their minds. They consider you as united with your servants against America; and know how to distinguish the sovereign and a venal parliament on one side, from the real sentiments of the English people on the other. Looking forward to independence, they might possibly receive you for their king; but if ever you retire to America, be assured they will give you such a covenant to digest as the presbytery of Scotland would have been ashamed to offer to Charles II. They left their native land in search of freedom, and found it in a desert. Divided as they are into a thousand forms of polity and religion, there is one point in which they all agree; they equally detest the pageantry of a king, and the supercilious hypocrisy of a bishop.

It is not, then, from the alienated affections of Ireland or America that you can reasonably look for assistance: still less from the people of England, who are actually contending for their rights, and in this great question are parties against you. You are not, however, destitute of every appearance of support; you have all the Jacobites, nonjurors, Roman Catholics, and Tories of this country; and all Scotland, without exemption. Considering from what family you are descended, the choice of your friends has been singularly directed; and truly, sir, if you had not lost the Whig interest of England, I should admire your dexterity in turning the hearts of your enemies. Is it possible for you to place any confidence in men who, before they are faithful to you, must renounce every opinion, and betray every principle, both in church and state, which they inherit from their ancestors, and are confirmed in by their education; whose numbers are so inconsiderable, that they have long since been obliged to give up the principles and language which distinguish them as a party, and to fight under the banners of their enemies? Their zeal begins with hypocrisy, and must conclude in treachery. At first, they deceive; at last, they betray.

As to the Scotch, I must suppose your heart and understanding so biased from your earliest infancy in their favour, that nothing less than your own misfortunes can undeceive you. You will not accept of the uniform experience of your ancestors; and when once a man is determined to believe, the very absurdity of the doctrine confirms him in his faith. A bigoted understanding can draw a proof of attachment to the house of Hanover from a notorious zeal for the house of Stuart; and find an earnest of future loyalty in former rebellions. Appearances are, however, in their favour; so strongly indeed, that one would think they had forgotten that you are their lawful king, and had mistaken you for a pretender to the crown. Let it be admitted, then, that the Scotch are as sincere in their present professions, as if you were in reality not an Englishman, but a Briton of the north; you would not be the first prince of their native country against whom they have rebelled, nor the first whom they have basely betrayed. Have you forgotten, sir, or has your favourite concealed from you, that part of our history when the unhappy Charles (and he, too, had private virtues) fled from the open avowed indignation of his English subjects, and surrendered himself at discretion to the good faith of his own countrymen? Without looking for support in their affections as subjects, he applied only to their honour as gentlemen for protection. They received him, as they would your majesty, with bows, and smiles, and falsehood; and kept him till they had settled their bargain with the English parliament; then basely sold their native king to the vengeance of his enemies. This, sir, was not the act of a few traitors, but the deliberate treachery of a Scotch parliament, representing the nation. A wise prince might draw from it two lessons of equal utility to himself: on one side he might learn to dread the undisguised resentment of a generous people who dare openly assert their rights, and who in a just cause are ready to meet their sovereign in the field; on the other side, he would be taught to apprehend something far more formidable—a fawning treachery, against which no prudence can guard, no courage can defend. The insidious smile upon the cheek would warn him of the canker in the heart.

From the uses to which one part of the army has been too frequently applied, you have some reason to expect that there are no services they would refuse. Here, too, we trace the partiality of your understanding. You take the sense of the army from the conduct of the Guards, with the same justice with which you collect the sense of the people from the representations of the ministry. Your marching regiments, sir, will not make the Guards their example either as soldiers or subjects. They feel and resent, as they ought to do, that invariable undistinguishing favour with which the Guards are treated; while those gallant troops, by whom every hazardous, every laborious service is performed, are left to perish in garrisons abroad, or pine in quarters at home, neglected and forgotten. If they had no sense of the great original duty they owe their country, their resentment would operate like patriotism, and leave your cause to be defended by those on whom you have lavished the rewards and honours of their profession. The prætorian bands, enervated and debauched as they were, had still strength enough to awe the Roman populace; but when the distant legions took the alarm, they marched to Rome and gave away the empire.

On this side, then, whichever way you turn your eyes, you see nothing but perplexity and distress. You may determine to support the very ministry who have reduced your affairs to this deplorable situation; you may shelter yourself under the forms of a parliament, and set your people at defiance; but be assured, sir, that such a resolution would be as imprudent as it would be odious. If it did not immediately shake your establishment, it would rob you of your peace of mind for ever.

On the other, how different is the prospect! how easy, how safe and honourable is the path before you! The English nation declare they are grossly injured by their representatives, and solicit your majesty to exert your lawful prerogative, and give them an opportunity of recalling a trust which they find has been scandalously abused. You are not to be told that the power of the House of Commons is not original; but delegated to them for the welfare of the people, from whom they received it. A question of right arises between the constituent and the representative body. By what authority shall it be decided? Will your majesty interfere in a question in which you have properly no immediate concern? It would be a step equally odious and unnecessary. Shall the Lords be called upon to determine the rights and privileges of the Commons? They cannot do it without a flagrant breach of the constitution. Or will you refer it to the judges? They have often told your ancestors that the law of parliament is above them. What party, then, remains, but to leave it to the people to determine for themselves? They alone are injured; and since there is no superior power to which the cause can be referred, they alone ought to determine.

I do not mean to perplex you with a tedious argument upon a subject already so discussed, that inspiration could hardly throw a new light upon it. There are, however, two points of view in which it particularly imports your majesty to consider the late proceedings of the House of Commons. By depriving a subject of his birthright, they have attributed to their own vote an authority equal to an act of the whole legislature; and though, perhaps, not with the same motives, have strictly followed the example of the Long Parliament, which first declared the regal office useless, and soon after, with as little ceremony, dissolved the House of Lords. The same pretended power which robs an English subject of his birthright, may rob an English king of his crown. In another view, the resolution of the House of Commons, apparently not so dangerous to your majesty, is till more alarming to your people. Not contented with divesting one man of his right, they have arbitrarily conveyed that right to another. They have set aside a return as illegal, without daring to censure those officers who were particularly apprised of Mr. Wilkes's incapacity—not only by the declaration of the house, but expressly by the writ directed to them—and who nevertheless returned him as duly elected. They have rejected the majority of votes, the only criterion by which our laws judge of the sense of the people; they have transferred the right of election from the collective to the representative body; and by these acts, taken separately or together, they have essentially altered the original constitution of the House of Commons. Versed as your majesty undoubtedly is in the English history, it cannot easily escape you how much it is your interest, as well as your duty, to prevent one of the three estates from encroaching upon the province of the other two, or assuming the authority of them all. When once they have departed from the great constitutional line by which all their proceedings should be directed, who will answer for their future moderation? or what assurance will they give you, that when they have trampled upon their equals, they will submit to a superior? Your majesty may learn hereafter how nearly the slave and the tyrant are allied.

Some of your council, more candid than the rest, admit the abandoned profligacy of the present House of Commons, but oppose their dissolution upon an opinion (I confess not very unwarrantable) that their successors would be equally at the disposal of the treasury. I cannot persuade myself that the nation will have profited so little by experience. But if that opinion were well founded, you might then gratify our wishes at an easy rate, and appease the present clamour against your government, without offering any material injury to the favourite cause of corruption.

You have still an honourable part to act. The affections of your subjects may still be recovered. But before you subdue their hearts, you must gain a noble victory over your own. Discard those little personal resentments which have too long directed your public conduct. Pardon this man [1] the remainder of his punishment; and if resentment still prevails, make it—what it should have been long since—an act not of mercy, but of contempt. He will soon fall back into his natural station—a silent senator, and hardly supporting the weekly eloquence of a newspaper. The gentle breath of peace would leave him on the surface,

---

[1] Mr. Wilkes, who was then under confinement in the King's Bench, on a sentence of a fine of a thousand pounds, and twenty-two months' imprisonment (from the 18th of June 1768), for the publication of the *North Briton* No. 45, and the *Essay on Woman*.

neglected and unremoved; it is only the tempest that lifts him from his place.

Without consulting your minister, call together your whole council. Let it appear to the public that you can determine and act for yourself. Come forward to your people; lay aside the wretched formalities of a king, and speak to your subjects with the spirit of a man, and in the language of a gentleman. Tell them you have been fatally deceived: the acknowledgment will be no disgrace, but rather an honour, to your understanding. Tell them you are determined to remove every cause of complaint against your government; that you will give your confidence to no man that does not possess the confidence of your subjects; and leave it to themselves to determine, by their conduct at a future election, whether or not it be in reality the general sense of the nation, that their rights have been arbitrarily invaded by the present House of Commons, and the constitution betrayed. They will then do justice to their representatives and to themselves.

These sentiments, sir, and the style they are conveyed in, may be offensive, perhaps, because they are new to you. Accustomed to the language of courtiers, you measure their affections by the vehemence of their expressions: and when they only praise you indirectly, you admire their sincerity. But this is not a time to trifle with your fortune. They deceive you, sir, who tell you that you have many friends whose affections are founded upon a principle of personal attachment. The first foundation of friendship is not the power of conferring benefits, but the equality with which they are received, and may be returned. The fortune which made you a king, forbade you to have a friend; it is a law of nature, which cannot be violated with impunity. The mistaken prince who looks for friendship will find a favourite, and in that favourite the ruin of his affairs.

The people of England are loyal to the house of Hanover, not from a vain preference of one family to another, but from a conviction that the establishment of that family was necessary to the support of their civil and religious liberties. This, sir, is a principle of allegiance equally solid and rational; fit for Englishmen to adopt, and well worthy of your majesty's encouragement. We cannot long be deluded by nominal distinctions. The name of Stuart of itself is only contemptible: armed with the sovereign authority, their principles are formidable. The prince who imitates their conduct should be warned by their example; and while he plumes himself upon the security of his title to the crown, should remember that as it was acquired by one revolution, it may be lost by another.

FRAMINGHAM WILLIS (fl. 1767)

The writer of this letter was an undergraduate at Caius College,
Cambridge. He was the son of Thomas Willis of Brancaster, Norfolk,
a well-to-do squire who sent his son to college and afterwards put him to
the Law. The letter was addressed to Thomas Kerrich, University
Librarian, and a man of much artistic knowledge and skill. It gives an
excellent sketch of an undergraduate's life in the mid-eighteenth century.

TO THOMAS KERRICH

CAIUS COLLEGE, JULY 18TH, 1767

DEAR SIR, Your last letter, bearing date the 3rd of June, I did not
receive till the 13th of this month. Sure Cooper's people must have been
strangely negligent in not putting it into the post office according to your
direction. Your questions are so very numerous that I am afraid I shall
not be able to answer them all in this epistle, for want of room: but to
begin with the first. I must take the liberty to say, that you asking me
what purpose my residence here during the vacation will answer, is
absurd enough. Pray what end do you think your residence here in
term-time will answer? You will tell me that you come with a design
to study. I stay here for just the same reason, and by the bye, I think
this time the most convenient for application. For though I like books
indifferently, yet I love to enjoy my friends, which it is most convenient
to do in term time, and there is an inconvenience you will be subject to at
your first outset, which you ought to guard against; that is the interruption of loungers. There are but few people of this stamp in the university now; they are all gone down into the country, and none are left
behind but those that are studiously inclined. Therefore, this is an evil
I am free from; and indeed I got a room up two pairs of stairs in order the
more to have it in my power to dip (?) the *non domi* upon them. They
are a set of people whom I much dislike; for they relish no scheme of
diversion that you can propose to them, but take a pleasure in ruining two
hours in a morning, by idle chit-chat, which may be applied to good
advantage. You desire to know the manner I spend my time in College;
but before I do this, I must tell you that you will be here your own master,
and may do just what you please (so it be nothing wicked) without control.

As I can do anything I please, at this time especially, I spend a part of my time in a manner very different from what the rest of my acquaintance here do, in a manner which perhaps you will call whimsical. I generally rise at five, and then read for an hour; at six I take a pretty long walk, but so as to be back to chapel at seven. After chapel is done, three times a week I go to the cold bath, and after that I come home to breakfast, which I take care to have over before nine. Then I sit down to read for three hours and a half, and at half-an hour after twelve my hairdresser comes to me, and I begin to dress for commons. You will be obliged to comply with the custom of putting on a clean shirt every day and of having your hair dressed. After commons, if ever, 'tis allowable to lounge away an hour at a friend's room and drink a glass of wine, but this is what I seldom do. At five I sometimes go to a coffee-house, where you meet with all the new pamphlets, magazines, newspapers, &c., and drink a dish of tea, coffee, or chocolate. At six I return to chapel, and after that I take a walk on the walks if it be fine weather, if not, in some college cloisters. At eight, your bed-maker comes to ask what you please to have for supper, and gives you a bill of fare, which they call here a size bill. They have always very good things, but they are exorbitantly dear, as you may guess by 3*d.* for a common tart. Persuade your father to let you have a good allowance; if you keep whole terms, an hundred pounds a year will not be·sufficient. You will be glad to hear that the custom of drinking is entirely exploded in polite company; but I would advise you never to seem afraid of drinking, for the bucks here will imagine by that, that they can make you drunk very easily; and to make a freshman drunk is excellent fun to them. Your Tutor or your Master will probably ask you to sup with them; if they do not I shall be glad to see you with me the night of your admission and then you will be in no danger to be led into any excess. Does not your father come up with you?

An old acquaintance ought not to be dropped abruptly; always be civil and complaisant to him, but never go to his room to sup or engage in any scheme with him. He is very expensive I am told, and the character that he bears in the University is that of a d—d polite fellow, one who is a blood in all respects, but that he cannot afford to spend so much money.

Make yourself master of all common arithmetic and decimal fractions, &c. There are many (other) questions to be answered but I must defer (them) till another opportunity.

I am, Dear Sir,

Your most assured friend and obedient servant,

FRAM. WILLIS

MARY DELANY (1700–88)

Mrs. Delany was one of the Bluestockings. A very close friend of the Royal Family, George III gave her a house in Windsor and a pension of £300 a year which enabled her to entertain her friends and a select circle of wits and lively souls, who fled to her house, very often, to escape the dullness of the staid Court.

TO MISS DEWES

1770

THE embroidery of the nankeen, etc., must be with the same knitting-thread as you knot with, cotton-thread is not strong enough to bear the working. I enclose you what I did it with, and generally worked it double; but you must judge by the effect when you try it.

Your brothers will miss Mr. G., I fear. I own I wished to have known how he would receive them, though upon the whole, perhaps, it is better as it is, and I believe they won't be sorry, but I hope they will meet with another friend (Mr. Port), and if they do that they will make my particular compliments.

Last Monday, I told you in my last, we were to dine at Lady Primrose's, and to perform the long-intended visit at Beaumont Lodge. Were at her ladyship's great gate at one o'clock, but no ladyship was there, but gone to Lady Frances Elliot's! In order to console ourselves for the disappointment we travelled on to Cooper's Hill, where the Duchess of Portland never had been, and when we came to the point from whence the prospect was to be seen, her Grace got out of the chaise and mounted a bank with as much alacrity as if she had been in pursuit of a plant or a butterfly; and after all, though the prospect is fine and extensive, its greatest beauties may be seen with less trouble—the Castle of Windsor and the Thames. We arrived at Lady Primrose's at half an hour after two, found her but indifferent, always glad to see her friends, and sorry you were not at the party. We were treated with a triumvirate of old maids—Mrs. Primrose and the two Mrs. Needhams. Returned by nine. A charming day; read Sir John Denham's poem on Cooper's Hill; admired some part and criticised others. Tuesday, a Bulstrode day. Wednesday, our engagement with the Garricks took place, and there my amiable niece was zealously wished for, and she would have been much pleased and entertained.   Mr. Garrick did the honours of his house very respectfully, and though in high spirits seemed sensible of the honour done them.   Nobody else there but Lady Weymouth and Mr. Bateman. As to Mrs. Garrick, the more one sees her the better one must like her; she seems never to depart from a perfect propriety of behaviour accompanied with good sense and gentleness of manners, and I cannot help looking on her as a wonderful creature, considering all circumstances relating to her.   The house is singular (which you know I like), and seems to owe its prettiness and elegance to her good taste; but I saw it so short a time, and only passed once through the rooms, that I can't well describe it, but on the whole it has the air of belonging to a genius.   We had an excellent dinner nicely served, and when over went directly into the garden—a piece of irregular ground sloping down to the Thames, very well laid out, and planted for shade and shelter; and an opening to the river which appears beautiful from that spot, and from Shakespeare's Temple at the end of the improvement, where we drank tea and coffee, and where there is a very fine statue of Shakespeare in white marble, and a great chair with a large carved frame, that was Shakespeare's own chair, made for him on some particular occasion, with a medallion of him fixed in the back.   Many were the relics we saw of the favourite poet. There was not a moment I did not wish for you, knowing how much you would have been entertained.   At six o'clock Lady Weymouth's fine group of children walked into the garden, which added to the agreeableness of the scene, and Mr. Garrick made himself as suitable a companion to the children as to the rest of the company, to their great delight.   We got home very well a little before ten.

Thursday, Friday, Saturday, *virtu* went on as usual.   Mr. Lightfoot here, and whilst the Duchess and he pursued their philosophical tracks I followed my own business.   All the difficult part of the cave is finished, and now there can, I think, no blunder be made in our absence, though my friend Davis is as liable to such a misfortune as any man alive!   The Duchess has engaged Mr. Lightfoot to come this evening to read prayers, etc., as Mr. Jones is obliged to go into Wales for a fortnight; he stays here to-morrow to settle some botanical affairs, and I shall have his company, and set him down on Tuesday in my way to town.

I must add I have had a letter from Mr. G, rather kind.   Mr. Cannon has been with him, and the deeds signed, so he has got rid of me! He is gone to Tunbridge, and says he was glad to hear by Mr. C that I looked so well, and that all were well.

Many thanks for your letter, which welcomed me on my arrival home.

I enclose you a yellow carnation, which is new to me, it grew at Bulstrode.   I hope the Duchess of Portland got yesterday as far as Salisbury; she was to stay a day there with the Dean.

Your box will be with you, I hope, by next Saturday.   I have sent Lady F. B's muslin, that you might deliver it yourself to Lady Cowper.

I have written this post to our Ravaud, to let her know our Duchess will spend a day with her on her return from Cornwall.   I believe Mrs. Mead's recipe for a cold a good one, if it does not clog the stomach.

PHILIP DODDRIDGE (1702–51)

Doddridge was a dissenting minister, pastor of various Independent congregations and tutor in a seminary for the education of dissenting ministers, at Northampton. To-day he is best known as the writer of some of our most popular hymns. This letter to one who had challenged his religious convictions is an able piece of advocacy.

TO THE REV. MR. BOURNE

NOVEMBER, 1742

HAD the letter which I received from you so many months ago been merely an address of common friendship, I hope no hurry of business would have led me to delay so long the answer which civility and gratitude would in that case have required; or had it been to request any service in my power to you, sir, or to any of your family or friends, I would not willingly have neglected it so many days or hours: but when it contained nothing material, except an unkind insinuation, that you esteemed me a dishonest man, who, out of a design to please a party, had written what he did not believe, or, as you thought fit to express yourself, had "trimmed it a little with the gospel of Christ," I thought all that was necessary, after having fully satisfied my own conscience on that head, which, I bless God, I very easily did, was to forgive and pray for the mistaken brother who had done me the injury, and to endeavour to forget it, by turning my thoughts to some more pleasant, important, and useful subject. I imagined, sir, that for me to give you an assurance under my hand that I meant honestly, would signify very little, whether you did or did not already believe it; and as I had little particular to say on the doctrines to which you referred, I thought it would be of little use to send you a bare confession of my faith, and quite burdensome to enter into a long detail and examination of arguments which have on one side and the other been so often discussed, and of which the world has of late years been so thoroughly satiated.

On this account, sir, I threw aside the beginning of a long letter, which I had prepared in answer to yours, and with it your letter itself:

320

and I believe I may safely say, several weeks and months have passed in which I have not once recollected anything relating to this affair. But I have since been certainly informed that you, interpreting my silence as an acknowledgment of the justice of your charge, have sent copies of your letter to several of your friends, who have been industrious to propagate them far and near! This is a fact which, had it not been exceedingly well attested, I should not have believed; but as I find it too evident to be questioned, you must excuse me, sir, if I take the liberty to expostulate with you upon it, which, in present circumstances, I apprehend to be not only justice to myself, but, on the whole, kindness and respect for you.

Though it was unkind readily to entertain the suspicions you express, I do not so much complain of your acquainting me with them; but on what imaginable humane or Christian principle could you communicate such a letter, and grant copies of it? With what purpose could it be done, but with a design of aspersing my character? and to what purpose could you desire my character to be reproached? Are you sure, sir, that I am not intending the honour of God and the good of souls, by my various labours of one kind and another—so sure of it, that you will venture to maintain at the bar of Christ, before the throne of God, that I was a person whom it was your duty to endeavour to discredit? for, considering me as a Christian, a minister, and a tutor, it could not be merely an indifferent action; nay, considering me as a man, if it was not a duty, it was a crime!

I will do you the justice, sir, to suppose you have really an ill opinion of me, and believe I mean otherwise than I write; but let me ask, what reason have you for that opinion? Is it because you cannot think me a downright fool, and conclude that every one who is not, must be of your opinion, and is a knave if he does not declare that he is so? or is it from anything particular which you apprehend you know of my sentiments contrary to what my writings declare? He that searches my heart, is witness that what I wrote on the very passage you except against, I wrote as what appeared to me most agreeable to truth, and most subservient to the purposes of His glory and the edification of my readers; and I see no reason to alter it in a second edition, if I should reprint my Exposition, though I had infinitely rather the book should perish than advance anything contrary to the tenor of the gospel, and subversive to the souls of men. I guard against apprehending Christ to be a mere creature, or another God, inferior to the Father, or co-ordinate with Him. And you will maintain that I believe Him to be so; from whence, sir, does your evidence of that arise? If from my writings, I apprehend it must be in consequence of some inference you draw from them, of laying any just foundation for which I am not at present aware; nor did I ever intend, I am sure, to say or intimate anything of the kind. If from report, I must caution you against rashly believing such reports. I have heard some stories of me, echoed back from your neighbourhood, which God knows to be as false as if I had been reported to have asserted the divine authority of the Alcoran! or to have written Hobbes's *Leviathan*; and I can account for them in no other way than by supposing, either that coming through several hands, every one mistook a little, or else that some people have such vivid dreams, that they cannot distinguish them from realities, and so report them as facts; though how to account for their propagating such reports so zealously, on any principles of Christianity or common humanity, especially considering how far I am from having offered them any personal injury, would amaze me, if I did not know how far *party* zeal debases the understandings of those who in other matters are wise and good. All I shall add with regard to such persons is, that I pray God this evil may not be laid to their charge.

I have seriously reflected with myself whence it should come that such suspicions should arise of my being in what is generally called the Arian scheme, and the chief causes I can discover are these two: my not seeing the arguments which some of my brethren have seen against it in some disputed texts, and my tenderness and regard to those who, I have reason to believe, do espouse it, and whom I dare not in conscience raise a popular cry against! Nor am I at all fond of urging the controversy, lest it should divide churches, and drive some who are wavering, as indeed I myself once was, to an extremity to which I should be sorry to see such worthy persons, as some of them are, reduced.

Permit me, sir, on so natural an occasion, to conclude with expressing the pleasure with which I have heard that you of late have turned your preaching from a controversial to a more practical and useful strain. I am persuaded, sir, it is a manner of using the great talents which God has given you, which will turn to the most valuable account with respect to yourself and your flock; and if you would please to add another labour of love, by endeavouring to convince some who may be more open to the conviction from you than from others, that Christian candour does not consist in judging the hearts of their brethren, or virulently declaring against their supposed bigotry, it would be a very important charity to them, and a favour to, reverend and dear sir, your very affectionate brother and humble servant,

P. Doddridge

P.S.—I heartily pray that God may confirm your health, and direct and prosper all your labours, for the honour of his name and the Gospel of his Son.

The multiplicity of my business has obliged me to write this with so many interruptions, that I hope you will excuse the inaccuracies it may contain. My meaning I am sure is good, and, I hope, intelligible; and I am heartily willing that, with what measure I mete, it may be measured to me again.

BENJAMIN STILLINGFLEET (1702–71)

Stillingfleet was a Norfolk naturalist and general dilettante, and carried on a long correspondence with Windham, who was his neighbour in the country and lived near him in town. This letter has been left in its original spelling as a curious example of how cultured men occasionally wrote so late as the mid-18th century.

TO WILLIAM WINDHAM

LONDON. DECEM^r ye 20, 1757

DEAR SIR, I am very much obliged to you for the very extraordinary case you were so kind as to communicate to me. I have shewn it to several people and amongst the rest physicians who seem to look on it as exceeding any thing of that kind they ever knew or heard of. The relation seems to be so particular that i cannot think of any thing further to be enquired into. All that is wanting is perhaps a more authentic attestation, which would certainly be judged necessary before it can be properly publish'd to the world. Dr Hill i remember calls Norwich the city of wonders, and some future wit will perhaps take occasion from this and Needham's case to give that denomination to the whole county. I rejoyce to find the spirit that reigns amongst you in relation to the Militia, tho' perhaps i ought to say in you, for i have heard of no body else who has taken the pains you have done, unless the great projector and promoter of the bill.[1] I am told you have publish'd upon the occasion and by the account i have had of it in a way perfectly well adapted to the purpose. Our people want to be made sensible of the blessings of this government not only on this but many other occasions, for tho' we have an infinite deal of corruption and selfish dirty conduct in many considerable people, yet still we enjoy many advantages which our neighbours want, and such as are very well worth preserving at any rate. The King of Prussia is growing into a prodigy. What a victory has he just gain'd! You have it

[1] Hon. George Townshend, afterwards first Marquess Townshend

under his own hand in his letter to the Queen.   Nothing is talk'd of but he and Mr Pit who made such a speech t'other day as rais'd a sort of Enthusiasm in every one.   Aldworth, whose connections you know, came so hot from the house, that he forgot all the indiscretions of it till the next day when he had leasure to reflect on the consequences. I was told that no business was done at the Exchange the day after ; they could talk of nothing but the speech.   It was universally extolled by men of all parties as the finest performance that ever was heard. The subject of great part was the want of spirit in our Generals and Admirals both on the coast of France and North America, from whence he took an opportunity of making econiums upon Clive and Pocock in the East Indies and made the finest contrast imaginable.   He called Clive "that heaven born general who from a clerk had done such things as equall'd any thing in Q. Curtius."

As to the odes [1] i think of them as you do.   Mere clinquant verbiage! without instruction or sentiment, or even ideas agreable, for they require as much thought to understand them as a mathematical problem.   The author can write for one and has done it but not in this gallimawfry stile.   I every day grow plainer and plainer in my tast.   There is enought in nature to furnish our description or senti- ment if men will look about them and watch either men or things with inquisitive eyes; but when people applaud such stuff, there will never be wanting writers to propagate this false tast.   But i expect this bold way of talking be confin'd to yourself, for of all things i should dislike to be used upon such an occasion.   I will always endeavour to keep clear of the genus *irritabile vatum*, who perhaps would think they might reasonably impute this opinion to envy; tho' were this the case i would certainly run down the Churchyard and the Prospect of Eaton as performances i should despair of coming up to were i to attempt it, but perhaps not these made flights, which some call Pindaric, as they do many bombast attempts in blank verse, Miltonic!

. . . I am rejoyc'd to find Marsham begins to think of Eaton for his son.   I did not choose to press the thing too much, for if any thing should happen, he would never bear to see me again.

I am sorry to hear of poor Mr Doughty's miserable condition.   I should not despair of a cure, from a remedy lately recommended to the world by one Mon^r Murelle physician to the King of Prussia.   He gives many cases of raving and melancholy madness cured by it.   'Tis

[1] Gray's "Odes," published in August, 1757 ("The Bard" and "The Progress of Poesy").

certainly worth trying, as a medicine very innocent and frequently given on other occasions. With my best respects to Mrs Windham, compliments to Sir W. Harbord and Lady, Tayleure and Jones when you see them, and love to all the young ones of your family i am

Dear Sir

Your most obliged and affectionate servant

Benj: Stillingfleet

JOHN WESLEY (1703–91)

Wesley was probably the busiest man in England. For years he travelled up and down the country on horseback, preached three or four times a day, wrote books, conducted meetings and organized his company of Methodists. At the same time he contrived to keep up an extensive correspondence and controlled his followers with vigour, though with a certain pleading patience, as can be seen from this letter, which was written when he was eighty-three.

(1786)

You know I love you. Ever since I knew you I have neglected no way of showing it that was in my power. And you know I esteem you for your zeal and activity, for your love of discipline, and for your gifts which God has given you; particularly quickness of apprehension and readiness of utterance; especially in prayer.

Therefore I am jealous over you, lest you should lose any of the things you have gained, and not receive a full reward. And the more so because I fear you are wanting in other respects. And who will venture to tell you so? You will scarce know how to bear it from me, unless you lift up your heart to God. If you do this, I may venture to tell you what I fear without any further preface. I fear you think of yourself more highly than you ought to think. Do not you think too highly of your understanding? Of your gifts, particularly in preaching? as if you were the very best preacher in the Connexion? Of your own importance? as if the work of God, here or there, depended wholly or mainly on you? And of your popularity? which I have found to my surprise far less, even in L—, than I expected.

May not this be much owing to the want of brotherly love? With what measure you mete men will measure to you again. I fear there is something unloving in your spirit; something not only of roughness but of harshness, yea, of sourness! Are you not also extremely open to prejudice, and not easy to be cured of it? so that whenever you are prejudiced you commence bitter, implacable, unmerciful? If so, that people are prejudiced against you is both the natural and judicial consequence.

I am afraid lest your want of love to your neighbours should spring from want of love to God; from want of thankfulness. I have sometimes heard you speak in a manner that made me tremble; indeed in terms that not only a weak Christian but even a serious Deist would scruple to use.

I fear you greatly want evenness of temper. Are you not generally too high or too low? Are not all your passions too lively, your anger in particular? Is it not too soon raised? And is it not too impetuous, causing you to be violent, boisterous, bearing down all before you?

Now lift up your heart to God, or you will be angry at me. But I must go a little farther. I fear you are greatly wanting in the government of your tongue. You are not exact in relating facts. I have observed it myself. You are apt to amplify; to enlarge a little beyond the truth. You cannot imagine, if others observe this, how it will affect your reputation.

But I fear you are more wanting in another respect: that you give a loose to your tongue when you are angry; that your language then is not only sharp, but coarse and ill-bred. If this be so, the people will not bear it. They will not take it either from you or me.

DAVID MALLET (c. 1705–65)

This Scotch poet made a name for himself in London by his plays and verses. He is best known to us perhaps as the friend and correspondent of Pope, to whom he wrote the following amusing letter. He was at this time tutor to a young gentleman named Knight.

TO ALEXANDER POPE

CHESTER, 2ND AUGUST (1734)

DEAR SIR, After a tedious ramble of six weeks through South and North Wales, I am just arrived at Chester; from whence I do myself the pleasure to send you some account of my troubles. I wish it may not prove altogether uninteresting to you, since it is to me a real refreshment to converse with you even at this distance.

I have seen Nature and human nature both in their undress, and, to say truth, the latter especially is infinitely the better for a little culture. If the golden age was stocked chiefly with such animals I heartily thank Heaven for having reserved me to these iron times.

The ordinary women in Wales are generally short and squat, ill-favoured, and nasty. Their headdress is a remnant of coarse blanket, and for their linen—they wear none, and they are all barefooted. But then they are wonderfully good-natured.

The parsons I have seen are beyond all description astonishing. One of them, who has a living of no less than £140 a year, having been asked by his patron, the day he was ordained priest, why we observe the 30th of January, answered seriously, on account of Our Blessed Lady's purification. Though the story is incredible, it is true. But then he kills more red game, and hollas louder to a pack of hounds than any other man in the country. A second, whose face no Dutch painter could deform by a caricature, had the impudence lately to attempt a rape on the body of his clerk; for what is as odd as the rest, the clerk of this parish is a woman. The squires are rather more admirable than they are in England, and distinguished by the same attributes—a gun on their shoulder, a leash of dogs at their heels, and three or four scoundrels for their bosom friends.

I saw nothing remarkable in South Wales except Tenby and Milford Haven. Tenby is a little seaport town, of a situation most delightfully romantic. It is built in form of a crescent on a very deep cleft, the sides of which towards the sea are all overgrown with ivy, as the bottom is washed by the tide. In the rock which runs out farthest into the sea are several natural arches of great height, and curiously adorned, with all the variety of fretwork and shells. Here, indeed, to atone for the rest of her countrywomen, I met with the greatest beauty I ever saw, and yet this plebeian angel, this goddess of low degree, was doing the humble office of a jack, or, in plain English, turning a spit. Milford Haven is certainly a very noble harbour, and several hundred ships of burden may ride safe at anchor in its numerous bays and windings.

In this country I became acquainted with Sir Arthur Owen, Knight and Baronet, who by his own authority, is Admiral of the Haven, and Viceroy of Pembrokeshire. He is for ever building and planting, and as he is his own gardener and architect, his performances are uncommon. Orielton, his manor house, is an enormous pile, built, I cannot say in a false taste, for there is no shadow of any taste at all. It has a very little porch, reaching one story high, and removed as far from the middle as possible, which is just such another beauty as the nose to a human face would be within half an inch of the left ear. The ceilings of his rooms are inverted keels of ships, painted black and brown. The fortress is defended by twenty pieces of cannon, which are fired on all rejoicing days; for the Knight is a passionate lover of the Court, and of a great noise. As he walked over his grounds, he ever and anon turned his head to survey it from several points of view, Heaven only can tell with what secret delight. You remember when Sancho was going to his government, how he would be looking back every moment to steal a glance at his beloved Dapple, when the grooms had made him so fine with ribbons and Brussels lace. The plantations are all detached without regularity or design. They consist of about two acres each, and are each of them strongly confined with stone walls. One part of his garden is wonderful. It is a grove of near an acre and a half; and here Sir Arthur desired me to mount my horse, as he did his, because, he said, it would take us a hour and a quarter to traverse it all: as, indeed, it did; for he rode two and thirty courses on it. You must know this grove is cut into thirty-two walks, to answer the number of points in the mariner's compass, with a tree in the centre, which he calls the needle. Each of these walks may be about six foot in length, and near two in latitude. Our horses and we threaded every one of these, and this, he told me, was boxing the compass.

This letter has already run into so great a length that I will say nothing of North Wales, but conclude at once with my best wishes for your health and happiness; and with assuring you that I am, in all places and on all occasions, dear sir, your most affectionate, humble servant.

RICHARD YATES (1706–96)

Yates and his wife were two of the favourite actors of the eighteenth century, he as a comedian and she in tragic roles. Mrs. Yates was, indeed, the leading tragic actress of her time: only when she was an old woman did her star wane and then it was before Sarah Siddons. The anger which inspired Yates to write the following letter was occasioned by a paragraph in a London newspaper.

TO THE PRINTER OF THE *PUBLIC ADVERTISER*

SATURDAY, 18TH OCTOBER, 1783

SIR, Though it is not my profession to write, but to retail the writings of others, yet I find the spirit move me to hazard some observations on a very good-humoured, sprightly, elegant paragraph in your paper of yesterday.

The facetious gentleman is pleased to say, that Yates and his wife have retired from the stage with £36,000 or £40,000, and that they are remarkable for their comely appearance, though one is, from theatrical dates, 70, the other above 60 years of age. 'Tis wonderful so wise a man should be mistaken, but the facts are,

They have not retired with £40,000.

They have not retired at all.

Theatrical dates do not prove them to be, the one 70, the other more than 60 years of age.

In respect to myself, that I am remarkable for my comely appearance; that I can (though not worth quite £40,000) eat my mutton without an engagement, and yet owe no man anything, are offences to which I am ready to plead guilty: if comeliness is a sin, heaven help me, I say! and as to owing no man anything, in these days when it is the genteelest thing in the world to pay no man any thing, I must e'en stand trial before a jury of honest tradesmen, who, I dare say, will acquit me, from the singularity of the case.

In respect to theatrical dates, I have, to be sure, told the chimes at midnight some five and thirty years ago, which, as I find myself just as healthy and alert as in those delightful days, I do not think at all disqualifies me from my general cast of characters, in which I have pleased as good judges as your correspondent; nor is it absolutely necessary that the Miser, Fondlewife, Gomez, Don Manuel, Sir Wilful Witwou'd, &c. should have the first down of a beard on their chins; but I will whisper something in the gentleman's ear, that whilst such writers as he are allowed to assassinate honest people in the dark, by abusive anonymous paragraphs, nobody that has mutton to eat will look out for theatrical engagements, but quietly let the stage fall into that happy state

> "When one Egyptian darkness covers all."

So much for myself; and now for Mrs. Yates.

That she is a pretty enough actress, as times go, and by no means uncomely, I willingly allow; but that she is more than 60, or will be these dozen years at least, may bear something of a doubt. As her first appearance was on Drury Lane stage, and in the full meridian of its glory, the date is easily ascertained; but to save the gentleman trouble, as he seems a bad calculator, I will inform him it was in Mr. Crisp's Virginia, in the year 1754, (29 years ago,) and that she was then as pretty a plump, rosy Hebe, as one shall see in a summer's day.

She had the honour (an honour never conferred on any other person) of being introduced, as a young beginner, by a prologue written and spoken by that great master, Mr. Garrick, in which the following lines are to the present purpose:

> If novelties can please, to-night we've two,—
> Tho' English both, yet spare 'em as they're new.—
> To one at least your usual favour show;
> A female asks it, can a man say no?
> Should you indulge our novice yet unseen,
> And crown her with your hands a tragic queen,
> Should you with smiles a confidence impart,
> To calm those fears which speak a feeling heart;
> Assist each struggle of ingenuous shame,
> Which curbs a genius in its road to fame;
> With one wish more her whole ambition ends—
> She hopes some merit to deserve such friends.

And now give me leave, sir, to tell your correspondent a story.— On the first coming to England of Signor Trebbi, a worthy gentleman, the editor of a newspaper, paid him a morning visit, and informed him he was a public writer, and had characters of all prices. "I understand you, Sir," said Trebbi, "and have heard of you: I have no guineas to throw away so ill; but I am a writer too; *et voila ma plume*!"—"This is my pen," showing him a good English oaken trowel. Signor Trebbi was so good as to leave me his pen, the only one I shall make use of against malevolence in future, where the writer does me the honour of making himself known to me.

I am, Sir,

Your most obedient humble servant,

RICHARD YATES

SAMUEL JOHNSON (1709–84)

The Doctor's letter to the Earl of Chesterfield is well known, yet it is such a remarkable document that the temptation to include it is irresistible. Chesterfield had talked so largely, had promised so much and had done nothing; how little did he think that the pock-marked literary drudge should have it in his power to pillory him for all time. And what a different aspect of the Great Cham of literature is shown in the other letters, to Mrs. Thrale and to Boswell! His letters, even at their lightest, show some of the Johnsonian stateliness, with his equally characteristic good sense and warm affection.

TO THE EARL OF CHESTERFIELD

FEBRUARY 7, 1755

MY LORD, I have been lately informed, by the proprietors of *The World*, that two papers, in which my Dictionary is recommended to the public, were written by your Lordship. To be so distinguished is an honour, which, being very little accustomed to favours from the great, I know not well how to receive, or in what terms to acknowledge.

When, upon some slight encouragement, I first visited your Lordship, I was overpowered, like the rest of mankind, by the enchantment of your address; and could not forbear to wish that I might boast myself *Le vainqueur du vainqueur de la terre*; that I might obtain that regard for which I saw the world contending; but I found my attendance so little encouraged, that neither pride nor modesty would suffer me to continue it. When I had once addressed your Lordship in public, I had exhausted all the art of pleasing which a retired and uncourtly scholar can possess. I had done all that I could; and no man is well pleased to have his all neglected, be it ever so little.

Seven years, my Lord, have now gone past, since I waited in your outward rooms, or was repulsed from your door; during which time I have been pushing on my work through difficulties, of which it is useless to complain, and have brought it, at last, to the verge of publication, without one act of assistance, one word of encouragement, or

335

one smile of favour. Such treatment I did not expect, for I never had a Patron before.

The shepherd in Virgil grew at last acquainted with Love, and found him a native of the rocks.

Is not a Patron, my Lord, one who looks with unconcern on a man struggling for life in the water, and, when he has reached ground, encumbers him with help? The notice which you have been pleased to take of my labours, had it been early, had been kind; but it has been delayed till I am indifferent, and cannot enjoy it; till I am solitary, and cannot impart it; till I am known and do not want it. I hope it is no very cynical asperity not to confess obligations where no benefit has been received, or to be unwilling that the Public should consider me as owing that to a Patron which Providence has enabled me to do for myself.

Having carried my work thus far with so little obligation to any favourer of learning, I shall not be disappointed though I should conclude it, if less be possible, with less; for I have been long wakened from that dream of hope, in which I once boasted with so much exultation, my Lord.

Your Lordship's most humble,
most obedient servant,
SAM: JOHNSON

TO MRS. THRALE

LICHFIELD, JULY 11TH, 1770

MADAM, Since my last letter nothing extraordinary has happened. Rheumatism, which has been very troublesome, is grown better. I have not yet seen Dr. Taylor, and July runs fast away. I shall not have much time for him if he delays much longer to come or send. Mr. Grene, the apothecary, has found a book which tells who paid levies in our parish, and how much they paid, above an hundred years ago. Do you not think we study this book hard? Nothing is like going to the bottom of things: many families that paid the parish rates are now extinct, like (race and Hercules. *Pulvis et umbra sumus.* What is nearest us touches us most.) passions rise higher at domestic than at imperial tragedies. I am not wholly unaffected by the revolutions of Sadler Street, nor can forbear to mourn a little when old names vanish away and new come into their place.

Do not imagine, Madam, that I wrote this letter for the sake of these philosophical meditations; for when I began it, I had neither

Mr. Grene nor his book in my thoughts, but was resolved to write and did not know what I had to send, but my respects to Mrs. Salusbury and Mr. Thrale, and Harry, and the Misses.

I am, dearest Madam, Yours etc.,
SAM: JOHNSON.

TO THE SAME

LICHFIELD, JULY 7 (?) 1771

DEAR MADAM, Once more I sit down to write, and hope you will once more be willing to read it.

Last Sunday an old acquaintance found me out, not, I think, a school-fellow, but one with whom I played perhaps before I went to school. I had not seen him for forty years, but was glad to find him alive. He has had, as he phrased it, *a matter of four wives*, for which neither you nor I like him much the better; but after all his marriages he is poor, and has now, at sixty-six, two very young children.

Such, Madam, are the strange things of which we that travel come to the knowledge. We see *mores hominum multorum*. You that waste your lives over a book at home, must take life upon trust.

I am, &c.
SAM: JOHNSON

TO THE SAME

LONDON, TUESDAY, JAN. 26, 1773

MADAM, The inequalities of human life have always employed the meditations of deep thinkers, and I cannot forbear to reflect on the difference between your condition and my own. You live upon mock turtle, and stewed rumps of beef; I dined yesterday upon crumpets. You sit with parish officers, caressing and caressed, the idol of the table, and the wonder of the day. I pine in the solitude of sickness, not bad enough to be pitied, and not well enough to be endured. You sleep away the night, and laugh or scold away the day. I cough and grumble, and grumble and cough. Last night was very tedious, and this day makes no promises of much ease. However I have this day put on my shoe, and hope that Gout is gone. I shall have only the cough to contend with, and I doubt whether I shall get rid of that without change of place. I caught cold in the coach as I went away, and am disordered by very little things. Is it accident or age?

I am, dearest Madam, &c.
SAM: JOHNSON

TO JAMES BOSWELL

MARCH 14, 1781

DEAR SIR, I hoped you had got rid of all this hypocrisy of misery. What have you to do with Liberty and Necessity? Or what more than to hold your tongue about it? Do not doubt but I shall be most heartily glad to see you here again, for I love every part about you but your affectation of distress.

I have at last finished my Lives, and have laid up for you a load of copy, all out of order, so that it will amuse you a long time to set it right. Come to me, my dear Bozzy, and let us be as happy as we can. We will go again to the Mitre, and talk old times over.

I am, dear Sir, yours affectionately,

SAM: JOHNSON

JOHN HOADLY (1711–76)

John was the youngest son of old Benjamin Hoadly, Bishop of Winchester. Like his father, he made a living in the Church and at his death was Master of St. Cross, Winchester. But Hoadly really found expression on the stage, and that he knew it well is shown in this letter to David Garrick.

TO MR. GARRICK

St. Marys, Jan. 14th, 1776

Dear David, I am told you are very soon to bring out Ben Jonson's "Silent Woman." There are a few things, I think, worth dropping upon paper concerning the play, which I submit to your consideration, if not too late. Do not slabber over the principal part, as has formerly been done. I hope Mr. King performs Old Morose. Though not the most brilliant, it requires, as your Kitely does, a judicious actor and a good speaker to support it, through so much *action* or rather *passion* i.e. suffering. I think, also, that the two knights are enough shamed before the ladies by the confession they make of having tasted the bride's favours. For that, and all other reasons in the world, I would by no means have Epicene acted by a woman. A young *smooth-face* certainly, if you have *one* in the company; the force is entirely lost by its being acted by a woman. *Sex* is so strong in everybody's mind, especially of your more vulgar hearers, that it is impossible to be separated.

To resume. *Truewit* is flat, by being overdone with plot and mechanical wit. I would cut out the whole almost of his exploits with the knights to prove them *cowards*, which the audience know before; and, as I said, they are exposed enough to their ladies, and the ladies to the world on their account, by their confession of the bride's favours. What will you do with the two Doctors of law, which is now obsolete; but they make such fun that I would let them stand, as well as Tom Otter's *bull, bear,* and *horse.* They are all good pictures of *the times.*

I have read the play lately, and with attention; and am astonished at the likeness to Congreve's writings, not only as to plot, but even the brilliancy of wit and conversation. The first act is as witty, as natural, nay, as *easy*, as any modern gentlemen upon the stage. The stiffness of Jonson so much complained of is almost entirely laid aside; and the introduction of the audience to the knowledge of his characters is admirable, and, what is more, natural. I am convinced Jonson was Congreve's great stagemaster, and not his own observations on nature. I see a great number of his *characters modernized* in Congreve. *Bobadil* is his Noll Bluff—Lady Haughty and her (Coterie) College is Lady *Wishfort* and her club) *Fast. Brisk* [in "Every Man out of his Humour"] is the original of his fops and wits, &c.

"Bon Ton," I find, I remember: I think it was acted by *children, and shocked* people to hear such sentiments out of the mouths of babes and sucklings.

Sir John Trotley's servant, Davy, is too like *Spy,* in "The Rival Candidates." The prologue is too good, and anticipates the piece, which Colman was always against, and so are most of yours. Another theatrical letter—and so I, or rather we, are your humble cum-dumble-dums.

J. HOADLY

CATHERINE CLIVE (1711–85)

Kitty Clive first came to the notice of London when Colley Cibber was managing Drury Lane. He started her in her career and for forty years and more she enjoyed the unfailing love of her audience, as a charming hoyden, a rattle, a madcap full of pranks. For twenty-three years she was a member of Garrick's company. This letter was written on his retirement from the theatre.

TO MR. GARRICK

TWICKENHAM, JAN. 23RD, 1776

DEAR SIR, Is it really true, that you have put an end to the glory of Drury Lane theatre? *If it is so,* let me congratulate my dear Mr. and Mrs. Garrick on their approaching happiness: *I know* what it will be; you cannot yet have an idea of it; *but* if you should still be so wicked not to be satisfied with that *unbounded,* uncommon degree of fame you have received as an actor, and which no other actor ever did receive —nor no other actor ever *can* receive;—I say, if you should still long to be dipping your fingers in their theatrical pudding (now without plums), you will be no Garrick for the Pivy [his nickname for her].

In the height of the public admiration for you, when you were never mentioned with any other appellation but the Garrick, the charming man, the fine fellow, the delightful creature, both by men and ladies; when they were admiring everything you did, and everything you scribbled,—at this very time, *I, the Pivy,* was a living witness that they did not know, nor could they be sensible, of half your perfections. I have seen you, with your magical hammer in your hand, *endeavouring* to beat your ideas into the heads of creatures who had none of their own—I have seen you, with lamb-like patience, endeavouring to make them comprehend you; and I have seen you, when that could not be done—I have seen your lamb turned into a lion. By this your great labour and pains the public was entertained; *they* thought they all acted very fine,—they did not see you pull the wires.

There are people *now* on the stage to whom you gave their consequence; they think themselves very great; now let them go on in

341

their new parts without your leading-strings, and they will soon convince the world what their genius is; I have always said this to everybody, even when your horses and mine were in their highest prancing. While I was under your control, I did not say half the fine things I thought of you, because it looked like flattery; and you know your Pivy was always proud; besides, I thought you did not like me then; but *now* I am sure you do, which makes me send you this letter.

What a strange jumble of people they have put in the papers as the purchasers of the patent! [of Drury Lane Theatre] I thought I should have died of laughing when I saw a man-midwife amongst them: I suppose they have taken him to prevent *miscarriages*! I have some opinion of Mr. Sheridan, as I hear everybody say he is very sensible; then he has a divine wife, and I loved his mother dearly. Pray give my love to my dear Mrs. Garrick; we all join in that. Your Jemmy is out of his wits with joy and grief; he rejoices at your escape, and cries from wanting to make his own to London; it is dreadful here, but I believe it is much worse there. Pray send me a line to let me know how you do, and how the world goes, for we are rather dull, though my neighbours do pick their way to come and see me. I have, since the snow, been once out in my carriage; did you not hear me scream?

Now let me say one word about my poor unfortunate friend Miss Pope: I know how much she disobliged you; and if I had been in your place, I believe I should have acted just as you did. But by this time I hope you have forgot your resentment, and will look upon her late behaviour as having been taken with a dreadful fit of vanity, which for that time took her senses from her, and having been tutored by an affected beast, who helped her to turn her head; but pray recollect her in the other light, a faithful creature to you, on whom you could always depend, certainly a good actress, amiable in her character, both in her being a very modest woman, and very good to her family; and, to my certain knowledge, has the greatest regard for you. Now, my dear Mr. Garrick, I hope it is not yet too late to reinstate her before you quit your affairs there; I beg it, I entreat it; I shall look upon it as the greatest favour you can confer on your

Ever obliged friend,

C. CLIVE

ALISON COCKBURN (1712–94)

This lady was famous in the Edinburgh of her day for her wit, but she is now best remembered as the author of "The Flowers of the Forest." She was the first to recognize the unusual qualities of young Walter Scott; what she thought of him is expressed in the second letter.

TO THE REV. ROBERT DOUGLAS

1788, 12 NOVEMBER

WHAT is become of you, Friend Douglas? It is just two months and four days since you wrote, and both Lady and I wrote to you after. We suspect our letters have miscarried. We are all anxious about our good King, and in expectation of a grand Comet. If it be commissioned to destroy this globe, no doubt we will be terrified; but when we reflect that we are promised a new Heaven and a new earth in which dwelleth righteousness, the change will be charming. Pray let us know how Mrs. Douglas is, and yourself, and all your concerns in which I wish you all good.

TO THE SAME

15 NOV. 1777

Saturday night 15 of the gloomy
month in which the people of England
Hang and drown themselves.

I RECEIVED your Sunday's oblation with pleasure. It is perhaps the best letter you ever wrote or will write in your life; and as I know you honest and sincere, I must really doubt your taste and judgment when you say it is cold and uninteresting! We cannot always be animated with passions: is not reason as good? And if we describe or paint portraits of manners and reason on them, is it not more useful and entertaining as Declamation? You really write *well*, Douglas. . . . I last night sup'd in Mr. Walter Scott's. He has the most extraordinary genius of a boy I ever saw. He was reading a poem to his mother when I went in. I made him read on. It was the descrip-

343

tion of a shipwreck. His passion rose with the storm: he lifted his eyes and hands. "There's the mast gone," says he, "crash it goes, they will all perish." After his agitation he turns to me, "That is too melancholy," says he, "I had better read you somewhat more amusing." I preferred a little chat, and asked his opinion of Milton and other books he was reading, which he gave me. Wonderful indeed. One of his observations was—how strange it was that Adam, just new come into the world, should know everything! "That must be poet's fancy," says he; but when he was told he was created perfect by God Himself, he instantly yielded. When he was taken to bed last night, he told his aunt he liked that lady. "What lady?" says she. "Why, Mrs. Cockburne, for I think she's a virtuoso like myself." "Dear Walter," says aunt, "what is a virtuoso?" "Don't ye know? Why, it's one who wishes and will know everything!" Now, sir, you will think this a very silly story. Pray, what age do you suppose this boy to be? Name it now, before I tell you. Why, 12 or 14?—no such thing. He is not quite six years old. He has a lame leg for which he was a year at Bath, and has acquired the perfect Eng: accent which he has lost since he came, and he reads like a Garrick. You will allow this an uncommon exotic? You will also allow this to be a pretty long letter. You owe it to laziness and to a certain tiredness that grows daily of that frivolous company that makes me yawn. I begin to like my own company best of any. I hope you will often through this winter be with Brother and Lady— I am sure they will be the better of your prayers and company.

Yours sincerely,

A. C.

I had a visit of Lord Advocate before he went to London.

The members are all summoned. I wonder if any news will come this night? Remember to put in all the S's and offs and ands I forget while I write. Remember I am old. I don't see well: read me fair. I must tell you of a wedding I have heard of—the Countess of Sutherland, 10 yrs old, to Mr. Weemy's son, 15. I leave you to make the remarks.

Have you read a history of—I forget his name—on the cause of the fall of the Roman Empire. By Gibbons, is the name. I wish you to read it and give me your sentiments of it.

No terrible news yet.

LAURENCE STERNE

LAURENCE STERNE (1713–68)

The lively author of "Tristram Shandy" kept up a long correspondence with many of his friends. These letters are delightful in their simplicity and all the pleasanter in that they shed a new light on the character of a rather over-witty parson that is usually associated with the name of Sterne.

TO LADY P——

MOUNT COFFEE HOUSE, TUESDAY, 3 O'CLOCK

THERE is a strange mechanical effect produced in writing a billet-doux within a stone-cast of the lady who engrosses the heart and soul of an inamorato—for this cause (but mostly because I am to dine in this neighbourhood) have I, Tristram Shandy, come forth from my lodgings to a coffee-house the nearest I could find to my dear Lady ——'s house, and have called for a sheet of gilt paper, to try the truth of this article of my creed—Now for it—

O, my dear lady, what a dish-clout of a soul hast thou made of me!—I think, by-the-bye, this is a little too familiar an introduction for so unfamiliar a situation as I stand in with you—where, Heaven knows, I am kept at a distance—and despair of getting one inch nearer you, with all the steps and windings I can think of to recommend myself to you.—Would not any man in his senses run diametrically from you—and as far as his legs would carry him, rather than thus carelessly, foolishly, and foolhardily expose himself afresh—and afresh, where his heart and his reason tells him he shall be sure to come off loser, if not totally undone?—Why would you tell me you would be glad to see me?—Does it give you pleasure to make me more unhappy —or does it add to your triumph that your eyes and lips have turned a man into a fool, whom the rest of the town is courting as a wit?— I am a fool—the weakest, the most ductile, the most tender fool that ever woman tried the weakness of—and the most unsettled in my purposes and resolutions of recovering my right mind.—It is but an hour ago that I kneeled down and swore I never would come near you— and, after saying my Lord's Prayer for the sake of the close, *of not being led into temptation*—out I sallied like any Christian hero, ready

to take the field against the world, the flesh, and the devil; not doubting but I should finally trample them all down under my feet—and
now I am got so near you—within this vile stone's cast of your house
—I feel myself drawn into a vortex, that has turned my brain upside
downwards, and though I had purchased a box-ticket to carry me to
Miss ——'s benefit, yet I know very well, that was a single line
directed to me to let me know Lady —— would be alone at seven,
and suffer me to spend the evening with her, she would infallibly see
every thing verified I have told her.—I dine at Mr. C——r's, in
Wigmore Street, in this neighbourhood, where I shall stay till seven,
in hopes you purpose to put me to this proof. If I hear nothing by
that time, I shall conclude you are better disposed of—and shall take
a sorry hack, and sorrily jog on to the play—Curse on the world. I
know nothing but sorrow—except this one thing, that I love you
(perhaps foolishly, but) most sincerely,

L. STERNE

TO MR. W.

COXWOULD, MAY 23, 1765

AT this moment I am sitting in my summer-house with my head and
heart full, not of my Uncle Toby's amours with the Widow Wadman,
but my Sermons—and your letter has drawn me out of a pensive mood
—the spirit of it *pleaseth me*, but, in this solitude, what can I tell or
write to you but about myself? I am glad that you are in love, 'twill
cure you at least of the spleen, which has a bad effect both on man
and woman—I myself must ever have some Dulcinea in my head, it
harmonizes the soul—and in those cases I first endeavour to make the
lady believe so, rather I begin first to make myself believe that I am
in love, but I carry on my affairs quite in the French way, sentiment-
ally—"*l'amour*," (say they) "*n'est rien sans sentiment*." Now notwithstanding they make such a pother about the *word*, they have no precise
idea annexed to it—And so much for that same subject called love.
I must tell you how I have just treated a French gentleman of fortune
in France, who took a liking to my daughter. Without any ceremony
(having got my direction from my wife's banker) he wrote me word
that he was in love with my daughter, and desired to know what *fortune* I would give her at present, and how much at my *death*—by the
bye, I think there was very little *sentiment* on *his side*. My answer
was, "Sir, I shall give her ten thousand pounds on the day of marriage
—my calculation is as follows—she is not eighteen, you are sixty-two

—there goes five thousand pounds,—then, sir, you at least think her not ugly—she has many accomplishments, speaks Italian, French, plays upon the guitar, and as I fear you play upon no instrument whatever, I think you will be happy to take her at my terms, for here finishes the account of the ten thousand pounds." I do not suppose but he will take this as I mean, that is, a flat refusal. I have had a parsonage-house burnt down by the carelessness of my curate's wife? as soon as I can I must rebuild it, I trow, but I lack the means at present—yet I am never happier than when I have not a shilling in my pocket— for when I have I can never call it my own. Adieu, my dear friend, may you enjoy better health than me, though not better spirits, for that is impossible. Yours sincerely,

                                                              L. STERNE

My compliments to the Colonel.

TO MR. FOLEY, AT PARIS

                                        TOULOUSE, AUGUST 14, 1762

MY DEAR FOLEY, After many turnings (*alias* digressions) to say nothing of downright overthrows, stops, and delays, we have arrived in three weeks at Toulouse, and are now settled in our house, with servants, &c., about us, and look as composed as if we had been here seven years. —In our journey we suffered so much from the heats, it gives me pain to remember it—I never saw a cloud from Paris to Nismes half as broad as a twenty-four sols piece.—Good God! we were toasted, roasted, grill'd, stew'd, and carbonaded on one side or other all the way—and being all done enough (*assez cuits*) in the day, we were eat up at night by bugs, and other unswept-out vermin, the legal inhabitants (if length of possession gives right) of every inn we lay at.—Can you conceive a worse accident than that in such a journey, in the hottest day and hour of it, four miles from either tree or shrub which could cast a shade of the size of one of Eve's fig-leaves—that we should break a hind wheel into ten thousand pieces, and be obliged, in consequence, to sit five hours on a gravelly road, without one drop of water, or possibility of getting any?—To mend the matter, my two postillions were two dough-hearted fools, and fell a-crying—Nothing was to be done! By heaven, quoth I, pulling off my coat and waistcoat, some-thing shall be done, for I'll thrash you both within an inch of your lives—and then make you take each of you a horse, and ride like two devils to the next post for a cart to carry my baggage, and a wheel to carry ourselves.—Our luggage weighed ten quintals—'twas the fair of Beaucaire—all the world was going or returning—we were asked by every soul who passed by us, if we were going to the fair of Beaucaire?— No wonder, quoth I, we have goods enough! *vous avez raison, mes amis.*

Well! here we are, after all, my dear friend, and most deliciously placed at the extremity of the town, in an excellent house, well furnished, and elegant beyond anything I look'd for.—'Tis built in the form of a hotel, with a pretty court towards the town—and behind, the best garden in Toulouse, laid out in serpentine walks, and so large that the company in our quarter usually come to walk there in the evenings, for which they have my consent—"the more the merrier."—The house consists of a good *salle à manger* above stairs, joining to the very great *salle à compagnie* as large as the Baron d'Holbach's; three handsome bed-chambers with dressing-rooms to them—below stairs two very good rooms for myself, one to study in, the other to see company.—I have, moreover, cellars round the court, and all other offices.—Of the same landlord I have bargained to have the use of a country-house which he has two miles out of town, so that myself and all my family have nothing more to do than to take our hats and remove from the one to the other.—My landlord is, moreover, to keep the gardens in order— and what do you think I am to pay for all this? neither more or less than thirty pounds a year—all things are cheap in proportion—so we shall live for very little.—I dined yesterday with Mr. H.; he is most pleasantly situated, and they are all well.—As for the books you have received for D——, the bookseller was a fool not to send the bill along with them—I will write to him about it.—I wish you were with me for two months; it would cure you of all evils ghostly and bodily— but this like many other wishes both for you and myself, must have its completion elsewhere.—Adieu, my kind friend, and believe that I love you as much from inclination as reason, for I am most truly yours,

L. STERNE

My wife and girl join in compliments to you—My best respects to my worthy Baron and d'Holbach all that society—Remember me to my friend Mr. Panchaud.

TO THE SAME

MONTPELLIER, JAN. 5, 1764

MY DEAR FRIEND, You see I cannot pass over the fifth of the month without thinking of you, and writing to you. The last is a periodical

habit—the first is from my heart, and I do it oftener than I remember
—however, from both motives together, I maintain I have a right to
the pleasure of a single line—be it only to tell me how your watch
goes—You know how much happier it would make me to know that
all things belonging to you went on well. You are going to have
them all to yourself (I hear), and that Mr. S—— is true to his first
intention of leaving business. I hope this will enable you to accomplish yours in a shorter time, that you may get to your long-wished-for
retreat of tranquillity and silence. When you have got to your fireside, and into your arm-chair (and, by the bye, have another to spare
for a friend), and are so much a sovereign as to sit in your furred cap,
if you like it, though I should not (for a man's ideas are at least the
cleaner for being dressed decently), why then it will be a miracle if I
do not glide in like a ghost upon you, and in a very unghost-like fashion
help you off with a bottle of your best wine.

    January 15.—It does not happen every day that a letter begun in
the most perfect health should be concluded in the greatest weakness.
I wish the vulgar high and low do not say it was a judgment upon me,
for taking all this liberty with *ghosts*.—Be it as it may—I took a ride
when the first part of this was wrote, towards Perenas—and returned
home in a shivering fit, though I ought to have been in a fever, for I
had tired my beast; and he was as immovable as Don Quixote's wooden
horse, and my arm was half dislocated in whipping him.—This, quoth
I, is inhuman.—No, says a peasant on foot behind me, I'll drive him
home,—so he laid on his posteriors, but 'twas needless—as his face
was turned towards Montpellier, he began to trot. But to return:
this fever has confined me ten days in my bed—I have suffered in this
scuffle with death terribly—but, unless the spirit of prophecy deceive
me—I shall not die, but live—in the mean time, dear F., let us live
as merrily, but *as innocently*, as we can. It has ever been as good, if
not better than a bishopric to me, and *I desire no other*. Adieu, my dear
friend, and believe me, yours,

                                                       L. S.

    Please to give the inclosed to Mr. T——, and tell him I thank
him cordially from my heart for his great *good-will*.

TO MRS. JAMES
                                                    TUESDAY

YOUR poor friend is scarce able to write—he has been at death's door
this week with a pleurisy—I was bled three times on Thursday, and

blistered on Friday—The physician says I am better—God knows, for I feel myself sadly wrong, and shall, if I recover, be a long while of gaining strength.   Before I have gone through half this letter, I must stop to rest my weak hand above a dozen times.   Mr. James was so good to call upon me yesterday.   I felt emotions not to be described at the sight of him, and he overjoyed me by talking a great deal of you. Do, dear Mrs. James, entreat him to come to-morrow or next day, for perhaps I have not many days or hours to live—I want to ask a favour of him, if I find myself worse—that I shall beg of you, if in this wrestling I come off conqueror—my spirits are fled—'tis a bad omen —do not weep, my dear lady—your tears are too precious to shed for me—bottle them up, and may the cork never be drawn.   Dearest, kindest, gentlest, and best of women! may health, peace, and happiness prove your handmaids!   If I die, cherish the remembrance of me, and forget the follies which you so often condemn'd—which my heart, not my head, betrayed me into.   Should my child, my Lydia, want a mother, may I hope you will (if she is left parentless) take her to your bosom;—You are the only woman on earth I can depend upon for such a benevolent action.   I wrote to her a fortnight ago, and told her what I trust she will find in you.——Mr. James will be a father to her—he will protect her from every insult, for he wears a sword which he has served his country with, and which he would know how to draw out of the scabbard in defence of innocence.   Commend me to him—as I now commend you to that Being who takes under His care the good and kind part of the world.   Adieu—All grateful thanks to you and Mr. James.   Your poor affectionate friend,

L. STERNE

TO MISS STERNE

COXWOULD, AUG. 24, 1767

I AM truly surprised, my dear Lydia, that my last letter has not reached thy mother and thyself—It looks most unkind on my part, after your having wrote me word of your mother's intention of coming to England, that she has not received my letter to welcome you both—and though in that I said I wished you would defer your journey till March, for before that time I should have published my sentimental work, and should be in town to receive you—yet I will show you more real politeness than any you have met with in France, as mine will come warm from the heart.—I am sorry you are not here at the races, but *les fêtes champêtres* of the Marquis de Sade have made you amends.—I know

B—— very well, and he is what in France would be called admirable
—that would be but so-so here—You are right—he studies nature more
than any, or rather most, of the French comedians. If the Empress
of Russia pays him and his wife a pension of twenty thousand livres
a year, I think he is very well off.—The folly of staying till after twelve
for supper—that you two excommunicated beings might have meat!—
"his conscience would not let it be served before." Surely the Marquis
thought you both, being English, could not be satisfied without it. I
would have given, not my gown and cassock (for I have but one), but
my topaz ring, to have seen the *petits maîtres et maîtresses* go to mass,
after having spent the night in dancing.—As to my pleasures, they are
few in compass. My poor cat sits purring beside me—your lively
French dog shall have his place on the other side of my fire—but if
he is as devilish as when I last saw him, I must tutor him, for I will
not have my cat abused—in short, I will have nothing devilish about
me—a combustion will spoil a sentimental thought.

Another thing I must desire—do not be alarmed—'tis to throw
all your rouge pots into the Sorgue before you set out—I will have
no rouge put on in England—and do not bewail them as —— did
her silver seringue or glister equipage, which she lost in a certain river
—but take a wise resolution of doing without rouge. I have been
three days ago bad again—with a spitting of blood—and that unfeeling
brute —— came and drew my curtains, and with voice like a trumpet, halloo'd in my ear— Z—ds, what a fine kettle of fish have you
brought yourself to, Mr. S——! In a faint voice I bade him leave
me, for comfort sure was never administered in so rough a manner—
Tell your mother, I hope she will purchase what either of you may
want at Paris—'tis an occasion not to be lost—so write to me from
Paris, that I may come and meet you in my post-chaise with my long-
tailed horses—and the moment you have both put your feet in it, call
it hereafter yours.—Adieu, dear Lydia—believe me what I ever shall
be, your affectionate father,

L. STERNE

I think I shall not write to Avignon any more, but you will find
one for you at Paris—once more adieu.

TO DODSLEY, THE BOOKSELLER

SIR, What you wrote to me in June last, in answer to my demand of
£50 for the "Life and Opinions of Tristram Shandy"—"that it was

too much to risk on a single volume, which, if it happened not to sell, would be hard upon your brother"—I think a most reasonable objection in him, against giving me the price I thought my work deserved. You need not be told by me how much authors are inclined to overrate their own productions: for my own part, I hope I am an exception; for, if I could find out, by any arcanum, the precise value of mine, I declare Mr. Dodsley should have it 20 per cent. below its value. I propose, therefore, to print a lean edition, in two small volumes, of the size of "Rasselas," and on the same paper and type, at my own expense, merely to feel the pulse of the world, and that I may know what price to set on the remaining volume, from the reception of these. If my book sells, and has the run our critics expect, I propose to free myself of all future troubles of the kind, and bargain with you, if possible, for the rest as they come out, which will be every six months. If my book fails of success, the loss falls where it ought to do. The same motives which inclined me first to offer you this trifle, incline me to give you the whole profits of the sale (except what Mr. Kirksman sells here, which will be a great many), and to have them sold only at your shop, upon the usual terms in these cases. The book shall be printed here, and the impression sent up to you; for, as I live at York, and shall correct every proof myself, it shall go perfect into the world, and be printed in so creditable a way, as to paper, type, &c., as to do no dishonour to you, who, I know, never choose to print a book meanly. Will you patronize my book upon these terms, and be as kind a friend to it as if you had bought the copyright? Be so good as to favour me with a line by the return; and believe me, Sir,

Your obliged and most

humble servant,
LAUR. STERNE

P.S. All locality is taken out of the book; the satire general; notes are added where wanted; and the whole made more saleable: about a hundred and fifty pages added; and to conclude, a strong interest formed and forming on its behalf, which, I hope, will soon take off the few I shall print in this *coup d'essai*.

EDWARD WORTLEY MONTAGU (1713–76)

*Montagu was the son of Lady Mary, who had taken him with
her to the East, and he has the distinction of being the first native of
the United Kingdom ever to be inoculated for small-pox. He was a
wild youth, constantly running away from home, and his parents even
thought him deranged. He wandered about the Continent and eventually got into trouble in Paris, as the following letter reveals.*

ABRAHAM PAYBA, a Jew, under the name of James Roberts, in his
complaint, dated the 25th of October 1751, gives an account of his
leaving England with Miss Rose, intending to make the tour both of
France and Italy, being provided with bills for considerable sums upon
the Bank of England, and several eminent bankers in London. He
then sets forth that, coming to lodge at the Hotel d'Orleans, he was
greatly surprised by my presuming to visit him, as he had no manner
of acquaintance with me. That next day, he set out for the country;
from whence returning on the 23rd of September, he found a card
from me inviting him to dine, which he was polite enough to comply
with; and that at my lodging he dined with a large company of English. That I forced him to drink (till I perceived he was fuddled) of
several sorts of wines and other liquors during dinner, which was not
over till about six in the evening, when the company retired to my
apartments to drink coffee. That after this, all the company went
away, excepting Mr. Taafe, my lord Southwell, and myself; and that
Mr. Taafe took a pair of dice, and, throwing them upon the table,
asked, Who would play? That the complainant Roberts at first excused himself, because he had no more than two crowns about him;
upon which the other said that he had no occasion for money, for he
might play upon his word of honour. He (Roberts) still excused himself, alleging that he had occasion for all his money for a journey on
which he was to set out on the Wednesday following: but that Mr.
Taafe, Lord Southwell, and I, insisted so strongly on his playing that,
being well flustered with wine, and not knowing what he did, he at
last yielded; and that, taking advantage of his situation, we made him

lose in less than an hour 870 Louis d'ors; that is, 400 to Mr. Taafe, 350 to Lord Southwell, and 120 to me; and that we then suffered him to go about his business.   That next day Mr. Taafe sent him a card inviting him to supper, but he excused himself; and on Sunday, the 26th of September, he received a letter from the same gentleman, desiring him to send the 400 Louis d'ors he had won of him; and that he (Roberts) wrote him in answer that he would pay him a visit on the Tuesday following: but that, on the 27th of September, between eleven and twelve at night, Mr. Taafe, Lord Southwell, and I, knocked with great violence, menaces, and imprecations, at his gate; where, getting admittance, we informed him that if he did not give each of us a draft for the several sums we had won of him, we would carry him instantly to the Bastile; the Archers [constables], with the Governor of the Bastile, waiting below for that purpose.   That we told him, it was a maxim in France that all gaming debts should be paid in 24 hours after they were contracted; and at the same time we threatened to cut him across the face with our swords if he should refuse to give us the drafts we demanded.   That, being intimidated with our menaces, and ignorant of the customs of France, he gave us drafts for our several sums upon Mr. Walters the younger, banker in Paris, though he had no money of his in his hands.   That the complainant, well knowing that the drafts would be refused, and thinking his life in danger, resolved next day, being the 28th, to set out for Lyons.   That there, and since his return to Paris, he understood that Mr. Taafe, Lord Southwell, and I, on the very day of his leaving Paris, came early to his lodging, where, meeting only with Miss Rose and her sister, Mr. Taafe persuaded the former to leave the complainant, and to go with him to the Hotel de Perou, promising to send her over to England in a short time.   After this, that he searched all the trunks, portmanteaus, and drawers belonging to the complainant, from whence he took out in one bag 400 Louis d'ors, and out of another to the value of 300 Louis, in French and Portuguese silver; from another bag 1200 livres in crown pieces, a pair of brilliant diamond buckles for which the complainant paid 8020 livres to the Sieur Pierre, and his own picture set round with diamonds to the amount of 1200 livres, besides the value of the picture which cost him ten Louis to the Sieur Marolle; a shirt buckle, set with diamonds, rubies, and emeralds, which cost him 650 livres to the Sieur Pierre; laces to the amount of 3000 livres; seven or eight women's robes or gowns valued at 4000 livres; two brilliant diamond rings; several gold snuff-boxes; a travelling chest containing his plate and china and divers other effects, which he cannot call to mind; all which Mr. Taafe packed up in one box, and by the help of his footman carried in a coach (which waited for him at the corner of the street of the Little Augustines) to his own apartment. That afterwards Mr. Taafe carried Miss Rose with her sister in another coach to his lodging, where they remained three days, and then sent them to London under the care of one of his friends.

On Sunday the 31st of October, 1751, when it was near one on the morning, as I was undressed and going to bed, with that security which ought to attend innocence, I heard a person enter my room; and upon turning round and seeing a man whom I did not know, I asked him calmly what he wanted? His answer was, that I must put on my clothes. I began to expostulate upon the motives of his appearance, when a commissary instantly entered the room, with a pretty numerous attendance; and told me with great gravity that he was come, by virtue of a warrant for my imprisonment, to carry me to the Grand Chatelet. I requested him again and again to inform me of the crime laid to my charge; but all his answer was, that I must follow him. I begged him to give me leave to write to Lord Albemarle, the English ambassador; promising to obey the warrant if his Excellency was not pleased to answer for my forthcoming. But the commissary refused me the use of pen and ink; though he consented that I should send a verbal message to his Excellency; telling me at the same time that he would not wait the return of the messenger, because his orders were to carry me instantly to prison. As resistance under such circumstances must have been unavailing, and might have been blameable, I obeyed the warrant by following the commissary, after ordering one of my domestics to inform my Lord Albemarle of the treatment I underwent.

I was carried to the Chatelet, where the gaolors, hardened by their profession, and brutal for their profit, fastened upon me as upon one of those guilty objects whom they lock up to be reserved for public punishment; and though neither my looks nor my behaviour betrayed the least symptom of guilt, yet was I treated as a condemned criminal. I was thrown into prison, and committed to a set of wretches who have no character of humanity but its form.

My residence (to speak in the gaol dialect) was in the *secret*, which is no other than the dungeon of the prison, where all the furniture was a wretched mattress, and a crazy chair. The weather was cold, and I called for a fire; but I was told I could have none. I was thirsty, and called for some wine and water, or even a draught of water by itself, but was denied it. All the favour I could obtain was a promise to be waited on in the morning; and then was left to myself, under a hundred locks and bolts, with a bit of candle, after finding that the words of my gaolers were few, their commands peremptory, and their favours unattainable. After a few moments of solitary reflection, I perceived myself shut up in a dungeon destined for the vilest male-factors; the walls were scrawled with their vows and prayers to Heaven, before they were carried to the gibbet or the wheel. Amongst other notable inscriptions I found one with the following note underneath; viz. "These verses were written by the priest who was burned and hanged in the year 1717, for stealing a chalice of the holy sacrament." At the same time I observed the floors were studded with iron staples, either to secure the prisoners, or to prevent the effects of their despair. I must own that the survey of my dreadful situation, deprived of the common comforts of life, even fire and water, must have got the better of conscience itself, irreproachable as mine was, and of all trust in the equity of my judges, had I not wrapped myself up in innocence, whose portion is fortitude, and whose virtue is tranquillity.

ELIZABETH VESEY (c. 1715–91)

Mrs. Vesey was one of the most prominent of the London Blue-stockings; but that her cleverness and erudition did not carry her beyond the interest of mundane things is shown in her letter to a sister Blue-stocking.

TO MRS. MONTAGU

WEDNESDAY, 28TH MAY, 1777

I RECEIVED your letter, my dear friend, last night too late to answer it, as I dined at Kew. Mrs. Hatten, acting Cleopatra, sailed under our windows to the sound of flutes—the day incessant rain, but had every nymph her Anthony I believe poor Cupid would have been heartily weary of being boxed up 12 hours where the company laboured under the call of diverting themselves. As there was no such demand in our little causerie I was very sorry when the Royal summons struck seven, especially as we talked a great deal of you. As there was only the family, I think I liked Lady Clive more than ever; nature has given her a good breeding which she has not embroidered because she did not want it; neither has she added the affected caution and reserve of a court. She and her mistress seem to confide in their own hearts for pleasing without imprudence or torturing the heaven-born gifts of unstudied attentive civility that looks so like truth and good nature. I cannot think of such a character without saying something of dear charming Gregory. Do you know, I envy her your letter? She would have it back again and it was not without something—I don't know what—that I returned it. Perhaps it was, however, that you wrote so well—how she loves you! and how pleasant it must be to you to see the heart you have snatched from a shipwreck so entirely devoted to you; it tells so much for both. My eyes fill—so I will proceed to my London *Gazette* which disdains a subject that promises so little fun.

All the *bon ton* Dames and Mess[rs] went last opera night to Bedlam, from thence adjourned to the Gallery of the Opera in their hats and half sacks and from thence to sup at Vauxhall, and a night of dreadful weather it was. The next day a lady asked another to call upon her at Marshes, the Dentists, to carry her to breakfast at Miss Floids, Kensington, as husband was going out of town and she had no carriage. The friend called at the appointed hour and found the Lady rushing out of Marsh's door all dishevelled, followed by her husband. Both of them went into the friend's coach, who was entreated by the husband to carry him and his lady home, which was performed in disconsolate silence. It is said the husband changed his mind about going out of town, and coming to Marsh's found a certain Captain, who had also occasion for the dentist. These are not acquaintance of yours or people who anybody cares about, so I will go on in acting the *Morning Post* by setting their names, lest the gentleman of the office may be curious. Don't let your nightingales hear these stories. As to Messrs the Cuckoo and Magpie, they are heartily welcome to it. Abbé Reynal is to be here this evening with 3 of his friends who go off Saturday to Oxford, Bath, Bristol, Ireland; but I shall not give them the least hint that Sandleford is in the way or I am sure you would have a visit and I am not sure you would like it. I shall also see Garrick and Burke; the first I shall flatter with your approbation of his Serenade, for the latter I wish I could find some enlivening cordial. Mr. William Burke went off last week to India overland to join a person at Paris who is going about the Company's service till Mr. Rumbold arrives, who goes by sea. I admire the spirit of the man who at once seizes the resolution (though past the meridian of life) to restore the drooping fortunes of his friend and kinsman. They have long made one common purse. Edmund is so touched with this generous act, and the loss of so dear a friend, that I could hardly keep from tears when I saw him.

THOMAS GRAY (1716–71)

The author of the famous "Elegy" and the close friend of Horace Walpole was a man of many accomplishments. This letter is addressed to an old friend, Nicholls, who had accompanied Gray on various tours; and it was with something of this in his mind that Gray wrote.

TO THE REV. NORTON NICHOLLS

PEMBROKE HALL, AUGUST 26, 1766

DEAR SIR, It is long since that I heard you were gone in haste into Yorkshire on account of your mother's illness; and the same letter informed me that she was recovered; otherwise I had then written to you, only to beg you would take care of her, and to inform you that I had discovered a thing very little known, which is, that in one's whole life one never can have any more than a single mother. You may think this is obvious, and (what you call) a trite observation. You are a green gosling! I was at the same age (very near) as wise as you, and yet I never discovered this (with full evidence and conviction, I mean) till it was too late. It is thirteen years ago, and seems but yesterday; and every day I live it sinks deeper into my heart. Many a corollary could I draw from this axiom for your use (not for my own), but I will leave you the merit of doing it yourself. Pray tell me how your own health is. I conclude it perfect, as I hear you offered yourself for a guide to Mr. Palgrave into the Sierra Morena of Yorkshire. For me, I passed the end of May and all June in Kent not disagreeably; the country is all a garden, gay, rich, and fruitful, and (from the rainy season) had preserved, till I left it, all that emerald verdure, which commonly one only sees for the first fortnight of the spring. In the west part of it from every eminence the eye catches some long winding reach of the Thames or Medway with all their navigation; in the east, the sea breaks in upon you, and mixes its white transient sails and glittering blue expanse with the deeper and brighter greens of the woods and corn. This last sentence is so fine, I am quite ashamed; but no matter; you must translate it into prose. Palgrave, if he heard it, would cover his face with his pudding sleeve. I went to Margate for a day; one would think it was Bartholomew Fair that had *flown* down from Smithfield to Kent in the London machine, like my Lady Stuffdamask: (to be sure you have read the New Bath Guide, the most fashionable of books) so then I did *not* go to Kingsgate, because it belonged to my Lord Holland; but to Ramsgate I did, and so to Sandwich, and Deal, and Dover, and Folkestone, and Hythe, all along the coast, very delightful. I do not tell you of the great and small beasts, and creeping things innumerable that I met with, because you do not suspect that this world is inhabited by anything but men and women and clergy, and such two-legged cattle. Now I am here again very disconsolate and all alone, even Mr. Brown is gone; and the cares of this world are coming thick upon me; I do not mean children. You, I hope, are better off, riding and walking with Mr. Aislaby, singing duets with my cousin Fanny, improving with Mr. Weddell, conversing with Mr. Harry Duncomb. I must not wish for you here; besides, I am going to town at Michaelmas, by no means for amusement. Do you remember how we are to go into Wales next year? well! Adieu, I am sincerely yours.

T. G.

P.S.   Pray how does poor Temple find himself in his new situation? Is Lord Lisburne as good as his letters were? What is come of the father and brother? Have you seen Mason?

DEANE SWIFT (*c.* 1717–83)

Swift was a connexion of the great Jonathan, and this letter was in answer to one from Lord Orrery, who had asked whether there was any truth in the story that one day, when he was an old man, the Dean had caught sight of himself in a looking-glass, and exclaimed, "Oh, poor old man!"

TO LORD ORRERY

DUBLIN, APRIL 4, 1744

MY LORD, As to the story of "O poor old man!" I inquired into it. The Dean did say something, upon his seeing himself in the glass, but neither Mrs. Ridgeway nor the lower servants could tell me what it was he said. I desired them to recollect it by the time when I should come again to the deanery. I have been there since, they cannot recollect it. A thousand stories have been invented of him within these two years, and imposed upon the world. I thought this might have been one of them, and yet I am now inclined to think there may be some truth in it, for on Sunday the 17th of March, as he sat in his chair, upon the housekeeper's moving a knife from him as he was going to catch at it, he shrugged his shoulders, and rocking himself, said, "I am what I am, I am what I am": and about six minutes afterwards, repeated the same words two or three times over.

His servant shaves his cheeks, and all his face as low as the tip of his chin, once a week: but under the chin, and about the throat, when the hair grows long, it is cut with scissors.

Sometimes he will not utter a syllable, at other times he will speak incoherent words, but he never yet, as far as I could hear, talked nonsense, or said a foolish thing.

About four months ago he gave me great trouble; he seemed to have a mind to talk to me. In order to try what he would say, I told him I came to dine with him, and immediately his housekeeper, Mrs. Ridgeway, said, "Won't you give Mr. Swift a glass of wine, sir?" He shrugged his shoulders, just as he used to do when he had a mind a friend should pass the evening with him. Shrugging his shoulders, your Lordship may remember, was as much as to say, "You'll ruin

361

me in wine." I own, I was scarce able to bear the sight. Soon after, he again endeavoured, with a good deal of pain, to find words to speak to me. At last, not being able, after many efforts, he gave a heavy sigh, and, I think, was afterwards silent. This puts me in mind of what he said about five days ago. He endeavoured several times to speak to his servant (now and then he calls him by name), at last, not finding words to express what he would be at, after some uneasiness he said, "I am a fool." Not long ago the servant took up his watch that lay upon the table to see what o'clock it was, he said, "Bring it here": and when it was brought, he looked very attentively at it: some time ago, the servant was breaking a large stubborn coal, he said, "That's a stone, you blockhead."

In a few days, or some very short time after guardians had been appointed for him, I went into his dining-room, where he was walking. I said something to him very insignificant, I know not what; but, instead of making any kind of answer to it, he said, "Go, go," pointing with his hand to the door, and immediately afterwards, raising his hand to his head, he said, "My best understanding," and so broke off abruptly, and walked away. I am, my Lord, Your Lordship's most obedient and most humble servant,

DEANE SWIFT

DAVID GARRICK (1717–79)

Garrick was a prolific letter-writer and corresponded with most people of note in his time. That he was a man not to be dismayed by any threats or bluff, is shown by his letter to Mr. Hawkins.

MEMORANDUM TO SIR W. YOUNG

JAN. 10, 1776

I HAVE ventured to produce "Hamlet," with alterations. It was the most imprudent thing I ever did in all my life; but I had sworn I would not leave the stage till I had rescued that noble play from all the rubbish of the fifth act. I have brought it forth without the Grave-digger's trick and the fencing-match. The alteration was received with general approbation, beyond my most warm expectations.

I shall play "Lear" next week, and "Macbeth" (perhaps) in the old dresses, with new scenes, the week after that, and then exit Roscius.

I wrote a farce, called "The Irish Widow," in less than a week.

TO THE REV. MR. HAWKINS

SEPT. 20, 1774

SIR, Though your threatening letter found me in a fit of the gout, which is a very peevish disorder, yet I assure you it added nothing to my ill-humour; nay I could have laughed, though in pain, had not the more humane sensation of pity prevented it.

Notwithstanding your former flattering letters to me, which I have luckily preserved, you now accuse me of pride, rancour, evil designs, and the Lord knows what, because I have refused your plays, which I most sincerely think unfit for representation, and which (some of them if not all) have had the same fortune with other managers. You are pleased to say that "of all animals a manager is the sorest." Pray, Mr. Hawkins, had you no feelings at the time you write this which contradicted the assertion? Can you really believe that this unprovoked, intemperate, behaviour can make me submit to your inquisitorial menaces? "Perform my plays or I'll appeal to the public!"

363

If you will publish your plays with your appeal, I will forgive you the rest.

Your insinuation that I formerly mortified you because you "once offended me in the business of 'Henry and Rosamond,'" is unworthy of an answer. It is very well known that I bear no malice; and the offence which *you* so well remember is as much forgotten by me as "Henry and Rosamond," the cause of it.

You value yourself much upon "laying a design to sound me," that is, to catch me tripping in order to expose me: a very liberal design truly for a scholar and a divine, and I wish you joy in your success; but to convince you, if possible, how much your intemperate zeal contradicts itself, you confess that "Alfred," your tragedy-trap, was not well prepared; that the play was (as you are pleased to express it) "improperly digested," and you "readily admit the justness of my exceptions": nay you go farther and say you "give up 'Alfred,' and acquiesce" in my judgment. Can anything I write vindicate my conduct more than your own words? Have I seen "Alfred" *since* your above confession; have I *refused* to see it? I know my duty too well—I am obliged by my situation to read all you are pleased to send me; but I have the same right to reject a play, which I think a bad one, as you have to compose it.

May I, without offence, differ in opinion with a gentleman who once was a credit to the Professorship of Poetry in Oxford? "It will be very hard, methinks" (these are your own words) "if that should not be a proper foundation of a fable which happens to be a matter of fact." Indeed, Sir, the best dramatic critics I have read tell me that matters of fact are *not* always proper foundations for dramatic fables.

You say I wrote a cavalier note: if it were so, your very cavalier letter produced it—I never begin first. Your last letter begot this, but I hope it is very unlike its father.

You conclude with saying you "do not desire to come to an open rupture" with me, and that you "wish not to exasperate, but to convince"; and you again tender me your friendship and your play. So far you seem to be returning to temper and reason;—but how was I deceived!—for in order to promote the good work and bring about a reconciliation, you add, that you have "too much knowledge of human nature in general and the particular pride" of my situation to look for any good from this amicable overture. Ought you not as a gentleman and a clergyman, and in justice, reason and good manners, to have waited for my answer, before you had been guilty of such outrageous behaviour?—or is it the Rev. Mr. Hawkins's method of convincing and not exasperating, to call names, while he is making a tender of his friendship?

I am, Sir, your humble servant,

D. GARRICK

Give me leave to make another observation upon your peculiar behaviour to me and to your friends. Though you seem to think me inexcusable for daring to differ with them, yet when they do not agree with you it is to stand for nothing. For example—Mr. Warton tells you that your present "Alfred" "is deficient in point of bustle according to the turn and taste of the times"; and you tell me "so far as the objection goes," Mr. Warton "seems to think the success of representation may be affected—but this opinion (supposing it to have ground) cannot," you presume, affect a right of representation. Indeed! I do not know which most to admire, your logic or politeness to your friend.

HORACE WALPOLE, 4TH EARL OF ORFORD (1717–97)

There is no equivalent in any literature to Horace Walpole, save, perhaps, Madame de Sevigné. Of his immense collection of letters the few given here are practically culled at random. They are to his intimate friends, men to whom he opened his heart and incidentally showed the whole workings of the world of his time.

TO GEORGE MONTAGU

ARLINGTON STREET, JULY 13, 1745

DEAR GEORGE, We are all *Cabob'd* and *Cacofagoed*, as my lord Denbigh says. We, who formerly you know, could any one of us beat three Frenchmen, are now so degenerated that three Frenchmen [1] can evidently beat one Englishman. Our army is running away, all that is left to run, for half of it is picked up by three or four hundred at a time. In short, we must step out of the high pantoufles that were made by those cunning shoemakers at Poitiers, and Ramillies, and go clumping about in perhaps wooden ones. My lady Hervey, who you know doats upon everything French, is charmed with the hopes of these new shoes, and has already bespoke herself a pair of pigeon wood. How did the tapestry at Blenheim look? Did it glow with victory, or did all our glories look overcast?

I remember a very admired sentence in one of my Lord Chesterfield's speeches, when he was haranguing for this war; with a most rhetorical transition, he turned to the tapestry in the House of Lords, and said, with a sigh, he feared there were no historical looms at work now! Indeed, we have reason to bless the good patriots, who have been employing our manufactures so historically. The countess of that wise earl, with whose two expressive words I began this letter, says, she is very happy now that my lord had never a place upon the coalition, for then all this bad situation of our affairs would have been laid upon him.

Now I have been talking of remarkable periods in our annals,

---

[1] Alluding to the success of the French army in Flanders, under the command of Marshal Saxe.

I must tell you what my Lord Baltimore thinks one:—He said to the prince t'other day: "Sir, your royal highness's marriage will be an *area* in English history."

If it were not for the life that is put into the town now and then by very bad news from abroad, one should be quite stupified. There is nobody left but two or three solitary regents; and they are always whisking backwards and forwards to their villas; and about a dozen antediluvian dowagers, whose carcasses have miraculously resisted the wet, and who every Saturday compose a very reverend catacomb at my old Lady Strafford's. She does not take money at the door for shewing them, but you pay twelvepence a-piece under the denomination of card-money. Wit and beauty indeed remain in the persons of Lady Townshend and Lady Caroline Fitzroy; but such is the want of taste of this age, that the former is very often forced to wrap up her wit in plain English before it can be understood; and the latter is almost as often obliged to have recourse to the same artifices to make her charms be taken notice of.

Of beauty I can tell you an admirable story: one Mrs. Comyns, an elderly gentlewoman, had lately taken a house in St. James Street. Some young gentleman went there t'other night. "Well, Mrs. Comyns, I hope there won't be the same disturbances here that were at your other house in Air Street."—"Lord, sir, I never had any disturbances there: mine was as quiet a house as any in the neighbourhood, and a great deal of good company came to me: it was only the ladies of quality that envied me."—"Envied you! why your house was pulled down about your ears."—"Oh dear, sir! don't you know how that happened?" —"No, pray how?"—"Why, dear sir, it was my lady who gave ten guineas to the mob to demolish my house, because her ladyship fancied I got women for Colonel Conway."

My dear George, don't you delight in this story? If poor Harry [Conway] comes back from Flanders, I intend to have infinite fun with his prudery about this anecdote, which is full as good as if it was true. I beg you will visit Mrs. Comyns when you come to town: she has infinite humour.   Adieu, dear George,
                                                                                Yours ever

TO THE SAME

ARLINGTON-STREET, AUG. 5, 1746

DEAR GEORGE, Though I can't this week accept your invitation, I can prove to you that I am most desirous of passing my time with you,

and therefore *en attendant* Harley house, if you can find me out any
clean, small house in Windsor, ready furnished, that is not absolutely
in the middle of the town, but near you, I should be glad to take it
for three or four months.   I have been about Sir Robert Rich's, but
they will only sell it.   I am as far from guessing why they send Sandwich
in embassy, as you are; and when I recollect of what various materials
our late embassadors have been composed, I can only say, *ex quovis
ligno fit Mercurius*.   Murray has certainly been discovering, and
warrants are out, but I don't yet know who are to be their prize.   I
begin to think that the ministry had really no intelligence till now.
I before thought they had, but durst not use it.   *A-propos* to not
daring; I went t'other night to look at my poor favourite Chelsea, for
the little Newcastle is gone to be dipped in the sea.   In one of the rooms
is a bed for her duke, and a press-bed for his footman; for he never dares
lie alone, and, till he was married, had always a servant sit up with him.
Lady Cromartie presented her petition to the king last Sunday.   He
was very civil to her but would not at all give her any hopes.   She
swooned away as soon as he was gone.   Lord Cornwallis told me
that her lord weeps every time any thing of his fate is mentioned to
him.   Old Balmerino keeps up his spirits to the same pitch of gaiety.
In the cell at Westminster he showed lord Kilmarnock how he must
lay his head; bid him not wince, lest the stroke should cut his skull
or his shoulders; and advised him to bite his lips.   As they were to
return, he begged they might have another bottle together, as they
should never meet any more till——and then pointed to his neck.   At
getting into the coach, he said to the jailer, "take care, or you will
break my shins with this damned axe."

I must tell you a *bon-mot* of George Selwyn's at the trial.   He
saw Bethel's sharp visage looking wistfully at the rebel lords; he
said, "What a shame it is to turn her face to the prisoners till they
are condemned."

If you have a mind for a true foreign idea, one of the foreign
ministers said at the trial to another, "*vraiment cela est auguste.*"
"*Oui,*" replied the other, "*cela est vrai, mais cela n'est pas royale.*"

I am assured that the old countess of Errol made her son lord
Kilmarnock go into the rebellion on pain of disinheriting him.   I
don't know whether I told you that the man at the tennis-court protests
he has known him dine with the man that sells pamphlets at Story's
gate: "and," says he, "he would often have been glad if I would have
taken him home to dinner."   He was certainly so poor, that in one

of his wife's intercepted letters she tells him she has plagued their steward for a fortnight for money, and can get but three shillings. Can one help pitying such distress? I am vastly softened too about Balmerino's relapse, for his pardon was only granted him to engage his brother's vote at the election of Scotch peers.

My lord chancellor has had a thousand pounds in present for his high stewardship, and has got the reversion of clerk of the crown (twelve hundred a-year) for his second son. What a long time it will be before his posterity are drove into rebellion for want like lord Kilmarnock.

The duke gave his ball last night to Peggy Banks at Vauxhall. It was to pique my lady Rochford in return for the prince of Hesse. I saw the company get into their barges at Whitehall stairs, as I was going myself, and just then passed by two city companies in their great barges, who had been a swan-hopping. They laid by and played "God save our noble King": and altogether it was a mighty pretty show. When they came to Vauxhall, there were assembled about five-and-twenty hundred people, besides crowds without. They huzzaed, and surrounded him so, that he was forced to retreat into the ball-room. He was very near being drowned t'other night going from Ranelagh to Vauxhall, by a politeness of the lord Cathcart's, who, stepping on the side of the boat to lend his arm, overset it, and both fell into the water up to their chins.

I have not yet got Sir Charles's ode; when I have, you shall see it: here are my own lines. Good-night.

TO RICHARD BENTLEY

STRAWBERRY-HILL, JUNE 10, 1755

MR. MÜNTZ is arrived. I am sorry I can by no means give any commendation to the hasty step you took about him. Ten guineas were a great deal too much to advance him, and must raise expectations in him that will not at all answer. You have entered into no written engagement with him nor even sent me his receipt for the money. My good sir, is this the sample you give me of the prudence and providence you have learned? I don't love to enter into the particulars of my own affairs; I will only tell you in one word, that they require great management. My endeavours are all employed to serve you; don't, I beg, give me reasons to apprehend that they will be thrown away. It is much in obscurity whether I shall be able to accomplish your re-establishment: but I shall go on with great discouragement, if I cannot promise myself that you will be a very different person after your return. I shall never have it in my power to do twice what I am now doing for you; and I choose to say the worst before-hand, rather than to reprove you for indolence and thoughtlessness hereafter, when it may be too late. Excuse my being so serious, but I find it is necessary.

You are not displeased with me, I know, even when I pout: you see I am not quite in good-humour with you, and I don't disguise it; but I have done scolding you for this time. Indeed I might as well continue it; for I have nothing else to talk of but Strawberry, and of that subject you must be well wearied. I believe she alluded to my disposition to *pout*, rather than meant to compliment me, when my lady Townshend said to somebody, t'other day, who told her how well Mrs. Leneve was, and in spirits, "Oh! she must be in spirits: why, she lives with Mr. Walpole, who is spirit of hartshorn!"

Princess Emily has been here:—Liked it? Oh no!—I don't wonder:—I never liked St. James's.—She was so inquisitive and so curious in prying into the very offices and servants' rooms that her captain Bateman was sensible of it, and begged Catherine not to mention it. He addressed himself well, if he hoped to meet with taciturnity! Catherine immediately ran down to the pond, and whispered to all the reeds, "Lord! that a princess should be such a gossip!"—In short, Strawberry-hill is the puppet-show of the times.

I have lately bought two more portraits of personages in Grammont, Harry Jermyn and Chiffinch: my Arlington-street is so full of portraits that I shall scarce find room for Mr. Müntz's works.

WEDNESDAY, 11TH

I was prevented from finishing my letter yesterday, by what do you think? By no less magnificent a circumstance than a deluge. We have had an extraordinary drought, no grass, no leaves, no flowers; not a white rose for the festival of yesterday.[1] About four arrived such a flood, that we could not see out of the windows; the whole lawn was a lake, though situated on so high an Ararat: presently it broke through the leads, drowned the pretty blue bed-chamber, passed through ceilings and floors into the little parlour, terrified Harry, and opened all Catherine's water-gates and *speech-gates*.—I had but just time to

[1] The Pretender's birthday.

collect two dogs, a couple of sheep, a pair of bantams, and a brace of gold-fish; for, in the haste of my zeal to imitate my ancestor Noah, I forgot that fish would not easily be drowned. In short, if you chance to spy a little ark with pinnacles sailing towards Jersey, open the skylight, and you will find some of your acquaintance. You never saw such desolation! A pigeon brings word that Mabland has fared still worse: it never came into my head before, that a rainbow-office for insuring against water might be very necessary. This is a true account of the late deluge.

Witness our hands,

HORACE NOAH.
CATHERINE NOAH, her × mark.
HENRY SHEM.
LOUIS JAPHET.
PETER HAM, &c.

I was going to seal my letter, and thought I should scarce have any thing more important to tell you than the history of the flood, when a most extraordinary piece of news indeed arrived—nothing less than a new gunpowder-plot—last Monday was to be the fatal day—There was a ball at Kew—Vanneschi and his son, directors of the opera, two English lords and two Scotch lords are in confinement at justice Fielding's.—This is exactly all I know of the matter: and this weighty intelligence is brought by the waterman from my housemaid in Arlington-street, who sent Harry word that the town is in an uproar; and to confirm it, the waterman says he heard the same thing at Hungerford-stairs. I took the liberty to represent to Harry, that the ball at Kew was this day se'nnight for the prince's birth-day; that, as the duke was at it, I imagined that the Scotch lords would rather have chosen that day for the execution of their tragedy; that I believed Vanneschi's son was a child, and that peers are generally confined at the Tower, not at justice Fielding's; besides, that we are much nearer to Kew than Hungerford-stairs are.—But Harry, who has not at all recovered the deluge, is extremely disposed to think Vanneschi is very like Guy Fawkes; and is so persuaded that so dreadful a story could *not* be invented, that I have been forced to believe it too: and in the course of our reasoning and guessing, I told him, that though I could not fix upon all four, I was persuaded that the late Lord Lovat who was beheaded must be one of the Scotch peers, and Lord A.'s son who is not begot, one of the English.—I was afraid he would think I treated so serious a business too ludicrously, if I had hinted at the scene of distressed friendship that would be occasioned by lord H***'s examining his intimate Vanneschi. Adieu! my dear sir—Mr. Fox and lady Caroline, and lord and lady Kildare are to dine here to-day; and if they tell Harry or me any more of the plot, you shall know it.

WEDNESDAY NIGHT

Well! now for the plot: thus much is true. A laundry-maid of the duchess of Marlborough, passing by the Cocoa-tree, saw two gentlemen go in there, one of whom dropped a letter; it was directed *to you*. She opened it. It was very obscure, talked of designs at Kew miscarried, of new methods to be taken; and as this way of correspondence had been repeated too often, another must be followed; and it told *you* that the next letter to him should be in a bandbox at such a house in the Haymarket. The duchess concluded it related to a gang of street-robbers, and sent it to Fielding. He sent to the house named, and did find a box and a letter, which, though obscure, had treason enough in it. It talked of a design at Kew miscarried; that the opera was now the only place, and consequently the scheme must be deferred till next season, especially as *a certain person* is abroad. For the other great person (the duke), they are sure of him at any time. There was some indirect mention too of gunpowder. Vanneschi and others have been apprehended: but a conclusion was made, that it was a malicious design against the lord high treasurer of the opera and his administration; and so they have been dismissed. Macnamara, I suppose you Jerseyans know, is returned with his fleet to Brest, leaving the transports sailing to America. Lord Thanet and Mr. Stanley are just gone to Paris, I believe to inquire after the war.

The weather has been very bad for showing Strawberry to the Kildares; we have not been able to stir out of doors: but to make me amends, I have discovered that lady Kildare is a true Sevignist. You know what pleasure I have in any increase of our sect; I thought she grew handsomer than ever as she talked with devotion of *Notre Dame des Rochers*. Adieu, my dear sir!

Yours ever

P.S. Tell me if you receive this; for in these gunpowder times to be sure the clerks of the post-office are peculiarly alert.

TO THE SAME

BATTLE, WEDNESDAY, AUGUST 5, 1752

HERE we are, my dear sir, in the middle of our pilgrimage; and lest we should never return from this holy land of abbeys and Gothic castles, I begin a letter to you, that I hope some charitable monk, when he has buried our bones, will deliver to you. We have had piteous distresses, but then we have seen glorious sights! You shall hear of each in their order.

Monday, Wind S.E.—at least that was our direction. While they were changing our horses at Bromley, we went to see the bishop of Rochester's palace; not for the sake of anything there was to be seen, but because there was a chimney, in which had stood a flower-pot, in which was put the counterfeit plot against Bishop Sprat. 'Tis a paltry parsonage, with nothing of antiquity but two panes of glass, purloined from Islip's chapel in Westminster Abbey, with that abbot's rebus, an eye and a slip of a tree. In the garden there is a clear little pond, teeming with gold fish. The bishop is more prolific than I am.

From Sevenoaks we went to Knowle. The park is sweet, with much old beech, and an immense sycamore before the great gate, that makes me more in love than ever with sycamores. The house is not near so extensive as I expected: the outward court has a beautiful decent simplicity that charms one. The apartments are many, but not large. The furniture throughout, ancient magnificence; loads of portraits, not good nor curious; ebony cabinets, embossed silver in vases, dishes, &c., embroidered beds, stiff chairs, and sweet bags lying on velvet tables, richly worked in silk in gold. There are two galleries, one very small; an old hall, and a spacious great drawing room. There is never a good staircase. The first little room you enter has sundry portraits of the times; but they seem to have been bespoke by the yard, and drawn all by the same painter: one should be happy if they were authentic; for among them there is Dudley Duke of Northumberland, Gardiner of Winchester, the Earl of Surrey the poet, when a boy, and Thomas Duke of Norfolk; but I don't know which. The only fine picture is of Lord Goring and Endymion Porter by Vandyke. There is a good head of the queen of Bohemia, a whole length of Duc d'Espernon, and another good head of the Clifford Countess of Dorset, who wrote that admirable haughty letter to secretary Williamson, when he recommended a person to her for member for Appleby: "*I have been bullied by an usurper, I have been neglected by a court, but I won't be dictated to by a subject:—your man shan't stand. Ann Dorset, Pembroke and Montgomery.*" In the chapel is a piece of ancient tapestry: Saint Luke in his first profession is holding an urinal. Below stairs is a chamber of poets and players, which is proper enough in that house; for the first earl wrote a play, and the last earl was a poet, and I think married a player. Major Mohun and Betterton are curious among the latter, Cartwright and Flatman among the former. The arcade is newly enclosed, painted in fresco, and with modern glass of all the family matches. In the gallery is a whole length of the unfortunate Earl of Surrey, with his device a broken column, and the motto *Sat superest.* My father had one of them, but larger, and with more emblems, which the Duke of Norfolk bought at my brother's sale. There is one good head of Henry VIII, and divers of Cranfield Earl of Middlesex, the citizen who came to be lord treasurer, and was very near coming to be hanged. His countess, a bouncing kind of lady mayoress, looks pure awkward amongst so much good company. A visto cut through the wood has a delightful effect from the front; but there are some trumpery fragments of gardens that spoil the view from the state apartments.

We lay that night at Tunbridge town, and were surprised with the ruins of the old castle. The gateway is perfect, and the inclosure formed into a vineyard by a Mr. Hooker to whom it belongs, and the walls spread with fruit, and the mount on which the keep stood, planted in the same way. The prospect is charming, and a breach in the wall opens below to a pretty Gothic bridge of three arches over the Medway. We honoured the man for his taste—not but that we wished the committee at Strawberry Hill were to sit upon it, and stick cypresses among the hollows. But, alas! he sometimes makes eighteen sour hogsheads, and is going to disrobe the *ivy-mantled tower*, because it harbours birds!

Now begins our chapter of woes. The inn was full of farmers and tobacco; and the next morning, when we were bound for Penshurst, the only man in the town who had two horses would not let us have them, because the roads, as he said, were so bad. We were forced to send to the Wells for others, which did not arrive till half the day was spent—we all the while up to the head and ears in a market of sheep and oxen. A mile from the town we climbed up a hill to see Summer Hill, the residence of Grammont's princess of Babylon. There is now scarce a road to it: the Paladins of those times were too valorous to fear breaking their necks; and I much apprehend that *la Monsery* and the fair mademoiselle Hamilton must have mounted their palfreys and rode behind their gentlemen-ushers upon pillions to the Wells. The house is little better than a farm, but has been an excellent one, and is entire, though out of repair. I have drawn the front of it to show you, which you are to draw over again to show me. It stands high, commands a vast landscape beautifully wooded, and has quantities of large old trees to shelter itself, some of which might be well spared to open views.

From Summer Hill we went to Lamberhurst to dine; near which, that is, at the distance of three miles, up and down impracticable hills, in a most retired vale, such as Pope describes in the last Dunciad,

Where slumber abbots, purple as their vines,

we found the ruins of Bayham abbey, which the Barrets and Hardings bid us visit. There are small but pretty remains, and a neat little Gothic house built near them by their nephew Pratt. They have found a tomb of an abbot, with a crosier, at length on the stone.

Here our woes increase. The roads grew bad beyond all badness, the night dark beyond all darkness, our guide frightened beyond all frightfulness. However, without being at all killed, we got up, or down, I forget which, it was so dark, a famous precipice called Silver Hill, and about ten at night arrived at a wretched village called Rother-bridge. We had still six miles hither, but determined to stop, as it would be a pity to break our necks before we had seen all we intended. But, alas! there was only one bed to be had: all the rest were inhabited by smugglers, whom the people of the house called mountebanks; and with one of whom the lady of the den told Mr. Chute he might lie. We did not at all take to this society, but, armed with links and lanthorns, set out again upon this impracticable journey. At two o'clock in the morning we got hither to a still worse inn, and that crammed with excise officers, one of whom had just shot a smuggler. However, as we were neutral powers, we have passed safely through both armies hitherto, and can give you a little farther history of our wandering through these mountains, where the young gentlemen are forced to drive their curricles with a pair of oxen. The only morsel of good road we have found, was what even the natives had assured us was totally impracticable; these were eight miles to Hurst Monceaux. It is seated at the end of a large vale, five miles in a direct line to the sea, with wings of blue hills covered with wood, one of which falls down to the house in a sweep of 100 acres. The building for the convenience of water to the moat sees nothing at all; indeed it is entirely imagined on a plan of defence, with draw-bridges actually in being, round towers, watch-towers mounted on them, and battlements pierced for the passage of arrows from long bows. It was built in the time of Henry VI and is as perfect as the first day. It does not seem to have been ever quite finished, or at least that age was not arrived at the luxury of white-wash; for almost all the walls, except in the principal chambers, are in their native *brickhood*. It is a square building, each side about two hundred feet in length; a porch and cloister, very like Eton College; and the whole is much in the same taste, the kitchen extremely so, with three vast funnels to the chimneys going up on the inside. There are two or three little courts for offices, but no magnificence of apartments. It is scarcely furnished with a few necessary beds and chairs: one side has been sashed, and a drawing-room and dining-room and two or three rooms wainscoted by the Earl of Sussex, who married a natural daughter of Charles II. Their arms with delightful carvings by Gibbons, particularly two pheasants, hang over the chimneys. Over the great drawing-room chimney is the coat armour of the first Leonard Lord Dacre, with all his alliances. Mr. Chute was transported, and called cousin with ten thousand quarterings. The chapel is small, and mean: the Virgin and seven long lean saints, ill done, remain in the windows. There have been four more, but seem to have been removed for light; and we actually found St. Catherine, and another gentlewoman with a church in her hand, exiled into the buttery. There remain two odd cavities, with very small wooden screens on each side the altar, which seem to have been confessionals. The outside is a mixture of grey brick and stone, that has a very venerable appearance. The drawbridges are romantic to a degree; and there is a dungeon, that gives one a delightful idea of living in the days of soccage and under such goodly tenures. They showed us a dismal chamber which they called *Drummer's* Hall, and suppose that Mr. Addison's comedy is descended from it. In the windows of the gallery over the cloisters, which leads all round to the apartments, is the device of the Fienneses, a wolf holding a baton with a scroll, *Le roy le veu* —an unlucky motto, as I shall tell you presently, to the last peer of that line. The estate is two thousand a year, and so compact as to have but seventeen houses upon it. We walked up a brave old avenue to the church, with ships sailing on our left hand the whole way. Before the altar lies a lank brass knight, hight William Feinis, chevalier, who obiit c.c.c.c.v. that is in 1405. By the altar is a beautiful tomb, all in our trefoil taste, varied into a thousand little canopies and patterns, and two knights reposing on their backs. These were Thomas Lord Dacre, and his only son Gregory, who died *sans issue*. An old grey-headed beadsman of the family talked to us of a blot in the scutcheon; and we had observed that the field of the arms was green instead of blue, and the lions ramping to the right, contrary to order. This and the man's imperfect narrative let us into the circumstances of the personage before us; for there is no inscription. He went in a Chevy-chace style to hunt in *a Mr. Pelham's* park at Lawton: the keepers opposed, a fray ensued, a man was killed. The haughty baron took the death upon himself, as most secure of pardon: but however, though there was no chancellor of the exchequer in the question he was condemned to be hanged: *Le roy le vouloist.*

Now you are fully master of Hurst Monceaux, I shall carry you on to Battle. By the way, we bring you a thousand sketches, that you may show us what we have seen. Battle Abbey stands at the end of the town exactly as Warwick Castle does of Warwick; but the house of Webster have taken due care that it should not resemble it in anything else. A vast building, which they call the old refectory, but which I believe was the original church, is now barn, coach-house, &c. The situation is noble, above the level of abbeys: what does remain of gateways and towers is beautiful, particularly the flat side of a cloister, which is now the front of the mansion house. A miss of the family has clothed a fragment of a portico with cockle-shells! The grounds, and what has been a park, lie in a vile condition. In the church is the tomb of Sir Antony Browne, master of the horse for life to Harry VIII, from whose descendants the estate was purchased. The head of John Hammond, the last abbot, is still perfect in one of the windows. Mr. Chute says, What charming things we should have done if Battle Abbey had been to be sold at Mrs. Chenevix's, as Strawberry was! Good-night!

TUNBRIDGE, FRIDAY.

We are returned hither, where we have established our head-quarters. On our way, we had an opportunity of surveying that formidable mountain, Silver Hill, which we had floundered down in the dark: it commands a whole horizon of the richest blue prospect you ever saw. I take it to be the individual spot to which the Duke of Newcastle carries the smugglers, and, showing them Sussex and Kent, says, "All this will I give you, if you will fall down and worship me." Indeed one of them, who exceeded the tempter's warrant, hangs in chains on the very spot where they finished the life of that wretched custom-house officer whom they were two days in murdering.

This morning we have been to Penshurst—but, oh! how fallen! The park seems to have never answered its character: at present it is forlorn; and instead of Sacharissa's cypher carved on the beeches, I should sooner have expected to have found the milk-woman's score. Over the gate is an inscription, purporting the manor to have been a boon from Edward VI to Sir William Sydney. The apartments are the grandest I have seen in any of these old palaces, but furnished in a tawdry modern taste. There are loads of portraits; but most of them seem christened by chance like children at a foundling hospital. There is a portrait of Languet, the friend of Sir Philip Sydney; and divers of himself and all his great kindred, particularly his sister-in-law with a vast lute, and Sacharissa, charmingly handsome. But there are really four very great curiosities, I believe as old portraits as any extant in England: they are, Fitzallen Archbishop of Canterbury, Humphrey Stafford the first duke of Buckingham, T. Wentworth, and John Foxle; all four with the dates of their commissions as constables of Queenborough Castle, from whence I suppose they were brought. The last is actually receiving his investiture from Edward the third, as Wentworth is in the dress of Richard the third's time. They are really not very ill done. There are six more, only heads; and we have found since we came home, that Penshurst belonged for a time to that Duke of Buckingham. There are some good tombs in the church, and a very Vandal one, called *Sir Stephen of Penchester*. When we had seen Penshurst, we borrowed saddles, and, bestriding the horses of our post-chaise, set out for Hever to visit a tomb of Sir Thomas Bullen, Earl of Wiltshire, partly with a view to talk of it in Anna Bullen's walk at Strawberry Hill. But the measure of our woes was not full; we could not find our way, and were forced to return; and again lost ourselves in coming from Penshurst, having been directed to what they called a better road than the execrable one we had gone.

Since dinner we have been to Lord Westmoreland's at Mereworth, which is so perfect in a Palladian taste, that I most own it has recovered me a little from Gothic. It is better situated than I had expected from the bad reputation it bears, and has some prospect, though it is in a moat, and mightily besprinkled with small ponds. The design, you know, is taken from the Villa del Capra by Vicenza, but on a larger scale; yet, though it has cost an hundred thousand pounds, it is still only a fine villa: the finishing of in and outside has been exceedingly expensive. A wood that runs up a hill behind the house is broke like an Albano landscape with an octagon temple and a triumphal arch; but then there are some dismal clipped hedges, and a pyramid, which by a most unnatural copulation is at once a grotto and a greenhouse. Does it not put you in mind of the proposal for your drawing a garden-seat, Chinese on one side and Gothic on the other? The chimneys, which are collected to a centre, spoil the dome of the house, and the hall is a dark well. The gallery is eighty-two feet long, hung with green velvet and pictures, among which is a fine Rembrandt, and a pretty La Hire. The ceilings are painted, and there is a fine bed of silk and gold tapestry. The attic is good, and the wings extremely pretty, with porticos formed on the style of the house. The earl has built a new church, with a steeple which seems designed for the latitude of Cheapside, and is so tall that the poor church curtsies under it, like Mary Rich in a vast high crown hat: it has a round portico like St. Clements', with vast Doric pillars supporting a thin shelf. The inside is the most abominable piece of tawdriness that ever was seen, stuffed with pillars painted in imitation of verd antique, as all the sides are like Siena marble: but the greatest absurdity is a Doric frieze, between the triglyphs of which is the Jehovah, the I.H.S. and the dove. There is a little chapel with Nevil tombs, particularly of the first Fane Earl of Westmoreland, and of the founder of the old church, and the heart of a knight who was killed *in the wars*. On the Fane tomb is a pedigree of brass in relief, and a genealogy of virtues to answer it. There is an entire window of painted-glass arms, chiefly modern, in the chapel, and another over the high altar. The hospitality of the house was truly Gothic; for they made our postillion drunk, and he overturned us close to a water, and the bank did but just save us from being in the middle of it. Pray, whenever you travel in Kentish roads, take care of keeping your driver sober.

ROCHESTER, SUNDAY

We have finished our progress sadly! Yesterday, after twenty mishaps, we got to Sissinghurst to dinner. There is a park in ruins, and a house in ten times greater ruins, built by Sir John Baker, chancellor of the exchequer to Queen Mary. You go through an arch of the stables to the house, the court of which is perfect and very beautiful. The Duke of Bedford has a house at Cheneys in Buckinghamshire, which seems to have been very like it, but is more ruined. This has a good apartment, and a fine gallery a hundred and twenty feet by eighteen, which takes up one side: the wainscot is pretty and entire; the ceiling vaulted, and painted in a light genteel grotesque. The whole is built for show; for the back of the house is nothing but lath and plaster. From thence we went to Bocton-Malherbe, where are remains of a house of the Wottons, and their tombs in the church: but the roads so exceedingly bad, that it was dark before we got thither—and still darker before we got to Maidstone. From thence we passed this morning to Leeds castle. Never was such disappointment! There are small remains: the moat is the only handsome object, and is quite a lake, supplied by a cascade which tumbles through a bit of a romantic grove. The Fairfaxes have fitted up a pert bad apartment in the fore-part of the castle, and have left the only tolerable rooms for offices. They had a gleam of Gothic in their eyes; but it soon passed off into some modern windows, and some that never were ancient. The only thing that at all recompensed the fatigues we have undergone, was the picture of the Duchess of Buckingham, la Ragotte, who is mentioned in Grammont—I say us; for I trust that Mr. Chute is as true a bigot to Grammont as I am. Adieu! I hope you will be as weary with reading our history, as we have been in travelling it.

Yours ever

TO THE HON. H. S. CONWAY

PARIS, OCT. 6, 1765

I AM glad to find you grow just, and that you do conceive at last that I could do better than stay in England for politics. *Tenez, mon enfant*, as the Duchess de la Ferte said to Madame Staal; *comme il n'y a que moi au monde qui aie toujours raison*, I will be very reasonable; and as you have made this concession to me, who knew I was in the right, I will not expect you to answer all my *reasonable* letters. If you send a bullying letter to the King of Spain, or to *chose* my neighbour here, I will consider them as written to myself, and substract so much from your bill. Nay, I will accept a line from Lady Aylesbury now and then in part of payment. I shall continue to write as the wind sets in my pen; and do own my babble does not demand much reply.

For so reasonable a person as I am, I have changed my mind very often about this country. The first five days I was in violent spirits—then came a dismal cloud of whist and literature, and I could not bear it. At present I begin, very *Englishly* indeed, to establish a right to my own way. I laugh, and talk nonsense, and make them hear me. There are two or three houses where I go quite at my ease, am never asked to touch a card, nor hold dissertations. Nay, I don't pay homage to their authors. Every woman has one or two planted in her house, and God knows how they water them. The old president Henault is the pagod at Madame du Deffand's, an old blind debauchee of wit, where I supped last night. The president is very near deaf, and much nearer superannuated. He sits by the table: the mistress of the house, who formerly was his, inquires after every dish on the table, is told who has eaten of which, and then bawls the bill of fare of every individual into the president's ears. In short, every mouthful is proclaimed, and so is every blunder I make against grammar. Some that I make on purpose, succeed; and one of them is to be reported to the queen to-day by Henault, who is her great favourite. I had been at Versailles; and having been much taken notice of by her majesty, I said, alluding to Madame de Sevigné, *La reine est le plus grand roi du monde*, You may judge if I am in possession by a scene that passed after supper. Sir James Macdonald had been mimicking Hume: I told the women, who, besides the mistress, were the Duchesse de la Valiere, Madame de Forcalquier, and a demoiselle, that to be sure they would be glad to have a specimen of Mr. Pitt's manner of speaking; and that nobody mimicked him so well as Elliot. They firmly believed it, teasted him for an hour, and at last said he was the rudest man in the world not to oblige them. It appeared the more strange, because here every body sings, reads their own works in public, or attempts any one thing without hesitation or capacity. Elliot speaks miserable French; which added to the diversion.

I had had my share of distress in the morning, by going through the operation of being presented to the whole royal family, down to the little Madame's pap-dinner, and had behaved as sillily as you will easily believe, hiding myself behind every mortal. The queen called me up to her dressing-table, and seemed mightily disposed to gossip with me; but instead of enjoying my glory like Madame de Sevigné, I slunk back into the crowd after a few questions. She told Monsieur de Guerchy of it afterwards, and that I had run away from her, but said she would have her revenge at Fontainbleau. So I must go thither, which I did not intend. The king, dauphin, dauphiness, mesdames, and the wild beast, did not say a word to me. Yes, the wild beast, he of the Gévaudan. He is killed, and actually in the queen's ante-chamber, where he was exhibited to us with as much parade as if it was Mr. Pitt. It is an exceedingly large wolf, and, the connoisseurs say, has twelve teeth more than any wolf ever had since the days of Romulus's wet-nurse. The critics deny it to be the true beast; and I find most people think the beast's name is *legion, for there are many*. He was covered with a sheet, which two chasseurs lifted up for the foreign ministers and strangers. I dined at the Duke of Praslin's with five-and-twenty tomes of the *corps diplomatique*; and after dinner was presented, by Monsieur de Guerchy, to the Duc de Choiseul. The Duc de Praslin is as like his own letters in D'Eon's book as he can stare; that is, I believe, a very silly fellow. His wisdom is of the grave kind. His cousin, the first minister, is a little volatile being, whose countenance and manner had nothing to frighten me for my country. I saw him but for three seconds, which is as much as he allows to any one body or thing. Monsieur de Guerchy, whose goodness to me is inexpressible, took the trouble of walking everywhere with me, and carried me particularly to see the new office for state papers—I wish I could send it you. It is a large building, disposed like an hospital, with the most admirable order and method. Lodgings for every officer; his name and business written over his door. In the body is a perspective of seven or eight large chambers: each is painted with emblems, and wainscoted with presses with wired doors and crimson curtains. Over each press, in golden letters, the country to which the pieces relate, as Angleterre, Allemagne, &c. Each room has a large funnel of bronze with *or moulu*, like a column, to air the papers and preserve them. In short, it is as magnificent as useful.

From thence I went to see the reservoir of pictures at Monsieur de Marigny's. They are what are not disposed of in the palaces, though sometimes changed with others. This *refuse*, which fills many rooms from top to bottom, is composed of the most glorious works of Raphael, L. da Vinci, Giorgione, Titian, Guido, Correggio, &c. Many pictures, which I knew by their prints, without an idea where they existed, I found there.

The Duc de Nivernois is extremely obliging to me. I have supped at Madame de Bentheim's, who has a very fine house, and a woeful husband. She is much livelier than any Englishwoman. The liveliest man I have seen is the Duc de Duras: he is shorter and plumper than Lord Halifax, but very like him in the face. I am to sup with the Dussons on Sunday. In short, all that have been in England are exceedingly disposed to repay any civilities they received there. Monsieur de Caraman wrote from the country to excuse his not coming to see me, as his wife is on the point of being brought to bed, but begged I would come to them. So I would, if I was a man-midwife: but though they are easy on such heads, I am not used to it, and cannot make a party of pleasure of a labour.

Wilkes arrived here two days ago, and announced that he was going minister to Constantinople. To-day I hear he has lowered his credentials, and talks of going to England, if he can make his peace. I thought, by the manner in which this was mentioned to me, that the person meant to sound me: but I made no answer; for, having given up politics in England, I certainly did not come to transact them here. He has not been to make me the first visit, which, as the last arrived, depends on him: so, never having spoken to him in my life, I have no call to seek him. I avoid all politics so much, that I had not heard one word here about Spain. I suppose my silence passes for very artful mystery, and puzzles the ministers, who keep spies on the most insignificant foreigner. It would have been lucky if I had been as watchful. At Chantilly I lost my portmanteau with half my linen; and the night before last I was robbed of a new frock, waistcoat, and breeches, laced with gold, a white and silver waistcoat, black velvet breeches, a knife, and a book. There are expenses I did not expect, and by no means entering into my system of extravagance.

I am very sorry for the death of Lord Ophaly, and for his family. I knew the poor young man himself but little, but he seemed extremely good-natured. What the Duke of Richmond will do for a hotel, I cannot conceive. Adieu!

Yours ever

TO GEORGE MONTAGU

ARLINGTON STREET, MAY 11, 1769

You are so wayward, that I often resolve to give you up to your humours. Then something happens with which I can divert you, and my good humour returns. Did not you say you should return to London long before this time? At least, could you not tell me you had changed your mind? Why am I to pick it out from your absence and silence, as Dr. Warburton found a future state in Moses's saying nothing of the matter! I could go on with a chapter of severe interrogatories, but I think it more cruel to treat you as a hopeless reprobate; yes, you are graceless, and as I have a respect for my own scolding, I shall not throw it away upon you.

Strawberry has been in great glory; I have given a *festino* there that will almost mortgage it. Last Tuesday all France dined there; Monsieur and Madame du Chatelet, the Duc de Liancour, three more French ladies, whose names you will find in the enclosed paper, eight other Frenchmen, the Spanish and Portuguese ministers, the Holdernesses,

Fitzroys, in short we were four-and-twenty. They arrived at two. At the gates of the castle I received them dressed in a cravat of Gibbons's carving, and a pair of gloves embroidered up to the elbows that had belonged to James the First. The French servants stared, and firmly believed this was the dress of English country gentlemen. After taking a survey of the apartments we went to the printing-house, where I had prepared some verses, with translations by Monsieur de Lille, one of the company. The moment they were printed off, I gave a private signal, and French horns and clarionets accompanied this compliment.

We then went to see Pope's grotto and garden, and returned to a magnificent dinner in the refectory. In the evening we walked, had tea, coffee, and lemonade in the gallery, which was illuminated with a thousand, or thirty candles, I forget which, and played at whist and loo till midnight. Then there was a cold supper, and at one the company returned to town saluted by fifty nightingales, who as tenants of the manor came to do honour to their lord.

I cannot say last night was equally agreeable. There was what they called a *ridotto al fresco* at Vauxhall, for which one paid half-a-guinea, though except some thousand more lamps and a covered passage all round the garden, which took off from the gardenhood, there was nothing better than on a common night. Mr. Conway and I set out from his house at eight o'clock; the tide and torrent of coaches was so prodigious that it was half an hour after nine before we got half way from Westminster Bridge. We then alighted, and after scrambling under bellies of horses, through wheels, and over posts and rails, we reached the gardens, where were already many thousand persons. Nothing diverted me but a man in a Turk's dress and two nymphs in masquerade without masks, who sailed amongst the company, and which was surprising seemed to surprise nobody. It had been given out that people were desired to come in fancied dresses without masks. We walked twice round and were rejoiced to come away, though with the same difficulties as at our entrance, for we found three strings of coaches all along the road, who did not move half a foot in half an hour. There is to be a rival mob in the same way at Ranelagh to-morrow, for the greater the folly and imposition the greater is the crowd. I have suspended the vestimenta that were torn off my back to the god of repentance, and shall stay away. Adieu; I have not a word more to say to you.

Yours, &c.

P.S.—I hope you will not regret paying a shilling for this packet.

STRAWBERRY HILL, MONDAY, JUNE 22, 1772

IT is lucky that I have had no dealings with Mr. F.; for, if he had ruined me, as he has half the world, I could not have *run* away.   I tired myself with walking on Friday; the gout came on Saturday in my foot; yesterday, I kept my bed till four o'clock, and my room all day—but, with wrapping myself all over with bootikins, I have scarce had any pain—my foot swelled immediately, and to-day I am descended into the blueth and greenth; and though you expect to find that I am paving the way to an excuse, I think I shall be able to be with you on Saturday.   All I intend to excuse myself from, is walking.   I should certainly never have the gout, if I had lost the use of my feet.   Cherubims that have no legs, and do nothing but stick their chins in a cloud and sing, are never out of order. Exercise is the worst thing in the world, and as bad an invention as gunpowder.

A propos to Mr. F., here is a passage ridiculously applicable to him, that I met with yesterday in the letters of Guy Patin: "Il n'y a pas long tems qu'un auditeur des comptes nommé Mons. Nivelle fit banqueroute; et tout fraichement, c'est-à-dire depuis trois jours, un tresorier des parties casuelles, nommé Sanson, en a fait autant; et pour vous montrer, qu'il est vrai que *res humanæ faciunt circulum,* comme il a été autrefois dit par Plato et par Aristote, celui-là s'en retourne d'où il vient. Il est fils d'un paisan; il a été laquais de son premier metier, et aujourd'hui il n'est plus rien, si non qu'il lui reste une assez belle femme."—I do not think I can find in Patin or Plato, nay, nor in Aristotle, though he wrote about everything, a parallel case to ――'s: there are advertised to be sold more annuities of his and his society, to the amount of five hundred thousand pounds a year!   I wonder what he will do next, when he has sold the estates of all his friends!

I have been reading the most delightful book in the world, the lives of Leland, Tom Hearne, and Antony Wood.   The last's diary makes a thick volume in octavo.   One entry is, "This day Old Joan began to make my bed."   In the story of Leland is an examination of a freemason, written by the hand of King Henry VI with notes by Mr. Locke.   Free-masonry, Henry VI and Locke make a strange heterogeneous olio; but that is not all.   The respondent, who defends the mystery of masonry, says it was brought into Europe by the Venetians— he means the Phœnicians.   And who do you think propagated it? Why, one Peter Gore.   And who do you think that was?   One Pythagoras, Pythagore.   I do not know whether it is not still more extraordinary, that this and the rest of the nonsense in that account made

Mr. Locke determine to be a free-mason: so would I too, if I could expect to hear of more *Peter Gores*.

Pray tell Lady Lyttleton that I say she will certainly kill herself if she lets Lady Aylesbury drag her twice a day to feed the pheasants; and you make her climb cliffs and clamber over mountains. She has a tractability that alarms me for her; and if she does not pluck up a spirit and determine never to be put out of her own way, I do not know what may be the consequence. I will come and set her an example of immoveability. Take notice, I do not say one civil syllable to Lady Aylesbury. She has not passed a whole day here these two years. She is always very gracious, says she will come when *you* will fix a time, as if *you* governed, and then puts it off whenever it is proposed, nor will spare one single day from Park Place—as if other people were not as partial to their own Park-Places! Adieu!

Yours ever

TUESDAY NOON

I wrote my letter last night; this morning I received yours, and shall wait till Sunday, as you bid me, which will be more convenient for my gout, though not for other engagements; but I shall obey the superior, as *nullum tempus occurrit regi et podagræ*.

TO THE SAME

STRAWBERRY HILL, JUNE 23, 1774

I HAVE nothing to say—which is the best reason in the world for writing; for one must have a great regard for anybody one writes to, when one begins a letter neither on ceremony nor business. You are seeing armies [in Germany], who are always in fine order and great spirits when they are in cold blood. I am sorry you thought it worth while to realize what I should have thought you could have seen in your mind's eye. However, I hope you will be amused and pleased with viewing heroes, both in their autumn and their bud. Vienna will be a new sight; so will the Austrian eagle and its two heads. I should like *seeing* too, if any fairy would present me with a chest that would fly up into the air by touching a peg, and transport me whither I pleased in an instant: but roads, and inns, and dirt are terrible drawbacks on my curiosity. I grow so old, or so indolent, that I scarce stir from hence; and the dread of the gout makes me almost as much a prisoner, as a fit of it. News I know none, if there is any. The papers tell me the city was to present a petition to the king against the Quebec-bill yesterday; and I suppose they will tell me to-morrow whether it was presented. The king's speech tells me there has nothing happened between the Russians and the Turks. Lady Barrymore told t'other day that nothing was to happen between her and Lord E. I am as well satisfied with these negatives, as I should have been with the contrary. I am much more interested about the rain, for it destroys all my roses and orange flowers, of which I have exuberance; and my hay is cut, and cannot be made. However, it is delightful to have no other distresses. When I compare my present tranquillity and indifference with all I suffered last year, I am thankful for my happiness, and enjoy it—unless the bell rings at the gate early in the morning—and then I tremble, and think it an express from Norfolk.

It is unfortunate, that when one has nothing to talk of but one's self, one should have nothing to say of one's self. It is shameful too to send such a scrap by the post. I think I shall reserve it till Tuesday. If I have then nothing to add, as is probable, you must content yourself with my good intentions, as I hope you will with this speculative campaign. Pray for the future remain at home and build bridges: I wish you were here to expedite ours to Richmond, which they tell me will not be passable these two years. I have done looking so forward.

Adieu!

ELIZABETH CARTER (1717–1806)

Miss Carter was the leading woman writer of the mid-eighteenth century. Poet, translator, and conversationalist, she was on friendly terms with all whose acquaintance was worth having in her time. She was friendly with Johnson for half a century, and the Doctor's opinion of her was so high that he observed "she ought to be celebrated in as many different languages as Louis le Grand." Her first letter, to Catherine Talbot, describes excitement at Deal in the days of the Young Pretender.

TO MISS TALBOT

CANTERBURY, DEC. 5, 1745

I MUST give you a little account, my dear Miss Talbot, of our great topic of conversation here, though possibly you know more about it than I do.

Two gentlemen and a messenger came in post chaises to Deal on Thursday; they went first on board the *Admiral*, and then all the other ships in the Downs, where the prisoners of note were dispersed. They returned on shore about eight at night, and in two hours despatched back the messenger to London. On Friday they went on board the *Admiral* again, in whose ship was Mr. Radcliffe and his pretended son. On Saturday they went to Dover Castle to look over the seamen of the *Soleil*, about forty in number. All this time a remarkable secrecy and mysteriousness were carried on. On Sunday arrived two horse guards and demanded billets for fourteen more just coming. Soon after came a coach and six with two gentlemen in it, and the messenger. An express came in Sunday night at nine, and immediately another was returned to fetch more guards, and fourteen more came on Monday. All this apparatus and affected reserve made our suspicions greatly increase, that young Radcliffe was the young Pretender. It blew hard yesterday, but boats at last went off, and with some hazard brought seven of the prisoners ashore: they were received by the soldiers under arms, and as it was past nine o'clock, it was agreed to keep them at Deal all night. The person suspected seems not above twenty years old, has fair hair, inclining to yellow, is fair and ruddy, short waisted, long chinned, six foot high, and appears dejected.

388

Thus far my account from Deal. The prisoners went through Canterbury this morning; I was in the room with them, and saw them very particularly. The young man who calls himself Mr. Radcliffe came first into the room, and looked with an air of authority upon the rest, and, without taking any notice of his pretended father, placed himself immediately by the fire; he looked extremely dejected, is fair, and has the look of a Polander; he is very tall, and looks extremely awkward and boyish in his make. His whole person was as unlike as it was possible to Mr. Radcliffe's. One of the other prisoners called himself Captain Macdonald, and has the most effronterie I ever saw in a countenance, and looks moreover as if he could eat up men, women, and children.

The mob made a great huzzaing for King George, but no insult was offered the prisoner. The Post is going out; I have been in a hurry all day with this uproar, so must finish, etc.

TO THE SAME

HILL STREET, AUGUST 9, 1769

THERE is something so seducing, dear Miss Talbot, in writing to you by the Penny-Post that I cannot resist it. Not that I think you would be under any great solicitude about my getting home quietly last night in spite of the bad character of the roads; for I reached London in such good time, that if I had been robbed I might have sued the county. Perhaps you will think it would have been worth while to have been robbed, for the satisfaction of suing the county of Middlesex.

I called at Mrs. A. Pitt's, she was not at home, and delivered Sir J. Yorke's Letter to Miss Finch, with the condition annexed, of her returning it herself.

I set out on my city expedition this morning, where I met with an adventure, which I believe you will think much more formidable than all the terrors of the Richmond road. I was to call on a person in my way, to accompany me to the South Sea House; and my nearest route was through Newgate. On going up Snow Hill I observed a pretty many people assembled, but did not much regard them, till, as I advanced, I found the crowd thicken, and by the time I was got into the midst of them I heard the dreadful toll of St. Sepulchre's bell, and found I was attending an execution. As I do not very well understand the geography of Newgate, I thought if I could push through the postern I should find the coast clear on the other side, but to my utter dismay I found myself in a still greater mob than before, and very little able to make my way

through them. Only think of me in the midst of such heat and suffoca-
tion, with the danger of having my arms broke, to say nothing of the
company by which I was surrounded, with near 100*l.* in my pocket. In
this exigency I applied to one of the crowd for assistance, and while he was
hesitating, another man, who saw my difficulty, very good-naturedly said
to me, "Come, madam, I will do my best to get you along." To this
volunteer in my service, who was tolerably creditable and clean, considering the corps to which he belonged, I most cordially gave my hand; and
without any swearing, or bawling, or bustle whatever, by mere gentle
persevering dexterity, he conducted me, I thank God, very safely
through. You will imagine that I expressed a sufficient degree of
gratitude to my conductor, which I did in the best language I could find;
a circumstance which is never thrown away upon the common people, as
you will acknowledge from the speech which he made me in return—
"That all he had done was due to my person, and all he could do was due
to my merit." This high strain of complimental oratory is really no
embellishment of my story; but literally what my hero said. What a
figure he would have made in the days of chivalry! In the midst of all
my perplexities, I could not help remarking a singular circumstance in the
discourse of the mob, in speaking of the unhappy criminal, that he was to
die to-day; and I scarcely once heard the expression of his being to be
hanged. To trace the cause of this delicacy, is a good problem for the
investigators of human nature.

As I thought this history of my city adventures would amuse Mrs.
Talbot and you, I ought to prevent any kind concern you might feel
from the apprehension of its having hurt me, which I do not think it has.
I was immoderately heated at first getting out of the crowd, but it soon
went off, and except being extremely tired, I am about as well as usual
to-night, though not equal to any more adventures. I hear but an
indifferent account of the poor young Duchess of Beaufort, the bruises
still continue very bad. The Lady Finches are inconsolable for their
father.

Mrs. Boscawen was the widow of the famous admiral and one of the four founders of the Bluestockings. Boswell said "her manners are the most agreeable, and her conversation the best of anybody with whom I ever had the happiness to be acquainted."

TO MRS. DELANY

GLAN VILLA, NOV. 9, 1773

IT is very true, my dear madam, I returned you scrap for your scrap, but I did by no means *pay in kind*, a most agreeable letter that preceded it, so that now I am in debt for two kind epistles; if I do not declare myself bankrupt it is because I will compound with you and send you empty covers instead of charming letters; but you are a gracious creditor, and will be content to take such as one can give. I will scrape together all the effects I can collect, and therefore tell you that I have sent Mrs. Chapone one of these same empty covers directed to you, with which poor coin I pay now, as she will fill it vastly well. I am at least the cause that you receive entertaining letters tho' I can write none myself.

And now, my dear madam, I will tell you a pleasant adventure I had last Friday, and which you will like. At the hour of breakfast, my kettle boiling upon the table, I took to feeding my robin-redbreast with almonds as you bid me, and very generously gave him his breakfast before I took my own; but at a second visit to him, behold—a tortoiseshell cat waiting with wicked leer to catch my sweet robin. I sallied out in a rage, arm'd with *a spud*, and cou'd have executed fearful vengeance if in that moment I had not heard my servant call, or rather scream out "Lady Gower." I left *cat*, and *bird*, and *spud* instantly, and *flew* to the other door, where I cou'd hardly discern her ladyship in her chaize for a fine tall *magnolia* which she had been so good to make her companion in it for my sake. I need not tell you how glad I was to see her, and that this honour was indeed a pleasure. She was glad to find the breakfast so ready that the tea was made and the chocolate arrived in a minute. She lik'd the brown bread, and eat very heartily, and chatted most agreeably. We sat long at our breakfast, and then went to the greenhouse with our magnolia, which was unpacked and treated after the direction of its noble mistress. She was pleased to bring also a basket full of carnations for Mrs. Leveson, from whom she had just received a letter that seemed to please her, so that after she had read parts of it to me she said, "I wish we had her here." Her ladyship approved my little guinguette exceedingly, but would have had me quit it now and go with her to Holkham, assuring me that Lady L. would like it mightily. I was much flattered by the invitation, but could not accept it for the same reason that withholds me from the honour and happiness of being now at Bulstrode. Lady Gower left me about one; I went with her as far as the turning off to Hampstead, whither she was bound on a visit to Lady Salisbury. I hope she got no cold by giving me this pleasure; at present she is on her way to Holkham. I hope there are no waters on the road, for *prodigious* rains have fallen since the day she was here, which luckily was a very fine one. I am exceedingly glad the *chicken* turtle [dove] arrived *at last*, I despaired and concluded it dead; what could they keep it for so long? in hopes 'twould be a *pullet*? I suppose it must have waited to recover its voyage. Poor Mrs. Walsingham has indeed had various pains of mind and body lately; I am glad she had such a holiday as I know her visit to Bulstrode must have given her. Adieu, my dearest madam.

GILBERT WHITE (1720–93)

Here are two charming letters from the delightful naturalist and chronicler of Selborne. Science may have disproved much of White's lore but what has it given us so dainty in its stead?

TO THE HONOURABLE DAINES BARRINGTON

12 APRIL, 1772

WHILE I was in Sussex last autumn my residence was at the village near Lewes from whence I had formerly the pleasure of writing to you. On the first of November I remarked that the old tortoise, formerly mentioned, began first to dig the ground in order to the forming its hybernaculum, which it had fixed on just beside a great tuft of hepaticas. It scrapes out the ground with its fore-feet, and throws it up over its back with its hind; but the motion of its legs is ridiculously slow, little exceeding the hour-hand of a clock; and suitable to the composure of an animal said to be a whole month in performing one feat of copulation. Nothing can be more assiduous than this creature night and day in scooping the earth, and forcing its great body into the cavity; but, as the noons of that season proved unusually warm and sunny, it was continually interrupted and called forth by the heat in the middle of the day; and though I continued there till the thirteenth of November, yet the work remained unfinished. Harsher weather, and frosty mornings would have quickened its operations. No part of its behaviour ever struck me more than the extreme timidity it always expresses with regard to rain; for though it has a shell that would secure it against the wheel of a loaded cart, yet does it discover as much solicitude about rain as a lady dressed in all her best attire, shuffling away on the first sprinklings, and running its head up in a corner. If attended to, it becomes an excellent weather-glass; for as sure as it walks elate, and as it were on tiptoe, feeding with great earnestness in a morning, so sure will it rain before night. It is totally a diurnal animal, and never pretends to stir after it becomes dark. The tortoise, like other reptiles, has an arbitrary stomach as well as lungs; and can refrain from eating as well as breathing for a great part of the year. When first awakened it eats nothing; nor again in the autumn before it retires:

through the height of the summer it feeds voraciously, devouring all the food that comes in its way.   I was much taken with its sagacity in discerning those that do it kind offices: for, as soon as the good old lady comes in sight who has waited on it for more than thirty years, it hobbles towards its benefactress with awkward alacrity; but remains inattentive to strangers.   Thus not only "the ox knoweth his owner, and the ass his master's crib," but the most abject reptile and torpid of beings distinguishes the hand that feeds it, and is touched with the feelings of gratitude!

P.S.—In about three days after I left Sussex the tortoise retired into the ground under the hepatica.

TO THE SAME

SELBOURNE, FEB. 26, 1774

THE sand-martin, or bank martin (*Hirundo riparia*, Linnæus), is by much the least of any of the British *hirundines*; and, as far as we have ever seen, the smallest known *hirundo*: though Brisson asserts that there is one much smaller, and that is the *hirundo esculenta*.

But it is much to be regretted that it is scarce possible for any observer to be so full and exact as he could wish in reciting the circumstances attending the life and conversation of this little bird, since it is *fera naturâ*, at least in this part of the kingdom, disclaiming all domestic attachments, and haunting wild heaths and commons where there are large lakes; while the other species, especially the swallow and house-martin, are remarkably gentle and domesticated, and never seem to think themselves safe but under the protection of man.

Here are in this parish, in the sand-pits and banks of the lakes of Wolmer Forest, several colonies of these birds; and yet they are never seen in the village; nor do they at all frequent the cottages that are scattered about in that wild district.   The only instance I ever remember where this species haunts any building is at the town of Bishop's Waltham, in this county, where many sand-martins nestle and breed in the scaffold holes of the back wall of William of Wykeham's stables: but then this wall stands in a very sequestered and retired enclosure, and faces upon a large and beautiful lake.   Indeed, this species seems so to delight in large waters that no instance occurs of their abounding but near vast pools or rivers: and in particular it has been remarked that they swarm in the banks of the Thames in some places below London Bridge.

It is curious to observe with what different degrees of architectonic skill Providence has endowed birds of the same genus, and so nearly correspondent in their general mode of life! For while the swallow and the house-martin discover the greatest address in raising and securely fixing crusts or shells of loam as *cunabula* for their young, the bank-martin terebrates a round and regular hole in the sand or earth, which is serpentine, horizontal, and about two feet deep. At the inner end of this burrow does this bird deposit, in a good degree of safety, her rude nest, consisting of fine grasses and feathers, usually goose-feathers, very inartificially laid together.

Perseverance will accomplish anything: though at first one would be disinclined to believe that this weak bird, with her soft and tender bill and claws, should ever be able to bore the stubborn sand-bank without entirely disabling herself; yet with these feeble instruments have I seen a pair of them make great dispatch: and could remark how much they had scooped that day by the fresh sand which ran down the bank, and was of a different colour from that which lay loose and bleached in the sun.

In what space of time these little artists are able to mine and finish these cavities I have never been able to discover, for reasons given above; but it would be a matter worthy of observation, where it falls in the way of any naturalist to make his remarks. This I have often taken notice of, that several holes of different depths are left unfinished at the end of summer. To imagine that these beginnings were intentionally made in order to be in the greater forwardness for next spring is allowing perhaps too much foresight and *rerum prudentia* to a simple bird. May not the cause of these *latebræ* being left unfinished arise from their meeting in those places with strata too harsh, and solid, for their purpose, which they relinquish, and go to a fresh spot that works more freely? Or may they not in other places fall in with a soil as much too loose and mouldering, liable to founder, and threatening to overwhelm them and their labours?

One thing is remarkable—that, after some years, the old holes are forsaken and new ones bored; perhaps because the old habitations grow foul and fetid from long use, or because they may so abound with fleas as to become untenable. This species of swallow, moreover, is strangely annoyed with fleas: and we have seen fleas, bed-fleas (*pulex irritans*), swarming at the mouths of these holes, like bees on the stools of their hives.

The following circumstance should by no means be omitted—that these birds do not make use of their caverns by way of hybernacula, as might be expected; since banks so perforated have been dug out with care in the winter, when nothing was found but empty nests.

The sand-martin arrives much about the same time with the swallow, and lays, as she does, from four to six white eggs. But as this species is *cryptogame*, carrying on the business of nidification, incubation, and the support of its young in the dark, it would not be so easy to ascertain the time of breeding were it not for the coming forth of the broods, which appear much about the time, or rather somewhat earlier than those of the swallow. The nestlings are supported in common like those of their congeners, with gnats and other small insects; and sometimes they are fed with *libellulæ* (dragon-flies) almost as long as themselves. In the last week in June we have seen a row of these sitting on a rail near a great pool as perchers; and so young and helpless, as easily to be taken by hand: but whether the dams ever feed them on the wing, as swallows and house-martins do, we have never yet been able to determine; nor do we know whether they pursue and attack birds of prey.

When they happen to breed near hedges and enclosures, they are frequently dispossessed of their breeding holes by the house sparrow, which is, on the same account, a fell adversary to house-martins.

These *hirundines* are no songsters, but rather mute, making only a little harsh noise when a person approaches their nests. They seem not to be of a sociable turn, never with us congregating with their congeners in the autumn. Undoubtedly they breed a second time, like the house-martin and swallow; and withdraw about Michaelmas.

Though in some particular districts they may happen to abound, yet on the whole, in the south of England at least, is this much the rarest species. For there are few towns or large villages but what abound with house-martins; few churches, towers, or steeples, but what are haunted by some swifts; scarce a hamlet or single cottage-chimney that has not its swallow; while the bank-martins, scattered here and there, live a seques-tered life among some abrupt sand-hills, and in the precipitous banks of some few rivers.

These birds have a peculiar manner of flying; flitting about with odd jerks, and vacillations, not unlike the motions of a butterfly. Doubtless the flight of all *hirundines* is influenced by, and adapted to, the peculiar sort of insects which furnish their food. Hence it would be worth inquiry to examine what particular genus of insects affords the principal food of each respective species of swallow.

Notwithstanding what has been advanced above, some few sand-martins, I see, haunt the skirts of London, frequenting the dirty pools in Saint George's Fields, and about Whitechapel. The question is where these build, since there are no banks or bold shores in that neighbourhood: perhaps they nestle in the scaffold holes of some old or new deserted building. They dip and wash and they fly sometimes, like the house-martin and swallow.

Sand-martins differ from their congeners in the diminutiveness of their size, and in their colour, which is what is usually called a mouse-colour. Near Valencia in Spain, they are taken, says Willughby, and sold in the market for the table; and are called by the country people, probably from their desultory jerking manner of flight, *Papilion de Montagna*.

ELIZABETH MONTAGU (1720–1800)

Mrs. Montagu was one of the choice spirits of the world of Walpole. The wife of a wealthy man, she entertained lavishly if somewhat ostentatiously. Doctor Johnson remarked that "her constant stream of conversation always impregnated, always had meaning . . . Sir," he added, "that lady exerts more mind *in conversation than any person I have ever met."*

TO THE DUCHESS OF PORTLAND

TUNBRIDGE, 1745

DEAR MADAM, I hope your Grace is sensible I should write oftener if it was consistent with drinking these waters; but really it is very inconvenient to apply a head to any business that cannot think without aching; I am not singular in this, for many people affirm thinking to be a pain at all times; I have more discretion than to declare as much any where but at Tunbridge. I have been in the vapours these two days, on account of Dr. Young's leaving us; he was so good as to let me have his company very often, and we used to ride, walk, and take sweet counsel together; a few days before he went away he carried Mrs. Rolt (of Hertfordshire) and myself, to Tunbridge, five miles from hence, where we were to see some fine old ruins; but the manner of the journey was admirable, nor did I, at the end of it, admire the object we went to observe more than the means by which we saw it; and to give your Grace a description of the place, without an account of our journey to it, would be contradicting all form and order, and setting myself up as a critic upon all writers of travels.   Much

> Might be said of our passing worth,
> And manner how we sallied forth;

but I shall, as briefly as possible, describe our progress, without dwelling on particular circumstances; and shall divest myself of all pomp of language, and proceed in as humble a style as my great subject will admit:—First rode the Doctor on a tall steed, decently caparisoned in dark grey; next ambled Mrs. Rolt, on a hackney horse, lean as the famed Rozinante, but in shape much resembling Sancho's ass; then followed your humble servant on a milk-white palfrey, whose reverence for the human kind induced him to be governed by a creature not half as strong, and, I fear, scarce twice as wise as himself. By this enthusiasm of his, rather than my own skill, I rode on in safety, and at leisure, to observe the company; especially the two figures that brought up the rear. The first was my servant, valiantly armed with two uncharged pistols; whose holsters were covered with two civil harmless monsters that signified the valour and courtesy of our ancestors. The last was the Doctor's man, whose uncombed hair so resembled the mane of the horse he rode, one could not help imagining they were of kin, and wishing that for the honour of the family they had had one comb betwixt them; on his head was a velvet cap, much resembling a black saucepan, and on his side hung a little basket. Thus did we ride, or rather jog on, to Tunbridge town, which is five miles from the Wells. To tell you how the dogs barked at us, the children squalled, and the men and women stared, would take up too much time; let it suffice, that not even a tame magpie, or caged starling, let us pass unnoted. At last we arrived at the King's-head, where the loyalty of the Doctor induced him to alight, and then, knight-errant like, he took his damsels from off their palfreys, and courteously handed us into the inn. We took this progress to see the ruins of an old castle; but first our divine would visit the churchyard, where we read that folks were born and died, the natural, moral, and physical history of mankind. In the churchyard grazed the parson's steed, whose back was worn bare with carrying a pillion-seat for the comely, fat personage, this ecclesiastic's wife; and though the creature ate daily part of the parish, he was most miserably lean. Tired of the dead and living bones, Mrs. Rolt and I jumped over a stile, into the parson's field, and from thence, allured by the sight of golden pippins, we made an attempt to break into the holy man's orchard. He came most courteously to us, and invited us to his apple trees; to shew our moderation, we each of us gathered two mellon codlings, one of which I put into my pocket, from whence it sent forth a smell that I uncharitably supposed to proceed from the Doctor's servant, as he waited behind me at dinner. The good parson offered to shew us the inside of his church, but made some apology for his undress, which was a true canonical dishabille. He had on a grey striped calamanco nightgown, a wig that once was white, but, by the influence of an uncertain climate, turned to a pale orange, a brown hat, encompassed by a black hatband, a band, somewhat dirty, that decently retired under the shadow of his chin, a pair of grey stockings, well mended with blue worsted, strong symptom of the conjugal care and affection of his wife, who had mended his hose with the very worsted she bought for her own; what an instance of exalted friendship, and how uncommon in a degenerate age.

"How rare meet now such pairs in love and honour join'd!"

When we had seen the church the parson invited us to take some refreshment at his house, but Dr. Young thought we had before enough trespassed on the good man's time, so desired to be excused, else we should, no doubt, have been welcomed to the house by Madam, in her muslin pinners, and sarsenet hood; who would have given us some mead, and a piece of a cake, that she had made in the Whitsun holidays to treat her cousins. However, Dr. Young, who would not be out-done in good offices, invited the divine to our inn, where we went to dinner; but he excused himself, and came after the meal was over, in hopes of smoking a pipe; but our Doctor hinted to him that it would not be proper to offer any incense, but sweet praise, to such goddesses as Mrs. Rolt and your humble servant. To say the truth, I saw a large horn tobacco box, with Queen Anne's head upon it, peeping out of his pocket, but I did not care to take the hint, and desire him to put in use that magnificent piece of furniture. After dinner we walked to the old castle, which was built by Richard de Clare, Earl of Gloucester, in William Rufus's days. It has been a most magnificent building; the situation is extremely beautiful; the castle made a kind of half moon down to the river; and where the river does not defend it, it has been guarded by a large moat. It is now in the hands of a country squire, who is no common sort of man; but having said so much of the parson, I will let the rest of the parish depart in peace, though I cannot help feeling the utmost resentment at him for cutting down some fine trees almost contemporary with the castle, which he did to make room for a plantation of sour grapes. The towers at the great gate are covered with fine venerable ivy.

It was late in the evening before we got home, but the silver Cynthia held up her lamp in the heavens, and cast such a light on the earth as shewed its beauties in a soft and gentle light. The night silenced all but our divine Doctor, who sometimes uttered things fit to be spoken in a season when all nature seems to be hushed and hearkening. I followed, gathering wisdom as I went, till I found, by my horse's stumbling, that I was in a bad road, and that the blind was leading the blind; so I placed my servant between the Doctor and myself, which he not perceiving, went on in a most philosophical strain to the great amazement of my poor clown of a servant, who not being wrought up to any pitch of enthusiasm, nor making any answer to all the fine things he heard, the Doctor wondering I was dumb, and grieving I was so stupid, looked round, declared his surprise, and desired the man to trot on before; and thus did we return to Tunbridge Wells. I can give your Grace great comfort in telling you Dr. Young will be with you in a week's time. The Duchess of Manchester is very high in my esteem; she has most generous qualities, delicate sentiments, and an expression that does honour to them. I am, Madam,

Your Grace's most affectionate, and obedient,

E. Montagu

TOBIAS SMOLLETT (1721–71)

It was through Smollett's good offices that Doctor Johnson was able to rescue his black servant from the Navy. Smollett knew Wilkes, a man whom the Doctor at that time abominated, and, as will be seen from this letter, used his influence to good effect.

TO JOHN WILKES

CHELSEA, MARCH 16, 1759

DEAR SIR, I am again your petitioner in behalf of that CHAM of Literature, Samuel Johnson. His black servant, Francis Barber, has been pressed on board the *Star* frigate, Captain Angel; and our lexicographer is in distress. He says the boy is a sickly lad, of a delicate frame, and particularly subject to a malady in his throat, which renders him very unfit for His Majesty's service. You know what matter of animosity the said Johnson has against you; and I daresay you will desire no other opportunity of resenting it, than that of laying him under an obligation. He was humble enough to desire my assistance on this occasion, though he and I were never cater-cousins; and I gave him to understand that I would make application to my friend Wilkes, who, perhaps, by his interest with Mr. Hay and Mr. Elliot, might be able to procure the discharge of his lacquey. It would be superfluous to say more on the subject which I leave to your own consideration; but I cannot let slip this opportunity of declaring that I am, with the most inviolable esteem and attachment, dear sir, your affectionate, obliged, humble servant,

T. SMOLLETT

HESTER CHAPONE (1727–1801)

Miss Mulso, or Mrs. Chapone as she became on her marriage, was undoubtedly the bluest of the Bluestockings. She wrote "Letters on the Improvement of the Mind" which Mrs. Delany considered "next to the Bible." In her epistle to a new-married lady there is quite a deal of sound wholesome advice, though how palatable to modern tastes is a more debateable point.

TO A NEW-MARRIED LADY

INDEED, my dear young friend, you have highly obliged me by such a distinguishing mark of friendship and consideration as that of finding time, on the most important day of your life, to inform me with your own hand of your marriage: an event most interesting to me, who wish your happiness with the sincerest ardour. You tell me you expect from me, not a letter of formal congratulation, but of serious and friendly advice on the new situations and duties in which you are going to be engaged. You wish I could be always with you to watch and direct your conduct, and seem full of that salutary fear and distrust of your own prudence which is the best security for youth and inexperience. Whilst you retain this, I may venture to answer for you, that you will not materially deviate from the paths of duty and happiness.

I am glad you are still to remain a few weeks under the parental roof, which has hitherto sheltered you from every evil, and where you have seen examples only of good; but, from this scene of regularity and quiet cheerfulness you will soon go to London, to become mistress of yourself and of a family, and to plunge at once into the hurry and bustle of a world to which you are almost a stranger. Thither will my anxious good wishes attend you; for, on the manner of your first setting out depends more than you can possibly imagine.

I know you have not been brought up in modish principles, and that you do not at present consider marriage as a title to unbounded liberty and perpetual dissipation, instead of a solemn engagement to subjection and obedience, to family cares and serious employments.

403

You will probably, indeed, meet with people who will endeavour to laugh you out of all such regards, and who will find something very ludicrous in the idea of authority in a husband. But, whatever your opinions may be on this head, it is certain that a man of Mr. B's generosity would be much mortified and distressed to find himself obliged to exert his authority in restraining your pleasures, particularly on his first setting out with you on the journey of life. He knows he would be universally condemned, as either jealous or covetous, should he interfere to stem the torrent of dissipation into which it will be the business of most of your acquaintance to see you fairly plunged; for well they know that when once you are drawn into the whirlpool, more than female strength is required to get out of it again. Curiosity and vanity will join their temptations. You have a new face and new finery to show, new flattery to hear, and every fine place about town to see and to be seen in.

Alas! poor Mr. B! What chance have you for a moment's attention! And what a sudden end is here of all that dear domestic happiness to which you both looked forward with rapture a few weeks ago! You have nothing for it but to engage as deeply in the same course, and leave to whining swains in the country all ideas of that union of heart, that sweet intercourse of tenderness and friendship of which "soft souls in love" are apt to dream, when they think of living with the object of their wishes.

Mr. B chose you from affection only: the superiority of his fortune, and the large field of choice which that fortune, joined with his amiable person and character, secured to him, precludes the possibility of any other motive. I—who know the disinterestedness of your nature, and the perfect freedom of rejection which your parents have always allowed you—have not the least doubt that your preference of him was the genuine effect of a real attachment, without any bias from his riches. Youth is naturally disinterested, and your heart is hitherto uncorrupted. But, my dear, the mode of living in this too civilized part of the world leaves scarce a single trace of nature, and even youth now grows a stranger to tenderness and truth, and pursues wealth (as the means of gratifying vanity) with all the rapacity of an old usurer. It is necessary, therefore, that you should prove to your husband the sincerity of your attachment, which he may justly doubt if he sees that your happiness arises from the enjoyment of his fortune rather than of him. By a reserved and moderate use of his indulgence, by always preferring his company and that of his particular friends to public diversions and assemblies, by studying his taste rather than your own, and making the gratification of it your highest pleasure, you must convince him that your heart is his own; a truth which should always appear in the general tenour of your conduct rather than in professions or in that officious parade of affection which designing women often substitute in the place of every genuine mark of tenderness and consideration. Dean Swift, in his coarse way, says very sensible things on the subject, which, however, may safely be left to your own natural delicacy: *l'amour, de sa nature, aime le secret*, and a person of sensibility is always averse to showing any passion or affection before those whose sympathy is not interested in it. An amiable author, of much more delicacy than the Dean, goes so far as to advise his daughters never to show the extent of their love, even to their husbands; a precept which does no honour to his own sex, and which would take from ours its sweetest charms, simplicity and artless tenderness. A haughty and imperious woman, who desired an undue power over her husband, would indeed do wisely to keep him always in suspense, and conceal from him an affection which must increase his power and diminish her own; but a gentle and truly feminine nature has no such desires, and consequently needs no such arts. A modest heart may trust its genuine feelings with a husband who has generosity and delicacy, and who, like yours, is untainted with that base opinion of women which a commerce with the worst of the sex always inspires.

Swift, (and almost every male writer on the subject), pronounces that the passion of love in men is infallibly destroyed by possession, and can subsist but a short time after marriage. What a dreadful sentence must this appear to you at this time! Your heart, which feels its own affection increased, knows not how to support the idea of such a change in the beloved object: but, my dear friend, the God of Nature, who provided the passion of love as the incitement to marriage, has also provided resources for the happiness of this his own institution, which kind and uncorrupted natures will not fail to find. It is not, indeed, intended that we should pass our lives in the delirium of passion, but whilst this subsides, the habit of affection grows strong. The tumult and anxiety of desire must of course be at an end when the object is secure; but a milder and more serene happiness succeeds, which in good hearts creates a tenderness that is often wanting amidst the fervours of violent passion. Before this palls, your business is to build the solid foundation of a durable friendship. This will best be done whilst the partiality of fondness places all your excellencies in the fairest point of view, and draws a veil over your defects. This season you should take care to prolong as far as is possible, that habit and esteem may have time to take deep root: to this end you must avoid every thing that can create a moment's disgust towards either your person or your mind. Keep the infirmities of both out of the observation of your husband more scrupulously than of any other man; and never let your idea in his imagination be accompanied with circumstances unpleasant or disgraceful. A mistress of a family cannot always be adorned with smiles. It will sometimes be incumbent on you to find faults, and human nature may sometimes fail of doing this with proper temper and dignity; therefore let it never be done in the presence of your husband. Do not disturb him with the detail of your grievances from servants or tradespeople, nor with your methods of family management. But above all, let nothing of this kind embitter his meals when you happen to be *tête-à-tête* at table. In mixing with the world and its affairs he will often meet with such things as cannot fail to hurt a mind like his, and which may sometimes affect his temper. But when he returns to his own house, let him there find everything serene and peaceful, and let your cheerful complacency restore his good humour and quiet every uneasy passion.

Endeavour to enter into his pursuits, catch his taste, improve by his knowledge; nor let anything that is interesting to him appear a matter of indifference to you. Thus will you make yourself delightful to him as a companion and friend, in whom he may be always sure to find that sympathy which is the grand cement of friendship. But if you affect to speak of his pursuits as beyond your capacity or foreign to your taste, you can be no longer pleasing to him in that light, and must rely merely on your personal attractions, of which, alas, time and familiarity must every day impair the value. When you are in the country, perhaps you may sometimes find hours, and even days, for each other's society, without any other company; in this case, conversation will hardly supply sufficient entertainment; and, next to displeasing or disgusting him, you should of all things dread his growing dull and weary in your company. If you can prevail upon him to read with you, to practise music with you, or to teach you a language or a science, you will then find amusement for every hour; and nothing is more endearing than such communications. The improvements and accomplishments you gain from him will be doubly valuable in his esteem; and certainly you can never acquire them so agreeably as from his lips.

And though you should not naturally be disposed to the same taste in reading or amusement, this may be acquired by habit, and by a hearty desire of conforming to his inclinations and sharing in his pleasures. With such a master you will find your understanding enlarge, and your taste refine to a degree far beyond your expectations; and the sweet reward of his praise will inspire you with such spirit and diligence as will easily surmount any natural inaptitude.

Your behaviour to his particular friends and near relations will have the most important effects on your mutual happiness. If you do not adopt his sentiments with regard to these, your union must be very incomplete, and a thousand disagreeable circumstances will continually arise from it. I am told that he is an excellent son to a mother, who, with many good qualities, has defects of temper which determined him to decline her continuing to live with him after his marriage. In this he is equally kind and prudent; for though he could himself meritoriously bear with failings to which he had been accustomed from his infancy, in a parent who doats upon him, yet this would have been too hard a task upon you, who have not an equal affection to support your duty, and to whom her ways would have been new and unusual. But though I thus far highly approve his consideration for you, yet you must remember how great a part of her happiness she is thus deprived of on your account, and make her all the amends in your power by your own attentions, as well as by promoting opportunities of indulging her in the company of her son. It would be a grievous charge on your conscience if, through your means, he should become less observant of her, or diminish aught of that duty and affection which has hitherto so amiably distinguished him. Be careful, therefore, that no dispute may ever happen between this lady and yourself, no complaint from either of you disturb his peace, to whom it would be so painful and unnatural to take part against either. Be armed against the sallies of her temper, and predetermined never to quarrel with her, whatever she may say or do. In such a relationship, this conduct would not be meanness but merit; nor would it imply any unworthy compliance or false assent; since silence and good-humoured steadiness may always preserve sincerity in your conversation, and proper freedom in your conduct. If she should desire to control your actions, or to intermeddle in the affairs of your family more than you think is reasonable, hear her advice with patience, and answer with respect, but in a manner that may let her see you mean to judge of your own duties for yourself. "I will consider of what you are so good to observe to me. I will endeavour to rectify whatever is amiss," or some such general answer, will probably for the time put a stop to her attempts of this kind.

Great care must be taken to proportion at least your outward regards with equity and good breeding between your husband's relations and your own. It would be happy if your feelings could be almost the same to both: but whether they are so or not, you are bound by duty and prudence to cultivate as much as possible the goodwill and friendship of the family into which you are now adopted, without prejudice to that affection and gratitude in which I am sure you can never be wanting towards your own.

If it is an important duty to avoid all dissentions and disobligations with those who are nearly connected with your husband, of how much greater consequence is it to avoid all occasions of resentment between yourselves? Whatever may be said of the quarrels of lovers, believe me those of married people have always dreadful consequences, especially if they are not very short and very slight. If they are suffered to produce bitter or contemptuous expressions, or betray an habitual dislike in one party of anything in the person or mind of the other, such wounds can scarcely ever be thoroughly healed: and though regard to principle and character lays the married couple under a necessity to make up the breach as well as they can, yet is their affiance in each other's affection so rudely shaken in such conflicts that it can hardly ever be perfectly fixed again. The painful recollection of what is past will often intrude upon the tenderest hours, and every trifle will awaken and renew it. You must even now be particularly on your guard against this source of misery. A new-married pair, from their very excess of fondness, sometimes give way to little jealousies and childish quarrels, which at first, perhaps, quickly end in the renewal and increase of tenderness, but, if often repeated, they lose these agreeable effects and soon produce others of a contrary nature. The dispute grows every time more serious—jealousies and distrusts take deeper root—the temper is hurt on both sides—habits of sourness, thwarting, and mutual misconstruction prevail, and soon overpower all that tenderness which originally gave them birth. Keep it, then, constantly in mind, that the happiness of marriage depends entirely upon a solid and permanent friendship, to which nothing is more opposite than jealousy and distrust. Nor are they less at variance with the true interests of passion. You can never be a gainer by taxing your husband's affection beyond its natural strength; the fear of alarming your jealousy, and bringing on a quarrel, may force him to feign a greater fondness than he feels; but this very effort and constraint will, in fact, diminish, and by degrees extinguish that fondness. If, therefore, he should appear less tender or attentive than you wish, you must either awaken his passion by displaying some new grace—some winning charm of sweetness and sensibility, or else conform (at least in appearance) to that rate of tenderness which his example prescribes; for it is your part rather modestly to follow as he leads, than make him feel the uneasiness of not being able to keep pace with you. At least one may pronounce that there is nothing less likely to increase affection than ill-humour and captiousness. The truth is, that pride rather than tenderness usually occasions the unreasonable expectations of an exceptious person, and it is rewarded as it deserves, with mortifications, and the cold dislike of those who suffer from it.

I am unwilling to sadden your present halcyon days, and the fair prospect of happiness before you, by supposing the possibility of any proper cause of jealousy—any real unkindness or infidelity on the part of Mr. B. As far as the human character can be known and relied on, you have reason to think yourself secure from this heaviest of calamities; and nothing but irresistible proof, unsought for, and obtruded upon your senses, should ever shake your confidence and esteem. If this were to happen—if my dear tender friend should be doomed to the heart-breaking trial of seeing those looks of love changed into

> —hard Unkindness altered eye,
> That mocks the tear it forc'd to flow:
>
> *Gray.*

What must then be your resource? Not rage and exclamation—not sullenness and pride—not an appeal to the world, which would laugh at your complaints—nor even to your friends, who cannot help you, unless by a separation, which would publish and complete your misfortune! The comforts and helps of religion, with a firm resolution not to be driven out of the path of duty, can alone support you under such a sorrow. The only hope of removing the cause of it must be derived from time and future contingencies, which you will watch for and improve. Sickness or disappointment may give him opportunity for reflection, and for observing the merit of that silent patience, the dignity of that uniform adherence to your duty, which must force his esteem, and may at length regain his heart. If not, yours will of course be cured of the exquisite pain of unrequited love, which cannot very long subsist in a mind of any dignity or strength. If you have children, they will supply the "aching void" with a passion not less lively than that which you will have subdued; for their sakes life will still be valuable to you, and entertained with cheerfulness. But let me hasten from a subject so unsuitable to your present situation, and to your most reasonable hopes.

I cannot but flatter myself that ladies are mightily improved since the time when Dean Swift (writing on the same occasion that I do now) exhorts his fair pupil to make no friendships with any of her own sex. This is, in effect, forbidding her to make any friendships at all; for the world, with very good reason, tolerates no male friends at your age, excepting your nearest relations. The rules of decorum, in such points, are founded on a knowledge of human nature, which young women cannot have attained and are therefore apt to despise such rules as founded on base ideas of the nature of friendship, or of the hearts that entertain it. But one would have supposed that the Dean had lived long enough in the world, and thought ill enough of mankind, to have been convinced of the impropriety of a young lady's making her strictest intimacies and confidential attachments with persons of the other sex. But, setting aside the danger to her reputation, and even to her morals, surely a woman who despised her own sex, and would converse with none but men, would be not less ridiculous than a man who should pass his whole time among women. Like the monkey in the fable, she would stand a chance of being rejected and disowned by both species. The reasons the Dean gives for this preposterous advice, if ever founded on truth, are certainly so no longer. You may find advantages in the conversation of many ladies, if not equal to those which men are qualified to give, yet equal at least to what you, as a female, are capable of receiving. Yet in one point the Dean and I agree; in recommending your husband to be your first and dearest friend, and his judgment to be consulted in the choice of every new one you may hereafter make. Those you already possess are, I believe, secure of some portion of his esteem, and he is too much interested in your constancy and fidelity of heart, to wish you to be fickle towards them. I shall therefore depend on his full consent to my having always the pleasure of styling myself

Your faithful

And affectionate friend,

H. CHAPONE

OLIVER GOLDSMITH (1728–74)

There are few better examples of the precariousness of a literary life than can be found in the career of poor Noll Goldsmith. A literary hack of the first order nothing came amiss to his pen; alas, that he should have had to indite such letters as the following.

TO MR. GRIFFITH

Sir, I know of no misery but a jail to which my own imprudence and your letter seems to point. I have seen it inevitable these three or four weeks, and, by heavens! request it as a favour,—as a favour that may prevent something more fatal. I have been some years struggling with a wretched being—with all that contempt that indigence brings with it—with all those passions which make contempt insupportable. What, then, has a jail that is formidable? I shall at least have the society of wretches, and such is to me true society. I tell you, again and again, that I am neither able nor willing to pay you a farthing, but I will be punctual to any appointment you or the jailor shall make; thus far, at least, I do not act the sharper, since, unable to pay my own debts one way, I would generally give some security another. No, sir, had I been sharper—had I been possessed of less good nature and native generosity, I might surely now have been in better circumstances.

I am guilty, I own, of meannesses which poverty unavoidably brings with it; my reflections are filled with repentance for my imprudence, but not with any remorse for being a villain; that may be a character you unjustly charge me with. Your books, I can assure you, are neither pawned nor sold, but in the custody of a friend from whom my necessities obliged me to borrow some money. Whatever becomes of my person, you shall have them in a month. It is very possible both the reports you have heard and your own suggestions may have brought you false information with respect to my character; it is very possible that the man whom you now regard with detestation may inwardly burn with grateful resentment.

It is very possible that, upon a second perusal of the letter I sent you, you may see the workings of a mind strongly agitated with grati-

411

tude and jealousy. If such circumstances should appear, at least spare invective till my book with Mr. Dodsley shall be published, and then, perhaps, you may see the bright side of a mind, when my professions shall not appear the dictates of necessity, but of choice.

You seem to think Dr. Milner knew me not. Perhaps so; but he was a man I shall ever honour; but I have friendship only with the dead! I ask pardon for taking up so much time; nor shall I add to it by any other professions than that I am, sir, your humble servant,

OLIVER GOLDSMITH

P.S. I shall expect impatiently the result of your resolutions.

LADY JANET GORDON (c. 1728–58)

> Lady Gordon, daughter of the 1st Earl of Fife, married Sir William Gordon, a Jacobite who was forced into hiding after Culloden. He took her abroad and for some years they lived at Douai, where he died a year after this letter was written. In spite of the tender state of her health Lady Janet survived her husband, returned with her three children to Scotland, and there married another Jacobite, George Hay, by whom she had several more children before she died at the age of 30.

TO LADY BRACO

DOUAI. MAY 19, 1750

MY DEAR MADAM, As I have the opportunity of Mr. Smith going to Scotland, I can't deny myself the happiness of writing your ladyship and to assure your Ladyship of the satisfaction it gives me to hear you and all your families being well; which I have the pleasure to hear pretty often as there are always people coming to this from Britain, which I think is a great advantage to this place our hearing often of our friends. We would live pretty reasonable here if it were not for some English families that have come here to settle. I don't mean merchants, but people of condition, some upon account of their health and others for reasons they choose to keep to themselves. There is only some of them that I choose to be acquainted with, but not to be intimate with either of them for it's not for company that we stay here, it's to live as cheap and private as possible. And even if I could afford it, I have no inclination, for the tender state of health I'm in, the only divertion I take is any day that I'm able to go out, which is not many, to go a little airing in the chaise as Mr. Johnston [1] is obliged to keep a chaise and horse upon the account of his travelling sometimes upon his business and it's cheaper than hiring horses. He leaves me tomorrow and is obliged to stay there till the 1st of November with his business. I would gladly hope he will get back for a few days when I am brought to bed, as at that time you may be sure it will be a great comfort to me his being in the same place, whatever be my

[1] This name was used by Sir William Gordon for purposes of concealment.

fate. Considering the tender state I am in it is no great surprise if the worst should happen me at such a time; but as I came through last in the same tender state of health, it ought to encourage me now. We was a good deal alarmed with a fever that they say was raging in Aberdeenshire; it gives me pleasure to hear no more of it. I was afraid it would come to Banffshire. I'll assure you, my dear Madam, that my thoughts are oftenest there and many an anxious wish have I for all your health and happiness. I think oftener on my friends than I ought to do, as it can be of no use to them and only serves to disturb my mind and can never bring me nearer them. Tho' Mr. Johnston is as often with me as formerly, yet it's impossible for me, when I think of being absent from all the friends I have, but it must make a very deep impression on me. I'll assure your ladyship all the other unconveniences I have is not near so hard upon me as being banished from you, and all my dearest friends, and to think I have parents but must be denied the blessing of seeing them—for even to have the happiness to be in the same country with you, it's impossible that it ever can happen. Everybody else has a chance, but we have none ever to be so happy. You may be sure the same thought is hard upon my friend and gives him more uneasiness than he cares to show. For my part, I never speak to him on the subject, as my sorrow and grief is more touching to him than his own, for my melancholy may be easily read in my face. You never saw such a change upon a person as there is on me every day, and I am afraid instead of time making it more easy, to people in our way it will rather make it the worse. I am afraid the *Maladie du Pays* will kill the most of us in spite of all the spirits the best of us have. The only happiness we can have is to hear sometimes from our friends. I beg, my dear Madam, if you will make me happy to let me have but a line from you now and then to keep up my spirits.

. . . .

I return your ladyship thanks for the dried fish, they came very soft here and are very good. I wrote my sister to see if possible there could be a cook-maid sent me to dress our meat and help wash our linen. The manservant I got over is learning to market for me and seems to be very honest. I want to keep no servant in a better way than a cook-maid. For a gentlewoman, I am not such a fool as to set up on that footing and I have been at a great loss with a drunken creature I have had some time by past.

My dear Madam, adieu
JANET JOHNSTON

A. WALLIS (fl. 1777)

In his collection of letters Garrick endorses the following epistle: "Wallis's letter from Wales—excellent." Who Wallis was it is difficult now to say, but the letter reveals a man with considerable powers of observation.

TO MR. GARRICK

ROBSTON HALL, AUG. 22ND, 1777

DEAR SIR,—(mind that,)

You have heard from the *niece* how we journeyed from the Adelphi to Bath, and of the dangers she escaped from thunder, lightning, rain, and spirits (of brandy) between Bath and Bristol, after her elopement from her fellow-traveller. Now you will expect to hear of the dangers I have passed, and the hair-breadth escapes in the dreadful Welsh precipices; how I have been taken by the friendly foe, and imprisoned whole days and nights, fed upon nothing but fish, venison, claret, and Welsh ale, in the finest country in the world. All these to hear will make your mouth water. Wales, for variety and beauty of scenery, plenty, and conveniency, exceeds every place which has come within my ken. From my leaving Bristol, to this place, I was scarce ever more than five miles distant from the sea, and never half-an-hour out of its sight, which, with mountains, rocks, rivers, cataracts, castles, valleys, &c., &c., form the most delightful of countries.

I am now in Milford Haven, at a good inn, after the manner of that at Hampton; my landlord keeps a yacht for the amusement of his guests. He took me a cruise into a thousand creeks; we hailed as many vessels, and took twice that number of prisoners, such as john dories, mullets, bretts, &c., which, according to the ancient laws and customs of Wales, we ate alive; and conformable to more modern customs, introduced from England, drink our claret, ate our pines, grapes, cherries, &c., all of the captain's own manufacture; and in the evening returned to our inn, where I am again a close prisoner, unable to pay my ransom, or to make my escape. I wish you and *Pen.* and my fair niece, would come to my relief, or you will lose my custom at Hampton.

This country affords remedies for all complaints, as you will see by

415

the enclosed, which my landlord sends you with his compliments, and an offer of his inn for your accommodation.   He is a very civil, obliging man; keeps a good larder; has laid in a large stock of the best wines, which he perfectly understands the management of, tastes them all himself; pays the utmost attention to his guests, whether they drink wine, sea-water or ——, as I have experienced.   In short, he is very clever in his way, having been long in business, and can only be excelled by the politeness of my two landladies, who, to their perfect knowledge in the management of the public business of the inn, add the benevolence of administering health to their neighbours; but have by that means introduced a most barbarous custom into the country, of not giving burial to the dead, under 100 years of age, for which reason the people never begin to be sick till 99.   The consequence is, the ladies are worshipped as divinities, the churchyard lies fallow, and the sexton is ruined, and must either dig a grave for himself, or lie above-ground.   His place, not like the places at St. James's, is not even solicited for; nor will anyone accept it, unless the parson take it as a sinecure, and then he must take the burial fees at the time of baptism, or he too will be ruined.

I have seen Newton, which commands the finest view in the Haven. But this is not the Newton whose landlord you are acquainted with, and which everyone says is not to be equalled.

The landlord of that Newton and this inn give each other a character; they drive to each other's houses, which are both pretty decent Welsh inns, make very reasonable bills, and have met with great encouragement from, and are well known to, the noblemen and gentlemen travelling this road.   They hope for your custom as you pass this way, having already secured that of your friend,

A. WALLIS

MRS. J. H. PYE (*fl.* 1777)

*This lady appears to have been a rather sprightly young person,
though fame knows her not except as a correspondent of Garrick.*

TO MR. GARRICK

HOTEL DE MALTHE, RUE ST. NICAISE, PARIS.

APRIL 15TH, 1777

I CANNOT let the post go out, my much honoured and worthy friend,
without a full vindication of myself in respect to those high crimes and
misdemeanours which in your long-wished-for favour I stood charged
with. I say, crimes, because in my opinion (and in yours, I am sure)
neglect and lukewarmness, whether in love or friendship, are most
unpardonable ones. Upon my honour then, and as I am a *gentlewoman*
and a *soldier's wife*, I have not seen your handwriting since Mrs. Beliard
left Paris; and what is more, in her very last letter, which I received four
days before yours, she makes heavy complaints that she never has been
able to get a sight of you. How may these things be? Why, I will tell
you: I do imagine that you made some mistake in the direction of your
letter, by which means it never reached me, and Mrs. Beliard's duncial
servants never told her that you had done her the favour of calling on her.

As to Mrs. Garrick; she may perhaps find it difficult to pay her debts
to me, for she owes me the return of such sincere sentiments of esteem and
affection as I cannot in reason expect from her, till I merit them as well as
she does. However, pray tell her that I will undertake no more commissions for her,—I do insist upon her coming and doing them herself.
Why should you delay? You will never be less persecuted by officious
friendship and admiration in England, were you to stay there for a
century: then e'en take post, and leave the gout and stone behind you;
they are contraband, and will not be suffered to pass at Calais.

I wish you would give me a commission to secure you the apartment
on the first floor of this hotel. It consists of a noble ante-chamber, a
handsome *salle à manger*, a superb *salon*, an excellent bed-chamber, out of
which a *boudoir* for Madam, and a dressing-room for Monsieur. A door
out of the *salon* into the garden; and out of the garden an iron gate, which

leads directly to the Tuileries; the opera so near, that it is scarcely worth while to get into a carriage. What think you of it? But indeed you ought to be a judge of the apartment, because old *Younge* told me you occupied it the last time you was at Paris.

Do be kind enough to write soon, and let me know how you stand affected to this salutary trip; and at the same time send me the address of the lady in question, whom I shall wait upon with the greater pleasure as I shall be secure of a good reception from such a recommendation.

Have you read the Quinzaine Anglaise? It has made a great noise here, and as, I am told, its fame has reached London—but I will send it you, with all the names written in it; for the work is nothing without the key.

I do most sincerely rejoice to find that you are not sunk into *Sir David*; for, as I said before, titles can add nothing to fame like yours. Indeed, I should never have supposed it to be a matter of your own seeking; for it has ever been remarked, to your honour, that you have never employed your ample fortune to excite envy and make fools stare, but in the rational and sober enjoyment of life. However, I will not allow you the whole merit of this neither; most men's follies are owing to their wives, and you have a wife whose judgment is as near infallible as ever fell to the lot of a mortal: *entre nous*, had my husband had such a one, we should not have lain so long on different sides of the Channel. However, as they say, everyone is to be fool or physician at forty, and I, having reached that dreaded era, have turned physician to my own mind, and by the help of some bitter doses of distress and deep draughts of adversity, begin to hope I shall establish a perfect cure beyond the fear of a relapse. And I am apt to believe my little volatile lord and master (should I be happy enough to recover him from the American hazards) will begin to think that there are some pleasures to be found in the names of husband and father, and will be glad to sit quietly down by his fireside with his ancient helpmate. In one thing we both agree, which is, that if ever we meet again, we separate no more "till death do us part." By the way, I was misled by a private letter about your baronetage, for I know our London papers too well to trust them.

I find they have been very busy, and very cruelly and falsely so, about a person who has lately left Paris,—I mean Lady Berkley; not one word which they have advanced about her being true. She has passed the winter in this hotel, and behaved as properly as any woman could. We all know what she was when she had a good stock-in-trade, and we none of us know what she would be yet if she had the same advantages; but she is now more eminently ugly than ever she was handsome, and she seems to have no other thought but for her daughter, of whom she is very careful. I cannot help speaking on this subject, because I hate unjust abuse; for, though we lived in the house together, I have no particular partiality for her.

Two months before Mr. Pye was ordered to America, I sent him "Gabriella de Vergy," which I wish you to read, and favour me with your judgment. It is shrunk down to a ballad about the length of "Eldred of the Bower"; I wish it had anything else in common with that sweet poem. I shall write to my brother and desire him to send it to you. It was very much approved by d'Arnaud, and several other Frenchmen who read English:—poor evidence in its favour, you will say; however, so I should say of almost any evidence save yours, because I equally rely on your judgment and sincerity.

When first I came to Paris, I had a seal with a tolerable cast of your profile from Wedgwood and Bently: it was stolen from me. I have since written to know if I could have another, but Mr. Pye told me it was not to be had;—truth is, I suspect, he never inquired. May I take the liberty of troubling you to that purpose? I have written a shameful long letter, but I hope to be forgiven, or to receive a rebuke in writing. I sincerely embrace dear Mrs. Garrick, and remain,

Dear Sir, your most sincere and affectionate friend and servant,

J. H. Pye

WILLIAM COWPER (1731–1800)

The gentle poet, who yet was sprightly enough to write "John Gilpin," suffered from religious melancholy, and on two occasions lost his reason. His letters on country life and about his tame hares are among the most delightful in the language.

TO THE REV. JOHN NEWTON

AUGUST 21, 1780

THE following occurrence ought not to be passed over in silence, in a place where so few notable ones are to be met with. Last Wednesday night, while we were at supper, between the hours of eight and nine, I heard an unusual noise in the back parlour, as if one of the hares was entangled, and endeavouring to disengage herself. I was just going to rise from table, when it ceased. In about five minutes, a voice on the outside of the parlour door inquired if one of my hares had got away. I immediately rushed into the next room, and found that my poor favourite Puss had made her escape.

She had gnawed in sunder the strings of a lattice work, with which I thought I had sufficiently secured the window, and which I preferred to any other sort of blind, because it admitted plenty of air.

From thence I hastened to the kitchen, where I saw the redoubtable Thomas Freeman, who told me that, having seen her, just after she had dropped into the street, he attempted to cover her with his hat, but she screamed out, and leaped directly over his head. I then desired him to pursue as fast as possible, and added Richard Coleman to the chace, as being nimbler, and carrying less weight than Thomas; not expecting to see her again, but desirous to learn, if possible, what became of her. In something less than an hour, Richard returned, almost breathless, with the following account: that soon after he began to run, he left Tom behind him, and came in sight of a most numerous hunt of men, women, children, and dogs; that he did his best to keep back the dogs, and presently out-stripped the crowd, so that the race was at last disputed between himself and Puss;—she ran right through the town, and down the lane that leads to Dropshort. A little before she came to the house, he got the start and turned her; she pushed for the town again, and soon after she entered it, sought shelter in Mr. Wagstaff's tanyard, adjoining to old Mr. Drake's. Sturges's harvest men were at supper, and saw her from the opposite side of the way. There she encountered the tanpits full of water; and while she was struggling out of one pit, and plunging into another, and almost drowned, one of the men drew her out by the ears, and secured her. She was then well washed in a bucket to get the lime out of her coat, and brought home in a sack at ten o'clock.

This frolic cost us four shillings, but you may believe we did not grudge a farthing of it.

The poor creature received only a little hurt in one of her claws, and in one of her ears, and is now almost as well as ever.

I do not call this an answer to your letter, but such as it is I send it, presuming upon that interest which I know you take in my minutest concerns, which I cannot express better than in the words of Terence a little varied—*Nihil mei a te alienum putas.*

Yours, my dear friend,

W. C.

TO THE SAME

Nov. 3, 1783

My dear Friend, My time is short, and my opportunity not the most favourable. My letter will consequently be short likewise, and perhaps not very intelligible. I find it no very easy matter to bring my mind into that degree of composure, which is necessary to the arrangement either of words or matter. You will naturally expect to receive some account of this confusion that I describe, some reason given for it. On Saturday night, at eleven o'clock, when I had not been in bed five minutes, I was alarmed by a cry of fire, announced by two or three shrill screams upon our staircase. Our servants, who were going to bed, saw it from their windows, and in appearance so near, that they thought our house in danger. I immediately rose, and putting by the curtain, saw sheets of fire rising above the ridge of Mr. Palmer's house, opposite to ours. The deception was such, that I had no doubt it had begun with *him*, but soon found that it was rather farther off. In fact, it was at three places;— in the outhouses belonging to George Griggs, Lucy and Abigail Tyrrel. Having broke out in three different parts, it is supposed to have been maliciously kindled. A tar-barrel and a quantity of tallow made a most tremendous blaze, and the buildings it had seized upon being all thatched, the appearance became every moment more formidable.　Providentially, the night was perfectly calm; so calm that candles without lanterns, of which there were multitudes in the street, burnt as steadily as in a house. By four in the morning it was so far reduced, that all danger seemed to be over; but the confusion it had occasioned was almost infinite.　Every man who supposed his dwelling-house in jeopardy, emptied it as fast as he could, and conveyed his movables to the house of some neighbour, supposed to be more secure.　Ours, in the space of two hours, was so filled with all sorts of lumber, that we had not even room for a chair by the fireside.　George Griggs is the principal sufferer.　He gave eighteen guineas, or nearly that sum, to a woman whom, in his hurry, he mistook for his wife; but the supposed wife walked off with the money, and he will probably never recover it.　He has likewise lost forty pounds' worth of wool.　London never exhibited a scene of greater depredation, drunkenness, and riot.　Everything was stolen that could be got at, and every drop of liquor drunk that was not guarded.　Only one thief has yet been detected; a woman of the name of J——, who was stopped by young Handscomb with an apron full of plunder.　He was forced to strike her down, before he could wrest it from her.　Could you visit the place, you would see a most striking proof of a Providence interposing to stop the progress of the flames.　They had almost reached, that is to say, within six yards of Daniel Raban's wood-pile, in which were fifty-pounds' worth of faggots and furze; and exactly there they were extinguished; otherwise, especially if a breath of air had happened to move, all that side of the town must probably have been consumed.　After all this dreadful conflagration, we find nothing burnt but the outhouses; and the dwellings to which they belonged have suffered only the damage of being unroofed on that side next the fire.　No lives were lost, nor any limbs broken.　Mrs. Unwin, whose spirits served her while the hubbub lasted, and the day after, begins to feel the effect of it now.　But I hope she will be relieved from it soon, being better this evening than I expected.　As for me, I am impregnable to all such assaults.　I have nothing, however, but this subject in my mind, and it is in vain that I invite any other into it.　Having, therefore, exhausted this, I finish, assuring you of our united love, and hoping to find myself in a frame of mind more suited to my employment when next I write.

Yours, my dear Friend,

W. C.

THE LODGE, MARCH 3, 1788

ONE day last week, Mrs. Unwin and I, having taken our morning walk and returning homeward through the wilderness, met the Throckmortons. A minute after we had met them, we heard the cry of hounds at no great distance, and mounting the broad stump of an elm which had been felled, and by the aid of which we were enabled to look over the wall, we saw them. They were all at that time in our orchard: presently we heard a terrier, belonging to Mrs. Throckmorton, which you may remember by the name of Fury, yelping with much vehemence, and saw her running through the thickets within a few yards of us at her utmost speed, as if in pursuit of something which we doubted not was the fox. Before we could reach the other end of the wilderness, the hounds entered also; and when we arrived at the gate which opens into the grove, there we found the whole weary cavalcade assembled. The huntsman dismounting, begged leave to follow his hounds on foot, for he was sure, he said, that they had killed him—a conclusion which I suppose he drew from their profound silence. He was accordingly admitted, and with a sagacity that would not have dishonoured the best hound in the world, pursuing precisely the same track which the fox and dogs had taken, though he had never had a glimpse of either after their first entrance through the rails, arrived where he found the slaughtered prey. He soon produced dead reynard, and rejoined us in the grove with all his dogs about him. Having an opportunity to see a ceremony, which I was pretty sure would never fall in my way again, I determined to stay and to notice all that passed with the most minute attention. The huntsman having by the aid of a pitchfork lodged reynard on the **arm** of an elm, at the height of about nine feet from the ground, there left him for a considerable time. The gentlemen sat on their horses contemplating the fox, for which they had toiled so hard; and the hounds assembled at the foot of the tree, with faces not less expressive of the most rational delight, contemplated the same object. The huntsman remounted, cut off a foot, and threw it to the hounds—one of them swallowed it whole like a bolus. He then once more alighted, and drawing down the fox by the hinder legs, desired the people, who were by this time rather numerous, to open a lane for him to the right and left. He was instantly obeyed, when, throwing the fox to the distance of some yards, and screaming like a fiend, "tear him to pieces," at least six times repeatedly, he consigned him over absolutely to the pack, who in a few minutes devoured him completely. Thus, my dear, as Virgil says, what none of the gods could have ventured to promise me, time itself, pursuing its accustomed course, has of its own accord presented me with.   I have been in at the death of a fox, and you now know as much of the matter as I, who am as well informed as any sportsman in England.

Yours,
W. C.

JOSEPH PRIESTLEY (1733–1804)

Born at Birstall in Yorkshire, Priestley became a Nonconformist minister and tutor at Warrington Academy. In his spare time he experimented in chemistry, particularly with gases, and in 1774 discovered oxygen. In politics, as in chemistry, his views were far in advance of his time, and in 1791 his house in Birmingham was stormed and burned by a mob, and all his scientific apparatus and manuscripts destroyed. He replied with this letter to his townsmen.

TO THE INHABITANTS OF THE TOWN
OF BIRMINGHAM

JULY 19, 1791

MY LATE TOWNSMEN AND NEIGHBOURS,

You have destroyed the most truly valuable and useful apparatus of philosophical instruments that perhaps any individual, in this or any other country, was ever possessed of, in my use of which I annually spent large sums with no pecuniary view whatever, but only in the advancement of Science, for the benefit of my country and mankind. You have destroyed the Library corresponding to that apparatus, which no money can re-purchase, except in course of time. But what I feel far more, you have destroyed manuscripts which have been the result of the laborious study of many years, and which I shall never be able to recompense; and this has been done to one who never did, or imagined, you any harm.

In this business we are the sheep and you the wolves. We will preserve our character and hope you will change yours. At all events we return you blessings for curses, and hope that you shall soon return to that industry and those sober manners for which the inhabitants of Birmingham were formerly distinguished.

Yours faithfully,

J. PRIESTLEY

ROBERT ROBINSON (1735–90)

Robinson was a Baptist minister whose preaching filled Cambridge with admiration. In this letter he describes a day's work in his country-house at Chesterton.

TO HENRY KEENE

CHESTERTON, MAY 26, 1784

OLD FRIEND, You love I should write folios: that depends upon circumstances, and if the thunderstorm lasts, it will be so: but what a sad thing it is to be forced t o write, when one has nothing to say? Well, you shall have an apology for not writing,—that is, a diary of one day.

Rose at three o'clock—crawled into the library—and met one who said, "Yet a little while is the light with you: work while ye have the light—the night cometh, when no man can work—my father worketh hitherto, and I work." Rang the great bell, and roused the girls to milking—went up to the farm, roused the horse-keeper—fed the horses while he was getting up—called the boy to suckle the calves, and clean out the cow-house—lighted my pipe, walked round the gardens to see what was wanting there—went up the paddock to see if the weanling calves were well—went down to the ferry, to see whether the boy had scooped and cleaned the boats—returned to the farm—examined the shoulders, heels, traces, chaff, and corn of eight horses going to plough—mended the acre staff—cut some thongs, whip-corded the boys' plough whips—pumped the troughs full—saw the hogs fed—examined the swill tubs, and then the cellar—ordered a quarter of malt, for the hogs want grains, and the men want beer—filled the pipe again, returned to the river, and bought a lighter of turf for dairy fires, and another of sedge for ovens—hunted up the wheelbarrows and set them a-trundling—returned to the farm, called the men to breakfast, and cut the boys' bread and cheese, and saw the wooden bottles filled—sent one plough to the three-roods, another to the three half-acres, and so on—shut the gates, and the clock struck five—breakfasted—set two men to ditch the five roods—two more to chop sads, and spread about the land—two more to throw up muck in the yard—and three men and six women to weed wheat—set on

426

the carpenter to repair cow-cribs, and set them up till winter—the wheeler to mend up the old carts, cart-ladders, rakes, etc., preparatory to hay-time and harvest—walked to the six-acres, found hogs in the grass—went back and sent a man to hedge and thorn—sold the butcher a fat calf, and the suckler a lean one—the clock strikes nine—walked into barley-field— barleys fine, picked off a few tiles and stones, and cut a few thistles—the peas fine, but foul; the charlock must be topped—the tares doubtful; the fly seems to have taken them—prayed for rain, but could not see a cloud —came round to the wheat-field—wheats rather thin, but the finest colour in the world—set four women on to the shortest wheats—ordered one man to weed the ridge of the long wheats—and two women to keep rank and file with him in the furrows—thistles many—blue-bottles no end—traversed all the wheat-field—came to the fallow-field—the ditchers have run crooked—set them straight—the flag-sads cut too much, rush-sads too little, strength wasted, shew the men how to three-corner them—laid out more work for the ditchers—went to the ploughs —set the foot a little higher; cut a wedge, set the coulter deeper, must go and get a new mould-board against to-morrow—went to the other plough —picked up some wool, and tied over the traces—mended a horse-tree, tied a thong to the plough-hammer—went to see which lands want ploughing first—sat down under a bush—wondered how any man could be so silly as to call me *reverend*—read two verses and thought of his loving-kindness in the midst of his temple—gave out, "Come all har-monious tongues," and set Mount Ephraim tune—rose up—whistled— the dogs wagged their tails, and on we went—got home—dinner ready— filled the pipe—drank some milk—and fell asleep—woke by the car-penter for some slats, which the sawyer must cut—the Reverend Messrs. A. in a coat, B. in a gown of black, and C. in one of purple, came to drink tea, and to settle whether Gomer was the father of the Celts and Gauls and Britons, or only the uncle—proof sheet from Mr. Archdeacon— corrected it—washed—dressed—went to meeting, and preached from, *The end of all things is at hand, be ye sober and watch unto prayer*—found a dear brother *reverence* there, who went home with me, and edified us all out of Solomon's Song, with a dish of tripe out of Leviticus, and a golden candlestick out of Exodus.—Really and truly we look for you and Mrs. Keene and Mr. Dore at harvest; and if you do not come I know what you all are.

Let Mr. Winch go where he can better himself.   Is not this a folio? And like many other folios? . . .

R. ROBINSON

EDWARD GIBBON (1737-94)

This letter was written to Garrick the year after Gibbon had brought out the first volume of his History. It is a pleasant little note, far removed from the somewhat pompous tone one might expect from such a writer.

TO MR. GARRICK

PARIS, AUG. 14, 1777

DEAR SIR, The other day Madame Necker made me very happy by the communication of your entertaining and obliging letter. It is pleasant to find one's-self mentioned with friendship by those whom posterity will mention with admiration. Foreign nations are a kind of posterity, and among them you already reap the full harvest of your fame. I can assure you that in every polite circle there is not any name so frequently repeated as the name of Garrick. The persons who have been in England before the fatal month of June, 1776 [when Garrick retired], describe with transport what they have seen and what they have felt; and those who propose to undertake the same journey, express the regret that the principal object of their curiosity no longer subsists. So much for your numerous admirers. Your friends, and they are many, who have enjoyed your social qualities, are sincere and earnest in their wishes that you would execute your promise of visiting this country; and I some-times hear them exclaim, with the good-natured vanity which constitutes no unamiable part of the French character: "Ce Monsieur Garrick étoit fait pour vivre parmi nous." In the meanwhile send us, without a moment's delay, your elegant fable. From the impartial account which I have given Madame Necker, she is impatient to see it; and, though a good subject, I will venture to say that she is as capable of tasting its beauties as any monarch in Christendom.

You have reason to envy me, for I can truly declare that I reckon the three months which I have now passed in Paris among the most agreeable of my life. My connection with a house, before which the proudest of the Gallic nobles bow the knee, my familiar acquaintance with the language, and a natural propensity to be pleased with the people and their manners, have introduced me into very good company; and, different in that respect from the traveller Twiss, I have sometimes been invited to the same houses a second time. If besides these advantages your partiality should ascribe any others to your friend, I am not proud enough entirely to disclaim them. I propose to stay at Paris about two months longer, to hook in (if possible) a little of the Fountainbleau voyage, and to return to England a few days before the meeting of Parliament, where I suppose we shall have some warm scenes. You cannot surely be satisfied with the beginning, or rather no beginning, of the American campaign, which seems to elevate the enemies as much as it must humble the friends of Great Britain.

At this time of year, the society of the Turk's Head [Literary Club] can no longer be addressed as a corporate body, and most of the individual members are probably dispersed: Adam Smith in Scotland; Burke in the shades of Beaconsfield; Fox, the Lord or the devil knows where, &c., &c. Be so good as to salute in my name these friends who may fall in your way. Assure Sir Joshua, in particular, that I have not lost my relish for *manly* conversation and the society of the brown table. I hope Colman has made a successful campaign. May I beg to be remembered to Mrs. Garrick? By this time she has probably discovered the philosopher's stone: she has long possessed a much more valuable secret, that of gaining the hearts of all who have the happiness of knowing her.

I am, dear Sir, most affectionately yours,

E. GIBBON

JONATHAN BOUCHER (1738–1804)

Jonathan Boucher left England for America early in the eighteenth century and became a clergyman in Virginia. He set up school, and among his pupils was Custis, the step-son of George Washington. Boucher remained a Loyalist and was driven out in 1775. After preaching his last sermon with pistols on his pulpit and the words "Long live the King," he withdrew to England and dedicated his work to Washington in the following letter, to which, for sake of completeness, Washington's reply is also given. Boucher was grandfather of Frederick Locker the poet.

TO GEORGE WASHINGTON

EPSOM, SURREY, NOV. 4, 1797

SIR, In prefixing your name to a work avowedly hostile to that Revolution in which you bore a distinguished part, I am not conscious that I deserve to be charged with inconsistency. I do not address myself to the General of a Conventional Army; but to the late dignified President of the United States, the friend of rational and sober freedom.

As a British subject I have observed with pleasure that the form of Government, under which you and your fellow-citizens now hope to find peace and happiness, however defective in many respects, has, in the unity of its executive, and the division of its legislative powers, been framed after a British model. That, in the discharge of your duty as head of this Government, you have resisted those anarchical doctrines, which are hardly less dangerous to America than to Europe, is not more an eulogium on the wisdom of our forefathers, than honourable to your individual wisdom and integrity.

As a Minister of Religion I am equally bound to tender you my respect for having (in your valedictory address to your countrymen) asserted your opinion that "the only firm supports of political prosperity are religion and morality"; and that "morality can be maintained only by religion." Those best friends of mankind, who, amidst all the din and uproar of Utopian reforms, persist to think that the affairs of this world

430

can never be well administered by men trained to disregard the God who made it, must ever thank you for this decided protest against the fundamental maxim of modern revolutionists, that religion is no concern of the State.

It is on these grounds, Sir, that I now presume (and I hope not impertinently) to add my name to the list of those who have dedicated their works to you. One of them, not inconsiderable in fame, from having been your fulsome flatterer, has become your foul calumniator; to such dedicators I am willing to persuade myself I have no resemblance. I bring no incense to your shrine even in a Dedication. Having never paid court to you whilst you shone in an exalted station, I am not so weak as to steer my little bark across the Atlantic in search of patronage and preferment; or so vain as to imagine that now, in the evening of my life, I may yet be warmed by your setting sun. My utmost ambition will be abundantly gratified by your condescending, as a private Gentleman in America, to receive with candour and kindness this disinterested testimony of regard from a private Clergyman in England. I was once your neighbour and your friend: the unhappy dispute, which terminated in this disunion of our respective countries, also broke off our personal connexion: but I never was more than your political enemy; and every sentiment even of political animosity has, on my part, long ago subsided. Permit me then to hope, that this tender of renewed amity between us may be received and regarded as giving some promise of that perfect reconciliation between our two countries which it is the sincere aim of this publication to promote. If, on this topic, there be another wish nearer to my heart, it is that you would not think it beneath you to co-operate with so humble an effort to produce that reconciliation.

You have shown great prudence (and in my estimation, still greater patriotism) in resolving to terminate your days in retirement. To become, however, even at Mount Vernon, a mere private man, by divesting yourself of all public influence, is not in your power. I hope it is not your wish. Unincumbered with the distracting cares of public life, you may now, by the force of a still powerful example, gradually train the people around you to a love of order and subordination; and, above all, to a love of peace. "Hae tibi erunt artes." That you possessed talents eminently well adapted for the high post you lately held friends and foes have concurred in testifying: be it my pleasing talk thus publicly to declare that you carry back to your paternal fields virtues equally calculated to bloom in the shade. To resemble Cincinnatus is but small praise: be it yours, Sir, to enjoy the calm repose and holy serenity of a Christian hero; and may "the Lord bless your latter end more than your beginning."

I have the honour to be, Sir, etc.

JONATHAN BOUCHER

GENERAL WASHINGTON'S REPLY

MOUNT VERNON, 15 AUG., 1798

REVD. SIR, I know not how it has happened, but the fact is that your favour of the 8th November, last year, is but just received, and at a time when both public and private business pressed so hard upon me as to afford no leisure to give the "View of the causes, and consequences of the American Revolution" written by you, and which you had been pleased to send me a perusal.

For the honour of its dedication, and for the friendly and favourable Sentiments which are therein expressed I pray you to accept my acknowledgements and thanks.

Not having read the book it follows of course that I can express no opinion with respect to its political contents; but I can venture to assert beforehand, and with confidence, that there is no man in either country, more zealously devoted to Peace, and a good understanding between the two Nations than I am—nor one who is more disposed to bury in oblivion all animosities which have subsisted between them and the Individual of each.

Peace with all the world is my sincere wish—I am sure it is our true policy, and am persuaded it is the ardent desire of the Government. But there is a Nation whose intermeddling and restless disposition, and attempts to divide, distract and influence the measures of other Countries, will not suffer us, I fear to enjoy this blessing long, unless we will yield to them our rights and submit to greater injuries and insults than we have already sustained, to avoid the calamities resulting from Wars.

What will be the consequences of our arming for self-defence, that Providence who permits these doings in the disturbers of Mankind, and who rules and governs all things, alone can tell. To its all powerful decrees we must submit, whilst we hope that the justice of our cause, if War must ensue, will entitle us to its protection.

Your most obedient Servant,

GEORGE WASHINGTON

SIR WILLIAM CODRINGTON (1739–1816)

Sir William was living in France when the Revolution broke out, and his letter describing the events at the height of the Terror is one of the most graphic documents of that time.

PARIS, 14 NIVOSE: 3ME ANNÉE REPUBLICAINE
Liberté, Egalité, Fraternité, ou la Morte

YOU may think perhaps that you have lived long enough to know how to date a letter, but I can show you that the wisest may learn. You may also learn that I am all alive again. How that comes about I am at a loss to tell you unless you've faith in predestination, and after all that's the best way of accounting for it, that my time was not come. Otherwise I presume I should have accompanied many of my companions. However, all's well that ends well, but would it (was) ended indeed. For though I've escaped one great storm, the weather still seems inclined to be squally.

To furnish a History of Fifteen months would be rather a bore, and would carry me beyond the limits of my paper, therefore if you please we will abridge it as much as possible.

To begin then, I was arrested because I was born in one kingdom instead of in another, and also it was taken much amiss, that my countrymen should accept of a town that was very kindly offered them; as I was about two hundred leagues distant from the town in question and that I had not been consulted whether the offer should have been accepted or refused, I thought they might as well have found out some other·person to have punished instead of me. However, I was conducted to a high tower upon the sea shore, built by William the Conqueror. I was there placed in a room where there was sure enough no glass to the windows, but that deficiency was made up by the number of bars. What added to the agreeableness of the *sejour*, was that it happened to be exactly at the equinox, so I could not complain for the want of air. After a few days' residence there an officer came into my room and told me he was ordered to accompany [me] to my house, which was about a mile from the town, in order for me to be present at the examination of my papers; I accord-

ingly followed him.   When I got into the street I was surprised to find
guards to escort me, sufficient in number to have defended the castle had
it been besieged by an enemy; in this stately manner I was conducted to
my house and back again.   After a few days I was informed they had
found nothing among my papers but family matters and an innocent
correspondence.   However, they were sent to the National Deputy who
was then at Rennes, who put a different construction upon my correspondence and he ordered me to be conducted thither.   I was then thrown
into a prison more disagreeable in every respect than that which I had
quitted.   After a few days there arrived a person from St. Malo with a
petition in my favour, and signed, also, by the Municipality of St. Servan.
The person that brought it got a reputable woman to present it to the
Deputy; she had no sooner done it, than he began by abusing her in a
most indecent manner and threatened to send her to prison.   She
defended herself by saying she was not acquainted with the contents of the
letter, and that it was left at her house by a person that did not leave his
name.   "I wish," says he, "I could find him out, I would commit him
directly, and as for the Municipality, I'll break them," says he, "as soon
as I return thither, for he's a conspirator and I have the proof in my
hands,"—holding up a paper.   When I found how the land laid, I
desired to be heard, but that was refused me and in a few days after I had a
visit from a Commissary of War, together with a National one, who
signified to me that I must prepare to set off for Paris, they having received
orders to conduct me thither.

At eleven o'clock at night came a guard and conducted me to the
Diligence, where I was chained like an assassin to two other unfortunate
people, and after travelling night and day during four days and a half, we
arrived at Paris where the Commissary at War got out of the coach,
thinking it beneath his dignity to be seen upon such an errand.   And,
sure enough, it was very unusual to send such a conductor upon such an
occasion: But Carrier had swelled up my importance by calling me a
milord, and *ci devant* this and *ci devant* that, and in order to keep up the
ball, he occasioned [me] to be accompanied in an extraordinary manner,
that he might gain the more credit to himself.   Our two other conductors
conveyed us to the fatal Conciergerie.   The entrance therein (at that
period) and death were nearly synonymous.   From the compliments we
met with upon the road I never thought we should have got so far, or
that we should have lived to have died honourable deaths; our conductors never attempted to quell the populace, excepting when they cried
out "rascals and conspirators," they answered that there was but one.

However, after so unpleasant and fatiguing a journey I comforted myself with the hopes of one good night's rest, but was sadly disappointed when the Concierge told us there was no private room vacant, and that we must sleep in the straw-room. "But," added he, "take care of your pocket-books and watches for you'll be among a den of thieves who will rob you of all you have." With such consolation we entered into the prison-court where there were some hundreds of unfortunate people of all denominations. Being tired and hungry we employed a commissioner of the prison to get us something to eat. When it came we were obliged to make use of a low parapet wall for a table (as the straw-rooms are kept shut during the day and those that inhabit them are obliged to stay in the open air all the day long, be the weather what it may).

The people in the court took compassion upon us, and lent us knives and forks: and informed us also that by applying to the superior turnkey in a *prevailing* manner we might possibly obtain a place in a room. That business was presently undertaken and two of us procured the seventh part of a small apartment. The beds were placed so near together that one was obliged to get in at the feet, and though we paid for them apart, I was three weeks before I could get any sheets, and when at length I had them, I could with great facility have crept through them. But the room being very small and the ceiling so very low, and so many persons stove in so narrow a compass that the air was so bad we could none of us sleep, at least not for more than an hour, often less, and sometimes not at all. As we were locked up every evening about five o'clock and the door not opened till near ten the next morning, a tub was placed in the room for those whose necessities obliged them to make use of it, and though that was avoided as much as possible, still it had been so long an inhabitant there and so impregnated with what it had been so used to contain, that it was almost as disagreeable as if it had been constantly made use of. We had in the room with us a tolerable good physician, who advised us to burn incense, etc., every night before we went to bed in order to purify the air, and to take a mouthful of brandy every morning as soon as we got up, as a preventative against infection. We all of us rose in the morning with a great dryness in the throat, or something of a soreness.

At twelve o'clock every night, we used to be visited by three or four turnkeys with as many great bull-dogs: with large staves they used to thump against the ceiling, open the windows, and with an iron hammer beat against the bars to see that all was safe and sound. Another visit we were also subject to, that was still more unpleasant though it came but seldom.   When we used to hear the jingling of keys upon our staircase in the evening we were sure it was to summon some one of us to appear the next morning at the fatal Tribunal.   As soon as the door opened, each was apprehensive of the lot falling upon himself.   The taking leave the next morning of the unfortunate person before he went to take his trial with so little hopes of ever seeing him again, was another melancholy proceeding.

Four months I passed in this pleasing abode, having seen half my room-companions quit me to take their final leave, and the half of that half have since shared the same fate.   One day with another we used to reckon upon five condemnations, and esteemed that sufficiently severe for those times, notwithstanding how much they have since increased upon that number.

Towards the latter part of my *sejour* we had thrown in among us upwards of an hundred prisoners from Nantes, most of them opulent people and some of them of a great age; they had travelled in a severe season forty days together and had been most miserably fed and lodged upon their journey.   Twenty-five died upon the road, as many were put into the infirmary prison upon their arrival, the rest were put in the straw-rooms for there was at that time no other vacancy, our numbers amounting at that time to about six hundred and fifty.   But notwithstanding the precaution of placing the most unhealthy of them apart, still the disorder they brought with them was so violent and so infectious that it began to spread in the prison.   As I preferred the chance of a short death to a lingering one, I made what interest I could to bring on my trial, contrary indeed to the advice of my council who would have had me wait for the chance of more lenient measures.   I, however, succeeded in my attempt.   But before one appears at the Tribunal one's accusation and papers are laid before a council of judges and they determine whether or no there is sufficient grounds for accusation; and luckily for me they determined that there were not; by that means I escaped the severity of that fatal court.

Though guiltless, still as a subject of Great Britain I was doomed to confinement; but by the assistance of some friends I got to be transferred to a *Maison de Santé* instead of to another prison.   A servant that waited upon us, and my hairdresser were both taken ill of the Nantes fever the day I left the place, and died a few days after.   I had begun to droop the few last days, but it was amazing the instantaneous effect that the change of air had upon me, like a fish out of water for some time, and thrown into it again.   In less than two hours I felt quite a different person.   I dined with some friends by the indulgence of my conductor, and eat with a very good appetite which had quite failed me latterly.   Awful as that abode was, you would scarcely believe that I have not been so cheerful since as I was there, nor have I since seen so many cheerful people.   One should think that nature had formed one's nerves according to the different situations that they may be exposed to, *on se fait à tout,* and one may accustom oneself to bad fortune as one does to good.   We used frequently to breakfast and dine at each other's room, which time generally passed in mirth.   Most of us thought that we had but a short time allotted to us and that it was better to enjoy that little as much as we could.   I don't recollect among the hundred that I both saw and spoke to after their condemnation, one single one of them except Madame Dubarré that showed any softness upon the occasion, and several seemed as cheerful as if nothing had happened to them.

After I had remained a few months at my new abode, where we were comfortable enough, things took another turn, and without beat of drum we were all conveyed in a hurry to another prison where we had not been long before we were visited by a part of the Municipality of Paris, attended by a numerous guard, and all ordered to our rooms, with sentinels placed at our doors to prevent us going out.   Each of us was visited by a Municipal and his attendants, who, as soon as they came into the room, told us with a threat to deliver all our money, knives, forks, scissors, and that whoever hid the least matter demanded should immediately be sent to the Conciergerie.   I was in a very small room and alone and yet they passed above an hour with me, to the amazement of my neighbours. They examined my trunks and my drawers a second time to see if there were not false bottoms to them, they were mean enough to stoop to take the buckles out of one's shoes.   This visit was soon followed by another to examine if our garden was not convenient to make a burying ground of. Though no small one they did not find it big enough.   They afterwards went to another prison a few doors from us where they found a part of the garden would suit them, where they occasioned to be dug a great hole in which in a very few days they stove in two thousand two hundred corpses, and afterwards proceeded to make another hole of the kind which they pallisaded round and was in a field opposite our prison.

Having been tried by the Council and acquitted, I concluded I had been out of harm's way, but from the above proceedings and unpleasant reports that went about we concluded that we were all of us destined for 'tother world.   But very lucky for us, Robespierre and many of his party were overthrown the 9th, and they had fixed on the 11th for a general massacre in the prisons.   (Thus—Thus and no nearer, as say the seamen).   After the event there was a general cry in favour of the prisoners and many were daily set at liberty, by which means my habitation became so thinned of its inhabitants that they transferred us to another prison. But they forgot me in the scramble and I remained alone for some time, having the whole house to range in, and thirty men that used to mount guard night and day to watch my person.   At length they found they had left me by myself and that it was not absolutely necessary to harrass such a number of men to guard a single harmless prisoner.   They ordered me to follow my companions to the Luxembourg, where I found G. O'Hara and his suite, Temple Luttrell, and there were many other English, but most of them of an inferior class.

As the Decree for the arrestation of the English had not been repealed I saw but little chance of obtaining my liberty before a peace.   However, it at length came by accident and when I the least expected it.   A friend of mine applied to a printer of his acquaintance to demand me as his journeyman; by that means together with a little interest of friends I slipped my neck out of the collar, after having remained near fifteen months in prison.

I shall remain here during the winter and perhaps for a longer term as this place all things considered is the best to reside in as long as the war lasts.   I take the same opportunity of sending you this as the inhabitant of Davies Street took when she wrote to me in the beginning of last June, which I received but a few days since, the person to whom it was directed not daring to deliver it, or even to enquire after me, such was the severity of those times.   As this epistle or rather narrative is already too long I shall not add to the length of it, especially as I think there is a degree of uncertainty of its ever reaching you.   But, that my packet may risk the loss, I have confided in my correspondence to females only: notwithstanding it is said that there never was a plot but that there was a woman in it.   If such be their ideas in this country, I shall have taken some pains and have used much ink and paper for nothing and had better have confined myself to merely saying if you are well.—I am so and hope you are so.—So Adieu Affectionately.

JAMES BOSWELL (1740–95)

The first of these letters affords an unconsciously amusing picture of Boswell courting a young lady, whom he styles the Princess, who was obviously exceedingly bored by his attentions. In these lines poor James reveals his character as truly as in every page of his immortal Life.

TO W. J. TEMPLE

EDINBURGH, 24TH DECEMBER, 1767

MY DEAREST FRIEND, In my last I told you that, after I had resolved to give up with the Princess for ever, I resolved first to see her. I was so lucky as to have a very agreeable interview, and was convinced by her that she was not to blame. This happened on a Thursday; that evening her cousin and most intimate friend, the Duchess of Gordon, came to town. Next day I was at the concert with them, and afterwards supped at Lord Kaimes's. The Princess appeared distant and reserved; I could hardly believe that it was the same woman with whom I had been quite easy the day before; I was then uneasy. Next evening I was at the play with them; it was "Othello." I sat close behind the Princess, and at the most effecting scenes I pressed my hand upon her waist; she was in tears, and rather leaned to me. The jealous Moor described my very soul. I often spoke to her of the torment she saw before her; still I thought her distant, and still I felt uneasy. On Sunday the Duchess went away. I met the Princess at church; she was distant as before. I passed the evening at her aunt's, where I met a cousin of my Princess, a young lady of Glasgow, who had been with us at Adamtown. She told me she had something to communicate, and she then said my behaviour to the Princess was such that Mrs. B. and her daughter did not know how to behave to me; that it was not honourable to engage a young lady's affections while I kept myself free; in short, the good cousin persuaded me that the Princess had formed an attachment for me, and she assured me the Nabob had been refused. On Monday forenoon I waited on Miss B. I found her alone, and she did not seem distant; I told her that I was most sincerely in love with her, and that I only dreaded those

439

faults which I had acknowledged to her. I asked her seriously if she now believed me in earnest. She said she did. I then asked her to be candid and fair as I had been with her, and to tell me if she had any particular liking for me. What think you, Temple, was her answer? "No, I really have no particular liking for you; I like many people as well as you." Temple, you must have it in the genuine dialogue.

Boswell.—Do you indeed? Well, I cannot help it; I am obliged to you for telling me so in time. I am sorry for it.

Princess.—I like Jeany Maxwell (Duchess of Gordon) better than you.

B.—Very well; but do you like no man better than me?

P.—No.

B.—Is it possible that you may like me better than other men?

P.—I don't know what is possible.

(By this time I had risen and placed myself by her, and was in real agitation.)

B.—I'll tell you what, my dear Miss Blair, I love you so much that I am very unhappy if you cannot love me. I must, if possible, endeavour to forget you. What would you have me do?

P.—I really don't know what you should do.

B.—It is certainly possible that you may love me; and if you shall ever do so, I shall be the happiest man in the world. Will you make a fair bargain with me? If you should happen to love me, will you own it?

P.—Yes.

B.—And if you should happen to love another, will you tell me immediately, and help me to make myself easy?

P.—Yes, I will.

B.—Well, you are very good (often squeezing and kissing her fine hand, while she looked at me with those beautiful black eyes).

P.—I may tell you, as a cousin, what I would not tell to another man.

B.—You may indeed. You are very fond of Auchinleck, that is one good circumstance.

P.—I confess I am. I wish I liked you as well as I do Auchinleck.

B.—I have told you how fond I am of you; but unless you like me sincerely, I have too much spirit to ask you to live with me, as I know that you do not like me. If I could have you this moment for my wife, I would not.

P.—I should not like to put myself in your offer though.

B.—Remember, you are both my cousin and my mistress, you must make me suffer as little as possible, as it may happen that I may engage your affections. I should think myself a most dishonourable man if I were not now in earnest, and, remember, I depend upon your sincerity; and whatever happens, you and I shall never have another quarrel.

P.—Never.

B.—And I may come and see you as much as I please?

P.—Yes.

My worthy friend, what sort of a scene was this? It was most curious. She said she would submit to her husband in most things. She said that to see one loving her would go far to make her love that person; but she would not talk anyhow positively, for she never had felt the uneasy anxiety of love. We were an hour and a half together, and seemed pleased all the time. I think she behaved with spirit and propriety. I admire her more than ever. She intended to go to her aunt's, twelve miles from town, next day: her jaunt was put off for some days. Yesterday I saw her again; I was easy and cheerful, and just endeavoured to make myself agreeable.

This forenoon I was again with her. I told her how uneasy I was that she should be three weeks absent. She said I might amuse myself well enough: she seemed quite indifferent. I was growing angry again, but I recollected how she had candidly told me that she had no particular liking for me.

Temple, where am I now? What is the meaning of this? I drank tea with her this afternoon, and sat near four hours with her mother and her. Our conversation turned all on the manner in which two people might live. She has the justest ideas. She said she knew me now; she could laugh me out of my ill-humour; she could give Lord Auchinleck a lesson how to manage me. Temple, what does the girl mean? We talked a good deal of you: you are a prodigious favourite. Now, my worthy friend, assist me. You know my strange temper and impetuous disposition; shall I boldly shake her off, as I fear I cannot be patient and moderate? or, am I not bound in honour to suffer some time, and watch her heart? How long must I suffer? how must I do? When she comes back, shall I affect any indifference, to try her? or, shall I rather endeavour to inspire her with my flame? Is it not below me to be made uneasy by her? or, may I not be a philosopher, and without uneasiness, take her, if she likes me, and if

not, let her alone? During her absence, I have time to get a return
from you. It is certainly possible that all she has said may be literally
true; but is not her indifference a real fault? Consult Mrs. Temple
and advise me. Amidst all this love, I have been wild as ever. . . .
Trust me in time coming; I give you my word of honour, Temple:
I have nothing else to save me.

I have this day received a large packet from Paoli, with a letter,
an elegant letter, from the University of Corte, and also an extract
of an oration pronounced this year at the opening of the University,
in which oration I am celebrated in a manner which does me the
greatest honour. I think, Temple, I have had my full share of fame;
yet my book is still to come, and I cannot doubt its doing me credit.
Come, why do I allow myself to be uneasy for a Scots lass? Rouse
me, my friend! Kate has not fire enough; she does not know the
value of her lover! If on her return she still remains cold, she does
not deserve me. I will not quarrel with her: she cannot help her
defects: but I will break my enchanting fetters. To-morrow I shall
be happy with my devotions. I shall think of you, and wish to be at
Mamhead. Could you assist me to keep up my real dignity among
the illiberal race of Scots lawyers? Adieu, my dearest friend! My
best compliments to your amiable spouse.

J. B.

TO THE SAME

LONDON, 10TH JANUARY, 1789

MY DEAR TEMPLE, Another sad interruption of our correspondence,
without any sufficient reason. Soon after receiving your last, long,
kind letter, I recovered my spirits pretty well, I know not how. A
letter from my wife, recommending me to take a house in a well-aired
situation, determined me not to sell my furniture; as my doing so, after
what she wrote, might appear like discouraging her from coming to
me, which, though I could hardly hope, would have made me very
happy. It is incredible what difficulty I found, in several weeks'
wandering, to find a house that would answer; and at last I fixed on
one at £50, in Queen Anne Street, West, Cavendish Square, very
small but neat. It, however, would not accommodate the whole of
my family, with even tolerable conveniency, but would serve as a
sort of camp-lodging till better could be had. In winter, the upholsterers and brokers take numbers of houses and furnish them
with old trash, and by letting them furnished get great profits. This

makes it very difficult to get choice of unfurnished houses at that
season. I am in a most illegal situation, and for appearance should
have cheap chambers in the Temple, as to which I am still enquiring.
But in truth I am sadly discouraged by having no practice, nor probable
prospect of it; and to confess fairly to you, my friend, I am afraid that,
were I to be tried, I should be found so deficient in the forms, the
quirks and the quiddities, which early habit acquires, that I should
expose myself. Yet the delusion of Westminster Hall, of brilliant
reputation and splendid fortune as a barrister, still weighs upon my
imagination. I must be seen in the Courts, and must hope for some
happy openings in causes of importance. The Chancellor, as you
observe, has not done as I expected; but why did I expect it? I am
going to put him to the test. Could I be satisfied with being Baron of
Auchinleck, with a good income for a gentleman in Scotland I might,
no doubt, be independent. But what can be done to deaden the
ambition which has ever raged in my veins like a fever? In the
country, I should sink into wretched gloom, or at best into listless
dullness and sordid abstraction. Perhaps a time may come when I
may by lapse of time be grown fit for it. As yet I really, from a
philosophical spirit, allow myself to be driven along the tide of life with
a good deal of caution, not to be much hurt; and still flattering myself
that an unexpected lucky chance may at last place me so, that the
prediction of a fortunate cap appearing on my head at my birth will be
fulfilled.

My two boys are still in the house with me. The eldest is advancing
both in Latin and Greek exceedingly well, by the assistance of one of
the ushers of the Soho Academy; and the other goes on in Latin with
him during this hard weather, but next week I am to send him again
to that academy. I am sensible that it is a great disadvantage to them
to be under my roof, as I am so much abroad; and then they must be
with my Scotch housekeeper and footman, whom I yet retain on
account of their fidelity and moderate wages, but I am afraid to send
my eldest to a public school with his rupture; the younger I shall send
to one when he is a year older.

I am now very near my rough draft of Johnson's Life. On
Saturday I finished the Introduction and Dedication to Sir Joshua,
both of which had appeared very difficult to be accomplished. I am
confident they are well done. Whenever I have completed the rough
draft, by which I mean the work without nice correction, Malone and
I are to prepare one-half perfectly, and then it goes to press, where I

hope to have it early in February, so as to be out by the end of May.
I do not believe that Malone's Shakespeare will be much before me:
his brother, Lord Sunderlin, with his Lady and two sisters, came home
from a long tour on the Continent in summer last, and took a country-
house about twenty miles from town, for six months. Malone lived
with them, and so his labour was much intermitted.

I am very sorry to find that it is the most difficult thing you can
imagine, to get a boy, not the son of a citizen, into Christ's Hospital.
Miss Palmer, whom I have solicited, cannot do it; and I am sure I
have not a tenth part of that kind of interest which is required. You
must think of something else for your nephew, and pray do not blame
me if I recommend aiming at humble situations. It is impossible, in
the nature of society, that every branch of every creditable family can
have that preference to others from generation to generation.

As to the Archbishop of York I had a letter to him from Dr. Ball,
one of his particular friends. He asked me to a private dinner; but a
number of company came, and I had very little of his conversation,
for he does not show away in talk at his table upon a Sunday. I was
at the dinner which he gives in form to the Judges and Counsel on the
Northern Circuit, and a splendid dinner it was; indeed his table is
princely. In the evening, departing, he whispered to me, "Don't go,
there's a bed for you." So I and Mr. Law, King's Counsel, whose
brother is married to his Lordship's eldest daughter, stayed. His
Lordship took me to walk with him through his delightful Seat and
was quite easy: his conversation turned chiefly on British antiquities,
in which he seemed to be deeply versed; and he said a good deal of
Scotland, a considerable part of which he had seen some years ago.
There is nothing of the pedagogue or the high-priest in his domestic
behaviour: he is all affability, and even playfulness with his children.
I believe I should leave a card at his door in town; I will do it.

As to my canvass in my own county, I started in opposition to a
junction between Lord Eglintoun and Sir Adam Fergusson, who were
violent opponents, and whose coalition is as odious there, as the Great
One is to the nation. A few friends and real independent gentlemen
early declared for me; three other noble lords, the Earls of Cassillis,
Glencairn, and Dumfries, have lately joined and set up a nephew of
the Earl of Cassillis. A Mr. John Whitefoord, who as yet stands as
I do, will, I understand, make a bargain with this last alliance. Supposing he does, the two great parties will be so poised that I shall have
it in my power to cast the balance. If they are so piqued that either

will rather give the seat to me than be beaten by the other, I may have it. Thus I stand, and I shall be firm. Should Lord Lonsdale give me a seat he would do well, but I have no claim upon him for it.

General Paoli's steady kindness is indeed highly to be valued.

I have said nothing about the Regency, because you have it all in the newspapers. (Pray, which do you read?) Do you know I was at first carried away with the notion of the right having devolved to the Prince, and had almost written one of my very warm popular pamphlets for it; but Lord Lonsdale having been taken ill with a feverish disorder, from which he is not yet quite free, so that I have not yet seen him for five weeks, so as to know his sentiments, I prudently refrained, and have become satisfied that I was wrong; for there is a King, though his faculties be suspended. Pitt has behaved very ill in his neglect of me. I now think Dundas a sad fellow in his private capacity; he has used honest David cruelly. I breakfasted to-day with Hawkins; he is, I believe, a good man, but mean for a man of his fortune. We depend on your coming to London in April or May; it will be impossible to bear another disappointment. Write soon to your ever affectionate,

JAMES BOSWELL

HESTER THRALE (1741–1821)

The first of these letters was written to Doctor Johnson some months after the death of Thrale, and before the estrangement took place. By the time of the next the widow had long been married to Piozzi, an Italian musician, and had settled with him in England. It is quite a good example of her easy flow of chatter.

TO DR. JOHNSON

NOVEMBER 2, 1781

DEAR SIR, There was no need to be enraged because I thought you might easily forget a transaction not at all pleasing to remember; nor no need that I should be enraged if you had indeed forgotten it—but you was always suspicious in matter of memory. Cummins don't forget it, however, as I can tell you more at large. My health is growing very bad to be sure. I will starve still more rigidly for a while, and watch myself carefully; but more than six months will I not bestow upon that subject. You shall not have in me a valetudinary correspondent who is always writing such letters that to read the labels tied on bottles by an apothecary's boy would be more eligible and amusing; nor will I live like Flavia in Law's "Serious Call," who spends half her time and money on herself with sleeping draughts and waking draughts and cordials and broths. My desire is always to determine against my own gratification, so far as shall be possible for my body to co-operate with my mind, and you will not suspect me of wearing blisters and living wholly upon vegetables for sport. If that will do, the disorder may be removed; but if health is gone, and gone for ever, we will act as Zachary Pearce, the famous bishop of Rochester, did when he lost the wife he loved so—call for one glass to the health of her who is departed, never more to return—and so go quietly back to the usual duties of life and forbear to mention her again from that time till the last day of it.

Susan is exceedingly honoured, I think, by Miss Seward's enquiries, and I would have Susan think so too; the humbler one's heart is, the more one's pride is gratified, if one may use so apparently Irish an

446

expression, but the meaning of it does not lie deep. They who are too proud to care whether they please or no, lose much delight themselves and give none to their neighbours. Mrs. Porter is in a bad way, and that makes you melancholy; the visits to Stowhill will this year be more frequent than ever. I am glad Watt's "Improvement of the Mind" is a favourite book among the Lichfield ladies: it is so pious, so wise, so easy a book to read for any person, and so useful, nay, necessary, are its precepts to us all, that I never cease recommending it to our young ones. 'Tis *à la portée de chacun* so, yet never vulgar; but Law beats him for wit; and the names are never happy in Watts, somehow. I fancy there was no comparison between the scholastic learning of the two writers; but there is prodigious knowledge of the human heart, and perfect acquaintance with common life, in the "Serious Call." You used to say you would not trust me with that author upstairs on the dressing-room shelf, yet I now half wish I had never followed any precepts but his. Our lasses, indeed, might possibly object to the education given her daughters by Law's "Eusebia."

That the ball did so little towards diverting you I do not wonder: what can a ball do towards diverting any one who has not other hopes and other designs than barely to see people dance, or even to dance himself? They who are entertained at the ball are never much amused by the ball, I believe; yet I love the dance on Queeney's birthday and yours, where none but very honest and very praiseworthy passions, if passions they can be called, heighten the mirth and gaiety. It has been thought by many wise folks that we fritter our pleasures all away by refinement, and when one reads Goldsmith's works, either verse or prose, one fancies that in corrupt life there is more enjoyment—yet we should find little solace from alehouse merriment or cottage carousals, whatever the best wrestler on the green might do, I suppose—mere brandy and brown sugar liqueur, like that which Foote presented the Cherokee kings with, and won their hearts from our fine ladies who treated them with sponge biscuits and Frontiniac. I am glad Queeney and you are to resolve so stoutly and labour so violently; such a union may make her wiser and you happier, and can give me nothing but delight.

We read a good deal here in your absence, that is, I do. It is better we sate all together than in separate rooms; better that I read what is not fit for the young ones to hear. Besides, I am sure they must hear that which I read out to them, and so one saves the trouble of commanding what one knows will never be obeyed—I can find no other way as well.

Come home, however, for 'tis dull living without you. Sir Philip and Mr. Selwyn call very often, and are exceedingly kind. I see them always with gratitude and pleasure; but as the first has left us now for a month, come home therefore. You are not happy away, and I fear I shall never be happy again in this world between one thing and another. My health, flesh, and complexion are quite lost, and I shall have a red face if I live, and that will be mighty detestable—a humpback would be less offensive, vastly.

This is the time for fading: the year is fading round us, and every day shuts in more dismally than the last did. I never passed so melancholy a summer, though I have passed some that were more painful: privation is indeed supposed to be worse than pain.

Instead of trying the *Sortes Virgilianae* for our absent friends, we agreed after dinner to-day to ask little Harriet what they were doing now who used to be our common guests at Streatham. "Dr. Johnson," (says she) "is very rich and wise; Sir Philip is drown'd in the water—and Mr. Piozzi is very sick and lame, poor man!" What a curious way of deciding! all in her little soft voice. Was not there a custom among the ancients in some country—'tis mentioned in Herodotus, if I remember right—that they took that method of enquiring into futurity from the mouths of infants under three years old?—but I will not swear to the book I have read it in. The Scriptural expression, however, "Out of the mouths of babes and sucklings," etc., is likely enough to allude to it, if it were once a general practice. In Ireland, where the peasants are mad after play, particularly backgammon, Mr. Murphy says they will even, when deprived of the necessaries for continuing so favourite a game, cut the turf in a clean spot of green sward, and make it into tables for that amusement, setting a little baby boy behind the hedge to call their throws for them, and supply with his unconscious decisions the place of box and dice.

Adieu, dear Sir, and be as cheerful as you can this gloomy season, I see nobody happy hereabouts but the Burneys; they love each other with uncommon warmth of family affection, and are beloved by the world as much as if their fondness were less concentrated. The Captain has got a fifty-gun ship now, and we are all so rejoiced. Once more farewell, and do not forget Streatham nor its inhabitants, who are all much yours—and most so of all

Your faithful Servant,
H. L. THRALE

We never name Mr. Newton of Lichfield: I hope neither he nor his fine China begin to break yet—of other friends there the accounts get very bad to be sure.

TO MRS. PENNINGTON

PENZANCE, SUNDAY, FEB. 25, 1821

MY last letter to dear Mrs. Pennington should be a pretty one, but it will only be dull; replete with Kitchen-griefs, and thanks to Heaven that they are my worst afflictions. Mr. Kenrick's insults have brought me civil letters from Lord and Lady Keith, kind ones from Mr. and Mrs. Hoare, and all will end—in nothing, as they hope, and as I firmly believe. Pray do not suffer your good husband, (so much younger than myself,) to grow old. He and I mean to keep on this many a day, and we will not *shew teeth* when *biting* is over with us.

Now for the Kitchen-griefs. James has behaved monstrously ill, "beaten the Maids a row," like the fierce fellow in Shakespeare, and forced reproofs even from *my acquaintance* by his *out-door* conduct. This has been going on a long while, but I forbore to speak to you about it, till it suited me to say—do, dear Mrs. Pennington, get me a footman. Not a fellow to wear *his own clothes*; I must have a *livery* servant, who will walk before the chair, and ride behind the coach, and be an old-fashioned, tho' not ill-looking servant. My little plate, so small in quantity, is easily cleaned, but *clean* it must be. For I will not live in a state of disgust when I have a decent mansion over my head, and James was too dirty and slovenly, even for a wretched smoky closet like that I inhabit at Penzance: he is a sad fellow . . .

& now

Let me tell you the sights that we have *seen*. I always like them better than the tales that we have *heard*; and to-day the tales are truly melancholy. Lord Combermere has lost his only child, a son; so his honours and titles are gone, and the estate will fall, I suppose, to Willoughby Cotton, son of the Admiral, my Uncle's *second* boy. He had nine. *This* young fellow was a Colonel in what regiment I know not, and married Lady Augusta Coventry, who brings babies every year:—but these are *not* the sights I meant to tell you of.

On last Wednesday, then, a memorable day, Mr. George Daubuz John undertook to show us the Land's End, and we did stand upon the last English stone, jutting out from the cliffs, 300 feet high, into the Atlantic Ocean, which lay in wild expanse before us, tempting our eyes towards the land Columbus first explored, Hispaniola. Dinner

E.L.   Q at a mean house, affording only eggs and bacon, gave us spirits to go, not forward, for we could go no further, but sideways to a tin and copper mine under the sea.   Aye! 112 fathom from the strange spot of earth we stood on, in a direct line downwards, where no fewer than three score human beings toil for my Lord Falmouth in a submarine dungeon, listening at leisure moments, if they *have* any, to the still more justly to be pitied mariner, who is so liable to be wrecked among those horrid rocks, proverbial over all the kingdom,—Cornish rocks! ruinous to approach, as difficult to avoid.   The men go up and down in buckets, with two lighted candles each, into a close path, long and intricate.   And should their lights go out before their arrival in the open space where their companions work, there they must remain till the hour of relieving one wretched set by another comes to set them free.   Billows, meanwhile, roaring over their heads, upon a stormy day most dreadful, threatening to burst the not very thick partition of solidity that divides them from the light of heaven, bestowed on all but miners.   This place is called Botalloch, whence we drove home our half-broken carriage but not even half-broken bones; having refreshed at the house on which is written "First Inn in England" on one side the board, and "Last Inn in England" on the other.   By "us" and "we" I mean Miss Willoughby and H.L.P., but we took our two maids, Bell and Hickford, on the dicky, and James rode.   Four horses were not too many for such an exploit, tho' one of them was a Waterloo warrior.

We will go to Conway's Benefit certainly, if I get home time enough: Miss Willoughby will wish herself of the party most truly. But for her I should have passed many a dreary hour. . . .

LADY SARAH BUNBURY (1745-1826)

Daughter of the 2nd Duke of Richmond, and successively the wife of Sir Thomas Charles Bunbury, Bart., and the Hon. George Napier, she was famous for her beauty, her vivacity, and her charming personality. Many of her letters were written to a life-long friend, Lady Susan Fox Strangways (afterwards O'Brien). Both girls were bridesmaids at the wedding of George III and Princess Charlotte.

TO LADY SUSAN O'BRIEN

PARIS, MAY 5, 1765

I ARRIVED here this day sevennight, my dear Netty, & am so taken up with everything I see, that I hardly know where I am. In the first place, the town is beautiful, and the people so genteel that it's a real amusement to drive about the streets. I have seen no beauties yet, for there being no assemblies 'tis ten to one if I should see them before I went, if 'twas not for Marli, where the Court now is; and I am to see the King play at cards (not to be presented). Louisa is here, she and I go back in a month to England; my sister, I fancy, stays longer. Ste. & Charles & Tatty were with us. We had a very pleasant journey, and I should like it vastly if my dear Charles was here too, but I own I am so impatient to get back that it takes off my pleasure. Lord and Lady Hertford [the Ambassador] are very civil to me. There was never anything so beautiful as their house is, it is quite a palace even here, where the style of houses in general are charming in my opinion. 'Tis true they are inconvenient & dirty, but for one's own appartments they are delightful. In the first place, they are mostly upon the groundfloor, & have every one a garden, (where there are horse-chestnuts for shade). The rooms are large, the windows immense & all down to the ground, the furniture very fine (if new), for there are comodes even in our lodgings, & looking-glasses in every part of the room & very large ones. The houses are dirty & cold, but yet I own I like the style of them infinitely.

The Opera is the most ridiculous music you can imagine; 'tis most

like to Mrs Clive when she imitates an Italian singer than to anything
I know; but the dances & the scenery is beyond anything I ever saw.
The actors have all been quarrelling, & Madamoiselle Clairon talks
of going into a convent: I have, however, seen Presilli, a charming
comedian I think, & the most like to Garrick of any actor I ever saw.
By the bye, I met him at Calais; he is grown to look very old & thin,
& I hear is grown mighty pert with the immense rout that has been
made with him here.   But that's *entre nous*, for I have no notion of
owning it is possible he can be spoiled to any but friends.   Louisa
sends her love to you, my dear Netty; my best compts to Mr O'Brien.
I mean to write to you from hence towards the end of my journey;
for, till I have seen all, it's very useless to write & 'tis but by slow
degrees I get to see anything.   Adieu.

Yours most sincerely & affectionately,

S. B.

TO THE SAME

BARTON, JULY THE 12TH, 1765

I CAME from Woburn the other day with Madame Bouffler, & brought
her to Newmarket & here.   She is just gone.   She liked Newmarket
vastly.   There was a meeting of two days this time of year, to see the
sweetest little horse run that ever was.   His name is Gimcrack, he is
delightful.   Lord Rockingham, the Duke of Grafton, & General
Conway kissed hands the day Gimcrack ran.   I must say I was more
anxious about the horse than the Ministry, which sounds odd, for
Sir Charles loses £4,000 a year by the Secretary's pay; but there
was such numberless reasons to object to it that I am quite comforted
for it.

I will give orders about your flower-roots & things very soon.   I
wish you would not leave it to me to chuse what you'd have, it's the
most difficult thing in the world; but if I must, the thing *I* would
choose for myself would be a very good horse; if the expense of keeping
it is not an objection I think it a very good thing, but pray tell me
your choice sincerely.

I have brought you a little French china white cup.   I think it
very pretty, but if you would like a coloured one better you shall have
it, if they come safe through the Custom house, & are not all broke.
I would have bought you something else, but tea things I know you
have, & upon my word china is so dear, & I spent so much more than

I meant before I knew what I was about, that I am absolutely ruined,
& now that the good *place* is gone, it's really serious.

Adieu, my dear Netty, my best compts to Mr O'Brien.   God
bless you.

Believe me yours most affecately,

S. BUNBURY

HANNAH MORE (1745–1833)

A woman of strong religious interests, Hannah More had a very vivid personality. That she was by no means narrow in her views is demonstrated by her letter to Garrick.

TO MR. GARRICK

BRISTOL, JUNE 10TH, 1776

MY DEAR SIR, I have devoured the newspapers for the last week with the appetite of a famished politician, to learn if my General had yet laid down arms; but I find you go on with a true American spirit, destroying thousands of his Majesty's liege subjects, breaking the limbs of many, and the hearts of all.

When I promised I would not plague you with any of my nonsense till you were disengaged, could I possibly divine you would be so good as to honour me with a letter?—ay, and a charming letter, too, albeit a little one—it made me so proud and so happy!—but you are so used to make folks proud and happy, that it is nothing to you; and what would be a violent effort to other people, slides naturally into your ordinary course of action.

I think by the time this reaches you I may congratulate you on the end of your labours, and the completion of your fame—a fame which has had no parallel, and will have no end. Yet, whatever reputation the world may ascribe to you, I, who have had the happy privilege of knowing you intimately, shall always think you derived your greatest glory from the temperance with which you enjoyed it, and the true greatness of mind with which to lay it down. Surely to have suppressed your talents in the moment of your highest capacity for exerting them, does as much honour to your heart, as the exertion itself did to your dramatic character: but I cannot trust myself on this subject, because, as Sterne says, I am writing to the man himself; yet I ought to be indulged—for, is not the recollection of my pleasures all that is left me of them? Have I not seen in one season that *man* act *seven-and-twenty* times, and rise each time in excellence, and shall I be silent? Have I not spent three months under the roof of that man

454

and his dear charming lady, and received from them favours that would take me another three months to tell over, and shall I be silent?

But highly as I enjoy your glory (for I do enjoy it most heartily, and seem to partake it too, as I think a ray of it falls on all your friends), yet I tremble for your health. It is impossible you can do so much mischief to the nerves of other people, without hurting your own—in Richard especially, where your murders are by no means confined to the Tower, but you assassinate your whole audience who have hearts;— I say, I tremble lest you should suffer for all this; but it is over now, as I hope are the bad effects of it to yourself. You may break your *wand* at the end of your trial, when you lay down the office of *haut intendant* of the passions; but the enchantment it raised you can never break, while the memories and feelings remain of those who were ever admitted into the magic circle.

This letter is already of a good impudent length, and to the person of all others who has the least time to read nonsense. I will not prolong my impertinence but to beg and conjure that I may hear a little bit about your finishing night. The least scrap, printed or manuscript, paragraph or advertisement, merry or serious, verse or prose, will be thankfully received and hung up in the temple of reliques.

Pray tell my sweet Mrs. Garrick I live in the hope of hearing from her; and tell her farther that she and you have performed a miracle, for you have loaded one person with obligations, and have not made an ingrate.

Viva V. M. Mille Años!

H. MORE

And has "The Nine" really been called for? What a comfort was that piece of flattery!

I send the Bristol play-bill "by the King's servants." Do not you think the King has a great many servants that neither he nor anybody else ever heard of?

SAMUEL PARR (1747-1825)

*Samuel Parr was a schoolmaster. He had been in the running
for the headmastership of Harrow but lost the appointment through
backstairs politics, so he opened another establishment at Stanmore.
Probably no one ever courted a wife with so curious a letter as the
following. But Jane Morsingale accepted; and as she was a woman
with a sharp temper and a keen tongue, there is little doubt that in
married life she made up in talking what had been missed when they
were courting.*

TO JANE MORSINGALE

MADAM, You are a very charming woman, and I should be happy to
obtain you as a wife. If you accept my proposal I will tell you who
was the author of Junius.

S. P.

CUTHBERT, ADMIRAL LORD COLLINGWOOD (1750–1810)

The first of these letters was written by the Admiral just after he had been paid off, following a cruise in the West Indies. He had gone North to get married and he writes to his old friend Captain Nelson, who was also at that time without employment. The other letters were written home while cruising off the coast of Spain.

TO CAPTAIN NELSON

MORPETH, NOV. 14, 1792

MY DEAR FRIEND, I am much obliged to you for your letter, which I received last month; it was particularly welcome to me, as it brought information of your and Mrs. Nelson's good health. You must not be displeased that I was so long without writing to you. I was very anxiously engaged a great part of the time, and perhaps sometimes a little lazy; but my regard for you, my dear Nelson, my respect and veneration for your character, I hope and believe will never be lessened. God knows when we may meet again, unless some chance should draw us to the sea-shore. I hope, however, to have long the happiness of hearing of your welfare. There are great commotions in our neighbourhood at present. The seamen at Shields have embarked themselves, to the number of 1,200 or 1,400, with a view to compel the owners of the coalships to advance their wages; and, as is generally the case when they consider themselves the strongest party, their demand has been exorbitant. Application was made to Government for such assistance as the remedy of this evil might require. They have sent the Drake and Martin sloops to join the Race-horse, which was here before, and some troops of dragoons, whose presence, I hope, will dispose the Johnnies to peace, without their having occasion to act. But the times are turbulent; and the enthusiasm for liberty is raging even to madness. The success of the French people in establishing their republic has set the same principle, which lurked in every state of Europe, afloat; and those who secreted it in their bosoms have now the boldness to avow a plan for adopting it in the government of this Country, and to recruit volunteers for carrying their purpose into

457

execution. In this neighbourhood we seem to be pacific. Misery will undoubtedly be the consequence of any commotion or attempt to disturb our present most excellent Constitution. My wife joins me in best regards to you and Mrs. Nelson; and pray, when you have leisure, let me hear from you. God bless you, and believe me, my dear Nelson, affectionately and faithfully yours.

TO LADY COLLINGWOOD

Ocean, off Cadiz, July 28, 1808

I HAVE just received your letter of the 25th June, out of the sea; for the Pickle schooner, which brought it out with all the public despatches, ran on a reef of rocks in the night, and is entirely lost. The despatches, being on weighty subjects, I am afraid are all lost; your lighter letter was saved from the wreck with some others, and gave me the happiness of hearing that you were well. The Spaniards have been in great spirits since their victory; but they have rather marred the business by allowing the French to capitulate. I shall mend it for them as much as I can.

I am sorry to find my picture was not an agreeable surprise: I did not say anything to you about it, because I would always guard you as much as I could against disappointment; but you see, with all my care, I sometimes fail. The painter was reckoned the most eminent in Sicily; but you expected to find me a smooth-skinned, clear-complexioned gentleman, such as I was when I left home, dressed in the newest taste, and like the fine people who live gay lives ashore. Alas! it is far otherwise with me. The painter was thought to have flattered me much: that lump under my chin was but the loose skin from which the flesh has shrunk away; the redness of my face was not, I assure you, the effect of wine, but of burning suns and boisterous winds; and my eyes, which were once dark and bright, are now faded and dim. The painter represented me as I am; not as I once was. It is time and toil that have worked the change, and not his want of skill. That the countenance is stern, will not be wondered at, when it is considered how many sad and anxious hours and how many heartaches I have. I shall be very glad when the war is over. If the other nations of Europe had resisted the French as the Spaniards have done, governments would not have been overturned nor countries despoiled. But Spain has had many favourable circumstances; they got rid of a weak court and licentious nobility. The invisible power that directs the present

Government is the priesthood; the people are their instruments, whom they raise to an enthusiasm that makes them irresistible. Buonaparte has not merely the Spanish army to combat, (indeed the best of them are prisoners either in the north or at Lisbon,) but it is the Spanish nation which is opposed to him. Every peasant is a soldier, every hill a fortress. As soon as I have settled affairs here, which will be as soon as the supplies come from England, I shall proceed up the Mediterranean again, where I have much to do in many points. I hope I am working them pretty well at this moment, and that my ships are actively employed.

—— writes to me that her son's want of spirits is owing to the loss of his time when he was in England, which is a subject that need give her no concern, for if he takes no more pains in his profession than he has done, he will not be qualified for a lieutenant in sixteen years, and I should be very sorry to put the safety of a ship and the lives of the men into such hands. He is of no more use here as an officer than Bounce is, and not near so entertaining. She writes as if she expected that he is to be a lieutenant as soon as he has served six years, but that is a mistaken fancy; and the loss of his time is while he is at sea, not while he is on shore. He is living on the navy, and not serving in it. —— too is applying to go home. If he goes he may stay; for I have no notion of people making the service a mere convenience for themselves, as if it were a public establishment for loungers.

TO HIS DAUGHTERS

VILLE DE PARIS, MINORCA, APRIL 17, 1809

I RECEIVED both your kind letters, and am much obliged for your congratulations on my being appointed Major-General of Marines. The King is ever good and gracious to me; and I dare say you both feel that gratitude to His Majesty which is due from us all, for the many instances of his favour which he has bestowed on me, and, through me, on you. Endeavour, my beloved girls, to make yourselves worthy of them, by cultivating your natural understandings with care. Seek knowledge with assiduity, and regard the instructions of Mrs. Moss, when she explains to you what those qualities are which constitute an amiable and honourable woman. God Almighty has impressed on every breast a certain knowledge of right and wrong, which we call conscience. No person ever did a kind, a benevolent, a humane, or charitable action, without feeling a consciousness that it was good; it creates a pleasure in the mind that nothing else can produce: and this pleasure is the greater, from the act which causes it being veiled from the eye of the world. It is the delight such as angels feel when they wipe away the tear from affliction, or warm the heart with joy. On the other hand, no person ever did or said an ill-natured, an unkind, or mischievous thing, who did not, in the very instant feel that he had done wrong. This kind of feeling is a natural monitor, and never will deceive if due regard be paid to it; and one good rule, which you should ever bear in mind, and act up to as much as possible, is, never to say anything which you may afterwards wish unsaid, or do what you may afterwards wish undone.

The education of a lady, and indeed of a gentleman too, may be divided into three parts; all of great importance to their happiness, but in different degrees. The first part is the cultivation of the mind, that they may have a knowledge of right and wrong, and acquire a habit of doing acts of virtue and honour. By reading history you will perceive the high estimation in which the memories of good and virtuous people are held; the contempt and disgust which are affixed to the base, whatever may have been their rank in life. The second part of education is to acquire a competent knowledge how to manage your affairs, whatever they may happen to be; to know how to direct the economy of your house; and to keep exact accounts of every thing which concerns you. Whoever cannot do this must be dependent on somebody else, and those who are dependent on another cannot be perfectly at their ease. I hope you are both very skilful in Arithmetic, which, independently of its great use to every body in every condition of life, is one of the most curious and entertaining sciences that can be conceived. The characters which are used, the 1, 2, 3, are of Arabic origin; and that by the help of these, by adding them, by subtracting or dividing them, we should come at last to results so far beyond the comprehension of the human mind without them, is so wonderful, that I am persuaded that if they were of no real use, they would be exercised for mere entertainment; and it would be a fashion for accomplished people, instead of cakes and cards at their routs, to take coffee and a difficult question in the rule of three, or extracting the square root.—The third part is, perhaps, not less in value than the others. It is how to practise those manners and that address which will recommend you .to the respect of strangers. Boldness and forwardness are exceedingly disgusting, and such people are generally more disliked the more they are known; but, at the same time, shyness and bashfulness, and the shrinking from conversation with those with whom you ought to associate, are repulsive and unbecoming.

There are many hours in every person's life which are not spent in any thing important; but it is necessary that they should not be passed idly. Those little accomplishments, as music and dancing, are intended to fill up the hours of leisure, which would otherwise be heavy on you. Nothing wearies me more than to see a young lady at home, sitting with her arms across, or twirling her thumbs, for want of something to do. Poor thing! I always pity her, for I am sure her head is empty, and that she has not the sense even to devise the means of pleasing herself. By a strict regard to Mrs. Moss's instruction you will be perfected in all I recommend to you, and then how dearly shall I love you! May God bless you both, my dearest children.

GILBERT ELLIOT, 1ST EARL OF MINTO (1751–1814)

It was in India that Minto made his name, but the letters chosen here show the breadth of the statesman's interests and his keen observation on general matters.

TO LADY MINTO

THURSDAY, FEBRUARY 20, 1793

I SAW a letter yesterday from the sister of Edgeworth, the King of France's confessor, giving a short account of his attendance on the King at his execution and the day before. Edgeworth made his will and delivered it to his sister the day on which he was sent for to the Temple, desiring his sister not to inform his mother of his having undertaken that service until it should be over, expecting at that time that his own death would immediately follow that of the King. He went to the Temple the evening before the execution. The King asked him what he should do. He answered that he must retract his signature or assent to any acts which had been extorted from him in prejudice of the Catholic religion. The King answered that he had foreseen that this would be required of him and had already provided for it by his will, which he then produced to Edgeworth and asked him if that would be sufficient to entitle him to the sacrament, to which Edgeworth assented. He then proposed to administer the sacraments at five o'clock next morning, and applied to the Commissioners on the subject. They at first objected that he might administer a poisoned wafer; but Edgeworth suggested that they might themselves provide the wafer and other necessaries, if they suspected that he or the King could be guilty of so great a crime, and this was agreed to. Edgeworth passed the night in the Temple, and administered the sacrament at five in the morning. From that time the King's behaviour was firm and composed to the last. Edgeworth was on the scaffold with him, contrary to the report which has commonly prevailed, that none but the executioners and officers were there. It is thought that this false account was circulated in order to facilitate any misrepresentation of his behaviour that his enemies might wish to make. It had accordingly been put about that the King expected an attempt to rescue him, and that when he was prevented from haranguing the people, he had

462

shown great emotion and had called out "Ah! je suis perdu!" This story seems to detract in some manner from the courage which his behaviour indicated. It appears, however, from the letter I am mentioning, that no such thing happened. It is true (the letter says) that he shrank when the executioner began to bind his arms, but Edgeworth said to him, "Il faut suivre votre modèle jusqu'à la fin,"—meaning our Saviour. The King answered, "Cela est vrai; c'est le dernier sacrifice." He was immediately extended and placed for execution. Edgeworth continued still to speak to him and pray; and he was so near him and so earnest, that the first notice Edgeworth had of the stroke, was receiving the King's blood on his clothes. Edgeworth then descended the scaffold, expecting to be massacred; but the people made a wide passage for him, and he walked slowly through the crowd, the people looking at him with a sort of awful respect. He is now in retreat in the neighbourhood of Paris. The King's shrinking from the touch of the executioner was owing to a notion of dishonour attached to that circumstance.

This is a melancholy subject, but I thought you would like to hear particulars so authentic.

TO THE SAME

PRAGUE, JANUARY 3, 1800

I AM here to see Suwarrow on business, and am not sorry for the opportunity of seeing one of whom one has heard so much and such extraordinary things. Indeed it is impossible to say how extraordinary he is. There is but one word that can really express it. I must not on any account be quoted, but he is the most perfect Bedlamite that ever was allowed to be at large. I never saw anything so stark mad, and as it appears to me so contemptible in every respect. To give you some little notion of his manners, I went by appointment to pay my first visit, which I was told would be only one of ceremony. I was full dressed of course, and although I did not expect him to be so I was not prepared for what I saw. After waiting a good while in an antechamber with some aides-de-camp, a door opened and a little old shrivelled creature in a pair of red breeches and his shirt for all clothing, bustled up to me, took me in his arms, and embracing me with his shirt sleeves, made me a string of high-flown flummery compliments which he concluded by kissing me on both cheeks, and I am told I was in luck that my mouth escaped. His shirt collar was buttoned but he had no stock, and it was made of materials, and of a fashion, and was about as clean and white, as you may have seen on some labourers at home. On his arrival here he was waited upon by the Commandant at the head of all the Austrian officers, and received them exactly in the same attire. His whole manner and conversation are as mad as his first appearance, and indeed those about him seem conscious of it, for nobody is suffered to see him alone. He is always attended by one or two nephews, who never take their eyes off him, and seem to me to keep him in the sort of subjection that a keeper generally does. They discover at the same time the greatest anxiety lest his extraordinary manner and still more extraordinary discourse should detect him and discover his real situation. This is mixed up with the extreme of exterior submission, and with an appearance of looking up to these eccentricities and all the nonsense he talks as the inspiration of an oracle. He pretends, or thinks at times, that he has seen visions; and I have seen an official note written, or rather dictated, by him to Mr. Wickham, in which he says his Master, Jesus Christ, has ordered him so and so. His head wanders so much that it is with great difficulty he recollects himself through two sentences, and in order to accomplish this he is always clapping his hand before his eyes, and applying to his nephews for a word, and for the subject he is speaking on. What he says is not by any means intelligible, at least it requires a great deal of thought and ingenuity to get a meaning out of it. His writing is exactly like his talk. In the midst of all this there is a sort of wild obscure meaning that seems to wander through his mad conversation, and there is a great deal of that sort of sagacity or cunning towards his own personal objects which is characteristic of madness. With all this he is the most ignorant and incapable officer in the world; does nothing, and can do nothing himself, hardly ever knowing what is going forward; never looks at a map, never visits a post, or reconnoitres the ground; dines at eight in the morning, goes to bed for the rest of the day, gets up muddled and crazy for a few hours in the evening; and has owed his whole success in Italy to the excellent Austrian officers who served under him. He is not so mad as not to know that, and accordingly he refuses positively to trust himself with a Russian army alone, or without both Austrian troops and Austrian officers. In difficulty and danger he totally loses his head and lets himself be led very submissively; the danger over, he begins to vapour and take all the honour.

Such are heroes, and thus the world is led, and such is fame and name. This is a correct picture of this mad mountebank.

I cannot help wondering at his having gained Lord Mulgrave, and several other Englishmen. They were mostly cured, however, on further acquaintance; but Lord Mulgrave, who saw him but twice, came

away an enthusiastic admirer.   This is all most strictly confidential.   I
am come, in spite of all this, to keep him in Germany and to arrange a
great Russian army on the Rhine.   A Russian army ought to be terrible
to the enemy, for it is dreadful to its friends.   It is like a great blight
coming over a country.   They live entirely at free quarters, to the utter
ruin of the country-people.   The officers are as bad and pay for nothing.
The Grand Duke Constantine himself would not pay for his post-
horses, and beat the waiters or landlords if they presented a bill for his
dinner or lodging.   The common soldiers, however, seem to make up for
everything by courage and hardiness and obedience in the field.

JANUARY 6

WE all got up yesterday at six in the morning to attend Suwarrow at Mass,
on their Christmas-day.   We saw him crawl on all fours to kiss the
ground, and hold his head on the ground almost a quarter of an hour, with
various other antics.   The vocal music, however, was good and entertained us.   After Mass we dined at about nine o'clock, and sat till twelve,
by which time all our heads were splitting.   Before dinner Frere and
Casamajor were presented to him.   The latter being extremely tall, and
Suwarrow very short, he jumped up on a chair to get at Casamajor's neck
and kiss him.   He began before we sat down to dinner by drinking a
tumbler full of rosolio or strong liqueur, the heat of which seemed to take
away his breath.   It is the sort of thing that people drink thimblefuls of.
At dinner he drank a variety of strong things, among others a cupful of
champagne which went round the table; and as the bottle was going
round, he held out his beer tumbler and had it filled again with champagne.   The bottle was set down by him at last.   Afterwards a servant
filled him a large tumbler of something which I did not know, but I presume it was not water.   You may imagine that he got fuddled pretty
early.   He talked incessantly and unintelligibly, becoming more and
more inarticulate.   As I sat next to him, and as most of his conversation
was addressed to me, I was really bored to death.   I got home about half-
past twelve and went to another great long dinner at the Governor's, at
two o'clock, after which I paid formal visits to ladies I had never seen;
altogether it was a long day.

TO THE SAME

MARCH 22, 1802

I WENT to Lord Nelson's [at Merton] on Saturday to dinner, and
returned to-day in the forenoon.   The whole establishment and way of

life is such as to make me angry, as well as melancholy; but I cannot alter it, and I do not think myself obliged or at liberty to quarrel with him for his weakness, though nothing shall ever induce me to give the smallest countenance to Lady Hamilton. She looks ultimately to the chance of marriage, as Sir W. [Hamilton] will not be long in her way, and she probably indulges a hope that she may survive Lady Nelson; in the meanwhile she and Sir William and the whole set of them are living with him at his expense. She is in high looks, but more immense than ever. She goes on cramming Nelson with trowelfuls of flattery, which he goes on taking as quietly as a child does pap. The love she makes to him is not only ridiculous, but disgusting: not only the rooms, but the whole house, stair-case and all, are covered with nothing but pictures of her and him, of all sizes and sorts, and representations of his naval actions, coats of arms, pieces of plate in his honour, the flagstaff of *L'Orient*, &c.—an excess of vanity which counteracts its own purpose. If it was Lady H.'s house there might be a pretence for it; to make his own a mere looking-glass to view himself all day is bad taste. Braham, the celebrated Jew singer, performed with Lady H. She is horrid, but he entertained me in spite of her. Lord Nelson explained to me a little the sort of blame which had been imputed to Sir Hyde Parker for Copenhagen; in the first place, for not commanding the attack in person, and in the next place, for making signals to recall the fleet during the action; and everything would have been lost if these signals had been obeyed. Lord Nelson said that he would trust to nobody sooner than to Sir Hyde against an enemy in deep water, but that he is not equal to shoals and responsibilities, and is too much afraid of losing ships to make the most of them.

RICHARD BRINSLEY SHERIDAN (1751–1816)

Here is an example of an airy note, delightfully turned but carrying its message none the less shrewdly.

TO MR. CREEVEY

RICHMOND HILL,
MONDAY—THE THIRD DAY OF PEACE AND TRANQUILLITY

MY DEAR CREEVEY, You must make my excuse to the Lord Mayor. Pray vouch that you should have brought me, but my cold is really so bad that I should infallibly lay myself up if I attempted to go.   Here are pure air, quiet and innocence, and everything that suits me.

Pray let me caution you not to expose yourself to the *air* after Dinner, as I find malicious people disposed to attribute to wine what was clearly the mere effect of the atmosphere.   My last hour to your Ladies, as I am certainly going to die; till when, however,

Yours truly,

R. B. S.

FRANCES BURNEY (1752–1840)

The sprightly author of "Evelina" is at her best when writing to her godfather, Daddy Crisp. Both the letters given here were written when she was at the height of her new-found fame, between the publication of "Evelina" and "Cecilia."

TO MR. CRISP

JANUARY, 1779

YOUR patience, my dear daddy, in being able to mention my name without invectives, as you have done in your letter to Hetty, forces me to write, because it makes me eager to thank you for not having taken offence at me. Indeed your last most excellent letter ought to have had my acknowledgments long since, but the fact is I received it when I was most violently out of sorts, and really had not spirits to answer it. I intended to have kept from you the subject of my uneasiness, because I know you will only scoff it, or, perhaps, think it should rather have gratified than dispirited me; and in truth I have been so plentifully lectured already upon my vexation, that I feel no *goût* for further lashing and slashing; and yet I will own to you the subject, because I had rather of the two you should think me a fool, than think I wanted gratitude sufficient to thank you for the many useful hints and the kind and excellent advice you took the trouble to give me.

In short, not to spend my whole letter in enigmatical preluding, just as I received your letter I had had information that my name had got into print, and what was yet worse, was printed in a new pamphlet.

I cannot tell you, and if I could you would perhaps not believe me, how greatly I was shocked, mortified, grieved, and confounded at this intelligence: I had always dreaded as a real evil my name's getting into print—but to be lugged into a pamphlet!

I must, however, now I have gone so far, tell you how it is, lest you should imagine matters worse. This vile pamphlet is called "Warley: a Satire"; it is addressed to the first artist in Europe, who proves to be Sir Joshua Reynolds. Probably it is to his unbounded partiality for "Evelina" that I owe this most disagreeable compliment, for he had been so eager to discover the author, that by what I had reason given me to conjecture, I fancy he has been not a little laughed at since the discovery, for divers *comique* sort of speeches which he had made while in the dark.

So now the murder's out! but, dear daddy, don't belabour me for my weakness, though I confess I was for more than a week unable to eat, drink, or sleep, for vehemence of vexation. I am now got tolerably stout again but I have been furiously lectured for my folly (as I see everybody thinks it) by all who have known it. I have, therefore, struggled against it with all my might, and am determined to aim at least at acquiring more strength of mind.

Yet, after all, I feel very forcibly that I am not—that I have not been—and that I never shall be formed or fitted for any business with the public. Yet now my best friends, and my father at their head, absolutely prohibit a retreat; otherwise I should be strongly tempted to empty the whole contents of my bureau into the fire, and to vow never again to fill it. But, had my name never got abroad with my book, ere this I question not I should again have tried how the world stood affected to me.

Now once again to your letter.

Why, my dear daddy, will you use so vile, so ill-applied a word as "officious" when you are giving me advice? Is it not of all favours the most valuable you can confer on me? and don't I know that if you had not somewhat of a sneaking kindness for me you would as soon bite off your own nose, as the Irishman says, as take so much trouble about me? I do most earnestly, seriously, and solemnly entreat that you will continue to me this first, best, greatest proof of regard, and I do, with the utmost truth and gratitude, assure you that it is more really flattering to me than all the flummery in the world. I only wish, with all my heart, you would be more liberal of it.

Every word you have urged concerning the spirit of gay, unrestrained freedom in comedies, carries conviction along with it,—a conviction which I feel, in trembling; should I ever venture in that walk publicly, perhaps the want of it might prove fatal to me. I do, indeed, think it most likely that such would be the event, and my poor piece, though it might escape cat-calls and riots, would be fairly slept off the stage. I cannot, however, attempt to avoid this danger, though I see it, for I would a thousand times rather forfeit my character as a writer, than risk ridicule or censure as a female. I have never set my heart on fame, and therefore would not, if I could, purchase it at the expense of all my own ideas of propriety. You who know me for a prude will not be surprised, and I hope not offended, at this avowal, for I should deceive you were I not to make it. If I should try, I must e'en take my chance, and all my own expectations may be pretty easily answered.

The Streathamites have been all re-assembled for these six weeks, and I have had invitation upon invitation to join them, or, in Mrs. Thrale's words, to go home. But Susan is at Howletts, and I can by no means leave town till her return. However, we correspond, and Mrs. Thrale's kindness for me promises to be as steady as it is flattering and delightful to me; but I never knew how much in earnest and in sincerity she was my friend till she heard of my infinite frettation upon occasion of being pamphleted; and then she took the trouble to write to me a long scolding letter; and Dr. Johnson himself came to talk to me about it, and to reason with me; and now I see that they have sufficient regard to find fault with me, I do indeed hope that I am well with them.

Yours affectionately,
F. B.

TO THE SAME

St. Martin's Street, January 22nd, 1780

My dearest Daddy, As this sheet is but to contain a sequel of what I writ last, not to aspire at being regarded as a separate or answer-claiming letter, I shall proceed without fresh preamble.

You make a *comique* kind of inquiry about my "incessant and uncommon engagements." Now, my dear daddy, this is an inquiry I feel rather small in answering, for I am sure you expect to hear something respectable in that sort of way, whereas I have nothing to enumerate that commands attention, or that will make a favourable report. For the truth is, my "uncommon" engagements have only been of the *visiting system*, and my "incessant" ones only of the *working party*;—for perpetual dress requires perpetual replenishment, and that replenishment actually occupies almost every moment I spend out of company.

"Fact! fact!" I assure you—however paltry, ridiculous, or inconceivable it may sound. Caps, hats, and ribbons make, indeed, no venerable appearance upon paper;—no more do eating and drinking;—yet the one can no more be worn without being made, than the other can be swallowed without being cooked; and those who can neither pay milliners nor keep scullions, must either toil for themselves, or go capless and dinnerless. So, if you are for high-polished comparison, I'm your man!

Now, instead of furbelows and gewgaws of this sort, my dear daddy probably expected to hear of duodecimos, octavos, or quartos! *Helas!*

I am sorry that is not the case,—but not one word, no, not one syllable did I write to any purpose, from the time you left me at Streatham, till Christmas, when I came home. But now I have something to communicate concerning which I must beg you to give me your opinion.

As my play was settled in its silent suppression, I entreated my father to call on Mr. Sheridan, in order to prevent his expecting anything from me, as he had had a good right to do, from my having sent him a positive message that I should, in compliance with his exhortations at Mrs. Cholmondeley's, try my fortune in the theatrical line, and send him a piece for this winter. My father did call, but found him not at home, neither did he happen to see him till about Christmas. He then acquainted him that what I had written had entirely dissatisfied me, and that I desired to decline for the present all attempts of that sort.

Mr. Sheridan was pleased to express great concern,—nay, more, to protest he would not accept my refusal. He begged my father to tell me that he could take no denial to seeing what I had done—that I could be no fair judge for myself—that he doubted not but it would please, but was glad I was not satisfied, as he had much rather see pieces before their authors were contented with them than afterwards, on account of sundry small changes always necessary to be made by the managers, for theatrical purposes, and to which they were loth to submit when their writings were finished to their own approbation. In short, he said so much, that my father, ever easy to be worked upon, began to waver, and told me he wished I would show the play to Sheridan at once.

This very much disconcerted me: I had taken a sort of disgust to it, and was myself most earnestly desirous to let it die a quiet death. I therefore cooled the affair as much as I conveniently could, and by evading from time to time the conversation, it was again sinking into its old state,—when again Mr. Sheridan saw my father, and asked his leave to call upon me himself.

This could not be refused.

Well,—I was now violently fidgeted, and began to think of alterations,—and by setting my head to work, I have actually now written the fourth act from beginning to end, except one scene. Mr. Sheridan, however, has not yet called, and I have so little heart in the affair that I have now again quite dropped it.

Such is the present situation of my politics. Now, I wish you much to write me your private opinion what I had best do in case of an emergency. Your letters are always sacred, so pray write with your usual sincerity and openness. I know you too well to fear your being offended if things should be so managed that your counsel cannot be followed; it will, at any rate, not be thrown away, since it will be a fresh proof of your interest in my affairs and my little self.

My notions I will also tell you; they are (in case I must produce this piece to the manager):—

To entirely omit all mention of the club;—

To curtail the parts of Smatter and Dabbler as much as possible;—

To restore to Censor his £5000 and not trouble him even to offer it;—

To give a new friend to Cecilia, by whom her affairs shall be retrieved, and through whose means the catastrophe shall be brought to be happy;—

And to change the nature of Beaufort's connexions with Lady Smatter, in order to obviate the unlucky resemblance the adopted nephew bears to our female pride of literature.

This is all I have at present thought of. And yet, if I am so allowed, even these thoughts shall all turn to nothing; for I have so much more fear than hope, and anxiety than pleasure, in thinking at all of the theatre, that I believe my wisest way will be to shirk—which, if by evasive and sneaking means I can, I shall.

Now concerning Admiral Jem;—you have had all the accounts of him from my mother; whether or not he has made any change in his situation we cannot tell. *The Morning Post* had yesterday this paragraph:—

"We hear Lieutenant Burney has succeeded to the command of Capt. Clerke's ship."

That this, as Miss Waldron said of her hair, is all a falsity, we are, however, certain, as Lord Sandwich has informed my father that the first lieutenant of poor Capt. Cook was promoted to the *Discovery*. Whether, however, Jem has been made first lieutenant of the *Resolution*, or whether that vacancy has been filled up by the second lieutenant of that ship, we are not informed. The letter from my admiral has not, it seems, been very clear, for I met the Hon. Capt. Walsingham last week on a visit, and he said he had been at court in the morning. "And the king," he continued, "said to me, 'Why, I don't think you captains in the navy shine much in the literary way!' 'No, sir,' answered I; 'but then, in return, no more do your Majesty's captains in the army'—except Burgoyne, I had a good mind to say!—but I did not dare."

I shall give you some further particulars of my meeting this Capt. Walsingham in some future letter, as I was much pleased with him.

I am sure you must have been grieved for poor Capt. Cook. How hard, after so many dangers, so much toil,—to die in so shocking a manner—in an island he had himself discovered—among savages he had himself, in his first visit to them, civilized and rendered kind and hospitable, and in pursuit of obtaining justice in a cause in which he had himself no interest, but zeal for his other captain! He was, besides, the most moderate, humane, and gentle circumnavigator who ever went out upon discoveries; agreed the best with all the Indians, and, till this fatal time, never failed, however hostile they met, to leave them his friends.

Dr. Hunter, who called here lately, said that he doubted not but Capt. Cook had trusted them too unguardedly; for as he always had declared his opinion that savages never committed murder without provocation; he boldly went among them without precautions for safety, and paid for his incautious intrepidity with his very valuable life.

The Thrales are all tolerably well,—Mr. Thrale, I think and hope, much better. I go to them very often, and they come here certainly once every week, and Mrs. Thrale generally oftener. I have had some charming meetings at their house, which, though in brief, I will enumerate.

At the first, the party was Mr. Murphy, Mr. Seward, Mr. Evans, Dr. Solander, and Lady Ladd. Dr. Johnson had not then settled in the borough.

Mr. Evans is a clergyman, very intimate with the Thrales, and a good-humoured and a sensible man.

Dr. Solander, whom I never saw before, I found very sociable, full of talk, information, and entertainment. My father has very exactly named him, in calling him a philosophical gossip.

The others you have heard of frequently.

Mr. Murphy "made at me" immediately;—he took a chair next mine, and would talk to me, and to me only, almost all the day. He attacked me about my play, entreated me most earnestly to show him the rest of it, and made it many compliments. I told him that I had quite given it up—that I did not like it now it was done, and would not venture to try it, and therefore could not consent to show it. He quite flew at this—vowed I should not be its judge.

"What!" cried he, "condemn in this manner!—give up such writing! such dialogue! such character! No, it must not be. Show it me—you shall show it me. If it wants a few stage-tricks trust it with me, and I will put them in. I have had a long experience in these matters. I know what the galleries will and will not bear. I will promise not to let it go out of my hands without engaging for its success."

This, and much more, he went on with in a low voice, obliging me by the nature of the subject to answer him in the same, and making everybody stare at the closeness of our confab, which I believe was half its pleasure to him, for he loves mischievous fun as much as if he was but sixteen.

While we were thus discoursing, Mr. Seward, who I am sure wondered at us, called out, "Miss Burney, you don't hear Dr. Solander." I then endeavoured to listen to him, and found he was giving a very particular account to the company of Captain Cook's appearance at Khamschatka—a subject which they naturally imagined would interest me. And so indeed it did; but it was in vain, for Mr. Murphy would not hear a word; he continued talking to me in a whisper, and distracted my attention in such a manner that I heard both and understood neither.

Again, in a few minutes, Mr. Seward called out, "Miss Burney, you don't hear this"; and yet my neighbour would not regard him, nor would allow that I should. Exhortation followed exhortation, and entreaty entreaty, till, almost out of patience, Mr. Seward a third time exclaimed:

"Why, Miss Burney, Dr. Solander is speaking of your brother's ship."

I was half ashamed, and half ready to laugh.

" Ay," said Mrs. Thrale, "Mr. Murphy and Miss Burney are got to flirtation, so what care they for Captain Cook and Captain Clerke."

"Captain Cook and Captain Clerke?" repeated Mr. Murphy,— "who mentioned them?"

Everybody laughed.

"Who?" said Mrs. Thrale. "Why Dr. Solander has been talking of them this hour."

"Indeed!" exclaimed he; "why, then, it's Miss Burney's fault: she has been talking to me all this time on purpose to prevent my listening."

Did you ever hear such assurance?

I can write no more particulars of my visit, as my letter is so monstrously long already; but in conclusion, Dr. Solander invited the whole party to the Museum that day week, and Lady Ladd, who brought me home, invited us all to dine with her after seeing it. This was by all accepted, and I will say something of it hereafter. I am very sorry I have forgot to ask for franks, and must not forget to ask your pardon.

And so God bless you, my dear daddy! and bless Mrs. Gast, Mrs. Ham, and Kitty, and do you say God Bless

Your ever loving and affectionate

F. B.

BATH, JUNE 9, 1780

My DEAREST SIR, How are you? where are you? and what is to come next? These are the questions I am dying with anxiety to have daily announced. The accounts from town [1] are so frightful, that I am uneasy, not only for the city at large, but for every individual I know in it. I hope to Heaven that ere you receive this, all will be once more quiet; but till we hear that it is so, I cannot be a moment in peace.

Does this martial law confine you quite to the house? Folks here say that it must, and that no business of any kind can be transacted. Oh, what dreadful times! Yet I rejoice extremely that the opposition members have fared little better than the ministerial. Had such a mob been confirmed friends of either or of any party, I think the nation must have been at their disposal; for, if headed by popular or skilful leaders, who and what could have resisted them?—I mean, if they are as formidable as we are here told.

Dr. Johnson has written to Mrs. Thrale, without even mentioning the existence of this mob; perhaps at this very moment he thinks it "a humbug upon the nation," as George Bodens called the parliament.

A private letter to Bull, the bookseller, brought word this morning that much slaughter has been made by the military among the mob. Never, I am sure, can any set of wretches less deserve quarter or pity; yet it is impossible not to shudder at hearing of their destruction. Nothing less, however, would do; they were too outrageous and powerful for civil power.

But what is it they want? who is going to turn papist? who, indeed, is thinking in an alarming way of religion—this pious mob, and George Gordon excepted?

I am very anxious indeed about our dear Etty. Such disturbance in her neighbourhood I fear must have greatly terrified her; and I am sure she is not in a situation or state of health to bear terror. I have written and begged to hear from her.

All the stage-coaches that come into Bath from London are chalked over with "No Popery," and Dr. Harrington called here just now, and says the same was chalked this morning upon his door, and is scrawled in several places about the town. Wagers have been laid that the popish chapel here will be pulled or burnt down in a few days; but I believe not a word of the matter, nor do I find that anybody is at all alarmed. Bath, indeed, ought to be held sacred as a sanctuary for invalids; and I doubt not but the news of the firing in town will prevent all tumults out of it.

[1] The Gordon Riots convulsed London during the first week of June, 1780.

Now, if, after all the intolerable provocation given by the mob, after all the leniency and forbearance of the ministry, and after the shrinking of the minority, we shall by-and-by hear that this firing was a massacre—will it not be villainous and horrible? And yet as soon as safety is secured—though by this means alone all now agree it can be secured—nothing would less surprise me than to hear the seekers of popularity make this assertion.

Will you, dear sir, beg Charlotte to answer this letter by your directions, and tell me how the world goes? We are sure here of hearing too much or too little. Mr. Grenville says he knows not whether anything can be done to Lord George; and that quite shocks me, as it is certain that, in all equity and common sense, he is either mad enough for Moorfields, or wicked enough for the Tower, and, therefore, that to one of these places he ought to go.

Friday Night.—The above I writ this morning, before I recollected this was not post-day, and all is altered here since. The threats I despised were but too well grounded, for, to our utter amazement and consternation, the new Roman Catholic chapel in this town was set on fire at about nine o'clock. It is now burning with a fury that is dreadful, and the house of the priest belonging to it is in flames also. The poor persecuted man himself has I believe escaped with life, though pelted, followed, and very ill used. Mrs. Thrale and I have been walking about with the footmen several times. The whole town is still and orderly. The rioters do their work with great composure, and though there are knots of people in every corner, all execrating the authors of such outrages, nobody dares oppose them. An attempt indeed was made, but it was ill-conducted, faintly followed, and soon put an end to by a secret fear of exciting vengeance.

Alas! to what have we all lived!—the poor invalids here will probably lose all chance of life, from terror. Mr. Hay, our apothecary, has been attending the removal of two, who were confined to their beds, in the street where the chapel is burning. The Catholics throughout the place are all threatened with destruction, and we met several porters, between ten and eleven at night, privately removing goods, walking on tiptoe, and scarcely breathing.

I firmly believe, by the deliberate villainy with which this riot is conducted, that it will go on in the same desperate way as in town, and only be stopped by the same desperate means. Our plan for going to Bristol is at an end. We are told it would be madness, as there are seven Romish chapels in it; but we are determined upon removing somewhere to-morrow; for why should we, who can go, stay to witness such horrid scenes?

Saturday Afternoon, June 10.—I was most cruelly disappointed in not having one word to-day. I am half crazy with doubt and disturbance in not hearing. Everybody here is terrified to death. We have intelligence that Mr. Thrale's house in town is filled with soldiers, and threatened by the mob with destruction. Perhaps he may himself be a marked man for their fury. We are going directly from Bath, and intend to stop only at villages. To-night we shall stop at Warminster, not daring to go to Devizes. This place is now well guarded, but still we dare not await the event of to-night; all the Catholics in the town have privately escaped.

I know not now when I shall hear from you. I am in agony for news. Our head-quarters will be Brightelmstone, where I do most humbly and fervently entreat you to write,—do, dearest sir, write, if but one word—if but only you name YOURSELF! Nothing but your own hand can now tranquillize me. The reports about London here quite distract me. If it were possible to send me a line by the diligence to Brighton, how grateful I should be for such an indulgence! I should then find it there upon our arrival. Charlotte, I am sure, will make it into a sham parcel, and Susy will write for you all but the name. God bless—defend—preserve you! my dearest father. Life is no life to me while I fear for your safety.

God bless and save you all! I shall write to-morrow from wherever we may be,—nay, every day I shall write, for you will all soon be as anxious for news from the country as I have been for it from town. Some infamous villain has put it into the paper here that Mr. Thrale is a papist. This, I suppose, is an Hothamite report, to inflame his constituents.

GEORGE CRABBE (1754–1832)

Born in the little Suffolk sea-town of Aldeburgh, Crabbe tried to earn a living by letters when his early studies as a surgeon proved vain. He moved up to London, by a lucky stroke of patronage was enabled to enter the Church, and was given the living of Trowbridge. His poem, "The Borough," is a masterpiece of character delineation. Among Crabbe's literary friends, who included all the people of culture in England, was Mary Leadbeater to whom the following letters were written.

TO MRS. LEADBEATER

TROWBRIDGE, 7TH SEPTEMBER, 1818

I KNOW very well, my dear lady, that the mind in its sorrows and troubles, besides that first and greatest support which it seeks, will likewise feel a secondary consolation in the sympathy of friends and even in awakening that sympathy. The children who sit in the market-place of this world of trial, say to their fellows, "We mourn for you," and they should be answered, "We weep." And so it should be; it would be miserable indeed if we had not some hearts to feel for us and with us.

I can most readily believe all that even a sister says of a brother, but I have nothing to add on the occasion, assured that your own mind has in itself every comfort that I could suggest, and many doubtless that I could not. You knew him intimately; I can have only the general ideas of a good man.

Your letter dated the 29th August did not reach me till the fifth of this month, and that in the evening. Yesterday I was too much engaged to write, for mine is a very populous parish, and requires much attendance, and this day I purpose to fulfil an engagement which will detain me till the 11th or 12th; and being unwilling that your kind and friendly letter should remain so long unacknowledged, I am sitting down with all my business and duties in contemplation,—to give you thanks, to ask you to excuse a hurried and confused reply, and to promise, like other naughty children, that I will do better for the time to come.

And it is this same hurry that put out of my mind what I was about to observe afore, when I was speaking of our claims to the sympathies of

478

our friends. I was going to mention that they are indeed our friends whom we then call upon; the mind turns to them, and if this be in any degree truth, then I am more obliged to you still; for however assured we are that those who profess to regard us are sincere, yet none of us dislike the proofs and evidences of their sincerity.

A description of your village society—for I must not slide but break into my subjects—would be very gratifying to me. How the manners differ from those in larger societies, or in those under different circumstances. I have observed an extraordinary difference in village manners in England; especially between those places, otherwise nearly alike, where there was, or where there was not, a leading man or a squire's family, or a manufactory near, or a populous vitiated town, &c.—all these and many other circumstances have great influence. Your quiet village with such influencing minds I am disposed to think highly of—no one perhaps very rich, none miserably poor, no girls from six years old to sixteen sent to a factory, where men, women, and children of all ages are continually with them breathing contagion: not all, however; we are not all so evil; there is a resisting power, and it is strong; but the thing itself, the congregating of so many minds and the intercourse it occasions will have its powerful and visible effect. But of this you have not; yet, as you mention your schools of both kinds, you must be more populous and perhaps not so happy as I was giving myself to believe.

We had a singular man—and I must have his name before I release you—from Ireland, and with your most inveterate accent and tone. He gave us (in a public meeting) a long, very long account of his efforts to convert Catholics by a communication of the Bible, and gave us instances of the avidity with which some Catholic poor people sought and read them. His zeal was the best of him; I can have no doubt of that, but much of the discretion of his avowed opposition to the Catholics, and his complaint, where I am not sure he was not the aggressor: he surely could not expect that a Catholic priest (who is sincere) will quietly give up the people whom he has guided. We have much of this zeal scattered about, of which I scarcely know what to think. Have you Bible Societies in Ireland? and do you send them about wherever you can? Is there not a text, "Let not your good be evil spoken of"? That is the misfortune and the frailty of unguided zeal: its good has evil spoken of it.

I will write my name and look for two lines; but complying with you, my dear lady, is a kind of vanity. I find, however, no particular vexation of spirit, and will do as you desire. Indeed your desire must be very unlike yours, if I were not glad to comply with it; for the world has not spoiled you, Mary, I do believe. Now it has me;—I have been absorbed in its mighty vortex, and gone into the midst of its greatness, and joined in its festivities and frivolities, and been intimate with its children. You may like me very well, my kind friend, while the purifying water, and your more effectual imagination are between us; but come you to England, or let me be in Ireland, and place us together till mind becomes acquainted with mind—and then! Ah! Mary Leadbeater! you would have done with your friendships with me! Child of simplicity and virtue, how can you let yourself be so deceived? Am I not a great fat rector living upon a mighty income, while my poor curate starves with six hungry children upon the scraps that fall from the luxurious table? Do I not visit that horrible London, and enter into its abominable dissipations? Am I not this day going to dine on venison and drink claret? Have I not been at election dinners, and joined the Babel confusion of a town hall? Child of simplicity, am I fit to be a friend to you, and to the peaceful, mild, pure, and gentle people about you? One thing is true—I wish I had the qualification. But I am of the world, Mary.

Though I hope to procure a free cover [for postage] for you, yet I dare not be sure, and so must husband my room.—I am sorry for your account of the fever among your poor. Would I could suggest anything. I shall dine with one of our representatives to-day; but such subjects pass off. All say, "Poor people! I am sorry"; and there it ends.

My verses are not yet entirely ready, but do not want much that I can give them. Some time in the passing year I believe some publisher will advertise them. If I had room, you should have some account of them. I return all your good wishes, and think of you with much regard, —more than indeed belongs to a man of the world. "Still be permitted occasionally to address thee!" Oh! my dear Mrs. Leadbeater, this is so humble that I am afraid it is in vain. Well, write soon then, and believe me sincerely and affectionately yours,

GEORGE CRABBE

TO THE SAME

TROWBRIDGE, WILTS, 5TH NOV., 1819

MY DEAR MADAM, Are you not a little naughty—more than a little—to write in a style so soothing to the vanity of authorship? Or do you believe me to be so correct, so conscious of balancing errors and infirmities, that your praises would only serve to give the moderate elevation of spirits which necessarily results from a friend's approbation? Alas! that vanity has its insinuations of so powerful a kind that they make their way into minds the most fortified by self-denial and guarded by humility! Yet I am sure you meant no more than to give that pleasure which your approval must afford, and I will not chide you for the pleasing feelings which stole upon me as I read your friendly and affectionate letter; but I will gladly accept the testimony of your regard, and set my failings and infirmities in battle-array against your joint and powerful commendation. In truth, my dear lady, something will and must be allowed for our satisfaction in a friend's approbation, and I will not suppress the honest avowal of that which you have given me.   I will own that there is a pleasure in the very act of composing verses, and there is (though of a more mixed kind) pleasure also in the submitting our efforts to the public; but the higher and more genuine satisfaction comes from the approving pen of the friends whom we love, and of whose judgment and power of deciding we are well informed.   As Sir Henry Englefield, one of your admirers, truly says—"The honest opinion of the author of the 'Cottage Dialogues' must ever have its value.   She who can so write must be a judge of what is written."

I have oftentimes thought and sometimes said how much I should love to see the whole fraternity of you in your commonwealth of Ballitore; and yet I am not fitted to be one of the members of that amiable society. I am a creature of this world, and mix too much with its people to be one of you; and yet I love you too, and am not so far a disciple of the relaxed philosophy of the great world as not to covet the enjoyments of simplicity, domestic affection, moral refinement, and unaffected sensibility; for so I appreciate your worth, and you may be sure that so thinking I am not so lost to nature and truth as to be indifferent to the worth of which I am able to form an estimate.   I very much love those young people of yours. You appear to be an agreeing and assorting kind of folk!   Would that seventy miles of water, and that salt and billowy water, were not between us!   In England, indeed—and yet I must not boast of my travelling energies neither, but there is a probability where there is a carriage-road and solid earth.   I am just returned from a visit to Cromer.

Money and versification have not of late that utter dissociation and repugnancy that they had of old.   Scott is wealthy.   Lord Byron might be.   Moore is indigent only by accident.   Rogers is rich and bountiful. The Lake Poets, if they have not money, say they want none; and I, who do not say so, have as much as does me good, and if I wish for one scrap of bank paper more, it is not for any indulgence to my own whims, appetites, or inclinations.   So it is a time of rich poets, but whether of rich poetry—No! that is another thing! A letter from Mr. Murray informs me that he is about to put me in splendid company, by engaging a celebrated artist to paint about thirty pictures for so many engravings to the verses which best afford scope and matter for his talents; and I am afraid in this case it will not be in my power to be a purchaser of my own rhymes.

I have at this time a house of sadness and suspense—our only little one, a girl, about two months old, appearing with a frame and constitution unsuited to the roughness of this world. She breathes with pain, and has often symptoms of decay. The parents are disappointed, but bear the evil with fortitude—patience I believe I should say. My elder son has two healthy children, so that the unpoetical and rude name is likely to live at least one generation longer. We are quiet in this part of the land, and in fact our tumults depend not upon politics, but the employment of the inhabitants. If they have work, they are peaceable and loyal; if not, they are whigs, rebels, and reformists.

17th Feb., 1820.—You see, my dear madam, how long since I thought of my debt to you. To-morrow we in this place look for an assembling of the people, and are doubtful whether they will be perfectly satisfied. George the Fourth is to be proclaimed king, and the silence so acceptable in general in a numerous assembly would here be dissatisfaction. How the event will be received in Ireland does not yet appear, but you are in a very quiet county, I believe.

Dear lady, forgive me my long silence. It would be unjust and ungenerous to ask that I might hear of you again, and that soon, after such an interval; but I have some little plea to make, and have hold upon your pity, for I have very much to do, and my spirits are not equal to my demands for them. My son is lost to me at this time, being with his wife in Suffolk. Our little baby died.

Accept our best respects and sincere good wishes. Present them to my younger friends, whom I should be glad to see, and, next that pleasure, to hear of. Teach thy friends to reckon amongst them yours affectionately,

G. CRABBE

SARAH SIDDONS (1755–1831)

That the divine Siddons could be graceful in the throes of a cold was only to be expected. That she should have been so kindly to a prosy gentleman like Mr. Windham is yet more to her credit.

TO MR. WINDHAM

FOUR O'CLOCK, THURSDAY MORNING, MAY 29, 1788

MY DEAR SIR, I take the earliest opportunity to thank you for your very obliging letter, and I should certainly put your kindness to the test were I not obliged to leave town to-morrow morning not without regret at having seen so little of you during my stay. I take my leave of you, my dear Sir, wishing you all the good you deserve, and above all things health of body and mind, for I think the langour of one enfeebles the other. It is lucky for me, however, that I have so pleasant an employment to beguile this tedious night as writing to you. "Past four o'clock," says the watch, and I have been unable to close my eyes to shut out the day, or to stop my ears to shut out the noise of my own terrible cough, which has tormented me four nights in the same way. I have this moment taken the resolution of getting all the business of the day done in an hour or two, and then taking a tolerable quantity of laudanum to procure a little sleep, for, though "Macbeth shall sleep no more," I fancy a little will be necessary to enable his lady to get through her bloody business to-night. I beg ten thousand pardons for troubling you with this history, but when a lady's in the talking vein, you know——

Adieu! my dear Sir. There is nothing of which I am more proud than the honour of being

Your affectionate and obliged humble servant,

S. SIDDONS

WILLIAM GODWIN (1756–1836)

The author of "Caleb Williams" was a man of strongly revolutionary principles, including a contempt for marriage, and he encouraged similar opinions in his friend and disciple Shelley. The fact gives added piquancy to the following letter to a woman friend, announcing his marriage to Mary Wollstonecraft, the feminist authoress, who professed the same views.

TO MARY HAYS

APRIL 10

MY fair neighbour desires me to announce to you a piece of news, which it is consonant to the regard that she and I entertain for you, you should learn rather from us than from any other quarter. She bids me remind you of the earnest way in which you pressed me to prevail upon her to change her name [1]; she directs me to add that it has happened to me, like many other disputants, to be entrapped in my own toils; in short, that we found that there was no way so obvious for her to drop the name of Imlay, as to assume the name of Godwin. Mrs. Godwin (who the devil is she?) will be glad to see you at No. 29 Polygon, Somers Town, whenever you are inclined to favour her with a call.

[1] *I.e.* To revert to her own name of Wollstonecraft, instead of Imlay.

WILLIAM BLAKE (1757–1827)

Blake is one of the strangest figures in English literature. A London engraver and painter who believed himself to be prophetically inspired, he was a poet of genius, and, in such works as "Jerusalem," had a very wide appeal. His letters illustrate his naïveté of character.

TO MR. BUTTS

Jan. 10, 1802

Dear Sir, Your very kind and affectionate letter, and the many kind things you have said in it, called upon me for an immediate answer. But it found my wife and myself so ill, and my wife so very ill, that till now I have not been able to do this duty. The ague and rheumatism have been almost her constant enemies, which she has combated in vain almost ever since we have been here; and her sickness is always my sorrow, of course. But what you tell me about your sight afflicted me not a little, and that about your health, in another part of your letter, makes me entreat you to take due care of both. It is a part of our duty to God and man to take due care of His gifts; and though we ought not think *more* highly of ourselves, yet we ought to think *as* highly of ourselves as immortals ought to think.

When I came down here, I was more sanguine than I am at present; but it was because I was ignorant of many things which have since occurred, and chiefly the unhealthiness of the place [Felpham]. Yet I do not repent of coming on a thousand accounts; and Mr. Hayley, I doubt not, will do ultimately all that both he and I wish—that is, to lift me out of difficulty. But this is no easy matter to a man who, having spiritual enemies of such formidable magnitude, cannot expect to want natural hidden ones.

Your approbation of my pictures is a multitude to me, and I doubt not that all your kind wishes in my behalf shall in due time be fulfilled. Your kind offer of pecuniary assistance I can only thank you for at present, because I have enough to serve my present purpose here. Our expenses are small, and our income, from our incessant labour, fully adequate to these at present. I am now engaged in engraving six

485

small plates for a new edition of Mr. Hayley's "Triumphs of Temper," from drawings by Maria Flaxman, sister to my friend the sculptor. And it seems that other things will follow in course, if I do but copy these well. But patience! If great things do not turn out, it is because such things depend on the spiritual and not on the natural world; and if it was fit for me, I doubt not that I should be employed in greater things; and when it is proper, my talents shall be properly exercised in public, as I hope they are now in private. For, till then, I leave no stone unturned, and no path unexplored that leads to improvement in my beloved arts. One thing of real consequence I have accomplished by coming into the country, which is to me consolation enough: namely, I have re-collected all my scattered thoughts on art, and resumed my primitive and original ways of execution, in both painting and engraving, which in the confusion of London I had very much lost and obliterated from my mind. But whatever becomes of my labours, I would rather that they should be preserved in your greenhouse (not, as you mistakenly call it, dunghill) than in the cold gallery of fashion. The sun may yet shine, and then they will be brought into open air.

But you have so generously and openly desired that I will divide my griefs with you that I cannot hide what it has now become my duty to explain. My unhappiness has arisen from a source which, if explored too narrowly, might hurt my pecuniary circumstances; as my dependence is on engraving at present, and particularly on the engravings I have in hand for Mr. Hayley: and I find on all hands great objections to my doing anything but the mere drudgery of business, and intimations that, if I do not confine myself to this, I shall not live. This has always pursued me. You will understand by this the source of all my uneasiness. This from Johnson and Fuseli brought me down here, and this from Mr. H. will bring me back again. For that I cannot live without doing my duty to lay up treasures in heaven is certain and determined, and to this I have long made up my mind. And why this should be made an objection to me, while drunkenness, lewdness, gluttony, and even idleness itself, do not hurt other men, let Satan himself explain. The thing I have most at heart—more than life, or all that seems to make life comfortable without—is the interest of true religion and science. And whenever anything appears to affect that interest (especially if I myself omit any duty to my station as a soldier of Christ), it gives me the greatest of torments. I am not ashamed, afraid, or averse to tell you what ought to be told—that I am under the direction of messengers from heaven, daily and nightly.

But the nature of such things is not, as some suppose, without trouble or care. Temptations are on the right hand and on the left. Behind, the sea of time and space roars and follows swiftly. He who keeps not right onwards is lost; and if our footsteps slide in clay, how can we do otherwise than fear and tremble? But I should not have troubled you with this account of my spiritual state, unless it had been necessary in explaining the actual cause of my uneasiness, into which you are so kind as to inquire: for I never obtrude such things on others unless questioned, and then I never disguise the truth. But if we fear to do the dictates of our angels, and tremble at the tasks set before us; if we refuse to do spiritual acts because of natural fears or natural desires, who can describe the dismal torments of such a state!—I too well remember the threats I heard!—"If you, who are organized by Divine Providence for spiritual communion, refuse, and bury your talent in the earth, even though you should want natural bread,—sorrow and desperation pursue you through life, and after death shame and confusion of face to eternity. Every one in eternity will leave you, aghast at the man who was crowned with glory and honour by his brethren, and betrayed their cause to their enemies. You will be called the base Judas who betrayed his friends!"—Such words would make any stout man tremble, and how then could I be at ease? But I am now no longer in that state, and now go on again with my task, fearless, though my path is difficult. I have no fear of stumbling while I keep it.

My wife desires her kindest love to Mrs. Butts, and I have permitted her to send it to you also. We often wish that we could unite again in society, and hope that the time is not distant when we shall do so, being determined not to remain another winter here, but to return to London.

> I hear a Voice you cannot hear, that says I must not stay,
> I see a Hand you cannot see, that beckons me away.

Naked we came here—naked of natural things—and naked we shall return: but while clothed with the Divine mercy, we are richly clothed in spiritual, and suffer all the rest gladly. Pray, give my love to Mrs. Butts and your family.

I am yours sincerely,
WILLIAM BLAKE

P.S.—Your obliging proposal of exhibiting my two pictures likewise calls for my thanks; I will finish the others, and then we shall judge of the matter with certainty.

TO THE SAME

23RD SEPTEMBER 1800

DEAR FRIEND OF MY ANGELS, We are safe arrived at our cottage without accident or hindrance, though it was between eleven and twelve
o'clock at night before we could get home, owing to the necessary
shifting of our boxes and portfolios from one chaise to another. We
had seven different chaises and as many different drivers. All upon
the road was cheerfulness and welcome. Though our luggage was
very heavy there was no grumbling at all. We travelled through a
most beautiful country on a most glorious day. Our cottage is more
beautiful than I thought it, and also more convenient, for though
small it is well proportioned, and if I should ever build a palace it
would only be my cottage enlarged. Please to tell Mrs. Butts that
we have dedicated a chamber for her service, and that it has a very
fine view of the sea. Mr. Hayley received me with his usual brotherly
affection. My wife and sister are both very well, and courting Neptune
for an embrace, whose terrors this morning made them afraid, but whose
mildness is often equal to his terrors. The villagers of Felpham are
not mere rustics; they are polite and modest. Meat is cheaper than in
London; but the sweet air and the voices of winds, trees and birds, and
the odours of the happy ground, make it a dwelling for immortals.
Work will go on here with God-speed. A roller and two harrows lie
before my window. I met a plough on my first going out at my gate
the first morning after my arrival, and the ploughboy said to the plough-
man, "Father, the gate is open." I have begun to work, and find
that I can work with greater pleasure than ever. Hoping soon to
give you a proof that Felpham is propitious to the arts.

God bless you! I shall wish for you on Tuesday evening as usual.
Pray give my and my wife's and sister's love and respects to Mrs. Butts.
Accept them yourself, and believe me, for ever, your affectionate and
obliged friend,

WILLIAM BLAKE

My sister will be in town in a week, and bring with her your
account, and whatever else I can finish.

Direct to me: Blake, Felpham, near Chichester, Sussex.

TO JOHN FLAXMAN

FELPHAM, 21ST SEPTEMBER 1800, SUNDAY MORNING
DEAR SCULPTOR OF ETERNITY, We are safe arrived at our cottage, which is more beautiful than I thought it, and more convenient. It is a perfect model for cottages, and I think for palaces of magnificence, only enlarging, not altering its proportions, and adding ornaments and not principles. Nothing can be more grand than its simplicity and usefulness. Simple without intricacy, it seems to be the spontaneous expression of humanity, congenial to the wants of man. No other formed house can ever please me so well; nor shall I ever be persuaded, I believe, that it can be improved either in beauty or use.

Mr. Hayley received us with his usual brotherly affection. I have begun to work. Felpham is a sweet place for study, because it is more spiritual than London. Heaven opens here on all sides her golden gates; her windows are not obstructed by vapours; voices of celestial inhabitants are most distinctly heard, and their forms more distinctly seen; and my cottage is also a shadow of their houses. My wife and sister are both well, courting Neptune for an embrace.

Our journey was very pleasant; and though we had a great deal of luggage, no grumbling. All was cheerfulness and good humour on the road, and yet we could not arrive at our cottage before half-past eleven at night, owing to the necessary shifting of our luggage from one chaise to another; for we had seven different chaises, and as many different drivers. We set out between six and seven in the morning of Thursday, with sixteen heavy boxes and portfolios full of prints.

And now begins a new life, because another covering of earth is shaken off. I am more famed in Heaven for my works than I could well conceive. In my brain are studies and chambers filled with books and pictures of old, which I wrote and painted in ages of eternity before my mortal life; and those works are the delight and study of archangels. Why, then, should I be anxious about the riches or fame of mortality? The Lord our Father will do for us and with us according to His divine will for our good.

You, O dear Flaxman! are a sublime archangel,—my friend and companion from eternity. In the Divine bosom is our dwelling place, I look back into the region of reminiscence, and behold our ancient days before this earth appeared in its vegetated mortality to my mortal vegetated eyes. I see our houses of eternity, which can never be separated, though our mortal vehicles should stand at the remotest corners of heaven from each other.

Farewell, my best friend! Remember me and my wife in love and friendship to our dear Mrs. Flaxman, whom we ardently desire to entertain beneath our thatched roof of rusted gold.—And believe me for ever to remain your grateful and affectionate

WILLIAM BLAKE

JAMES CARLYLE (1757–1832)

The father of Thomas Carlyle was one of those manful, earnest types that flourish in Scotland.   In this letter to his famous son there is a tragic poignancy at the spectacle of the old Calvinist facing the End.

TO HIS SON, THOMAS CARLYLE

MY DEAR SON, I cannot write you a letter, but just tell you that I am a frail old sinner that is very likely never to see you any more in this world.   Be that as it may, I could not help telling you that I feel myself gradually drawing towards the hour appointed for all living. And, O God! may that awful change be much at heart with every one of us.   May we be daily dying to sin and living to righteousness.   And may the God of Jacob be with you and bless you, and keep you in his ways and fear.   I add no more, but leave you in his hands and care.

JAMES CARLYLE

HORATIO LORD NELSON (1758–1805)

Nelson was commanding the frigate "Albemarle" when he wrote this letter to one of his fellow-officers. He was twenty-four at the time, and the letter was prophetic.

"ALBEMARLE," NEW YORK.

NOV. 14TH, 1782

DEAR PILFORD, Since I saw you yesterday I have changed my mind about appointing Edwards as boatswain but will ask Lord Hood to give him the rating in some other ship, this I hope will do as well. I am to dine with the Admiral today and very likely shall not be on board till nine; will you sup with me at ten. I will speak with you about Ross and what can be done. My interest at Home you know is next to nothing, the name of Nelson being little known, it may be different one of these days, a good chance only is wanting to make it so.

Yours sincerely,

HORATIO NELSON

MARY LEADBEATER (1758–1826)

Mrs. Leadbeater was a Quaker, and the author of some rather charming little works, typical of the period. Her first publication was "Extracts and Original Anecdotes for the Improvement of Youth"; some time later this was followed by "Cottage Dialogues among the Irish Peasantry." The dialogues are on such subjects as dress, a wake, a spinning match, cookery, marriage, and other incidents of peasant life.

TO MRS. TRENCH

BALLITORE, 24TH OF SEVENTH-MONTH, 1812

JOHN CUMMING, the Dublin bookseller, who published the last edition of the Cottage Dialogues, lately proposed that I should write a series of dialogues between men. I caught at the idea, and framed the histories of Thady and Martin. Thady begins with playing pitch and toss, because he was prevented amusing himself with a garden; he contracts a love of gaming and idleness; gets to be servant in the families of fox-hunting squires, and occasionally associates with Larry and Kit, some of his idle companions. At last he is humbled by the death of a young woman whom he had seduced; is taken into a clergyman's family, and becomes sensible of the advantage of his situation till Larry and Kit beguile him, and take him with them to Dublin under pretence of getting him a better place. Here they inveigle him into a robbery, one of his comrades escapes, the other is taken with him, turns king's evidence, and Thady is condemned to Botany Bay.

Martin loves his garden, is encouraged by his parents to cultivate it, it becomes a source of pleasure and profit, and he marries happily. Most of these dialogues are between Martin and Thady. I send thee two for a specimen.

We have extraordinary fine weather now, and I have spent much of the day watching our bees, while our old gardener was otherwise employed, he having left near me the frying-pan and weeding-knife, to sound the alarm, according to ancient custom, should the swarm issue out. Seated in a bower, I enjoyed the sweets of solitude. I felt much released from care. I thought how peculiarly favoured I

493

was in husband, children, friends; I beheld the simple garden blooming in the pride of summer; I saw the trees expanding which I had planted myself; the tinkling of the river, the hum of the bees, and occasional voices and sounds increased my quiet pleasure. I saw old James, the gardener, coming; I went to meet him, and we stood opposite the hives conjecturing whether or no the bees had a mind to swarm; and we stood, unconscious of danger, till I felt one of my enemies alight on my forehead. "Mistress, 'tis a bee coming home, and you were in its way; but here's the sting, however." The bee made a terrible bustle in my cap. James released him, and I walked into the house, holding my hand to my forehead, which began to pain severely. My eyes, my ears, my nose, my throat partook of the venom. I sneezed, grew hoarse, one eye presently closed, and I had serious fears for the other. The pain abated, but stupor, uneasiness, and inconvenience lasted for days, and the swelling is not yet quite gone.

Many beautiful poems leave an uncomfortable sensation on the mind, from the evident anxiety, depression, or sorrow of the writer; but the sentiments of thine accord with that of the virtuous Addison:

> Ten thousand thousand precious gifts
> My daily thanks employ,
> Nor is the least a cheerful heart,
> Which tastes these gifts with joy.

My father, who was one of the best men I ever knew, was also one of the happiest; he enjoyed his comforts, and diffused around him the glow of his cheerful gratitude. While I was thus pondering on the thoughts thy lines excited, I received a letter from a friend so much in unison with them that I must quote her:—"I doubt whether any incense is more acceptable than that which ascends from a grateful spirit. Clouds we must expect, because they are necessary for us; but we may safely wait till they come, and I am fully persuaded we often suffer more from anticipated evils than from real ones."

M. LEADBEATER

TO THE SAME

BALLITORE, 29TH OF NINTH-MONTH, 1813

MY ESTEEMED FRIEND, Thy apology for my "want of religion" is so kind and so grateful to me that I intend to shelter myself under it from the attacks of reviewers who in fact compliment me by noticing me at all, though I am conscious it is to Maria Edgeworth I owe this notice. Borne on her wing the first series of my "Dialogues" has crossed the line, and is read in India, and with peculiar pleasure by natives of Ireland.

We are greatly gratified by thy mention of Madame de Staël. The Princess Charlotte affords still more gratification, especially as we had heard strange accounts of her temper. One improbable story was that she carried on a correspondence with a young man; the relater thought it was the Prince of Orange, and that one of her ladies was picking the lock of her bureau, *by order*, to obtain his letters, when the princess entered the room, and snatching up one of the candles which were being borne before her flung it at her governess. Also we heard that she was accustomed to throw her books at the heads of her tutors, and disregard their instructions. So far for royalty.

Canst thou tell me whether Lord Byron and Lord Strangford are one and the same person? and what character does Lord Byron bear? There is fine poetry in "Childe Harold," but being, like Beattie's "Minstrel," neither narrative nor didactic, it causes some confusion in my head to comprehend it. Lord Byron seems very melancholy, and bewails his Thyrza in beautiful numbers. Ever thy obliged friend,

M. LEADBEATER

MARY WOLLSTONECRAFT (1759–97)

Here we meet one of the tragic characters of literature. A woman with strong feminist ideas, Mary Wollstonecraft lived for some time with an American named Imlay, who basely deserted her and their child, leaving the girl a victim to melancholia. Happily for her sanity she met and married William Godwin; but the birth of their child, who was in her turn to play a sinister part in the life of the poet Shelley, proved fatal to her. The letter below was written to Imlay from Paris and describes the last scenes in the life of Louis XVI.

TO GILBERT IMLAY

PARIS, DECEMBER 26, 1792

I SHOULD immediately on the receipt of your letter, my dear friend, have thanked you for your punctuality, for it highly gratified me, had I not wished to wait till I could tell you that this day was not stained with blood. Indeed the prudent precautions taken by the National Convention to prevent a tumult, made me suppose that the dogs of faction would not dare to bark, much less to bite, however true to their scent; and I was not mistaken; for the citizens, who were called out, are returning home with composed countenances, shouldering their arms. About nine o'clock this morning, the king passed by my window, moving silently along (excepting now and then a few strokes on the drum, which rendered the stillness more awful) through empty streets, surrounded by the national guards, who, clustering round the carriage, seemed to deserve their name. The inhabitants flocked to their windows, but the casements were all shut, not a voice was heard, nor did I see anything like an insulting gesture. For the first time since I entered France, I bowed to the majesty of the people, and respected the propriety of behaviour so perfectly in unison with my own feelings. I can scarcely tell you why, but an association of ideas made the tears flow insensibly from my eyes, when I saw Louis sitting, with more dignity than I expected from his character, in a hackney coach, going to meet death, where so many of his race have triumphed. My fancy instantly brought Louis XIV before me, entering the capital with all his pomp, after one of the victories most flattering to his pride, only to see the sunshine of prosperity overshadowed by the sublime gloom of misery. I have been alone ever since; and, though my mind is calm, I cannot dismiss the lively images that have filled my imagination all the day. Nay, do not smile, but pity me; for, once or twice, lifting my eyes from the paper, I have seen eyes glaring through a glass-door opposite my chair, and bloody hands shook at me. Not the distant sound of a footstep can I hear. My apartments are remote from those of the servants, the only persons who sleep with me in an immense hotel, one folding door opening after another. I wish I had even kept the cat with me! I want to see something alive; death in so many frightful shapes has taken hold of my fancy. I am going to bed— and, for the first time in my life, I cannot put out the candle.

M. W.

JOHN JAMES (1760–86)

This young man was the son of Boucher's great friend, Doctor James. He was an undergraduate at Queen's College, Oxford, in 1778, and took Holy Orders, but a very promising career was cut short when he died at the early age of twenty-six. One of his mother's letters is also given below.

TO J. BOUCHER

QUEENS. OCTOBER 7, 1779

DEAR SIR, I have once more arrived safe under the wing of Alma Mater, and am doing all in my power to forget the liveliness of Paddington in the solitary walls of a college, though the transition is not very abrupt either, from a Hermitage to a cloister. The cold which detained me a few days longer in town than I expected after bidding you adieu, has ended in the complaint that was so prevalent at the departure of the hot weather. I am now, however, clear of both and become as stout and as stupid as ever; for I begin to consider the latter as a symptom of good health with me, as I seldom am in such spirits as when out of order. Upon my arrival I found a letter just come from home. It contained little else than domestic good news, without a syllable of the sick Bishop [of Carlisle]. Upon the presumption that he is still in the land of the living, I have ventured to detain your frank a week longer and intend to stretch his lordship's privilege as far as it will go by stuffing it within a scruple of the prescribed weight.

The university is yet thin and desolate. As the term does not commence till the tenth, few of the absentees will think of returning till the last minute. A few solitary tutors, that drop in one by one, are all you meet in an evening, and these by a certain woefulness of countenance seem not too well pleased with the exchange of a good table and merry circle of friends for spare diet and prayers twice a day. There is such an uncharitableness in the manners of a college, such an unsociable reserve, and disregard of each other's welfare, that I never can think of them without growing out of humour with all about me. The fellows of a college, that spend half their lives in poring over

498

newspapers and smoking tobacco, seem to live to no end, to be cut off from all the dearer interests of society, to possess, or at least to exert, no benevolence. What in the name of wonder can these men think of themselves when they look back upon a life that has been spent without either receiving or communicating pleasure? 'Tis like living on the side of a Scotch fell, or in the middle of a huge morass. "Peace to all such!"

In leaving your house I (*ut meus est mos*) forgot two or three very material things: to pay my hairdresser for a fortnight's, or odd, attendance. The debt is small, but the fellow may not like to wait for his money till the next time I see him. May I beg of you then to discharge it? Another slip of the memory was the leaving behind me the poems of that sweet swan of Wigton, Evan Clarke. A copy of these has been lately presented in great form to the Taberdor's Library here. However, as it would be troublesome and expensive to send me them, I shall let them remain till next I wait upon you, and endeavour in the meantime to console myself with the productions of other wits. I can remember nothing more except it was the omission of a thousand thanks for numerous civilities. I shall not attempt to put them down here, but leave you to conjecture what, believe me, you will hardly exaggerate.

I am at a loss how to procure an answer to Mr. Addison's enquiry about the Bodleian Catalogue. My Tutor is as much a stranger to these matters as myself, and all my other friends are absent. I shall however make application in some way or other and communicate the result. The weather which regularly makes a part of an Englishman's dis(course) has changed from bright and pure to foggy and unwholesome. Mrs. Boucher will by this time, I hope, be too well to care a farthing for the uncertainty of this month or the gloominess of the next. With my compliments to her, Mr. Addison, and all my friends among the fry below stairs.

I am, dear Sir,
Your very obliged and humble servant,
J. James

TO MRS. JAMES

Oxford, March 3, 1779

MY DEAR AND HONOURED MOTHER, I have long thrown away the schoolboy's excuse of "I did not do it on purpose," and frankly acknowledge that I am in debt to you for, I believe, three letters. What! and is that all? Reflect once more, and confess (Lent being of all the most proper time for confession) that thou art involved over head and ears for benefits, and tendernesses and carefulnesses, without a possibility of discharging them. You must e'en suffer them to run on, my dear mother. They are debts of so peculiar a kind that parents and children seem to have been in a league ever since Adam's day to be perpetually accumulating without any thoughts of paying them. I am already bankrupt.

I have often thought how charming a thing it would be if it were possible for a man to lose his sight upon some raw day in winter, and not recover it till the middle of June or July. You smile at my idea of pleasure. But the sudden and wondrous change in the face of nature from her winter to her summer dress would strike one prodigiously. What suggested this at present was the forwardness of our spring. Some trees are already in leaf, and the little boys and girls have tricked themselves out with primroses a good while ago. It was but last Friday that I was quite overpowered with heat in labouring up Heddington Hill, and though in February was exclaiming Pope's "Come gentle air!" and with all the languor of July or August. Now could you but step over from the top of Arthuret hills hither you would suppose you had been cheated out of a few months, and return with the same impressions as the Turkish Sultan in the story. My father will set you right in your geography. I do verily believe you will be able to conduct me through the streets of Oxford with as much skill as at London, and purposely shall throw in now and then the name of a place near Oxford, in order to make you repair to the map over the chimney-piece in the study. I see that you have been all along surprized that I never mentioned a syllable about my music. I have avoided it hitherto purposely till I was able to give you a creditable account of myself. To tell you the truth, I only entered on my music lectures the 16th of last month. I could not have the master I wished before that time. My hour is between dinner and prayers, a good time, you say, as it will digest the one and put me in tune for the other. I have got into Corelli, and he gives me hopes of being able to play after a while. Pick seems to have known very little about the matter. I am, however, getting the better of some of my habits, though you must not expect to find me capital. There are a good number of musical men here, with whom I could *scrape* acquaintance if I pleased, but they are not perhaps the most eligible. We keep Lent, as you may have heard, very religiously. I ate the best dinner I remember upon the first Sunday, and starve every day on roast beef and plum pudding.

You fear, perhaps, th(at) my wit will grow too fat. My letters, indeed, may give you reason to think so. I keep it as low as I can, however, by reading and writing French and talking nonsense. Of the first, I shall give my father a specimen some day. The other you have had enough of. I heard from town last week, where all friends were well. My love to my father, brothers, and sisters, with all relations at Breckon-hill and elsewhere. Compliments as usual. I sent off a little parcel for Arthuret last week in a box of Goldings, which he was a sending home. Adieu.

> I am, my honoured Mother,
> Your very affectionate and dutiful son,
> J. James

MRS. JAMES TO HER SON

ARTHURET, NOVEMBER 6TH, 1778

MY DEAR JOHN, We have been made very happy by two letters from you this week, one to your father on Monday, the other to your sister this morning without a postmark, so that we are ignorant how it came, but suppose it might be inclosed to Mr. Nicolson. 'Tis seven weeks to-night since we parted with you at Penrith, and I have thought myself long in answering your favour of the 2nd of October from London; but as your father wrote, it made it of less moment to you. You may believe me when I tell you that my heart has dictated more or less to you every day. From the spirits you write in I hope your health has not suffered from your journey, nor from the change of air; and as you have got good rooms, I doubt not you will be very happy after you have formed connexions, which I hope will be both useful and agreeable, as much depends upon the acquaintance you make. You will not, I daresay, think it an impertinent admonition to be nice in this particular. Suspicion is said to dwell only in low minds, and I believe it is generally the case; but I hope prudence and caution may be admitted into the most generous breasts. My dear child will excuse a mother's anxiety. I have not the smallest reason to doubt your conduct; I only wish you to be upon your guard, as young people are too apt to be deceived by professions and appearances.

. . . We think the sooner you begin French the better, if it don't interfere with any particular scheme which you might chuse to pursue at this season; and if it don't crowd too much upon you at once, a lesson in musick once a week (we suppose the French master will only attend thrice) might, with your own practice, enable you by-and-by to join in the concerts, or at least introduce you amongst the performers, which might be a means of your learning with more ease and pleasure; but these are only hints, it is left entirely to yourself whether you chuse to begin now, or not till after Christmas, or when you judge most convenient. We would by no means debar you on account of the expense, as we have no doubt of your making the best use of the instructions you receive.

Nor for some enquiries about your house-keeping. You have got china and glasses; have you got spoons? or a tea-chest; any green tea for your genteeler company? or how do you manage? You seem to breakfast upon milk, shall we send you any oat-meal, or is there anything we can get you? . . .

Our best compliments wait on the Doctor and Mr. Radcliffe. All the family join in love and best wishes for your health and happiness, with,

My dear son's ever affectionate mother,

ANN JAMES

WILLIAM CAREY (1761–1834)

Carey did more than any other Englishman to waken the conscience of British Christendom to the obligation of World-Missions, and to bring to Asia the knowledge of Christ. He reached India in November, 1793, and through more than the next four decades lived for his calling. With the help of pundits he translated the whole Bible into six of India's chief languages, including Sanskrit, the New Testament into twenty-three other Indian languages, and separate Gospels into five more. He and his colleagues, Joshua Marshman and William Ward, built in Serampore the first Christian College for the sons of India, which alone had and still has the right there to confer Divinity degrees. In the first letter he describes a widow-burning at Calcutta.

CALCUTTA

1799

DEAR MR. FULLER, We saw a number of people assembled on the river-side. I asked for what they were met, and they told me—to burn the body of a dead man. I inquired if his wife would die with him; they answered "Yes," and pointed to her. She was standing by the pile of large billets of wood, on the top of which lay her husband's dead body. Her nearest relative stood by her; and near her was a basket of sweetmeats. I asked if this was her choice, or if she were brought to it by any improper influence. They answered that it was perfectly voluntary. I talked till reasoning was of no use, and then began to exclaim with all my might against what they were doing, telling them it was shocking murder. They told me it was a great act of holiness, and added, in a very surly manner, that if I did not like to see it, I might go further off, and desired me to do so. I said I would not go, that I was determined to stay and see the murder, against which I should certainly bear witness at the tribunal of God. I exhorted the widow not to throw away her life; to fear nothing, for no evil would follow her refusal to be burned. But in the most calm manner she mounted the pile, and danced on it with her hands extended, as if in the utmost tranquillity of spirit. Previous to this, the relative, whose office it was to set fire to the pile, led her six times round it—thrice at

503

a time.   As she went round she scattered the sweetmeats amongst the people, who ate them as a very holy thing.   This being ended, she lay down beside the corpse, and put one arm under its neck, and the other over it, when a quantity of dry cocoa-leaves and other substances were heaped over them to a considerable height, and then ghî was poured on the top.   Two bamboos were then put over them, and held fast down, and fire put to the pile, which immediately blazed very fiercely owing to the dry and combustible materials of which it was composed. No sooner was the fire kindled than all the people set up a great shout of joy, invoking Siva.   It was impossible to have heard the widow, had she groaned, or even cried aloud, on account of the shoutings of the people, and again it was impossible for her to stir or struggle, by reason of the bamboos held down on her, like the levers of a press.   We made much objection to their use of these, insisting that it was undue force, to prevent her getting up when the fire burned.   But they declared that it was only to keep the fire from falling down.   We could not bear to see more, and left them, exclaiming loudly against the murder, and filled with horror at what we had seen.

Yours truly,

WILLIAM CAREY

TO HIS SON JABEZ CAREY

CALCUTTA, JAN. 15, 1814

MY DEAR JABEZ, Trust always in Christ.   Be pure of heart.   Live a life of devotedness to God.   Be gentle and unassuming, yet firm and manly.

You are now married.   Esteem your wife highly that she may highly esteem you.   The first impressions of love arising from form or beauty will soon wear off, but the trust arising from character will endure and increase.

Behave affably to all, cringingly and unsteadily to none.   Feel that you are a man, and always act with that dignified sincerity, which will command men's respect.   Seek not the society of worldly men, but when called to be with them, act and converse with propriety and dignity.   To this end labour to gain a good acquaintance with men and things.   A gentleman is the next best character after a Christian, and the latter includes the former.   Money never makes a gentleman, much less a fine appearance: but an enlarged understanding joined to engaging manners.

As soon as you are settled, get a Malay, who can speak a little

English, and make a tour of your islands, visiting every school. Keep a journal of each, and encourage all you see worthy. Compare their periodic progress. Consider yourself more than a Director of schools,— even their Christian instructor, and devote yourself to their good.

Shun all indolence and love of ease, and never try to act the part of the great and gay in this world. Labour incessantly to become a perfect master of the Malay. With this in view, associate with the native people, walk with them, ask the name of everything you see, visit them when they are sick. Every night arrange your new words in alphabetical order, and use them as soon as you can. Learn correctly the number, size and geography of your islands: the number and character of their inhabitants, their manners and customs, and regularly communicate with me. Be sure to send me every possible vegetable production. Plant tubers and bulbs in a box so thickly as to touch one another, or hang them dry in a well-covered basket in an airy part of the ship. Send, if you can, two or three hundred of each sort. I shall be glad of the smallest as well as the largest common plants. Think none insignificant. Plant the small in boxes, and always keep some rooted and ready; if too recently planted, they die on the way. Just before despatching them, sow very thickly amongst them seeds of trees, fruits and shrubs, covered with a finger's thickness of fresh soil. They should be watered a little on the voyage. You must often send the same thing, as it will be ten to one that they arrive alive. Do send abundant seeds of every sort, perfectly ripe and dry, in named paper packets, in a box or basket, secured from the rats; and, if possible, cite the due soil. Parasitical plants, such as you have seen me tie on trees, need only be shipped where they grow, and hung in baskets in any airy part of the ship, or even at the main top. All boxes of plants must have strips of wood over them, to keep out the rats. Nothing must be put in the hold. Send me as many live birds as possible; also small quadrupeds, monkeys, etc. Beetles, lizards, frogs, serpents may be put in a small keg of rum. I have much confidence in you to add greatly to my stock of natural productions. But you must persevere in both collecting and sending.

May you be kept amid all temptations, and supported under every trial. Write by every opportunity. Now, my dear son, I commit you and Eliza to God and to the word of His grace. Should I never see you again on earth, I trust we shall meet with joy before God's Throne.

Your very, very affectionate

FATHER

GEORGE DUFF (1764–1805)

This letter was written by Captain Duff to his wife on the morning of the Battle of Trafalgar. He commanded the "Mars" in the action, and was one of the two British captains, killed. His head was taken off by a French cannon-ball, and his death was witnessed by his young son Norwich. The latter was only thirteen years old, but he stood on the quarter-deck during the heat of the battle, and the next day wrote to his mother an account of all that had taken place. The cannon-ball was taken home and is still preserved in the family. A further adventure of Norwich Duff's is narrated in the letter from Dalrymple; it is interesting to note that the young man survived all these events and lived to be an admiral. He died in 1862.

TO MRS. DUFF

MONDAY MORNING, 21ST OCT. 1805

MY DEAREST SOPHIA, I have just had time to tell you we are just going into action with the combined (fleets). I hope and trust in God that we shall all behave as becomes us, and that I may yet have the happiness of taking my beloved wife and children in my arms. Norwich is quite well and happy. I have, however, ordered him off the quarter deck.

Yours ever and most truly,
GEO. DUFF

NORWICH DUFF TO THE SAME

22 OCT., 1805

MY DEAR MAMA, You cannot possibly imagine how unwilling I am to begin this melancholy letter. However as you must unavoidably hear of the fate of dear Papa, I write you these few lines to request you to bear it as patiently as you can. He died like a hero, having gallantly led his ship into action, and his memory will ever be dear to his king, his country and his friends. It was about 15 minutes past 12 in the afternoon of the 21st Oct. when the engagement began, it was not finished till 5. Many a brave hero sacrificed his life upon that occasion to his king and country. You will hear that Lord Viscount Nelson was wounded in the commencement of the engagement and only survived long enough to learn that the victory was ours—"then," said that brave hero "I die happy since I die victorious," and in a few minutes expired.

I have written my uncle a long letter and have enclosed one to my Aunt Grace, containing a short narrative of some particulars of the action.

We are now all aboard the *Euryalus* with the Hon. Captain Blackwood and in compliance with the wish of Admiral Collingwood are now on our way to England that we may have an opportunity of more readily knowing your wishes respecting the arrangement of our future conduct. Captain Blackwood has indeed been very polite and kind to me and has requested Mr. Dalrymple to let my uncle know that on account of his acquaintance with my papa he will feel himself very happy in keeping me on board his ship and to acquaint him that his annual allowance to young gentlemen in his ship and under his charge is 50 pounds, half of which he wishes to be deposited in the hands of his agent once in six months; however I would much rather wish to see you and to be discharged into the guardship at Leith for two or three months. My dear Mama, I have again to request you to endeavour to make yourself as happy and as easy as possible. It has been the will of Heaven and it is our duty to submit.

Believe me your obedient and affectionate son,

NORWICH DUFF

Mr. Dalrymple, the purser and instructor of the midshipmen on board the "Euryalus" and afterwards the "Ajax," wrote two years later to Norwich Duff's mother.

FEB. 1807

LEST my letter of the 17th should have miscarried, I do myself the honour of preparing another against the earliest opportunity. Before this reach you the *Gazette* will have publicly announced the loss of the *Ajax* off the mouth of the Dardanelles on the evening of the 14th inst. about 9 o'clock. She took fire in the starboard side of the Breadroom, and it is generally thought it was occasioned by the carelessness of the Purser's steward, who was much addicted to drinking and was seen drunk a few minutes before the fire was discovered. Everything being dry, the flames raged with incredible fury and tho' repeated attempts were made to get them under every exertion availed us nothing; yet till I saw the flames rolling on the quarter deck and everything round me in a blaze I had not the most distant idea that the ship would be burnt, but then I was forced to rush forward to the forecastle and consult my safety. You will easily conceive how much I was rejoiced to find Norwich there (he was one of the midshipmen of the watch) but my joy was soon interrupted when he told me he had not seen Mr. David Clerk or Mr. Manners from the time the fire broke out. We stood on the sprite sail yard for some minutes thinking we might discover them lurking in some place which the flames had not reached, but no, the poor little fellows had leapt overboard, as we afterwards understood, soon after the accident happened. At this time there was no boat near us nor any prospect of our preservation, as neither of us can swim; however I bless God Almighty that I continued as cool and collected as I am at this moment and exhorted the dear partner of my misfortune to keep up his spirits, depend upon the mercy of God and we might be saved. For since I had found him I was resolved to save him or perish in the attempt. We shook hands and bid adieu to Capt. Blackwood who at that moment plunged into the waves with a Mr. Sibthorp, a worthy young man who perished with cold, struggling against the current. We had not waited above ten minutes when a boat from the *Windsor Castle* came under the bows into which I made Norwich immediately go down. Even then we were far from being safe; the flames had taken such full possession of the ship that the guns which were loaded being made hot, were discharging the shot in every quarter and several flew over our heads when in the boat rowing towards the *Canopus*, which ship we got safe on board, when we had the good fortune to find the Captain and several other shipmates among whom I am happy to include Mr. Thomas Duff who was saved in the half of the Captain's boat which in lowering was cut in two upon the anchor. From what I have said, I daresay you already perceive that my unfortunate young friends, Mr. Clerk and Mr. Manners, are included among the lost. I hope you will receive my first letter and answer it, as I am particularly perplexed what to do with Norwich after this service is finished. By going home he will lose much practical knowledge of his profession which he perhaps may never again have as good an opportunity of acquiring and by staying here without a thread of clothes but what the generosity of a shipmate may bestow, is very inconvenient and may in the end hurt his health.

JOHN NYREN (1764–1837)

Nyren was one of the fathers of cricket as we know it to-day. One of the "Hambledon Men," he is said to have kept the Bat and Ball inn at Hambledon, and looked after the Broad Halfpenny, as the cricket-field was called. In 1833 he published "The Young Cricketer's Tutor," to which the first following letter was a preface.

TO WILLIAM WARD

BROMLEY, MIDDLESEX, MARCH, 1833

DEAR SIR, You have kindly consented to my wish of dedicating my little book to you, and I am much pleased that you have done so: first, because you are a countryman of my own—having lived in Hampshire; and secondly, and chiefly, because, as a CRICKETER, I consider you the most worthy man of the present day to reflect credit upon my choice as a patron.

It would ill become me, Sir, in this place to allude to other weighty reasons for congratulating myself upon this point—an insignificant book of instruction—as to the best mode of excelling in an elegant relaxation, not being the most fitting medium for digressing upon unquestionably high public worth and integrity, or private condescension and amenity: at the same time, I cannot but feel how happily such a combination of qualities in a patron must redound to my own advantage.

I have not seen much of your playing—certainly not so much as I could have wished; but so far as my observation and judgement extend, I may confidently pronounce you to be one of the *safest* players I remember to have seen. The circumstances of your rising so much above the ordinary standard in stature (your height, if I recollect, being six feet one inch), your extraordinary length of limb, your power and activity: to all which, I may add, your perfect judgement of all points in the game, have given you the superior advantages in play, and entitle you to the character I have given. As a proof of its correctness, the simple fact will suffice of your having gained the "*longest hands*" of any player upon record. This circumstance occurred upon the 24th and 25th of July, 1820, at Maryle-bone, when the great number of 278 runs appeared against your name,

509

108 more than any player ever gained: and this, be it remembered, happened after the increase of the stumps in 1817.

May you long live, Sir, to foster and take your part in our favourite amusement; and may you never relax your endeavours to restore the game to the good old principles from which, I regret to say, it has in some instances departed since the time I used to be an active member of the fraternity. You are aware that I principally allude to the practice that the modern bowlers have introduced of *throwing* the ball, although in direct infringement of a law prohibiting that action.

I beg to subscribe myself, Dear Sir, Your faithful Countryman, And obedient humble Servant,

JOHN NYREN

TO THE EDITOR OF THE *LONDON JOURNAL*

BROMLEY, MIDDLESEX, JUNE 25, 1834

MY DEAR SIR, The wise men of the East invited me to stand umpire at a cricket match, the married men against the bachelors. The day was highly interesting, and I cannot forbear giving you a short account of it. If you can take anything from the description I give you for your paper, do it any way you like; this will be only a rough sketch. I call these gentlemen "the wise men of the East," as they will not suffer their names in print, and they live at the East End of London.

When we arrived at the place of our destination I was both surprised and delighted at the beautiful scene which lay before me. Several elegant tents, gracefully decked out with flags and festoons of flowers, had been fitted up for the convenience of the ladies; and many of these, very many, were elegant and beautiful women. I *am not* seventy; and "the power of beauty I remember yet." I am *only* sixty-eight! Seats were placed beneath the wide-spreading oaks, so as to form groups in the shade. Beyond these were targets for ladies, *who love archery*, the cricket ground in front.

The carriages poured in rapidly, and each party as they entered the ground was received with loud cheers by such of their friends as had arrived before them. At this time a band of music entered the ground, and I could perceive the ladies' feathers gracefully waving to the music, and quite ready for dancing. However, the band gave us that fine old tune "The Roast Beef of Old England."

We entered a large booth, which accommodated all our party; a hundred and thirty sat down to the *déjeuner*. Our chairman was *young*, but old in experience. Many excellent speeches were made; and ever and anon the whole place rang with applause. After this the dancing commenced—quadrilles, gallopade, etc., etc. It was, without exception, the most splendid sight that I ever witnessed, and reminded one far more of the descriptions we read of fairyland than of any scene in real life. The dancing was kept up with great spirit, till the dew of heaven softly descended on the bosoms of our fair countrywomen.

Not a single unfortunate occurrence happened to damp the pleasure of this delightful party. Had you been with us you would have sung "Oh, the Pleasures of the Pains," etc., etc. How is it that we have so few of these parties? Can any party in a house compare with it? God bless you and yours.

JOHN NYREN

P.S.—The cricket match was well contested, the bachelors winning by three runs only.

SIR WILLIAM FREEMANTLE (1766–1850)

Sir William was famous in his time for his knowledge of Irish affairs, and he became a figure in Parliament. This letter was written to Francis Horner, a generally useful man, whom we shall meet in these pages before long.

TO FRANCIS HORNER

STANHOPE STREET, MARCH 16, 1813

DEAR HORNER, I wrote a note to you yesterday, not recollecting you were on the circuit: my object was to speak to you on the subject of a seat in Parliament. I have reason to know that a seat will be vacant in the course of ten days, which I am authorized to offer you, begging you to understand it to be without stipulation or pledge of any sort or kind, saving that which, of course, you would feel it just to admit, namely, to resign whenever your politics should differ from the person who has the means of recommending you to the seat. The expense will be merely the dinner, which I rather think does not usually amount to more than £30 or £40. If this meets with your wishes, I will trouble you to let me know, as I am sure it has long been an object with the person whose sentiments I speak, to place you where your character and abilities have before rendered you so useful; and it has only been from unavoidable circumstances that the offer was delayed.

Ever believe me, my dear Horner

MELESINA TRENCH (1768–1827)

Mrs. Trench was one of those witty Irishwomen who sparkle, like gems, in the galaxy of English letters. In this letter to Mrs. Leadbeater she talks of Paris as it was in the days succeeding Waterloo.

TO MRS. LEADBEATER

JUNE, 1815

I HAVE just received your long and delightful letter—delightful I must call it, though it contains so many melancholy details, as it shows the blue serene which smiles above the temporary clouds and storm. I saw the death of one of the assistants in Ballitore school, and I feared you were in affliction, for I know you can always say with Miranda, "Oh, I have suffered with those whom I saw suffer." As to me, my last alarm has confirmed me in that state of constant recollection of that frail tenure of all earthly goods which some moralists recommend, but which I cannot think was intended by Providence; as everything in nature seems designed to prevent us from dwelling on it; and as our not thinking of it perpetually in spite of all the veils thrown over it seems to me a constant miracle, and one of the strongest proofs that the great Disposer "wills the happiness of His creatures." Madame de Staël justly says, "*La vie ne va, que parcequ'on oublie la mort.*"

Since I wrote to you we were at a morning concert of sacred music, given for a charitable purpose, in the beautiful Gothic cathedral of Gloucester. This is a truly national amusement—polished, pure, and dignified. It owes nothing to the glare of tapers, the false spirits of the evening hour, the splendour of ornaments, or any theatrical illusion. The performance of Handel's "Dead March in Saul" was singularly affecting, and as the double drum echoed, reverberated, and died away along the aisles, it had to the imagination the effect of cannon among distant hills—while the sounds of the wind instruments floated through the lofty roof with the most plaintive sweetness.

Sunday (June 25th). All here are in the tears and triumph of a dear bought victory [Waterloo]. The ecstasy with which it is said to be received exists but in the papers. Bonaparte abdicates, forced to this act by the senate he himself convened. This is the most remarkable event, perhaps, of this eventful time.

Your amusing packets always diffuse cheerfulness over my horizon, or rather increase that which, I thank heaven, does not often forsake me. Indeed I do consider that moment as most fortunate to me which made us acquainted. You know not of how much use you have been to my mind, nor what moral benefit is derived from intercourse with you, dear friend.

Paris, November, 1815. I can give you no account of Paris. I came only to see Charles, and I have seen nothing else, except what forces itself on a traveller. I have seen women holding the plough, and men selling caps, trying them on their customers with the assurance of their being perfectly becoming. One of those amphibious creatures, highly dressed and ornamented, inflames a milliner's bill prodigiously—on which an English lady here said, "I never deal at shops where they are to be found, as I hate paying for the sight of a man." I inhabit an apartment that affects to be luxurious. In one of the rooms there are seven large looking-glasses inserted in the walls. But my bed-room is without a carpet or a bell, and the curtains both of my bed and windows are of unlined tambour muslin; so I shiver in state; and when I want any attendance in my bed-room, I must either run or roar for my maid, which is not accordant to the dignified appearance of the first *coup d'œil* of my apartment. A thousand such contrasts offer themselves. None are more disagreeable to me than those springing from affected politeness and real coarseness of habits.

You asked me in a former letter about Mrs. Piozzi. She is about sixty or seventy, lively, animated, agreeable in countenance, and, as far as I could judge in a mixed company, in manners also. You may judge of her vigor and spirits, when I tell you that two years since she went to a masquerade, disguised as a constable, attended by the Dowager Lady Bellmore and Miss Caldwell as watchmen; and they amused themselves throwing the whole assembly into consternation by pretending they had a warrant to imprison them as engaged in an illegal amusement. In my youth I used to hear that "cards were better than scandal," as if there was no *third* manner of passing the evening. Adieu, my dear Mrs. Leadbeater. Ever yours, *de pres et de loin, l'été et l'hyver.*

M. T.

THOMAS CREEVEY (1768–1838)

There is something very amusing in the tittle-tattle Creevey loved to record. This letter, scribbled at various times, and telling of the early days of Victoria's reign is, in its way, inimitable.

TO MISS ORD

BROOK'S, SEPT. 6TH, 1837

. . . Lady Tavistock and I had a most confidential walk and talk. You have heard me say what a gaby she is; but she is all truth and daylight. She told me she was in the second carriage after Vic on Sunday at Windsor; and that the Queen according to her custom, being cold in the carriage, had got out to walk, and of course all her ladies had to do the same; and the ground being very wet their feet soon got into the same state. Poor dear Lady Tavistock, when she got back to the Castle, could get at no dry stockings, her maid being out and her clothes all locked up. I am sure from Lady Tavistock that she thinks the Queen a resolute little tit. . . .

SEPT. 22

I have taken to Wellington and his despatches again, and the more I read of him the fonder I am of him. He really is in every respect a *perfect man.* . . . Palmerston was very communicative at Stoke as to the great merits of the Queen. He said that any Ministers who had to deal with her would soon find she was no ordinary person; and when Lady Sefton observed what credit it did the Duchess of Kent to have made her what she was, Palmerston said the Duchess of Kent had every kind of merit, but that the Queen had an understanding of her own that could have been made by no one.

Lady Charlemont succeeded Lady Tavistock the other day [in waiting at Windsor]. She is very, very blue, and asked Lady T. if she might take any books out of the library. "Oh, yes, my dear," said Lady Tavistock, not knowing what reading means; "as many as you like"; upon which Lady Charlemont swept away a whole row, and was carrying them away in her apron. Passing thro' the gallery in this state, whom should she meet but little Vic! Great was her perturbation, for

515

in the first place a low curtsy was necessary, and what was to come of the books, for they must curtsy too. Then, to be found with all this property within the first half hour of her coming, and before even she had seen Vic! . . . But Vic was very much amused with the thing altogether, laughed heartily and was as good humoured as ever she could be.

BRIGHTON, OCT. 9TH

Now for Brighton! It is *detestable*: the crowd of unknown human beings is not to be endured. Whether it is a natural sentiment or not, I don't know, or whether I mistake *ennui* for it, but I have a strong touch of melancholy in comparing Brighton of the present with times gone by. Death has made great havoc in a very short time with our Royalties of the Pavilion—Prinney [Prince Regent] and "brother William," Duke of York and Duke of Kent, all gone, and all represented now by little Vic only. Is it not highly dramatic that the Duke of Kent should have announced to me in 1818, upon Princess Charlotte's death, that he was going to marry for the succession, and named his bride to me; and here she is, with the successor by her side, and what is to become of her, or how she is to turn out, who shall say?

In talking to Lady Cowper of Lord Melbourne, and, as I suppose, of his health, Vic said: "He eats too much, and I often tell him so. Indeed I do so myself, and my doctor has ordered me not to eat luncheon any more." "And does your Majesty quite obey him?" asked Lady Cowper. "Why yes, I think I do," said Vic, "for I only eat a little broth." Now I think a little Queen taking care of her Prime Minister's stomach, he being nearly sixty, is everything one could wish! If the Tory press could get hold of this fact, what fun they would make of it. The Duchess of Kent plays whist every night, and a horrible player she is. Vicky, I am happy to say, always plays chess with Melbourne when he is there.

OCT. 13TH

Yesterday Lady Sefton, her two eldest daughters and myself, sallied forth in the yellow coach to dine with the Queen at our own old Pavilion. Lord Headfort, a chattering, capering, spindle-shanked gaby, was in waiting, and handed Lady Sefton into the drawing-room, where I was glad to see Glenelg, and besides him were Tom Bland and a Portuguese diplomat, as black in the face as one's hat, but with a star on his stomach, I assure you! Presently Headfort was summoned away, and on his return he came up to me with his antics and said:—"Mr. Creevey, you are to sit on the Duchess of Kent's right hand at dinner." Oh, the fright I was in about my right ear. Here comes in the Queen, the Duchess of Kent the least bit in the world behind her, all her ladies in a row still more behind; Lord Conyngham and Cavendish one on each flank of the Queen. She was told by Lord Conyngham that I had not been presented, upon which a scene took place that to me was most truly distressing. The poor little thing could not get her glove off. I never was so annoyed in my life; yet what could I do? But she blushed and laughed and pulled, till the thing was done, and I kissed her hand. Then to dinner. The Duchess of Kent was agreeable and chatty, and she said: "Shall we drink some wine?" My eyes, however, all the while were fixed upon Vic. To mitigate the harshness of any criticism I may pronounce upon her manners, let me express my conviction that she and her mother are one. I never saw a more pretty or natural devotion than she shows to her mother in everything, and I reckon this as by far the most amiable, as well as *valuable*, disposition to start with in the fearful struggle she has in life before her. Now for her appearance—but all in the strictest confidence. A more homely little thing you never beheld, *when she is at her ease*, and she is evidently dying to be always more so. She laughs in real earnest, opening her mouth as wide as it can go, showing not very pretty gums. She eats as heartily as she laughs, I think I may say she gobbles. She blushes and laughs every instant in so natural a way as to disarm anybody. Her voice is perfect, and so is the expression of her face, when she means to say or do a pretty thing. At night I played two rubbers of whist, one against the Duchess of Kent, and one as her partner. The Queen, in leaving the room at night, came across quite up to me, and said:—"How long do you stay at Brighton, Mr. Creevey?" Which I presume could mean nothing else than another rubber for her mother. So it's all mighty well.

ARTHUR WELLESLEY, DUKE OF WELLINGTON (1769–1852)

This brief little note, written during the stress of the Peninsular War, is, perhaps, more characteristic of the Iron Duke than many of his more elaborate epistles.

TO GENERAL H. M. W. GORDON

FUENTE GUINALDO, MAY 29TH, 1812

MY DEAR GORDON, I received yesterday your letter of the 14th for which I am much obliged. The death of Mr. Perceval is indeed an unfortunate event; and I consider the manner of it as unfortunate almost as the fact itself, from being so very disgraceful to the country.

I'll keep you informed of all events while you will be at Madeira. In the meantime I write to Mr. Stewart to request he would send you the Portuguese newspapers by every occasion, in which you will see the principal events. Hill has struck a very important blow lately at Almaraz.

I hope you won't drink all the Madeira in the island, as the Duke Littlehales & Pole do all the Liffey Champaign in Dublin. I cannot get a Drop for love or Money!

Beresford is here and very well.

Believe me, my dear Gordon, yours most sincerely,

WELLINGTON

JANET CARLYLE (1769–1853)

Janet was the second wife of James Carlyle, the stone-mason of Ecclefechan. Only in the last few years of her life did she learn to write, though always with great difficulty. She was the mother of Thomas Carlyle. Her staunch spirit reveals itself in this letter to her sons telling them of their father's death.

TO THOMAS CARLYLE

IT is God that has done it; be still, my dear children.

Your affectionate Mother

JAMES HOGG (1770–1835)

*The Ettrick Shepherd is one of the high lights of Scottish literature.
What need to speak of him to those who know "Noctes Ambrosianae"?
This letter to Professor John Wilson, so much better known to us all as
Christopher North, is typical of the man, fresh from his Ettrick forests.*

TO PROFESSOR JOHN WILSON

MOUNT BENGER, AUGUST, 1829

MY DEAR AND HONOURED JOHN, I never thought you had been so uncon-
scionable as to desire a sportsman on the 11th or even the 13th of August
to leave Ettrick Forest for the bare scraggy hills of Westmoreland!—
Ettrick Forest, where the black cocks and white cocks, brown cocks and
grey cocks, ducks, plovers and peasesweeps and whilly-whaups are as
thick as the flocks that cover her mountains, and come to the hills of
Westmoreland that can nourish nothing better than a castril or a stone-
chat!   To leave the great yellow-fin of Yarrow, or the still larger grey-
locher for the degenerate fry of Troutbeck, Esthwaite, or even Wast-
water!   No, no, the request will not do; it is an unreasonable one, and
therefore not unlike yourself, for besides, what would become of Old
North and Blackwood, and all our friends for game, were I to come to
Elleray just now?   I know of no home of man where I could be so
happy within doors with so many lovely and joyous faces around me;
but this is not the season for indoor enjoyments; they must be reaped on
the wastes among the blooming heath, by the silver spring, or swathed
in the delicious breeze of the wilderness.   Elleray, with all its sweets,
could never have been my choice for a habitation, and perhaps you are the
only Scottish gentleman who ever made such a choice, and still persists in
maintaining it, in spite of every disadvantage.—Yours most respectfully,

JAMES HOGG

THOMAS WALLIS

Wallis was Lord Nelson's secretary, and when an old man was appealed to by Haydon, the painter, for particulars he needed in painting one of his historical tableaux.

TO BENJAMIN ROBERT HAYDON

BRIGHTON, 11TH OCTOBER, 1843

DEAR SIR, I shall be most happy to give you all the information in my power relative to the Copenhagen affair, especially the circumstances attending that important event, the sending on shore in the midst of the action Lord Nelson's celebrated note addressed to the "Brothers of Englishmen, the Danes."

Lord Nelson wrote the note at the casing of the rudder-head, and as he wrote I took a copy, both of us standing. The original was put in an envelope and sealed with his arms. At first I was going to secure it with a wafer, but he would not allow this to be done, observing that it "must be sealed," or the enemy "would think it was written and sent on shore in a hurry." The man I sent below for a light never returned, having been killed on his way.

To the best of my recollection the admiral wore a plain, blue, sort of great coat, without epaulettes or gold lace, but on his breast were his several orders, and he wore a plain cocked-hat.

Civilians in those days were not required to wear a uniform. My dress was a plain blue coat, blue trousers, with a white kerseymere waistcoat.

The decks, as you observe, were perfectly clear fore and aft, and the place where the note was written was on the extreme after part of the ship. Captain Foley commanded the *Elephant*. Captain Thesiger, to the best of my remembrance held no command, but was merely a volunteer on board Sir Hyde Parker's flag-ship, and in consequence of his knowledge of Copenhagen and the Danish language he was considered the fittest officer to be entrusted with the flag of truce.

I shall be very glad to see you on Wednesday, and shall be delighted to give you any further information.

I am, dear Sir,

THOS. WALLIS

LADY HOLLAND (1770–1845)

Lady Holland was one of the greatest hostesses of the nineteenth century, and her salon was the resort of all the wits and wise men of her time. Before her marriage to Lord Holland she had been the wife of Sir Godfrey Webster, and it was during this period that she wrote the following letter to her friend Lady Sheffield, the mother of Lady Stanley of Alderley.

TO LADY SHEFFIELD

NAPLES, MARCH 5, 1793

I HAVE not heard from you for months, which tho' distressing is not alarming, as I hear of you from other quarters. . . . My child is a Phenomenon, really the most wonderful Natural Production I ever beheld, so much so that I think it quite unjust not to pickle him, to send to John Hunter's Museum which he would adorn. He is little beyond belief. He is certainly bigger than a geometrical point, and "c'est tout dire." When he has learnt the art of sucking he will live and thrive.

Poor Louis! How hard has been thy fate! I still struggle with my reason to believe the perpetration of so horrid a Deed; and can hardly credit the Reality of it. Events of this dreadful sort that come immediately within one's own time are more difficult to believe than those equally horrible (if such there are) in remote Periods. None of us doubt the Execution of Charles I, and yet the murder of Louis appears Impossible. . . . Nothing can be quieter than we are here, which makes me fear you will think my letter sadly stupid; as one from the Continent without Massacres, Insurrections or Invasions must be the dullest of all dull things. However, we have had our day, for in the course of one month we either have been Bombarded by the French, Smothered by the Mountain, or Swallowed up in an Earthquake, and one of these three would have been a Fine Catastrophe. I felt two shocks of the Earthquake, and a most unpleasant undulating motion it was; it was slight here, but at Salerno the inhabitants quitted their homes . . . say everything kind to dear Lord S. and Maria, and believe me,

faithfully yours,

E. W.

SIR WALTER SCOTT (1771–1832)

This charming letter was written to the artist Haydon, who had inquired about some costumes for one of his pictures. It shows the immense amount of knowledge Scott had at his finger-tips and is more familiar in its friendliness than many of his other letters.

TO BENJAMIN ROBERT HAYDON

EDINBURGH, 7TH JANUARY, 1821

DEAR SIR, I just scribble a few lines to thank you for your letter, and to add in reply that at any time you may command any information I have about either incident or costume, should you find a Scottish subject which hits your fancy. In general there is a great error in dressing ancient Scottish men like our Highlanders, who wore a dress, as they spoke a language, as foreign to the Lowland Scottish as to the English. I remember battling this point with poor Bird, who had a great fancy to put my countrymen, the spearmen of Tiviotdale, who fought and fell at Chevy Chase, into plaids and filabegs. I was obliged at last to compound for one Highland chief, for the tartan harmonised so much with some of the other colours, the artist would not part with him.

Adieu, my dear Sir; proceed to exert your talents in prosecution and in representation of what is good and great, and so, as Ophelia says, "God be with your labour!" I am very happy to have seen you, and hope to show you one day some of our scenery.

By the way, there is a tale of our country which, were the subject, well known as it is, but in a local and obscure tradition, strikes me as not unfit for the pencil, and I will tell it you in three words.

In ancient times there lived on the Scottish frontier, just opposite to England, a champion belonging to the clan of Armstrong called the Laird's Jock, one of the most powerful men of his time in stature and presence, and one of the bravest and most approved in arms. He wielded a tremendously large and heavy two-handed sword, which no one on the west border could use save himself. After living very many [years] without a rival, Jock-of-the-Side became old and bedridden, and could no longer stir from home. His family consisted of a son and

523

daughter, the first a fine young warrior, though not equal to his father; and the last a beautiful young woman. About this time an English champion of the name of Foster, ancient rivals of the Armstrongs, and Englishmen to boot, gave a challenge to any man on the Scottish side to single combat. These challenges were frequent among the Borderers, and always fought with great fairness, and attended with great interest. The Laird's Jock's son accepted the challenge, and his father presented him on the occasion with the large two-handed sword which he himself had been used to wield in battle. He also insisted on witnessing the combat, and was conveyed in a litter to a place called Turner's Holm, just on the frontier of both kingdoms, where he was placed, wrapped up with great care, under the charge of his daughter. The champions met, and young Armstrong was slain; and Foster, seizing the sword, waved it in a token of triumph. The old champion never dropped a tear for his son, but when he saw his renowned weapon in the hands of an Englishman, he set up a hideous cry, which is said to have been heard at an incredible distance, and exclaiming, "My sword! my sword!" dropped into his daughter's arms, and expired.

I think that the despair of the old giant, contrasted with the beautiful female in all her sorrows, and with the accompaniments of the field of combat, are no bad subject for a sketch *à la mode* of Salvator, though perhaps better adapted for sculpture.

Yours, at length,

WALTER SCOTT

SYDNEY SMITH (1771–1845)

Smith was the wit of his time. His bon mots were passed with glee in every drawing-room in London, and as an after-dinner speaker he has seldom had an equal. There was, however, a more serious side to him, and his essays were of considerable importance and weight in their day. He was consulted by politicians of all shades, and gave sound advice that was rarely taken.

TO LADY MARY BENNETT

FOSTON, DECEMBER 20TH, 1821

MY DEAR LADY MARY, In the first place I went to Lord Grey's, and stayed with them three or four days; from thence I went to Edinburgh, where I had not been for ten years. I found a noble passage into the town, and new since my time; two beautiful English chapels, two of the handsomest library-rooms in Great Britain, and a wonderful increase of shoes and stockings, streets and houses. When I lived there, very few maids had shoes and stockings, but plodded about the house with feet as big as a family Bible, and legs as large as portmanteaus. I stayed with Jeffrey. My time was spent with the Whig leaders of the Scotch bar, a set of very honest, clever men, each possessing thirty-two different sorts of wine. My old friends were glad to see me; some had turned Methodists—some had lost their teeth—some had grown very rich—some very fat—some were dying—and, alas! alas! many were dead; but the world is a coarse enough place, so I talked away, comforted some, praised others, kissed some old ladies, and passed a very riotous week.

From Edinburgh I went to Dunbar,—Lord Lauderdale's—a comfortable house, with a noble sea-view. I was struck with the great goodnature and vivacity of his daughters.

From thence to Lambton. And here I ask, what use of wealth so luxurious and delightful as to light your house with gas? What folly, to have a diamond necklace or a Correggio, and not to light your house with gas! The splendour and glory of Lambton Hall make all other houses mean. How pitiful to submit to a farthing-candle existence, when science puts such intense gratification within your reach! Dear lady, spend all your fortune in a gas-apparatus. Better to eat dry bread by the splendour of gas, than to dine on wild beef with wax-candles; and so good-bye, dear lady.

SYDNEY SMITH

TO JOHN MURRAY

COMBE FLOREY, SEPT. 12TH, 1842

MY DEAR MURRAY, How did the Queen receive you? What was the general effect of her visit? Was it well managed? Does she show any turn for metaphysics? Have you had much company in the Highlands?

Mrs. Sydney and I are both in fair health,—such health as is conceded to moribundity and caducity.

Horner applied to me, and I sent him a long letter upon the subject of his brother, which he likes, and means to publish in his Memoirs. He seeks the same contribution from Jeffrey. Pray say to Jeffrey that he ought to send it. It is a great pity that the subject has been so long deferred. The mischief has all proceeded from the delays of poor Whishaw, who cared too much about reputation to do anything in a period compatible with the shortness of human life. If you have seen Jeffrey, tell me how he is, and if you think he will stand his work.

We have the railroad now within five miles. Bath in two hours, London in six,—in short, everywhere in no time! Every fresh accident on the railroads is an advantage, and leads to an improvement. What we want is an overturn which would kill a bishop, or at least a dean. This mode of conveyance would then become perfect. We have had but little company here this summer. Luttrell comes next week. I have given notice to the fishmongers, and poulterers, and fruitwomen! Ever, dear Murray, your sincere friend,

SYDNEY SMITH

TO MRS. HOLLAND

DECEMBER 11TH, 1835

MY DEAREST CHILD, Few are the adventures of a Canon travelling gently over good roads to his benefice. In my way to Reading I had, for my companion, the Mayor of Bristol when I preached that sermon in favour of the Catholics. He recognized me, and we did very well together. I was terribly afraid that he would stop at the same inn, and that I should have the delight of his society for the evening; but he (thank God!) stopped at the Crown, as a loyal man, and I, as a rude one, went on to the Bear.   Civil waiters, wax candles, and off again the next morning, with my friend and Sir W. W., a very shrewd, clever, coarse, entertaining man, with whom I skirmished *à l'aimable* all the way to Bath.   At Bath, candles still more waxen, and waiters still more profound.   Being, since my travels, very much gallicized in my character, I ordered a pint of claret; I found it incomparably the best wine I ever tasted; it disappeared with a rapidity which surprises me even at this distance of time.   The next morning in the coach by eight, with a handsome valetudinarian lady, upon whom the coach produced the same effect as a steam-packet would do.   I proposed weak warm brandy and water; she thought, at first, it would produce inflammation of the stomach, but presently requested to have it warm and *not* weak, and she took it to the last drop, as I did the claret.   All well here.   God bless you, dearest child!   Love to Holland.

SYDNEY SMITH

TO ROBERT MONCKTON MILNES,
1ST LORD HOUGHTON

33 CHARLES STREET, BERKELEY SQUARE,
JUNE 20TH, 1838

MY DEAR SIR, I began years ago to breakfast with Rogers, and I must go on unless he leaves off asking me, but I must not make any fresh alliances of this sort, for it deranges me for the whole day, and I am a very old gentleman, and must take care of myself, a duty I owe to my parish, or, rather, I should say, two parishes.   But you have, luckily for you, no such plea, and therefore you must come and breakfast with me on Saturday morning next, at ten o'clock precisely.   Say that you will do this.

Yours truly,
SYDNEY SMITH

TO THE SAME
JUNE 9TH, 1838

MY DEAR SIR, If you want to get a place for a relation, you must not delay it till he is born. . . .   The same thing with any smaller accommodation.   You ask me for tickets on Wednesday to go to St. Paul's on Thursday.   My first promise dated 1836.   I would, however, have done my possible, but your letter did not arrive till Saturday (Paulo post).   The fact is, I have been wandering about the coast for Mrs. Sydney's health and am taken by the Preventive Service for a brandy merchant waiting an opportunity of running goods on a large scale. I wish you many long and hot dinners with lords and ladies, wits and poets, and am always truly yours,

SYDNEY SMITH

TO THE SAME

JULY 23RD, 1840

MY DEAR MILNES, If you have really any intention of paying me a visit, I must describe the *locale*. We live six miles from Taunton, on the Minehead Road. An inn at Taunton is the London Inn. I shall be at home from the end of July to the end of October, or rather the 20th of October. You must give me good notice, and wait my answer, for we are often full and often sick. It is but fair to add that nothing can be more melancholy than Combe Florey; that we have no other neighbours than the parsonism of the country, and that in the country I hibernise, and live by licking my paws. Having stated these distressing truths, and assuring you that (as you like to lay out your life to the best advantage) it is not worth your while to come, I have only to add that we shall be very glad to see you.

Yours very truly,

SYDNEY SMITH

MARIA JOSEPHA, LADY STANLEY OF ALDERLEY
(1771–1863)

Maria Josepha Holroyd was the daughter of the Earl of Sheffield. In her youth she saw a lot of interesting society and became an intimate correspondent of Gibbon, who called her "a most extraordinary young woman." Our first two letters were written to an old family retainer, a year or two before Maria's marriage to Edward Stanley, later Lord Stanley of Alderley. No less characteristic are the letters from her Aunt Serena; the first was written when Maria had just given birth to twins; the second chats about Paris at the time of the First Empire.

TO MISS FIRTH

SHEFFIELD PLACE: JULY 11TH, 1793

MRS. SARAH HOLROYD [1] calls you by very unseemly names, which still having some regard for you, I will not shock your ears with. But I am perfectly satisfied that no appellation is too bad for you, you villainous Grimalkin! I am all Impatience to hear what you think of your House, and in this hot weather Impatience is a bad thing! . . . Papa is very busy settling the things in the Garret. The chairs that were in the best Drawing room are to come down here for the Winter Drawing room. . . . What a D—— of a Cat you are! When I send you so many interesting particulars about House etc. that you should not express gratitude. Unless indeed it is too great to find utterance. I do begin to be convinced you are gone to shades below. I hope your Executors will not be surprised at my Style of writing!

It is too hot to swear any more.

Ever sincerely yours,

M. J. H.

TO THE SAME

MARCH 21ST, 1793

. . . Papa has got into Guy's Hospital four Frenchmen, Gentlemen and Officers who perhaps you may recollect something of their having been a

---

[1] The writer's aunt.

long time confined on board a ship, and at last escaped by swimming to shore; I forget the particulars. How melancholy to think that these Gentlemen are most thankful for admittance to the hospital! but one of them, a very genteel young man, is almost eat up by the "Itch", and as it is a most extraordinary complaint, and they have no other proper place to put him into, he is now in the same apartment with the lunatics. They have hardly a Shirt to their Backs and neither Shoes nor Stockings. With the greatest difficulty they (four in a Hackney Coach) collected amongst them two pence to pay the turnpike. James went to the Hospital to receive them and recommend them to the Steward and offered them money by Papa's desire. They refused accepting it, saying they should want for nothing there. What uncommon generosity of mind! for Men who are not above entering into an Hospital cannot be accused of false pride. Papa has sent Walpole to-day to get a lodging for the Itchy man if he finds himself at all incommoded by his situation among the madmen. It really makes one's blood run cold to think what extremities hundreds are reduced to, and what a number of melancholy stories there are that come to our ears.

Adieu. I am in haste, but ever,

Yours affectionately,

M. J. H.

TO HER SISTER, LOUISA, AFTERWARDS LADY CLINTON

JANUARY 21, 1802

A GOOD child you was to mention books to me; mind you always pick up knowledge in that way when you can. I have not got Miss Hamilton's two volumes yet. The first is, I think, by far the most sensible work upon Education I have seen, and by no means difficult of comprehension to middling capacities. Such, however, have so little business to study any system of education, or, if they do, are so little likely to make any hand of it, that it is rather a good thing when a work of this kind is in language above their comprehension that the few ideas they have may not be bothered. It would be a happy thing for the community at large if nine tenths of the young gentlemen and ladies who are turned out into the world, thoroughly well educated, had never been taught more than to write a good hand, read their Bible, be taught what some would call a "religion of prejudice"—by which I mean, not led to make inquiries, which has mischievous effects on ordinary minds—the Hes to be instructed in regard to the profession they are about to enter, and the Shes made perfect in plain work.

I am writing in the midst of such tempests and storms that the barn only can stand unmoved in the commotion.

FROM AUNT SERENA TO HER MARIA

BATH, MONDAY, NOV., 1802

I CAN'T belive it.   It is all a dream!   I am shaking away and reading the letter over and over, and I did not come in till near four; but write I will, to bless the dear precious mother of boys.   Heaven bless them!   There is no danger.   They will live and do well, as many other twins have done; and it was but right, for it would have been nothing to follow Lady Sheff and Louisa in the common vulgar way of one at a time.   Maria shows her superior spirit.   I will rejoice that there are two.   A thousand congratulations to dear Mr. Stanley!   May these dear boys be worthy of him and never give him anything but pleasure and honour!   I should delight were I to live to see how he will educate sons—but I must not talk of that before the poor dears know how to see or breathe.   A thousand thanks to the dear Firth [old family servant] for all her intelligence!   My heart beats to think how near she was to not being with you, and somehow I should not think them well born without her. . . . Only to think how lately no boy in the family and now four!   How very grand it sounds!   I am no longer forced to say, "O, Maria has girls enough!"   My servants shall positively get tipsy this good day.   As for Alderley, I expect to hear there was not a sober person in the county, and at least a dozen houses made into bonfires.   Best wishes to all who care for me, and a thousand blessings of my own.

Ever and ever,

yours,

S. H.

THE SAME TO THE SAME

APRIL 23RD, 1804

As I have seen a letter from an intimate friend of mine to Lady Hesketh, lamenting, with only too true affection and kindness, my death—which she knew to be true from undoubted authority—you may perhaps like some news from the next world, and be glad to find my spirit still hovering about you with affection.   As I passed through the Inferno I met crowds hurrahing.   Buonaparte and his myrmidons, and particularly rejoicing in the murder of Duc d'Enghien and Pichegru. Some among them, however, muttered how *poor* his inventions were to cover his deceit and wickedness, for that none but idiots could possibly believe his fabrications; and, as Pride and Barbarity were pushing him on so fast, they feared he might be destroyed before he had done all the mischief the great prince intended him to do. As I went a little further they showed me a high seat of honour intended for him, but I saw through a mist the horrid tortures he was to suffer, with the never dying worm of remorse, in which he had many associates, such as Robespierre, etc. I wasn't glad to leave that scene of horror and go to the next place, where I saw the victims of those monsters waiting for judgment, hoping they had atoned for their sins, and by repentance might be fitted for Heaven. I wanted to join them, but I was told I must not yet be admitted; and this is all I am permitted to tell you. In some of the passages I met people about whom I have been puzzled. In Heaven they would meet nothing to suit them. . . No employment on earth but cards, dress, scandal and folly, what enjoyment can their poor souls find even in Heaven, if, through mercy they should be admitted there. These people I met chattering and disputing for place, and I was not allowed to see the end of their destination, though I wished to do. I feel in a great fright lest I should be reckoned in that class; for though I may never have been exactly like them, yet, if I had been taught better and have more advantages without making the use I ought to have made of them I may be glad enough to get even into those passages without the hope of no worse punishment than such associates would be. . . . If I can now recollect anything that happened before my death I will tell it you. . . . I remember I was very pleasantly situated at Clifton, and was greatly delighted with the third volume of "Cowper's Letters" which I read to Lady Hesketh before it was published.

I was so well at Clifton that my death must have been very unexpected. I wish I had the privilege from these regions to see you and your children and your dear husband; for, were I admitted among the blessèd, I should still take pleasure and interest in you all. In the last year of my life my greatest regret was not having visited you. Heaven bless you ever.

S. HOLROYD

SAMUEL TAYLOR COLERIDGE (1772–1834)

Coleridge and Southey were regular correspondents long before they settled in the Lakes. In this letter Coleridge describes his new home at Keswick.

TO ROBERT SOUTHEY

GRETA HALL, KESWICK; APRIL 13, 1801

MY DEAR SOUTHEY, I received your kind letter on the evening before last, and I trust that this will arrive at Bristol just in time to rejoice with them that rejoice. Alas! you will have found the dear old place sadly *minus*ed by the removal of Davy. It is one of the evils of long silence, that when one recommences the correspondence, one has so much to say that one can say nothing. I have enough, with what I have seen, and with what I have done, and with what I have suffered, and with what I have heard, exclusive of all that I hope and all that I intend—I have enough to pass away a great deal of time with, were you on a desert isle, and I your *Friday*. But at present I purpose to speak only of myself relatively to Keswick and to you.

Our house stands on a low hill, the whole front of which is one field and an enormous garden, nine-tenths of which is a nursery garden. Behind the house is an orchard, and a small wood on a steep slope, at the foot of which flows the river Greta, which winds round and catches the evening lights in the front of the house. In front we have a giant's camp—an encamped army of tent-like mountains, which by an inverted arch gives a view of another vale. On our right the lovely vale and the wedge-shaped lake of Bassenthwaite; and on our left Derwentwater and Lodore full in view, and the fantastic mountains of Borrodale. Behind us the massy Skiddaw, smooth, green, high, with two chasms and a tent-like ridge in the larger. A fairer scene you have not seen in all your wanderings. Without going from our own grounds we have all that can please a human being. As to books, my landlord, who dwells next door, has a very respectable library, which he has put with mine; histories, encyclopædias, and all the modern gentry. But then I can have, when I choose, free access to

533

the princely library of Sir Guilfred Lawson, which contains the noblest collection of travels and natural history of, perhaps, any private library in England; besides this, there is the Cathedral library of Carlisle, from whence I can have any books sent to me that I wish; in short, I may truly say that I command all the libraries in the county.

Our neighbour is a truly good and affectionate man, a father to my children, and a friend to me. He was offered fifty guineas for the house in which we are to live, but he preferred me for a tenant at twenty-five; and yet the whole of his income does not exceed, I believe, £200 a year. A more truly disinterested man I never met with; severely frugal yet almost carelessly generous; and yet he got all his money as a common carrier, by hard labour, and by pennies and pennies. He is one instance among many in this country of the salutary effect of the love of knowledge——he was from a boy a lover of learning. The house is full twice as large as we want; it hath in it more rooms than Allfoxen; you might have a bed-room, parlour, study, &c. &c., and there would always be rooms to spare for your or my visitors. In short, for situation and convenience,——and when I mention the name of Wordsworth, for society of men of intellect,——I know no place in which you and Edith would find yourselves so well suited.

FRANCIS, LORD JEFFREY (1773–1850)

Jeffrey was one of the leading men in the Edinburgh of his day. Editor of the "Edinburgh Review" throughout its opposition to the Romantic movement in poetry, he was notorious as the fiercest critic of the Lake Poets and their younger followers. He provoked Byron's "English Bards and Scotch Reviewers" and was challenged to a duel by Tom Moore, which was, however, prevented by the police.

TO HIS SISTER MARY

OXFORD, QUEEN'S COLLEGE, NOV. 2, 1791

. . . .

WHENCE arises my affection for the moon. I do not believe there is a being, of whatever denomination, upon whom she lifts the light of her countenance, who is so glad to see her as I am! She is the companion of my melancholy, and the witness of my happiness. There are few people for the sake of whose society I should be glad to shut her out. I went half a mile yesterday to see her on the water, and to-night I have spent the most pleasant hour that I have known these six weeks in admiring her from my back window. This place should never be looked on but by moonlight, and then, indeed, what place does not look well! But there is something striking here—you recollect it—the deep and romantic shades on the sculptured towers—the sparkle of their gilded vanes—their black and pointed shadows upon the smooth green turf of our courts—the strong shades of the statues over the library—the yellow and trembling heads of the trees beyond them! Could I find anybody here who understood these matters, or who thought them worth being understood, I should regain my native enthusiasm and my wonted enjoyment; but they are all drunkards, or pedants, or coxcombs.

How little does happiness depend upon ourselves! Moralists may preach as they please, but neither temperance, nor fortitude, nor justice, nor charity, nor conscious genius, nor fair prospects, have power to make anybody happy for two days together. For the little power they have they are indebted to their novelty. In short, all our

535

enjoyment here seems to depend upon a certain energy and vigour of mind, which depend upon—we know not what. What has happened to me since the morning? that I am now as cheerful and gay as I was then discontented and unhappy! I believe I have written nonsense, for I have written wholly from myself.

I have almost put out my eyes, and can hardly see to tell you that I am your amiable brother.

TO A GRANDCHILD

CRAIGCROOK, 20TH JUNE, 1848

MY SONSY NANCY! I love you very much, and think very often of your dimples, and your pimples; and your funny little plays, and all your pretty ways; and I send you my blessing, and wish I were kissing, your sweet rosy lips, or your fat finger tips; and that you were here, so that I could hear, your stammering words, from a mouthful of curds; and a great purple tongue (as broad as it's long); and see your round eyes, open wide with surprise, and your wondering look, to find yourself at Craigcrook! To-morrow is Maggie's *birthday*, and we have built up a great bonfire in honour of it; and Maggie Rutherfurd (do you remember her at all?) is coming out to dance round it; and all the servants are to drink her health, and wish her many happy days with you and Frankie; and all the mammys and pappys, whether grand or not grand. We are very glad to hear that she and you love each other so well, and are happy in making each other happy; and that you do not forget dear Tarley or Frankie, when they are out of sight, nor Granny either—or even old Granny pa, who is in most danger of being forgotten, he thinks. We have had showery weather here, but the garden is full of flowers; and Frankie has a new wheel-barrow, and does a great deal of work, and *some mischief* now and then. All the dogs are very well; and Foxey is mine, and Froggy is Tarley's, and Frankie has taken up with great white Neddy—so that nothing is left for Granny but old barking Jacky and Dover when the carriage comes. The donkey sends his compliments to you, and maintains that you are a cousin of his! or a near relation, at all events. He wishes too, that you and Maggie would come, for he thinks that you will not be so heavy on his back as Tarley and Maggie Rutherfurd, who now ride him without mercy. This is Sunday, and Ali is at church— Granny and I taking care of Frankie till she comes back, and he is now hammering very busily at a corner of the carpet, which he says does not lie flat.   He is very good, and really too pretty for a boy, though I think his two eyebrows are growing into one—stretching and meeting each other above his nose!   But he has not near so many *freckles* as Tarley—who has a very fine crop of them—which she and I encourage as much as we can.   I hope you and Maggie will lay in a stock of them, as I think no little girl can be pretty without them in summer.   Our pea-hens are suspected of having young families in some hidden place, for though they pay us short visits now and then, we see them but seldom, and always alone.   If you and Maggie were here with your sharp eyes, we think you might find out their secret, and introduce us to a nice new family of young peas.   The old papa cock, in the meantime, says he knows nothing about them, and does not care a farthing!   We envy you your young peas of another kind, for we have none yet, nor any asparagus either and hope you will bring some down to us in your lap.   Tarley sends her love, and I send mine to you all; though I shall think most of Maggie to-morrow morning, and of you when your birth morning comes.   When is that, do you know?   It is never dark now here, and we might all go to bed without candles.   And so bless you ever and ever, my dear dimply pussie.— Your very loving GRANDPA.

SIR CHARLES BELL (1774–1842)

Bell was a famous surgeon of his time and will ever be remembered as the discoverer of the distinct functions of the nerves. This description of the medical side of Waterloo throws a remarkable side-light on the horrors of war before the introduction of anæsthetics and ordinary cleanliness.

TO FRANCIS HORNER

JULY, 1815

MY DEAR HORNER, I write this to you, after being some days at home, engaged in my usual occupations, and consequently disenchanted of the horrors of the battle of Waterloo. I feel relief in this, for certainly if I had written to you from Brussels, I should have appeared very extravagant. An absolute revolution took place in my economy, body and soul; so that I who am known to require eight hours sleep, found first three hours, and then one hour and a half sufficient, after days of the most painful excitement and bodily exertion.

After I had been five days engaged with the prosecution of my object, I found that the best cases, that is, the most horrid wounds left totally without assistance, were to be found in the hospital of the French wounded. This hospital was only forming; they were even then bringing these poor creatures in from the woods. It is impossible to convey to you the picture of human misery continually before my eyes. What was heartrending in the day, was intolerable at night; and I rose and wrote, at four o'clock in the morning, to the chief surgeon Gunning, offering to perform the necessary operations upon the French. At six o'clock I took the knife in my hand, and continued incessantly at work till seven in the evening; and so the second day, and again the third day.

All the decencies of performing surgical operations were soon neglected. While I amputated one man's thigh, there lay at one time thirteen, all beseeching to be taken next; one full of entreaty, one calling upon me to remember my promise to take him, another execrating. It was a strange thing to feel my clothes stiff with blood, and my arms powerless with the exertion of using the knife; and more extraordinary still, to find my mind calm amidst such variety of suffering; but to give one of these objects access to your feelings was to allow yourself to be unmanned for the performance of a duty. It was less painful to look upon the whole, than to contemplate one object.

When I first went round the wards of the wounded prisoners, my sensations were very extraordinary. We had every where heard of the manner in which these men had fought—nothing could surpass their devotedness. In a long ward, containing fifty, there was no expression of suffering, no one spoke to his neighbour. There was a resentful, sullen rigidness of face, a fierceness in their dark eyes, as they lay half-covered in the sheets.

Sunday. I was interrupted, and now I perceive I was falling into the mistake of attempting to convey to you the feelings which took possession of me, amidst the miseries of Brussels. After being eight days among the wounded, I visited the field of battle. The view of the field, the gallant stories, the charges, the individual instances of enterprise and valour, recalled me to the sense which the world has of victory and Waterloo. But this was transient, a gloomy uncomfortable view of human nature is the inevitable consequence of looking upon the whole as I did—as I was forced to do.

It is a misfortune to have our sentiments so at variance with the universal sentiment. But there must ever be associated with the honours of Waterloo, to my eyes, the most shocking signs of woe; to my ear, accents of entreaty; outcry from the manly breast, interrupted forcible expressions of the dying, and *noisome smells*. I must show you my note books, for as I took my notes of cases generally by sketching the object of our remarks, it may convey an excuse for this excess of *sentiment*.

Faithfully yours,

C. BELL

ROBERT SOUTHEY (1774–1843)

Southey was a man to whom Fate dealt many a hard blow. It was while smarting from some of these that he wrote to his friend Bedford, pouring into his ears the story of his woes. Duppa was an artist and author who, on occasions, wrote to Southey for help and advice.

TO GROSVENOR C. BEDFORD

BRISTOL, APRIL 3, 1803

I HAVE been thinking of Brixton, Grosvenor, for these many days past, when more painful thoughts would give me leave. An old lady whom I loved greatly, and have for the last eight years regarded with something like a filial veneration, has been carried off by this influenza. She was mother to Danvers, with whom I have so long been on terms of the closest intimacy.

Your ejection from Brixton has very long been in my head as one of the evil things to happen in 1803, though it was not predicted in Moore's Almanack. However, I am glad to hear you have got a house, and still more, that it is an old house. I love old houses best, for the sake of the odd closets and cupboards and good thick walls that don't let the wind blow in, and little out-of-the-way polyangular rooms with great beams running across the ceiling,—old heart of oak, that has outlasted half a score generations; and chimney pieces with the date of the year carved above them, and huge fire-places that warmed the shins of Englishmen before the house of Hanover came over. The most delightful associations that ever made me feel, and think, and fall a-dreaming, are excited by old buildings—not absolute ruins, but in a state of decline. Even the clipt yews interest me; and if I found one in any garden that should become mine, in the shape of a peacock, I should be as proud to keep his tail well spread as the man who first carved him. In truth, I am more disposed to connect myself by sympathy with the ages which are past, and by hope with those that are to come, than to vex and irritate myself by any lively interest about the existing generation.

Your letter was unusually interesting, and dwells upon my mind.

I could, and perhaps will some day, write an eclogue upon leaving an old place of residence. What you say of yourself impresses upon me still more deeply the conviction, that the want of a favourite pursuit is your greatest source of discomfort and discontent. It is the pleasure of *pursuit* that makes every man happy; whether the merchant, or the sportsman, or the collector, the philobibl, or the *reader-o-bibl*, and *maker-o-bibl*, like me,—pursuit at once supplies employment and hope. This is what I have often preached to you, but perhaps I never told you what benefit I myself have derived from resolute employment. When Joan of Arc was in the press, I had as many legitimate causes for unhappiness as any man need have,—uncertainty for the future, and immediate want, in the literal and plain meaning of the word. I have often walked the streets at dinner-time for want of a dinner, when I had not eighteen-pence for the ordinary, nor bread and cheese at my lodgings. But do not suppose that I thought of my dinner when I was walking— my head was full of what I was composing; when I lay down at night I was planning my poem; and when I rose up in the morning the poem was the first thought to which I was awake. The scanty profits of that poem I was then anticipating in my lodging-house bills for tea, bread and butter, and those little &cs which amount to a formidable sum when a man has no resources; but that poem, faulty as it is, has given me a Baxter's shove into my right place in the world.

So much for the practical effects of Epictetus, to whom I hold myself indebted for much amendment of character. Now,—when I am not comparatively, but positively, a happy man, wishing little, and wanting nothing,—my delight is the certainty that, while I have health and eyesight, I can never want a pursuit to interest. Subject after subject is chalked out. In hand I have Kehama, Madoc, and a voluminous history; and I have planned more poems and more histories; so that whenever I am removed to another state of existence, there will be some *valde lacrymabile hiatus* in some of my posthumous works.

We have all been ill with La Gripe. But the death of my excellent old friend is a real grief, and one that will long be felt: the pain of amputation is nothing,—it is the loss of the limb that is the evil. She influenced my every-day thought, and one of my pleasures was to afford her any of the little amusements, which age and infirmities can enjoy.

When do I go to London? If I can avoid it, not so soon as I had thought. The journey, and some unavoidable weariness in tramping over that overgrown metropolis, half terrifies me; and then the thought of certain pleasures, such as seeing Rickman, and Duppa, and Wynn, and Grosvenor Bedford, and going to the old book-shops, half tempts me. I am working very hard to fetch up my lee-way; that is, I am making up for time lost during my ophthalmia. Fifty-four more pages of Amadis, and a preface—no more to do—huzza! land! land! God bless you!

R. S.

TO THE SAME

KESWICK, NOV. 24, 1807

MY DEAR GROSVENOR, Mine is a strong spirit, and I am very desirous that you should not suppose it to be more severely tried than it is. The temporary inconvenience which I feel is solely produced by unavoidable expenses in settling myself, which will not occur again; and if Espriella slides into a good sale, or if one edition of our deplorable Specimens should go off, I shall be floated into smooth water. Bear this in mind, also, that I can command an income, fully equivalent to all my wants, whenever I choose to write for money, and for nothing else. Our Fathers in the Row would find me task-work to undertake, and I could assuredly make £300 a-year as easily as I now make half that sum, simply by writing anonymously, and doing what five hundred trading authors could do just as well. This is the worst which can befall me.

Old John Southey dealt unjustly with me,—but it was what I expected, and his brother will, without doubt, do just the same. In case of Lord Somerville's death without a son, a considerable property devolves to me or my representatives—encumbered, however, with a lawsuit to recover it; and, as I should be compelled to enter into this, I have only to hope his Lordship will have the goodness to live as long as I do, and save me from the disquietude which this would occasion. I used to think that the reputation which I should establish would ultimately turn to marketable account, and that my books would sell as well as if they were seasoned with slander or obscenity. In time they will; it will not be in my time. I have, however, an easy means of securing some part of the advantage to my family, by forbearing to publish any more corrected editions during my lifetime, and leaving such corrections as will avail to give a second lease of copyright, and make any book-seller's editions of no value. As for my family, I have no fears for them; they would find friends enough when I am gone; and having this confidence, you may be sure that there is not a lighter-hearted man in the world than myself.

Basta,—or, as we say in Latin, Ohe jam satis est. My eyes are better, which I attribute to an old velvet bonnet of Edith's, converted without alteration into a most venerable studying cap for my worship; it keeps my ears warm, and I am disposed to believe that having the sides of my head. cold, as this Kamschatka weather needs must make it, affected the eyes. Mr. Bedford, you may imagine what a venerable and, as the French say, penetrating air this gives me. Hair, forehead, eyebrows, and eyes are hidden,—nothing appears but nose; but that is so cold that I expect every morning when I get out of bed to see the snow lie on the summit of it. This complaint was not my old Egyptian plague, but pure weakness, which makes what I have said probable. . . .

We had an interesting guest here a few evenings ago, who came to visit Tom,—Captain Guillem, Nelson's first lieutenant at Trafalgar, a sailor of the old Blake and Dampier breed, who has risen from before the mast, was in Duncan's action, and at Copenhagen, &c. He told us more of Nelson that I can find time to write. God bless you.

R. S.

TO RICHARD DUPPA

MARCH 31, 1809

MY DEAR DUPPA, I am sorry for your loss,—a heavy one under any circumstances, and particularly so to one who, being single at your time of life, will now feel more entirely what it is to have no person who intimately loves him. It is not in the order of nature that there should ever be a void in the heart of man,—the old leaves should not fall from the tree till the young ones are expanding to supply their place.

I have now three girls living, and as delightful a playfellow in the shape of a boy as ever man was blest with. Very often, when I look at them I think what a fit thing it would be that Malthus should be hanged.

You may have known that I have some dealings, in the way of trade, with your bookseller, Murray. One article of mine is in his first "Quarterly," and he has bespoken more. Whenever I shall have the satisfaction of seeing you once more under this roof, it will amuse you to see how dextrously Gifford emasculated this article of mine of its most forcible parts. I amused myself one morning with putting them all in again, and restoring vigour, consistency, and connection to the whole. It is certainly true that his Majesty gives me a pension of £200 a-year, out of which his Majesty deducts £60 and a few shillings;

but, if his Majesty trebled or decupled the pension, and remitted the whole taxation, it would be the same thing. The treasury should never bribe, nor his judges deter me from delivering a full and free opinion upon any subject which seems to me to call for it. If I hate Bonaparte, and maintain that this country never ought to accept of any peace while that man is Emperor of France, it is precisely upon the same principle that I formerly disliked Pitt, and maintained that we never ought to have gone to war.

I am glad you have been interested by the "Cid"; it is certainly the most curious chronicle in existence. In the course of the summer —I hope early in it,—you will see the first volume of my "History of Brazil," of which nine-and-twenty sheets are printed. This book has cost me infinite labour. The "Cid" was an easy task; of that no other copy was made than what went to the press; of this every part has been twice written, many parts three times, and all with my own hand. For this I expect to get a sufficient quantity of abuse, and little else; money is only to be got by such productions as are worth nothing more than what they fetch per sheet. I could get my thousand a year, if I would but do my best endeavours to be dull, and aim at nothing higher than Reviews and Magazines. God bless you,

Yours very truly,

R. Southey

JANE AUSTEN (1775–1817)

In these letters we catch a glimpse of the Austen family as seen through the eyes of Jane. Cassandra was her elder sister; Henry a brother whose health was the cause of considerable anxiety; Edward another brother, who inherited the property and took the name of their second cousin Knight. Edward was the father of Fanny, to whom the second letter is addressed.

TO CASSANDRA AUSTEN

HANS PLACE, SATURDAY (DEC. 2), 1815

MY DEAR CASSANDRA, Henry came back yesterday, and might have returned the day before if he had known as much in time. I had the pleasure of hearing from Mr. T. on Wednesday night that Mr. Seymour thought there was not the least occasion for his absenting himself any longer.

I had also the comfort of a few lines on Wednesday morning from Henry himself, just after your letter was gone, giving so good an account of his feelings as made me perfectly easy. He met with the utmost care and attention at Hanwell, spent his two days there very quietly and pleasantly, and, being certainly in no respect the worse for going, we may believe that he must be better, and he is quite sure of being himself. To make his return a complete gala Mr. Haden was secured for dinner. I need not that our evening was agreeable.

But you seem to be under a mistake as to Mr. H. You call him an apothecary. He is no apothecary; he has never been an apothecary; there is not an apothecary in this neighbourhood—the only inconvenience of the situation perhaps—but so it is; we have not a medical man within reach. He is a Haden, nothing but a Haden, a sort of wonderful nondescript creature on two legs, something between a man and an angel, but without the least spice of an apothecary. He is, perhaps, the only person *not* an apothecary hereabouts. He has never sung to us. He will not sing without a pianoforte accompaniment.

Mr. Meyers gives his three lessons a week, altering his days and hours, however, just as he chooses, never very punctual, and never giving good measure. I have not Fanny's fondness for masters, and Mr. Meyers does not give me any longing after them. The truth is, I think, that they are all, at least music-masters, made of too much consequence and allowed to take too many liberties with their scholars' time.

We shall be delighted to see Edward on Monday, only sorry that you must be losing him. A turkey will be equally welcome with himself. He must prepare for his own proper bedroom here, as Henry moved down to the one below last week; he found the other cold.

I am sorry my mother has been suffering, and am afraid this exquisite weather is too good to agree with her. *I* enjoy it all over me, from top to toe, from right to left, longitudinally, perpendicularly, diagonally; and I cannot but selfishly hope we are to have it last till Christmas —nice, unwholesome, unreasonable, relaxing, close, muggy weather.

Oh, thank you very much for your long letter; it did me a great deal of good. Henry accepts your offer of making him nine gallon of mead thankfully. The mistake of the dogs rather vexed him for a moment, but he has not thought of it since. Today he makes a third attempt at his strengthening plaster, and, as I am sure he will now be getting out a great deal, it is to be wished that he may be able to keep it on. He sets off this morning by the Chelsea coach to sign bonds and visit Henrietta St., and I have no doubt he will be going every day to Henrietta St.

Fanny and I were very snug by ourselves as soon as we were satisfied about our invalid's being safe at Hanwell. By manœuvring and good luck we foiled all the Malins' attempts upon us. Happily I caught a little cold on Wednesday, the morning we were in town, which we made very useful, and we saw nobody but our precious and Mr. Tilson.

This evening the Malins are allowed to drink tea with us. We are in hopes—that is, we *wish*—Miss Palmer and the little girls may come this morning. You know, of course, that she could *not* come on Thursday, and she will not attempt to *name* any other day.

God bless you. Excuse the shortness of this letter, but I must finish it now that I may save you 2d. Best love.

Yours affectionately,
J. A.

It strikes me that I have no business to give the P.R. a binding, but we will take counsel upon the question.

I am glad you have put the flounce on your chintz; I am sure it must look particularly well, and it is what I had thought of.

CHAWTON: FEB. 20, 1817

MY DEAREST FANNY, You are inimitable, irresistible. You are the delight of my life. Such letters, such entertaining letters, as you have lately sent! such a description of your queer little heart! such a lovely display of what imagination does. You are worth your weight in gold, or even in the new silver coinage. I cannot express to you what I have felt in reading your history of yourself—how full of pity and concern, and admiration and amusement, I have been! You are the paragon of all that is silly and sensible, commonplace and eccentric, sad and lively, provoking and interesting. Who can keep pace with the fluctuations of your fancy, the capprizios of your taste, the contradictions of your feelings? You are so odd, and all the time so perfectly natural—so peculiar in yourself, and yet so like everybody else!

It is very, very gratifying to me to know you so intimately. You can hardly think what a pleasure it is to me to have such thorough pictures of your heart. Oh, what a loss it will be when you are married! You are too agreeable in your single state—too agreeable as a niece. I shall hate you when your delicious play of mind is all settled down in conjugal and maternal affections.

Mr. B. frightens me. He will have you. I see you at the altar. I have *some* faith in Mrs. C. Cage's observation, and still more in Lizzy's; and, besides, I know it *must* be so. He must be wishing to attach you. It would be too stupid and shameful in him to be otherwise; and all the family are seeking your acquaintance.

Do not imagine that I have any real objection; I have rather taken a fancy to him than not, and I like the house for you. I only do not like you should marry anybody. And yet I do wish you to marry very much, because I know you will never be happy till you were; but the loss of a Fanny Knight will be never made up to me. My "affec. niece F.C.B——" will be but a poor substitute. I do not like your being nervous, and so apt to cry—it is a sign you are not quite well; but I hope Mr. Scud—as you always write his name (your Mr. Scuds amuses me very much)—will do you good.

I enjoy your visit to Goodnestone, it must be a great pleasure to you; you have not seen Fanny Cage in comfort so long. I hope she represents and remonstrates and reasons with you properly. Why should you be living in dread of his marrying somebody else? (Yet, how natural!) You did not choose to have him yourself, why not allow him to take comfort where he can? You cannot forget how you felt under the idea of its having been possible that he might have dined in Hans Place.

Mrs. Deedes is as welcome as May to all our benevolence to her son; we only lamented that we could not do more, and that the £50 note we slipped into his hand at parting was necessarily the limit of our offering. Good Mrs. Deedes! Scandal and gossip; yes, I dare say you were well stocked, but I am very fond of Mrs. —— for reasons good. Thank you for mentioning her praise of "Emma," &c.

Your objection to the quadrilles delighted me exceedingly. Pretty well for a lady irrecoverably attached to *one* person! Sweet Fanny, believe no such thing of yourself, spread no such malicious slander upon your understanding within the precincts of your imagination. Do not speak ill of your sense merely for the gratification of your fancy; yours is sense which deserves more honourable treatment. You are *not* in love with him; you never *have* been really in love with him.

Yours very affectionately,

J. AUSTEN

CHARLES LAMB (1775-1834)

An East India Office clerk, dividing his leisure between the care of his tragic sister Mary, and the presidency of a "ragged regiment" of friends, Lamb was the king of a company which included Wordsworth, Hazlitt, and all the choicest spirits of the time, and an essayist of unique delicacy and charm. As might have been expected, Elia is his own charming self in his letters. The one to Bernard Barton, the Quaker poet of Woodbridge, is especially delightful in its sound common sense, offered by probably the least common-sense writer in English literature.

TO MR. COLERIDGE

NOV. 14TH, 1796

COLERIDGE, I love you for dedicating your poetry to Bowles: Genius of the sacred fountain of tears, it was he who led you gently by the hand through all this valley of weeping, showed you the dark green yew trees, and the willow shades, where, by the fall of waters, you might indulge an uncomplaining melancholy, a delicious regret for the past, or weave fine visions of that awful future,

> When all the vanities of life's brief day
> Oblivion's hurrying hand hath swept away,
> And all its sorrows, at the awful blast
> Of the archangel's trump, are but as shadows past.

I have another sort of dedication in my head for my few things, which I want to know if you approve of, and can insert. I mean to inscribe them to my sister. It will be unexpected, and it will give her pleasure; or do you think it will look whimsical at all? as I have not spoken to her about it, I can easily reject the idea. But there is a monotony in the affections, which people living together, or, as we do now, very frequently seeing each other, are apt to give in to; a sort of indifference in the expression of kindness for each other, which demands that we should sometimes call to our aid the trickery of surprise. Do you publish with Lloyd, or without him? in either case my little portion may come last, and after the fashion of orders to a country correspondent, I will give directions how I should like to have 'em done. The title-page to stand thus:—

POEMS,

BY

CHARLES LAMB, OF THE INDIA HOUSE.

Under this title the following motto, which, for want of room, I put over leaf, and desire you to insert, whether you like it or no.   May not a gentleman choose what arms, mottoes, or armorial bearings the herald will give him leave, without consulting his republican friend, who might advise none?   May not a publican put up the sign of the Saracen's Head, even though his undiscerning neighbour should prefer, as more genteel, the Cat and Gridiron?

[MOTTO.]

This beauty, in the blossom of my youth,
When my first fire knew no adulterate incense,
Nor I no way to flatter but my fondness,
In the best language my true tongue could tell me,
And all the broken sighs my sick heart lend me,
I sued and served. Long did I love this lady.

MASSINGER.

THE DEDICATION.

THE FEW FOLLOWING POEMS,
CREATURES OF THE FANCY AND THE FEELING
IN LIFE'S MORE VACANT HOURS,
PRODUCED, FOR THE MOST PART, BY
LOVE AND IDLENESS,
ARE,
WITH ALL A BROTHER'S FONDNESS,
INSCRIBED TO

MARY ANNE LAMB,

THE AUTHOR'S BEST FRIEND AND SISTER.

This is the pomp and paraphernalia of parting, with which I take my leave of a passion which has reigned so royally (so long) within me; thus, with its trappings of laureateship, I fling it off, pleased and satisfied with myself that the weakness troubles me no longer.   I am wedded, Coleridge, to the fortunes of my sister and my poor old father.   Oh! my friend, I think sometimes, could I recall the days that are past, which among them should I choose? not those "merrier days," not the "pleasant days of hope," not "those wanderings with a fair hair'd maid," which I have so often and so feelingly regretted, but the days, Coleridge, of a *mother's* fondness for her *school-boy*.   What would I give to call her back to earth for *one* day, on my knees to ask her pardon for all those little asperities of temper which, from time to time, have given her gentle spirit pain; and the day, my friend, I trust, will come; there will be "time enough" for kind offices of love, if "Heaven's eternal year" be ours. Hereafter, her meek spirit shall not reproach me. Oh, my friend, cultivate the filial feelings! and let no man think himself released from the kind "charities" of relationship: these shall give him peace at the last; these are the best foundation for every species of benevolence. I rejoice to hear, by certain channels, that you, my friend, are reconciled with all your relations. 'Tis the most kindly and natural species of love, and we have all the associated train of early feelings to secure its strength and perpetuity. Send me an account of your health; *indeed* I am solicitous about you. God love you and yours.

C. LAMB

TO MR. MANNING

JAN. 2ND, 1810

DEAR MANNING, When I last wrote you I was in lodgings. I am now in chambers, No. 4, Inner Temple-lane, where I should be happy to see you any evening. Bring any of your friends, the Mandarins, with you. I have two sitting-rooms: I call them so *par excellence*, for you may stand, or loll, or lean, or try any posture in them, but they are best for sitting; not squatting down Japanese fashion, but the more decorous mode which European usage has consecrated. I have two of these rooms on the third floor, and five sleeping, cooking, &c., rooms, on the fourth floor. In my best room is a choice collection of the works of Hogarth, an English painter, of some humour. In my next best are shelves containing a small, but well-chosen library. My best room commands a court, in which there are trees and a pump, the water of which is excellent cold, with brandy, and not very insipid without. Here I hope to set up my rest, and not quit till Mr. Powell, the undertaker, gives me notice that I may have possession of my last lodging. He lets lodgings for single gentlemen. I sent you a parcel of books by my last to give you some idea of the state of European literature. There comes with this two volumes, done up as letters, of minor poetry, a sequel to "Mrs. Leicester": the best you may suppose mine; the next best are my coadjutor's; you may amuse yourself in guessing them out; but I must tell you mine are but one-third in quantity of the whole. So much for a very delicate subject. It is hard to speak of one's self, &c. Holcroft had finished his life when I wrote to you, and Hazlitt has since finished his life; I do not mean his own life, but he has finished a life of Holcroft, which is going to press. Tuthill is Dr. Tuthill. I continue Mr. Lamb. I have published a little book for children on titles of honour: and to give them some idea of the difference of rank and gradual rising, I have made a little scale, supposing myself to receive the following various accessions of dignity from the King, who is the fountain of honour—As at first, 1, Mr. C. Lamb; 2, C. Lamb, Esq.; 3, Sir C. Lamb, Bart.; 4, Baron Lamb of Stamford [1]; 5, Viscount Lamb; 6, Earl Lamb; 7, Marquis Lamb; 8, Duke Lamb. It would look like quibbling to carry it on further, and especially as it is not necessary for children to go beyond the ordinary titles of sub-regal dignity in our own country, otherwise I have sometimes in my dreams imagined myself still advancing, as 9th, King Lamb; 10th, Emperor Lamb; 11th, Pope Innocent, higher than which is nothing. Puns I have not made many (nor punch much), since the date of my last; one I cannot help relating. A constable in Salisbury Cathedral was telling me that eight people dined at the top of the spire of the cathedral, upon which I remarked that they must be very sharp set. But in general I cultivate the reasoning part of my mind more than the imaginative. I am stuffed out so with eating turkey for dinner, and another turkey for supper yesterday (Turkey in Europe and Turkey in Asia), that I can't jog on. It is New-year here. That is, it was New-year half-a-year back, when I was writing this. Nothing puzzles me more than time and space, and yet nothing puzzles me less, for I never think about them. The Persian Ambassador is the principal thing talked of now. I sent some people to see him worship the sun on Primrose Hill, at half-past six in the morning, 28th November; but he did not come, which makes me think the old fire-worshippers are a sect almost extinct in Persia. The Persian Ambassador's name is Shaw Ali Mirza. The common people call him Shaw nonsense. While I think of it, I have put three letters besides my own three into the India post for you, from your brother, sister, and some gentleman whose name I forget. Will they, have they, did they come safe? The distance you are at, cuts up tenses by the root. I think you said you did not know Kate *********. I express her by nine stars, though she is but one. You must have seen her at her father's. Try and remember her. Coleridge is bringing out a paper in weekly numbers, called the *Friend*, which I would send, if I could; but the difficulty I had in getting the packets of books out to you before deters me; and you'll want something new to read when you come home. Except Kate I have had no vision

---

[1] Where my family came from. I have chosen that, if ever I should have my choice.

of excellence this year, and she passed by like the queen on her coronation day; you don't know whether you saw her or not. Kate is fifteen: I go about moping, and sing the old pathetic ballad I used to like in my youth—

> She's sweet fifteen,
> I'm *one year more*.

Mrs. Bland sung it in boy's clothes the first time I heard it. I sometimes think the lower notes in my voice are like Mrs. Bland's. That glorious singer, Braham, one of my lights, is fled. He was for a season. He was a rare composition of the Jew, the gentleman, and the angel, yet all these elements mixed up so kindly in him, that you could not tell which preponderated; but he is gone, and one Phillips is engaged instead. Kate is vanished, but Miss B—— is always to be met with!

> Queens drop away, while blue-legged Maukin thrives;
> And courtly Mildred dies while country Madge survives.

That is not my poetry, but Quarles's; but haven't you observed that the rarest things are the least obvious? Don't show anybody the names in this letter. I write confidentially, and wish this letter to be considered as *private*. Hazlitt has written a *grammar* for Godwin; Godwin sells it bound up with a treatise of his own on language, but the *grey mare is the better horse*. I don't allude to Mrs. ——, but to the word *grammar*, which comes near to *grey mare*, if you observe, in sound. That figure is called paranomasia in Greek. I am sometimes happy in it. An old woman begged of me for charity. "Ah, sir"! said she, "I have seen better days"; "So have I, good woman," I replied; but I meant literally, days not so rainy and overcast as that on which she begged: she meant more prosperous days. Mr. Dawe is made associate of the Royal Academy. By what law of association I can't guess. Mrs. Holcroft, Miss Holcroft, Mr. and Mrs. Godwin, Mr. and Mrs. Hazlitt, Mrs. Martin and Louisa, Mrs. Lum, Capt. Burney, Mrs. Burney, Martin Burney, Mr. Rickman, Mrs. Rickman, Dr. Stoddart, William Dollin, Mr. Thompson, Mr. and Mrs. Norris, Mr. Fenwick, Mrs. Fenwick, Miss Fenwick, a man that saw you at our house one day, and a lady that heard me speak of you; Mrs. Buffam that heard Hazlitt mention you, Dr. Tuthill, Mrs. Tuthill, Colonel Harwood, Mrs. Harwood, Mr. Collier, Mrs. Collier, Mr. Sutton, Nurse, Mr. Fell, Mrs. Fell, Mr. Marshall, are very well, and occasionally inquire after you.

I remain yours ever,

Сн. Lamb

TO BERNARD BARTON

9TH JANUARY, 1823.

THROW yourself on the world without any rational plan of support, beyond what the chance employ of booksellers would afford you!!!

Throw yourself rather, my dear sir, from the steep Tarpeian rock, slap-dash headlong upon iron spikes. If you had but five consolatory minutes between the desk and the bed, make much of them, and live a century in them, rather than turn slave to the booksellers. They are Turks and Tartars, when they have poor authors at their beck. Hitherto you have been at arm's length from them. Come not within their grasp. I have known many authors want for bread, some repining, others envying the blessed security of a counting-house, all agreeing they had rather have been tailors, weavers—what not? rather than the things they were. I have known some starved, some to go mad, one dear friend literally dying in a workhouse. You know not what a rapacious, dishonest set these booksellers are. Ask even Southey, who (a single case almost) has made a fortune by book-drudgery, what he has found them. Oh, you know not, may you never know! the miseries of subsisting by authorship. 'Tis a pretty appendage to a situation like yours or mine; but a slavery, worse than all slavery, to be a booksellers' dependant, to drudge your brains for pots of ale, and breasts of mutton, to change your free thoughts and voluntary numbers for ungracious task-work. Those fellows hate *us*. The reason I take to be, that contrary to other trades, in which the master gets all the credit (a jeweller or silver-smith for instance), and the journeyman, who really does the fine work, is in the background: in *our* work the world gives all the credit to us, whom *they* consider as *their* journeyman, and therefore do they hate us, and cheat us, and oppress us, and would wring the blood of us out, to put another sixpence in their mechanic pouches! I contend that a book-seller has a *relative honesty* towards authors, not like his honesty to the rest of the world.

Keep to your bank, and the bank will keep you. Trust not to the public; you may hang, starve, drown yourself, for anything that worthy *personage* cares. I bless every star, that Providence, not seeing good to make me independent, has seen it next good to settle me upon the stable foundation of Leadenhall. Sit down, good B. B., in the banking-office; what! is there not from six to eleven p.m. six days in the week, and is there not all Sunday? Fie, what a superfluity of man's-time, if you could think so! Enough for relaxation, mirth, converse, poetry, good thoughts, quiet thoughts. O the corroding, torturing, tormenting thoughts, that disturb the brain of the unlucky wight, who must draw upon it for daily sustenance! Henceforth I retract all my fond complaints of mercantile employment; look upon them as lovers' quarrels. I was but half in earnest. Welcome dead timber of a desk, that makes me live. A little grumbling is a wholesome medicine for the spleen, but in my inner heart do I approve and embrace this our close, but unharassing way of life. I am quite serious. If you can send me Fox, I will not keep it *six weeks*, and will return it, with warm thanks to yourself and friend, without blot or dog's-ear. You will much oblige me by this kindness.

Yours truly,

C. Lamb

WALTER SAVAGE LANDOR (1775–1864)

*The first of these letters was written to the editor of the "Examiner"
newspaper against whom Lord Brougham had brought an action on the
ground that the paper had accused him of having insinuated that Cobden
advised private assassination. As a piece of merciless denunciation it is
remarkable. Frederick Paynter was one of Landor's intimate friends,
and it was to the niece of another friend, Rose Alymer, that the last letter
was written, within a few days of his eighty-first birthday.*

TO THE EDITOR OF THE *EXAMINER*

AUGUST 17, 1843

SIR, The prosecution with which you are threatened by Lord Brougham
might well be expected from every facette of his polygonal character. He
began his literary and political life with a scanty store of many small
commodities. Long after he set out, the witty and wise Lord Stowell
said of him, that, that he wanted only a little law to fill up the vacancy.
His shoulders were not over-burdened by the well-padded pack he bore
on them; and he found a ready sale, where such articles find the readiest,
in the town of Edinburgh. Here he entered into a confederacy (the
word *conspiracy* may be libellous) to defend the worst atrocities of the
French, and to cry down every author to whom England was dear and
venerable. A better spirit now prevails in the *Edinburgh Review*, from
the generosity and genius of Macaulay. But in the days when Brougham
and his confederates were writers in it, more falsehood and malignity
marked its pages than any other Journal in the language. And here is
the man who cries out he is wounded! the recreant who, screaming for
help, aims a poisoned dagger at the vigorous breast that crushes him to the
ground.

Had he no respect for the tenets by which he made his fortune?
Has he none for a superiority of intellectual power which leaves to him
superiority of station? This eminently bad writer and reasoner brings
an action for slander on many counts, at the summit of which is "because
it is *despicable*." Now did ever man or cat fly at the eyes for a thing,
beneath his notice: and such is the meaning of *despicable* among us who
have learnt Latin and who write English. What other man within the
walls of Parliament, however hasty, rude, and petulant, hath exhibited

such manifold instances of bad manners, bad feelings, bad reasonings, bad language, and bad law? They who cannot be what they want to be, resolve on notoriety in any shape whatever. Each House exhibits a specimen of this genus, pinned to the last pages of its Journals. Such notoriety can in no manner be more readily attained than by suddenly turning round on one leg, showing how agile is old age in this step, and then appealing to you whether the Terpsichorist has ever changed countenance or colour, from youth upwards. Meanwhile the toothless jaws are dropping, on both sides, the slaver of wrath and dotage.

How many things are published with impunity which are more injurious to a man's character, more detrimental to his fortune and interest, than a great proportion of those which the law calls libellous! Suppose an author, who has devoted his whole life to some particular study, writes a book upon it; suppose it is in any manner displeasing to Lord Brougham, whether on its own account or the author's; would he hesitate, has he ever hesitated, to inflict an irremediable wound? Dexterity in mischief is applauded; the sufferer is derided. Easily may a weaker, who watches the opportunity, trip up a stronger. Similar feats are the peculiar gratification of coarse and vulgar minds. Has no virtuous man of genius bled to death under the scourge of such a critic as Brougham? Years of application, if years were yet allowed him, would be insufficient to place him in the festive seat, which a crueller hand than a murderer's made vacant. On the contrary, the accusations brought against Lord Brougham, by the *Examiner*, could be shown by his Lordship to be true or false within a single hour, and the fact be rendered apparent to the whole nation before nightfall. But here no vindictive spirit can exert its agency: no lightning of phosphorus runs along the benches of the Lords; no thunder as awful shakes the Woolsack.

Wavering as he is by habit, malicious as he is by nature, it is evident that Lord Brougham says and does the greater part of his sayings and doings for no other purpose than to display his ability in defending them. He dazzles us by no lights of eloquence, he attracts us by not even a fictitious flue-warmth but he perplexes and makes us stare and stumble by his angular intricacies and sudden glares. Not a sentence of his speeches or writings will be deposited in the memory as rich and rare; and even what is strange will be cast out of it for what is stranger, until this goes too. Is there a housewife who keeps a cupboardfull of cups without handle or bottom; a selection of brokages and flaws?

I am, Sir, etc.,

W. S. LANDOR

TO FREDERICK PAYNTER

BATH, OCTOBER 22ND, 1839

DEAR FRED, You do not seem to place a proper and fair value on your letter; for the devil himself with all his ingenuity and knowledge of languages could not read the specimen with which you favoured me. However, I am heartily glad to get it, because it shows that you have not forgotten an old friend, and because it is a proof that your ideas run on with such rapidity, no pen can follow them up with any hope of catching them. I will deliver your message to the Miss. Do not wonder nor fight me if taking advantage of your absence I have cut you out. I shall be glad to see you in Bath again. Meanwhile, Believe me, Very sincerely yours,

W. S. LANDOR

TO A. DE NOÉ WALKER

(The references are to "Heroic Idylls," then in the press.)

FLORENCE, 1863

DEAR ARTHUR, A folded sheet is come leaving a blank between pp. [sic] 240 and 257. I am made to write (in note to 158 which is numbered wrong), endurated for indurated, p. 262, v. 13, sprad for spread, and p. 264, v. 7, ptolemies for Ptolemais. God has preserved me from cutting my throat after this. . . .

May you be happier than your affectionate

W. L.

TO ROSE PAYNTER

BATH, JAN. 18, 1856

CONFINEMENT by a troublesome cold has not made me forget the 19th January. On more than half your birthdays I have had the pleasure of drinking your health. On this one, so near, I think I may indulge in the hope of doing so. Alas! I am gone very far down the vale of years, a vale in which there is no fine prospect on the other side, and the few flowers are scarcely worth gathering. But it is pleasant to turn round in the midst of one's weariness and look on the verdant declivity behind;

pleasant to see pure white images on either hand, and to distinguish here and there a capital letter on the plinth. Dim as my eyes are become, I do think I can peruse the letter R on the one nearest to me. Old people, it is said, are apt to be verbose, so I must not authenticate it. . . .

My dear friend, I beg you to believe me,

Your ever affte old friend,

W. S. L.

JOHN CONSTABLE (1776–1837)

Constable had been offered the sum of £70 for "The Hay Wain," which had been exhibited in the Royal Academy in 1821 under the title of "A Landscape—Noon." He borrowed money from his friend, John Fisher, to enable him to tide over his financial difficulties without selling at such a price. Eventually the Frenchman did buy it, together with two others for £250, and exhibited the picture at the Salon.

TO THE REV. JOHN FISHER

KEPPEL STREET, APRIL 17TH, 1822

MY DEAR FISHER, Accept my thanks for yᵣ very kind letter. The contents will be useful, for as I told you, I had been so long upon unprofitable canvas that I was getting hard run. But I am now busy on some minor works which will bring things soon about again. My writing requires much apology, but I seldom sit down till I am already fatigued in my painting-house, and near the post hour, and I must say of my letters, as Northcote says of his pictures, "I leave them for the ingenious to find out." I made 2 or 3 fruitless attempts to read the last I sent you, and the postman ringing his bell at the moment, I dismissed it. I must work hard this summer, but I should like much to take the Windsor coach to hear your sermon, though I can ill spare a day, and now that I have an opportunity of earning a little money, I must make it a religious duty to do it. I shall not let the Frenchman have my picture. It would be too bad to allow myself to be knocked down by a Frenchman. In short, it may fetch my family something, sometime or other, and it would be disgracing my diploma to take so small a sum, less by near one-half than the price I asked.

Several cheering things have lately happened to me—professionally. . . . I am anxious about this picture. My neighbour ——, who expects to be an Academician before me, called to see it. He has always praised me; now he said not a word, till on leaving the room, he looked back and said "he hoped his picture would not hang near it."

. . . I am about Farrington's house: I think this step necessary. I shall get more by it than my family, in conveniences, though I am loth to leave a place where I have had so much happiness, and where I painted my four landscapes; but there is no giving way to fancies; occupation is my sheet anchor. My mind wd soon devour me without it. I felt as though I had not my arms after my picture was gone to the exhibition. I dare not read this letter over, take it as one of my sketches.

LADY HESTER STANHOPE (1776–1839)

This was a very remarkable woman. Daughter of Earl Stanhope, and niece of William Pitt, whose household she managed and to whom she acted as private secretary, she left England on Pitt's death and went to Mount Lebanon where she founded a little State of her own. When Ibraham Pasha was going to invade Syria he had to secure her neutrality first. Lady Hester's style of trouncing Lord Palmerston is characteristic. It had been decided that a pension she enjoyed should be stopped to pay her debts. Furious at the insult, she wrote to the Queen a letter which Palmerston " explained."

TO LORD PALMERSTON

JULY, 1838

MY LORD, If your diplomatic dispatches are as obscure as the one which now lies before me, it is no wonder that England should cease to have that proud preponderance in her foreign relations which she once could boast of.

Your Lordship tells me that you have thought it your duty to explain to the Queen the subject which caused me to address Her Majesty; I should have thought, my Lord, that it would have been your duty to have made those explanations prior to having taken the liberty of using Her Majesty's name, and alienated from her country a subject who, the great and small must acknowledge (however painful it may be to some), has raised the English name in the East higher than anyone has yet done, besides having made many philosophical researches of every description for the advantage of human nature at large, and this without having spent one farthing of the public money. Whatever may be the surprise created in the minds of statesmen of the old school respecting the conduct of Government towards me, I am not myself in the least astonished; for when the son of a king, with a view of enlightening his own mind and the world in general, had devoted part of his private fortune to the purchase of a most invaluable library at Hamburgh, he was flatly refused an exemption from the custom-house duties; but, if report speaks true, had an application been made to pass band-boxes, millinery, inimitable wigs, and invaluable rouge, it would have been instantly granted by Her Majesty's ministers, if we may judge by precedents. Therefore, my Lord, I have nothing to complain of; yet I shall go on fighting my battles, campaign after campaign.

Your Lordship gives me to understand that the insult which I have received was considerately bestowed upon me to avoid some dreadful unnameable misfortune which was pending over my head. I am ready to meet with courage and resignation every misfortune it may please God to visit me with, but certainly not insult from man. If I can be accused of high crimes and misdemeanours, and that I am to stand in dread of the punishment thereof, let me be tried, as I believe I have a right to be, by my peers; if not, then, by the voice of the people. Disliking the English because they are no longer English—no longer that hardy, honest, bold people that they were in former times—yet, as some few of this race must remain, I should rely in confidence upon their integrity and justice when my case had been fully examined.

It is but fair to make your Lordship aware that, if by the next packet there is nothing definitely settled respecting my affairs, and that I am not cleared in the eyes of the world of aspersions intentionally or unintentionally thrown upon me, I shall break up my household and build up the entrance gate to my premises, there remaining, as if I was in a tomb, till my character has been done justice to, and a public acknowledgment put in the papers, signed and sealed by those who have aspersed me. There is no trifling with those who have Pitt blood in their veins upon the subject of integrity, nor expecting that their spirit would ever yield to the impertinent interference of consular authority.

Meanly endeavouring (as Colonel Campbell has attempted to do) to make the origin of this business an application of the Viceroy of Egypt to the English Government, I must, without having made any inquiries upon the subject, exculpate his highness from so low a proceeding. His known liberality in all such cases, from the highest to the lowest class of persons, is such as to make one the more regret his extraordinary and reprehensible conduct towards his great master, and that such a man should become totally blinded by vanity and ambition, which must in the end prove his perdition, an opinion I have loudly given from the beginning.

Your Lordship talks to me of the capitulations with the Sublime Porte: what has that to do with a private individual's having exceeded his finances in trying to do good? If there is any punishment for that, you had better begin with your ambassadors, who have often indebted them-

selves at the different courts of Europe as well as at Constantinople. I
myself am so attached to the Sultan that, were the reward of such conduct
that of losing my head, I should kiss the sabre wielded by so mighty a
hand, yet, at the same time, treat with the most ineffable contempt your
trumpery agents, as I shall never admit of their having the smallest power
over me; if I did, I should belie my origin.

WILLIAM WARDEN (1777-1849)

Warden was a naval surgeon, who in 1815 was appointed to the "Northumberland" which conveyed the Emperor Napoleon to St. Helena. During the voyage Warden talked as much as he could with the prisoner, and reported his conversations at great length to the lady whom he afterwards married. His letter is as interesting on account of its style as for the matter it contains.

LETTER FROM ST. HELENA

AT SEA

MY DEAR MISS HUTT, I renew my desultory occupation—*la tache journalière, telle que vous la voulez.* On the first day of his [Napoleon's] arrival on board, our distinguished passenger displayed rather an eager appetite; I observed that he made a very hearty dinner, which he moistened with claret. He passed the evening on the quarter-deck, where he was amused by the band of the 53rd Regiment; when he personally required them to give the airs of "God save the King" and "Rule Britannia." At intervals he chatted in a way of easy pleasantry with the officers who were qualified to hold a conversation with him in the French language. I remarked, that on these occasions he always maintains what seems to be an invariable attitude which has somewhat of importance in it, and probably such as he had been accustomed to display at the Tuileries when giving audience to his marshals or officers of State. He never moves his hands from their habitual places in his dress, but to apply them to his snuff-box; and it struck me as a particular circumstance, to which I paid an observing attention, though it might have been connected with his former dignity—that he never offered a pinch to anyone with whom he was conversing.

On the subsequent day he breakfasted at eleven. His meal consists of meat and claret, which is closed with coffee.—At dinner, I observed that he selected a mutton cutlet, which he contrived to dispose of without the aid of either knife or fork.

He passed much of the third day on deck, and appeared to have paid particular attention to his toilette. He received no other mark of respect from the officers of the ship than would be shown to a private gentleman, nor does he seem to court or expect more than he receives. He is probably contented with the homage of his own attendants, who always appear before him uncovered, so that if a line were drawn round them, it might be supposed that you saw an equal space in the Palace of St. Cloud.

He played at cards in the evening; the game was whist, and he was a loser. It was not played in the same way as is practised at our card-tables in England; but I am not qualified to explain the varieties.

The whole of the next day Napoleon passed in his cabin. It was generally perceived by his attendants that he was sea-sick; but he was either so little of a sailor, if that can be supposed, as not to know the ordinary effects of a ship's motion on persons unused to the sea, or he suspected that his megrim arose from some other cause; for it seems he would by no means allow the salt-water origin of it. None of his people, I presume, would venture on the occasion, to repeat to him his brother Canute's practical Lecture to his Courtiers on the unmannerly power of the ocean.

Among his baggage were two camp-beds, which had accompanied him in most of his campaigns. One of them, a very improbable destination when it was first constructed, was now an essential article of his cabin; the other was now no longer to give repose to some military hero, in the hurry of a campaign, but is pressed by such a marine heroine as Madame Bertrand, amidst the dashing of waters. They are, however, altogether as comfortable as the combined skill of the upholsterer and the machinist could make them. They are about six feet long and three feet wide, with strong, green silk furniture: the frames are of steel, and so worked and shaped as to surprise by their lightness and the consequent ease with which they are moved. When I happened to be seated on one of them, I could not but reflect on the battles of Wagram, Austerlitz, Friedland, etc. etc.

This was a situation where the politician and the sage might be inspired, as it were, to contemplate the changes and the chances of the world; but as I do not presume to possess enough of those characters, either distinctly or collectively, to justify my engaging in a train of reflection on these affecting subjects, I shall leave such employment to your better thoughts, and the exercise of your enthusiastic propensity.

Notwithstanding it blew fresh, and there was considerable motion, Bonaparte made his appearance upon deck between three and four p.m., when he amused himself with asking questions of the Lieutenant of the Watch: such as, how many leagues the ship went in an hour? whether the sea was likely to go down? what the strange vessel was on the bow of the *Northumberland*? In short, enough to prove that nothing escaped his notice. But I could not help smiling when I beheld the man who had stalked so proudly, and with so firm a step over submissive countries, tottering on the deck of a ship, and catching at any arm to save himself from falling; for he has not yet found his sea-legs. Among other objects of his attention, he observed Mr. Smith, who was taking the usual to-and-fro walk with his brother midshipmen, to be much older than the rest; and, on this account he appears to have asked him how long he had been in the service; and being answered nine years, he observed: "That surely is a long time." "It is, indeed," said Mr. Smith; "but part of it was passed in a French prison; and I was, sir, at Verdun when you set out on your Russian campaign." Napoleon immediately shrugged up his shoulders with a very significant smile, and closed the conversation.

I must here tell you, once for all, if I have not already made the observation, that he seldom or ever omitted an opportunity of asking a question; and it was about this time that he made a most unexpected enquiry of our orthodox Chaplain—whether he was not a Puritan? I need not tell you what would be the reply; and you may conjecture, probably, what might be the feelings of a gentleman clothed in canonical orders, and firm in canonical principles, when he was saluted with such an interrogatory.

He wished also to have his curiosity gratified respecting a religious community in Scotland called Johnsonians, who, he understood, were a very active sect in that part of Britain. His conversation at all times consisted of questions, which never fail to be put in such a way as to prohibit a return of them. To answer one question by another, which frequently happens in common discourse, was not admissible with him. I can conceive that he was habituated to this kind of colloquy, when he sat upon such a throne as that which supported him, and before which no one spoke but when he commanded utterance; nor does he seem disposed to lay it aside when he sits in the cabin, stands in the gangway, or patrols the deck of a ship, where he is subject to the control of its commander. The foundation of this singular question, therefore, was not attainable. As in the various plans he had laid for invading our tight little Island, as the song has it, it is not improbable that he might have looked towards the Hebrides, as capable of favouring his design; and, if so, Doctor Johnson's tour thither might have been curiously consulted, and may I not deduce these Johnsonians from such a combination of circumstances? Many a doubt has been reconciled by more vague conjectures; that eminent writer's opinions, however, as you will probably suggest, are not altogether calculated to form a sect on the other side of the Tweed. But, badinage apart, I should be glad to know the origin of these Johnsonians; and if we should be tossed and tumbled in the course of our voyage, into a sufficient degree of familiarity for me to ask a question of the ex-Emperor, I will endeavour to be satisfied.

He appeared to be very much struck by two long-boats (gigs) placed with their bottom upwards on our launch on the booms; their singular length attracted his notice, while their particular use and application produced such a succession of enquiries on his part as almost to suggest an opinion that he entertained a suspicion of their being a part of the naval apparatus, peculiarly provided to prevent his escape from the Island to which he was destined. The answer he received was a quiet remark as to their general employment in the British Fleets; to which he made no reply.

The name of Talleyrand happening to occur in the course of conversation with our Franch shipmates, the high opinion entertained of his talents by the Bonapartists was acknowledged without reserve. On my asking at what period he was separated from the councils and confidence of Napoleon, it was replied, "At the invasion of Spain." I then observed that the reports in England, respecting that circumstance, were correct as to time, and I presumed were equally so as to the cause; his unreserved disapprobation of that bold and adventurous enterprise. This met with an instant contradiction; which was followed by a most decisive assertion that the Prince of Benevento approved of the Spanish War, and founded his recommendation of that measure on his unalterable opinion, which he boldly communicated to the Emperor, that his life was not secure while a Bourbon reigned in Europe.

I entered further on this subject with Madame Bertrand, and she actually and most unequivocally asserted that Talleyrand was in secret communication with Napoleon when they were last at Paris, and that he would have joined them in a month. His proposed departure from Vienna to take the waters at Aix la Chappelle was under the cloak of indisposition to conceal his duplicity. "Can you persuade yourself, Madame," I said, "that Talleyrand, if he had the inclination, possessed the power to influence the Court of Vienna in favour of the son-in-law?" "The Court of Vienna!" she exclaimed; "O yes, yes; he has the capacity to influence all the courts of Europe! If he had but joined the Emperor, we should at this instant have been in Paris, and France would never more have changed its master." Of this man's virtues I heard no eulogium; but you will now be a competent judge how his political talents were appreciated in the French circle on board the *Northumberland*.

On my asking Count Bertrand which of the French Generals had amassed the greatest portion of wealth, he without the least hesitation mentioned Masséna; though, he added, they have all made very considerable fortunes. Macdonald, Duke of Tarentum, he appeared to think, had made less than any other. Of Davout, Duke d'Eckmuhl, he spoke, to our extreme astonishment, in an animated strain of panegyric, which was instantly met with an outcry from all who heard it, respecting the conduct of that officer at Hamburg, which we represented as atrocious beyond example. This he would not allow; on the contrary, he described him as a zealous, correct, and faithful commander, and far from being destitute of humanity; as notwithstanding his notions of military obedience, which were known to be of the most rigid kind, he did not act up to the severity of his instructions. As for his taking a bribe, Bertrand declared him to be incapable of such baseness; and asserted, from his own knowledge, that a very large sum had been offered him to connive at the sailing of some ships from Hamburg in the night, which he refused with the disdain of a faithful soldier and an honourable man.

Count de Las Cases also took up the subject of the Marshals of France, and spoke of them with very little reserve. He described Masséna as having been originally a fencing-master; but that previous to his campaign in the Peninsula, he was considered by the French nation as equal, if not superior to, Bonaparte in his military capacity. From that period the Count represented him as having dwindled into absolute insignificance. He is avaricious, he said, in the extreme, though he has only one child—a daughter—to inherit his enormous wealth. He then proceeded to relate the following circumstance of the Marshal, as the accidental topic of the moment.

The preservation of the Army, on crossing the Danube, was boldly attributed by the soldiers who composed it, and consequently re-echoed as the opinion of the nation, to the superior skill and persevering courage of Masséna. It appears that a sudden and impetuous inundation of the river had destroyed all possible communication between its right and left bank when half the French force had passed it. The remaining half were without ammunition, when Masséna threw himself into the village of Essling, where he withstood fifteen repeated attacks of the Austrians, and effected the escape of that part of the French Army from the destruction which threatened it. The eulogiums which the army and the nation lavished on Masséna for his conduct and the success which crowned it, partook of that clamorous character which implied no inconsiderable degree of blame and censure on Bonaparte himself. This he was supposed to have felt. But he contrived, nevertheless, to dissipate it, by conferring the title of Prince of Essling on Masséna, as the merited reward, and magnanimous acknowledgment of a service on which depended, for the moment, the success and honourable issue of the campaign. Soult, he said, is an excellent officer, and Ney, brave to a fault; but Suchet possesses a more powerful intellect, with more enlarged information, and political sagacity, as well as more conciliatory manners, than any of the Marshals of France.

He then mentioned Admiral Ganteaume, and asked what character was assigned in the English newspapers to that naval officer. I replied that they gave him no small credit for his spirit in advancing out of port, and his success in getting back again. "Yes," he answered, with a significant look and tone, "good at hide-and-seek. He was the friend of Louis, and then of Napoleon, and then of Louis again; he is, in fact, what you call the Vicar of ——" I assisted him in completing the proverbial expression, by adding the word "Bray," which he immediately caught and exclaimed, "Aye, aye. He is the Vicar of Bray. He is an old man," the Count added, "but his indiscretions," which, however, he did not particularise, "were rather of a juvenile character."

In the afternoon our chief passenger continued longer on deck than he had done before, and his countenance denoted a feeling of disquietude. His questions all related to the state of our progress, and marked an impatience to arrive at the termination of his voyage. He probably experienced some degree of inconvenience from his confined situation, having been long accustomed to exercise that bordered upon violence. His appearance, I understand, was rather meagre, till about the time that he became First Consul. If he had been otherwise, his campaigns in Egypt were sufficient to have reduced him; but though his exertions, both mental and corporeal, have since been such as to destroy any constitution but his own, which must have been of an extraordinary, internal texture, to have enabled him to sustain them, his health has rather been improved than impaired; and, during the last ten years, he has gradually advanced into corpulence.

It is a singular circumstance that Count Montholon, whom I have already mentioned as one of the Imperial Aides de Camp, is the son of a General Officer of that name, whom Bonaparte served in the same capacity during the Revolutionary War. All the family, except his father and himself, have been decided Royalists, and are possessed of large property: but the General is dead, while the son has sacrificed fortune and abandoned his family, to share, with his wife and child, the exiled state of his former Sovereign; whom it is his pride still to love and serve under that title, and with all the feelings of duty and loyalty which his enthusiastic fidelity attaches to it.

I give you Madame Bertrand's description of young Napoleon as very beautiful, in order to introduce his father's laconic English account of him. The boy, he says, resembles him only in the upper part of his form. "He has one grand, big head." The same Lady, speaking of the Bonaparte family, represents the female part in terms of no common admiration. With the exception of the Princess Piombino she describes the sisters as possessed of extraordinary beauty: with these charming women, therefore, and to use the expression of the grand, big head of them all, I shall conclude my second grand, big Letter.

Etc. Etc. Etc.,

W. W.

FRANCIS HORNER (1778–1817)

A London lawyer, acquainted with all who counted in the world of letters, Horner was one of the founders of the "Edinburgh Review," for the first number of which he wrote four articles. His life was spent in the hurly-burly of politics, but this letter to his mother shows that he had keen appreciation for the world outside Westminster.

TO HIS MOTHER

KILLARNEY, 13TH SEPTEMBER, 1810

MY DEAR MOTHER, We came here last night, having made two days of it from Limerick, and rather tiresome ones; I had the pleasure, upon my arrival, to find your letter of the 5th instant, which had been forwarded to me from Dublin, together with one from Warwick.

I hope you got the note from Dublin, which I wrote immediately after I landed, that you might be relieved from your fears about the deep sea. I was very lucky in being able to reach it, the day we had fixed as the first that we had a chance of meeting; by travelling two nights in the mail, and being fortunate enough to get on without delay either at Birmingham or Shrewsbury; at both which places I changed coaches. I left Bristol on Monday evening at seven, and was at Holyhead on Wednesday about two in the afternoon. The packet sailed about an hour afterwards; but we were three-and-twenty hours upon the passage, and near twenty of those were to me hours of mortal sickness: I thought of poor Jonah in the whale's belly, and fancied myself in as bad a plight, as I lay in my crib with nothing to relieve me in my nausea but the sighs of sympathising Welsh, Irish, and Scotch around me, men, women, and children. I had just retired to my berth, and was in my first pangs, when I heard the loud, good-natured, vulgar voice of a raw-boned Scotch lad, asking the cabin-boy, for information only, if "ony body was seek yet?" I cannot say that I had not some satisfaction for a moment, when I heard this bumpkin, about an hour afterwards, expressing himself in very different tones, as if he was about to render up his very entrails. For all this, however, I was fully compensated by the view of the bay of Dublin, as we sailed into it. It is very deep and broad, the coast all round appears lined with woods, great houses or villages, and the Wicklow mountains, which rise on the left hand, have quite a Highland form and character.

We spent the best part of two days in Dublin. It is rather a handsome town; the quay along the Liffey, with the bridges one after another, four or five of them, gives a fine town view; and there is one point where several public buildings are assembled together, the College, the Parliament House, and some others, to which I should be at a loss to say what there is in London that is equal; Whitehall I think is not. The public offices in Dublin are all very ornamental buildings; the Custom House is most talked of, but I would praise the Parliament House, now the Bank, more highly. We went a few miles out of Dublin to see the Phœnix Park, and a gentleman's seat called Luttrel's Town. The last is always recommended to strangers, but is hardly worth their while; we were much more pleased with the grounds of the Duke of Leinster, a little farther on, and with the situation of the village of Leixlip.

From Dublin we went to Limerick by the mail-coach; through a tame country, level the greater part of the way, all (except where there is bog) under cultivation, and passing (in the county of Tipperary particularly) some wild villages. The cultivation of every thing but potatoes seemed to be sorry; but its extent is so great as to give the idea of an immense produce, even if we did not see the multitudes who crowd the whole country. All that I had heard in description of the numbers of the Irish, and of their dirt, rags, and beggary, seems to me now to have been short of the truth. The streets of Limerick were like a great fair; though it was not even market day; and this from morning to night. It seemed as if every house had poured out its inhabitants; yet every cellar we looked into seemed full. It was more or less the same in all the towns and villages we came through and we never went a mile upon the highway, without seeing a great many persons. None of them seem to have anything to do; through all that we should call the working hours of the day we saw large lasses, and lads six feet high, lounging round the cabin doors. It is literally true that the only appearance of industry we saw was in the number of schools that we observed on this side of Limerick; schools for the ragged children of those same cabins: and we two or three times passed a little swarm of them sitting on the outside, to all appearance because it was quite full of them within, reading, writing, and ciphering. Murray got into conversation with one of the schoolmasters, in a village where there was not a hovel better than a hog-sty, who was a young man, and who told him that Telemachus was one of the books he read with the children. All this, when one sees the idleness of the people and the backwardness of the country, is a little puzzling. With this idleness, and dirt, and nakedness, they look a much happier people than I have seen in any part of England or Scotland; the English peasant is a torpid animal, and the Scotch one eaten with care, compared with the light-hearted cheerful people of this country. They seem for ever talking, and in a high tide of spirits; their volubility is somewhat distressing, and their language is more full of submission than is pleasant, because it reminds one how they have been taught it by oppression; but among themselves, they seem to have a great deal of merriment and enjoyment. They have all of them a real share of sharp drollery and imagery; enough to mark them as entirely a different race of people from those on our side of the Channel. I have seen but very little in the course of these few days; but all this, I think, I have observed distinctly. It is very likely they have not the same steadiness of understanding, which makes the Englishman always a master of his own particular profession, and which makes the Scotchman (who seldom knows one profession thoroughly) ready to turn his hand to almost any one, and to get through it well enough to thrive by it; but the Irish have a quickness, readiness, and sharpness, which the others seldom possess.

Nothing has surprised me so much in Ireland as the excellence of the roads. All the way from Dublin, even into this unfrequented country, they are most admirable, and must have been made at a great expense. Probably, there has been particular attention paid to this since the rebellion, from political considerations; it is a care well bestowed, and must assist very rapidly the civilization of the country. We came from Limerick by Adair, Newbridge, Glyn, Tarbert, Listowel, and Tralee. The views we had of the Shannon going down to Glyn, and of the mountains at Tralee, were very fine. We have spent this day upon the lower and middle lakes here; I must write another letter about this place: we have the best of it yet to see, but I would say already, that it exceeds greatly all the scenery with which I have been hitherto acquainted.

With kindest love to my father and my sisters,
I am, my dear mother,
Most affectionately yours,
FRA. HORNER

LADY FRANCES DILLON (c. 1778–1819)

Lady Fanny Dillon was daughter of the twelfth Viscount, and some four years after writing this letter she married Sir Thomas Webb. Her friend Charlotte had just left to marry Sir Richard Bedingfield.

TO LADY BEDINGFIELD

TUESDAY, YOU HAVE BEEN GONE AN HOUR!

O! MY Charlotte, are you gone!—have you left your poor Fanny. I have lost a most beloved cousin—My dearest and best friend—My all—my everything! You that for these two years past have shewed me every mark of goodness care and friendship—more than a stranger could expect. O! My dearest cousin, notwithstanding the certainty of seeing you shortly at Bodney, I cannot bear to think my Charlotte's gone. . . .

Good news, oh how happy I am. I was interrupted just now by my aunt's coming into my room. Oh what do you think she told me? We are to go to Oxburgh before Bodney!—Perhaps stay there a day or two—if our fair hostess will allow it.—How good is Providence. I was in one of my fits of despair—this news has been the greatest joy to me—but I must not forget to tell you. Cousin, when you got into carriage my aunt *cried*—and who would not? but we were all amazingly provoked to see *little Saisseval* should get into the carriage and crowd you up—when Mademoiselle Dossier was quite alone,— for my part I was vexed at it because it is not comfortable to you two to talk—while that brat is there—but I hope she will get out at the first stage—

I have desired your two parcels to be sent as soon as possible—I have been into your room—like that Roman (I forget his name) sitting on the ruins of Carthage—your room was no less dear to me than Carthage could be to him. (I suppose through forgetfulness) you have left your portfolio of drawings behind you—I have put it in my room— and when the happy hour comes of my *seeing* you—you will see it. This sheet of paper is out of your room—I have seized upon all I could lay hands upon that you have left—primo—that *red bag* you

575

used to keep letters in, and write upon, and a *blue* piece *of music* book cover, like that you used to have in it—I have put in the bag (which I am writing upon at present) then all your letters I received at Bodney are likewise in it—the little steel seal, &c.—and it shall in future accompany me everywhere—your long and constant use of it has endeared it ten thousand times more to me—than the finest presents I could receive—I have also taken possession of a little saucer for paint—I found in your room—I would not touch the *wax bougie*— as I do not choose to appear taking things out of interest (like five years ago when you was going abroad, in Prince's Street I seizing upon everything I saw) whilst it is Only out of affection for you I love everything that has belonged to the dearest of all creatures—I have barricaded both *the doors*—which *till now* would have been the greatest punishment you could have inflicted upon me—and now, Cousin—that you are already so many miles from me and *every instant farther.* O! Cousin, if you knew how those *five words* you left wrote on my table made me cry—the longest letter could not have done more—I discovered in them—affection, pity, regret—&c. and a thousand *other Sentiments* which in you

.   .   .   .

My Aunt has brought me a pair of that little girl's stockings to mark—which I *don't relish* much, I own—but I will offer up to God for you the dislike I have to them. George has just been in my room, *making faces* and talking such things! Enough to make one die of laughing. I mean those that have not *their dearest* . . . gone from them.

WILLIAM HAZLITT (1778–1830)

Here is a letter written when the great master critic was fourteen years of age, showing the course of his studies at Hackney College. How different was the school regime of those days from what is now the fashion!

TO HIS FATHER

HACKNEY COLLEGE, 1793

DEAR FATHER, I received your kind letter on Monday evening at five o'clock, the usual time. I was very much pleased you liked the plan of my essay. You need not fear for the execution of it, as I am sensible that, after I have made it as perfect as I can, it will have many imperfections, yet I know that I can finish in a manner equal to the introduction. I have made some progress, since I wrote last. The essay on laws will make a part of it. I will here give you an account of my studies, &c. On Monday I am preparing Damien's lectures from seven until half-past eight, except the quarter of an hour in which I say Corrie's grammar lecture, and from nine till ten. From ten till twelve we are with him. His lectures are Simpson's elements of grammar and Bonnycastle's algebra. By the bye, the Ass's bridge is the tenth proposition of the geometry. From twelve to two I am preparing Belsham lectures in shorthand, and the Hebrew grammar, which I am saying till then. The shorthand is to write out eight verses, (of the) Bible. From half-past three till five I walk. From five to six, I have my Greek grammar for the morning. At liberty from six to seven. From seven to eight, preparing Belsham's evening lecture in L(eviticus?) and Hebrew. With them from eight to nine. And from half after nine till eleven I am reading Dr. Price's lecture for the next day. On Tuesday I am from seven till half-past eight preparing Corrie's classical lecture, only the time that I am saying my grammar. And again from nine to half-past ten, from which time to half-past eleven I attend Dr. Priestley's lecture in history. From then till a little after twelve is Corrie's classical lecture, which is Sophocles one week and Quintilian the next. In the Greek we have two of the old students, in the Latin five. J(oseph) S(wanwick) is now in my classes, at first he was not. But on his requesting it, he is now with me. You will take care not to mention this. From twelve till one, I am at Corrie's lecture in Greek antiquities. With him till half-past one. From which till three I study my essay. Walking as before. From five till six, preparing my evening lecture in geography with Corrie, and my Greek for the next day. And from seven to nine, except about half-an-hour at geography with Corrie, I again studying my essay. From half-past nine to eleven, reading David Hartley. I go on in the same course rest of the week, except the difference that not having Dr. Price's lecture on Saturday night. On Sundays, too, I am always idle. I like Hebrew very well, the mathematics very much. They are very much suited to my genius. The Reid whom I mentioned is about eighteen, a Bristol lad, and a pupil of Mr. Eslin. I was in town to-day. I was glad to hear of the increase of my yearly allowance, and of what Corrie told Rowmann. They are very well. I am sorry to hear that my mother is poorly. My love to her and Peggy.

I am,

Your affectionate son,

W. HAZLITT

I forgot to give you an account of my expenses, and, as I am tired, shall defer till next time. I have spent only 8s. since Thursday fortnight, though I have had everything I wanted. Adieu.

THOMAS MOORE (1779–1852)

The "Irish Anacreon" went to New York from Bermuda, when he found that his post as Admiralty Registrar at the latter place was not worth his while. In our first letter Moore tells how he went sight-seeing; the subject of the other letter was a fête he attended where Royalty, in the shape of the Prince Regent, was present.

TO HIS MOTHER

NIAGARA, JULY 24, 1804

MY DEAREST MOTHER, I have seen the Falls, and am all rapture and amazement. I cannot give you a better idea of what I felt than by transcribing what I wrote off hastily in my journal on returning. Arrived at Chippewa, within three miles of the Falls, on Saturday, July 21, to dinner. That evening walked towards the Falls, but got no farther than the rapids, which gave us a prelibation of the grandeur we had to expect. Next day, Sunday, July 22, went to visit the Falls. Never shall I forget the impression I felt at the first glimpse of them which we got as the carriage passed over the hill that overlooks them. We were not near enough to be agitated by the terrific effects of the scene; but saw through the trees this mighty flow of waters descending with calm magnificence, and received enough of its grandeur to set imagination on the wing: imagination which, even at Niagara, can outrun reality. I felt as if approaching the very residence of the Deity; the tears started into my eyes; and I remained, for moments after we had lost sight of the scene, in that delicious absorption which pious enthusiasm alone can produce. We arrived at the New Ladder and descended to the bottom. Here all its awful sublimities rushed full upon me. But the former exquisite sensation was gone. I now saw all. The string that had been touched by the first impulse, and which *fancy* would have kept for ever in vibration, now rested at *reality*. Yet, though there was no more to imagine, there was much to feel. My whole heart and soul ascended towards the Divinity in a swell of devout admiration, which I never before experienced. Oh! bring the atheist here, and he cannot return an atheist! I pity the man who

579

can coldly sit down to write a description of these ineffable wonders; much more do I pity him who can submit them to the admeasurement of gallons and yards. It is impossible by pen or pencil to convey even a faint idea of their magnificence. Painting is lifeless, and the most burning words of poetry have all been lavished upon inferior and ordinary subject. We must have new combinations of language to describe the Fall of Niagara.

So much for my journal; but if, notwithstanding all this enthusiastic contempt for matter-of-fact description, you still should like to see a particular account of the Falls, Weld, in his Travels, has given the most accurate I have seen. On the Sunday morning before I left Chippewa, I wrote you a letter, darling mother, which I entrusted to the waggoner (who was going back) to have it forwarded. Oh! if the stupid scoundrel should have neglected it. Since the day I left New York (July 4) this is the fourth letter I have written to you. How dreadfully provoking if they have miscarried. Never was I in better health than I have been during my journey. This exercise is quite new to me, and I find the invigorating effects of it. My heart, too, feels light with the idea that the moment is approaching when I shall fly on the wings of the wind to the dear embrace of all that is dear to me. God bless you, loves. I pray for you often and fervently; and I feel that Heaven *will* take care of us. A thousand kisses to dear father and the girls, from their own boy on the banks of Lake Ontario. Again God bless you, dearest mother. Ever, ever your

                                                                      TOM

TO THE SAME

FRIDAY, JUNE 21, 1811

MY DEAREST MOTHER, I ought to have written yesterday, but I was in bed all day after the fête, which I did not leave till past six in the morning. Nothing was ever half so magnificent; it was in *reality* all that they try to imitate in the gorgeous scenery of the theatre; and I really sat for three quarters of an hour in the Prince's room after supper, silently looking at the spectacle, and feeding my eyes with the assemblage of beauty, splendour, and profuse magnificence which it presented. It was quite worthy of a prince, and I would not have lost it for any consideration. There were many reports previous to it (set about, I suppose, by disappointed *aspirants*), that the company would be mixed, etc. etc.; but it was infinitely less so than could possibly be expected from the strange hangers-on that all the Royal Brothers have about them, and of course everything high and noble in society was collected there. I saw but two unfortunate ladies in the group (mother and daughter) who seemed to "wonder how the devil they got there," and everybody else agreed with them. While all the rest of the women were outblazing each other in the richness of their dress, this simple couple, with the most philosophic contempt of ornament, walked about in the unambitious costume of the breakfast-table, and I dare say congratulated each other, when they went home, upon the great difference between their becoming simplicity and the gaudy nonsense that surrounded them. It was said that Mr. Waithman, the patriotic linendraper, had got a card; and every odd-looking fellow that appeared, people said immediately, "That's Mr. Waithman." The Prince spoke to me, as he always does, with the cordial familiarity of an old acquaintance.

This is a little *gossiping* for you, dearest mother, and I expect some in return from Kate very soon. God bless you. Ever your own,

TOM

ELIZABETH FRY (1780–1845)

Mrs. Fry was one of the old Quaker families, the Gurneys of Earlham. From an early age she devoted herself to good works, and even when the mother of eleven children she found time and opportunity to do an immense amount of good. In 1813 she began her great work in the prisons, and it was largely through her representations that the era of prison reform was inaugurated.

TO PRISCILLA BUXTON

UPTON LANE, FEBRUARY 16, 1832

THY mother, and indeed all of you, are so much on my mind that I must write a few words of love. I have feared lest the cholera being in London should have much tried thy dearest mother or any of you. I wish, therefore, to express my hope that you will none of you admit any undue fears about it. With all outward discouragements, which at times I acutely feel, and even this cholera *weightily*, I have at times a strong sense that these trials are not in vain here, especially as regards some of the afflicted, disappointed, and abused ones. My belief is, we fret ourselves too much as to what the future may produce as to the things of this life, and, because we do not sufficiently fix our attention upon that which is to come, cannot estimate or enjoy the blessings given to us while we are unworthy pilgrims in a probationary state. . . . Yet we ought to be satisfied if we find *at times* a rest in the wilderness.

TO HER SONS

[1813]

I CANNOT help longing to see you, my very dear little John and Willy, and give you each a kiss. I am so very fond of my little children, and often feel thankful I have so many; and if they grow better and better as they grow older, they will comfort and please their parents. I have lately been twice to Newgate prison to see after the poor prisoners, who had little infants almost without clothing. If you saw how small a piece of bread they are allowed every day, you would be very sorry,

582

for they have nothing else to eat, unless their friends give them a trifle. I could not help thinking when in the prison, what sorrow and trouble those have who do wrong; and they have not the comfort of feeling amidst all their trials that they have endeavoured to do their duty. Good people are, no doubt, often much tried, but they have so much to comfort them when they remember that the Almighty is their Friend, and will care for them. We may also hope that if the poor wicked people are really sorry for their faults, God will pardon them for His mercy is very great. If you were to grow up, I should like you to go to visit the poor sad people, to try to comfort them and do them good. I hope you will endeavour to be very useful, and not spend all your time in pleasing yourselves, but try to serve others and prefer them before yourselves. How very much I love you. Let me have letters written by yourselves. Farewell, my darling children. Remember the way to be happy is to do good.

Your tender mother,

E. F.

LUCY AIKIN (1781–1864)

Miss Aikin was one of those clever women who flourished so conspicuously at the opening of the last century. She wrote a number of memoirs of royal people, though when she had completed "Memoirs of the Court of Charles I," she said she was going to stop, as "Charles II is no theme for me; it would make me contemn my species." These two chatty letters are written to her brother Edmund, an architect of some repute.

TO MR. E. AIKIN

STOKE NEWINGTON: NOVEMBER, 1815

MY DEAR EDMUND, I am glad of this opportunity to thank you for your letter by H. K., and to tell you how glad we all are that you have got this new job. It seems to have been by an odd sort of chance at last, though Mr. Roscoe always hoped to be able to procure it for you without difficulty. You must now have your hands quite full of business—all the better, though it removes and lessens the chance of your return hither. We have not seen Mr. Roscoe, who is extremely engaged, but he has promised us a visit at the end of the week. Judge how impatient I am to see him; I shall be able to give him a tolerable account of Elizabeth, with whom I converse regularly several hours in the day. I am now pretty near the end of Edward's time, and I feel myself more and more interested in my subject.

Benger has been spending part of two days with us. She is pretty well for one who will never let herself alone, and full of curious anecdote as usual.

Charles Wesley, a while ago, took a queer very fat old Mrs. S. to see the queen go to the drawing-room. In the ante-chamber, in which they waited, were no seats, and the fat lady, becoming tired of standing, at last spread her handkerchief on the floor, and seated herself in a picturesque manner upon it. Charles, being a great blunderer, and somewhat wicked besides, gave the alarm several times that the Queen was coming, and as often poor Mrs. S. made incredible efforts to get up and see her. At last, he had cried wolf so often that she did not heed him, and when the Queen came indeed, she was not able with the help

584

of all his tugging, to rise from the ground till Her Majesty was past; and one end of her hoop was all that blessed the eyes of this loyal and pains-taking subject. To complete the misfortune, she was kept waiting for her carriage, owing to Charles's stupidity, till her dinner was spoiled, and the friends she had invited to eat it were quite out of patience; and to mend all, this rare composition of wit and goose tells the whole story as a good joke, mimicking her to admiration!

Pray read, when you can meet with it, a tragedy called "Fazio," by a very clever young Mr. Milman [later Dean Milman], whom I once saw at Allerton. The language is the best imitation of our old dramatists that I have ever seen; it is brilliant with poetry, and contains fine scenes and situations, though the plot is shocking and improbable. If I mistake not, this is a rising star, destined to blaze far and wide. Talking of choice people, to be sure, I ought to tell you that we have had a call from Mr. Rogers, who was very agreeable and entertaining with his accounts of Italy. What a beau King Murat is! The morning Mr. Rogers was presented to him, he was standing in the middle of a large room, displaying his fine figure in a Spanish cloak, hat and feather, yellow boots, pink pantaloons, and a green waistcoat! In the evening he appears in a simpler costume, but still wearing roses on his shoes, a white plume in his hat, and his hair prodigiously curled and frizzed, with a long love-lock hanging down on each side. He does not dress above five times a day. Then, no king in Europe, probably, cuts such high capers in the dance— but for other qualifications for reigning, I hear nothing of them. Naples is beautiful, says Mr. Rogers, and the court very gay and pretty; but after all, Florence is the place one longs to live in. No city of its size has half so many fine domes and towers; then the beautiful Arno meets your eye at every turn, and beyond it the finest woods and distant mountains. His descriptions quite set me longing; such gales of myrtle, such groves of orange trees, stuck as full of fruit, he says, as the trees you see sometimes painted by a child!

To-day being Sunday, William Taylor dines with my aunt, and I suppose will call here. As my letter cannot go till to-morrow, I will leave it open, in hopes of some sayings of his. He was very agreeable the short time he stayed; with his usual calculating spirit, he said that if it was necessary to have a war with France, better now than three years hence, when two or three more conscriptions would have grown up. It was to be wished that such a balance could be re-established as would allow the ten years' peaces in Europe which there had been formerly— we could not well bear longer ones, for man was essentially a fighting

animal, and a twenty years' peace would turn any republic into a
monarchy. He is visiting Dr. Southey, who is thriving greatly, and
about to marry again, and to our great regret, he cannot promise us a day.
We have likewise had a call from Mr. J. Taylor. Great joy to see him
again in London, looking tolerably, and able to walk from Islington
hither. We are all quite well here, and all send love to you.

Your affectionate sister,

L. A.

TO THE SAME

STOKE NEWINGTON: MAY 9, 1815

DEAR EDMUND, I hope you will allow that everybody loves ten times
better to receive what you call a gossiping letter than to write one—
judge, then, by the size of paper I have taken to fill, how welcome are
your epistles to me!

Well! the beginning of last week I was, as I told you, in town. An
evening party on Monday at the N.'s, rather too grave and presbyterian;
but to make amends we had an alderman, a person excellent in his way,
thinner indeed than alderman beseems (but his wife atones for that), and
he had a red face, hair powdered snow-white, and one of those long
foolish noses that look as if they thrust themselves into everything.
Then, ye gods! he is musical; summoned Miss N. to the instrument by
touching a few call-notes, and would fain have sung with her, but wicked
H. had left her duets behind, and would not patronise his proposal of
taking *two-thirds* of a glee for three voices, so, to my unspeakable
mortification, he had no opportunity of exhibiting. Have I got thus far
in my letter and said nothing of last Friday? It is a great proof of my
methodical and chronological habits of writing that I did not jump to this
period of my history in the first paragraph. Know, that on Thursday last
arrived an invitation from the Carrs to my father and my aunt to dine
with them the next day, to meet Walter Scott—apologies at the same
time that their table would not admit us all. Well! nothing could
persuade my father to go, so my aunt said she would take me instead,
and I had not the grace to say no. A charming day we had. I did not,
indeed, see much of the great lion, for we were fourteen at dinner, of
whom about half were constantly talking, and neither at table nor after
was I very near him; but he was delighted to see my aunt, and paid her
great attention, which I was very glad of. He told her that the "Tramp,
tramp," "Splash, splash," of Taylor's "Lenora" which she had carried
into Scotland to Dugald Stewart many years ago, was what made him a

poet. I heard him tell a story or two with a dry kind of humour, for which he is distinguished; and though he speaks very broad Scotch, is a heavy-looking man, and has little the air of a gentleman, I was much pleased with him—he is lively, spirited, and quite above all affectation. He had with him his daughter, a girl of fifteen, the most naive child of nature I ever saw; her little Scotch phrases charmed us all, and her Scotch songs still more. Her father is a happy minstrel to have such a lassie to sing old ballads to him, which she often does by the hour together, for he is not satisfied with a verse or two, but chooses to have *fit* the first, second, and third. He made her sing us a ditty about a border *reiver* who was to be hanged for stealing the bishop's mare, and who dies with the injunction to his comrades,

> If e'er ye find the bishop's cloak,
> Ye'll make it shorter by the hood.

She also sung a lullaby in Gaelic—very striking novelties both, in a polished London party. Nobody could help calling this charming girl pretty, though all allowed her features were not good, and we thought her not unlike her father's own sweet Ellen. I had the good fortune to be placed at dinner between Mr. Whishaw and Sotheby, better known by Wieland's "Oberon" than by his own "Saul." He is a lively, pleasant, elderly man; his manners of the old school of gallantry, which we women must ever like. A lady next him asked him if he did not think we could see by Mr. Scott's countenance, if "Waverley" were mentioned, whether he was the author? "I don't know," said Mr. S., "we will try." So he called out from the bottom of the table to the top, "Mr. Scott, I have heard there is a new novel coming out by the author of 'Waverley,' have you heard of it?" "I have," said the minstrel, "and I believe it." He answered very steadily, and everybody cried out directly, "O, I am glad of it!" "Yes," said Mr. Whishaw, "I am a great admirer of those novels"; and we began to discuss which was the best of the two, but Scott kept out of this debate, and had not the assurance to say any handsome things of the works, though *he* is not the author—O no! for he denies them.

Mr. Whishaw was lamenting that his friend Dumont is returning to Geneva; "but he has the *maladie du pays*, like all Swiss. Talleyrand says that to a Genevois, Geneva is *la cinquième partie du monde*, and Dumont has a prospect of being Secretary of State, with a salary of £50 per annum. And they do not give cabinet dinners there, but *goûters*." "Of what?" "Peach tart, I suppose." He asked me what was become of that Roscoe who was under Smyth at Cambridge some years ago? "A pretty romantic young man, and the gods had made him poetical. There were verses to a lily by moonlight." "Oh," said I, "he is a steady banker now." "A *steady* banker?" "Yes; there is something of the old character left, certainly, but he is more a man of the world than he was then." "O, of course; a banker is *of the earth, earthy*." I greatly doubt whether *the lion* of the day uttered any roarings equal to these. But the latter part of the evening, our laughing philosopher fell in love with the little Scotch lassie, and only "roared like any sucking dove." . . .

I positively must chatter no longer, I am so busy to-day.

Your affectionate,

L. AIKIN

SIR CHARLES NAPIER (1782–1853)

Napier will always be remembered as the conqueror of Sind. It was in 1842 that he was ordered to capture Sind, and this he did after a brilliant campaign, announcing his success to the authorities by the single word "Peccavi"—I have sinned—one of the best puns in literature. Napier's mother was the same Lady Sarah Bunbury whom we have already met with in these letters, she having married Sir George Napier as her second husband.

TO LADY CAMPBELL

CAMP AT LUCK, JAN. 18TH, 1843

*From I in the Desert of Scinde
To She in the Bog of Allen.*

MY DEAR COUSIN, Paper, pen and ink are very scarce, so are clean shirts; but that don't matter, as nobody sees us but your namesakes the camels, and they are not nice. However, we are clean, though we look dirty. The sand scours us; it pours into the nape of one's neck, and so progresses downwards to the toes of one's boots in a constant succession of little avalanches from rib to rib, till it locates or squats under the soles of our feet. Our mouths, ears, eyes, noses, and hair are all full—our teeth all ground quite short, our skin growing daily into excellent fish-skin texture, our shirts growing black and our boots brown, and I have (as indeed have most of us) a beard that would do honour to Moses himself. Some of our fat-faced, red-faced, rosy-gilled, plump-cheeked, inveterate John Bulls do shave yet, and pretty examples of decency they are. They use thin jagged razors, for the sand on the strops makes all the razors into accomplished and talented saws; and so the "apple-faced heroes" have faces that look as if they and all their race had an hereditary leprosy. "And what the devil brings you into the desert?" you will say. Oh, that is a story as long as my beard, and I have no time to tell you; and I suppose when the Tories have skinned Lord Auckland alive, the Whigs will skin Lord Ellenborough in revenge; and then I, as one of his slaves, will be hanged up, and I will leave a true and posthumous history of my

589

life, and one chapter shall be "How the General got into the Sandy Desert—How his beard grew Long and his Shirt Dirty, and other Strange Things." Then you will see all about it, and how I got out again; but of that I cannot at present speak with propriety, seeing as how that I am not out yet! which I assure you is a very interesting affair. Your friend Captain Archer is at Belgar, somewhere about 1,500 miles distant; but if I come across him, be assured I will show him all the attention in my power; as to my wife and girls, they are 1,000 miles from me, but I hope are well. I have not seen them since August last, and God knows when I shall! for into this infernal climate I cannot bring them: nothing but sucking devils can live here! However, I suppose I shall be let back to India in time; at present I cannot go. I must settle Scinde, or Scinde settle me; and I think the former, for I never was so well or so strong in my life, at least not for the last ten years, "but ould, my dear, ould," a complaint not to be got rid of. My "threescore" are gone and my "ten" fast going. However, at this particular moment I find no want of "sand" in my glass. The whole of the desert is full of sea-shells, and it looks like an ocean of sand, which lies all in ridges, steep on the north side, and sloping towards the south, very like great waves just ready to curl and tumble over; it is very curious, we are all tired of it, and of dragging cannon up and down the sand waves.

And so God bless you and all your dear bright-eyed brood of beauties, is the prayer of your affectionate Coz.,

C. Napier

ROBERT PEMBERTON MILNES (1784–1858)

A brilliant young man, who entered Parliament at the age of twenty-two, Milnes had every promise of rising high in the world of politics. But he was fastidious by nature, to the extent, even, of refusing Palmerston's offer of a peerage. He was the father of the 1st Lord Houghton. This letter was written to his wife just after the battle of Waterloo.

TO HIS WIFE

BRUXELLES, JULY 2, 1815

MY DEAREST HARRIETTE, We arrived here yesterday evening. We had an unprosperous voyage of thirty hours to Ostend. I suffered extremely from sickness, but recovered the moment I landed.

We found Ostend full of English people just landed to join the army. Lord Rendlesham was there, who, remembering me at Cambridge, made himself known to me. We slept at Bruges, and arrived here to dinner the day after. From Ostend to this place they know nothing whatever of public events. Here we were furnished with the last intelligence from Paris, which has determined us to set out for that city to-morrow morning. The moment we arrived we went to the park, as it is called, which is more like Vauxhall than anything else, and where all the people promenade. There we saw Sir James Gambier and Sir Hew Dalrymple, Hamilton, Lord Cuningham, Lambe and Lady Caroline, &c.

As we determined to set off for Paris, there was not time to lose in seeing Waterloo, and Sir J. G. borrowed for us horses belonging to Colonel Vigoureux, who is wounded and laid up. We set off at nine in the morning to view the field of this dreadful combat, and we passed several hours there. Colonel Dashwood, who was in action, accompanied us. The battle was fought in a large open field sown with rye, so that the whole plain is now covered with straw. There were some hundred women and children collecting whatever fragments they could pick up, and we have brought away several scraps ourselves, such as tricoloured cockades, feathers, and French song-books, &c., &c., which I will give you on my return. The immense number of graves are evidence of the carnage; but we did not require the sight of them to

591

convince us of it, for the air was quite pestilential, and at one time made me quite ill. There is nothing now remaining on the field of battle but the French cannon, of which I counted 133 pieces, and military caps, which the country people do not think worth taking away. The situation of these caps showed where the battle had raged most violently. I am so little of a soldier, I do not see the advantage of our position over that of the French, who attacked us. The ascent to it is so gradual. The Duke of Richmond, who was Wellington's aide-de-camp, told Beckford that the Duke actually laughed when the French came up to attack our squares, his confidence was such of their invincibility; and nothing can better show you his extraordinary calmness than that when he first was told of Buonaparte's attack, and that he was within fifteen miles of Brussels, when he got the despatch at a ball, he went out for a couple of hours, gave every order requisite for the movements of the army, and then joined the dance, and kept it up all night. This extraordinary coolness had the effect of calming much of the alarm Buonaparte's incursion had created. Brussels is full of wounded. I have only seen Vigoureux, who was shot in the leg. At every window in this town there is sitting a wounded soldier. You would be sorry to hear of poor Henry Milnes's death; it was throughout very affecting. He was brought in on the Monday, quite naked, having been stripped in the night by the Belgians and thrown into a ditch. Sir J. Gambier was with him frequently. He lived a week. Dashwood, who was in the same regiment, says he behaved most gallantly. Through the day he defended the farmhouse of Hougoumont, which you may remember Wellington says the French could never take. He was shot through the back as he was turning round.

It may be some time before I write again, as the communications between Paris and England are not restored. I saw Louis's first entrée, and don't doubt I shall see this. It is undeniable that the wonderful valour of the English at Waterloo has seated him on the throne, and yet you cannot talk here to one of any party, but they laugh at the simplicity of the Bourbons.

In great haste,
Ever your affectionate husband,
R. P. MILNES

LEIGH HUNT (1784-1859)

Keats died in the arms of his friend Severn, on February 23, 1821, but Leigh Hunt did not learn this until he had despatched the following letter. The Hunts had nursed the dying poet until shortly before his journey to Italy, and had shown him every kindness, though Leigh Hunt was himself ill with overwork.

TO JOSEPH SEVERN

VALE OF HEALTH, HAMPSTEAD, MARCH 8, 1821

DEAR SEVERN, You have concluded, of course, that I have sent no letters to Rome, because I was aware of the effect they would have on Keats' mind; and this is the principal cause,—for besides what I have been told of his emotions about letters in Italy, I remember his telling me on one occasion, that, in his sick moments, he never wished to receive another letter, or ever to see another face however friendly. But still I should have written to *you* had I not been almost at death's-door myself. You will imagine how ill I have been when you hear that I have but just begun writing again for *The Examiner and Indicator*, after an interval of several months, during which my flesh wasted from me in sickness and melancholy. Judge how often I thought of Keats, and with what feelings. Mr. Brown tells me he is comparatively calm now, or rather quite so. If he can bear to hear of us, pray tell him—but he knows it all already, and can put it in better language than any man. I hear he does not like to be told that he may get better; nor is it to be wondered at, considering his firm persuasion that he shall not recover. He can only regard it as a puerile thing, and an insinuation that he cannot bear to think he shall die. But if this persuasion should happen not to be longer strong upon him, or if he can now put up with such attempts to console him, remind him of what I have said a thousand times, and that I still (upon my honour, Severn), think always, that I have seen too many instances of recovery from apparently desperate cases of consumption, not to indulge in hope to the very last. If he cannot bear this, tell him— tell that great poet and noble-hearted man—that we shall all bear his memory in the most precious part of our hearts, and that the world shall bow their heads to it, as our loves do. Or if this again will trouble his spirit, tell him we shall never cease to remember and love him, and, that the most sceptical of us has faith enough in the high things that nature puts into our heads, to think that all who are of one accord in mind and heart, are journeying to one and the same place, and shall unite somehow or other again, face to face, mutually conscious, mutually delighted. Tell him he is only before us on the road, as he was in everything else; or, whether you tell him the latter or no, tell him the former, and add that we shall never forget he was so and that we are coming after him. The tears are again in my eyes, and I must not afford to shed them. The next letter I write shall be more to yourself, and a little more refreshing to your spirits, which we are very sensible must have been greatly taxed. But whether our friend dies or not, it will not be among the least lofty of our recollections by-and-by that you helped to smooth the sick-bed of so fine a being.

God bless you, dear Severn.

Your sincere friend,
LEIGH HUNT

DAVID WILKIE (1785–1841)

Wilkie studied painting in Edinburgh, though with what encourage-
ment from his parents is best illustrated by the story of his father, who,
upon being shown one of the boy's sketches of a human foot, exclaimed
"A foot! it's mair like a fluke!" But in 1805 he went to London where
he sold several pictures quite successfully and made a number of friends.
His success with "The Blind Fiddler" enabled him to return home, and
it was during this visit that he wrote the letter about Edinburgh; the
second letter is quite an amusing description of the Duke of Wellington's
visit to his studio.

TO BENJAMIN ROBERT HAYDON

Cults, N.B., 3rd June, 1807

My dear Friend, Considering that writing to you is the first duty I
have to discharge on my arrival in Scotland, I have taken this as the first
opportunity that my time would allow since I came to my father's house.
I left London, as I purposed when I saw you, on the day following, and,
after a favourable passage of five days, during which I was sick almost
from the beginning to the end, we arrived at Leith the Friday following.
I stopped in Edinburgh ten days, which I spent in calling on a number
of my friends; and amongst them my old master, Mr. Graham, who was
very glad to see me, and who was the only person I have met in Scotland
who could talk reasonably about the art, for I must confess the people of
Edinburgh seem to be far behind in their knowledge of that subject. I
find nothing so remarkable in Edinburgh as to merit being mentioned to
you, except that Mr. Geddes is flourishing at a great rate, and making
money in the portrait-line; and from the speeches he occasionally makes,
he is considered by some, who think themselves connoisseurs, as a great
genius. From Edinburgh I came on to my father's house on Monday
last. I have not yet had time to begin anything, as my painting apparatus
is not yet come to hand; but I have been looking about in the village for
subjects of study, and I have the satisfaction to find a great number of
scenes almost superior to anything I have yet seen, that combine the most
interesting sweetness with the most picturesque effect.

On my first landing in Scotland, the effect which the Scottish dialect had on my ear was very surprising. All my friends seemed to speak a language which I had never heard before, and so great is the contrast between my mode of speaking and theirs, that they think I speak the English language in all its purity, an opinion in which I am very much inclined to agree. I request you will remember me particularly to Mr. Jackson; say that I am exceedingly sorry at not having seen him before I left London, and that I will probably write him. Let me know what progress you make with your picture, and

Believe me, my dear Haydon, yours truly,

DAVID WILKIE

TO THE SAME

18TH AUGUST, 1816

YESTERDAY morning Lord Lynedoch (Sir Thomas Graham that was) called upon me, and said that if I should be at home at four o'clock the Duke of Wellington and a party that came to meet at his house previous to that would then call on me with him. Upon this information I set to work for the rest of the day to get my rooms put to rights, put all my pictures in order for view, and last, though not least, had to arrange it so that my mother and sister might see the great man from the parlour windows as he came in.

Matters being thus settled, we waited in a sort of breathless expectation for their arrival, and at half-past four they accordingly came. The party consisted of the Duke and Duchess of Bedford, Lady Argyle and another lady, the Duke of Wellington and Lord Lynedoch, to all of which the latter introduced me as they came in. When they went upstairs they were first occupied in looking at the pictures severally, but without entering into conversation further than by expressing a general approbation. The Duke, on whom my attention was fixed, seemed pleased with them, and said in his firm voice, "Very good," "Capital," &c., but said nothing in the way of remark, and seemed indeed not much attended to by the company, of whom the ladies began to talk a good deal. They went on in this way for a considerable time, and I had every reason to feel satisfied with the impression my works seemed to make on the Duke and Duchess of Bedford and the others, but though the Duke of Wellington seemed full of attention, I felt disappointed with his silence. At last Lady Argyle began to tell me that the Duke wished me to paint him a picture, and was explaining what the subject was, when the Duke, who was at that time seated on a chair and looking at one of the pictures that happened to be on the ground, turned on us, and swinging back upon the chair turned up his lively eyes to me, and said that the subject should be a parcel of old soldiers assembled together on their seats at the door of a public-house, chewing tobacco and talking over their old stories. He thought they might be in any uniform, and that it should be at some public-house in the King's Road, Chelsea. I said this would make a most beautiful picture, and that it only wanted some story or a principal incident to connect the figures together: he said perhaps playing at skittles would do, or any other game, when I proposed that one might be reading a newspaper aloud to the rest, and that in making a sketch of it many other incidents would occur. In this he perfectly agreed, and said I might send the sketch to him when he was abroad. He then got up and looked at his watch, and said to the company his time was nearly out, as he had to go and dine with the Duke of Cambridge.

After they had proposed to go, he made me a bow, and as he went out of the room, he turned to me, and said, "Well, when shall I hear from you?" To which I replied that my immediate engagements, and the time it would take to collect materials for his Grace's subject, would prevent me being able to get it done for two years. "Very well," said he, "that will be soon enough for me." They then went downstairs, and as they went out our people were all ready to see him from the parlour windows. When he got to the gate, he made me a bow again, and seeing at the same time my family at the parlour windows, he bowed to them also. As he got upon his horse he observed all the families and the servants were at the windows, and I saw two lifeguardsmen, the rogues, just behind the pillar at the corner, waiting to have a full view of him.

The sensation this event occasioned quite unhinged us for the rest of the day. Nothing was talked about but the Duke of Wellington; and the chair he happened to sit upon has been carefully selected out, and has been decorated with ribbons, and there is talk of having an inscription upon it, descriptive of the honour it has received.

With respect to the appearance of the man, none of the portraits of him are like him. He is younger and fresher, more active and lively, and in his figure more clean-made and firmer built than I was led to expect. His face is in some respects odd; has no variety of expression, but his eye is extraordinary, and is almost the only feature I remember, but I remember it so well that I think I see it now. It has not the hungry and devouring look of Bonaparte, but seems to express in its liveliness the ecstasy that an animal would express in an active and eager pursuit.

THOMAS DE QUINCEY (1785–1859)

The "Confessions of an English Opium-eater" appeared in 1821, but when De Quincey wrote his note to Haydon he was preparing the new and greatly enlarged edition of 1856, among what difficulties his letter reveals. He had a morbid love of storing documents; when he was so cluttered up with papers and manuscripts that he knew not how to turn he would simply move to other lodgings, locking the door of the old rooms behind him. At the time of his death there were six of these former lodgings thus full of papers.

TO B. R. HAYDON

MY DEAR SIR, There is a great confusion this day in Mrs. Wilson's lodgings, from the repairing, sweeping, painting, &c. And moreover the landlady's sister, who it is that chiefly communicates with strangers at the door, is deaf. At the moment (I believe between 7 and 8 a.m.) of appointing 12 as the hour for the return of your messenger, I was quite unaware that by a mistake natural in the confusion of yesterday's sudden clearance, most of the papers belonging to the "Confessions" had been placed within a set of drawers against which is now reared the white-washer's scaffolding. That will be withdrawn, I understand, so far as to give me access about 5 p.m. But that will be too late for me to have them in a state for the press till to-morrow morning. I am exhausted by the twenty-four hours' labour of the separation and *sorting* of such innumerable papers. The sorting could not be evaded, under the necessity of removing them at all; else I should have been *lost* irrecoverably in the resulting confusion. I am just at the last point of my *innovations* in the "Confessions." After those I fall back into the old current, so that pretty nearly a mere reprinting will be all. Except, however, as to the final *Suspiria*.

TO HIS DAUGHTER FLORENCE

FRIDAY, FEBRUARY 9TH, 1855

MY DEAR FLORENCE, I heard with great concern from Ellen on (was it not?) Friday evening last—i.e., this day week—of your toothache sufferings. Every day I have been on the point of writing to you about the remedy; and I reproach myself heavily for having suffered my own miserable want of energy to interfere with the *instant* suggestion of so much practical counsel as my own bitter experience enables me to offer. This counsel divides into three sections—A, B, C. A relates to the *cause* of toothache. I pass to B and C. B indicates what relates to *clothing*. Warm coverings for the feet (lamb's wool fleecy hosiery, &c.), and above all, for the chest and shoulders, are indispensable; and therefore if from any cause you are not immediately in possession of the right kind, I will buy whatever you direct me, pay for them, and forward them at once to Lasswade. Have you and Emily muffs and fur tippets? C stands for *diet*. Now, I remember most distinctly a long course of atrocious wretchedness from a fit of toothache that never intermitted night or day through nearly three weeks, and, behold! suddenly within two minutes, as if the angel of Bethesda had cried *halt*! it gave way, fled, vanished, and did not return through half a year, simply under the accident of a dinner more stimulant than usual. From dreadful ignorance—ignorance that was bovine, canine, bestial—I had been systematically feeding and nursing this accursed torment, under the fatal conceit that I was starving it, by a low vegetable diet. Fortunately, I had at length become infuriated by ill success. I resolved on trying the opposite system; and, by mere chance, on this day there happened to have been dressed for dinner a superb sirloin of beef. This I supported by a bottle of old port, and, as I am a living man, not one full glass had I drunk (simultaneously eating a square inch, not a cubic inch, of beef, and its reasonable proportion of gravy), when the foul fiend of toothache flapped his gloomy wings, and like a gorged vulture, rose heavily, vanished, and for six months did not return. Now, comparing the three weeks' unrelenting persecution with the absolutely instantaneous flight of the monster, you will hardly feel a doubt but that this mere hint of a generous diet, falling on a system that by previous starvation had been disqualified for offering any resistance to a strong impulse, must have been the magic that worked the sudden revolution. "Take up thy bed and walk!" was the summons, that would not be refused, of this memorable dinner. Not for vain carnal amusement do I rehearse this instructive fact, but for thy practical conversion, O daughter of lukewarm faith! Promise me that, if I send out a bottle of the oldest port, you will order for dinner a sirloin of beef (roasted), and will drink at the said dinner two glasses of the wine, undiluted; or, if a little diluted, not to reckon the water as part of the two glasses.

I am in deadly depression of nervousness; spite of which, however,

I meditate great exertions; and with the benefit of a daily nine or ten miles' exercise; I believe that I could accomplish my plans. Towards these it is important for me to return home; and in the course of next week without fail I will do so. Meantime a wonderful sally of ingenuity has suggested to me that, by means of a previous concert between us, my return might be made available for a visit on your part to Edinburgh. You might come in by means of Cuthbert's carriage, for which, of course, I will pay, and take me up with my small quantum of baggage at *any* hour that suited you; i.e., any hour from one to six. But let me know forty-eight hours before taking any final step in the matter. If one of the Miss Widnells should chance to find any motive for coming in on the same day, it would be easy for me to make room by taking my seat on a box of papers.

Do not suppose that my delays in returning argue any uncertainty of plans. The plain reason is simply my immeasurable incapacity for business—above all, for that sort of business which lies in arranging papers or packing up books. However, if you or Emily will concert some scheme, I, on *my* part, will really make an effort.

I have suffered much from my eyes since the influenza; some days all but blind, and on some nights roused up for hours by the pain, and still more by the nervous uneasiness besieging them. Sulphate of zinc is all the remedy I have applied.

Send my love to little Eva three times a week. Good night!

Ever affectionately yours

BENJAMIN ROBERT HAYDON (1786–1846)

Haydon's correspondence is intensely interesting as showing a man of vigorous mind and keen interest. The first of those published here was written to Leigh Hunt, when the latter was in prison with his brother for libelling the Prince Regent, whom he had called "a violater of his word, a libertine over head and ears in disgrace, a despiser of domestic ties," etc. Haydon's letter to a pupil is typical of a generous mind and a sympathetic nature.

TO LEIGH HUNT

FRIDAY NIGHT, 12TH FEBRUARY, 1813

MY DEAR HUNT, I am most anxious to see you, but have been refused admittance, and was told yesterday you would write to your friends when you wished to see them, by Mr. Cave, the Under-Governor or gaoler. I really felt my heart ache at every line of your last week's effusion. All your friends were affected, and all complained of the cruelty and severity of your sentence. I am delighted Mrs. Hunt and the children are now admitted to you, and if they ultimately relax, with respect to your friends, I hope in God the pressure of your imprisonment will be greatly lightened. I must say I have been excessively irritated at not having seen you yet; and had I gone to you as I intended the day on which the committee sat, I find, my dear fellow, I should have been allowed to see you; but I suffered myself to be *advised* out of my intention. I have never yet acted by the advice of others, in opposition to my own judgment, without having cause to repent it. I assure you, my dear Hunt, I think of you often, with the most melancholy and exquisite sensations. After my day's study I generally lay my head on my hand, draw near the fire, and muse upon you till midnight, till I am completely wrapped in the delusion of my fancy. I see you, as it were, in a misty vision. I imagine myself quietly going to you in the solemnity of evening; I think I perceive your massy prison, erect, solitary, nearly lost in deep-toned obscurity, pressing the earth with supernatural weight, encircled with an atmosphere of enchanted silence, into which no being can enter without a shudder. As I advance with whispering steps I imagine, with an acuteness that amounts to reality, I hear oozing on the evening wind, as it sweeps along with moaning stillness, the strains of your captive flute; I then stop and listen with gasping agitation, and with associations of our attachment, and all the friendly affecting proofs I have had of it; afraid to move, afraid to stir, lest I might lose one melancholy tone, or interrupt by the most imperceptible motion one sweet and soothing undulation. My dear fellow, I am not a man of tears, nor do I recollect ever yielding to them but when my mother died. But I declare I felt a choking sensation when I rose to retire to rest after this waking abstraction. I have no doubt we shall talk over this part of our existence when we are a little advanced in life, with excessive interest. Let misfortune confirm instead of shake your principles, and you will issue again into the world as invulnerable as you left it. Take care of your health; use as much exercise as you can. Send me word by your nephew, or through Mrs. Hunter, when I can see you, for which I am very anxious; and believe me, unalterably your faithful and attached friend,

B. R. HAYDON

TO JOHN HUNT

PARIS, 10TH JUNE, 1814

MY DEAR HUNT, I wrote your brother just after our arrival, and told him to show my letter to you; so that you will have had a correct journal of my proceedings to the moment I entered Paris. We passed over the field of battle, and saw very little remains of a fight, except the Russian batteries. About two we got to Paris, through one of the most infernal entrances, I think, I ever witnessed—St. Giles's is an Elysium to it. The gate of St. Denis, built by Louis XIV, is at the end of the street we came through; it struck me as being high and grand, but the bas-reliefs in a wretched French taste. The first appearance of Paris, to one accustomed to the streets of London, is a feeling of unutterable confusion——houses, horses, carriages, carts; men, women, children, and soldiers; Turks, Jews, Christians, Cossacks, and Russians, all mingled together, without comfort, without system, in dirt and dreariness, hot, fatigued, and in haste. After pushing our way through this chaos dire, we put up at a dirty golden hotel——gilt this and gilt that, satin beds and satin sofas, but embalmed with grease and worn with age. Never was such misery as an Englishman suffers at first from the mode of lodging and living in Paris. You have your breakfast from one place and your dinner from another; who is the master or where the mistress no human creature can tell. We got lodgings next day, and were extremely lucky to fall into respectable hands. The Louvre, of course, was our first object, and by the next day we were there. The first sight is grand, but yet I was disappointed; it is too long to impress one, and it affected me (as I have mentioned to another friend) as if I was looking through the wrong end of a spy-glass. The "Transfiguration" is a proof that had Raphael lived, he would have completed all the requisites of art. It is powerfully coloured, and in many parts will bear comparison with Titian. The expressions distinctly tell the story, they really speak to one's soul; and yet, from forming, in my own imagination, something beyond nature, as we always do, I must own I was disappointed at its first impression. It has a little and rather an insignificant appearance, and the female heads are certainly not beautiful. In sweetness, Correggio, who hangs opposite, is very much superior— indeed I cannot say enough of the works of this divine painter. There is a magical, a trembling sensitiveness; he has caught all those fleeting, delicate expressions which you see illumine the face of a beautiful woman while you are telling her anything peculiarly interesting. All such refinements he has caught and realized. You can trace nowhere but in Nature any remains of a hint from others, either ancient or modern. He felt what he painted in his own way, and has touched a chord which every other being had passed and neglected. His pictures affected me like the strains of an angel's harp, and have all the loveliness of an angel's dream. They won't permit us to copy yet, or most assuredly I should do my best to bring home something of this man's delightful fancy. Reynolds had studied him well, in colour and in expression, and his whole life was spent in aiming at making a new discovery in the road which Correggio had opened. The statues below are beautiful, but I can assure you the Elgin "Theseus" is superior in style and in principles to anything in this superb collection. I have spent hours there, day after day, and shall spend hours yet till I depart. All my principles of art are confirmed by the practice of these men, and I hope to return with my mind and feelings enlarged after having seen their highest efforts.

Wilkie and I yesterday spent the day in surveying Montmartre; and from the top of the telegraph the old soldier who has the direction of it pointed out every particular of the battle, and told us every interesting thing before it. It is amazingly strong, and had it been properly defended and properly fortified, would certainly never have been taken. But all was confusion, and everything done in terror and dismay. The prospect from it is immense, and Paris below has a beautiful look, with its intermingled trees and gilded domes, though in size it certainly bore no comparison with London. I observe everywhere old soldiers are employed where the duty is not difficult. You find them in all parts of Paris, taking money at bridges, &c., and nearly everybody has served in some way or other. Last night we went to the Théatre Français to see Talma, and were very much entertained. The mob at the door was regulated by a gendarme, which, though disagreeable in an Englishman, certainly prevented a squeezing and confusion. The audience made the orchestra play the favourite air "Vive Henri Quatre," and received it with shouts of enthusiasm. The French mob possesses great patience and good nature. They bear from each other what I am sure in England would produce the most furious quarrels. The manners of the women are very sweet, but they soon begin to look old, and the children have the appearance of being prematurely formed in their features. The race of men is certainly smaller than ours; in the soldiers it is particularly apparent. All the old soldiers that have served in the most celebrated campaigns are active, energetic, little fellows. At the Hotel des Inválides I met an old soldier who had lost his leg at the battle of Marengo, and inquired about Bonaparte with great interest. He was quietly watching the departure of a body of Russians, and observed to me, "This is all owing to the campaign of Moscow." They all say, "He was a great general, a great genius, but a bad sovereign." This is the feeling in every quarter. The artists and the army, being those who suffer the most, are of course the most outrageous and disaffected; but I have no doubt when they perceive that Louis is as likely as Bonaparte to protect their efforts, he will be as great a patron and they as good loyal subjects as king could wish. We have seen very little of private society. Indeed, our objects being entirely different, we intend to avoid all invitations. Our landlady and her husband are temperate, frugal and industrious. They seem, like all the middle class, to be indifferent who governs them so long as they are quiet. This indifference is one great cause of their sufferings. Had the people felt the value of having a voice in public matters, they would never have suffered a parcel of scoundrels to torment them at their leisure. They know hardly any events they have passed, and inquire about them in a manner betraying an amount of ignorance that makes me stare. Paris, in every way, looks like the residence of a despotic monarch, and the country round Paris uncultivated and dreary. From the top of Montmartre the villages are distinctly seen; but there are no straggling houses as in England, giving the whole a social look. Each village seemed to fear the other, and each was surrounded by a sort of wall or ditch. In one road I saw old chateaux, but dirty and neglected. In every part of

Paris are traces of the change that has taken place. Great buildings, begun by republicans and left unfinished when they lost their power; palaces and temples in ruins, though but half built—monuments of Bonaparte's ambition and fall. The most interesting exhibition—except the Louvre—is that of monuments of French kings and great men, collected and saved during the Revolution by a private gentleman. Here are monuments from the earliest ages; here, contained in sarcophagi, are the remains of Molière, La Fontaine, Boileau, and in a secret grove that of Abélard and Héloïse. The monuments are not so defaced in France as in England, and the people have evidently more feeling for things of this sort. Paris is certainly a very interesting place, and you, my dear Hunt, would derive great pleasure from a visit. The officers I contrive to bungle out a conversation with, all talk of recovering their conquests without the least hesitation, when the country has had a little repose. As I was walking by the Seine on Sunday I went accidentally into a sort of open house, and to my surprise saw three dead bodies lying inside a sort of glasshouse; here they lie till they are owned, as I found. Women and children, playing battledore on the other side, when the shuttlecock was down would quietly walk over and take a peep, and when they had satisfied their curiosity resume their game, repeating the process at intervals. I must own I never was so shocked—such palpable indifference and indecency. If this be not a way to use the people to blood I know none more effectual. There are no squares equal to ours in Paris—that is, public squares. The square of the Tuileries is grand, but this belongs to the monarch. In Paris they are much more refined than in London in the luxuries and comforts of gluttony, but in cleanliness and thorough enjoyment I think they are very far behind us, and certainly are nearly altogether ignorant of every moral feeling. The people in the coffee-houses have a spirited air, but at the same time the air of bravoes. Something I heard this morning gave me a complete idea of their military notions. An officer, crossing a bridge where a toll was taken, was stopped to pay, and expressed the greatest surprise that the *military* should have to do so as well as the others! Adieu, my dear Hunt. Kind remembrances to your wife and brother. I forgot to send him my direction which you can now give him—No. 6, Rue St. Benoit, Faubourg St. Germain, Paris.

Most truly and affectionately your friend,

B. R. HAYDON

TO A PUPIL

London, 21st January, 1840

My dear Sir, I regret to hear of your friend's difficulties. As I passed my word to your landlord to pay your rent due if you could not, so that you might be able to return home and help your father; and as you now wrote to me that you and your father are really unable to pay the rent, I will undoubtedly pay it, so make your mind easy, and don't let it press on you as a debt.   I release you from it entirely.   You obeyed me strictly, you advanced rapidly, you kept your word of following my instructions, and I kept mine of educating you if you were supported.   But do not despair because you are this moment unfortunate.   Take adversity always as a correction, and success more to be feared.

I shall be most happy to see you again as soon as your circumstances and the help of your friends will enable you to come to London; but you must act with energy, and not forget the precepts I gave you when here.

Yours faithfully,

B. R. Haydon

MARY RUSSELL MITFORD (1787-1855)

Miss Mitford was an inveterate letter-writer, scribbling her epistles on all sorts of little bits of paper. The curious thing about it is that she never met the majority of those with whom she corresponded. Her letter to Mrs. Ouvry, mother of the antiquary, is characteristic of her happy style.

TO MRS. OUVRY

[Undated]

No! dearest Mrs. Ouvry, I am afraid there is no chance of my being in town this Christmas, and yet I don't know, it will depend upon when a play, by a dear friend of mine, is to be brought out at the Surrey—an odd place! but my friend, who lives much among very fine people, says that he rather likes the idea of a *Faubourg* audience (people not fine),—it is a very favourite friend, whose dramatic power I have always rated highly, for whom I have always predicted a dramatic success,—so I feel bound to go and see it. How I may stand the light and the heat I don't know, although much better than this time last year. I have not regained anything like my old powers of going into company, have not been at a lecture these two winters, and never mean if I can help it to go to a dinner party again. Except for this play, I should not go to town till the spring upon the chance of seeing Mrs. Browning then . . . at all events, if I be in London, the seeing you would be among my chief pleasures; and I should be sure to give you notice. I suppose you will stay a month or so. Just now we are under quarantine, having had a very heavy case of small-pox after vaccination in the house, and it has been so rife about (I have just counted up twenty-nine cases of my own knowledge, three of whom have died)—it has been so prevalent, and so serious, that we have been shunned as if we had the plague, and could not get a nurse for love or money. It was my man, gardener, coachman, etc., John, a steady good servant, who was ill, and my own dear little maid (an old servant who has left a much better place to return and live with me), having luckily had the disorder the natural way, has devoted herself to the sick man—she is a true sister of charity in all illnesses. The man is recovering, my own excellent maid is getting over the fatigue, but it has been a sensible anxiety. Now for "Shirley." I liked it very much, better than "Jane Eyre." It has not the melodramatic interest, and is all the better for the want of it; but to me it seems a racy, poignant, pungent book—and with one admirable character, Shirley herself. None but a woman would have made so fine a portrait of a self-willed, spoilt, charming creature, who gives her heart to the only being whom she has ever learnt to fear and to look up to. No man of equal ability would have made love the be-all and end-all of life. It must be a woman. Besides, there is governess French in it, and a thousand small indications which you will find in reading; among others she gives the sort of social predominance to the clergy (writing of manufacturing district among mill-owners and great squires) which women, who claim them as their own would do, and men would not. A friend of mine, who is more than anyone behind the curtain in literary society, says that it is by the daughter of a Yorkshire clergyman, and that seems likely. You are quite right about the want of objects for single women. In France, the rank just below the gentry is made at once happy, and useful by keeping the shop books. In England even that resource is wanting, and that class is added to the idle and the wretched worsted-working young ladies. Among the other evils, too, the want of better occupation drives girls to write bad verse—the quantity of trash of that sort that I see would amuse you. But it is easier to point out the evil than to find the remedy. There is however a spirit of improvement abroad in the world, and I am hopeful. How are your Irish friends? I have just been reading Thomas Davis's admirable life of Curran, prefixed to his edition of those matchless speeches; and I am wanting to read all about the rebellion of '98. Can you give me a list of books?—a long list—I love to read down a subject. Did you know Mr. Lever in England? He and I have been exchanging tender messages through Mrs. Browning. I always liked his books, but hardly expected that he would like mine. What an excellent subject Mr. Stevenson chose for his lecture! I delight in topography, and am just now reading eight volumes of Border History—of Northumberland chiefly, our own country.

GEORGE GORDON, LORD BYRON (1788–1824)

The correspondence of Byron shows in every line the vehemence and vigour that mark his verse. The first letter of those below was written in his Cambridge days; the last is from Greece and was penned shortly before his death.

TO MR. PIGOT

LONDON, AUGUST 18TH, 1806

I AM just on the point of setting off for Worthing, and write merely to request you will send that *idle scoundrel Charles* with my horse immediately; tell him I am excessively provoked he has not made his appearance before, or written to inform me of the cause of his delay, particularly as I supplied him with money for his journey. On no pretext is he to postpone his *march* one day longer; and if, in obedience to Mrs. B., he thinks proper to disregard my positive orders, I shall not, in future, consider him as my servant. He must bring the surgeon's bill with him, which I will discharge immediately on receiving it. Nor can I conceive the reason of his not acquainting Frank with the state of my unfortunate quadrupeds. Dear Pigot, forgive this *petulant* effusion, and attribute it to the idle conduct of that *precious* rascal, who, instead of obeying my injunctions, is sauntering through the streets of that *political Pandemonium*, Nottingham. Present my remembrances to your family and the Leacrofts, and believe me, &c.

P.S. I delegate to *you* the unpleasant task of dispatching him on his journey—Mrs. B.'s orders to the contrary are not to be attended to: he is to proceed first to London, and then to Worthing, without delay. Every thing I have *left* must be sent to London. My *Poetics you* will *pack up* for the same place, and not even reserve a copy for yourself and sister, as I am about to give them an *entire new form*: when they are complete, you shall have the *first fruits*. Mrs. B. on no account is to *see* or touch them. Adieu.

TO LORD HOLLAND

ST. JAMES'S STREET, MARCH 5TH, 1812

MY LORD, May I request your Lordship to accept a copy of the thing which accompanies this note? You have already so fully proved the truth of the first line of Pope's couplet,

Forgiveness to the injured doth belong,

that I long for an opportunity to give the lie to the verse that follows. If I were not perfectly convinced that any thing I may have formerly uttered in the boyish rashness of my misplaced resentment had made as little impression as it deserved to make, I should hardly have the confidence—perhaps your Lordship may give it a stronger and more appropriate appellation—to send you a quarto of the same scribbler. But your Lordship, I am sorry to observe to-day, is troubled with the gout; if my book can produce a *laugh* against itself or the author, it will be of some service. If it can set you to *sleep*, the benefit will be yet greater; and as some facetious personage observed half a century ago, that "poetry is a mere drug," I offer you mine as a humble assistant to the "eau medicinale." I trust you will forgive this and all my other buffooneries, and believe me to be, with great respect,

Your Lordship's obliged and Sincere servant,

BYRON

TO MR. MURRAY

RAVENNA, 8BRE 16°, 1820

THE Abbot has just arrived; many thanks; as also for the *Monastery*— *when you send it*!!!

The Abbot will have a more than ordinary interest for me, for an ancestor of mine by the mother's side, Sir J. Gordon of Gight, the handsomest of his day, died on a scaffold at Aberdeen for his loyalty to Mary, of whom he was an imputed paramour as well as her relation. His fate was much commented on in the Chronicles of the times. If I mistake not, he had something to do with her escape from Loch Leven, or with her captivity there. But this you will know better than I.

I recollect Loch Leven as it were but yesterday. I saw it on my way to England in 1798, being then ten years of age. My mother, who was as haughty as Lucifer with her descent from the Stuarts, and her right line from the *old Gordons, not the Seyton Gordons*, as she disdainfully termed the ducal branch, told me the story, always reminding me how superior *her* Gordons were to the southern Byrons, notwithstanding our Norman, and always masculine descent, which has never lapsed into a female, as my mother's Gordons had done in her own person.

I have written to you so often lately, that the brevity of this will be welcome.

Yours &c.

TO THE SAME

RAVENNA, 8BRE 25°, 1820

PRAY forward the enclosed to Lady Byron. It is on business.

In thanking you for the Abbot, I made four grand mistakes, Sir John Gordon was not of Gight, but of Bogagicht, and a son of Huntley's. He suffered *not* for his loyalty, but in an insurrection. He had *nothing* to do with Loch Leven, having been dead some time at the period of the Queen's confinement: and, fourthly, I am not sure that he was the Queen's paramour, or no, for Robertson does not allude to this, though *Walter Scott does*, in the list he gives of her admirers (as unfortunate) at the close of "The Abbot."

I must have made all these mistakes in recollecting my mother's account of the matter, although she was more accurate than I am, being precise upon points of genealogy, like all the aristocratical Scotch. She had a long list of ancestors, like Sir Lucius O'Trigger's, most of whom are to be found in the old Scotch Chronicles, Spalding, &c., in arms and doing mischief. I remember well passing Loch Leven, as well as the Queen's Ferry: we were on our way to England in 1798.

Yours

You had better not public Blackwood and the Roberts' prose, except what regards Pope:—you have let the time slip by.

TO MR. BOWRING

IOBRE 26, 1823

LITTLE need be added to the enclosed, which arrived this day, except that I embark to-morrow for Missolonghi. The intended operations are detailed in the annexed documents. I have only to request that the Committee will use every exertion to forward our views by all its influence and credit.

I have also to request you *personally* from myself to urge my friend and trustee, Douglas Kinnaird (from whom I have not heard these four months nearly), to forward to me all the resources of my *own* we can muster for the ensuing year; since it is no time to menager *purse*, or, perhaps, *person*.   I have advanced, and am advancing, all that I have in hand, but I shall require all that can be got together;—and (if Douglas has completed the sale of Rochdale, *that* and my year's income for next year ought to form a good round sum),—as you may perceive that there will be little cash of their own amongst the Greeks (unless they get the Loan), it is the more necessary that those of their friends who have any should risk it.

The supplies of the Committee are, some, useful, and all excellent in their kind, but occasionally hardly *practical* enough, in the present state of Greece; for instance, the mathematical instruments are thrown away—none of the Greeks know a problem from a poker—we must conquer first, and plan afterwards.   The use of the trumpets, too, may be doubted, unless Constantinople were Jericho, for the Hellenists have no ears for bugles, and you must send us somebody to listen to them.

We will do our best—and I pray you to stir your English hearts at home to more *general* exertion; for my part, I will stick by the cause while a plank remains which can be honourably clung to.   If I quit it, it will be by the Greeks' conduct, and not the Holy Allies or holier Mussulmans —but let us hope better things.

Ever yours

P.S.   I am happy to say that Colonel Leicester Stanhope and myself are acting in perfect harmony together—he is likely to be of great service both to the cause and to the Committee, and is publicly as well as personally a very valuable acquisition to our party on every account.   He came up (as they all do who have not been in the country before) with some high-flown notions of the sixth form at Harrow or Eton, &c.; but Col. Napier and I set him to rights on those points, which is absolutely necessary to prevent disgust, or perhaps return; but now we can set our shoulders *soberly* to the *wheel*, without quarrelling with the mud which may clog it occasionally.

I can assure you that Col. Napier and myself are as decided for the cause as any German student of them all; but like men who have seen the country and human life, there and elsewhere, we must be permitted to view it in its truth, with its defects as well as beauties—more especially as success will remove the former *gradually*.

P.S.   As much of this letter as you please is for the Committee, the rest may be *entre nous*.

RICHARD HARRIS BARHAM (1788–1845)

Barham will always be remembered as the inimitable author of the "Ingoldsby Legends." As a canon of St. Paul's he saw quite a lot of London life. At the time of writing this letter to his friend Mrs. Hughes he had just published "My Cousin Nicholas" in "Blackwood's Magazine" and was enjoying his first taste of literary fame.

TO MRS. HUGHES

St. Paul's Churchyard, March 29, 1834

MY DEAR MADAM, By the time this reaches you, you will, I trust, have seen in print the reason why I have not before availed myself of the permission to address you occasionally, which you were kind enough to continue to me when last I had the pleasure of seeing you in London. Blackwood can be, whether you know it or not, a great "worry"; and having put all he had of "My Cousin Nicholas" into type, he has ever since been uproarious, what he calls "stirring me up," and crying with the horse-leech's daughter "Give! Give!" though I must in all honesty avow he is quite as ready to impart on his side, as he is insatiable in demanding. All the spare time therefore that I have had in this, as you will know it to be, the busiest period of the parson's year, has been devoted to copying and rewriting for him, till I am really grown almost to hate the sight of a pen. Last night I received his number for the ensuing month, which contains "Nicholas," or at least the first four chapters of his memoirs, and the "Tale of the Rhine." The latter is a pretty literal, but of course burlesque, version of a remarkably absurd, but showy, piece brought out at the Adelphi, the success of which has induced half the theatres in London—Covent Garden, which ought to scorn such piracy, among the number—to exhibit the same thing with little more of change than that of name. Perhaps there is more excuse for the practice in this instance than in many others, as there is a common source, from which all have been pilfered, in a mediocre French opera by Auber, whose music, flimsy as it is, the good lieges of Cockaigne do not disdain to admire. The same parcel conveyed a note to me from "Ebony" [John Wilson] in which he threatens us with a new "Noctes" next month, and asks for

613

"some *jeux d'esprit* if I have any by me," to help him out.   But, alas, as a drysalter of this kind of commodity I am lamentably off for stock, and find myself obliged to confess the truth of your old acquaintance L.'s observation when he told Mr. Sydney Smith last Sunday, in animadversion on the want of general co-operation in "the body" that they "had no *jeu d'esprit* among them."   His reverend host, without admitting or denying the fact, hinted that it was not their only want, and that a French Dictionary, to some of them, was not at least as great a desideratum.

Poor L. has experienced a severe loss in the sudden death of one of his children, a fine boy about a year old, who was carried off by the prevailing influenza in a few hours.   This disorder seems to be precisely that which was last year so fatal to young children, whom it attacks in the chest and throat, and appears to be of the scarlatina kind, and of no common malignity.   In this case the poor child was bled, a mode of practice which, both for children and grown persons, last year's experience has proved to be, in almost every case, the worst that could be adopted.   Should it make its way into Berkshire, pray impress upon Mr. Hughes, and all your friends who have children, a strong caution against phlebotomy.   Poor Dr. Dean, my old friend, who was head of St. Mary's Hall, Oxford, lost his life entirely by having recourse to this expedient when he had caught the complaint.

The name of Oxford reminds me that I have to communicate, what I am sure you will sympathize with me in, my great satisfaction and delight at having got Mr. Dick fairly on the books at Oriel.   This I owe solely to the goodness of the Bishop, who has on this as on every other occasion acted towards me with a degree of kindness my sense of which I really want words to express.   Not content with writing to Dr. Hawkins on the subject for me, when he found that the college was so full that, in the ordinary course of rotation, so long a period must elapse that the "exhibition" from St. Paul's School would necessarily be forfeited, he applied a second and a third time, till he not only got him on the Provost's private list, but even at the top of that list, for the very first vacancy; and two days after a vacancy actually took place.   Within an hour after this announcement the new candidate for Alma Mater and myself were on the top of the Oxford Coach, which deposited us in six hours safe at the Angel.   The next day we dined in Hall at Oriel with the Bishop's nephew, Mr. Edward Copleston, who gave Dick a good rattling examination more than an hour long, and one which would have made my hair stand on end in my best days.   He got through it, however, I am happy to say, so that after breakfasting with the Provost the next morning, the hero of the "Long-tailed Coat" was enabled to say in verity, "Upon my life I am a *man* indeed, and not a schoolboy, nor Christophero Sly." If Lavater's system be not altogether a dream—if there be any faith at all to be placed in the expression of the human face divine then was the newly matriculated "*man* of Oriel" as high in the seventh heaven as the ennobled tinker; and I must question whether the imposition of a mitre ever imparted greater satisfaction to the wearer than did that of the trencher cap (the one which of all in the shop had the longest tassel) in the instance. "Hostess, a cup of the smallest ale!" quoth I, as the similarity of what the dramatic folks call "situation" struck me most forcibly. We drank it at the Angel door, while the clock of St. Mary's was striking eleven, and at six o'clock I was seated at Vivian's, in Guildford Street, at dinner with a party to which I had been for some time engaged. The absolute necessity of my being in London the following day indeed, and the suddenness of our call to the University, alone prevented my carrying into execution a plan I had very much at heart, viz. that of taking the liberty of calling at Kingston Lisle on my way home.

I have little or no news to tell you, though we are not quite so dull here just at present as we, or at least I, have been. I have had two dinners lately, both of them amusing enough in their way, and the more so perhaps from the contrast they offer to each other. The one was with my Lord Mayor, whom I attended in my capacity as chaplain to the Worshipful Company of Vintners (of which he is a member) on the occasion of his presenting the livery of that company and the freedom of the City, in an *oak* box (for the precious metals are rarely now called into play on these occasions), to the redoubted Captain [Nares], who prosed in a style decidedly hyper*bore*an, and who, though he has found out the magnetic pole, seems as far as I can judge, little likely to discover the longitude. The gold plate was superb and the banquet faultless. The few speeches that were made were of the most approved fashion— "Unaccustomed as I am to speaking, I should be unworthy the name of a man and a Briton," etc., etc. And as the *Morning Post* saith, "The evening concluded with the utmost festivity."

The other was a small quiet party at the Garrick, where a dozen persons sat down to a "leg of mutton and trimmings," the latter end of last week.

Hook and Mathews, who were of the party, worried John Murray— whom the former named (from his incautiously giving his opinion of a book of which, it came out, he had only seen the back) "the Hind-Quarterly Reviewer"—in a manner that, as "Ebony" would say, "It was just a curiosity to see!" About the small hours Hook started off, as he often does when in his happiest vein, in an improvisatory gallopade, and gave every one in the room his extempore stanza, and every stanza, as usual, an epigram. This is a most extraordinary proof of talent, as, from the fact of every point he made relating to something which has passed in the course of the evening, you saw at once that it was impossible he could have come previously prepared.

And now, my dear Madam, having bestowed all my tediousness upon you, let me take my leave while you have any patience left. You will be glad to hear that Mrs. Barham has wonderfully improved in her health of late, and has so far got rid of her lameness that she walked with me the other day to Jermyn Street and back, without feeling the slightest inconvenience either at the time or since. She begs to join with me in kindest regards to you and yours. Dick is now spending his Easter vacation with his uncle, Colonel Smart, at Dover; and, from a letter which I received yesterday, seems to be enjoying himself there not a little. The rest of the family, thank God, are all in excellent health and spirits, and we are looking forward with hope to a pleasant summer, in spite of Joe Hume and the Trades Unions. Mr. Capel, who was of the party at the Mansion House, inquired earnestly after you, and, when I told him I was about to write, begged me to add his kindest remembrances to those of, my dear Madam,

Your ever obliged servant,

R. H. BARHAM

GEORGE LIONEL DAWSON-DAMER (1788–1856)

The writer of this letter was the third son of the 1st Earl of Portarlington. He joined the army at a very early age, and in 1812 went to Russia as aide-de-camp to Sir Robert Wilson, arriving in time to see the retreat of the Grande Armée. The following is his first letter home.

TO HIS MOTHER

KRASSNOI, 19TH NOVEMBER, 1812

I ARRIVED at the headquarters of the Russian Army yesterday, and am most happy to say at a most glorious moment, the French Emperor having in his retreat from Moscow lost nearly three parts of his army. He is still in full retreat, and was in this village the day before yesterday. There are daily actions with the enemy in which he always comes off worst. During the last three days he has lost 12,000 men, besides cannons, etc. etc. So rapid is his flight that he has been obliged to sacrifice everything for personal safety, having with him only the Imperial Guards and one other corps. All his baggage has been taken, even his *portefeuille*, and, of course, many valuable papers; but in fact, almost the whole of the baggage of the army has fallen into the hands of the Russians. I have seen a number of excessively curious and valuable papers belonging to different officers. You may suppose what spirit everybody is in here. The quantity of booty, between gold and silver, for the payment of his army, to an immense amount, plate and jewels, lace, coats, etc., that have been taken is such that it is almost incredible; literally the Cossacks asking you to give them some paper money for a handful of the French gold. Anybody having a sum of money might really have made enormous profit by buying the gold, that will not pass among the shopkeepers that follow an army. The French have had nothing to eat for months but horseflesh; every dead horse we meet with on the road had part of him cut off; I think the rump and the shoulder appear the most favourite bits.

Notwithstanding one's being glad to see the French so well beaten, they are still very much to be pitied. *Rushy* has none for them. . . .

From famine and cold, thousands surrender themselves voluntarily, and every night when the fires are lighted, they come literally into *this* village to get food, and are, of course, taken. The soldiers in general strip them almost naked, and of course in this climate many perish.

. . . .

The prisoners all say there have been disturbances in Paris. Bonaparte, they say, vents his rage on Murat, whom he kicks at all hours of the day.

. . . .

The French have begged for peace over and over, but I do not think at present that event can take place.

MICHAEL FARADAY (1791–1867)

Faraday was originally apprenticed as a bookbinder, but before he was twenty-one he determined to spend his life in scientific research. He obtained through Sir Humphrey Davy a post in the laboratory of the Royal Institution, where he worked till 1861, succeeding Davy in the control of the laboratories. In 1831 Faraday discovered the principle of electro-magnetic induction. This discovery opened the door to all the subsequent utilization of electricity which may be said to have changed the face of our civilization. The following letter was written to Sarah Barnard, whom he afterwards married.

ROYAL INSTITUTION, THURSDAY EVENING

MY DEAR SARAH, It is astonishing how much the state of the body influences the powers of the mind. I have been thinking all the morning of the very delightful and interesting letter I would send you this evening, and now I am so tired, and yet have so much to do, that my thoughts are quite giddy, and run round your image without power of themselves to stop and admire it. I want to say a thousand kind and, believe me, heartfelt things to you, but am not master of words fit for the purpose; and still, as I ponder and think on you, chlorides, trials oil, Davy, steel, miscellanea, mercury, and fifty other professional fancies swim before me farther and farther into the quandary of stupidness.

Ever your affectionate,

MICHAEL

PERCY BYSSHE SHELLEY (1792–1822)

When Shelley wrote the following he had gone to Italy with Mary Godwin on his last visit, and was living at Naples, where, at the time this letter was written, he had composed the "Lines Written in Dejection." Shelley's letters to Peacock place him, according to Richard Garnett, "at the head of English epistolographers" of a descriptive style.

TO THOMAS LOVE PEACOCK

NAPLES, DECEMBER 22, 1818

MY DEAR PEACOCK, I have received a letter from you here, dated November 1st; you see the reciprocation of letters from the term of our travels is more slow. I entirely agree with what you say about *Childe Harold.* The spirit in which it is written is, if insane, the most wicked and mischievous insanity that ever was given forth. It is a kind of obstinate and self-willed folly, in which he hardens himself. I remonstrated with him in vain on the tone of mind from which such a view of things alone arises. For its real root is very different from its apparent one. Nothing can be less sublime than the true source of these expressions of contempt and desperation. The fact is, that first, the Italian women with whom he associates, are perhaps the most contemptible of all who exist under the moon—the most ignorant, the most disgusting, the most bigoted; countless smell so strongly of garlic, that an ordinary Englishman cannot approach them. Well, L. B. is familiar with the lowest sort of these women, the people his gondolieri pick up in the streets. He associates with wretches who seem almost to have lost the gait and physiognomy of man, and who do not scruple to avow practices which are not only not named, but I believe seldom even conceived in England. He says he disapproves, but he endures. He is heartily and deeply discontented with himself; and contemplating in the distorted mirror of his own thoughts the nature and the destiny of man, what can he behold but objects of contempt and despair? But that he is a great poet, I think the address to Ocean proves. And he has a certain degree of candour while you talk to him, but unfortunately it does not outlast your departure. No,

I do not doubt, and, for his sake, I ought to hope, that his present career must end soon in some violent circumstance.

Since I last wrote to you, I have seen the ruins of Rome, the Vatican, St. Peter's, and all the miracles of ancient and modern art contained in that majestic city. The impression of it exceeds anything I have ever experienced in my travels. We stayed there only a week, intending to return at the end of February, and devote two or three months to its mines of inexhaustible contemplation, to which period I refer you for a minute account of it. We visited the Forum and the ruins of the Coliseum every day. The Coliseum is unlike any work of human hands I ever saw before. It is of enormous height and circuit, and the arches built of massy stones are piled on one another, and jut into the blue air, shattered into the forms of overhanging rocks. It has been changed by time into the image of an amphitheatre of rocky hills overgrown by the wild olive, the myrtle, and the fig-tree, and threaded by little paths, which wind among its ruined stairs and immeasurable galleries: the copsewood overshadows you as you wander through its labyrinths, and the wild weeds of this climate of flowers bloom under your feet. The arena is covered with grass, and pierces, like the skirts of a natural plain, the chasms of the broken arches around. But a small part of the exterior circumference remains—it is exquisitely light and beautiful; and the effect of the perfection of its architecture, adorned with ranges of Corinthian pilasters, supporting a bold cornice, is such as to diminish the effect of its greatness. The interior is all ruin. I can scarcely believe that when encrusted with Dorian marble and ornamented by columns of Egyptian granite, its effect could have been so sublime and so impressive as in its present state. It is open to the sky, and it was the clear and sunny weather of the end of November in this climate when we visited it, day after day.

Near it is the arch of Constantine, or rather the arch of Trajan; for the servile and avaricious senate of degraded Rome ordered that the monument of his predecessor should be demolished in order to dedicate one to the Christian reptile, who had crept among the blood of his murdered family to the supreme power. It is exquisitely beautiful and perfect. The Forum is a plain in the midst of Rome, a kind of desert full of heaps of stones and pits, and though so near the habitations of men, is the most desolate place you can conceive. The ruins of temples stand in and around it, shattered columns and ranges of others complete, supporting cornices of exquisite workmanship, and vast vaults of shattered domes distinct with regular compartments, once filled with sculptures of ivory or brass. The temples of Jupiter, and Concord, and Peace, and the Sun, and the Moon, and Vesta, are all within a short distance of this spot. Behold the wrecks of what a great nation once dedicated to the abstractions of the mind! Rome is a city, as it were, of the dead, or rather of those who cannot die, and who survive the puny generations which inhabit and pass over the spot which they have made sacred to eternity. In Rome, at least in the first enthusiasm of your recognition of ancient time, you see nothing of the Italians. The nature of the city assists the delusion, for its vast and antique walls describe a circumference of sixteen miles, and thus the population is thinly scattered over this space, nearly as great as London. Wide wild fields are enclosed within it, and there are grassy lanes and copses winding among the ruins, and a great green hill, lonely and bare, which overhangs the Tiber. The gardens of the modern palaces are like wild woods of cedar, and cypress, and pine, and the neglected walks are overgrown with weeds. The English burying-place is a green slope near the walls, under the pyramidal tomb of Cestius, and is, I think, the most beautiful and solemn cemetery I ever beheld. To see the sun shining on its bright grass, fresh, when we first visited it, with the autumnal dews, and hear the whispering of the wind among the leaves of the trees which have overgrown the tomb of Cestius, and the soil which is stirring in the sun-warm earth, and to mark the tombs, mostly of women and young people who were buried there, one might, if one were to die, desire the sleep they seem to sleep. Such is the human mind, and so it peoples with its wishes vacancy and oblivion.

I have told you little about Rome; but I reserve the Pantheon, and St. Peter's, and the Vatican, and Raphael, for my return. About a fortnight ago I left Rome, and Mary and Claire followed in three days, for it was necessary to procure lodgings here without alighting at an inn. From my peculiar mode of travelling I saw little of the country, but could just observe that the wild beauty of the scenery and the barbarous ferocity of the inhabitants progressively increased. On entering Naples, the first circumstance that engaged my attention was an assassination. A youth ran out of a shop, pursued by a woman with a bludgeon, and a man armed with a knife. The man overtook him, and with one blow in the neck laid him dead in the road. On my expressing the emotions of horror and indignation which I felt, a Calabrian priest, who travelled with me, laughed heartily, and attempted to quiz me, as what the English call a flat. I never felt such an inclination to beat any one. Heaven knows I have little power, but he saw that I looked extremely displeased, and was silent. This same man, a fellow of gigantic strength and stature, had expressed the most frantic terror of robbers on the road: he cried at the sight of my pistol, and it had been with great difficulty that the joint exertions of myself and the vetturino had quieted his hysterics.

But external nature in these delightful regions contrasts with and compensates for the deformity and degradation of humanity. We have a lodging divided from the sea by the royal gardens, and from our windows we see perpetually the blue waters of the bay, forever changing, yet forever the same, and encompassed by the mountainous island of Capreae, the lofty peaks which overhang Salerno, and the woody hill of Posilipo, whose promontories hide from us Misenum and the lofty isle Inarime, which, with its divided summit, forms the opposite horn of the bay. From the pleasant walks of the garden we see Vesuvius; a smoke by day and a fire by night is seen upon its summit, and the glassy sea often reflects its light or shadow. The climate is delicious. We sit without a fire, with the windows open, and have almost all the productions of an English summer. The weather is usually like what Wordsworth calls 'the first fine day of March'; sometimes very much warmer, though perhaps it wants that 'each minute sweeter than before,' which gives an intoxicating sweetness to the awakening of the earth from its winter's sleep in England. We have made two excursions, one to Baiae and one to Vesuvius, and we propose to visit, successively, the islands, Paestum, Pompeii, and Beneventum.

We set off an hour after sunrise one radiant morning in a little boat; there was not a cloud in the sky, nor a wave upon the sea, which was so translucent that you could see the hollow caverns clothed with the glaucous sea-moss, and the leaves and branches of those delicate weeds that pave the unequal bottom of the water. As noon approached, the heat, and especially the light, became intense. We passed Posilipo, and came first to the eastern point of the bay of Puzzoli, which is within the great bay of Naples, and which again incloses that of Baiae. Here are lofty rocks and craggy islets, with arches and portals of precipice standing in the sea, and enormous caverns, which echoed faintly with the murmur of the languid tide. This is called La Scuola di Virgilio. We then went directly across to the promontory of Misenum, leaving the precipitous island of Nesida on the right. Here we were conducted to see the Mare Morto, and the Elysian fields; the spot on which Virgil places the scenery of the Sixth *Aeneid*. Though extremely beautiful, as a lake, and woody hills, and this divine sky must make it, I confess my disappointment. The guide showed us an antique cemetery, where the niches used for placing the cinerary urns of the dead yet remain. We then coasted the Bay of Baiae to the left, in which we saw many picturesque and interesting ruins; but I have to remark that we never disembarked but we were disappointed—while from the boat the effect of the scenery was inexpressibly delightful. The colours of the water and the air breathe over all things here the radiance of their own beauty. After passing the Bay of Baiae, and observing the ruins of its antique grandeur standing like rocks in the transparent sea under our boat, we landed to visit lake Avernus. We passed through the cavern of the Sibyl (not Virgil's Sibyl) which pierces one of the hills which circumscribe the lake, and came to a calm and lovely basin of water, surrounded by dark woody hills, and profoundly solitary. Some vast ruins of the temple of Pluto stand on a lawny hill on one side of it, and are reflected in its windless mirror. It is far more beautiful than the Elysian fields— but there are all the materials for beauty in the latter, and the Avernus was once a chasm of deadly and pestilential vapours. About half a mile from Avernus, a high hill, called Monte Novo, was thrown up by volcanic fire.

Passing onward we came to Pozzoli, the ancient Dicaearchea, where there are the columns remaining of a temple to Serapis, and the wreck of an enormous amphitheatre, changed, like the Coliseum, into a natural hill of the overteeming vegetation. Here also is the Solfatara, of which there is a poetical description in the *Civil War* of Petronius, beginning—'Est locus,' and in which the verses of the poet are infinitely finer than what he describes, for it is not a very curious place. After seeing these things we returned by moonlight to Naples in our boat. What colours there were in the sky, what radiance in the evening star, and how the moon was encompassed by a light unknown to our regions!

Our next excursion was to Vesuvius. We went to Resina in a carriage, where Mary and I mounted mules, and Claire was carried in a chair on the shoulders of four men, much like a Member of Parliament after he has gained his election, and looking, with less reason, quite as frightened. So we arrived at the hermitage of San Salvador, where an old hermit, belted with rope, set forth the plates for our refreshment.

Vesuvius is, after the glaciers, the most impressive exhibition of the energies of nature I ever saw. It has not the immeasurable greatness, the overpowering magnificence, nor, above all, the radiant beauty of the glaciers; but it has all their character of tremendous and irresistible strength. From Resina to the hermitage you wind up the mountain, and cross a vast stream of hardened lava, which is an actual image of the waves of the sea, changed into hard black stone by enchantment. The lines of the boiling flood seem to hang in the air, and it is difficult to believe that the billows which seem hurrying down upon you are not actually in motion. This plain was once a sea of liquid fire. From the hermitage we crossed another vast stream of lava, and then went on foot up the cone—this is the only part of the ascent in which there is any difficulty, and that difficulty has been much exaggerated. It is composed of rocks of lava, and declivities of ashes; by ascending the former and descending the latter, there is very little fatigue. On the summit is a kind of irregular plain, the most horrible chaos that can be imagined; riven into ghastly chasms, and heaped up with tumuli of great stones and cinders, and enormous rocks blackened and calcined, which had been thrown from the volcano upon one another in terrible confusion. In the midst stands the conical hill from which volumes of smoke, and the fountains of liquid fire, are rolled forth forever. The mountain is at present in a slight state of eruption; and a thick heavy white smoke is perpetually rolled out, interrupted by enormous columns of an impenetrable black bituminous vapour, which is hurled up, fold after fold, into the sky with a deep hollow sound, and fiery stones are rained down from its darkness, and a black shower of ashes fell even where we sat. The lava, like the glacier, creeps on perpetually, with a crackling sound as of suppressed fire. There are several springs of lava; and in one place it rushes precipitously over a high crag, rolling down the half-molten rocks and its own overhanging waves; a cataract of quivering fire. We approached the extremity of one of the rivers of lava; it is about twenty feet in breadth and ten in height; and as the inclined plane was not rapid, its motion was very slow. We saw the masses of its dark exterior surface detach themselves as it moved, and betray the depth of the liquid flame. In the day the fire is but slightly seen; you only observe a tremulous motion in the air, and streams and fountains of white sulphurous smoke.

At length we saw the sun sink between Capreae and Inarime, and, as the darkness increased, the effect of the fire became more beautiful. We were, as it were, surrounded by streams and cataracts of the red and radiant fire; and in the midst, from the column of bituminous smoke shot up into the air, fell the vast masses of rock, white with the light of their intense heat, leaving behind them through the dark vapour trains of splendour. We descended by torch-light, and I should have enjoyed the scenery on my return, but they conducted me, I know not how, to the hermitage in a state of intense bodily suffering, the worst effect of which was spoiling the pleasure of Mary and Claire. Our guides on the occasion were complete savages. You have no idea of the horrible cries which they suddenly utter, no one knows why; the clamour, the vociferation, the tumult. Claire in her palanquin suffered most from it; and when I had gone on before, they threatened to leave her in the middle of the road, which they would have done had not my Italian servant promised them a beating, after which they became quiet. Nothing, however, can be more picturesque than the gestures and the physiognomies of these savage people. And when, in the darkness of night, they unexpectedly begin to sing in chorus some fragments of their wild but sweet national music, the effect is exceedingly fine.

Since I wrote this, I have seen the museum of this city. Such statues! There is a Venus; an ideal shape of the most winning loveliness. A Bacchus, more sublime than any living being. A Satyr, making love to a youth: in which the expressed life of the sculpture, and the inconceivable beauty of the form of the youth, overcome one's repugnance to the subject. There are multitudes of wonderfully fine statues found in Herculaneum and Pompeii. We are going to see Pompeii the first day that the sea is waveless. Herculaneum is almost filled up; no more excavations are made; the king bought the ground and built a palace upon it.

You don't see much of Hunt. I wish you could contrive to see him when you go to town, and ask him what he means to answer to Lord Byron's invitation. He has now an opportunity, if he likes, of seeing Italy. What do you think of joining his party, and paying us a visit next year; I mean as soon as the reign of winter is dissolved? Write to me your thoughts upon this. I cannot express to you the pleasure it would give me to welcome such a party.

I have depression enough of spirits and not good health, though I believe the warm air of Naples does me good. We see absolutely no one here.

Adieu, my dear Peacock,
Affectionately your friend,
P. B. S.

FREDERICK MARRYAT (1792–1848)

Captain Marryat was already a writer of fame when he sent this letter to Lady Blessington. It reflects in characteristically breezy terms his pleasure at doing nothing, and his dislike, amounting to disgust, of Democracy.

TO LADY BLESSINGTON

SPA, JUNE 17, 1836

MY DEAR LADY BLESSINGTON, . . . Of course I do see the English papers, and I am very much disgusted. Nothing but duels and blackguardism. Surely we are extremely altered by this reform. Our House of Lords was the beau ideal of all that was aristocratical and elegant. Now we have language that would disgrace the hustings. In the House of Commons it is the same, or even worse. The gentlemen's repartee, the quiet sarcasm, the playful hit, where are they? all gone; and in exchange for them, we have *you* lie, and *you lie*. This is very bad, and, it appears to me, strongly smacking of revolution; for if the language of the lower classes is to take precedence, will not they also do the same? I am becoming more Conservative every day; I cannot help it: I feel it a duty as a lover of my country. I only hope that others feel the same, and that Peel will soon be again what he ought to be. I don't know what your politics are, but all women are Tories in their hearts, or perhaps Conservatives is a better word, as it expresses not only their opinion but their feelings.

I never thought that I should feel a pleasure in idleness; but I do now. I had done too much, and I required repose, *or rather repose to some portions of my brain.* I am idle here to my heart's content, and each day is but the precursor of its second. I am like a horse, which has been worked too hard, turned out to grass, and I hope I shall come out again as fresh as a two-year-old. I walk about and pick early flowers with the children, sit on a bench in the beautiful *allées vertes* which we have here, smoke my cigar, and meditate till long after the moon is in the zenith. Then I lie on the sofa and read French novels, or I gossip with anyone I can pick up in the streets. Besides which,

627

I wear out all my old clothes; and there is a great pleasure in having a coat on which gives you no anxiety. I expect that by October I shall be all right again.

I am afraid this will be a very uninteresting letter; but what can you expect from one who is living the life of a hermit, and who never even takes the trouble to wind up his watch; who takes no heed of time, and feels an interest in the price of strawberries and green peas, because the children are very fond of them? I believe that this is the first epoch of real quiet that I have had in my stormy life, and every day I feel more and more inclined to dream away my existence.

Farewell! my dear Lady Blessington; present my best wishes to the Count D'Orsay *beau et brave*. I have found out a fly-fisher here, and I intend to be initiated into the sublime art. There is a quiet and repose about fly-fishing that I am sure will agree with me. While your line is on the water, you may be up in the clouds, and everything goes on just as well. Once more, with many thanks, adieu.

F. MARRYAT

LORD JOHN RUSSELL (1792–1878)

In addition to his great political activities Lord John was a man of considerable literary abilities and tastes. One of his early friendships was with the poet Thomas Moore, whose life and correspondence he later edited.

TO THOMAS MOORE

STEBBING, OCTOBER 23, 1827

DEAR MOORE, I was very sorry to find you had declined coming to Chatsworth when I was there. But I suppose Clio and Mrs. Moore have beckoned you back to Sloperton. However, I have no right to complain, as I altered my plan of going to Bowood for the purpose of keeping a previous engagement to visit the Duke of Devon this autumn.

I have been several times considering what I could furnish you about Lord Byron, and it is so little that it is not worth making a separate paper of.

I recollect he shows in the beginning of the memoirs that extreme sensitiveness about his leg, which he always retained. I think he says that when he was in love with Miss Chaworth, being about twelve years old, he was mortally offended by hearing she had said to her maid, "What! Do you think I can care about that lame boy?" he directly set off home some seven or eight miles without taking leave of her or any of the family. We may remember that he was always afterwards very touchy about this leg, and no doubt he fancied himself the Black Dwarf and other things.

I recollect that when in Greece he speaks of the delight he had in swimming and in sitting naked upon a rock, looking upon the port of Athens. When he comes home he does not at first think of "Childe Harold," but of something else he had written, and when he shows the Childe to his friends, Rogers and one or two others, they agree that it won't do. Someone told him it was too good for the age. Rogers says it was not him. The success was, we all know, prodigious—a rage. Rogers says he used to be asked by ladies to get him to sit next to them at supper, &c., &c., &c. He describes the blue-stocking parties, with a number of young ladies at the back "trying hard to look wise, and all the prettier for not succeeding."

About his married life, the less you say the better. And there are more reasons than one why I wish you to be tender of his wife and sister, not to praise them unduly, of course, but to respect their feelings in the unpleasant situation in which they stand to the world.

In the latter part of his life I do not remember anything, and indeed the whole merit of his MSS. was, as Lady H. says, in the impression; he praises Lady Byron very much for her acquirements, and says they were only diminished by the unjustly low opinion she had of them herself.

One of his poems, "The Giaour," I think, was entirely written after he returned home from balls in London at 2 or 3 in the morning.

Write to Lady Blessington to get you the papers from the merchant at Genoa, and also the lines he addressed to her, which are some of them very good.

All that scene about his marriage, which has been often alluded to, I suppose you will leave out. You may say, however, that he denied having said he would be revenged on her for refusing him, when he got into the carriage. Perhaps he said it in joke.

If I recollect more I will write again. I think, on the whole, with Greece at the beginning and the end, London life, Venice, and Ravenna, you may work up a pretty story enough.

I see W. Scott, in his "Life of Napoleon," emulates your love of similes and poetical ornament. But he fails most egregiously, and his writing is as bad as the substance of his history—bad stuff altogether!

Mrs. Arkwright delighted us at Chatsworth by her singing. But we missed you the more. Remember me kindly to Mrs. Moore. What does she think of the present administration, and the chance of its lasting?

Yours faithfully,
J. RUSSELL

Pray write—to St. James's Square.

FELICIA DOROTHEA HEMANS (1793-1835)

Here is a very characteristic letter written by Mrs. Hemans during a visit to Scotland, where she had met the great Sir Walter and had fallen a victim to his delightful personality.

CHIEFSWOOD, JULY 20, 1829

WHETHER I shall return to you all "brighter and happier," as your letter so kindly prophesies, I know not: but I think there is every prospect of my returning more fitful and wilful than ever; for here I am leading my own free native life of the hills again, and if I could but bring some of my friends, as the old ballad says, "near, near, *near* me," I should indeed enjoy it. But that strange solitary feeling which I cannot chase away, comes over me too often like a dark sudden shadow, bringing with it an utter indifference to all things around. I lose it most frequently, however, in the excitement of Sir Walter Scott's society. And with him I am now in constant intercourse, taking long walks over moor and woodland, and listening to song and legend of other times, until my mind quite forgets itself, and is carried wholly back to the days of the Slogan and the fiery cross, and the wild gatherings of border chivalry. I cannot say enough of his cordial kindness to me; it makes me feel when at Abbotsford, as if the stately rooms of the proud ancestral-looking place, were old familiar scenes to me. Yesterday he made a party to show me the "pleasant banks of Yarrow," about ten miles from hence. I went with him in an open carriage, and the day was lovely, smiling upon us with a *real blue* sunny sky, and we passed through I know not how many storied spots, and the spirit of the master-mind seemed to call up sudden pictures from every knoll and cairn as we went by—so vivid were his descriptions of the things that had been. The *names* of some of those scenes had, to be sure, rather savage sounds; such as "*Slain Man's Lea*," "*Dead Man's Pool*," etc., etc.; but I do not know whether these strange titles did not throw a deeper interest over woods and waters now so brightly peaceful. We passed one meadow on which Sir Walter's grandfather had been killed in a duel; "had it been a century earlier," said he, "a bloody feud would have been transmitted to me, as Spaniards bequeath

631

a game of chess to be finished by their children." And I do think, that had *he* lived in those earlier days, no man would have more enjoyed what Sir Lucius O'Trigger is pleased to call "*a pretty quarrel.*" The whole expression of his benevolent countenance changes if he has but to speak of the dirk or the claymore: you see the spirit that would "say amidst the trumpets, ha! ha!" suddenly flashing from his grey eyes, and sometimes, in repeating a verse of warlike minstrelsy, he will spring up as if he sought the sound of a distant gathering cry. But I am forgetting beautiful Yarrow, along the banks of which we walked through the Duke of Buccleugh's grounds, under old rich patrician trees; and at every turn of our path the mountain stream seemed to assume a new character, sometimes lying under steep banks in dark transparence, sometimes

> crested with tawny foam,
> Like the mane of a chestnut steed.

And there was Sir Walter beside me, repeating, with a tone of feeling as deep as if *then* only first wakened—

> They sought him east, they sought him west,
> They sought him far with wail and sorrow;
> There was nothing seen but the coming night,
> And nothing heard but the roar of Yarrow.

It was all like a dream. Do you remember Wordsworth's beautiful poem "Yarrow visited"? I was ready to exclaim, in its opening words— "And is this Yarrow?" There was nothing to disturb the deep and often solemn loveliness of the scenery: no *rose-coloured* spencers such as persecuted the unhappy Count Forbin amidst the pyramids. Mr. Hamilton, and Mrs. Lockhart, and the boys, who followed us, were our whole party; and the sight of shepherds, real, not Arcadian shepherds, sleeping under their plaids to shelter from the noon-day, carried me at once into the heart of a pastoral and mountain country. We visited Newark tower, where, amongst other objects that awakened many thoughts, I found the name of Mungo Park (who was a native of the Yarrow vale), which he had inscribed himself, shortly before leaving his own bright river never to return. We came back to Abbotsford, where we were to pass the remainder of the day, partly along the Ettrick, and partly *through* the Tweed; on the way, we were talking of trees, in his love for which Sir Walter is a perfect Evelyn. I mentioned to him what I once spoke of to you, the different sounds they give forth to the wind, which he had observed, and he asked me if I did not think that a union of music and poetry, varying in measure and expression, might in some degree imitate or represent those "voices of the trees"; and he described to me some Highland music of a similar imitative character, called the "notes of the sea-birds," barbaric notes truly they must be! In the evening we had a good deal of music: he is particularly fond of national airs, and I played him many, for which I wish you had heard how kindly and gracefully he thanked me. But, O! the bright swords! I must not forget to tell you how I sat, like Minna in "The Pirate" (though *she* stood or moved, I believe), the very "queen of swords." I have the strongest love for the flash of glittering steel—and Sir Walter brought out I know not how many gallant blades to show me; one which had fought at Killicrankie, and one which had belonged to the young Prince Henry, James the First's son, and one which looked of as noble race and temper as that with which Cœur de Lion severed the block of steel in Saladin's tent. What a number of things I have yet to tell you! I feel sure that my greatest pleasure from all these new objects of interest will arise from talking them over with you when I return. . . .

Ever faithfully yours,

F. H.

JOSEPH SEVERN (1793–1879)

Severn the painter will ever be remembered as the last and loyal friend of John Keats. This letter was written the day before the poet died. It was in Severn's arms that Keats breathed his last, murmuring, "Thank God, it has come."

TO JOHN HASLAM

FEBRUARY 22ND.

MY DEAR HASLAM, O, how anxious I am to hear from you! I have nothing to break this dreadful solitude but letters. Day after day, night after night, here I am by our poor dying friend. My spirits, my intellect, and my health are breaking down. I can get no one to change with me—no one to relieve me. All run away, and even if they did not, Keats would not do without me. Last night I thought he was going, I could hear the phlegm in his throat, he bade me lift him up on the bed or he would die with pain. I watched him all night, expecting him to be suffocated at every cough. This morning by the pale daylight, the change in him frightened me; he has sunk in the last three days to a most ghastly look. Though Dr. Clark has prepared me for the worst, I shall ill bear to be set free even from this, my horrible situation, by the loss of him. I am still quite precluded from painting, which may be of consequence to me. Poor Keats has me ever by him, and shadows out the form of one solitary friend; he opens his eyes in great doubt and horror, but when they fall upon me they close gently, open quietly and close again, till he sinks to sleep. This thought alone would keep me by him till he dies; and why did I say I was losing my time? The advantages I have gained by knowing John Keats are double and treble any I could have won by any other occupation.

WILLIAM WHEWELL (1794–1866)

Master of Trinity and the leading Cambridge scholar of his time, Whewell was a man of very wide interests and of deep domestic affection. In the following letter he speculates as to the authorship of "Jane Eyre."

TO HIS WIFE

TRINITY LODGE : NOV. 8, 1849

I HAVE been considering how much of their interest all the letters which I have opened lose by your not being here to read them and talk them over with me. I am disposed to think that if I were to say they lose nine-tenths of their charm it would be saying too much; but if I were only to say that they lose five-sixths, it would certainly be saying too little. But you do not comprehend these fractional ways of talking of such matters!

I had a very pleasant breakfast at Dr. Holland's with Mrs. Holland and the two girls, and Lord Lansdowne, with whom I afterwards walked down to Berkeley Square. Then at the Athenæum I met James Ross, just rushing in from Baffin's Bay. I was sorry to find that he had no belief in the Esquimaux stories which they have put in the newspapers, and very little hope about Sir J. Franklin. I was glad to see him safe and well, and also to hear from him that Sir J. Richardson was safely arrived at Liverpool.

I am glad you find the "Lives of the Lindsays" better, or at least less factitious and fictitious, and more real, than you at first expected. I, on my part, have been somewhat disturbed at having to send on "Shirley" without your reading it. For a good novel which we both read is like a new and clever acquaintance which we have in common, and "Shirley" is, I think, much cleverer and more dramatic than "Jane Eyre." Then it puzzles me much as to the sex of the writer. It has even more of the cleverness, largeness of speculation and audacity, which made me think "Jane Eyre" a masculine performance; but then there are some ways of dealing with male and female relations which look like feminine workmanship. For instance, all the women fall in love with the men, which I think a female characteristic. But if it be a woman's book, women are growing to be very strange and alarming creatures.

There goes the fly, rumbling, rumbling, rumbling, across the court with Sedgwick's female creatures. I told you he had a party to-night.

JOHN KEATS (1795–1821)

Lord Houghton has said that the life of Keats "may be summed up in the composition of three small volumes of verse, some earnest friendships, one passion, and a premature death." He himself asked that his epitaph should be

HERE LIES ONE WHOSE NAME WAS WRIT IN WATER

but critics have united ever since in acclaiming him as one of the most gifted of all our poets. The close of his life is described in a letter by Joseph Severn, printed three pages earlier. His own letters are particularly self-revealing.

TO B. R. HAYDON

[MARGATE, MAY 1817]

MY DEAR HAYDON,

> Let Fame, that all pant after in their lives,
> Live registered upon our brazen tombs,
> And so grace us in the disguise of death;
> When, spite of cormorant devouring Time,
> The endeavour of this present breath may bring
> That honour which shall bate his scythe's keen edge,
> And make us heirs of all eternity.

To think that I have no right to couple myself with you in this speech would be death to me, so I have e'en written it, and I pray God that our "brazen tombs" be nigh neighbours. It cannot be long first; the "endeavour of this present breath" will soon be over, and yet it is as well to breathe freely during our sojourn—it is as well if you have not been teased with that money affair, that bill-pestilence. However, I must think that difficulties nerve the spirit of a man, they make our prime objects a refuge as well as a passion; the trumpet of Fame is as a tower of strength, the ambitious bloweth it, and is safe. I suppose, by your telling me not to give way to forebodings, George has been telling you what I have lately said in my letters to him; truth is, I have been in such a state of mind as to read over my lines and to hate them. I am one that "gathereth samphire, dreadful trade"; the

637

cliff of Poetry towers above me; yet when my brother reads some of Pope's "Homer," or Plutarch's Lives, they seem like music to mine. I read and write about eight hours a-day. There is an old saying, "Well begun is half done"; 'tis a bad one; I would use instead, "Not begun at all till half done"; so, according to that, I have not begun my Poem ["Endymion"], and consequently, *a priori*, can say nothing about it; thank God, I do begin ardently, when I leave off, notwithstanding my occasional depressions, and I hope for the support of a high power while I climb this little eminence, and especially in my years of more momentous labour. I remember your saying that you had notions of a good Genius presiding over you. I have lately had the same thought, for things which, done half at random, are afterwards confirmed by my judgment in a dozen features of propriety. Is it too daring to fancy Shakespeare this presider? When in the Isle of Wight I met with a Shakespeare in the passage of the house at which I lodged. It comes nearer to my idea of him than any I have seen; I was but there a week, yet the old woman made me take it with me, though I went off in a hurry. Do you not think this ominous of good? I am glad you say every man of great views is at times tormented as I am.

(*Sunday after.*) This morning I received a letter from George by which it appears that money troubles are to follow up for some time to come—perhaps for always: those vexations are a great hindrance to one; they are not, like envy and detraction, stimulants to further exertion, as being immediately relative and reflected on at the same time with the prime object; but rather like a nettle-leaf or two in your bed. So now I revoke my promise of finishing my Poem by Autumn, which I should have done had I gone on as I have done. But I cannot write while my spirit is fevered in a contrary direction, and I am now sure of having plenty of it this summer; at this moment I am in no enviable situation. I feel that I am not in a mood to write any to-day, and it appears that the loss of it is the beginning of all sorts of irregularities. I am extremely glad that a time must come when everything will leave not a wrack behind. You tell me never to despair. I wish it was as easy for me to observe this saying: truth is, I have a horrid morbidity of temperament, which has shown itself at intervals; it is, I have no doubt, the greatest stumbling-block I have to fear; I may surer say, it is likely to be the cause of my disappointment. However, every ill has its share of good; this, my bane, would at any time enable me to look with an obstinate eye on the very devil himself; or, to be as proud to be the lowest of the human race, as Alfred would be in being of the highest. I am very sure that you do love me as your very brother. I have seen it in your continual anxiety for me, and I assure you that your welfare and fame is, and will be, a chief pleasure to me all my life. I know no one but you who can be fully aware of the turmoil and anxiety, the sacrifice of all that is called comfort, the readiness to measure time by what is done, and to die in six hours, could plans be brought to conclusions; the looking on the sun, the moon, the stars, the earth, and its contents, as materials to form greater things, that is to say, ethereal things—but here I am talking like a madman,—greater things than our Creator himself made.

I wrote to —— yesterday: scarcely know what I said in it; I could not talk about poetry in the way I should have liked, for I was not in humour with either his or mine. There is no greater sin, after the seven deadly, than to flatter one's self into the idea of being a great poet, or one of those beings who are privileged to wear out their lives in the pursuit of honour. How comfortable a thing it is to feel that such a crime must bring its heavy penalty, that if one be a self-deluder, accounts must be balanced! I am glad you are hard at work; it will now soon be done. I long to see Wordsworth's, as well as to have mine in; but I would rather not show my face in town till the end of the year, if that would be time enough; if not, I shall be disappointed if you do not write me ever when you think best. I never quite despair, and I read Shakespeare,—indeed, I shall, I think, never read any other book much; now this might lead me to a very long confab, but I desist. I am very near agreeing with Hazlitt, that Shakespeare is enough for us.

You should have heard from me before this, but, in the first place, I did not like to do so, before I had got a little way in the first Book, and in the next, as G. told me you were going to write, I delayed till I heard from you. So now in the name of Shakespeare, Raphael, and all our Saints, I commend you to the care of Heaven.

Your everlasting friend,

JOHN KEATS

TO HIS PUBLISHER

10TH JULY, 1817

MY DEAR SIR, A couple of Duns that I thought would be silent till the beginning, at least, of next month, (when I am certain to be on my legs, for certain sure,) have opened upon me with a cry most "untunable." Never did you hear such "ungallant chiding." Now, you must know, I am not desolate, but have, thank God, twenty-five good notes in my fob. But then, you know, I laid them by to write with, and would stand at bay a fortnight ere they should quit me. In a month's time I must pay, but it would relieve my mind if I owed you, instead of these pelican duns.

I am afraid you will say I have "wound about with circumstance," when I should have asked plainly. However, as I said, I am a little maidenish or so, and I feel my virginity come strong upon me, the while I request the loan of a £20 and a £10, which, if you enclose to me, I would acknowledge and save myself a hot forehead. I am sure you are confident of my responsibility, and in the sense of squareness that is always in me.

Yours obliged friend,

JOHN KEATS

TO J. H. REYNOLDS

HAMPSTEAD, FEB. 3, 1818

MY DEAR REYNOLDS, I thank you for your dish of filberts. Would I could get a basket of them by way of dessert every day for the sum of twopence (two sonnets on Robin Hood sent by the twopenny post). Would we were a sort of ethereal pigs, and turned loose to feed upon spiritual mast and acorns! which would be merely being a squirrel and feeding upon filberts; for what is a squirrel but an airy pig, or a filbert but a sort of archangelical acorn? About the nuts being worth cracking, all I can say is, that where there are a throng of delightful images ready drawn, simplicity is the only thing. It may be said that we ought to read our contemporaries, that Wordsworth, etc., should have their due from us. But, for the sake of a few imaginative or domestic passages, are we to be bullied into a certain philosophy engendered in the whims of an egotist? Every man has his speculations, but every man does not brood and peacock over them till he makes a false coinage and deceives himself. Many a man can travel to the very bourne of Heaven, and yet want confidence to put down his half-seeing. Sancho will invent a journey heavenward as well as anybody. We hate poetry that has a palpable design upon us, and, if we do not agree, seems to put its hand into its breeches pocket. Poetry should be great and unobtrusive, a thing which enters into one's soul, and does not startle it or amaze it with itself, but with its subject. How beautiful are the retired flowers! How would they lose their beauty were they to throng into the highway crying out, "Admire me, I am a violet! Dote upon me, I am a primrose!" Modern poets differ from the Elizabethans in this: each of the moderns, like an Elector of Hanover, governs his petty state, and knows how many straws are swept daily from the causeways in all his dominions, and has a continual itching that all the housewives should have their coppers well scoured. The ancients were emperors of vast provinces; they had only heard of the remote ones, and scarcely cared to visit them. I will cut all this. I will have no more of Wordsworth or Hunt in particular. Why should we be of the tribe of Manasseh, when we can wander with Esau? Why should we kick against the pricks when we can walk on roses? Why should we be owls, when we can be eagles? Why be teased with "nice-eyed wagtails," when we have in sight "the cherub Contemplation"? Why with Wordsworth's "Matthew with a bough of wilding in his hand," when we can have Jacques "under an oak," etc.? The secret of the "bough of wilding" will run through your head faster than I can write it. Old Matthew spoke of him some years ago on some nothing, and because he happens in an evening walk to imagine the figure of the old man, he must stamp it down in black and white, and it is henceforth sacred. I don't mean to deny Wordsworth's grandeur and Hunt's merit, but I mean to say we need not be teased with grandeur and merit when we can have them uncontaminated and unobtrusive. Let us have the old Poets and Robin Hood. Your letter and its sonnets gave me more pleasure than will the Fourth Book of "Childe Harold," and the whole of anybody's life and opinions.

In return for your dish of filberts, I have gathered a few catkins. I hope they'll look pretty.

No, those days are gone away, etc.

I hope you will like them—they are at least written in the spirit of outlawry. Here are the Mermaid lines:

Souls of Poets dead and gone, etc.

In the hope that these scribblings will be some amusement for you this evening, I remain, copying on the hill,

Your sincere friend and co-scribbler,

JOHN KEATS

E.L.   Y

TO THE SAME

[HAMPSTEAD, FEB. 19, 1818]

MY DEAR REYNOLDS, I had an idea that a man might pass a very pleasant life in this manner—let him on a certain day read a certain page of full poesy or distilled prose, and let him wander with it, and muse upon it, and reflect from it, and bring home to it, and prophesy upon it, and dream upon it, until it becomes stale. But will it do so? Never. When man has arrived at a certain ripeness of intellect, any one grand and spiritual passage serves him as a starting post towards all "the two-and-thirty palaces." How happy is such a voyage of conception—what delicious diligent indolence! A doze upon a sofa does not hinder it, and a nap upon clover engenders ethereal finger-pointings; the prattle of a child gives it wings, and the converse of middle-age a strength to beat them; a strain of music conducts to "an odd angle of the Isle," and when the leaves whisper, it puts a girdle round the earth. Nor will this sparing touch of noble books be any irreverence to their writers; for perhaps the honours paid by man to man are trifles in comparison to the benefit done by great works to the "spirit and pulse of good" by their mere passive existence. Memory should not be called knowledge. Many have original minds who do not think it: they are led away by custom. Now it appears to me that almost any man may, like the spider, spin from his own inwards, his own airy citadel. The points of leaves and twigs on which the spider begins her work are few and she fills the air with a beautiful circuiting. Man should be content with as few points to tip with the fine web of his soul, and weave a tapestry empyrean—full of symbols for his spiritual eye, of softness for his spiritual touch, of space for his wanderings, of distinctness for his luxury. But the minds of mortals are so different, and bent on such diverse journeys, that it may at first appear impossible for any common taste and fellowship to exist between two or three under these suppositions. It is however quite the contrary. Minds would leave each other in contrary directions, traverse each other in numberless points, and at last greet each other at the journey's end. An old man and a child would talk together, and the old man be led on his path and the child left thinking. Man should not dispute or assert but whisper results to his neighbour, and thus by every germ of spirit sucking the sap from mould ethereal, every human (being) might become great, and humanity, instead of being a wide heath of furze and briars, with here and there a remote oak or pine, would become a grand democracy of forest trees! It has been an old comparison for our urging on—the bee-hive; however, it seems to me that we should rather be the flower than the bee. For it is a false notion that more is gained by receiving than giving—no, the receiver and the giver are equal in their benefits. The flower, I doubt not, receives a fair guerdon from the bee. Its leaves blush deeper in the next spring. And who shall say, between man and woman, which is the most delighted? Now it is more noble to sit like Jove than to fly like Mercury:—let us not therefore go hurrying about and collecting honey, bee-like buzzing here and there for a knowledge of what is to be arrived at; but let us open our leaves like a flower, and be passive and receptive, budding patiently under the eye of Apollo and taking hints from every noble insect that favours us with a visit. Sap will be given us for meat, and dew for drink.

I was led into these thoughts, my dear Reynolds, by the beauty of the morning operating on a sense of idleness. I have not read any books—the morning said I was right—I had no idea but of the morning, and the thrush said I was right—seeming to say,

> O thou! whose face hath felt the Winter's wind,
> Whose eye hath seen the snow-clouds hung in mist
> And the black elm-tops among the freezing stars
> To thee the Spring will be a harvest-time.
> O thou! whose only book hath been the light
> Of supreme darkness which thou feddest on
> Night after night, when Phoebus was away,
> To thee the Spring will be a triple morn.
> O fret not after knowledge!—I have none,
> And yet my song comes native with the warmth.
> O fret not after knowledge! I have none,
> And yet the evening listens. He who saddens
> At thought of idleness cannot be idle,
> And he's awake who thinks himself asleep.

Now I am sensible all this is a mere sophistication (however it may neighbour to any truths), to excuse my own indulgence. So I will not deceive myself that man should be equal with Jove—but think himself very well off as a sort of scullion-mercury, or even a humble-bee. It is no matter whether I am right or wrong, either one way or another, if there is sufficient to lift a little time from your shoulders.

Your affectionate friend,

JOHN KEATS

TO HIS PUBLISHER

9TH OCT., 1818

MY DEAR HESSEY, You are very good in sending me the letters from *The Chronicle*, and I am very bad in not acknowledging such a kindness sooner: pray forgive me. It has so chanced that I have had that paper every day. I have seen to-day's. I cannot but feel indebted to those gentlemen who have taken my part. As for the rest, I begin to get a little acquainted with my strength and weakness. Praise or blame has but a momentary effect on the man whose love of beauty in the abstract makes him a severe critic of his own works. My own domestic criticism has given me pain without comparison beyond what *Blackwood* or *The Quarterly* could inflict: and also when I feel I am right, no external praise can give me such a glow as my own solitary reperception and ratification of what is fine. J. S. is perfectly right in regard to the "slip-shod *Endymion*." That it is so is no fault of mine. No! though it may sound a little paradoxical, it is as good as I had power to make it by myself. Had I been nervous about it being a perfect piece, and with that view asked advice, and trembled over every page, it would not have been written; for it is not in my nature to fumble. I will write independently. I have written independently *without judgment*. I may write independently, and with *judgment*, hereafter. The Genius of Poetry must work out its own salvation in a man. It cannot be matured by law and precept, but by sensation and watchfulness in itself. That which is creative must create itself. In *Endymion* I leaped headlong into the sea, and thereby have become better acquainted with the soundings, the quicksands, and the rocks, than if I had stayed upon the green shore, and piped a silly pipe, and took tea and comfortable advice. I was never afraid of failure; for I would sooner fail than not be among the greatest. But I am nigh getting into a rant; so, with remembrance to Taylor and Woodhouse, etc., I am,

Yours very sincerely,
JOHN KEATS

TO HIS FRIEND WOODHOUSE

[HAMPSTEAD, 27 OCT. 1818]

MY DEAR WOODHOUSE, Your letter gave me great satisfaction, more on account of its friendliness than any relish of that matter in it which is accounted so acceptable in the "genus irritable." The best answer

I can give you is in a clerklike manner to make some observations on two principal points which seem to point like indices into the midst of the whole *pro* and *con* about genius, and views, and achievements, and ambition, *et cætera*. 1st. As to the poetical character itself (I mean that sort, of which, if I am anything, I am a member; that sort distinguished from the Wordsworthian, or egotistical sublime; which is a thing *per se*, and stands alone), it is not itself—it has no self—it is every thing and nothing—it has no character—it enjoys light and shade—it lives in gusts, be it foul or fair, high or low, rich or poor, mean or elevated,—it has as much delight in conceiving an Iago as an Imogen. What shocks the virtuous philosopher delights the cameleon poet. It does no harm from its relish of the dark side of things, any more than from its taste for the bright one, because they both end in speculation. A poet is the most unpoetical of anything in existence, because he has no identity; he is continually informing, and filling, some other body. The sun, the moon, the sea, and men and women, who are creatures of impulse, are poetical, and have about them an unchangeable attribute; the poet has none, no identity. He is certainly the most unpoetical of all God's creatures. If, then, he has no self, and if I am a poet, where is the wonder that I should say I would write no more? Might I not at that very instant have been cogitating on the characters of Saturn and Ops? It is a wretched thing to confess, but it is a very fact, that not one word I ever utter can be taken for granted as an opinion growing out of my identical nature. How can it, when I have no nature? When I am in a room with people, if I am free from speculating on creations of my own brain, then, not myself goes home to myself; but the identity of every one in the room begins to press upon me, so that I am in a very little time annihilated—not only among men; it would be the same in a nursery of children. I know not whether I make myself wholly understood: I hope enough to let you see that no dependence is to be placed on what I said that day.

In the second place, I will speak of my views, and of the life I purpose to myself. I am ambitious of doing the world some good: if I should be spared, that may be the work of future years—in the interval I will assay to reach to as high a summit in poetry as the nerve bestowed upon me will suffer. The faint conceptions I have of poems to come bring the blood frequently into my forehead. All I hope is, that I may not lose all interest in human affairs—that the solitary indifference I feel for applause, even from the finest spirits, will not blunt any acuteness of vision I should write from the mere yearning and fondness I have for the beautiful, even if my night's labours should be burnt every morning, and no eye ever shine upon them. But even now I am perhaps not speaking from myself, but from some character in whose soul I now live.

I am sure, however, that this next sentence is from myself.—I feel your anxiety, good opinion, and friendship, in the highest degree, and am,

Yours most sincerely,

JOHN KEATS

JULIUS CHARLES HARE (1795–1855)

Hare was archdeacon of Lewes and had been at college with Whewell. When the latter wrote to him for advice as to whether he should leave Cambridge or not, Hare wrote the following letter, which is a delightful piece of common sense and practical Christianity.

TO PROFESSOR WHEWELL

HURSTMONCEUX: DEC. 17, 1840

YOUR letter is not an easy one to answer, but so you must have known when you wrote it. Even those who know you best can only form a partial judgment on such a question. There will be much in you, there will probably be much in your outward circumstances, which ought of right to be taken into account, but of which they will be ignorant. However, I will give you my thoughts, such as they are, confident that you will not be offended if I intimate any doubt of your having the universality of the Admirable Crichton. I doubt whether any great man ever had, least of all when he was approaching to fifty. Most fully do I agree with you that college rooms are not a home for one's latter years, and in my late visits to Cambridge I have felt that you were outliving your contemporaries. It seemed to me too, at least last March, that the intercourse with your juniors, many of whom had been your pupils, was not altogether wholesome to you. One of the greatest delights I had during my stay at Cambridge last year was to perceive that the vehemence of your nature had been greatly subdued. This year, on the contrary—I know not whether anything had happened in the interval—you seemed to me to have become quite as vehement as ever. And this reason, along with others, such as the departure of most of your friends, led me to wish that some change should take place in the outward form of your life. And yet I have never been able to think with satisfaction of your undertaking a parochial cure. I can neither fancy that you would suit it, nor that it would suit you. It *hardly* seems to me right to enter upon such a cure unless one does so with the purpose of making it the primary object of one's thoughts and interests. At least, I am sure no man of

647

right feeling can enjoy peace of mind unless he has a satisfactory conviction that the people committed to his spiritual charge are duly taken care of.   Much may, indeed, be done by an able and zealous curate; such a one you may find, and if you take the living you must unquestionably have one.

Thus, since so large a part of my own time has been withdrawn from my parish by my new office, I have felt a daily increasing comfort and blessing in Simpkinson; and you too would be rightfully withdrawn from your parish by the duties of your professorship, which, from their great importance to the Church and to the whole nation, might most justly take the precedence.   At the same time, unless you could feel a considerable sympathy with the new objects of your care, unless you do feel a strong interest in your new duties, and not merely in your regular Sunday ministrations, but in the schools, in visiting the sick, in talking to the poor about the petty concerns of their daily life, your life would be a very unsatisfying one.   Many blessings attend on these labours when one does take a hearty interest in them; but when one does not, they become an intolerable weariness, until by degrees one grows to neglect them.

Now at your age it is most difficult for a man to change the whole current of his daily thoughts and interests—above all, when the mind has been constantly habituated to look at all things from a speculative point of view.   You who stand atop of a mountain cannot see the clouds in the valley, still less can you care for them.   Nor is it desirable that you should.   All are not meant to be pastors; some are to be apostles, some doctors.   This is what our blundering Church-reformers could not understand.   Your ministry in this world seems to me to be that of a doctor, rather than a pastor; and what I should wish for would be a post where you might fulfil that ministry—the Mastership of Trinity, a deanery, or something of this sort.   I would have you pursue your work in moral philosophy; there is an ample field, a noble one; and it would be an evil thing for England that you should abandon it.

But you would not.   True, you would not give up literature and philosophy as I have done.   My course in this matter has not been determined by my own will; it has been forced upon me by causes which I could not resist.   Some of them lie merely in individual peculiarities.   I have always been called exclusive; Ma Man told Miss Ferrier: "Mr Hare cannot care about anybody except Kate"; and I believe there is a narrowness in me that disqualifies me for taking a deep interest in more than one thing at once. Besides, as you know from my etymological vagaries, I can never rest satisfied until a thing is done as thoroughly as my faculties and means will enable me. This is almost a disease; and hence I have been forced to leave so many things incomplete. But you are not so hyperscrupulous about petty details, nor do you allow yourself so easily to be monopolized. Therefore I doubt not that you might be able to pursue your speculative studies amid the cares of your parish. Thirlwall has done so, and his work is perfect. A. has done so; B. has done so, even with the case of a London parish and the distractions of London society. But then their books seem to be much as if a painter were to dash his brush across his pallet, after which, if he were wise, his next thought would probably be to obliterate his daub. However, Thirlwall's example is an encouragement; and I know your energy. I doubt not you would find time. But I do doubt whether you could ever refashion your mind according to your new calling—whether you could unravel the whole network of your thoughts, to weave them anew; whether you could descend, like Apollo, to become a shepherd.

I am the more urgent on this point, because I myself felt the misery of the distraction occasioned by an uncongenial calling during the two years I was in the Temple. And many a hard struggle have I had, many a long fit of despondency, since I came to Hurstmonceux, from the reluctance to forsake my old pursuits, from the difficulty of adapting myself to my new ones, and from the impossibility of reconciling the two. From my misery in the Temple you rescued me, and so were one of the greatest benefactors of my life; but from my struggle here I have gradually been freed by God's grace, and by the infinite blessing He has given me in my sister-in-law. Still it was an exceeding delight to return to Cambridge, and to recur to the speculations of former years, and to find the opportunity of using the knowledge it had been the chief business of my life to acquire. And now it seems to me that the habits and frame of my mind qualify me better for pastoral ministrations. Hence my happiness in these last years has greatly increased. The great lesson of my life has been that there can be no true happiness except when one is walking in the path of duty. Then alone "can love be an unerring light, and joy its own security."

I have written unconnectedly, it may be contradictorily, as the thoughts have risen up. You would not expect a determinate answer; and no one can determine the question but yourself. I have merely suggested such reflexions as my knowledge of you and of your present position, as well as of that of a parochial minister, called forth. Whatever your decision may be, you must keep in mind that your calling is rather to be a doctor than a pastor, and you are bound not to do what would hinder your efficiency in that calling. At the same time God may give you strength to fulfil both. And humanly speaking, with a good curate, and a wife, such as there are many, well fitted for a charge of a parish, you might look with contentment on the condition of your own flock, at least in some measure, even while your thoughts are mainly turned toward that larger flock who have been more especially committed to you. Whatever you decide, may it be right, and may the blessing of God prosper it!

There is another consideration which I would just hint at. A country parson's life is almost infallibly one almost devoid of everything like intellectual society. This to me, who was always a good deal of a recluse, is no intolerable loss. But how would you reconcile yourself to it?

If the alternative lay between continuing in college and taking a living, I should indeed feel little hesitation. A college life seems to me so unwholesome for a man after he has outlived his contemporaries, and abandoned practical work, that I would quit it, trusting that I might be enabled to discharge my new duties, without abandoning those which the whole course of my life had imposed upon me. But, as I said before, I should wish to see you in a different post.

You talk of discussing things with me "face to face." It will always be a very great pleasure to me to see you; but I feel some scruples about inviting my friends in winter; because then my sister is away (she always goes to her father); and I fancy she must be the charm of the place to others, as she is to me. However, if you like to come now, you shall be received with much joy, only I must leave home in January, having to preach at Chichester on two Sundays in that month.

J. C. H.

Was not the removal of Golgotha and the inversion of the pulpit in St. Mary's effected in our time? I have an indistinct notion that I remember the change. My imprudence, I suppose, will exclude me from it henceforward.

THOMAS CARLYLE (1795–1881)

Of all people in this book Carlyle needs the least introduction. There is a strength about his most casual words that carries conviction beyond need of comment.

TO HIS MOTHER

4, AMPTON STREET,
MECKLENBURGH SQUARE,
LONDON.
OCTOBER 20, 1831

MY DEAR MOTHER, . . . I dare say you have not seen in the news-papers, but will soon see something extraordinary about poor Edward Irving. His friends here are all much grieved about him. For many months he has been puddling and muddling in the midst of certain insane jargonings of hysterical women, and crack-brained enthusiasts, who start up from time to time in public companies, and utter confused stuff, mostly "Ohs" and "Ahs," and absurd interjections about "the body of Jesus"; they also pretend to "work miracles," and have raised more than one weak bedrid woman, and cured people of "nerves," or as they themselves say, "cast devils out of them." All which poor Irving is pleased to consider as the "work of the Spirit," and to janner about at great length, as making *his* church the peculiarly blessed of Heaven, and equal to or greater than the primitive one at Corinth. This, greatly to my sorrow and that of many, has gone on privately a good while, with increasing vigour; but last Sabbath it burst out publicly in the open church; for one of the "Prophetesses," a woman on the verge of derangement, started up in the time of worship, and began to speak with tongues, and, as the thing was encouraged by Irving, there were some three or four fresh hands who started up in the evening sermon and began their ragings; whereupon the whole congregation got into foul uproar, some groaning, some laughing, some shrieking, not a few falling into swoons: more like a Bedlam than a Christian church. Happily, neither Jane nor I were there, though we had been the previous day. We had not even heard of it; when going next evening to call on Irving, we found the house all decked

651

out for a "meeting," (that is, about the same "speaking with tongues"), and as we talked a moment with Irving, who had come down to us, there rose a shriek in the upper story of the house, and presently he exclaimed, "There is one prophesying; come and hear her!" We hesitated to go, but he forced us up into a back room, and there we could hear the wretched creature raving like one possessed; *hoo*ing, and *ha*ing, and talking as sensibly as one would do with a pint of brandy in his stomach, till after some ten minutes she seemed to grow tired and became silent.

TO JOHN CARLYLE

CHELSEA: APRIL 16, 1839

MY heart silently thanks Heaven that I was not tried beyond what I could bear. It is quite a new sensation, and one of the most blessed, that you will actually be allowed to live *not* a beggar. As to the praise, &c., I think it will not hurt me much; I can see too well the meaning of what that is. I have too faithful a dyspepsia working continually in monition of me, were there nothing else. Nevertheless, I must tell you of the strangest compliment of all, which occurred since I wrote last—the advent of Count d'Orsay. About a fortnight ago, this Phoebus Apollo of dandyism, escorted by poor little Chorley, came whirling hither in a chariot that struck all Chelsea into mute dazzlement with splendour. Chorley's under jaw went like the hopper or under riddle of a pair of fanners, such was his terror on bringing such a splendour into actual contact with such a grimness. Nevertheless, we did amazingly well, the Count and I. He is a tall fellow of six feet three, built like a tower, with floods of dark-auburn hair, with a beauty, with an adornment unsurpassable on this planet; withal a rather substantial fellow at bottom, by no means without insight, without fun, and a sort of rough sarcasm rather striking out of such a porcelain figure. He said, looking at Shelley's bust, in his French accent, "Ah, it is one of those faces who weesh to swallow their chin." He admired the fine epic, &c., &c.; hoped I would call soon, and see Lady Blessington withal. Finally he went his way, and Chorley with reassumed jaw. Jane laughed for two days at the contrast of my plaid dressing-gown, bilious, iron countenance, and this Paphian apparition. I did not call till the other day, and left my card merely. I do not see well what good I can get by meeting him much, or Lady B. and demirepdom, though I should not object to see it once, and then oftener if agreeable.

T. C.

TO THE SAME

CHELSEA, MARCH 17, 1840

THERE, at the dear cost of a shattered set of nerves and head set whirling for the next eight-and-forty hours, I did see lords and lions—Lord Holland and Lady, Lord Normanby, &c.—and then, for soirée upstairs, Morpeth, Lansdowne, French Guizot, the Queen of Beauty, &c. Nay, Pickwick, too, was of the same dinner party, though they do not seem to heed him over-much. He is a fine little fellow—Boz, I think. Clear blue, intelligent eyes, eyebrows that he arches amazingly, large protrusive rather loose mouth, a face of most extreme *mobility*, which he shuttles about—eyebrows, eyes, mouth and all—in a very singular manner while speaking. Surmount this with a loose coil of common-coloured hair, and set it on a small compact figure, very small, and dressed à la D'Orsay rather than well—this is Pickwick. For the rest a quiet, shrewd-looking, little fellow, who seems to guess pretty well what he is and what others are. Lady Holland is a brown-skinned, silent, sad, concentrated, proud old dame. Her face, when you see it in profile, has something of the falcon character, if a falcon's bill were straight; and you see much of the white of her eye. Notable word she spake none—sate like one wont to be obeyed and entertained. Old Holland, whose legs are said to be almost turned to *stone*, pleased me much. A very large, bald head, small, grey, invincible, composed-looking eyes, the immense tuft of an eyebrow which all the Foxes have, stiff upper lip, roomy mouth and chin, short, angry, yet modest nose. I saw there a fine old *Jarl*—an honest, obstinate, candid, wholesomely limited, very effectual and estimable old man. Of the rest I will not say a syllable, not even of the Queen of Beauty, who looked rather withered and unwell.

WRITING HOME FROM GHENT

AUGUST, 1842

How the ear of man is tortured in this terrestrial planet! Go where you will, the cock's shrill clarion, the dog's harsh watch note, not to speak of the melody of jackasses, and on streets, of wheel-barrows, wooden clogs, loud-voiced men, perhaps watchmen, break upon the hapless brain; and, as if all was not enough, "the Piety of the Middle Ages" has founded tremendous bells; and the hollow triviality of the present age—far worse—has everywhere instituted the piano! Why are not at least all those cocks and cockerels boiled into soup, into ever-lasting silence? Or, if the Devil some good night should take his hammer and smite in shivers all and every piano of our European world, so that in broad Europe there were not one piano left soundable, would the harm be great? Would not, on the contrary, the relief be consider-able? For once that you hear any real music from a piano, do you not five hundred times hear mere artistic somersets, distracted jangling, and the hapless pretence of music? Let him that has lodged wall neighbour to an operatic artist of stringed music say.

This miserable young woman that now in the next house to me spends all her young, bright days, not in learning to darn stockings, sew shirts, bake pastry, or any art, mystery, or business that will profit herself or others; not even in amusing herself or skipping on the grass-plots with laughter of her mates; but simply and solely in raging from dawn to dusk, to night and midnight, on a hapless piano, which it is evident she will never in this world learn to render more musical than a pair of barn-fanners! The miserable young female! The sound of her through the wall is to me an emblem of the whole distracted misery of this age; and her barn-fanners' rhythm becomes all too significant.

TO HIS WIFE

LONDON: SEPTEMBER 23, 1831 (?)

MY POOR GOODY, All yesterday my thoughts were with thee in thy lone voyage, which now I pray the great Giver of Good may have terminated prosperously. Never before did I so well understand my mother's anxious forecasting ways. I felt that my best possession was trusted to the false sea, and all my cares for it could avail nothing. Do not wait a moment in writing. I shall have no peace till I know that you are safe. Meanwhile, in truth there is no use in tormenting myself; the weather, here at least, was good. I struggle what I can to believe that it has all passed without accident, and that you are now resting in comparative safety in your uncle's house among friends.

Of rest I can well understand you have need enough. I grieve to think how harassed you have been of late, all which, I fear, has acted badly on your health; these bustlings and tossings to and fro are far too rough work for you. I can see, by your two last letters especially, that it is not well with you; your heart is, as it were, choked up, if not depressed. You are agitated and provoked, which is almost the worst way of the two. Alas! and I have no soft Aladdin's Palace here to bid you hasten and take repose in. Nothing but a noisy, untoward lodging-house, and no better shelter than my own bosom. Yet is not this the best of all shelters for you? the only safe place in this wide world? Thank God, this still is yours, and I can receive you there without distrust, and wrap you close with the solacements of a true heart's love. Hasten thither, then, my own wife. Betide what may, we will not despair, were the world never so unfriendly. *We* are indivisible, and will help each other to endure its evils, nay to conquer them.

TO THE SAME

SCOTSBRIG: SEPTEMBER 13, 1847

THE mills! oh the fetid, fuzzy, ill-ventilated mills! And in Sharp's cyclopean smithy do you remember the poor "grinders" sitting underground in a damp dark place, some dozen of them, over their screeching stone cylinders, from every cylinder a sheet of yellow *fire* issuing, the principal light of the place? And the men, I was told, and they themselves knew it, and "did not mind it," were all or mostly *killed* before their time, their lungs being ruined by the metal and stone dust! Those poor fellows, in their paper caps with their roaring grindstones, and their yellow *oriflammes* of fire, all grinding themselves so quietly to death, will never go out of my memory. In signing my name, as I was made to do, on quitting that Sharp establishment, whose name think you stood next to be succeeded by mine? In a fine flowing character, *Jenny Lind's*! Dickens and the other Player Squadron (wanting Forster, I think) stood on the same page.

I will tell you about Bright, and Brightdom, and the Rochdale Bright mill some other day. Jacob Bright, the younger man, and actual manager at Rochdale, rather pleased me—a kind of delicacy in his features when you saw them by daylight—at all events, a decided element of "hero-worship," which of course went for much. But John Bright, the Anti-Cornlaw member, who had come across to meet me, with his cock nose and pugnacious eyes and Barclay-Fox-Quaker collar—John and I discorded in our views not a little. And, in fact, the result was that I got to talking occasionally in the Annandale accent, and communicated large masses of my views to the Brights and Brightesses, and shook peaceable Brightdom as with a passing earthquake; and, I doubt, left a very questionable impression of myself there! The poor young ladies (Quaker or ex-Quaker), with their "abolition of Capital Punishment"—*Ach Gott!* I had great *remorse* of it all that evening; but now begin almost to think I served them right. Any way *we cannot help it*; so there it, and Lancashire in general, may lie for the present.

T. C.

TO THE RIGHT HON. B. DISRAELI

(In reply to Disraeli's letter offering the Bath, see page 704).

5, CHEYNE ROW, CHELSEA, DECEMBER 29, 1874

SIR, Yesterday, to my great surprise, I had the honour to receive your letter containing a magnificent proposal for my benefit, which will be memorable to me for the rest of my life. Allow me to say that the letter, both in purport and expression, is worthy to be called magnanimous and noble, that it is without example in my own poor history; and I think it is unexampled, too, in the history of governing persons towards men of letters at the present, or at any time; and that I will carefully preserve it as one of the things precious to memory and heart. A real treasure or benefit *it*, independent of all results from it.

This said to yourself and reposited with many feelings in my own grateful mind, I have only to add that your splendid and generous proposals for my practical behoof, must not any of them take effect; that titles of honour are, in all degrees of them, out of keeping with the tenour of my own poor existence hitherto in this epoch of the world, and would be an encumbrance, not a furtherance to me; that as to money, it has, after long years of rigorous and frugal, but also (thank God, and those that are gone before me) not degrading poverty, become in this latter time amply abundant, even superabundant; more of it, too, now a hindrance, not a help to me; so that royal or other bounty would be more than thrown away in my case; and in brief, that except the feeling of your fine and noble conduct on this occasion, which is a real and permanent possession, there cannot anything be done that would not now be a sorrow rather than a pleasure.

With thanks more than usually sincere,
I have the honour to be, Sir,
Your obliged and obedient servant,

T. CARLYLE

FROM A LETTER TO LORD HOUGHTON

SHE [his wife] wrapped me round like a cloak, to keep all the hard and cold world off me. When I came home sick with mankind, there she was on the sofa, always with a cheerful story of something or somebody, and I never knew that she, poor darling, had been fighting with bitter pains all day.

To think that little dog should have been the instrument to take the light of life away from me! What would it be for me now to have the fame of Trismegistus, without her to be glad at it?

She never had a mean thought or word from the day I first saw her, looking like a flower out of the window of her mother's old brick house, my Jeanie, my queen.

EDWARD RUSHTON (1796–1851)

Rushton was a leading member of the Reform Party in Liverpool; "Roaring Rushton" old Cobbett called him. Brought up a printer, at Canning's suggestion he studied for the Bar and was eventually appointed stipendiary magistrate of Liverpool.

TO HIS WIFE

LONDON, 5TH FEBRUARY, 1830

THE distress seems to have reached the lawyers. We have very little to do in comparison with the last term, but we are as well off as our neighbours.

I should like to read Moore's "Life of Byron" right well, but I must postpone it. I agree about the poet, and you will see how I feel by reading a hasty letter signed "Scotus" in a late *Chronicle*, headed "Lord Byron." There is no species of impertinence which galls me so much as that of the little-minded strictly-righteous crew, who, having not the power to comprehend the minds of such men as Byron, judge them by a severe code in which deviations from the market morality are denounced and punished as if they were sins against the Holy Ghost. No doubt Byron would have been a better man if he had not done some things which he did do, but I take it, considering who and what he was, that he was a wonderful example of splendid genius, industry and self-denial. God rest his soul, I pray, and save his memory from the insulting pity of the base and timid. Had Byron lived until age had tamed his fancy and ripened his judgement, he would have ranked as high among politicians as among poets, and he might have done great and good service in the stirring times which are, I fear, very near us.

THOMAS HOOD (1799–1845)

Hood was quite a young man when he wrote the long letter to his sister-in-law, Charlotte, the humour and detailed description of which are reminiscent of Boz. All his letters, indeed, are very live and full of merriment. What better could have been written than that note to little Dunnie Elliott?

TO CHARLOTTE REYNOLDS

ISLINGTON, SUNDAY MORNING (1823)

MY DEAR LOTTE, Once more I write to you out of pity—for I know that the very sight of a letter must make you move your ears like Baby's rabbit,—or as Mr. Darley doth, I have observed, in little twitches before he speaks. But those who listen to him feel as if theirs were turning inside out with impatience—which I hope is not your case with me, for I could never hope to fill the double drums of your female curiosity. You must gaze your fill, therefore upon Jane's or Marianne's letters before you venture upon mine; though I do suppose that in your parts, the least scrap is a godsend, and that you lick every word off the butter papers. It must be a comfort to you then to know that here we have Marianne Longmore, and have seen brides and brides' groom by pairs, but I will not meddle with these matters. Jane and Marianne will describe their dresses and trimmings to a nicety, with endless quotations, as it were of Mr. Harvey's shop-bills,—and I do not expect till you have read these letters twice over that you will turn your blue eyes upon mine. Heaven, however, has kindly blown up something like an incident for your amusement,—and according to your desire to draw all the particulars of so extraordinary an occurance (as Browne the novelist would begin) though indeed you have expressed no such desire—I commence my narrative. It was on Wednesday, the 16th inst., at half past six p.m., squally with rain, that I set off for a dance at Hackney, with my sister and two others—(your sisters were no party to my party so have this slice of news to myself)—but the wind was so high that whether we *sailed* or rode thither I have some doubts.—If it had been a boat I should have thought we rowed; but

it was in a coach—Number 1776. There was a large party when we
arrived, I think it was said there were 16 or 18 ladies arrived, and the
entertainment was given by the *single* unmarried daughter of Mr. and
Mrs. Gouldsmith—late our neighbours of Islington. She is a young
girl of a very solemn aspect,—giving the lie to the proverb about old
heads and young shoulders—and of a very *pious* turn, and, when she
complains, of the most whining and melancholy voice possible. Then we
all had tea and coffee in the back parlour—I could send you a cut of
the house and grounds like Probert's but for want of time;—yet suffice
it that there are two large rooms communicating by folding-doors, and
both entered from a large hall on the left. I sat in the back room close
to the garden window,—with my feet in the fourth position—talking
of I know not what to a young lady with very lobster-like eyes. I
only remember that she said, with a flirt of her fan, that she liked "the
simplicity of the country," and I thought of you when she said it. In
the meantime the gale roared without and the gentlemen came dropping
in like windfalls. And I remember remarking—the only remark I
made aloud—that the hurricane without made a most pleasant contrast
to the comforts within,—for the wind was making sort of Pan's pipes
of our stack of chimneys, and played such a air in a little ante-chamber
behind the hall, where all the fruit and custards, &c., were laid out,
that the grate would hold no fire within its bars. And now a game of
bagatelle was proposed, before dancing,—and all the company adjourned
to the front room, except myself, who took that opportunity of examining a picture which hung in the extreme corner. It represented a
group in a hayfield during a storm,—watching the sky, as it seemed,
in awful expectation of a thunderbolt. When just then, at that very
moment,—in the silent pause, just on the eve of the bagatelle,—I
heard a most tremendous fall overhead—right on the ceiling—as if a
lady in practising her steps upstairs, some dowager—only as loud as
twenty dowagers—had tripped and fallen. But it was not as I thought
a lady, but a whole stack of chimneys that had tumbled—beating through
the roof and stamping on the first floor like the very giant of the Castle
of Otranto. The explosion was tremendous; and might aptly be compared, yes, most aptly—for this *was* to have been a Ball—to the first
awful cannon-shot at Brussels!

> —Hackney had gather'd then
> Her beauty and her chivalry all bright,
> And there were well-dressed women and brave men,

but now—at a blow—the glory of the Ball was demolished for ever!—

I looked through the folding doors, and it was like a glimpse of L filled with smoke and darkness palpable, and in the midst moved shapes of men and ladies;—demons and soiled angels,—whilst the huge grate continually spit forth its flames in fiery tongues towards the infernal centre. And the soot whirled round and round with the wind and the smoke, like black bandalores[1],—so that some fled into "the wide gusty hall";—and others stopped not until they had reached the fore-court or garden—where they stood, shaking and blowing out of all shape. Among these I found my sister, planted in the mid-walk, with a white pocket handkerchief pulled round her white face!—"each lent to each a double charm" and waiting as if for a tile from above. Then I pulled her into the hall, and looked round me on the grimly company.—O, how Beauty (if any beauty *was* there) was soiled and dimmed! What lustres were quenched! What silks were tarnished! What fair faces were rawncely'd by filthy smoke and soot! It was like a May-day in high life!—The rich Sweep's Jubilee!—or a revel among the blacks! Only there was no "white lass" for Black Man to kiss;—they were all Wowskis.—I looked for the lady with lobster-eyes, whom I had conversed with, but she was run away out of the House, and like De Quincey's Ann—with all my search I could never find her again. I spoke to another, but she only stared and could make no answer, and then the Lady of the Mansion came to me, with her hands flapping up and down with wonder and fright, and asked me which way the wind blew. Then came a little old Lady from over the way, to offer beds for the family but in reality to slack the quicklime of her own curiosity,—and then came an old gentleman, hastily fetched over by one of the daughters who thought he was a surveyor,—but he turned out to be an old stockbroker. This is he who would not come,—though the young woman said that her ma was dying of terror—till he had put on his best gaiters. Of course he was of no service, so he went off with as many of us as lived near, but some were forced to wait for their coaches. Thus we stood all about, and for some of the ladies we wiped chairs—in that little back room you wot of—behind which perchance we stood like Pompey or Mungo, and served them with wine and tarts. I only, owing to my fortunate station at the time of the fall, showed off amongst these grimed Othellos like—forgive the comparison—like a swan amongst ravens. I believe

---

[1] The bandalore was a toy containing a coiled spring, which caused it, when thrown down, to rise again to the hand by the winding of the string by which it was held.

they would have been glad to smut me out of envy and spite.—I asked one, a Frenchman, how long he had been from Africa, but he mistook my drift, and replied he was not from Africa, but the United States. Another, unmannerly, had stood between the ladies and the fire, and the spurting flames had singed his pantaloons to a nice crisp brown;— but the object of all objects was the young lady our invitress—who with mingled soot and disappointment, looked blacker than black, and in a crow's voice croaked a thousand regrets for this uncomfortable entertainment. Then she rated her brother for stuffing at the tarts and custards when he might be dusting the chairs, or blowing the soot off the pictures. As for the relics of us—the guests—we were invited to the next house—a Madhouse—till our Coaches came to us, and thither we went, and were formally introduced to the family. We were quite strangers to each other—but to be sure had we been friends they could scarcely have known us—and here we were provided with houseroom, coal and candle and young ladies till half past eleven. They did not offer us any refreshment however,—thinking perhaps that we had brought our own grub—and might sup off each other's faces—but for the rest we were very comfortable, and I met with amusement enough for another chapter.

II

OF THE PEOPLE AT THE MADHOUSE: THEIR APPEARANCE AND BEHAVIOUR

On entering the Madhouse, we were ushered into a very handsome large room, with a fine blazing fire, that seemed to crackle and enjoy its safe and sound chimney. Indeed the fall of ours seemed to have cleared up the weather, which had settled into a fine moonlight; nevertheless we all sat at a respectful distance from the fireplace, protesting that we were not cold, and the corners were occupied by the family. The Lady of the House was a goodly well-grown dame, I guess Welsh,— and opposite her sat two daughters who took after their mother in size—and might have visited the great Cattle show at Sadler's without any very humiliating sense of their own insignificance. They kept all their conversation in the family, so that I cannot speak of them beyond their looks, but I should take them to be young and good-tempered—the first because they had very girlish faces, with sleek combed braided hair, and altogether rather a bread-and-butter look, and the last because they seemed to thrive so well on their victuals.

The father was a very respectable kind of man but rather homely betwixt his nose and chin, and there were three Brothers, one tall, nothing uncommon in appearance except that he wore spectacles, the other ditto except the spectacles, and the third—but of him more anon. We—the Accidentals—were five in number,—myself, two ladies, their brother, the gentleman of the scorched pantaloons—and the Frenchman. The latter—I should tell you—had suffered most in complexion and sat with his grim black face in most agreeable relief, between the two white busts of Paris, and Canova's Venus, which stood upon the chiffonières. He addressed most of his animated discourse to the mother, and she received it with a most polite and inflexible gravity, in spite of all the smoky workings of his face and fingers, by which he illustrated his meaning. But the consciousness of her stiff crisp immaculate double and triple frills and smooth white-kidlike face, by the side of his dingy flesh and cravat might account for some part of her complacency. I sat silently watching them, till I believe the Father, thinking I wanted some amusement, sends his youngest son, who anchored himself in a seat beside me and began to pour in a regular flood of talk, great and small. He had been a sailor and the climate had tanned his face into a mahogany brown which advantageously set off his curly flax-coloured hair. He had too, a strange crooked upper lip to his mouth that twisted and worked whenever he spoke enough to turn all his letters to an S. Of his discourse as well as I can, I will give you a sample. He began with his last voyage to Jamaica. The captain was a Scotchman and pinched his crew very much—hoped I was not a Scotchman, he was a Welshman. That gentleman opposite (the Frenchman) was talking of Deal boats, so he described the Deal boats. He had been in the Downs in a storm—very bad anchorage in a storm—and the ship ran down another with a cargo of ivory on board, but they had a freight of timber, but the crew of the ivory ship were all ashore but two—what a providence it was. How should I climb up a mast? Really I could not tell. Why, when he tried, he endeavoured to get up the pole, but it was greased and he slipped down again—you should lay hold of the two backstays and *warp* yourself up, hand over hand. Begged I would excuse his nautical phrases and then explained what a hobb-de-hoy was. Really *those* black girls (not our ladies) but the negresses in Jamaica, were very humane, he had a deep cut once in his ankle and they healed it. Did I ever wake at a thunderstorm? No; or very seldom. No more should he if it was not for that fellow (pointing to the manservant who came in with coals) who waked him always and said, "See, sir, what beautiful light-ning." Did I ever see a dolphin? but he forgot they were not by law allowed to be brought into England. What did I think Bill would do for (pointing to his Brother)? I guessed a Doctor—from the spectacles.—No, he was to be a parson. Dick, pointing to the other, was a painter and poet, and played on the flute and keyed-bugle—and in this very candid ingenuous way he ran on till we parted, when he shook my hand and bid God bless me and I parted from one of the most amusing openhearted little Boy-men that ever twaddled about ships and canvas. There! feast upon him in your fancy. I am sure such a mere shadow of a young Tar as I have given you must be a comfort in your country. I wished I could have packed him up and sent him to you per Canal. He would out-talk Mrs. H.!—and make you quite enjoy the Barges.

We have had Mr. Green here with three of your ribbons in his hat, beating up for recruits to go abroad with him to Upwell—but he can get no one to take your shilling. I have however volunteered some riddles for Mr. Hardwicke which you shall receive per first opportunity, and my next letter will be to Eliza; provided she will from this sample condescend to take it in. If she please I will pay the postage. I could write a deal of nursy-pursy for Baby, but I will not take it out of your mouth. I am quite delighted with the accounts I hear of her mimicry—and count her already as clever as Clara Fisher—but as she imitates it behoves you who are so much with her to be very guarded in your own conduct—that she may profit by her pattern. I own I should be sorry to see her, on being paid a compliment by a young gentleman, sidle off, and hold down her head, and shake it, like a pony about to *shy*—or when she begins to talk, to hear her fumbling and poking out her explanations, like broken corks picked piecemeal out of the necks of bottles;—a comparison which, to be candid, I have known to be inspired by yourself. I know you will not be offended at my telling you of all your little faults, since I do it only for that dear child's benefit;—and I shall not have room in this letter or I would tell you of all the rest which I have observed in you with the affectionate vigilance of a Friend. I would also favour you with a few of her Mother's—if I could just now remember what they were—but I abstain lest they should seem easier invented than recalled. I merely suspect in the meantime that that dirty little trick Miss has, of poking her mutton-bones into other people's eyes, must have been learnt of her mother, for I do not recollect that you had any such practice when

I have sat with you at dinner. If such be the case, however much it may divert and entertain you for the present, and tend to her Father's amusement, yet I cannot but consider her talent for imitation rather as a *bane* (the Scotch for bone) than as a blessing to her, if it is to lead to such consequences. But I will not school you in your own duty and province—only I must send a kiss thro' you to your little charge—and I wish it were a bullet for your sake. Do give a little hug to her then for my sake, and kiss her mouth—so pretty and little as Rowland Prince says of *his* child "that it might be covered with a sixpence." But give her a shilling kiss! Her aunts have sent her some toys. I did not think she would take to the rabbit; but perhaps by rubbing it over with a little parsley and butter at the beginning she may be tempted to lick (like) it. Do, do take care that she doesn't get the ninepins under her little feet and so fall, in which caution I have got the start of her grandmother. I went with Jane for the toys—and our purchases were, oddly enough, as follows,—*Pins* for Baby, *Pegs* for Ma, and *stumps* for Marianne! Can you club together such another set of commissions? I have no news but that I am learning quad.

. . . .

A parcel-knock at the door and a general skuttle! Your letter is come, and I have got thus far,—so you must give me credit for writing all in advance of this without being *coaxed*. But I am grieved to hear that our good Eliza is unwell; if anything I could wish would cure her it is entirely hers. I believe I like her better and better, as Baby grows—and you may tell her so for me, and very sincerely. I hope I do not need Jane's or Marianne's affidavits to confirm this assurance, and so venture to offer my simple love to her, and pray present it in your kindest manner. I need but to mention George for I know she will box your ears or mine for forgetting him, but as I am out of reach of her gentle hands he will receive my remembrances as from regard more than fear. And now, dear Lotte, accept my own love and this long letter in token of my desire to please you, but do not presume upon it, or presume upon me by sending up all Mr. Hardwicke's notes for you. Such a wish is not expressed,—but I have guessed it. God bless you. Your affectionate brother,

THOS. HOOD

P.S.—*Have the goodness to turn over a new leaf!*
I had nigh forgot to wish a "Merrie Christmas" to you all my dear good Masters and Mistresses and also the Young Lady from London. So in the name of the Bellman, "God bless your House and all the

wery worthy people as is in it."—Have you heard the Bellman yet, and what time do your Waits play at Upwell? I do suppose by this, that little Miss has ate up all the plums from your pudding. A little dear, to seem to know so naturally what Xmas means!

So you have been to hear the new Bells for the sake of their tongues. Did you make any conquests among the Triple Bob Majors!

TO THE SAME

JULY 11, 1828

My dear Lot,
There's a blot!—
This is to write
That Sunday night
By the late
Coach at eight,
We shall get in
To Little Britain,—
So have handy
Gin, rum, Brandy,
A lobster,—may be—
Cucumbers, they be
Also in season
And within reason
Porter, by Gum!
Against we come—
In lieu of Friday
Then we keep high day
And holy, as long as
We can. I get strong as
A horse—i.e. pony.
Jane tho keeps boney.
How is your mother,
Still with your brother?
And Marian too—
And that good man too
Called your papa, Miss
After these, ah Miss
Don't say I never
Made an endeavour
To write you verses.

Tho this lay worse is
Than any I've written.
The truth is I've sitten
So long over letters
Addressed to your betters
That—that—that
Somehow—
My pen,
                 Amen,
                                T. HOOD

TO DUNNE ELLIOTT

DEVONSHIRE LODGE, NEW FINCHLEY ROAD, ST. JOHN'S WOOD,
          JULY 1ST (1ST OF HEBREW FALSITY)

MY DEAR DUNNIE, I have heard of your doings at Sandgate, and that
you were so happy at getting to the sea, that you were obliged to be
flogged a little to moderate it, and keep some for next day. I am
very fond of the sea, too, though I have been twice nearly drowned
by it; once in a storm in a ship, and once under a boat's bottom when
I was bathing. Of course you have bathed, but have you learned to
swim yet? It is rather easy in salt water, and diving is still easier, even
that at the *sink*. I only swim in fancy, and strike out new ideas.

Is not the tide curious? Though I cannot say much for its tidiness;
it makes such a slop and litter on the beach. It comes and goes as
regularly as the boys of a proprietary school, but has no holidays. And
what a rattle the waves make with the stones when they are rough;
you will find some rolled into decent marbles and bounces: and sometimes you may hear the sound of a heavy sea, at a distance, like a giant
snoring. Some people say that every ninth wave is bigger than the
rest. I have often counted, but never found it come true, except
with tailors, of whom every ninth is a man. But in rough weather
there are giant waves, bigger than the rest, that come in trios, from
which, I suppose, Britannia rules the waves by the rule of three. When
I was a boy, I loved to play with the sea, in spite of its sometimes getting
rather rough. I and my brother chucked hundreds of stones into it,
as you do; but we came away before we could fill it up. In those days
we were at war with France. Unluckily it's peace now, or with so
many stones you might have good fun for days in pelting the enemy's
coast. Once I almost thought I nearly hit Boney! Then there was
looking for an island like Robinson Crusoe! Have you ever found

one yet, surrounded by water? I remember once staying on the beach, when the tide was flowing, till I was a peninsula, and only by running turned myself into a continent.

Then there's fishing at the seaside. I used to catch flat fish with a very long string line. It was like swimming a kite? But perhaps there are no flat fish at Sandgate—except your shoe-soles. The best plan, if you want flat fish where there are none, is to bring codlings and hammer them into dabs. Once I caught a plaice, and, seeing it all over red spots, thought it had caught the measles.

Do you ever long, when you are looking at the sea, for a voyage? If I were off Sandgate with my yacht (only she is not yet built), I would give you a cruise in her. In the meantime you can practise sailing any little boat you can get. But mind that it does not flounder or get squamped, as some people say instead of "founder" and "swamp." I have been swamped myself by malaria, and almost foundered, which reminds me that Tom junior, being very ingenious, has made a cork model of a diving-bell that won't sink!

By this time, I suppose, you are become, instead of a land-boy, a regular sea-urchin; and so amphibious, that you can walk on the land as well as on the water—or better. And don't you mean, when you grow up, to go to sea? Should you not like to be a little midshipman? or half a quarter-master, with a cocked hat, and a dirk, that will be a sword by the time you are a man? If you do resolve to be a post-captain, let me know; and I will endeavour, through my interest with the Commissioners of Pavements, to get you a post to jump over of the proper height. Tom is just rigging a boat, so I suppose that he inclines to be an Admiral of the Marines. But before you decide, remember the port-holes, and that there are great guns in those battle-doors that will blow you into shuttlecocks, which is a worse game than whoop and hide—as to a good hiding!

And so farewell young "Old Fellow," and take care of yourself so near the sea, for in some places, they say, it has not even a bottom to go to if you fall in. And remember when you are bathing, if you meet with a shark, the best way is to bite off his legs, if you can, before he walks off with yours. And so, hoping you will be better soon, for somebody told me you have the shingles, I am, my dear Dunnie, your affectionate friend,

THOMAS HOOD

P.S.—I have heard that at Sandgate there used to be *lob*sters; but some ignorant fairy turned them all by a spell into *bol*sters.

MY DEAR PHILLIPS, What the devil do you mean? Have you no concern for the nerves of editors—the nourishment of magazine readers? It may be horseplay to you, but death to us. What business had you in the saddle at all? Have I not said in print, that sedentary persons never have a good seat? Is it not notorious that authors from Coleridge down to Poole are bad riders? And you must go proving it again by being run away with; not by vanity, in a very writerlike way, but by the brute quadruped, never well pick-a-backed by seamen and the literati. Do you want a hole in your head as well as in your lungs? And are you not contented with the Neck, crying "lost, lost," but you must break your own? Is your head no better than a common pumpkin, that you must go pitching on it, and grazing the "dome of thought and palace of the soul"? I think I see you getting up—not content with expectorating blood—spitting mud! And, plague take you, all through trotting on an earthly roadster, when you might have been soaring so celestially on Pegasus, after his feed of "husk and grain." Do you really expect, though you die of riding, that you will get an equestrian statue for it at Trafalgar Square, Cockspur Street, or in front of the new Exchange? Not a bronze pony! Nor will you get a shilling a sheet the more from Hood's or Blackwood's, no, nor from any of the Sporting Magazines, for going at a gate without hounds or fox! And a father, too, with a baby and a boy, and a young lord to bring up! And a friend, with such friends as a Blair, a Salomans, and a Hood, and all the Pratts, to expose himself to be kicked out of such society by a hoof. Oh! Philippus, you deserve a Philippic—and here it is! Seriously, I am glad you escaped, and hope "you will not do so any more." If you must run risks, do it as I do, on two legs, and at a walk—for such invalids, a damp clothes-horse is danger enough— or if you must go pick-a-back, get acquainted with some sheriff that can lend you a quiet nag.

I am come back here from Vanburg House for good—much better; and have resumed the driving of the Magazine. I am sorry to have had the last of the "Sea-side Lore": but your beautiful poem was some consolation. It has been much admired by my friends. Don't get too proud with your Marchionesses for the muses. My bust is modelled and cast. It is said to be a correct likeness: two parts Methodist, to one of Humourist, and quite recognizable in spite of the Hood all over the face.

To-morrow I take a trip to Calais, for a day only, with Fanny, for the sake of the voyage and sea air. We are a brace in need of bracing, as you know. If I can catch a sea-horse, I will, for you to ride in the Race of Portland. Ward accompanies to edit the main sheet, and return the whole packet if unsuitable. I only hope he won't be sick without "Notice to Correspondents."

Pray for us, and for peace, for if a war breaks out while we are there, the Magazine will be as bad as blown up, and I might as well be cased full-length in plaster of Paris.

By the bye, have you read the "Mysteries of Paris"? Very bad! Or the "Amber Witch," which is very good? Or do you read nothing but Burke and Debrett to the young Peerage? Do you like my novel? or do you prefer "Rookwood" for the sake of the ride to York?—advertises "Revelations of London," in imitation of the Parisian mysteries, of course! Won't they be very full of the slang of the Rookery? The mere idea gives me the back-Slumbago!

Write soon, and tell me how you like your new position, and how you live. Aristocratically enough I guess, and spitting nothing under high blood. Your stomach a mere game bag, or pot for the preserves, eh? And some fine day you will come and triumph over us with your corpulence, and "Phillips me like a three-man beadle." For you drink the choicest of wines of course—your smallest beer old double X ale. What a change for an author! And then you lie I warrant in a down bed, with such sheets! everyone equal to forty-eight pages of superfine cambric margined with lace and hot-pressed with a silver warming-pan! Nevertheless come some day and see us—some day when you are ordered to live very low and then perhaps our best holiday diet may be good enough for you. We are very poor and have only seventy-two thousand a-year (pence mind, not pounds), and our names not even in the Post-office Directory, much less the Court Guide!

Well, if it isn't too great a liberty, God bless you! Mrs. Hood hopes you will forgive her offering her kind regards; and Fanny and Tom presume to join in the same. And if you would condescend to present my kind regards and respects to Mr. Salomans, it would exceedingly oblige, dear Phillips, yours very truly, and hoping no offence,

THOS. HOOD

WILLIAM CLARKE (1799–1856)

The following letter, written to the Hon. Frederick Ponsonby, by Clarke, Slow Bowler and Secretary to the All England Eleven, was used by him as a dedication to his "Practical Hints on Cricket"; thus following the example of John Nyren.

TO THE HON. FREDERICK PONSONBY

UNDATED

SIR, In making a few observations to my Brother Cricketers and the rising generation, I don't say that I lay down the only true method; but from many years' experience I have had (having played from my earliest years, and studied the game in all its various branches), I am able to declare that it will generally be found pretty correct. There are instructions out, such as for keeping your right shoulder up, and your left elbow forward, and your right foot fixed firm on the ground, but so that you can turn round on it like a swivel. I shall pass over these, and place my remarks in as plain and simple manner as possible; so that they will not only be intelligible to the Peer and the Squire, but also to the Artisan, the Peasant, and my Brother Cricketers; and if there be some things they don't agree with, there perhaps will be others that will take their attention. At any rate they are given with a good feeling; and when I am called to that bourn from whence no Cricketer returns, people won't have to say, "what he knew he took with him."

WM. CLARKE

THOMAS BABINGTON, LORD MACAULAY (1800-59)

Macaulay was one of the most brilliant essayists and historians of English literature. But his activities were by no means confined to his study, for he was an active politician, and rose to high rank in the cabinet. From 1834 until 1838 he was a member of the Supreme Council in India, and it was while in the East that he wrote the letter to Ellis which is here printed. The other note, addressed to his sister Hannah, who subsequently married Sir Charles Trevelyan, gives an interesting picture of the famous salon of Holland House.

TO THOMAS FLOWER ELLIS

OOTACAMUND; JULY 1, 1834

DEAR ELLIS, You need not get your map to see where Ootacamund is: for it has not found its way into the maps. It is a new discovery; a place to which Europeans resort for their health, or, as it is called by the Company's servants,—blessings on their learning!—a *sanaterion*. It lies at the height of 7,000 feet above the sea.

While London is a perfect gridiron, here am I, at 13° North from the equator, by a blazing wood-fire, with my windows closed. My bed is heaped with blankets, and my black servants are coughing round me in all directions. One poor fellow in particular looks so miserably cold that, unless the sun comes out, I am likely soon to see under my own roof the spectacle which, according to Shakespeare, is so interesting to the English,[1]—a dead Indian.

I travelled the whole four hundred miles between this and Madras on men's shoulders. I had an agreeable journey on the whole. I was honoured by an interview with the Rajah of Mysore, who insisted on showing me all his wardrobe, and his picture gallery. He had six or seven coloured English prints not much inferior to those which I have seen in the sanded parlour of a country inn; "Going to Cover," "The Death of the Fox," and so forth. But the bijou of his gallery, of which he is as vain as the Grand Duke can be of the Venus, or Lord

---

[1] *The Tempest*, Act ii, scene 2.

Carlisle of the Three Maries, is a head of the Duke of Wellington, which has, most certainly, been on a sign-post in England.

Yet, after all, the Rajah was by no means the greatest fool whom I found at Mysore. I alighted at a bungalow appertaining to the British Residency. There I found an Englishman who, without any preface, accosted me thus: "Pray, Mr. Macaulay, do not you think that Bonaparte was the Beast?" "No, Sir, I cannot say that I do." "Sir, he was the Beast. I can prove it. I have found the number 666 in his name. Why Sir, if he was not the Beast, who was?" This was a puzzling question, and I am not a little vain of my answer. "Sir," said I, "the House of Commons is the Beast. There are 658 members of the House; and these, with their chief officers,—the three clerks, the Sergeant and his deputy, the Chaplain, the doorkeeper, and the librarian,—make 666." "Well, Sir, that is strange. But I can assure you that, if you write Napoleon Bonaparte in Arabic, leaving out only two letters, it will give 666." "And pray, Sir, what right have you to leave out two letters? And, as St. John was writing Greek and to Greeks, is it not likely that he would use the Greek rather than the Arabic notation?" "But, Sir," said this learned divine, "everybody knows that the Greek letters were never used to mark numbers." I answered with the meekest look and voice possible: "I do not think that everybody knows that. Indeed I have reason to believe that a different opinion,—erroneous no doubt,—is universally embraced by all the small minority who happen to know any Greek." So ended the controversy. The man looked at me as if he thought me a very wicked fellow; and, I dare say, has by this time discovered that, if you write my name in Tamul, leaving out T in Thomas, B in Babington, and M in Macaulay, it will give the number of this unfortunate Beast.

I am very comfortable here. The Governor-General is the frankest and best-natured of men. The chief functionaries who have attended him hither are clever people, but not exactly on a par as to general attainments with the society to which I belonged in London. I thought, however, even at Madras, that I could have formed a very agreeable circle of acquaintance; and I am assured that at Calcutta I shall find things far better. After all, the best rule in all parts of the world, as in London itself, is to be independent of other men's minds. My power of finding amusement without companions was pretty well tried on my voyage. I read insatiably; the Iliad and Odyssey, Virgil, Horace, Cæsar's Commentaries, Bacon "de Augmentis," Dante, Petrarch, Ariosto, Tasso, Don Quixote, Gibbon's

Rome, Mill's India, all the seventy volumes of Voltaire, Sismondi's History of France, and the seven thick folios of the Biographia Britannica. I found my Greek and Latin in good condition enough. I liked the Iliad a little less, and the Odyssey a great deal more, than formerly. Horace charmed me more than ever; Virgil not quite so much as he used to do. The want of human character, the poverty of his supernatural machinery, struck me very strongly. Can anything be so bad as the living bush which bleeds and talks, or the Harpies who befoul Æneas's dinner? It is as extravagant as Ariosto, and as dull as Wilkie's Epigoniad. The last six books which Virgil had not fully corrected pleased me better than the first six. I like him best on Italian ground. I like his localities; his national enthusiasm; his frequent allusions to his country, its history, its antiquities, and its greatness. In this respect he often reminded me of Sir Walter Scott, with whom, in the general character of his mind, he had very little affinity. The Georgics pleased me better; the Eclogues best,—the second and tenth above all. But I think that the finest lines in the Latin language are those five which begin:

Sepibus in nostris parvam te roscida mala—

I cannot tell you how they struck me. I was amused to find that Voltaire pronounces that passage to be the finest in Virgil.

I liked the "Jerusalem" better than I used to do. I was enraptured with Ariosto; and I still think of Dante, as I thought when I first read him, that he is a superior poet to Milton, that he runs neck and neck with Homer, and that none but Shakespeare has gone decidedly beyond him.

As soon as I reach Calcutta I intend to read Herodotus again. By the bye, why do you not translate him? You would do it excellently; and a translation of Herodotus, well executed, would rank with original compositions. A quarter of an hour a day would finish the work in five years. The notes might be made the most amusing in the world. I wish you would think of it. At all events I hope you will do something which may interest more than seven or eight people. Your talents are too great, and your leisure-time too small, to be wasted in inquiries so frivolous, (I must call them,) as those in which you have of late been too much engaged; whether the Cherokees are of the same race with the Chickasaws; whether Van Diemen's Land was peopled from New Holland, or New Holland from Van Diemen's Land; what is the precise mode of appointing a headman in a village in Timbuctoo.

I would not give the worst page in Clarendon or Fra Paolo for all that ever was, or ever will be, written about the migrations of the Leleges and the laws of the Oscans.

I have already entered on my public functions, and I hope to do some good. The very wigs of the Judges in the Court of the King's Bench would stand on end if they knew how short a chapter my Law of Evidence will form. I am not without many advisers. A native of some fortune at Madras has sent me a paper on legislation. "Your honour must know," says this judicious person, "that the great evil is that men swear falsely in this country. No judge knows what to believe. Surely if your honour can make men to swear truly, your honour's fame will be great, and the Company will flourish. Now, I know how men may be made to swear truly; and I will tell your honour for your fame, and for the profit of the Company. Let your honour cut off the great toe of the right foot of every man who swears falsely, whereby your honour's fame will be extended." Is not this an exquisite specimen of legislative wisdom?

I must stop. When I begin to write to England, my pen runs as if it would run on for ever.

Ever yours affectionately,

T. B. M.

TO HANNAH MORE MACAULAY

London: May 30, 1831

Well, my dear, I have been to Holland House. I took a glass coach and arrived through a fine avenue of elms, at the great entrance towards seven o'clock. The house is delightful;—the very perfection of the old Elizabethan style;—a considerable number of very large and very comfortable rooms, rich with antique carving and gilding, but carpeted and furnished with all the skill of the best modern upholsterers. The library is a very long room,—as long, I should think, as the gallery at Rothley Temple,—with little cabinets for study branching out of it, warmly and snugly fitted up, and looking out on very beautiful grounds. The collection of books is not, like Lord Spencer's, curious; but it contains almost everything that one ever wished to read. I found nobody there when I arrived but Lord Russell, the son of the Marquess of Tavistock. We are old House of Commons friends: so we had some very pleasant talk, and in a little while in came Allen, who is warden of Dulwich College, and who lives almost entirely at Holland

House. He is certainly a man of vast information and great conversational powers. Some other gentlemen dropped in, and we chatted till Lady Holland made her appearance. Lord Holland dined by himself on account of his gout. We sat down to dinner in a fine long room, the wainscot of which is rich with gilded coronets, roses, and portcullis. There were Lord Albemarle, Lord Alvanley, Lord Russell, Lord Mahon,—a violent Tory, but a very agreeable companion, and a very good scholar. There was Cradock, a fine fellow who was the Duke of Wellington's aide-de-camp in 1815, and some other people whose names I did not catch. What however is more to the purpose, there was a most excellent dinner. I have always heard that Holland House is famous for its good cheer, and certainly the reputation is not unmerited. After dinner Lord Holland was wheeled in, and placed very near me. He was extremely amusing and good-natured.

In the drawing-room I had a long talk with Lady Holland about the antiquities of the house, and about the purity of the English language, wherein she thinks herself a critic. I happened, in speaking about the Reform Bill, to say that I wished that it had been possible to form a few commercial constituencies, if the word constituency were admissible. "I am glad you put that in," said her ladyship. "I was just going to give it you. It is an odious word. Then there is *talented*, and *influential*, and *gentlemanly*. I never could break Sheridan of *gentlemanly*, though he allowed it to be wrong." We talked about the word *talents* and its history. I said it had first appeared in theological writing, that it was a metaphor taken from the parable in the New Testament, and that it had gradually passed from the vocabulary of divinity into common use. I challenged her to find it in any classical writer on general subjects before the Restoration, or even before the year 1700. I believe that I might safely have gone down later. She seemed surprised by this theory, never having, so far as I could judge, heard of the parable of the talents. I did not tell her, though I might have done so, that a person who professes to be a critic in the delicacies of the English language ought to have the Bible at his fingers' ends.

She is certainly a woman of considerable talents and great literary acquirements. To me she was excessively gracious; yet there is a haughtiness in her courtesy which, even after all that I had heard of her, surprised me. The centurion did not keep his soldiers in better order than she keeps her guests. It is to one "Go," and he goeth; and to another "Do this," and it is done. "Ring the bell, Mr. Macaulay." "Lay down that screen, Lord Russell; you will spoil it." "Mr. Allen, take a candle and show Mr. Cradock the picture of Buonaparte. Lord Holland is, on the other hand, all kindness, simplicity, and vivacity.   He talked very well both on politics and on literature.   He asked me in a very friendly manner about my father's health and begged to be remembered to him.

When my coach came, Lady Holland made me promise that I would on the first fine morning walk out to breakfast with them, and see the grounds;—and, after drinking a glass of very good iced lemonade, I took my leave, much amused and pleased.   The house certainly deserves its reputation for pleasantness, and her ladyship used me, I believe, as well as it is her way to use anybody.

Ever yours,
T. B. M.

JANE WELSH CARLYLE (1801–66)

Brilliant wife of a brilliant husband, Jane Welsh Carlyle survives to our days chiefly by reason of her letters. The couple printed here exhibit something of the wit and liveliness of her nature; they have been selected as showing the woman herself, rather than her attainments.

TO A FRIEND

OCT. 1847.

Times Newspaper

"If W., who went by rail to L. on Saturday night, will return to house he started from, no questions will be asked, and every exertion made to meet his views. If this appeal to his feelings fails to move him, let him send back to his afflicted friends the key of the linen-chest."

DEAR W, The above was written to send to the *Times*, but I bethink me an advertisement will cost five and sixpence, a letter only a penny, and so I take the cheaper course. Why don't you write to me, for God's sake? (That is not swearing, is it?) I should hardly have looked for a letter from you in such a press of business, and other things, had it not been for the fact of the key . . . but why don't you send back my key?

I fancy there must be some new worry to have driven that out of your mind. Not that I have wanted the key any more than if it had been the key of Blue Beard's closet . . . but you did not know whether I should want it or not, and you are always so considerate. Pray write me two lines just to quieten my imagination, which has a faculty of self-tormenting that beats the world.

Emerson is here—has been here since Monday night. I have seen him face to face and (over) soul to (over) soul, and (I may just as well speak the truth and shame the devil) I do *not* like him the least bit. Carlyle says he is a most polite and gentle creature, a man really of a seraphic nature; and all that may be true; at all rates, C. has good cause to say it, for Emerson, with a tact as laudable as prudent, avoids all occasions of dispute, and when dragged into it by the hair of his head, so to speak, he receives the most provoking contradictions with the softness of a feather bed, gives under them for the moment, and so no dreadful collision takes place, such as I was looking for. But with his politeness and tolerance, my approbation ends. The man has no "Natur" about him, his geniality is of the head not the heart, a theoretic systematic geniality, that as Mazzini would say, leaves me cold. In fact, you can get no hold of him nor yet feel held by him, he is neither impressive nor impressionable; a sort of man I cannot get on with, that.

His face is two, or rather half a dozen faces, that change into one another like dissolving views; he has one face, young, refined, almost beautiful, radiant with "virtue its own reward" and another that is old, hatchet-like, crochety, inclusive; like an inscrutability of one of his own poems; whichever way you take him, he slips through your fingers, "like water that cannot be gathered" . . . fine, pure spring water, but water all the same. C. and he will end, I predict, in disliking one another pretty well, though C. under the first restraining grace of hospitality and a certain regard for consistency, makes the best of him as yet; and though the other (in confidence with me) calls C. a good child in spite of his love of the positive, the practical which must be very astonishing to all who have learnt to know him through his books.

Very astonishing indeed, thou American Seraph. You will find many things to astonish you on this side the "Atlantic" I guess. I never saw much come of men who wait upon what is called elevation; your elevated man, *par excellence*, is always, as far as my experience goes, a sort of moral reed, has run all to height without taking breadth along with him. Oh give me "Natur Natur," nobody is loveable without that, however he may strike the stars with his sublime head. I am rather satisfied that he is going away to-morrow night to commence his orations in the North.

He will return to London when the town fills, to lecture here, but then I fancy he will go into lodgings.

Dear W. you are worth a cartload of Emersons, so God bless you with calm in all good things

ever your true friend
JANE CARLYLE

TO THOMAS CARLYLE

TEMPLAND: DECEMBER 30, 1828

GOODY, GOODY, DEAR GOODY, You said you would weary, and I do hope in my heart you are wearying. It will be so sweet to make it all up to you in kisses when I return. You will *take me* and hear all my bits of experiences, and your heart will beat when you find how I have longed to return to you. Darling, dearest, loveliest, "The Lord bless you." [1] I think of you every hour, every moment. I love you and admire you, like—like anything. My own Good-Good. But to get away on Sunday was not in my power: my mother argued, entreated, and finally *grat* [wept]. I held out on the ground of having appointed Alick to meet me at church; but that was untenable. John Kerr could be sent off at break of day to tell that I could not come. I urged that the household would find themselves destitute of every Christian *comfort*, unless I were home before Wednesday. That could be taken care of by sending anything that was wanted from here. Tea, sugar, butchers' meat, everything was at my service. Well, but I wanted, I said, to be your *first foot* on New Year's Day. I might be gratified in this also. She would hire a post-chaise and take me over for that day on condition that I returned at night!

In short, she had a remedy for everything but death, and I could not without seeming very unkind and ungracious, refuse to stay longer than I proposed. So I write this letter "with my own hand" (Ed. Irving) that you may not be disappointed from day to day; but prepare to welcome me "in your choicest mood" on Sunday. If the day is at all tolerable, perhaps Alick or you will meet me at church. Mrs. Crichton of Dabton, was very pressing that you and I should spend some days with them just now, "when their house was full of company." But I assured her it would be losing labour to ask you. However, by way of consolation, I have agreed to "refresh" a party for her with my presence on Friday, and held out some hope that you would visit them at your leisure. "I am sure the kindness of those people——" "The Lord bless them."

Dearest, I wonder if you are getting any victual. There must be cocks at least, and the chickens will surely have laid their eggs. I have many an anxious thought about you: and I wonder if you sleep at nights, or if you are wandering about—on, on—smoking and killing mice. Oh, if I was there I could put my arms so close about your neck, and hush you into the softest sleep you have had since I went away. Good night. Dream of me.

I am ever,
Your own Goody

---

[1] Carlyle noted against this phrase and its repetition later in the letter, "Poor Edward Irving's practice and locution, suspect of being somewhat too solemn.—T. C."

ABRAHAM HAYWARD (1801–84)

Politician, lawyer, and above all, conversationalist, Hayward knew everyone in London and was in the innermost circles of the political and literary world. His dinners in his chambers were famous for their fare no less than for the distinguished company that partook of them: Macaulay, Sydney Smith, Lockhart and many others were constant guests.

TO LADY CHATTERTON

BRIDGEWATER, AUGUST 3, 1845

MY DEAR LADY CHATTERTON, Don't attribute my long silence to indifference, for it is quite the contrary. I kept the writing to you as a *bonne bouche*—as a resource for a melancholy morning; and I now congratulate myself on my prudence, for Heaven knows what I should do with or *to* myself to-day if I had not something agreeable to set about. The course of circuiteering brought me to this place yesterday. It is the ugliest and dirtiest you can fancy; and, being situated on a navigable river, has all the *disagreeables* of a fishing town without the sea. Changes of places are good illustrations of life. I passed part of Thursday and the whole of Friday at Torquay, the most beautiful place in Devonshire, though they have done their best to ruin it by building. You should make a tour to Devonshire and sketch. This one county could match most continental countries for beauty, and Ilfracombe has something of the sublime. Apropos of tours, now provoking it was of Lockhart not to give you a place among the *Lady Travellers* [a quarterly review]. I was quite disappointed at the omission and can only attribute it to forgetfulness. They have left out Mrs. Shelley too. I left London more than three weeks ago, and the only conversable people I have met are Sir William and Lady Molesworth far down in Cornwall, and the Fords at Exeter. He has at last finished his handbook [to Spain], which is full of pleasant and instructive matter, but very thick and close printed. To illustrate a passage, he produced the other day one of the knives the Madrid women wear in their garters. In case a lover is faithless, they draw it and cut him across the face, saying: "I have marked you now." Some lady-killers would have their faces scored like a hot-cross-bun. Lockhart reviewed Ford's book in the *Quarterly*. I also reviewed Mrs. Norton's poem. The short review of it in the *Edinburgh* is by me. Sedgwick's article on the "Vestiges" in the *Edinburgh* has made a noise, but it is too violent and far from well written. The most curious case on Circuit was that of the Brazilian slavers, which you probably saw in the newspapers. They were tried for the murder of their captors, a midshipman and seven sailors. I had a brief for the prosecution, and was occupied three long days about it. The criminals were ten in number, each a picture. Only two looked like pirates or murderers. The man who stabbed the midshipman behind the back was a handsome, soft-looking person, and all the young ladies were for saving him. I am not quite sure that some of them were not for rewarding him too. It is not yet known whether they are to be hanged or no. I go to Lyme Regis to see my family in two or three days, and shall be in town about the 18th. I shall stay there about a fortnight. Pray write to me again, and tell me what you are doing and planning, and I will answer on the instant. Regards to Sir William.

Ever yours faithfully

A. HAYWARD

SARA COLERIDGE (1802–52)

As daughter of the poet, Sara was brought up at Keswick in the constant society of Southey and Wordsworth. She soon showed great literary abilities and wrote many books for children.

TO MRS. FARRER

12 CLIFF TERRACE, MARGATE, SEPT. 5TH, 1843

MY DEAR FRIEND, Here we are, my children, and nurse, and self, on the East Cliff at Margate, a few miles from the spot where I sojourned with you in June. That fortnight is marked among the fortnights of this my first year of widowhood with a comparative whiteness, in the midst of such deep (though never, I must thankfully acknowledge, never, even at the earliest period of my loss, quite unrelieved) blackness. I fixed upon this place, instead of Broadstairs or Ramsgate, on account of its greater cheapness, and because it could be reached with rather less exertion. Lodgings certainly *are* cheaper than I could have got them in an equally good situation at more genteel sea-bathing places; but provisions are dear enough—lamb 8½*d.*, and beef 9*d.*! I am so often twitted with my devotion to intellectual things, that I am always glad of an opportunity of sporting a little beef and mutton erudition, though I cannot help thinking that, as society is now constituted in the professional middle rank of life—still more in a higher one—women may get on and make their families comfortable, and manage with tolerable economy—by which I mean economy that does not cost more than it is worth of time and devotion of spirit —with less knowledge of details respecting what we are to eat, and what to put on, than used to be thought essential to the wise and worthy matron. I dare say your dear C. will make her loved and honoured S. as comfortable as if she had been studying butchers' and bakers' bills, and mantua-making, and upholstery in a little way, for the last seven years, instead of reading Dante, and Goethe, and Richter, and Wordsworth, and Tennyson. But to return to this place, it is a contrast to Broadstairs as looked out upon from the White Hart, where we took up our abode the first night; but the East Cliff, where, by medical recommendation, we have settled ourselves for a fortnight or three weeks, is neither more nor less than the Broadstairs Cliffery continued; and as we return from the gully leading down to the sands (the very brother to that which I so often went down and up with you), Edy and I might fancy that we were returning to the Albion Street lodgings, if it were not for the tower of the handsome new church, where we attended morning service last Sunday, which reminds us that we are at Margate.

We were delayed in coming hither for some days by Herbert's prolonged stay at Rickmansworth, where he spent nearly three weeks in a sort of boys' paradise, bathing two or three times a day. Both Baron and Lady A. wrote about him to me in very gratifying terms. It is perhaps not right to repeat things honourable to our children without being equally communicative about their faults and ill-successes. But you have been so specially friendly with me, and shown such kind interest about all that concerns me, that I think I should withhold a pleasure from you in not telling you what has very much pleased me. Herbert thinks this place very *seedy*, and despises the bathing. The tide seems never in a state to please him; but the truth is, he wants companions, and does not like to be a solitary Triton among the minnows, or rather, as those are fresh-water fish, among the crabs and seaweed. However, he has got "Japhet in Search of a Father" from the circulating library, reads a portion daily of Euripides, and has begun learning French; and it is quite right that a little *seediness* should come in its turn after "jollity," and quietness and plain fare after "splendid lark," with "Sock" of all sorts, that he may learn to cut out interests and amusements for himself out of home materials.

I must tell tales of the vessel that brought us hither, in order to deter you, dear friend, from ever trusting yourself to it in future. The "Prince of Wales" does certainly make its way fast over the water, but the vibration of its disproportionately small frame under the energy of its strong steam-engine is such that it fatigued me much more than a slower voyage would have done, and gave both nurse and me a headache. The motion almost prevented me, too, from reading. Carlyle's "Hero-worship" trembled in my hand like a culprit before a judge; and as the book *is* very full of paradoxes, and has some questionable matter in it, this shaking seemed rather symbolical. But oh! it is a book fit rather to shake (take it all in all) than to be shaken. It is very full of noble sentiments and wise reflections, and throws out many a suggestion which will not waste itself like a blast blown in a wilderness, but will surely rouse many a heart and mind to a right, Christian-like way of acting and of dealing with the gifted and godlike in man and of men. Miss Farrer lent me the work, and many others. Very pleasant to me was her stay at Gloucester Terrace, if *pleasant* is a fit word for an intercourse which awakened thoughts and feelings of "higher gladness" than are commonly so described. She is one who loves to reveal her mind, with all its "open secrets," to those who care at all for the one thing which is, and which she happily has found to be, needful; and few indeed are the minds which will so well bear such inspection as she invites; few can display such a pure depth of sunny blue without a cloud, such love for all men, and Christ above all—ascending from them whom she has seen to God whom she has not seen, and again honouring them and doing good to them, on principle, for His sake. My doctrinal differences from her (and *some* doctrine we all must have in this world) are considerable; but I could almost say, that were all men like her, no Christian *doctrine* would be needed. She has much knowledge, too, of men and things—has read and seen much; and pray tell you T. H. that I learned to thread the at first bewildering labyrinth of her discourse, after a while much better than at first. Even to the last her rapid transitions confounded me very often, and some of her replies to objections are rather appeals to the imagination and affections than properly answers. But she has a logic of her own; and though I do maintain that Christendom would fall abroad if it were not knit together by a logic of another sort, the want of which would be felt sorely, if it were possible that it could ever be wholly wanting, which the nature of man prevents; yet this logic of the heart and spiritual nature is more than sufficient to guide every individual aright that possesses it in such high measure as she does.

MARJORIE FLEMING (1803–11)

Pet Marjorie, the favourite of Scott, the wonderful little creature who only lived to be eight, yet found her way into the ponderous "Dictionary of National Biography," is unique in English literature, perhaps in any literature. Yet she was no Infant Phenomenon; Marjorie was just a clever little girl who had the gift of writing just what she thought. This, her first letter, was written when she was five years old.

TO HER COUSIN ISABELLA KEITH

MY DEAR ISA, I now sit down on my botom to answer all your kind and beloved letters which you was so good as to write to me. This is the first time I ever wrote a letter in my life.

There are a great number of Girls in the Square and they cry just like a pig when we are under the painfull necessity of putting it to Death.

Miss Potune, a lady of my acquaintance, praises me dreadfully. I repeated something out of Deen Swift and she said I was fit for the stage, and you may think I was primmed up with majestick Pride, but upon my word I felt myselfe turn a little birsay—birsay is a word which is a word that William composed which is as you may suppose a little enraged. This horid fat Simpliton says that my Aunt is beautiful which is intirely impossible for that is not her nature.

GERALD GRIFFIN (1803-40)

Dramatist and poet, Griffin was an Irishman who lived in the full swing of the literary and social world of Dublin. He was a great friend of Tom Moore, and it is largely on account of his references to him that the following letter is of interest.

MONDAY MORNING, MARCH 31, 1833
TAUNTON

MY DEAR L. Procrastination—it is all the fruit of procrastination. When Dan and I returned to the inn at Devizes, after our first sight and speech of the Irish Melodist, I opened my writing case to give L. an account of our day's work: then I put it off, I believe, till morning: then as Dan was returning, I put it off till some hour when I could tell you about it at full leisure: then Saunders and Otley set me to work, and I put it off until my authorship should be concluded for the season, at least; and now it is concluded, for I am not to publish *this* year; and here I come before you with my news, my golden bit of news, stale, flat, and unprofitable. I saw the poet! and I spoke to him, and he spoke to me, and it was not to bid me "get out of his way," as the King of France did to the man who boasted that his majesty had spoken to him; but it was to shake hands with me, and to ask me "How I did, Mr. Griffin," and to speak of "my fame." *My* fame! Tom Moore talk of my fame! Ah, the rogue! he was humbugging, I'm afraid. He knew the soft side of an author's heart, and, perhaps, he had pity on my long melancholy-looking figure, and said to himself, "I will make this poor fellow feel pleasant, if I can"; for which, with all his roguery, who could help liking him and being grateful to him. But you want to know all about it step by step, if not for the sake of your poor dreamy-looking *Beltard*, at least for that of fancy, wit, and patriotism. I will tell you then, although Dan has told you before, for the subject cannot be tiresome to an Irishwoman. I will tell you how we hired a great, grand cabriolet, and set off—no, pull in a little. I should first tell you how we arrived at the inn at Devizes, late in the evening, I forget the exact time, and ordered tea (for which,

by the bye, we had a prodigious appetite, not having stopped to dine
in Bath or Bristol), when the waiter (a most solid-looking fellow, who
won Dan's heart by his precision and the mathematical exactness of
all his movements) brought us up, amongst other good things, fresh
butter prepared in a very curious way.   I could not for a long time
imagine how they did it.   It was in strings just like vermicelli, and
as if tied in some way at the bottom.   King George, not poor *real*
King George, but Peter Pindar's King George, was never more puzzled
to know how the apple got into the dumpling; but at last, on applying
to the waiter, he told us it was done by squeezing it through a linen
cloth; an excellent plan, particularly in frosty weather, when it is actually
impossible to make the butter adhere to the bread on account of its
working up with a coat of crumbs on the under side, but that's true
—Tom Moore—and, besides, it is unfashionable now to spread the
butter, isn't it?   I'm afraid I *exposed* myself, as they say.   Well, we
asked the waiter, out came the important question, "How far is Sloperton
Cottage from Devizes?"   "Sloperton, sir? that's Mr. Moore's place,
sir, *he is a poet, sir*.   We do all Mr. Moore's work."   What ought
I to have done?   To have flung my arms about his neck for knowing
so much about Moore, or to have knocked him down for knowing
so little?   Well, we learned all we wanted to know, and, after making
our arrangements for the following day, went to bed and slept soundly.
And in the morning it was that we hired the grand cabriolet, and set
off to Sloperton; drizzling rain, but a delightful country; such a gentle
shower as that through which *he* looked at Innisfallen—his farewell
look.   And we drove away until we came to a cottage, a cottage of
gentility, with two gateways and pretty grounds about it, and we alighted
and knocked at the hall-door; and there was dead silence, and we
whispered one another; and my nerves thrilled as the wind rustled in
the creeping shrubs that graced the retreat of—Moore.   Oh, there's
no use in talking, but I must be fine.   I wonder I ever stood it at
all, and I an Irishman, too, and singing his songs since I was the height
of my knee—"The Veiled Prophet," "Azim," "She is far from the
Land," "Those Evening Bells."   But the door opened, and a young
woman appeared.   "Is Mr. Moore at home?"   "I'll see, sir.   What
name shall I say, sir?"   Well, not to be too particular, we were shown
upstairs, when we found the nightingale in his cage; in honester language,
and more to the purpose, we found our hero in his study, a table before
him covered with books and papers, a drawer half opened and stuffed
with letters, a piano also open at a little distance; and the thief himself,

a little man, but full of spirits, with eyes, hands, feet, and frame for ever
in motion, looking as if it would be a feat for him to sit for three minutes
quiet in his chair. I am no great observer of proportions, but he seemed
to me to be a neat-made little fellow, tidily buttoned up, young as fifteen
at heart, though with hair that reminded me of "Alps in the sunset";
not handsome, perhaps, but something in the whole *cut* of him that
pleased me; finished as an actor, but without an actor's affectation;
easy as a gentleman, but without *some* gentlemen's formality: in a word,
as people say when they find their brains begin to run aground at
the fag end of a magnificent period, we found him a hospitable, warm-
hearted Irishman, as pleasant as could be himself, and disposed to make
others so. And is this enough? And need I tell you the day was
spent delightfully, chiefly in listening to his innumerable jests and
admirable stories and beautiful similes—beautiful and original as those
he throws into his songs—and anecdotes that would make the Danes
laugh? and how we did all we could, I believe, to get him to stand for
Limerick; and how we called again the day after, and walked with
him about his little garden; and how he told us that he always wrote
walking, and how we came in again and took luncheon, and how I
was near forgetting that it was Friday (which you know I am rather
apt to do in pleasant company), and how he walked with us through the
fields, and wished us a "good-bye" and left us to do as well as we could
without him?

THOMAS LOVELL BEDDOES (1803–49)

Beddoes had given promise of a great literary career when he decided to take up medicine as a profession. In July, 1825, he went to study at Göttingen, and in this letter to his old friend Kelsall he describes his impressions of the place.

TO THOMAS FORBES KELSALL

GÖTTINGEN

[OCT. 5, 1826]

Lieber Kelsall, Der, den du so eifrig die schönen Wissenschaften und Lituratur treibst, der in "des Lebens goldenen Baum," den sängenden Baum von den Tausend und einen Nächten suchest, der dem Anbeter der saligen Gottheiten den Musen u.s. w. war unterhaltender kann der Liebhaber von Knaben der flussiger Botaniker und Physiolog mittheilen? u.s.w.

Well, I hope that has frightened you: however, as I can still write a little English and it will be a profitable exercise I will continue in that be-L.E.L.-ed and be-Milmaned tongue. That I have not sent you a letter sooner, will be scarce a cause of complaint or discontent when you learn that all my sublunary excursions this summer have been botanical ones, and my transluscary (it is a good word and I only recollect it in Drayton's "Epistle to Reynolds"—has Johnson it?) a thought or two for a didactic Boem (is that *richtig?*) on Myology, which I was prevented from executing by finding that a preceding genius of the scalpel had led the Muses a dance to his marrow-bones and cleaver.

I wish you would come and see me: not only because it would save me the chagrin of dosing you (the shop!) with superfluous solutions of nonsense in ink: but that you might look over my unhappy devil of a tragedy, which is done and done for; its limbs being scattered and unconnected as those of the old gentleman whom Medea minced and boiled young. I have tried twenty times at least to copy it fair, but have given it up with disgust, and there is no one here for whose judgement in such things I would give a fig or a teacup without a handle (I have one at the critic's service), consequently neither their praise

690

nor blame can lure or sting me onwards. However we must disappoint disappointments by taking them coolly, and throw a chain-bridge across impossibilities or dig a passage under them, or Rubiconize them if one has the good saddle-horse Pegasus to ride—and I will find out some way of bestowing my dullness on you in its ore of illegibility.

I gave you (or did I not?) a caricature of three professors last letter, and now you shall have a little more Göttingen scandal. Tobias Mayer is professor of nat. philosophy, a little fellow in top-boots, with a toothless earthquake of a mouth, and a frosty grey coat; he never can find words, repeats his *alsos*, etc., and by endeavouring to make up for want of eloquence by violent action, he literally swims through his subject. His dad was a good astronomer and published a famous map of the moon. This "Wife for a month" of the earth revenged the publication of her secret hiding-places on the most natural object of female heavenly malice, his wife, thus ingeniously. Top-booted Toby in his lecture was talking of her sonnetship; and came to the subject of her portrait. "Among others," said he, "Tobias—To-bi-as Mayer—who was—a-mong others was my father."

Tiek has published in the "Urania Taschenbuch" for 1826 a story called "Dichterleben" which is a very well worked adventure of Marlowe and Green's with Shakespeare. The latter is however, too German, and he announces an English translation, probably by himself, to be published at Leipsig under the title of the "Lives of Poets." But you are a bad Marlowite or none at all—I like the man on many scores. Here is a Dr. Raupach who lays a tragedy or two in the year —mostly windeggs—but he's the wit of the folks about Melpomene's sepulchre in Germany. Schiller, you know, took her out of the critical pickle she lies in and made a few lucky galvanic experiments with her, so that the people thought she was alive when she was only kicking. Do you know that a French doctor of medicine, too, has published a gossiping tour in England in letters, in which he criticizes our late friend Barry Cornwall under the name of Proctor! The fellow's book is all out of *Blackwood* excepting a plate or two of autographs out of the forgotten *Forget-me-not*. Goethe is preparing a new edition of his rhymed and prosy commissions, XXXX vols. for ten dollars; who'll buy, who'll buy? They are as cheap as oysters if not so swallowable.

In the neighbourhood of Göttingen is a slightly Chalybeate spring and a little inn with a tea garden whither students and Philistines (i.e. townsmen who are not students) resort on Sundays to dance and ride on the Merry-go-round, an instrument of pleasure which is always to be found on such places, and is much ridden by the German students, perhaps because it, as well as waltzing, produces mechanically the same effects as the week-day hobby-horse, the philosophy of Schelling, etc., doth physically, i.e. a giddiness and confusion of the brain.

Behind this Terpsichorean τέμενος rises a woody rocky eminence on which stands a fair high tower and some old mossy and ivy-hugged walls, the remains of an old castle called the Plesse. The date of the tower is said to be 963. If this be true it may have earned a citizenship among the semi-eternal stony populace of the planet: at all events it will be older than some hills which pretend to be natural and carry trees and houses—e.g. Monte Nuovo.

On this hill and in the hole and vaults of the old building resides a celebrated reptile, which we have not in England—the salamander. He is to a lizard what a toad is to a frog, slow, fat and wrinkled—of a mottled black and yellow. It is true that under his skin one finds a thick layer of a viscid milky fluid of a peculiar not disagreeable smell, which the beast has the power of ejecting when irritated and by this means might for a short time resist the power of fire.

Where the vulgar fable has its origin I am altogether ignorant. I believe it comes from the Middle Ages; from the monkish writers of natural history perhaps—and they might have had a spite against the poor amphibium because he is unorthodox enough to live a long while after you have removed his stomach and intestines—and therefore condemned him to the flames for impiety against the belly gods Ἀδηφαγία and Ἀκρατοπότης. The servants at the altars of these thundering deities (v. Euripides "Cyclops," 327) may aduce physiological authority for the immateriality of their adored Paunch. J. Baptista van Helmont placed the soul, which he nicknamed Archæus, in the stomach and whatever the clergy knew more about the spirit in question I do not think they are inclined to let the cat out of the bag. This is a pleasant doctrine for aldermen and Kings, the dimensions of the soul perhaps corresponding with the size of its habitation: only they must beware of purges. It would be a mishap to leave one's soul in a close-stool-pan, like George the 2nd.

To return to our Maria-spring, the aforesaid tenement or tenements of fantastictoeness, and what I had intended to tell you. It was here that an unhappy Hungarian who came to Göttingen three or four years ago to study medicine, and had wandered to propitiate his Archüus with beer and tobacco at this place, was smitten with the charms of the tavern-keeper's daughter. She was insensible and he desperate.

He left Göttingen and built a hut under a rock in the Plesse wood where he lived two years, descending occasionally to feed his eyes upon the beauties of the cruel one.   But either the lady departed or his passion burnt out, for at the end of this time the hermitage was left by its love-lorn founder and it now remains as an object of curiosity for folks, who see it, hear his tale and laugh at it.

Such is alas! the state of sentiment in this part of Germany: and probably if Werter's hermitage stood here it would be equally profaned; hard-heartedness and worldly prudence has its paw upon the poor planet; and as Chaucer sung long ago, Pity is dead and buried in gentle heart—but we have lost the sepulchre.   And we fellows who cannot weep without the grace of onions or hartshorn, who take terror by the nose, light our matches with lightning, have plucked the "tempest-winged chariots of the deep" of its winds and impeded its pinions with steam.   We who have little belief in heaven and still less faith in man's heart, are we fit ministers for the temple of Melpomene?   O age of crockery! no—let Scandal and Satire be the only reptiles of the soul-abandoned corse of literature.

DOUGLAS JERROLD (1803-57)

A century ago Jerrold's name was one to conjure with. "Black-eyed Susan, or All in the Downs" was a play known throughout England. When "Punch" came out, in 1841, Jerrold became one of its principal contributors and "Mrs. Caudle's Curtain Lectures" has taken its definite place in literature. The "Weekly Newspaper" mentioned below was short-lived, but some years later he started "Lloyds Weekly Newspaper" with better success.

TO CHARLES DICKENS

[OCTOBER 1846]

MY DEAR DICKENS, Let me break this long silence with heartiest congratulations. Your book ["Dombey and Son"] has spoken like a trumpet to the nation, and it is to me a pleasure to believe that you have faith in the sincerity of my gladness at your triumph. You have rallied your old thousands again; and, what is most delightful, you have rebuked and for ever "put down" the small things, half knave, half fool, that love to make the failure they "feed on." They are under your boot—tread 'em to paste.

And how is it that your cordial letter, inviting me to your cordial home, has been so long unanswered? Partly from hope, partly from something like shame. Let me write you a brief penitential history. When you left England I had been stirred to this newspaper [*Weekly Newspaper*] ('tis forwarded to you, and, I hope arrives). Nevertheless, the project was scarcely formed, and I had not the least idea of producing it before October—perhaps not until Christmas. This would have allowed me to take my sunny holiday at Lausanne. Circumstances, however, too numerous for this handbill, compelled me to precipitate the speculation or to abandon it. I printed in July, yet still believed I should be able to trust it to sufficient hands, long enough to enable me to spend a fortnight with you. And from week to week I hoped this—with fainter hopes, but still hopes. At last I found it impossible, though compelled, by something very like conjestion of the brain, to abscond for ten days' health and idleness. And

694

I went to Jersey, when, by heavens, my heart was at Lausanne. But why not *then* answer this letter? The question I put to myself—God knows how many times—when your missive, every other day, in my desk, smote my ungrateful hand like a thistle. And so time went on, and "Dombey" comes out, and now, to be sure, I write. Had "Dombey" fallen apoplectic from the steam-press of Messrs. B[radbury] and E[vans], of course your letter would still have remained unanswered. But, with all England shouting "Viva Dickens," it is a part of my gallant nature to squeak through my quill "brayvo" too.

This newspaper, with other allotments, is hard work; but it is independence. And it was the hope of it that stirred me to the doing. I have a feeling of dread—a something almost insane in its abhorrence of the condition of the old, worn-out literary man; the squeezed orange (lemons in my case, sing some sweet critics); the spent bullet; the useless lumber of the world, flung upon literary funds while alive, with the hat to be sent round for his coffin and his widow. And therefore I set up this newspaper, which—I am sure of it—you will be glad to learn, is a large success. Its first number went off 18,000 it is now 9,000 (at the original outlay of about £1,500), and is within a fraction three-fourths my own. It was started at the dullest of dull times but every week it is steadily advancing. I hope to make it an engine of some good. And so much for my apology—which, if you resist, why, I hope Mrs. Dickens and Miss H[ogarth] (it's so long ago —is she still Miss?) will take up and plead for me. . . .

You have heard, I suppose, that Thackeray is big with twenty parts, and, unless he is wrong in his time, expects the first instalment at Christmas. *Punch*, I believe, holds its course. . . . Nevertheless, I do not very cordially agree with its new spirit. I am convinced that the world will get tired (at least I hope so) of this eternal guffaw at all things. After all, life has something serious in it. It cannot all be a comic history of humanity. Some men would, I believe, write the Comic Sermon on the Mount. Think of a Comic History of England; the drollery of Alfred; the fun of Sir Thomas More in the Tower; the farce of his daughter begging the dead head, and clasping it in her coffin on her bosom. Surely the world will be sick unless *Punch* goes a little back to his occasional gravities.

And so you are going to Paris? I'm told Paris in the spring is very delectable. Not very bad sometimes at Christmas. Do you know anybody likely to ask me to take some *bouilli* there? In all seriousness, give my hearty remembrances to your wife and sister.

I hope that health and happiness are showered on them, on you, and all. And believe me, my dear Dickens,

Yours ever truly and sincerely,
DOUGLAS JERROLD

(For Dickens's answer see page 740.)

TO MISS SABILLA NOVELLO

PUTNEY GREEN, JUNE 9, 1849

DEAR MISS NOVELLO, I thank you very sincerely for your present, though I cannot but fear its fatal effect upon my limited fortunes, for it is so very handsome that whenever I produce it I feel that I have thousands a year, and, as in duty bound, am inclined to pay accordingly. I shall go about, to the astonishment of all *omnibii* men, insisting upon paying sovereigns for sixpences. Happily, however, this amiable insanity will cure itself (or I may always bear my wife with me as a keeper).

About this comedy [*The Cat's Paw*]. I am writing it under the most significant warnings. As the Eastern King—name unknown, to me at least—kept a crier to warn him that he was but a mortal and must die, and so to behave himself as decently as it is possible for any poor King to do, so do I keep a flock of eloquent geese that continually, within earshot, cackle of the British public. Hence, I trust to defeat the birds of the Haymarket by the birds of Putney.

But in this comedy I do contemplate such a heroine, as a set-off to the many sins imputed to me as committed against woman, whom I have always considered to be an admirable idea imperfectly worked out. Poor soul! she can't help that. Well, this heroine shall be woven of moonbeams—a perfect angel, with one wing cut to keep her among us. She shall be all devotion. She shall hand over her lover (never mind his heart, poor wretch!) to her grandmother, who she suspects is very fond of him, and then, disguising herself as a youth, she shall enter the British Navy, and return in six years, say, with epaulets on her shoulders, and her name in the Navy List, rated Post-Captain. You will perceive that I have Madame Celeste in my eye—am measuring her for the uniform. And young ladies will sit in the boxes, and with tearful eyes, and noses like rose-buds, say, "What magnanimity!" and when this great work is done—this monument of the very best gilt gingerbread to women set up on the Haymarket stage—you shall, if you will, go and see it, and make one to cry for the "Author," rewarding him with a crown of tin-foil, and a shower of sugar-plums.

In lively hope of that ecstatic moment, I remain,

Yours truly,

DOUGLAS JERROLD

TO CHARLES KNIGHT

PUTNEY, AUGUST 11 [1849]

MY DEAR KNIGHT, A friend of darkness or a spirit of light has, I incline to believe, assumed my form (which of the two do you think it would best fit?) and is going up and down, seeking what dinner it may devour. We are dwelling in the green wildness of Putney, and receive assurance that I am in Paris. If really there, in any shape, I hope I am behaving myself. I have been only once to town since I saw you. All London is in my present thoughts a reeking grave-yard; pray you, avoid it. Sit in your wicker-chair, get your wife and daughter to cover your thistle-down with vine-leaves, and quaff imaginary quarts of nut-brown—since the real, however particular, is denied you.

Nothing stirring in London but the cholera and murder. It will be proved that certain proprietors of Sunday newspapers hired the respited Mannings to murder Fergus O'Connor. The *Observer* intends to present the deceased man and wife, when duly hanged, with two silver coffin-plates. They are now to be seen at the office (with blanks for date of demise) on purchase of a paper. But don't let even *this* bring you to town.

Do you stay another week? If so, at the risk of crowding you (I have but a little body, as Queen Mary said of her neck), I will come to-morrow week, if I can return on the Sunday. I can sleep any-where—upon a boot-jack or a knife-board.

Mind you insist upon your wife to insist upon your remaining from St. Bride's. Go to the top of Box Hill, and "with nostril well-upturned, scent the murky air" of London—and keep away from it.

Remember me to Mrs. Knight and daughter, single and double. Mr. Kerr (is there one *r* too many here? if so, I'll take it back) talked some eloquent Gaelic about some whiskey. . . .

BENJAMIN DISRAELI, EARL OF BEACONSFIELD (1804-81)

The greatest of nineteenth-century Conservative statesmen and the favourite prime minister of Queen Victoria, Disraeli will, despite all this, live to posterity rather as a man of letters. While still young he travelled on the Continent and his letters home form one of the most charming collections of descriptive writing that we possess. His letter to Carlyle offering the Bath and a pension called forth the answer given on page 656.

TO HIS MOTHER

GRANADA: AUGUST 1, 1830

MY DEAR MOTHER, Although you doubtless assist, as the French phrase it, at the reading of my despatches, you will, I am sure, be pleased to receive one direct from your absent son. It has just occurred to me that I have never yet mentioned the Spanish ladies, and I do not think that I can address anything that I have to say upon this agreeable subject to any one more suitable than yourself. You know that I am rather an admirer of the blonde; and, to be perfectly candid, I will confess to you that the only times which I have been so unfortunate as to be captivated, or captured, in this country were both by English-women. But these Espagnolas are nevertheless very interesting personages. What we associate with the idea of female beauty is not common in this country. There are none of those seraphic countenances, which strike you dumb or blind, but faces in abundance which will never pass without commanding a pleasing glance. Their charm consists in their sensibility; each incident, every person, every word touches the far eye of a Spanish lady, and her features are constantly confuting the creed of Mahomet, and proving that she has a soul: but there is nothing quick, harsh, or forced about her. She is extremely unaffected, and not at all French. Her eyes gleam rather than sparkle, she speaks with quick vivacity but in sweet tones, and there is in all her carriage, particularly when she walks, a certain dignified grace which never leaves her, and which is very remarkable. The general female dress in this country is a black silk, called a *basquiña*, and a

698

black silk shawl, with which they usually envelop their head, called a *mantilla*. As they walk along in this costume in an evening, with their soft dark eyes dangerously conspicuous, you willingly believe in their universal beauty. They are remarkable for the beauty of their hair; of this they are very proud, and indeed its luxuriance is only equalled by the attention which they lavish on its culture. I have seen a young girl of fourteen whose hair reached her feet, and was as glossy as the curl of a Lady Caroline [Lamb]. All day long, even the lowest order are brushing, curling, and arranging it. A fruit-woman has her hair dressed with as much care as the Duchess of Ossuna. At this time of the year they do not wear the mantilla generally over the head, but show their combs, which are of immense size. The fashion of their combs varies constantly, every two or three months, though the part of the costume of which the Spanish female is most proud. The moment that a new comb appears, even the servant wench will have her old one melted down, and thus, with the cost of a dollar or two, appear the next holiday in the newest style. These combs are worn at the back of the head. They are of tortoiseshell, the very fashionable wear them of the white. I sat next to a lady of high distinction at a bull-fight at Seville. She was the daughter-in-law of the Captain-General, and the most beautiful Spaniard I have yet met. Her comb was white, and she wore a mantilla of blonde, I have no doubt extremely valuable, for it was very dirty. The effect, however, was charming. Her hair was glossy black, and her eyes like an antelope's, but all her other features deliciously soft; and she was further adorned, which is rare in Spain, with a rosy cheek, for here our heroines are rather sallow. But they counteract this defect by never appearing until twilight, which calls them from their bowers, fresh, though languid, from the late siesta. To conclude, the only fault of the Spanish beauty is that she too soon indulges in the magnificence of embonpoint. There are, however, many exceptions to this. At seventeen a Spanish beauty is poetical, tall, lithe, and clear, though sallow. But you have seen Mercandotti. As she advances, if she does not lose her shape, she resembles Juno rather than Venus. Majestic she ever is; and if her feet are less twinkling than in her first career, look on her hand and you'll forgive them all.

There is calm voluptuousness about the life here that wonderfully accords with my disposition, so that if I were resident, and had my intellect at command, I do not know any place where I could make it more productive. The imagination is ever at work, and beauty and grace are not scared away by those sounds and sights, those constant cares and changing feelings, which are the proud possession of our free land of eastern winds. You rise at eight, and should breakfast lightly, although a table covered with all fruits renders that rather difficult to one who inherits, with other qualities good and bad, that passion for the most delightful productions of nature, with which my beloved sire can sympathize. I only wish I had him here over a medley of grape and melon, gourd and prickly-pear. In the morning you never quit the house, and these are hours which might be profitably employed under the inspiration of a climate which is itself poetry, for it sheds over everything a golden hue which does not exist in the objects themselves illuminated. At present I indulge only in a calm reverie, for I find the least exertion of mind instantly aggravate all my symptoms; and even this letter is an exertion, which you would hardly credit. My general health was never better. You know how much better I am on a sunny day in England; well, I have had two months of sunny days infinitely warmer. I have during all this period enjoyed general health of which I have no memory during my life. All the English I have met are ill, and live upon a diet. I eat everything, and my appetite each day increases. I have constantly ridden eight hours a day on horseback. I travelled through three successive nights, and saw the sun set and rise, without quitting my saddle, which few men can say, yet have I never known fatigue. This is literally the fact. A feverish feeling, of which all travellers complain, I have not known for an instant, so extraordinary and so beneficial is the influence of this climate upon me, and so entirely does my frame sympathize with this expanding sun. But is all a subject of congratulation when the great evil does not proportionately—I should say, does not at all amend? The great hope, that with the improvement of my general health it would disappear, seems vanishing. To what am I to cling? Enough of this: it is three o'clock, and nearly dinner; I doff my dressing-gown and slippers, my only costume, and prepare my toilette. The Spanish cuisine is not much to my taste, for garlic and bad oil preponderate; but it has its points: the soups are good, and *the most agreeable dish* in the world is an olio. I will explain it to you, for my father would delight in it. There are two large dishes, one at each end of the table. The one at the top contains bouilli beef, boiled pork sausage, black-pudding; all these not mixed together, but in their separate portions. The other dish is a medley of vegetables and fruits, generally French beans, caravanseras, slices of melons, and whole pears. Help each person to a portion of the meats, and then to the medley. Mix them in your plate together, and drown them in tomato sauce. There is no garlic and no grease of any kind. I have eaten it thus every day, it is truly delightful. Of course you can fix upon those ingredients most at hand. I have described a usual olio. The tomato sauce here is very light, piquant and pleasant. It is thin. We have it with us too thick and rich. The Spaniards eat the tomato in all possible ways. I obtained the receipt for one dish, which infinitely pleased me, and with which I think my father would be charmed. It is very simple. Take four pounds of tomatos, fry them very small, add four eggs, yolk and all. Mix them well. They should be served up very dry, and indeed on the whole like a dry soup, but of a very pretty colour. I need not tell the mistress of so experienced a cuisine as you, to add a small quantity of onion in frying the tomatos. By-the-bye, Adams, I hope, is well.

After dinner you take your siesta. I generally sleep for two hours. I think this practice conducive to health. Old people, however, are apt to carry it to excess. By the time I have risen and arranged my toilette it is time to steal out, and call upon any agreeable family whose Tertullia you may choose to honour, which you do, after the first time, uninvited, and with them you take your tea or chocolate. This is often *al fresco*, under the piazza or colonnade of the *patio*. Here you while away the time until it is cool enough for the *alameda* or public walk. At Cadiz, and even at Seville, up the Guadalquivir, you are sure of a delightful breeze from the water. The sea breeze comes like a spirit. The effect is quite magical. As you are lolling in listless languor in the hot and perfumed air, an invisible guest comes dancing into the party and touches them all with an enchanted wand. All start, all smile. It has come; it is the sea breeze. There is much discussion whether it is as strong, or whether weaker, than the night before. The ladies furl their fans and seize their mantillas, the cavaliers stretch their legs and give signs of life. All rise. I offer my arm to Dolores or Florentina (is not this familiarity strange?), and in ten minutes you are in the *alameda*. What a change! All is now life and liveliness. Such bowing, such kissing, such fluttering of fans, such gentle criticism of gentle friends! But the fan is the most wonderful part of the whole scene. A Spanish lady with her fan might shame the tactics of a troop of horse. Now she unfurls it with the slow pomp and conscious elegance of a peacock. Now she flutters it with all the languor of a listless beauty, now with all the liveliness of a vivacious one. Now, in the midst of a very tornado, she closes it with a whir which makes you start, pop! In the midst of your confusion Dolores taps you on the elbow; you turn round to listen, and Florentina pokes you in your side. Magical instrument! You know that it speaks a particular language, and gallantry requires no other mode to express its most subtle conceits or its most unreasonable demands than this slight, delicate organ. But remember, while you read, that here, as in England, it is not confined alone to your delightful sex. I also have my fan, which makes my cane extremely jealous. If you think I have grown extraordinarily effeminate, learn that in this scorching clime the soldier will not mount guard without one. Night wears on, we sit, we take a *panal*, which is as quick work as snapdragon, and far more elegant; again we stroll. Midnight clears the public walks, but few Spanish families retire till two. A solitary bachelor like myself still wanders, or still lounges on a bench in the *warm* moonlight. The last guitar dies away, the cathedral clock wakes up your reverie, you too seek your couch, and amid a gentle, sweet flow of loveliness, and light, and music, and fresh air, thus dies a day in Spain.

Adieu, my dearest mother. If possible, I write to my father from this place. 1,000 loves to all.

B. DISRAELI

MALTA : SATURDAY, 27TH

I SCRIBBLE, until the return of the packet, a daily bulletin. We landed yesterday for breakfast, and are quartered in a capital hotel, Beverley's. I assure you I look forward to some repose here, after all my exertions, with great zest. We did not find this at Gibraltar, where our quarters were horrid. To our surprise we find James Clay here, immensely improved, and quite a hero. He has been here a month, and has already beat the whole garrison at rackets and billiards and other wicked games, given lessons to their prima donna, and seccatura'd the primo tenore. Really he has turned out a most agreeable personage, and has had that advantage of society in which he had been deficient, and led a life which for splendid adventure would beat any young gentleman's yet published in three vols. post 8vo. Lord Burghersh wrote an opera for him, and Lady Normanby a farce. He dished Prince Pignatelli at billiards, and did the Russian Legation at écarté. I had no need of letters of introduction here, and have already "troops of friends." The fact is, in our original steam-packet there were some very agreeable fellows, officers, whom I believe I never mentioned to you. They have been long expecting your worship's offspring, and have gained great fame in repeating his third-rate stories at second hand: so in consequence of these messengers I am received with branches of palm. Here the younkers do nothing but play rackets, billiards, and cards, race and smoke. To govern men, you must either excel them in their accomplishments, or despise them. Clay does one; I do the other, and we are both equally popular. Affectation tells here even better than wit. Yesterday, at the racket court, sitting in the gallery among strangers, the ball entered, and lightly struck me, and fell at my feet. I picked it up, and observing a young rifleman excessively stiff, I humbly requested him to forward its passage into the court, as I really had never thrown a ball in my life. This incident has been the general subject of conversation at all the messes to-day!

I call on the Governor to-morrow. He is reputed a very *nonchalant* personage, and exceedingly exclusive in his conduct to his subjects. Clay had no letter to him, but his Excellency is a great racket player, and so he addressed our friend one day with condescending familiarity, but did not ask him to dinner till he had been here some time, which so offended our friend—who is excessively grand, and talks of nothing but Burghersh, Normanby, Lady Williamson, and various princes—that he refused, and is in opposition.

The city is one of the most beautiful, for its architecture and the splendour of its streets, that I know: something between Venice and Cadiz.

We dined yesterday with Clay, to meet Captain Anstruther, our principal steamboat friend, and some of the officers.

TO THOMAS CARLYLE

(Confidential)

BOURNEMOUTH: DECEMBER 27, 1874

SIR, A Government should recognize intellect. It elevates and sustains the tone of a nation. But it is an office which, adequately to fulfil, requires both courage and discrimination, as there is a chance of falling into favouritism and patronizing mediocrity, which, instead of elevating the national feeling, would eventually degrade or debase it. In recommending Her Majesty to fit out an Arctic Expedition, and in suggesting other measures of that class, her Government have shown their sympathy with Science; and they wish that the position of High Letters should be equally acknowledged; but this is not so easy, because it is in the necessity of things that the test of merit cannot be so precise in literature as in science. When I consider the literary world, I can see only two living names which I would fain believe will be remembered, and they stand out in uncontested superiority. One is that of a poet—if not a great poet, a real one; the other is your own.

I have advised the Queen to offer to confer a baronetcy on Mr. Tennyson, and the same distinction should be at your command if you liked it; but I have remembered that, like myself, you are childless, and may not care for hereditary honours. I have, therefore, made up my mind, if agreeable to yourself, to recommend to Her Majesty to confer on you the highest distinction for merit at her command, and which, I believe, has never yet been conferred by her except for direct services to the State, and that is the Grand Cross of the Bath.

I will speak with frankness on another point. It is not well that in the sunset of your life you should be disturbed by common cares. I see no reason why a great author should not receive from the nation a pension, as well as a lawyer or statesman. Unfortunately, the personal power of Her Majesty in this respect is limited; but still it is in the Queen's capacity to settle on an individual an amount equal to a good fellowship; and which was cheerfully accepted and enjoyed by the great spirit of Johnson and the pure integrity of Southey.

Have the goodness to let me know your feelings on these subjects.

I have the honour to remain, Sir,

Your faithful Servant,

B. DISRAELI

JOHN STERLING (1806–44)

Sterling is best known to modern readers as the subject of one of Carlyle's most personal biographies. He was, however, a poet of considerable genius and a writer deserving of a higher place in literature than he holds. Ill-health necessitated his living in a warm climate for a while, and he started sugar-planting in the West Indies. Thus it happened that he experienced the terrific hurricane of 1831, which is described in the following letter.

TO HIS MOTHER

BRIGHTON, ST. VINCENT, 28TH AUGUST, 1831

MY DEAR MOTHER, The packet came in yesterday; bringing me some Newspapers, a Letter from my Father, and one from Anthony, with a few lines from you. I wrote, some days ago, a hasty Note to my Father, on the chance of its reaching you through Grenada sooner than any communication by the packet; and in it I spoke of the great misfortune which had befallen this Island and Barbadoes, but from which all those you take an interest in have happily escaped unhurt.

From the day of our arrival in the West Indies until Thursday the 11th instant, which will long be a memorable day with us, I had been doing my best to get ourselves established comfortably; and I had at last bought the materials for making some additions to the house. But on the morning I have mentioned, all that I had exerted myself to do, nearly all the property both of Susan and myself, and the very house we lived in, were suddenly destroyed by a visitation of Providence far more terrible than any I have ever witnessed.

When Susan came from her room, to breakfast, at eight o'clock, I pointed out to her the extraordinary height and violence of the surf, and the singular appearance of the clouds of heavy rain sweeping down the valleys before us. At this time I had so little apprehension of what was coming, that I talked of riding down to the shore when the storm should abate, as I had never seen so fierce a sea. In about a quarter of an hour the House-Negroes came in, to close the outside shutters of the windows. They knew that the plantain-trees about the Negro houses had been blown down in the night; and had told the maid-servant Tyrrell, but I had heard nothing of it. A very few minutes after the closing of the windows, I found that the shutters of Tyrrell's room, at the south and commonly the most sheltered end of the House, were giving way. I tried to tie them; but the silk handkerchief which I used soon gave way; and as I had neither hammer, boards nor nails in the house, I could do nothing more to keep out the tempest. I found, in pushing at the leaf of the shutter, that the wind resisted, more as if it had been a stone wall or a mass of iron, than a mere current of air. There were one or two people outside trying to fasten the windows, and I went out to help; but we had no tools at hand: one man was blown down the hill in front of the house, before my face; and the other and myself had great difficulty in getting back again inside the door. The rain on my face and hands felt like so much small shot from a gun. There was great exertion necessary to shut the door of the house.

The windows at the end of the large room were now giving way; and I suppose it was about nine o'clock, when the hurricane burst them in, as if it had been a discharge from a battery of heavy cannon. The shutters were first forced open, and the wind fastened them back to the wall; and then the panes of glass were smashed by the mere force of the gale, without anything having touched them. Even now I was not at all sure the house would go. My books, I saw, were lost; for the rain poured past the bookcases, as if it had been the Colonarie River. But we carried a good deal of furniture into the passage at the entrance; we set Susan there on a sofa, and the Black Housekeeper was even attempting to get her some breakfast. The house, however, began to shake so violently, and the rain was so searching, that she could not stay there long. She went into her own room; and I stayed to see what could be done.

Under the forepart of the house, there are cellars built of stone, but not arched. To these, however, there was no access except on the outside; and I knew from my own experience that Susan could not have gone a step beyond the door, without being carried away by the storm, and probably killed on the spot. The only chance seemed to be that of breaking through the floor. But when the old Cook and myself resolved on this, we found that we had no instrument with which it would be possible to do it. It was now clear that we had only God to trust in. The front windows were giving way with successive crashes, and the floor shook as you may have seen a carpet on a gusty day in London. I went into our bed-room; where I found Susan, Tyrrell, and a little coloured girl of seven or eight years old; and told them that we should probably not be alive in half an hour. I could have escaped, if I had chosen to go alone, by crawling on the ground either into the kitchen, a separate stone building at no great distance, or into the open fields away from trees or houses; but Susan could not have gone a yard. She became quite calm when she knew the worst; and she sat on my knee in what seemed the safest corner of the room, while every blast was bringing nearer and nearer the moment of our seemingly certain destruction.

The house was under two parallel roofs; and the one next the sea, which sheltered the other, and us who were under the other, went off, I suppose about ten o'clock. I was sitting in an arm-chair, holding my Wife; and Tyrrell and the little Black child were close to us. We had given up all notion of surviving: and only waited for the fall of the roof to perish together.

Before long the roof went. Most of the materials, however, were carried clear away: one of the large couples was caught on the bed-post, and held fast by the iron spike; while the end of it hung over our heads: had the beam fallen an inch on either side of the bed-post, it must necessarily have crushed us. The walls did not go with the roof; and we remained for half an hour, alternately praying to God, and watching them as they bent, creaked, and shivered before the storm.

Tyrrell and the child, when the roof was off, made their way through the remains of the partition, to the outer door; and with the help of the people who were looking for us, got into the kitchen. A good while after they were gone, and before we knew anything of their fate, a Negro suddenly came upon us, and the sight of him gave us a hope of safety. When the people learned that we were in danger, and while their own huts were flying about their ears, they crowded to help us; and the old Cook urged them on to our rescue. He made five attempts, after saving Tyrrell, to get to us; and four times he was blown down. The fifth time he, and the Negro we first saw, reached the house. The space they had to traverse was not above twenty yards of level ground, if so much. In another minute or two, the Overseers and a crowd of Negroes, most of whom had come on their hands and knees, were surrounding us; and with their help Susan was carried round to the end of the house; where they broke open the cellar window, and placed her in comparative safety. The force of the hurricane was, by this time, a good deal diminished, or it would have been impossible to stand before it.

But the wind was still terrific; and the rain poured into the cellars through the floor above. Susan, Tyrrell, and a crowd of Negroes remained under it, for more than two hours: and I was long afraid that the wet and cold would kill her, if she did not perish more violently. Happily we had wine and spirits at hand, and she was much nerved by a tumbler of claret. As soon as I saw her in comparative security, I went off with one of the Overseers down to the Works, where the greater number of the Negroes were collected, that we might see what could be done for them. They were wretched enough, but no one was hurt; and I ordered them a dram apiece, which seemed to give them a good deal of consolation.

Before I could make my way back, the hurricane became as bad as at first; and I was obliged to take shelter for half an hour in a ruined Negro house. This, however, was the last of its extreme violence. By one o'clock, even the rain had in a great degree ceased; and as only one room of the house was standing, and that rickety, I had Susan carried in a chair down the hill, to the Hospital; where, in a small paved unlighted room, she spent the next twenty-four hours. She was far less injured than might have been expected from such a catastrophe.

Next day, I had the passage at the entrance of the house repaired and roofed; and we returned to the ruins of our habitation, still encumbered as they were with the wreck of almost all we were possessed of. The walls of the part of the house next the sea were carried away, in less I think than half an hour after we reached the cellar: when I had leisure to examine the remains of the house, I found the floor strewn with fragments of the building, and with broken furniture; and our books all soaked as completely as if they had been for several hours in the sea.

In the course of a few days I had the other room, which is under the same roof as the one saved, rebuilt; and Susan stayed in this temporary abode for a week,—when we left Colonarie, and came to Brighton. Mr. Munro's kindness exceeds all precedent. We shall certainly remain here till my Wife is recovered from her confinement. In the mean while we shall have a new house built, in which we hope to be well settled before Christmas.

The roof was half blown off the kitchen, but I have had it mended already; the other offices were all swept away. The gig is much injured; and my horse received a wound in the fall of the stable, from which he will not be recovered for some weeks: in the mean time I have no choice but to buy another, as I must go at least once or twice a week to Colonarie, besides business in Town. As to our own comforts, we can scarcely expect ever to recover from the blow that has now stricken us. No money would repay me for the loss of my books, of which a large proportion had been in my hands for so many years that they were like old and faithful friends, and of which many had been given to me at different times by the persons in the world whom I most value.

But against all this I have to set the preservation of our lives, in a way the most awfully providential; and the safety of every one on the Estate. And I have also the great satisfaction of reflecting that all the Negroes from whom any assistance could reasonably be expected, behaved like so many Heroes of Antiquity; risking their lives and limbs for us and our property, while their own poor houses were flying like chaff before the hurricane. There are few White people here who can say as much for their Black dependents; and the force and value of the relation between Master and Slave has been tried by the late calamity on a large scale.

Great part of both sides of this Island has been laid completely waste. The beautiful wide and fertile Plain called the Charib Country, extending for many miles to the north of Colonarie, and formerly containing the finest sets of works and best dwelling-houses in the Island, is, I am told, completely desolate: on several estates not a roof even of a Negro hut standing. In the embarrassed circumstances of many of the proprietors, the ruin is, I fear, irreparable.—At Colonarie the damage is serious, but by no means desperate. The crop is perhaps injured ten or fifteen per cent. The roofs of several large buildings are destroyed, but these we are already supplying; and the injuries done to the cottages of the Negroes are, by this time, nearly if not quite remedied.

Indeed, all that has been suffered in St. Vincent appears nothing when compared with the appalling loss of property and of human lives at Barbadoes. There the Town is little but a heap of ruins, and the corpses are reckoned by thousands; while throughout the Island there are not, I believe, ten estates on which the buildings are standing. The Elliotts, from whom we have heard, are living with all their family in a tent; and may think themselves wonderfully saved, when whole families round them were crushed at once beneath their houses. Hugh Barton, the only officer of the Garrison hurt, has broken his arm, and we know nothing of his prospects of recovery. The more horrible misfortune of Barbadoes is partly to be accounted for by the fact of the hurricane having begun there during the night. The flatness of the surface in that Island presented no obstacle to the wind, which must, however, I think, have been in itself more furious than with us. No other island has suffered considerably.

I have told both my Uncle and Anthony that I have given you the details of our recent history,—which are not so pleasant that I should wish to write them again. Perhaps you will be good enough to let them see this, as soon as you and my Father can spare it. . . . I am ever, dearest Mother,—your grateful and affectionate,

JOHN STERLING

SIR GEORGE CORNEWALL LEWIS (1806–63)

Lewis was a statesman and author of considerable repute in the mid-nineteenth century, holding the offices of Chancellor of the Exchequer, Home Secretary and Secretary for War. His letter to Twisleton on the outbreak of the American Civil War is of peculiar interest.

TO THE HON. EDWARD TWISLETON

KENT HOUSE: JANUARY 21, 1861

MY DEAR TWISLETON, I read with much interest the articles in the New York papers which you had the kindness to send me. It is certain that this break up of the Union, for such it apparently is, has taken the world by surprise. When the Prince of Wales was at Washington in last October, nobody thought that Buchanan would be the last President of the old Union. The greatest events seem to be the least anticipated. Nobody in England expected that the great rebellion would end in the execution of the king; and when Charles II was in exile, nobody expected that he would be restored. When Napoleon was at the height of his power, nobody expected that he would be deposed; and when he was at Elba nobody expected that he would again be Emperor of France. The French Revolution itself was clearly a universal and complete surprise, both to France and the rest of Europe. Everybody thought that the old French monarchy rested on an immovable basis. Revolutions, as Aristotle has remarked, spring from small causes, but they are made on account of great interests. The immediate cause in this case is small. The importance of Lincoln's election was not great one way or the other. But it is clear that the feelings and interests about slavery have been gradually growing to the point of difference at which common discussion and decision by vote of a joint Assembly becomes impossible. The assault upon [Fort] Sumner was not, if properly regarded, a proof of the brutal manners of the Southern gentlemen—it was the first blow in a civil war. It was an outward sign that the Hall of Congress was not a place where slavery and anti-slavery could settle their disputes. Olmsted's third volume, which I have been reading with great interest and profit,

711

shows the width of the chasm between the North and the South on the subject of federal compacts, if it is resisted by the Slave-holding States.

However, so far the practical problem is clear. There is no doubt that free labour is preferable to slave labour, if the option exists. But there is a point at which the heat is such that white labour in the open air becomes impossible. I want to know what the Northern States propose to do from that point. What is their slavery legislation south of the line, where none but niggers can work in the fields? Olmsted's book does not, so far as I see, contain a vestige of an attempt to answer this question, and yet, if the United States are to remain in their present extent, it must receive a practical answer. Buchanan's conduct has been weak and impolitic in the extreme—the natural result of a position of political dishonesty. One of the strongest objections to the present political state of the Union seems to me to be that every leading public man is almost of necessity driven to disgraceful compromises and to dishonest compliances and professions. If he had used coercion at first, before the other States of the South were committed, he might possibly have succeeded. I doubt, even so, whether he would have brought South Carolina back, but this was the only chance. Now, however, that six or seven States have virtually joined, coercion can lead to nothing but an armed struggle; and an armed struggle will not hold the Union together. The means are inconsistent with the end. It is the most singular action for restitution of conjugal rights which the world ever heard of. You may conquer an insurgent province, but you cannot conquer a seceding State. The Roman *plebs* used secession as a means of extorting concessions from the patricians, but they would not have returned until they had gained their end. In this case the seceders are to be brought back by force, the concession of the point at issue is to be refused, and the two contending parties are to live harmoniously and happily ever after in the tender embraces of federal union. Such an idea seems to me utterly absurd and extravagant.

The progress of events is so rapid that I confess I cannot see my way at all as to the probable form of the new system which is to emerge from the chaos. Head thinks it not impossible that the Western States will form a Union of their own.

Ever yours sincerely,

G. C. LEWIS

HELEN SELINA, LADY DUFFERIN (1807–67)

Lady Dufferin was one of the famous Sheridan beauties and grand-daughter of the dramatist. In her youth she had met and been friendly with all the famous people of London, and in this letter to Abraham Hayward she narrates her reminiscences of the poet Rogers. Lady Dufferin will always be remembered for her songs.

TO MR. HAYWARD

DUFFERIN LODGE, HIGHGATE, FEBRUARY 8, 1858

MY reminiscences of Rogers? Yes, I will endeavour to rub them up for your service. To the best of my recollection, he was a fine, robust-looking man, with a florid complexion and something of a rollicking manner. The heartiness and cordiality of his address had perhaps a tinge of rusticity, which, combined with his peculiar costume (top-boots and cords), and the unkempt luxuriance of his shaggy locks—or am I thinking of the late Archbishop of Canterbury? There is a slight confusion in my ideas on this subject, so I had best go straight to my less material souvenir of your old friend.

Jesting apart—I wish I could find anything either in my papers or my recollections to add to your own interesting details about Rogers. I am loth to say, now that he is gone (what I often said in his lifetime), that I never could *lash myself* into a feeling of affection or admiration for him. This may account for the paucity of my stock of recollections respecting a really remarkable man, to whom my grandfather [R. B. Sheridan, the dramatist] had obligations, and who always professed to feel a great attachment to me and my family. To tell the truth, there was a certain *unreality* in him which repelled me. I have heard him say many graceful things, but few kind ones, and he never seemed to me thoroughly in earnest save in expressing contempt or dislike. I have always heard that he was very liberal in pecuniary matters—although the instances you give (or rather, which your friend gives) do not appear to me to merit the term generous. He gave what he valued least—*money*; he never gave what he valued most—admiration. It seemed a positive pain to him to hear any modern poet praised, and I remember

713

his treating me with rudeness almost bearish because I indiscreetly avowed how much I admired Tennyson's "Princess." He was certainly witty: it was wit in the strictest estimation of the term: the produce of a keen and polished intellect sharpened by long contact with the world and hardened by a just confidence in his own powers; but there was little or no *humour* in him, nothing that warmed or kindled fun or sympathy in others, much that provoked retort.

The only "funny" thing I remember his saying was, on one occasion when we were accidentally left alone in the dark, after some jesting remark on the danger of my reputation—"Ah! my dear, if sweet 78 could come again! *Mais ces beaux jours sont passés.*"

He told gracefully, with his usual elaborate simplicity and studied artlessness, a little anecdote about himself. "They were playing at forfeits. Miss S. had to pay a kiss. 'Oh! it was to my uncle, so I paid gladly.' 'Suppose it had been to me?' 'I should have paid it *cheerfully!*' Was not that a bitter-sweet adverb?"

I can remember nothing more, and fear that *this* is hardly worth remembering. I have had in the course of my life many notes from him, much in the style of one you have already adverted to. They generally begin with "Pray, pray!" A form of exordium which alternated with, "What shall I say?" I have preserved none of them, and the only *letter* I ever received from him is mislaid at present, so I am unable even to subscribe that much to your pleasant article. Pray forgive my poverty—it extends even to my powers of invention, or you should have had some sparkling "mots" which no one else ever heard of.

I return the proofs with many thanks.

Yours very truly,

HELEN DUFFERIN

FELIX BEDINGFIELD (1808–84)

In after years the writer of this letter became a prominent states-man and was Colonial Secretary for the island of Mauritius. There is something very charming about this schoolboy epistle from Ghent.

TO HIS MOTHER

GHENT, NOVEMBER 1, 1819

On Monday Cadet (a favourite dog) underwent a great operation: a little piece of his tail was obliged to be taken of. His muzzle was put on and his head wrapped up in a cloth, that he might not *see who did it.* The great gate stood open also, that the blacksmith might run out as soon as he had finished the operation. Mrs. Parke held Cadet's head, whilst the blacksmith cut his tail. She was fit to die with fear, and blacksmith was as much afraid as her; he was some minutes before he could get Cadet's tail in the machine. Silence was kept that he might not hear any voices. He was left to bleed an hour and the blacksmith then came and bound up his tail with a composition of burnt tinder, whilst Mrs. Parke had to hold him again. He went on pretty well till Thursday when he was very bad indeed and we thought he was going to die; but now he is getting much better. Mrs. Parke gives him everything the blacksmith orders. He is washed 2 a day with a hot bath made of herbs and other things.—I hope in my next letter I shall be able to say he is quite well.

CHARLES DARWIN (1809–82)

*In 1859 the great scientist published "On the Origin of Species,"
and in this letter he tells Wallace, who might almost be called his rival,
that a copy of the book had been sent on to him. In his letter to the
naturalist Carpenter, Darwin foreshadows the application of this
principle to the study of Man.*

TO A. R. WALLACE

ILKLEY, NOVEMBER 13TH, 1859

MY DEAR SIR, I have told Murray to send you by post (if possible) a
copy of my book, and I hope that you will receive it at nearly the
same time with this note. (N.B. I have got a bad finger, which
makes me write extra badly.) If you are so inclined, I should very
much like to hear your general impression of the book ["Origin of
Species"], as you have thought so profoundly on the subject, and in
so nearly the same channel with myself. I hope there will be some
little new to you, but I fear not much. Remember it is only an abstract,
and very much condensed. God knows what the public will think.
No one has read it, except Lyell, with whom I have had much correspondence. Hooker thinks him a complete convert, but he does not
seem so in his letters to me; but is evidently deeply interested in the
subject. I do not think your share in the theory will be overlooked
by the real judges, as Hooker, Lyell, Asa Gray, &c. I have heard
from Mr. Sclater that your paper on the Malay Archipelago has been
read at the Linnean Society, and that he was *extremely* much interested
by it.

I have not seen one naturalist for six or nine months, owing to the
state of my health, and therefore I really have no news to tell you.
I am writing this at Ilkley Wells, where I have been with my family
for the last six weeks, and shall stay for some few weeks longer. As
yet I have profited very little. God knows when I shall have strength
for my bigger book.

I sincerely hope that you keep your health; I suppose that you will
be thinking of returning [from Malaya] soon with your magnificent

collections, and still grander mental materials. You will be puzzled how to publish. The Royal Society fund will be worth your consideration. With every good wish, pray believe me,

Yours very sincerely,

CHARLES DARWIN

P.S.—I think that I told you before that Hooker is a complete convert. If I can convert Huxley I shall be content.

TO W. B. CARPENTER

ILKLEY, YORKSHIRE, DECEMBER 3RD (1859)

MY DEAR CARPENTER, I am perfectly delighted at your letter. It is a great thing to have got a great physiologist on our side. I say "our" for we are now a good and compact body of really good men, and mostly not old men. In the long-run we shall conquer. I do not like being abused, but I feel that I can now bear it; and, as I told Lyell, I am well convinced that it is the first offender who reaps the rich harvest of abuse. You have done an essential kindness in checking the odium theologicum in the E.R. [Edinburgh Review]. It much pains all one's female relations and injures the cause.

I look at it as immaterial whether we go quite the same lengths; and I suspect, judging from myself, that you will go further, by thinking of a population of forms like Ornithorhynchus, and by thinking of the common homological and embryological structure of the several vertebrate orders. But this is immaterial. I quite agree that the principle is everything. In my fuller MS. I have discussed a good many instincts; but there will surely be more unfilled gaps here than with corporeal structure, for we have no fossil instincts, and know scarcely any except of European animals. When I reflect how very slowly I came round myself, I am in truth astonished at the candour shown by Lyell, Hooker, Huxley, and yourself. In my opinion it is grand. I thank you cordially for taking the trouble of writing a review for the "National." God knows I shall have few enough in any degree favourable.

TO A. R. WALLACE

DOWN, FEBRUARY 26 (1867)

MY DEAR WALLACE, Bates was quite right; you are the man to apply to in a difficulty. I never heard anything more ingenious than your suggestion,[1] and I hope you may be able to prove it true. That is a splendid fact about the white moths; it warms one's very blood to see a theory thus almost proved to be true. With respect to the beauty of male butterflies, I must as yet think that it is due to sexual selection. There is some evidence that dragon-flies are attracted by bright colours; but what leads me to the above belief, is so many male Orthoptera and Cicadas having musical instruments. This being the case, the analogy of birds makes me believe in sexual selection with respect to colour in insects. I wish I had strength and time to make some of the experiments suggested by you, but I thought butterflies would not pair in confinement. I am sure I have heard of some such difficulty. Many years ago I had a dragon-fly painted with gorgeous colours, but I never had an opportunity of fairly trying it.

The reason of my being so much interested just at present about sexual selection is that I have almost resolved to publish a little essay on the origin of Mankind, and I still strongly think (though I failed to convince you, and this, to me, is the heaviest blow possible) that sexual selection has been the main agent in forming the races of man.

By the way, there is another subject which I shall introduce in my essay, namely, expression of countenance. Now, do you happen to know by any odd chance a very good-natured and acute observer in the Malay Archipelago, who you think would make a few easy observations for me on the expression of the Malays when excited by various emotions? For in this case I would send to such person a list of queries. I thank you for your most interesting letter, and remain,

Yours very sincerely,

CH. DARWIN

[1] That conspicuous caterpillars or butterflies which are distasteful to birds are protected by being easily recognized and avoided.

EDWARD FITZGERALD (1809–83)

*The translator of "Omar Khayyám" was a constant correspondent
of his friend and neighbour, Bernard Barton, the Quaker poet of Woodbridge—that same Barton to whom Charles Lamb wrote the letter
printed on page 554. The Charles Eliot Norton to whom he wrote
the third letter was professor of Art at Harvard, and editor, with
J. R. Lowell, of the "North American Review."*

TO BERNARD BARTON

BEDFORD, JULY 24, 1839

DEAR BARTON, I have brought down here with me Sydney Smith's
Works, now first collected: you will delight in them: I shall bring
them to Suffolk when I come: and it will not be long, I dare say, before
I come, as there is to be rather a large meeting of us at Boulge this
August. I have got the fidgets in my right arm and hand (how the
inconvenience redoubles as one mentions it)—do you know what the
fidgets are?—a true ailment, though perhaps not a dangerous one.
Here I am again in the land of old Bunyan—better still in the land
of more perennial Ouse, making many a fantastic winding and going
much out of his direct way to fertilize and adorn. Fuller supposes
that he lingers thus in the pleasant fields of Bedfordshire, being in
no hurry to enter the more barren fens of Lincolnshire. So he says.
This house is just on the edge of the town: a garden on one side skirted
by the public road which again is skirted by a row of such Poplars as
only the Ouse knows how to rear—and pleasantly they rustle now
—and the room in which I write is quite cool and opens into a greenhouse which opens into said garden: and it's all deuced pleasant. For
half an hour I shall seek my Piscator [W. Browne], and we shall go
to a village two miles off and fish, and have tea in a pot-house, and
so walk home. For all which idle ease I think I must be damned.
I begin to have dreadful suspicions that this fruitless way of life is
not looked upon with satisfaction by the open eyes above. One really
ought to dip for a little misery: perhaps however all this ease is only
intended to turn sour bye and bye, and so to poison one by the very

719

nature of self-indulgence. Perhaps again as idleness is so very great a trial of virtue, the idle man who keeps himself tolerably chaste, etc., may deserve the highest award; the more idle, the more deserving. Really I don't jest: but I don't propound these things as certain.

There is a fair review of Shelley in the new Edinburgh: saying the truth on many points where the truth was not easily enunciated, as I believe.

Now, dear Sir, I have said all I have to say: and Carlyle says, you know, it is dangerous to attempt to say more. So farewell for the present: if you like to write soon, direct to the Post Office, Bedford: if not, I shall soon be at Woodbridge to anticipate the use of your pen.

TO THE SAME

LONDON, FEBRUARY 21, 1842

I HAVE just got home a new coat for my Constable: which coat cost 33 shillings: just the same price as I gave for a Chesterfield wrapper (as it is called) for myself some weeks ago. People told me I was not improved by my Chesterfield wrapper: and I am vext to see how little my Constable is improved by his coat of Cloth of Gold. But I have been told what is the use of a frame lately: only as it requires nice explanation I shall leave it till I see you. Don't you wish me to buy that little Evening piece I told you of? worth a dozen of your Paul Veroneses put together.

When I rate you (as you call it) about shewing my verses, letters, etc., you know in what spirit I rate you: thanking you all the time for your ge...ious intention of praising me. It would be very hard, and not desirable, to make you understand why my Mama need not have heard the verses: but it is a very little matter: so no more of it. As to my doing anything else in that way, I know that I could write volume after volume as well as others of the mob of gentlemen who write with ease: but I think unless a man can do better, he had best not do at all; I have not the strong inward call, nor cruel-sweet pangs of parturition, that prove the birth of anything bigger than a mouse. With you the case is different, who have so long been a follower of the Muse, and who have had a kindly, sober, English, wholesome, religious spirit within you that has communicated kindred warmth to many honest souls. Such a creature as Augusta—John's wife—a true Lady, was very fond of your poems: and I think that is no mean praise: a very good assurance that you have not written in vain. I

am a man of taste, of whom there are hundreds born every year: only
that less easy circumstances than mine at present are compel them to
one calling: that calling perhaps a mechanical one, which overlies all
their other, and naturally perhaps more energetic, impulses. As to an
occasional copy of verses, there are few men who have leisure to read,
and are possessed of any music in their souls, who are not capable of
versifying on some ten or twelve occasions during their natural lives:
at a proper conjunction of the stars. There is no harm in taking
advantage of such occasions. This letter-writing fit (one must suppose)
can but happen once in one's life: though I hope you and I shall
live to have many a little bargain for pictures. But I hold communion
with Suffolk through you. In this big London all full of intellect
and pleasure and business I feel pleasure in dipping down into the
country, and rubbing my hand over the cool dew upon the pastures,
as it were. I know very few people here: and care for fewer; I believe
I should like to live in a small house just outside a pleasant English
town all the days of my life, making myself useful in a humble way,
reading my books, and playing a rubber of whist at night. But England
cannot expect such a reign of inward quiet as to suffer men to dwell
so easily to themselves. But Time will tell us:

Come what come may,
Time and the Hour runs through the roughest day.

It is hard to give you so long a letter, so dull an one, and written
in so cramped a hand, to read in this hardworking part of your week.
But you can read a bit at odd times, you know: or none at all. Anyhow 'tis time to have done. I am going to walk with Luisa. So
farewell.

P.S. I always direct to you as "Mr. Barton" because I know
not if Quakers ought to endure Squiredom. How I long to shew
you my Constable!

Pray let me know how Mr. Jenney is. I think that we shall get
down to Suffolk the end of next week.

TO C. E. NORTON

WOODBRIDGE, AUGUST 5, 1881

MY DEAR NORTON, I am sorry that you felt bound to write me so
fully about the Play when, as you tell me, you had much other work
on your hands. Anyhow, do not trouble yourself to write more. If

you think my Version does as well, or better, without any introduction, why, tear that out; all, except (if you like the Verse well enough to adopt it) the first sentence of Dedication to yourself: adding your full name and Collegiate Honours whenever you care so to do.

Your account of your Harvard original in the *Alantic Monthly* was quite well fitted for its purpose: a general account of it for the general reader, without going into particulars which only the Scholar would appreciate.

I believe I told you that thirty years ago at least I advised our Trinity's Master, then only Greek Professor, to do the like with one of the Greek Tragedies, in what they call their Senate-house, well fitted for such a purpose. But our Cambridge is too well fed, and slow to stir; and I not important enough to set it a-going.

By the way, I have been there for two days; not having seen the place for those same thirty years, except in passing through some ten years ago to Naseby Field, for the purpose of doing Carlyle's will in setting up a memorial Stone with his Inscription upon it. But the present owners of the Place would not consent: and so that simple thing came to nothing.

Well, I went again, as I say, to Cambridge a month ago; not in my way to Naseby, but to my friend George Crabbe's (Grandson of my Poet) in Norfolk. I went because it was Vacation time, and no one I knew up except Cowell and Aldis Wright. Cowell, married, lives in pleasant lodging with trees before and behind, on the skirts of the town; Wright, in "Neville's Court," one side of which is the Library, all of Wren's design, and (I think) very good. I felt at home in the rooms there, walled with Books, large, and cool: and I was lionized over some things new to me, and some that I was glad to see again. Now I am back again, without any design to move; not even to my old haunts on our neighbouring Sea-coast. The inland Verdure suits my Eyes better than glowing sand and pebble: and I suppose that every year I grow less and less desirous of moving.

I will scarce touch upon the Carlyle Chapter: except to say that I am sorry Froude printed the Reminiscences; at any rate, printed them before the Life which he has begun so excellently in the *Nineteenth Century* for July. I think one can surely see there that Carlyle might become somewhat crazed, whether by intense meditation or Dyspepsy or both: especially as one sees that his dear good Mother was so afflicted. But how beautiful is the Story of that home, and the Company of Lads travelling on foot to Edinburgh; and the monies which he sends home for the paternal farm: and the butter and cheese which the Farm returns to him. Ah! it is from such training that strength comes, not from luxurious fare, easy chairs, cigars, Pall Mall Clubs, etc. It has all made me think of a very little Dialogue ["Euphranor"] I once wrote on the matter, thirty years ago and more, which I really think of putting into shape again; and, if I do, will send it to you, by way of picture of what our Cambridge was in what I think were better days than now. I see the little tract is overdone and in some respects in bad taste as it is. Now, do not ask for this, nor mention it as if it were of any importance whatsoever: it is not, but if pruned, etc., just a pretty thing, which your Cambridge shall see if I can return to it.

By the by, I had meant to send you an emendation of a passage in my Tyrannus which you found fault with. I mean where Œdipus, after putting out his eyes, talks of seeing those in Hades he does not wish to see. I knew it was not Greek: but I thought that a note would be necessary to explain what the Greek was: and I confess I do not care enough for their Mythology for that. But, if you please, the passage (as I remember it) might run:

Eyes, etc.,

Which, having seen such things, henceforth, he said,
Should never by the light of day behold
Those whom he loved, nor in the after-dark
Of Hades, those he loathed, to look upon.

All this has run me into a third *screed*, you see: a word we used at School, only calling it "*screet*"—"I say, do lend me a screet of paper," meaning, a quarter of a foolscap sheet.

FRANCES ANNE KEMBLE (1809–93)

Fanny Kemble was the daughter of the famous actor Charles Kemble. She made her first public appearance in 1829 and was an immediate success; a few years later, however, she settled in America, though her visits to England were frequent. That she had grown accustomed to American ways of life is shown by the chatty letter addressed to one of her friends.

23 PORTMAN STREET, PORTMAN SQUARE,
WEDNESDAY, APRIL 18, 1877

MY small troubles are swelled by the addition of poor F——'s, and hers are complicated with my own incessant and unsuccessful efforts to obtain two out of the four servants I require. I feel quite addled with a sort of cook, kitchen, and housemaid idiotcy, and as if I should address my friends and visitors with, "What wages do you expect?" or, "Why did you leave your last situation?" I do not quite understand who does the work in English houses now. I hire a cook, and she demands a kitchen-maid under her. I look for a kitchen-maid, and she asks for a scullery-maid under her; and I suppose the least the latter functionary would expect would be a turnspit dog *under her*. Used this to be all so, or do I dream that it was otherwise? And how did my father and mother and four children contrive to exist upon their small income? and six servants—which we never had; a cook, a house-maid, and a footman forming our modest establishment. But to be sure that was a long time ago, for I was young then!

The manners and general demeanour, too, of the lady domestics are very novel and surprising to me. They stand close up to one, with their hands thrust into their jacket pockets, and before you can ask them a single question, enquire if your house is large or small, how many servants you keep, if you keep a man-servant; until I quite expect that the next thing I shall hear will be, and "how many back teeth have you left?"

Certainly things and people have greatly changed since I had anything to do with housekeeping in England. Not pleasantly, I think, for the employers. I hope the employed find it more agreeable.

724

Yesterday, directly after breakfast, I drove to the Army and Navy Co-operative Stores, hoping at an early hour to find it empty, and so it was comparatively; but still there were some exemplary lords and ladies even then buying their own groceries. To come and make their own purchases in these dirty, crowded, most inconvenient, most troublesome, and most ill-mannered shops has become the high fashion and a daily amusement of the great and gay London folk; and the Haymarket in the afternoon is as full of fine carriages, opposite the Co-operative store, as it used formerly to be on a gala night at the Opera House, and friends and acquaintances make appointments for meeting at the Co-op, as they vulgarly abbreviate it.

After my luncheon, I took an American gentleman, an acquaintance of mine, and a friend of my dear S——'s, to call on my very old and kind friend, Mrs. Proctor. She is now, I believe, very near eighty, but has two days a week appointed for the reception of her friends, when she appears in a becoming and elegant old lady's toilet and does the honours of her afternoon tea, which her daughter pours out, with wonderful sprightliness and vivacity.

Here, my dearest H——, I was interrupted by a visit from Lady M——, who told me, that Sir Anthony's servants' wages alone in Australia cost him a thousand pounds a year. To be sure he is a governor! But Lord Mayo, remonstrating with a man who asked him a hundred pounds a year as his butler, to whom Lord Mayo said, "Why, my son and many other young gentlemen of his social position don't get more than that as curates!" "Poor young gentlemen," said the man, "I am really very sorry for them!"

I am going to see Fanny Cobbe this afternoon. She paid me a visit the other day, but my little old (eighty-eight years old), Dr. Wilson, who is as brisk as a bee, and runs up the stairs into my room before the servant can announce him, was here, so that I had but half the good of half her visit.

When he was gone we had free talk; and she told me, among other things, what did not surprise me at all—that her devotion to this vivisection cause had estranged many of her former acquaintances, and that she now saw comparatively few of her former pleasant intellectual associates: "*ainsi va le monde.*"

I go to see her at her office sometimes, and find the table strewed with *pictorial* appeals to the national humanity—portraits of dogs and horses, etc, by famous [*sic*] masters, coarsely reproduced in common prints, with, "Is this the creature to torture?" printed above them.

All this seems *small*; but "despise not the day of small things," is the true motto for those who mean to achieve great ones; and "many a mickle makes a muckle" is a good saying, and hers are assuredly good doings.

God bless you, dear.

WILLIAM EWART GLADSTONE (1809–98)

Of the vast mass of correspondence left by the great Victorian statesman this early letter of his, addressed to the electors of Newark, is perhaps as typical as any that could be found. Not always did he express himself so succinctly; not always was the great principle of Emancipation so clearly put. The second, a masterpiece of brevity, was written to a political opponent who said that he had seen Gladstone talking to a woman of the street, not far from the House of Commons. The reply, written on a postcard, was as scathing as such an imputation deserved.

TO THE ELECTORS OF NEWARK

OCTOBER 9, 1832

HAVING now completed my canvass, I think it my duty as well to remind you of the principles on which I have solicited your votes, as freely to assure my friends that its result has placed my success beyond a doubt.

I have not requested your favour on the ground of adherence to the opinions of any man or party, further than such adherence can be fairly understood from the conviction I have not hesitated to avow, that we must watch and resist that unenquiring and indiscriminating desire for change amongst us which threatens to produce, along with partial good, a melancholy preponderance of mischief; which, I am persuaded, would aggravate beyond computation the deep-seated evils of our social state, and the heavy burthens of our industrial classes; which, by disturbing our peace, destroys confidence, and strikes at the root of prosperity. Thus it *has done already*; and thus, we must therefore believe, it *will do*.

For the mitigation of those evils, we must, I think, look not only to particular measures, but to the restoration of sounder general principles. I mean especially that principle on which alone the incorporation of Religion with the State in our Constitution can be defended; that the duties of governors are strictly and peculiarly religious; and that legislatures, like individuals, are bound to carry throughout their acts the spirit of the high truths they have acknowledged. Principles

727

are now arrayed against our institutions; and not by truckling nor by temporizing—not by oppression nor corruption—but by principles they must be met.

Among their first results should be a sedulous and special attention to the interests of the poor, founded upon the rule that those who are the least able to take care of themselves should be most regarded by others. Particularly is it a duty to endeavour, by every means, that *labour may receive adequate remuneration*; which, unhappily, among several classes of our fellow-countrymen is not now the case. Whatever measures, therefore—whether by correction of the poor laws, allotment of cottage grounds, or otherwise—tend to promote this object, I deem entitled to the warmest support, with all such as are calculated to secure sound moral conduct in any class of society.

I proceed to the momentous question of Slavery, which I have found entertained among you in that candid and temperate spirit which alone befits its nature, or promises to remove its difficulties. If I have not recognized the right of an irresponsible society to interpose between me and the electors, it has not been from any disrespect to its members, nor from unwillingness to answer theirs or any other questions on which the electors may desire to know my views. To the esteemed secretary of the society I submitted my reasons for silence; and I made a point of stating these views to him, in his character of a voter.

As regards the abstract lawfulness of Slavery, I acknowledge it simply as importing the right of one man to the labour of another; and I rest it upon the fact that Scripture, the paramount authority upon such a point, gives directions to persons standing in the relation of master to slave, for their conduct in that relation; whereas, were the matter absolutely and necessarily *sinful*, it would not regulate the manner. Assuming sin as the cause of degradation, it strives, and strives most effectually, to cure the latter by extirpating the former. We are agreed, that both the physical and the moral bondage of the slave are to be abolished. The question is as to the *order*, and the order only; now Scripture attacks the moral evil *before* the temporal one, and the temporal *through* the moral one, and I am content with the order which Scripture has established.

To this end I desire to see immediately set on foot, by impartial and sovereign authority, an universal and efficient system of Christian instruction, not intended to resist designs of individual piety and wisdom for the religious improvement of the negroes, but to do thoroughly what they can only do partially.

As regards immediate emancipation, whether with or without compensation, there are several minor reasons against it; but that which weighs with me is, that it would, I much fear, exchange the evils now affecting the negro for others which are weightier—for a relapse into deeper debasement, if not for bloodshed and internal war. Let *fitness* be made a condition for emancipation; and let us strive to bring him to that fitness by the shortest possible course. Let him enjoy the means of earning his freedom through honest and industrious habits; thus the same instruments which attain his liberty shall likewise render him competent to use it; and thus, I earnestly trust, without risk of blood, without violation of property, with unimpaired benefit to the negro, and with the utmost speed which prudence will admit, we shall arrive at that exceedingly desirable consummation, the utter extinction of slavery.

And now, gentlemen, as regards the enthusiasm with which you have rallied round your ancient flag, and welcomed the humble representative of those principles whose emblem it is, I trust that neither the lapse of time nor the seductions of prosperity can ever efface it from my memory. To my opponents my acknowledgments are due for the good-humour and kindness with which they have received me; and while I would thank my friends for their zealous and unwearied exertions in my favour, I briefly but emphatically assure them, that if promises be an adequate foundation of confidence, or experience a reasonable ground of calculation, our victory *is sure.*

I have the honour to be, Gentlemen,

Your obliged and obedient Servant,

W. E. GLADSTONE

A POSTCARD

(*To a correspondent who saw him in talk with a "lady of the town."*)

IT may be true, that the honourable gentleman saw me in such conversation. But the object of it was not what he assumed or, as I am afraid, hoped.

WILLIAM MAKEPEACE THACKERAY (1811-63)

Thackeray was at the height of his fame, after the publication of "Vanity Fair" and "Pendennis," when he was put up for the Athenæum by Macaulay, Croker, Milman, Abraham Hayward and others. The opposition of one member of the committee was sufficient, however, to hinder his election, though he became a member of the club in the following year.

TO ABRAHAM HAYWARD

KENSINGTON, FEB. 1, 1850

MY DEAR HAYWARD, Thank you for your kind note. I was quite prepared for the issue of the kind effort made at the Athenæum in my behalf; indeed, as a satirical writer, I rather wonder that I have not made more enemies than I have. I don't mean enemies in a bad sense, but men conscientiously opposed to my style, art, opinions, impertinences, and so forth. There must be thousands of men to whom the practice of ridicule must be very offensive; doesn't one see such in society, or in one's own family? persons whose nature was not gifted with the sense of humour? Such a man would be wrong not to give me a black-ball, or whatever it is called—a negatory nod of his honest, respectable, stupid old head. And I submit to his verdict without the slightest feeling of animosity against my judge. Why, Doctor Johnson would certainly have black-balled Fielding, whom he pronounced "a dull fellow—Sir, a dull fellow!" and why shouldn't my friend at the Athenæum? About getting in I don't care twopence: but indeed I am very much pleased to have had such sureties as Hallam and Milman, and to know that the gentlemen whom you mention were so generous in their efforts to serve me. What does the rest matter? If you should ever know the old gentleman (for old I am sure he is, steady and respectable) who objects to me, give him my best compliments, and say I think he was quite right to exercise his judgment honestly, and to act according to that reason with which heaven has mercifully endowed him. But that he would be slow I wouldn't in the least object to meet him; and he in his turn would think me flippant, etc.—Enough of these egotisms. Didn't I tell you once before, that I feel frightened almost at the kindness of people regarding me? May we all be honest fellows, and keep our heads from too much vanity. Your case was a very different one: yours was a stab with a sharp point; and the wound, I know, must have been a most severe one. So much the better in you to have borne it as you did. I never heard in the least that your honour suffered by the injury done you, or that you lost the esteem (how should you?) of any single friend, because an enemy dealt you a savage blow. The opponent in your case exercised a right to do a wrong: whereas, in the other, my Athenæum friend has done no earthly harm to any mortal, but has established his own character and got a great number of kind testimonials to mine.

Always, dear Hayward, yours very truly,

W. M. THACKERAY

JOHN BRIGHT (1811–89)

The great Corn Law reformer and Liberal orator was one of the leading statesmen of the Victorian Era. In the letter printed below he comments with characteristic vigour on a speech by one of his opponents. In March, 1879, a member of the Barrow Conservative Club had spoken about the Liberal Repeal of the Corn Laws, alleging that the employers wanted cheap labour as well as cheap bread. He referred to Bright's having lowered wages because the working men had got cheap bread. This was John Bright's reply:—

132, PICCADILLY, LONDON,
MARCH 28, 1879

DEAR SIR, I thank you for your note and for your newspaper. I do not know which is more apparent among the Tory speakers—their ignorance or their faculty for lying. The man whose speech you send me is largely guilty of both. He may not know that he is ignorant, but he cannot be ignorant that he lies. And after such a speech the meeting thanked him,—I presume because they enjoyed what he had given them. I think the speaker was named Smith. He is a discredit to the numerous family of that name.

I am, Very truly yours,
JOHN BRIGHT

ROBERT LOWE, VISCOUNT SHERBROOKE (1811–92)

Lowe had had a distinguished career both in Parliament and as a colonial administrator when he was raised to the peerage by Gladstone. The letter to his brother on the occasion is characteristic of his dry wit.

34 LOWNDES SQUARE: MAY 21, 1880

MY DEAR HENRY, As Vespasian said when he was dying, I am beginning to be a god. That the process is proceeding you will see from the enclosed document, the amount of which I have paid, and which I advise you to keep among your muniments to cool the courage of any of your descendants who may be seized with the desire for similar honours. N.B. The Heralds are still to be paid. I am to be gazetted on Tuesday next, but there is something else, I really have forgotten what, before I can take my seat. I will write as soon as I know myself. I am very much flattered and honoured by your wish to attend the function. For myself, I feel very much as if I had got again into the company of the four neuter verbs of the Latin Grammar,—

Vapulo—I am beaten

Veneo—I am sold

Exulo—I am banished.

Fio—I am done.

Your affectionate brother

R. LOWE

CHARLES DICKENS (1812–70)

Few authors have reflected their work so much in their letters as Charles Dickens, as the following notes will demonstrate.

Early in 1838 Dickens paid that visit to the north of England which resulted in "Nicholas Nickleby" and the exposure of the Yorkshire schools. The first letter, written to his wife, breathes much of the spirit of "Nickleby" and the coach ride to the North. The next letter, to young Master Hughes, is about the same book, and is couched in the sprightly style that made its writer as popular with the young as with the old. Four years later we have one of his letters from America, and here we are in the world of "Martin Chuzzlewit." The answer to the now unknown Mr. Dickson was occasioned by one of the thousands of reproofs Dickens was constantly receiving from humourless cranks who were eager to find fault with his writing. He had written "The Battle of Life" and was busy on "Dombey" when he indited the letter to Douglas Jerrold.

TO HIS WIFE

GRETA BRIDGE, THURSDAY, FEB. 1ST, 1838

MY DEAREST KATE, I am afraid you will receive this later than I could wish, as the mail does not come through this place until two o'clock to-morrow morning. However, I have availed myself of the very first opportunity of writing, so the fault is that mail's, and not this.

We reached Grantham between nine and ten on Thursday night, and found everything prepared for our reception in the very best inn I have ever put up at. It is odd enough that an old lady, who had been outside all day and came in towards dinner time, turned out to be the mistress of a Yorkshire school returning from a holiday stay in London. She was a very queer old lady, and showed us a long letter she was carrying to one of the boys from his father, containing a severe lecture (enforced and aided by many texts of Scripture) on his refusing to eat boiled meat. She was very communicative, drank a great deal of brandy and water, and towards evening became insensible, in which state we left her.

Yesterday we were up again shortly after seven a.m., came on upon our journey by the Glasgow mail, which charged us the remarkably low sum of six pounds fare for two places inside. We had a very droll male companion until seven o'clock in the evening, and a most delicious lady's-maid for twenty miles, who implored us to keep a sharp look-out at the coach-windows, as she expected the carriage was coming to meet her and she was afraid of missing it. We had many delightful vauntings of the same kind; but in the end it is scarcely necessary to say that the coach did not come, but a very dirty girl did.

As we came further north the snow grew deeper. About eight o'clock it began to fall heavily, and, as we crossed the wild heaths hereabout, there was no vestige of a track. The mail kept on well, however, and at eleven we reached a bare place with a house standing alone in the midst of a dreary moor, which the guard informed us was Greta Bridge. I was in a perfect agony of apprehension, for it was fearfully cold, and there were no outward signs of anybody being up in the house. But to our great joy we discovered a comfortable room, with drawn curtains and a most blazing fire. In half an hour they gave us a smoking supper and a bottle of mulled port (in which we drank your health), and then we retired to a couple of capital bedrooms, in each of which there was a rousing fire halfway up the chimney.

We have had for breakfast, toast, cakes, a Yorkshire pie, a piece of beef about the size and much the shape of my portmanteau, tea, coffee, ham, and eggs; and are now going to look about us. Having finished our discoveries, we start in a postchaise for Barnard Castle, which is only four miles off, and there I deliver the letter given me by Mitton's friend. All the schools are round about that place, and a dozen old abbeys besides, which we shall visit by some means or other to-morrow. We shall reach York on Saturday I hope, and (God willing) I trust I shall be home on Wednesday morning.

I wish you would call on Mrs. Bentley and thank her for the letter; you can tell her when I expect to be in York.

A thousand loves and kisses to the darling boy, whom I see in my mind's eye crawling about the floor of this Yorkshire inn. Bless his heart, I would give two sovereigns for a kiss. Remember me too to Frederick, who I hope is attentive to you.

Is it not extraordinary that the same dreams which have constantly visited me since poor Mary died follow me everywhere? After all the change of scene and fatigue, I have dreamt of her ever since I left home, and no doubt shall till I return. I should be sorry to lose such visions, for they are very happy ones, if it be only the seeing of her in one's sleep.

I would fain believe, too, sometimes, that her spirit may have some
influence over them, but their perpetual repetition is extraordinary.
Love to all friends.

Ever, my dear Kate,

Your affectionate Husband,

CHARLES DICKENS

TO MASTER HASTINGS HUGHES

DOUGHTY STREET, LONDON, DEC. 12TH, 1838

RESPECTED SIR, I have given Squeers one cut on the neck and two on
the head, at which he appeared much surprised and began to cry, which,
being a cowardly thing, is just what I should have expected from him—
wouldn't you?

I have carefully done what you told me in your letter about the
lamb and the two "sheeps" for the little boys. They have also had
some good ale and porter, and some wine. I am sorry you didn't say
what wine you would like them to have. I gave them some sherry,
which they liked very much, except one boy, who was a little sick and
choked a good deal. He was rather greedy, and that's the truth, and I
believe it went the wrong way, which I say served him right, and I
hope you will say so too.

Nicholas had his roast lamb, as you said he was to, but he could not
eat it all, and says if you do not mind his doing so he should like to have
the rest hashed to-morrow with some greens, which he is very fond of,
and so am I. He said he did not like to have his porter hot, for he
thought it spoilt the flavour, so I let him have it cold. You should have
seen him drink it. I thought he never would have left off. I also
gave him three pounds of money, all in sixpences, to make it seem more
and he said directly that he should give more than half to his mamma and
sister, and divide the rest with poor Smike. And I say he is a good
fellow for saying so; and if anybody says he isn't I am ready to fight him
whenever they like—there!

Fanny Squeers shall be attended to, depend upon it. Your drawing
of her is very like, except that I don't think the hair is quite curly enough.
The nose is particularly like hers, and so are the legs. She is a nasty
disagreeable thing, and I know it will make her very cross when she sees
it; and what I say is I hope it may. You will say the same I know—
at least I think you will.

I meant to have written you a long letter, but I cannot write very fast when I like the person I am writing to, because that makes me think about them, and I like you, and so I tell you. Besides, it is eight o'clock at night, and I always go to bed at eight o'clock, except when it is my birthday, and then I sit up to supper. So I will not say anything more besides this—and that is my love to you and Neptune; and if you will drink my health every Christmas Day I will drink yours—come,

I am, Respected Sir, Your affectionate Friend,
CHARLES DICKENS

P.S. I don't write my name very plain, but you know what it is you know, so never mind.

TO THOMAS MITTON

BALTIMORE, UNITED STATES, MARCH 22ND, 1842

MY DEAR FRIEND, We have been as far south as Richmond in Virginia (where they grow and manufacture tobacco, and where the labour is all performed by slaves), but the season in those latitudes is so intensely and prematurely hot, that it was considered a matter of doubtful expediency to go on to Charleston. For this unexpected reason, and because the country between Richmond and Charleston is but a desolate swamp the whole way, and because slavery is anything but a cheerful thing to live amidst, I have altered my route by the advice of Mr. Clay (the great political leader in this country), and have returned here previous to diving into the far West. We start for that part of the country—which includes mountain travelling, and lake travelling, and prairie travelling—the day after to-morrow, at eight o'clock in the morning; and shall be in the West, and from there going northward again, until the 30th of April or 1st of May, when we shall halt for a week at Niagara before going further into Canada. We have taken our passage home (God bless the word) in the *George Washington* packet-ship from New York. She sails on the 7th of June.

I have departed from my resolution not to accept any more public entertainments; they have been proposed in every town I have visited—in favour of the people of St. Louis, my utmost western point. That town is on the borders of the Indian territory, a trifling distance from this place—only two thousand miles! At my second halting-place I shall be able to write to fix the day; I suppose it will be somewhere about the 12th of April. Think of my going so far towards the setting sun to dinner!

E.L. BB

In every town where we stay, though it be only for a day, we hold a regular levee or drawing-room, where I shake hands on an average with five or six hundred people, who pass on from me to Kate, and are shaken again by her. Maclise's picture of our darlings stands upon a table or sideboard the while; and my travelling secretary, assisted very often by a committee belonging to the place, presents the people in due form. Think of two hours of this every day, and the people coming in by hundreds, all fresh, and piping hot, and full of questions, when we are literally exhausted and can hardly stand. I really do believe that if I had not a lady with me, I should have been obliged to leave the country and go back to England. But for her they never would leave me alone by day or night, and as it is, a slave comes to me now and then in the middle of the night with a letter, and waits at the bedroom door for an answer.

It was so hot at Richmond that we could scarcely breathe, and the peach and other fruit trees were in full blossom; it was so cold at Washington next day that we were shivering; but even in the same town you might often wear nothing but a shirt and trousers in the morning, and two greatcoats at night, the thermometer very frequently taking a little trip of thirty degrees between sunrise and sunset.

They do lay it on at the hotels in such style! They charge by the day, so that whether one dines out or dines at home makes no manner of difference. T'other day I wrote to order our rooms at Philadelphia to be ready on a certain day, and was detained a week longer than I expected in New York. The Philadelphia landlord not only charged me half rent for the rooms during the whole of that time, but board for myself and Kate and Anne during the whole time too, though we were actually boarding at the same expense during the same time in New York! What do you say to that? If I remonstrated, the whole virtue of the newspapers would be aroused directly.

We were at the President's drawing-room while we were in Washington. I had a private audience besides, and was asked todinner, but couldn't stay.

Parties—parties—parties—of course, every day and night. But it's not all parties. I go into the prisons, the police-offices, the watch-houses, the hospitals, the work-houses. I was out half the night in New York with two of their most famous constables; started at midnight, and went into every brothel, thieves' house, murdering hovel, sailors' dancing-place, and abode of villainy, both black and white, in the town. I went *incog.* behind the scenes to the little theatre where

Mitchell is making a fortune.   He has been rearing a little dog for me, and has called him "Boz."   I am going to bring him home.   In a word, I go everywhere, and a hard life it is.   But I am careful to drink hardly anything, and not to smoke at all.   I have recourse to my medicine-chest whenever I feel at all bilious, and am, thank God, thoroughly well.

When I next write to you, I shall have begun, I hope, to turn my face homeward.   I have a great store of oddity and whimsicality, and am going now into the oddest and most characteristic part of this most queer country.

Always direct to the care of David Colden, Esq., 28 Laight Street, Hudson Square, New York.   I received your Caledonia letter with the greatest joy.

Kate sends her best remembrances.

And I am always,
CHARLES DICKENS

P.S.   Richmond was my extreme southern point, and I turn from the South altogether the day after to-morrow.   Will you let the Britannia [Insurance Co.] know of this change—if needful?

TO MR. DAVID DICKSON

1 DEVONSHIRE TERRACE, YORK GATE, REGENT'S PARK,
MAY 10TH, 1843

SIR, Permit me to say, in reply to your letter, that you do not understand the intention (I daresay the fault is mine) of the passage in the "Pickwick Papers" which has given you offence.   The design of "the Shepherd" and of this and every other allusion to him is to show how sacred things are degraded, vulgarized, and rendered absurd when persons who are utterly incompetent to teach the commonest things take upon themselves to expound such mysteries, and how, in making mere cant phrases of divine words, these persons miss the spirit in which they had their origin. I have seen a great deal of this sort of thing in many parts of England, and I never knew it lead to charity or good deeds.

Whether the great Creator of the world and the creature of his hands, moulded in his own image, be quite so opposite in character as you believe, is a question which it would profit us little to discuss.   I like the frankness and candour of your letter, and thank you for it. That every man who seeks heaven must be born again, in good thoughts of his Maker, I sincerely believe. That it is expedient for every hound to say so in a certain snuffling form of words, to which he attaches no good meaning, I do not believe. I take it there is no difference between us.

Faithfully yours,
CHARLES DICKENS

TO DOUGLAS JERROLD

(In answer to Jerrold's letter given on page 694.)

[GENEVA, OCTOBER 1846]

MY DEAR JERROLD, This day week I finished my little Christmas book (writing towards the close the exact words of a passage in your affectionate letter, received this morning; to wit, "After all, life has something serious in it"), and ran over here for a week's rest. I cannot tell you how much true gratification I have had in your most hearty letter. F[orster] told me that the same spirit breathed through a notice of "Dombey" in your paper; and I have been saying since to K. and G.[1] that there is no such good way of testing the worth of a literary friendship as by comparing its influence on one's mind with any that literary animosity can produce. Mr. W. will throw me into a violent fit of anger for the moment, it is true; but his acts and deeds pass into the death of all bad things next day, and rot out of my memory; whereas a generous sympathy, like yours, is ever present to me, ever fresh and new to me—always stimulating, cheerful and delightful. The pain of unjust malice is lost in an hour. The pleasure of a generous friendship is the steadiest joy in the world. What a glorious and comfortable thing that is to think of.

No, I don't get the paper regularly. To the best of my recollections I have not had more than three numbers—certainly not more than four. But I knew how busy you must be, and had no expectation of hearing from you until I wrote from Paris (as I intended doing), and implored you to come and make merry with us there. I am truly pleased to receive your good account of that enterprise. I feel all you say upon the subject of the literary man in his old age, and know the incalculable benefit of such a resource. . . . Anent the Comic (History) and similar comicalities I feel exactly as you do. Their effect upon me is very disagreeable. Such joking is like the sorrow of an undertaker's mute, reversed, and is applied to serious things, with the like propriety and force. . . .

[1] His wife and sister.

Paris is good both in the spring and in the winter. So come, first at Christmas, and let us have a few jolly holidays together at what Mr. Roland of Hatton Garden calls "that festive season of the year," when the hair is peculiarly liable to come out of curl unless, etc. I hope to reach there, bag and baggage, by the twentieth of next month. As soon as I am lodged I will write to you. *Do* arrange to run over at Christmas-time, and let us be as English and as merry as we can. It's nothing of a journey, and you shall write "o' mornings," as they say in modern Elizabethan, as much as you like. . . .

The newspapers seem to know as much about Switzerland as about the Esquimaux country I should like to show you the people as they are here, or in the Canton de Vaud—their wonderful education, splendid schools, comfortable homes, great intelligence, and noble independence of character. It is the fashion among the English to decry them because they are not servile. I can only say that, if the first quarter of a century of the best general education would ever rear such a peasantry in Devonshire as exists about here, or about Lausanne ('bating their disposition towards drunkenness), it would do what I can hardly hope in my most sanguine moods we may effect in four times that period. The revolution here just now (which has my cordial sympathy) was conducted with the most gallant, true and Christian spirit—the conquering party moderate in the first transports of triumph, and forgiving. I swear to you that some of the appeals to the citizens of both parties, posted by the new government (the people's) on the walls, and sticking there now, almost drew the tears into my eyes as I read them; they are so truly generous, and so exalted in their tone—so far above the miserable strife of politics, and so devoted to the general happiness and welfare. . . .

I have had great success again in magnetism. E[lliotson], who has been with us for a week or so, holds my magnetic powers in great veneration, and I really think they are, by some conjunction of chances, strong. Let them, or something else, hold you to me by the heart. Ever, my dear Jerrold,

Affectionately your friend,
C. D.

TO EDMUND YATES

TAVISTOCK HOUSE, TUESDAY, FEB. 2ND, 1858

MY DEAR YATES, Your quotation is, as I suppose, all wrong. The text is *not* "which his 'owls was organs." When Mr. Harris went into an empty dog-kennel, to spare his sensitive nature the anguish of overhearing Mrs. Harris's exclamations on the occasion of the birth of her first child (the Princess Royal of the Harris family), "he never took his hands away from his ears, or came out once, till he was showed the baby." On encountering that spectacle, he was (being of a weakly constitution) "took with fits." For this distressing complaint he was medically treated; the doctor "collared him, and laid him on his back upon the airy stones"—please to observe what follows—"and she was told, to ease her mind, his 'owls was organs."

That is to say, Mrs. Harris, lying exhausted on her bed, in the first sweet relief of freedom from pain, merely covered with the counterpane, and not yet "put comfortable," hears a noise apparently proceeding from the back-yard, and says, in a flushed and hysterical manner: "What 'owls are those? Who is a-'owling? Not my ugebond?" Upon which the doctor, looking round one of the bottom posts of the bed, and taking Mrs. Harris's pulse in a reassuring manner, says, with much admirable presence of mind: "Howls, my dear madam?—no, no, no! What are we thinking of? Howls, my dear Mrs. Harris? Ha, ha, ha! Organs, ma'am, organs. Organs in the streets, Mrs. Harris; no howls."

Yours faithfully,

CHARLES DICKENS

EDWARD LEAR (1812–88)

Lear was on a visit to Corfu when he wrote this letter, brimming over with enthusiasm at the glory of that island. Tennyson and Chichester Fortescue, Lord Carlingford, were among his intimate friends and it was to them, especially the latter, that his most ecstatic letters were addressed.

TO CHICHESTER FORTESCUE

PALEOKASTRIZZA,
EASTER SUNDAY, APRIL 20, 1862

I WISH you were here for a day, at least to-day:—only that you are at "Red House," which is a properer and Abercrombier. I have been wondering if on the whole the being influenced to an extreme by every-thing in natural or physical life, i.e. atmosphere, light, shadow, and all the varieties of day and night,—is a blessing or the contrary—and the end of my speculations has been that "things must be as they may," and the best is to make the best of what happens.

I should however have added "quiet and repose" to my list of influences, for at this beautiful place there is just now perfect quiet, excepting only a dim hum of myriad ripples 500 feet below me, all round the giant rocks which rise perpendicularly from the sea:—which sea, perfectly calm and blue, stretches right out westward unbrokenly to the sky, cloudless that, save a streak of lilac cloud on the horizon. On my left is the convent of Paleokastrizza, and happily, as the monkery had functions at 2 a.m. they are all fast asleep now and to my left is one of the many peacock-tail-hued bays here, reflecting the vast red cliffs and their crowning roofs of Lentish Prinari, myrtle and sage— far above them—higher and higher, the immense rock of St. Angelo rising into the air, on whose summit the old castle still is seen a ruin, just 1,400 feet above the water. It half seems to me that such life as this must be wholly another from the drumbeating bothery frivolity of the town of Corfu, and I seem to grow a year younger every hour. Not that it will last. Accursed picnic parties with miserable scores of asses male and female are coming to-morrow, and peace flies—as I shall to . . .

743

Enough of myself for the present, only as one wants one's friends to write about theirselves, one goes and does likewise. I shall be anxious now every letter to hear something of your destinies—though perhaps they must rather be talked of than written.

A great drawback to these Islands is the once a week post: there is a tension and a vacuum for six days—and a horrid smash of disappointment if the 7th brings nothing.

I hope this summer we may get a quiet two or three days together, for I take it after a short time you, the last of the Mohicans, will cease also to be single, at least I hope so, though the fact of your doubling yourself would cut you off more from my intercourse. . . . In your old age I suppose you will be a minister, and won't go near Ireland,— or I might settle to die at Flurrybridge or Dundalk (!!), and get good studies at Newcastle and Ravensdale. But I shall—or should—have a chapel of my own. Belfast Protestantism, Athanasian creeds, and all kinds of moony miracles should have no entrance there: but a plain worship of God, and a perpetual endeavour at progress. (Which reminds me of Tennyson's little poem of "Will," which I have been trying to translate, and part of which I send you.)

One thing, under all circumstances I have quite decided on—I unconditionally refuse when I go to heaven "if indeed I go"—and am surrounded by thousands of polite angels,—I shall say courteously "please leave me alone!—you are doubtless all delightful, but I do not wish to become acquainted with you:—let me have a park and a beautiful view of the sea and hill, mountain and river, valley and plain, with no end of tropical foliage:—a few well-behaved small cherubs to cook and keep the place clean—and—after I am quite established—say for a million or two of years—an angel of a wife. Above all, let there be no hens! No, not one! I give up eggs and roast chicken for ever!"—which rhapsody arises from a cursed, infernal hen having just laid an egg under my window, and she screeches! O Lord! how she screeches and will screech for an hour! Wherefore, Goodbye. No more, dear friend, for at a screech I stop.

TO LADY WALDEGRAVE

15 Stratford Place, Oxford Street, W.,
17 October 1866

My dear Lady Waldegrave, It is orfle cold here, and I don't know what to do. I think I shall go to Jibberolter, passing through Spain, and doing Portigle later. After all one isn't a potato—to remain always in one place.

A few days ago in a railway as I went to my sister's a gentleman explained to two ladies (whose children had my "Book of Nonsense"), that thousands of families were grateful to the author (which in silence I agreed to) who was not generally known—but was really Lord Derby: and now came a showing forth, which cleared up at once to my mind why that statement has already appeared in several papers. Edward Earl of Derby (said the Gentleman) did not choose to publish the book openly, but dedicated it as you see to his relations, and now if you will transpose the letters L E A R you will read simply EDWARD EARL.— Says I, joining spontanious in the conversation—"That is quite a mistake: I have reason to know that Edward Lear the painter and author wrote and illustrated the whole book." "And I," says the Gentleman, says he—"have good reason to know, Sir, that you are wholly mistaken. *There is no such a person* as Edward Lear." "But," says I, "there is— and I am the man—and I wrote the book!" Whereon all the party burst out laughing and evidently thought me mad or telling fibs. So I took off my hat and showed it all round, with Edward Lear and the address in large letters—also one of my cards, and a marked handkerchief: on which amazement devoured those benighted individuals and I left them to gnash their teeth in trouble and tumult.

Believe me, Dear Lady Waldegrave,

Yours sincerely,

EDWARD LEAR

ROBERT BROWNING (1812–89)

ELIZABETH BARRETT BROWNING (1806–61)

*Browning was undoubtedly the most robust of the Victorian poets,
and expressed his ideas with vigour in "Paracelsus," "Sordello,"
"Bells and Pomegranates," "Dramatis Personæ," etc. In 1844
Elizabeth Barrett published a volume of poems which contained an
appreciation of Browning's work. His gratification led him to write to
her, and this was followed by a meeting, which led very shortly to
their engagement. She had been an invalid for years, but Browning's
vehement wooing and zest of life helped her to recover, and in 1846
they were secretly married and eloped. The letters given below are
the first he wrote to her, and her reply; and others in which they discuss
their plans for going to Italy.*

ROBERT BROWNING TO ELIZABETH BARRETT

New Cross, Hatcham, Surrey,
January 10th, 1845

I LOVE your verses with all my heart, dear Miss Barrett—and this
is no off-hand complimentary letter that I shall write,—whatever
else, no prompt matter-of-course recognition of your genius, and there
a graceful and natural end of the thing. Since the day last week when
I first read your poems, I quite laugh to remember how I have been
turning and turning again in my mind what I should be able to tell
you of their effect upon me, for in the first flush of delight I thought
I would this once get out of my habit of purely passive enjoyment,
when I do really enjoy, and thoroughly justify my admiration—
perhaps even, as a loyal fellow-craftsman should, try and find fault
and do you some little good to be proud of hereafter!—but nothing
comes of it all—so into me has it gone, and part of me has it become,
this great living poetry of yours, now a flower of which but took root
and grew—Oh, how different that is from lying to be dried and pressed
flat, and prized highly, and put in a book with a proper account at
top and bottom, and shut up and put away . . . and the book called

746

a "Flora," besides!   After all, I need not give up the thought of doing that, too, in time; because even now, talking with whoever is worthy, I can give a reason for my faith in one and another excellence, the fresh strange music, the affluent language, the exquisite pathos and true new brave thought; but in thus addressing myself to you—your own self, and for the first time, my feeling rises altogether.   I do, as I say, love these books with all my heart—and I love you too.   Do you know I was once not very far from seeing—really seeing you?   Mr. Kenyon said to me one morning "Would you like to see Miss Barrett?" then he went to announce me,—then he returned . . . you were too unwell, and now it is years ago, and I feel as at some untoward passage in my travels, as if I had been close, so close, to some world's-wonder in chapel or crypt, only a screen to push and I might have entered, but there was some slight, so it now seems, slight and just sufficient bar to admission, and the half-opened door shut, and I went home my thousands of miles, and the sight was never to be?

Well, these Poems were to be, and this true thankful joy and pride with which I feel myself,

Yours ever faithfully,

ROBERT BROWNING

HER REPLY

50 WIMPOLE STREET,

JAN. 11TH, 1845

I THANK you, dear Mr. Browning, from the bottom of my heart. You meant to give me pleasure by your letter—and even if the object had not been answered, I ought still to thank you.   But it is thoroughly answered.   Such a letter from such a hand!   Sympathy is dear—very dear to me: but the sympathy of a poet, and of such a poet, is the quintessence of sympathy of me!   Will you take back my gratitude for it?—agreeing, too, that of all the commerce done in the world, from Tyre to Carthage, the exchange of sympathy for gratitude is the most princely thing!

For the rest you draw me on with your kindness.   It is difficult to get rid of people when you once have given them too much pleasure —*that* is a fact, and we will not stop for the moral of it.   What I was going to say—after a little natural hesitation—is, that if ever you emerge without inconvenient effort from your "passive state," and will *tell* me of such faults as rise to the surface and strike you as important in my poems (for of course, I do not think of troubling you with criticism in detail), you will confer a lasting obligation on me, and one which I shall value so much, that I covet it at a distance. I do not pretend to any extraordinary meekness under criticism and it is possible enough that I might not be altogether obedient to yours. But with my high respect for your power in your Art and for your experience as an artist, it would be quite impossible for me to hear a general observation of yours on what appear to you my master-faults, without being the better for it hereafter in some way. I ask for only a sentence or two of general observation—and I do not ask even for *that*, so as to tease you—but in the humble, low voice, which is so excellent a thing in women—particularly when they go a-begging! The most frequent general criticism I receive, is, I think, upon the style,—"if I *would* but change my style"! But *that* is an objection (isn't it?) to the writer bodily? Buffon says, and every sincere writer must feel, that "Le style c'est l'homme"; a fact, however, scarcely calculated to lessen the objection with certain critics.

Is it indeed true that I was so near to the pleasure and honour of making your acquaintance? and can it be true that you look back upon the lost opportunity with any regret? *But*—you know—if you had entered the "crypt," you might have caught cold, or been tired to death, and *wished* yourself "a thousand miles off"; which would have been worse than travelling them. It is not my interest, however, to put such thoughts in your head about its being "all for the best"; and I would rather hope (as I do) that what I lost by one chance I may recover by some future one. Winters shut me up as they do dormouse's eyes; in the spring, *we shall see*: and I am so much better that I seem turning round to the outward world again. And in the meantime I have learnt to know your voice, not merely from the poetry but from the kindness in it. Mr. Kenyon often speaks of you—dear Mr. Kenyon!—who most unspeakably, or only speakably with tears in my eyes,—has been my friend and helper, and my book's friend and helper! critic and sympathizer, true friend of all hours! You know him well enough, I think, to understand that I must be grateful to him.

I am writing too much,—and notwithstanding that I am writing too much, I will write of one thing more. I will say that I am your debtor, not only for this cordial letter and for all the pleasure which came with it, but in other ways, and those the highest: and I will say that while I live to follow the divine art of poetry, in proportion to my love for it and my devotion to it, I must be a devout admirer and student of your works.   This is in my heart to say to you—and I say it.

And for the rest, I am proud to remain,

Your obliged and faithful

ELIZABETH B. BARRETT

ROBERT BROWNING TO ELIZABETH BARRETT

TUESDAY, JUNE 30, 1846

I HAVE looked in the map for "L——," the place praised in the letter, and conclude it must be either Ceva (La Ceva, between Nocera and Salerno, about four miles from the latter, and on the mountain-side, I suppose . . . see a map, my Ba!)—or else Lucera, (which looks very much like the word) . . . and which lies at about sixty miles to the N.E. of Naples, in a straight line over the mountains and roadless country, but perhaps twice as far by the mainway through Avellino, Ariano, Bevino, and Savia—(exactly 120 Italian miles now that I count the posts).   So that there would be somewhat of a formidable journey to undertake after the sea voyage.   I daresay at Ceva there is abundance of quietness, as the few who visit Salerno do not go four miles inland, —can you enquire into this?

How inexpressibly charming it is to me to have a pretext for writing thus . . . about such approaches to the real event—these business-like words, and names of places!   If at the end you should bring yourself to say "But you never seriously believed this would take place"— what should I answer, I wonder?

Let me think on what is real, indisputable, however . . . the improvement in the health as I read it on the dear, dear cheeks yesterday.   This morning is favourable again . . . you will go out, will you not?

Mr. Kenyon sends me one of his kindest letters to ask me to dine with him next week—on Wednesday.   I feel *his* kindness, just as you feel in the other case, and in its lesser degree, I feel it,—and then I know,—dare think I know whether he will be so sorry in the end, —loving you as he does.   I will send his letter that you may understand here as elsewhere.

I think my head is dizzy with reading the debates this morning —Peel's speech and farewell.   How exquisitely absurd, it just strikes me, would be any measure after Miss Martineau's own heart, which should introduce women to Parliament as we understand its functions at present—how essentially retrograde a measure!   Parliament seems no place for originating creative minds—but for second-rate minds influenced by and bent on working out the results of these—and the most efficient qualities for such a purpose are confessedly found oftener with men than with women—physical power having a great deal to do with it beside. So why shuffle the heaps together which, however arbitrarily divided at first, happen luckily to lie pretty much as one would desire—here the great flint stones, here the pebbles—and diamonds too. The men of genius knew all this, said more than all this, in their way and proper place on the outside, where Miss M. is still saying something of the kind—to be taken up in its time by some other Mr. Cobden and talked about, and beleagured. But such people cannot or will not see where their office begins and advantageously ends; and that there is such a thing as influencing the influencers, playing the Bentham to the Cobden, the Barry to a Commission for Public Works, the Lough to the three or four industrious men with square paper caps who get rules and plummets and dot the blocks of marble all over as his drawings indicate. So you and I will go to Salerno or L—— (not to the L—akes, Heaven forefend!) and if we "let sail winged words, freighted with truth from the throne of God"—we may be sure—

Ah, presumption all of it! Then, you shall fill the words with their freight, and I will look on and love you,—is that too much? *Yes*—for any other—*No*—for one you (know) is *yours*—

Your very own,

For the quick departing yesterday our day was not spoken of . . . it is Saturday, is it not?

ELIZABETH BARRETT TO ROBERT BROWNING

Tuesday morning, June 30, 1846

The gods and men call you by your name, but I never do—never dare. In case of invocation, tell me how you should be called by such as I? not to be always the "inexpressive *He*" which I make of you. In case of courage for invocation!

Dearest . . . (which is a name too) read on the paper inside what I have been studying about Salerno since we parted yesterday. Forsyth is too severe in his deductions, perhaps, from the apothecaries, but your Naples book will not help me to contradict him, saying neither the one thing nor the other. The word we could not read in the letter yesterday, was *La Cava*—and La Cava is a town on the way between Naples and Salerno, which Mrs. Stark describes as "a large town with porticoes on each side of the High Street, like those at Bologna!" To which the letter adds, remember, "enchantingly beautiful, very good air and no English." Then there is Vietri, mentioned by Forsyth, between La Cava and Salerno, and *on the bay*. It is as well to think of all three. Were you ever at either? Amalfi itself appears to be very habitable. Oh—and your Naples book says of Salerno, that it is illuminated by fireflies, and that the chanting of frogs covers the noises of the city. You will like the frogs, if you don't the apothecaries, and I shall like the fireflies if I don't the frogs —but I *do* like frogs, you know, and it was quite a mistake of yours when you once thought otherwise.

Now I am going out in the carriage, to call on Mr. Kenyon, and perhaps to see Mr. Boyd. Your flowers are more beautiful than they were yesterday, if possible: and the fresh coolness helps them to live, so, that I hope you may see some of them on Saturday when you come. On Saturday! What a time to wait! if not for *them*, yet for *me*. Of the two, it is easier for them, certainly. *They* only miss a little dew and air.

I shall write again to-night,—but I cannot be more then than now, or less *ever* than now.

Your own
BA.

TO THE SAME

TUESDAY EVENING, JULY 1ST, 1846

THANK you for letting me see dear Mr. Kenyon's letter. He loves you, admires you, trusts you. When what is done cannot be undone, then he will forgive you besides—that is, he will forgive both of us, and set himself to see all manner of good where now he would see evil if we asked him to look. So we will not, if you please, ask him to look on the encouragement of ever so many more kind notes, pleasant as they are to read, and worthy to trust to, under certain conditions. Dear Mr. Kenyon—but how good he is! And I love him more (shall it be under-love?) because of his right perception and understanding of *you*—no one among men sets you higher than he does as a man and as a poet—even if he misses the subtle sense, sometimes.

So you dine with him—don't you? And I shall have you on Wednesday instead of Thursday! yes, certainly. And on Saturday, of course, next time.

In the carriage to-day, I went first to Mr. Kenyon's, and as he was not at home, left a card for a footstep. Then Arabel and Flush and I proceeded on our way to Mr. Boyd's in St. John's Wood, and I was so nervous . . . so anxious for an excuse for turning back . . . that . . . can you guess what Arabel said to me? "Oh Ba," she said; "such a coward as *you* are, never will be . . . married, while the world lasts." Which made me laugh if it did not make me persevere—for you see by it what her notion is of an heroic deed! So, there, I stood at last, at the door of poor Mr. Boyd's dark little room, and saw him sitting . . . as if he had not moved these seven years—these seven heavy, changeful years. Seeing him, my heart was too full to speak at first, but I stopped and kissed his poor bent-down forehead, which he never lifts up, his chin being quite buried in his breast. Presently we began to talk of Ossian and Cyprus wine, and I was forced, as I would not have Ossian for a god, to take a little of the Cyprus,— there was no help for me nor alternative; so I took as little as I could, while he went on proving to me that the Adamic fall and corruption of human nature (Mr. Boyd is a great theologian) were never in any single instance so disgustingly exemplified as in the *literary controversy about Ossian*; every man of the Highland Society having a lost soul in him; and Walter Scott . . . oh, the woman who poisoned all her children the other day, is a saint to Walter Scott . . . so we need not talk of him any more. "Arabel!—how much has she taken of that wine? not half a glass." "But Mr. Boyd, you would not have me be obliged to carry her home."

That visit being over, we went into the Park, Hyde Park, and drove close to the Serpentine, and then returned. Flush would not keep his head out of the window (his favourite pleasure) all the way, because several drops of rain trickled down his ears Flush has no idea of wetting his ears—his nose so near, too!

Right you are, I think, in opposition to Miss Martineau, though your reasons are too gracious to be right . . . except indeed as to the physical inaptitude, which is an obvious truth. Another truth (to my mind) is, that women, as they *are* (whatever they *may be*) have not mental strength any more than they have bodily; have not instruction, capacity, wholeness of intellect enough. To deny that women, as a class, have defects, is as false I think, as to deny that women have wrongs.

Then you are right again in affirming that the creators have no business *there*, with the practical men—*you* should not be *there* for instance.   And *I* (if I am to be thought of) would be prouder to eat cresses and macaroni (Dearest—there is a manufactory of macaroni and writing-paper at Amalfi close by—observe that combination! macaroni and writing-paper!) *I* would be prouder to eat cresses and macaroni with *you* as *you*, than to sit with diamonds in my ears, under the shelter of the woolsack, *you* being a law-lord and parliamentary maker of speeches!   By the way, I *couldn't* have diamonds in my ears: they never were *bored* for it . . . as I never was *born* for it.   A physical inaptitude, here too!

Shall I say what you tell me . . . "You never seriously believed" . . . shall I?   I will, if you like.   But it is not *C*eva, if you like—it is Cava . . . La Cava . . . in my map, and according to my authorities. Otherwise, the place is the same—four miles from Salerno, I think, and "enchantingly beautiful."   It is worth an inquiry certainly, this enchanting place which has no English in it, with porticoes like Bologna, and too little known to be spelt correctly by the most accomplished geographers.

Ah—your head is *"dizzy"* my beloved!   Tell me how it is now. And tell me how your mother is.   I think of you—love you.   I, who am discontented with myself . . . self-condemned as unworthy of you, in all else . . . am yet satisfied with the *love* I have for you —it seems worthy of you, as far as an abstract affection can go, without taking note of the personality loving.

Do you see the meaning through the mist?   Do you accept

Your very own

BA?

DAVID LIVINGSTONE (1813–73)

This devoted missionary and intrepid explorer was the son of poor parents who lived near Glasgow. Having qualified in medicine, he was sent out to Africa by the London Missionary Society in 1840. He discovered Lakes Ngami and Moerio, the source of the Congo, and the Victoria Falls on the Zambesi. In 1865 he exposed the scandals of the Portuguese slave-trade. Alarmed by the total absence of news of Livingstone, in 1871 an agitation was got up at home to send a party to his rescue and H. M. Stanley was sent out by the "New York Herald" to find him. How Stanley penetrated the African forests with a large convoy, eventually discovered the missionary, and greeted him with, "Dr. Livingstone, I presume!" is now matter of history. Shortly after he left, Livingstone succumbed to fever. His body was brought home and buried in Westminster Abbey.

TO THE REV. WILLIAM THOMPSON, OF CAPETOWN

SEKELETU'S TOWN, 17TH SEPTEMBER 1853

MY DEAR MAN, Your letters are "necessarily brief" so you say, and I am bound to believe the Reverend Father William Capeton seeing he hath received two students from Hankey into his ghostly care. Ah, mine are necessarily long, long winded or flatulent, as a follower of Esculapius expresseth it, the reason whereof lieth in an immense sheet of paper which must be filled, for Nature abhorreth a vacuum, and want of time to shorten them . . . here I am after my 8th attack of fever, the last very severe being accompanied with large discharges of blood. It has made me quite thin, but as I am becoming old and skinny per process of time that does not matter much. I never laid by, but vertigo from exhaustion compelled me to give up some of my sedentary work.

Please retain the medal [1] in Capetown till you hear from me. It is not likely I shall ever come your way again. Here one of your questions holds up its phiz at me "Unless you discover a good way to

[1] The silver medal of the French Geographical Society.

the sea either to the East or West how are we in future to send men to the region of the Lake or to the parts beyond? For Lobale?" *"In future,"* the dear man! how many has he sent in time past? "Unless you discover a good," &c. an indifferent one will do for those who have any pluck in them, and for those who have none the old overland route may be safely recommended for they will discover some important and very large field of labour a long way South of the Orange River in which they will be associated with a Wesleyan, a church of England clergyman, a Dutch Predicant and a Government schoolmaster, each of whom considers the 10 shanties and 8 shopkeeper's houses as his "sphere of labour" involving the most exacting responsibility.

I was delayed long at Kuruman by . . . want of people, for all feared to go North, but having got over these difficulties we made very good progress till we came to Lat. 19° 16′ South. There all my people were knocked down by fever except our Bakwain lad. I managed the hospital and he the oxen, and by God's mercy none were cut off. When we were able to move Northwards, the poor Bakwain lad took it too. I had to drive and cut a path too, for keeping more to the Eastward in order to avoid the Tsetse we travelled through a densely wooded country in which the axe was in constant operation. But for two bushmen who managed to loose the oxen and otherwise assisted we could not have moved. Some were still so weak we had to lift them out and into the waggon. When we came near the Chobe the adjacent country was flooded for fifteen miles out. Valleys appeared like deep rivers with hippopotami in them. We tried long in vain to get a ford through one large river called Sanshureh, our bushmen decamped too. So I took a small pontoon and the strongest of my weak crew, crossed the Sanshureh, half a mile wide and went North to find the Chobe and people. We waded among reed and high grass for three days trying to obtain a passage into the Chobe through the dense masses of reed, &c., which line its banks. On the fourth day we obtained our object, launched the pontoon and after passing along about 20 miles we reached a Makololo village. In their figurative language they said I "had come upon them as if I had dropped out of a cloud, yet I came riding upon the back of a hippopotamus." A rumour had reached the Makololo previously and two parties had been sent out in search of us. All our difficulties were now at an end. Canoes were soon sent down by the chief, our waggons, &c., were transported across the country and river and after proceeding North in order to avoid flooded lands on the other side, we turned

S.W. and reached the town. Our reception was far more flattering than I could have anticipated. The chief,[1] just over 18 years of age, said he rejoiced to obtain another father instead of Sebituane and repeatedly requested me to name whatever I wished and he would shew his affection by giving it, cattle, money, &c. &c., and he seemed distressed when I refused to name anything. He is not equal in appearance or abilities to his father but there is nothing weak or childish in his conduct or conversation and several executions which have taken place on account of conspiracy shew that he is not destitute of Sebituane's energy. He is afraid to learn to read at present, "Lest it should change his heart and make him content with one wife," as in the case of Sechele. I like a frank objector. . . .

I have just returned from a nine weeks' tour through the country in search of a suitable location for a mission. Went up the Barotse River, or as it is universally called by the Makalaka—the aboriginal inhabitants—the black race of whom I spoke—the Leeamby or "The River" [Zambesi].

[We] reached the confluence of the Loeti with its light coloured water, also that of the Leeba or Londa. Londa is the proper name because it comes from Londa the capital of a large state. The confluence of the Londa and the Leeamby is in 14° 11′ South, this is a point of great importance for the Leeamby turns thence away to the East N. East. The Londa about 150 yards wide (the Lecamby 250 beyond it), the Londa coming from the N. and by W. or N.N.W. is I dream yet to form part of our way West. Conveyance by water is of great importance with 6 paddlers; we went forty-four miles o Latitude in one day of 10½ hours and taking into account the windings of the river and our course being what sailors term a two and a half point one the actual distance must have been upwards of fifty Geographical miles. The river is one of very great beauty and breadth. It is often more than a mile broad with islands 3 or four miles long in it. These are covered with sylvan vegetation, the rounded masses of which seem to recline on the bosom of the water. The Tsetse spoils the most beautiful and healthful spots. I must reserve details, but after a laborious search have not found a spot that I could pronounce salubrious. We must brave the fever. It is God, not the Devil that rules our destiny. Surely we may when slave traders do. I met Arabs from Zanguebar, subjects of the Maum of Muscat, who

---

[1] The old chief Sebituane had died, and Livingstone did not know if his successor, Sekeletu, was favourable to him.

could write readily, and Portuguese from the farthest trading station inland on the West.   The latter probably through the influence of the chevalier Du Pratt's letter and passport shewed me every civility. An intrigue with an underchief who had pretensions to the chieftainship enabled the latter to drive a brisk trade in slaves in the Northern half of the Makololo country.   Nothing was done here to encourage them to call again.   A stockade was erected in the Barotse country, a flagstaff for the Portuguese banner set up, a small cannon given to the pretender who it is supposed gave authority for the prosperity of the slave trade contrary to the orders of the chief.   The conduct on the part of the merchant was very silly, for no sooner was the intrigue known, than the chief conspirators were cut off and their bodies tumbled into the River. . . .   They would have repelled the slave merchant too, but refrained on my representing that their doing so might injure me in the West and their departure is to take place soon.   I go Westward as soon as the rains commence.   I have preached in many spots where the name of Christ was never heard before. This is a matter for gratitude.   Hope the gospel will yet be established in these savage lands.   I travelled in a company of 160 in 33 canoes.   From the chief downwards all strove to shew kindness.   Nine weeks intimate intercourse, hearing their conversation, anecdotes, quarrelling, roaring, dancing, singing, and murdering, have imparted a greater disgust at heathenism than I ever had before, and in comparison with Southern tribes a firm belief that missionaries effect a great deal more than they are aware of even when there are no conversions. . . .

Ever affectionately yours,

DAVID LIVINGSTON

TO JAMES GORDON BENNETT

UJIJI, ON TANGANYIKA,
EAST AFRICA, NOVEMBER, 1871

MY DEAR SIR, It is in general somewhat difficult to write to one we have never seen—it feels so much like addressing an abstract idea —but the presence of your representative, Mr. H. M. Stanley, in this distant region takes away the strangeness I should otherwise have felt, and in writing to thank you for the extreme kindness that prompted you to send him, I feel quite at home.

If I explain the forlorn condition in which he found me, you will easily perceive that I have good reason to use very strong expressions of gratitude. I came to Ujiji off a tramp of between four hundred and five hundred miles beneath a blazing vertical sun having been baffled, worried, defeated, and forced to return, when almost within sight of the end of the geographical part of my mission, by a number of half-caste Moslem slaves sent to me from Zanzibar instead of men. The sore heart made still sorer by the woful sights I had seen of man's inhumanity to man reacted and told on the bodily frame and depressed it beyond measure. I thought that I was dying on my feet. It is not too much to say that almost every step of the weary, sultry way was in pain and I reached Ujiji a mere "ruckle" of bones.

There I found that some five hundred pounds sterling worth of goods which I had ordered from Zanzibar had unaccountably been entrusted to a drunken half-caste Moslem tailor who after squandering them for sixteen months on the way to Ujiji finished up by selling off all that remained for slaves and ivory for himself. He had "divined" on the Koran and found that I was dead. He had also written to the Governor of Unyanyembe that he had sent slaves after me to Manyema who returned and reported my decease and begged permission to sell off the few goods that his drunken appetite had spared.

He, however, knew perfectly well from men who had seen me that I was alive and waiting for the goods and men, but as for morality he is evidently an idiot, and there being no law here except that of the dagger or musket, I had to sit down in great weakness destitute of everything except a few barter-cloths and beads which I had taken the precaution to leave here in case of extreme need. The near prospect of beggary among Ujijians made me miserable. I could not despair because I laughed so much at a friend who, on reaching the mouth of the Zambezi, said that he was tempted to despair on breaking the photograph of his wife. We could have no success after that. Afterward the idea of despair had to me such a strong smack of the ludicrous that it was out of the question.

Well, when I had got to the lowest verge, vague rumours of an English visitor reached me. I thought of myself as the man who went down from Jerusalem to Jericho; but neither priest, Levite nor Samaritan could possibly pass my way. Yet the good Samaritan was close at hand and one of my people rushed up at the top of his speed and in great excitement gasped out, "An Englishman coming. I see him," and off he darted to meet him.

The American flag, the first ever seen in these parts, at the head of a caravan, told me the nationality of the stranger. I am as cold and non-demonstrative as we islanders are usually reputed to be, but your kindness made my frame thrill. It was indeed overwhelming, and I said in my soul—

"Let the richestest blessings descend from the Highest on you and yours."

The news Mr. Stanley had to tell me was thrilling. The mighty political changes on the Continent; the success of the Atlantic cables; the election of General Grant and many other topics riveted my attention for days together and had an immediate and beneficial effect on my health. I had been without news from home for years save what I could glean from a few *Saturday Reviews* and *Punch* of 1868. The appetite revived, and in a week I began to feel strong again. . . . The watershed of South Central Africa is over 700 miles in length. The fountains thereon are almost innumerable—that is, it would take a man's lifetime to count them. From the watershed they converge into four large rivers and these again into two mighty streams in the great Nile Valley which begins in ten degrees to twelve degrees South Latitude. It was long ere light dawned on the ancient problem and gave me a clear idea of the drainage. I had to feel my way and every step of the way and was generally groping in the dark. For who cared where the waters ran? We drank our fill and let the rest run by.

The Portuguese who visited Cazemba asked for slaves and ivory and heard of nothing else. I asked about the waters, questioned and cross-questioned until I was almost afraid of being set down as afflicted with hydrocephalus.

My last work in which I had been greatly hindered from want of suitable attendants was following the central line of drainage down through the country of the cannibals, called Manyema. This line of drainage has four large lakes in it. The fourth I was near when obliged to turn. It is from one to three miles broad and never can be reached at any point or at any time of the year. . . . Now I know about 600 miles of the watershed, and unfortunately the seventh hundred is the most interesting of the whole, for in it, if I am not mistaken, four fountains arise from an earthen mound and the last of the four becomes at no great distance off a large river. Two of these run north to Egypt, Lupira and Louraine, and two run south into Inner Ethiopia as the Liambai or Upper Zambezi and the Kaforeare, but these are but the sources of the Nile mentioned by the Secretary of Minerva in the city of Sais to Herodotus. I have heard of them so often and at great distances off that I cannot doubt their existence, and in spite

of the sore longing for home that seizes me every time I think of my
family, I wish to finish up by their discovery . . . and if my disclosures
regarding the terrible Ujijian slavery should lead to the suppression
of the east coast slave trade, I shall regard that as a greater matter by
far than the discovery of all the Nile sources together. Now that
you have done with domestic slavery for ever, lend us your powerful
aid for this great object. This fine country is blighted as with a
curse from above in order that the slavery privileges of the petty Sultan
of Zanzibar may not be infringed, and the rights of the Crown of
Portugal, which are mythical, should be kept in abeyance till some
future time when Africa will become another India to Portuguese
slave traders.

I conclude by again thanking you most cordially for your great
generosity, and am,

                                        Gratefully yours,
                                        DAVID LIVINGSTONE

CHARLOTTE BRONTË (1816–55)

When Charlotte wrote this letter fourteen years had still to go before the publication of "Jane Eyre," but much of her power of writing is discernible in its lines. Her father was curate of Haworth, at that time a country village, and was ruling his family with a discipline that almost verged on madness. His children were fed on potatoes and no meat, to make them hardy. He burnt their boots to cure them of vanity; and when overwrought by religious emotion would ease his temper by firing pistols out of the back door. Ellen Nussey was one of Charlotte's school-fellows and remained throughout her life an intimate friend and constant correspondent. The letter to Lewes was written when "Jane Eyre" was still the work of the mysterious "Currer Bell," though Lewes had at least detected the author's sex.

TO ELLEN NUSSEY

HAWORTH, FEBRUARY 20TH, 1834

YOUR letter gave me real and heartfelt pleasure, mingled with no small share of astonishment. Mary had previously informed me of your departure for London, and I had not ventured to calculate on any communication from you while surrounded by the splendours and novelties of that great city, which has been called the merchantile metropolis of Europe. Judging from human nature, I thought that a little country girl, for the first time in a situation so well calculated to excite curiosity, and to distract attention, would lose all remembrance, for a time at least, of distant and familiar objects, and give herself up entirely to the fascination of those scenes which were then presented to her view. Your kind, interesting, and most welcome epistle showed me, however, that I had been both mistaken and uncharitable in these suppositions. I was greatly amused at the tone of nonchalance which you assumed, while treating of London and its wonders. Did you not feel awed while gazing at St. Paul's and Westminster Abbey? Had you no feeling of intense and ardent interest, when in St. James's you saw the palace where

761

so many of England's kings have held their courts, and beheld the representations of their persons upon the walls? You should not be too much afraid of appearing *country-bred*; the magnificence of London has drawn exclamations of astonishment from travelled men, experienced in the world, its wonders, and beauties. Have you yet seen anything of the great personages whom the sitting of Parliament now detains in London, the Duke of Wellington, Sir Robert Peel, Earl Grey, Mr. Stanley, Mr. O'Connell? If I were you, I would not be too anxious to spend my time in reading whilst in town. Make use of your eyes for the purposes of observation now, and, for a time, at least, lay aside the spectacles with which authors would furnish us.

P.S.—Will you be kind enough to inform me of the number of performers in the King's military band?

TO G. H. LEWES

Nov. 1st, 1849

MY DEAR SIR, It is about a year and a half since you wrote to me; but it seems a longer period, because since then it has been my lot to pass some black milestones in the journey of life. Since then there have been intervals when I have ceased to care about literature and critics and fame, when I have lost sight of whatever was prominent in my thoughts at the first publication of "Jane Eyre"; but now I want these things to come back vividly, if possible: consequently, it was a pleasure to receive your note. I wish you did not think me a woman. I wish all reviewers believed "Currer Bell" to be a man; they would be more just to him. You will, I know, keep measuring me by some standard of what you deem becoming to my sex; where I am not what you consider graceful, you will condemn me. All mouths will be open against that first chapter; and that first chapter is as true as the Bible, nor is it exceptionable. Come what will, I cannot, when I write, think always of myself and of what is elegant and charming in feminity; it is not on those terms, or with such ideas, I ever took pen in hand: and if it is only on such terms my writing will be tolerated, I shall pass away from the public and trouble it no more. Out of obscurity I came, to obscurity I can easily return. Standing afar off, I now watch to see what will become of "Shirley." My expectations are very low, and my anticipations somewhat sad and bitter; still, I earnestly conjure you to say honestly what you think; flattery would be worse than vain; there is no consolation in flattery.

As for condemnation I cannot, on reflection, see why I should much fear it; there is no one but myself to suffer therefrom, and both happiness and suffering in this life soon pass away.   Wishing you all success in your Scottish expedition,

I am, dear Sir,
Yours sincerely,
C. BELL

RICHARD, 1ST EARL LYONS (1817–87)

*Few diplomats in the mid-nineteenth century saw more interesting
service than Lord Lyons. He was at Washington during the difficult
days of the American Civil War; and was at Paris when the Second
Empire fell. There is something prophetic in this letter describing
German aims.*

TO LORD DERBY

PARIS, FEB. 5, 1877

IT is believed here that Bismarck is determined to produce at least such
a scare as he did two years ago, if not to do more. The idea provokes
some anger, but more fear. Nevertheless, the danger is greater now
than it was last time; for although France is very far from being ready
for even a defensive war, she does feel so much stronger than she did in
1875, as not to be willing to bear quite as much from Germany as she
would have borne then.

The impressions prevalent here are:

That Bismarck is very much disappointed by the result of the
Constantinople Conference, which he had hoped would have ended by
setting all Europe by the ears.

That he is very much irritated by the cordiality which existed
between the English, French, and Russian Plenipotentiaries, and by the
considerable part taken by Chaudordy in the proceedings.

That he is very much annoyed by the number of Socialist votes given
in the recent German elections, and is eager to destroy Paris as the hotbed
of socialism.

That he wants a cry to make the Germans pay their taxes willingly.

That he looks with an evil eye upon the material prosperity of France.

That he considers the Exhibition of 1878 as a sort of defiance of
Germany, and is ready to go to great lengths to prevent its taking place.

These are French views, not mine; but I do agree with the conclusion
which the greater and the wiser part of the French nation drawn from
them: namely, that it behoves France to be more than ever prudent and
cautious, and more than ever careful not to give Germany any pretext for
a quarrel.

France is certainly not at all likely to oppose Russia in anything that country may undertake in the East; but she is still less likely to give her any military assistance there. She might not be able to resist the bait, if Russia held it out, of an offensive and defensive alliance against Germany, but in that case she would more than ever want her own forces on this side of Germany. This contingency, however, is too improbable to be worth considering.

It is quite true that France has a large force on her Eastern Frontier, and that she is hard at work there, but considering the difficulty of guarding that frontier, such as it has been left by the Treaty of 1871, her objects may well be supposed to be purely defensive.

Lord Salisbury is to arrive this evening and to go on to London without stopping.

SIR WILLIAM STIRLING-MAXWELL (1818–78)

This letter gives an extraordinarily vivid picture of Paris in the revolution of 1848 when the "bourgeois king" Louis Philippe was dethroned and the Second Republic proclaimed.

TO ABRAHAM HAYWARD

PARIS, JULY, 1848

MY DEAR HAYWARD, We arrived here with the mail this morning in due course of post, seeing nothing indicative of revolution or outrage (although they said at Boulogne 1,000 rails had been torn up on Thursday or Friday), till we drew up opposite the blackened shell of the refreshment-room at Pontoise. The streets were quite quiet as we drove to Meurice's, and with the exception of a piece of pavement in the Rue de Trieste of which the youthful complexion hinted that it had lately served for a barricade, we saw and heard nothing that was inconsistent with the ordinary aspect of Sunday, Paris, and peace. In the afternoon we made a tour of many of the scenes of action. The Boulevards, as you go towards the Place de la Bastille, get every hundred yards more disturbed in their roadways and foot-pavements; heaps of stones piled up out of the way hinder the crowds of passengers; then you see smashed a window or *jalousie*, or a splintered shutter; then a few marks of balls on the houses, or on the barks of the wretched little new trees, or poplars of liberty; next, you come on a row of unfinished houses, with their carved door-ways and balconies sadly gashed, and finally every house-front wears a rueful countenance marked like a pugilist's with severe punishment. All that cluster of corner houses which forms one side of the Place de la Bastille has been severely handled: some have been actually levelled to the ground; and the rest have their angles here and there shot away, or two or more windows smashed into one. A certain great magazine there with the sign "Au Bélier Merinos," the whole façade of which ten days ago seems to have been painted a bright chocolate, looked like a breadth of cloth, tattered with uncertain holes, and spotted with mud, so effectually have the windows been confused with cannon-shot, and the wall small-poxed with musket-balls. We called it the *Battered Ram*.

The Place was full of people, jabbering and grimacing, and the top of the Column of July crowded with soldiers and sightseers. The winding Rue St. Antoine is in parts almost a ruin. One of the houses which had suffered most severely was an *Estaminet-Billard*; not an inch of glass was left in any of the windows, and hardly a window-frame; but we saw the cigars and the cues of the players within, making their cannons as coolly as if revolution and artillery were unknown. The Church of St. Gervais had been severely peppered, and we found in one of its chapels a little crowd visiting and sprinkling holy water on the bodies of three dead officers, lying in state there, with bullet-holes and blood-stains on the breasts of their uniforms. The Pantheon is not much punished: the pillars are chipped a little, but so far as I could see with an opera-glass, the gods and goddesses in the pediment are unwounded. The space in front of it was a bivouac; and so were many parts of the quays, where a sort of stage had been erected which enabled the poor weary *gardes-nationaux* and *mobiles* to sleep in two tiers one above another, like rabbits in a hutch. We afterwards dined at the Café de Paris, and took our coffee at Torloni's in company with a very pleasant socialist friend of Coningham's. The Boulevard was crowded with its usual bearded idlers and unbonneted *grisettes*, and I did not see a single face or object to remind one of the fact, that a battle bloodier than Eylau had been fought a few days before in the streets of Paris—except a jolly, laughing beggar with a wooden leg which, he told me, replaced one that he had left in the massacre at Rouen! Where can the Rachels be, who are weeping for their children, lovers, husbands or brothers? They had not heard the story of Mrs. H—— H—— being taken in arms and men's clothes at the Embassy, so it is no doubt a London lie. Lamartine, they say, is as deeply implicated as anybody in the revolt, which I hope is a Paris lie.

Ever yours very truly,

WM. STIRLING

GEORGE ELIOT (1819–80)

Mary Ann Evans was born at Arbury Farm, near the Forest of Arden. Much of her early life is described in "The Mill on the Floss" and "Adam Bede." She was largely influenced by George Herbert Lewes, whom she subsequently married; he persuaded her to write the "Scenes from Clerical Life," and encouraged her in her work until his death, in 1878. George Eliot died two years later, seven months after her marriage to J. W. Cross. The first letter printed below refers to a translation of Strauss undertaken for some friends named Bray. This led to work on the "Westminster Review", and ultimately to her meeting with Lewes.

APRIL 10

THE other day I received a letter from an old friend in Warwickshire, containing some striking information about the author of "Adam Bede." I extract the passage for your amusement:

"I want to ask you if you have read 'Adam Bede,' or the 'Scenes of Clerical Life,' and whether you know that the author is Mr. Liggins? . . . A deputation of Dissenting parsons went over *to ask him to write for the 'Eclectic,'* and they found him washing his slop-basin at a pump. He has no servant, and does everything for himself; but one of the said parsons said that he inspired them with a reverence that would have made any impertinent question impossible. The son of a baker, of no mark at all in his town, so that it is possible you may not have heard of him. You know he calls himself 'George Eliot.' It sounds strange to hear the *'Westminster'* doubting whether he is a woman, when *here he is so well known.* But I am glad it has mentioned him. *They say he gets no profit out of 'Adam Bede,' and gives it freely to Blackwood, which is a shame.* We have not read him yet, but the extracts are irresistible."

Conceive the real George Eliot's feelings, conscious of being a base worlding—not washing his own slop-basin, and *not* giving away his MS.! not even intending to do so, in spite of the reverence such a course might inspire. I hope you and Major Blackwood will enjoy the myth.

Mr. Langford sent me a letter the other day from Miss Winkworth, a grave lady, who says she never reads novels—except a few of the most famous, but that she has read "Adam" three times running. One likes to know such things: they show that the book tells on people's hearts, and may be a real instrument of culture. I sing my Magnificat in a quiet way, and have a great deal of deep, silent joy; but few authors, I suppose, who have had a real success, have known less of the flush and the sensations of triumph that are talked of as the accompaniments of success. I think I should soon begin to believe that *Liggins* wrote my books—it is so difficult to believe what the world does *not* believe, so easy to believe what the world keeps repeating.

TO CHAS. BRAY

BROADSTAIRS, JULY 21, 1852

Do not be anxious about me—there is no cause. I am profiting, body and mind, from quiet walks and talks with nature, gathering "Lady's Bedstraw" and "Rest-Harrow," and other pretty things; picking up shells (not in the Newtonian sense, but literally); reading Aristotle, to find out what is the chief good; and eating mutton-chops, that I may have strength to pursue it. If you insist on my writing about "Emotions," why, I must get some up expressly for the purpose. But I must own I would rather not, for it is the grand wish and object of my life to get rid of them as far as possible, seeing they have already had more than their share of my nervous energy. I shall not be in town on the 2d of August—at least I pray heaven to forbid it.

TO MRS. BRAY

THE PRIORY, MARCH 18, 1865

I BELIEVE you are one of the few who can understand that in certain crises direct expression of sympathy is the least possible to those who most feel sympathy. If I could have been with you in bodily presence, I should have sat silent, thinking silence a sign of feeling that speech, trying to be wise, must always spoil. The truest things one can say about great Death are the oldest, simplest things that everybody knows by rote, but that no one knows really till death has come very close. And when that inward teaching is going on, it seems pitiful presumption for those who are outside to be saying anything. There is no such thing as consolation when we have made the lot of another our own. I don't know whether you strongly share, as I do, the old belief that made men say the gods loved those who died young. It seems to me truer than ever, now life

E.L.   C C has become more complex, and more and more difficult problems have to be worked out. Life, though a good to men on the whole, is a doubtful good to many, and to some not good at all. To my thought, it is a source of constant mental distortion to make the denial of this a part of religion—to go on pretending things are better than they are. To me early death takes the aspect of salvation; though I feel, too, that those who live and suffer may sometimes have the greater blessedness of *being* a salvation. But I will not write of judgments and opinions. What I want my letter to tell you is that I love you truly, gratefully, unchangeably.

TO MISS SARA HENNELL

FOLESHILL, SUNDAY, MAY, 1844

To begin with business, I send you on the other side the translations you wished (Strauss), but they are perhaps no improvements on what you had done. I shall be very glad to learn from you the particulars as to the mode of publication—who are the parties that will find the funds, and whether the manuscripts are to be put into the hands of any one when complete, or whether they are to go directly from me to the publishers? I was very foolish not to imagine about these things in the first instance, but ways and means are always afterthoughts with me.

You will soon be settled and enjoying the blessed spring and summer time. I hope you are looking forward to it with as much delight as I. One has to spend so many years in learning how to be happy. I am just beginning to make some progress in the science, and I hope to disprove Young's theory that "as soon as we have found the key of life, it opes the gates of death." Every year strips us of at least one vain expectation, and teaches us to reckon some solid good in its stead. I never will believe that our youngest days are our happiest. What a miserable augury for the progress of the race and the destination of the individual, if the more matured and enlightened state is the less happy one! Childhood is only the beautiful and happy time in contemplation and retrospect: to the child it is full of deep sorrows, the meaning of which is unknown. Witness colic and whooping-cough and dread of ghosts, to say nothing of hell and Satan, and an offended Deity in the sky, who was angry when I wanted too much plum-cake. Then the sorrows of older persons, which children see but cannot understand, are worse than all. All this to prove that we are happier than when we were seven years old, and that we shall be happier when we are forty than we are now, which I call

a comfortable doctrine, and one worth trying to believe! I am sitting
with father, who every now and then jerks off my attention to the history
of Queen Elizabeth, which he is reading.

TO THE SAME

ST. LEONARDS, JUNE 4, 1848

ALAS for the fate of poor mortals which condemns them to wake up some
fine morning and find all the poetry in which their world was bathed,
only the evening before, utterly gone!—the hard, angular world of chairs
and tables and looking-glasses staring at them in all its naked prose! It is
so in all the stages of life: the poetry of girlhood goes—the poetry of love
and marriage—the poetry of maternity—and at last the very poetry of
duty forsakes us for a season, and we see ourselves, and all about us, as
nothing more than miserable agglomerations of atoms—poor tentative
efforts of the *Natur Princip* to mould a personality. This is the state of
prostration—the self-abnegation through which the soul must go, and to
which perhaps it must again and again return, that its poetry or religion,
which is the same thing, may be a real everflowing river, fresh from the
windows of heaven and the fountains of the great deep—not an artificial
basin, with grotto-work and gold-fish. I feel a sort of madness growing
upon me—just the opposite of the delirium which makes people fancy that
their bodies are filling the room. It seems to me as if I were shrinking
into that mathematical abstraction, a point. But I am wasting this "good
Sunday morning" in grumblings.

JOHN RUSKIN (1819–1900)

The first of these letters was written by Ruskin in early days. It congratulates Severn on his success in the cartoon competition for the Westminster frescoes. The great writer's letters to Dr. John Brown reveal the man in his most amiable mood. The first was written on the publication of "Horæ Subsecivæ," and Ruskin's cordial appreciation of that book will be endorsed by the many thousands who still find it a source of constant joy.

TO DR. JOHN BROWN

DENMARK HILL, 16TH JANUARY '62

DEAR DR. BROWN, There's no use in telling you these lay sermons are delicious, for everybody will be telling you as much, but you may be glad to know, at least, that I'm getting the good of them.   And partly the Bad of them, for all such wise and good sayings make me very selfishly sorrowful, because I had them not said to me thirty years ago.   All good knowledge seems to come to me now

> As unto dying eyes
> The casement slowly grows a glimmering square.

But you yourself, I remember, were despondent about yourself when you went (to Spain was it not?), and now you're able to write these jolly things and preach them too!

Am I not in a curiously *unnatural* state of mind in this way—that at 43, instead of being able to settle to my middle-aged life like a middle-aged creature, I have more instincts of youth about me than when I was young, and am miserable because I cannot climb, run, or wrestle, sing, or flirt—as I was when a youngster because I couldn't sit writing metaphysics all day long.   Wrong at both ends of life. . . .

TO THE SAME

1862

DEAR DR. BROWN, Yes, indeed, I shall always regard you as one of the truest, fondest, faithfullest friends I have.   It was precisely because I did and do so that your letters made me so despondent. "If Dr. Brown thinks this of me, if *he* supposes that my strong, earnest words on a subject of this mighty import are worth no more than the Editor of the *Scotsman's* or (who is it?—Mr. Heugh's?), and that they can be seen to the bottom of in a day's reading, what must others think of me?" You say I have effected more revolution than other writers. My dear Doctor, I have been useful, in various accidental minor ways, by pretty language and pleasant hints, chiefly to girls (I don't despise girls, I love them, and they help me, and understand me often better than grown women), but of my intended work I have done nothing. I have not yet made people understand so much as my first principle that in art there is a Right and Wrong.

At this instant nineteen thousand Turner sketches are packed in tin cases without one human being in Europe caring what happens to them. Why, again, should you suppose that I would be unjust in any such serious work as this,[1] if I could help it? Those expressions of mine may do me harm, or do me good; what is that to me? They are the only true, right, or possible expressions. The Science of Political Economy *is* a Lie,— wholly and to the very root (as hitherto taught). It is also the damnedest, that is to say, the most Utterly and to the Lowest Pit condemned of God and His Angels, that the Devil, or Betrayer of Men, has yet invented, except his (the Devil's) theory of Sanctification. To this "science" and to this alone (the Professed and organized pursuit of Money) is owing *All* the Evil of modern days. I say All. The Monastic theory is at an end. It is now the Money theory which corrupts the church, corrupts the household life, destroys honour, beauty, and life throughout the universe. It is *the* Death incarnate of Modernism, and the so-called science of its pursuit is the most cretinous, speechless, paralysing plague that has yet touched the brains of mankind.

There is no "state of mind" indicated in my saying this. I write it as the cool, resolute result of ten years' thought and sight. I write it as coolly as I should a statement respecting the square of the hypothenuse. If my hand shakes, it is from mere general nervousness, vexation about my mother (who, however, is going on quite well as far as the accident admits), and so on. The matter of this letter is as deliberate as if I were stating an equation to you, or a chemical analysis. You say I should "go and be cheerful." I don't know what your Edinburgh streets afford of recreative sight. Our London ones afford not much. My only way of being cheerful is precisely the way I said, to shut myself up and look at

---

[1] Ruskin's *Cornhill* papers.

weeds and stones; for as soon as I see or hear what human creatures are suffering of pain, and saying of absurdity, I get about as cheerful as I should be in a sheepfold strewed hurdle-deep with bloody carcases, with a herd of wolves and monkeys howling and gibbering on the top of them. I am resting now from all real work and reading mineralogy and such things, amusing myself as I can, and hope to get rid of nervousness and so on in good time, and then have it well out with these economical fellows.

It puzzles me not a little that you should not *yet* see the drift of my first statement in those *Cornhill* papers. I say there is *no* science of Political Economy yet, because no one has defined wealth. They don't know what they are talking about. They don't even know what Money is, but tacitly assume that Money is desirable,—as a sign of wealth, without defining Wealth itself. Try to define Wealth yourself, and you will soon begin to feel where the bottom fails.

TO JOSEPH SEVERN

VENICE, SEPTEMBER 21ST, 1843 (45?)

MY DEAR SIR, I am sure you will not excuse my not having answered your kind letter before, when I tell you that I have been altogether unhinged by the condition in which I found Venice, and that every time I stir out of doors I return too insensible to write or almost to speak to anyone. But I cannot longer defer expressing my sincere gladness at your well deserved success, and my sympathy in all the enthusiasms of your hopes, so far as regards your own aims and prospects, and I am glad for the sake of our national honour, that you are to be one of its supporters. But with your hopes for the elevation of English art by means of fresco, I cannot sympathize. I have not the remotest hope of anything of the kind. It is not the material nor the space that can give us thoughts, passions or powers. I see on our Academy walls nothing but what is ignoble in small pictures, and would be disgusting in large ones. I never hear one word of genuine feeling issue from anyone's mouth but yours, and the two Richmonds', and if it did, I don't believe the public of the present day would understand it. It is not the love of *fresco* that we want: it is the love of God and his creatures: it is humility, and charity, and self-denial, and fasting, and prayer, it is a total change of character. We want more faith and less reasoning, less strength and more trust. You want neither walls, nor plaster nor colours—*ça ne fait rien à l'affaire*—it is Giotto and Ghirlandajo and Angelico that you want, and that you will and must want, until this disgusting nineteenth century has, I can't say breathed, but steamed, its last. . . .

It isn't of any use to try and do anything for such an age as this. We are a different race altogether from the men of old time; we live in drawing rooms instead of deserts; and work by the light of chandeliers instead of volcanoes. I have been perfectly prostrated these two or three days back by my first acquaintance with Tintoret; but then I feel as if I had got introduced to a being from a planet a 1,000,000 of miles nearer the sun, not to a mere earthly painter. As for our little bits of R.A.'s calling themselves painters, it ought to be stopped directly. One might make a mosaic of R.A.'s perhaps; with a good magnifying glass, big enough for Tintoret to stand with one leg upon . . . if he balanced himself like a gondolier.

I thought the mischief was confined to architecture here, but Tintoret is going quite as fast. The Empire of Austria is his Geo. Robins. I went to see the Senora di San Rocco the other day, in heavy rain, and found the floor half under water, from large pools from droppings *through* the *pictures* on the ceiling, not through the side or mouldings, but the pictures themselves. They won't take care of them, nor sell them, nor let anybody else take care of them.

I beg your pardon for this hurried sulky scrawl, but conceive how little one is fit for when one finds them covering the marble palaces in stucco and painting them in *stripes*.

Allow me again to thank you for your kind letter, and to express my delight at the good news it contains, and believe me, with compliments to Mrs. Severn,

Ever most truly yours,

J. RUSKIN

VICTORIA (1819–1901)

The letters of the Great Queen are too well known to need comment or eulogy. The first of those printed below was written some ten days before her marriage, and it shows with what clarity she viewed her position and her own relative importance even to the man she loved. The second letter was addressed to her uncle and unfailing counsellor, the King of the Belgians. It describes one of the foolish attempts on her life and reveals with what indomitable pluck Victoria pursued the course of her duty.

TO THE PRINCE ALBERT

BUCKINGHAM PALACE, 31ST JANUARY 1840

You have written to me in one of your letters about our stay at Windsor, but, dear Albert, you have not at all understood the matter. You forget, my dearest Love, that I am the Sovereign, and that business can stop and wait for nothing. Parliament is sitting, and something occurs almost every day, for which I may be required, and it is quite impossible for me to be absent from London; therefore two or three days is already a long time to be absent. I am never easy a moment, if I am not on the spot, and see and hear what is going on, and everybody, including all my Aunts (who are very knowing in all these things), says I must come out after the second day, for, as I must be surrounded by my Court, I cannot keep alone. This is also my own wish in every way.

Now as to the Arms: as an English Prince you have no right, and Uncle Leopold had no right to quarter the English Arms, but the Sovereign has the power to allow it by Royal Command: this was done for Uncle Leopold by the Prince Regent, and I will do it again for you. But it can only be done by Royal Command.

I will, therefore, without delay, have a seal engraved for you.

You will certainly feel very happy too, at the news of the coming union of my much-beloved Vecto with Nemours. It gives me quite infinite pleasure, because then I can see the dear child more frequently.

I read in the newspaper that you, dear Albert, have received many Orders; also that the Queen of Spain will send you the Golden Fleece. . . .

Farewell, dearest Albert, and think often of thy faithful

VICTORIA R.

BUCKINGHAM PALACE, 31ST MAY 1842

MY DEAREST UNCLE, I wish to be the first to inform you of what happened yesterday evening, and to tell you that we are *saines et sauves*. On returning from the chapel on Sunday, Albert was observing how civil the people were, and then suddenly turned to me and said it appeared to him as though a man had held out a pistol to the carriage, and that it had hung fire; accordingly, when we came home he mentioned it to Colonel Arbuthnot, who was only to tell it to Sir J. Graham and Sir Robert Peel, and have the police instructed, and *nobody else*. No one, however, who was with us, such as footmen, etc., had seen anything at all. Albert began to doubt what he believed he had seen. Well, yesterday morning (Monday) a lad came to Murray (who of course knew nothing) and said that he saw a man in the crowd as we came home from church, present a pistol to the carriage, which, however, did not go off, and heard the man say, "Fool that I was not to fire!" The man then vanished, and this boy followed another man (an old man) up St. James's Street who repeated twice, "How very extraordinary!" but instead of saying anything to the police, asked the boy for his direction and disappeared. The boy accordingly was sent to Sir Robert Peel, and (doubtful as it still was) every precaution was taken, still keeping the thing completely secret, not a soul in the house knowing a word, and accordingly after some consultation, as *nothing* could be done, we drove out—many police then in plain clothes being distributed in and about the parks, and the two Equerries riding so close on each side that they must have been hit, if anybody had; still the feeling of looking out for such a man was not *des plus agréables*; however, we drove through the parks, up to Hampstead, and back again. All was so quiet that we almost thought of nothing—when, as we drove down Constitution Hill, very fast, we heard the report of a pistol, but not at all loud, so that had we not been on the alert we should hardly have taken notice of it. We saw the man seized by a policeman *next to whom he was standing when he* fired, but we did not stop. Colonel Arbuthnot and two others saw him take aim, but we only *heard* the report (looking both the other way). We felt both very glad that our drive had had the effect of having the man seized. Whether it was loaded or not we cannot yet tell, but we are again full of gratitude to Providence for invariably *protecting* us! The feeling of horror is very great in the public, and great affection is shown us. The man was yesterday examined at the Home Office, is called John Francis, is a cabinet-maker, and son of a machine-maker of Covent Garden Theatre, is good-looking (they say). I have never seen him at all close, but Arbuthnot gave the description of him from what he saw on Sunday, which exactly answered. Only twenty or twenty-one years old, and *not* the *least* mad—but very cunning. The boy identified him this morning, amongst many others. Everything is to be kept secret *this* time, which is very right, and altogether I think it is being well done. Every further particular you shall hear. I was really not at all frightened, and feel *very* proud at dear Uncle Mensdorff calling me "*sehr muthig*," which I shall ever remember with peculiar pride, coming from so distinguished an officer as he is! Thank God, my Angel is also well! but he says that had the man fired on Sunday, he must have been hit in the head! God is merciful; that indeed we must feel daily more! Uncle and cousins were quite horrified. . . . Ever your devoted Niece,

VICTORIA R.

You will tell Louise *all*, of course.

These letters are printed by permission, from "The Letters of Queen Victoria," published by Mr. John Murray.

FLORENCE NIGHTINGALE (1820–1910)

The Crimean War was at its height when Florence Nightingale decided to go out to Russia. Her letter to Mrs. Herbert, wife of Sidney Herbert, the secretary at war, announcing this intention is given below.

TO MRS. HERBERT

1 UPPER HARLEY STREET,
OCTOBER 14TH 1854

MY DEAREST, I went to Belgrave Square this morning for the chance of catching you or Mr. Herbert even, had he been in town.

A small private expedition of nurses has been organized for Scutari, and I have been asked to command it. I take myself out and one nurse.

Lady Maria Forester has given £200 to take out three others. We feed and lodge ourselves there, and are to be no expense whatever to the country. Lord Clarendon has been asked by Lord Palmerston to write to Lord Stratford for us, and has consented. Dr. Andrew Smith of the Army Medical Board, whom I have seen, authorizes us, and gives us letters to the Chief Medical Officer at Scutari.

I do not mean to say that I believe the *Times* accounts, but I do believe that we may be of use to the wounded wretches.

Now to business.

(1) Unless my Ladies' Committee feel that this is a thing which appeals to the sympathies of all, and urge me, rather than barely consent, I cannot honourably break my engagement here. And I write to you as one of my mistresses.

(2) What does Mr. Herbert say to the scheme itself? Does he think it will be objected to by the authorities? Would he give us any advice or letters of recommendation? And are there any stores for the Hospital he would advise us to take out? Dr. Smith says that nothing is needed.

I enclose a letter from E. Do you think it any use to apply to Miss Burdett Coutts?

We start on Tuesday if we go, to catch the Marseilles boat of the 21st for Constantinople, where I leave my nurses, thinking the Medical

Staff at Scutari will be more frightened than amused at being bombarded by a parcel of women, and I cross over to Scutari with some one from the Embassy to present my credentials from Dr. Smith, and put ourselves at the disposal of the Drs.

(3) Would you or some one of my Committee write to Lady Stratford to say, "This is not a lady but a real Hospital Nurse," of me? "And she has had experience."

My uncle went down this morning to ask my father and mother's consent.

Would there be any use in my applying to the Duke of Newcastle for his authority?

Believe me, dearest, in haste, ever yours,

F. NIGHTINGALE

Perhaps it is better to keep it quite a private thing, and not apply to Govt. *qua* Govt.

LUCY, LADY DUFF-GORDON (1821–69)

This lady was the daughter of the well-known translator and writer, Sarah Austin; so, when she married Duff-Gordon and opened her drawing-room in Queen's Square, Westminster, she soon gathered around her a circle of friends of amazing interest. Dickens, Thackeray, Tennyson, Kinglake, among many others, were constantly to be found there, and every foreigner of talent and renown naturally gravitated to her house. For reasons of health Lady Duff-Gordon went to Egypt in 1862, and the rest of her life was spent there. The extraordinarily vivid descriptions embodied in her letters ensured their fame immediately on their publication.

TO HER MOTHER

LUXOR, MARCH 22, 1864

THE whole of the European element has now departed from Thebes, save one lingering boat on the opposite shore, belonging to two young Englishmen,—the same who lost their photographs and all their goods by the sinking of their boat in the cataract last year. They are an excellent sample of our countrymen, kind, well-bred, and straightforward.

I am glad my letters amuse you. Sometimes I think they must breathe the unutterable dullness of Eastern life,—not that it is dull to me, a curious spectator, but how the men with nothing on earth to do *can* endure it is a wonder. I went yesterday evening to call on a Turk at El-Karnak; he is a gentlemanlike man, the son of a former *mudeer* who was murdered, I believe, for his cruelty and extortion. He has a thousand *feddáns* (acres, or a little more) of land, and lives in a mud house, larger, but no better, than that of a Fellah, and with two wives, and the brother of one of them; he leaves the farm to his Fellaheen altogether, I fancy. There was one book, a Turkish one; I could not read the title-page, and he did not tell me what it was. In short, there were no means of killing time but the *nargheeleh*; no horse, no gun, nothing; and yet they don't seem bored. The two women are always clamorous for my visits, and very noisy and schoolgirlish, but apparently excellent friends, and very good-natured. The gentleman gave me a *kuffeeyeh* (thick head-kerchief for the sun), so I took the ladies a bit of silk I happened to have. You never heard anything like his raptures over M.'s portrait. "Másháalláh! it is the will of God! and, by God, he is like a rose." But I can't take to the Turks; I always feel that they secretly dislike and think ill of us European women, though they profess huge admiration and pay *personal* compliments, which an Arab very seldom attempts.

I heard Seleem Efendi and Omar discussing English ladies one day lately, while I was inside the curtain with Seleem's slave-girl, and they did not know I heard them. Omar described J., and was of opinion that a man who was married to her could want nothing more. "By my soul, she rides like a Bedawee, she shoots with the gun and pistol, rows the boat; she knows many languages and what is in their books; works with the needle like an Efreet, and to see her hands run over the teeth of the music-box (keys of the piano) amazes the mind, while her singing gladdens the soul. How, then, should her husband ever desire the coffee-shop? *Walláhee!* she can always amuse him at home. And as to *my* lady, the thing is not that she does not know. When I feel my stomach tightened, I go to the divan and say to her, 'Do you want anything—a pipe or sherbet or so-and-so?' and I talk till she lays down her book and talks to me, and I question her and amuse my mind; and by God! if I were a rich man and could marry one English *hareem* like these, I would stand before her and serve her like her *memlook*. You see I am only this lady's servant, and I have not once sat in the coffee-shop, because of the sweetness of her tongue. Is it not true, therefore, that the man who can marry such *hareem* is rich more than with money?"

Seleem seemed disposed to think a little more of good looks, though he quite agreed with all Omar's enthusiasm, and asked if J. were beautiful. Omar answered with decorous vagueness, that she was "a moon"; but declined mentioning her hair, eyes, etc. (It is a liberty to describe a woman minutely.) I nearly laughed out at hearing Omar relate his manœuvres to make me "amuse his mind." It seems I am in no danger of being discharged for being dull. On the other hand, frenchified Turks have the greatest detestation of *femmes d'esprit*.

The weather has set in so hot that I have shifted my quarters out of my fine room to the south-west, into a room with only three sides, looking over a lovely green view to the north-east, and with a huge sort of solid verandah, as large as the room itself, on the open side; thus I live in the open air altogether. The bats and swallows are quite sociable; I hope the serpents and scorpions will be more reserved.

El-Khamáseen (the fifty days) has begun, and the wind is enough to mix up heaven and earth; but it is not distressing, like the Cape south-easter, and though hot, not choking like the *khámaseen* in Cairo and Alexandria. Mohammad brought me some of the new wheat just now. Think of harvest in March and April! These winds are as good for the crops here as a "nice steady rain" is in England. It is not necessary to water as much when the wind blows strong.

As I rode through the green fields along the dyke, a little boy sang, as he turned round on the musically-creaking *Sákiyeh* (water-wheel turned by an ox), the one eternal *Sákiyeh* tune. The words are *ad libitum*, and my little friend chanted: "Turn, O *Sákiyeh*, to the right, and turn to the left; who will take care of me if my father dies? Turn, O *Sákiyeh*, etc. Pour water for the figs and the grapes, and for the water-melons. Turn," etc., etc. Nothing is so pathetic as hat *Sákiyeh* song.

I passed the house of the Sheykh-el-Abab'-deh, who called out to me to take coffee. The moon rose splendid, and the scene was lovely: the handsome black-brown sheykh in dark robes and white turban, Omar in a graceful white gown and red turban, the wild Abab'deh with their bare heads and long black ringlets, clad in all manner of dingy white rags, and bearing every kind of uncouth weapon in every kind of wild and graceful attitude, and a few little brown children quite naked, and shaped like Cupids. And there we sat and looked so romantic, and talked quite like ladies and gentlemen about the merits of Sákneh and Almas, the two great rival women singers of Cairo. I think the sheykh wished to display his experience of fashionable life.

The Copts are now fasting, and cross. They fast fifty-five days for Lent (old style; no Coptic style); no meat, fish, eggs, or milk, no exception of Sundays, no food till after twelve at noon, and no intercourse with the *hareem*. The only comfort is plenty of *arakee*; and what a Copt can carry discreetly is an unknown quantity; one seldom sees them drunk, but they imbibe awful quantities. They always offer me wine and *arakee*, and can't think why I don't drink it; I believe they suspect my Christianity, in consequence of my preference for Nile water. As to that though, they scorn all heretics (i.e. all Christians but themselves and the Abyssinians) more than they do the Muslims, and dislike them more. The procession of the Holy Ghost question divides us with the Gulf of Jehannum.

The gardener of this house is a Copt, such a nice fellow! and he and Omar chaff one another about religion with the utmost good humour;

indeed they seldom are touchy with the Muslims. There is a pretty little man called Meekaeel, a Copt, *wakeel* to M. M. I wish I could draw him, to show you a perfect specimen of the ancient Egyptian race; his blood must be quite unmixed. He came here yesterday to speak to Alee Bey, the *mudeer* of Kiné, who was visiting me (a splendid, handsome Turk he is); so little Meekaeel crept in to mention his little business under my protection, and a few more followed, till Alee Bey got tired of holding a Durbar in my divan, and went away to his boat. You see the people think the *kurbáj* is not quite so handy in the presence of an English spectator.

The other day Mustafa Agha got Alee Bey to do a little job for him—to let the people in the Gezeereh (the island), which is Mustafa's property, work at a canal there, instead of at the canal higher up, for the Pasha. Very well; but down comes the *Názir* (the *mudeer's* sub), and *kurbájes* the whole Gezeereh; not Mustafa, of course, but the poor Fellahs who were doing his *corvée* instead of the Pasha's, by the *mudeer's* order. I went to the Gezeereh, and thought that the first-born in every house were killed as of yore, by the crying and wailing; when up came two fellows, and showed me their bloody feet, which their wives were crying over, as if for their death.

Wednesday. Last night I bored Sheykh Yoosuf with Antara and Aboo-Zeyd, maintaining the greater valour of Antara, who slew ten thousand men for the love of Ibla; (you know Antar). Yoosuf looks down on such profanities, and replied, "What are the battles of Antara and Aboo-Zeyd, compared with the combats of our Lord Moses with Og, and other infidels of might; and what is the love of Antara for Ibla, compared to that of our Lord Solomon for Balkees (Queen of Sheba), or their beauty and attractiveness to that of our Lord Joseph?" And then he related the combat of Seyyidna Moosa with Og, and I thought, "Hear, O ye Puritans! and learn how religion and romance are one to those whose manners and ideas are the manners and ideas of the Bible, and how Moses was not at all a gloomy fanatic, but a gallant warrior." There is a Homeric character in the religion here: the *Nebee*, the Prophet, is a hero like Achilles, and like him, directed by God,—Allah instead of Athene. He fights, prays, teaches, makes love, and is truly a man, not an abstraction; and as to wonderful events, instead of telling one to shut one's eyes and gulp them down, they believe them and delight in them, and tell them to amuse people. Such a piece of deep-disguised scepticism as *credo quia impossibile* would find no favour here; "What is impossible to God?" settles everything. In short, Mohammad has somehow left the stamp of romance on the religion, or else it is in the blood of the people, though the Koran is prosy and "common-sensical," compared to the Old Testament. I used to think Arabs intensely prosaic, till I could understand a little of their language; but now I can trace the genealogy of Don Quixote straight up to some Sheykh-el-Arab.

A fine handsome woman with a lovely baby came to see me the other day. I played with the baby, and gave it a cotton handkerchief for its head. The woman came again yesterday, to bring me a little milk and some salad as a present, and to tell me my fortune with date-stones. I laughed, so she contented herself with telling Omar about his family, which he believed implicitly. She is a clever woman, evidently, and a great Sibyl here; no doubt, she has faith in her own predictions. Superstition is wonderfully infectious here, especially that of the evil eye; which, indeed, is shared by many Europeans, and even by some English. The fact is, that the Arabs are so impressionable and so cowardly about inspiring any ill will, that if a man looks askance at them it is enough to make them ill; and as calamities are by no means unfrequent, there is always some mishap ready to be laid to the charge of somebody's "eye." A part of the boasting about property, etc., is politeness,—so that one may not be supposed to be envious of one's neighbour's nice things. My *sakka* (water-carrier) admired my bracelets yesterday as he was watering the verandah floor, and instantly told me of all the gold necklaces and earrings he had bought for his wife and daughters,—that I might not be uneasy and fear his envious eye. He is such a good fellow! For two shillings a month, he brings up eight or ten huge skins of water from the river a day, and never begs or complains, is always merry and civil; I shall enlarge his *baksheesh*.

A number of camels sleep in the yard under my verandah; they are pretty and smell nice, but they growl and swear at night abominably. I wish I could draw you an Egyptian farmyard—men, women, and cattle. But what no one can draw is the amber light—so brilliant and so soft; not like the Cape sunshine at all, but equally beautiful—hotter and less dazzling. There is no glare in Egypt as in the south of France, and I suppose, in Italy.

Thursday. I went yesterday afternoon to the island again, to see the crops and farmer Omar's house and Mustafa's village. Of course we had to eat, and did not come home till the moon had long risen. Mustafa's brother, Abd-er-Rahman, walked about with us,—a noble-looking man, tall, spare, dignified, and active; grey-bearded and hard-featured, but as lithe and bright-eyed as a boy; scorning any conveyance but his own feet, and quite dry, while we ran down with perspiration. He was like Boaz the wealthy gentleman-peasant; nothing except the Biblical characters give any idea of the rich Fellah.   We sat and drank new milk in a "lodge in a garden of cucumbers" (the lodge is a neat hut of palm-branches), and saw the moon rise over the mountains and light up everything like a softer sun.   Here you see all colours as well by moonlight as by day; hence it does not look as brilliant as the Cape moon, or even as I have seen it in Paris, where it throws sharp black shadows and white light.   The night here is a tender, subdued, dreamy sort of enchanted-looking day.   *Ya Leyl! ya Leyl! ya Leyl!* etc.

My Turkish acquaintance from El-Karnak has just been here, and he boasted of his house at Damascus, and invited me to go with him after the harvest here; also of his beautiful wife in Syria, and then begged me not to mention her to his wives here.   It is very hot now; what will it be in June?   It is now 86° in my shady room at twelve o'clock, noon; it will be hotter at two or three.   But the mornings and evenings are delicious.   I am shedding my clothes by degrees—stockings are unbearable—I feel much stronger, too; the horrible feeling of exhaustion has left me; I suppose I must have salamander blood in my body to be made lively by such heat.

Saturday.   This will go by Mr. B. and Mr. C., the last winter swallows.   We went together yesterday afternoon to the Tombs of the Kings on the opposite bank; the mountains were red-hot, and the sun went down into Amenti all on fire.   We met Herr Dümmichen, the German who is living in the Temple of Ed-Deyr-el-Bahree, translating inscriptions, and went down Belzoni's tomb.   Herr Dümmichen translated a great many things for us which were very curious, and I think I was more struck with the beauty of the drawing of the figures than last year.   The face of the goddess of the western shore, Amenti,— Athor or Hecate,—is ravishing, as she welcomes the king to her regions; Death was never painted so lovely.   The road is a long and most wild one, truly through the valley of the shadow of death; not an insect nor a bird.

Our moonlight ride home was beyond belief beautiful.   The Arabs who followed us were extremely amused at hearing me interpret between German and English, and at my speaking Arabic.   One of them had droll theories about "Amellica"—as they always pronounce it; e.g. that the Americans are the *fellaheen* of the English; "they talk so loud." "Was the king very powerful, that the country was called El Melekeh (the queens)?" I said.   "No, all are kings there; you would be a king like the rest." My friend disapproved of that utterly. "If all are kings, they must all be taking away every man the other's money";—a delightful idea of the kingly vocation.

I wish I could send you my little Ahmad, just of R.'s size, who "takes care of the *Sitt*" when riding or walking. He is delicious, so wise and steady, like a good little terrier. When we landed on the opposite shore, I told him to go back in the ferry-boat which had brought over my donkey; a quarter of an hour after I saw him by my side. The guide asked why he had not gone as I told him. "Who would take care of the lady?" said he. Of course he got tired, and on the way home, seeing him lagging, I told him to jump up behind me *en croupe*, after the *fellah* fashion. I thought the Arabs would never have done laughing, and saying, "*Wallah*" and "*Másháalláh*."

Sheykh Yoosuf talked about the excavations; he is shocked at the way in which the mummies are kicked about; he said one boy told him, as an excuse, that they were not Muslims. Yoosuf rebuked him severely, and told him it was *haram* (accursed) to do so to any of the children of Adam.

The harvest is about to begin here, and the crops are splendid this year; Old Nile pays his damages. I went to Mustafa Agha's farm two nights ago to drink new milk, and saw the preparations for harvest— baking bread, and selecting a young bull to be killed for the reapers—all just like the Bible. I reckon it will be Easter here in a fortnight. All eastern Christendom adheres to the old style; the Copts, however, have a reckoning of their own—probably that of ancient Egypt.

It is not hot to-day; only 84° in a cool room. The dust is horrid; with the high wind everything is gritty, and it obscures the sun; but the wind has no evil quality in it.

I am desired to eat a raw onion every day during the *Khamáseen*, for health and prosperity. This too must be a remnant of ancient Egypt.

FREDERICK LOCKER-LAMPSON (1821–95)

This poet and man of letters was the author of "London Lyrics" and some of the most charming vers de société. One or other of his verses will continue to appear in anthologies for many years. He was one of the first collectors of 16th-century books, and formed the famous Rowfant Library, which has since been dispersed. Here is a letter in verse to his second son, a boy at Cheam School.

DEAR OLLY, it has been my joy
To know you as a baby boy.
I've often had you on my lap,
A little cosy, chirping chap.
And now they tell me to my sorrow
That you are to be ten to-morrow.

F. LOCKER

MATTHEW ARNOLD (1822–88)

The famous critic, poet, and essayist was the son of the well-known Doctor Arnold, Headmaster of Rugby. His "Scholar Gipsy," "Forsaken Merman," "Thyrsis" and other poems rank high in English literature; and in these, as in his essays, he is the staunch upholder of the classical spirit. The letter printed below was written to his sister while on holiday abroad; he was at that time Professor of Poetry at Oxford.

TO HIS SISTER

STRASBOURG, JUNE 25, 1859

A REAL summer day without a cloud in the sky has come at last to make travelling pleasant, and to light up the charming old town with its high roofs and great houses, the old ones of white plaster, and the new ones of the most beautiful pink stone in the world. The whole country round, the plain of Alsace, is to me one of the pleasantest anywhere, so genially productive, so well cultivated, and so cheerful, yet with the Vosges and the Black Forest and the Alps to hinder its being prosaic. And one is getting near Switzerland, and I shall see the Lake of Como, I hope and trust, before the month of June quite ends. I had promised myself to see it in May with the spring flowers out in the fields, but that could not be managed. And the news of another great French victory has just come, and every house has the tricolour waving out of its windows, and to-night, this beautiful night that it is going to be, every window will be lighted up, and the spire of the Cathedral will be illuminated, which is a sight. I shall go down towards the Rhine and Desaix's monument to see the effect from there. . . . You know the people here are among the Frenchest of the French, in spite of their German race and language. It strikes one as something unnatural to see this German town and German-speaking people all mad for joy at a victory gained by the French over other Germans. The fact speaks much for the French power of managing and attaching its conquests, but little for the German character. The Rhine provinces in 1815, after having belonged to France for only ten years, objected exceedingly to being given back to Germany. The truth is that, though French occupation is very detestable, French administration since the Revolution is, it must be said, equitable and enlightened, and promotes the comfort of the population administered. They are getting very angry here with Prussia, and if Prussia goes to war there will be a cry in this country to compel the Emperor to take the limit of the Rhine whether he wishes it or no. That the French will beat the Prussians all to pieces, even far more completely and rapidly than they are beating the Austrians, there cannot be a moment's doubt; and they know it themselves. I had a long and very interesting conversation with Lord Cowley, tête-à-tête for about three-quarters of an hour the other day. He seemed to like hearing what I had to say, and told me a great deal about the French Emperor, and about the Court of Vienna, and their inconceivable infatuation as to their own military superiority to the French. He entirely shared my conviction as to the French always beating any number of Germans who come into the field against them. They will never be beaten by any nation but the English, for to every other nation they are, in efficiency and intelligence, decidedly superior. I shall put together for a pamphlet, or for *Fraser* a sort of *resumé* of the present question as the result of what I have thought, read, and observed here about it. I am very well, and only wish I was not so lazy; but I hope and believe one is less so from forty to fifty, if one lives, than at any other time of life. The loss of youth ought to operate as a spur to one to live more by the head, when one can live less by the body. Have you seen Mill's book on Liberty? It is worth reading attentively, being one of the few books that inculcate tolerance in an unalarming and inoffensive way.

ALFRED RUSSEL WALLACE (1823–1913)

Here is a very charming little note from the great scientist to his granddaughter, explaining a simple point for a simple mind.

TO MISS VIOLET WALLACE

PARKSTONE, DORSET, OCTOBER 22, 1897

MY DEAR VIOLET, In your previous letter you asked me the conundrum, Why does a wagtail wag its tail? That's quite easy, on Darwinian principles. Many birds wag their tails. Some Eastern flycatchers— also black and white—wag their long tails up and down when they alight on the ground or on a branch. Other birds with long tails jerk them up in the air when they alight on a branch. Now these varied motions, like the motions of many butterflies, caterpillars, and many other animals, must have a use to the animal, and the most common, or rather the most probable, use is, either to frighten or to distract an enemy. If a hawk was very hungry and darted down on a wagtail from up in the air, the wagging tail would be seen most distinctly and be aimed at, and thus the bird would be missed or at most a feather torn out of the tail. The bird hunts for food in the open, on the edges of ponds and streams, and would be especially easy to capture, hence the wagging tail has been developed to baffle the enemy.

COVENTRY PATMORE (1823-96)

No one who has read Coventry Patmore's verse can have failed to appreciate his intense love for, and sympathy with children; how admirably is this expressed in this first little note, written to his eldest daughter when she was a child. There is something very vivid in the next letter, in the picture he draws of Leigh Hunt; as also in that to his second wife describing life at Houghton and the "thirty-three fish" there to be caught.

TO HIS ELDEST DAUGHTER

BUXTED HALL, SEPTEMBER 14TH, 1866

MY DEAR LITTLE GIRL, I am very much pleased with your letter, which is longer and better written, and which expresses your feelings with more credit to yourself than your letters usually do. I shall certainly be in town in a few days and then I will come and see you, and bring you some apples and nuts out of the orchard. The squirrels are always scampering about the filbert trees, but there are plenty for them and us. Langley told me yesterday "they wanted shooting." But I told them they wanted no such thing, and that they were to live, even though they ate all the nuts.

Your affectionate Father,
C. PATMORE

HASTINGS, FEBRUARY 6TH, 1889

MY first sight of Leigh Hunt—concerning which you enquire—was in this wise. I, being at 17 or 18 years of age, or perhaps younger, an admirer of the "Indicator" and "Rimini," set off with a letter from my Father, an old friend of the Poet, informing him of my ambition to see him. Arriving at his house, a very small one in a small square somewhere in the extreme west, after a walk of some five or six miles, I was informed that the poet was at home, and asked to sit down until he came to me. This he did after I had waited in the little parlour at least two hours, when the door was opened and a most picturesque gentleman, with hair flowing nearly or quite to his shoulders, a beautiful velvet coat and a Vandyke collar of lace about a foot deep, appeared, rubbing his hands and smiling ethereally, and said, without a word of preface or notice of my having waited so long, "This is a beautiful world, Mr. Patmore!" I was so struck by this remark that it has eclipsed all memory of what occurred during the remainder of my visit.

Yours very truly,
C. Patmore

TO HIS WIFE

Houghton, Stockbridge
Thursday Morning.
Friday, May 23rd, 1890

Your yesterday's letter come, Dear. I'm very glad you feel so well: I am doing splendidly; the weather is exquisite and the river the loveliest thing in water I ever saw. I can look at it all day. I am walking seven hours or so a day and feel no fatigue—eat immensely and am already of a beautiful brownish-red complexion. Tell Piffie (his youngest son, Francis) about the fishing: it is quite unlike anything I have seen. There are eight miles of river, rented by fifteen gentlemen, each paying £25 a year, that is £375. No one is allowed to catch any fish unless it weighs a pound and a half or over. In the eight miles of river there are thirty-three fish of the lawful weight, that is, from $1\frac{1}{2}$ to $8\frac{1}{2}$ lb. They are all known by name, and are always to be found in the same place, unless one is caught, and then all the rest move up a step, so that their names are still known. Everybody for ten miles round knows when a fish is caught, and if it weighs more than $3\frac{1}{4}$ lbs., it is telegraphed to all the London papers, and to Portsmouth, where there is a salute fired, one gun every half-pound. Seven gents have been fishing there two days, but Mr. Champneys alone has come off with any glory. To-day, after four hours' fishing, he hooked "Sir William Harcourt," a fish of $1\frac{1}{2}$ lbs., but looking bigger than he is. We got him nearly to land, but, by some paltry trick, he managed to get off the hook, just as we were putting the landing-net under him. All the gentlemen of the Club are to have a champagne dinner to-night at the "Boot Inn," to celebrate this event. Piffie would perhaps like to hear the names of the thirty-three fish which it is lawful to catch— if you can. They are, Vernon Harcourt, Tom Browne, Cobden ($6\frac{1}{2}$ lbs.), Strafford, Pym, Tom Paine, Bright (5 lbs.), Palmerston, Holbein, Hobbes (8 lbs.), Cromwell ($8\frac{1}{2}$ lbs.), Voltaire, Bob Sawyer, Boz, Burke, Lever, Tom Thumb (7 lbs.), Victor Hugo, Macready,

Lever, W. Pitt, Kean, Boanerges ($7\frac{1}{2}$ lbs.), Jack Straw, Thurtell, Hookey Walker (so-called because he has walked off with so many hooks), General Gordon ($6\frac{1}{2}$ lbs.), Bismarck (8 lbs.), Talleyrand, Wat Tyler, Pecksniff, Gladstone, Dr. Manning, Shaftesbury, Labouchere, and Sir William Temple. All these fish let you stand close by and stare at them without the least concern. I watched Dr. Manning and Tom Paine at play together ever so long this morning. Sir William Temple is the only one of these fish who has never risen to an artificial fly. Indeed, he is so prudent, that he will scarcely take a real fly; so that he is not so big as he ought to be for his age. A good fisherman knows all these fish by sight: the only two they can scarcely distinguish are Shaftesbury and Gladstone. These are both large fish, but they are habitually what the fishermen call "unclean" and "lousy," so they don't try to catch them. They also leave Bismarck alone, for they know it's of no use trying. He only winks at the flies, and once or twice when he has been hooked, he has given a jump, and snap goes the line or the rod.

We think of going away to Winchester or Salisbury for a couple of days, in order to get away from the numerous visitors and deputations who will be waiting on us to congratulate us on the glory of having hooked Sir William Harcourt. I come in for a share of the glory, for everyone knows I had the landing net ready to land him, had he not behaved so shabbily. I am sorry I did not bring my best clothes, for I am to dine with the Club in recognition of my share in the event of the week, and everyone else will be in white ties and swallow-tails. The dinner is to cost 25s. a head, including wine—which I do not think is extravagant, considering the occasion. Give my love to the girls and tell them I am sure they will excuse my not writing a separate letter to them, under these exciting circumstances.

As always, your Lover,

C. P.

I open my letter to say that at a meeting of the Committee of the Club, to-morrow, Sir William Clay is to propose and Captain Head to second the following motions:

"That in consideration of his eminence as a Poet and of his intending services in landing Sir William Harcourt, this Committee do decide that the next fish which shall attain to the legal weight of one and a half pounds shall be called 'Patmore.' "

FRANK BUCKLAND (1826–80)

This great naturalist and journalist was for some time Inspector of Fisheries. When dying he humorously remarked that God was so good to the little fishes that he hoped he would not allow their Inspector to suffer shipwreck at the last. In his official capacity he protested against the creation of weirs, which hampered salmon in their ascent of streams. The following letter to these friends of his was found pinned one day to a weir belonging to the Duke of Northumberland, who agreed to make a ladder for Buckland's "dear fish."

TO THE SALMON AND BULL-TROUT

GENTLEMEN, No road at present over this weir. Go down stream, take the first turn to the right, and you will find good travelling water up stream, and no jumping required.

Yours truly,

F. T. BUCKLAND

SIR WILLIAM HARCOURT (1827–1904)

Sir William was one of the greatest Liberal statesmen of his time and leader of the House of Commons under Lord Rosebery. The following amusing letter to the painter Millais, who had written to tell him that he had shot a very fine stag, needs no comment.

TO J. E. MILLAIS

STUDLEY ROYAL, RIPON,
OCTOBER 3RD, 1866

MY DEAR MILLAIS, I received your insane letter, from which I gather that you are under the delusion that you have killed a stag. Poor fellow, I pity your delusion. I hope the time is now come when I can break to you the painful truth. Your wife, who (as I have always told you) alone makes it possible for you to exist, observing how the disappointment of your repeated failures was telling on your health and on your intellect, arranged with the keepers for placing in a proper position a *wooden* stag constructed like that of . . . You were conducted unsuspectingly to the spot and fired at the *dummy*. In the excitement of the moment you were carried off by the gillie, so that you did not discern the cheat, and believed you had really slain a "hart of grease." Poor fellow, I know better; and indeed your portrait of the stag sitting up *smiling*, with a head as big as a church door on his shoulders, tells its own tale. I give Mrs. M. great credit on this, as on all other occasions, for her management of you. I am happy to hear that the result of the pious fraud has been to restore you to equanimity and comparative sanity, and I hope by the time I see you again you may be wholly restored.

Pray remember me to Mrs. M.

Yours ever,
W. V. HARCOURT

I see that, in order to keep up the delusion, puffs of your performance have been inserted in all the papers.

GEORGE MEREDITH (1828–1909)

The letter selected below was written to one of his friends who had just become engaged to be married; it is characteristic of Meredith and the intense interest he took in all around him. The references to Swinburne and Dante Gabriel Rossetti are of considerable interest.

TO A FRIEND

COPSHAM, ESHER, SURREY, 1861

MY DEAR ——, "Tannhauser" was in yesterday's "Post," and exceedingly well done. I read the extracts also. They produce on me the effect, after three lines, of too much sugar on the palate: something rich, certainly, but of a base richness. I don't agree with you that they have brought Venus sensibly to the reader at all, tho' it's fair to say that with Elizabeth it is less so than Venus. The former is a prim good miss, a shrew when in passion; she quite justifies (to me) Tannhauser's choice of the dear voluptuous Goddess whom they call such naughty names, and who, I begin to think, is the favourite daughter of Mother Earth.

This to you, who are in love!—Do you know, I have seldom seen anything with so much pleasure as your honest, modest manly love for her. You don't tire me in telling me about it, and of your feelings, and your thoughts about her. The fonder and the deeper your emotions reach, the more I see and admire the large nature you are gifted with.

I trust it may be that Heaven brings the other half of her. She is, I am sure, a very sweet person: but how strong she is, or can be made, my instinct does not fathom. I am so miserably constituted now that I can't love a woman if I do not feel her soul, and that there is force therein to wrestle with the facts of life (called the Angel of the Lord). But I envy those who are attracted by what is given to the eye;—yes, even those who have a special taste for woman flesh, and this or that particular little tit-bit—I envy them! It lasts not beyond an hour with me.

Happy you with all the colour of life about you! Has she principle? Has she any sense of responsibility? Has she courage? Enough that you love her. I believe that this plan of taking a woman on the faith of a mighty wish for her, is the best, and the safest way to find the jewel we are all in search of. As to love "revealing" all the qualities in one great flash—do you believe it even in your present state? Still of so fair and exquisite a person it is just to augur hopefully; and when one comes to read her face, surely that is a book with plates of virgin silver. Well! of her face I will tell you, without trying to make you too happy, that I don't know any face the memory of which leaves with me the unique impression of music so completely. There is that softness in the curves, and purity of look, which move like music in my mind.

As to her singing qualities, that is another matter, and really I had forgotten. But on coming to consider this, there's something right in one—a woman—who knows her capabilities to be not brilliant, sitting down to do her duty at the piano to pass the evening properly. Some fair ones would have declined resolutely. For my part I like simple, gentle, unpretending songs, and shall be always glad of the privilege of hearing them.

Health somewhat better. Working on pomes. You will find some alterations, much for the better, I think.

Rossetti admires your beloved, tho' she has not green eyes and carrots; which, I tell him, astonishes me.

He sent me a book of MSS. original poetry the other day, and very fine are some of the things in it. He is a poet, without doubt. He would please you more than I do, or can, for he deals with essential poetry, and is not wild, and bluff, and coarse; but rich, refined, royal-robed! Swinburne read me the other day his French novel "La Fille du Policeman"; the funniest rampingest satire on French novelists dealing with English themes that you can imgaine. One chapter, "Ce qui peut se passer dans un Cab Safety," where Lord Whitestick, Bishop of Londres, ravishes the heroine, is quite marvellous. But he is not subtle; and I don't see any internal centre from which springs anything that he does. He will make a great name, but whether he is to distinguish himself solidly as an Artist, I would not willingly prognosticate.

Rossetti is going to illustrate my Cassandra, which pome has taken his heart.

I am obliged to make money as I can, to meet these new claims on me, and so all my pieces must be published before they're collected. Your name, you know, may be withheld from the Dedication then if you please.

BOX HILL, DORKING, MAY 11, 1902

MY DEAR LESLIE, We two have looked at the world and through men, and to us the word consolation is but a common scribble, for there is none under a deep affliction that can come from without, not from the dearest of friends. What I most wish for you I know you have, fortitude to meet a crisis, and its greater task, to endure. We have come to the time of life when the landscape surrounding, *haec data poena diu viventibus*, the tombstones of our beloved and the narrowing of our powers throws a not unpleasant beam on the black gateway, as we take it to be in the earlier days. And those young ones, whom Nature smites with the loss of us, she will soon bring into her activities, if they are the healthy creatures we wish them to be. I find nothing to regret in the going, at my age, and only a laughing snarl when I look about on the deprivations, which make the going easy. So I see things in your mind as well. If you can come in perfect certainty that the journey will be harmless, prescribe diet (soups and light puddings, I suppose), and don't kick when I say my fly shall be sent for you.

GEORGE MEREDITH

LADY MARY SIBYLLA HOLLAND (d. 1891)

Lady Holland was the daughter of the philosopher and traveller, Alfred Lyall; her husband was chaplain to Queen Victoria and a canon of Canterbury. The nature of the writer reveals itself with a striking clarity in the letter printed below.

TO HER SISTER

ST. DUNSTAN'S, APRIL 1861

IT is half-past seven and yet I have plenty of light whereby to begin a letter to you, sitting at this window with my writing-book on the ledge and my ink-pot in the flower-stand outside. The strong east wind has also departed from us, glory be! and the south-west breeze which you doubtless have been enjoying all day, blew before it reached Suffolk over the primroses and budding bells in the woods of Kent. If it only could blow me to Blacklands! It has been a lovely day, but with these spring days a melancholy fastens upon me. I alternately hang my depression upon your absence and our approaching change, but I well know that without these real causes my spirits would flag. Spring is more melancholy to me than autumn. I am always full of self-reproaches and longings for I know not what. I long to be and to do better, but I have no courage to begin. I know too well what is right and wise, but I am unstable as water and cannot excel. My resolution is as weak as my standard is high. I am happy in my pleasant pottering life, and at the same time angry with myself for being happy. A squirrel born in his comfortable little cage, and used to it, and with plenty to eat and drink, is stupidly happy, but, at times, my Cathy, he must have dim instincts and yearnings for the tops of the trees and the open sky. And, at times, I too seem to have a glimpse of heaven opened, so to speak, but it is but for a moment, and I rattle round and round in my cage again.

I know what it is. It is this sleepiness, this leprosy of indolence which sticks to and grows upon us all, and upon me above all. And one day I am convinced it will be a body of death to me, for to me it is like some dreadful body clogging me, from which I cannot escape.

And it is not my real body which is at fault. That is well worked and little indulged. Indeed I think I could make my body submit to any discomfort if only that *something* which is neither my mind nor my heart nor my soul but which is *me myself*, could be left at peace, to dream and to sleep, and at last to die, nothing attempted and nothing done. Wretched state, and yet true. And in London things will be worse—there I shall live in a dream. I daresay you will think all this morbid and depressed, but it is not. It is the result of honest reflection. Do not try to argue with anything I say unless you really feel as I do. Your friendship will be and is so precious to me, and I desire with all my heart that it should be sincere. It is possible to have the closest intimacy with independence of thought. Both of us, I think, are too apt to *try* to agree with other people. One ought to try to see what truth there is in what things they say, but not try to warp one's own clear conviction for the sake of agreeing. . . . The woods are charming now, the cutting down this year at Faulkner's has thrown open the prettiest views. When you get to the end of the deep lane, and stand at the point where the old pilgrim's road emerges from its copse, the whole rising ground to the right hand is a blue mountain of blue bells, blue already, though they are not fully out. Yet I agree with you that the cowslip is by far the most delightful flower to pick. There is something so pleasant to touch and eye in the shape of the fragrant and delicate clean stalk—and then to shut one's eyes and bury one's face in a great bunch is joy indeed. I wish there were more here.

Two days ago, I walked into the wood beyond Mount Ephraim, where there is a pretty little clearing and faggots piled up like little houses. There I sat by the tiny brook, among the anemones and ladysmock, and for the last time leisurely lingered gathering up the threads of my past life and retracing many scenes and sensations. By next spring we shall be quite gone, and the place will know strangers' feet and voices.

SIR JOHN EVERETT MILLAIS (1829-96)

Millais was one of the founders of the Pre-Raphaelite Brotherhood. The following letter to Mrs. Combe, whose husband was of the Clarendon Press, at Oxford, describes the difficulties which attended the painting of "Ophelia." The artist was staying at the time with Holman Hunt and other Brethren in lodgings in Kingston.

TO MRS. COMBE

SURBITON HILL, KINGSTON, JULY, 1851

MY DEAR MRS. PAT, I have taken such an aversion to sheep, from so frequently having mutton chops for dinner, that I feel my very feet revolt from the proximity of woollen socks.

. . . .

We are getting on very soberly, but have some suspicions that the sudden decrease of our bread and butter is occasioned by the C—— family (under momentary aberration) mistaking our fresh butter for their briny. To ascertain the truth, we intend bringing our artistic capacity to bear upon the eatables in question by taking a careful drawing of their outline. Upon their reappearance we shall refer to the portraits, and thereby discover whether the steel of Sheffield has shaven their features. . . . In the field where I am painting there is haymaking going on; so at times I am surrounded by women and men, the latter of which remark that mine is a tedious job, that theirs is very warm work, that it thundered somewhere yesterday, and that they *feel thirsty, very thirsty.* An uneasiness immediately comes over me; my fingers tingle to bestow a British coin upon the honest yeomen to get rid of them; but no, I shall not indulge the scoundrels after their rude and greedy applications. Finding hints move me not, they boldly ask for money for a drop of drink. In the attitude of Napoleon commanding his troops over the Alps, I desire them to behold the river, the which I drink. Then comes a shout of what some writers would call honest country laughter, and I, coarse brutality. Almost every morning Hunt and I give money to children; so all the mothers send their offspring (amounting by appearance to 12 each) in the line of our road; and in rank and file they stand curtseying with flattened palms ready to receive the copper donation. This I like; but men with arms larger round than my body hinting at money disgusts me so much that I shall paint some day (I hope) a picture laudatory of Free Trade.

Goodnight to yourself and Mr. Combe, and believe that I shall ever remain

Most faithfully yours,
JOHN EVERETT MILLAIS

THOMAS EDWARD BROWN (1830–97)

For many years Brown was a master at Clifton. He was born in the Isle of Man and chose the dialect of that charming entity as the medium for much of his poetry. His vivacious unconventional letters reflect a boundless delight in his beloved isle.

TO MRS. WORTHINGTON

MARCH 5TH, 1894

You will readily understand that there is little going on here with which I might hope to *oblect* you. There are fitful advances of the spring and the ordinary transitions "from" blue to the brown, but that is all. The Vicar's alternation of chambers is literally carried out on these premises. The perpetual storms compel us to have two bedrooms, one behind and one before (I had almost said, "And one behind the parlour door"). At the very top, and in the exact centre of the house, there is a sky-light which raves like a bacchanal or a pythoness. Do what you like, you must lay your account with the fiend, No. 3 central.

I have had an old colleague staying with me for a week-end. He came in a storm, and left in a hurricane. I wish you and Mr. Worthington knew him. The neighbours here are full of it that he has invented a "New Religion." To this they add that *I* (Mr. Brown) am his only convert. You should have seen us at it.

TO MISS GRAVES

ARMITAGE RECTORY, RUGELEY,
MAY 13, 1894

A GENIUS! that's it. And they are all like that, almost all. Those little falsetti, and affectations, and posings, and putting the best foot foremost; those cravings for appreciation, the egotism, the self-consciousness (go ahead!) all characterize the genius. You must take him with them—take him or leave him alone. But you seem to seek a portent! A man of genius and a man of hard practical commonsense knocked into one. The world has produced half a dozen such men. They are tremendous. But—Heaven help us!—you must be content with something less than this, or Nature will never get her great men off her hands. "Sell me a genius," say you. "Here you are," says Nature, handing over a lot, "plenty of choice: marked in figures; read—Byron, Shelley, Keats, Coleridge——" "Oh, I want——" "Well, what do you want?" "A strong, powerful, healthy intellect, and genius as a dhooragh! [luck-penny, make-weight]." "Oh, thank you for nothing! We don't make them. You had better try the shop over the way, or give a special order. Order, and we can try, provided you are willing to wait a thousand years or so!" . . . This "rift within the lute" of genius is the inseparable accident. I have long learnt to bear with it, and I earnestly desire, for your own sake, that you will make up your mind to it. . . . They (geniuses) are all divine babies, and will kiss and scratch in a breath. That is the divine thing in them. Now, don't be impatient with me. They *must be borne with*; and remember what compensation we have. *Nulla rosa sine spina:* but what a glorious rose blooms among the thorns!

I have no doubt that to many of us it were better if we never got to know men of genius privately. You may depend upon it that, throughout the history of literature, they offended their contemporaries by their airs and their bosh, their pettiness and their *asinine conceit.*

Never mind! The world has taken its hat off to these men: and so must we. We need not stroke the quills on the "back of the fretful porpentine"; let us avoid coming into close contact. Perhaps some of them had better be kept in cages. But chance may domesticate you with one; you may, for instance, marry one. Poor Mrs. Carlyle! And she too a genius. "Oh, it is a glorious thing! Marry me to the lightning!" Well, just think a bit first But don't mistake the matter, don't ignore genius, and don't complain of it when you find its silly and shabby adjuncts.

TO MR. RYDINGS

RAMSEY, JUNE 3, 1896

YOUR idea of forcing, or fostering, the sale of my little books is most amusing. But it shows the kindness of your heart.

It is odd, but do you know? I have a perfectly serene confidence in their future. How it will come to pass I am not prepared to say, nor does it much matter. A child, perhaps yet unborn, will do it.

A great poet is yet to be, a Manx poet, transcending all our small doin's! He will be called Kewish, Shimmin, Quayle, Cottier—All right! He will stumble across my *old ditties,* he will love them, he will wonder, he will muse, the fire will be kindled, and at the last he will speak with his tongue.　And he will say—"This man was my brother, my father, my own real self."　Through Kewish I shall find utterance, through Shimmin, through Quayle, through Cottier.　Even so my heart goes stretching back to some possible progenitor whom I'd give worlds to find.　I cannot find him; but I shall be found, though after many days—found of Cottier, Quayle, Shimmin, Kewish.　You'll see! Ah no, you'll not.

Dear friend, you and I will be far away.　At any rate, under the sweet Manx sod we knew and cherished we shall sleep the last sleep. And Kewish will be the *boee!* (Manx, "boy").　He will be the poet of the twentieth century.　How he will yearn towards us!　He will handle loftier themes, and broader branches will issue from his stem; but his roots will be in our ashes, in the bed of dialectic homeliness which we have laid.

Theer now!

And I shall be perfectly satisfied, feeding the young native genius with racy sap, sending up the blossoms to blow in Manx air, and make all Manx men and women happy.　Kewish will, I doubt not, give readings of our booklets, just to give the people a notion of what this old stuff was like.　Kewish will shed the tear of sympathetic divination. Leave it to KEWISH!　"A gran' chap—KEWISH."

CHARLES STEWART CALVERLEY (1831–84)

The following letter was written to Calverley's poet friend, on returning to London from the country. As a comment on noses Calverley might have recalled the fact that the failure of Fielding's "Amelia," in 1752, was attributed by Dr. Johnson to the fact that her nose was broken in a carriage accident, and the public of that day would not stand such a heroine.

TO FREDERICK LOCKER-LAMPSON

17 DEVONSHIRE TERRACE, HYDE PARK,
NOV. 6, 1872

MY DEAR LOCKER, We have just got back to London and I promptly went in quest of your picture which I found at Bell and Daldy's *quondam* shop opposite the Temple. They now inhabit York Street.

I think it is very good, very clever as a picture and very satisfactory as a likeness, and so does my Wife, I am much obliged to you for sending it, nor shall I by any means bury it under a bushel as you suggested.

I also found "Gareth and Lynette" awaiting me, sent thoughtfully by Bumpus, and I have just read it with much delight. I agree (myself) with the *Saturday* upon one point, viz., that we hear too much about the maiden's nose, and I dislike the Epithet "tiptilted" as much as they seem to do.

I have no idea why it is (if it is) that the human nose cannot be introduced into serious poetry. I think it cannot, and I imagine Tennyson wishes to protest against my notion, and the received notion, by steadily mentioning it by name, not by subterfuge such as "nostrils."

I cannot quarrel with the "tears coursing down his innocent nose"— but then that was a stag's nose. "The glory of his nose is terrible," would sound rather horrible, it just struck me. I am not, however, prepared to say why.

My kind regards and my Wife's, Yours,

C. S. CALVERLEY

JOHN BELLOWS (1831–1902)

The son of a Friend and brought up in the Society, Bellows was trained for the printing trade, and introduced the first steam printing-press into Gloucester. He was an able student of philology, and as such a correspondent of Max Muller and Prince Lucien Bonaparte. He was also a keen lexicographer. Among his friendships, that with Oliver Wendell Holmes, to whom the first of our letters was addressed on the occasion of Holmes sending him "Over the Teacups," lasted for a quarter of a century. In 1892 Bellows and another Quaker went to Russia to visit the Dukhobortsi, a much persecuted sect. They travelled as far as the Persian frontier, and on their way home met Tolstoi, with whom Bellows corresponded to the end of his life. Bellows was a strict Friend, and always wore the distinctive Quaker dress.

TO OLIVER WENDELL HOLMES

DEAR FRIEND, Which chord shall I touch to begin with, as I rise from the first few delightful hours reading of thy book? So many are answering to the master vibration that I can scarcely decide!

No. This is no winter night out into which I have been looking through its pages, but belated Autumn with all its colours; not summer, but Indian summer, the last of the seasons we would part with, if we might but retain one!

I have been reading aloud to my wife; and again and again in the pauses some lines of Runeberg, the poet of Finland, have kept coming back to me in gentle refrain, although I have not read them for years:—

> Shall the land that saw thy morning bloom,
> That saw thy noonday bright,
> Not also see thy evening come
> With its calm sweet sunset light?

One mystery thy volume has set me further away than ever from solving, and that is, where is the boundary between childhood and boyhood; or boyhood and manhood and age? This I have never been able to find. . . . Only this very evening I was wheedled into an interlude from the "Teacups" by a deputation of four Gallios who care for none of these things, to entreat that I would "give them a chase." Seven-year-old put the request in a very low voice, for a chase, in this house, is forbidden by the Mistress on the ground that it makes a Dust; it Destroys the Carpets; it leaves Finger-Marks on the Walls; it Tears the Clothes; it Upsets the Furniture; with other high crimes and misdemeanours which are duly set forth in the manifesto that forbids chasing indoors. So, like Shelley's "sweet child, Sleep" seven-year-old "murmurs like a noontide bee"; while ten-year-old and five-year-old and eight-year-old keep furtively glancing at the Arbitress of their fate to make sure that she does not overhear what is going on. And so

A spirit in my feet
Has led me, who knows how,

out of the room—these four stealing silently after me till we get to the foot of the stairs, when off they go like hares, I following—into the bathroom, and the day nursery, and the night nursery, and down the back stairs, for dear life! Everyone I can catch is swept off to prison, either tucked under my arm, or dragged by the heels along the floor, according to size and weight. (It doesn't hurt the carpets a bit! It's only a superstition of the mistress. They look fresher than ever after it.) And all this time there is a din of voices in calls and shouts and shrieks, à tue-tête as the French say!

By and by a message comes from the Mistress that the chase ha lasted long enough; that we must all come into the dining-room, an that it is Dorothy's bedtime. Which is followed by a sudden hush and then a suppressed "Oh!" of disappointment and injured resignation and we five come slinking in very red and hot, I to resume my place as an invalid in the arm-chair by the fire, for I have been laid up severa days with a cold and bronchitis, which I should have pleaded as a weight excuse for not chasing, only that the children could not understand it So, being obliged to go, I went, and once in the game, even five-year old herself could not throw herself heart and soul into it more entire Boy! Why, I never was more of a boy in my life! What boy in whole world ever cared about carpets in the midst of a chase? A I care one straw whether they were old sacks, or cloth of g High Priest of Mecca's prayer-rugs, if by racing ov catch two of those hares at one hit? Why, here i Adam! The old hunting instinct of the ca author has shown, come down to us by here scores of times transformed me into a cave-

table, and which only the counterbalancing forces of civilized life kept from transforming me into an elephant after our chase was over just now, crawling into the room with three men on my back, and one leading me!

I do not think that anything in this life has more puzzled me than this consciousness that the bound between boyhood and manhood

> Is marked by no distinguishable line
> The turf unites; the pathways intertwine.

The secret is this? That we go on adding to our existing ring of life as the ammonites do with their spiral shells. *We include all that has gone before.* Hence we can keep more fully in touch or in sympathy *with children than they can with us.*

Now and then in my morning walk to Gloucester I have enjoyed the company of Freddie Matthews, aged eight, on his way to school. No ceremony is needed to step into conversation with him, any more than to step into a horse-car while it is going; and the like freedom prevails in leaving the one as the other. Observe that in stepping into the tram-car we at once surrender our volition as to the direction in which we are carried; and Freddie Matthews no more thinks of adapting his subject to my ideas than the car-driver does of running off his track to take me down a side street.

"We killed our pig last week."

"Was he fat?"

"Ay, ten score. Father weighed 'un back in June and he was ght score, and then he weighed 'un again in a bit-a-while and he as more'n nine score. So, soon as he was ten score, Father killed un."

"Indeed! And what has he done with him?"

"Salted 'un in. He've put the sides in Grandfather Ponting's."

"What's that for?"

"Cause hee's house is drier'n ourn."

Before I could assert this information and store it away for reference mind under the article "Pig," Freddie suddenly whipped out of top and held it up triumphantly under my eye.

"

Harry made 'un out of a bobbin for Syd."

yd?"

e made the peg with a nail he found."

(*Scornfully*.) "Ay! a lot better than them there boughten ones."
"But why is he *better* than a boughten one?"

"Cause when they goes down they lies there, but after he's down HE'LL JUMP UP AGAIN IF YOU GIVES 'UN A GOOD HARD HIT and go on just the same as he was afore! . . . LOOK-EE HERE!" and he hopped off the path into the middle of the road, and gave the transformed bobbin a twirl and a tremendous smack. It gave a feeble stagger and fell. One more rousing smack—I looking on in breathless excitement to see it jump up again—but it lay still as if stunned by the blow.

In a bated tone Freddie said, "He didn't do it *that* time, but HE WILL!" and slipped it into his pocket as he sprang back to my side on the footpath.

I had not gone many yards, and was still under the sting of disappointment at the failure of the top to jump up again when he was down, when I suddenly became aware that I was alone. Turning round I was dazzled by the full blaze of the sun shining over the Cotteswold Hills behind. We were under the giant elms of Saintbridge. Right in the midst of the resplendence that filled up the vista were three figures. Two, facing each other, were bending low towards the earth; the third stood facing them with his head bowed in rapt observation. It was Freddie Matthews, watching the struggle for supremacy between the tops of two of his schoolfellows, who had just come out of a cottage gateway.

Nearing the town I pass group after group of children tending towards school in alternations of stopping to whip their tops and running to make up lost time. Amid the din of voices and pattering feet the lashes whirl and flip in every direction in fashion very hazardous to one's eyes, and making a vizor of my fingers I see between them a throng of figures, growing tiny and tinier, and the darting up and down of innumerable points till they are lost in the sunlit haze of the distance; a picture of cadence and rhythm, a poem of life, transient but beautiful beyond words.

A fortnight after this I was again walking to Gloucester. I met Grandfather Ponting, as I often do, at the bottom of Matson Pitch (all gentle slopes in Gloucestershire are "pitches"), carrying two buckets of mash for the nephews of the pig who was salted in. In the garden gateway of Matthews's cottage stood a little boy with a perfectly circular face, large-eyed, and very red in the cheeks, a sort of cherubo-rustic. I found this was Syd. Freddie's face is oval, not quite so ruddy or so perfectly free from all trace of care.

In a few moments I overtook the latter, and the instant I was abreast of him I broached the subject that had often been in my thoughts since our last walk.

"How's the top going on that Harry made out of the bobbin?"

"Oh! he's lost. Syd's got a new 'un."

"*Lost?*"

"Ay! he lost 'un . . . and then he found 'un . . . and then he lost 'un again."

Before I could recover from the strain put on me by the vivid realization of the alternations of trouble and hope and disappointment involved in this series of changes, Freddie drew from his pocket a bright magenta-tinted top with a glittering tintack at its point. I saw at a glance that this was no home made article. There was a professional touch about it that told of the toy factories of the Black Forest.

"What did it cost?"

"A farthin'. Syd found a farthin' by the pigsty and our Harry went into Gloucester to spend 'un for 'im, and bought HE." (Four miles, two each way, for Harry.)

I remembered the comparison that had been made between the now lost top and "boughten ones," to the disadvantage of the latter, and I felt some misgiving as I asked:

"Will he spin as well as the one Harry made with the bobbin and the nail?" But I had misjudged the forces of optimism in this ever fresh state of the human mind.

"Ay! A LOT BETTER'N HE."

Optimism? It is not a strong word to describe the continual flow of cheeriness which carries this boy of eight through the ups and downs of his career. It was with a smile he told me of his week's stay home from school "because Mother's bad, got the Brown Kitis, and her head's bad"; with a smile that he related how "Father chopped open his hand with the bill-hook, and had to go into the Infirmary to have it sewed up, and to-day he's gone in again to have the tackin' took out."

Is his father digging potatoes? Freddie gives me some to put in my pocket that I may boil them and see what they are like.

"Well, they look fine large ones."

"But they be nothin' to them's father got from the sid what he gave sixpence a tatur for. Them taturs be as big as your shoe!"

"And were they good?"

"Ay! Them as haves them allus wants six sacks more."

I must say it gave me a start when he told me with a delighted grin—"We're goin' to have a holiday this afternoon cause it's Will ——'s funeral," poor Will —— being a boy in the same class at school.

Two or three years have slipped away since this, and I see Grandfather Ponting's hair getting whiter, as my own is becoming what his used to be. Syd's face is distinctly no longer quite round, but I one day caught sight, inside the gate, of one just like it only smaller, and more than a circle in its outline. Freddie, standing near, had a bandage over one eye.

"What's the matter?"

He looked up, quite pleased, with the other, and replied, "A ball hit 'un."

When some weeks had gone by and the bandage was still in its place, I felt a hearty sorrow for the boy; but he showed no sign of sharing it, for as I was driving past I slackened the reins to ask, "How is thy eye, Fred? Any better?"

"No, nor never won't be, no more!" and turned away in undisguised pleasure.

I have run on to greater length than I should have planned had I followed any plan at all in this letter, but once on this sketch of this English village boy, I lacked the skill to draw it in fewer strokes, and yet make it as complete as it looks to myself. Yet I feel sure of thy finding room in the wide outer court of thy sympathies for these two little fellows and the story of their tops, and of making it a matter of interest to Oliver Wendell Holmes to learn that Freddie Matthews has been kindly dealt with by nature (our quieter term for Providence), and is after all allowed to steer his barque over the sea of life with two eyes instead of one.

Eleven days have passed since I began this letter, during which I have been a close prisoner from bronchitis, and now coughing and sneezing in varied keys warns me that many others of the family are following. The winter is exceptionally severe for *Old* England, for it is rare for us to look down for a whole fortnight from our mountain home upon a white world below. This gap taken out of my business life recalls the riots in the middle of last century when the London masses went about the streets shouting, "Give us back our eleven days!" (taken from them by the new act establishing the Gregorian Calendar). The Old Style, singularly enough, lingers on in the hearts of the old folk in our rural districts, who keep up "Old May Day," and the like, one point in connection with which is the care to make the day begin at midnight, and end at noon.

Now here is a case of *cerebricity*. I started this morning for Gloucester for the first time since my stay-in, and a little before reaching Matson Pitch exchanged greetings with a hale old farmer, to whom I muttered from under my comforter something about the sharpness of the weather. "Ay," he answered, "and 'twas sharp afore Christmas; but my father wouldn't never allow as Christmas was over till the fifth o' Jannywerry. That's the day as the Rosemary blows. I had a uncle as gathered it at twelve o'clock at night, and wer it in his jacket to church."

With which item of folk-lore I will close, and again thanking thee for thy kind gift,

I remain

Thy friend very affectionately,

JOHN BELLOWS

TO THE SAME

UPTON KNOLL, GLOUCESTER, 9–4–1891

NOTHING is harder to realize than the flight of time. It seems but as the vivid yesterday that I was passing swiftly through the streets of London in a cab with thy daughter, who was on her way to take thee from one friend's house to that of another, in the crowd of engagements that filled up thy brief visit to England. Suddenly we turned out of the throng and bustle, and in a few moments drew up before the mansion of James Russell Lowell, from whose company I had to send up a message to summon thee. As I stood in the hall I heard his voice in a cheery leave-taking on the stair: the only time I ever heard it, though I had had some kindly written words from him anent my dictionary. The next moment I was shaking hands with thyself and receiving the greeting that was thereafter renewed in Gloucestershire. The scene is before me: the tall, many-storied, many-windowed houses; the silent street making its silence felt by contrast with the roar of the great tide of life so near yet now inaudible; the lofty elms in the Park close by; and the glinting of the summer afternoon sun on the sward below. *This* is the picture that makes it hard to realize that already two out of the three principal figures in it have passed away from time.

I recollect thy telling me that Russell Lowell reversed thy own figure of "76," and I realize, not without pain, that seventy-six has in turn given way to other numbers, and that each of these bournes, as it is left behind, marks a more lonely path to the summit of the hill! *More* lonely—yet never wholly companionless. If the Father of All appoints us sorrow, He yet tempers it with some gleam of love; and that thirty-third verse of the eighty-ninth Psalm is as true of us as it was of those earlier children of men, to whom, as to us, the three preceding verses apply. If our very sorrow itself were not mingled with somewhat that is of a different nature, we should not cherish as we do our saddest bygone moments, or so willingly, more than willingly, recall

> The touch of a vanished hand,
> And the sound of a voice that is still.

There is one *adoucissement* that tells on us with increasing force as life advances—the society of little children. Their resistless self-assertion, their uncompromising insistence on our entering into their ideas and ways, to the utter ignoring of our riper experience, their dead incapacity of sympathy with our daily anxieties, and their perennial freshness of imagination, all help us.

I come home jaded and careworn from my work, and tempted to think my lot heavier than other men's: when my boy Jack comes marching up to me with a sort of box in his hand—four bits of board nailed together with brads and tin-tacks, and two thick wooden discs that he had routed out of some cupboard, to make a baker's cart. I wanted to sit and "rest"—that is, to brood over the miseries of my lot; but Jack cannot stay for brooding or anything else. He has been "waiting such a long time" for my coming home, to tell him how to saw these two wheels edgeways so as to make them into four; and how to put axles to them; and the end of it is that I have to set to work in good earnest, and, after long application of blunt tools and tool substitutes—the baker's cart is finished.

By this time I have begun to take a real interest in it. Next morning I buy a wooden horse that fits it; and another spell of work ensues in the fitting of his harness. Dorothy (five) has been busy in the kitchen making loaves to go in it for a load; and he and she and I drag it for miles along the sideboard and the dining table and the hall floor. In the course of the evening Jack asks me whether a mouse could pull the baker's cart. I tell him I think it could. Later on he wants to know how many flies are as strong as one mouse. Not foreseeing the bearing of the question, I reply somewhat carelessly, "Perhaps a hundred." Next morning I meet him marching about with a pasteboard box in his hand. "How do people feed flies?" "With sugar." "How much sugar would a hundred flies eat?" Now in strict truth I could not tell; but an answer must be given at once, and so I say, "Oh, I should think a lump would last them three days." In a few minutes he is at my side again with the box. The lid is cautiously raised, and I am desired to look in. "I'm going to catch a hundred flies and tame them like the man did the fleas, and make them draw the baker's cart. I've caught *one*. There he is!" I looked in. There was a large lump of sugar in the centre, and the fly pacing up and down past it with a nonchalant air as if it did not concern *him* what was done. Light streamed in through a number of pinholes in the ceiling of the apartment, intended for ventilation. A doll's saucer full of water stood in the corner, so that the sanitation of the place, and the arrangements for the comfort of the hundred flies, left nothing to be desired.

The time at breakfast passed quickly, for I was plied with a variety of questions about the team of fleas I had at some time mentioned, that were trained by a man at Plymouth to draw a little coach, and with one of their own species sitting on the box as driver.

I must say I began to get uneasy, for I knew not whereunto this would grow, and I slipped off to the office with some new anxieties in my mind. At dinner the crisis came. "Papa, how do they *tame* flies?" I was in a dilemma; and at last, humiliated at having to show my ignorance, I was forced to confess that I did not know. "And, besides," I hurried on to add, "I don't know how we can harness them. I could not tie knots small enough to hold them without hurting them." There was a pause of disappointment. Jack's whole scheme was breaking down. He had looked upon me as able to do *any*thing, if I only tried; and now I had failed him. Revolving the whole altered position in his mind, he at last said: "What had I better do with the fly that is in the box? Perhaps I had better let him go?" I caught at the idea and assented. The fly himself had come to the same conclusion a little earlier, for when Jack lifted the lid he had already gone! I heaved a sigh of relief. But it was premature. "Wouldn't a mouse be easier to harness than a hundred *flies*?" "Well, yes, I think it would." "Then I'll go and ask William to set the trap in the stable and catch me one."

Many days passed. Many times during their passing I heard the enquiry, "Is my mouse caught yet?" I began to hope the stable was free from anything smaller than cats. In the evening our talk was of the baker's cart, and of the speed at which a mouse could make it go; of the danger that the mouse, when harnessed, might turn round in the shafts and eat the loaves instead of helping to deliver them; of the other danger of his being eaten himself by the black cat; or of his bolting, cart and all, no one knows where, to save his life! . . .

Suddenly, one afternoon, we were startled by a shout from a number of voices in different high keys, "*Jack's mouse is caught!*" and Jack himself was rushing to and fro in a state of wild excitement, with a tiny cage in his hand, in which the future motor of the cart crouched, frightened at his surroundings. The vehicle itself was near, ready, with nothing in the shafts; and a glance on the floor showed that

> *There* lay the steed with his nostril all wide,
> But through it there rolled not the breath of his pride.

In fact that was his weak point, lack of life; and it was this which suggested his being replaced by a creature in which the mysterious force existed, if not by a multitude aggregating it.

All the rest of the day "my mouse" was the object of lavish attentions; and when I last saw him before he retired for the night, he had, stacked by his side, as much cheese and tallow-candle ends as it would take him four days to eat. "Does he like being in the box?" I was asked. "Well—yes; he's comfortable enough there." "Would he as soon be there as running about in the stable like he was before?" "Well—*no*. He would rather be able to run about. *Thou* might be happy up in the playroom; but if someone came and locked the door, and thou could not get out into the garden, wouldst thou like it?" Jack looked very thoughtful, but only said "No, papa!"

In the morning he brought me the box, stored as it had been overnight with cheese and ends of candle; but no occupant was in it. "Why, Jack! where's the mouse?" "Oh, I thought it would be ra'r cruel to keep him in; so I took him to the stable and let him go!" And so ended the scheme for propelling the baker's cart by vital force at first hand.

TO HIS WIFE

Train, Petersburg to Moscow, 19–3–93

The snow is nearly cleared from the streets of Petersburg, but here on the line there has been a little fresh fall: just enough to make everything dazzling white and clean again. The trees are beautiful in their last winter beauty. The spring will come almost suddenly on them.

We are told that the change is much more rapid than with us, the growth of the leaves being almost magical.   I expect the change at Upton will be so to *me*!

TRAIN, RETURNING MOSCOW TO PETERSBURG, 20–3–93

I have now, I believe, finally done with Moscow.   It has been a time of great exercise of spirit with me: of special anxiety, such as I can more fully make clear verbally than by letter.   Three or four visits have filled up the time, but by far the larger part of it has been spent at Count Tolstoi's.   He was exceedingly glad to see me, and I feel bound up in him more than I can express.   There are some things in which we see eye to eye; and others that I know to a certainty he is mistaken in, and which I would give much to open his eyes to.   To-day, besides the conversation at his own house, he accompanied me for many miles over Moscow on foot and in the trams.   I had a call to make at a house outside the city on the opposite side to his house and he came there first with me: afterwards to a bookseller's and finally to the hotel, till nearly the train-time.

After lunch this morning, before we started on this round, he took a nap, as is his custom.   A friend of his, who seems a very thoughtful earnest man, and one of his daughters (Countess Mary Tolstoi) remained at table, asking me about Friends' doctrines.   They were deeply interested; and Mary Tolstoi said it was of great interest to them that one should come from so far off, who held the same doctrines they believed, on the universality of the light of God, and other points. She asked if I believed in the Divinity of Christ.   I said "I do believe in it; but I do not think it would be of any benefit to thee to force thyself into it, or into any other belief: for it is only as the thing is Divinely made manifest to us, that it is true or real to us.   The great thing is for all of us to be faithful to the light we already have.   That will lead us to all truth."   She interpreted each point to the visitor as we proceeded; and then she mentioned some difficulty that seemed to her to stand in the way of her accepting Christ as God.   I advised her to leave this at present; for if the true revelation of His character came to her, the seeming difficulty would disappear.   I put the differences of creed, and yet their compatibility with our holding some truths notwithstanding, and the unity of spirit resulting from this, as follows:— each of us—i.e. every one—has a *double* vision in these matters.   We see the real truth in a manner comparable to seeing, say, the trees in the garden, through the window.   This I will call our spiritual sense, or that which we have through immediate revelation. But we have also an intellectual or merely human apprehension of them also, which may be compared to our holding a coloured glass between our eyes and the window. My glass may be red; my neighbour's, blue, or some other colour. Now it is human nature, or a law of the human mind, that we should imagine this coloured glass to be of capital importance, and try to force our neighbour to change his colour for ours. But a mistake here may injure his sight. The main thing is to direct him to that which is beyond, and leave *his* glass alone unless we are clearly called to touch it. I find I have put this less distinctly, here, in writing, than I believe I was enabled to do *vivâ voce*; for they were satisfied that it is the truth.

Presently the two youngest children came in, and began to coax me to get them some English postage stamps: for my carte, etc., etc. Little Ivan is five: his sister Alexandra, a most lovely child of eight. . . . The two little ones dragged me off, at this point, to the nursery, to shew me their toys and their brother's puppy. "An English pointer, Mr. Bellows." "What is his name?" "O, he has not got a name yet. You see it is—a little girl—and my brother would rather have a little *boy*: so it will be changed." Ivan's English is hardly so perfect as his sister's. It was delightful to see his earnestness as he strove after words to say what he wanted. Their governess is a young [English] lady, and the nurse a motherly old Russian who was sorely exercised to keep them from making too much noise. "I think Mr. Bellows will be tired with your taking him about so," said their sister Mary, coming into the nursery—adding some suggestion about shewing me to her brother's room, if I wished some rest. I declared that I would rather play with the little ones: but Ivan dragged me to a couch—and pushing my head towards the pillow, said "Repose. Now—you can—repose—yourself"—but I was to go on, *while* I reposed myself, telling them stories about dogs, *bien entendu!* My heart fairly ached, in the vivid remembrance of our own Jack and Dorothy, as these two little things stood in the porch shouting "Good-bye!" after me—and promising to come to Upton to play with my children.

As we left the house, Mary Tolstoi slipped on her outdoor wraps and went on before us. Three hours after, when her father and I reached the hotel, I found a little parcel of toys for our children, with the enclosed note.

"Your wife will not like you to come back looking so thin," said Count Tolstoi, this evening, as he was bidding me farewell on the hotel stairs. "You must tell her that you are not feeding yourself enough on this journey: and that if you had stayed with us, we would have looked after you better than you are doing yourself." Again and again he said with emphasis: "How *glad* I am that you came over. O, how *glad* I am of your visit!" . . .

I made one call yesterday on an elderly lady who has had a great fight of trials and doubts; and when I told her she was not alone in some of the things she mentioned, and told her of the full cup that I had had to drink of in the past week, she said, after a pause, "Perhaps it has been permitted in order that you might be better able to say a word of comfort and encouragement to others." It *may* be so. I hardly know. What I do know is that I am ready to sink under the discouragements of the whole position; and the impossibility of hoping, humanly speaking, for any material alteration in the Russian system of persecution. Joseph Neave is more hopeful; but I cannot test his hope so as to hold on to its margin myself.

LEWIS CARROLL (CHARLES LUTWIDGE DODGSON)
(1832–98)

Lewis Carroll was never so happy as when surrounded with little girls or writing to them. He had a huge circle of correspondents and the following is typical of the notes he used to send these little folk.

CHRIST CHURCH, OXFORD, OCTOBER 15, 1875

MY DEAR GERTRUDE, I never give birthday *presents*, but you see I *do* sometimes write a birthday *letter*: so, as I have just arrived here, I am writing this to wish you many and many a happy return of your birthday to-morrow. I will drink your health, if only I can remember, and if you don't mind—but perhaps you object? You see, if I were to sit by you at breakfast, and to drink your tea, you wouldn't like *that*, would you? You would say "Boo! Hoo! Here's Mr. Dodgson's drunk all my tea, and I haven't got any left!" So I am very much afraid, next time Sybil looks for you, she'll find you sitting by the sad sea-wave, and crying, "Boo! Hoo! Here's Mr. Dodgson has drunk my health, and I haven't got any left!" And how it will puzzle Dr. Maund when he is sent for to see you! "My dear madam, I am very sorry to say your little girl has got *no health at all*! I never saw such a thing in my life!" "Oh, I can easily explain it!" your mother will say. "You see, she would go and make friends with a strange gentleman, and yesterday he drank her health!" "Well, Mrs. Chataway," he will say, "the only way to cure her is to wait till his next birthday and then for *her* to drink *his* health."

And then we shall have changed healths. I wonder how you will like mine! Oh, Gertrude, I wish you wouldn't talk such nonsense!

Your loving friend,
LEWIS CARROLL

CHRIST CHURCH, OXFORD, DECEMBER 9, 1875

MY DEAR GERTRUDE, This really will *not* do, you know, sending one more kiss every time by post: the parcel gets so heavy it is quite expensive. When the postman brought in the last letter, he looked quite grave. "Two pounds to pay, Sir!" he said. *"Extra weight,* Sir!" (I think he cheats a little, by the way. He often makes me pay two *pounds,* when I think it should be *pence.*) "Oh, if you please, Mr. Postman!" I said going down gracefully on one knee (I wish you could see me go down on one knee to a postman—it's a very pretty sight), "do excuse me just this once! It's only from a little girl!"

"Only from a little girl!" he growled. "What are little girls made of?" "Sugar and spice," I began to say, "and all that's ni——" but he interrupted me. "No! I don't mean *that.* I mean, what's the good of little girls, when they send such heavy letters?" "Well, they're not *much* good, certainly," I said, rather sadly.

"Mind you don't get any more such letters," he said, "at least, not from that particular little girl. *I know her well, and she's a regular bad one!*" That's not true, is it? I don't believe he ever saw you, and you are not a bad one, are you? However, I promised him we would send each other *very* few more letters—"Only two thousand four hundred and seventy, or so," I said. "Oh!" he said, "a little number like *that* doesn't signify. What I meant is, you mustn't send *many.*"

So you see we must keep count now, and when we get to two thousand, four hundred and seventy, we mustn't write any more, unless the postman gives us leave.

I sometimes wish I was back on the shore at Sandown; don't you?

Your loving friend,

Lewis Carroll

Why is a pig that has lost its tail like a little girl on the seashore? Because it says, "I should like another tale, please!"

CHARLES GEORGE GORDON (1833–85)

"Chinese Gordon" as the General was called, from his victories over the Taeping rebels, was sent out to the Sudan in 1884 to assist the Khedive of Egypt in withdrawing the garrisons of the country which could no longer stand against the Mahdi. During the siege of Khartum, Gordon kept a record of events, which he sent from time to time, as occasion offered, to the commander of the relief force. Below are printed the letter sent with the final instalment of this record and extracts from his journal which was written in letter form.

TO THE CHIEF OF STAFF, SUDAN EXPEDITIONARY FORCE

KHARTUM, 10 NOV., 1884

SIR, Since departure, 10 Sept., of Lt.-Colonel Stewart, C.M.G., I have kept a daily journal of all events at Khartum, which contains also my *private* opinions upon certain facts, which perhaps it is just as well you should know confidentially. You can of course make extracts of all official matter, and will naturally leave my private opinions out in the case of publication. I have already sent five portions of this journal, and now send the sixth portion.

I have the honour to be, Sir,

Your most obedient servant,

C. G. GORDON

FROM THE JOURNAL

IT is not a small thing for a European for fear of death to deny our faith; it was not so in old times and it should not be regarded as if it was taking off one coat and putting on another. If the Christian faith is a myth then let men throw it off but it is mean and dishonourable to do so merely to save one's life if one believes it is the true faith. ... Treachery never succeeds and however matters may end, it is better to fall with clean hands than to be mixed up with dubious acts and dubious men. ... I am using this argument with them, in saying: "You ask me to become a Mussulman to save my life and you yourself acknowledge Mahomet Achmet as the Mahdi to save your lives; why, if we go on this principle we will be adopting every religion whose adherents threaten our existence, for you know and own when you are safe that Mahomet Achmet is *not* the Mahdi."

.   .   .   .   .   .

During our blockade we have often discussed the question of being frightened which, in the world's view a man should never be. For my part I am always frightened and very much so. I fear the future of all engagements. It is not the fear of death; that is past, thank God; but I fear defeat and its consequences. I do not believe a bit in the calm unmoved man. I think it is only he does not show it outwardly. Thence I conclude no commander of forces ought to live closely in relation with his subordinates who watch him like lynxes, for there is no contagion equal to that of fear.

.   .   .   .   .   .

I dwell on the joy of never seeing Great Britain again with its horrid wearisome dinner parties and miseries. How we can put up with those things passes my imagination. It is a perfect bondage. At those dinner parties we are all in masks saying what we do not believe, eating and drinking things we do not want and then abusing one another. I would sooner live like a Dervish with the Mahdi than go out to dinner every night in London.

.   .   .   .   .   .

(*Finally, on December* 13*th, he writes*)
The steamers went up and attacked the Arabs at Bourré (certainly this day-after-day delay has a most disheartening effect on every one. To-day is the 276th day of our anxiety). The Arabs appear, by all accounts, to have suffered to-day heavily at Bourré. We had none wounded by the Arabs; but one man, by the discharge of a bad cartridge, got a cut in the neck: this was owing to the same cause as nearly blew out my eyes the other day. We are going to send down the *Bordeen* the day after to-morrow, and with her I shall send this Journal. *If some effort is not made before ten days' time the town will fall.* It is inexplicable, this delay. If the Expeditionary Forces have reached the river and met my steamers, one hundred men are all that we require, just to show themselves.

I send this Journal, for I have little hopes of saving it if the town falls. I put in the sort of arrangement I would make with Zubair Pasha for the future government of the Soudan. Ferratch Pasha is really showing an amount of vigour I did not give him credit for. Even if the town falls under the nose of the Expeditionary Force, it will not, in my opinion, justify the abandonment of Sennaar and Kassala, or of the Equatorial Province, by Her Majesty's Government. All that is absolutely necessary is, for fifty of the Expeditionary Force to get on board a steamer and come up to Halfeyeh, and thus let their presence be felt; this is not asking much, but it must happen *at once*; or it will (as usual) be too late. • A soldier deserted to the Arabs to-day from the North Fort. The buglers on the roof, being short of stature, are put on boxes to enable them to fire over the parapet; one with the recoil of rifle was knocked right over, and caused considerable excitement. We thought he was killed, by the noise he made in his fall. The Arabs fire their Krupps continually into town from the South Front, but no one takes any notice of it. The Arabs at Goba only fired one shell at the Palace to-day, which burst in the air.

December 14. Arabs fired two shells at the Palace this morning; 546 ardebs dhoora! in store; also 83,525 okes of biscuit! 10.30 a.m. The steamers are down at Omdurman, engaging the Arabs, consequently I am on *tenterhooks*! 11.30 a.m. Steamers returned. The *Bordeen* was struck by a shell in her battery; we had only one man wounded. We are going to send down the *Bordeen* to-morrow with this Journal. If I was in command of the two hundred men of the Expeditionary Force, which are all that are necessary for the movement, I should stop just below Halfeyeh, and attack the Arabs at that place before I came on here to Kartoum. I should then communicate with the North Fort, and act according to circumstances. Now MARK THIS, if the Expeditionary Force, and I ask for no more than two hundred men, does not come in ten days, *the town may fall*; and I have done my best for the honour of our country. Good-bye.

C. G. GORDON

You send me no information, though you have lots of money.

C. G. G.

JOHN, LORD ACTON (1834-1902)

Acton was one of the most striking figures in the circle of Gladstone's friends. A brilliant historian and essayist, a Catholic of liberal tendencies, a man with wide-spreading Continental interests and connexions, Acton never achieved the full anticipated promise of the lifelong dedication to a book on liberty, which he never wrote. Matthew Arnold used to say, "Gladstone influences all around him but Acton; it is Acton who influences Gladstone."

TO MARY GLADSTONE

TEGERNSEE, JUNE 21, 1880

THE Tennysons came and went, I am sorry to say, prematurely. They spent two days with us, and would have gone by Achensee to Innsbruck, but the rain sent them back to Munich, where they took the train for Italy. You will be surprised to learn that the Poet made a favourable impression on my ladies and children. He was not only a gracious Poet, but he told us lots of good stories, read aloud without pressure, walked repeatedly with M., and seemed interested in the books he carried to his room. Lady Acton took him to Kreuth and round the lake, and liked him very well. Yet our ways were very strange to him, and he must have felt that he stood on the far verge of civilization, without the enjoyments proper to savage life. Even I was tamed at last. There was a shell to crack, but I got the kernel, chiefly at night, when everybody was in bed. His want of reality, his habit of walking on the clouds, the airiness of his metaphysics, the indefiniteness of his knowledge, his neglect of transitions, the looseness of his political reasonings—all this made up an alarming *cheval de frise.*

But then there was a gladness—not quickness—in taking a joke or story, a comic impatience of the external criticism of Taine and others found here, coupled with a simple dignity when reading ill-natured attacks, a grave groping for religious certainty, and a generosity in the treatment of rivals—of Browning and Swinburne, though not of Taylor—that helped me through. He was not quite well, in consequence of the damp and of the mountain fare.

I write for news of your hôtel at Venice, the weather having been against the Dolomites.

Hallam is a much better and clearer politician than his father, and the only time we differed he was the truer Blue. If I add that I discovered why he refused a baronetcy, I suspect it is no more than you know very well already.

I have made Liddon's acquaintance at last. Nothing but Tennyson prevented me from seeing more of him, for I found in him all that I love Oxford for, and only a very little of what I dislike in it.

TO THE SAME

CANNES, DEC. 27

YOUR patient and forgiving letter is my best Xmas gift. It will be a joy indeed to see you again next week. I hope not only in the midst of gilded ceremonial.

It is so like you to take my nonsense kindly and only to dispute the praise. But I am not quite so far off as you imagine. In speaking of home I must have indicated by a—break, that there was a change of key; that I could not stay among the lofty entities that surround Tennyson even when he butters toast, that I was coming down from the silver side of the clouds and gropings for things of earth. So that my climax is not quite literally meant. Having thus paved the way to retreat from an exposed position, let me take my stand for a moment, and say that I think it not quite untenable. . . . You yourself, who have shared so much of your father's thoughts and confidence, have hardly adapted yourself to his chosen tastes and special pursuits? In more than one of the later phases of his life, I fancy you hardly recognized the secret laws of the growth of his mind, and join him sometimes by an effort, over a gap. There is an ancient scholar at Cannes, who told me that he has such confidence in the P.M. that he feels sure he will succeed in defending his policy. I partly said and partly thought that anybody can be on Mr. Gladstone's side who waits to be under the thrall of his speech. The difficulty is to hear the grass growing, to know the road by which he travels, the description of engine, the quality of the stuff he treats with, the stars he steers by. The scholar is old and ugly, and, it may be, tiresome. It is impossible to be less like you. But is there not one bit of likeness—in the stars?

Really it is time for me to adopt the Carey tactics and run away from my post of defiance.

You know one of the two subjects. You will know the other on the last night of the debate on the address. I am only listening to the grass.

You will not resist what I said of our five Ministers if you will consider one word. I think I spoke of their best qualities, not of all their qualities. Pitt's art of making himself necessary to the King and the constituencies is unapproached. But then it is a vice, not a merit, to live for expedients, and not for ideas. Chatham was very successful as a War Minister. Mr. Gladstone has not rivalled him in that capacity. I fancy that both Pitt and Peel had a stronger hold than he has on the City. Please remember that I am possessed of a Whig devil, and neither Peel nor Pitt lives in my Walhalla. The great name of Mr. Canning and the greater name of Mr. Burke [1] are the only names that I hold in highest honour since party government was invented.

You could hardly imagine what Burke is for all of us who think about politics, and we are not wrapped in the blaze and the whirlwind of Rousseau. Systems of scientific thought have been built up by famous scholars on the fragments that fell from his table. Great literary fortunes have been made by men who traded on the hundredth part of him. Brougham and Lowe lived by the vitality of his ideas. Mackintosh and Macaulay are only Burke trimmed and stripped of all that touched the skies. Montelambert, borrowing a hint from Döllinger, says that Burke and Shakespeare were the two greatest Englishmen.

But when I speak of Shakespeare the news of last Wednesday[2] comes back to me, and it seems as if the sun had gone out. You cannot think how much I owed her. Of eighteen or twenty writers by whom I am conscious that my mind has been formed, she was one. Of course I mean ways, not conclusions. In problems of life and thought, which baffled Shakespeare disgracefully, her touch was unfailing. No writer ever lived who had anything like her power of manifold, but disinterested and impartially observant sympathy. If Sophocles or Cervantes had lived in the light of our culture, if Dante had prospered like Manzoni, George Eliot might have had a rival.

.   .   .   .

I do think that, of the three greatest Liberals, Burke is equally good in speaking and writing; Macaulay better in writing, and Mr.

---

[1] An allusion to Mr. Gladstone's speech on the Reform Bill of 1866.
[2] The death of George Eliot.

Gladstone better in speaking. I doubt whether he feels it; and if he does not feel it, then I should say that there is a want of perfect knowledge and judgment. That want I see clearly in his views as to other men. He hardly ever, I think, judges them too severely. Sometimes I am persuaded he judges with an exceeding generosity, and I fancy it is because he will not charge his mind with uncharitableness, because he does not allow for the wind, that he does not always make bull's eyes.

SIR EDWARD MALET (1837–1908)

Malet held many diplomatic appointments in Europe and America. He accompanied Lord Lyons to Paris in 1867 and was sent by him on a mission to Count Bismarck after the battle of Sedan. He was in charge of the Paris embassy during the Commune, and was awarded the C.B. His letter to Lord Lyons throws an interesting light on Bismarck.

TO LORD LYONS

PARIS, SEPTEMBER 17, 1870

DURING my two interviews with Count Bismarck on the 15th he said some things which it may not be uninteresting to Your Lordship to know, although from the confidential familiar manner in which they were uttered, I did not feel justified in including them in an official report.

He stated it was the intention to hang all persons not in uniform who were found with arms. A man in a blouse had been brought before him who had represented that he was one of the Garde Mobile: Count Bismarck decided that as there was nothing in his dress to support his assertion he must be hung, and the sentence was forthwith carried into effect. His Excellency added, "I attach little value to human life because I believe in another world—if we lived for three or four hundred years it would be a different matter." I said that although some of the Mobile wore blouses, each regiment was dressed in a uniform manner and that they all bore red collars and stripes on their wrist-bands. His Excellency replied that that was not enough, at a distance they looked like peasants and until they had a dress like other soldiers those who were taken would be hung.

He said, "When you were a little boy you wanted your mother to ask a lady, who was not of the best position in society, to one of her parties; your mother refused, on which you threw yourself on the ground and said you would not rise till you had got what you wanted. In like manner we have thrown ourselves on the soil of France and will not rise till our terms are agreed to." In speaking of the surrender of the Emperor he observed, "When I approached the carriage in which the Emperor was His Majesty took off his cap to salute me. It is not the custom for us when in uniform to do more than touch the cap—however I took mine off and the Emperor's eyes followed it till it came on a level with my belt in which was a revolver, when he turned quite pale—I cannot account for it. He could not suppose I was going to use it, but the fact of his changing colour was quite unmistakable. I was surprised that he should have sent for me; I should have thought I was the last person that he would wish to receive him, because he has betrayed me. All that has passed between us made me feel confident that he would not go to war with Germany. He was bound not to do so and his doing it was an act of personal treachery to me. The Emperor frequently asked whether his carriages were safe out of Sedan, and a change indicating a sense of great relief came over him when he received the news of their arrival in our lines." M. de Bismarck talked in the most contemptuous terms of M. de Gramont, allowing him only one merit, that of being a good shot. He touched on the publication of the secret treaty, but his arguments in defence of it were rather too subtle for me to seize them clearly. He said the secret should have died with him had France had a tolerable pretext for going to war, but that he considered her outrageous conduct in this matter released him from all obligation.

"If," he remarked, "a man asked the hand of my daughter in marriage and I refuse it I should consider it a matter of honour to keep the proposal a secret as long as he behaved well to me, but if he attacked me I should be no longer bound. This is quite a different question from that of publishing a secret proposition at the same time that you refuse it; you must be a Beust or an Austrian to do that."

In talking of the scheme to replace the Emperor on the throne by the aid of Bazaine and the French prisoners in Germany, I asked whether His Majesty was now in a state of health to be willing to undertake such a work. He answered that he never in his life had seen the Emperor in the enjoyment of better health and he attributed it to the bodily exercise and the diet which late events had forced upon him.

Count Bismarck spoke of Italy and appeared to think that it was in immediate danger of Republican revolution. He said "If," as appeared likely at the beginning, "Italy had sided with France such a movement would have broken out at once; we had everything prepared, and could have forced on a revolution within three days after a declaration of war."

On leaving him he asked me if I had a horse, saying, "I would offer you mine but the French are in the habit of firing on our Parlementaires, and as I have only one I cannot afford to lose it."

SIR ROBERT STAWELL BALL (1840–1913)

It would be curious to glance through a collection of the amazing questions asked of scientists by the unlearned. When Halley's Comet revisited the sky, in 1910, a nervous friend, apprehensive of the end of the world, wrote to the famous astronomer for reassurance. This was his answer.

FEBRUARY 10, 1910

A RHINOCEROS in full charge would not fear collision with a cobweb, and the earth need not fear collision with a comet. In 1861 we passed through the tail of a comet and no one knew anything about it at the time. For a hundred million years life has been continuous on this earth, though we have been visited by at least five comets every year. If comets could ever have done the earth any harm they would have done it long ago, and you and I would not have been discussing comets or anything else. I hope this letter will give you the assurance you want. So far as I can learn we may be in the tail of Halley about May 12th; and I sincerely hope we shall. I think Sir John Herschel said somewhere that the whole comet could be squeezed into a portmanteau.

THE SHUCKBURGH CORRESPONDENCE

Anne, Lady Shuckburgh, was the wife of Sir Francis Shuckburgh, a Northamptonshire baronet. To her wrote Lady Seymour, aforetime Queen of Beauty at the famous Eglinton Tournament, for the character of Mary Stedman, a maid who had applied for a situation.

LADY SEYMOUR presents her compliments to Lady Shuckburgh, and would be obliged to her for the character of Mary Stedman, who states that she lived twelve months, and still is, in Lady Shuckburgh's establishment. Can Mary Stedman cook plain dishes well? make bread? and is she honest, good-tempered, sober, willing, and cleanly? Lady Seymour would also like to know the reason why she leaves Lady Shuckburgh's service. Direct, under cover to Lord Seymour, Maiden Bradley.

To this Lady Shuckburgh replied:

Lady Shuckburgh presents her compliments to Lady Seymour. Her ladyship's note, dated October 28, only reached her yesterday, November 3. Lady Shuckburgh was unacquainted with the name of the kitchen-maid until mentioned by Lady Seymour, as it is her custom neither to apply for or to give characters to any of the under servants, this being always done by the housekeeper, Mrs. Pouch—and this was well knnow to the young woman; therefore Lady Shuckburgh is surprised at her referring any lady to her for a character. Lady Shuckburgh having a professed cook, as well as a housekeeper, in her establishment, it is not very likely she herself should know anything of the abilities or merits of the under servants; therefore she is unable to answer Lady Seymour's note. Lady Shuckburgh cannot imagine Mary Stedman to be capable of cooking for any except the servants'-hall table.

But Sheridan's granddaughter was quite the wrong subject for these experiments in fine ladyism, and she lost no time in replying as follows:

Lady Seymour presents her compliments to Lady Shuckburgh, and begs she will order her housekeeper, Mrs. Pouch, to send the girl's character without delay; otherwise another young woman will be sought for elsewhere, as Lady Seymour's children cannot remain without their dinners because Lady Shuckburgh, keeping a "professed cook and a housekeeper," thinks a knowledge of the details of her establishment beneath her notice. Lady Seymour understands from Stedman that, in addition to her other talents, she was actually capable of dressing food fit for the little Shuckburghs to partake of when hungry.

> *To this note was appended a pen-and-ink vignette by Lady Seymour representing the three "little Shuckburghs," with large heads and cauliflower wigs, sitting at a round table and voraciously scrambling for mutton chops dressed by Mary Stedman, who was seen looking on with supreme satisfaction, while Lady Shuckburgh appeared in the distance in evident dismay.*

THOMAS HARDY (1840–1928)

The novelist and poet of the Wessex countryside outlived the early bitter criticism of his work, to be recognized as the foremost literary artist of his time. His letter to a clergyman who had asked his views on field-sports, is typical of his indignant compassion for suffering and, in its conclusion, of the sombre outlook that repelled so many of his early readers.

TO THE REV. S. WHITTELL

I AM not sufficiently acquainted with the many varieties of sport to pronounce which is, quantitatively, the most cruel. I can only say generally that the prevalence of those sports which consist in the pleasure of watching a fellow-creature, weaker or less favoured than ourselves, in its struggles, by Nature's poor resources only, to escape the death-agony we mean to inflict by the treacherous contrivances of science, seems one of the many convincing proofs that we have not yet emerged from barbarism.

In the present state of affairs there would appear to be no logical reason why the smaller children, say, of over-crowded families, should not be used for sporting purposes. Darwin has revealed that there would be no difference in principle; moreover, these children would often escape lives intrinsically less happy than those of wild birds and other animals.

TO EDWARD CLODD

AUG. 28, 1914

MY DEAR CLODD, I fear we cannot take advantage of your kind invitation, and pay you a visit just now—much as in some respects we should like to. With the Germans (apparently) only a week from Paris, the native hue of resolution is sicklied o'er with the pale cast of thought. We shall hope to come when things look brighter.

Trifling incidents here bring home to us the conditions of affairs not far off—as I daresay they do to you still more—sentries with gleaming bayonets at unexpected places as we motor along, the steady flow of soldiers through here to Weymouth, and their disappearance across the Channel in the silence of night, and the 1,000 prisoners whom we get glimpses of through chinks, mark these fine days. The prisoners, they say, have already mustered enough broken English to say "Shoot Kaiser!" and oblige us by playing "God Save the King" on their concertinas and fiddles. Whether this is "meant sarcastic," as Artemus Ward used to say, I cannot tell.

I was pleased to know that you were so comfortable, when I was picturing you in your shirt sleeves with a lot of other robust Aldeburghers digging a huge trench from Aldeburgh church to the top of those steps we go down to your house, streaming with sweat, and drinking pots of beer between the shovellings (English beer of course).

Sincerely yours,
Thomas Hardy

P.S.—Yes; everybody seems to be reading "The Dynasts" just now—at least, so a writer in the "Daily News" who called here this morning tells me.—T. H.

SIR HENRY MORTON STANLEY (1841–1904)

The 80's and 90's rang with the name of Stanley. Not only had he found Livingstone; he had made great discoveries in Central Africa; had rescued Emin Pasha; and exposed the horrors of the African slave trade. This letter from Uganda was written during Stanley's exploration of the Great Lakes.

MTESA'S CAPITAL, UGANDA, APRIL 14, 1875

I MUST not forget to inform you and your readers of one very interesting subject connected with Mtesa, which will gratify many a philanthropic European and American.

I have already told you that Mtesa and the whole of his court profess Islamism. A long time ago—some four or five years—Khamis bin Abdullah (the only Arab who remained with me three years ago, as a rear-guard, when the Arabs disgracefully fled from Mirambo) came to Uganda. He was wealthy, of noble descent, and a fine, magnificent personal appearance, and brought with him many a rich present for Mtesa, such as few Arabs could afford. The king became immediately fascinated with him, and really few white men could be long with the son of Abdullah without being charmed by his presence, his handsome proud features, his rich olive complexion, and his liberality. I confess I never saw an Arab or Mussulman who attracted me so much as Khamis bin Abdullah, and it is no wonder that Mtesa, meeting a kindred spirit in the noble youth of Muscat, amazed at his handsome bearing, and splendour of his apparel, the display of his wealth, and the number of his slaves, fell in love with him. Khamis stayed with Mtesa a full year, during which time the king became a convert to the creed of his visitor—namely, Mohammedanism. The Arab clothed Mtesa in the best that his wardrobe offered; he gave him gold embroidered jackets, fine white shirts, crimson slippers, swords, silk sashes, daggers, and a revolving rifle, so that Speke and Grant's presents seemed of necessity insignificant.

Now, until I arrived at Mtesa's Court, the king delighted in the idea that he was a follower of Islam; but by one conversation I flatter myself that I have tumbled the newly-raised religious fabric to the ground, and, if it were only followed by the arrival of a Christian mission here, the conversion of Mtesa and his Court to Christianity would, I think, be complete. I have indeed undermined Islamism so much here that Mtesa has determined henceforth, until he is better informed, to observe the Christian Sabbath as well as the Moslem Sabbath, and the great captains have unanimously consented to this. He has further caused the ten commandments of Moses to be written on a board for his daily perusal—for Mtesa can read Arabic—as well as the Lord's Prayer and the golden commandment of our Saviour, "Thou shalt love thy neighbour as thyself." This is great progress for the few days that I have remained with him, and, though I am no missionary, I shall begin to think that I might become one if such success is feasible. But oh! that some pious, practical missionary would come here! What a field and a harvest ripe for the sickle of civilization! Mtesa would give him anything he desired—houses, lands, ivory, etc.; he might call a province his own one day. It is not the mere preacher, however, that is wanted here. The Bishops of Great Britain collected, with all the classic youth of Oxford and Cambridge, would effect nothing by mere talk with the intelligent people of Uganda. It is the practical Christian tutor, who can teach people how to become Christians, cure their diseases, construct dwellings, understand and exemplify agriculture, and turn his hand to anything, like a sailor—this is the man who is wanted. Such an one, if he can be found, would become the saviour of Africa. He must be tied to no Church or sect, but profess God and His Son and the moral law, and live a blameless Christian, inspired by liberal principles, charity to all men, and devout faith in heaven. He must belong to no nation in particular, but the entire White race. Such a man, or men, Mtesa, King of Uganda, Usoga, Umgoro, and Karagwe—a kingdom three hundred and sixty geographical miles in length by fifty in breadth— invites to repair to him. He has begged me to tell the white men that if they will only come to him he will give them all they want. Now, where is there in all the Pagan world a more promising field for a mission than Uganda? Colonel Linant de Bellefonds is my witness that I speak the truth, and I know he will corroborate all I say. The colonel, though a Frenchman, is a Calvinist, and has become as ardent a well-wished for the Waganda as I am. Then why further spend needlessly vast sums upon black Pagans of Africa who have no example of their own people becoming Christians before them? I speak to the Universities' Mission at Zanzibar, and to the Free Methodists at Mombasa, to the leading philanthropists, and the pious people in England. Here, gentlemen, is your opportunity—embrace it! The people on the shores of the Nyanza call upon you. Obey your own generous instincts, and listen to them; and I assure you that in one year you will have more converts to Christianity than all other missionaries united can number. The population of Mtesa's kingdom is very dense; I estimate the number of his subjects at two millions. You need not fear to spend money upon such a mission, as Mtesa is sole ruler, and will repay its cost tenfold with ivory, coffee, otter skins of a very fine quality, or even in cattle, for the wealth of this country in all these products is immense. The road here is by the Nile, or via Zanzibar, Ugogo, and Unyanyembe. The former route, so long as Colonel Gordon governs the countries of the Upper Nile, seems the most feasible.

With all deference I would suggest that the mission should bring to Mtesa as presents three or four suits of military clothes, decorated freely with gold embroidery; together with half-a-dozen French *kepis*, a sabre, a brace of pistols, and suitable ammunition; a good fowling-piece and rifle of good quality, for the king is not a barbarian; a cheap dinner-service of Britannia ware, an iron bedstead and counterpanes, a few pieces of cotton print, boots, etc. For trade it should also bring fine blue, black, and grey woollen cloths, a quantity of military buttons, gold braid and cord, silk cord of different colours, as well as binding; linen and sheeting for shirts, fine red blankets, and a quantity of red cloth, with a few chairs and tables. The profit arising from the sale of these things would be enormous.

For the mission's use it should bring with it a supply of hammers, saws, augers, chisels, axes, hatchets, adzes, carpenters' and blacksmiths' tools, since the Waganda are apt pupils; iron drills and powder for blasting purposes, trowels, a couple of good-sized anvils, a forge and bellows, an assortment of nails and tacks, a plough, spades, shovels, pickaxes, and a couple of light buggies as specimens, with such other small things as their own common sense would suggest to the men whom I invite. Most desirable would be an assortment of garden seed and grain; also white-lead, linseed oil, brushes, a few volumes of illustrated journals, gaudy prints, a magic lantern, rockets, and a photographic apparatus. The total cost of the whole equipment need not exceed five thousand pounds sterling.

HENRY M. STANLEY

MANDELL CREIGHTON (1843–1901)

The future Bishop of London was a master at Marlborough when he wrote this letter to the lady who became his wife the following year. It shows something of the man's firmness and purity of character, and the intense zealousness of his nature.

TO MISS VON GLEHN

MARLBOROUGH COLLEGE, JUNE 24, 1871

I DON'T know what you would call a regular life, but I mean by it a life in which one habitually breakfasts at eight: try as you will to escape, that one fact pins you down to hopeless regularity: the whole day must centre round that. Now, an irregular life is one in which one breakfasts when one gets up, and gets up when one likes, occasionally choosing to sit up late and meditate lazily, occasionally choosing to do so when about three-quarters awake in the morning. It is a pleasant but mischievous life, provocative of much sweetness of character, but absolutely destructive of energy. By an energetic man I mean always a man who gets up the moment he is awake. It costs me a severe struggle every morning to get up at all. I commence my day with a serious moral conflict, which acts as a tonic to my whole nature. If I did not undergo that battle, I should be unnerved for the day. I am glad you did see my view that the object of life after all is to live—conscious energizing in the world comes to nothing. St. Francis certainly was not guilty of it: he wished to lead the life to which his natural sympathies attracted him. His "marriage with poverty" is no mere allegorical expression. The life he led was the only one he wanted to lead: there is no conscious struggle to adapt his life to the purpose of teaching others. I don't find any self-conscious effort about St. Paul: do you think he thought that the simple record of his life would be read by all civilized men for all time? Do you think his letters would be what they are if he had thought that out of his stray admonitions to struggling erring Christian communities millions of men would form their views of life and its duties? What a mess he would have made if he had thought it his duty to sit down and write

840

a philosophical and moral treatise setting forth Christianity in a plain and clear form so as to commend it to everybody! We can never do anything except by the fact of our lives: and to lead a good life is quite enough to do. The only class of people I know who go in for consciously doing good and producing great things in the world are the Jesuits: their reputation answers for the effect upon themselves, the results they have wrought for the desirability of their method. . . . If you are doing any work it will be recognizable enough; if you are not, begin contentedly in a little way at first. Such is my theory of life: it took me a long while to learn; but since I have given up regenerating mankind by the million, I find it very hard to satisfy myself about my own wisdom in the smallest duties of life, still more about the goodness of my intentions and the singleness of heart in the process. It is very hard to get rid of one's lower self—to be utterly unpretentious, truthful, and charitable all at once.

ANDREW LANG (1844–1912)

Scholar and man of letters, Lang did much fine work as a writer on history and anthropology. He is perhaps best known for his admirable translations, ranging from Homer and Theocritus to "Aucassin and Nicolete," and, to a younger audience, as the compiler of the famous books of fairy tales.

TO A YOUNG JOURNALIST

DEAR SMITH, You inform me that you desire to be a journalist, and you are kind enough to ask my advice. Well, be a journalist, by all means, in any honest and honourable branch of the profession. But do not be an eavesdropper and a spy. You may fly into a passion when you receive this very plainly worded advice. I hope you will; but, for several reasons, which I now go on to state, I fear that you won't. I fear that, either by natural gift or by acquired habit, you already possess the imperturbable temper which will be so useful to you if you do join the army of spies and eavesdroppers. If I am right, you have made up your mind to refuse to take offence, as long as by not taking offence you can wriggle yourself forward in the band of journalistic reptiles. You will be revenged on me, in that case, some day; you will lie in wait for me with a dirty bludgeon, and steal on me out of a sewer. If you do, permit me to assure you that I don't care. But if you are already in a rage, if you are about tearing up this epistle, and are starting to assault me personally, or at least to answer me furiously, then there is every hope for you and for your future. I therefore venture to state my reasons for supposing that you are inclined to begin a course which your father, if he were alive, would deplore, as all honourable men in their hearts must deplore it. When you were at the University (let me congratulate you on your degree) you edited, or helped to edit, *The Bull-dog*. It was not a very brilliant nor a very witty, but it was an extremely "racy" periodical. It spoke of all men and dons by their nicknames. It was full of second-hand slang. It contained many personal anecdotes, to the detriment of many people. It printed garbled and spiteful versions of private conversations on private affairs. It did not even spare to make comments on ladies, and on the details of domestic life in the town and in the University. The copies which you sent me I glanced at with extreme disgust.

In my time, more than a score of years ago, a similar periodical, but a much more clever periodical, was put forth by members of the University. It contained a novel which, even now, would be worth several ill-gotten guineas to the makers of the *Chronique scandaleuse*. But nobody bought it, and it died an early death. Times have altered, I am a fogey; but the ideas of honour and decency which fogies hold now were held by young men in the sixties of our century. I know very well that these ideas are obsolete. I am not preaching to the world, nor hoping to convert society, but to *you*, and purely in your own private, spiritual interest. If you enter on this path of tattle, mendacity, and malice, and if, with your cleverness and light hand, you are successful, society will not turn its back on you. You will be feared in many quarters, and welcomed in others. Of your paragraphs people will say that "it is a shame, of course, but it is amusing." There are so many shames in the world, shames not at all amusing, that you may see no harm in adding to the number. "If I don't do it," you may argue, "some one else will." Undoubtedly; *but why should you do it?*

You are not a starving scribbler; if you determine to write, you can write well, though not so easily, on many topics. You have not that last excuse of hunger, which drives poor women to the streets, and makes unhappy men act as public blabs and spies. If *you* take to this *métier*, it must be because you like it, which means that you enjoy being a listener to and reporter of talk that was never meant for any ears except those in which it was uttered. It means that the hospitable board is not sacred for you; it means that, with you, friendship, honour, all that makes human life better than a low smoking-room, are only valuable for what their betrayal will bring. It means that not even the welfare of your country will prevent you from running to the Press with any secret which you may have been entrusted with, or which you may have surprised. It means, this peculiar kind of profession, that all things open and excellent, and conspicuous to all men, are with you of no account. Art, literature, politics, are to cease to interest you. You are to scheme to surprise gossip about the private lives, dress, and talk of artists, men of letters, politicians. Your professional work will sink below the level of servants' gossip in a public-house parlour. If you happen to meet a man of known name, you will watch him, will listen to him, will try to sneak into his confidence, and you will blab, for money, about him, and your blab will inevitably be mendacious. In short, like the most pitiable outcasts of woman-kind, and, without their excuse, you will live by selling your honour. You will not suffer much, nor suffer long. Your conscience will very speedily be seared with a red-hot iron. You will be on the road which leads from mere dishonour to crime; and you may find yourself actually practising chantage, and extorting money as the price of your silence. This is the lowest deep: the vast majority, even of social mouchards, do not sink so low as this.

The profession of the critic, even in honourable and open criticism, is beset with dangers. It is often hard to avoid saying an unkind thing, a cruel thing, which is smart, and which may even be deserved. Who can say that he has escaped this temptation, and what man of heart can think of his own fall without a sense of shame? There are, I admit, authors so antipathetic to me, that I cannot trust myself to review them. Would that I had never reviewed them! They cannot be so bad as they seem to me: they must have qualities which escape my observation. Then there is the temptation to hit back. Some one writes, unjustly or unkindly as you think, of you or your friends. You wait till your enemy has written a book, and then you have your innings. It is not in nature that your review should be fair: you must inevitably be more on the lookout for faults than merits. The *éreintage*, the "smashing" of a literary foe is very delightful at the moment, but it does not look well in the light of reflection. But these deeds are mere peccadilloes compared with the confirmed habit of regarding all men and women as fair game for personal tattle and the sating of private spite. Nobody, perhaps, begins with this intention. Most men and women can find ready sophistries. If a report about any one reaches their ears, they say that they are doing him a service by publishing it and enabling him to contradict it. As if any mortal ever listened to a contradiction! And there are charges—that of plagiarism, for example—which can never be disproved, even if contradictions were listened to by the public. The accusation goes everywhere, is copied into every printed rag; the contradiction dies with the daily death of a single newspaper. You may reply that a man of sense will be in-different to false accusations. He may, or may not be,—that is not the question for you; the question for you is whether you will circulate news that is false, probably, and spiteful, certainly.

In short, the whole affair regards yourself more than it regards the world. Plenty of poison is sold; is it well for you to be one of the merchants? Is it the business of an educated gentleman to live by the trade of an eavesdropper and a blab? In the Memoirs of M. Blowitz he tells you how he began his illustrious career by procuring the publication of remarks which M. Thiers had made to him. He then "went to see M. Thiers, not without some apprehension." Is that the kind of emotion which you wish to be habitual in your experience? Do you think it agreeable to become shame-faced when you meet people who have conversed with you frankly? Do you enjoy being a sneak, and feeling like a sneak? Do you find blushing pleasant? Of course you will soon lose the power of blushing; but is that an agreeable prospect? Depend on it, there are discomforts in the progress to the brazen, in the journey to the shameless. You may, if your tattle is political, become serviceable to men engaged in great affairs. They may even ask you to their houses, if that is your ambition. You may urge that they condone your deeds and are even art and part in them. But you must also be aware that they call you, and think you, a reptile. You are not one of those who will do the devil's work without the devil's wages; but do you seriously think that the wages are worth the degradation?

Many men think so, and are not in other respects bad men. They may even be kindly and genial. Gentlemen they cannot be, nor men of delicacy, nor men of honour. They have sold themselves and their self-respect, some with ease (they are the least blamable), some with a struggle. They have seen better things, and perhaps vainly long to return to them. These are "St. Satan's Penitents," and their remorse is vain:

Virtutem Videant, intabescanique relicta.

If you don't wish to be of this dismal company, there is only one course open to you. Never write for publication one line of personal tattle. Let all men's persons and private lives be as sacred to you as your father's, —though there are tattlers who would sell paragraphs about their own mothers if there were a market for the ware. There is no half-way house on this road. Once begin to print private conversation, and you are lost—lost, that is, to delicacy and gradually, to many other things excellent and of good report. The whole question for you is, Do you mind incurring this damnation? If there is nothing in it which appals and revolts you, if your conscience is satisfied with a few ready sophisms, or if you don't care a pin for your conscience, fall to!

Vous irez loin! You will prattle in print about men's private lives, their hidden motives, their waistcoats, their wives, their boots, their business, their incomes. Most of your prattle will inevitably be lies. But go on! Nobody will kick you, I deeply regret to say. You will earn money. You will be welcomed in society. You will live and die content, and without remorse. I do not suppose that any particular inferno will await you in the future life. Whoever watches this world "with larger other eyes than ours" will doubtless make allowance for you, as for us all. I am not pretending to be a whit better than you; probably I am worse in many ways, but not in your way. Putting it merely as a matter of taste, I don't like the way. It makes me sick—that is all. It is a sin which I can comfortably damn, as I am not inclined to it. You may put it in that light; and I have no way of converting you, nor, if I have not dissuaded you, of dissuading you from continuing, on a larger scale, your practices in *The Bull-dog.*

Yours faithfully,
ANDREW LANG

A DAUGHTER OF OLD WALES

The following letter was received by Gladstone early in 1893, when a Bill was introduced into the House of Commons for the suspension of the Welsh Church.

CANNES, MARCH 15TH, 1893

FAR away from my native Land, my bitter indignation as a *Welshwoman* prompts me to reproach you, you *bad, wicked, false, treacherous* Old Man! for your iniquitous scheme to *rob* and overthrow the dearly-beloved Old Church of my Country. You have no conscience, but I pray that God may even yet give you one that will sorely *smart* and trouble you before you die. You pretend to be religious, you old hypocrite! that you may more successfully pander to the evil passions of the lowest and most ignorant of the Welsh people. But you neither care for nor respect the principles of Religion, or you would not distress the minds of all true Christian people by instigating a mob to commit the awful sin of Sacrilege. You think you will shine in History, but it will be a notoriety similar to that of *Nero*. I see someone pays you the unintentional compliment of comparing you to Pontius Pilate, and I am sorry, for Pilate, though a political time-server, was, with all his faults, a very respectable man in comparison with you. And he did not, like you, profess the Christian Religion. You are certainly *clever*. So also is your lord and master the Devil. And I cannot regard it as sinful to hate and despise you, any more than it is sinful to abhor him. So, with full measure of contempt and detestation, accept these compliments from

A DAUGHTER OF OLD WALES

SIR FRANK LOCKWOOD (1846–97)

Lockwood had already made himself a name at the Bar when he was elected Liberal member for York. His career in politics was eminently successful for, nine years after taking his seat, he was appointed Solicitor-General. His pen-pictures from the House were highly amusing, and the imaginary "Moses" whom he depicted in hurriedly drawn sketches on scraps of paper is no less delightful.

TO HIS SISTER, MRS. ATKINSON

SEPTEMBER 18, '72

My dear Loo, I trust it is well with yourself, John, and the childer. It is an off-day. We are resting on our legal oars after a prolonged and determined struggle yesterday. Know! that near our native hamlet is the level of Hatfield Chase, whereon are numerous drains. Our drain (speaking from the Corporation of Hatfield Chase point of view) we have stopped, for our own purposes. Consequently, the adjacent lands have been flooded, are flooded, and will continue to be flooded. The landed gentry wish us to remove our dam, saying that if we don't they won't be worth a d——n. We answer that we don't care a d——n.

This interesting case has been simmering in the law courts since 1820. The landed gentry got a verdict in their favour at the last Lincoln Assizes, but find themselves little the better, as we have appealed, and our dam still reigns triumphant. Yesterday an application was made to the Judge to order our dam to be removed. In the absence of Mellor, I donned my forensic armour and did battle for the Corporation. After two hours' hard fighting we adjourned for a week; in the meantime the floods may rise, and the winds blow. The farmers yelled with rage when they heard that the dam had got a week's respite. I rather fancy that they will yell louder on Tuesday, as I hope to win another bloodless victory. It is a pretty wanton sport, the cream of the joke being that the dam is no good to us or to anybody else, and we have no real objection to urge against its removal, excepting that such a measure would be informal, and contrary to the law as laid down some hundred years ago by an old gentleman who never heard of a steam-engine, and who would have fainted at the sight of a telegraph post.   As we have the most money on our side, I trust we shall win in the end.   None of this useful substance, however, comes my way, as it is Mellor's work.   But I hope to reap some advantage from it, both as to experience and introduction. I make no apology for troubling you with this long narration.   I wish it to sink into your mind, and into that of your good husband.   Let it be warning to you and yours.   And never by any chance become involved in any difficulties which will bring you into a court of law of higher jurisdiction than a police court.   An occasional "drunk and disorderly" will do you no harm, and only cost you 5s.   Beyond a little indulgence of this kind—Beware!   In all probability I shall be in the North in a few weeks.   Sessions commence next month.   I will write to the Mum this week.

> With best love to all, I am,
> Your affectionate brother,
> FRANK LOCKWOOD

TO HIS SISTER AGNES

> 1 HARE COURT, TEMPLE: 28–11–72

MY DEAR AGNES, I do not know whether you have ever heard of a strike.   They are very fashionable just now—policemen strike, curates strike, organ-grinders strike.   In fact, all people that on earth do dwell strike, excepting, of course, lawyers, who know better, and act accordingly.   But of all the strikes, the one which strikes my mind as being the most disgraceful is the one which I have endeavoured to depict on the other side of this page.   Fancy, a girls' school has struck.   They put the globes into the grand piano, and hung the harp on a willow tree in the back garden.   As I passed by the house, and saw what I have drawn, I thought of you, and at once sat down in the middle of the road to write this letter.   As I see the water-cart coming round the corner, I think I had better get up.   So with best love,

> Believe me, your affectionate brother,
> FRANK

HOUSE OF COMMONS, FEBRUARY 26, 1894

MY DEAR MADGIE, Moses is here to-night, sitting next to Mr. Glad-

stone.   He is **very conceited** about it.   I am sorry you won't see Lucy in her finery.

Your loving father,
FRANK LOCKWOOD

THE EARL OF ROSEBERY (1847–1929)

The Liberal statesman wrote the first of these letters on the death of his friend Sir Frank Lockwood. The second letter acknowledges receipt of what he praises as "the second biography in the English language."

As a crushing reply it would be difficult to find anything to parallel the note to the gentleman who described himself as "a writer of political tracts and family short stories."

TO AUGUSTINE BIRRELL

MY DEAR BIRRELL, You ask me to write something about Frank Lockwood. It is a labour of love, but a labour of despair. The more I think of it, the more hopeless a task it seems, to convey to those who did not know him what he was to his friends and to society at large. For his position reminds me faintly of that which was occupied by George Selwyn in the last century, who seems to have possessed a fascination, different perhaps in kind, but alike in effect.

What, then, constituted Lockwood's charm? I believe it to be impossible to express this in words, but one may at least touch on one or two obvious points.

In the first place he was a splendid specimen of humanity, and humanity loves to see itself well embodied. His tall, powerful frame, his fine head crowned with picturesque, premature white hair, his handsome, healthy face, with its sunshine of genial, not vapid, good-nature, made him notable everywhere. So powerful was this personality that his entrance into a room seemed to change the whole complexion of the company, and I often fancied that he could dispel a London fog by his presence.

Secondly, his humour, whether in conversation or in caricature, was signal and memorable, for it was as spontaneous and exuberant, though not so brilliant, as Sydney Smith's. Whether any record can give the least idea of it seems to me more than doubtful. Considered apart from the circumstances of the occasion and the personality of the man, his sayings might seem little worthy of publication, and indeed, as I write, I can think of nothing of his that is really worthy of separate record. It would seem as if his reputation for humour will have to rest on his drawings and on the affidavits of his friends.

But there was this about his humour, which is probably unique— it never made him an enemy. He was too much of a man, and too successful a man, not to have had enemies (though I never came across one); but I feel confident that his humour, whether expressed in speech or in drawing, never made him one. Those whom he most loved to rally cherished him all the more. It was, indeed, the peculiarity of his pencil to delineate the humorous aspects of his intimate friends. There was probably an unconscious motive for this—that of these men he was sure —they knew him and would not misunderstand him. This was his instinct: they would appreciate his motive; and to make this quite clear he would frequently associate with the sketch his own portrait, the most burlesque of all.

His sketches speak for themselves, as can be seen in the exhibition which was lately held. But even these do not explain themselves as do those of Gillray or Rowlandson or Leech or the Doyles (to cite only dead artists). To understand their charm, one must understand the appositeness, the spontaneousness, the apropos. One must put oneself in the position of a correspondent opening a letter in the welcome hand-writing and finding a note summed up with an irresistible sketch; or a lawyer who has had a heavy case enlivened by a succession of droll portraits; or a colleague in the House of Commons who has seen a tedious orator reproduced on a notice paper during a prosaic speech. Frank Lockwood's sketches were the oases of serious life, and it would often need a column of letterpress to explain their full bearing and popularity.

So, too, with his jokes. Written down in black and white they are not like Sheridan's or Canning's, which make the librarian laugh as he takes down the volumes in which they are enshrined. Nor are they like those of Disraeli or Luttrell, elaborate, saturnine, desperately cynical. But then did Disraeli or Luttrell's conversation ever make anyone laugh? Lockwood's well-spring was mirth—his mirth gushed out of him and affected everyone else—it was a general enjoyment, irresistible, contagious, eminently natural. He was of the order of wit who, enjoying his joke himself, conveys at the same time his enjoyment to others. But each was possessed by this exuberant irrepressible drollery. Let me say this last capital word: Lockwood was never coarse.

But, as I said, I can give no specimens. I am writing here alone, far from England, and cannot appeal to his friends for assistance; nor would I if I could, as you want the single impression that he made no one individual. I can only appeal to all who met him as to the impression he made on them as to the quality of his humour, and (to use a dubious expression) as to his magnetism. For one instance I would appeal to those who dined on a certain occasion with Lord Burghclere, if they will ever forget the war of wits between Lockwood and Haldane and yourself. It is pitiful not to be able to quote, for I seem to give away the case, but I cannot; I can only again point to George Selwyn as some parallel to our friend, and remind you that his reputation certainly does not rest on his surviving letters and jokes.

Withal, there is something more to be said of Lockwood which could also be said of Selwyn—he was a good friend. When a man who has shown exceptional qualities of head (especially that of acute and humorous perception) displays also exceptional qualities of heart, he irresistibly attracts his fellow-men. This was the final, subtlest touch of Lockwood's fascination, for it gave the charm to his manners. His manners were the mirror of his soul: the clear, pure, sympathetic mirror of a clear, pure, sympathetic soul.

But I am running on—saying nothing but what all who knew him know as well as I do, and what those who did not know him will not appreciate. He is gone, cut off in the flower of a vigorous life, in the spring-tide of success, in the triumph of popularity. What that means to those who loved him, only those can realize who witnessed the congregation of sorrow that assembled at the little Chelsea church to bid him farewell.

Yours sincerely,
R.

TO SIR GEORGE TREVELYAN

HOTEL BRISTOL, PARIS, OCT. 1, 1908

MY DEAR G., As I passed through London yesterday I found your precious gift, for which I return my warmest thanks. Apart from your friendship, I am glad to receive from you the second biography in the English language, which has this advantage over the first, that its author is not a Boswell, and is free from his degradations and humiliations and fatuous-fawning. One would not be a Boswell to have written his immortal book; one would gladly be a Trevelyan even had he not written the Life of Lord Macaulay.

And yet Boswell, a ludicrous composition of every sort of imbecility, with his instinct of delineation and his consciousness of a great achievement, is profoundly interesting. I was asked to unveil his statue at

Lichfield, and wish that I had done it, as the task seems to have been the final cause of poor Churton Collins's suicide. It would not have driven me to take my own life, but I should have found it difficult to place Boswell's on the heroic plane required for such an effigy, though I am a devout admirer of his incomparable portraiture.

I am on my way to Naples, and if I find it hotter there than here shall certainly be cooked.

yours ever
R.

TO A WRITER OF POLITICAL TRACTS

DEAR SIR, I have received your letter this morning.

I am at a loss to understand the following sentence,

"Your promised aid in recognition of services rendered."

This contains two propositions which are quite new to me.

I am, Yours respectfully,
R.

ARTHUR JAMES, EARL OF BALFOUR (1848–1930)

*Here is the famous Balfour Note, written by the Conservative states-
man on behalf of the British Government and addressed to the French
Ambassador and the representatives of other European Powers. It
would be difficult to find a complicated case put with greater clarity.*

FOREIGN OFFICE, AUGUST 1ST, 1922

YOUR EXCELLENCY, As your Excellency is aware, the general question
of the French debt to this country has not as yet been the subject of any
formal communication between the two Governments, nor are His
Majesty's Government anxious to raise it at the present moment.
Recent events, however, leave them little choice in the matter, and they
feel compelled to lay before the French Government their views on
certain aspects of the situation created by the present condition of
international indebtedness.

Speaking in general terms, the war debts, exclusive of interest, due to
Great Britain at the present moment amount in the aggregate to about
£3,400,000,000, of which Germany owes £1,450,000,000, Russia
£650,000,000, and our Allies £1,300,000,000. On the other hand,
Great Britain owes the United States about a quarter of this sum—say,
£850,000,000 at par of exchange, together with interest accrued since
1919.

No international discussion has yet taken place on the unexampled
situation partially disclosed by these figures; and, pending a settlement
which would go to the root of the problem, His Majesty's Government
have silently abstained from making any demands upon their Allies,
either for the payment of interest or the repayment of capital. But, if
action in the matter has hitherto been deemed inopportune, this is not
because His Majesty's Government either underrate the evils of the
present state of affairs or because they are reluctant to make large sacrifices
to bring it to an end. On the contrary, they are prepared, if such a
policy formed part of a satisfactory international settlement, to remit all
the debts due to Great Britain by our Allies in respect of loans, or by
Germany in respect of reparations. Recent events, however, make such
a policy difficult of accomplishment.

855

With the most perfect courtesy, and in the exercise of their undoubted rights, the American Government have required this country to pay the interest accrued since 1919 on the Anglo-American debt, to convert it from an unfunded to a funded debt, and to repay it by sinking fund in twenty-five years. Such a procedure is clearly in accordance with the original contract. His Majesty's Government make no complaint of it. They recognize their obligations, and are prepared to fulfil them. But, evidently, they cannot do so without profoundly modifying the course which, in different circumstances, they would have wished to pursue. They cannot treat the repayment of the Anglo-American loan as if it were an isolated incident in which only the United States of America and Great Britain had any concern. It is but one of a connected series of transactions in which this country appears sometimes a debtor, sometimes as creditor; and, if our undoubted obligations as a debtor are to be enforced, our not less undoubted rights as a creditor cannot be left wholly in abeyance.

His Majesty's Government do not conceal the fact that they adopt this change of policy with the greatest reluctance. It is true that Great Britain is owed more than it owes, and that if all inter-Allied war debts were paid the British Treasury would on balance be a large gainer by the transaction. But can the present world situation be looked at only from this narrow financial standpoint? It is true that many of the Allied and Associated Powers are as between each other creditors or debtors or both, but they were and are much more. They were partners in the greatest international effort ever made in the cause of freedom, and they are still partners in dealing with some at least of its results. Their debts were incurred, their loans were made, not for the separate advantage of particular States, but for a great purpose common to them all, and that purpose has been in the main accomplished. To generous minds it can never be agreeable, although for reasons of State it may perhaps be necessary to regard the monetary aspect of this great event as a thing apart, to be torn from its historical setting and treated as no more than an ordinary commercial dealing between traders who borrow and capitalists who lend. There are, moreover, reasons of a different order to which I have already referred which increase the distaste with which His Majesty's Government adopt so fundamental an alteration in method of dealing with loans to Allies.

The economic ills from which the world is suffering are due to many causes, moral and material, which are quite outside the scope of this dispatch. But among them must certainly be reckoned the weight of international indebtedness, with all its unhappy effects upon credit and exchange, upon national production and international trade. The peoples of all countries long for a speedy return to the normal. But how can the normal be reached while conditions so abnormal are permitted to prevail? And how can these conditions be cured by any remedies that seem at present likely to be applied? For, evidently, the policy hitherto pursued by this country of refusing to make demands upon its debtors is only tolerable so long as it is generally accepted. It cannot be right that one partner in the common enterprise should recover all that she has lent, and that another, while recovering nothing, should be required to pay all that she has borrowed. Such a procedure is contrary to every principle of natural justice, and cannot be expected to commend itself to the people of this country.

They are suffering from an unparalleled burden of taxation, from an immense diminution in national wealth, from serious want of employment, and from the severe curtailment of useful expenditure. These evils are courageously borne, but were they to be increased by an arrangement which, however legitimate, is obviously one-sided, the British taxpayer would inevitably ask why he should be singled out to bear a burden which others are bound to share.

To such a question there can be but one answer, and I am convinced that Allied opinion will admit its justice. But while His Majesty's Government are thus regretfully constrained to request the French Government to make arrangements for dealing, to the best of their ability, with Anglo-French loans, they desire to explain that the amount of interest and repayment for which they ask depends, not so much on what France and other Allies owe to Great Britain, as on what Great Britain has to pay America.

The policy favoured by His Majesty's Government is, as I have already observed, that of surrendering their share of German reparation and writing off, through one great transaction, the whole body of inter-Allied indebtedness. But if this be found impossible of accomplishment, we wish it to be understood that we do not in any event desire to make a profit out of any less satisfactory arrangement. In no circumstances do we propose to ask more from our debtors than is necessary to pay to our creditors. And while we do not ask for more, all will admit that we can hardly be content with less; for it should not be forgotten, though it sometimes is, that our liabilities were incurred for others, not for ourselves.

The food, the raw material, the munitions required by the immense naval and military efforts of Great Britain, and half the £2,000,000,000 advanced to Allies were provided, not by means of foreign loans, but by internal borrowing and war taxation. Unfortunately, a similar policy was beyond the power of other European nations; appeal was therefore made to the Government of the United States, and under the arrangement then arrived at the United States insisted, in substance if not in form, that though our Allies were to spend the money, it was only on our security that they were prepared to lend it. This co-operative effort was of infinite value to the common cause, but it cannot be said that the rôle assigned in it to this country was one of special privilege or advantage.

Before concluding, I may be permitted to offer one further observation in order to make still clearer the spirit in which His Majesty's Government desire to deal with the thorny problem of international indebtedness.

In an early passage of this dispatch I pointed out that this, after all, is not a question merely between Allies; ex-enemy countries are also involved, for the greatest of all international debtors is Germany. Now, His Majesty's Government do not suggest that either as a matter of justice or expediency Germany should be relieved of her obligation to the other Allied States. They speak only for Great Britain, and they content themselves with saying once again that so deeply are they convinced of the economic injury inflicted on the world by the existing state of things that this country would be prepared (subject to the just claims of other parts of the Empire) to abandon all further right to German reparation and all claims to repayment by Allies provided that this renunciation formed part of a general plan by which this great problem could be dealt with as a whole, and find a satisfactory solution. A general settlement would, in their view, be of more value to mankind than any gains that could accrue even from the most successful enforcement of legal obligations.

I have, etc.,

BALFOUR

ALEXANDER MURDOCK MACKAY (1849–90)

Mackay went to Uganda with the original party of the Church Missionary Society, who were sent out largely as a result of Stanley's letter to the "Daily Telegraph" challenging Christendom to plant a mission in Uganda. Mackay never returned, but spent the remainder of his life teaching "that true wisdom which alone can elevate a man from a brute to a son of God." His last message from Uganda embodies one from Mwanga, a hitherto cruel heathen king, who asks for teachers to preach the Gospel to his people.

MSALALA, JUNE 6TH, 1885

YOUR very welcome letter of March 3rd has just come. How many letters you have sent me since last August I cannot tell, as I am waiting for them to be sent back here from Kagei, where they have gone.

All these long, weary months, how have we longed for news from home! Trouble and danger and illness with gloomy prospects would have been much relieved, had we got a line or two from our friends; but that could not be. Still we were borne up in it all by a mightier Hand than our own. And now I am here alive and well, to ask you to join us in praising our Father in heaven, who has not left us even in great danger, and who is in it all, leading us closer to Himself, and guiding His own work through blood and fire.

Our first martyrs have won the martyr's crown. On January 30th three Christian lads were burnt alive, after being terribly mutilated, for their reception of and adherence to the faith of Jesus Christ. They were snatched from our very presence, accused of no crime but that they were learning from us, and first tortured, then roasted alive.

Both Ashe and I suffered a deal of personal violence, but that was soon over, and was nothing to the anxiety of mind which we suffered on account of the cruel death of the dear lads, and the threats of determined persecution against the whole of the native Christians; the threats of robbery and expulsion of ourselves; and later on a rebellion of the chiefs, whose aim was to make a complete end of us. But by a sharp stroke the king arrested the ringleaders and deposed the others. Since then we have had less to fear; and though the king is young and unstable, he has again and again asserted his determination to stand by us, probably because in doing so he finds a way of escape from the demands made upon him by the old chiefs and sorcerers, which he finds irksome.

There are some of the chiefs by no means friendly to us, but doubtless their day of power will be short.   Of course, as in many similar cases, their suspicion of us arises from pure ignorance.   We only must endeavour to enlighten them; but whether the powers are friendly or not, we must put no confidence in their favour or dislike.   The work of God will stand and grow quite independently of their patronage or opposition.

I believe that a work has been begun in Uganda which has its origin in the power of God, and which never can be uprooted by all the forces of evil.

Some young Christians are very bold, sometimes I think more courageous than prudent.   While many of them have gone into hiding through natural alarm for their lives, others we have to urge to keep out of the way, knowing that they are in great danger.   But whether their retirement has been voluntary or compulsory, I myself do not know of a single case in which any one preferred to draw back and renounce Christianity.

Doubtless you will recall passages in Christian history in Europe, when persecution seemed to be infectious, and many were led to stand together from feelings of a new enthusiasm.   History but repeats itself. The powers arrayed against Christianity in Nero's reign are just the same as those fighting against it to-day in Central Africa.   It is with the same weapons, too, that the battle has to be fought and won.

Your remarks on the Soudan campaign I cannot agree with.   The Madhi, a Mohammedan Messiah, cannot, by the nature of his claims, rest content with only the Soudan, or even part of it.   His demands are like those of Christianity, " No compromise."   It is not any more to-day a struggle for liberty and independence than were the wars of Mohammed and his successors the Caliphs.   They may use these words, but we know they are false.   The question is simply a mutiny among the Moham- medans.   Who is the true successor of the Prophet, the new Mahdi or the Sultan of Turkey?   We care nothing for the religious pretensions of either the one or the other; but when the problem has to be solved by arms, and has far-reaching influences through the whole Mohammedan world, we have a right to reduce the usurping power, which is a wild fanaticism.   What liberty will the poor Soudanese have under the Mahdi and his successors?   Surely such Governors as Gordon, acting in the name of the Khedive, will exercise a more humane sway on these great provinces than a wild fanatic.

We know what Islam has been in the past, and to-day it is not different. It has been the ruin of many fair lands, and besides has this strange venom in it, that people may, with comparative ease, be led to embrace Christianity when simply heathen, but when Islam has put its vile name on them, though ever so superficially, there is no doing anything with them after that. The universal failure of missions to Moslems throughout the world proves this incontrovertibly. Since I came to the East, I have been familiar with the genius of the Moslem creed, as I never was in England.

Its sole reliance for conversion has ever been the sword, and that power has done everything for it in the past. Christianity cannot use these means for its promulgation, and wherever it does it ceases to be Christianity. But the sword has ever been used of God in subduing that terrible evil, and thus preparing the way for teachers of Christianity to use peaceful powers of persuasion.

Gordon was right in disclaiming an army to relieve himself. It is the loyal, peaceful people of the Soudan that must be relieved from their enemies, the Mahdists. But to take them out of the country is not to relieve them, any more than loyal Irish should be taken away from their homes because the Fenians demand to be allowed to rule. The surest way, and the most merciful way to protect the good is to crush by a sharp stroke the indomitable evil.

TO HIS FATHER

UGANDA, 28TH JUNE, 1886

AGAIN I have sorrowful news to tell, even more distressing than before. Only a month ago a violent persecution against the Christians broke out, and they have been murdered right and left. The origin was an act of splendid disobedience and brave resistance to this negro Nero's orders to a page of his, who absolutely refused to be made the victim of an unmentionable abomination. The lad was a Christian, and was threatened with instant death, but was ultimately only cruelly beaten. But there the matter did not end. "These Christians are disobedient, and learn rebellion from the white man. I shall kill them all." So said our Nero. At once the order was given for their arrest. Those in the palace grounds, and the more conspicuous and well-known Christians, were first seized. About a dozen were hacked to pieces the first day, and their members left lying in all directions on the road.   Bands were sent out to catch and kill.   Over thirty were thus slain.   As in the case of the murder of Bishop Hannington, we were helpless, and expected every moment our own arrest.   We cannot yet realize the awful loss we have sustained.   Nearly all our best friends arrested suddenly, and murdered almost before our very eyes.   For the scattered remnant we must appeal to Christian England, and for all who may yet embrace our faith.   We ourselves, too, are in a position of the gravest danger.   This tyrant is rash and vain, and fancies that there is no power in the world that can call his vilest and most cruel acts in question.   If this part of the world is longer neglected, and if effective measures are not at once taken to bring this bloodshed to an end, the indelible disgrace of abandoning our fellow Christians to torture and the stake will remain a blot on every land of freedom.   We believe it to be necessary that we be enabled to leave this country—our withdrawal will only be temporary—until this eccentric potentate be brought to reason.   He has given out that he means to hold us as hostages, fearing that the white men will be upon him for the murder of the bishop with his fifty porters, besides all his other cruelties.   It is not now the cry of the heathen for the gospel, but the eloquent, unremitting appeal of severed limbs and writhing bodies for help and deliverance from their persecutors.   There is a greater bondage than slavery to be grappled with here, and it must be grappled with.   If single power will interfere to demand freedom of faith for East Africa let the concert of Europe take up the subject, and proclaim an East African Free State, as has been done on the Congo.   If on the Congo, why not on the Nile?

LORD RANDOLPH CHURCHILL (1849–94)

Lord Randolph was son of the sixth Duke of Marlborough. He entered Parliament in 1874 as a Conservative and subsequently was a member of Lord Salisbury's Cabinet and leader of the House of Commons. In this letter, written at the age of 14, he describes the wedding of the Prince of Wales (Edward VII) to Princess Alexandra of Denmark.

TO HIS FATHER

ETON COLLEGE, MARCH 11, 1863

IT was not my fault that my letter did not reach you before, for I gave it to the servant the same day to post, and she forgot all about it. I have written to you about the reception on Saturday; I will now tell you about the fireworks on Monday and the wedding yesterday.

On Monday night we were all ordered to be present in the school-yard at nine o'clock. When we were all there we formed fours and marched up Windsor with a large body of police before us (which rather spoilt the fun) to clear the way. Then we got into the Home Park by the South Western Station, just under the windows of the State Rooms, and there we stood all the time the fireworks were going on. I luckily had the forethought to take my great-coat, or else I do not believe I should have got home, it was so dreadfully cold. The fireworks were very pretty, only there was such an awful lot of rockets and too few catherine-wheels and all that sort of fun.

The Princess Alexandra having never seen fireworks before, they were on Monday night instead of on Tuesday night, because she wanted to see them. We did not get home till nearly twelve o'clock. There was no illumination that night. Yesterday morning was a whole holiday without any early school or chapel. We were all mustered in the school-yard about eleven o'clock, and then marched up Windsor into the Castle by Henry VIIIth's gate. There we had to stand for a tremendous time without anything coming. (It luckily was fine and not very cold.) At last the first procession came; it was the King of Denmark and all those people. We had a beautiful view of all the people. Then we had to wait about a quarter of an hour, and then came the Princess Royal. She was sitting on our side, and she bowed away as hard as she could go. (I think her neck must have been stiff.) And then came the Prince; he looked extremely gracious. I never saw him put his hat on, and he held it about an inch from his head, and kept bowing, always in the same place. And last of all came the Princess. And then there was such a row, in spite of the Queen's express commands that there was to be no cheering. I never heard such an awful noise in all my life. I think, if the Queen heard it, she must have had a headache for a long time afterwards. We were not allowed to go into the chapel, or into the courtyard by the chapel. A whole lot of us charged the policemen and soldiers to get in, but it was no use; they managed to keep us back that time. But we had our revenge afterwards. After they had come back we went back into college. Then at three o'clock we all came to see the Princess go away. She did not come till about a quarter past four in the afternoon—the Prince and Princess in an open carriage; and then came the squashing. We all rushed after the carriage. (I was right in the front of the charge; it was a second Balaclava.) Nothing stood before us; the policemen charged in a body, but they were knocked down. There was a chain put across the road, but we broke that; several old *genteel* ladies tried to stop me, but I snapped my fingers in their face and cried "Hurrah!" and "What larks!" I frightened some of them horribly. There was a wooden palisade put up at the station (it was the Great Western), but we broke it down; and there, to my unspeakable grief, I was bereaved of a portion of my clothing, viz. my hat. Somebody knocked it off. I could not stop to pick it up. I shrieked out a convulsive "Oh, my hat!" and was then borne on. I got right down to the door of the carriage where the Prince of Wales was, wildly shouting "Hurrah!" He bowed to me, I am perfectly certain; but I shrieked louder. I am sure, if the Princess did not possess very strong nerves, she would have been frightened; but all she did was to smile blandly. At last the train moved off while the band played "God save the Queen." I am sure I wonder there were no accidents, we were all so close to the carriage. There I was, left in the station "hatless." I met Lord Churchill there, who told me Lady Churchill was in waiting. I was introduced to lots of soldiers by one of the masters who caught me. And then I began to search for my hat; but it was in vain, for I never saw it again. I was told to get another one, for I had no other to wear. At last I got home, and in the evening we went out again to see the illumination. There was not much to see. I think I have given you a full account of the wedding and the reception.

Believe me to remain,
Your affectionate son,
RANDOLPH CHURCHILL

P.S. My holidays begin on the 27th March.

ROBERT LOUIS STEVENSON (1850–94)

The letters of R. L. S. and his wife have long been treasured by all who love to read beautiful things well said. Those reprinted here are, perhaps, in a lighter vein than some of their more exquisite work; but they are characteristic of the writers.

TO EDMUND GOSSE

THE COTTAGE (LATE THE LATE MISS M'GREGOR'S)
CASTLETON OF BRAEMAR, AUGUST 10, 1881

MY DEAR GOSSE, Come on the 24th, there is a dear fellow. Everybody else wants to come later, and it will be a godsend for, sir—Yours sincerely.

You can stay as long as you behave decently, and are not sick of, sir—Your obedient, humble servant.

We have family worship in the home of, sir—Yours respectfully.

Braemar is a fine country, but nothing to (what you will also see) the maps of, sir—Yours in the Lord.

A carriage and two spanking hacks draw up daily at the hour of two before the house of, sir—Yours truly.

The rain rains and the winds do beat upon the cottage of the late Miss Macgregor and of, sir—Yours affectionately.

It is to be trusted that the weather may improve ere you know the halls of, sir—Yours emphatically.

All will be glad to welcome you, not excepting, sir—Yours ever.

You will now have gathered the lamentable intellectual collapse of, sir—Yours indeed.

And nothing remains for me but to sign myself, sir—Yours,

ROBERT LOUIS STEVENSON

N.B. Each of these clauses has to be read with extreme glibness, coming down whack upon the "Sir." This is very important. The fine stylistic inspiration will else be lost.

I commit the man who made, the man who sold, and the woman who supplied me with my present excruciating gilt nib to that place where the worm never dies.

The reference to a deceased Highland lady (tending as it does to foster unavailing sorrow) may be with advantage omitted from the address, which would therefore run—The Cottage, Castleton of Braemar.

TO HIS FATHER

2 SULYARDE TERRACE, TORQUAY, THURSDAY (APRIL, 1866)

RESPECTED PATERNAL RELATIVE, I write to make a request of the most moderate nature. Every year I have cost you an enormous—nay, elephantine—sum of money for drugs and physician's fees, and the most expensive time of the twelve months was March.

But this year the biting Oriental blasts, the howling tempests, and the general ailments of the human race have been successfully braved by yours truly.

Does not this deserve remuneration?

I appeal to your charity, I appeal to your generosity, I appeal to your justice, I appeal to your accounts, I appeal, in fine, to your purse.

My sense of generosity forbids the receipt of more—my sense of justice forbids the receipt of less—than half-a-crown. Greeting from, Sir, your most affectionate and needy son,

R. STEVENSON

MRS. STEVENSON TO SIDNEY COLVIN

TAIOHAE HIVA-OA
MARQUESAS ISLAND,
AUGUST 18, 1888

DEAR AND NEVER-FORGOTTEN CUSTODIAN, Oh, that you and a few— a very few friends were with us in these enchanted Isles to stay for ever and ever, and live and die with these delightful miscalled savages. That they are cannibals may be true, but that is only a freak of fashion, like the taste for decayed game, and not much more unpleasant. Last evening we had a savage queen to dine with us; I say savage, because her son, who came with her, continually referred to themselves as "we savages." The old lady has presided at many a sacrificial feast, and ordered many a poor witch to instant execution, and yet a more gracious, affection-compelling person I did not expect to see until I again met Lady Shelley, of whom she greatly reminded us. Not a word of any tongue could she speak but her own, and she was deaf besides, but we managed to pass more than three hours very pleasantly in her charming society. She wore a white dress made like a night-gown, of very fine material, no underclothes, and a white china crêpe shawl heavily embroidered and fringed.   Her hands and what could be seen of her feet and legs were elaborately tattooed.   Even Mrs. Stevenson has grown to dislike the look of untattoed hands.   The queen, they say, is entirely covered with the most beautiful tattooing that has ever been done in the Islands. On Monday next, Stanilao, the heir apparent, has invited us to a picnic. We are to go on horses, natives having gone on ahead to prepare a meal. I am rather curious as to what will take place, as the point of interest, a balancing rock, has been tabooed for many years, though it stands in full sight of the village, and even Stanilao has never been near it.   He made a little speech to us last evening thanking us formally for our sympathetic treatment of "his savages."

It was a sad business when we left Amaho.   We had eight particular friends there whom, I suppose, we shall never see again.   When we first arrived they swarmed over the vessel like flies, clothed in breech cloths and tattooing only.   For their farewell visit the beachcomber had made them all white trousers and shirts.   Every man was as clean as a new pin, and shining with cocoanut oil, their finger nails, even, as carefully looked after as our own.   We gave them what keepsakes we could find among our things, and they presented us with tappa cloth beaten out of the bark, oranges, cocoanuts prepared for drinking, some rare shells, and to Lloyd one of them gave a carving done on the bone of one of his ancestors.   We had gingerbread and a glass of rum all round, the whole party took a last walk through the vessel, we shook hands, and parted.   Hoka, the beautiful dancer and the most graceful person I have ever seen, dropped all his usual airs and graces, and sat most of the time staring on the floor just as we do when we are very unhappy and distressed; sighing heavily, when he had shaken hands he turned his head away, and never once looked back.   Typee, the chief, on the contrary, stood up in the midst of his men, waving his hand and making gestures of farewell as long as he could see us.   As the canoe went off the captain saluted Typee, when all the men uncovered.   Our cannibal friend, Koamoa, was, I am sorry to say, too drunk to come aboard, and was left on the beach hanging over the branch of a tree. It seems that a Corsican had come over in a boat with a demijohn of rum, which was more than the old chief could stand.   Our own Hoka, I fear, believes in eating one's enemies.   He had had a quarrel with the Corsican, who called him "cochon" and "sauvage."   Hoka's reply was "you are more of a savage than I am," whereupon the man struck him a boxer's blow of which Hoka had no understanding.   He said he was going to get a gun soon, and then he could go over to the Island where the Corsican lives and shoot him, after which he meant to cut off and eat one of his arms. In the next Island we are going to visit, a man whom the whole population hated was killed for vengeance. The question was how should every man have a taste of his enemy without the authorities finding it out. This was solved by filling matchboxes with the cooked flesh, and passing them about. I think the combination of the civilized matchbox and the "long pig" very interesting.

Three months ago, a little boy was called for at the school by a couple of people who were decoying him into a quiet spot for the purpose of killing and eating him, but he discovered their vile intentions in time to call for help. Three of the townspeople have disappeared mysteriously: they are supposed to have fallen victims to private vengeance. Lloyd has had given him by a native woman an ornament to wear in the war dance. It is composed of locks of women's hair made into a sort of gigantic fringe. As many as ten women were killed to make this ghastly ornament, their bodies being cooked for the dancers' feast.

I am glad to tell you that quite suddenly Louis' health took a change for the better, and he is now almost as well as he ever was in his life. It has been a mistake about the cold places, warmth and hot sun is what he needs. Certainly we have found the right place for him; and we both love it. It is hard that we should ever have to go away. Stanilao says that Dominique is still better, and if we conclude to come back here to stay that is the Island for us. I think it very nice of Stanilao to praise another Island when he would so much like to have us here. Our next point is Hiva-oa, for which we start in three days, taking with us a most delightful person called Frère Michel, who builds churches not to be conceived of. I have made awful drawings of one which will delight your soul, and fill you with pleased laughter. My dearest love to you, best beloved friends. Louis is away walking in the hills, Lloyd playing on the fiddle.—Ever yours affectionately,

F. V. DE G. STEVENSON

THE SAME TO SIDNEY COLVIN AND MRS. SITWELL

HONOLULU, JUNE 18, 1889

MY DEAR ONES, This is about the last chance for a word of good-bye. The seachests are all corded up, Mr. Strong is just finishing a last transparency for the magic lantern, Louis is resting prior to the fatigue of bidding farewell to his gracious majesty (Kalakaua), and we are all in our travelling clothes, while Ah Foo scans the horizon for what he can clap his eyes on. I wish you could see the preparations Ah Foo and Lloyd have made in case of shipwreck. Mysterious parcels of garden seeds and carpenter's tools are stowed away in all sorts of inaccessible places. I am sure they will both be disappointed if we are not cast ashore on a desolate island, though I believe Ah Foo would really prefer to trust to his own hands unaided by the arts of civilization: he can make fire by rubbing two sticks together; he can catch fish without any hook or line, and bring birds down with a stone, to say nothing of being able to use a bit of stone for a knife or hatchet, in the native fashion, or walk up the stem of the tallest cocoa-nut tree. In fact he is civilized just so much as we should like to have him, and a savage just as far as it is useful. He has fallen heir to rice lands, houses, and bullocks in China, and his presence is urgently demanded by his relatives. After much weeping and tribulation and sleepless nights it was finally arranged that he would start on the cruise with us, remain so long as he was necessary to our comfort, and then branch off towards China.

His is a sad case; he has almost forgotten his own tongue, and has entirely fallen out of sympathy with his own countrymen: he is much more like an emotional pirate in manners and appearance than the suave, soft-speaking elegant gentleman that a man of property in China should be. I am afraid his mother, who seems a stiffly conventional person, will loathe the very sight of him. The second son is holding the property pending Ah Foo's return, and in the meantime is ill-treating and cheating the family. It is that, and not the money that is taking Ah Foo home. He proposes to go home and "lick um my bludder" until he is brought to a proper sense of his duty, then turn over everything to his mother and come back to the white man's country again. I hope he may come back to us, but where may such will-o'-the-wisps be by that time? With you, I trust. Had we known the truth about our dear friend we should not be here now. We only learned it too late, after we were committed to the cruise. That is the only person in the world for whom I should be willing to have Louis sacrifice himself in any way. I do not mean to say that Louis is not continually offering himself up on unworthy altars; but it is not with my consent.

Louis is coming round now to my view of his book of travels, and I think that by the time we arrive in Sydney he will have forgotten entirely that he ever held any other and will look as coldly upon the scientific aspect as ever I have done. It should be the most entrancing reading that man has ever engaged in.

And if you could only see him! I do not think he is much below his own good average of health. If I can only take him back to you like this! But even if that is not to be, for a time he has lived the life of a free man, and that is something gained for him. It is a delight to me beyond words, as it would be to you, to see him, bare-footed, and half clothed, flying about with his usual impetuosity, accompanied by no fear of danger.

I must stop now for other things. With dearest and best love to you all, including our dear Henry James, to whom I hope to write yet this evening.

TO THE SAME

(After the death of R. L. Stevenson.)

I BELIEVE, for him, all is for the best; he went as he wished to go, when he wished to go, leaping off from the highest pinnacle with the great drums beating behind him. Could he have arranged his own life and death how little things would have been changed. With such thoughts I try to console myself and pretend that I am to go on and on indefinitely and always alone; it seems impossible. After all these years of preparation I was not ready when the time came. That very day I said to him, "I am not a coward; for a woman I am brave." Vain words; where is my courage now? I am not altogether selfish in my grief, for I do think of the others who loved him—more particularly of you.

THOMAS SHAW, LORD CRAIGMYLE

Lord Shaw of Dunfermline, as he was when these letters to his daughter were written, was created Baron Craigmyle of Craigmyle in 1929. He was Solicitor-General for Scotland 1894–5, and Lord Advocate 1904–5. He sat in Parliament for the Hawick Division, and as a member of the Scottish Universities Committee of the Privy Council. He is the author of several books, and the "Letters to Isabel" which were published in 1921.

TO HIS DAUGHTER ISABEL

CRAIGMYLE, SEPTEMBER 1, 1919

MY DEAR ISABEL, Alas! This week has brought the news of Mr. Andrew Carnegie's death.

Carnegie had a daring, adventurous spirit, and he was able to punctuate the record of his astounding successes, in business, in finance, in manufacture, with vivid dramatic detail. But I am sure I am one of very many of those whom he gathered about him who heard his record with a rather unintelligent wonder. I once frankly told him so. He was giving an account of an installation of two new blast furnaces, their enormous output, their saving in cost, and the like. I said to him:

"It all sounds very wonderful. But honestly I cannot grasp it: I have no standard by which to measure these things."

"What do you mean?" said he.

"Well," I replied, "how, for instance, do these two blast furnaces compare with the Baird's?"

"I think," he said, "that the output of these two new furnaces alone is equal to the output of all the furnaces in Scotland!"

In short, on all that material side of things, we had, as I say, nothing in common.

Yet he had a great heart; and he had a good heart. Far and wide he voyaged—to Confucius, to Zoroaster, to the world's sages—seeking the truth if haply he might find it. And I do believe that, after all those voyagings, and storms of argufying, and declamatory monologue, into which an uneasiness of mind seemed ever to draw him, that at last his bark landed on the Christian shore. Surely, it could not be otherwise: he revered conscience, sought truth, loved and helped mankind, and was honest. Many a time he was wrathful with me, because I would not yield. But he is gone, and I want you to know that that is my testimony of him.

Of course there were points of contact between us. The most real of these were in our dreams. And there we came together, helping, co-operating, companioning each other. The dream of my life was to have the educational ladder free to the ability of Scotland wherever real ability could be found, down to the humblest and poorest dwelling in the land. That was something for Scotland. And he helped my dream to come true by giving ten millions of dollars for free University education.

The dream of his life was to be the Laird of Pittencrieff, that sweet enclosure of the ruins of monastery and Royal palace from which as a boy he and his townsmen of Dunfermline had been always debarred. His dream came true; at a critical moment he besought my help and I bought for him the picturesque Glen; and he gifted it to the lucky old town. That was something for Dunfermline.

Who says there is no romance in life?

I hope that I was numbered among his friends till the last. But for two years he was unable to re-visit Skibo, and I never visited New York. During that period I learned with deep regret of his failing powers, and I was sad, but not surprised, at having no letter from him.

He was in some ways a quite distinct type of the remarkable man. I never quite understood him. We fished together: but even on that we differed. He had a delusion that a good basket of trout was like a loss of capital and made a loch so much the poorer—a delusion not unnatural to a millionaire and a non-sportsman.

He liked literary men about him: and they listened. Your mother and I once lunched with him at the Langham to meet Mr. and Mrs. Clemens. He got on to a familiar tack and declaimed against people getting mixed up as directors with business they know nothing about, against speculation, and all in favour of a man sticking whole-heartedly to his trade.

At that luncheon we got what I have often thought is a double characteristic of Americans: I mean about their telling of stories. For twenty years the *Century Magazine* was the only magazine that entered my library, just as for your nursery the only one was the *St. Nicholas*. There could hardly be a higher testimonial to the United States of America than that. For a short written story, select in matter, and in treatment vivid, dramatic, and done with, America whips the world. But set an American on his legs, allowing him to pad up a speech with a story, and it is only the special restraint of a forgiving Providence that prevents every auditor making for the door. The detail, the elaboration of nothing at all, the visibility of the point far far off—why, in a country of revolver practice, is it allowed?

Clemens was a good illustration of both sides of it. At lunch he told us a story of a gloom-faced fellow-traveller whom he found to be reading—the "Innocents Abroad"! But before he got to the climax we had to be worked up to the smiling scenery of England, the anxiety of mind of the author, the personal appearance of the reader, and course pursued course in the lunch, and then all was over—all but the story: it was still running.

But now see the other side of it. Some time after that luncheon appeared "Puddenhead Wilson." And there, by the way of preface to one of the chapters, I found that Clemens had put into a tabloid all the doctrine about sense in business of which we had heard so much from Carnegie.

It runs something like this: "The wise man sayeth: 'Put not all thine eggs into one basket.' And the wiser man sayeth, 'Put all thine eggs into one basket, and *watch that basket!*' "

Now a truce to irrelevances. "I have a tale to tell, oh!"

Of course you girls knew the rich man pretty well both at Cluny and at Skibo. Elsie's singing pleased him and so did your violin-playing. He was certainly fond of music, had heard good music in various lands; and he was genuinely anxious to give it a lift as a "sweetness and light" instrument. He used to join with gusto, keeping good time and tune, in any American chorus that was hit on of an evening, but naturally he had no expert knowledge of the subject and he depended in that, as in so many other things, upon his impulses as the motive for his benefactions.

Good impulses they were, however; they leaned to the sentimental side. Great and noble benefactions they were, and of some of them an ungrateful world was not worthy. Naturally, having had so much to do with it, I think that his ten millions of dollars for the Scotch University Trust was the least rash and the most fruitful of them all.

Often and often you have asked me to put down the true story of the origin of that great gift. Well, here goes.

In other letters you have had a peep of what romancers would call the "early struggles." Well, they *were* struggles, and they made a deep impression on my mind. Once I made a singular discovery. In my second year at the University, I happened, one week-end at home in Dunfermline, to be let loose among old books and papers. There were a good many of these about. The notes under my father's beautiful hand showed signs of real scholarship. He had had his bit of Latin, too, in his day, but the necessity of earning a living by the sweat of his brow had shut up for him most of the upper doors of life. Suddenly I came upon a private ledger kept by my mother, and my attention was arrested by a long column of items headed by some title like "Tom's College." There were the entries, advances for board and lodging, advances for books, and then one damning entry froze into my mind. It was "University Class Fees," say, somewhere about fifteen guineas. The column was for five months' session and ran over £100.

She had never whispered a word to me about keeping a record; she had never denied me the money required—absolutely trusting me to disburse it honestly and legitimately—never a complaint had passed her lips, not even when she realized that after working at the law for three years out of four for nothing, I was in for another four or five years at college without earning a shilling, all the on-cost and the upkeep to be out of her slender bank account. Faith and hope and love were her portion, and therewith, and without any blindness to the struggle—therewith she was content.

All the entries except one were honourable; but the entry of "Class Fees" seemed to me, knowing all that it signified to her, to be indefensibly mean. And in the renewing of my vows—for there are such occasions in life, my dear—I vowed that that item should go, that great corporations like Universities should no longer close their doors to those with straitened means, should no longer work their institutions and give their endowments making entrance and enjoyment easy for the rich and relatively harder for the poor.

Were there not, you ask, bursaries, and could not the poor win these? There, my dear, was another hardship, making the inequality cruel. The "well-off" parent had the means to secure for his sons the questionable advantages of cramming or the solid advantages of a full Secondary School education. Thus and thereby even the bulk of the bursaries went past the poor. The world and the world's law seemed on every side against him.

I felt somehow that some universal bursary was required for everyone who had the knowledge and the brains to enable him to matriculate. That was the idea; a universal bursary; won by matriculation; won as a right. Nothing but that could bring strength and restore equality into the system. Otherwise there was more than meanness in it; there was social cruelty and national loss.

So there you are; the whole of these thoughts swept dimly through my mind as I read the modest yet tragic ledger sheet. Of none of them have I seen any reason to repent; nay, time and experience have deepened and strengthened my conviction of their truth, and I have seen them shine and spread until they have become the commonplaces of enlightened statecraft.

They were sizzling in my mind when I entered Parliament, and then one vacation I was fishing on Loch Laggan when suddenly they became very active and vivid. That, so to speak, would be Chapter Two of the University story. What I have written to you this morning may be called Chapter One—what the writers of stories would head, "The Birth of a Notion."

Quite enough at present,

From your very own,

S. OF D.

TO THE SAME

CRAIGMYLE, AUGUST 18, 1920

MY DEAR DAUGHTER ISABEL, Tired of exciting epistles? Well, then, let me write you a restful letter.

These two months in town have been lonely enough in all conscience. Yet the judicial work was engrossing, and it had that interest which sprang from being an aftermath of the Great War.

Why did great vessels, for instance, steam through the darkness without lights, and add in this and many ways new perils to the deep: Why? Simply because they had to, by order of the Admiralty. They and their cargo were precious to our people. Hundreds of millions of pounds of sterling were afloat on seas infested by German submarines. And the enemy had abjured the duties of capture and condemnation of ship and cargo as prize, and of the rescue of shipwrecked passengers and crew. Germany had abandoned the traditions of civilized war and made a new code of terror for the traffic of the sea.

To meet this code, a vast energy of watchfulness was developed by our fleet and a vast energy of heroism by our beloved sailormen: while from places like the Moray Firth, over there across the hills, there went one of the glories of the war—those great crews of mine-sweepers—modest, patient, skilled, unwearied men, who by day and night, in calm and in storm, showed the stuff of which patriotism is made and were the saviours of our country.

All these things, remember, were disciplined. Without that, all would have been lost. Thus there came stern, clever, minute Regulations of the Admiralty, supported alike by prudence, by the common interest, and by the instant sanction of force. Courses were changed: sailing orders were given for traversing great spaces of the sea which in normal times the prudent navigator would avoid: lights on shore and on shipboard were dowsed: vessels were put under convoy—taking their course and points of the compass from its commander. And that commander had the power and had the right to fire on, and to sink, offending, disobedient craft.

This vast new code or counter-code of the sea produced—as every new code does—a crop of problems of its own. So our dear bright friend Sir Samuel Evans earned a great renown, in shaping and applying old codes and new, and so he wore out his brilliant life. And to us in the Privy Council and the House of Lords there came difficulties neither few nor slight in solving puzzles, such as, for instance: which ship was to blame, or were both, for a collision when both were sailing without lights, or under convoy? Did the calamities spring from marine risks, or from warlike operations? and so on and so on; millions hanging in the balance of this way or that in the solutions, with sometimes great insurance corporations in the background, and always in the foreground the most brilliant of advocacy. And even as we fingered the bulky volumes, a hint, a reference, an allusion, would suddenly touch a spring; and, away beyond law cases, and codes and codeless destruction, tragedies unfolded to imagination's eye and ear: the watchers' straining senses, the tearing of the torpedo in the entrails of the innocent, heroic merchantmen, the wrestling with doom, and even

> The cry
> Of some strong swimmer in his agony.

Then in a moment the spring recoiled and one was back again to duty and to legal issues. They were not tiresome, but they were troublesome and tough. And *that*, my dear, must be my excuse if

I have failed to keep my promise to go on writing and telling you about things long past.

. . . .

If I remember rightly, my recountings had not reached the period when you arrived on the scene to brighten all our lives. The legal years of the 'eighties have left few impressions which are vivid. I have no memory for drudgery. I suppose it would be possible by consulting fee-books and the like to make up a kind of record; but with all the respect to some very, very eminent lawyer friends of mine, now deceased, what would be the use of that to any mortal? Was I earning more money from year to year? Were there fine solicitors standing by me? and had they good businesses? and had I compliments from this quarter or rebukes from that? Oh! dear, dear, the idea of any sensible man, even a father, taking the trouble to write down the like of that!

I do not deny that drudgery there was. Yes, indeed; but why not? There are two ways of it to a practising lawyer: either to treat work as duty, and to tackle it accordingly, preserving equanimity and if possible, a gaiety of mind; or to shirk it as an undeserved sentence of penal servitude. This last means "giving in," and I was not brought up that way. Whereas the other way—what happy inducements there were that I should follow it! "Fame," says Milton,

> Fame is the spur that the clear spirit doth raise
> To scorn delights and live laborious days.

There is something in that, no doubt, but not so much as men think. There are two passages in Burns which come nearer to the actual life of the barrister both north and south of the Tweed than most people unacquainted with the early struggles of such men would dream of:

> To gather gear by every wile
> That's justified by honour.

That, of course, stamps character upon achievement. But the other is a tenderer and more inspiring wish:

> To mak' a happy fireside clime
> For weans and wife—
> That's the true pathos and sublime
> Of human life.

"Oh! hoity, toity," exclaim the miraculous persons, applauded by all sorts of affectation and the shallow mind. "We believe in genius;

it is for such that the professions were made; but stuff like that: never!"
And, mark you: all the time they believe nothing of the sort; all the
time they know that hard work, drudgery if you will, and drudgery
manfully faced, that the rub is *there*.

For fame's sake? Well, perhaps so, in one case out of a score.
And the other nineteen cases? What do they say about them? Year
in, year out, the steadfast shouldering of work and care, what was
its secret? Ah! it is the Latin tag that tells the truth: "*Res angustæ
domi.*" Yes, my dear, that is it. That is the secret, that is the spur.
It accounts for the nineteen cases.

Upon the whole, the Bench of the United Kingdom has sufficient
experience to know this, and so has sufficient imagination to feel that
an advocate's task, faithfully performed and thus inspired, demands
and deserves respect, consideration, sympathy. And for that reason,
as well as for the sake of jurisprudence as the marshalled search for
justice, it has always appeared to me that the treatment by a great
Bench of the presentment of an uphill case by a great Bar is a study
in those higher ethics where truth and courtesy are rich and shining
things. And when again, either in the case of judge or counsel, to
knowledge and fidelity are added culture and imagination, then indeed
justice is justified of her children and jurisprudence comes to its own.

Sometimes through the 'eighties and through all that drudgery of
which I have no memory, thoughts of that sort, in the watching and
measuring of judical procedure, drifted through the mind, and ideals
were revealed. "Who is sufficient for these things?" I said it so
often during those toilsome years: and I say so still.

Have I told you nothing in this letter? Have I drifted unwarrant-
ably from what the philosophers call the objective to the subjective?
Well, the mist is on the hills and great clouds are drifting down the
valley from Braemar, and the grouse are too wild, and, as I have been
sitting in the library, my memory has yielded little to recount from a
decade which is blank. So the thoughts have turned inward, and
instead of description and action you have simply musing: musing,
not on the outward bewildering events of to-day's bewildered world,
but musing just as the thoughts deploy from the past and as they are
felt in the quiet by a thankful heart.

Your loving
FATHER

GEORGE BERNARD SHAW

These two very characteristic letters need no comment.

TO THE EDITOR OF THE *PALL MALL GAZETTE*

OCCURRED ON SATURDAY, FEBRUARY 20TH, 1892, AT OXFORD.
REVOLUTIONARY PROGRESS AT OXFORD.

SIR, Will you be so good as to allow me to use your columns to thank the members of Magdalen College, Oxford, for the very enthusiastic welcome which they have just accorded to the first Socialist who has ever lectured within their walls?

The greatest difficulty with which a public speaker has to struggle is the tendency of the audience to leave before the close of his remarks. I therefore desire especially to thank the thoughtful and self-sacrificing body of undergraduates who voluntarily suffered exclusion from the room in order that they might secure the door on the outside and so retain my audience screwbound to the last syllable of the vote of thanks. I desire to explain, however, that I do not advocate the indiscriminate destruction of property as a first step towards Socialism, and that their action in entirely wrecking the adjoining chamber by a vigorous bombardment of coals, buckets of water and asafoetida, though well meant, was not precisely on the lines which I was laying down inside. Nor, though I expressed myself as in favour of a considerable extension of Communism in the future, did I contemplate the immediate throwing of all the portable property in the lobby into a common stock, beginning with my own hat, gloves and umbrella. Not that I grudge these articles to Magdalen College, but that I wish them to be regarded as an involuntary donation from myself to the present holders rather than as having been scientifically communized.

Speaking as a musical critic, I cannot say that the singing of the National Anthem which accompanied these modest beginnings of revolution was as sincere as that of Ta-ra-ra boom-de-ay which one of my friends within the room loudly supported at the general request by a pianoforte accompaniment. It is injurious to the voice, I may add, to sing in an atmosphere rendered somewhat pungent by the projection of red pepper on a heated shovel.

I need not dwell on the friendly care which was taken not to unscrew the door until our proceedings were entirely over. I wish to say, however, that we should not have incommoded our friends by crowding the staircase had not the rope formed of two blankets, by which we were originally intended to proceed from the apartment directly into the open air, unhappily given way under the strain of being energetically steadied at one end by the outside and at the other by the inside party. There was really no chance of the friction igniting the blankets; so that the pains of the attack posted at an upper window to keep them drenched with water was unnecessary. The gentleman who rendered me a similar attention from the landing above as I descended the stairs also wasted most of his moisture through infirmity of aim; but his hospitable desire to speed the parting guest was unmistakable.

Although my admirers mustered in such numbers that there were at least three times as many persons outside the door as inside (including a don), I am credibly assured that if I had lectured in Brasenose my reception would have been still more overwhelming, and I quite believe it. I was the more overcome as I visited Magdalen under the impression that I was to pass a quiet hour chatting with a few friends and had no idea until I arrived that I was expected to address a meeting or that my advent had roused so deep an interest.

(Sgd.) GEORGE BERNARD SHAW

TO HENRY ARTHUR JONES

22ND MARCH, 1902

MY DEAR H.A.J., I have read *The Princess's Nose* and I am shocked —profoundly shocked. I positively forbid any more La Turbie. You will lose your public if you do not reform at once. Fast, pray, forswear meat and alcohol, turn your back for ever on Monte Carlo, or you are lost.

None of the criticisms I have read have really touched the black spot in this most turpitudinous play. I have often said, when Socialists talk Free Love, that Marriage is invincible as men are at present, because it is the most licentious of all human institutions; and I shall perhaps yet write a play to illustrate that fact. I quite admit that the proposition of your infamous old *raisonneur*, that a man's wife is simply his whore, and must compete with all the other whores if she is to retain her hold of him, is as a matter of fact true of a considerable number of marriages, especially those to be observed at Monte Carlo. But that you of all men should embrace this position and make comedy capital out of it, as if it were an entirely satisfactory and sensible one, and exhibit the old scoundrel, who deliberately preaches it to the young wife, as virtuously horsewhipping the infinitely less repulsive artistic ass who makes love to her, is utterly unendurable. That the author of the scene between Palsam and Rusper should descend to the horse-whipping of Eglinton Pyne (at odds of five to one) is evidence of the most frightful moral decay. I hoped to the last the Pyne would lick the Prince and draw the moral; but in vain. The dialogue writer is still there; but the dramatist's soul is gone; and the public is chilled and horrified without knowing why. These characters are the ghosts of old successes—I except from this the Prince, who is delicately done, and only needs to be placed in his proper moral bearings to be a fine piece of work. The Princess is interesting too, until she turns whore and does a seduction scene which puts her far below the other woman —flogged into theatrical activity by mere brutalities, poultices, and horsewhips and cantharidean *négligées* and so on. The Wyndham plays were immoral (as their climax in *The Princess's Nose* now shows); but they had character in them and humour; and they made money. But this thing will damage you more than a thousand murdered *Michaels*; it piles moral bankruptcy on top of pecuniary bankruptcy—adds Hell to Kentish Town, so to speak. By this I mean that you will have to live in Kentish Town and in Hell hereafter if you do not make your peace with outraged British morality. If you do it again, you are done for.

All this is in the interest of the next play—the Lena Ashwell one, I suppose. If you are mad enough to write it at La Turbie, at least send me the MSS. and let me invest it with moral grandeur. But why not write it in Chiddingfold or wherever you wrote *The Crusaders?* I am now a respectable married man, and, as such, I positively decline to tolerate any more of these stalking horses for smart harlots. You can't really be morally dead; you talk all right and you look all right. You shall have one more chance; but if you miss that, I disown you for ever.

Yours on the highest moral ground,

G. BERNARD SHOCKED

OSCAR WILDE (1856–1900)

*Even as an undergraduate Wilde was a poet of importance and his
novel "The Picture of Dorian Gray" (1891), followed by the play "Lady
Windermere's Fan" (1892), made him the most provocative literary
personality of the time. He was the leader of the "Decadents" and will
perhaps be longest remembered by the "Ballad of Reading Gaol" and
some of his Fairy Stories. Wilde was a casual letter-writer, and not
many good examples of his style in this medium are extant. The following letter is characteristic of his pose and pleasantry.*

TO ROBERT ROSS

Berneval-sur-Mer, June 5, 1897

My dear Robbie, I propose to *live* at Berneval. I will *not* live in
Paris, nor in Algiers, nor in Southern Italy. Surely a house for a year,
if I choose to continue there, at £32 is absurdly cheap! I could not live
cheaper in a hotel. You are penny foolish and pound foolish—a dreadful state for any financier to be in. I told Monsieur Bonnet that my
bankers were Messrs. Ross et Cie., banquiers célèbres de Londres: and
now you suddenly show me that you have really no place among the
great financial people, and are afraid of any investment over £31 10s.
It is merely the extra ten shillings that baffles you.

As regards people living on me in the extra bedroom: dear boy, there
is no one who would stay with me but you, and you will pay your own
bill at the hotel for meals; and as for your room, the charge will be
nominally fr. 2.50 a night, but there will be *lots* of extras, such as *bougie*,
bain and hot water: all cigarettes smoked in the bedroom are charged
extra: washing is extra: and if any one does not take the extras, of course
he is charged more. *Bain* 25c., *pas de bain* 50c. *Cigarette dans la
chambre à coucher* 10c. *pour chaque cigarette; pas de cigarette dans la
chambre à coucher* 20c. *chaque cigarette*. This is the *système* in all good
hotels. If Reggie comes, of course he will pay a little more. I cannot
forget that he gave me a dressing-case. Sphinxes pay a hundred per cent.
more than any one else: they always did in ancient Egypt. Architects,

on the other hand, are taken at a reduction. I have special terms for architects.

But seriously, Robbie, if any people stayed with me, of course they would pay their *pension* at the hotel. They would have to, except architects. A modern architect, like modern architecture, doesn't pay. But then I know only one architect, and you are hiding him somewhere from me. I am beginning to believe that he is as extinct as the dado, of which now only fossil remains are found, chiefly in the vicinity of Brompton, where they are sometimes discovered by workmen excavating. They are usually embedded in the old Lincrusta-Walton strata, and are rare consequently.

I visited Monsieur le Curé to-day. He has a charming house and a *jardin potager*: he showed me over the church: to-morrow I sit in the choir by his special invitation. He showed me all his vestments—to-morrow he really will be charming in red. He knows I am a heretic, and believes that Pusey is still alive. He says that God will convert England on account of England's kindness to *les prêtres exilés* at the time of the Revolution. It is to be the reward of that sea-lashed island.

Stained-glass windows are wanted in the church: he has only six: fourteen more are needed. He gets them at 300 francs—£12—a window in Paris! I was nearly offering half-a-dozen, but remembered you, and so only gave him something *pour ses pauvres*. You had a narrow escape, Robbie. You should be thankful.

I hope the £40 is on its way, and that the £60 will follow. I am going to hire a boat. It will save walking, and so be an economy in the end. Dear Robbie, I must start well. If the life of St. Francis awaits me I shall not be angry. Worst things might happen.

Yours,
OSCAR

NANNIE FOX

The little daughter of Mrs. Charles Fox, one of the leaders of Dublin society in the fifties, was seven years old when she wrote this letter.

MY DEAR MAMA, I am very sorry for touching that stinking little cat. I'll try to-morrow and Teusday if I can do as happy and as well without touching Dawny. I had once before my birthday a little holiness in my heart and for two days I was trying to keep it in and I exceeded a little in it but alas one day Satan tempted me and one day I kept it out of my heart and then I did not care what I did and I ware very bold. One day the week after that I tried without touching Dawny and I thought myself every bit as much happy but I was tempted tempted tempted another day: but I hope to-morrow morning I may be good Mama and that there will be one day that I may please Mama.

Your affectionate daughter,

NANNIE FOX

JOSEPH CONRAD (1857–1924)

The author of "Typhoon," "The Nigger of the Narcissus," etc., was of Polish birth, his original surname being Korzeniowski. He joined the English merchant service as a young man, and thereafter adopted British nationality, eventually revealing himself as a master of English prose, and one of the greatest creative novelists of modern England. This letter was written to his cousin on the death of her husband.

STANFORD-LE-HOPE, ESSEX, 6.2.98

MY DEAREST ANGÈLE, It is still more painful and hard to think of you than to realize my loss; if it was not so, I would pass in silence and darkness these first moments of suffering. Neither you, nor he, know—can know—what place you occupy in my life—how my feelings, my thoughts and my remembrances have been centred round you both and your children. And perhaps I myself did not know until now how much I depended on his memory, his sympathy and his personality—who, even when seen only once, could arouse such feelings of devotion and confidence. He had the gift of drawing all hearts to him and from the moment when I first saw him for the first time, fourteen years ago, I was overcome with affection for him, as the man most akin to me in thought and by blood—after my Uncle, who took the place of my parents. Not a single day passed but I found myself thinking of you both—and during the most painful moments *l'idée qu'il y aurait un jour où je pourrais lui confesser ma vie toute entière et être compris de lui: cette pensée était ma plus grande consolation. Et voilà que cet espoir—le plus précieux de tous—s'est éteint pour toujours.*

The sound of human words does not bring consolation—there is no consolation on this earth. Time can soften but not efface sorrow. I have never felt so near to you and your little girls until this moment when we feel together the injustice of Fate which has loaded you with the burden of life without any support. In the presence of your grief I dare not speak of mine. I only ask you to believe in my attachment to you and to the memory of the mourned husband and father who, with you, was my whole family.

886

My wife said to me with tears in her eyes: "I felt as if I knew him"— and seeing her tears, it seemed to me that never had I cared for him as much as now. Unfortunately she never knew him—altho' she had often heard me speak of him—for I was not capable of appreciating the worth of such a man. I did not know him thoroughly; but I believe that I understood him. I had a profound affection for him, I always went to him in my thoughts. And now I feel alone—even as you.

I kiss your hands, my poor Angèle, I also kiss your little daughters, for whose sake you must be courageous. My affection and my sympathy are always yours.

C. KORZENIOWSKI

TO SIR SIDNEY COLVIN

Written during Lady Colvin's last illness, and shortly before Conrad's death.

WITH all my heart and soul, with all the strength of affection and admiration for her, who is about to leave this hard world, where all the happiness she could find was in your devotion, I am with you every moment of these black hours it is yours to live through. Pray kiss her hands for me in reverence and love. I hope she will give blessing thoughts to those who are dear to me, my wife and children, to whom she always was the embodiment of all that is kind and gracious and lovable on earth.

EDWARD VERRALL LUCAS

Most readers of these letters already know the author of "The Open Road," "A Wanderer in London," and numerous other books.

TO GEORGE WHERRY

AUGUST, 1924

DEAR MR. WHERRY, I was very sorry to read of the death of Charles Sayle, whom I shall always think of as the best kind of self-effacing enthusiastic book-man. On the morning after the Charles Lamb Dinner of 1910 I went round the Trinity Library with him and Aldis Wright, and I remember noticing with what reverence he came to every treasure, although to handle them was, I suppose, his constant task.

It has amused me, at this distance of fourteen years, to set down such impressions as I retain of that visit to Cambridge, hoping that they may amuse you too.

I stayed on that occasion at Trinity College with the Master, the late Dr. Butler, and I was honoured by being given a bedroom with historical associations of a somewhat formidable character, for a brass plate recorded the fact that it had been once occupied, many years before, by Queen Victoria and her Consort. The servant who showed me to it expressed the wish that I would not smoke as I dressed; but he need not have troubled: I should never have dreamed of desecrating such a sanctuary.

I had not yet seen the Master, whom I found waiting in the hall ready to drive to the University Arms Hotel in a brougham; and I was struck by the disparity between his fine great authoritative head, as of a Biblical patriarch, and the soft caressing, almost deferential, voice.

And so we started for the slaughter, I nervous as all public occasions —even so friendly a one as this—make me, and not in the least fortified by the circumstances that directly we arrived the Master changed his boots; for I wondered if this was one of those sacred Cambridge customs which even strangers ought to know about; and I had but the one pair I was wearing!

I was placed on the Master's right ; with you on my other side, and I remember realizing that I had never met a student of Lamb with so much

888

knowledge, zeal and generosity.   Later in the evening I had some talk with one whose work I had long admired and even fattened on——Dr. Giles of the "Chinese Biographical Dictionary."   I also met A. C. Benson for the first time, in the not inconsiderable flesh.

The actual dinner, which piously included sucking-pig, would have been more alluring if the knowledge was not weighing upon me that, when it was finished, I should have, as the guest of the evening, to stand and deliver; but the fact that I had prepared something which could frankly be read made it possible to eat a mouthful here and there and to drink, with less difficulty, the wine that you provided.   The Suffragettes were then at the height of their revolt, and I remember creating, before I began to read, a fairly good impression as one who knew his Lamb by suggesting that if they carried out their threat to burn down the Houses of Parliament, they should not waste them but roast a pig or two in the process.

This pleasantry going well, I started to read with the more confidence, but my reading aloud is, as a matter of fact, merely another way of keeping matters secret; and the circumstance that the Master was sleeping softly by my side did not heighten my spirits.   As the paper, however, was printed in the following number of the *Cambridge Review* (February 17th, 1910), under the title "Cambridge and Charles Lamb," in course of time some idea of my drift got about.

When I had finished reading, the Master made a few apposite remarks in perfectly turned phrases, which showed either that he could slumber with one ear open, or that years and years of familiarity with public speakers had provided him with very definite and accurate data as to their line of attack.

On our return to the Lodge we found Bishop Montgomery, another guest (also of Harrow and Trinity), waiting up for us, in a room to which tobacco might penetrate, and the Master, now wide awake, the Bishop and I, sat on for an hour talking not about Charles Lamb but about one of the few subjects to which Lamb never makes any reference whatever, either in his works or correspondence—in short, to cricket: a subject on which the Bishop is an authority.   As we talked, the Master, with perfect urbanity, brought the conversation round to some verses of his own which I had unhappily misquoted in a recent book.   The famous Harrow poem, in praise of Frederick Ponsonby and the Hon. Robert Grimston, begins thus:

> Old Damon and Old Pythias,
> They always found together;

but I, being not an Harrovian but only a busybody, had changed the second line to:

Were always found together.

I am glad of the error, because it led to a long digression on Harrow slang and other early reminiscences.   The Master's references to cricket ranged from his school days to the banquet in honour of Ranjitsinhji at which he had taken the chair, and, as usual, he seemed to know all.

The next morning Aldis Wright and Charles Sayle came to breakfast, and Aldis Wright filled me with complacency and pride by trusting me to take away the original exercise book in which Edward FitzGerald had written down his notes on Charles Lamb.   I assure you that it was punctually returned.

I see from your list that Walter Raleigh was the guest of the evening in the following year.   No one could speak about Charles Lamb better than he, and I have always regretted that the notes of an address he delivered at the Times Book Club were irrecoverable.

Believe me, dear Mr. Wherry,

Yours sincerely,
E. V. Lucas

SIR JAMES BARRIE

*This eminent Scottish novelist and playwright, the author of "Peter
Pan," has introduced into our literature a new type of whimsical humour
peculiar to himself. The following letter, inspired by a remark in the
correspondence-page of "The Times," is an excellent illustration of this
quality.*

TO THE EDITOR OF *THE TIMES*

SIR, Now that May and the Australians are upon us is it permissible, for
just this once, to make use of *The Times* as a means of inviting an attractive
man to dinner? I don't know him, but he is a Brigadier and he says in
The Times of to-day that he realizes his cricketing days are over; surely
this is a combination that will melt even your stubborn heart. In this
hope I ask you to forward my invitation to him, and to take note that I
leave it open as a guarantee of good faith.

DEAR BRIGADIER, Though I don't know you I wish I did, and that is the
only excuse I can offer for my presumption in begging you to dine with
me at any time or place that is seemly to you. I have already known one
brigadier, which makes me the more desirous to know another, but it is
to-day's confession in *The Times* about your last cricket exploit that makes
me long to see you sitting opposite me at a table for two. This, however,
can create no similar craving in you, and so I hasten to offer you my
credentials.

Though I am not a brigadier (through no fault of my own) I, too,
can look back upon days when I led my men into the tented field, and to
the last match of all when I performed so differently from you that
ordinary civility prevents my stating at this early period of our acquaintance what I did, though it may come out at our little dinner. As
cricket teaches most things and being a brigadier must teach the rest, you
will, I am sure, pardon me for pointing out that on the great occasion
you made a regrettable mistake in going in last. I gather indeed (reluctantly) that it was your practice to be tenth man or so, for the same reason
that always made me go in first. Modesty, of course, was at the root of it
in both cases, but I had evidently thought the matter out more elaborately

891

than you.   You were no doubt influenced by the reflection that with a little luck you might carry out your bat, though you should have known (I say it with all deference) that when the ninth wicket falls there are always four more balls to that over.   Furthermore, you were playing for the glory of the moment when you should have been thinking of posterity. No one seeing you go in last, or hearing that you go in last, or noticing in *The Times* that you went in last, will ever credit you with being a bats-man, not even if you get into double figures.   Now, having thought the matter out profoundly, I always as captain went in first.   This did not deceive the onlookers, and still less my side, as to my prowess, but I was intentionally playing a waiting game.   Readers of the local weekly see-ing that I opened the innings, same as Hobbs does, took for granted that I was an accomplished bat who on this occasion happened to be "unfor-tunate."   I never got into *The Times*, but I became vaguely known to its readers as a man who went in first.   The result of the match would have been the same, but very likely the reporters (hoodwinked) would have said it was owing to my not making my usual stand.

The things we can talk about if you will only come to dinner!   The Australians, for instance.   I must admit that I have a leaning to them, being such a young side and having, all the time they are batting or hold-ing out their hands for a catch, to remember the 67 rules they have sworn not to break about wives and autographs.   This puts me into an awkward position, which I shall ask your opinion of at dinner, and is briefly this. I daresay when you were a captain (I mean a real captain, not a military one) you had my experience about tossing?   The opposing captain, after looking me over, always told me to toss, and he called "The Bird," and then, whether the coin came down head or tail, he said, "The Bird it is; we shall go in."   I often felt there was something wrong about this, but could never quite see what it was.   Now do you think that, as the Australians are such a young side and have so many things to remember, I would be justified in dropping a line to Mr. Woodfull, saying that the toss is very important, and putting him up to calling "The Bird"?

Another thing, ought I to give him or Mr. Hornibrook a tip about slow left-hand bowling?   Mr. Hornibrook I understand is their only slow left-hand bowler, and I am a slow left-hand bowler myself.   I was elated to read of Mr. J. C. White's success in Australia, and as soon as he came back I hurried to Lord's to see him.   To my horror I discovered that he did not know what slow left-hand bowling is.   I would have called it (and did so) fast left-hand bowling.   You say nothing of bowling in *The Times* except that you were out first ball, so that perhaps you find

TO THE EDITOR OF *THE TIMES* 893

all bowling alike and inclined to be fast. Now my left-hand bowling is so slow that it exasperates the batsman, who has gone through all his flourishes by the time the ball reaches the middle of the pitch. My bowling does not so much take the wickets as lie against them. If I think I have sent down a bad delivery I can pursue the ball, recapture it, and send it down again. Ought I to tell Mr. Hornibrook about this, or would it be more patriotic to tell Mr. White, or should they be left to go on in the old way?

Do you feel a special interest in the very young Australians? I do, especially in Master McCabe, who is so young that his schoolmaster has had to sign 34 rules not to appear on the field and take him back to school. There are also Mr. Jackson and Mr. Bradman. I know something that is going to happen to all three of them, besides centuries. At some period in a Test Match they will be found in a dressing-room, each one drooping on a seat and murmuring in anguish: "Oh gosh, oh gosh, why did I play forward to that ball!" Ought I to prepare them for this, or leave them looking happy with 97 on the board?

Perhaps wisest to give them no tips. A side that can leave out Macartney needs them not or is mad. Did you ever see a swallow with a sense of humour chased by dogs? It would come down close to them to tempt them, then soar, then down again and soar again, and so round and round the lawn. That was Macartney with his bowlers. They say Jackson is such another. How splendid! I mean, Oh, dear! Such a talk we will have if you will dine with me.

J. M. BARRIE

APRIL 29, 1930

SIR *WALTER RALEIGH* (1861–1922)

Raleigh was, in his time, one of the leading critical writers on English literature, and occupied the post of professor of English Literature with distinction. He had a peculiar grace and elegance of style, and his gift of adapting his views and expression to the writer he had in mind at the moment is excellently exemplified in this very successful imitation of Burns.

TO PROFESSOR H. A. STRANG, LL.D.

DEAR STRANG,

> On this your natal day,
> We Glaisgie bodies wish to say
> We're sorry that we cannot gae
>> That far to see ye;
> But though oor bodies here maun stay,
>> In hairt we're wi' ye.

> The Northern clans, wi' pipes and drones—
> The "Scotswhahaes" and brave "Hechmons,"
> The "Hootsawas" and "Sodascones"—
>> Are here thegither;
> And ilka ane in joyful tones
>> Proclaims you brither.

> We're fine and glad ye didna scorn
> The fashious wark o' being born,
> Whilk wad ha' left us sair forlorn;
>> But noo—Losh guide us!—
> Ye're found, this braw November morn,
>> On airth beside us.

> 'Twas in this toon ye first assayed
> The ancient gerund-grinding trade,

Wi' Latin in a spune ye gaed
                The fowk to feed them;
And eh! the bonny jokes ye made—
                Deil kens wha seed them!

Oor thochts hae dwelt upon you aft,
The climate's turned a wee thing saft,
Oor college noo wi' gowks is staffed,
                Wi' gomerals deevit;
But, Lord be praised there's Heaven alaft
                And here, Glenleevit.

For Scotland nane need droop or dwine;
For them that feel their stren'th decline
The certain cure (it's just divine)
                Each year returns,
(Whilk mony a lassie had lang syne)
                —A nicht wi' Burns.

We twa hae strayed ower Brownlow Hill,
And pu'd lang faces on the sill,
While toddling ben to yon auld mill
                That still plays clatter,
—And auld Mackay is there, and still
                As daft's a hatter.

Lang may the flags o' Bedford Street
Resound beneath your honoured feet!
Lang may ye hauld your annual treat
                For a' the leddies!
Lang may ye flout and jink and cheat
                The Laird o' Hades.

                                    W. A. R.

Dec. 1, 1900

TO MISS C. A. KER

The junction worked beautifully at Crian Larich. There was a
young stout athletic Englishwoman ordering porters about in a high
superior voice that just fascinated me. I followed her about gaping
like a fish. When she'd got all she wanted, the rest of us crawled out

of corners with our poor luggage, to see if anyone would take it up too. No one could move or speak till she had finished. We were birds to a snake. Tremendous! The porters just trembled. She was not beautiful. About 30. O, very stout! Hale. It's the De Vere voice. I wondered whether it would work in a real shipwreck. "These two in the life-boat, and the wraps and the cloak in my seat in the Captain's cutter, and the two large trunks in the jolly boat, and get them all off at once, please." Suppose someone laughed? No one does. She'd die of apoplexy on the spot.

TO EDWARD ARNOLD

UFFINGTON, FARINGDON, BERKS, 6–v–02

I AM content to leave the matter of the American "Milton" wholly in your hands. What does the delightful P. mean by "cancelling the books as waste"? Does he mean destroying them? I hope so. But I have a lurking suspicion that he is in treaty with a Butter or Margarine Trust. Or does he mean that they cease to have a legal existence as copyright works, and that he is to do as he pleases with them?

I am full of sympathy for him. I never thought the American people wanted my works. But I had heard, from natives of that continent, that America is a large place; and I had supposed that 720 copies of my little work (which would take exactly 1 cubic yard of storage space) might have room made for them somewhere on those billowy savannahs. The rent of a cubic yard of America is beyond my means, it appears.

The outward appearance of the book produced by P. (especially the tail-pieces borrowed from some evangelical agency) is—not to put too fine a point on it—beastly; and I should be glad to hear, on good authority, that the copies had all been burned. Why did you not (why do you not?) take my advice and produce an edition of 12 copies of each of my works, in the form of a penny railway guide, as an American edition? Put them up at 10 dollars each, and (as I said) I will write an "Ode to the American people," to make the book a bibliographical rarity. My Ode shall be in the metre of the "Psalm of Life" by Henry Wadsworth Longfellow. Is it credible that there would be no demand for this?

DAVID LLOYD GEORGE

*The following is an extract from a letter written by the great states-
man when he was eighteen years of age and on his first visit to London.*

NOVEMBER 12, 1881

WENT to the Houses of Parliament. Very much disappointed with
them. Grand buildings outside, but inside they are crabbed, small
and suffocating, especially the House of Commons. I will not say
but that I eyed the assembly in a spirit similar to that in which William
the Conqueror eyed England on his visit to Edward the Confessor,
as the region of his future domain. Oh, vanity!

BERKELEY, LORD MOYNIHAN

This eminent surgeon, undoubtedly one of the greatest of our day, wrote the following amusing letter to the golf correspondent of "The Times." What echoes will it awaken in the heart of every "rabbit."

TO THE EDITOR OF *THE TIMES*

Sir, This will never do! For five days in the week we avail ourselves of *The Times* as it so competently deals with the less important affairs of life, politics, domestic or foreign, the imminence, hopes, fears of a General Election, the arrivals or departures of great people, the steady depreciation of our scanty investments, another century or two by Hobbs, or a stupendous break by Smith. But on the sixth day *The Times* is exalted in our eyes, for then your Golf Correspondent, in a column of wisdom, humour, and unmatched literary charm, deals with the one real thing in life. This week for the first time he has deeply shocked and disappointed us all. I am but a "rabbit." I confess to a handicap of 24 (at times) and a compassionate heart (always). I cannot bear to see a fellow creature suffer, and it is for this reason among others that I rarely find myself able to inflict upon an opponent the anguish of defeat. To-day I suffer for the whole world of caddies, wounded in the house of their friend. They learn in a message almost sounding a note of disdain that the verb which signifies their full activity is "to carry." By what restriction of mind can anyone suppose that this is adequate? Does not a caddy in truth take charge of our lives and control all our thoughts and actions while we are in his august company? He it is who comforts us in our time of sorrow, encourages us in moments of doubt; inspires us to that little added effort which, when crowned with rare success brings a joy that nothing else can offer. It is he who with majestic gravity and indisputable authority hands to us the club that he thinks most fitted to our meagre power, as though it were not a rude mattock but indeed a royal sceptre. It is he who counsels us in time of crisis, urging that we should "run her up" or "loft her" or "take a lie a wee bit to the left, with a shade of a slice." Does he not enjoin us with magisterial right not to raise our head? Are **we** not most properly rebuked when our left knee sags, or our right elbow soars, or our body is too rigid while our eyes go roaming?   Does he not count our strokes with remorseless and unpardonable accuracy, keeping all the while a watchful eye upon our opponent's score?   Does he not speak of "our" honour, and is not his exhortation that "we" must win this hole?   Does he not make us feel that some share of happiness, or of misery, will be his in our moment of victory or defeat? Does he not with most subtle but delicious flattery coax us to a belief that if only we had time to play a "bit oftener" we should reach the dignity of a single figure handicap?   Does he not hold aloft the flag as though it were indeed our standard, inspiring a reluctant ball at last to gain the hole?   Does such a man do nothing but "carry" for us? Of course he does infinitely more.   He "caddies" for us, bless him!

MOYNIHAN

THE OAKS WIDOWS

A terrible explosion occurred in the Oaks Colliery, near Barnsley, in 1866; twenty-five years later the widows of those who lost their lives wrote this letter of condolence to the Queen, on the death of the Prince of Wales's eldest son, the Duke of Clarence, who died January 14, 1892.

TO OUR BELOVED QUEEN, VICTORIA

DEAR LADY, We, the surviving widows and mothers of some of the men and boys who lost their lives by the explosion which occurred in the Oaks Colliery, near Barnsley, in December, 1866, desire to tell your Majesty how stunned we all feel by the cruel and unexpected blow which has taken "Prince Eddie" from his dear Grandmother, his loving parents, his beloved intended, and an admiring nation. The sad news affected us deeply, we all believing that his youthful strength would carry him through the danger. Dear Lady, we feel more than we can express. To tell you that we sincerely condole with your Majesty and the Prince and Princess of Wales in your and their sad bereavement and great distress is not to tell you all we feel; but the widow of Albert the Good and the parents of Prince Eddie will understand what we feel when we say that we feel all that widows and mothers feel who have lost those who were dear as life to them. Dear Lady, we remember with gratitude all that you did for us Oaks widows in the time of our great trouble, and we cannot forget you in yours. We have not forgotten that it was you, dear Queen, who set the example, so promptly followed by all feeling people, of forming a fund for the relief of our distress—a fund which kept us out of the workhouse at the time and has kept us out ever since. We wish it were in our power, dear Lady, to dry up your tears and comfort you, but that we cannot do. But what we can do, and will do, is to pray to God, in His mercy and goodness, to comfort and strengthen you in this your time of great trouble.—Wishing your Majesty, the Prince and Princess of Wales, and the Princess May all the strength, consolation, and comfort which God alone can give, and which He never fails to give to all who seek Him in truth and sincerity, we remain, beloved Queen, your loving and grateful though sorrowing subjects,

THE OAKS WIDOWS

GEORGE WILLIAM RUSSELL (Æ)

Æ embodies, perhaps more than any other writer, the Irish spirit of to-day.

I WILL try to write more clearly. I am sorry my notes were so difficult to read. My printers are accustomed to them and I am afraid their subservience to my manner of writing has encouraged me to write for all as I do for them.

You ask how I escaped the Ancient Darkness—by renewing every day my old habit of meditation on the Spirit, every day setting aside a time for it, and rarely allowing it to be encroached on. There were some years in which I was so absorbed in external activities that my meditations were intermittent. I have, with some effort of will, brought myself round to a state where when I began meditation I had myself in some relation to a spiritual nature. You ask about "Resurrection" and "Promise." Both poems depend on the same fundamental idea perceived in different moods. Emerson once wrote echoing the sacred books; "we live in succession, in division, in perils (?), meantime within man is the soul of the whole, the wise silence." That is, there is an Everliving in which all that ever was, or is, or perhaps will be, exists in some transcendental fashion. I cannot go into the metaphysic of it. But I have been forced by spiritual experiences to believe that there is a life in which, if we enter it, what was past is what we live over again. You will find this idea in many of my verses. Perhaps the most coherent expression of the idea is in the verses beginning: "Through the blue shadowy valley I hastened in a dream." The feeling which prompted me to write "Resurrection" has been with me for thirty years or more. I felt somewhere in the immortal memory there was some tragedy of my heart and the very thought of it made me feel faint and terrified at things I had done, and I dared not explore it lest I might bring it all back. The first two lines of the poem were in my mind for at least thirty years, but I did not dare to face the subject, and it was only a couple of years ago I continued the opening skirting round the idea rather than exploring it to find what that tragedy was.   The idea in "Promise" is that all that is beautiful to our vision is in that immortality when we come to it.   The idea in "Resurrection" is that all that was terrible in our heart has also to be faced when we come to our own immortal city (?). It is an obscure part of the psychology of the spirit about which I find it difficult to write, as intuitions about it are fragmentary and I could speak about it with more ease than I can write.   It is in another sense an expression of the Indian Karma or the Greek Nemesis "that you cannot escape the consequences of your thoughts or actions good or bad, and if you go to the Heaven-world they will meet you there."

I write in my office without the poems but I think I know the verses you name.   Does not one poem begin—"Not by me these feet were led"? and "Promise" with—"Be not so desolate"?

I wrote two poems with more profound feeling than "Resurrection" and "Promise," but one passes away from oneself and I cannot at the moment restore to myself that deep consciousness and write to you out of it.   I have done the best I can now to hint what was behind them.

Yours ever

Æ

ENOCH ARNOLD BENNETT

This great author and critic took up literature as a profession in 1900, after a period of journalism. A Staffordshire man by birth, he is best known as the chronicler of the Five Towns, though his later work has covered a very wide field. The letter which appears below, now printed for the first time, was written to a friend.

11 NOVEMBER, 1895.

YOUR letter came exactly at the moment when I wanted something. I have just returned from "putting the paper to bed," and don't reckon to work seriously on Monday nights; I was trying to bring myself to write a col. of reviews in advance so as to leave the week clear for the novel. After I have written this, I shall no doubt get through the col. smoothly enough: the atmosphere will have been created.

My dear *Globe* contributor, I find a novel the damnedest nerve-shattering experience as ever was. Nothing but my strong aversion to being beaten by anything on God's earth that I set myself to whip, prevents me from throwing up the present one. And this, mind you, in spite of the facts that I have all my material in hand, and that I am not short of inspiration—as I believe they call it! It is the *arrangement* that kills one, the mere arrangement of "sensation and event" which—in a manner o' speaking, one knows by heart. Conversations are the very devil to me,—at present; I eschew them all I can, and when I can't avoid jaw, keep it short and *très select*. This is à la de Maupassant, who could, however, do conversations *à merveille*, when he felt that way. I have developed so strangely this last three years—my first attempt at fiction was made exactly 2½ years ago—that I don't know what may happen in the future, but at present I do "sensations" best, leaving events alone.

With regard to the impression abroad that pages undiversified by dialogue are apt to be dull, I am persuaded that the dullness, apparent dullness, can be done away with by a judicious arrangement of paragraphs. The effect of a separate line of 4 or 5 words in the middle of two longish paragraphs must be seen to be believed. The French know this—they taught it me. Probably you are aware of it, but unless you have consciously meditated upon it, I venture to think that you have not grasped (excuse my cheek) the tremendous effect, even on an educated and trained reader, of paragraph arrangement.

Of course a determined attempt to write for the eye (the eye which reads a whole page in one flash, as it were—am I clear?) influences materially the details of style which are meant to appeal to the intellect only. If you have a long paragraph, you can't offhandedly cut it in two, or shove a short line into the middle of it. You must deliberately, from the beginning of the par, work up to the short line, or the short par. (If, as is probable, you have thought out all this for yourself kindly excuse my exuberance, but I am interested in the little matter.)

In my new vol. of the Edinburgh Stevenson, there is a luminous essay, reprinted for the first time from a *Fortnightly Review* of 1881: on "Some technical elements of style in literature." You must read it when you come up; it is profoundly interesting to a craftsman. He deals chiefly with the sweet uses of alliteration—subtle, concealed alliteration of course—and he dam well knows what he is talking about. The essential "stylistic" (his word) differences between prose and verse are also finely set out. I read the thing last night in bed—after an evening at Chapman's—and was made to think thereby.

(I don't know whether you have seen any of Chapman's verse, but he is an accomplished artist—unlikely to express himself through fiscal troubles.)

Curious: My style has altered (improved, I trust) so much during the progress of this bally novel, that one reason for writing the whole thing again, is the difference between the earlier and later portions. I feel more sure than ever I did in my life before, that I can *write* in time, and "make people care," too, as Hy. James says—though perhaps only a few people. Still, to have made fellow artists care—that is the thing! That is what will give ultimate peace of mind. Do you ever suddenly stand still and ponder: "Suppose, after all, I am an artist, rather a fine one! But it can't be true. What am *I* that *I* should be an artist? Every dabbler thinks he is—till he learns better. And yet, and yet. . . ."

I have never been in love (wish to God I had, when I am struggling with a love scene!) but I imagine that the joy of the artist when he first *knows* that he is an artist, is similar to the joy of the lover when he first knows that he is in love and loved; and the thought of both, after the first scepticism has gone, is: "What the hades have I done to deserve this ineffable happiness?"

I have boasted to at least one person (another of my indiscretions) that I know I am an artist. I know no such thing When I have read my first novel in print, I think I shall know.

Yes, I am well aware that this farrago, coming from a youthful person who has nothing to show, nothing done, is absurdly self-conscious and egotistic. But my dear villager, one writes to please oneself, after all, not to please the correspondent addressed. Is not this a great truth?

À propos des bottes, have you got Roget's "Thesaurus of English Words and Phrases"? It is the most wonderful machine for getting at words that you know but can't think of at the moment, that I have encountered. Even when you have only an adumbrated notion of the idea itself, this precious volume will help you to define it, and end up by giving you the word to describe the idea it has itself defined. I bought it about a year ago, and wonder now how I ever did without it. If I had to choose between Shakespeare and Roget, I would let Billy go, upon my word.

I would advise you not to read my dramatic criticisms—yet. I am feeling my feet, and incidentally coming to the conclusion that although I can tell a good play from a bad one with some certainty, I know nothing whatever about acting. Besides, this work is not paid well enough, and I have too many distractions, to tempt me to let myself go on it. Further, my criticisms are not seldom disingenuous. For sufficiently weighty reasons I praised "Trilby" to the skies though privately I am convinced that it is a silly worthless namby-pamby piece.

(By the way, the MS. of "Trilby" can now be viewed in Bond Street, in a glass case, on payment of 1s.! Such is the force of the Trilby boom.)

Tree was so enchanted with my notice of Trilby that he asked me to write a couple of short articles describing Trilby as seen by a deaf man and as heard by a blind man—and I shared the Royal box with my editor's wife, at a second witnessing of the play. I was surprised and deeply gratified, when I came to write the article, at the ease with which I could produce in myself the illusion of being blind and being deaf. The actual articles were, however, rot; I had no time to do them for one thing, and deliberately did them badly for another. My editor is very pleased with them. Behold then the temptations which beset my path!

You might, if you care, read my criticism of Hardy's new novel in Wednesday next's *Woman*. Though it contains little actual criticism, I imagine it to give a sort of impression of the book.

I am very sorry about the bankrupt and your £100. That sort of thing dries up the fountains quicker than anything. .

I haven't yet seen the *Globe*. The "W.G." article was competent journalism—all you intended it to be, I guess. I am told that the *Globe* article is "delicious."

I must return to technics: I believe in short chapters, 2000 to 3000 words, and in making, as a rule, each chapter a complete scene, and detached—of course there are exceptions. I learnt this from the brothers de Goncourt. I must get you to read their "Renée Mauperin." To study the principles of its construction is both "entertaining and instructive."

My favourite masters and models: (1) Turgeneff, a royal first (you must read "On the Eve"—*flawless*, I tell you. Bring back such books of mine as you have; I have others you must read); (2) de Maupassant; (3) de Goncourts; (4) George Moore—the great author who can neither write nor spell!

Stevenson only helps me in minute details of style.

Excuse prolixity,

Yours ever,

ARNOLD BENNETT

GEORGE SLYTHE STREET

Author of much that will live in literature and for some years Reader of Plays, G. S. Street has occupied a position of his own in English letters. His observations on the passing craze of the decivilizing car are expressed in his own matchless style.

TO THE EDITOR OF *THE TIMES*

SIR, This is a futile letter and quite probably unworthy of publication; yet I think that a public wail may express the emotion of some of your readers. Some time ago you published a letter from me on "the sacrifice to speed," in which I called attention to the disproportion of fatal and other accidents to the convenience of people who wish to travel rapidly. The number of these accidents has gone up considerably since, and you have called attention to it in a leading article. But it seems that the authorities and the public are indifferent in the matter. I regret this, believing it to be a setback in civilization, the more deplorable because in other ways we are becoming more civilized, in general kindness and amiability of manners. But since this callousness about human life, which no war has ever produced, seems to be established, it is useless to go on protesting. It is useless also, no doubt—but since I did not urge it before I should like to do so now—to point out how not only human life but everything which makes life worth living to civilized people is sacrificed to "transport." Cities are no longer regarded as places in which to live agreeably, if possible, and to transact business, but as places in which it is possible to go from one end to the other with rapidity. You published recently a letter from a correspondent advocating, with an air of expecting unqualified congratulation, a scheme for facility of transport which would render uninhabitable the street in which I have found comparative peace for 25 years. It did not occur to him that the sufferings of its inhabitants, deprived of sleep, meditation, and rational conversation, are worth a thought. So in the country. Peace does not matter ; beauty does not matter; what is wanted is roads, roads, and more roads. Into the sociological or political merits of this latter idea

I do not propose to enter, but I notice—in my futile way—that the amenities of life do not come into the account.

Surely in all this, Sir, I am right in seeing a decivilizing influence in the invention of the petrol engine as it is used at present? And I have not touched on aeroplanes, which in the summer make life hideous over a large part of England. With foresight and patience this invention might have been good for humanity; in its present exploitation it is a curse.

I suggest, in conclusion, that the sacrifice to traffic is needless. In the matter of human life the loss might certainly be diminished by regulations as to speed, whatever automobile associations or clubs may say, because a fast moving object will strike another with greater impact than a less fast-moving one, and the latter may be stopped more quickly. And in regard to the amenities of life destroyed by new roads and so on, I suggest that the greater part of the present traffic is not due to necessary business but to the contemporary craze for continually rushing about, which, like other and less stupid crazes, will pass.

I am, Sir, your obedient servant,

G. S. STREET

OSWALD BARRON ("THE LONDONER")

For thirty years under the title "The Londoner," Oswald Barron has written daily in the "Evening News" his whimsical, wise, contemplative causeries.   He has a personal following of hundreds of thousands who turn each evening in tram or train or by the fireside to his peaceful page.   He is a discriminating and deep reader; a mediævalist in his love of the lost and the old; and one of our great experts on heraldry.

TO THE PUBLIC

WHICHEVER way the road may go, I know now that it will never lead at the end to my country house, nor even to my country cottage.   In the country I cannot be more than a pilgrim, a peeping wanderer.

That is why, now that I am once more upon the hill in the upland village, I find myself looking at all the common country sights with a sort of envy.   To-day I saw the day's last lights radiant upon the trees of a hillside spinney.   To-night I looked long at the stars from a bleak road and was naming them with a sort of rapture.

It is my misfortune that I can name so few stars.   There are times when I cannot call friends with any but the Pole Star and the Plough that drives about the Pole Star.   When, as to-night, I can point with my hand to the studded belt of Orion, to red Mars and to Cassiopeia, I have all the superior emotions of a star-gazing high priest.   What a piece of luck was it that all the stars of any quality were named so long ago that they bear the names of the old gods and heroes and goddesses: those bright stars that hung below the young moon were surely Venus and Jupiter.

If we were to name them nowadays we should do terrible things, we who could land upon a coral island and call it after a cotton-spinning factory town, who name a demi-detached villa in West Kensington with the name of a mountain of the northern Highlands.   When we came to naming that august peak of the Himalayas where the foot of man may climb nearest to high heaven, our geographers did not hesitate.   They fter the gentleman who had completed the trigonometrical It is well for the world that his surname was Everest, for Everest is calm and stately of sound. Everest might have been a mountain's name from the beginning, instead of the surname of a respectable family in Brecknockshire. But if Sir George Everest had been Sir George Tomlinson, our world would have been capped by Mount Tomlinson.

There was a planet discovered by an English telescope in the seventeen-eighties. The loyal astronomer at once honoured the new planet by making it the godchild of King George III; such loyalty would have seen a fuff of court hair-powder in the star-dust of the Milky Way. Let it be to our credit that we have found another name for the Georgium Sidus, else we should be still as the Chinamen whose emperors were cousins of the moon.

I am so ignorant that I cannot remember much from the list of the lesser stars. It may be that they have suffered indignities. The astronomer is a man of science and science has honourable children. But the botanist is also a man of science, and we know what he has done with the flowers that we used to name so happily, our honeysuckle and heartsease and foxglove and ladysmock. The botanist who, looking at the tender flower of the clematis, could stick good Mr. Jackman's surname to it, may have an industrious astronomer for his brother. Somewhere in the broad fields of heaven may twinkle a twinkling Jackman.

It is hard to make such people understand the nature of their sacrilege. You could not have persuaded Mr. Herschel that King George III, that shape of majesty, all royal from his wig to his shoe-buckles, might not be raised to heaven as a star. And *Clematis Jackmanii!* Surely that Mr. Jackman who brought the flower from overseas, or with his own hands laboured it to grow, deserved that the clematis should always remember him gratefully? As well try to explain why an English family inheriting an English name written in a family Bible, should not dip into that Bible at christening times and bring up Ebenezer and Jehoshaphat as likely names for baby.

But we should learn reverence when we look up at the stars. I look upward ignorantly but reverently at the white host of heaven. Even the astronomer who peers through the magic glasses must go in peril of losing his mysterious awe in a tangle of mathematical calculations. I remember a buoyant astronomer who used to teach much star-craft to children at holiday time; I did not love the jokes that he cracked about planets and wandering stars. You must not pretend to pull the comet's fiery tail; the night sky ought not to set us giggling.

Rather than get our astronomy with the help of a comic primer of

astronomy, it were better to be ignorant with the children whose knowledge went no further than the nursery rhyme, whose hymn to the star
was on the note of "how I wonder what you are." And if we must
tell fortunes, let us tell them with the pack of cards and cut and see what
the Dark Woman and the Fair Man promise us. I am intolerant of
all astrologers; the Law is just that makes rogues and vagabonds of them.

Yet there is always with us that odd little sect of heretics which
believes that the stars are busy with the little business of our lives. You
bring out your grubby little astrological calendars, you set up your
planetary figures, and then you can wring from the shining ones the
secret of what will befall Edwin in his courtship of Angelina, or Demos
in his adventure among stocks and shares.

All such twopenny sorceries I put behind me. Through the clean
air on the top of a hill I have once again seen the multitude of the skies,
and like the child I have wondered what they are, not asking for an
astronomer's playful wisdom nor for an astrologer's solemn nonsense.
For in this quiet place of night silences it is enough to know that these
are lamps lit before the highest mystery, before the secret of secrets
that shall never be told to any man.

"THE LONDONER"

ELIZABETH ATWATER (d. 1900)

Mrs. Atwater was one of the missionary victims of the Boxer Rising in China in 1900. She and a number of other missionaries were being escorted by soldiers from the city of Fen-chau on August 15, 1900, when they were attacked and murdered. This letter, written twelve days before the tragedy, gives a vivid picture of conditions at the time.

TO HER RELATIVES

FENCHOUFU, AUGUST 3, 1900

MY DEAR, DEAR ONES, I have tried to gather courage to write to you once more. How am I to write all the horrible details of these days? I would rather spare you. The dear ones at Shouyang, seven in all, including our lovely girls, were taken prisoners and brought to T'aiyuan in irons, and there by the Governor's orders beheaded, together with the T'aiyuan friends, thirty-three souls. The following day the Roman Catholic priests and nuns from T'aiyuan were also beheaded, ten souls yesterday. Three weeks after these had perished, our Mission at Taku was attacked, and our six friends there, and several brave Christians who stood by them, were beheaded. We are now waiting our call home. We have tried to get away to the hills, but the plans do not work. Our things are being stolen right and left, for the people know that we are condemned. Why our lives have been spared we cannot tell. The Proclamation says that whoever kills us will be doing the Governor a great service. Our Magistrate has kept peace so far, but if these men come from Taku there is not much hope, and there seems none any way we turn. The foreign soldiers are in Pao-ting-fu, and it is said that peace is made. This would save us in any civilized land, no matter what people may say. The Governor seems to be in haste to finish his bloody work, for which there is little doubt he was sent to Shansi.

Dear ones, I long for a sight of your dear faces, but I fear we shall not meet on earth. I have loved you all so much, and know you will not forget the one who lies in China. There never were sisters and brothers like mine. I am preparing for the end very quietly and calmly. The Lord is wonderfully near, and He will not fail me. I was very restless and excited while there seemed a chance of life, but God has taken away that feeling, and now I just pray for grace to meet the terrible end bravely. The pain will soon be over, and oh the sweetness of the welcome above!

My little baby will go with me. I think God will give it to me in Heaven, and my dear mother will be so glad to see us. I cannot imagine the Saviour's welcome. Oh, that will compensate for all these days of suspense. Dear ones, live near to God and cling less closely to earth. There is no other way by which we can receive that Peace from God which passeth all understanding. I would like to send a special message to each of you, but it tries me too much. I must keep calm and still these hours. I do not regret coming to China, but I am sorry I have done so little. My married life, two precious years, has been so very full of happiness. We will die together, my dear husband and I.

I used to dread separation. If we escape now it will be a miracle. I send my love to you all, and the dear friends who remember me.—Your loving sister,

LIZZIE

ROBERT FALCON SCOTT (1868–1912)

The story of Captain Scott's dash to the South Pole and its tragic ending need no recapitulation. This last message, written in his tent with Death standing at the door, is a piece of prose that will endure as long as language lasts.

TO THE BRITISH PUBLIC

WE should have got through but for the sickening of a second companion, and a shortage of fuel for which I cannot account, and the storm which has fallen on us within eleven miles of the depot at which we hoped to secure our final supplies. Surely misfortune could scarcely have exceeded this last blow.

We arrived within eleven miles of our old One Ton Camp with fuel for one last meal and food for two days. For four days we have been unable to leave the tent, the gale howling about us. We are weak, writing is difficult, but for my own sake I do not regret this journey, which has shown that Englishmen can endure hardships, help one another, and meet death with as great a fortitude as ever in the past. We took risks, we knew we took them; things have come out against us, and therefore we have no cause for complaint, but bow to the will of Providence, determined still to do our best to the last. But if we have been willing to give our lives to this enterprise, which is for the honour of our country, I appeal to our countrymen to see that those who depend on us are properly cared for.

Had we lived I should have had a tale to tell of the hardihood, endurance, and courage of my companions which would have stirred the heart of every Englishman. These rough notes and our dead bodies must tell the tale, but surely, surely, a great rich country like ours will see that those who are dependent on us are properly provided for.

"BULLY" HAYES

"Bully" Hayes was a pirate in the South Seas. When the missionary ship "John Williams II" was wrecked on the island of Niué, the missionaries on board chartered Hayes's boat, the brig "Rona," to carry them over to Samoa. For his own reasons Hayes took the opportunity of exhibiting the utmost piety and after he had landed the missionaries wrote them the following letter. It is an ironical comment on this note that the day after the missionaries landed Hayes nearly killed one of his crew by striking him on the head with the bag containing the missionaries' passage money.

TO MR. AND MRS. SAVILL

BRIG. "RONA" AT SEA, APRIL 27TH, 1867

MY DEAR FRIENDS, Altho' the way and place of our becoming acquainted is connected with many sad recollections to you, yet I trust the time we have known each other, and the pleasant trips we have had in the *Rona* may carry pleasant reminiscences in years to come.

I feel it my duty to sincerely thank you for the good you have endeavour'd to do to my Officers and men and I do not think it has been all thrown away.

Mrs. Hayes joins me in kindest wishes to Mrs. Savill and yourself, and trusting you may enjoy the best of health in your probable long stay at Huahine and have the satisfaction of seeing your labours fully and thankfully appreciated,

I remain,

My dear Friends,

Yours very truly,

W. H. HAYES

ARTHUR CLUTTON-BROCK (1868–1924)

The following letter has never before been published; it reveals the author and critic in a characteristic mood of quiet gaiety.

CHRISTMAS, 1917

DEAR BELL

    It is very pleasant
To read your very pretty Christmas present,
Got up so delicate and clean—
And I reply on this machine.
Even my verses on a "Yost"
Are as incongruous almost
As music on a Gramophone.
But, to return to yours, I own,
I have enjoyed your last and most.
And much I wish that I could dance
As nimbly as the lucky chance
Of sense and rhyme at Christmas time.
I wish to God that I could be
From all seriousness set free;
For who has given this imperious
Command that we should all be serious?
God? Nature? Nowhere do I find
A proof convincing to my mind
That either likes us as we are;
And since God's heaven is very far,
It may be that divines are wrong.

Why not assume His taste in art
Is rather for our own Mozart.
And that He has but little patience
With the whole book of Revelations,
And with the nuisances who bawl
Skyward that Jesus is their all?

917

How if, at last, we all awoke
To find this present world a joke,
And entered on the great hereafter
Greeted by celestial laughter?
God himself could never find
A better purging for mankind.
That were heaven indeed, but I
Can't keep off theology.
You must bear my little weakness
With what you can of Christian meekness;
Since I, suspecting you of treason,
Still send you greetings of the season.

A. CLUTTON-BROCK.

WINSTON SPENCER CHURCHILL

WINSTON SPENCER CHURCHILL

*This document was written in circumstances surely unique in litera-
ture. Mr. Churchill had not at that time attained the fame and
reputation that have since made him a commanding figure in English
literature and politics, and considerable confusion had been caused
by the identity of name borne by a well-known American writer of
eminence.*

TO MR. WINSTON CHURCHILL

LONDON, JUNE 7, 1899

MR. WINSTON CHURCHILL presents his compliments to Mr. Winston
Churchill and begs to draw his attention to a matter which concerns
them both. He has learnt from the Press notices that Mr. Winston
Churchill proposes to bring out another novel, entitled "Richard
Carvel," which is certain to have a considerable sale both in England
and America. Mr. Winston Churchill is also the author of a novel
now being published in serial form in *Macmillan's Magazine*, and for
which he anticipates some sale both in England and America. He also
proposes to publish on the 1st of October another Military Chronicle
on the Soudan War. He has no doubt that Mr. Winston Churchill
will recognize from this letter—if indeed by no other means—that
there is grave danger of his works being mistaken for those of Mr.
Winston Churchill. He feels sure that Mr. Winston Churchill desires
this as little as he does himself. In future to avoid mistakes as far as
possible, Mr. Winston Churchill has decided to sign all published articles,
stories, or other work, "Winston Spencer Churchill," and not "Winston
Churchill" as formerly. He trusts that this arrangement will commend
itself to Mr. Winston Churchill, and he ventures to suggest, with a
view to preventing further confusion which may arise out of this
extraordinary coincidence, that both Mr. Winston Churchill and Mr.
Winston Churchill should insert a short note in their respective publica-
tions explaining to the public which are the works of Mr. Winston
Churchill and which those of Mr. Winston Churchill. The text of
this note might form a subject for future discussion if Mr. Winston

Churchill agrees with Mr. Winston Churchill's proposition.   He takes this occasion of complimenting Mr. Winston Churchill upon the style and success of his works, which are always brought to his notice whether in magazine or book form, and he trusts that Mr. Winston Churchill has derived equal pleasure from any work of his that may have attracted his attention.

MAX BEERBOHM

Max Beerbohm is equally famous as author and caricaturist, and must have written many letters which breathe the same fragrance as his essays. He treats here of a political issue which is remote from the scope of his other work.

TO HENRY ARTHUR JONES

14TH MAY, 1926

MY DEAR HENRY ARTHUR, I have been thinking of you much during the past horrible week or so[1]—and now I write to say how glad I am with you that England has done well. I suppose there may be difficulties yet; but they won't matter so much: the long-impending big fight has been fought and won. England has all sorts of faults—dullnesses, stupidities, heavy frivolities, constantly pointed out by you. But in politics somehow she always is—somehow slowly, dully, but splendidly—all right. I have often thought, in reading your brilliant and violent rebukes of her, that you hadn't quite as much faith in her as she deserves. You didn't overstate her dangers; but I felt that you believed not quite enough in her power to meet these and deal with these successfully in her own fumbling and muzzy way, by her own dim (damnably dim, you would say) lights. You are a die-hard, and she is a die-soft. She says mildly, "No violence, pray! I quite see your points of view, dear gentlemen all! I'm full of faults. Really I rather doubt whether I deserve to survive. Yet I hope, I even intend, to do so" . . . and she *does*—the dear old thing! *Brava, bravissima*, dear silly old thing!

Dear Henry Arthur, I know how happy you are feeling—and I write to add my happiness to yours. The past week has made for my wife and me "a goblin of the sun," and the big roses in our small garden looked horrible. In writing to me at about Christmas-time, you said I did well to be out here, because of all the trouble brewing in England. But really out here, in this alien golden clime, one feels more acutely any dangers to England. What a relief it was to us both, my wife

[1] An allusion to the General Strike of 1926.

and me, when, early in 1915, we settled down into England! And Civil War is of course much more distressing to the heart and to the imagination than war with any number of more or less natural enemies. And of, what pæans our hearts sing that the wretched affair is, to all intents and purposes, over—and that the right side has won.

I think King George's Message to the people very finely composed, I read it with emotion. Had you been he, the message would have been still finer, and I should have read it with still greater emotion. But it wouldn't have been so exactly right for the occasion. For the purpose of interpreting the deepest feelings of the British People, I back Hanover against Bucks every time!—though I sometimes wish Hanover had a little of Buck's sparkle all the same.

Your affectionate,

MAX BEERBOHM

P.S. I never can remember the Christian or surname of anybody I haven't met constantly. Thus I forget those of the charming and gifted young man who was my fellow-guest when I dined with you last May at the Athenæum. Otherwise I would ask you to give him my kindest regards. The name of DORIS does not escape me. And to her I send my love.

P.P.S. Old friendship—there's nothing very much better than that. I am reminded of this truism by my P.S. about dining with you last May at the Athenæum. I have my faults (like England), but am sensitive to impressions and retentive of these. I do so well remember being ushered in by a waiter to that Writing-Room to the right of the hall. Up from a table rises H. A., and quickly advances, with that forward thrust of the head (that I have so often caricatured), and looking not a day older, though it was long since I had met him; and with just the same kind eager look in his eyes. And, as we shook hands, he placed his left hand over my right hand—and then I placed *my* left hand over *his*, in glad response.

Whatever happens to the world, things of this kind will go on. Life will always have dear good moments.

M. B.

FREDERICK EDWIN, 1ST EARL OF BIRKENHEAD (1872–1930)

Since this volume of letters went to press after Lord Birkenhead's death, he was not able to make the final revision of the proofs. He would not, of course, have chosen one of his own letters; but those who have helped in the production of this volume would like to pay to the author's memory the homage of inclusion.

TO THE EDITOR OF *THE DAILY TELEGRAPH*

SIR, In the discussions which are proceeding upon this subject it appears to me that the decisive considerations are being rather surprisingly ignored. The question is not whether the German Government have any right to request a censorship over the British film. Most evidently they have no such right.

The question is not whether our present system—such as it is—of censorship is satisfactory. Very likely it is not. The question is not whether any films heretofore exhibited in Germany have been calculated to give offence in Allied countries.

The issues (for there are two) cut far deeper.

The first is: Is it in the interests of peace and international good-will that we should perpetuate by public exhibition those incidents of the war which most embitter its memories? Do we desire, or do we not desire, that a new era of peace should dawn in Europe?

Do we, or do we not, desire by every means in our power to increase that mutual good feeling which must be established in Europe unless all alike are to perish in ruin? Do we serve any useful purpose by exasperating and humiliating a Government which has shown by its repudiation of the Hohenzollern dynasty its opinion of that dynasty and of its works?

Is it really our wish that while attempting to complete the Locarno edifice, Baralong films, true or false, should be exhibited in Germany; and Nurse Cavell films in the Allied countries?

I should myself have thought it was a commonplace that every man and, still more, every woman, of good intention, who does not wish to see his son or her son involved in another war, would strive by every effort to put away the memory of these old unhappy things in the effort to establish a new and more humane relationship.

We are told that the existence in London of a statue to the heroic and incomparable woman whom it commemorates for ever, is inconsistent with these views. It is not. A dignified memorial to the immortal dead has as little relation to the incidents of a hectic film as a classical picture of the crucified Jesus to the attempt to commercialize His anguish for the purposes of Hollywood.

The second point seems to me to be even more decisive. What would Nurse Cavell herself have said about this proposal? The true purposes of this sainted woman—her only message to the world—are engraved on her memorial:

> Patriotism is not enough. I must have no hatred or bitterness for anyone.

Does anyone suppose that the woman who, at the very moment of her agony, could speak like this, would permit her death to be commercialized, with the certain result that the bitter memories associated with it would be kept alive and fertilized so as to prevent the sweet restoration of friendship and good relationship between the nations of the world?

And what is the object of this adventure, over the frustration of which we are invited to shed tears? Is it to preach a Holy message? Are the profits to be devoted to some charitable purpose? Will they establish foundation scholarships to train a new generation of women to the Nurse Cavell standards?

Or are they intended to bring in profit to the producer and those associated with him? If this, indeed, be the purpose, is it decent so to exploit the agony and the sacrifice of the noblest woman whom the war produced? And so to exploit it in circumstances which, as I have shown, make it almost certain that nothing in the world could have seemed more horrible to that brave, proud and sensitive nature?

Yours faithfully,

BIRKENHEAD

GEORGE SAMPSON

A critic and author of very wide knowledge and experience, George Sampson is one of the most discriminating devotees of music of the twentieth century. In this letter he describes his experiences at the Salzburg Festival.

HOTEL DE L'EUROPE, SALZBURG,
21ST AUGUST, 1928

WERE you ever in Salzburg? It is new to me, and I find it a perfect duck of a place. It is twice blessed. It has all the gifts of God and not a few gifts of men. It isn't medieval: it is too gracious for that; it is just seventeen-something, and you feel that if there had been no Mozart born here he would have had to be invented. Happily, the Birthplace is rather a sweet old house, perfectly becoming to the dear creature, and not in the least shocking, like that bescribbled Horror at Stratford-on-Avon.

We—meaning the Festival visitors—are rather conscious of ourselves, and anxious not to resemble the Nonconformists who go to gratify their Dissent at Ober-Ammergau. No, no! we are not disciples of the late W. T. Stead, to whom, I like to think, Mozart would have meant nothing. We—meaning now our two selves—had a curious foretaste of present joys last week in Vienna, where we heard "Così fan tutte" broadcast from the Festspielhaus here. Our first Show in Salzburg itself was the "Flute," which I grow more and more to think the greatest as it is certainly the loveliest of operas. It is gospel, grace, and gaiety made one—a blessed Trinity indeed. Do you remember a precious utterance of George Moore's?—"No one has written many operas successfully—none, except Wagner. Mozart is *next best*." Next best, indeed! I think George is no more than a dear old frump after all, gullible too, as sparkish frumps usually are. How he clings to his Wagner, that idol of the advanced suburbs! I wonder if the dread secret is that George is really vulgar at heart? Wouldn't it be more distinguished if he admired say "Robert le Diable"?

Yesterday we had "Fidelio" with Lotte Lehmann. She is a dear; but we remember Ternina, you and I, don't we, and even the earlier,

925

pre-historic Lehmann, the great Lilli! "Fidelio" has many faults, not all of 'em Beethoven's; but it has also that about it which makes most other operas sound trashy. "Mir ist so wunderbahr" is alone worth coming halfway across Europe to hear. The producer (and I am getting violent against the arrogant fatuity of producers and long to make a Smithfield of some of them) committed the blunder of setting Act II in a prison court about as cheerful as Mr. Dorrit's Marshalsea and dressing the prisoners in a dirty-drab convict-uniform, so that these Spanish politicals looked like a lot of jugged Charley Peaces. Their joy at being let out into the all-hailed Light and Sun and Air of this dismal and slummy backyard seemed a trifle excessive. The man should have remembered Goya, and given us blazing Spanish sunlight and picturesque raggedness. I record my conviction that Leonora III, great and wonderful as it is, ought not to be played *any-where* in this opera. After all, Beethoven himself deliberately took it out.

As we came for music I suppose I ought not to complain of the encircling sounds; but here in this hotel I am compassed about with the two most detestable of noises—the American snarl and the English haw-haw. Almost at my elbow as I write are two dear compatriots, a woman, mouthy and excessive, and a young man with the flat, wooden, expressionless public-school voice—"vice," as he would felicitously call it. I hear snatches—"neow thet he had retah'd and left Injah" —"M'yahriel's new flet, soo *mach* nace-ah than the eould, electric fahz in all the rooms, and not too fratefully deah." "And Ahris, you will be glad to h'yah, now that her bebby is grooing ap, is gooing to tek ap penting rairly quate sairiously." My boy, surely for such there is a place prepared!

We have a pleasant garden room here, and after late performances and midnight suppers I continue to evade the burden of health, wealth and wisdom by lying late abed. In a few days we are off to Munich, where we shall have still another "Così fan tutte," and thereafter to Nuremburg for the Dürers. We live, we live!

Good-bye! Love me, and wish me well, as R. B. says.

Yours,

G. S

GILBERT KEITH CHESTERTON

A buccaneering essayist and robust poet, G. K. Chesterton should shine in correspondence. The following example reveals him as a tender and devoted friend.

TO SIDNEY COLVIN

1903

DEAR MR. COLVIN, Things do sometimes occur in this world so beautiful and sensible that in thinking or speaking of them one forgets all about oneself. In the reality induced by my genuine feeling I will not conceal from myself or you that I have long been afraid that I have from time to time distressed you, both by things due to my detestable negligence and by other things which I really could not have avoided. But the news I have just heard about you is the kind of thing that in my eyes makes my short-comings quite as microscopic and irrelevant as my merits. I have as much right to look on at your new arrangements with delight as a criminal has to admire a sunset.

I will not say anything more about yourself or Mrs. Sitwell, because congratulations upon these real things always seem to me to be quite unsuited to this nasty and elegant language in which we write letters. If we could write a page of very exquisite blank verse, it might be all right, or erect an altar and slaughter a thousand oxen. As a milder form of burnt-offering, the only thing that occurs to me is to send you the copy of the Browning I had long marked off for you. Of what I owe you in that connection I need not speak. You will, I think, find that in the later part your most generous suggestions have borne fruit: the earlier part, I am sorry to say, had gone to Macmillan's, just too soon to be recalled or revised.

I think it must be something atmospheric connected with the news about you that has kept me reading "Across the Plains" for hours when I ought to have been working.

Yours always most gratefully,

G. K. CHESTERTON

MAURICE BARING

Trained for the diplomatic service but forsaking that for journalism, Baring made a name for himself in the world of literature by his masterly letters while a war correspondent for one of the principal London newspapers. When the Great War broke out he was gazetted to the Royal Flying Corps, in which he performed distinguished service. These two letters were sent home from the Front during the War.

R.F.C., H.Q.,
JANUARY 1, 1916

. . . I returned from Italy last night. It was one of the most exhausting journeys I have ever done. We motored all day to Paris, then we rushed to the Gare de Lyons, and thence rushed to Turin. Then the next morning we got up at five and went by train, changing five or six times, to Vezzola, with two Italian officers, who discussed a point of higher mathematics during the journey. We got out at Adine, hired a motor, drove across the Ticino, and for all I know the Rubicon, and the Tiber, and Lake Maggiore, through Lombarda, and Novara and Arona, to Gallerata, where the Italians learn to fly. There we inspected the Caproni machine in a shed, and saw Pinsuti, the stunt Caproni pilot, and thence we drove to Malpensa, where Dante was born and Virgil died, and there we were introduced to 45 flying officers, who each one said his name and use and clicked his heels. Then we had luncheon with the Flying School, which was commanded by Captain Falchi. At the end of luncheon the Captain made a speech about delicious England and the adorable English people, and I made a speech about divine Italians, quoting Browning, Dante, and D'Annunzio. Then an Italian pilot called Pellegrini, Cooper and myself went up into the sky. Into the grey, misty, sunless, lampless, sullen, unpeopled sky. And, as the machine climbed, the curtains of heaven were rent asunder, and through and over oceans of mist and rolling clouds, naked, majestic, white, shining and glorious, rose the Alps, like a barrier; and at our feet, dark as a raven's wing, loomed the waves of Lake Maggiore, fringed with foaming breakers; and the earth was outspread beneath us like a brown and purple carpet. And we climbed and banked, and banked and climbed, and far beneath us a little Maurice Farman fluttered like a white dove. Then suddenly the three engines stopped buzzing, and we turned and banked and turned and banked and turned and banked and dived and turned sheer and steep till we gently rolled on to the ground.

Then we spent a few hours in technical conversation, and then we went by train to Milan and dined. After dinner we nearly missed the train, and finally got back to Turin at midnight. The next day we started for Paris. A Frenchman sitting next to us in the train whom I knew said: "Il y a seulement quatorze personnes qui voyagent en temps de guerre et on est sûr de les rencontrer. Vous êtes l'une des quatorze." General de Castelnau was also one of the *quatorze.*

We reached Paris the next morning, and thence hither in the fastest motor in the world.

R.F.C., H.Q.,
The Eve of Christmas Eve, 1917

We started at 8 and got to the place where the Empress Eugénie used to give her famous little parties, at a quarter to 12. Then, after a quarter of an hour's conversation . . . (This was Compiègne, and the conversation was with Colonel Duval) we had luncheon. After luncheon, a Conference, which lasted till half-past two, and then we started home.

We reached a sharp turning when a *camion automobile* ran into us, but the icy road on which we skidded saved us from the worst, and the axle was undamaged and the only damage done was to the mudguard. A little further on we met two lorries at right angles across a steep and slippery hill. We managed to get round them, but having done so, the wheels of the Rolls-Royce refused to turn round and we had to dig in, get stones and sand and chains and spades and ropes, and persuade the vehicle to go uphill, an arduous and long task. It was in the end successfully accomplished, but the result was we took five hours to get home. At dinner an allied Major told me a long story, which was unfortunately interrupted long before the point had been reached. The cold is beyond all words.

. . . To-morrow is Christmas Eve, and one naturally wonders how many more Christmas Eves we shall have to endure darkened by the shadow of war and overhung by the threats of air-raids. Let us hope not many more. As for me, I am finished. My spirit is broken, my moral is deplorable, my feet are covered with chilblains, my fingers

E.L.   H H are stained with the nicotine of Virginian cigarettes, my hairs, which are grey and few in number, want cutting, my shoes, worn in the evening, have got holes in the soles of them, my boots pinch me and are as cold as vaults. Apart from all this, I am in very good spirits, and I think the war prospects are much better than they were last Sunday. Why? I cannot tell.

LORD DUNSANY

This hitherto unpublished letter is of great interest, revealing as it does a poet's view of the War.

TO HERBERT E. PALMER

DEAR MR. PALMER, Thank you very much for so kindly sending me your book. Poetry is, I think, the chief interest in my life, and I always delight in reading it. I should have written to thank you sooner only that your book arrived here while I was in France, and it was not sent on to risk the chances of that country. I enjoyed reading your verses very much, particularly, of course, "Two Fishers" after which you name the book. There are, I think, too many people who, when there are only one or two poets, abuse them for eccentricity, asking why they write poetry when nobody else does; and who, when there are many poets, rage more angrily still, asking why in Heaven's name there should be so many poets. I think that the hatred of poetry is pretty widespread and takes many forms, particularly that of discouraging living poets, which is easier than hurting the dead; and so, if I say I believe the pursuit of any of the arts to be desirable, if only done with sincerity and single purpose, and that it is these same arts that the Earth most remembers and treasures, I shall do no harm, for very few will believe me.

Yet it is perhaps worth while telling you this belief, for but a few years ago we came out of an age of commerce and entered an age of war; and neither amongst the materialism of commerce nor the necessary violence of war has there been any room for poetry in men's recognition. Lest you should despair during these few years, as I sometimes do, I repeat that, looking out over broad ages, not dazzled by the fluctuations of one particular age, the arts appear as mankind's supreme achievement.

Having seen the misery of active battlefields, and the dirt and rubbish and ruin of old ones, I think that the poets should do all that can be done to draw from the war what is glorious and noble and to preserve it. For the world needs some splendour for a compensation after four lamentable years.

Yours truly,

DUNSANY

OLIVER LOCKER-LAMPSON

During the Great War Commander Oliver Locker-Lampson (a son of Frederick Locker-Lampson) commanded a unit of armoured cars in Russia and elsewhere. The following letter purports to have been written by a Morris motor-car to one of the writer's many nieces.

THE MORRIS TO HIS MISTRESS

UNDER THE KEEPER'S TREES,

SUNDAY, 1 A.M. AUG. 15TH, 1927

DEAREST LADY LEARNER, I am under the oak trees, near the pheasant coops, and patches of moonlight dapple my battered sides. The doorway of the hut stands a square of crimson against the heath, and only the purr of the night-jar makes gaps in the silence.

I am thinking of a far-away bronze-haired friend who sat so lately in my leather arms and guided me—rather wobblingly at times—through street and lane. It was a stunning experience for me, and I quiver still at the remembrance.

You may not have been experienced but I treasure the touch of your hand beyond that of the deftest driver. How cosily you nestled against the cushions; how confidingly you took the wheel—and my pedals ache for two muffled gummers [1] which played the piano there adorably.

I may be battered about the flanks and asthmatic about the carburettor and otherwise bruised by the impact of walls and hedges which I sought to avoid. But I would take any risk if only a pair of little feet I know controlled my speed and a pair of pink fists I love decided my destination. What champion comings and goings were ours! Do you remember your first drive . . . interrupted, you will recall, and oh! your last (*our* last, I mean) still more disturbed, nay! stopped altogether. Beloved pupil, thou didst thrill back then in magic communion.

---

[1] India-rubber boots.

932

And now I lie marooned beneath the stars this midnight—solitary and ·sad.

Farewell, fond fairy of my dreams and wakings.   Do not fruit-lessly engage the gears of other cars forgetful of me, but return, darling mistress of my motion, and be mine once again soon.

I remain,

With palpitating cylinders,

Marjorie's devoted

MORRIS

RUPERT BROOKE (1887–1915)

This promising poet set out in 1913 *on a long tour round the world, visiting North America, Oceania and New Zealand, and had hardly returned to England when the Great War broke out. In September,* 1914, *he was commissioned in the Royal Naval Division, with which he sailed to Gallipoli early the following year and while there he died of blood-poisoning, in April,* 1915. *Rupert Brooke's posthumous* "1914 *and Other Poems" made his name familiar to all who love their country and cherish the memory of those who died for it.*

TO EDWARD MARSH

SOMEWHERE NEAR FIJI,
NOVEMBER 15 (?), 1913

DEAR EDDIE, I'm conscious I haven't written to you for a long time: —though, indeed, my last letter was *posted* only a short time ago. When it, or when this, will get to you, God knows. About Christmas, I suppose, though it seems incredible. My *reason* tells me that you'll be slurring through London mud in a taxi, with a heavy drizzle falling, and a chilly dampness in the air, and the theatres glaring in the Strand, and crowds of white faces. But I can't help *thinking* of you trotting through crisp snow to a country church, holly-decorated, with little robins picking crumbs all around, and the church-bells playing our brother Tennyson's *In Memoriam* brightly through the clear air. It may not be: it never has been:—that picture-postcard Christmas. But I shall think of you so. You think of me, in a loin-cloth, brown and wild in the fair chocolate arms of a Tahitian beauty, reclining beneath a bread-fruit tree, on white sand, with the breakers roaring against the reefs a mile out, and strange brilliant fish darting through the pellucid hyaline of the sun-saturated sea.

Oh, Eddie, it's all true about the South Seas! I get a little tired of it at moments, because I am just too old for Romance. But there it is: there it wonderfully is: heaven on earth, the ideal life, little work, dancing and singing and eating, naked people of incredible loveliness, perfect manners, and immense kindliness, a divine tropic climate, and intoxicating beauty of scenery. I came aboard and left Samoa two days ago. Before that I had been wandering with an "interpreter"—entirely genial and quite incapable of English—through Samoan villages. The last few days I stopped in one, where a big marriage-feast was going on. I lived in a Samoan house (the coolest in the world) with a man and his wife, nine children, ranging from a proud beauty of 18 to a round object of 1 year, a dog, a cat, a proud hysterical hen, and a gaudy scarlet and green parrot, who roved the roof and beams with a wicked eye; choosing a place whence to ——, twice a day, with humorous precision, on my hat and clothes. The Samoan girls have extraordinarily beautiful bodies, and walk like goddesses. They're a lovely brown colour, without any black Melanesian admixture; their necks and shoulders would be the wild envy of any European beauty; and in carriage and face they remind me continually and vividly of my incomparable heartless and ever-loved X. Fancy moving among a tribe of X's! Can't you imagine how shattered and fragmentary a heart I'm bearing away to Fiji and Tahiti? And, oh dear! I'm afraid they'll be just as bad.

And Eddie, it's all True about, for instance, Cocoanuts. You tramp through a strange vast dripping tropical forest for hours, listening to weird liquid hootings from birds and demons in the branches above. Then you feel thirsty, so you send your boy up a great perpendicular palm. He runs up with utter ease and grace, cuts off a couple of vast nuts and comes down and makes holes in them. And they are chock-full of the best drink in the world.

Romance! Romance! I walked 15 miles through mud and up and down mountains, and swam three rivers, to get this boat. But if ever you miss me, suddenly, one day, from lecture-room B. in King's, or from the Moulin d'Or at lunch, you'll know that I've got sick for the full moon on these little thatched roofs, and the palms against the morning, and the Samoan boys and girls diving thirty feet into a green sea or a deep mountain pool under a waterfall—and that I've gone back.

ROMANCE? That's half my time. The rest is Life—Life, Eddie, is what you get in the bars of the hotels in 'Frisco, or Honolulu, or Suva, or Apia, and in the smoking-rooms in these steamers. It is incredibly like a Kipling story, and all the people are very self-consciously Kiplingesque. Yesterday, for instance, I sat in the Chief Engineer's cabin, with the first officer and a successful beach-comber lawyer from the white-man's town in Samoa, drinking Australian champagne from breakfast to lunch. "To-day I am not well." The

RUPERT BROOKE

beach-comber matriculated at Wadham, and was sent down. Also, he rode with the Pytchley, quotes you Virgil, and discusses the ins and outs of the Peninsular campaign. And his repertoire of smut is enormous. Mere Kipling, you see, but one gets some good stories. Verses, of a school-boy kind, too. . . . *Sehr primitiv.* The whole thing makes a funny world.

I may pick up some mail, and hear from you, when I get to New Zealand. I'm afraid your post as my honorary literary agent, or grass-executor, is something of a sinecure. I *can't* write on the trail.

There's one thing I wanted to consult you about, and I can't remember if I mentioned it. I want some club to take an occasional stranger into, for a drink, and to read the papers in, and, sometimes, to have a quiet meal in. Where do you think I should go? . . . I want somewhere I needn't always be spick and span in, and somewhere I don't have to pay a vast sum.

There's nothing else in the way of my European existence, I think. That part of it which is left, out here, reads Ben Jonson. Kindly turn up his "New Inn" (which is sheer Meredith) and read Lovel's Song in Act IV. The second verse will dispel the impression of the first, that it is by Robert Browning. The whole thing is pure beauty.

No more. My love to everyone, from Jackson down to ——— if you've made her acquaintance yet—Helena Darwin Cornford.[1] And to such as Wilfrid (Gibson) and Denis (Browne) and yourself and a few more poor, pale-skinned stay-at-homes, a double measure. I have a growing vision of next summer term spent between King's and Raymond Buildings: a lovely vision. May it be.

Manina! Tofa!

Thy

RUPERT

---

[1] Professor Henry Jackson, O.M.—and a baby born since his departure.

GERTRUDE BELL (d. 1926)

Gertrude Bell was the gifted daughter of Sir Hugh Bell. In 1913 she travelled alone, except for native guides, from Damascus by a circuitous route to Bagdad. At that time she was the only woman traveller in Arabia. Her knowledge of the East was invaluable in the complicated situation produced by the Great War. She was employed in Mesopotamia in a diplomatic capacity and drafted a remarkable state paper upon the political questions of that district.

TO HORACE MARSHALL

GULAHEK, JUNE 18, 1892

DEAR COUSIN MINE, Are we the same people I wonder when all our surroundings, associations, acquaintances are changed. Here that which is me, which womanlike is an empty jar that the passer by fills at pleasure, is filled with such wine as in England I had never heard of, now the wine is more important than the jar when one is thirsty, therefore I conclude, cousin mine, that it is not the person who danced with you are Mansfield St. that writes to you to-day from Persia. Yet there are dregs, English sediments at the bottom of my sherbet, and perhaps they flavour it more than I think. Anyhow, I remember you as a dear person in a former existence, whom I should like to drag into this one and to guide whose spiritual coming I will draw paths in ink. And others there are whom I remember yet not with regret but as one might remember people one knew when one was an inhabitant of Mars 20 centuries ago. How big the world is, how big and how wonderful. It comes to me as ridiculously presumptuous that I should dare to carry my little personality half across it and boldly attempt to measure with it things for which it has no table of measurements that can possibly apply. So under protest I write to you of Persia: I am not me, that is my only excuse. I am merely pouring out for you some of what I have received during the last two months.

Well, in this country the men wear flowing robes of green and white and brown, the women lift the veil of a Raphael Madonna to

937

look at you as you pass; wherever there is water a luxuriant vegetation springs up and where there is not there is nothing but stone and
desert. Oh, the desert round Teheran! miles and miles of it with
nothing, *nothing* growing; ringed in with bleak bare mountains snow
crowned and furrowed with the deep courses of torrents. I never
knew what desert was till I came here; it is a very wonderful thing to
see; and suddenly in the middle of it all, out of nothing, out of a little
cold water, springs up a garden. Such a garden! trees, fountains, tanks,
roses and a house in it, the houses which we heard of in fairy tales when
we were little: inlaid with tiny slabs of looking-glass in lovely patterns,
blue tiled, carpeted, echoing with the sound of running water and
fountains. Here sits the enchanted prince, solemn, dignified, clothed
in long robes. He comes down to meet you as you enter, his house
is yours, his garden is yours, better still his tea and fruit are yours, so
are his kalyans (but I think kalyans are a horrid form of smoke, they
taste to me of charcoal and paint and nothing else). By the grace of
God your slave hopes that the health of your nobility is well? It is
very well out of his great kindness. Will your magnificence carry
itself on to this cushion? Your magnificence sits down and spends
ten minutes in bandying florid compliments through an interpreter
while ices are served and coffee, after which you ride home refreshed,
charmed, and with many blessings on your fortunate head. And all
the time your host was probably a perfect stranger into whose privacy
you had forced yourself in this unblushing way. Ah, we have no
hospitality in the west and no manners. I felt ashamed almost before
the beggars in the street—they wear their rags with a better grace
than I my most becoming habit, and the veils of the commonest women
(now the veil is the touchstone on which to try a woman's toilette)
are far better put on than mine. A veil should fall from the top of
your head to the soles of your feet, of that I feel convinced, and it
should not be transparent.

Say, is it not rather refreshing to the spirit to lie in a hammock
strung between the plane trees of a Persian garden and read the poems
of Hafiz—in the original mark you!—out of a book curiously bound
in stamped leather which you have bought in the bazaars. That is
how I spend my mornings here; a stream murmurs past me which
Zoroastrian gardeners guide with long handled spades into tiny sluices
leading into the flower beds all around. The dictionary which is
also in my hammock is not perhaps so poetic as the other attributes
—let us hide it under our muslin petticoats!

This also is pleasant: to come in at 7 o'clock in the morning after a two hours' ride, hot and dusty, and find one's cold bath waiting for one scented with delicious rose water, and after it an excellent and longed-for breakfast spread in a tent in the garden.

What else can I give you but fleeting impressions caught and hardened out of all knowing? I can tell you of a Persian merchant in whose garden, stretching all up the mountain side, we spent a long day, from dawn to sunset, breakfasting, lunching, teaing on nothing but Persian foods. He is noted for his hospitality; every evening parties of friends arrive unexpectedly "he goes out, entertains them," said the Persian who told me about it, "spreads a banquet before them and relates to them stories half through the night. Then cushions are brought and carpeted mattresses and they lie down in one of the guest houses in the garden and sleep till dawn when they rise and repair to the bath in the village." Isn't it charmingly like the Arabian nights; but that is the charm of it all and it has none of it changed; every day I meet our aged calenders and ladies who I am sure have suits of swans' feathers laid up in a chest at home, and some time when I open a new jar of rose water I know that instead of a sweet smell, the great smoke of one of Suleiman's afreets will come out of its neck.

In the garden there are big deep tanks where in the evenings between tennis and dinner I often swim in the coldest of cold water. Before we left Teheran when it was too hot to sleep, I used to go out at dawn and swim under the shadow of the willows. We were very glad to leave Teheran though we liked the house there. It began to be very stuffy and airless; here, though we are only 6 miles away, there is always air, except perhaps between two and four in the afternoon when one generally sleeps. We are much higher up and much nearer the hills and all round us are watered fields where the corn is almost ripe for cutting. The joy of this climate! I don't think an English summer will be very nice after it.

I learn Persian, not with great energy, one does nothing with energy here. My teacher is a delightful old person with bright eyes and a white Turban who knows so little French (French is our medium) that he can neither translate the poets to me nor explain any grammatical difficulties. But we get on admirably nevertheless and spend much of our time in long philosophic discussions carried on by me in French and by him in Persian. His point of view is very much that of an oriental Gibbon, though with this truly oriental distinction, that he would never dream of acknowledging in words or acts his scepticism to one of his own countrymen.   It would be tacitly understood between them and their 'intercourse would be continued on the basis of perfect agreement.   Now this is a great simplification and promotes, I should imagine, the best of good manners. . . .

Good-bye, write to me and tell me how the world goes with you.

TO HER FATHER

BAGDAD, AUGUST 28TH, 1921

WE have had a terrific week but we've got our King crowned and Sir Percy and I agree that we're now half seas over, the remaining half is the Congress and the Organic Law. . . .   The enthronement took place at 6 a.m. on Tuesday, admirably arranged.   A dais about 2 ft. 6 in. high was set up in the middle of the big Sarai courtyard; behind it are the quarters Faisal is occupying, the big Government reception rooms; in front were seated in blocks, English, Arab officials, townsmen, Ministers, local deputations, to the number of 1,500.

Exactly at 6 we saw Faisal in uniform, Sir Percy in white diplomatic uniform with all his ribbons and stars, Sir Aylmer, Mr. Cornwallis, and a following of A.D.C.s descend the Sarai steps from Faisal's lodging and come pacing down the long path of carpets, past the guard of honour (the Dorsets, they looked magnificent) and so to the dais. . . . We all stood up while they came in and sat when they had taken their places on the dais.   Faisal looked very dignified but much strung up—it was an agitating moment.   He looked along the front row and caught my eye and I gave him a tiny salute.   Then Saiyid Hussain stood up and read Sir Percy's proclamation in which he announced that Faisal had been elected King by 96 per cent. of the people of Mesopotamia, long live the King! with that we stood up and saluted him.   The national flag was broken on the flagstaff by his side and the band played "God save the King"—they have no national anthem yet.   There followed a salute of 21 guns. . . .   It was an amazing thing to see all Iraq, from North to South gathered together.   It is the first time it has happened in history. . . .

Sir Percy had been unwell but on the day of the Coronation he began to recover and is now quite fit again, so I who had kept all people off him for a week quietly arranged for the deputations to pay their respects to him.   We had two days of it Friday and Saturday morning. It would be difficult to tell you how many people there are in the office one and the same time. It was immensely interesting seeing them—there were people I had never seen before and a great many who had never seen Bagdad before. Basrah and Amarah came on Friday, Hillah and Mosul on Saturday; they were the big deputations, of these Mosul was the most wonderful. I divided it into three sections—first the Mosul town magnates, my guests and their colleagues, next the Christian Archbishops and Bishops—Mosul abounds in them—and the Jewish Grand Rabbi. . . .

The third group was more exciting than all the others; it was the Kurdish chiefs of the frontier who have elected to come into the Iraq state until they see whether an independent Kurdistan develops which will be still better to their liking. . . .

After they had had their quarter of an hour with Sir Percy all in turn came down to me. The Kurds came last and stayed longest. The Mayor . . . said that they hadn't had an opportunity to discuss with Sir Percy the future of Kurdistan, what did I think about it? I said that my opinion was that the districts they came from were economically dependent on Mosul and always would be however many Kurdistans were created. They agreed, but they must have Kurdish officials. I said I saw no difficulty there. And the children must be taught in Kurdish schools. I pointed out that there would be some difficulty about that as there wasn't a single school book—nor any other—written in Kurdish. This gave them pain and after consideration they said they thought the teaching might as well be in Arabic, but what about local administrative autonomy. . . . I said, "Have you talked it over with Saiyidna Faisal—our Lord Faisal?" "No," they said. "Well, you had better go and do it at once," I suggested. "Shall I make an appointment for you?" "Yes," they said. So I telephoned to Rustam Haidar and made an appointment for yesterday afternoon—I'm longing to hear from Faisal what came of it. Fun, isn't it? . . . Faisal . . . asked me to tea.

We spent a happy hour discussing (a) our desert frontier to South and West and (b) the National Flag and Faisal's personal flag. For the latter we arranged provisionally this, i.e. the Hijaz flag with a gold crown on the red triangle. The red I must tell you is the colour of his house so he bears his own crown on it. Father, do for heaven's sake tell me whether the Hijaz flag is heraldically right. You might telegraph. It's a very good flag and we could differentiate it for the Iraq by putting a gold star on the black stripe or on the red triangle.

The Congress will settle it directly it meets. *Do* let me know in time. Also whether you have a better suggestion for Faisal's standard. . . .

There's no doubt that this is the most absorbing job that I've ever taken a hand in. . . .

JAMES STEPHENS

There is something of great beauty in this letter from one poet to another. It needs little comment; it shows a depth of sympathy and feeling far removed from the petty disparagements so commonly to be found among men of letters in previous times.

18TH MAY, 1920

DEAR——, Print, or use in any way anything of mine that you think will help. I am not sanguine, myself, that it will be of much assistance, and I would urge you not to let any (apparent) failure worry you. After all, the great thing is that you can write such good verse—that is, your part is faithfully performed. If publishers, or others, do not perform their part, you cannot help it. You remember Whitman's phrase, "The Song returns to the Singer." I quote from memory, and always misquote. It is already a great thing to be a poet. Success lies simply in that fact. Even if recognition does not come to you, the truth is unaltered, and you must bear, or rather, be utterly careless of the whips and scorns of time, and all the other calamities which may seem to be piling on you. Some of us get into print more easily, but, after that, we are almost utterly neglected. Try, I beg you, to be content with your great gift; it is personal to you, and within your control, and all the rest is vanity. This may all seem priggish to you: but is essentially true. The poem returns to the poet—that is his, and your, reward; any other success than that is not his business. Is it nothing that you can walk along repeating the poems that you have actually made yourself, or that you can delight your friends with them? I think your work is excellent; you, I am sure, know that it is, and that certitude may be all the reward you will ever get, but it should be sufficient for a poet. You ought to be proud and happy, and you ought to let public success or failure go as they please. Yours very truly,

JAMES STEPHENS

943

LETTERS DURING THE GREAT WAR

The letters printed below were written home by officers who died in the war. They, show, if the showing be needed, what rising talent was lost for ever in the tragedy of that great holocaust.

CAPTAIN SIR EDWARD HAMILTON WESTROW HULSE, BART., SCOTS GUARDS

Educated Eton and Balliol College, Oxford, Regular Army. Killed in action, France, March 12, 1915, at the age of 25.

28/12/14

MY DEAREST MOTHER, Just returned to billets again, after the most extraordinary Christmas in the trenches you could possibly imagine. Words fail me completely in trying to describe it, but here goes!

On the 23rd we took over the trenches in the ordinary manner, relieving the Grenadiers, and during the 24th the usual firing took place, and sniping was pretty brisk. We stood to arms as usual at 6.30 a.m. on the 25th, and I noticed that there was not much shooting; this gradually died down, and by 8 a.m. there was no shooting at all, except for a few shots on our left (Border Regt.). At 8.30 a.m. I was looking out, and saw four Germans leave their trenches and come towards us; I told two of my men to go and meet them, unarmed (as the Germans were unarmed), and to see that they did not pass the half-way line. We were 350–400 yards apart, at this point. My fellows were not very keen, not knowing what was up, so I went out alone, and met Barry, one of our ensigns, also coming out from another part of the line. By the time we got to them, they were ¾ of the way over, and much too near our barbed wire, so I moved them back. They were three private soldiers and a stretcher-bearer, and their spokesman started off by saying that he thought it only right to come over and wish us a happy Christmas, and trusted us implicitly to keep the truce. He came from Suffolk where he had left his best girl and a 3½ h.p. motor-bike! He told me that he could not get a letter to the girl, and wanted to send one through me. I made him write out a postcard in front of me, in English, and I sent it off that night. I told him that she probably would not be

944

a bit keen to see him again. We then entered on a long discussion on every sort of thing. I was dressed in an old stocking-cap and a man's overcoat, and they took me for a corporal, a thing which I did not discourage, as I had an eye to going as near their lines as possible. . . . I asked them what orders they had from their officers as to coming over to us, and they said *none*; they had just come over out of goodwill.

They protested that they had no feeling of enmity towards us at all, but that everything lay with their authorities, and that being soldiers they had to obey. I believe that they were speaking the truth when they said this, and that they never wished to fire a shot again. They said that unless directly ordered, they were not going to shoot again until we did. . . . We talked about the ghastly wounds made by rifle bullets, and we both agreed that neither of us used dum-dum bullets, and that the wounds are solely inflicted by the high-velocity bullet with the sharp nose, at short range. We both agreed that it would be far better if we used the old South African round-nosed bullet, which makes a clean hole. . . .

They think that our Press is to blame in working up feeling against them by publishing false "atrocity reports." I told them of various sweet little cases which I have seen for myself, and they told me of English prisoners whom they have seen with soft-nosed bullets, and lead bullets with notches cut in the nose; we had a heated, and at the same time, good-natured argument, and ended by hinting to each other that the other was lying!

I kept it up for half an hour, and then escorted them back as far as their barbed wire, having a jolly good look round all the time, and picking up various little bits of information which I had not had an opportunity of doing under fire! I left instructions with them that if any of them came out later they must not come over the half-way line, and appointed a ditch as the meeting place. We parted after an exchange of Albany cigarettes and German cigars, and I went straight to H.-qrs. to report.

On my return at 10 a.m. I was surprised to hear a hell of a din going on, and not a single man left in my trenches; they were completely denuded (against my orders), and nothing lived! I heard strains of "Tipperary" floating down the breeze, swiftly followed by a tremendous burst of "Deutschland über Alles," and as I got to my own Coy. H.-qrs. dug-out, I saw, to my amazement, not only a crowd of about 150 British and Germans at the half-way house which I had appointed opposite my lines, but six or seven such crowds, all the way down our lines, extending towards the 8th Division on our right.   I bustled out and asked if there were any German officers in my crowd, and the noise died down (as this time I was myself in my own cap and badges of rank).

I found two, but had to talk to them through an interpreter, as they could neither talk English nor French. . . .   I explained to them that strict orders must be maintained as to meeting half-way, and everyone unarmed; and we both agreed not to fire until the other did, thereby creating a complete deadlock and armistice (if strictly observed). . . .

Meanwhile Scots and Huns were fraternizing in the most genuine possible manner.   Every sort of souvenir was exchanged, addresses given and received, photos of families shown, etc.   One of our fellows offered a German a cigarette; the German said, "Virginian?"   Our fellow said, "Aye, straight-cut": the German said, "No thanks, I only smoke Tur-kish!"   (Sort of 10s. a 100 me!)   It gave us all a good laugh.   A German N.C.O. with the Iron Cross, gained, he told me, for conspicuous skill in sniping,—started his fellows off on some marching tune.   When they had done I set the note for "*The Boys of Bonnie Scotland, where the heather and the bluebells grow*," and so we went on singing every-thing from "*Good King Wenceslaus*" down to the ordinary Tommies' song, and ended up with "*Auld Lang Syne*," which we all, English, Scots, Irish, Prussian, Wurtembergers, etc., joined in.   It was absolutely astounding, and if I had seen it on a cinematograph film I should have sworn that it was faked! . . .

From foul rain and wet, the weather had cleared up the night before to a sharp frost, and it was a perfect day, everything white, and the silence seemed extraordinary, after the usual din.   From all sides birds seemed to arrive, and we hardly ever see a bird generally.   Later in the day I fed about 50 sparrows outside my dug-out, which shows how complete the silence and quiet was.

I must say that I was very much impressed with the whole scene, and also, as everyone else, astoundingly relieved by the quiet, and by being able to walk about freely.   It is the first time, day or night, that we have heard no guns, or rifle-firing, since I left Havre and convalescence!   Just after we had finished "*Auld Lang Syne*" an old hare started up, and seeing so many of us about in an unwonted spot, did not know which way to go.   I gave one loud "View Holloa," and one and all, British and Germans, rushed about giving chase, slipping up on the frozen plough, falling about, and after a hot two minutes we killed in the open, a German and one of our fellows falling together heavily upon the completely baffled hare. Shortly afterwards we saw four more hares, and killed one again; both were good heavy weight and had evidently been out between the two rows of trenches for the last two months, well-fed on the cabbage patches, etc., many of which are untouched on the "no-man's land." The enemy kept one and we kept the other. It was now 11.30 a.m. and at this moment George Paynter arrived on the scene, with a hearty "Well, my lads, a Merry Christmas to you! This is d——d comic, isn't it?" . . . George told them that he thought it only right that we should show that we could desist from hostilities on a day which was so important in both countries; and he then said, "Well, my boys, I've brought you over something to celebrate this funny show with," and he produced from his pocket a large bottle of rum (not ration rum, but the proper stuff). One large shout went up, and the nasty little spokesman uncorked it, and in a heavy unceremonious manner, drank our healths, in the name of his "camaraden"; the bottle was then passed on and polished off before you could say knife. . . .

During the afternoon the same extraordinary scene was enacted between the lines, and one of the enemy told me that he was longing to get back to London: I assured him that "So was I." He said that he was sick of the war, and I told him that when the truce was ended, any of his friends would be welcome in our trenches, and would be well-received, fed, and given a free passage to the Isle of Man! Another coursing meeting took place, with no result, and at 4.30 p.m. we agreed to keep in our respective trenches, and told them that the truce was ended. They persisted, however, in saying that they were not going to fire, and as George had told us not to, unless they did, we prepared for a quiet night, but warned all sentries to be doubly on the alert.

During the day both sides had taken the opportunity of bringing up piles of wood, straw, etc., which is generally only brought up with difficulty under fire. We improved our dug-outs, roofed in new ones, and got a lot of very useful work done towards increasing our comfort. Directly it was dark, I got the whole of my Coy. on to improving and re-making our barbed-wire entanglements, all along my front, and had my scouts out in front of the working parties, to prevent any surprise; but not a shot was fired, and we finished off a real good obstacle un-molested.

On my left was the bit of ground over which we attacked on the 18th, and here the lines are only from 85 to 100 yards apart.

The Border Regiment were occupying this section on Christmas Day, and Giles Loder, our Adjutant, went down there with a party that morning on hearing of the friendly demonstrations in front of my Coy., to see if he could come to an agreement about our dead, who were still lying out between the trenches. The trenches are so close at this point, that of course each side had to be far stricter. Well, he found an extremely pleasant and superior stamp of German officer, who arranged to bring all our dead to the half-way line. We took them over there, and buried 29 exactly half-way between the two lines. Giles collected all personal effects, pay-books and identity discs, but was stopped by the Germans when he told some men to bring in the rifles; all rifles lying on their side of the half-way line they kept carefully!

They apparently treated our prisoners well, and did all they could for our wounded. This officer kept on pointing to our dead and saying, "*Les Braves, c'est bien dommage.*" . . .

When George heard of it he went down to that section and talked to the nice officer and gave him a scarf. That same evening a German orderly came to the half-way line, and brought a pair of warm woolly gloves as a present in return for George.

The same night the Borderers and we were engaged in putting up big trestle obstacles, with barbed wire all over them, and connecting them, and at this same point (namely, where we were only 85 yards apart) the Germans came out and sat on their parapet, and watched us doing it, although we had informed them that the truce was ended. . . . Well, all was quiet, as I said, that night; and next morning, while I was having breakfast, one of my N.C.O's came and reported that the enemy were again coming over to talk. I had given full instructions and none of my men were allowed out of the trenches to talk to the enemy. I had also told the N.C.O. of an advanced post which I have up a ditch, to go out with two men, *unarmed*; if any of the enemy came over, to see that they did not cross the half-way line, and to engage them in pleasant conversation. So I went out, and found the same lot as the day before; they told me again that they had no intention of firing, and wished the truce to continue. I had instructions not to fire till the enemy did; I told them; and so the same comic form of temporary truce continued on the 26th, and again at 4.30 p.m. I informed them that the truce was at an end. We had sent them over some plum-puddings, and they thanked us heartily for them and retired again, the only difference being that instead of all my men being out in the "no-man's zone," one N.C.O. and two men only were allowed out, and the enemy therefore sent fewer.

Again both sides had been improving their comfort during the day, and again at night I continued on my barbed wire and finished it right off. We retired for the night all quiet and were rudely awakened at 11 p.m. A H.-qr. orderly burst into my dug-out, and handed me a message. It stated that a deserter had come into the 8th Division lines, and stated that the whole German line was going to attack at 12.15 midnight, and that we were to stand to arms immediately, and that reinforcements were being hurried up from billets in rear. I thought, at the time, that it was a d——d good joke on the part of the German deserter to deprive us of our sleep, and so it turned out to be. I stood my Coy. to arms, made a few extra dispositions, gave out all instructions, and at 11.20 p.m. George arrived. . . . Suddenly *our* guns all along the line opened a heavy fire, and all the enemy did was to reply with 9 shell (heavy howitzers), *not one of which exploded*, just on my left. Never a rifle shot was fired by either side (except right away down in the 8th Division), and at 2.30 p.m. we turned in half the men to sleep, and kept half awake on sentry.

Apparently this deserter had also reported that strong German reinforcements had been brought up, and named a place just in rear of their lines, where, he said, two regiments were in billets, that had just been brought up. Our guns were informed, and plastered the place well when they opened fire (as I mentioned). The long and the short of it was that absolutely *nixt* happened, and after a sleepless night I turned in at 4.30 a.m., and was woken again at 6.30, when we always stand to arms before daylight. I was just going to have another sleep at 8 a.m. when I found that the enemy were again coming over to talk to us (Dec. 27th). I watched my N.C.O. and two men go out from the advanced post to meet, and hearing shouts of laughter from the little party when they met, I again went out myself.

They asked me what we were up to during the night, and told me that they had stood to arms all night and thought we were going to attack them when they heard our heavy shelling; also that our guns had done a lot of damage and knocked out a lot of their men in billets. I told them a deserter of theirs had come over to us, and that they had only him to thank for any damage done, and that we, after a sleepless night, were not best pleased with him either! They assured me that they had heard nothing of an attack, and I fully believed them, as it is inconceivable that they would have allowed us to put up the formidable obstacles (which we had on the two previous nights) if they had contemplated an offensive movement.

Anyhow, if it had ever existed, the plan had miscarried, as no attack was developed on any part of our line, and here were these fellows still protesting that there was a truce, although I told them that it had ceased the evening before.   So I kept the same arrangement, namely, that my N.C.O. and two men should meet them half-way, and strict orders were given that no other man was to leave the lines. . . .   I admit that the whole thing beat me absolutely.   In the evening we were relieved by the Grenadiers, quite openly (not crawling about on all fours, as usual), and we handed on our instructions to the Grenadiers in case the enemy still wished to pay visits! . . .

LIEUTENANT ARTHUR GEORGE HEATH, QUEEN'S OWN ROYAL WEST KENT REGIMENT

Educated Grocers' Company's School and New College, Oxford (scholar).   Fellow and Tutor of New College.   Killed in action, France, October 8, 1915, at the age of 28.

(FLANDERS) JULY 11TH, 1915

MY DEAR MOTHER, It is Sunday, and though we shall be working all the same in a few hours, I feel that I should like to take the opportunity of telling you some things I've wanted to say now for a long time.   You remember that I told you when I was going that nothing worried me so much as the thought of the trouble I was causing you by going away, or might cause you if I was killed.   Now that death is near I feel the same.   I don't think for myself that I've more than the natural instinct of self-preservation, and I certainly do not find the thought of death a great terror that weighs on me.   I feel rather that, if I were killed, it would be you and those that love me that would have the real burden to bear, and I am writing this letter to explain why, after all, I do not think it should be regarded as merely a burden.   It would, at least, ease my feelings to try and make the explanation.   We make the division between life and death as if it were one of dates—being born at one date and dying some years after.   But just as we sleep half our lives, so when we're awake, too, we know that often we're only half alive.   Life, in fact, is a quality rather than a quantity, and there are certain moments of real life whose value seems so great that to measure them by the clock, and find them to have lasted so many hours or minutes, must appear trivial and meaningless.   Their power, indeed, is such that we cannot properly tell how long they last, for they can colour all the rest of our lives, and remain a source of strength and joy that you know not to be exhausted, even though you cannot trace exactly how it works. The first time I ever heard Brahms' *Requiem* remains with me as an instance of what I mean.   Afterwards you do not look back on such events as mere past things whose position in time can be localized; you still feel as living the power that first awoke in them.   Now if such moments could be preserved, and the rest strained off, none of us could wish for anything better. . . .   And just as these moments of joy or elevation may fill our own lives, so, too, they may be prolonged in the experience of our friends, and, exercising their power in those lives, may know a continual resurrection.   You won't mind a personal illustration.   I know that one of the ways I live in the truest sense is in the enjoyment of music.   Now just as the first hearing of the *Requiem* was for me more than an event which passed away, so I would like to hope that my love of music might be for those who love and survive me more than a memory of something past, a power rather that can enhance for them the beauty of music itself.   Or, again, we love the South Down country.   Now I would hate to think that, if I died, the "associations" would make these hills "too painful" for you, as people sometimes say.   I would like to think the opposite, that the joy I had in the Downs might not merely be remembered by you as a fact in the past, but rather be, as it were, transfused into you and give a new quality of happiness to your holidays there. . . .   Will you at least try, if I am killed, not to let the things I have loved cause you pain, but rather to get increased enjoyment from the Sussex Downs or from J—— singing folk songs, because I have such joy in them, and in that way the joy I have found can continue to live.

And again, do not have all this solemn funeral music, Dead Marches, and so on, played over me as if to proclaim that all has now come to an end, and nothing better remains to those who loved one than a dignified sorrow.   I would rather have the Dutch Easter Carol, where the music gives you the idea of life and joy springing up continually.

And if what I have written seems unreal and fantastic to you, at least there's one thing with which you'll agree.   The will to serve now is in both of us, and you approve of what I'm doing.   Now that is just one of the true and vital things that must not be, and is not, exhausted by the moment at which it is dealt or expressed.   My resolution can live on in yours, even if I am taken, and, in your refusal to regret what we know to have been a right decision, it can prove itself undefeated by death.

Please forgive me if I have worried you by all this talk. If we loved one another better I could not have written this, and just because we love one another, I cannot bear to think that, if I died, I should only give you trouble and sorrow.

LIEUTENANT RICHARD DONALDSON, M.C., R.N.V.R.

Educated Glasgow University.   Joined R.N.V.R. while a student. Killed in Action, France, 5 September, 1918, at the age of 25.

(FLANDERS) 14.11.17

MY DEAR MOTHER, When I come home on leave you must not marvel if I am restless. This is a restless life of ours out here, and the wonder should be that I am able to sit down even for five consecutive minutes. Yesterday we moved; and on the day before, we moved; and on Saturday (two days previous) we moved. But be content. At each step we have moved back, away from the line, by easy stages, and last night I slept out of earshot of the guns in the most clean and picturesque village I have ever seen in this benighted country.

Up to the present I have seen only one aspect of this part of France —mud! Of course even the mud can startle by its beauty on occasions, as when I looked from my hut through what might have been a porthole of a ship and saw a stretch of grey water, as sombre and still a sea as any sailor gazed on. And last Wednesday morning, just a week ago as I write, I stood by an old German trench and watched the blessed sun dawning on still another sea of mud. And that too was beautiful! Sunrise, gold and orange and purple fading into an ultra violet that the eye could not discern, and under it mud and swamp and brimming shell-holes, all reflecting the gaudy colours of the sky. Only there was no life about it, no men, no birds, no creeping things; and the stillness was painful because the guns were suddenly silent.

But now I have seen another aspect of the country and a more familiar beauty.

The village is reminiscent of Rosebank at its prettiest, only it seems scarcely so fragile and considerably bigger. The villagers are kind, there are green fields and trees and cattle and the Battery is settling down for a real rest. . . .

*Educated Licensed Victuallers' School, clerk in a shipping firm.
Served in Gallipoli, East Africa, Egypt, Palestine, and South Russia.
Accidentally killed, Russia, August 15, 1919, at the age of 24.*

TO HIS MOTHER

(PALESTINE) 17/8/18

MY DEAR, . . . It's topping to see the war again.   The star-shells are
faintly visible at night and the guns are distinct.   I have trodden the
road over which Mary and Joseph fled into Egypt, and saw Jaffa from
the train 3 days ago.   From my tent, and as I write, I see the low clouds
hanging over the blue mountains which surround the Holy City, and
from a height of 6,000 feet this morning saw the Dead Sea, and all
the land of Palestine.   A mile or so from the camp an ancient tower
stretches leanly up from its surrounding bed of olive trees.   It is a relic
of the brave Crusader and bears upon its breast the effigy of St. George.
How amazed the armoured saint must be to see, after all these centuries,
British soldiers sweating past, marching on towards his Master's Tomb.
And across the fields there is an old Bedouin and his family, and on this
land our fast scouts lie waiting for the call!   He, with his dark skin,
his hooked nose, his Koran and his knowledge of the Turkish Regime,
sees the "infidels" making tennis-courts and playing football between
their bloody combats!

Heaven, this is a fair country!   Mother, after the sand and flies,
to see mountains, and fields, ploughs and corn, olive and orange groves,
and to get your legs stung by thistles and nettles.   Clouds and in the
distance the blue sea. . . .

Now, isn't all this ridiculous!   I'm relapsing into my old senti-
mentality.   Me!   The cold-blooded me who races up after the poor
unfortunate Hun!   He (the Hun) is getting such a thick time here,
dear.   We shot one down yesterday.   Shot his observer in cold blood
and then shot off one of his planes, and then his fuselage—like a boy
picking off flies' legs one by one!   All my love, dear.

MODELS OF BREVITY

Royal Duke to Irish Bishop

DEAR CORK, Please ordain Stanhope.

Yours,
YORK

Irish Bishop to Royal Duke

DEAR YORK, Stanhope's ordained.

Yours,
CORK

*   *   *   *   *

Mr. Rogers to Lady Dufferin

WILL you dine with me on Wednesday?

Lady Dufferin to Mr. Rogers

WON'T I?

*   *   *   *   *

From a Schoolboy to his Father

S.O.S.   L.S.D.   R.S.V.P.

*   *   *   *   *

Sir Herbert Beerbohm Tree, to a would-be Dramatist

MY DEAR SIR, I have read your play.

Oh, my dear Sir,
Yours Faithfully,

*   *   *   *   *

INDEX

I

WRITERS OF LETTERS

II

THOSE TO WHOM THE LETTERS WERE WRITTEN

Printed in Great Britain by Butler & Tanner Ltd., Frome and London
F.60.331.